Bremen Public Library
Bremen, Indiana
9/06

D1128422

Bremen Public Library
Bremen, Indiana
9/06

Newsmakers®

Bremen Public Library
Bremen, Indiana
ISSN 0899-0417

Newsmakers®

The People Behind Today's Headlines

Laura Avery

Project Editor

2006
Cumulation

Includes Indexes from
1985 through 2006

THOMSON

GALE

Detroit • New York • San Francisco • New Haven, Conn. • Waterville, Maine • London • Munich

THOMSON ™

GALE

Newsmakers 2006, Cumulation

Project Editor
Laura Avery

Image Research and Acquisitions
Leitha Etheridge-Sims

Editorial Support Services
Emmanuel T. Barrido

Rights Acquisition and Management
Margaret Chamberlain-Gaston, Jackie Jones, Shalice Shah-Caldwell

Imaging
Lezlie Light, Mike Logusz

Composition and Electronic Capture
Gary Leach, Carolyn A. Roney

Manufacturing
Rita Wimberley

© 2007 Thomson Gale, a part of The Thomson Corporation.

Thomson and Star Logo are trademarks and Gale is a registered trademark used herein under license.

For more information, contact
Thomson Gale
27500 Drake Rd.
Farmington Hills, MI 48331-3535
Or you can visit our Internet site at
http://www.gale.com

ALL RIGHTS RESERVED
No part of this work covered by the copyright herein may be reproduced or used in any form or by any means—graphic, electronic, or mechanical, including photocopying, recording, taping, Web distribution, or information storage retrieval systems—without the written permission of the publisher.

For permission to use material from the product, submit your request via the Web at http://www.gale-edit.com/permissions, or you may download our Permissions Request form and submit your request by fax or mail to:

Permissions Department
Thomson Gale
27500 Drake Rd.
Farmington Hills, MI 48331-3535
Permissions Hotline:
248-699-8006 or 800-877-4253, ext. 8006
Fax 248-699-8074 or 800-762-4058

Cover photographs reproduced by permission of Kyodo/Landov (portrait of Shizuka Arakawa) and Phil Han/ZUMA/Corbis (portrait of Steve Carell).

While every effort has been made to secure permission to reprint material and to ensure the reliability of the information presented in this publication, Thomson Gale neither guarantees the accuracy of the data contained herein nor assumes any responsibility for errors, omissions, or discrepancies. Thomson Gale accepts no payment for listing; and inclusion in the publication of any organization, agency, institution, publication, service, or individual does not imply endorsement of the editors or publisher. Errors brought to the attention of the publisher and verified to the satisfaction of the publisher will be corrected in future editions.

ISBN 0-7876-8086-9
ISSN 0899-0417

This title is also available as an e-book.
ISBN 1-4144-1886-8
Please contact your Thomson Gale sales representative for ordering information.

Printed in the United States of America
10 9 8 7 6 5 4 3 2 1

Contents

Obituaries

Introduction

Newsmakers provides informative profiles of the world's most interesting people in a crisp, concise, contemporary format. Make *Newsmakers* the first place you look for biographical information on the people making today's headlines.

Important Features

- **Attractive, modern page design** pleases the eye while making it easy to locate the information you need.

- **Coverage of all the newsmakers** you want to know about: people in business, education, technology, law, politics, religion, entertainment, labor, sports, medicine, and other fields.

- **Clearly labeled data sections** allow quick access to vital personal statistics, career information, major awards, and mailing addresses.

- **Informative sidelights essays** include the kind of in-depth analysis you're looking for.

- **Sources for additional information** provide lists of books, magazines, newspapers, and internet sites where you can find out even more about *Newsmakers* listees.

- **Enlightening photographs** are specially selected to further enhance your knowledge of the subject.

- **Separate obituaries section** provides you with concise profiles of recently deceased newsmakers.

- **Publication schedule and price** fit your budget. *Newsmakers* is published in three paperback issues per year, each containing approximately 50 entries, and a hardcover cumulation, containing approximately 200 entries (those from the preceding three paperback issues plus an additional 50 entries), *all at a price you can afford!*

- And much, much more!

Indexes Provide Easy Access

Familiar and indispensable: The *Newsmakers* indexes! You can easily locate entries in a variety of ways through our four versatile, comprehensive indexes. The Nationality, Occupation, and Subject Indexes list names from the current year's *Newsmakers* issues. These are cumulated in the annual hardbound volume to include all names from the entire *Contemporary Newsmakers* and *Newsmakers* series. The Newsmakers Index is cumulated in all issues as well as the hardbound annuals to provide concise coverage of the entire series.

- **Nationality Index**—Names of newsmakers are arranged alphabetically under their respective nationalities.

- **Occupation Index**—Names are listed alphabetically under broad occupational categories.

- **Subject Index**—Includes key subjects, topical issues, company names, products, organizations, etc., that are discussed in *Newsmakers*. Under each subject heading are listed names of newsmakers associated with that topic. So the unique Subject Index provides access to the information in *Newsmakers* even when readers are unable to connect a name with a particular topic. This index also invites browsing, allowing *Newsmakers* users to discover topics they may wish to explore further.

- **Cumulative Newsmakers Index**—Listee names, along with birth and death dates, when available, are arranged alphabetically followed by the year and issue number in which their entries appear.

Available in Electronic Formats

Licensing. *Newsmakers* is available for licensing. The complete database is provided in a fielded format and is deliverable on such media as disk or CD-ROM. For more information, contact Thomson Gale's Business Development Group at 1-800-877-GALE, or visit our website at www.gale.com/bizdev.

Online. *Newsmakers* is available online as part of the Gale Biographies (GALBIO) database accessible through LexisNexis, P.O. Box 933, Dayton, OH 45401-0933; phone: (937) 865-6800, toll-free: 800-227-4908.

Suggestions Are Appreciated

The editors welcome your comments and suggestions. In fact, many popular *Newsmakers* features were implemented as a result of readers' suggestions. We will continue to shape the series to best meet the needs of the greatest number of users. Send comments or suggestions to:

The Editor
Newsmakers
Thomson Gale
27500 Drake Rd.
Farmington Hills, MI 48331-3535

Or, call toll-free at 1-800-877-GALE

Paige Adams-Geller

Fashion designer and model

Born c. 1969, in Wasilla, AK; married Michael. *Education:* Earned degree in broadcast arts from the University of Southern California.

Addresses: *Office*—c/o Paige Premium Denim, 116 N. Robertson Blvd., Ste. B, Los Angeles, CA 90048.

Career

Competed as a teen beauty pageant contestant, early 1980s; won Alaska title in the Miss Charm pageant, c. 1982; signed with the Elite modeling agency, and worked as a petite-division model in New York City after 1985; won California title for the Miss America pageant, 1991; appeared in television commercials and in guest spots on *Evening Shade* and *Baywatch*; worked as a fit model, c. 1999-2004; launched own denim line, Paige Premium Denim, 2005.

Sidelights

Former model Paige Adams-Geller launched her own jeans line, Paige Premium Denim, in 2005. Though her name is unknown to most, Adams-Geller was the curvy secret weapon among jeans manufacturers for a number of years prior to that as the industry's top "fit model." Designers of such high-end lines like Lucky Brands and Seven for All Mankind considered her body type ideal, and so bringing out her own line of jeans seemed a natural career progression, she told Nola Sarkisian-Miller in *WWD*. "I've always loved fashion, and I definitely had a voice and shared my opinions as a fit model. It only made sense to try my hand at this."

Michael Buckner/Getty Images

Born in the late 1960s in Wasilla, Alaska, Adams-Geller never imagined a career as a model. "I knew I was smart, a straight-A student, but I had never identified myself as pretty," she recalled in an interview with a writer for London's *Independent Sunday* newspaper, Mark Ellwood. "In a nutshell, I was an overweight, chubby kid—I used to be called Pudgy Paigey. I wouldn't have labelled myself fat, but other kids poked fun at me and teased me because I had very chubby cheeks and a pear-shaped figure."

As she entered her teens, Adams-Geller shed some pounds and began entering beauty pageants. At the age of 13, she won the Alaska title and went on to represent her state in the Miss Charm pageant, and later competed in the Miss National Teenager and America's Junior Miss pageants. Modeling-agency talent scouts were regulars at such contests, and while some showed interest in signing her, they suggested she lose more weight. She took their advice, but veered into anorexia thanks to a 600-calorie-a-day eating plan and heavy exercise. After graduating from high school at the age of 16, she moved to New York City and signed with the Elite agency. Because she was relatively short for a model, at five feet, seven inches, she was slotted in the petite division, and worked steadily for the next few years.

But the pressure of staying thin in order to work was ruinous to her health, Adams-Geller told Michelle Tan in *People*. "It became a sickness that I couldn't stop. Everyone's controlling you—agents, manager and parents. I couldn't deal with what everyone else was telling me, but I could control how much I weighed." She finally quit the modeling business, and enrolled at the University of Southern California, where she majored in broadcast arts with a minor in theater. Drawn into the pageant world once again, she won the Miss California title in 1991, and went on represent her adopted state in the Miss America contest. Though she did not place in the national event, her state title win opened many other doors, and she soon found work in television commercials, daytime dramas, and as a guest star on series that included *Evening Shade* and *Baywatch*.

Adams-Geller's eating disorder continued to be a problem for her, however. "I starved myself so much I didn't have enough energy to get out of bed," she told Tan in the *People* interview. "I couldn't eat with normal people. I couldn't really be normal." Finally in 1999, she entered an in-patient treatment facility to learn how to eat normally and come to terms with her body image. When she emerged, her measurements of 36-27-37 led to a new career as a fit model. "For print and runway work, you need to be 10 to 15 [pounds] under weight," she explained to Ellwood in the *Independent Sunday* interview. "I was always fighting the 15 [pounds] that never wanted naturally to stay off my body. It was tough for me—I had to treat my body abusively to get that weight off, restrict myself from eating or exercising too much. With fit modelling you can't get a job if you're too skinny—you need to be a nice, healthy, American size."

By then, a new fashion trend for high-end designer denim had taken hold of the women's apparel market in the United States, and Adams-Geller became the most sought-after fit model in the sub-industry when Jerome Dahan, the former denim designer for Lucky Brand, hired her when he was working on what would become the Seven for All Mankind line. Dahan believed that if he could get the fit exactly right on Adams-Geller, his jeans would look right on any woman. By 2001, Dahan's low-rise, dis-

tressed Seven jeans had developed a cult following among women for their perfect fit, and were selling out in stores despite a price tag of $100. The Seven line launched a denim craze, and a slew of other premium-priced lines hit the market. Adams-Geller found herself in high demand for a few years, working as a fit model for Hard Tail, Guess, True Religion, Lucky, Habitual, and Liquid, among others. She also worked with Dahan again on his next venture, the Citizens of Humanity jeans label, which arrived on the market in 2003.

Adams-Geller learned a lot in five years, she told Adam Tschorn in the *Daily News Record*. "I'd get to look at the patterns, see how fabrics draped, hear them talk about problems with shrinkage and production tolerance, and experience firsthand what happens when things go into production," she said. With the expertise of her husband, Michael, she set up a deal with a manufacturer, and Paige Premium Denim was introduced in early 2005. The jeans quickly attracted a devoted celebrity following, including actress Eva Longoria from television's *Desperate Housewives*, fashion model Amber Valletta, and singer Mandy Moore. Estimated sales for the first year were pegged as high as $3 million the first year, with retail prices between $75 to $270.

Adams-Geller works full-time on her denim business, after having officially retired from modeling. In late 2005, she opened Paige, situated in Los Angeles' trendy shopping mecca along Robertson Boulevard. What would be her fifth major career move seemed a perfect fit for Adams-Geller, who still attends support-group meetings to stay healthy. "I'm feeling good about myself," she told *WWD*'s Sarkisian-Miller, "and hope to make other women feel the same way."

Sources

Daily News Record, November 28, 2005, p. 11.
Independent Sunday (London, England), November 7, 2004, p. 25.
People, June 13, 2005, pp. 131-32.
WWD, September 9, 2004, p. 18; April 7, 2005, p. 8; November 17, 2005, p. 8.

—*Carol Brennan*

Jonathan Adler

Home-furnishings designer and ceramicist

Born in 1966, in New Jersey; son of Harry (an attorney) and Cynthia (an artist) Adler; partner of Simon Doonan (creative director of Barneys New York) since 1994. *Education:* Attended Brown University, 1984-88, and Rhode Island School of Design.

Addresses: *Home*—New York, NY. *Office*—c/o Jonathan Adler Soho, 47 Greene St., New York, NY 10013.

Career

Worked for a talent agency in New York City, after 1990, and for a film producer; launched own line of pottery, 1993; opened first store in New York City, 1998; introduced furniture collection, 2002, and home-furnishings line, 2004; published *My Prescription for Anti-Depressive Living*, 2005.

Sidelights

Jonathan Adler's fresh, modern ideas about interior design found their outlet in a mini-empire he oversees in New York City. Adler entered the market as a potter, making high-end, hand-crafted ceramics that soon won over an impressive roster of style-conscious celebrities and tastemakers. In 2004, his full range of home furnishings—from bed linens to tableware—joined his already-successful furniture line. "My career has been completely serendipitous," Adler told *Atlanta Journal-Constitution* writer Danny C. Flanders. "When I chose to become

a potter, I feared I was sacrificing any kind of financial security and would spend my life just peddling my work at rain-soaked crafts fairs."

Born in 1966, Adler grew up in the southern New Jersey community of Bridgeton. His father was an attorney, while his artist-mother had a keen sense of style she put to use collecting modernist furniture for their contemporary home. Adler's future career direction grew out of a summer-camp experience at age 12, when he first encountered a potter's wheel. Within a year, he had convinced his parents to buy him a wheel as well as the kiln oven used to fire ceramics. Adler's official Web site biography gives a chronological timeline of his career, and for the years 1980-84 it reads, "spends entire adolescence in basement … throwing pots."

In 1984, Adler went off to Brown University in Rhode Island, where his plan was to study semiotics and art history. He also took classes in ceramics at the nearby Rhode Island School of Design, one of the top art schools in the United States. His wares were whimsical, and included a teapot that paid homage to Chanel couture, with the interlocking "C"s-logo, but his more conservative teachers dismissed his work as superficial. As he recalled in an interview with Dominic Lutyens for London's *Independent*, one instructor cautioned him against pursuing the creative arts as a career plan. "'I don't think you have what it takes,'" Adler said he was told. "I was crushed."

After college, Adler settled in New York City and took a job at a talent agency. He went on to work in the office of a well-known producer, but came to intensely dislike the entertainment industry. Dejected after a few years, he ventured back into ceramics full-time around 1993, with some financial support from his parents. He made starkly chic vases and other wares, in mostly black and white shades, with a signature vertical-stripe design. His first break came when Aero, a home design store in SoHo, began selling his work, which was followed by an order from Barneys New York, the high-end retailer.

Adler's wares drew celebrity buyers, such as French film star Catherine Deneuve, and fashion designers from Geoffrey Beene to Cynthia Rowley. By 1998, he was able to open his own store in SoHo, though he was no longer making every piece by hand. A non-profit organization called Aid to Artisans had put him in touch with pottery-makers in Peru, and thanks to this he was able to launch a more affordable line called "Pot au Porter." By the end of the 1990s, his business was earning more than $2 million annually, and both Adler and his wares were regularly mentioned in the shelter-magazine press (magazines that target the home and home design).

In 2002, Adler introduced a furniture line under his name, and also began taking interior design jobs for private clients, which led to larger-scale hotel-renovation projects. One was in Palm Beach, the wealthy Florida enclave, and another followed in the California desert resort of Palm Springs. For the restaurant of the Parker Palm Springs assignment, he summed up his design concept in an interview with Nancy Hass of the *New York Times Magazine,* with a few characteristically insouciant words that had made him such a favorite of the design-world press. "If the hotel is where your elegant great-aunt lives, the restaurant is where her wastrel husband spends his time," Adler said. "I wanted to do a baronial Mick Jagger castle in the 'Let It Bleed' era. Lurid, slightly menacing with a psychedelic overlay Gothic chairs with mod upholstery."

By 2005, Adler presided over a veritable home-décor empire, with seven stores and a full line of accessories for the bed, bath, and dining room. He still made the occasional ceramic piece, with his higher-end wares sold under the "Couture" line of limited-edition works. His inspiration, as always, came from somewhat unusual sources, such as the architecture of Reform synagogues. "I have always been driven by and fantasized about moving into those synagogues," he told *New York Times* writer Jennifer Steinhauer. "They have such a groovy, brutalist, modern thing going on. Growing up, we went to a Conservative synagogue, and I was always jealous of those kids who went to Reform."

The year 2005 also saw the publication of Adler's first book, a how-to guide for do-it-yourself decorating and entertaining. *My Prescription for Anti-Depressive Living,* published by ReganBooks, was built around the ideas enshrined in the Manifesto section of his company Web site, such as "minimalism is a bummer," and "We believe that when it comes to decorating, the wife is always right. Unless the husband is gay."

Adler is frequently profiled along with his partner, Simon Doonan, also a renowned stylesetter. The British-born Doonan is the creative director for Barneys New York, as well as an author and occasional judge on the reality series *America's Next Top Model.* The two share a Norwich terrier named Liberace, and homes in Greenwich Village, the Long Island resort of Shelter Island, and in Palm Beach. All feature Adler's signature look, with vivid colors and a mix of styles and periods. "My entire philosophy," Adler told Guy Trebay in a *New York Times* article, "is that when you come home, your house should have the effect of Zoloft." He put it in more detailed terms in the *Atlanta Journal-Constitution* interview with Flanders. "I truly believe that good decorating can cure a lot of psychological ills," he told the paper, "and make you feel good about yourself as well as your home."

Selected writings

My Prescription for Anti-Depressive Living, Regan Books, 2005.

Sources

Periodicals

Advocate, June 21, 2005, p. 160.
Atlanta Journal-Constitution, December 7, 2005, p. E1.
Domino, September 2005, p. 38.
HFN: The Weekly Newspaper for the Home Furnishing Network, January 6, 2003, p. 22.
Independent (London, England), April 1, 2000, p. 18.
New York Times, August 9, 1998; April 3, 2005, p. ST1.
New York Times Magazine, October 10, 2004, p. 86; February 13, 2005.
Times (London, England), November 29, 2003, p. 81.

Online

Jonathan Adler company Web site, http://www.jonathanadler.com/shop/index.php (February 21, 2006).

—*Carol Brennan*

Albert, Prince of Monaco

Monika Graff/UPI/Landov

Prince of Monaco

Born Albert Alexandre Louis Pierre Grimaldi, March 14, 1958, in Monaco; son of Rainier III (a prince and head of state) and Grace (a princess; maiden name, Kelly); children: Alexandre (with Nicole Coste). *Education:* Amherst College, B.A., 1981.

Addresses: *Home*—Monte Carlo, Monaco. *Office*—c/o Consulate General of Monaco, 565 Fifth Ave., New York, NY 10017.

Career

Inherited the title His Serene Highness, the Hereditary Prince of Monaco, at birth, 1958; Marquis of Baux, 1958-2005; became His Most Serene Highness, the Sovereign Prince of Monaco, 2005. Served in Monaco's Royal Navy, 1981-82, and reached rank of first-class ensign; internships with Morgan Guaranty Trust's New York City and Paris offices, with Moët-Hennessy's Paris office, with the New York City advertising firm of Wells, Rich & Greene, and the New York City law firm of Rogers & Wells, 1983-85. Also member, International Olympic Committee, 1985—.

Sidelights

Monaco's Prince Albert II ascended to the throne of this tiny European principality in 2005 after the death of his father, Prince Rainier III. The 47-year-old ruler, considered one of Europe's most eligible bachelors, heads one of the world's oldest extant royal houses; he is also one of the handful of hereditary rulers left in the world who wield absolute power over their subjects. More benevolent than tyrannical, Albert is very much a scion of the modern era, a pro-environment prince unafraid to sit for press interviews. Not long after becoming head of state, Albert ridded the palace of his late father's phalanx of advisors, and announced a number of initiatives whose goal was to infuse Monaco's economy with a new vigor.

Albert is a scion of the long-reigning Grimaldi family, who originally hailed from Genoa, Italy. They fled strife there—neighborhoods were clannish and went to war with one another at alarmingly frequent intervals—and in 1270 settled on a tiny, seaside spit of land perched between Italy and France. Within a generation, a deal was struck with France that gave the Grimaldis royal status. The line continued down to Albert's father, Rainier, who in 1956 married the American film star Grace Kelly in a lavish royal ceremony that was one of the most major press events of the year. A daughter, Princess Caroline, was born to the couple in 1957, followed 13 months later by Albert, whose full name is Albert Alexandre Louis Pierre Grimaldi. He was born in Monte Carlo, the city which has nearly the same borders as the principality of Monaco.

When Rainier inherited the throne in 1949, Monaco was nearly bankrupt, and had a reputation for being nothing more than a lavish but somewhat dissolute playground on the French Riviera. The British writer W. Somerset Maugham famously dubbed the principality "a sunny place for shady people." Before Rainier's time, its landmark casino had been the source of so much revenue that taxes in Monaco were abolished entirely, and it became known as a haven for the rich and powerful—as well as for the rich and secretive, whose wealth may have been obtained via illicit means. Monaco also had some famously lax banking laws, which allowed for an unusual degree of secrecy.

Both Rainier and Princess Grace did much to revive Monaco's fortunes over the next quarter-century. Rainier did little to reform the secretive banking laws, but did work to enhance Monaco's reputation in the world, and reasserted his control over the once-again profitable casino after a lease deal with Greek shipping tycoon Aristotle Onassis. Princess Grace, a devoted mother to Albert, Caroline, and Albert's younger sister, Princess Stephanie, was an active patron of the arts in Monaco and hosted a lavish annual charity gala for the International Red Cross aid organization.

As a teenager, Albert attended Monte Carlo's Albert I High School, named after his illustrious ancestor, Prince Albert I. After graduating in 1976, he spent a year in preparation for his future royal duties as heir to the throne, and entered Amherst College in Massachusetts. He proved a talented athlete in several sports, including tennis, javelin-throwing, and skiing, and pledged a campus fraternity, Chi Psi. He graduated in 1981 with a degree in political science, and went on to serve stints in Monaco's Royal Navy and with Morgan Guaranty Trust, the Wall Street banking house. Gossip columnists across Europe and in North America, too, speculated on his future and who he might marry.

The exploits of Monaco's royal offspring had already been well-chronicled in the international media. Albert's sister Caroline had recently divorced her first husband, a Paris banker several years her senior, which was a somewhat scandalous event back in 1980 in light of the fact that she was the scion of a devoutly Roman Catholic royal family. In 1982, a far greater tragedy struck the Grimaldi household, when Albert's mother, Princess Grace, died in an automobile accident on a perilous stretch of road that linked Monte Carlo to a family retreat just across the border with France. Stephanie, 17 years old at the time, was also in the car, but survived the crash. The funeral coverage, broadcast around the world, showed a Prince Rainier and his children seemingly paralyzed by grief.

Albert spent the next two decades preparing for his future role as the prince of Monaco, the title he would inherit upon the death of his father or, as some predicted, if his father chose to retire and abdicate the throne. Still an avid athlete, he participated in five Winter Olympiads between 1988 and 2002 as a member of Monaco's Olympic bobsled team. He also continued to confound the press with his perennial bachelor status. Though he dated a legion of beauties, including model Claudia Schiffer, he seemed disinclined to make a more permanent match. His sisters continued to provide fresh stories for the tabloids, however. Princess Caroline remarried in 1983, to wealthy Italian businessman and speedboat racer Stefano Casiraghi, and was already expecting her first child with him at the time of the ceremony. Casiraghi died in a 1990 speedboat accident, leaving Caroline a widow at age 33 with three young children. In 1999, she wed a German prince, Ernst of Hanover, whom her mother had reportedly once hoped to fix her up with back in the 1970s. They had a daughter together, Alexandra, again born shortly after their nuptials. Princess Stephanie's exploits were far more salacious: she had a number of failed careers, including a run as a pop singer and swimsuit designer, and dated a number of decidedly non-royal types. In the 1990s, she had two children by her former bodyguard, but the pair were divorced in 1996 after a short-lived marriage. She later took up with a circus trainer, and had a third child, whose father she steadfastly refused to identify by name.

Rainier, known for his autocratic temperament as a ruler, was said to have been disappointed with the choices his children made as adults, and there were also rumors that he had voiced doubts about Albert's leadership capabilities. As Rainier's health declined, there was some speculation that he might abdicate, but instead became Europe's longest-serving living monarch. Albert formally became regent in early 2005 when Rainier's health took a turn for the worse. Hospitalized in early March, the prince died on April 6, 2005, at the age of 81. That same day, Albert's title changed from Hereditary Prince Albert to Albert II, Sovereign Prince of Monaco.

An official three-month mourning period ensued, and Albert was enthroned as the Prince of Monaco in a formal Roman Catholic ceremony at Monte Carlo's Cathedral of the Immaculate Conception on July 12, 2005. The ceremony formally conferred his powers as an absolute monarch, responsible for all decision-making over his 32,000 subjects—known as Monegasques—and he was one of the few royals left in the world to wield such authority. He shares legislative power with a National Council, and appoints a minister of state; otherwise all executive and judicial power rests with him.

Albert's first actions as sovereign prince seemed to set the tone for a new era in Monaco. Inside the royal Palace of Monaco—part of a complex of buildings whose original foundation was dug around 1215—he informed his father's longtime advisors that he expected their resignations shortly. Some Monaco royal-watchers had speculated that the longstanding rumors that Albert was gay may have originated among some of Prince Rainier's coterie who were hostile to the heir.

Most of those doubts about Albert's private life were assuaged a month after his father's death, when a former Air France flight attendant named Nicole Coste gave an interview detailing her relationship with the prince and providing photographs of the child that resulted from it. The two had met in 1997, and were occasionally seen together in public until Rainier reportedly objected to Coste. She became pregnant after that, and a son, Alexandre, was born in August of 2003. Coste was a native of Togo, a west African nation with colonial ties to France, and therefore Alexandre was of mixed race, but bore a clear resemblance to his father. Coste gave a tell-all interview to the French tabloid magazine *Paris-Match*, which published photographs of Albert holding a child that was immediately dubbed "the black prince." Headlines from other sources teased readers with speculation that Alexandre might one day become ruler of Monaco, but there was a longtime law on the books that only a direct male descendant of the reigning prince could inherit the throne, meaning Albert needed to be married to Coste for their son to rule.

Coste claimed that Albert had submitted to a DNA test that confirmed his paternity, but could not provide any evidence. She did tell *Paris-Match* that the prince had been quietly supporting her and Alexandre, and quite generously, too. By going to the press, she said, she hoped to force Albert to publicly acknowledge his son, which she asserted was in the child's best interests. Her tactic seemed to work, for in early July Albert's lawyer issued a statement confirming he was the father of Alexandre Coste. "It's not a very pleasant situation," Albert told *New York Times* journalist Craig S. Smith two months later. "My only concern now is the well-being of the kid."

Albert had already earned the nickname "the Green Prince" for himself for enacting a series of pro-environment measures. He drives a hybrid gas-and-electric sport-utility vehicle, and shortly after his enthronement took part in a scientific mission to the Arctic Circle that planned to measure the effects of global warming on the Earth's surface. He followed the trail of his dynamic, intelligent namesake, Prince Albert I, whose same journey to Spitsbergen was one of several scientific research trips he made during his 1889-1922 reign. Albert also followed in his mother's footsteps by establishing himself as an active philanthropist and patron of humanitarian causes. He also was keenly interested in turning Monaco into a center for biotechnology, and working to increase the principality's leisure-activity revenue via sporting events.

Though Albert had yet to produce a legitimate male heir to the Grimaldi line—which for centuries had been threatened with the loss of its sovereignty to France if there was no male heir to Monaco's throne—that dilemma was resolved in 2002 with a new constitutional law stating that if a reigning prince died without any surviving legitimate direct descendants, the throne would pass on to his siblings and their children, with male heirs first in line for the throne. This made Princess Caroline the presumptive heiress to the Grimaldi title, with her son Andrea Casiraghi, born in 1984, the future prince of Monaco should Albert remain a bachelor.

Forty-seven years old when he became ruler of Monaco, Albert hosted a number of international political leaders and other luminaries for a second formal enthronement ceremony in November of 2005. He was still quite boyish, though his hairline had receded over the past decade, and was proving himself an active, athletic ruler known for the occasional press interview in which he came across as a likable, rather down-to-earth royal. He still hoped to marry, he would reply when asked, and often said that like many others, he had simply not met the right person yet. His princely status, and the legacy of a mother who was one of the twentieth century's greatest style icons, would daunt the most intrepid potential partner, he also liked to point out. Any woman who dated him would inevitably be compared to the late Princess Grace. And that, Albert told Smith in the *New York Times* interview, "has not only scared me, but also many women I have known."

Sources

Independent (London, England), May 6, 2005, p. 34; July 13, 2005, p. 20.

New York Times, April 7, 2005; September 10, 2005, p. A4.

People, September 28, 1987, p. 84; May 16, 2005, p. 23; July 25, 2005, p. 74.

Sports Illustrated, November 4, 2002, p. R20.

Sunday Times (London, England), May 8, 2005, p. 26; July 10, 2005, p. 26.

Time International (Europe Edition), July 18, 2005,
  p. 11.
Times (London, England), December 23, 1987.

—*Carol Brennan*

Jeremy Allaire

Photo courtesy of Brightcove, Inc.

Founder, president, and CEO of Brightcove, Inc.

Born May 13, 1971, in Philadelphia, PA; son of Jim (a psychologist) and Barb (a press editor) Allaire; married Marjorie; children: two sons. *Education:* Macalester College, St. Paul, MN, B.A. (political science), 1993.

Addresses: *Office*—Brightcove, Inc., One Cambridge Center, Cambridge, MA 02142. *Website*—http://www.brightcove.com.

Career

Consultant for Global Internet Horizons, 1993-94; co-founder and chief technology officer, Allaire Corp., 1995-2001; chief technology officer, Macromedia, Inc., 2001-03; technologist and entrepreneur-in-residence, General Catalyst, 2003; founder, president, and CEO of Brightcove, Inc., 2004—.

Awards: Young Entrepreneurs of the Year (shared with brother, J.J. Allaire), Massachusetts Interactive Media Council, 1999; named *Business 2.0* magazine's "Smartest Entrepreneur of the Year," 2006.

Sidelights

Back in the early 1990s, before most people even knew what a home page was, Jeremy Allaire set his sights on the Internet, believing it would grow at such a fast rate that a company providing Net software would earn fistfuls of money. He was right.

In 1995, he co-founded Allaire Corp., which created web development software. Six years later, he sold the company for $360 million.

In 2004, Allaire spotted another high-tech market opportunity and founded Brightcove, Inc., an Internet television and video distribution service. Brightcove allows networks and producers the opportunity to distribute their media directly to the consumer through multitudes of websites. While the idea of Internet TV may seem peculiar to some, Allaire believes in its future. "We are trying to create a new kind of online media distribution business that has the scale of Google, an Amazon or an eBay," he told *New York Times* reporter Saul Hansell.

Allaire was born on May 13, 1971, in Philadelphia, Pennsylvania, to Jim and Barb Allaire. His father is a retired psychologist and his mother, a retired press editor. Raised in Winona, Minnesota, Allaire was an enterprising youth. When he was 13, he persuaded his parents to give him $5,000 so he could start a baseball-card venture. He bought cards and traded them, eventually doubling the initial investment.

In 1983, his family acquired an early model Apple, touching off his long-term fascination with computers. Allaire studied political science at Macalester

College in St. Paul, Minnesota. His roommate worked for the college's computer services group and finagled an Internet connection for their dorm room, giving Allaire the opportunity to log onto the web in its early days.

By the time Allaire graduated in 1993, the web had become "the central passion" in his life, he told *VAR Business* magazine's Rob Wright, though he was not sure what to do about it. "I really wasn't in a great position to get a job," he recalled. "But I did know a lot about the Internet and, at that time, the commercialization of the Internet was a very real thing."

From 1993 to 1994, Allaire took web consulting jobs. He helped the *Utne Reader* establish its website and also developed a web archive of political theorist Noam Chomsky's essays. Allaire had studied Chomsky's works during his college days.

These early endeavors got Allaire thinking about the potential of the Internet way before other entrepreneurs. Eventually, Allaire and his brother, J.J., formed their own company (J.J. Allaire was an expert in software development). Melding their talents, they founded Allaire Corp. in 1995, initially operating out of a one-bedroom apartment in St. Paul with $18,000 in startup money from J.J. Allaire's savings. Their business plan was simple—create easy-to-use web development tools. In 1996, the company moved to Massachusetts on the heels of a $2.5 million funding injection from Boston-based Polaris Venture Partners. In 1999, Allaire Corp. went public.

The company developed ColdFusion, which had commercial web applications. The software was purchased by companies such as Lockheed, Boeing, and Intel, allowing them to use the web for various applications, including customer websites and internal communications. ColdFusion also makes online purchasing possible. It is the guts that powers millions of websites, online services, and business applications on the Internet.

Allaire Corp. also created HomeSite, a highly popular HTML editor used for web development. During the Internet boom, the company's products earned legions of fanatical devotees. At one point, Allaire Corp. boasted some 1.5 million web developers as customers. The brothers sold the company to Macromedia, Inc., in 2001 for $360 million and Jeremy Allaire became Macromedia's chief technology officer. He left in 2003 to join the Massachusetts-based venture capital firm General Catalyst.

In the early 2000s, Jeremy Allaire hit upon another bright idea and in 2004 founded Brightcove with hopes of earning money in the emerging Internet video programming market. Brightcove lets consumers order movies or programs online. They are then sent over high-speed Internet connections to the consumer's hard drive or set-top box, ready for viewing at any time. Purchased videos can be burned onto a CD, creating a disc that is viewable on a DVD player.

Besides helping consumers, Brightcove benefits producers by allowing them to upload their programs directly to Brightcove. Content owners can catalog, package, and market their products on the site for consumption by Internet surfers. Allaire says Brightcove will allow a whole new generation of filmmakers to distribute their creations. In the past, film and television producers relied on networks and cable companies to get their shows out to the public. Brightcove allows pretty much anyone to get their programming out, including amateurs shooting home videos, media moguls with extensive libraries, and niche video suppliers. Through Brightcove, they can all put their programs on the Internet and rake in some money if someone watches. Brightcove also hopes to make money on advertising by selling quick commercials that run before the videos. Some content is ad-supported and free to view.

Allaire says the name Brightcove is part metaphor—he likens his company to a "cove" that helps producers locate an audience for their particular program in the enormous sea called the Internet. While Brightcove has a handful of competitors, it has received cash backings from prominent media players, including Time Warner Inc. and America Online. In addition, several media companies have agreed to let Brightcove distribute their video content to various websites. Brightcove clients include cable television's Oxygen Media Inc., Reuters, and the New York Times Co. CBS was looking to negotiate a deal. "We have so much content and so little of it is seen," Larry Kramer of CBS Digital Media told the *Wall Street Journal*'s Peter Grant. "News, entertainment, and sports can all be sliced and diced for different markets."

Clearly, Allaire was successful in his first Internet venture back in the 1990s, though he says he is better positioned now to lead a company. "This time around I have a much more sophisticated understanding of what it takes to put together teams," he told *Boston Globe* staffer Robert Weisman. "I have a very strong understanding of the financing opportunities that are available to companies and what attracts investors. And I still have a lot of fire in the belly as to what we're trying to accomplish, which is to transform multimedia distribution."

Sources

Periodicals

Boston Globe, February 28, 2005, p. B7; February 6, 2006, p. E1.
Broadcasting & Cable, January 16, 2006, p. 45.
Mass High Tech, November 1, 1999, p. 22.
New York Times, October 6, 2005, p. C7.
Television Week, July 18, 2005, p. 12.

VAR Business, December 11, 2000, p. 44.

Online

"Gate Crashers: Online Video Goes Mainstream, Sparking an Industry Land Grab," Dow Jones Web Reprint Service (reprinted from the *Wall Street Journal*), http://webreprints.djreprints.com/1413650118976.html (May 24, 2006).
"Jeremy Allaire," Brightcove, http://www.brightcove.com/management-allaire.cfm (May 1, 2006).

—Lisa Frick

Judd Apatow

Michael Germana/Landov

Writer, producer, and director

Born December 6, 1967; married Leslie Mann (an actress); children: Maude, Iris. *Education:* Attended the University of Southern California, mid- to late 1980s.

Addresses: *Agent*—United Talent Agency, 9560 Wilshire Blvd., Ste. 500, Beverly Hills, CA 90212-2427.

Career

Director of films, including: *The 40-Year-Old Virgin,* 2005; *Knocked Up,* 2007. Executive producer of films, including: *Heavyweights,* 1995; *Celtic Pride,* 1996. Producer of films, including: *The Cable Guy,* 1996; *The Whistleblower,* 1999; *Anchorman: The Legend of Ron Burgundy,* 2004; *The 40-Year-Old Virgin,* 2005; *Talledega Nights: The Ballad of Ricky Bobby,* 2006; *Knocked Up,* 2007. Associate producer of films, including: *Crossing the Bridge,* 1992; *Kicking and Screaming,* 2005. Film appearances include: *Heavyweights,* 1995; *Anchorman: The Legend of Ron Burgundy,* 2004. Uncredited author of screenplays for *Happy Gilmore,* 1996; *The Cable Guy,* 1996; *The Wedding Singer,* 1998. Received story credit for *Celtic Pride,* 1996. Author of screenplays for *Fun with Dick and Jane,* 2005; *Knocked Up,* 2007. Television work includes: co-creator and executive producer, *The Ben Stiller Show,* FOX, 1992; series co-creator and executive producer, *Freaks and Geeks,* NBC, 1999-2000; executive producer, *Undeclared,* FOX, 2001; co-executive producer, *The Larry Sanders Show,* HBO, 1997-98; consulting producer, *The Critic,* FOX, 1994; also directed episodes of *The Larry Sanders Show* and *Freaks and Geeks;* writer for *The Ben Stiller Show, The Larry Sanders Show, The Critic, Freaks and Geeks,* and *Undeclared.*

Awards: Co-recipient of an Emmy Award for writing, Academy of Television Arts and Sciences, for *The Ben Stiller Show,* 1993.

Sidelights

Judd Apatow's career as a film and television writer had several false starts before he scored with the 2005 comedic film, *The 40-Year-Old Virgin.* As the creator of the television critics' favorite *Freaks and Geeks* for NBC in 1999, and another much-lauded series, *Undeclared* that was also cancelled after its first season, Apatow was one of Hollywood's best-known writers, but had a difficult time producing a winner for nearly a decade before finding his niche in R-rated comedies. An appreciation for life's underdogs and a sharp sense of the absurd was evident in his projects as well as interviews he gave. "I always wonder, why will people watch a guy slowly die of a brain tumor on a hospital show but they don't want to see a kid get beat up in high school?" he reflected when discussing what clicked with viewers on network television in an interview with *Entertainment Weekly*'s Josh Rottenberg. "I have no answers for that."

Apatow was determined to forge a career in comedy all the way back at Syosset High School on Long Island in the early 1980s. He hosted his own show on the school radio station, which utilized interviews he conducted on his own time with soon-to-be famous comics as well as a few well-known names. When he managed to book a subject for his show, rarely would he tell them that they had agreed to do an interview for a high school radio station, and they were surprised to find a teenager with a tape recorder in hand. As he recalled in the *Entertainment Weekly* article, "I'd go to Jerry Seinfeld's house and he would look at me like, I can't believe I have to do this," he told Rottenberg.

One of Apatow's first jobs was as a dishwasher at the Eastside Comedy Club on Long Island. Eventually he started doing his own stand-up act, and went on to the University of Southern California's film school to study screenwriting. He abandoned his degree plans after becoming immersed in the Hollywood stand-up scene, and forged friendships with a number of other struggling performers and writers who achieved fame more quickly than he would. Adam Sandler was a roommate for a time, and Apatow opened for Jim Carrey and then began writing material for him, some of which found its way into the comedy-sketch series *In Living Color.* From there, he progressed into writing jobs for Roseanne Barr, Tom Arnold, and Garry Shandling, and Shandling even used some of Apatow's material when he hosted the Grammy and Emmy awards ceremonies.

In 1991, Apatow met Ben Stiller, who was pitching a sketch-comedy series to the FOX network. Stiller hired him as the show's executive producer and writer, though Apatow had virtually no television experience. "We were completely winging it," Apatow recalled in an interview with David Handelman for the *New York Times* some years later. "I would sit in my office and read books on how to have a staff." *The Ben Stiller Show* lasted just 13 episodes before FOX pulled the plug, but Apatow and his writing team shared an Emmy Award for their work. Around this same time, he left the stand-up circuit for good, realizing he had better luck writing material for others.

Apatow went on to serve as a writer and consulting producer for Shandling's highly acclaimed HBO series, *The Larry Sanders Show.* His work there netted him four Emmy nominations with the other writers, but Apatow had decided to branch out into film by then. He was an associate producer for the 1992 Mike Binder movie, *Crossing the Bridge,* and served as executive producer for the 1995 comedy about overweight youngsters at a sadistic weight-loss camp, *Heavyweights.* A year later, he and *Saturday Night Live* star Colin Quinn wrote the sports caper *Celtic Pride,* for which Apatow also served as executive producer.

Apatow spent the rest of the 1990s switching back and forth between writing for films and the occasional television job. He was involved, either as a producer or script doctor, on movies that served as vehicles for both Carrey and Sandler, including *Happy Gilmore, The Cable Guy,* and *The Wedding Singer.* He also wrote and served as consulting producer for *The Critic,* the animated FOX series that featured the voice of Jon Lovitz. Apatow was also still working with *The Larry Sanders Show,* and served as co-executive producer in its final 1997-98 season. His next project teamed him with Paul Feig, who had been part of the L.A. comedy circuit in the late 1980s. Feig wanted to mine his late 1970s Midwest suburban background for an hour-long comedy-drama, and NBC agreed to a deal with Apatow serving as the executive producer.

Freaks and Geeks debuted in September of 1999 and starred a number of unknown teen actors. The series revolved around Lindsay (Linda Cardellini), a good student and "mathlete" who finds herself drawn to a less-ambitious group of high-school pals. Subplots revolved around the exploits of Lindsay's younger brother, Sam, and his moderately geeky friends. Critics loved *Freaks and Geeks,* with *Entertainment Weekly*'s Ken Tucker calling it "one of the most fully realized pieces of comic entertainment in any medium of the past few years."

Apatow's show was hampered by the network's lack of faith in it, however, which started when NBC decided to make it part of its Saturday-night lineup. "They always tell you that's a good time slot," Apatow joked with *Mediaweek* writer Alan James Frutkin. "You don't have to do well because they don't expect anyone to do well. And then you don't do well, and they're very upset." After an intermittent fall run—preempted by major-league baseball games and pulled off for the November sweeps—NBC moved *Freaks and Geeks* to a Monday-night prime-time slot at the beginning of 2000. Then they cancelled it altogether. A cable outlet, Fox Family, picked it up for re-broadcast later that year, and the 18-episode run posted impressive ratings. The show went on to accumulate a devoted cult following in subsequent reruns on the ABC Family cable network.

Freaks and Geeks was also hamstrung by comparisons with a lighter-hearted series about teens also set during that era, *That '70s Show.* Tucker compared the two in an *Entertainment Weekly* article in 2001, and noted the surge in popularity of the latter show, thanks in part to its quickly paced sitcom wisecracks and rising star, Ashton Kutcher. "I wish Apatow and his crew," he concluded, "could somehow rescue the '70s cast and bring them over to a series that's fresh and unafraid to take its characters seriously."

By then, Apatow was working on a new project, *Undeclared*, which had a brief one-season run on FOX before it, too, was axed. The show was set in the present day, at the fictional University of North Eastern California, and centered around incoming freshman Steven (Jay Baruchel), and his new dormitory-mates. Apatow described its concept to Dan Snierson in *Entertainment Weekly* as "a way to find out what happened to the geeks after high school, because the freaks aren't going to get into college." Once again, critics gave the series high marks, with *New York Times* writer Caryn James finding it "wonderfully cast and acted, with a tone of larger-than-life realism. Its humor comes from the instantly believable characters who try to behave like grownups but have a complete lack of social assurance." This time, Apatow's creation even enjoyed a solid time slot—following *That '70s Show* and just before the first season of *24*—but FOX canned the show after ordering 22 episodes.

Apatow spent some of 2002 and 2003 on two other series that never made it onto a network. In 2004, the long-lamented *Freaks and Geeks* was released on DVD, thanks in part to an online petition submitted by the show's dedicated fan base. Writing in *Variety*, Josef Adalian gave the six-disc set unstinting praise, claiming it could "serve as a more than sufficient time capsule of a show that demonstrated just how good network TV can get when producers with passion are allowed to execute their vision."

Returning once more to the film industry, Apatow scored a minor hit when he served as producer for *Anchorman: The Legend of Ron Burgundy*, the 2004 Will Ferrell comedy. Some of its supporting players were cast in Apatow's next project, *The 40-Year-Old Virgin*, which also marked his big-screen directorial debut. He wrote this script about a nebbish, inexperienced guy heading into middle age along with *Daily Show* veteran Steve Carell, who also played the lead. The movie was part of a new trend toward R-rated comedies, including *The Wedding Crashers*, and pulled in strong box-office numbers after its August of 2005 release. It was a hit with critics, too. Writing in *Entertainment Weekly*, Rottenberg called it "a blissfully refreshing alternative to typical studio summer fare." *Rolling Stone*'s Peter Travers commended Apatow's first run as a director in a similarly laudatory review. "What he doesn't yet grasp about framing a scene he makes up for with his intuitive grasp of the architecture of a joke," Travers noted, and predicted "Apatow has a big future making movie comedies … [b]ecause he knows that laughs fly higher and wilder when the characters keep it real."

Later that year another film that Apatow had co-written, *Fun with Dick and Jane*, appeared in theaters. This Jim Carrey-Tea Leoni comedy was a re-make of 1977 classic that starred George Segal and Jane Fonda as a middle-class couple who resort to a life of crime. His next project was *Knocked Up*, tentatively scheduled for a 2007 release, and he would once more direct his own script. Again, he cast familiar faces, including Seth Rogen, one of the "Freaks" from *Freaks and Geeks* whom Apatow had also cast in *Undeclared* and *The 40-Year-Old Virgin*.

Another star of *Knocked Up* was Leslie Mann, Apatow's wife, whom he met on the set of *The Cable Guy* back in 1996. Mann played the drunk date in *The 40-Year-Old Virgin*. She and Apatow have two daughters, and she was briefly mentioned in a notorious e-mail exchange that made the rounds in Hollywood before being reprinted in its entirety in the March 2002 issue of *Harper's*. The correspondence was between Apatow and Mark Brazill, creator of *That '70s Show*, and initially began over a guest appearance by one of the latter show's stars, Topher Grace, on *Undeclared*. It quickly devolved into an argument over a comedy-series pilot Brazill had been discussing ten years earlier with MTV about a hapless rock band, which he accused Apatow of stealing for *The Ben Stiller Show* in the e-mails. "Nobody has ever goofed on rock bands, not *Spinal Tap* or The Rutles or 800 *Saturday Night Live* sketches," Apatow responded with characteristic dry wit in one of the messages. "I should have told everyone on the show, no rock band sketches, that's Brazill's area."

The e-mail exchanges provided an unusual behind-the-scenes glimpse into the insular world of Hollywood writers, many of whom, like Apatow and his cohorts, had all known one another at varying stages of their career struggle. Apatow himself summed up the sometimes-brutal nature of the entertainment industry from a writer's perspective in the interview with Frutkin for *Mediaweek*. "In a lot of ways, you're like a runway model," he reflected. "You have a window of success, but you don't know when that window closes."

Sources

Entertainment Weekly, September 21, 2001, p. 48, p. 67; August 5, 2005, p. 29; August 26, 2005, pp. 30-33.

Film Journal International, August 2004, p. 55.

Harper's, March 2002, p. 23.

Mediaweek, September 3, 2001, p. 19.

New York Times, December 28, 1997; September 25, 2001, p. E8.

Rolling Stone, August 25, 2005, p. 111.

Variety, September 20, 1999, p. 43; August 23, 2004, p. 31.

—*Carol Brennan*

Fiona Apple

AP Images

Singer and songwriter

Born Fiona Apple McAfee-Maggart, September 13, 1977, in New York, NY; daughter of Brandon Maggart (an actor) and Diane McAfee (a dancer and singer).

Addresses: *Home*—Venice Beach, CA. *Record company*—Sony Music Entertainment, 550 Madison Ave., New York, NY 10022-3211. *Website*—http://www.fiona-apple.com.

Career

Landed record deal with Work Group, a Sony Music label, early 1990s; released debut album, *Tidal*, 1996; released *When the Pawn*, 1999; released *Extraordinary Machine*, 2005.

Awards: Best new artist in a video, MTV Video Music Awards, for "Sleep to Dream," 1997; MTV Video Music Awards, best cinematography of the year, for "Criminal," 1998; Grammy Award, best female rock vocal performance, for "Criminal," 1998.

Sidelights

Fiona Apple soared into the rock-world limelight with her 1996 triple-platinum debut album *Tidal* when she was only 19 years old. She captured a Grammy, then followed with 1999's *When the Pawn*. Despite her talents, Apple gained more notoriety for her tormented life story than for her music. On-stage and during interviews she was so frank and temperamental that many in the music world re-fused to take her seriously and instead viewed her as a self-absorbed drama queen who was exploiting her deep-seated emotional wounds. Sick of being vilified and misunderstood, Apple faded from the music scene and at one point quit altogether before releasing 2005's comeback album *Extraordinary Machine*. This album, released when Apple was a confident and stable 28 years old, shows maturity and depth. Speaking to *Entertainment Weekly*'s Karen Valby, Apple acknowledged her rocky beginnings in the business. "I was cast in the crazy role and I was perfect for it."

The future singer-songwriter was born Fiona Apple McAfee-Maggart on September 13, 1977, in New York City. Her parents, Diane McAfee and Brandon Maggart, had forged a relationship while performing in a musical together. Apple's mother was a singer and dancer; her father was an actor. They never married but had two daughters together before splitting up when Apple was four. Afterward, Apple and her older sister, Amber, lived with their mother. Apple turned to music at a young age and took piano lessons. By the age of eight, she was playing her own compositions at piano recitals. Apple's thirst for musical knowledge eventually drove her beyond her classical training. She learned to play piano chords by taking sheet music and translating the guitar tablature into the corresponding notes. As a result, her piano-backed music has its own unique, robust feel.

Raised in Manhattan schools, Apple had a hard time early on and was teased with taunts of being an ugly duckling. Later on, classmates called her a dog. By fifth grade, signs of Apple's inner darkness and turmoil began to surface. One day, Apple told a friend that she was going to kill herself—and take her sister's life, too. Apple was taken for a psychiatric evaluation, where a therapist recognized her obvious signs of depression. The therapist also said Apple had a problem with thinking too much.

Apple's father noticed her darkness seeping to the fore before she even entered adolescence. Apple always spent summers with her father in Los Angeles and he noticed she was becoming unsettled, even by the age of ten. "She had trouble sleeping at night—and she had written these inaccessible lyrics about darkness," her father told Rolling Stone's Chris Heath. "It kind of scared me in the beginning."

As a child Apple developed bizarre, compulsive rituals to help with her anxiety. Sometimes she played Bob Dylan's "Like a Rolling Stone" and skated around the dining room 88 times—there are 88 keys on a piano. Afterward, she felt safe and knew she would be OK until someone got home. When Apple got mad she would take her step-father's Boy Scout knife and stab the walls of her closet. Once, she carved the word "strong" on the wall. She wrote poetry and essays as an emotional outlet and was obsessed with journaling. When she grew older, she turned her rants into songs. For Apple, writing was a way to express herself. She did not do it with songwriting in mind—that came later.

At the age of 12, Apple was raped in the hallway of her apartment building after walking home from school. The gripping emotions and lyrics expressed in the song "Sullen Girl," from her debut album, are a result of that experience. Apple has said that coping with the ordeal became a defining moment in her life and pushed her to excel in music because she needed to express herself and wanted the world to know how she felt. Apple also turned to music because she struggled so much in school she did not feel confident she could do anything else with her life.

Apple's break came in the early 1990s when a friend passed along one of her tapes to a New York publicist she baby-sat for. This woman passed it on to Andy Slater, a Los Angeles-based producer and manager of such clients as Don Henley and Lenny Kravitz. Impressed with what he heard, Slater got Apple a music contract with Work Group, an upstart Sony Music label. However, when Slater first met Apple he was skeptical that someone so young could write songs expressing such a sultry, jaded outlook on life. "I was not entirely convinced that this person sitting in front of me—who was clearly 17—had written those words," he recalled in an interview with the New York Times' Dimitri Ehrlich. "At first I thought it was a Milli Vanilli thing," he said, in reference to the 1980s duo that won a Grammy for songs made by pre-recorded studio singers, which they tried to pass off as their own through lip-synching.

Immediately, producers insisted that Apple change her name, believing her given name, Fiona Apple McAfee-Maggart, was too long and awkward. At first, when the record company suggested Apple, she balked. Instead, she wanted to find a completely new name—that is what one of her heroes, author Maya Angelou, did. Apple's mother suggested Fiona Lone because she was a loner. In the end, when her contract arrived, it listed her stage name as Fiona Apple so she went with it.

Apple's first album, 1999's Tidal, which had sold three million copies by 2005, contains a lot of angst-ridden emotions bottled up from the breakup with her first real boyfriend. Making the album proved arduous and was a tumultuous affair for Apple. For starters, Apple had so much self-doubt that she believed her backup musicians felt she was wasting their time. In addition, Apple was becoming waif-thin because she was having trouble eating as she began to obsess over the color and textures of her food. Still dealing with the effects of her rape, Apple also felt uncomfortable sitting alongside the men on her production team.

At one point, production stopped so Apple could return to therapy. Finally, Apple was helped though her doubts by a visit from singer Lenny Kravitz, who came to the studio one night. He assured Apple that the album sounded promising. She believed him, and the two forged a close friendship filled with telephone calls whenever Apple began to doubt herself. She made it through and the album became a hit. The quality of the tracks was inconsistent, but the album was well-received and piqued many a listener's curiosity with its stark, sinister and confessional lyrics. The fierce-sounding album clearly captures an adolescent's dramatic take on life.

In an article in the New Yorker, Sasha Frere-Jones noted that the album, despite its drawbacks and awkward pseudo-literary language, was successful because Apple "had a lusciously capable voice, a unique sense of melody, and a percussive style at the piano—her main accompaniment," which gave the album a unique feel. Apple created some waves in her MTV video for the song "Criminal," in which she appeared in her underwear, exposing her rail-thin body. Critics said the video did not promote a healthy image for young women, and Apple later agreed and lamented the choice, saying the video ended up being disturbing rather than sexy. It did, however, receive lots of play on MTV.

Apple became most famous for her 1997 MTV Video Music Award acceptance speech for best new artist where she said the world was "bull****." At the time, Apple said she felt superficial, like she had become a paper doll, molded to play the famous rock-star image the world wanted to see. She felt as though she had betrayed herself, and she warned viewers not to play the game. Speaking to *Entertainment Weekly*'s Valby, Apple acknowledged her angst from that time. "I felt like it wasn't my music that had gotten me there, and I felt very resentful of that and of myself for that. It had been so important to me to get to this point, to be in this crowd, and once I got there I saw it wasn't anything I could really feel proud of."

Despite waves of criticism, Apple moved on and followed with *When the Pawn* in 1999, another album that explores the world of unsettled relationships. Full of feisty, yet humorous lyrics, this album was more sophisticated and clearly showed influences from Apple's love of jazz, the Beatles, and Joan Armatrading. Many of the songs, instead of focusing on relationships lost, delved into the intricacies of maintaining healthy bonds with a signicant other. Despite the more mature sound, it sold one-third fewer albums than *Tidal*. There were other disappointments as well. Apple's frail emotional state came to the forefront again in 2000 when she ran off the stage in tears during the middle of a concert at the Roseland Ballroom in New York after complaining that she could not hear herself. Fans waited, but she never returned.

Apple has spent her whole life struggling to escape from the grips of depression and at times has taken medication to help with her condition. She also had years of psychotherapy. Speaking to the *Rolling Stone*'s Heath, Apple acknowledged her suicidal tendencies. "I truly did want to die before. I remember I would be sitting in my shrink's office, looking at his computer with one of those screen savers on, and they have all these cubes in different colors, and I swear my mood would change.... A purple square would come up and I'd feel, 'Every-

thing's OK,' then a green one would come up and I'd be, 'Everything's terrible.' It would make no sense to me. I still don't understand it."

Six years passed before the release of her third album, *Extraordinary Machine*, in 2005. In the interim, Apple spent time getting herself together. For a while, she lived in Venice Beach, California, in a house with nothing but a twin bed, television, VCR, boombox, some green dog pillows, and her Staffordshire Terrior, Janet. She spent the time taking walks and sitting in silence on the lawn. By the time the album was released, Apple felt well enough to end therapy and quit taking her anti-anxiety medication, which she had been on for a decade. She began starting her days with long walks to clear her head and has kept up the routine.

Apple's third album barely made it to release. At one point, during her retreat from the music world, Apple actually called her manager and told him she was done with music. She then spent her days sitting around in her robe at her mother's house watching *Columbo* reruns and trying to figure out what to do with her life. The problem stemmed from a rift with Sony over production of the album. When Apple began work on the album in 2002, she recorded several songs with Jon Brion, who had produced her second album. After hearing the tracks, Sony did not think the album had been made with radio listeners in mind and wanted the songs remixed.

Apple, herself, did not feel the album was quite right and she wanted to re-record with bassist Mike Elizondo. He had played on her second album and helped produce albums for Eminem and 50 Cent. Apple says Sony wanted her to record one song at a time and then submit it for approval but she felt the company wanted too much control. Part of the album had been leaked to the Internet and fans were eager for its arrival. They were so upset with Sony they created a website called freefiona.com and through the mail bombarded Sony with hundreds of foam apples. Apple was moved by her fans' actions and for the first time in her life felt wanted and needed. She decided to finish the album and worked out a deal with Sony, which said it had all been a misunderstanding.

Extraordinary Machine hit the shelves in October of 2005. This album, full of hypnotic grooves and cabaret piano vamps, reflects Apple's own transformation to maturity and stability. As Frere-Jones noted in the *New Yorker*, the songs have a nice balance of attacks and retreats: "The album contains many moments both of lushness and of restraint.... *Extraordinary Machine* is just 50 minutes, and it feels short;

you want to replay it immediately. It's the kind of album that makes an artist's previous work sound better, a record that makes converts out of doubters."

Selected discography

Tidal, Sony BMG, 1996.
When the Pawn, Sony BMG, 1999.
Extraordinary Machine, Sony BMG, 2005.

Sources

Periodicals

Billboard, October 8, 2005, pp. 47-48.
Entertainment Weekly, September 30, 2005, pp. 28-35.

New Yorker, October 10, 2005, pp. 88-89.
New York Times, January 5, 1997, sec. 2, p. 34.
Rolling Stone, January 22, 1998, p. 30; October 6, 2005, pp. 64-66.

Online

"Bio," Fiona Apple, http://www.fiona-apple.com/html_content/bio.html (February 1, 2006).
"My Happy Ending," Blender, http://www.blender.com/guide/articles.aspx?id=1809 (February 1, 2006).

—Lisa Frick

Shizuka Arakawa

Figure skater

Kyodo/Landov

Born December 29, 1981, in Tokyo, Japan; daughter of Koichi and Sachi Arakawa. *Education:* Graduated from Waseda University, 2004.

Addresses: *Contact*—Champions on Ice, 3500 American Blvd. W, Minneapolis, MN 55431. *Home*—Sendai, Japan. *Website*—http://shizuka-arakawa.com.

Career

Began skating at the age of five and by age ten had been selected for a special summer camp sponsored by the Japan Skating Federation; at age 16 competed in her first Olympics, 1998; won Olympic figure-skating gold, 2006; retired from competition and turned pro, 2006; skated for the Champions on Ice series, 2006—.

Awards: Gold medal, Japanese National Championships, 1999; silver medal, Japanese National Championships, 2001; silver medal, Four Continents, Jeonju, South Korea, 2002, China, 2003; bronze medal, Japanese National Championships, 2003, 2004; gold medal, World Championships, Dortmund, Germany, 2004; first place, NHK Trophy, Nagoya, Japan, 2004; second place, Cup of Russia, Moscow, 2004; second place, Campbell's International Skating Challenge, New York City, 2004; ninth place, World Championships, 2005; second place, ISU Grand Prix Final, Beijing, 2005; bronze medal, Japanese National Championships, 2005; gold medal, Olympics, Turin, Italy, 2006.

Sidelights

As the 2006 Olympics began, the figure-skating world focused its attention on Russian world champion Irina Slutskaya and U.S. national champion Sasha Cohen, believing one of them would walk away with the gold. Japanese skater Shizuka Arakawa entered the final night of competition in third place behind the two but emerged in first place, becoming the first Asian to win a figure-skating gold and the first Japanese woman to win Olympic gold. Both Cohen and Slutskaya fell, but Arakawa skated with skill and poise, executing a flawless performance in the face of intense pressure, a feat that eluded her competitors. At 24, she was the oldest woman to win the event since 1920.

"Right now I'm just so surprised about all of this that I'm speechless," she told Tokyo's *Daily Yomiuri* after winning her medal, the first of the Games for Japan. "I never expected that I would be the first one to win a medal for Japan, so I didn't feel that pressure. But I'm very happy that I'm the one who won it."

An only child, Arakawa was born on December 29, 1981, in Tokyo, Japan, to Koichi and Sachi Arakawa, and was raised in Sendai, in northeastern Japan. Arakawa began skating at the age of five, lured into the sport by the prospect of wearing fancy costumes. She started ballet lessons at the age of seven and at age eight landed her first triple jump, a Salchow. By age ten, Arakawa was known as the "girl wonder from Miyagi," which was the prefecture where she lived, and she was selected for an elite summer camp hosted by the Japan Skating Federation. Growing up, she trained at the local rink until she graduated from Sendai's Tohoku High School.

Arakawa got her first major break in 1998 when she earned a chance to represent Japan at the Olympics, which it was hosting. Just 16, Arakawa placed 13th. When the 2002 Olympics rolled around, Arakawa did not even make the team. As the 2004 skating season progressed, Arakawa decided she would retire at the end of it. She took part-time jobs at a fast-food restaurant and a convenience store with plans of getting a full-time job after graduating with her social sciences degree from Waseda University in March of 2004. But Arakawa came alive at the 2004 World Championships in Dortmund, Germany, in a display of athleticism that saw her landing triple-triple combinations no woman had ever completed before, including one combination that required her to complete 14 revolutions in 30 seconds. She easily took first.

After winning the World Championship, Arakawa felt pressured to continue skating. She floundered through the 2004-05 season, though, plagued with skate trouble, homesickness, and injuries. Arakawa had lost her drive. "It was very difficult to motivate myself," she recalled in an interview, according to *USA Today*'s Kelly Whiteside. "It took a full year to regain my motivation." When the 2005 World Championships rolled around, Arakawa placed a disappointing ninth. The outcome, however, seemed to be a turning point for Arakawa, who decided she could not retire after a ninth-place finish. As Kyodo News Service reporter Shinsuke Kobayashi told *Sports Illustrated*'s E.M. Swift, "Afterward I saw a glint in her eyes that had been missing. She told me, 'I can't finish like this.' Something ignited inside her."

Arakawa re-dedicated herself to the sport. Just two months before the 2006 Olympics—and after an intensive bout of soul-searching—Arakawa made a gutsy, dramatic move by switching coaches, music, costumes, and programs. Most skaters spend a year getting comfortable with their programs before an event like the Olympics, but Arakawa knew she needed a change. At the time, Arakawa was working with Russian coach Tatiana Tarasova, who had coached seven skaters to Olympic gold. Just before

the Olympics, Arakawa began working with Nikolai Morozov, an Olympic ice dancer from Belarus and former choreographer for Tarasova. Morozov was surprised that Arakawa wanted to make changes that close to the Olympics but was delighted to work with her and impressed by her elegance. Many skaters "scratch" across the ice, but Arakawa seems to whisper. "When you watch her, it's like a feather. No noise," Morozov told *San Francisco Chronicle* writer Gwen Knapp. "It's very rare that you have that."

Prior to the Olympics, at the Japanese nationals in December of 2005, Arakawa took third, placing behind 15-year-old Japanese phenom Mao Asada. Arakawa may not have even made the Olympic team if Asada had not missed the age cutoff. Going into the competition, all eyes were focused on Slutskaya and Cohen, with many analysts believing a gold dangled out of reach for Arakawa. Going into the final night of competition—the free skate—Cohen stood in first place, just .03 of a point in front of Slutskaya. Arakawa trailed the leader by just .71 of a point. But Cohen and Slutskaya both fell during their final programs.

Arakawa skated her free skate to Puccini's "Violin Fantasy of Turandot." "I like to skate to music with a story," Arakawa once remarked, according to Goldenskate.com's Barry Mittan. "Something big that I can skate to. If you compare skating to ballet, there's a story you have to follow in ballet. But in skating, I can tell my own story by performing whatever feels best with the music."

Arakawa pulled off spectacular spirals and skated a cautious program that did not showcase her athleticism. She held back on two planned triple-triple jump combinations, downgrading them to triple-doubles, but also chose to double a solo triple. In sum, she landed five triple jumps, some in combination. The 5-foot-6-inch Arakawa, who is tall for a female skater, wowed the crowd with a stunning move called the Ina Bauer. It is a spread eagle variation where the performer skates on two parallel blades, with the heels pointing toward each other, while bending over backward. Arakawa's head nearly grazed the floor as she held the position, coasting across the ice.

While many critics said Arakawa's performance failed to dazzle the crowd—and suggested she only won because the others fell—1984 Olympic gold medalist and American Scott Hamilton suggested otherwise. As Jack Gallagher reported in the *Japan Times*, after Arakawa's performance, Hamilton remarked, "Shizuka Arakawa skated a wonderful program tonight. I am convinced it will stand the test of time."

After the Olympics, coaches around the world were left to wonder if Arakawa's gold marked a new era of dominance in the sport by the Japanese. It was the first time since 1994 that the United States did not win the gold. Arakawa, however, had no intention of staging a repeat. Following the Olympics, Arakawa retired from competition and turned professional, signing a deal to perform at certain venues of the Champions on Ice series.

Sources

Periodicals

Daily Yomiuri (Tokyo, Japan), February 25, 2006, p. 1.
Japan Times (Tokyo, Japan), March 16, 2006.
New York Times, February 24, 2006, p. S1.
San Diego Union-Tribune, February 26, 2006, Special Section, p. 2.
San Francisco Chronicle, February 25, 2006, p. D1.
Sports Illustrated, March 6, 2006, pp. 42-44.
USA Today, February 24, 2006, p. F6.

Online

"Shizuka Arakawa," Golden Skate, http://www.goldenskate.com/articles/2003/083003.shtml (April 17, 2006).
"Shizuka Arakawa," NBCOlympics.com, http://www.nbcolympics.com/athletes/5072356/detail.html (April 17, 2006).
"Slip Sliding Away," SI.com, http://sportsillustrated.cnn.com/2006/olympics/2006/02/23/figure.skating.gold.ap/index.html (February 24, 2006).

—Lisa Frick

Jim Balsillie and Mike Lazaridis

AP Images

Co-heads of Research in Motion

Born Jim L. Balsillie, February 3, 1961, in Seaforth, Ontario, Canada; son of Raymond (an electronics technician) and Laurel Balsillie; married Heidi; children: two. Born Michael Lazaridis, March 14, 1960, in Istanbul, Turkey; son of Nick (a salesman and factory worker) and Dorothy (a seamstress) Lazaridis; married Celia; children: one son, one daughter. *Education:* Balsillie: Graduated from the University of Toronto, 1984; Harvard School of Business, M.B.A., 1989; Wilfrid Laurier University, Waterloo, Ontario, Ph.D. Lazaridis: Attended the University of Waterloo.

Addresses: *Office*—Research in Motion, Ltd., 295 Phillip St., Waterloo, Ontario N2L 3W8 Canada.

Career

Balsillie: Worked for the Entrepreneur Services Group at Clarkson Gordon, 1984-87; Sutherland and Schultz, Kitchener, Ontario, Canada, vice president of finance, then executive vice president and chief financial officer, 1989-92; joined RIM, 1992; donated funds to found the Centre for International Governance Innovation, 2002. Lazaridis: Won contract to create project for GM, 1984; founded Research in Motion, Ltd. (RIM), 1984; created Digi-Sync Film KeyKode reader, c. 1992; created the Interactive Pager, 1996; wrote "white paper" for concept behind the BlackBerry, 1997; launched the BlackBerry to marketplace, 1999; used wealth to fund the Perimeter Institute for Theoretical Physics, Canada, 2000; funded the Institute for Quantum Computing at the University of Waterloo; added new features to BlackBerry, 2001, 2002.

Awards: Lazaridis: Emmy Award for the development of a high-speed barcode reader for film, Academy of Television Arts and Sciences, 1994; Academy Award for the development of a high-speed barcode reader for film, Academy of Motion Picture Arts and Sciences, 1998; Canadian-American Business Achievement Award, 1999; honorary Doctor of Engineering degree, University of Waterloo, 2000; Visionary Award, Office for Partnerships for Advanced Skills, 2001; Greater Kitchener-Waterloo Chamber of Commerce Community Leader of the Year Award, 2001; Canada's Nation Builder of the Year, readers of *Globe and Mail,* 2002. Both: Ontario High Technology Entrepreneur Award, c. 1997; Canadians of the Year, Canadian Club, 2006.

Sidelights

As the heads of Research in Motion (RIM), Jim Balsillie and Mike Lazaridis are best known for bringing the innovative BlackBerry wireless device to the market. Balsillie serves as RIM's chairman and co-chief executive officer, primarily handling the business side of the company. Lazaridis, the founder of RIM, focuses on product development and research and development, and is the company's visionary. Though RIM faced some difficult legal challenges regarding patents and the BlackBerry in the United States, the success of that device made them both extremely rich and their company quite successful. The pair used their wealth for philanthropic endeavors in their native Canada.

Lazaridis was born in 1960 in Istanbul, Turkey, into a Greek family. He is the son of Nick and Dorothy Lazaridis. The family left Turkey when Lazaridis was quite young. After living for a short time in West Germany, the family moved to Canada in 1966. They came on a ship to Montreal, and eventually settled in Windsor, Ontario. His father, who had worked as a clothing salesman in Turkey, found employment at a local Chrysler automotive factory. His mother worked as a seamstress.

Lazaridis was an intelligent child and greatly enjoyed school, especially reading and science. The gift of an electric train led to the growth of his interest in science and as he got older, he built rockets and radios, and did chemistry experiments. By high school, Lazaridis enjoyed both shop and academic classes. With a friend, Doug Fregin, he won the Windsor science fair. The pair created a solar-powered water heater. During the summers, he did work in his school's electronics lab, counting his teacher, John Micsinszki, as an early mentor. Micsinszki inspired Lazaridis' business, once telling his student that whoever puts together wireless and computer technology will be important.

After graduation, Lazaridis entered the University of Waterloo in Ontario, where he studied electrical engineering. He paid for his first year of school with the profits he earned from an improved buzzer system he created for his high school. Though Lazaridis took school seriously, he left a month before graduation in 1984. He had a contract with General Motors (GM) lined up that was worth $600,000, and could not go to school and complete the project at the same time. His parents gave him the money to start a company so he could fulfill the contract. With his childhood friend Fregin, Lazaridis founded RIM. The pair completed the project for GM, which involved creating a display system for LED signs at General Motors factories which could scroll messages.

In 1987, RIM landed a contract that changed the course of their company. Rogers Cantel Mobile Communications hired RIM to look at the possibilities of wireless digital networks. This contract led to the company designing wireless local area networks. By the early 1990s, Lazaridis realized that he needed to find someone to handle the business side of RIM because he knew engineering was his specialty. That is when Jim Balsillie stepped in to run RIM.

Balsillie was born in 1961 in Seaforth, Ontario, Canada, the son of Raymond and Laurel Balsillie. His father worked as an electronics technician for Ontario Hydro. From an early age, Balsillie was interested in business as well as athletics. By the time he was a teenager, he held numerous summer jobs such as camp manager, trailer park maintenance man, and manager of a painting company which hired students. During winters, he worked at a ski hill. He also held a number of paper routes.

Scholarships allowed Balsillie to enter the University of Toronto's Trinity College, where he studied commerce. He graduated in 1984, and spent the next three years working at Clarkson Gordon for their Entrepreneur Services Group. Balsillie then entered Harvard's business school in 1987. While a student, he held several jobs on campus, including editor of the student handbook. Balsillie graduated in 1989 with his M.B.A., and later earned his Ph.D. from Wilfrid Laurier University.

When Balsillie completed his M.B.A., he chose to take a job at Sutherland and Schultz in Kitchener, Ontario, though he could have had a higher-paying, higher-profile job on Wall Street. Sutherland and Schultz was a small technology company that created a ground-breaking product which allowed computers to be linked. Balsillie chose to work there so he could learn everything abut running a company. He was originally named the vice president of finance, before being promoted to executive vice president and chief financial officer. Balsillie spent three years learning much about business, including how to deal with a patent suit when Sutherland and Schultz took on Rockwell International Corp.

Balsillie's job at Sutherland and Schultz ended when the company was sold and he was replaced. Balsillie had previously met Lazaridis when the latter did some contract work for Sutherland and Schultz. Balsillie joined RIM in 1992, and believed in Lazaridis' vision, even though RIM was lacking in funds. Balsillie put up much of his own money and even mortgaged his home. They first worked in a small office with just one employee, Mike Barnstijn.

At RIM, Lazaridis and Balsillie shared duties. Lazaridis focused on the creative side: research and development, product strategy, and manufacturing. Balsillie focused on finance, the development of the business, and the strategy of the company. As Balsillie told Erin Anderssen of the *Globe and the Mail*, "My job is to get the money. Mike's job is to spend it."

By the early 1990s, Lazaridis was already working on his idea to bring together the technology of pagers and computers to make a device for exchanging e-mails over a wireless network. He decided to use Internet standards, which later helped with his device's popularity. He also developed other wireless products like interactive pagers, wireless modems for laptop computers, and wireless terminals for credit card and debit card purchases.

Lazaridis also created other significant devices for RIM's clients. In the early 1990s, under a contract RIM won from the National Film Board of Canada, he worked on technology that proved to be important in film, the DigiSync Film KeyKode reader. This piece of equipment automated the process of putting together film negatives. Bar codes were printed on the film's edges, and Lazaridis' product was a high speed bar code reader. The device cut down dramatically on the time it took for a film editor to do the work, and became used on a widespread basis in the film industry. His creation of the DigiSync Film KeyKode reader earned Lazaridis an Emmy Award and an Academy Award. Though not a particularly financially lucrative invention, the reader brought prestige to RIM and put the company in the news.

By 1996, Lazaridis had created a predecessor to the BlackBerry, the rather large Interactive Pager. A year later, the same year that RIM went public, he put down the idea for the BlackBerry itself. One night, working in his basement, Lazaridis typed up a "white paper" (a document espousing the benefits of particular technologies and products) entitled "Success Lies in Paradox" and e-mailed it to his office. In the paper, he explored the idea that a small keyboard could be just as efficient as a large one. He saw that thumbs could be used to type on a tiny keyboard. Lazaridis then created a handheld device which could produce and send e-mail simply on a small keyboard and securely over a wireless network. The device would always been on. It also had an address book, memo pad, and calculator. Originally, the BlackBerry was used by RIM's employees as the company's engineers figured out how to keep the amount of power the device needed on the small side while ensuring a large capacity.

The original BlackBerry was launched in 1999, and was an instant hit with corporations who could now reach their employees anywhere. Stockbrokers and celebrities were early fans of the device. Lazaridis and RIM continued to improve the BlackBerry over the years. By 2001, it could also be used as a cellular telephone and had voice capabilities. A year later, the BlackBerry had hands-free capabilities as well. Such improvements only added to its popularity. RIM sold BlackBerries to corporate clients and often created custom packages for software, servers, and airtime. Within a few years, BlackBerries were being used in many countries around the world.

The success of the BlackBerry made Balsillie and Lazaridis rich men. They used their wealth for a number of philanthropic causes. Lazaridis donated at least $100 million for programs to encourage educational research in the Waterloo, Ontario, region. In 2000, he used some of the wealth he accumulated to found the Perimeter Institute for Theoretical Physics, which focused on cutting-edge scientific research in experimental physics. Lazaridis wanted to make it the largest such physics institution in the world. He loved physics and was intrigued by its possibilities. A physicist at the institute, Ray Laflamme, told Erin Anderssen of the *Globe and Mail,* "His curiosity is beyond bounds. He wants to know the little details of how things work and the big pictures of where things are going. And he wants to connect the dots in between."

Lazaridis also funded the Institute for Quantum Computing at the University of Waterloo. At both the Perimeter Institute for Theoretical Physics and the Institute for Quantum Computing, he wanted to contribute to future technical innovations. To support such research, Lazaridis wanted to get the best professors and researchers at both places. Michele Mosca, the deputy director of the Institute for Quantum Computing, told Kevin McLaughlin of CRN, "What you quickly realize about Mike's philanthropic efforts is that he's trying to give back to the research community because he realizes that much of RIM's success has been built on the scientific discoveries of 50 to 100 years ago."

Balsillie also used his wealth from RIM to support research. In 2002, he donated $17 to $20 million to found the Centre for International Governance Innovation. This is a research institute which seeks to affect the structure of international governance, particularly economic and financial institutions. His interest in international affairs and public policy also extended to hosting international conferences like one on United Nations reform. Balsillie also founded a website, the International Governance Leadership Organizations Online, for public policy groups to discuss their research.

BlackBerries continued to make both men wealthy in the early 2000s. By 2005, there were more than three million BlackBerry users and the company had a market value of $14.3 billion. Yet RIM was facing legal difficulties that had the potential to affect its long-term viability. In 2001, a lawsuit was filed in the United States, where RIM did about 70 percent of its business. RIM was sued by NTP, Inc., a patent-holding firm based in Virginia, for patent infringement. RIM lost the initial rounds in court and refused to settle with NTP for several years. By

May of 2005, RIM finally agreed to pay NTP $450 million to end the legal battle. A month later, the deal fell apart and NTP threatened to enforce a court order which would shut down all BlackBerries in the United States. In March of 2006, an agreement was reached in which RIM paid NTP $612.5 million.

In addition to other potential lawsuits, RIM faced increasing competition for BlackBerries and other products they produced, but Lazaridis and Balsillie remained committed to their vision and continued innovation. Mark Guibert, the vice president of corporate marketing for Rim told McLaughlin of CRN, "Mike has a passion for excellence that is driven by a deep understanding of science and engineering and grounded by his own pragmatism. He wants RIM designing products for the real world—it can't just sound good on paper." Balsillie believed no matter what happened, RIM would keep going. He told David Paddon of the *Toronto Sun*, "We carry on anyway. One way or another, our services are staying running. One way or another, we're going to keep selling and growing."

Sources

Books

Contemporary Canadian Biographies, Thomson Gale, 2002.

Periodicals

BusinessWeek, April 19, 2004, p. 55; November 7, 2005, p. 52.
BusinessWeek Online, September 15, 2005.

CA Magazine, March 1997, p. 6.
Canadian Corporate News, April 24, 2006.
Financial Times (London, England), August 12, 2005, p. 11.
Globe and Mail (Toronto, Canada), June 29, 2002, p. 1.
InformationWeek, March 13, 2006.
Ottawa Citizen, February 14, 2002, p. B2; May 5, 2005, p. F1; December 20, 2005, p. D3.
Toronto Star, February 22, 2004, p. C1.
Toronto Sun, December 24, 2005, p. 58.

Online

"BlackBerry co-creator a national icon," CNN.com, http://www.cnn.com/2005/TECH/ptech/10/24/blackberry.bounty.ap/index.html (October 25, 2005).
"Executive Biographies," Research in Motion—News, http://www.rim.net/news/kit/media/bios/index.shtml (May 1, 2006).
"Jim Balsillie," *GlobeandMail.com*, http://www.theglobeandmail.com/servlet/story/RTGAM.20060221.gtrbalsillie20-;rimspec/BNStory/RIM2006/home/?pageRequested=all (May 1, 2006).
"Michael Lazaridis, Research in Motion," CRN, http://www.crn.com/sections/special/reports/hof.jhtml?ArticleID=174907165 (May 1, 2006).
"Research in Motion," *Businessweek.com*, http://www.businessweek.com/it100/2005/executive/RIMM.htm (May 1, 2006)

—A. Petruso

Bremen Public Library

Traian Băsescu

© Brooks Kraft/Corbis

President of Romania

Born November 4, 1951, in Basarabi, Romania; married Maria. *Education:* Graduated from the Navy Institute of Constan'''a, 1976.

Addresses: *Office*—Palatul Cotroceni, Strada Geniului nr. 1-3, Sector 5—Bucuresti, Romania 060116.

Career

Merchant marine officer, Navrom, 1976-81; oil tanker captain, Navrom, 1981-87; headed the Navrom office in Antwerp, Belgium, 1987-89; general manager of the State Inspectorate for the Civil Navigation within the Romanian Ministry of Transportation, 1989-90; Undersecretary of State, Chief of the Shipping Department within the Ministry of Transportation, 1990-91; elected to Romanian parliament on the Democratic Party ticket, 1992; transportation minister, 1991-92, and 1996-2000; elected mayor of Bucharest, 2000; elected president of Romania on the Alian'''a DA slate, December, 2004.

Sidelights

In a surprising turn of political events, Traian Băsescu became president of Romania in December of 2004. Romanians and international observers alike declared his victory a sign of the genuine end of Romania's communist era some 15 years after what turned out to be its merely symbolic finish back in 1989. While the Eastern European nation's human-rights record had improved considerably in the interim, the political life in this nation of 23 million continued to be dominated by the former Communists, who led new political parties. Băsescu rose to prominence as an opponent of the corruption and cronyism of that post-Communist aftermath.

Born in November of 1951, Băsescu spent his earliest years in a village called Basarabi, not far from Constan'''a, Romania's Black Sea port. He graduated from the Navy Institute of Constan'''a in 1976, and joined Navrom, the state-owned shipping company, as a merchant marine officer. Romania during the first four decades of Băsescu's life was a tightly controlled socialist state under longtime president Nicolae Ceauşescu, in power since 1965. The Romanian Communist Party (PCR) dominated life in the country, which enjoyed a relatively high standard of living until the 1980s, when Ceauşescu's grandiose building projects resulted in drastic food rationing rules and fuel shortages.

Băsescu joined the PCR, a move essential for any career advancement in Romania during the Ceauşescu era. He spent five years as an officer, and in 1981 was made captain of an oil tanker, the *Birun'''a*, that was the largest vessel in the Romanian fleet. In 1987, he was posted to Antwerp, Belgium, to run Navrom's foreign office in this North Sea-linked port city. He remained there until 1989, the same year that the Ceauşescu regime came to a violent but relatively swift end: in December of that year, the army fired on protesters in Timişoara, and Ceauşescu condemned the uprising as the work of foreign agents. A planned pro-Ceauşescu demonstration in Bucharest quickly erupted into an anti-government one; the military and Securitate (secret police) abandoned Ceauşescu, who was executed with his wife after a sham trial on Christmas Day.

A new political organization, the Frontul Salvării Na¨ionale (National Salvation Front, or FSN), arose to fill the power vacuum, and Băsescu soon joined it. During that first year, he held a management position in the Romanian Ministry of Transportation, and in 1990 was named undersecretary of state in the Ministry's shipping department. In 1992, the FSN split in two, and one of the parties that came out of its ashes was the Social Democratic Party (PSD) of Romania. The PSD was led by Ion Iliescu, a high-ranking Communist official who had fallen out with the Ceauşescu regime some years earlier. Băsescu joined the other party that emerged from the split, the Democratic Party (PD) of Romania. In 1991 he became the country's Minister of Transportation, but it was a time when Romania was busy selling off its merchant fleet, and there were charges that Băsescu may have personally benefited from the sales he helped to arrange. He served in the cabinet until 1992, but was elected to Romania's parliament that same year.

The *Dosarul Flota* (Fleet Affair) became an increasingly prominent story in Romania's press in the mid-1990s, and an official investigation began. Băsescu took the unusual step of formally renouncing his parliamentary immunity in 1996. This meant that he could be fully investigated for his former role as Minister of Transportation, and was a clear effort to vindicate his name before the public. He was the first member of Romania's parliament ever to renounce his immunity. Re-elected that same year, he was named Minister for Transportation once again, a cabinet post he held for the next four years. In 2000, he entered the Bucharest mayor's race, and won by a narrow margin. He went on to achieve a number of notable reforms within the capital city, and improve the standard of living for its two million residents over the next four years. One of the city's more bizarre problems was a large stray-dog population that was estimated to be at least 150,000 and perhaps as high as 300,000 when he took office; some 1,500 dog bites were reported daily. Băsescu enacted strong measures to reduce the population, but animal-rights activists, including 1950s French film star Brigitte Bardot, objected; he dismissed their complaints with the retort, "I am elected by the people of Bucharest, not the dogs," according to *Times* correspondent Adam LeBor.

Băsescu was elected his party's president in 2001, and two years later was instrumental in forming the *Alian¨a DA* (Justice and Truth Alliance) with another of Romania's political parties to oppose the PSD, which had been in power for much of the post-Communist era but was largely made up of former Communist elites. In 2004, he became the presidential candidate on the Alian¨a DA ticket, and ran a campaign that urged voters to oust the former Communists. In the run-up to the election, Băsescu lagged in opinion polls, and his opponent Adrian Năstase—PSD leader as well as incumbent prime minister—took the first round of balloting. International observers, however, found multiple instances of vote fraud. A second round of voting was held on December 12 and judged by the monitors to have been more fairly conducted, and Băsescu won the presidency.

With his victory at the polls, Băsescu became the leader of the country's first genuinely truly non-Communist government since the World War II era. During his first months in office, he enacted a new flat tax in an attempt to curb Romania's thriving black-market economy, and met with British Prime Minister Tony Blair and U.S. President George W. Bush. With Romania scheduled to become a member of the European Union (EU) in 2007, there were several drastic reforms—some in the realm of justice and human rights, others economic—that the country would have to enact before formal entry into the EU, but Băsescu reassured Romanians and the rest of the world that he was ready to lead. "I've been the sea captain of large oil tankers," a *Newsweek International* report from Andrei Postelnicu and Michael Meyer quoted him as saying, "and I always reach my destination."

Sources

Periodicals

BusinessWeek, December 17, 2001, p. 4.
Guardian (London, England), December 14, 2004, p. 13; December 15, 2004, p. 16.
New Statesman, January 31, 2005, p. 11.
Newsweek International, March 21, 2005, p. 20.
Times (London, England), December 14, 2004, p. 26.

Online

"Biography: Traian Băsescu," President of Romania, http://www.presidency.ro/?_RID=htm&id= 4&lang=en (October 12, 2005).

—*Carol Brennan*

Deborah Bedford

Author

Born June 12, 1958, in Fort Worth, TX; daughter of Calvin and Tommie Pigg; married Jack Bedford, 1982; children: Jeff, Avery. *Education:* Texas A&M University, B.A.

Addresses: *Publisher*—Warner Books, 1271 Avenue of the Americas, New York, NY 10020. *Website*—http://www.deborahbedfordbooks.com.

Career

Editor for *Evergreen Today,* a weekly newspaper in Evergreen, CO, early 1980s; worked for ad agency in Colorado, 1982-84; began writing fiction, 1984; published first novel, *Touch the Sky,* 1985; first inspirational story, the novella "The Hair Ribbons," published in the collection *The Story Jar,* 2001; first inspirational novel, *A Rose by the Door,* published by Warner Faith, 2001.

Awards: Reviewer's Choice Award, *Romantic Times,* for *Touch the Sky,* c. 1985; Colorado Romance Writers' Award of Excellence; Wyoming Writers' Milestone Award.

Sidelights

Deborah Bedford, author of more than a dozen novels, is "a star in the burgeoning Christian fiction genre," according to *People*'s Sue Corbett. Accolades like that are especially striking, since Bedford set out on a dramatic mid-career change at the end of the 1990s that left her without a publisher for three years. After 12 years as a successful romance writer, Bedford decided her relationship with God called her to write inspirational Christian fiction. Since 2001, her novels have focused on characters who find forgiveness and renewal when they face up to painful experiences and decisions.

Bedford was born in Fort Worth, Texas, and grew up in Richardson, Texas. During college, she channeled her dreams of being a writer into a journalism degree. After college, Bedford's first job was with a small newspaper in Evergreen, Colorado, where she worked as the editor, writing, reporting, laying out pages, and even distributing the paper. She and her husband, Jack, married in 1982, and Bedford took a job at an ad agency in Colorado. In 1984, she began to write fiction, mostly late at night and early in the morning. A year later, Harlequin, a leading publisher of romance novels, accepted her book *Touch the Sky,* about a woman who goes to a ranch to grieve after her airplane pilot husband dies in a crash, and meets a cowboy with whom she falls in love. The book set a new sales record for a Harlequin author's first book and won a reviewer's choice award from *Romantic Times.*

She wrote for Harlequin until 1993, producing about one romance novel a year as well as *Blessing,* a historical novel. She signed with HarperCollins Publishers, wrote four more books, and appeared on the *USA Today* best-seller list. Some of her books reflected her faith by mentioning God and Jesus. But, like many romance novels, her work included sex scenes with unmarried characters, a fact that came to trouble her.

A turning point in Bedford's career came when a biblical allegory in a sermon by her minister convinced her that books with premarital sex scenes in them did not serve God and that she had compromised her religious beliefs for success as a romance novelist. She decided she wanted to write inspirational, Christian romances from then on. She left her publisher and her agent and sent out new manuscripts to Christian publishers, but at first her search did not go well; she went three years without publishing a new book. She says she looked at the difficulties as God testing her convictions, so she lived off her credit cards for a while.

Eventually, her perseverance paid off. One of her new stories, "The Hair Ribbons," was published in 2001 in Multnomah Press' *The Story Jar*, a collection of three novellas about motherhood accompanied by letters and anecdotes from other authors. Bedford read from the story at the Jackson Hole Writer's Conference (a gathering she co-founded) and described her decision to move from mass-market fiction to Christian fiction. In the audience was Jamie Raab, publisher of Warner Books, who invited Bedford to become an author for the company's new imprint of Christian books, Warner Faith. Her first book for Warner, *A Rose by the Door*, was released in November of 2001. "It's wonderful writing for Warner," Bedford told Sarah Sawyer, a writer for *Today's Christian*. "So many of the letters I've gotten say, 'This is the first Christian book I have ever read and I want to read more like it.' And I'm getting so many letters, maybe ten times as many as I got before."

The new novels Bedford wrote confronted difficult topics. In 2001's *A Rose by the Door*, for instance, the main character is a woman who prays for her son to come home, only to find out he has died. The protagonist of her next book, 2002's *A Morning Like This*, discovers that her husband has had an affair and secretly fathered a child. *When You Believe*, published in 2003, tells the story of a high school counselor who is in love with a teacher, and then hears from a student that the teacher abused her. "All of my earlier career, I had thought that writing for the Lord would mean that I had to put parameters around my stories," she told an interviewer for the website Focus on Fiction. "Almost from the first page of writing, I realized how wrong I had been about that. In the market today, anything goes as long as it's handled right."

In 2004, Bedford published *If I Had You*, which dealt with the issue of abortion. "I'm not a preacher," she told a conference of booksellers, according to Sawyer of *Today's Christian*. "I'm not a speaker, but I wrote this book because I had an abortion and I want to share how God healed me." In the book, Nora, a mother, convinces her daughter, Tess, to bring her pregnancy to term. Nora is hard on Tess, but eventually confronts her own long-denied secret, which had hurt her for years.

Bedford's determination to write redemptive stories seems inspired by her own past and her spiritual journey. "I grew up in Texas, in a town where everybody talked about Jesus," she said in her interview with Focus on Fiction. "If something went wrong with someone, people lived under a strange code of silence.... I grew up believing that everyone had to stay 'good' all the time and if you slipped a little then, well, you might as well fall all the way." That is exactly what she did in her early college years, she told the Focus on Fiction interviewer, so that when she became a mother and a regular church-goer again, she spent a long time feeling she "had a lot to make up for." But then she had a religious awakening, when she prayed to God to tell her directly how to believe in Him, instead of hearing about Him from others. Her decision to switch to Christian fiction came soon after.

Bedford's next book, *Remember Me*, told the story of Sam Tibbits, a middle-aged minister who, facing burnout after a death in his family, takes a sabbatical and returns to the place in the Pacific Northwest where he spent his summers as a child, and he runs into the woman he was in love with as a teenager, who disappeared before he could propose marriage to her. *Publishers Weekly* called the novel "a multilayered, rewarding read" and praised Tibbits' character as "beautifully drawn."

In 2005, Bedford was busily acquiring the rights to her older books and rewriting them, or redeeming them, as she put it, replacing the premarital sex scenes with different plot points. First to be republished, in 2004, was her 1992 Harlequin romance *Just Between Us*, followed by her 1993 historical novel *Blessing* the next year, both published this time by Harlequin's new Christian publishing house, Steeple Hill Books. But for Bedford, replacing sex with God did not mean getting rid of romance. The reason "we're fascinated with secular romance," Bedford asserted in the Focus on Fiction interview, is that "God physiologically designed us to be drawn to a romance with Him."

Selected writings

Touch the Sky, Harlequin Superromance, 1985.
A Distant Promise, Harlequin Superromance, 1986.
To Weave Tomorrow, Harlequin Superromance, 1989.
Passages, Harlequin, 1990.
Just Between Us, Harlequin, 1992; Steeple Hill Books, 2004.

After the Promise, Harlequin Superromance, 1993.

Blessing, Harlequin Historical, 1993; Steeple Hill Books, 2005.

A Child's Promise, HarperCollins, 1995.

Chickadee, HarperTorch, 1995.

Timberline, HarperCollins, 1996.

Harvest Dance, HarperCollins, 1997.

"The Hair Ribbons," published in *The Story Jar,* Multnomah Press, 2001.

A Rose by the Door, Warner Faith, 2001.

A Morning Like This, Warner Faith, 2002.

When You Believe, Warner Faith, 2003.

If I Had You, Warner Faith, 2004.

Remember Me, Warner Faith, 2005.

Sources

Periodicals

People, November 21, 2005, p. 57.

Publishers Weekly, August 29, 2005, p. 32.

Today's Christian, May/June 2005.

Online

"Biography," Deborah Bedford, http://www.deborahbedfordbooks.com/bedford_bio.html (March 4, 2006).

"Deborah Bedford," FaithfulReader.com, http://www.faithfulreader.com/authors/au-bedford-deborah.asp (March 4, 2006).

"Deborah Bedford interview," Focus on Fiction, http://www.focusonfiction.net/deborahbedford.html (March 4, 2006).

"Deborah Bedford: 1958," American Collection Educators, http://www.ncteamericancollection.org/litmap/bedford_deborah_wy.htm (March 5, 2006).

"*When You Believe* by Deborah Bedford," Powells.com, http://www.powells.com/cgi-bin/biblio?inkey=17-0446690414-0 (March 4, 2006).

—*Erick Trickey*

Gail Berman

AP/Wide World Photos

President of Paramount Studios

Born c. 1957, in Bellmore, NY; married Bill Masters (a television scriptwriter); children: two. *Education:* University of Maryland, theater degree, 1978.

Addresses: *Home*—Pacific Palisades, CA. *Office*—Paramount Pictures, 5555 Melrose Ave., Hollywood, CA 90038.

Career

Play producer, beginning 1978; supervising producer, then executive producer, The Comedy Channel, c. late 1980s-early 1990s; executive producer, Sandollar, *All-American Girl, Buffy The Vampire Slayer,* and *Angel;* founding president, executive producer, Regency Television, 1998-2000; president of entertainment division, FOX Broadcasting Network, 2000-05; president, Paramount Studios, 2005—.

Awards: Ranked at number 25 on *Fortune* magazine's "50 Most Powerful Women in American Business" list, 2003; Lucy Award, Women in Film, 2003; ranked number 49 on *Forbes* magazine's "100 Most Powerful Women in the World" list, 2004.

Sidelights

Gail Berman has led the life of which many people dream. After seeing a production of *Joseph And The Amazing Technicolor Dreamcoat,* she and a partner decided to bring the show to Washington,

D.C. Having no experience in producing plays, the partners hounded a financier until he helped them. The show was a success, and soon moved to Broadway. Years later, she was given the chance to work for a new cable channel, The Comedy Channel, though she had zero experience in television. This foot in the door, however, soon led her to Hollywood and the opportunity to work on such shows as *Buffy the Vampire Slayer,* its spin-off *Angel,* and *All-American Girl.* Her rising star was noticed by the FOX Network, and she was hired as the president of entertainment. She turned the struggling network around, and then stepped up to motion pictures by agreeing to run Paramount Studios.

Berman was born in the late 1950s in the city of Bellmore on Long Island, New York. She grew up in this small suburb which is an hour away from Manhattan. Very little is known about her childhood, but she did graduate from the University of Maryland in 1978, where she majored in theater.

Berman saw a production of *Joseph And The Amazing Technicolor Dreamcoat* in Maryland and together with classmate Susan Rose decided to bring the show to Washington, D.C. They aggressively pursued the producer of the show, Robert Stigwood. He agreed to sell them the rights to the show. They began to raise the money, "like Girl Scouts selling cookies," Berman told Bernard Weinraub in the *New York Times*, and were helped along by Washington businessman Melvyn J. Estrin. *Joseph And The Amazing Technicolor Dreamcoat* was slated for a six-week run. Six weeks turned into nine months. The partners soon moved the production to New York. After spending two months Off Broadway, the show ran for two and a half years at the Royale Theater on Broadway. The production also received seven Tony Award nominations during its run.

Berman went on to produce a few more plays, including *Hurlyburly*, before deciding to change directions. She was offered a supervising producer position on a new cable channel launched by HBO Networks, The Comedy Channel, which would later become Comedy Central. She was promoted to executive producer. "I didn't know anything about television.... But I did know how to read a script. I did know how to work with writers. I did know how to work with production people. And what I learned eventually was that producing is the same, in whatever medium," Berman told Weinraub in the *New York Times*.

Berman's husband is scriptwriter Bill Masters, who worked on such shows as *Murphy Brown* and *Seinfeld*. His work called for him to spend his time on the West Coast. The couple decided to move to Los Angeles, and Berman found employment with production company Sandollar, which was co-owned by singer Dolly Parton. She produced several shows, including *All-American Girl*, *Buffy the Vampire Slayer*, and *Angel*. She worked for Sandollar for more than six years before leaving. However, she stayed on as executive producer of both *Buffy* and *Angel*. She worked with the Regency company which later became Regency Television, a joint venture between Regency and FOX Television Studios. Berman was named founding president, and the new company created such hits as *Malcolm in the Middle* and *The Bernie Mac Show*.

Those two shows both aired on the FOX Network. With her proven track record of producing hit shows, Berman was tapped to head the entertainment division at FOX. Sandy Grushow, chairman of FOX Television Entertainment, told *Electronic Media* that Berman has "an innate ability to create programming that taps into what appeals to younger viewers.... Simply put, Gail has her finger on very contemporary sensibilities and that is echoed by her involvement in *Buffy* and *Malcolm*." Berman had a great challenge ahead of her. Though FOX had many hits under its belt since it first aired in 1987, including *21 Jump Street*, *Married ... With Children*,

Beverly Hills 90210, *The X-Files*, and *Ally McBeal*, by 2000 many of its hits were either no longer on the air or in decline. FOX also had jumped on the reality show bandwagon, and produced a large number of controversial shows, including *Who Wants to Marry a Millionaire?*, *Married By America*, and *When Animals Attack*. The network continually lost in the ratings, and also failed to reach its target audience of viewers aged 18-34 who were coveted by advertisers who purchased airtime. Without its target audience, FOX could not get top dollar for its airtime.

Berman, the seventh president in eight years, helped the company climb out of the muck and mire it found itself in by choosing shows, both scripted and unscripted, that were innovative and "pushe[d] the envelope," she told *Electronic Media*. In addition to looking to Regency Television for programs, Berman was instrumental in bringing to the FOX family such shows as *American Idol*, which won its time slot since it began airing. It was also number one in its targeted audience of viewers aged 18-34. *American Idol* also saw the return of female viewers to FOX. Other shows that garnered high ratings included *Titus*, *Temptation Island*, and *24*.

With *American Idol*, which began as a summer show in 2002, Berman began to develop a style of programming that changed the way networks would do business. Normally all the networks would air first-run episodes of their shows in the fall, with a few shows beginning in January or February as midseason replacements. While reality shows could be aired at any time due to the ease of putting together this style of show, none of the networks aired first-run scripted shows or even introduced new scripted shows during the summer. Berman and her team, however, began pursuing introducing new programming year-round, especially since the network was always behind due to baseball's World Series, which aired on FOX, and the 2004 Summer Olympics which pre-empted all new programming on all of the networks since it would draw the most ratings. In 2003, FOX began airing episodes of a new dramedy, *The O.C.*, in early August. The show was a hit among young viewers, especially in the targeted audience age range and among women.

With the success of *The O.C.*, and *American Idol* continually staying atop the ratings charts, Berman prepped for the first full year of new programming, which began in June of 2004. Thanks to this creative strategy, FOX consistently won the top spot ratings for a handful of its shows, both new and returning. The summer of 2005 saw a couple of new hits that happened as the result of her tenure at FOX.

As her contract with FOX came to an end, Berman began talks with Paramount Studios to become president of the fledgling company. She was offered a contract, and she began a new era in the spring of 2005. Many were critical of her hiring, but she told *Daily Variety*, "I recognize that there is some skepticism so I come into this with a great deal of humility. The bottom line is going to be fostering an environment where creative ideas will transfer into great films." Before stepping down as FOX's president, Berman helped the network unveil its upcoming season. She also took some time to introduce herself to Paramount employees and partners. Upon completion of this task, she began to work in earnest to return Paramount to its ranking as one of the top studios, a place the company had lost. She began seeking scripts that went against the norm. Berman also struck deals with various writers, producers, and production companies, something that Paramount had been reluctant to do in the past. The studio also wanted to chase after films with bankable stars, and release more films in a year.

While Paramount's slump seemed to be ending with the previous regime's slate of films in the summer of 2005, no one can discredit what Berman will do for the studio during her time there. Paramount Studio chairman Brad Grey told *Daily Variety*, "Gail is one of the most respected and talented executives in the entertainment industry.... She brings to the studio the best of all the skills she has developed over the years and I'm sure she will be as success-

ful in this transition as others before her have been." It is likely that Berman will face this new challenge with the same tenacity she has utilized in both the theater and television.

Sources

Books

Marquis Who's Who, Marquis Who's Who, 2005.

Periodicals

Broadcasting & Cable, January 19, 2004, p. 6A.
Daily Variety, March 28, 2005, p. 2; March 31, 2005, p. 1.
Electronic Media, May 29, 2000, p. 2.
Mediaweek, April 12, 2004, p. 26.
New York Times, July 24, 2000, p. B1.

Online

"Paramount taps Berman to run studio," CNN Money, http://money.cnn.com/2005/03/30/news/fortune500/paramount_berman.reut/index.htm (March 31, 2005).

—*Ashyia N. Henderson*

Dorrit J. Bern

Photo courtesy of Dorrit Bern

Chief Executive Officer of Charming Shoppes

Born c. 1950; married Steve Bern (a business consultant); children: Chad, Collier, Tyler. *Education:* University of Washington, B.S. (business), 1972.

Addresses: *Home*—Barrington, IL. *Office*—Charming Shoppes, 450 Winks Lane, Bensalem, PA 19020.

Career

Buyer for The Bon Marché and Joske's, both divisions of the now-defunct Allied Department Stores, 1970s; divisional vice president of misses/junior sportswear, dresses, outerwear, petite and large size sportswear and dresses and maternity, Sears, Roebuck & Co., 1987; group vice president of Women's Apparel and Home Fashions, Sears, Roebuck & Co., 1993; vice chairman of the board, Charming Shoppes, 1995-97; CEO, president, Charming Shoppes, 1995—; chairman of the board, Charming Shoppes, 1997—.

Member: Fashion Group International; America's Women Business Leaders Committee of 200; board of directors, Southern Co.

Awards: Pennsylvania's Best 50 Women in Business Award, 1997; Women of Distinction Award from the *Philadelphia Business Journal*, National Association of Women's Business Owners and Forum for Executive Women, 1998; Greater Philadelphia Ernst & Young Entrepreneur of the Year Award, 2001; Moore College of Art and Design Visionary Woman Award, 2004; Intimate Apparel Square Club HUG (Help Us Give) Award, 2005; Greater Philadelphia Chamber of Commerce Paradigm Award, 2006.

Sidelights

When Dorrit J. Bern took over Charming Shoppes in 1995, the retailer, which operated the nationwide Fashion Bug stores, was hemorrhaging money to the tune of $100 million per year. "This company was so desperate—just a moment away from bankruptcy—that it wasn't anything that anyone else wanted," Bern acknowledged to *Chain Store Age.* Bern welcomed the challenge and after a massive restructuring returned the retailer to profitability in two years' time. Realizing the growing market for plus-size fashions, Bern then used the company's healthy balance sheets to purchase plus-size competitors Lane Bryant and Catherine's Plus Sizes, turning Charming Shoppes into the nation's leading plus-size retailer with 40 percent of the market share. Revenues, which stood at $1 billion in 1995, hit $3 billion in 2005.

A native of Spokane, Washington, Bern was born in the early 1950s and was named after the Dorrit family from the Charles Dickens novel *Little Dorrit.*

Bern's mother worked for the retail clothing chain Grayson-Robinson's. On Sunday afternoons, while her mother did the payroll, Bern entertained herself by re-arranging the store displays. Bern's mother also spent time as a buyer for The Bon Marché, Seattle's oldest and largest department store. She took Bern along on business trips to New York's garment center. "When other people went to summer camp, I went to Seventh Avenue with my mother on market trips," Bern recalled to the *Seattle Times'* Sylvia Wieland Nogaki.

In 1972, Bern earned a business degree from the University of Washington, then worked as an assistant golf pro at a country club for a while before following in her mother's footsteps and becoming a buyer for The Bon Marché and its sister company, Dallas-based Joske's. In 1987, Sears, Roebuck & Co., looking to revamp its fledgling women's fashion division, lured Bern aboard and made her a divisional vice president overseeing women's wear. Known for its Craftsman tools and DieHard batteries, Sears had a hard time luring women into its stores. To remedy the situation, Sears launched the "Softer Side of Sears" campaign in the early 1990s; Bern played a key role in the campaign's success, ultimately turning Sears into a player in the women's retail market. By 1993, Bern was group vice president of Women's Apparel and Home Fashions.

Bern's work impressed top executives at the fledgling Charming Shoppes. The company offered Bern its chief executive officer position in a deal that included a million-dollar annual salary, stock options, and a million-dollar signing bonus. Bern said no because she did not want to relocate her family—her three sons and husband were thriving in the Chicago area. Eventually, Charming Shoppes struck a deal allowing Bern to commute from the family home in Barrington, Illinois, to its Bensalem, Pennsylvania, headquarters. Charming Shoppes agreed to pay her weekly airfare and pay for an apartment for use during the workweek. "It was a job made in heaven," Bern quipped to *Wall Street Journal Online* reporter Joann S. Lublin. "All I had to do was save the company."

In August of 1995, Bern began her pre-dawn Monday morning flights to Charming Shoppes headquarters. She replaced most of the company's top management, then fiddled with the manufacturing process. To keep costs down, Fashion Bug used overseas factories but the lag time between order placement and delivery meant that the merchandise was often out of style by the time it arrived and did not sell without markdowns. Bern turned to domestic manufacturers for the newest, hippest items because of their faster turnaround time. Bern also shuttered hundreds of the retailer's stores, laying off about 2,500 people—nearly one-third of its workforce.

Bern's bold moves put the company on solid ground by 1997 and Bern began looking toward the future. Realizing that plus-size fashions brought in the most revenue at Fashion Bug, Bern decided to expand that niche and acquired the Modern Woman chain in 1999. In 2000, Charming Shoppes bought Catherine's Plus Sizes and in 2001 it purchased Lane Bryant, the premier plus-size shop. These acquisitions gave Charming Shoppes a powerful hold on the plus-size market. In 2003, Charming Shoppes launched *Figure,* a magazine for plus-size women. In 2005, the company acquired Crosstown Traders Inc., a catalog operation that sells apparel, shoes, and gifts. The acquisitions positioned Charming Shoppes as a three-channel business, selling its merchandise in stores, on e-commerce sites, and through catalogs. Analysts expect sales in plus-size clothing to grow five percent a year, and Charming Shoppes is positioned to gobble up more of the market.

When department stores tried to jump on the plus-size bandwagon by offering lines such as Liz Claiborne Woman, Bern remained unfazed. "Our advantage is that we own this woman," Bern told *Forbes'* Mark Tatge. "We aren't like the department store that still buries the plus sizes on the third floor next to the maternity department." Part of Bern's success comes from catering to her customers. Her store walls, decorated with pictures of attractive, plus-size models, are meant to boost customers' self-esteem.

Over the years, Bern's innovations have moved beyond business concerns. Bern launched the Keeping Kids Warm campaign, which, over a ten-year period, gave away some 50,000 new coats to needy kids across the United States. Bern also supports Philadelphia's Working Wardrobe, a non-profit that outfits welfare recipients with workplace attire when they re-enter the job market. Bern also writes a "Speaking Woman to Woman" marketing letter several times a year, which is mailed to customers. The letters deal with women's issues, such as domestic abuse, welfare-to-work and voting. Customers respond by writing back and this has opened up a dialogue between Bern and her clients. Bern receives 3,000 pieces of correspondence a month.

The Greater Philadelphia Chamber of Commerce presented Bern with a 2006 Paradigm Award for her philanthropic efforts. "Dorrit Bern is a positive force in the Greater Philadelphia region," chamber president Mark S. Schweiker said, according to a PR Newswire report. "She has incredible business savvy and also sets a fine example of how business leaders should give back to the community." The award came with a $50,000 gift for her to donate to charity.

Bern, herself, is an anomaly in the business world. She is one of about 20 female CEOs running Fortune 1000 companies. Bern regularly travels to business schools across the United States to encourage women entering the field. Her advice, according to *Chain Store Age:* "Don't be afraid to take the hard jobs that no one else wants." It is advice that has served her well.

Sources

Periodicals

Chain Store Age, December 2001, p. 70.
Forbes, March 18, 2002, pp. 82-84.
Philadelphia Inquirer, August 18, 2005, p. C1.
PR Newswire, December 5, 2005.
Seattle Times, April 12, 1994, p. D1.
Women's Wear Daily, January 9, 2006, p. 8.

Online

"Corporate Governance," Charming Shoppes, http://www.charmingshoppes.com/aboutus/corp/ceo.asp (February 1, 2006).
"Dorrit Bern Turns Retail Operations Around," *Philadelphia Business Journal,* http://www.bizjournals.com/philadelphia/stories/1998/12/07/focus2.html (February 1, 2006).
"How One CEO Juggles A Job and a Family Miles Apart," *Wall Street Journal Online,* http://www.careerjournal.com/columnists/edchoice/19971008-lublin.html (February 1, 2006).

—Lisa Frick

Paul Biya

Martial Trezzini/EPA/Landov

President of Cameroon

Born February 13, 1933, in Mvomeka'a, Cameroon; married Jeanne Atyam, 1960 (divorced); married Chantal, 1994; children: three. *Education:* University of Paris, law and political science, Paris, France, 1960; diplome, Institut d'Etudes Politiques, Paris, 1961; diplome, Institut des Hautes Etudes d'Outre-Mer, 1962; diplome, Etudes Superieures en Droit Public, 1963.

Addresses: *Office*—Office of the President, care of Central Post Office, Yaounde, Cameroon.

Career

Head, Department of Foreign Development Aid, 1962-63; director, Cabinet in Ministry National. Education, 1964-65; member, Goodwill mission to Ghana and Nigeria, 1965; secretary-general, Ministry Education, Youth and Culture, 1965-67; director, Civil Cabinet of Head of State, 1967-68, secretary-general to president, 1968-75, minister of state, 1968-75, prime minister, 1975-82; president, Republic of Cameroon, 1982—.

Member: Union Nat. Camerouaise; decorated chevalier, Order de la Valeur Ccmerounaise; commander, Nat. Order Fed. Republic Germany, Nat. Order Tunisia; Grand-Croix Nat. Order of Merit Senegal; grand officer, Legion of Honor (France).

Sidelights

From a childhood in a small Cameroonian village where he lived in poverty, Paul Biya has raised himself to the head of his country, taking over first the job of prime minister and then in 1982 the role of president of Cameroon. He has held that position ever since, retaining power in a series of elections— every seven years—that were boycotted by some and called fraudulent by others. He is known as a sometimes hard and oppressive leader.

Biya was born on February 13, 1933, in Mvomeka'a, Cameroon, a village in the southern part of the country. He grew up rather poor. When he was seven he was sent to a Catholic mission in Ndem to go to school. While he was studying he excelled and one of his French tutors thought his work was so good that he determined that Biya should become a priest. He was admitted to Edea and Akono Junior Seminaries when he was 14, which were run by the Saint Esprit fathers. He next won a place at the Lycee General Leclerc school in Yaounde, the capital of Cameroon. The Lycee Leclerc is French Cameroon's most prestigious high school. While there Biya studied—among other things—Latin, Greek, and philosophy. Because of his continued good work, Biya was accepted to the University of Paris where he studied law and political science. He obtained his law degree in 1960. He stayed on in France for a couple years after graduation to study public law.

While Biya was in Paris the Republic of Cameroon managed to gain independence. Its population was somewhere between 16 and 17 million. The national languages were English, French, and 24 African language groups. The main religions of the country were Indigenous, Christian, and Muslim. Geographically the country is located between West and Central Africa, between Nigeria, Chad, Central African Republic, Congo, Gabon, and Equatorial Guinea. The nation's economy was based on oil production and refining, food production, light consumer goods, textiles, and lumber. Its chief crops were coffee, cocoa, cotton, rubber, bananas, oilseed, and grains.

Biya returned to Cameroon in 1962 just in time to take part in one of the most important times in Cameroon's history. The country had been split into French and British territories, and was further split into Christian and Muslim areas. In January 1, 1960, the French half of the country won their independence and Ahmadou Ahidjo was named president. The English section won independence on October 1, 1961. Part of that section joined Nigeria and the rest joined with the French zone. When they joined together the country was renamed the Federal Republic of Cameroon. So when Biya returned he was able to join a newly constructing government as part of the Department of Foreign Development Aid, of which he was put in charge. He reported directly to Ahidjo.

The president became Biya's mentor despite the disparities in their pasts and personalities. Under Ahidjo, Biya held several positions including director of the cabinet, secretary general of the presidency, and minister of state—the highest ranking minister in Cameroon's government. He was named prime minister in 1975, a position that made him the legal successor to the presidency. At the same time that Biya was moving up in the government he was advancing in the single party that made up Cameroon's government, the Cameroon National Union (CNU). He proved to be skilled at party politics, a trait that would serve him well later on.

Ahidjo resigned his presidency on November 6, 1982, for health reasons and Biya took over as president. Because he was still the head of the CNU, Ahidjo assumed he would still retain control over the country—because there was only one party, many thought the position as leader of the party (the organization that made policies and laws) was actually more important than president. That was all to change. At first Biya seemed to be deferring to Ahidjo, but then he started to make some changes. When he did this some of the ministers and close

aides refused to follow his lead, preferring to remain loyal to Ahidjo. When he saw this, Biya began to replace them with men loyal to him rather than to Ahidjo. For this and other reasons Biya had a falling out with Ahidjo causing Ahidjo to leave the country, at which time Biya took over his position as party leader as well. After Biya became head of the CNU he abolished it and instead set up the Cameroon People's Democratic Movement (CPDM). It was around this time that some put forth the idea of allowing multiple parties in the country, but Biya would not allow it.

There were two coup attempts in Biya's early days in office, one in August of 1983 and one the following April. When both failed, Biya's power became more palpable and established. Because of Ahidjo's earlier arguments with Biya he was believed to be behind the coup attempts and he was officially accused. Biya's popularity grew, and he won his first real election on January 14, 1984.

The 1980s passed rather well for Biya's new cabinet, but starting in the early 1990s popular discontent started to rise. Because of these complaints, according to *Funk & Wagnalls*, "Biya slowly and reluctantly began to implement political reforms." Even then Biya's reign was not approved of by all his countrymen. He refused to allow any other political parties to work in Cameroon until the mid-1990 elections when, because of increasing demonstrations, he finally gave in and allowed other parties to form and vie for the presidency. The elections were a disaster. Most historians agree that Biya was defeated in the election by John Fru Ndi, but Biya had himself declared the winner and then declared a state of emergency and released troops to fight the massive demonstrations that followed the pronouncement. Loads of Fru Ndj supporters were arrested, and Amnesty International, the human rights organization, documented many instances of illegal arrests, torture, and death at the hands of Cameroonian police.

Fru Ndj and his party boycotted the 1997 elections, refusing to take part in something they called a charade. Biya, they have said, runs an authoritarian government, not a democracy, and many have complained that he only supports and helps members of his own community, the Francophones. Issues between northern Francophones and Southern Anglophones have done nothing but increase since Biya took over the presidency. Biya has been pushing all Anglophones out of office.

Despite internal conflicts, Biya has been working to bring Cameroon into a better financial situation. In 2000 Biya set up a deal with Chad president Idriss

Deby to install a pipeline from Chad to the Cameroon port of Kribi to transport oil. The oil wells were thought to be feasibly ready to distribute by 2005. The World Bank helped fund a small part of the operation, its "first foray into supporting oil production," according to the *New York Times*.

In March of 2003 Biya visited with President George W. Bush at the White House in the United States to discuss trade between the two countries. Cameroon had been attracting more foreign investment and its economy was growing. With an eye to continuing this trend, Biya visited Shanghai, China, in September of 2003 and met with Mayor Han Zheng to discuss strengthening the ties of friendship between Cameroon and Shanghai, and even with the entirety of China. Imports and exports between the two nations had increased by 300% at the beginning of 2003.

Yet things inside Cameroon were still unsettled. "[Biya's] main failing, I believe, was a lack of dynamism, which meant that, too often, there was a disparity between the policies he professed and what actually happened," William Quantrill, British Ambassador from 1991 to 1995, was quoted as having said in the Africa News Service. Biya has become well known for being unwilling to delegate even the smallest of tasks, causing great delays in the resolution of small matters.

In 2004 Biya was again reelected to Cameroon's presidency, although again opposition parties claimed that the elections were rigged. After he was elected he chose a prime minister to help clean up the public sector. Things had gotten a bit slovenly with government employees coming in later and later and many not doing their work at all. The first step was to lock the door at the ministry offices and refuse admittance to anyone who was late. Director of General Administration Johnson Doh Okie told the *New African*, "This is just part of efforts to modernize the Cameroon administration, maintain discipline and order, and ensure that people are punctual. Things will not be the same again. The president has decided there will be a change. The time of recreation is over."

In May of 2005 Biya met with Nigerian President Olusegun Obasanjo in Geneva, Switzerland, to resolve disputes over the Bakassi Peninsula, something that had been going on since the split up of the British section of Cameroon in the 1960s. The meeting was held by the United Nations. Nigeria, in accordance with a 2002 dictate, was supposed to withdraw their troops from the area, but by 2005 they still had not done so. Biya asked the United States to help encourage Nigeria to withdraw from the area (which is rich in oil) by applying pressure on the country since they are one of Nigeria's biggest trading partners.

These were not Biya's only concerns for his new term. Biya's new government was to focus on five points. First, he wanted to modernize the democratic system and fight corruption. Second, he planned on improving the five percent economic growth rate by improving agricultural systems and examining industrial and tourism policies. Third, he wanted to more evenly distribute the growth rate as there were sectors who did not benefit from the growth. Fourth, he wanted to ensure peace and security and better equip law-enforcement agencies so they could more successfully fight crime, insecurity, and terrorism. And fifth, he wanted to improve Cameroon's image internationally.

Unfortunately, Cameroon's citizens in 2005 were still feeling unrest, largely due to the problems between the Francophones and the Anglophones, which Biya has seemed unwilling to fix. He reorganized his entire cabinet when he entered his new term of office in 2005, but rather then give more seating to the underrepresented Anglophones, he gave less. People have expressed a concern that if this continues there will be a civil war. There are other problems in the government as well. According to the Africa News Service, an organization called Transparency International published a report called the Global Corruption Barometer. In 2004 they listed Biya's government as being one of the most corrupt in Africa. They did a study and found that 51 percent of Cameroonians admitted to having paid a bribe at some point in the year previous to the report's release. That was higher than anywhere else in the world.

Biya's private fortune is estimated to be somewhere near $75 million. He also owns two planes, two mansions in Cameroon, and homes in France and Switzerland. Biya has been married twice. His first wife, whom he divorced, died in 1992. He remarried in 1994. Biya has three children. The world looks on eagerly to see Biya implement his new plans for Cameroon to bring the country more firmly into the 21st century.

Sources

Books

Almanac of Famous People, 8th ed., Gale Group, 2003.
Contemporary Black Biography, vol. 28, Gale Group, 2001.
Current Leaders of Nations, Gale Research, 1998.
Encyclopedia of World Biography Supplement, vol. 18, Gale Research, 1998.
Funk & Wagnalls New Encyclopedia, 2005.
World Almanac and Book of Facts, 2005.
Worldmark Encyclopedia of the Nations: World Leaders, Gale, 2003.

Periodicals

Africa News Service, December 9, 2004; December 14, 2004; April 11, 2005; May 9, 2005; May 17, 2005; June 17, 2005.
Independent (London, England), March 20, 2003, p. 6.
New African, March 2005, p. 25.
New York Times, October 19, 2000, p. A15.
Xinhua News Agency, September 25, 2003.

—*Catherine Victoria Donaldson*

Black Eyed Peas

Pop group

Group formed in Los Angeles, CA in 1995; members include apl.de.ap (born Alan Pineda Lindo, November 20, 1974, in the Philippines), rapper, dancer; Fergie (born Stacey Ferguson, March 27, 1975, in Hacienda Heights, CA; joined group, 2001), singer, dancer; Kim Hill (left group, 2001), singer; Taboo (born Jaime Gomez, July 14, 1975, in Los Angeles, CA; children: Joshua), rapper, dancer; will.i.am (born William Adams, March 15, 1975, in Los Angeles, CA), rapper, dancer.

Addresses: *Agent*—William Morris Agency, 1325 Avenue of the Americas, New York, NY 10019. *Record company*—A&M Records, 2220 Colorado Ave., Santa Monica, CA 90404. *Website*—http://www.-blackeyedpeas.com.

John Rogers/Getty Images

Career

Apl.de.ap and will.i.am were members of Tribal Nation and later formed Atban Klann, which signed with Ruthless Records; Taboo joined the group and the named changed to the Black Eyed Peas; Kim Hill joined the group; released debut album, *Behind the Front*, 1998; released *Bridging the Gap*, 2000; Hill was replaced by Fergie, 2001; released *Elephunk*, 2003; released *Monkey Business*, 2005.

Sidelights

The Black Eyed Peas burst onto the music scene in 1998, drawing attention not only for their music, but for their politically and socially conscious lyrics that shied away from the more predominant gangsta sounds of the day, which were laced with violence, drugs, and abuse. They put out a couple of albums before they added a vocalist who seemed to give them just the edge they needed to become very popular. At that time, according to the Sing365 website, they "transcended their vigilant hip-hop roots and have become a global phenomenon, the likes of which the music world has rarely seen." The members of the group are will.i.am, apl.de.ap, Taboo, and Fergie.

Apl.de.ap was born Alan Pineda Lindo on November 20, 1974, in the Philippines. He was raised by adoptive parents in Los Angeles, California. Will.i.am was born William Adams on March 15, 1975, also in Los Angeles. Will.i.am and apl.de.ap met in that city in 1989 when they were in the eighth grade. They became instant friends, discovering a mutual interest in dancing—especially street dancing—and singing. They joined a break-dancing group, Tribal Nation, which was something that would later inform their stage shows after they created the Black Eyed Peas. After high school they formed their own group, Atban Klann. The Atban part of the name stood for A Tribe Beyond a Nation, and was a nod of respect to their starting group Tribal Nation. It was a difficult career to become a success in, but the two friends were determined. Many of their childhood friends who had been involved in music quit the scene for a life of selling drugs instead, but this was something that the duo refused to do. They stayed clear of the drug scene and rather than give up when they did not achieve instant success, steadfastly followed their dreams. They played at different venues around the Los Angeles area and tried to do what all bands do: come to the attention of a record label.

In 1992 Atban Klann had garnered enough attention to get will.i.am and apl.de.ap a record deal with Ruthless Records. They recorded an entire album, but unfortunately it was never released because of problems with marketing. Ruthless Records was accustomed to promoting the more violent gangsta groups and did not know what to do with a more laid-back, peace-loving, break-dancing group. The only person at Ruthless Records who really believed in the group was rapper Eazy-E, the person who had signed them in the first place. Unfortunately for the duo, Eazy-E died of AIDS in 1995 and Atban Klann's hopes were dashed. As soon as the one person who supported them had died, Ruthless Records let the group go.

With their chances of making it with Ruthless Records gone, will.i.am and apl.de.ap decided to start a new band with an additional member, Taboo, whom they had met at a break-dancing club named Ballistics. Taboo was born Jaime Gomez on July 14, 1975, and had been dancing and singing for just as long as will.i.am and apl.de.ap had been. He gladly joined the two friends and together they started the first incarnation of the Black Eyed Peas. The new trio began to play around Los Angeles. As luck would have it, two college students who were interning at different record labels heard the group and brought representatives from their companies back with them to hear the Black Eyed Peas perform. The group was soon invited to sign with Interscope Records in July of 1997.

Looking for a new sound to add to their record, they got singer Kim Hill to perform backup vocals and in 1998 the Black Eyed Peas released their first album, *Behind the Front*. The band consisted of the four front-liners and then four musicians in back playing live. Upon the album's release, the band was compared to the Roots, another hip-hop group that used live musicians rather than recorded tracks and synthesizers. The Black Eyed Peas preferred to do their music live, and it was this live sound that gave the group a more spontaneous and fresh sound that listeners appreciated. After the release of their first album, the band toured for almost two years, basking in popularity. What with their unique sound and their refreshingly clean and thought-provoking lyrics, the Black Eyed Peas were a welcome change in the rap and hip-hop worlds. Will.i.am spoke with Lorraine Ali of *Newsweek* about their lyrics: "The challenge was how to make feel-good albums with substance, but not come off like we were preaching. Nobody wants to be jamming at a party and be preached to. It's a real fine line between 'Oh, wow! Did you hear that?' And 'This guy needs to shut up.'" The group somehow managed to straddle that line successfully and the huge audiences at their performances showed that violence was not the only way to sell rap and hip-hop music.

In 2000 the Black Eyed Peas released their second album, *Bridging the Gap*, so named because the group felt they were bridging the gap between rock and hip-hop. "The album melds hip-hop, trip-hop, and jungle influences on a flowing, twitching release that may be one of the better urban releases of the year," stated Erin Brosha on the CanEHdian website. Macy Gray was one of several guest artists to join the group on the CD.

In 2001 Hill left the Black Eyed Peas and the band had to find itself another singer. The trio happened upon Fergie, born Stacey Ferguson, and not long after Hill left the band, Fergie filled the space. She had been a former cast member of the television program *Kids Incorporated* and a member of the teen-pop band Wild Orchid, so she had the experience the band wanted, plus a look and feel that seemed to blend well with the Black Eyed Peas. She admitted to being extremely nervous at first because she was taking the place of someone that fans had accepted and loved, but she put her best foot forward and threw herself into helping the Black Eyed Peas become an even better band than they already were.

Fergie need not have worried: She was an instant success, as was the band's third album, 2003's *Elephunk*. This album was not only successful, it made it to number one on *Billboard*'s Top 40 list. The record went gold in September of that year. Critics and audiences alike put part of the album's success down to Fergie having joined the group. She was seen as having added the depth of her vocals to the band's already hip sound. Also on this album, the band continued to bring in outside stars to perform with them. Unlike other hip-hop groups, the Black Eyed Peas were not afraid to team up with decidedly un-hip-hop stars. For instance, the song "Where is the Love," which made it to number one on the charts, was recorded with pop star Justin Timberlake. Not only did the inclusion of other artists add a different and interesting dynamic to some of the band's songs, but it also helped expand their fanbase.

The Black Eyed Peas went on tour with Timberlake and fellow pop star Christina Aguilera, spreading their music even further. The band was nominated for their first *Billboard* award for *Elephunk*, winning the Mainstream Top 40 Track of the Year for "Where is the Love." They were also nominated for four Grammy Awards, including Record of the Year for "Where is the Love." The song topped the U.S. Top 100 at #8, and went all the way to #1 in the United Kingdom where it also became the best-selling single of 2003. The group sold 7.5 million albums around the world. The Sing365 website said of *El-*

ephunk: "the album ... heralded a new sound for the modern age—one that is inspired by hip-hop, eschews boundaries and inhibitions, and cuts across ages, races, and backgrounds." It seemed like the Black Eyed Peas and their songs were everywhere. An alternate version of one of their tracks became the theme song for the NBA Finals.

Monkey Business, the band's fourth album, was recorded while the group was on tour for *Elephunk*. This album was like a piece of therapy for the band and helped connect the four of them together like never before. It was the first album the quartet wrote and designed together, something that was reflected in the deeper, more mature and thought-provoking songs. Timberlake reappeared on the album with the song "My Style." Singers Sting, Jack Johnson, and James Brown also contributed to the album. The song "Don't Phunk With My Heart" made it to #3 on the *Billboard* Hot 100, the highest any of their songs has gone in the United States to date. The album itself debuted at #2 on the *Billboard* chart.

In 2005 the Black Eyed Peas won the Grammy Award for Best Rap Performance for "Let's Get It Started." When talking about their success, will.i.am told the Black Eyed Peas Official Web Site, "I think the fact that we just have fun with music is the reason why it works for us. We love music and melodies and don't try to distinguish ourselves from regular music fans. It's really that simple."

Outside of music the members of the Black Eyes Peas are involved with many projects. In 2004, during the Black Eyed Peas' concert tour in Asia, apl.de.ap's life story was made into a television dramatic special called *Do You Think You Can Remember?*, which took a look at his childhood with his poor family in the Philippines and his eventual adoption and move to the United States. Plus, he was working on an album that features rapping in both Tagalog and English. Fergie was working on her own solo album, which had been in the works before she joined the group. Taboo started a martial arts and break-dancing after-school program in Los Angeles and worked on his solo album, which mixed Spanish and English rap with reggaeton. Will.i.am was involved with designing a clothing line and producing albums for other artists. After the 2004 tsunami disaster in Asia, he organized a relief benefit and went to areas in Malaysia to help rebuild homes. The socially conscious band did not just spout words about how to make the world a better place, they tried to help make it one. It is expected that the trend will continue and that fans, hungry for music minus the violence, will eagerly snap it up.

Selected discography

Behind the Front, Interscope, 1998.
Bridging the Gap, Interscope, 2000.
Elephunk, A&M, 2003.
Monkey Business, A&M, 2005.

Sources

Books

Contemporary Musicians, vol. 45, Gale Group, 2004.

Periodicals

Crain's Detroit Business, September 26, 2005, p. 46.
Entertainment Weekly, November 22, 2002, p. 74; June 27, 2003, p. 138; May 27, 2005, p. 22, p. 44; June 3, 2005, p. 81; October 7, 2005.
InStyle, August 1, 2005, p. 202.
Interview, July 2005, p. 40.
Keyboard, October 1, 2005, p. 30.
Newsweek, May 16, 2005, p. 66.
People, July 14, 2003, p. 39; June 27, 2005, p. 154.

Teen People, September 1, 2004, p. 159; June 3, 2005, p. 42.
Variety, February 5, 2001, p. 47.

Online

"Biography," Black Eyed Peas Official Web Site, http://www.blackeyedpeas.com (November 24, 2005).
"Black Eyed Peas," AOL Music, http://music.aol.com-artist-main.adp?tab=bio&artistid=302855&albumid=0 (November 24, 2005).
"Black Eyed Peas," VH1.com, http://www.vh1.com-artists-az-black_eyed_peas-bio.jhtml.pdf (November 24, 2005).
"Black Eyed Peas Biography," CanEHdian, http://www.canehdian.com-non-artists-b-black eyedpeas-biography.html.pdf (November 24, 2005).
"Black Eyed Peas Biography," Sing365.com, http://www.sing365.com-music-lyric.nsf-Black-Eyed-Peas-Biography-6747F9726428AE2748256A17000 B4062 (November 24, 2005).

—Catherine Victoria Donaldson

John A. Boehner

Joe Marquette/Bloomberg News/Landov

U.S. House Majority Leader

Born November 17, 1949, in Cincinnati, OH; married Debbie Gunlack; children: Lindsay, Tricia. *Education:* Xavier University, B.S., 1977.

Addresses: *Home*—West Chester, OH. *Office*—1011 Longworth House Office Building, Washington, DC 20515-3508.

Career

Worked at his family's business, Andy's Cafè, as a minor, and as a janitor at Xavier University in Cincinnati, OH; joined Nucite Sales in the 1970s, becoming part-owner and then president; elected township trustee in Union, OH, 1982; won a seat in the Ohio House of Representatives, 1984, and reelected in 1986 and 1988; elected to the House of Representatives from Ohio's Eighth Congressional District, 1990, and reelected every two years; chaired the House Republican Conference, 1995-99; named chair of the House Committee on Education and the Workforce House, 2000; Majority Leader, 2006—.

Sidelights

John A. Boehner won a tight race to become Majority Leader in the U.S. House of Representatives in early 2006. The Ohio Republican succeeded his ousted House colleague, Tom DeLay, as holder of one of the most powerful positions in Washington.

Born in 1949 in Cincinnati, Ohio, Boehner—whose surname is pronounced "bay-ner"—grew up in the suburb of Reading. His father ran a bar in Cincinnati, Andy's Cafe, that he had inherited from his own father. Like his eleven siblings, Boehner began working at the bar at an early age, mopping floors when he was still in elementary school. He attended Archbishop Moeller High School in Cincinnati, an all-male Roman Catholic academy whose football teams consistently dominated regional athletics. Boehner played football for the Crusaders and went on to Xavier University, another Roman Catholic institution in Cincinnati, and became the first in his family to enter college.

Midway through his college career, Boehner enlisted in the U.S. Navy during the height of the Vietnam War. "The people with long hair who were protesting against the war I thought were un-American at the time," he recalled in an interview with Weston Kosova in the *New Republic.* He never saw combat duty, however, after aggravating a back problem dating back to his high school football years. Discharged after six weeks, he returned to Ohio to complete his education.

Boehner worked several jobs in order to put himself through Xavier, including one as a campus janitor. By the time he graduated in 1977, he had become part-owner of Nucite Sales, a manufacturers' representative firm that served the packaging and plastics industry. Boehner eventually became president of Nucite, and his professional advancement coincided with a switch in political allegiances. He had been raised in a staunchly Democratic family, but became a Republican in the late 1970s when he realized he had just paid more in taxes on his annual earnings for his first full-time, post-collegiate job than he had grossed for the 1976 tax year.

In 1982, Boehner ran for and won his first political office, as a township trustee in Union, Ohio, which later became West Chester Township. Two years later, he was elected to the state house of representatives, and won re-election for two additional two-year terms. In 1990, he made a bid for Congress as a representative of the Eighth District of Ohio after a sex scandal tarnished the Republican incumbent. Despite being heavily outspent by a second, more experienced challenger in the Republican primary, Boehner won the first race, and bested his Democratic opponent that November by a wide margin.

Boehner emerged as one of the most prominent freshman House members in Washington that first year. He teamed with several other new Republican lawmakers to launch an ethics crusade against some House veterans. Boehner and the others, who became known as the Gang of Seven, made national headlines for calling attention to abuses involving the House Bank. The scandal resulted in felony charges for some of the 350 lawmakers involved, 77 of whom either resigned or did not run for reelection. Many of those singled out were Democrats, the party that had enjoyed a majority in the House of Representatives since 1954.

Boehner had a powerful mentor in the House in Georgia's Newt Gingrich, and was involved in drafting the GOP's "Contract With America," the set of legislative and policy goals presented in time for the 1994 Congressional elections. Democratic control of the House ended with that election, which became known as the "Republican Revolution." House Republicans elected Gingrich the new Speaker of the House. Boehner was chosen to serve as chair of the House Republican Conference in 1995, an influential caucus of GOP lawmakers.

Three years later, GOP lost five seats in the House, and Gingrich was blamed for the debacle. He resigned his seat, and though some speculated that Boehner might resign from office as well after being replaced as House Republican Conference chair, he remained on the job. In 2000, he was made chair of the House Committee on Education and the Workforce, and a year later newly elected President George W. Bush selected him to shepherd the No Child Left Behind bill through Congress. The education bill passed, and as a show of gratitude Bush formally signed it into law in early 2002 while visiting Hamilton, Ohio, in Boehner's district. Voters there had consistently reelected him to Congress by large margins every two years, with the 2004 results tallying 195,000 for Boehner and just 87,000 for his Democratic challenger.

Boehner reemerged on the national political scene early in 2006, when Representative Tom DeLay of Texas announced he would resign from his seat and his post as House Majority Leader because of the criminal indictments he was facing for violating campaign finance laws. The Majority Leader title is the second most powerful one in the chamber, after Speaker of the House, and its holder is integral in setting the legislative agenda for the annual session. Boehner put his name in for election, and lost in the first round of voting to Missouri's Roy Blunt. The votes were split three ways, however, and a run-off contest took place on February 1, which Boehner won by a count of 122-109.

After the scandal that had ended DeLay's political career, the GOP's opponents countered that the selection of Boehner by House Republicans signaled an unwillingness to reform, for Boehner was known to have extensive ties to tobacco political-action-committees and lobbyists for student-loan providers. The Democratic National Committee chair, Howard Dean, joked that "with Boehner in power, lobbyists won't have to wait in the lobby anymore, because they'll have their own back door into the majority leader's office," according to *Plain Dealer* journalist Sabrina Eaton.

Boehner is father to two daughters with his wife, Debbie, whom he met in college. An avid golfer, he is known in the Beltway for the annual beach-themed party he hosts. Despite the warnings from Democratic lawmakers, Boehner assured his district and the nation that his party was committed to ethics-reform issues in Congress. "The elected representatives of Congress must always be respectful of the public's right to know," he wrote in an editorial for *USA Today* in April of 2006, "and attentive to the guidelines governing public officials' conduct."

Sources

Christian Science Monitor, February 6, 2006, p. 3.
Cincinnati Post, January 27, 2006, p. A1.
New Republic, February 20, 1995, p. 22.

Plain Dealer (Cleveland, OH), February 3, 2006,
  p. A1.
USA Today, April 25, 2006, p. 12A.

—*Carol Brennan*

Jonathan Borofsky

Sculptor

Born in 1942, in Boston, MA; son of Sydney (a musician and music teacher) and Frances (an architect, artist, and gallery owner) Borofsky; married Francine Bisson (a teacher). *Education:* Carnegie Mellon University, B.F.A. 1964; studied at the Ecole de Fontainebleau, France, 1964; Yale School of Art and Architecture, M.F.A., 1966.

Addresses: *Agent*—Paula Cooper Gallery, 155 Wooster St., New York, New York 10012-3159. *Home*—Ogunquit, ME.

Career

Independent artist, 1966—. Teacher, School of Visual Arts, New York, 1969-77, and California Institute of the Arts, Valencia, 1977-80.

Sidelights

Jonathan Borofsky's oversized sculptures are a prominent feature of many European cities, but the American artist came to wider attention in his native country only with a well-received temporary installation at New York City's Rockefeller Center in the fall of 2004. His immense *Walking to the Sky,* a steel pole featuring a series of life-like figures striding up it, was viewed by some as an unofficial tribute to the victims of 9/11. It was part of a series that had been replicated elsewhere, and while Borofsky was heartened by the response, he asserted that he simply wanted the piece to represent all humankind. "These are human beings around the world; they represent all kinds of humanity," he explained to Carol Vogel in the *New York Times.* "They are not New Yorkers, not Americans. This piece can stand anywhere—Africa, India, Hawaii."

Born in Boston, Massachusetts, in 1942, Borofsky grew up in Newton, Massachusetts. His father was known for his storytelling talents, and as a child Borofsky's favorite was about a giant who lived in the sky, which would later inspire his *Walking to the Sky* series. Borofsky was drawn to art at an early age and was moved by certain images he encountered back then. One of these works was from French post-Impressionist painter Paul Gauguin, an 1897 painting titled "Where Do We Come From? What Are We? Where Are We Going?". The piece hung in the Boston Museum of Fine Arts, and as Borofsky recalled in the interview with Vogel, "I remember being very affected by that title," he told the *New York Times.* "It seemed so philosophical and psychological. I started thinking: 'This is what art can do. It can ask questions or it can answer them.'"

Borofsky went on to study art at Carnegie-Mellon University in Pittsburgh, spent time in France after graduating in 1964, and then earned his graduate art degree from the Yale School of Art and Architecture in 1966. He spent the next eleven years in New York City, laying the foundation for his artistic career, but seemed diverted for a time by a fascination with numbers. "I ended up in my studio a lot, thinking a lot, writing thoughts down," he told Ann Curran in *Carnegie Mellon Magazine.* "Less making of things and more thinking about things. I looked for a way to simplify the thought processes. I began to do little ... number sequences on paper almost as a way to pass the time and not have to think so deeply."

Borofsky wrote down numbers in his studio for three hours a day for a period between 1968 and 1969. Occasionally, he came up with an idea for something to draw, and sketched it out next to the number he was on. When he drew that image on its own, he signed it with the number instead of his name. He eventually amassed a stack of paper with numbers on it that was nearly three feet tall and reached the figure 2,346,502. His first major show in New York City, "Counting," featured this stack and the related drawings. By the late 1970s, he was showing regularly at the Paula Cooper Gallery in New York but had moved out of the city and settled in Maine.

The next phase of Borofsky's artistic output was inspired by his dreams, which he began to write down with the same fervent dedication he had earlier given to numbers. He started working on larger-than-life three-dimensional pieces in the mid-1980s, and his works were commissioned by civic cultural committees in several European cities. His immense *Hammering Man,* a silhouetted figure with a moving arm that stood as high as many buildings, was a series that he replicated for permanent public installations in Frankfurt, Germany; Basel, Switzerland; Seoul, South Korea; and Seattle and Dallas in the United States. Its stark simplicity was Borofsky's homage to what he considered the worker in every human being.

Borofsky's first *Walking to the Sky* piece was installed in 1992 at the prestigious European contemporary art event, Documenta, held every five years in Kassel, Germany. It featured an 80-foot steel pole and a lone figure striding up it. A similar work, this one with a woman, was installed two years later in Strasbourg, France. The figures were cast with a special foam into fiberglass, and they harkened back to his father's stories about the giant in the sky. "What was unique about this giant is that he did good things for people," Borofsky explained to Vogel in the *New York Times* interview. "We'd visit him in the sky and discuss what good things we could do down on earth. That got me thinking: 'How do you go to the sky? How do you get up there?'"

The nonprofit organization known as the Public Art Fund commissioned Borofsky to install a *Walking to the Sky* in its regular art space at the plaza within Rockefeller Center, a major-media headquarters hub as well as a favorite tourist destination in New York City. It was the first outdoor work of Borofsky's ever to appear in the city, and it was a hit with the public. This time, he put two more figures at the base, a man and a small boy, and included some steps near the concrete base so that visitors could climb it. Even the tabloid daily newspapers weighed in with approving remarks. The *New York Post* asserted that "There's something so disconcertingly strange about the spectacle played around the flagpole … that the work sears itself into your memory."

Art critics have not always been kind to Borofsky's works, the artist told Curran in *Carnegie Mellon Magazine.* Oftentimes, he noted, "this person has totally not got a clue as to what I'm doing. I mean I barely have a clue," he said. "So they're hurting me, they're hurting art; that's the worst thing. People care so little about art these days anyhow. If you can't write something nice, don't write anything at all. People walk away with an angry attitude toward art because they don't get it."

Sources

Books

Contemporary Artists, 5th ed., St. James Press, 2001.

Periodicals

Carnegie Mellon Magazine, Spring 2002.
Nation, February 2, 1985, p. 121.
New York Post, September 18, 2004, p. 26.
New York Times, September 13, 2004, p. E1.
People, October 4, 2004, p. 139.

Online

Jonathan Borofsky Website, http://www.borofsky.com/info.htm (April 21, 2006).

—*Carol Brennan*

Kate Bosworth

AP Images

Actress

Born Catherine Bosworth, January 2, 1983, in Los Angeles, CA; daughter of Hal (a business executive) and Patti Bosworth.

Addresses: *Agent*—c/o United Talent Agency, 9560 Wilshire Blvd., Ste. 500, Beverly Hills, CA 90212.

Career

Actress in films, including: *The Horse Whisperer*, 1998; *The Newcomers*, 2000; *Remember the Titans*, 2000; *Blue Crush*, 2002; *The Rules of Attraction*, 2002; *Wonderland*, 2003; *Advantage Hart*, 2003; *Win a Date with Tad Hamilton!*, 2004; *Beyond the Sea*, 2004; *Bee Season*, 2005; *Superman Returns*, 2006; *Seasons of Dust*, 2006. Television appearances include: *Young Americans*, The WB, 2000. Spokesperson for Revlon Cosmetics, 2004—.

Awards: Young Hollywood Award for next generation—female, 2003.

Sidelights

Blond, petite actress Kate Bosworth made her mark in a number of films, including her breakout role in the surfer girl hit *Blue Crush* and a lead in *Win a Date with Tad Hamilton!*. Acting had not been a particular interest of young Bosworth until she won a role in *The Horse Whisperer* because of her equestrian skills. After the experience, she became committed to acting as a career and deliberately chose to vary her roles so that she would never work in the same genre in back-to-back films. Of her potential in Hollywood, the director of *Win a Date*, Robert Luketic, told Allison Hope Weiner of *Entertainment Weekly*, "Kate Bosworth is a movie star in every sense of the word. There is something incredibly paper-thin about some of these Next Big Things, but Kate has the talent to back the fame up."

Born in 1983 in Los Angeles, Bosworth is the only child of Hal and Patti Bosworth. Her father worked as a fashion retailing executive for companies such as Ermenigildo Zegna and Talbots. Because of her father's career, she moved regularly throughout her childhood. When she was six years old, the family moved to San Francisco. In this period, Bosworth began singing at county fairs in the state of California. She also began competing in equestrian events and was a champion for many years. At the age of nine, Bosworth moved with her family to Connecticut. She already had a passing interest in acting, appearing in a community theater production of *Annie*.

When Bosworth was in eighth grade, she filmed her debut role in *The Horse Whisperer*. Bosworth applied for the role in an unusual fashion: she brought a photo from a family Christmas card instead of a standard headshot. For the film, casting directors were looking for a young girl who had experience with horses. Because her equestrian abilities, she was cast as Judith, the friend of the character played by Scarlett Johansson. Judith is killed in the first few scenes of the movie, and her horse-related death prompts the need for the title character, played by Robert Redford. Though Bosworth had only a small role, she found a new calling. She told Cindy Pearlman of the *Chicago Sun-Times*, "One of the biggest highs is when I did that role because I fell in love with acting. It was almost like when you meet that person you want to be with for the rest of your life. You're like, 'This is it. This is where I belong.'"

Bosworth did not immediately pursue an acting career after the 1998 release of *The Horse Whisperer*. Her family moved to Cohasset, Massachusetts, a suburb of Boston, after the film was shot. Bosworth decided to focus on school and family, and to complete her education at the local public school she had been attending. She also continued to compete as an equestrian as well as play soccer. When Bosworth was 15 years old, she began auditioning again, but was selective in what roles she would accept. School and a normal life remained important. When she was a senior in high school, for example, she was cast in her first leading role in an independent film. However, because the producers would not agree to let her go to her prom and graduation, she declined the role.

While still in high school, Bosworth did take on a few parts. She had a role in the short-lived television series *Young Americans*, set primarily at a fictional New England prep school, Rawley Academy. Bosworth played Bella Banks, a local girl who works at a gas station near campus. Bella becomes involved with a rich student at the academy, Scout. Though most of the cast was supposed to be high school age, she was the only cast member actually still in high school. *Young Americans* did not catch on with audiences; it only lasted one summer on the WB network.

Young Americans was one of the few television roles Bosworth would take in her young career. She focused primarily on film, though most of her roles remained small. She played Courtney Docherty in 2000's *The Newcomers*, a children's film. A more high profile role that same year came in *Remember the Titans*, a movie about a newly racially integrated high school football team. Set in 1971, *Remember the Titans* starred Denzel Washington as a football coach.

As her film career was developing, Bosworth graduated from Cohasset High School and was accepted to Princeton University. However, Bosworth took a deferred enrollment. As her acting career took off, Bosworth repeatedly stated her intention to go to school there. She was assured by Princeton that she would have a place there whenever she was ready to enter. Bosworth returned to the city of her birth, Los Angeles, to more fully pursue acting.

Within a few years, Bosworth was being cast in leading roles in Hollywood films. Her breakthrough role came in 2002's *Blue Crush*, directed by John Stockwell. Bosworth played Anne Marie Chadwick, a talented surfer with the skills to become a world-class champion. However, Anne Marie faces difficulties reaching her potential as a surfer related to a previous injurious accident and a problematic personal life. Her mother has abandoned Bosworth's Anne Marie, leaving her to support both herself and her younger sister. She works as a maid in a hotel, where she meets and becomes involved with a professional football player named Matt. Over the course of the film, Anne Marie conquers her fears and successfully competes in the Pipeline Masters competition.

When Bosworth first read the script for *Blue Crush*, she was certain she could play Anne Marie. She learned surfing basics just to audition. Despite what she considered poor casting sessions, she was given the role. She and the actresses who played her friends underwent intense training to hone surfing skills and develop the bodies of surfers. Bosworth told Susan Wloszczyna of *USA Today*, "At the height of training in Hawaii, I got pretty good. I was in 20-foot waves, and when you're thrown into a situation where you either deal with it or suffer consequences, you learn quickly." The shoot proved slightly hazardous for Bosworth who was knocked out for a short amount of time when a heavy surfboard hit her in the head. The pain aside, *Blue Crush* was a minor hit in the summer of 2002.

Bosworth's next two roles were supporting efforts in very different films. In 2002, she appeared in *The Rules of Attraction*, a film version of the novel by Bret Easton Ellis. It was directed and adapted by Roger Avary. Set in the 1980s, the plot explored the sex lives of college students. The film co-starred James Van Der Beek and Jessica Biel. Bosworth played a love interest of Van Der Beek's character. Bosworth's next film also took place in the 1980s. In 2003's *Wonderland*, Bosworth played Dawn Schiller, the teenaged girlfriend of John Holmes, played by Val Kilmer. The film was based on actual events in 1981 in which Holmes, a pornography industry insider, played a peripheral role in the Wonderland murders in Los Angeles. Both parties involved with the actual murders sold drugs to Holmes, who was arrested for the murder of one drug trafficker. Bosworth's Dawn was a drug addict living in Holmes' home with him and his Christian wife. Bosworth lost most of the muscle she gained for *Blue Crush* for this role.

Reviewing *Wonderland* in the *Toronto Sun*, Jim Slotek was dismissive of the part of the film related to Holmes and his personal life, but not Bosworth's performance. Slotek wrote, "The standout in the Holmes half of the tale is Kate Bosworth…. Tormented and stupidly faithful, it's the sort of character that actresses are obliged to learn how to play, and Bosworth carries it off with a touching innocence that suggests reserves of still-untapped talent."

For Bosworth's next two major film roles, she played characters far removed from Dawn Schiller. In 2004, she had a leading role in *Win a Date with Tad Hamilton!*. Bosworth played Rosalee Futch, a naive, big-hearted girl from small town America. In an interview with Evan Henderson of the *Houston Chronicle*, the actress explained her approach for developing the character. She told him, "What I tried to do is take all of my best qualities and eliminate the bad ones, to take the qualities I admire in other people and roll it all up in one person. She sees the best in people, really wanting to see the good in situations. That's her sweet naiveté and innocence. She's just kind of a kindhearted soul." Rosalee works as a grocery store clerk in Fraziers Bottom, West Virginia, when she wins a date with the title character, a famous movie actor. The contest was created to improve the bad-boy image of Tad, played by Josh Duhamel. After their date, the actor follows Rosalee home and competes for her affections with one of her best friends, Pete Monash, played by Topher Grace, who has had a long-time crush on her. (Coincidentally, Bosworth and Grace were acquainted as children, from the years she lived in Connecticut, where he spent his childhood.)

The same year *Win a Date with Tad Hamilton!* was released, Bosworth played a real icon in *Beyond the Sea*. Bosworth portrayed actress Sandra Dee, who was a star in the late 1950s and early 1960s, in the biopic about singer Bobby Darin, whom Dee married. Darin was played by Kevin Spacey, who also directed the film. Spacey had been working on getting the project off the ground for 12 years. Darin was a star whose career dimmed and whose alcoholism contributed to a tragic end, death due to heart failure in 1973. *Beyond the Sea* focuses on the sometimes troubled marriage between Dee and Darin. Though the film was a box office and critical flop, Spacey was sure from the first that Bosworth was the perfect Dee. He told Jane Stevenson of the *Toronto Sun*, "I met her at dinner. I never saw her work. And I cast her. I just knew. She had all the qualities I needed…. The chemistry just worked instantly and she was incredibly enthusiastic about it and I just looked at her and thought 'She could be America's Sweetheart.'"

Bosworth continued to take interesting roles in the early 2000s. After *Beyond the Sea*, Bosworth played Chali, a follower of Hare Krishna, in 2005's *Bee Season*. Her next major role had the potential to be a blockbuster. She was cast as Lois Lane in the 2006 release of the next *Superman* movie. In addition to her acting career, Bosworth also received a significant amount of press attention for her on-again, off-again relationship with British actor Orlando Bloom.

Bosworth continued to be careful about the roles she chose as an actress. She told Paul Fischer of *Sunday Herald Sun*, "I would never take a role for the money. I just think that is probably a bad way to go and I just listen to a combination of my heart and my mind." Yet acting was not her whole life. She continued to ride horses as a hobby and greatly enjoyed reading. Bosworth wanted to study literature or psychology when she was ready to go to college. Education remained important to her, though she kept deferring her enrollment at Princeton. Bosworth told Bruce Kirkland of the *Toronto Sun*, "I'm totally in love with what I do but [acting is] not the only thing that fulfils me. I mean, I'd love to be enriched by going to [college] and having that experience in learning. It's a great life experience."

Sources

Books

Celebrity Biographies, BASELINE II, Inc., 2005.

Periodicals

Boston Globe, July 12, 2000, p. C4; January 23, 2004, p. C1; December 31, 2004, p. C1.
Boston Herald, July 9, 2000, p. 53; August 13, 2002, p. 43.
Business Wire, August 13, 2004.
Chicago Sun-Times, January 18, 2004, p. 4; January 30, 2004, p. 24.
Courier Mail (Queensland, Australia), June 17, 2005, p. 3.
Entertainment Weekly, August 1, 2003, pp. 34-35.
Houston Chronicle, January 31, 2004, p. 9.

InStyle, October 1, 2003, p. 335.

Ottawa Citizen, August 12, 2002, p. D3.

Seattle Times, August 16, 2002, p. H19.

Sunday Herald Sun (Melbourne, Australia), December 8, 2002, p. 98.

Toronto Star, August 16, 2002, p. D3.

Toronto Sun, August 11, 2002, p. S14; August 13, 2002, p. 35; October 24, 2003, p. E5; January 18, 2004, p. S25; January 9, 2005, p. S14.

USA Today, August 15, 2002, p. 3D.

Vogue, November 2004, p. 247.

Online

"Kate Bosworth," Internet Movie Database, http://www.imdb.com/name/nm0098378/ (January 24, 2006).

—A. Petruso

Francois Bozize

AP Images

President of the Central African Republic

Born in 1946 in Gabon; children: Francois, Jr. *Education:* Attended a college for military officers in Bouar in the Central African Republic, early 1970s.

Addresses: *Office*—Presidence de la Republique, Bangui, Central African Republic.

Career

Named a brigadier general, 1978; became defense minister, 1979; became information and culture minister, 1981; ran unsuccessfully for president, 1991; appointed army chief, 1996; fired and left the country, 2001; unsuccessfully attacked Central African capital, Bangui, 2002; overthrew president and took control of the country, 2003; called elections and announced he would run for the presidency, 2004; won presidential election, 2005.

Sidelights

Francois Bozize, president of the Central African Republic starting in 2003, rose to prominence early. Appointed a general at age 32, he served in two governments in the late 1970s and early 1980s before going into exile after a failed coup. Imprisoned and tortured under a military dictatorship, he was released and rejoined his country's politics after its return to civilian rule in 1991 and became chief of the Central African armed forces in 1996. During an economic crisis, he organized a revolt against the country's president, and took over in a coup in 2003. He proved to be more popular than

the predecessor he removed; he called presidential elections, which he won in 2005. A profile of Bozize by Lucy Jones of BBC News described him as a "short, pot-bellied general" who was "widely respected for being a simple man" who "could often be seen chugging around Bangui in a battered ... car waving to people he knew."

Bozize was born in Gabon, a country southwest of the Central African Republic (CAR), where his father was a policeman. His family was from the Bossangoa region in the northwest corner of the CAR. He went to school for military officers in Bouar, distinguished himself early, and became a captain before he turned 30. The CAR's dictator, Jean-Bedel Bokassa, named him a brigadier general in 1978.

When ex-president David Dacko overthrew Bokassa in 1979, he named Bozize defense minister. The next president, Andre Kolingba, who overthrew Dacko in 1981, made Bozize the information and culture minister as part of his effort to have several ethnic groups represented in the government. However, Bozize left the country in 1982 after Ange-Felix Patasse attempted to overthrow Kolingba. Bozize announced the news of the coup attempt in a radio broadcast so confusing it was not clear which side he was on. While living in exile in various African countries, Bozize developed a friendship with Patasse, who later became president. Bozize was accused of being part of the coup attempt, was arrested in Benin and extradited to the CAR in 1989, and was tortured while in prison, but a court acquitted him in 1991. When Kolingba's dictatorship ended, Bozize ran for president, but lost to Patasse. Still, Patasse named him chief of the army in 1996, and Bozize helped defend the government against mutinies by unpaid soldiers in 1996 and 1997. Patasse was reelected in 1999.

In May of 2001, Patasse survived a coup attempt. Some suspected Bozize of being involved in it. A commission formed to investigate the rebellion summoned him to answer questions, but he would not. He was fired in October, but when government troops tried to arrest him in November, five days of violence broke out. Bozize fled to Chad, north of the CAR, with about 300 people loyal to him. In October of 2002, Bozize's forces attacked the CAR's capital, Bangui, but Patasse's forces pushed them back into the northern part of the country with the help of troops from Libya (which Patasse had promised a monopoly on extracting diamonds from the CAR) and a Congolese rebel force.

By the time Bozize pushed toward the capital city of Bangui again in March of 2003, at a time when Patasse was out of the country at a summit in Niger, the CAR was in an economic crisis that had made the president very unpopular. The government had been unable to pay the army or civil workers for months. The Congolese rebels that had helped Patasse keep power had raped women and stolen from people across the country. When Bozize's forces, which only numbered about 1,000, reached the capital on March 15, they met little resistance, and some CAR residents danced in the streets. However, members of Bozize's forces and allied troops from Chad were also accused of rape and looting on a smaller scale. Patasse attempted to fly back to Bangui, but his plane was shot at when it tried to land, so he went into exile in Togo.

When Bozize took power, he declared that he would restore democracy and not run for president in the next election. "I came to save my people. My mission ends here," he said, as quoted by IRIN, a news service run by the United Nations. The Bozize government created a national human rights commission, though some members of the military resisted its work by preventing it from talking to prisoners. A one-month national dialogue in September of 2003 resulted in a call for a constitution that split power between the president and a prime minister,

as well as apologies from former leaders such as Kolingba and members of Patasse's party for past mistakes and violence. In November of 2004, the government passed a new law ensuring freedom of the press, abolishing prison terms for libel and slander. Since then, newspapers in the CAR have criticized the government, but the country's radio and TV stations are state-owned and do not often cover the opposition, except for one station sponsored by the United Nations.

Bozize set up an electoral commission to oversee the transition back to democracy. Voters ratified a new constitution in December of 2004, and Bozize set up elections for March and May of 2005. Despite his earlier pledge, Bozize announced he would run in the presidential election. "In my capacity as a soldier, I'm serving my people," he announced at a political rally in Bangui in December, according to IRIN. "When I'm called I have no choice but to obey."

In May of 2005, Bozize won the presidency with 64 percent of the vote in the second round, beating former prime minister Martin Ziguele. His supporters won 42 out of 105 seats in the legislature. Foreign observers pronounced the elections fair, though the British magazine the *Economist* disagreed, saying there had been intimidation and ballot-stuffing.

As 2005 drew to a close and the country's years-long financial crisis dragged on, pressure on Bozize mounted. Corruption, rampant under Patasse, was reportedly still a serious problem, and the country was close to broke. Civil servants, still waiting for back pay, went on strike in October, and in December, riot police surrounded a union headquarters to stop workers from holding a rally. That month, Bozize asked the legislature for the power to rule by decree for nine months, saying it would help him deal with the financial crisis and make reforms urged by international lenders (which had been slow to send new aid to the country). Although human rights groups protested the move, the legislature granted him the power at the end of December. He used it in early January of 2006 to increase the price of paraffin, which is widely used as a fuel in the CAR.

Bozize faced other problems as 2006 began. The African Union warned that armed groups in the north of the country, possibly including soldiers loyal to Patasse, might be preparing for an offensive. Also, in February of 2006, Bozize's son, Francois Bozize Jr., was sentenced to four months in jail in France for defrauding a bank.

Sources

Periodicals

Agence France Presse, December 23, 2005.

AP Worldstream, December 10, 2005.

Economist, November 2, 2002, p. 50; March 22, 2003, p. 42; March 19, 2005, p. 54.

New York Times, March 14, 2005, p. A5; June 12, 2005.

Time International, November 19, 2001, p. 18.

UN Integrated Regional Information Networks, December 13, 2004; December 30, 2005; January 4, 2006.

Online

"Bozize, Francois," MSN Encarta, http://fr.encarta.msn.com/text_941550365___0/Bozize_Francois.html (February 25, 2006).

"Central African Republic (Report 2005)" Amnesty International, http://web.amnesty.org/report 2005/Caf-summary-eng (February 25, 2006).

"Central African Republic (Report 2004)" Amnesty International, http://web.amnesty.org/report 2004/Caf-summary-eng (February 25, 2006).

"Country profile: Central African Republic," BBC News, http://news.bbc.co.uk/1/hi/world/africa/country_profiles/1067518.stm (February 25, 2006).

"Profile of Francois Bozize," BBC News, http://news.bbc.co.uk/2/hi/africa/2854669.stm (February 25, 2006).

Transcripts

"French court jails Central African president's son for fraud," Radio France Internationale (transcribed by BBC Monitoring Africa), February 23, 2006.

—Erick Trickey

Adrien Brody

Robyn Beck/AFP/Getty Images

Actor

Born April 14, 1973, in New York, NY; son of Elliot Brody (a history teacher) and Sylvia Plachy
(a photojournalist). *Education:* Studied at the American Academy of Dramatic Arts, and at Queens College, early 1990s.

Addresses: *Agent*—Creative Artists Agency, 9830
Wilshire Blvd., Beverly Hills, CA 90212-1825.

Career

Actor in films, including: *New York Stories,* 1989;
King of the Hill, 1993; *Angels in the Outfield,* 1994;
Nothing to Lose, 1996; *Six Ways to Sunday,* 1997; *The
Thin Red Line,* 1998; *Summer of Sam,* 1999; *Bread and
Roses,* 2000; *Love the Hard Way,* 2001; *The Pianist,*
2002; *The Village,* 2004; *The Jacket,* 2005; *King Kong,*
2005; *Manolete,* 2006. Television appearances include:
Home at Last (movie), 1988; *Annie McGuire,* 1988.

Awards: Academy Award for best actor, Academy
of Motion Picture Arts and Sciences, for *The Pianist,*
2003.

Sidelights

In 2003, 29-year-old Adrien Brody became the
youngest actor to win an Academy Award for
Best Male Actor in a Lead Role. The New Yorker
won the Oscar for his title role in *The Pianist,* the
moving World War II-set drama from Roman Polanski that took two other Academy Awards that night.
In the film, Brody played the real-life Wladyslaw

Szpilman, a well-known Warsaw musician of Jewish roots who managed to survive the six-year Nazi
occupation of Poland. Often mentioned as the successor to Al Pacino and Robert De Niro, Brody possesses a rather unconventional handsomeness that
has made him one of the top leading men in Hollywood, a status confirmed by his appearance in the
2005 blockbuster *King Kong.*

Born in 1973, Brody grew up an only child in
Woodhaven, a community in the New York City
borough of Queens. His mother, Sylvia Plachy, was
a Hungarian-born photojournalist long associated
with the pages of the *Village Voice,* New York City's
award-winning alternative newspaper. Elliot Brody,
his father, was a history teacher whose family roots
were in Poland, where several of his Jewish relatives perished in the Holocaust.

Encouraged by his parents to find and express his
creative side, Brody took acting classes as a kid and
even worked as a birthday-party magician. He also
attended summer acting camps, and by the time he
reached his teens had appeared in an off-Broadway
play. "I was doing theatre in junior high school,"
Brody recalled in an interview with Jamie Painter
Young for *Back Stage West.* "I was taking the train
after school, going into the East Village, doing

avant-garde plays Off-Broadway, and getting beaten up on the way to work. I mean, that was my life."

At the age of 15, Brody was cast in a television movie that aired on the Public Broadcasting Service (PBS) about nineteenth-century orphans shipped out to farm families in the Midwest, and he also appeared that same year as Mary Tyler Moore's stepson in a short-lived sitcom, *Annie McGuire.* A year later, in 1989, he had a brief part in an acclaimed Woody Allen/Francis Ford Coppola collaboration, *New York Stories.* By then he was a student at Fiorello La Guardia High School for the Performing Arts, the same New York City high school made famous by the movie and television series *Fame.* Getting past its rigorous entrance requirements saved him from having to attend his local public high school in Queens, "which would have been probably disastrous," Brody told *Back Stage West's* Young. "It has one of the highest dropout levels; there's a ton of gang violence."

After high school, Brody won admission to the prestigious American Academy of Dramatic Arts in Manhattan, but had a difficult time with his acting classes, after having made it through so much classroom and professional training already. For a time, he took classes at Queens College, but dropped out at age 19 and moved to Los Angeles in 1992, where he knew one person—a friend he had made when they appeared in a television commercial a few years before. Not long afterward, he was in a serious motorcycle accident, and spent months recovering from his injuries.

Roles came sporadically for Brody over the rest of the decade. He assumed success was around the corner when he was cast in a 1993 film by Steven Soderbergh, *King of the Hill,* but the movie did poorly and was quickly forgotten. He appeared in a handful of projects over the next five years, but none of them were box-office hits. Finally, Brody believed his break had finally come when director Terrence Malick cast him in the critically lauded World War II-era drama, *The Thin Red Line.* Brody was cast opposite veteran actors Sean Penn and Nick Nolte, endured an army-style boot camp training period to prepare for the role, and then spent six months on location in a remote part of Australia, wearing the same filthy uniform for weeks. He was billed as one of the leads before its release, but then much of his performance was left on the editing-room floor at the last minute. As a result, Brody found himself in the uncomfortable position of having to do publicity for a film in which he barely appeared.

The letdown was especially trying because Brody had been struggling financially for a number of years. As he recalled in an interview with Tiffany

Rose in London's *Independent,* during *Thin Red Line's* filming, "I only owned one pair of Nikes. They shrunk, and I didn't even realize that they were killing me, but I wore them for the entire movie. Those were my sneakers. I would be in costume or I would be in my sneakers."

Brody traded in those on-screen army boots for a pair of Doc Martens when he took the lead role in *Summer of Sam,* the 1999 Spike Lee film about the summer of 1977, when a serial killer kept much of New York City on edge. Leonardo DiCaprio had originally been considered for the role of Ritchie, but Brody's borough roots made him an excellent fit for the part of a Bronx teen who was in the midst of rejecting his working-class neighborhood roots— and its rock and disco soundtrack—for the newly emerging punk scene. The film proved to be Brody's breakout role entirely by accident, for in the last fight scene that Lee filmed, Brody's nose was broken, and he later decided against reconstructive surgery to fix the bump. That minor flaw lent his already somewhat sorrowful face a further measure of character, and would become his trademark.

After *Summer of Sam,* Brody appeared in a Ken Loach film in 2000, *Bread and Roses,* and in a dark psychological drama called *Love the Hard Way* a year later. Once Polish-born director Roman Polanski saw some of his work, he immediately cast Brody in *The Pianist.* The epic, highly anticipated film from the sometimes-controversial director recounted the real-life story of a Polish Jew who hides out in Warsaw during World War II thanks to a combination of sympathetic friends and sheer luck. The script, a tale of survival against incredible odds, was based on the memoirs of Wladyslaw Szpilman, an acclaimed pianist in Warsaw in the 1930s, whose Jewish family did not survive the Nazi occupation of the country. Of the 350,000 Jews living in Warsaw when Germany invaded in 1939, Szpilman was one of just 200 found alive when the war ended six years later.

In his review of the 2002 movie for the *New Yorker,* David Denby asserted that Brody "gives Szpilman elements of vanity and weakness as well as a persevering obstinacy. At first, the pianist, a member of a loving, quarrelsome family, refuses to take the Occupation seriously—he shrugs it off as an irritation." Brody manages to get out of the infamous Warsaw Ghetto, where the city's Jews were walled in and left to starve, and then the forced deportations to the extermination camps. Corralled with his family at the train station, Brody's Szpilman is plucked from the line by someone he knows, and told to walk away. He hides out in a series of apartments until the war's horrors come, quite literally, crashing into the building.

In the next scene, an emaciated Szpilman emerges from the rubble and staggers down the streets of his hometown after a long period when he could not go outside. The city's immense apartment houses are now gaping, bombed-out skeletons, and the sense of devastation is immediate. Brody had lost 30 pounds on his already lean frame in order to play the starving pianist convincingly, and this was the scene that was shot first. Brody recalled that Polanski expected much of him, both that day and during the subsequent weeks of shooting. As he recalled in an interview with Christine Muhlke of *Paper*, when he was informed what was on schedule that first day, "I told them, I have *no* energy. I'm delirious. And Roman was like 'What do you need energy for? Just do it. *Do it!*' It made me cry. So I knew it wasn't going to be an easy journey."

When *The Pianist* premiered at the 2002 Cannes Film Festival, the roll of the credits at its end were greeted with a 15-minute standing ovation. It also won the Palm d'Or award at the Festival, and had a limited release in Europe and the United States in the build-up to the Academy Awards. Brody won laudatory reviews for his work, though some critics noted the overall effect of the movie was best described as flat. "Without his soulful performance," noted Ryan Gilbey in his critique for London's *Independent*, "it might also be drained of life. So richly does he inhabit Szpilman that the picture has no need to engineer our sympathy—the simple sight of Brody wasting away before our eyes, his initial haughtiness crumbling into humility, is in itself distressing enough."

As expected, *The Pianist* was nominated in several Academy Award categories, and Brody found himself in the unenviable position of being a contender for the Best Actor in a Lead Role along with four other stars who were all previous Oscar-winners at least once before: Jack Nicholson, Daniel Day-Lewis, and Nicolas Cage, who had won in the same category, and Michael Caine who owned two Oscars for supporting roles. But *The Pianist* beat out *Chicago*, the odds-on favorite, for Best Director and Best Screenplay, and Brody was the surprise winner of the Best Actor award. The presenter was Halle Berry, and when he accepted it he delivered a cinema-worthy kiss that made the front pages of newspapers around the country the next day as the emblematic image of that year's Academy Awards.

Brody's next films were in the psychological-thriller genre. He appeared in M. Night Shyamalan's *The Village* in 2004, and turned up as a persecuted veteran of the 1991 Gulf War in 2005's *The Jacket*. Later that year, he played the romantic lead in the highly anticipated remake of *King Kong*, from *Lord of the Rings* director Peter Jackson. *Manolete*, a biopic chronicling the life of Manuel Rodriguez Sanchez, one of Spain's greatest matadors, was next on Brody's agenda, and scheduled for a 2006 release.

Despite his motorcycle accident several years back, Brody is still enthralled by motor sports and speed. He drove a Porsche 911 Turbo across parts of Europe and North Africa for a 3,000-mile car race known as the Gumball Rally in 2004. He has been linked romantically with a number of prominent starlets or models, but is most frequently photographed with Ceelo, his chihuahua. He lives in both New York City and the Los Angeles area, and his California home features a studio where he writes and records quasi-hip-hop tracks.

Not until the day after his Oscar win did Brody realize how much his life had suddenly changed. That next evening, he dined out with his parents—whom he often brings along to his movie premieres or awards ceremonies—"and as we walked into the restaurant, everyone stood up and applauded," he recalled in the interview with Rose in the *Independent*. "It was the most surreal experience I've ever had in my life." In a later interview, he offered some reflections on the fickle and sometimes award-driven nature of the entertainment business. "After I did *The Pianist*, nothing changed," he told Kevin West in *W*. "Since I won an Academy Award, a lot has changed. There was a tremendous amount of support for me as an actor when *The Pianist* came out, and even before that. But it would be a different story without winning an Academy Award. Realistically, it really wasn't about the work."

Sources

Back Stage West, February 24, 2005, p. 1.
Entertainment Weekly, February 21, 2003, p. 29; June 24/July 1, 2005, p. 58.
Independent (London, England), December 6, 2002, p. 10; July 30, 2004, p. 8.
Newsweek, April 7, 2003, p. 58.
New Yorker, January 13, 2003, p. 90.
Paper, February 2003, pp. 44-48.
People, January 20, 2003, p. 85; July 14, 2003.
W, August, 2004, p. 100.

—*Carol Brennan*

Kurt Busch

Streeter Lecka/Getty Images

Race car driver

Born August 4, 1978, in Las Vegas, NV; son of Tom (a salesperson) and Gaye (a public schools employee) Busch. *Education:* Attended the University of Arizona.

Addresses: *Office*—Roush Racing, 4600 Roush Place, Concord, NC 28207.

Career

Began racing dwarf cars, c. 1994; won Nevada state championships for racing dwarf cars, 1994-95; won Nevada Dwarf Car championship, 1995; Legend Cars Western States champion, 1996; competed on the NASCAR Featherlite Southwest Series, 1997-99; NASCAR Featherlite Southwest Series champion, 1999; signed with Roush Racing, 1999; competed in Craftsman Truck Series, 2000; joined NASCAR's Winston Cup series, 2001; won first pole at a NASCAR race, Mountain Dew Southern 500, 2001; won first NASCAR race, Food City 500, 2002; won Nextel Cup, 2004; signed with Penske Racing South team, 2005.

Awards: National Rookie of the Year, 1996; Rookie of the Year Award, NASCAR Southwest Series, 1998.

Sidelights

Racing on the NASCAR leading series for only five short years, Kurt Busch rose from obscurity to win the first Nextel Cup title in 2004. Driving the number 97 Ford car for Roush Racing, Busch earned more than $20 million from racing alone by 2005. Though his ascent to the top of NASCAR has not been easy, especially because of conflicts with other drivers, he has been praised for his growing maturity and ability to adjust mid-race.

Busch was born on August 4, 1978, in Las Vegas, Nevada, to a father who had his own interests in racing. Though Tom Busch was a local racing champion in Las Vegas, he supported his family by selling MAC Tools. Kurt Busch's mother, Gaye, supported her husband, and later her sons' interests, in the sport. Busch has a younger brother, Kyle, who also turned pro and later competed against his brother on the NASCAR circuit.

By the time he was a teenager, Busch was interested in racing. While attending middle school, he decided he wanted to become a race car driver. Tom Busch promised to consider letting him race dwarf cars when he was 16 if he earned good grades at school. Busch held up his end of the promise and began racing when he was around 14. He raced in several series in Nevada with his family's help. Busch did well, winning whole series championships on several occasions. Busch won the Nevada Dwarf Car championship in 1995 and he won the Legend Cars Western States championship in 1996.

By the late 1990s, he was competing in the Western States Dwarf Car Association Nationals held in his hometown.

Though Busch had aspirations of becoming a professional driver, he also had other goals. When he graduated from Durango High School, he entered the University of Arizona. There, he studied pharmacy because he wanted to be a pharmacist. His inspiration was his mother; since she suffers from rheumatoid arthritis, he hoped to help her with his knowledge. While a college student, Busch continued to race. He only attended school for about a year, however, before deciding to focus exclusively on racing.

In 1997, Busch began racing full time. He competed in the NASCAR Featherlite Southwest Series, a semi-professional series. Again, Busch proved up to competition. He was named the rookie of the year in 1998. The following year, he won the Featherlite Southwest Series title, the youngest driver ever to win the honor. His success also showed that it was possible for drivers who come from Nevada to do well.

Busch continued to prove this point when he signed with Roush Racing in 1999. By signing with Roush, he was able to move up to a higher racing series. In 2000, he spent the majority of the racing season competing in the Craftsman Truck Series. This was an entry-level NASCAR series for young drivers. Busch won four races that year; he also finished second in the series' point standings and set several records. Among them was the fact that he was the youngest driver to both win a pole in the series and win a race in the series.

In 2000, Busch competed in seven NASCAR Winston Cup series races. However, he did not win or earn a pole in any races. Despite this lack of success, Roush Racing moved him to NASCAR's Winston Cup Series full time in 2001. Busch proved he was ready; that same year, he won his first pole at the Mountain Dew Southern 500. He finished in the top five in three races, though he also did not finish seven races. Busch earned more than $2 million during the 2001 season.

Busch continued to improve in the 2002 season. He won his first race in 2002, the Food City 500 in Tennessee. Jack Roush, owner of Roush Racing, told Jeff Wolf of the Las Vegas Review-Journal, "I'd never been prouder of ... a young driver. He has adapted quicker to all the things presented to him in racing [than] anybody I've ever worked with." Busch also

won three other races: Old Dominion 500, NAPA 500, and Ford 400. In addition, Busch finished in the top five 12 times. He earned more than $3.7 million. Busch's success led to endorsement deals, which brought him more income. By 2003, he was endorsing companies such as Ford, Rubbermaid products, and Coca-Cola.

In 2003, Busch posted four more victories and nine top five finishes, along with eight did not finishes. His victories came in the Food City 500, Auto Club 500, Sirius 500, and Sharpie 500. Busch ended the NASCAR season struggling. He only had one top ten finish after August, a fourth place showing in the Checker Auto Parts 500 in early November. Questions about his character continued to dog him. Busch had several confrontations with another driver, Jimmy Spencer, both on the track and off. Busch also feuded with other drivers, including Terry Labonte and Sterling Marlin.

After the 2003 season ended, NASCAR changed sponsorship of its title series and how the series would determine its champion. The name changed from the Winston Cup to the Nextel Cup. To win the Nextel Cup, drivers had to be in the top ten, based on points, before the last ten races of the season. These ten drivers would be the only ones competing for the Cup, dubbed "The Chase for the Cup," though all the drivers would still be competing in races.

Busch did well under the new system in 2004. He was one of those drivers able to compete for the Cup. By the end of the season, he had five wins, including the last two races of the season. He also had ten finishes in the top five. However, his season was not always easy. There were several key races where something went wrong with his car. Despite these setbacks, Busch won the inaugural Nextel Cup with his win of the last race of the season.

When Busch returned to racing in 2005, he started out slow with many early season struggles. He crashed in four straight events in March and April. Still, Busch was able to win twice—at the Subway Fresh 500 and Pennsylvania 500—through the first 21 races. His success early in the season put him in position to have a chance at repeating as champion.

During the 2005 season, Busch decided to make a change in who he raced for. Instead of Roush Racing, with whom he had a contract through 2006, Busch signed with Roger Penske and his Penske Racing South team. The contract was to begin in 2007. Busch would be replacing legendary driver

Rusty Wallace, who was retiring. Busch asked Roush to release him from his contract so he could race for Penske's group in 2006, but Roush refused. Busch promised to continue to focus on racing for Roush in 2006.

As Busch found success on NASCAR, his immaturity faded and he became more recognized for his abilities as a driver. Roush teammate Carl Edwards told Fluto Shinzawa of the *Boston Globe*, "He's a guy who can break down a racetrack and run perfect laps repeatedly. I don't think it's his setup specifically. I know Jimmy Fenning [Busch's crew chief] is awesome, but Kurt is just that good of a race car driver. He's truly talented...."

Sources

Periodicals

Associated Press State & Local Wire, August 18, 2004; July 27, 2005.

Atlanta Journal-Constitution, October 31, 2004, p. 7H.

Boston Globe, July 16, 2005, p. C1.

Denver Post, February 20, 2005, p. BB1.

Las Vegas Review-Journal (Nevada), April 16, 1999, p. 10C; July 14, 2000, p. 2C; March 26, 2002, p. 1C; August 3, 2003, p. 1C; March 4, 2004, p. 1DD; November 19, 2004, p. 11C; December 2, 2004, p. 1C; April 22, 2005, p. 1C.

New York Times, December 2, 2004, p. D3.

People, April 11, 2005, p. 139.

Sports Illustrated, November 1, 2004, p. 91.

St. Petersburg Times (Florida), November 21, 2004, p. 1C.

Tampa Tribune (Florida), November 12, 2004, p. 7.

Toronto Sun, November 20, 2004, p. S15.

Online

"Busch dominates in Phoenix," *SI.com,* http://sportsillustrated.cnn.com/2005/racing/04/23/nascar.phoenix.ap/index.html (May 13, 2005).

"Kurt Busch splitting with Roush," *USA Today,* http://www.usatoday.com/sports/motor/nascar/2005-08-09-busch -roush_x.htm?POE=SPOISVA (August 13, 2005).

"Kurt Busch," Yahoo! Sports, http://sports.yahoo.com/nascar/nextel/drivers/156 (August 8, 2005).

"Roush Refuses to Release Busch for 2006," *New York Times,* http://www.nytimes.com/2005/08/13/sports/othersports/13nascar.html (August 13, 2005).

"Roush to consider releasing Busch," *SI.com,* http://sportsillustrated.cnn.com/2005/racing/08/15/bc.car.nascar.roush.busch.ap/index.html (August 18, 2005).

—*A. Petruso*

Nick Cannon

© Axel Koester/Corbis

Actor

Born Nicholas Scott Cannon, October 8, 1980, in San Diego, CA; son of James Cannon (a televangelist) and Beth Gardner (an accountant).

Addresses: *Agent*—Endeavor Agency, 9601 Wilshire Blvd., 10th Fl., Beverly Hills, CA 90212.

Career

Began career as a stand-up comic in the Los Angeles area, and as a warm-up performer for the Nickelodeon cable channel's studio audiences; appeared on the Nickelodeon show *All That*, 1998-2000; series writer for the Nickelodeon shows *Kenan & Kel* and *Cousin Skeeter*; series creator, performer, and writer for *The Nick Cannon Show*, Nickelodeon, 2002-03; star and sketch director for *Nick Cannon Presents: Wild 'N Out*, MTV, 2005—. Film appearances include: *Whatever It Takes*, 2000; *Men in Black II*, 2002; *Drumline*, 2002; *Love Don't Cost a Thing*, 2003; *Garfield* (voice), 2004; *Roll Bounce*, 2005; *Underclassmen*, 2005; *Weapons*, 2006; *Bobby*, 2006. Released debut album, *Nick Cannon*, on Jive Records, 2003.

Sidelights

Nick Cannon emerged as a rising, multitalented performer when he was barely out of his teens. A talented stand-up comic, he was writing for Nickelodeon kids' shows at a time when his peers were finishing their high school credits, and went on to star in the surprisingly well-received marching-band movie, *Drumline*, in 2002. In 2005 he began hosting his own hip-hop improv comedy series for MTV,

which he followed by releasing his second album, *Stages*. He told journalist Aidin Vaziri of the *San Francisco Chronicle* that he needed a bit of help keeping track of appointment-heavy weeks. "I've got four different schedules that I work off of," he admitted. "It can be a little hectic sometimes."

Born in San Diego, California, on October 8, 1980, Cannon was raised partly by his grandmother while his mother, Beth Gardner, finished her education and established her career as an accountant. He also spent time with his father, James, who was an assistant pastor of a church in Charlotte, North Carolina, and hosted his own television ministry. An energetic child, Cannon was diagnosed with attention-deficit disorder (ADD) in elementary school, but both his parents and his grandmother encouraged his obvious love of performing in front of others as an outlet for his liveliness. Reflecting back on his childhood and other relatives in an interview with *Philadelphia Daily News* writer Gary Thompson, he believes his ADD was inherited, but was grateful he realized that "if you learn how to channel it, it can work for you."

Cannon's first exposure before an audience came thanks to the cable public-access show his father hosted in Charlotte. He wrote some jokes for it, and his father gave him a regular stand-up slot. At the age of 15, he was picked to appear on the long-running dance show *Soul Train* to compete on its Scramble Board. By that point he was already performing in Southern California comedy clubs, and went on to work as a pre-show comic who warmed up the young audiences for the Nickelodeon cable network shows. He admitted to nearly being waylaid by clothes, cars, and the popularity race during his first years at Monte Vista High School in San Diego, but once he had his first taste of professional success he realized he needed to keep focused on his studies. "Suddenly, it wasn't about being popular or what other people thought," he told *Boston Herald* writer Stephen Schaefer.

Cannon graduated a year ahead of schedule, and landed writing gigs for such Nickelodeon fare as *Kenan & Kel* and *Cousin Skeeter*. He also appeared on another Nickelodeon show, *All That*, between 1998 and 2000. His film debut came as the chess-club kid in a 2000 teen comedy, *Whatever It Takes*. But Cannon was determined to break into Hollywood's upper echelons, and concocted a scheme to pitch a movie idea to actor/comedian Eddie Murphy by pretending he was a television reporter. He made it into the room, but his ruse was quickly discovered. "His people tried to shoo me away," Cannon recalled in a *People* interview, "but Eddie wanted to play. He gave me a high-five when I left."

Cannon had better luck in finding a high-profile show-business connection when he met actor, rapper, and producer Will Smith, who bought him a drum machine and gave him a small part in *Men In Black II* as the autopsy agent. Cannon also wrote and appeared in his own show on Nickelodeon, *The Nick Cannon Show*, which ran for two seasons beginning in 2002. His first genuine break, however, came when he was cast in the lead for *Drumline*, the sleeper hit of the 2002 holiday-movie season. Reportedly based on the real-life experiences of music producer-songwriter Dallas Austin—also the film's executive producer—*Drumline* featured Cannon as Devon Miles, a hotshot New York City musical prodigy who wins a scholarship to a prestigious Atlanta college. He joins the school's marching band, but chafes at the tough, military-style discipline under the leadership of the respected band director, Dr. Lee (Orlando Jones). Devon's arrogance covers some flaws, including his inability to read music, and the coming-of-age story follows him on that journey of self-discovery.

Drumline pulled in impressive box-office numbers, and scored well with critics, too. Writing in *Entertainment Weekly*, Owen Gleiberman declared that

the film "does more than capture the excitement of marching bands; it gets their clockwork beauty as well." *Chicago Sun-Times* critic Roger Ebert lauded it as "a movie that celebrates black success instead of romanticizing gangsta defeatism. Nick Cannon plays Devon as a fine balance between a showoff and a kid who wants to earn admiration." Ebert also commended the film's writers for avoiding "all the tired old cliches in which the Harlem kid is somehow badder and blacker than the others, provoking confrontations."

Despite his impressive rise, Cannon claimed that he received no star treatment from his family. "My grandmother don't care about none of this stuff," he told a reporter for the E! Online website in 2003. "I went home yesterday, and I had to take out the trash, I had to mow the lawn." His next project was a remake of a 1987 movie, *Can't Buy Me Love*. Refashioned as *Love Don't Cost a Thing* and starring Cannon as a nerdy high schooler who pays a girl to hang out with him, the 2003 movie was the No. 5 box-office draw for its December opening weekend.

Love Don't Cost a Thing featured Cannon as the goofy Alvin Johnson, an automotive whiz and high-school nobody, who hatches a plan to boost his profile by bartering with one of his most popular classmates, cheerleader Paris Morgan (Christina Milian), to fix the family SUV that she smashed. In exchange, she must pretend to be his girlfriend for two weeks. "Gawky and guileless, Cannon makes a good case for Alvin's social awkwardness," noted Carla Meyer in the *San Francisco Chronicle*. Citing its Eighties-era predecessor, Meyer also noted that "the biggest difference in this version is the leads are African American. Otherwise, it's your basic rich-girl-transforms-nerd story, made relatively fresh by lanky … Cannon." Robert Koehler, writing in *Daily Variety*, singled the movie out for its portrayal of modern life, commenting that what he found "intriguing" was "the prickly interaction between barely middle-class blacks like Alvin and the ultra-upscale blacks like Paris. This kind of commingling is rare in American movies, as is the depiction of a casually integrated Los Angeles student body that is past racial issues."

Cannon had said in interviews that he turned down many film roles after the success of *Drumline*, and was determined to keep writing his own material and even produce his own projects when possible. "As a young African-American man, there aren't too many quality scripts out there," he told Schaefer in the *Boston Herald* article. "There are scripts where you can be drug dealers or [there are] hood movies or degrading comedies, but I'd rather do some quality things that are catered to me." Cannon was also busy with other projects, most notably his music career. After a few months of delay, his self-titled debut CD was released the same month as *Love Don't Cost a Thing*, and featured an impressive roster of guests, including Mary J. Blige and R. Kelly. The tracks were divided between a shady alter-ego character he called Fillmore Slim ("Gigolo" and "Feelin' Freaky") and more wholesome R&B crooner fare. Reviewing it for *Billboard*, Rashaun Hall found a middle ground in the themes with the track "Get Crunk Shorty," which Hall termed "the perfect balance of crunk and old-school hip-hop."

The success of *Drumline* helped Cannon score a deal with the Miramax film studio, which paid him $1.5 million for one of his movie ideas, which he then finessed with two other screenwriters and executive-produced. Filming began once he finished his commitment to other projects, including the voice of Louis the Mouse in *Garfield* in 2004 and an appearance as Bernard in the 2005 roller-skating comedy *Roll Bounce*. That next major project, which he wrote and produced, was *Underclassmen*. It was the number-three box-office draw for the September 4, 2005, weekend that it opened, but critics were merciless. Cannon played a new member of the Los Angeles police force, a rookie whose brash, impulsive nature keeps bringing him trouble until he convinces his bosses to give him an undercover assignment: his youthful appearance lets him pass as a new student in an elite private high school to crack a murder investigation there. The film critic for the *New York Times*, A. O. Scott, conceded that Cannon "has a loose, quick-talking charm ... but in this picture he tries on a series of secondhand movie star identities, trying so hard to be the next Will Smith or Eddie Murphy that his own personality all but dissolves."

Cannon finished his second LP, *Stages*, just before *Underclassmen* was released. Its breakout single proved to be the track "Can I Live?" in which an unborn child asks its mother to rethink her decision to terminate the pregnancy. Cannon based it on his own story, as he told many journalists once the song was adopted as an unofficial anthem by pro-life groups. "My mother was pregnant with me at 17 years old," he explained to Thompson, the *Philadelphia Daily News* writer. "A lot of people were telling her she wasn't married, she was still in high school, so she should probably get an abortion. But she said that like a voice spoke to her, and said she should have this child. I used to say to her, that was my voice! I was talking to you!"

The video for "Can I Live?" featured former *Fresh Prince of Bel Air* cast member Tatyana Ali as his mother, and became one of the top-requested clips on BET and MTV. Anti-abortion groups promoted it as a positive artistic expression of their moral message. Yet Cannon refused to take a side in the debate, saying only that he was opposed to abortion as a method of birth control. "It's a tough choice for a woman to make, and people who have all these opinions about it should put themselves in her shoes," he told Elon D. Johnson in *Essence*.

By mid-2005 Cannon was also hosting his own improv-comedy series for MTV, *Nick Cannon Presents: Wild 'N Out*, for which he also served as executive producer and sketch director. The show was arranged in contest format, with competing teams led by such guest stars as rappers Kanye West and Method Man. The improvisational challenges were largely the pranksterish Cannon's ideas, and he reveled in exposing the big names. "When somebody's really good at improv, that's entertaining," he told *Entertainment Weekly*'s Dan Snierson, "but it's not as much fun."

Selected discography

Nick Cannon, Jive Records, 2003.
Stages, Motown/Can I Ball, 2006.

Sources

Periodicals

Billboard, December 20, 2003, p. 62.
Boston Herald, December 9, 2003, p. 39.
Chicago Sun-Times, December 13, 2002.
Daily Variety, December 12, 2002, p. 14; Dec 12, 2003, p. 6; April 30, 2004, p. 4.
Ebony, February 2004, p. 22.
Entertainment Weekly, January 3, 2003, p. 47; June 27, 2003, p. 53; June 10, 2005, p. 65.
Essence, October 2005, p. 90.
New York Times, December 22, 2002, p. ST4; September 2, 2005.
People, January 20, 2003, p. 86.
Philadelphia Daily News, September 1, 2005.
Philadelphia Inquirer, August 4, 2005.
San Francisco Chronicle, December 12, 2003; December 28, 2003, p. 44.
Variety, September 5, 2005, p. 32.

Online

"Nick Cannon," E! Online, http://www.eonline.com/Features/Features/Sizzlin2003/Guys/index.html (May 10, 2006).

—*Carol Brennan*

Steve Carell

© Phil Han/ZUMA/Corbis

Actor and writer

Born August 16, 1963, in Concord, MA; married Nancy Walls (a comedian), 1995; children: Elisabeth, John. *Education:* Earned degree from Denison University, 1984.

Addresses: *Agent*—Endeavor Agency, 9601 Wilshire Blvd., 10th Fl., Beverly Hills, CA 90212.

Career

Actor on television, including: *The Dana Carvey Show* (also writer), ABC, 1996; *Over the Top,* ABC, 1997; *The Daily Show,* Comedy Central, 1999-2005; *Watching Ellie,* NBC, 2002-03; *The Office* (also writer), 2005—. Film appearances include: *Curly Sue,* 1991; *Tomorrow Night,* 1998; *Suits,* 1999; *Bruce Almighty,* 2003; *Anchorman: The Legend of Ron Burgundy,* 2004; *Bewitched,* 2005; *The 40-Year-Old Virgin* (also writer and executive producer), 2005; *Over the Hedge* (voice), 2006; *Get Smart,* 2006; *Little Miss Sunshine,* 2006.

Awards: Golden Globe award for best performance by an actor in a television series (musical or comedy), Hollywood Foreign Press Association, for *The Office,* 2006.

Sidelights

Actor and comedy writer Steve Carell was a favorite of viewers on Comedy Central's *The Daily Show* for several years, but in 2005 suddenly emerged as Hollywood's hottest new box-office draw thanks to the success of *The 40-Year-Old Virgin.* Carell's innocuous face was plastered all over America's urban centers as part of the film's marketing blitz on billboards that reprised the movie poster—a knock-off of a cheesy high-school senior photo. Carell did admit "it's a little jarring seeing it everywhere," he told *Newsweek* writer Devin Gordon. "I always think, 'God, is that what I really look like? I'm an idiot.'"

Born in 1963, Carell grew up in Newton, Massachusetts, and went on to Denison University in Ohio. After graduating, he decided against law school, and moved to Chicago in 1985, where he took acting classes and eventually joined the acclaimed improvisational comedy group, Second City. He made his feature-film debut in the 1991 comedy *Curly Sue,* and by the mid-1990s was living in New York City. His first break seemed to arrive when he was hired as a writer on *The Dana Carvey Show,* which debuted on ABC in the spring of 1996. Carell also appeared in the show's skits, along with another member of the writing team, Stephen Colbert, whom he knew from Second City.

Just five episodes of *The Dana Carvey Show* aired before ABC cancelled it. Carell later recalled in an interview with *Entertainment Weekly*'s Josh Wolk that the bad news "floored me. How could it not work? It was too funny for people not to watch it." Carell decided to relocate once again, this time to Los Angeles, and spent nearly three years being bypassed at the audition stage or working on projects that never made it into production. He was in an extremely shortlived series, *Over the Top*, with Tim Curry and Annie Potts in 1997, and had small roles in two little-seen films, including one in which he was credited as "Mail Room Guy Without Glasses."

Carell's career fortunes changed when Colbert suggested him for a correspondent's slot on Comedy Central's *The Daily Show*. Colbert had been appearing on the fake-news show and broadcast-journalism spoof since 1997, and the series was boosted by the arrival of comedian Jon Stewart as host in 1999, the same year that Carell joined the team. As a roving news correspondent, Carell appeared in sketches that scored high marks for their originality and deadpan delivery. His on-air demeanor, he told Richard Rushfield in *Daily Variety*, was that of someone he imagined was possibly a former "national news reporter and had been demoted to this Podunk local show and had kind of a chip on his shoulder."

Carell had a recurring role as the annoying ex-boyfriend of Julia Louis-Dreyfus in her sitcom *Watching Ellie*, which aired in 2002 and 2003, and was cast as Jim Carrey's on-screen nemesis in *Bruce Almighty*. His scenes as smarmy newscaster Evan Baxter were some of the funniest in that film, and led to his next role, in *Anchorman: The Legend of Ron Burgundy*, as meteorologist Brick Tamland.

Anchorman gave Carell a chance to work with writer-director Judd Apatow, and Carell pitched him a story idea based on a skit he had done years before with Second City. The premise involved a group of men telling risqué stories, but there was "one guy who just couldn't keep up," Carell recounted to Gordon in the *Newsweek* article. "It becomes quickly apparent that he's never done any of the things he's talking about." The "bag of sand" comment from that sketch made it into the screenplay for *The 40-Year-Old Virgin*, which Carell co-wrote with Apatow, who also directed him in his first lead role.

In the surprise hit of 2005, Carell played the titular virgin Andy Stitzer, a nice-enough guy but a loner who collects action figures and gave up on dating long ago. When his co-worker buddies at the electronics store discover his situation, they decide to help him find a girlfriend. A series of misadven-

tures ensues, but Carell's Andy eventually clicks with a single mom played by Catherine Keener. The movie garnered enthusiastic reviews and took in $20.6 million its first weekend in August of 2005 as the number-one box-office draw. *Entertainment Weekly* writer Owen Gleiberman called the film "buoyantly clever and amusing, a comedy of horny embarrassment that has the inspiration to present a middle-aged virgin's dilemma as a projection of all our romantic anxieties." Gleiberman also commended Carell's performance, remarking that "Andy may be a light caricature of a clueless, repressed loser ... but Carell plays him in the funniest and most surprising way possible: as a credible human being."

Carell's turn in *The 40-Year-Old Virgin* had a somewhat unexpected effect in boosting the chances of a new series on NBC, *The Office*. The American version of a hit British series of the same name that lured a cult following on cable's BBC America channel, the show had a brief run in the spring of 2005, with Carell as Michael Scott, the much-loathed boss of a paper company. By the time it returned for full season in the fall, Carell's *Virgin* was still in theaters, and ratings for the *The Office* spiked impressively.

Projects for 2006 included a reprisal of the Evan Baxter role for *Evan Almighty*, and a film version of the 1960s spy-spoof television series *Get Smart*. For 2007, Carell was scheduled to star in *Juvenile* as an average, 30-ish suburbanite who learns he must serve time for a crime he committed as a teen. The avalanche of film and television projects coming his way forced Carell to give up his *Daily Show* job in 2005. He made a few appearances on its "Indecision 2004" election reports, but politically disillusioned viewers began tuning into the show in record numbers that year. Carell conceded that "in the year and a half since I left, it's gone through the roof and won all kinds of accolades," he said in an interview with Joel Stein in *Time*. "I guess they needed to get rid of some dead weight."

Sources

Daily Variety, April 21, 2005, p. B2.
Entertainment Weekly, August 26, 2005, p. 40; February 24, 2006, p. 20.
Esquire, September 2005, p. 76.
Newsweek, August 15, 2005, p. 47.
New York Times, August 19, 2005.
Time, March 21, 2005, p. 72; August 22, 2005, p. 69.

—*Carol Brennan*

Mike Cassidy

AP/Wide World Photos

Chief Executive Officer of Xfire

Born Michael Cassidy, c. 1963. *Education:* Attended Berklee College of Music; Massachusetts Institute of Technology, B.S. (aerospace engineering), 1985, M.S. (aerospace engineering), 1986; Harvard Business School, graduate studies, 1991.

Addresses: *Website*—http://www.xfire.com.

Career

Founded Stylus Innovation, c. 1990; named chief executive officer of Direct Hit, 1997; founder and chief executive officer of Xfire, 2004.

Awards: First place, MIT business-plan contest, c. 1990.

Sidelights

In the world of online gaming, Michael Cassidy has become like a high-tech, high-powered matchmaker. By founding Xfire in 2004, and serving as its chief executive officer since, Cassidy has provided online gamers with the opportunity to easily and quickly find online playmates. Whereas online gamers used to have to prearrange gaming times with one another, setting up future games with friends well in advance, Xfire has largely eased this burden. Under the watchful and business-savvy eye of Cassidy, and supported by the expertise of chief gaming officer Dennis "Thresh" Fong, Xfire has flourished into a business that, according to *Forbes*, serves as "the *TV Guide*, maitre d', and instant mes-

senger of the gaming world." Specifically, Cassidy's company "can point you to a buddy who is ready to play the game you want at any moment of the day or night."

By tapping into the instant messaging and search engine technology already used by such online social networking services as Friendster and LinkedIn, Xfire has increased the ease with which online gamers can participate in nearly 75 role-playing and strategy games. For Xfire users, gone are the days of relying on conference calling and luck to schedule and execute play dates. And so far, nearly 1.5 million people have registered to use Xfire's services, making Cassidy himself a friend to online gamers. However, Cassidy's game plan for Xfire has involved not a single dollar of advertising money. According to Matt Slagle of the Associated Press, Cassidy has generated business "almost exclusively by word-of-mouth." Because Xfire users are eager to increase the number of buddies in their online gaming networks, they serve as Xfire's most powerful advertising tool. In this sense, then, customer satisfaction is what has propelled Cassidy's success.

However, this kind of success was not a sudden development in Cassidy's career. Rather, it was the result of a prolonged interest and investment in the intersection of computer technology and business innovation. As a student at Harvard Business School, Cassidy launched his first entrepreneurial endeavor. By entering and winning a business-plan contest hosted by MIT, where he had earlier earned both his Bachelor's and Master's degrees in aerospace engineering, Cassidy secured a portion of the seed money necessary to put into action what he was learning in the Harvard classroom. Along with two business partners, Cassidy combined his MIT winnings with an additional $125,000 and started Stylus Innovation. Devoted largely to developing fax and telephony software, this first of Cassidy's start-ups is best known for having produced Visual Voice. Although Cassidy sold Stylus Innovation in 1996 to Artisoft for $13 million, it was the invaluable experience and sterling reputation that he gained in running this 22-employee company that aided him in subsequent start-ups, most notably Xfire.

Cassidy has maintained close associations with both MIT, in general, and MIT's business-plan contest, in particular. Recognizing the catapulting effect that MIT's underwriting his fledgling business plan had upon his career, Cassidy has remained a staunch supporter of the business-plan contest. In 1997, specifically, Cassidy helped to launch a business plan proposed by a contest entrant. Feeling in need of a new project after having sold Stylus Innovation, Cassidy turned to MIT's website and the 84 student-proposed business plans published there. In Gary Culliss' blueprint for Direct Hit Technologies, which proposed a search engine that would list websites in the order of their popularity, Cassidy saw both a spark of business innovation and a match with his own interests. The business plan had lost in a warm-up round of the MIT competition. Quickly, Cassidy signed on as the CEO of Direct Hit and, according to *Inc.*, fleshed it out "from the wisp of an idea to a full-fledged upstart backed by $1.4 million in venture capital." With Cassidy's backing, Culliss and fellow MIT student Steven Yang won $30,000 from the MIT competition, were offered a one-year licensing pact with Wired Digital, and attracted the attention—and investment money—of the venture capital firm Draper Fisher Jurvetson.

Thus, Cassidy has not only carved out success for himself in the world of online technology and business, but has also helped spread this success to others. Lending his prestige and his knowledge to fellow MIT students, and supporting the business-plan competition that helped him, he has enjoyed personal triumph and shared in the triumph of up-and-coming business and technology innovators. This said, however, Cassidy's entrepreneurial involvement has hardly been worry-free. In February

of 2005, most notably, Xfire found itself being sued by Yahoo!. At the heart of the litigation is Yahoo!'s claim that Xfire has infringed Patent No. 6,699,125 by utilizing an only slightly modified version of the technology originally used by Yahoo!'s Game-Prowler IM application. Pointing to the technology used by Xfire in allowing gamers to chat online with one another, Yahoo! representatives have alleged that Xfire has relied upon Yahoo! technological innovation without garnering the appropriate permission or license.

Predictably, Cassidy has consistently refuted these claims against Xfire and has even initiated a countersuit against Yahoo!. According to Cassidy, these charges are more reflective of Yahoo!'s discomfort with free market competition than of any wrongdoing committed by Xfire. Cassidy feels that Yahoo! is using its economic clout in a blatant attempt to put Xfire out of business. Consequently, Xfire is asking that Yahoo!'s lawsuit be dismissed with prejudice and that Yahoo! be forced to compensate Xfire for any damage that the lawsuit causes to its business. Standing firmly on his remarkable history of award-winning and profitable innovation—first with Stylus Innovation and then with Direct Hit and Xfire—Cassidy has strongly defended the legality of the company's patent and the originality of the company's product. And Xfire users seem to be in agreement with this stance taken by Cassidy: An online petition urging Yahoo! to drop its charges had already gathered more than 25,000 signatures by mid-2005. Certainly, this indicates a great deal of support for both Xfire as a company and Cassidy as an entrepreneur.

Sources

Periodicals

Associated Press, May 13, 2005.
Forbes, September 6, 2004, pp. 146-47.
Inc., December 1998.
USA Today, February 16, 2004, p. 3B.

Online

"Mike Cassidy," Advertising in Games West, http://www.advertisingingames.com/west.speakers/mikecassidy.html (August 17, 2005).
"Mike Cassidy," Web 2.0 Conference 2005, http://www.web2con.com/cs/web2005/view/e_spkr/2387 (August 17, 2005).
"Xfire Countersuit Against Yahoo! Gaining Support," Game Daily Biz: Newsletter for Game Industry," http://biz.gamedaily.com/features.asp?article_id=9225 (August 17, 2005).

—*Emily Schusterbauer*

Jimmy Choo

Dave Hogan/Getty Images

Shoe designer

Born c. 1957, in George Town, Penang, Malaysia; married Rebecca; children: Emily. *Education:* Studied at Cordwainers' Technical College, London, England, early 1980s.

Addresses: *Office*—Jimmy Choo, 169 Draycott Ave., London SW3 3AJ, England.

Career

Worked for the family business as an apprentice shoemaker in George Town, Malaysia, in the 1970s; moved to London, England, 1980; first footwear designs sold under the brand name Lucky Shoes, 1984; opened custom shoe business, 1986; involved in a business partnership that launched the Jimmy Choo retail empire, 1996-2001; returned to custom-shoe business in London, 2001.

Awards: Accessory Designer of the Year, British Fashion Council, 1999; Order of the British Empire.

Sidelights

British shoemaker Jimmy Choo lent his name to the line of elegant women's footwear that quickly developed a cult following in the 1990s, despite their exorbitant prices. But there are actually two designer-shoe companies that bear his name— his own custom atelier in London, and the wholesale business with which he was once involved. Thanks to the public-relations savvy of his former partners, Choo's name joined the roster of ultra-fashionable luxury brands name-checked by R&B stars like Beyoncé Knowles and on the television series *Sex and the City.*

Choo hails from Penang, a province of Malaysia, and grew up in Penang's capital city, George Town. His family was of Chinese heritage, and he followed his father into shoemaking as a youngster. He made his first pair at the age of 12, and was soon working regularly in the family business that operated out of the first floor of their home. Around 1980, Choo traveled to London to visit relatives, and while there learned about a venerable shoemaking school in the city's East End called Cordwainers' Technical College. The term "cordwainer" had been used since 12th-century Britain to denote artisans who made shoes from new leather, as opposed to cobblers who worked with used material. Choo decided to stay, and rounded out his education in shoemaking at the school before attempting to return to Penang. "I went home for a year," he recalled in an interview with James Fallon for *Footwear News,* "but I had gotten used to the life here and came back."

Choo sold his first shoe designs under the brand name Lucky Shoes in 1984. Two years later, he started a custom shoe business using his own name, which operated out of the former Metropolitan Hospital in the east London neighborhood of Hackney. The building had been converted into a series of stalls for artisans and small-scale clothing retailers, and future Gucci creative director Alexander McQueen sold some his earliest designs there at the time. In 1989, Choo was joined in the business by his niece, Sandra Choi.

Over the next few years Choo built a small but profitable business making handmade shoes for style-conscious women who could afford his custom wares. He worked in leather, as well as python and even fish skin—which took color dyes quite well, he found—but his shoes were actually less expensive than traditional handmade shoes, which involve a pair of custom "lasts," or shoe forms, for each client. Choo had a strong sense for fashion and embellishment, and his designs became a favorite of Diana, the Princess of Wales. Fashionistas were also devoted clients, and in 1996 a stylist for British *Vogue* named Tamara Yeardye Mellon suggested they start a larger-scale shoe business together. Mellon's father, who had made part of his fortune overseeing the expansion of the Vidal Sassoon hair-care empire in the 1970s, agreed to bankroll the start-up costs.

Choo's new line was manufactured at an Italian factory, and then shipped to top department stores such as Neiman Marcus and Bergdorf Goodman. There was also a chic new London boutique with his name on it, but there was some sniping over who had actually designed the Jimmy Choos—the designer himself, or Choi and Mellon—and the partnership soured. Thomas Yeardye, Tamara Mellon's father, had been impressed with how well the $400-a-pair shoes were selling, and funded an ambitious expansion plan involving an increase in production and the number of freestanding Jimmy Choo stores. The partnership grew even more acrimonious, as Choi, the niece, told Evgenia Peretz in *Vanity Fair.* She and her uncle, she noted, "were just trying to be sure that, whatever we're investing in, we're not going backwards. To be fair, on Jimmy's side, he's got responsibility. He's got family that he needs to bring up…. Whereas, on the other side, the Yeardye family, they're all set up. To them, it's a gamble, and it could go sky-high and everything could be wonderful, or it could be in shambles. But it doesn't quite affect them."

Choi eventually joined the Yeardye side, and the partnership rearranged in 2001, with Choo retaining the name to his own custom line, while the Yeardye-managed retail line carried on. By then the Jimmy Choo name had become as prominent as that of another high-end women's footwear designer, Manolo Blahnik, and was mentioned frequently in the fash-

ion press. Characters on the hit HBO series *The Sopranos* and *Sex and the City* referenced the brand. The Jimmy Choo line also gained some priceless press attention when the 19-year-old twin daughters of U.S. president George W. Bush wore Jimmy Choo cashmere stiletto boots on their father's inauguration day in 2001. Later that year, the brand earned a somewhat more infamous distinction when a well-known Manhattan publicist, Lizzie Grubman, crashed her car into a crowd outside a nightclub in the posh resort town of Southampton in what witnesses said was a temper tantrum behind the wheel. According to other bystanders, one of the accident victims asked her friend to remove her Jimmy Choo heels from her feet, so that paramedics would not have to cut them off in their haste to treat her injuries.

Choo, who married a fellow student from Cordwainers' College and has a daughter, still makes about five pairs of custom shoes weekly at his by-appointment-only workshop in central London. These Jimmy Choos bear the "handmade" designation on their soles, unlike those sold at top retailers and in the 30 Jimmy Choo stores around the world. He is the recipient of an Order of the British Empire (OBE) designation, as well as a *Dato* title, the Malaysian equivalent of a peerage. His rather old-fashioned style of business, much in the style of his father's artisanry, suits him better than designing full-scale, fashion-driven collections. "Shoes are a personal thing, a personal touch," he said in an interview with Rose Shepherd of London's *Mail on Sunday.* "Everyone can sketch them, but to understand where they're comfortable, where they fit, where's the balance, that's important."

Sources

Books

Contemporary Fashion, second ed., St. James Press, 2002.

Periodicals

Footwear News, July 29, 1991, p. 64; December 6, 2004, p. 22.
Mail on Sunday (London, England), April 23, 2000, p. 7.
Mirror (London, England), December 22, 2001, p. 6.
New York Times Magazine, December 1, 2002, p. 102.
Times (London, England), July 16, 2001, p. 7.
Vanity Fair, August 2005, p. 124.

—Carol Brennan

Stephen Chow

Evan Agostini/Getty Images

Actor, director, and screenwriter

Born Stephen Chow Sing-chi, January 22, 1962, in Hong Kong, China. *Education:* Studied at a professional acting school, sponsored by local TVB television station.

Addresses: *Home*—Hong Kong, China. *Office*—Sony Pictures Classics, 550 Madison Ave., 8th flr., New York, NY 10022.

Career

Actor in more than 60 films, including: *Final Justice,* 1988; *All for the Winner,* 1990; *From Beijing With Love,* 1994; *God of Cookery,* 1996; *Forbidden City Cop,* 1996; *Shaolin Soccer,* 2001; *Kung Fu Hustle,* 2004. Director and writer of films, including: *King of Destruction* 1994; *From Beijing With Love,* 1994; *God of Cookery,* 1996; *Forbidden City Cop,* 1996; *The King of Comedy,* 1999; *Shaolin Soccer,* 2001; *Kung Fu Hustle,* 2004. Films produced include: *God of Cookery,* 1996; *Kung Fu Hustle,* 2004. Television appearances include: *Sou hat yi,* 1982; *The Legend of the Condor Heroes,* 1982; *Wut lik sap jat,* 1982; *430 Space Shuttle,* 1983-88; *The Justice of Life,* 1983; *Joi geen sup gao sui,* 1983; *But dou san hung,* 1983; *Sung meng chi loi,* 1987; *Mo min kap sin fung,* 1988; *Final Combat,* 1989.

Awards: Best supporting actor, Taiwanese Film Awards; Hong Kong Film Awards, six awards for various films; best film, Hong Kong Film Awards, for *Kung Fu Hustle,* 2005.

Sidelights

Stephen Chow seems to be Hong Kong's best-kept secret when it comes to making films. By American standards, he would be considered a superstar and an icon. While American movie audiences may be more familiar with such Asian stars as Jackie Chan, Jet Li, and Chow Yun Fat, Stephen Chow has out-shined them all in Hong Kong and most of the Asian countries. Chow, however, would love to cross over to international audiences. His first attempt, *Shaolin Soccer,* would have succeeded if it had not been botched by film studio Miramax. But his second effort, *Kung Fu Hustle,* helped Chow to finally achieve what he has long to become: an international star.

Stephen Chow Sing-chi was born on June 22, 1962, in Hong Kong. After his parents' divorce, he was raised in a government housing project by his mother and grandmother. As a boy, he watched many kung fu movies, and idolized martial-arts stars Bruce Lee and Wang Yu. After watching Lee's *Fists of Fury,* he decided to follow in his idols' footsteps and become an actor. He began studying wing chun, a form of kung fu, but never became a master. After graduating from high school, Chow auditioned to take acting classes, sponsored by TVB, a Hong Kong television station. Upon completion, he was given a role on *430 Space Shuttle*, a children's television show in 1983. He stayed with the program until 1988.

Chow grew in popularity and soon was given other television roles. He appeared on several television series, mainly in dramatic roles. He also had several supporting roles in a few movies. Chow's first starring role in 1990's *All for the Winner*, a parody of director-actor Chow Yun Fat's *God of the Gambler*, established him as a comedy star. He followed up *All for the Winner* with a number of films, and soon began drawing in not only huge Hong Kong audiences, but also crossed over in other Asian countries. Chow stuck with making parodies, including doing a parody of Bruce Lee's *Fists of Fury*. He also satirized James Bond films with 1994's *From Beijing With Love*, which also marked his directorial debut.

Chow's list of box-office smashes grew, and he soon out-grossed a number of Asian stars, including Chan and Li. However, these two stars crossed over to international audiences, especially American audiences. Chan became a major Hollywood player with hit movies such as *Rush Hour* and *Shanghai Noon*. Li crossed over with a role in the popular *Lethal Weapon 4*. He went on to a number of starring roles in films, including *Romeo Must Die, The One,* and *Hero.*

Many based Chow's failure to cross over due to "mou lei tau," which is translated as "nonsense" or "meaningless talk." According to the *Independent*'s Kaleem Aftab, mou lei tau are "action films mixed with slapstick comedy, in which the characters would frequently converse in a seemingly incomprehensible tongue that was a bizarre mix of Monty Python-speak and Shakespearean rhyming couplets." In addition to mou lei tau, in Chow's parodies were a number of pop culture references that only the Hong Kong and/or the Asian audiences would understand.

Chow continued moving forward, and tried to move to Canada. He was refused on the grounds of an affiliation with The Triads, Hong Kong's version of the Mafia. Chow denied any affiliation, and resigned himself to continuing to make films in Hong Kong. He began writing his films, and continued to achieve box office success with *God of Cookery* and *Forbidden City Cop*. In one year, four of the five films with the highest grosses were his movies. However, his next few films were flops, and many thought Chow was on the decline.

Chow came up with the idea to combine the popular sport of soccer with kung fu and *Shaolin Soccer* was born. *Shaolin Soccer* told the story of a former soccer player who teams up with a shaolin master who wants to share his special form of kung fu with the world and has a powerful kick that sends a soccer ball through objects. Together with the master's five brothers they form a soccer team to try to win a million dollars. The film was also heavy on the special effects. The *Independent* described the film as "the greatest martial arts football movie ever made, and the silliest."

Shaolin Soccer, Chow's 50th film, grossed $8 million in Hong Kong, $21 million in neighboring Japan, and $40 million throughout the rest of Asia. *Shaolin Soccer* also brought Chow to the attention of Hollywood. Miramax studios bought the distribution rights and planned a 2002 release of the film. However, the studio would severely cut the film down and sit on it for an extra two years, releasing it in 2004. By then, many had seen a pirated version of the film. Chow's debut to American audiences was a failure.

Chow, however, was still very much on the minds of Hollywood. Though he had planned a follow-up to *Shaolin Soccer*, Sony Pictures Classics approached him to direct a different feature. With Sony's backing and money, *Kung Fu Hustle* was created. The film, which starred Chow as a small-time thug who wanted to become a member of the Axe gang, was also loaded with special effects, and numerous American pop culture references including the Road Runner, and a dance scene a la *West Side Story* and a horror scene that mimicked *The Shining*. The fight scenes were choreographed by Yuen Wo Ping, who also choreographed *The Matrix* films. *Kung Fu Hustle* premiered in 2004, and made $7.7 million in Hong Kong its opening weekend. It replaced *Shaolin Soccer* as the highest grossing film of all time in Hong Kong. *Kung Fu Hustle* continued breaking records as it debuted at the Sundance Film Festival where it became a fan favorite and won rave reviews from all over the United States. It grossed more than $15 million in the United States alone in 2005.

Chow finally achieved his goal of showing his films to an international audience. *Kung Fu Hustle* won the Best Film award at the 24th Hong Kong Film Awards. Chow also began work on a sequel to *Kung Fu Hustle*. With constant comparisons to actor/director Charlie Chaplin, Chow will continue to wow international audiences for years to come.

Sources

Periodicals

Entertainment Weekly, April 15, 2005, p. 61.
Independent (London, England), November 12, 2004, p. 7; June 29, 2005, p. 45.
Los Angeles Times Weekly, March 25-31, 2005.
People, June 27, 2005, p. 94.
Post-Standard (Syracuse, New York), April 22, 2005, p. E2.
New York Times, September 22, 2002, p. 52L.
Rocky Mountain News (Denver, Colorado), April 16, 2005, p. 3D.
Variety, July 23, 2001, p. 41.

Online

"Doing the Hustle," E! Online, http://www.eonline.com/News/firstlook.html?news (March 28, 2005).
"Not-So-Hidden Master Stephen Chow steps out of the shadows," *Los Angeles Times Weekly,* http://www.laweekly.com/ink/05/18/films-chute.php (August 11, 2005).
"Rising martial-arts star Stephen Chow scores big with the non-stop bustle of *Kung Fu Hustle,*" SciFi.com, http://www.scifi.com/sfw/issue416/interview2.html (August 11, 2005).

—Ashyia N. Henderson

Kim Clijsters

Clive Brunskill/Getty Images

Professional tennis player

Born June 8, 1983, in Bilzen, Belgium; daughter of Leo Clijsters (a soccer coach) and Els Vandecaetsbeek.

Addresses: *Office*—c/o Women's Tennis Association, Bank Lane, Roehampton, London SW15 5XZ England.

Career

Began playing tennis at the age of five; won Belgian Junior Championship at age of eleven; made debut on the International Tennis Federation circuit, 1997; won doubles tournament at Roland Garros, 1998; debuted on the Women's Tennis Association (WTA) tour, 1999; won first title on WTA tour in Luxembourg, 1999; won Sparkassan Cup, 2000; finished in top 20 of WTA tour, 2000; member of the Belgian Fed Cup team, 2000-05; won three WTA tour events, 2001; won WTA Tour championship tournament, 2002, 2003; signed sponsorship deal with Fila, 2002; won nine titles, 2003; won seven doubles titles, 2003; ranked number one on the WTA tour for the first time, 2003; won the Pacific Life Open, 2005; won the NASDAQ-100, 2005; won the JPMorgan Chase title, 2005; won the U.S. Open women's single title, 2005.

Awards: Named Belgian sportswoman of the year, Belgian Sports Journalists Association, 1999, 2000, 2002, 2005; Most Promising Newcomer, Women's Tennis Association, 1999; Karen Krantzke Sportsmanship Award, Women's Tennis Association, 2000, 2003; National Trophy for Merit in Sport, Belgian government, 2001; Trophée National du Merite Sportif, Belgian government, 2002; named Tour Player of the Month, International Tennis Writers Association, November, 2002, May, 2003, August, 2003, and October/November 2003; ASAP Best Ambassador for the Sport of Tennis, International Tennis Writers Association, 2003; Great Cross of the Order of the Crown, Belgium, 2004; Ambassador for the Sport Award, Inaugural Lawn Tennis Association, 2005.

Sidelights

Belgian tennis player Kim Clijsters (pronounced KLEYE-sters) emerged as one of the premiere women's players in the world in the early 2000s. Through early 2006, she had won at least 30 singles titles and eleven doubles titles on the WTA (Women's Tennis Association) tour. Her prize money in this time period totaled nearly $13 million. After reaching the finals of several grand slam tournaments, she won her first slam, the U.S. Open, in 2005. For several weeks in the fall of 2005 and early 2006, Clijsters was the number-one-ranked female player in the world, a position she first held in 2003. Clijsters is a power player who likes to play from the baseline.

Born in 1983 in Belgium, Clijsters is the daughter of athletic parents. Her father, Leo, also known as Lei, was a soccer star in his native country. In 1988, he was player of the year in Belgium. Leo Clijsters played internationally and later became the coach of a team in Belgium. Clijsters' mother, Els, was a champion gymnast in Belgium. She was the national junior champion, but was forced to retire when back problems sidelined her career. Of her parents' contribution to her career, Clijsters told Ronald Atkin of the *Independent*, "I inherit power and perseverance from my dad. My thighs are very muscular and people say I have legs just like his. I don't have a body like Anna Kournikova but that's no problem. I have suppleness, which comes from my mother's side."

Clijsters chose to learn to play tennis, beginning at the age of five. She began competing in tournaments in Genk, Belgium, at the age of six. When she was eleven years old, she won the Belgian Junior championship. This win led to her being coached by Bart Van Kerchkhove. He remained her coach until 1996. That year, Clijsters entered a tennis academy in Antwerp, Belgium. There, she was able to combine academics with tennis, and began to compete internationally. She also gained a new coach in Carl Maes, whom she worked with until June of 2002.

In 1997, while Clijsters was still a student and competing in junior grand slams, she also began competing on the ITF (International Tennis Federation) circuit. Her first ITF tournament was in Koksijde, Belgium, where she made the quarter finals before losing. In 1998, Clijsters was the runner-up in the junior Wimbledon tournament. That same year, in doubles at Roland Garros in France, she won with Jelena Dokic. As Clijsters' career took off, her father played a pivotal role in her career by taking care of his daughter's contracts and finances. He also helped her mental game, though because of his lack of tennis knowledge, his role was limited. Clijsters was ranked 409th in the world in 1998.

In 1999, Clijsters began appearing on the WTA tour, though she still primarily competed in challenger and satellite tournaments. She was only 16 years old. Her first WTA event was in Antwerp, Belgium, where she lost the quarterfinals match. Clijsters soon won her first ITF singles tournament in Sheffield, England. In 1999, Clijsters began winning tournaments on the WTA tour. She won her first WTA women's singles tour event in Luxembourg, defeating fellow Belgian Dominique Van Roost. This event also marked the first time two Belgians played each other in a WTA event final. That same year, Clijsters also won the doubles title with fellow Belgian Laurence Courtois in Bratislava, Slovakia.

Clijsters made some progress in grand slams in 1999. After competing as a qualifier, she reached the fourth round of Wimbledon. There, Clijsters lost to her former idol, Steffi Graf, 6-2, 6-2. Clijsters saw the match as significant in her career. She told John Roberts of the *Independent*, "The honor of being one of the last players to play Steffi is my best memory of 1999." Clijsters also reported to Roberts, "After the match Steffi said to me I played the tennis of the future. That meant so much to me." Clijsters also reached the third round of the U.S. Open, where she came close to defeating Serena Williams, who later won the title. Clijsters had shown she could compete with the best. She finished the year ranked number 47.

In 2000, Clijsters played in 16 WTA tour events, winning two. One victory came in Leipzig, Germany. There, Clijsters won the Sparkassan Cup by defeating Elena Likhovtseva. She also had some success in grand slams, albeit in mixed doubles. She reached the finals of Wimbledon mixed doubles with then boyfriend and Australian champion men's player Lleyton Hewitt. (The couple became engaged in 2003, but ended their relationship in 2004.) In addition, she reached the quarter finals of the WTA championship tournament. Clijsters also played for Belgium in the Fed Cup for the first time, a tradition that would continue at least through 2005. By the end of 2000, Clijsters was ranked 18th in the world.

Over the next two years, Clijsters continued to improve and nearly won her first grand slam. She won three WTA tour events in Stanford, Leipzig, and Luxembourg, in 2001. Clijsters also reached the quarterfinals of the U.S. Open. That same year, she competed in the finals of the French Open. Though she nearly upset her opponent, Jennifer Capriati, Clijsters lost in the end. However, by reaching the finals of the French Open, she became the first Belgian woman to reach a Grand Slam final. Along the way to the finals, Clijsters had to defeat countrywoman Justine Henin in the semi-finals. This match made tennis popular again in Belgium, with Clijsters representing the Flemish side of the country, and Henin, the French-speaking side. The pair claimed they were friends to the public, but actually had a growing rivalry. In 2002, Clijsters won the WTA tour championship event as well as three other titles. That same year, she signed a sponsorship deal with Fila. By this time she was one the top five women in the world.

Clijsters won the most titles of her young career in 2003. She won nine titles that year, including a repeat victory at the WTA tour championship. She also had success competing in doubles. Clijsters won the Wimbledon women's double title with Ai Sugiyama. This was one of seven women's doubles titles Clijsters won that year. Clijsters also began working with a new coach, Marc Dehous.

Her track record in singles grand slams was less impressive in 2003. She reached the semi-finals of the Australian Open, facing Serena Williams. Though Clijsters nearly won the match, she eventually lost to Williams. At the French Open, Clijsters again reached the finals, facing Henin, now known as Justine Henin-Hardenne. Clijsters lost badly, 6-0, 6-4. At Wimbledon, Clijsters lost in three sets to Venus Williams in the semi-finals. While Clijsters reached the finals of the U.S. Open, she lost to Henin-Hardenne again, 7-5, 6-1. Clijsters knew that she had to improve her mental preparation at such events and become more selective at events she played in before slams, but claimed she did not have a problem with Henin-Hardenne. Clijsters told Scott Gullan of the *Herald Sun,* "That's always something that they're going to keep saying, if you lose against her. I definitely don't think [it is the case]. In those matches I knew where the problem was laying and I knew it wasn't psychological."

At the end of 2003, Clijsters was the number-two-ranked woman in the world. She had even spent some time at number one in August of 2003, knocking off long-time number one Serena Williams. When the first grand slam of 2004 came around, however, Clijsters found herself in a now familiar position. She reached the finals of the Australian Open, again playing Henin-Hardenne. Clijsters lost again, but had been suffering from ankle problems throughout the tournament. She did put up a better fight, losing 6-3, 4-6, 6-3. Some commentators believe that Clijsters' sunny demeanor contributed to her failing to win big events. L. Jon Wertheim of *Sports Illustrated* wrote, "The knock on Clijsters has been that her sweet nature exacted a price on her tennis, a sport that all but requires streaks of self-absorption and nastiness."

Clijsters never fully recovered in 2004. She won only two events, in Antwerp and Paris, mostly because the year was filled with injury. Clijsters had wrist problems after tearing a tendon in March. She continued to play for a while, but did not do well. Clijsters had surgery in June to remove a cyst from her wrist, but it did not help. She tried to play again in October, but the wrist was re-injured. Clijsters did not play for about eight months and there was some uncertainty over if she could have a career again. Clijsters told John Roberts of the *Independent,* "There were days when the doctors said, 'It's going

to be very tough for you to reach the same level again.' There have been a lot of boring weeks when I was in plaster, trying to recover, and doing all these crazy exercises.... You just have to be patient. You just try to think positive."

Clijsters did not play in tournaments again until February of 2005. She rebounded in 2005 with a new attitude and nasty edge. The result was nine victories in tournaments, including wins at the Pacific Life Open, NASDAQ-100, and the JPMorgan Chase title. Clijsters told Wertheim of *Sports Illustrated* "You realize that one injury can end your career tomorrow, so you should just enjoy playing. But you also realize that tennis is important to you, so you want to do everything possible to win." At the JPMorgan Chase event, Clijsters pulled off an unexpected athletic move with her vertical jump which threw off her opponent, Daniela Hantuchova. Clijsters later told Lisa Dillman of the *Los Angeles Times,* "The more you keep pushing them to go for more and the more they know they're going to go for more risk and you get them out of their comfort zone." Clijsters was improving both offensively and defensively.

Clijsters also won her first-ever grand slam event in 2005, at the U.S. Open. She began as the number-four seed in the tournament, and faced difficulties along the way. In the semifinals against Maria Sharapova, Clijsters dropped five match points in the second set, but rebounded in the third to win the match. In the finals, Clijsters soundly defeated Mary Pierce, 6-3, 6-1. Clijsters lost the label of being "the best player never to win a Grand Slam." She told the *Los Angeles Times'* Dillman, "I had the idea that the media was making more of it [the label], like a bigger deal of it than I was. I was very motivated and working hard to try to do it."

Early in 2006, Clijsters again faced injury issues. She developed ankle problems at the Australian Open which forced her to withdraw from the semifinals. Despite having take some time off to heal, she was again ranked number one in the world. Though Clijsters was at her peak as a player, she was not planning on playing more than two or three more years. She was not sure her body could take it, and wanted to start a family. Clijsters was involved with American basketball player Brian Lynch, who played college ball at Villanova and professionally in Belgium. She told S.L. Price of *Sports Illustrated* after her U.S. Open win, "Brian's the most important thing in my life now. I would give up this title, straight away, just to have him. Because at the end of the day when you go home, the trophies are not talking to you. They're not going to love you. I want the people I love with me."

Sources

Periodicals

Advertiser (Australia), October 23, 2004, p. 7.

Austin American-Statesman (Austin, TX), February 2, 2006, p. C2.

Australian, December 3, 2005, p. 51.

Express on Sunday (London, England), November 5, 2000.

Guardian (London, England), June 25, 2001, p. 16.

Herald (Glasgow, Scotland), January 30, 2004, p. 36.

Herald Sun (Melbourne, Australia), January 31, 2004, p. 36.

Independent (London, England), June 28, 1999, p. 5; January 5, 2000, p. 19; December 31, 2000, p. 14; September 12, 2005, pp. 70-71.

Los Angeles Times, August 15, 2005, p. D4; September 10, 2005, p. D1; September 11, 2005, p. D1; November 9, 2005, p. D3.

Newsday (New York, NY), September 11, 2005, p. B2.

New York Times, September 4, 2001, p. D5; August 29, 2005, p. F4.

San Diego Union-Tribune, August 28, 2005, p. C2.

Sports Illustrated, April 11, 2005, p. 87; September 19, 2005, p. 106.

Sunday Telegraph (Sydney, Australia), February 1, 2004, p. 49.

Online

"Kim Clijsters (BEL)," Sony Ericcson WTA Tour, http://www.wtatour.com/players/playerprofiles/PlayerBio2.asp?PlayerID=30458 (January 24, 2006).

Kim Clijsters Website; http://www.kimclijsters.com (January 24, 2006).

"Kim Clijsters," Who2.com, http://www.who2.com/kimclijsters.html (January 24, 2006).

—*A. Petruso*

Anderson Cooper

Ethan Miller/Reuters/Landov

Television journalist

Born June 3, 1967, in New York, NY; son of Wyatt Cooper (a writer) and Gloria Vanderbilt (an entrepreneur). *Education:* Earned degree in political science and international relations from Yale University, 1989.

Addresses: *Home*—New York, NY. *Office*—CNN, 1 Time Warner Center, New York, NY 10019-8012.

Career

Began at Channel One as a fact-checker c. 1989, became freelance news correspondent, c. 1990-93, and chief international correspondent, 1993-95; ABC News, correspondent after 1995 and co-anchor of *World News Now*; host of the ABC reality show *The Mole*, 2000-01; correspondent and substitute anchor, Cable News Network, 2002; host of his own weeknight news hour, *Anderson Cooper 360*, CNN, 2003—.

Sidelights

Anderson Cooper hosts *Anderson Cooper 360*, an hour-long newscast on Cable News Network (CNN) that quickly accrued an audience for its intelligent, sometimes bemused take on the day's top stories. Prior to joining CNN, Cooper worked for ABC and served several years in the trenches as a war correspondent. "To me the news is not a joke, especially in the times we live in now," he told *Atlanta Journal-Constitution* writer Jill Vejnoska. "But I think people are really smart and want something that doesn't assume that they don't get it. I think people get it. They get how news is put together."

Cooper possesses a rather impressive pedigree for a television journalist. His father, Wyatt Cooper, was a writer from Mississippi who married the heiress to one of America's greatest fortunes, Gloria Vanderbilt, in 1964. Anderson Cooper's mother was the great-great-granddaughter of shipping and railroad tycoon Cornelius Vanderbilt, who died in 1877 and left a fortune estimated at $100 million. In her own youth, Vanderbilt had been the subject of a vicious, well-publicized custody battle, and as a young woman led a glittering social life that was also avidly chronicled in the newspapers of the day. Wyatt Cooper was her fourth husband, and Anderson was their second child, born in 1967 two years after his brother, Carter. The family lived in Manhattan.

Despite the family fortune, Cooper was determined to earn his own money. He began modeling at the age of eleven, and in his teens worked as a waiter at Mortimer's, a famed Manhattan eatery frequented by Park Avenue society types. He was sent to Dalton, a private Manhattan school, primarily because his mother thought its emphasis on the arts over athletics would provide a firmer grounding. His father died when he was eleven, after a series of heart attacks in 1977. "I think, given my mom's background, people have some idea of what my life must have been like, but the reality is very different," he told Brad Goldfarb in *Interview.* "Certainly, growing up, there was a nice apartment and nice things in the apartment, but for me, one of the greatest privileges of my background was realizing that what a lot of people think they want will not ultimately make them happier."

Cooper was able to graduate a semester early from Dalton and satisfied a wanderlust by traveling through Africa for a few months before he entered Yale University. He earned a degree in political science and international relations in 1989, but his senior year was preceded by a tragedy of almost unimaginable sorrow: his brother, Carter, who had been under treatment for depression, jumped out of the 14th-floor window of their mother's New York City apartment in front of her, and fell to his death. When Cooper finished his degree, he considered taking the U.S. Foreign Service examination, a common career choice given his Ivy-League major, but opted instead to become a news correspondent. He was especially eager to get into the war zone, which he admitted was indirectly linked to the family tragedy. "Suicide is such an odd, taboo sort of thing, and my brother's death is still sort of a mystery, so I became interested in questions of survival: why some people survive and others don't," he explained to Goldfarb in *Interview*. "Covering wars just seemed logical."

Cooper's first job was as a fact-checker at Channel One, a news network that broadcast daily reports into American classrooms. Bored by the desk job and unable to get an interview at any of the major networks' news departments, he decided to go to Vietnam to study the language, and took a video camera with him. He stopped off in Myanmar first, and was able to film some footage about that country's internal strife thanks to some faked press credentials a friend had made for him on a computer. After that, he went back to Africa, and filed stories for Channel One as a freelancer on such topics as a spreading famine in Somalia. By 1993, the network had promoted Cooper to chief international correspondent. His reports from international danger zones like the Balkans and central Africa attracted the attention of the major news organizations, and in 1995 Cooper was hired by ABC News.

Cooper served as a correspondent for the network and then the co-anchor of *World News Now*, its overnight-news broadcast. After a while, he tired of the arduous schedule—the show aired from 3 a.m. to 5 a.m.—and took a break by accepting a job in 2000 as host of a new ABC reality series, *The Mole*.

After the September 11, 2001, attacks on the World Trade Center and Pentagon, Cooper was eager to return to hard news, however, and was hired by CNN in January of 2002 as a correspondent and substitute anchor.

Cooper seemed to score well with viewers when he took over Paula Zahn's two-hour nightly newscast, and so in mid-2003 his CNN bosses decided to give him his own newscast. Zahn held the 8 p.m. slot, where she covered stories in-depth, with Cooper leading in at the 7 p.m. hour with *Anderson Cooper 360*, which featured broader coverage of the day's major stories. The show debuted on September 8, 2003, and Cooper quickly gained a cult following thanks in part to his sardonic, sometimes bemused delivery. Furthermore, the show's pre- and post-commercial lead-in musical bits were drawn from obscure alternative rock acts, some dating back to the late 1970s, and established Cooper as one of the hipper personalities in mainstream network news. The host, however, maintains that his far more well-informed staffers choose the music.

Cooper's looks also attracted a fair amount of fans among both genders. Known for impeccably tailored suits, prematurely silver hair, and blue eyes, he became the target of a major Internet fan following. He still reports from the field on occasion, surveying the after-effects of the Asian tsunami in the first days of January of 2005, just after hosting the nationally telecast New Year's Eve celebrations from Times Square in New York. He realizes that both jobs might someday pass to others. "I've never expected to be anywhere," he confessed to *New York Observer* media critic Joe Hagan. "People love you one day and the next they don't. I ultimately find it depressing. I just try to focus on being smarter and better than I currently am."

Sources

Atlanta Journal-Constitution, November 23, 2003, p. MS1.
Electronic Media, June 30, 1997, p. 18.
Entertainment Weekly, July 12, 2002, p. 65; August 6, 2004, p. 36.
InStyle, November 1, 2004, p. 422.
Interview, October 2004, p. 122.
New York Observer, March 15, 2004, p. 1; January 10, 2005, p. 23.
People, May 6, 1996, p. 54; January 15, 2001, p. 77; December 2, 2002, p. 102.
TelevisionWeek, September 8, 2003, p. 5.

—*Carol Brennan*

Rhonda Cornum

AP Images

U.S. Army surgeon

Born October 31, 1954, in Dayton, OH; married first husband (divorced); married Kory Cornum (an Air Force colonel and orthopedist), 1983; children: Regan (from first marriage). *Education:* Cornell University, Ph.D. (biochemistry and nutrition), c. 1978; Uniformed Services University of the Health Sciences, M.D., 1986; National War College, 2003.

Addresses: *Publisher*—Presidio Press, 1745 Broadway, New York, NY 10019.

Career

Joined U.S. Army, 1978; worked at Letterman Army Institute of Research, c. 1978-82; general surgery intern at Walter Reed Army Medical Center, 1986-87; joined Army Aeromedical Center at Fort Rucker, 1987; assigned as flight surgeon to a helicopter battalion in the Persian Gulf, 1990; attended Air Command and Staff College at Maxwell Air Force Base, 1991-92; started training in urology surgery, 1993; named staff urologist, Eisenhower Army Medical Center, 1998; given command of a support hospital at Fort Bragg, 2000; served in Bosnia as a medical task force commander, 2000-01; commander of the Army's Landstuhl military hospital, 2003-05; reassigned to an Army position in Atlanta, GA, 2005.

Awards: Legion of Merit, Distinguished Flying Cross, Bronze Star, Meritorious Service Medal, Air Medal, POW Medal and Purple Heart, U.S. Army. Ten Outstanding Young Americans Award, U.S. Junior Chamber of Commerce, 1993.

Sidelights

When U.S. Army flight surgeon Rhonda Cornum became one of two American servicewomen taken prisoner in the 1991 Persian Gulf War against Iraq, her story of resilience helped convince Americans that female soldiers could serve in expanded roles in wartime. Her memoir about the conflict and her eight days in captivity, *She Went to War: The Rhonda Cornum Story*, was published to critical acclaim in 1992. When the attention the war brought her faded, Cornum continued her military career, training as a urologist and serving in Bosnia. In 2003, during the second war between the United States and Iraq, Cornum attracted media attention again as the first female commander of the military hospital in Germany that treated many soldiers wounded in Iraq.

Cornum was born in Dayton, Ohio, and grew up in East Aurora, New York, near Buffalo. She earned a Ph.D. in biochemistry and nutrition at Cornell University in Ithaca, New York, while living in a wood-heated cabin with her first husband and their daughter, Regan. She was recruited into the Army in 1978, and worked at an Army research facility in San Francisco. She took to the Army quickly, she told Jennifer Allen of *Good Housekeeping*, even though she had been a solitary child: "Everything I had ever done was very individual," she told Allen. "Maybe I hadn't realized I was missing it, but working for something bigger than yourself just appealed to me." In 1982, Cornum went to medical school at a military school in Bethesda, Maryland, where she met her second husband, Kory, who was in the Air Force; they married in 1983.

She first got the attention of the press in 1987, when she was selected as a finalist for becoming an astronaut. At the time, she was a captain in the Army, working at the Walter Reed Army Medical Center as an intern and living on a horse farm in Olney, Maryland. She was not selected, but went on instead to serve as a flight surgeon at Fort Rucker in Alabama.

In 1990, when the United States was preparing to go to war to reverse the Iraqi invasion of Kuwait, Cornum agreed to go to the Persian Gulf as a flight surgeon with the 101st Airborne Division. The war began in January of 1991, followed by a ground assault in February. During a failed attempt to rescue a fighter pilot with a broken leg, Cornum's helicopter was shot down over Iraq. As the copter fell, "I remember thinking, 'at least I'm dying doing something honorable,'" Cornum told Joellen Perry for a special "heroes" issue of *U.S. News and World Report.* "We crashed at 140 miles per hour—there's no way I should have survived that crash. But then I looked up and I saw five Iraqi guys with their rifles pointed at me," she recalled to Adam Ramirez of the military newspaper *Stars and Stripes.* "I knew I wasn't dead."

Five of the eight crew members died in the crash. Cornum had a bullet lodged in her shoulder, both her arms were broken, and she could not stand on her knee because of a blown ligament. The Iraqi soldiers pulled her out of the copter by one of her broken arms, threw her into a circle with another survivor, and threatened to shoot them, but did not. Instead, they drove them to a prison in the Iraqi city of Basra. During the drive, an Iraqi solider molested Cornum. She was unable to fight him off because of her broken arms. Held prisoner for eight days, Cornum was interrogated but did not reveal anything classified. Other Iraqi soldiers were more respectful, helping her take off her flight suit and giving her a gown to wear.

Cornum was released March 5, 1991, a week after the war ended. She and other prisoners were flown to Riyadh, the capital of Saudi Arabia, where Gen.

Norman Schwarzkopf greeted them. Cornum had her arms in slings. The press paid special attention to Cornum and Melissa Rathbun-Nealy, the other U.S. servicewoman taken prisoner by the Iraqis. Cornum's memoir, *She Went to War,* was published a year later. It told the story of her time as a prisoner of war. Barton Gellman, a *Washington Post* writer, praised the book, which begins with her helicopter flying over the desert in Iraq. "From its first sentence it is vivid and concrete," he wrote. Cornum, he added, "displays a resourcefulness and courage that would do credit to any soldier." The *New York Times* named it as one of the most notable books of 1992.

Washington Post profiler Henry Allen described her this way: "She has green eyes, brown hair and a distaste for being photographed from the left because of the narrow, high-bridged nose she has broken twice riding horses. She is a licensed steeplechase jockey. She used to fox-hunt when she was a medical student in Washington.... She wore a big wristwatch with a calculator and a compass on it. Aviators are known for wearing big wristwatches. She has flown everything from helicopters to F-15s, and she once built her own plane." Cornum, Allen noted, stayed out of the debate about the role of servicewomen in the military and the sexual harassment scandals, such as the Navy's Tailhook incident, that seemed part of an early-1990s backlash against military women. "She has mastered neither the confessional anguish nor the defiant boasting of the daytime talk shows and congressional hearings where our nation hammers out its moral certitudes of the moment," Allen noted.

Others may have seen her experience as an example of why women should be protected from combat's front lines, but Cornum did not. In June of 1992, Cornum made headlines when she revealed in advance of her book's publication that she had been molested while in Iraqi custody. She said she did not want to make light of sexual assault, but she did not seem to consider it the worst part of her imprisonment. "Since everything that happens to you as a prisoner of war is non-consensual, then the fact that one thing they did was non-consensual is not very relevant," she told the *Washington Post*'s Allen. "So then you have to organize the bad things that can happen to you in some other hierarchy. My hierarchy was, is it going to make me stay here longer, is it life-threatening, is it disabling or is it excruciating. If it's none of those things, then it took on a fairly low level of significance."

Though she never identified with the feminist movement, Cornum insisted that women in the military should be judged on their own talents, and she dismissed those who would use her experience as an argument for keeping women out of jobs on the front lines. "Every 15 seconds in America, some woman is assaulted. Why are they worried about a woman getting assaulted once every 10 years in a war overseas? It's ridiculous," she told Cathy Booth Thomas of *Time.* "Clearly it's an emotional argument they use ... because they can't think of a rational one."

When defense secretary Les Aspin opened many new military roles to women in April of 1993, the service of women such as Cornum in the Gulf War was credited with proving that women could serve capably in important roles and brave the dangers of war. Cornum's conduct as a prisoner "was a validation that if women are in combat and something like this happens ... they do have the strength, the stamina, the mental courage to meet the demands," retired Air Force Brig. Gen. Wilma Vaught told Perry of *U.S. News and World Report.*

Though most former prisoners of war end up leaving the military, Cornum stayed. She trained in urology surgery and became staff urologist at an Army medical center. By 2001, she had been promoted from major to colonel and was commanding a medical unit in Tuzla, Bosnia. She was well-respected by her staff there, in part because most members of the Army know her story, Maj. Richard Meaney, the hospital's executive officer, told Ramirez of *Stars and Stripes.* "But even if she didn't have that history, she's still a top physician and a fantastic commander," Meaney said.

In 2003, when the second Iraq war began, Cornum was stationed at Fort McNair in Washington, D.C. and studying at the National War College there. As American soldiers, including women, were taken prisoner, reporters spoke to Cornum again about her experience 12 years earlier. That summer, Cornum graduated from the War College—often considered a step toward higher positions in the military—and became commander of the Army's Landstuhl military hospital in Germany, its largest hospital outside the United States, with more than 1,800 staff members. She was the first woman to hold the position. Landstuhl often treated soldiers injured in Iraq, so her new position put her back in the spotlight, talking to reporters and conducting press conferences. She took over a few months after the invasion of Iraq, just before an insurgency broke out, prolonging the war. "There were some days when the workload was light," Rhonda recalled to Jim Warren of the *Lexington Herald-Leader* after leaving the position. "But you really couldn't relax because you knew that the next day you might be completely overwhelmed." When 16 soldiers were sent to Landstuhl that November after their Chinook helicopter was attacked, Cornum compared their experience to her wartime crash for Mark Landler of the *New York Times.* "At least we had the ability to shoot back," she said. "The guys in the Chinook just had to sit there and watch what was happening to them. That must have been the hardest part."

Good Housekeeping's Allen noted that Cornum sometimes still worked as a doctor when many wounded soldiers arrived at Landstuhl at once. After the battles in Fallujah, Iraq, in April of 2004, Cornum admitted patients and assisted in the operating room. "When you first meet her, you might say, 'Wow, she's kind of a tough bird,'" Col. Steven Older, Landstuhl's chief medical officer, told Allen. "But under that is a soft, compassionate person. She's a very caring physician." Patients often knew about her experience in the first Gulf War, since her memoir was available in the hospital store. She often consoled patients and their families. "Don't be discouraged," she told wounded soldiers, according to Allen. "It's going to take you a long time, but you're going to come back if you want to."

Cornum and her husband, Kory, an Air Force colonel and orthopedist, spent several years at the same posts. He was stationed at Fort McNair while she studied at the War College, and he was also stationed at Landstuhl while she commanded it; he coordinated a volunteer doctor program that brought in neurosurgeons from the United States to compensate for a shortage of military neurosurgeons. In June of 2005, the Cornums left Germany for the 320-acre horse farm they bought in 1998 in Kentucky, to take a break before their next assignment. Warren of the *Lexington Herald-Leader* found them resting and taking calves to market. Cornum was scheduled to report to a new assignment in Atlanta in July of 2005. Though press reports had speculated she might eventually become a general, Cornum said she might retire to the farm if their daughter, Regan, who looks after it while Cornum and her husband are on active duty, were to go to veterinary school.

Selected writings

She Went to War: The Rhonda Cornum Story (with Peter Copeland), Presidio Press, 1992.

Sources

Periodicals

Cincinnati Post, April 30, 1993, p. 1A.
Good Housekeeping, December 2004, pp. 58-60.

Lexington Herald-Leader, June 27, 2005, p. A1.
Miami Herald, December 6, 1993, p. 5B.
New York Times, November 4, 2003, p. A11.
Stars and Stripes, April 8, 2001.
Time, March 28, 2003.
U.S. News and World Report, August 20, 2001.
Washington Post, March 8, 1987, p. D2; March 6, 1991, p. A21; March 7, 1991, p. A25; June 11, 1992, p. A4; August 8, 1992, p. F1; December 13, 1992; March 30, 2003, p. F1; April 15, 2003, p. C1; April 25, 2005, p. A15.

Online

"Meet the Commander," U.S. Army Europe Healthcare, http://www.landstuhl.healthcare.hqus areur.army.mil/command/commandbio.htm (February 26, 2006).
"War Stories: Rhonda Cornum," PBS Frontline, http://www.pbs.org/wgbh/pages/frontline/ gulf/war/5.html (February 25, 2006).

—Erick Trickey

Paula Creamer

Kyodo/Landov

Professional golfer

Born August 5, 1986, in Mountain View, CA; daughter of Paul (an airline pilot) and Karen Creamer.

Addresses: *Contact*—c/o Ladies Professional Golf Association, 100 International Golf Dr., Daytona Beach, FL 32124-1092.

Career

Began playing golf, c. 1996; began competing on the junior and amateur circuits, c. 1997; took first-place medal at the Ladies Professional Golf Association Qualifying School Tournament, 2004; turned professional, 2004; won first tournament as a professional, Sybase Classic, 2005; won Evian Masters tournament, France, 2005; won NEC Karuizawa tournament, Japan, 2005; won Masters GC tournament, Japan, 2005; played for the United States on the winning Solheim Cup team, 2005.

Awards: Player of the Year, American Junior Golf Association, 2003; Nancy Lopez Award, Ladies Professional Golf Association, 2005; Louise Suggs Rolex Rookie of the Year, Ladies Professional Golf Association, 2005.

Sidelights

While still a teenager, Paula Creamer built on her strong amateur golf career and became a professional competing on the Ladies Professional Golf Association (LPGA) tour. Creamer found im-

mediate success in the 2005 season, winning at least three tournaments and rookie of the year honors. The young golfer is known as the "Pink Panther" for her favorite color, which she often wears while playing. Creamer is one of many sound young female golfers who have emerged in the early 2000s, including potential rival Michelle Wie.

Creamer was born on August 5, 1986, in Mountain View, California, and raised in Pleasanton, California, a suburb of San Francisco. She was an only child and competitive from an early age. Her first interest was dance. Creamer had the goal of becoming a cheerleader. As a child, Creamer was on a team of acrobatic dancers that toured the United States.

By the time Creamer was ten years old, she was playing golf. Creamer's father, airline pilot Paul Creamer, played the game on a daily basis. The family home was next to Castlewood Country Club, where Creamer learned to play. It was immediately obvious that the young girl had talent. She soon left the dance team behind and began competing in tournaments. When Creamer was eleven years old, she was victorious in 18 successive junior tournaments.

To further Creamer's career, the family moved to Florida in 2000. The young golfer honed her golf game at the David Leadbetter Golf Academy. She also became a student at the Pendleton School, a private high school which primarily educated elite athletes. While focusing on her education, Creamer continued to compete in amateur and junior tournaments as a young teenager. She also played in select elite golf events around the world such as in 2002, when she was the female U.S. representative at the R&A Junior Open in Royal Musselburgh, England. Creamer finished sixth in the combined finals totals.

Creamer's breakout year as an amateur was 2003. She reached the semi-finals of two major events: the U.S. Girls Amateur Championship and the U.S. Women's Amateur Championship. Creamer also qualified for the U.S. Women's Open, but missed the cut. However, she did later make the cut in two LPGA tour events. In 2003, she was named the player of the year by the American Junior Golf Association.

What made Creamer improve so much was the addition of a strong short game. From the beginning, she had a strong mental game and could work well under pressure. She also did exceptionally well at hitting the ball off the tee to the green. The great short game gave her the tool she needed to succeed as a professional. Such a short game would allow Creamer to earn the kind of low scores that win tournaments.

Creamer continued to compete on a high level as an amateur in 2004. She played in a number of amateur and junior events and finished thirteenth in the U.S. Women's Open. Creamer also competed in seven LPGA tour events, usually on sponsor's exemptions, and made the cut each time. She tied for second at the ShopRite LPGA Classic and was eighteenth at the Canadian Women's Open.

Creamer also represented the United States in several international team tournaments. She was a part of the Curtis Cup team, which beat Ireland and Great Britain. In addition, Creamer also played on Team USA at the World Amateur Team Championship, which finished second.

Her success in 2004 led to her winning the sixth annual Nancy Lopez Award. This honor is given to the best female amateur golfer. By the time Creamer won the award, she was already on the way to becoming a professional. She had entered the LPGA Tour Qualifying School (known as Q School) as an amateur. She could go through Q School as an amateur and retain that status if she did not do well. She planned on going to college if that happened.

Of making her decision, Creamer told Brian Murphy of the San Francisco Chronicle, "I've done pretty much all of the junior and amateur things you can do. And once you cross that big boundary, and know you can play out there, the sky's the limit..... It was time for me to say: Paula, you can play out there. You belong."

Creamer never entered college. After tying for first in the qualifier for the lesser Futures Tour (a developmental circuit run by the LPGA), Creamer dominated the LPGA Tour's Q School. She won the final qualifying tournament's first place medal by five shots. Creamer's victory marked the first time an amateur won the Q-School Tournament. Creamer turned professional soon after the victory, which came in December of 2004. Her first LPGA season began in February of 2005.

While Creamer was competing as a professional in the spring of 2005, she was completing her senior year at the Pendleton School. She missed her senior prom playing in a tournament. Creamer succeeded right away on the LPGA tour. In at least 21 starts, she missed only one cut and had ten top-ten finishes. Her first victory came in the Sybase Classic, only her ninth even as a professional. With this victory, she became the youngest to win a multi-round event in the history of the LPGA tour. Creamer was also the second-youngest player ever to win a LPGA event. Not since 1952 had an 18-year-old woman won.

In a short time, Creamer had her second victory as a professional. She won the Evian Masters in France by eight shots. This victory made her the youngest winner on the Ladies European Tour ever. Creamer also won two tournaments in Japan, the NEC Karuizawa tournament and the Masters GC, on the Japan LPGA tour. In addition, she finished third at the McDonald's LPGA Championship.

Over the course of her rookie season, Creamer won more than $1.2 million, making her the youngest player as well as the quickest person to make a million on the LPGA tour in its history. She also played her way onto the United States' Solheim Cup team, which won over Europe. Her play contributed to the victory. By August of 2005, Creamer's play had tied up the Louise Suggs Rolex Rookie of the Year title. She had at least 1,246 points, outpacing her nearest competitor by more than 600 points.

Despite her success on the women's tour, Creamer had no real desire to play in the men's Professional Golf Association (PGA) tour. Creamer's goal was to become the best player in the world in women's golf. She told Damon Hack of the *New York Times*, "I know what it takes to win events. I've won from behind, I've won from tied and I've won from in the lead. I've won all three ways you can win. Once you're there and you've done it, it becomes kind of routine. For me, I think the most important thing is to know how to win and how to compete under pressure."

Sources

Periodicals

Daily News (New York, NY), May 23, 2005, p. 78.
Denver Post, February 24, 2005, p. D1.
Los Angeles Times, September 12, 2005, p. D3.
New York Times, May 21, 2005, p. D2.
San Francisco Chronicle, September 4, 2004, p. D3; December 13, 2004, p. G1; June 23, 2005, p. A1.

Sports Illustrated, December 13, 2004, p. G19; May 30, 2005, p. 20.
St. Petersburg Times (St. Petersburg, FL), September 18, 2005, p. 1C.
UPI NewsTrack, July 23, 2005.
USA Today, December 14, 2004, p. 3C.

Online

"It's Official, Creamer Wins Louise Suggs Rolex Rookie of the Year Award," LPGA.com, http://www.lpga.com/conent_1.aspx?pid=4900&mid=2 (October 15, 2005).
"Paula Creamer," LPGA.com, http://www.lpga.com/player_results.aspx&id=3438 (October 15, 2005).
"Paula Creamer Named Winner of Sixth Annual Nancy Lopez Award," LPGA.com, http://www.lpga.com/content_1.aspx?pid=3884&mid=2 (October 15, 2005).

—A. Petruso

Sidney Crosby

Professional hockey player

Mario Anzuoni/Reuters/Landov

Born August 7, 1987, in Halifax, Nova Scotia, Canada; son of Troy (a law firm facilities manager) and Trina (Forbes) Crosby.

Addresses: *Contact*—Pittsburgh Penguins, One Chatham Center, Ste. 400, Pittsburgh, PA 15219-3516. *Home*—Cole Harbour, Nova Scotia, Canada. *Management*—International Management Group, Pat Brisson, 520 Broadway Ste. 660, Santa Monica, CA 90401. *Website*—http://www.crosby87.com.

Career

Began playing professional hockey after being drafted by the Pittsburgh Penguins as the first pick in the National Hockey League draft, 2005.

Awards: Canadian Hockey League Player of the Year, 2003-04; Canadian Hockey League scoring title, 2003-04; Canadian Hockey League Rookie of the Year, 2003-04; silver medal, Team Canada, World Junior Championships, Helsinki, Finland, 2004; Canadian Hockey League Player of the Year, 2004-05; Canadian Hockey League scoring title, 2004-05; gold medal, Team Canada, World Junior Championships, Grand Forks, ND, 2005.

Sidelights

Sidney Crosby picked up his first hockey stick as a toddler and began playing organized hockey at the age of five. By the time he entered his teens, Crosby was drawing comparisons to hockey great

Wayne Gretzky for his ability to make the puck dance. In July of 2005, the Pittsburgh Penguins chose Crosby as the No. 1 pick in the National Hockey League (NHL) draft, generating a buzz in the hockey world. The NHL, which had missed its entire 2004-05 season due to a labor dispute, hoped Crosby's presence would infuse some excitement and help revive its disheartened fan base. "We're always looking for guys to be the cornerstones, and he's a guy that has all that potential," Gretzky noted during an interview, according to the *Pittsburgh Tribune-Review.* "He's obviously the future of the National Hockey League." While Gretzky was known as "The Great One," Crosby has been dubbed "The Next One."

Crosby was born on August 7, 1987, in Halifax, Nova Scotia, Canada, to Troy and Trina Crosby, though he grew up in the fishing village of Cole Harbour, Nova Scotia, alongside a younger sister. He wears jersey No. 87 in honor of his birth year. Crosby began skating as a preschooler, pushed along by his hockey-crazed father who had been a goalie in the Quebec Major Junior Hockey League and, though drafted by the Montreal Canadiens, never signed. At three and a half, Crosby spent many afternoons skating at the nearby Halifax Forum. At the end of each session, the attendants tossed out plastic sticks and balls for the kids to play with. Even though Crosby was so young, he knew just what to do. "He seemed to know instinctively how to hold a stick, and he could keep the ball away from the other kids," his father recalled in an interview with Charlie Gillis of *Maclean's*.

As a youngster Crosby practiced his skills on a 22-by-15-foot roller-blade rink his father designed in the basement. Whenever Crosby's shots missed the net, the puck smacked the dryer, which over the years lost its knobs and buttons and became speckled with dents. "It was nothing to go down there in the morning and have a puck still stuck in the door," Trina Crosby told the *Pittsburgh Post-Gazette*'s Robert Dvorchak. The Crosby basement became the neighborhood hangout. "On a rainy day, everybody came over," Trina Crosby recalled. "There was room enough for a goaltender and one-on-one with roller blades."

Crosby began playing organized hockey at the age of five. Speaking to the *Pittsburgh Post-Gazette*'s Chuck Finder, Crosby's former coach, Paul Gallagher, recalled his awe at his first sight of Crosby. "When he first stepped on the ice … I thought he might have registered in the wrong group because of his ability to skate. Even at age five. Tremendous skater. Hands above the other guys." Within a year, Crosby was playing kids two to three years older. He gave his first hockey interview at age seven, to a reporter from the Halifax *Daily News*. When Crosby was 14, he pounded in 106 goals and had 111 assists in 81 games playing 17- and 18-year-olds in a Nova Scotia league. That same year, he appeared on the CBC sports show *Hockey Day in Canada*. At 15 Crosby signed with an agent and by 17 he had multimillion-dollar deals with Gatorade and Reebok.

Crosby spent his sophomore year of high school playing for Shattuck-St. Mary's, a Faribault, Minnesota-based prep school where hockey rules. While there, from 2002-03, Crosby scored 72 goals in 57 games. Teammates from the boarding school remembered Crosby as a devoted athlete. When they were out horsing around and having fun, Crosby was in the gym strengthening his quadriceps, hamstrings, and abdominal muscles. At practice, he was the first on the ice and the last off.

Next, Crosby played for Rimouski Oceanic in the Quebec Major Junior Hockey League, one of the top junior leagues in North America. The team was coming off a season with an 11-58-3 record and a dwindling fan base when Crosby entered the picture and pulled the team to the top of its division for the 2003-04 season. During two seasons with the Oceanic, Crosby had 120 goals and 183 assists in 121 regular-season games. These stats stack up nicely against some of hockey's greats. Hockey legend Mario Lemieux averaged 2.8 points per game over three seasons during the 1980s while playing in the Quebec juniors. Crosby was just behind, averaging 2.5 points per game. In addition, Gretzky played one season in the juniors, in 1977-78, scoring 70 goals and 112 assists in 64 games for a point average of 2.8 per game.

It was not surprising when the Pittsburgh Penguins scooped up the 5-foot-11-inch, 193-pound Crosby with the first pick of the 2005 NHL draft. Because of rookie rules, his salary was capped at $850,000 that first season. Crosby, barely 18 years old, played his first professional game in October of 2005. When he skated onto the ice, the opposing team's fans heckled him with shouts of "overrated." Crosby had an assist that game, earning his first NHL point, though the Penguins lost. Fans and teammates were pleased with his progress that first season. When the NHL began its 2006 Olympic break in mid-February, Crosby stood in second place in rookie scoring, behind the Washington Capitals' Alexander Ovechkin. At the time, Crosby had a point total of 65, from 28 goals and 37 assists. Ovechkin had 69 points on 36 goals and 33 assists. In a game against the New York Islanders on April 17, 2006, Crosby set up two goals to became the youngest player in NHL history to score 100 points in a season. With those goals, he also tied Lemiux's team record for most points in a season by a rookie. Plus, he joined Dale Hawerchuk as the only 18 year olds in league history to get 100 points in a season.

Despite his success and the constant praise, Crosby will not rest on his laurels. Speaking to *Sports Illustrated*'s Michael Farber, Crosby said that he was concentrating on the moment and trying not to get caught up in all the hype. "I realize a lot of guys have been tagged with that 'next great player' thing. Some have gone on to be great players, some have fallen. I don't want to be one of the guys who disappears. I remind myself of that every day."

Sources

Periodicals

Maclean's, May 9, 2005, p. 34.
New York Times, October 6, 2005, p. 6.
Pittsburgh Post-Gazette, July 31, 2005, p. A1; October 6, 2005, p. A1.

Pittsburgh Tribune-Review, May 27, 2005.
Sports Illustrated, November 10, 2003, p. 54.

Online

"Players: Sidney Crosby," Pittsburgh Penguins, http://www.pittsburghpenguins.com/team/bio.php?id=151 (February 2, 2006).
"The Rookie," *Globe and Mail* (Toronto), http://www.theglobeandmail.com/servlet/story/ RTGAM.20050914.wcrosby14/BNStory/Sports,Front/home (February 22, 2006).
Sidney Crosby Website, http://www.crosby87.com/web/guest/bio (February 5, 2006).
"Young gun," *SI.com*, http://sportsillustrated.cnn.com/2006/hockey/nhl/04/17/bc.hkn.crosby.100points.ap /index.html (April 20, 2006).

—*Lisa Frick*

Neda DeMayo

Animal rights activist

Born c. 1960; divorced.

Addresses: *Home*—California. *Office*—Return to Freedom, P.O. Box 926, Lompoc, CA 93438. *Website*—http://www.returntofreedom.org.

Career

Worked as a celebrity fashion stylist; established Return to Freedom, a sanctuary for wild horses in Lompoc, CA, 1997.

Sidelights

Neda DeMayo founded Return to Freedom, a sanctuary for wild horses in Lompoc, California, in 1997, and has emerged as one of the most ardent campaigners for the protection of what many consider a unique national living treasure. "We are here to point out that wild horses are a nation," DeMayo asserted in a *Los Angeles Times* interview with Ann Marsh. "They have a civilization and a community unto themselves."

DeMayo grew up in the 1960s in the New Haven, Connecticut, area, and rode horses from an early age. She began formal lessons at the age of five, and at eight years old received her own horse, whom she called Sam. "I'd ride him into town and to the Dairy Queen," she told *People* magazine. She and her cohorts were fascinated by horse lore, and one day some friends told her that she had just missed a pack of horses trotting down the street. "In my mind I thought they were wild horses," she said in an interview with the *Santa Maria Times* many years later, "and I looked everywhere for them. Everywhere."

Wild horses have captured the imagination of many other animal-lovers over the years, too. The sight of hundreds of mustangs or other breeds of wild horse racing across America's western landscape has become an iconic image signifying the national character and the country's immense, untainted majesty. Conservation groups estimate that between 40,000 to 100,000 wild horses roam freely in ten American states. The mustang—a small, elegant, and intensely fast runner—is one of the breeds known to possess a bloodline linked back to the horses that Spanish conquistadors brought over to the continent in the 1500s. Even the word "mustang" is derived from the Spanish *mestengo*, which is a term for "an ownerless beast."

DeMayo recalled seeing television footage of wild horses being rounded up by helicopter when she was seven or eight years old. This was probably related to a save-the-mustang campaign that gained ground in the early 1970s. Ranchers in western states had long considered wild horses a nuisance because of the grass they grazed for their diet—as the ranchers' cattle must do as well—and since the early twentieth century the wild-horse population had steadily declined thanks to tactics that included chasing the packs with aircraft until they dropped dead from exhaustion. The protection movement finally resulted in the Wild, Free-Roaming Horse and Burro Act (PL 92-195), a federal law passed by Congress in 1971 that banned the sale or slaughter of wild horses and burros. Since then, their numbers have been overseen by the U.S. Bureau of Land Management (BLM), part of the U.S. Department of the Interior.

DeMayo eventually moved away from her equestrian enthusiasm and the East Coast. She traveled extensively as a young woman, studied theater, and eventually settled in the Los Angeles area, where she found work as a fashion stylist to entertainment personalities who included Sandra Bullock and David Duchovny. In 1994, she was involved in two serious car accidents within months of one another, and she decided to make some changes. "I realized that I needed to get clear about what I really wanted to do with my life," she said in the *Santa Maria Times* interview. "Because you don't know how long it's gonna last."

DeMayo's early passion for horses was reawakened when she learned about canned hunts, which allow hunters to shoot their prey on organized outings for a hefty fee. Such hunts take place on private property, and DeMayo was stunned to learn that the BLM allowed some wild horses to be hunted if certain criteria were met. This was a capture program designed to thin out certain herds, and was enthusiastically supported by the ranching industry. DeMayo began to devote her attention to the anti-hunt cause, and submerged herself in an intensive educational effort. She studied with Carolyn Resnick, a noted horse expert, and worked with horse rescuers who took the captured mustangs and other wild horses and tried to place them in adoptive homes, or gave them shelter in specially created sanctuaries.

DeMayo spent two years learning about wild horse breeds and behaviors, and decided to use what she had learned to teach others. She set up Return to Freedom as a nonprofit organization in 1997. This sanctuary near Santa Barbara, California—on a former chicken farm—was acquired with the help of DeMayo's parents, who bought the land as a retirement property. The rest of the 300 acres were given over to the horses that DeMayo began taking in, often in family groups. DeMayo is adamant that mustangs and other wild-horse breeds need to be allowed to roam freely, and in their own herds. As she explained to *People*, "they live in social groups just like humans.... They are born to live in herds. Why would we want to take that away from anyone?"

DeMayo also took a more public role when she challenged the Burns Amendment, passed by Congress in December of 2004 as an attachment to another bill. Named after a Montana Republican senator, Conrad Burns, the law rescinded some of the protections of the 1971 Wild Horse and Burro Act and allowed the BLM to thin out the herds by the thousands. It allowed for the sale of some of the captured horses, ostensibly to private owners who would find homes for them, but at least 40 of them were instead immediately sold to slaughterhouses, because horse meat is considered a culinary delicacy in Japan and some parts of Europe. In April of 2005, thanks to efforts by DeMayo and others, the BLM ordered any pending sales halted until an inquiry into the Burns Amendment program was completed.

DeMayo does not receive a salary for her work, and her Return to Freedom foundation raises funds to pay the salaries for a staff of caretakers and other expenses; the monthly bill for hay for the 200 or so horses she had taken in by 2005 runs to $8,000. Local veterinarians donate their services, and some revenue comes from the educational camps for youngsters that Return to Freedom runs. DeMayo hopes to one day establish a historical land trust for the protection of wild horses. "These horses are unique to the United States," she said in the *People* interview. "They represent the pioneer spirit of the American West."

Sources

Periodicals

California Riding Magazine, May 2005.
Grit, March 2005.
Los Angeles Times, July 20, 2001.
People, May 9, 2005, pp. 219-20.
Santa Maria Times, June 22, 2002.

Online

Return to Freedom, http://www.returntofreedom. org (October 21, 2005).

—*Carol Brennan*

Patrick Dempsey

Peter Kramer/Getty Images

Actor

Born January 13, 1966, in Lewiston, ME; son of William (an insurance salesman) and Amanda (a high school secretary) Dempsey; married Rocky Parker, 1987 (divorced, 1993); married Jillian Fink (a celebrity makeup artist), July 31, 1999; children: Tallulah Fyfe.

Addresses: *Contact*—c/o The Burstein Co., 15304 Sunset Blvd., Ste. 208, Pacific Palisades, CA 90272.

Career

Actor in films, including: *Heaven Help Us*, 1985; *Meatballs III: Summer Job*, 1987; *Can't Buy Me Love*, 1987; *In the Mood*, 1987; *Some Girls*, 1988; *Lover-boy*, 1989; *Happy Together*, 1989; *Coupe de Ville*, 1990; *Run*, 1991; *Mobsters*, 1991; *Bank Robber*, 1993; *Face the Music*, 1993; *Ava's Magical Adventures* (also director), 1994; *With Honors*, 1994; *Outbreak*, 1995; *Hugo Pool*, 1997; *The Treat*, 1998; *There's No Fish Food in Heaven*, 1998; *Denial*, 1998; *Me and Will*, 1999; *Scream 3*, 2000; *Sweet Home Alabama*, 2002; *The Emperor's Club*, 2002. Television appearances include: *Fast Times*, CBS, 1986; *A Fighting Choice* (movie), ABC, 1986; *Merry Christmas Baby*, 1991; *For Better and For Worse* (movie), 1993; *J.F.K.: Restless Youth* (miniseries), ABC, 1993; *Bloodknot*, Showtime, 1995; *A Season of Purgatory* (miniseries), CBS, 1996; *The Right to Remain Silent*, Showtime, 1996; *The Escape*, TMC, 1997; *20,000 Leagues Under the Sea* (movie), CBS, 1997; *Dostoevsky's Crime and Punishment* (movie), NBC, 1998; *Jeremiah*, PAX TV, 1998; *Once and Again*, ABC, 2000-02; *Will & Grace*, NBC, 2000-01; *Blonde* (miniseries), CBS, 2001; *The Practice*, ABC, 2004; *Iron Jawed Angels*, HBO, 2004; *Grey's Anatomy*, ABC, 2005—. Stage appearances include: *On Golden Pond*, Maine Acting Company, c. 1983; *Torch Song Trilogy*, San Francisco, c. 1983; *Brighton Beach Memoirs*, touring group, c. 1985; *The Subject was Roses*, Roundabout Theatre, New York, 1991.

Awards: Young Artist Award for best young actor in a motion picture comedy, for *Can't Buy Me Love*, 1988.

Sidelights

For awhile it looked like Patrick Dempsey would never amount to much more than a distant memory as one of yesterday's forgotten teen idols. During the late 1980s Dempsey graced the pages of *Tiger Beat* magazine and drew teenage audiences to theaters playing sophomoric, underdog boys in a series of hits that included 1987's *Can't Buy Me Love* and 1989's *Loverboy*. In the 1990s Dempsey struggled to find breakthrough roles and faded from view. He returned with a matured vengeance in 2002's *Sweet Home Alabama*, opposite Reese Witherspoon. In 2005, Dempsey earned a role as Dr. Derek Shepherd on ABC's doctor drama *Grey's Anatomy*. Thanks in part to Dempsey's winsome onscreen chemistry, the show became an instant hit and returned Dempsey to pinup status. Older, more muscular and mature, Dempsey was named to *TV Guide*'s list of the 50 sexiest men on television.

The youngest of three children, Dempsey was born in 1966 in the rural Maine town of Lewiston. His father, William, sold insurance and his mother, Amanda, worked as a secretary. The Dempsey family was Catholic. As such, Dempsey attended St. Dominic's Regional High School, as well as Buckfield High. As a child Dempsey struggled academically, leaving teachers to conclude he was lazy. In seventh grade, however, Dempsey was diagnosed with dyslexia. The experience made Dempsey feel like an outsider and he turned to skiing as a diversion for his loneliness. He was good enough to win a state downhill championship. Over time—and in a roundabout way—Dempsey's love for skiing led him off the slopes and onto the stage.

As a young adolescent, Dempsey felt driven to perfect his skiing and often tuned into *Wide World of Sports* to study the pros. One day the show featured a ski champ who demonstrated unicycle riding, claiming it improved his skills. Dempsey had to try it, too. Once he mastered the unicycle, juggling seemed like a natural progression. "Learning how to juggle changed my life," Dempsey told the *New York Times*' Lawrence Van Gelder. "It gave me a purpose. It led me toward performance."

At 15, Dempsey won second place in the junior division of the International Jugglers' Competition. He added magic and puppetry to his repertoire and developed his own act, performing locally. In the early 1980s Dempsey's act caught the attention of the Maine Acting Company and he was cast in its summer production of *On Golden Pond* playing Billy, a teenage boy forced to spend the summer with an aging couple. Dempsey traveled to New York during the summer of 1983 to compete in a talent competition and snagged an agent. Within months he earned a role in a San Francisco production of Harvey Fierstein's Tony Award-winning play *Torch Song Trilogy*. Just 17, Dempsey quit school.

Spending several months onstage with professional actors convinced Dempsey that he did not want to attend college or acting school. "I think it's better to learn from actors who are working than study with actors who aren't working," he told the *Washington Post*'s Megan Rosenfeld. Next, he spent a year touring in the leading role of Eugene Jerome in Neil Simon's coming-of-age comedy *Brighton Beach Memoirs*. In 1985, Dempsey made his first film appearance in *Heaven Help Us* and in 1987 scored a

starring role in *Meatballs III*. Success followed with 1987's teen cult-classic *Can't Buy Me Love*, which featured Dempsey as a high school geek who tries to improve his status by paying a cheerleader to be his girlfriend. Dempsey followed with 1989's *Loverboy*, where he played a pizza delivery boy who offered customers more than just pizza.

At the age of 21, Dempsey married his 48-year-old manager, Rocky Parker. "I was a bit of a Freudian nightmare at the time," he admitted to *TV Guide*'s Steve Pond. "Those type of relationships are fun and exciting and sort of rebellious, but they just don't work out." Dempsey and Parker divorced in 1993, about the time his career began to stall. For the next decade Dempsey struggled to convince directors he had matured as an actor capable of moving beyond his earlier, juvenile roles. In 1994 Dempsey met then-salon owner Jillian Fink at her Los Angeles hair salon. After three years of haircuts they finally started dating and married in 1999. Meanwhile, Dempsey, with his career in the dumps, returned home to Maine, where he bought and restored a farm.

Once Dempsey relaxed, the roles started coming and he was able to project a more confident, mature person onscreen. In 2000 Dempsey earned a recurring role as Sela Ward's schizophrenic brother on the ABC drama *Once and Again* and earned a 2001 Emmy nomination for his performance. He also made repeated appearances on shows like *Will & Grace* and *The Practice*. Dempsey's career revived on the big screen as well in 2000's *Scream 3* and 2002's *Sweet Home Alabama*.

In 2005 *Grey's Anatomy*, a pilot in the waiting, hit the television lineup as a midseason replacement. The show centers around a set of surgical interns at a fictional Seattle hospital. One key character is Meredith Grey, played by Ellen Pompeo, a first-year intern who has a one-night stand with a stranger at a party the night before she begins her internship. When she shows up at the hospital, she discovers that the man she shared a bed with is her supervisor, surgeon Derek Shepherd, played by Dempsey. The show became an unexpected hit, drawing an average of 17 million viewers, making it the most-watched new midseason drama since 1993's *Dr. Quinn, Medicine Woman*.

The show's success catapulted Dempsey back into heartthrob status. In 2005 *TV Guide* named Dempsey one of the 50 hottest men on television. Speaking in that issue of *TV Guide*, co-star Pompeo summed up Dempsey's allure this way: "Dr. Mc-

Dreamy, that's what I call Patrick's character, Derek Shepherd. He's gorgeous, he's got a great body, and he's got [fantastic] hair."

As an actor who has been around the block, Dempsey is taking success in stride these days. He told *TV Guide*'s Pond that following the success of *Grey's Anatomy*, people kept asking him if he was excited. "And it's funny, [because] mostly it's just a big sigh of relief that now I have some opportunities. I don't need to be a huge superstar."

Sources

Periodicals

Entertainment Weekly, June 24/July 1, 2005, p. 78.

New York Times, October 2, 1987, p. C32.

People, October 21, 2002, pp. 111-12.

Sunday Herald Sun (Melbourne, Australia), August 7, 2005, p. X12.

TV Guide, May 15-21, 2005, pp. 36-38; June 5-11, 2005, p. 28.

Washington Post, December 24, 1984, p. B7.

Online

"Sweet Home Harpswell: Patrick Dempsey's Maine," *Portland* magazine, http://www.aroundmaine.com/Around_Town/features2002/portlandmag/dempsey/default.asp (July 31, 2005).

—*Lisa Frick*

Marc Ecko

© Nancy Kaszerman/ZUMA/Corbis

Fashion designer and business executive

Born Marc Milecofsky, in 1972, in New Jersey; married Allison; children: one daughter. *Education:* Attended Rutgers University.

Addresses: *Office*—Ecko Unlimited, 40 W. 23rd St., 2nd Flr., New York, NY 10010.

Career

Began designing and customizing clothing while in high school; founded Ecko Unlimited with partners, c. 1993; adopted rhino logo; company nearly folded, 1998; signed licensing deal with the National Football League, 1999; launched magazine *Complex,* 2002; signed licensing deal with Skechers, 2003; opened Ecko Unlimited flagship store, 2004; introduced tailored clothing line, Marc Ecko "Cut & Sew" collection, 2004; launched video game with Atari, *Marc Ecko's Getting Up: Contents Under Pressure,* 2005.

Sidelights

Fashion designer Marc Ecko is a modern Renaissance man, moving from a variety of clothing pieces into publishing, skateboards, and video games, most of which are products of his own company Ecko Unlimited (also written as Ecko Unltd. and ecko unltd.). While his trendy clothes reflected street and hip-hop influences and were marketed to a youthful audience, as Ecko has aged, he has brought mature influences into some of his fashions for men and added lines for women and children. Recognized by many observers as a powerful businessman and marketing genius, Ecko told the *New York Times Magazine*'s Rob Walker, "I want people to think of me almost as Willy Wonka. A pop-culture Willy Wonka, crossed with [wealthy businessman] Richard Branson."

Ecko was born Marc Milecofsky in 1972 in New Jersey with his twin sister, Marci. (The name Ecko comes from a family story about the twins' birth. Only his sister was physically on an ultrasound; Ecko appeared as just an echo. His parents did not know they were having twins until he was born.) The twins and their sister were raised in Lakewood, New Jersey, where their parents worked as real estate agents. They attended public schools, which were ethnically diverse, with many white, black, and Latino kids in the same class. From an early age, as young as elementary school, Ecko noticed that the way someone dressed allowed entrance to a social group. He also liked drawing and comic books.

As Ecko entered his teens, he became interested in hip-hop culture, rap music, and graffiti art. What became his career began while Ecko was still a high school student at Lakewood High School. Hip-hop and rap music were still relatively underground and the songs and clothes were hard to come by. In the mid-1980s, Ecko began doing clothing design in the family garage, using it as both a studio and showroom to design T-shirts. Because of the importance of customization of clothing in hip-hop, he also began offering this service as well. He made money on the side by customizing clothes for people from his school. Ecko even airbrushed girls' fingernails.

After graduating from Lakewood High School, Ecko studied pharmacy at the Rutgers School of Pharmacy. He did a little graffiti, but mostly created elaborate drawings in books. It was at this time that he took the tag name of Ecko, which he later adopted as his last name. Ecko soon believed that selling T-shirts would be profitable. With investments from his twin sister and friend Seth Gerszberg of several thousand dollars, Ecko founded Ecko Unlimited with them and had some success with the company's first six T-shirt designs. He became known nationwide when this first line of T-shirts was featured on the popular morning show *Good Morning America* in 1993. In the early days, he primarily focused on making T-shirts, some of which were worn by some of the leading artists of the day like Chuck D., founder of rap group Public Enemy, and filmmaker Spike Lee.

In this time period, urban clothing was not yet embraced by major retailers, but Ecko Unlimited was able to sell its T-shirts in boutiques. They sold well, and Ecko moved into more hip-hop and skater styles. A few years after its founding, the partners adopted the company's signature rhino logo. Ecko decided that his company needed a logo after it appeared at a fashion industry event in Las Vegas, the M.A.G.I.C. Show, for the first time. The choice of the rhino was both personal and symbolic. It was inspired by Ecko's father's collection of rhino statues. Ecko told Julee Greenberg of *WWD*, "People thought I was crazy. They had no idea why I would pick such a strange-looking animal for my logo. At first it was just an animal, but through time it has taken on new meanings. It is the only four-legged animal that can't walk backwards and by nature it is known as clumsy, which I think has come to represent us as a company."

Ecko Unlimited began having financial problems as it expanded into other types of clothing, such as jeans and jackets, and faced difficulties with manufacturers. While Ecko's clothes were popular, Ecko Unlimited lost about $6 million over the first six years of its existence. By 1998, Gerszberg and Ecko wondered if they should fold Ecko Unlimited or listen to advisors who told them to apply for bankruptcy. They tried to make a deal with another, more-established clothing company in an effort to save their company, but no one was interested. Gerszberg and Ecko managed to save themselves for the short term by having their largest creditor give them a loan to attempt a revitalization of Ecko Unlimited by using better suppliers and more designers than just Ecko.

After the 1998 low, Ecko Unlimited soon rebounded. The retail industry was changing with large retailers embracing the urban/hip-hop look. The company's clothing was featured in hip-hop magazines, not just on rap artists, but also on white and Latino stars as well as sports stars. The use of the rhino as the symbol came to be seen as particularly innovative. Walker of the *New York Times Magazine* found the choice inspired, writing, "In retrospect, Ecko says that using a visual symbol that had no connective tissue to hip-hop and leaving it open to interpretation were crucial. It looked cool as a graphic, was backed by marketing that played up individuality and achievement rather than you'll-never-be-this-cool exclusivity and yet was unspecific enough that made it made sense on rappers like RZA and Fat Joe, but also on [television character] A.J. Soprano, an archetype of the smirky teen suburbs."

Within several years, sales for Ecko Unlimited were in the hundreds of millions of dollars. While sales in 1998 totaled $36 million, two years later they more than doubled to $96 million and the company was able to pay off all its debts. In 2002, the men's sportswear division of Ecko Unlimited had revenues of at least $300 million. By 2004, Ecko's company's retail sales were more than a half a billion dollars, not including the licensing fees for some products like shoes and baby clothes. Sales grew over this time in part because Ecko Unlimited continually added more products and brands to become a lifestyle company.

Ecko Unlimited served as an umbrella for at least 12 distinct brands. The Ecko Unlimited name was attached to men's wear, while Eckored and Femme Arsenal were for women. Outerwear was sold under the name Ecko Unlimited Function, while Mark Ecko Leather focused on leather goods. Children's wear was sold under the names Ecko Unlimited Boys and Eckored Girls. There were also Marc Ecko watches, Marc Ecko gloves, Marc Ecko Footwear for men, women and children, and a line of cosmetics. Ecko also owned Zoo York, a brand of skateboards and related clothing and gear, and made the clothes for G-Unit, a clothing line for the rapper 50 Cent.

While not every deal Ecko has tried has worked out—for example, he negotiated with female rapper Eve to do her clothing line, but failed to reach an agreement—the contracts he did reach were sometimes quite high profile. In 1999, he inked a licensing deal with the National Football League (NFL) to create a sportswear line targeted at young men and women. The NFL wanted Ecko to bring a youthful appeal to its apparel. In 2003, Ecko signed a footwear licensing deal with Skechers to create shoes for both men and women. He also had a line of products specifically created for discount retailer Target.

As Ecko Unlimited continued to grow, he signed a lease in 2004 for the company's flagship store on 42nd Street in New York City. Ecko himself was a husband and father by this time, and in his early thirties. As he aged, he wanted his clothes to evolve with him. In 2004, he introduced the Marc Ecko "Cut & Sew" collection. This line focused on tailored clothing for men and a different logo. Instead of the trademark rhino, "Cut & Sew" featured a pair of sewing shears. Of this evolution, Ecko told Samantha Critchell of the Associated Press, "I design for people I know. They [the garments] are for myself, following my consumption tendencies. I am growing up with our customer.... The moment in your life when you throw your back out, you realize you can't do slinky, clingy fabrics anymore."

Ecko used the success of his fashion empire to try to conquer new worlds. In 2002, he launched a magazine called *Complex*. With a circulation of about 325,000, it was a lifestyle magazine targeted at young men which was advertised on the tags of his clothing. Three years after the launch of *Complex*, Ecko reached another goal with the launch of his first video game. A big fan of video games himself, Ecko had already allowed his clothing and the rhino logo to appear in a number of other games. Created in conjunction with Atari, Ecko had a hands-on role in the creation of *Marc Ecko's Getting Up: Contents Under Pressure*.

This game returned to Ecko's love of graffiti art. In *Contents Under Pressure*, gamers play a graffiti artist who is practicing his craft in the fictional city of New Radius. The artist must tag walls with the assistance of well-known graffiti artists like Future while dodging cops. Creating non-fashion works like video games helped further publicize Ecko's name and made him a celebrity in his own right. Ecko particularly took video games seriously, with strong opinions on what was wrong with the industry and what worked from the perspective of a serious gamer. He hoped to make more video games in the future, developing the "Getting Up" name as a brand. Ecko told the publication *Official US Playstation*, "I think ultimately, as we build the brand, we'll move the product toward [more customization]. I even see derivative products we can take with the Getting Up brand and do more free-form, open-environment, multiplayer experiences—pit one crew against another. We can get there, but first I wanted to put the flag in the ground and create a really cool graffiti experience, and I knew to do that, I needed to have some other hook that would get the cynic on board."

As a successful businessman, Ecko also believed in charity work. He worked on both a national and international level with less-fortunate young people. Ecko funded an orphanage in the Ukraine and also gave funds to maintain the world's rhino population. Though a philanthropist, he liked movies and music as well, owning five iPods with around 30,000 songs total. He also collected toys and sneakers. Yet Ecko still thought of himself as a graffiti artist, albeit on a bigger scale. He told *Official US Playstation*, "My whole career is the ultimate form of graffiti. There are going to be people that hate just like there are the skaters that hated on Tony Hawk, but there are also these artists out there that the broader part of pop culture should be honoring. There's not a set aesthetic that has had more influence on popular culture than graffiti over the years.... I'm taking this culture and putting it on a pedestal. Yeah, I'm making a commercial product, but I'm bombing the system.... I make blazers and woven shirts—to me, getting my name inside that label is the same ... high that I used to get when I tagged the backseat of a bus. It's the same hustle and swagger that a kid has, to want to make something from nothing."

Sources

Periodicals

ANSA English Media Service, January 9, 2004.

Associated Press, May 10, 2004.

Brandweek, May 14, 2001.

DNR, August 16, 1999, p. 8; November 19, 2001, p. 24.

Entertainment Weekly, April 8, 2005, p. 16.

Footwear News, November 3, 2003, p. 4; December 1, 2003, p. 4.

New York Times, May 4, 2003, p. ST13.

New York Times Magazine, July 10, 2005, p. 24.

Official US Playstation, June 1, 2005, p. 34.

WWD, August 28, 2003, p. 9.

Online

"Bios," Marc Ecko Enterprises, http://www.marc eckonenterprises.com/bios/bios1.shtml (February 12, 2006).

"The Company," eckounltd.com, http://www.ecko unltd.com/abouteckounltd/thecompany.shtml (February 12, 2006).

"Mark Ecko," nymag.com, http://www.newyork metro.com/fashion/fashionshows/designers/ bios/marcecko/ (February 12, 2006).

—A. Petruso

Mohamed ElBaradei

Herwig Prammer/Reuters/Landov

Director general of the International Atomic Energy Agency

Born June 17, 1942, in Cairo, Egypt; son of Mostafa ElBaradei (an attorney); married Aida Elkachef (a preschool teacher); children: Laila, Mostafa. *Education:* University of Cairo, bachelor's degree, 1962; New York University School of Law, doctorate, 1974.

Addresses: *Office*—International Atomic Energy Agency, PO Box 100, Wagramer Strasse 5, A-1400 Vienna, Austria.

Career

Worked with Egyptian Diplomatic Service, 1964-80; for the service, twice served as part of the Permanent Missions of Egypt to the United Nations; served as a special assistant to Egypt's Foreign Minister, 1974-78; senior fellow in charge of International Law Program, United Nations Institute for Training and Research, New York, NY, 1980-87; adjunct professor of international law, New York University, New York, NY, 1981-87; hired as a senior staff member of the International Atomic Energy Agency Secretariat, 1984; became the agency's legal advisor and later assistant director general for external relations; appointed director general of the International Atomic Energy Agency, 1997; appointed to third term as agency head, 2005.

Member: International Law Association, American Society of International Law.

Awards: Nobel Peace Prize (with the International Atomic Energy Agency), 2005; High Nile Sash, Egyptian government, 2006.

Sidelights

After beginning his career serving the Egyptian government as a diplomat and aide, Mohamed ElBaradei eventually became the head of the United Nations' International Atomic Energy Agency (IAEA). This group is the world's watchdog on all thing nuclear, and a continual source of controversy among nations already possessing nuclear capacities as well as countries who want to join their ranks. Though a somewhat contentious public figure because of his job, ElBaradei was elected to his third term as the head of IAEA in 2005. He and the agency were also awarded the Nobel Peace Prize that year for their work.

Born in 1942, in Cairo, Egypt, ElBaradei was one of four children born to an attorney, Mostafa ElBaradei. His father was once the president of the Egyptian Bar Association. He was also a supporter of democratic rights in Egypt, supporting a free press and a legal system that was independent. ElBaradei followed in his father's footsteps, graduating from the University of Cairo with a bachelor's degree in law in 1962.

Two years later after earning his degree, ElBaradei began working with the Egyptian Diplomatic Service. For the next sixteen years, he was employed in the service and lived abroad. ElBaradei was twice a part of the Permanent Missions representing Egypt in the United Nations (UN), stationed in both New York City and Geneva, Switzerland. He primarily dealt with issues related to arms control, as well as political and legal questions. As a member of the diplomatic service, ElBaradei was a part of the Egyptian-Israeli peace talks at Camp David in the United States in the late 1970s.

While living in New York, ElBaradei continued his education. In 1974, he earned his doctorate in international law from New York University. That year, ElBaradei began working for the Foreign Minister of Egypt as a special assistant. ElBaradei held that post for four years, before returning to the Egyptian Diplomatic Service.

In 1980, ElBaradei began a new phase of his professional life when he was hired by the UN in New York. He worked for the United Nations Institute for Training and Research as a senior fellow and headed the International Law Program. While living in New York City, he also worked for the New York University School of Law as an adjunct professor of International Law. Four years later, ElBaradei was hired as a senior staff member of the International Atomic Energy Association Secretariat and then made his primary home in Vienna, Austria, where its headquarters were located.

The IAEA had been founded in 1957 as nuclear capabilities were being developed by countries around the world and their deadly potential being realized. The organization was charged not only with a regulation function, but also encouraged the use of nuclear technology to solve problems in the world like hunger, disease, and environmental issues. By the 1990s and early 2000s, the IAEA's inspections to ensure that countries only used nuclear technology for peaceful means, not weapons, became controversial. While the organization could alert the UN and world at large that countries were in breach of international agreements and limitations, the IAEA and its director general could not control or sanction countries in violation.

ElBaradei continued to work for this arm of the UN for a number of years, holding powerful policy positions. They included acting as legal advisor and later Assistant General for External Relations. In 1997, ElBaradei was elected to his first term as director general of IAEA. He replaced the controversial Hans Blix, but was not Blix's first choice as his successor. ElBaradei was not even the primary choice among Egyptians, let alone most other coun-

tries. He was given the post primarily as a compromise candidate everyone could agree on, in part because he could work behind the scenes to build a consensus to solve problems. It was also seen as a good public relations move to have an Arab in charge of such an agency as a number of the world's nuclear hot spots were Arab countries. Like all of the director generals before him, he was only as powerful as the member nations of the UN let him and IAEA be.

ElBaradei proved to be a generally effective director general in his attempts to limit the number of nations with nuclear weapons and keep those nations who already have nuclear weapons to their promise to reduce the number of weapons in their possession. Yet he faced a number of problems as well. For example, in 2002 and 2003, the United States government insisted that Iraq possessed weapons of mass destruction, including nuclear arms, or, at the very least, the technology to build them. The work of ElBaradei and Blix, then employed as a chief inspector for the IAEA, proved in 2003 that Iraq did not have this technology. The IAEA did admit that Iraq had the same nuclear ambitions as many other Arab countries. ElBaradei argued against the war in Iraq at the UN. He wanted his inspectors to finish their final reports before the United States invaded, but his wishes were ignored. It was later shown that Iraq did not have any such nuclear weapons.

Another key initiative that ElBaradei worked on was modernizing the 1968 Nuclear Non-Proliferation Treaty. Many countries that had not originally signed the agreement now either had nuclear powers or the technical ability to do so. ElBaradei also promoted an additional protocol. He wanted inspectors to have access to any location with little notice in member states at the UN. By the early 2000s, 69 countries had signed on.

In September of 2005, ElBaradei was re-elected to a third term by the IAEA board of governors. Though he was the only candidate, not all UN members wanted his return, especially the United States. The administration of U.S. President George W. Bush did not want ElBaradei in office again for several reasons. In addition to ElBaraei's controversial stance on Iraq, the Americans also believed he did not challenge Iran, with its wide-open nuclear ambitions. Bush went as far as to have the Central Intelligence Agency bug his phone. Referring to the bug, ElBaradei told a reporter from *Der Spiegel* in an interview published in translation on the IAEA website, "I knew I had nothing material to hide. Nevertheless, it was unpleasant not to be able to chat with my children without unwanted eavesdroppers listening in."

Despite such difficulties, ElBaradei remained committed to his vision. He wanted to make the world a better place by strengthening the IAEA safeguards and using them as a standard worldwide. He also wanted more UN-mandated sanctions for countries that do not want safeguards. ElBaradei told Lally Weymouth in an interview published on the IAEA website shortly before he was elected to a third term, "If reelected, I will continue to do things the way I see best. It's very important to me that this multinational institution continue to be impartial and independent. I will not compromise on this.... I have spent almost 30 years of my life doing this, and before I cross to the other side, I want to get the Iran issue out of the way and get to the bottom of the A.Q. Khan [former head of Pakiston's nuclear program] network—he provided the complete kit [for a nuclear weapon] to Libya."

Secure in his position, ElBaradei set these kinds of ambitious goals for his third term. He wanted to rein in the nuclear ambitions of Iran as well as deal with the uncertainties surrounding the North Korean nuclear program. ElBaradei was proud of what he had accomplished in Iran. In 2003, the IAEA was unsure what was happening in Iran with their nuclear capabilities. By early 2005, the IAEA had been in Iran and knew exactly where that country stood. ElBaradei hoped to reach a diplomatic solution shortly, though he understood there were complex issues at hand. Discussing the way to prevent Iran from becoming a nuclear country, ElBaradei acknowledged the need for American support, but also told Weymouth in the interview published on the IAEA website, "You need inspections, but you need to also work with them diplomatically. If a country is suspected of going nuclear, you need to understand why. Why does it feel insecure? You need to address [Iran's] sense of isolation and its need for technology and economic [benefits]. They have been under sanctions for 20 years."

ElBaradei also had grave concerns about nuclear arms and terrorists. He wanted to ensure that terrorists could not get their hands on nuclear arms, believing this could put the world as we know it in jeopardy. ElBaradei believed that export controls have not worked and nuclear materials could be bought with relative ease on the black market by both terrorists and rogue nations. Another key goal centered around the question of how to give nuclear energy capabilities to countries eager to produce nuclear power but not let them be able to take the next step to produce nuclear weapons. ElBaradei's idea was to allow countries to build nuclear reactors and related technologies. However, he believed that fuel cycles should be controlled by an international group, like the IAEA, to ensure the removal of spent fuel. By removing this fuel, it cannot be enriched or processed again to make nuclear arms.

ElBaradei's work with the IAEA soon became lauded by the international community. In October of 2005, it was announced that ElBaradei and the IAEA had won the Nobel Peace Prize. The award was unexpected, though they were favorites, and the prize money was split equally between ElBaradei and his employer. The win also marked only the eighth time a native of Africa had won the Nobel Peace Prize. The award had a profound affect on ElBaradei. He was quoted by CNN.com as saying, "The award basically sends a very strong message, which is: Keep doing what you are doing. It's a responsibility, but it's also a shot in the arm."

As IAEA director, ElBaradei lives in an apartment in Vienna with his wife, Aida Elkachef. (Their two adult children live in London.) He tries to live as normal a life as possible. Yet his job and its importance weighs heavily on him on a daily basis. He told a reporter from *Der Spiegel* in an interview published in translation on the IAEA web site, "I am afraid that the memory of Hiroshima is beginning to fade. I am afraid that nuclear weapons will fall into the hands of dictators or terrorists. And I am also afraid of the nuclear arsenals of democratic countries, for as long as these weapons exist there can be no security against the catastrophic consequences of theft, sabotage, or accident.... I firmly believe the IAEA can make the difference between war and peace."

Sources

Periodicals

Africa News, February 7, 2006.
Asia Africa Intelligence Wire, October 7, 2005; January 30, 2006.
Guardian (London, England), January 27, 2003, p. 4.
Herald (Glasgow, Scotland), October 8, 2005, p. 17.
M2 Presswire, June 14, 2005.

Online

"DG's Biography," IAEA.org, http://www.iaea.org/About/DGC/dgbio.html (February 12, 2006).
"Diplomacy and Force: *Newsweek* Interview with Mohamed ElBaradei," IAEA.org, http://www.iaea.org/NewsCenter/Transcripts/2006/newsweek12012006.html (February 12, 2006).

"Director General Interview, World Economic Forum," IAEA.org, http://www.iaea.org/NewsCenter/Transcripts/2005/wp300105.html (February 12, 2006).

"Director General's interview on winning the 2005 Nobel Peace Prize," IAEA.org, http://www.iaea.org/NewsCenter/Transcripts/2005/nobel07102005.html (February 12, 2006).

"IAEA, ElBaradei win peace prize," CNN.com, http://www.cnn.com/2005/WORLD/europe/10/07/nobel.peace.main/index.html (October 7, 2005).

"Statements of the Director General," IAEA.org, http://www.iaea.org/NewsCenter/Statements/2005/ebsp2005n020.html (February 12, 2006).

"Superman and Sisyphus: Der Spiegel Interview with Mohamed ElBaradei," IAEA.org, http://www.iaea.org/NewsCenter/Transcripts/2005/derspiegel08122005.html (February 12, 2006).

—A. Petruso

Enrico Fabris

Robert Laberge/Getty Images

Speed skater

B orn October 5, 1981, in Asiago, Italy.

Addresses: *Contact*—Italian National Olympic Committee, Foro Italico 00194, Rome, Lazio, Italy. *Home*—Roana, Italy. *Website*—http://www.enrico-fabris.com.

Career

B egan competing in short-track speed-skating competitions at age six; took up long-track skating at age 12; joined the Italian national team, 2001; made his Olympic debut, 2002; earned Olympic gold, 2006.

Awards: Silver medal, Italian Allround Championships, 2001; bronze medal, Italian Allround Championships, 2002; gold medal, Italian Allround Championships, 2003, 2004, 2005, 2006; gold medal, 5,000 meter, gold medal, 1,500 meter, bronze medal, 1,000 meter, World Winter University Games, 2005; silver medal, 5,000 meter, bronze medal, 1,500 meter, World Cup Final, 2006; gold medal, Allround, European Championships, 2006; silver medal, Allround, World Championships, 2006; bronze medal, 5,000 meter, gold medal, 1,500 meter, gold medal, team pursuit, Olympic Games, 2006.

Sidelights

B efore the 2006 Winter Olympics, hosted by his own country, Italian speed skater Enrico Fabris was a virtual unknown, even in his homeland. The four-time national champion skated in relative anonymity in a country where soccer and cycling reign supreme. Fabris' performance at the Olympics, however, catapulted him to hero status when he became the first Italian in history to win a long-track speed-skating medal. Over the course of the Games, Fabris earned two gold medals and a bronze, making him the host nation's top medal-winner. His most glorious moment came in the men's 1,500 meter, when Fabris defeated American pre-race favorites Shani Davis and Chad Hedrick to earn the gold.

Born October 5, 1981, in the northern Italian city of Asiago, Fabris (pronounced Fah-BREEZE) grew up alongside two brothers. He caught the skating bug early on and honed his skills on the city's natural ice track. By the age of six, he was competing in short-track speed-skating races. At 12, Fabris started competing in long-track competitions, continuing in both until he was 17, when he decided to concentrate on long-track skating. As Fabris devoted himself to the sport and to his training, he received encouragement from his priest uncle, who continually cheered him on.

Fabris made his debut with the Italian national team in 2001. That year, he placed second at the Italian Allround Championships. In the allround event, participants skate four distances and receive an overall rank based on times for each distance. Fabris made his Olympic debut the following year, at the 2002 Salt Lake City Games, where he placed 16th in the 5,000 meter and 26th in the 1,500 meter. When Fabris won the European Championship in the allround in January of 2006, no one from his homeland was even following the story. Fabris phoned the Italian sports daily, the *Gazzetta dello Sport,* to report his win.

Fabris skated in four events at the 2006 Games. His first event was the 5,000 meter race, held the first day of Olympic competition. As he approached the halfway mark of the race, Fabris gazed up at the giant television screen to find himself in seventh place. The arena was packed with Italians, who began cheering wildly. Fabris dug in and came out the bronze medalist after completing his last lap in a blistering 29.25 seconds, which was 1.45 seconds faster than Hedrick, who took the gold. "In the middle of the race, the crowd pushed me on. I don't have any words to describe this medal," Fabris commented later, according to the NBC Olympics website. The medal was the first of the Games for the host country, but more important, it marked the first time an Italian had won an Olympic long-track speed-skating medal. Five days later, Fabris earned gold in the team pursuit, a new Olympic event.

Five days after his second medal win, Fabris was back on the ice, competing in the men's 1,500 meter, which insiders believed would be won by either Hedrick or Davis. The two Americans had been bickering since the start of the Games. Fabris skated against the Netherlands' Simon Kuipers in the 17th of 21 heats. Italians packed the Lingotto Oval for the event, waving their flags in the air alongside signs that read, "Forza, Enrico." The crowd's enthusiasm prompted Fabris to skate with heart and soul. When Fabris finished, he knew his time of 1:45.97 seconds was good, but he did not know if it would stand against the remaining eight skaters, including world record holder Hedrick. Hedrick breezed across the finish line at 1:46.22 at which point Fabris figured he had the silver because Davis still had to skate in the final heat. During his race, Davis' splits looked like they were good enough for gold, but in the end, he swept over the line with a time of 1:46.-13, giving Fabris the gold. The crowd went wild. It was an amazing accomplishment for someone who had finished 26th in the event at the previous Olympics.

Fabris' blazing performances surprised even his own country. "We knew that Fabris was improving," Italian sports columnist Gianni Merlo told the *San Francisco Chronicle*'s Carl T. Hall. "We knew that he was very strong. Some people in my field, track and field, they told me he was an incredible talent. And I must say they were completely right."

With three Olympic medals, the demure and boyishly handsome 6-foot-2, 165-pound skater became a national hero, garnering calls of congratulations from the Italian prime minister and president. Italy won five gold medals at the Olympics—and two belonged to Fabris. Countless women posted kisses on his website and a headline in the *Gazzetta dello Sport* proclaimed, "Fabris, the Man of the Games."

When Fabris is not skating, he takes university courses over the Internet, mostly in science. He also unwinds by playing the electric guitar. Prior to the Olympics, Fabris lived with his parents in Roana as skaters in Italy earn just a modest living compared to their soccer star counterparts. He has also worked as a police officer for the Italian army, but spent most of his time training and could not afford to live on his own. However, it was anticipated that Fabris' Olympic medals would bring him 300,000 euros in compensation from the Italian government. Fabris said he intended to take a vacation, perhaps to the United States or Norway, and buy a house.

While Fabris enjoyed the attention his wins brought and spent time joking with the press that he would finally be able to get a girlfriend, he also remained steadfast in his commitment to stay true to himself. After his win, Fabris turned down a lucrative deal to appear on an Italian reality television show. As Fabris told the *San Francisco Chronicle* during the Olympic Games: "After this I am for sure more famous, but I am sure I will stay with my feet on the ground, you know, and not change my inside life. I want to stay the same as before. But I would like to enjoy this moment."

Sources

Periodicals

Los Angeles Times, February 26, 2006, p. S2.
San Francisco Chronicle, February 26, 2006, p. C9.
Washington Post, February 25, 2006, p. E10.

Online

"A Star Is Reborn: Italy's Fabris Stole Thunder from Supposed Showdown," SI.com, http://sportsillustrated.cnn.com/2006/olympics/2006/writers/02/21/speed.fabris/index.html (February 27, 2006).

"Enrico Fabris," NBCOlympics.com, http://www.nbcolympics.com/athletes/5084383/detail.html (April 17, 2006).

"Enrico Fabris," SkateResults.com, http://www.skateresults.com/skater/show/1386 (May 22, 2006).

"Fabris Wins First Medal for Host Italy," NBC Olympics.com, http://www.nbcolympics.com/speedskating/5100620/detail.html (May 15, 2006).

"Italy Toasts Its Man of the Games," *Italy* magazine, http://www.italymag.co.uk/2006/news-from-italy/italy-toasts-its-man-of-the-games/ (May 15, 2006).

—Lisa Frick

Niall Ferguson

Historian, professor, and author

DPA/Landov

Born April 18, 1964, in Glasgow, Scotland; son of Campbell (a physician) and Molly (a physicist) Ferguson; married Sue Douglas (a media executive), 1994; children: three. *Education:* Earned degree (first-class) in history from Magdalen College, Oxford University, 1985.

Addresses: *Office*—Harvard University, Center for European Studies, 27 Kirkland St., Cambridge, MA 02138.

Career

Hanseatic scholar in Hamburg and Berlin, West Germany, 1986; junior research fellow, Christ's College, Cambridge University, 1989-90; lecturer and fellow, Peterhouse College, Cambridge, 1990-92; fellow and tutor in modern history, Jesus College, Oxford University, 1992-2000; first book, *Paper and Iron: Hamburg Business and German Politics in the Era of Inflation, 1897-1927,* published in Britain, 1995; professor of political and financial history, Jesus College, Oxford, 2000-02; Herzog Professor in Financial History, New York University, Stern School of Business, 2002-04; professor of international history, Harvard University, 2004—. Also Houblon-Norman fellow, Bank of England, 2000-01; Hoover Institution, Stanford University, senior fellow, 2002. Writer of op-ed articles for the *New York Times.* His books *Empire* and *Colossus* were both the basis of British television series.

Sidelights

British historian Niall Ferguson has produced a number of well-reviewed books examining the economic, political, and social forces that propel historical change, particularly in the modern civilization of the Western world. The Harvard University professor first rose to prominence in Britain for his well-developed assertions that imperialism—the extension of one nation's power over another, often by force—has not been entirely detrimental to the world's citizenry. Subsequent books by Ferguson, such as *Colossus: The Price of America's Empire,* critique the United States' foreign policy. That 2004 work, he told Victoria James in *Geographical,* "is a book designed to make people uncomfortable. It says to liberals, 'American hegemony may potentially be a force for good.'"

Born in 1964, Ferguson is a native of Glasgow, Scotland. His father was a physician, and his mother a physicist, but it was his grandfather, a journalist, who encouraged his career as a writer. Ferguson's first book was a tinfoil-covered tome that featured his parodies of ancient Greek myths, which he completed at the age of ten. He was schooled at Glasgow Academy, and went on to Oxford University, where he studied English and history. After earning his degree in 1985, he spent the remainder of the decade researching German economic history in Berlin and Hamburg, while writing articles for British newspapers.

During the 1990s, Ferguson held a series of academic posts at Oxford and Cambridge universities before advancing to a professorship at Jesus College at Oxford in 2000. His first book, *Paper and Iron: Hamburg Business and German Politics in the Era of Inflation, 1897-1927*, was published in Britain in 1995, but it was 1998's *The Pity of War* that secured his reputation as the rebel among a new generation of British historians. In it, he sought to shatter the ten great myths of World War I, including the long-cherished assertion that Britain was forced to go to war with imperial Germany because of the latter nation's aggressive actions. Ferguson theorized that had Britain stayed out of the conflict, the course of history in Europe would have certainly been much different, and likely would have led to a union of European nations in the 1920s, which would have prevented subsequent world war.

Two more books—a history of the legendary Rothschild banking family, and *The Cash Nexus: Money and Power in the Modern World, 1700-2000*, which became a bestseller in Britain in 2001—appeared before Ferguson began dividing his time between England and the United States. As a visiting professor of financial history at New York University, he became increasingly intrigued by the influence of American foreign policy and economic power on world events. Several weeks after the al-Qaeda attacks on the World Trade Center and Pentagon on September 11, 2001, he penned a cover story for the *New York Times Magazine* in which he imagined what New York City would be like ten years into the future. "You need only visit one of those cities—Jerusalem or Belfast—that have been fractured by terrorism and religious strife to get a glimpse" of what life would be like for New Yorkers in 2011, he asserted. "Imagine a segregated city, with a kind of Muslim ghetto in an outer borough that non-Muslims can enter only—if they dare—with a special endorsement on their ID cards. Imagine security checkpoints at every tunnel and bridge leading into Manhattan, where armed antiterrorist troops check every vehicle for traces of explosives and prohibited toxins."

Ferguson's 2003 book, *Empire: How Britain Made the Modern World*, aroused some controversy in Britain for his argument that British imperialism, which at one point controlled a quarter of the world's land surface and more than 400 million inhabitants thereof, was not wholly negative in its impact. Reviewing it for the *National Review*, David Harsanyi called it "ambitious, provocative, and entertaining.... While acknowledging the sins of British colonialism, this illustrated volume gives an enthusiastic nod to the Empire's high moral character and its role in bringing a sometimes regressive and antagonistic world kicking and screaming into modernity's fold."

In 2004 Ferguson took a permanent post as a professor of history at Harvard University, a defection from Britain's academic ranks that was judged to be as much the result of his star power as it was an admission that American academics of his reputation can command astronomical salaries. His 2004 book, *Colossus*, was made into a television series in Britain, as had *Empire* before it. The writer of regular articles for the opinion-editorial pages of the *New York Times*, Ferguson is continually bemused by Americans' lack of historical perspective about its foreign policy. "The lesson of history is that countries such as Afghanistan and Iraq are tremendously difficult to democratise," he explained to James in the *Geographical* interview. "Transforming their institutions in your image will take decades and will cost a lot of money."

In the spring of 2005, Ferguson wrote an op-ed piece for the *New York Times* that warned against a premature pullout of U.S. troops in Iraq, as public opinion for such a move began to gather support. He reminded readers of the British military experience in the Middle East during the earlier part of the twentieth century, which failed to quell regional tensions despite a well-equipped and relatively ruthless military machine for the time. Britain's abrupt departure from the area, Ferguson noted, only exacerbated the problems among competing religious and ethnic groups. "No one should wish for an over-hasty American withdrawal from Iraq," he wrote. "It would be the prelude to a bloodbath of ethnic cleansing and sectarian violence, with inevitable spillovers into and interventions from neighboring countries."

Ferguson is married to former journalist Sue Douglas, with whom he has three children. Though he once wavered in his career between journalism and academia, he believes he made the correct decision. "My parents weren't disappointed by my choice," he reflected in an interview with the *Guardian*'s John Crace, "though my father would have preferred me to play rugby for Scotland. Come to think of it, I'd have preferred to play rugby for Scotland."

Selected writings

Paper and Iron: Hamburg Business and German Politics in the Era of Inflation, 1897-1927, Cambridge University Press (Cambridge, UK), 1995; Basic Books (New York City), 2001.

(Editor) *Virtual History: Alternatives and Counterfactuals*, Picador (London), 1997; Basic Books, 1999.

The Pity of War, Allen Lane (London), 1998.

The World's Banker: The History of the House of Rothschild, Weidenfeld & Nicolson (London), 1998; published in the United States as *The House of Rothschild*, Viking (New York City), 1998.

The Cash Nexus: Money and Power in the Modern World, 1700-2000, Penguin Press, 2001; Allen Lane, 2001.

Empire: How Britain Made the Modern World, Allen Lane, 2003; published in the United States as *Empire: The Rise and Demise of the British World Order and the Lessons for Global Power*, Basic Books, 2003.

Colossus: The Price of America's Empire, Penguin Books (New York City), 2004.

Sources

Geographical April 2005, p. 51.
Guardian (London, England), February 13, 2001; March 1, 2001; January 9, 2003, p. 16.
Independent Sunday (London, England), September 1, 2002, p. 3.
National Review, May 5, 2003.
New York Times, May 24, 2005, p. A21.
New York Times Magazine, December 2, 2001, p. 76.
Sunday Times (London, England), March 18, 2001, p. 5.

—*Carol Brennan*

America Ferrera

© Lisa O'Connor/ZUMA/Corbis

Actress

Born America Georgina Ferrera, April 18, 1984, in Los Angeles, CA. *Education:* Theater and international-relations major at the University of Southern California, 2003—.

Addresses: *Home*—Los Angeles, CA.

Career

Actress in television, including: *Touched by an Angel,* 2002; *Gotta Kick It Up* (movie), 2002; *$5.15/Hr.* (movie), 2004; *Plainsong* (movie), 2004. Film appearances include: *Real Women Have Curves,* 2002; *Darkness Minus Twelve,* 2004; *The Sisterhood of the Traveling Pants,* 2005; *Lords of Dogtown,* 2005; *How the Garcia Girls Spent Their Summer,* 2005; *3:52,* 2005; *Steel City,* 2006.

Awards: (With cast) Special jury prize for acting, Sundance Film Festival, for *Real Women Have Curves,* 2002.

Sidelights

America Ferrera broke the mold for Latina film stars thanks to her acclaimed performance in 2002's *Real Women Have Curves.* Ferrera's figure perfectly embodied the title's sentiment, and she went on to appear in a number of major Hollywood projects, while still working toward her undergraduate degree at the University of Southern California. The daughter of Honduran immigrants, Ferrera is happy to serve as a role model for women of all shapes and colors, especially when she recalled her own formative years. "I went through a lot of self-doubt" in her younger days, she told Elizabeth Weitzman in *Interview.* "I never turned on the TV and saw a Latina woman with an average body."

Some of Ferrera's own biography echoes that of Ana, her character in *Real Women Have Curves.* She was born in 1984 in Los Angeles, the first of six children, and grew up in a single-parent household headed by a protective and determined mother. Unlike Ana's parent, however, the elder Ferrera was emphatic about the possibilities that higher education offered in the United States for her children. As Ferrera explained in an interview with Jamie Painter Young in *Back Stage West,* her mother had come north "for the sole purpose that my siblings and I could get an education, could have every opportunity in the business world, and whatever we wanted to pursue would be at our fingertips."

Ferrera lived up to those expectations by excelling in school. But she was also a talented stage performer in her after-school hours as a member of community and youth theater ensembles, and began auditioning for entertainment-industry roles at the age of 15, despite her mother's wariness. Ferrera endured numerous rejections, partly because of her less-than-lithe figure. "There was a point … where I auditioned for a year and never got a single callback," she recalled in the *Back Stage West* interview with Young. "I started to question, 'What is wrong with me? Why don't they want me?' Either it breaks you completely or it makes you stronger."

Ferrera's first real role was a supporting one in a Disney Channel television movie in 2002, *Gotta Kick It Up,* and then she landed the lead in *Real Women Have Curves.* The movie was adapted from a play of the same name by Josefina Lopez, and cast Ferrera alongside veteran Latina actor Lupe Ontiveros as Carmen, her on-screen mother. Carmen rules over a Mexican-American family in East Los Angeles, and is adamant that her daughter forego college and join the seamstress staff along with her and Ana's older sister at a dress factory; Ana is heartbroken to think that she may have to turn down an Ivy League scholarship offer.

The story arc in *Real Women Have Curves,* some critics felt, was a predictably triumphant one—along with a subplot about celebrating the full-figured female form—but reviewers were nonetheless appreciative of its charms. Elvis Mitchell, writing in the *New York Times,* singled out Ferrera's debut achievement, calling her "a young actress who is at once prickly, self-confident, and transparent. When Ana is stimulated—angry, hurt, or excited—the skin under her eyes often goes dark, a blush that goes past radiant to radioactive." *Entertainment Weekly* writer Missy Schwartz also commended the new star for "radiating a sassy confidence and smart defiance rarely displayed on screen by a teenage girl."

Ferrera noted in interviews that there were similarities between the *Real Women* tale and her own life. The movie was filmed during her senior year of high school in Woodland Hills, California, and her mother had strong opinions about her future plans and which college she chose to attend. After graduating first in her class, Ferrera decided to delay college for a year in order to pursue her acting career. She landed parts in two television movies as well as roles in *Darkness Minus Twelve,* and *The Sisterhood of the Traveling Pants,* a long-anticipated adaptation of a best-selling young-adult novel.

In *The Sisterhood of the Traveling Pants,* Ferrera played one of a quartet of female friends forced to endure a summer-long separation. Though all are built differently, they decide to share a pair of jeans over their vacations by mailing them to one another. Ferrera's character, Carmen, goes to visit a father in another state whom she barely knows; another, Lena (Alexis Bledel of *Gilmore Girls*), visits her extended family in Greece and falls in love; Bridget (Blake Lively, an industry newcomer), heads to Mexico for soccer camp, while the fourth young woman, Tibby (Amber Tamblyn of *Joan of Arcadia*) stays at home, befriends a younger girl with a very real problem, and makes a film about her.

The Sisterhood of the Traveling Pants did well at the box office, and resonated with the book's legions of fans. Lisa Schwarzbaum of *Entertainment Weekly* commended the entire cast and predicted that Ferrera would likely have an impressive career ahead of her in a variety of non-ethnic-slotted roles, but noted further that "the longer she goes on representing the interests of Hispanic Americans with such flair, and speaking out for young women who are totally at home in their full flesh, the greater the opportunity for women of all colors and sizes to see beauty on screen that looks like theirs."

Ferrera's next movie, *Lords of Dogtown,* opened on the same June day in 2005 as *The Sisterhood of the Traveling Pants.* By then, she was deeply involved in her double major, theater and international relations, at the University of Southern California. She also made *How the Garcia Girls Spent Their Summer,* released later that year, and was set to appear in two planned *Sisterhood* sequels. Her mother seemed to be coming to terms with her dual career goals, but Ferrera did tell Young in the *Back Stage West* interview that "I think every morning my mom waits for me to wake up and say, 'I'll be a doctor,' because she wants security for me; she wants me to have a good life, and what I have had to do is prove to her that this is what the [good] life is for me."

Sources

Back Stage West, October 17, 2002, p. 1.
Entertainment Weekly, December 20, 2002, p. 84; June 10, 2005, p. 40, p. 82.
Film Journal International, July 2005, p. 106.
Interview, October 2002, p. 108.
New Republic, November 11, 2002, p. 22.
New York Times, March 22, 2002.
Seattle Times, November 8, 2002, p. H22.
Teen People, September 1, 2002, p. 160.

—*Carol Brennan*

Jasper Fforde

David Levenson/Getty Images

Author and filmmaker

Born January 11, 1961, in London, England; companion of Mari Roberts; children: twin daughters, two sons.

Addresses: *Contact*—PO Box 165, Hay on Wye HR3 5WU United Kingdom. *E-mail*—jasperjasperfforde.-com.

Career

Began working in film industry, c. early 1980s; received first film credits as a production runner for *The Ploughman's Lunch*, 1983; production officer runner, *The Pirates of Penzance*, 1983; camera focus, *GoldenEye*, 1995; first assistant cameraman, *The Saint*, 1997; first assistant cameraman, *The Mask of Zorro*, 1998; cinematographer, *Lift*, 1998; cinematographer, *Passengers*, 1999; cinematographer, *Engaged*, 1999; focus puller, *Entrapment*, 1999; focus puller, *Quills*, 2000; published first novel, *The Eyre Affair*, 2002; began "Nursery Crimes" series with *The Big Over Easy: A Nursery Crime*, 2005.

Awards: Bollinger Everyman Wodehouse Prize for Comic Writing, for *The Well of Lost Plots*, 2004.

Sidelights

After beginning his career working on films, Jasper Fforde embraced his long-time interest in writing and published his first novel in 2002, *The Eyre Affair*. It took Fforde more than a decade to find a publisher for his work; he had written several rejected manuscripts for novels before *The Eyre Affair* was finally accepted. This novel was the first of many popular titles for Fforde, who wrote pun-filled fantasy books for adults which are often compared to J.K. Rowling's Harry Potter books. Of his strategy as a writer, Fforde told Mervyn Rothstein of the *New York Times*, "I love facts, and whenever I see something interesting I like to use it. I take little bits from here and there and mix them together, make them interlock like a jigsaw puzzle, try to weave the strands together in a logic that could be understood."

Fforde was born in 1961 in London. His father was a prominent economist, while his mother did charity work and was a passionate reader. Fforde and his four siblings were raised in London and Wales. Like his father, Fforde's siblings also became academic scholars. As a child, he shared his mother's love of reading, and by the age of eleven, had become quite interested in film and television as well. While the young Fforde liked to watch Monty Python, he was particularly influenced by a commercial he saw when he was 12 years old. The commercial was for milk and starred actor Roger Moore. It showed what happened behind the scenes on a production set. This commercial inspired Fforde's aspirations as a filmmaker.

When Fforde was 12 years old, he was sent to a boarding school for the next six years. While attending the Darlington School, a progressive school in Devon, he was rather unhappy because he did not like the school's environment. However, because he wanted to work in film, he was able to work on photography and unfinished short films while he was at the school. When Fforde was 18, he left school and decided not to go to college. Instead, he began working on his film career.

Fforde began his film career in the early 1980s. Among his early credits was work as a production runner on films like 1983's *The Ploughman's Lunch* and production office runner on *The Pirates of Penzance*, also released that year. For the latter film, his job essentially consisted of making beverages for the set. While Fforde's film career was growing, he thought about doing fiction, so he began writing short stories to help him become better in the form. As his skills developed, the stories grew longer and longer and he was soon writing full-length novels.

While writing his novel manuscripts on his own time, Fforde continued to develop his film career. By the 1990s, he was primarily working with cameras on film sets. He began doing camera focus on 1995's *GoldenEye*. Fforde was the first assistant cameraman on 1997's *The Saint* and 1998's *The Mask of Zorro*. He was also the focus puller on two films at the end of that decade, *Entrapment* and *Quills*. In addition, Fforde was a cinematographer on three films, 1998's *Lift* and two films in 1999, *Passengers* and *Engaged*.

While Fforde had many film credits to his name, he was sure he would not make it as a director, his original goal when he began working in the film business. He knew that he did not have the right personality for the job. However, his writing career was also not going well. His first full-length novel manuscript was *Nursery Crime*. The story concerned the circumstances under which Humpty Dumpty was found dead at the base of a wall. This manuscript was rejected repeatedly. However, Fforde would not let the rejections get him down for long because he wrote to amuse himself, inspired in part by his love of Douglas Adams and his Hitchhiker series, including *The Hitchhiker's Guide to the Galaxy*. Fforde produced four more novel manuscripts and had his works rejected a reported 76 times before one was accepted for publication.

His first published novel took years to write. Titled *The Eyre Affair* when it was published in 2002, Fforde began penning the book in 1993. He stopped for several years because he was concerned about how fans of the classic novel *Jane Eyre* might respond to his toying with its characters. In total, it took around five to six years to complete before it was published, including a last minute change from third person to first person point of view. *The Eyre Affair* is hard to categorize because the novel is a combination of fantasy, science fiction, satire, criminal thriller, and comedy, with many puns, inside jokes, and references to popular culture thrown in as well. At its core, Fforde created a novel around a complicated "what if" take on British history.

Though *The Eyre Affair* is set in Great Britain in 1985, the Crimean War is still being fought, nearly 130 years after it began, and Wales has been an independent, socialist country since 1848. Fforde also imagines British society differently as well. People make pets of endangered animals that have been cloned and literature is taken so seriously the people riot over disagreements about who wrote the plays of William Shakespeare. The primary character in Fforde's novel world is Thursday Next, a literary investigator working for a special unit in the police force. Because people can time travel and her uncle invented a means of physically entering the world of novels and affecting their contents (the "Prose Porter"), Next's job focuses on ensuring such classic novels remain in their original form. With partner Bowden Cable, Next is pursuing a rogue English professor, Acheron Hades, who has stolen important manuscripts and kidnapped her uncle. Hades has taken *Jane Eyre*, entered the world of the story, and kidnapped the title character, affecting all the copies of the book in existence. In the end, however, Next chooses to change the story's ending herself.

When originally published in Great Britain, *The Eyre Affair* was popular with both critics and readers alike. In the United States, the novel reached the *New York Times* Top Ten best-seller list. Many critics commented positively on the character of Next, comparing her to Bridget Jones, Nancy Drew, and Dirty Harry, as she brought down Hades. While Fritz Lanham of the *Houston Chronicle* took issue with the characters and dialogue, he also wrote, "Give first-time British novelist Jasper Fforde his due: For sheer inventiveness his book is hard to beat." *The Eyre Affair* was eventually translated into six languages.

Fforde's motivation for writing *The Eyre Affair* and its sequels was born out of his own appreciation of the classics. He told James Macgowan of the *Ottawa Citizen*, "I love literature. I love stories, actually. The point of using the classics in this kind of playful reverence is that I always felt the classics had become stuffy through being academized—is that what the word is? *Jane Eyre* is a study text, and it should never have been made a study text, as has *Wuthering Heights* and Shakespeare. I think people are in danger of seeing them as only that, when they aren't, they're just great stories."

By the time *The Eyre Affair* was published, Fforde had moved to a place near his childhood home in Wales, where he continued to write his books. With the success of the novel, he now had the luxury of writing full-time. He wrote a series of books featuring Next and her continuing adventures, all of which continued to defy categorization but remained popular with readers and critics. In 2003's *Lost in a Good Book*, Next has become well known for her literary investigations. She has discovered that within the fictional realm, there is another police group to take care of the fictional world called the Justification Section to ensure that no bad activities happen in novels. For example, this group stops the assassination of Heathcliff in *Wuthering Heights*. Next ends up helping the character Miss Havisham from the novel *Great Expectations* as they work to free someone from the story *The Raven* by Edgar Allan Poe. Next also has to deal with difficulties in her personal life. In Fforde's previous book, Next pined for a love she thought she lost, Landen Parke-Laine, whom she ended up marrying. In this book, she becomes pregnant by him, but he is removed from reality after they have only a few months together.

Two more novels complete this phase of Next's story. In 2004's *Well of Lost Plots*, the pregnant Next is on maternity leave and forced to run from reality into the fictional world. She hides in the Well of Lost Plots, where unpublished books in progress are kept. She tries to help the characters make their books better so they can be published. Next is specifically hiding in the unpublished novel *Caversham Heights*, which is under the control of Jurisfiction, the agency responsible for keeping the books organized. However, Jurisfiction personnel are being killed off, a black market thrives off of the buying and selling of ideas and words from the works in progress, and parasites and viruses are infecting books. Next is also looking for her still-missing husband.

Fforde wraps up the plot threads of the first three novels in the "Thursday Next" series in 2004's *Something Rotten: A Thursday Next Novel*. Next is back in reality, and is now the mother of a daughter named Friday. Her husband, Landen, has re-appeared as well. Next's professional life is more complicated as she has to deal with more literature issues, including a mutiny in *Hamlet* and an evil tyrant in a space-ship who crashes into a pulp western. She also has even larger problems as the fate of the world hangs in the balance of a croquet match, and Next must also save England. Reviewing this book in the *Independent*, Christina Hardyment wrote, "*Something Rotten* is, arguably, Fforde's best book yet. It shows him firmly in the authorial saddle, whipping in his glorious but unruly horde of characters to create a well-balanced story that stands in its own right, and has a definite plot."

While Fforde's Next books remained popular, he took a break from the character for his next books, though he planned to revisit her at a later date. Fforde focused his satirical, surreal, and playful eye on mystery writing and detective fiction, specifically crimes from fairy tales and nursery rhymes. The novels were among the first full-length manuscripts that Fforde produced, but originally rejected by publishers. The first novel, published in 2005, was his first novel idea. In *The Big Over Easy: A Nursery Crime*, Detective Inspector Jack Spratt of the Nursery Crime Division, working with assistant Mary Mary, is struggling to close cases and convict criminals. He has failed to convict the Three Pigs, for example. The pair are now working on the murder of Humpty Stuyvesant Van Dumpty III, who was found broken at the bottom of the wall.

The same pattern is repeated in 2006's *The Fourth Bear: A Nursery Crime*. Though Jack and Mary have resigned their commission, they are drawn into an investigation when Goldilocks, also known as investigative reporter Henrietta Hachett, goes missing just before her story comes out about a series of murders. Among the last to see her alive were the Three Bears, though the Gingerbread Man, a convicted murderer, is also loose and around at questionable times. Like the Next books, the "Nursery Crime" books proved popular with reviewers and sold well.

Though a long time in coming, Fforde appreciated his success as a writer and that audiences enjoyed his books. He told the *Independent*'s Hardyment, "I have no mission to educate or moralise. I see myself as in the entertainment business first and foremost. I'm just having terrific fun—and getting paid for it."

Selected writings

The Eyre Affair, Viking (New York City), 2002.
Lost in a Good Book, Viking, 2003.
The Well of Lost Plots, Viking, 2004.

Something Rotten: A Thursday Next Novel, Viking, 2004.

The Big Over Easy: A Nursery Crime, Viking, 2005.

The Fourth Bear: A Nursery Crime, Viking, 2006.

Sources

Periodicals

Bookseller, June 4, 2004, p. 6.

Courier Mail (Queensland, Australia), September 21, 2002, p. M5.

Entertainment Weekly, July 29, 2005, p. 73.

Guardian (London, England), July 26, 2003, p. 22.

Houston Chronicle, February 17, 2002, p. 16.

Independent (London, England), July 19, 2003, pp. 21-22; July 21, 2004, p. 11; August 5, 2004, p. 29.

New York Times, April 1, 2002, p. E1; August 5, 2004, p. E9; July 22, 2005, p. E35.

Ottawa Citizen (Ottawa, Ontario, Canada), November 2, 2003, p. C11.

People, August 23, 2004, p. 49.

Rocky Mountain News (Denver, CO), July 22, 2005, p. 24D.

Star Tribune (Minneapolis, MN), February 22, 2004, p. 16F.

Sunday Oregonian, February 22, 2004, p. D7.

Time Out, July 10, 2002, p. 8; July 21, 2004, p. 60.

Toronto Star, October 28, 2003, p. C5.

USA Today, February 21, 2002, p. 14B.

Washington Post, March 21, 2004, p. T15.

Weekend Australian, September 21, 2002, p. B10.

Online

"The Big Over Easy," Jasper Fforde.com, http://www.jasperfforde.com/nextbook.html (February 12, 2006).

"Jasper Fforde," Internet Movie Database, http://www.imdb.com/name/nm0275532/ (February 12, 2006).

"Meet the Writers: Jasper Fforde," Barnes & Noble, http://www.barnesandnoble.com/writers/writer/asp.?cid=1022595 (February 12, 2006).

—A. Petruso

Patrick J. Fitzgerald

© John Gress/Reuters/Corbis

Prosecutor

Born December 22, 1960, in New York, NY; son of Patrick Sr. (a doorman) and Tillie Fitzgerald. *Education:* Earned degrees in mathematics and economics from Amherst College; Harvard University School of Law, J.D., 1985.

Addresses: *Office*—United States Attorney's Office, 219 S. Dearborn St., Rm. 500, Chicago, IL 60604.

Career

Worked as a doorman, deckhand, and janitor in the early 1980s; in private practice as an attorney, 1985-88; Office of the U.S. Attorney for the Southern District of New York, assistant attorney, 1988-96, and National Security Coordinator, 1996-2001; U.S. Attorney for the Northern District of Illinois, 2001—; appointed special counsel for a U.S. Department of Justice Investigation, 2003.

Sidelights

Patrick J. Fitzgerald was a relatively unknown government attorney in late 2003 when he was appointed special counsel in charge of a criminal investigation that, two years later, would implicate senior staffers at the White House. He was charged with uncovering the source of a leak, or disclosure of classified information, involving the identity of a Central Intelligence Agency operative. Fitzgerald, who had served as U.S. Attorney for the Northern District of Illinois since 2001, won praise from both sides of the ideological fence for his handling of the investigation that became known as "Plamegate," after the agent, Valerie Plame.

Born in December of 1960, Fitzgerald grew up in the Flatbush neighborhood of Brooklyn, New York. His parents were Irish immigrants, and his father worked as a doorman for a Manhattan residential building. One of four siblings in the Roman Catholic family, Fitzgerald attended Regis High School in Manhattan, known for its rigorous academic program. At Regis he emerged as a talented member of the debate team before heading on to Amherst College, where he majored in economics and mathematics. He earned tuition money during the summer months by working as a doorman at a building down the street from his father's post, and also by serving as a deckhand on the commuter ferries that plied New York harbor.

Fitzgerald went on to Harvard Law School, and practiced at a firm for three years after earning his degree in 1985. In 1988, he was hired as an assistant U.S. Attorney for the district that includes New York City, and spent the next several years prosecuting drug-trafficking and organized-crime cases. He was involved in the trials related to the Gambino crime family, which resulted in several convictions, including that of notorious mob boss John Gotti. Fitzgerald soon developed a reputation as a brilliant legal strategist who possessed a photographic memory as well as a talent for unearthing obscure laws on the books which inevitably resulted in jury convictions.

One of the prime examples of that latter skill was Fitzgerald's work on the 1993 World Trade Center bombing case. With a blind Egyptian cleric, Sheikh Omar Abdel Rahman, and eleven other defendants in the dock, Fitzgerald applied a rarely used sedition law dating back to the Civil War era to convict them. The prosecutor eventually became somewhat of an expert in Islamic fundamentalist groups, and in 1996 was named National Security Coordinator for the Office of the U.S. Attorney for the Southern District of New York. An early predictor of the dangers posed by Osama bin Laden and the al-Qaeda network, Fitzgerald was designated to serve as chief counsel in prosecutions of those suspected of carrying out bombings on U.S. embassies in Africa in 1998, which again resulted in successful convictions.

Fitzgerald was nominated to become U.S. Attorney for the Northern District of Illinois on September 1, 2001. His appointment was confirmed by the Senate several weeks later, and Fitzgerald moved to Chicago, where he and his team of 160 attorneys launched a major probe of government corruption in the state. Less than five years later, former Illinois governor George Ryan had been prosecuted and faced up to 20 years in prison for bribery and lying to investigators. Fitzgerald's campaign, which netted a bipartisan roster of wrongdoers, also reached into the Chicago mayor's office, and in this case he relied on a mail-fraud statute usually deployed for organized-crime cases in order to prosecute some of the defendants.

Fitzgerald was still technically in charge of the U.S. Attorney's office in the northern half of Illinois when he was named special counsel for the White House leak investigation in December of 2003, which the U.S. Department of Justice had launched at the request of the Central Intelligence Agency (CIA). The Plamegate story had unfolded over several months, beginning in February of 2002, when Vice President Dick Cheney asked Joseph Wilson, a former U.S. ambassador with a distinguished career, to undertake a secret mission to Niger in order to confirm reports that in the late 1990s Iraqi leader Saddam Hussein had purchased uranium yellowcake from the country. The material is a lightly processed ore that can be refined into making weapons-grade plutonium. Wilson made the trip and found no truth to the report, which he delivered to administration officials. The claims persisted, however, and were repeated by Cheney and President George W. Bush, and became one of the Administration's series of justifications for the invasion of Iraq in March of 2003. Four months later, irate that the yellowcake rumors were still being repeated by the White House, Wilson penned a blistering op-ed piece for the July 6, 2003, edition of the *New York Times* headlined, "What I Didn't Find in Africa."

Within days, conservative commentator Robert Novak had mentioned the name of Wilson's wife, Valerie Plame, in his widely syndicated column, noting that she worked for the Central Intelligence Agency. But Plame was a covert operative—in other words, under no circumstances was it to be revealed that she worked for the agency, lest the lives of foreign nationals who provide intelligence information to the United States be endangered—and it was a violation of federal law to reveal such identities. Fitzgerald's investigation into who leaked her name to Novak resulted in the indictment of Lewis "Scooter" Libby, chief of staff for U.S. Vice President Dick Cheney, in October of 2005 on multiple counts of giving false statements to investigators, perjury, and obstruction of justice. Libby resigned, and Fitzgerald's team prepared for trial. The leak investigation also threatened to involve Karl Rove, a high-ranking White House official.

Fitzgerald rarely makes statements to the press or gives interviews. Friends and former colleagues divulge that he works long hours, once owned a cat but was rarely home to feed it, and occasionally takes mountain climbing or hang-gliding vacations. Unmarried, Fitzgerald is the subject of speculation that he may one day seek public office, but others note a more likely scenario is a future appointment as head of the Federal Bureau of Investigation.

Sources

National Review, November 21, 2005, p. 20.
Newsweek, July 25, 2005, p. 32.
New York Times, July 6, 2003.
Observer (London, England), February 12, 2006, p. 14.
People, November 14, 2005, p. 71.
Time, November 7, 2005, p. 39.
U.S. News & World Report, July 4, 2005, pp. 23-24.

—*Carol Brennan*

Foo Fighters

© *Martin Philbey/ZUMA/Corbis*

Rock group

Group formed in 1995; members include William Goldsmith (left band, March, 1997), drums; David Grohl (born January 14, 1969, in Warren, OH; son of James and Virginia Grohl; married Jennifer Youngblood, c. 1994 [divorced, 1997]; married Jordyn Blum, 2003), guitar, vocals; Taylor Hawkins (born Oliver Taylor Hawkins, February 17, 1972, in Laguna Beach, CA; joined band, 1997), drums; Nate Mendel (born December 2, 1968; children: one son), bass; Chris Shiflett (born Christopher Shiflett, May 6, 1971, in Santa Barbara, CA; married; children: Liam; joined band, 1999), guitar; Pat Smear (born Georg Ruthenberg, August 5, 1959, in Los Angeles, CA; left band, 1997), guitar; Franz Stahl (joined band, 1997; left band, 1999), guitar.

Addresses: *Record company*—RCA Records, 1540 Broadway, New York, NY 10036. *Website*—http://www.foofighters.com.

Career

Grohl was a member of the bands Nirvana, Scream, Dain Bramage, Freakbaby, and Mission Impossible; as a solo artist he recorded an album, playing all instruments; released *Foo Fighters* on Roswell/Capitol, 1995; Grohl recruited band members for a tour, 1995; Smear was a founding member of the Germs; Goldsmith and Mendel were former members of Sunny Day Real Estate, and Mendel was earlier a founder of Product of Rape and Christ on a Crutch; Hawkins spent 1995 and 1996 touring as Alanis Morissette's drummer; Shiflett was a member of No Use For A Name and Me First & the Gimmie Gimmies; recorded first album

as a group, *The Colour and the Shape*, 1997; released *There Is Nothing Left To Lose*, 1999; toured with Red Hot Chili Peppers, 2000; released *One By One*, 2002; toured worldwide, 2002-03; released *In Your Honor*, 2005; toured United States and Europe, 2005-06.

Awards: Video Music Award for best group video, MTV, for "Big Me," 1996; Grammy Award for best short form music video, Recording Academy, for "Learn To Fly," 2001; Grammy Award for best rock album, Recording Academy, for *There Is Nothing Left To Lose*, 2001; Grammy Award for best hard rock performance, Recording Academy, for "All My Life," 2003; Grammy Award for best rock album, Recording Academy, for *One By One*, 2004.

Sidelights

Although the Foo Fighters came out of the ashes of the same fire that incinerated the grunge rock scene, their sound more closely resembles popular, less hard-hitting rock groups. Led by Dave Grohl, the former drummer for Nirvana, the Foo Fighters rely on simple, energetic pop-rock tunes to get their point across. Although there was a lot of turnover in the band initially, the band finally formed a cohesive group after a few album releases.

Grohl grew up in Washington, D.C., the son of a single working mother. Too poor to buy a record player, Grohl listened to his Minor Threat and Bad Brains albums on a record player borrowed from the public school where his mother taught English. Moreover, he did not even possess his own drum kit when he started playing with DC hardcore bands like Dain Bramage, Freakbaby, and Mission Impossible. By the time he was 17, Grohl had joined a lauded punk ensemble called Scream, leaving high school before completing his senior year when the opportunity to tour Europe arose.

After Scream disbanded in 1990, a friend (Buzz Osbourne of the Melvins) put Grohl in touch with an up-and-coming Seattle band in need of a drummer. Grohl joined Kurt Cobain and Krist Novoselic in Nirvana in the fall of 1990, and a year later he was part of one of the biggest phenomenons in rock history. With a slew of successful releases and album sales in the tens of millions, Nirvana built a bridge between punk and rock. That winning streak ended in April of 1994 when Cobain committed suicide, a subject Grohl has been reluctant to discuss. He does confess to still being haunted by his friend's death. "It's hard not to think about something that everybody wants to talk about all the time," he told Mike Rubin in *Spin*.

After the dissolution of Nirvana, Grohl toyed with the idea of joining Tom Petty and the Heartbreakers and toured with them for a time. But instead, Grohl went into a recording studio by himself and began starting to tape a couple dozen of the songs he had written over several years. His only help came from his friend Barrett Jones, who produced the album, and Greg Dulli of the Afghan Whigs, who played guitar on one song. The result was 1995's *Foo Fighters*, which was also the name of Grohl's memberless band. (The name originated from unidentified flying objects [UFOs] encountered by the U.S. Army Air Force near the end of World War II; the UFOs were called "Foo Fighters" or "Kraut Balls" by those who believed the objects were a secret German weapon.) The debut was released on Roswell Records, a vanity label which Capitol Records had given Grohl, named after the famed New Mexico site on which some believe extraterrestrials crash-landed in 1947.

Grohl assembled a band in order to go out on the road in support of the record, which was receiving a healthy advance buzz. His first pick was Pat Smear, a beloved eccentric who had been a founding member of the Germs, the first Los Angeles punk band to record an entire album. Smear, facing hard times financially, had made ends meet by playing punk rocker roles on television during the 1980s, as well as adding some verve to the last days of Nirvana. Joining Smear and Grohl in the Foo Fighters line-up were two members of a much-lauded and recently disbanded Seattle act, Sunny Day Real Estate. Drummer William Goldsmith and bass player Nate Mendel found themselves adrift after Sunny Day Real Estate's lead singer had become a fervent born-again Christian.

The Foo Fighters toured as an opening act for Mike Watt in the spring of 1995. However, the band was headlining after only a few months as record sales took off. Critics often made much of the odd, abstruse lyrics in songs like "Big Me" and "This Is a Call." Given Grohl's ties to Nirvana, reviewers looked for hidden meanings everywhere, but he later admitted they were purposefully nonsensical. "It was for fear of writing something that might reveal too much," Grohl told *Spin*'s Rubin, "or actually reveal something at all.... I don't want to let everyone else in on my problems or my personal crisis or my misery. They're mine." He also pointed out that many of the songs had been written long before Nirvana became famous.

The Foo Fighters also exhibit a decidedly non-grunge demeanor on stage, in their playing, and in interviews. They shot a video for "Big Me" that spoofed the silly Mentos commercials and then were pelted by the candies at shows for months. The video went on to win the award for Best Group Video at the MTV Video Music Awards in 1996. As the Foo Fighters record issued one well-charting single after another, and they toured for more than a year-and-a-half, the band grew increasingly reticent about the fame that came with their success. "There does come a point where it's totally out of your control," Grohl told *Rolling Stone*'s Chris Mundy, "but I learned a lot of lessons from Nirvana. We don't want to spend too much time whoring ourselves around because not only does it make everyone else sick of you, eventually you get sick of yourself."

While Grohl appreciates his privacy, Smear appeared well-suited for the limelight. The guitarist, who loves to wear dresses and often outfitted himself in outlandish stage gear, began appearing on MTV's *House of Style*. Despite the band's success and popularity, Goldsmith left the Foo Fighters' vaulted orbit after a falling-out with Grohl. In recording their second album, Grohl expressed dissatisfaction with Goldsmith and re-recorded the drum parts himself. He was replaced by Taylor Hawkins, the former drummer for Alanis Morissette's world tour, after the Foo Fighters record was completed in early 1997.

The double album *The Colour and the Shape* was recorded in both Los Angeles and Seattle with Gil Norton as producer. Released in May of 1997 on Roswell, it took a slightly different path away from the light power-pop mood of Grohl's first record. This was a concept album, and its subject was the death of a relationship. Not surprisingly, Grohl's marriage to his high-school sweetheart dissolved around the time of the record's release. The songs sounded the same as the previous release, but the lyrics were suddenly trenchant—a marked contrast to the tracks on their debut. The Foo Fighters' development as a band, wrote *Entertainment Weekly*'s David Browne, "is clearly evident throughout *The Colour and the Shape*, but it isn't always a pretty sight or sound."

Though its subject matter was definitely more weighty, Grohl's penchant for building songs along the soft-verse/rocking-chorus structure hadn't changed on cuts like the first single, "Monkey Wrench." Chuck Crisafulli of *Request* noted that "Grohl is turning out to be something of a master builder when it comes to constructing pop hooks," and the musician admitted to loving pure pop music like Abba, as well as punk rock bands. As *Spin*'s Rubin pointed out, "Foo tunes are more hummers than bummers." Christina Kelly, reviewing *The Colour and the Shape* for *Rolling Stone*, asserted the record "has a big, radio-ready, modern-rock sound." In the *New York Times*, Jon Pareles opined that "timing, ingenuity, and conviction can be all it takes to make rock's common materials ring with passion. That's what happens on *The Colour and the Shape*, as Grohl balances power and tenderness, whipsaw riffing and wistful tunes."

The Foo Fighters embarked on another lengthy tour for *The Colour and the Shape*, and Grohl directed his first video for the "Monkey Wrench" single, an assignment that grew out of his penchant for amateur film making. At the 1997 MTV Music Video Awards, Smear announced he was leaving the group; he was replaced by guitarist Franz Stahl. However, Stahl was not a member for long; the group's 1999 album, *There Is Nothing Left To Lose*, was recorded as a three-piece. The album was recorded in Grohl's home shortly after the band left Capitol. The group signed with RCA and set off on a few club dates to break in its newest member, guitarist Chris Shiflett, who replaced Stahl. Grohl wrote the album's first single, "Learn to Fly," about his fear of flying. "Being afraid of flying isn't convenient when you are a band that seems to take two planes a day," Mendel told *Billboard*'s Carrie Bell. Instead, Grohl decided to learn about how planes stay in the air to get over his fear; the song is about that learning process. The album's variety of song styles "reveal a sensitive

streak that meshes nicely with Grohl's more aggressive inclinations," wrote *Entertainment Weekly*'s Scott Schinder.

After touring in 2000, the Foo Fighters began working on an album in October of that next year, but after working on it for three and a half months, the group realized that things were not clicking. "It didn't feel right. With our band, the most important thing is that the songs feel right and the recordings feel good.... Spontaneity and energy have a lot to do with rock, and rock records shouldn't take that long," Grohl told *Billboard*'s Andrew Katchen. To help spark their creativity, the band members went their separate ways for a short time. Grohl worked with the hard rock band Queens of the Stone Age, contributed to Tony Iommi's 2000 solo album, and created a death-metal compilation called Probot (he played all the instruments and had guest singers); Shiflett returned to his pre-Foo Fighters band, Me First & the Gimmie Gimmies; Hawkins worked on songs in his home studio, and Mendel recorded with the Fire Theft. "We'd never taken a substantial break," Grohl told Katchen. "It only made sense that after seven or eight years we do that—to step back and look at the big picture, especially when you're lost in the process of making a new album that seems like it's going nowhere." After taking a breather, Grohl and Hawkins reworked the album's tracks and then had Shiflett and Mendel record their parts; the second version of the album was completed in about two weeks.

Of the finished album, titled *One By One*, *Billboard*'s Katchen remarked that there was a shift in the band's sound and that the group's "current agenda [is] to kick out visceral, driving jams that are big on volume, speed, and airtight drum and guitar salvos throughout." Declaring that listening to the album resulted in "unexpected exhilaration," *Entertainment Weekly*'s Ken Tucker stated that the songs' "near-constant exploration of various relationships—those between lovers, or friends, or Foos-to-their-fans—never" got tiresome. In 2003, the song "All My Life" from the album won the Grammy Award for Best Hard Rock Performance. That next year, *One By One* won a Grammy Award for Best Rock Album.

Grohl continued to keep busy with projects outside the group, including playing drums on Killing Joke's self-titled 2003 album. "The great thing about being a musician is being free to jam with other musicians, and as with any musician you learn from each other," Grohl told Gary Graff of United Press International. It was three years before the public saw another release from the Foo Fighters. *In Your Honor*, released in 2005, was a two-disc set. When

Grohl began writing the music for the album, he planned on doing it as a solo project, envisioning a film score which then evolved into acoustic songs. However, realizing the resulting material had a Foo Fighters-type sound, he called his bandmates in to contribute. However, Grohl told *Billboard*'s Melinda Newman that the group "couldn't live without rock 'n roll," so it became a double album. The first disc featured hard-driving tunes and the second disc showcased a more "atmospheric, acoustic-guitar-driven affair marked by movie-score string arrangements and mandolins," wrote Scott Galupo in the *Washington Times. All Music Guide*'s Stephen Thomas Erlewine declared that the risk of creating such an album paid off: "By stretching out, the Foo Fighters not only have expanded their sound, but they've found the core of why their music works, so they now have better songs and deliver them more effectively." In support of the album, the band began a U.S. tour in the fall of 2005 which then moved to Europe in 2006. The album was nominated for five Grammy Awards, including one for Best Rock Album.

Besides their Foo Fighters recording and touring, the band members continued to work on side projects. Grohl was still involved with Queens of the Stone Age and did some drumming for Nine Inch Nails, Hawkins worked with former Jane's Addiction bassist Chris Chaney on a glam-prog album scheduled for 2006 release, Shiflett's punk group, Jackson United, released an album in 2005 and toured the United Kingdom that summer, and Mendel continued working with Fire Theft and another band called Ghost Wars. The Foo Fighters regrouped on September 9, 2005, to participate in the nationally televised *Shelter From the Storm: A Concert for the Gulf Coast*, which was broadcast on ABC, CBS, FOX, NBC, The WB, and UPN to raise funds for people affected by the effects of Hurricane Katrina.

Grohl avoids licensing the Foo Fighters' music for advertising (aside from one Japanese beer ad). "It kind of breaks my heart when I hear a classic song that changed my life in a car commercial," he told *Billboard*'s Newman. "Integrity means a lot to me. The ... tiny shred that we've maintained over the last ten years, I guard with my life." Grohl remains the definitive anti-grunge poster boy. "I've covered a lot of ground, but I still feel like a pathetic 17-year-old dropout," Grohl told *Spin*. "My spirit is still young." As for those fans who may be con-

cerned about the end of the Foo Fighters, Grohl told *Entertainment Weekly*'s Leah Greenblatt, "I've been traveling around the world since I was 18, and after every record I always think, Okay, after this I'm going to get on with real life and start a family and get fat and bald and do all the things most everyone does after they're finished running around. But, I don't think I'm finished running around yet."

Selected discography

Foo Fighters, Roswell/Capitol, 1995.
The Colour and the Shape, Roswell/Capitol, 1997.
There Is Nothing Left To Lose, Roswell/RCA, 1999.
One By One, Roswell/RCA, 2002.
In Your Honor, Roswell/RCA, 2005.

Sources

Periodicals

Alternative Press, June 1997.
Amusement Business, February 2000, p. 7.
Billboard, May 3, 1997; May 17, 1997; October 16, 1999, p. 14; November 27, 1999, p. 83; October 19, 2002, p. 10; June 11, 2005, p. 43.
Entertainment Weekly, May 9, 1997, p. 38; May 23, 1997, p. 62; November 5, 1999, p. 82; October 25, 2002, p. L2T8; October 25, 2002, p. 75; June 17, 2005, p. L2T8.
Guitar World, July 1997.
New York Times, May 18, 1997.
Request, July 1997.
Rolling Stone, October 5, 1995; March 21, 1996; May 29, 1997.
Spin, July 1997.
United Press International, May 27, 2003.
Us, July 1997.
Washington Times, June 14, 2005, p. B5; Oct 12, 2005, p. B5.

Online

Grammy.com, http://www.grammy.com/awards/ (January 4, 2006).
"In Your Honor," *All Music Guide*, http://www.allmusic.com (January 4, 2006).
Official Foo Fighters, http://www.foofighters.com (January 4, 2006).

Matthew Fox

WENN/Landov

Actor

Born July 14, 1966, in Crowheart, WY; son of Francis (a rancher) and Loretta (a teacher) Fox; married Margherita Ronchi, August, 1992; children: Kyle Allison, Byron. *Education:* Columbia University, B.A. (economics), 1989; studied acting at Atlantic Theater Company, New York, NY, and The School for Film and Television, New York, NY.

Addresses: *Office*—c/o Touchstone Television, 500 South Buena Vista, Production Building #343, Burbank, CA 91521.

Career

Actor in television, including: *Wings*, NBC, 1992; *Freshman Dorm*, CBS, 1992; *If I Die Before I Wake* (special), 1993; *Party of Five*, FOX, 1994-2000; *Survival of the Yellowstone Wolves* (special), TBS, 1996; *Behind the Mask* (movie), CBS, 1999; *Haunted*, UPN, 2002; *Lost*, ABC, 2004—. Film appearances include: *My Boyfriend's Back*, 1993. Member of a repertory company in Los Angeles, CA, 2000-2002. Also worked as a model and appeared in television commercials.

Sidelights

Though American actor Matthew Fox came to international prominence with his role as Charlie on the hit FOX television series *Party of Five*, he later admitted he did not handle the fame that came with it really well. After the show ended its six-season run, he took time off, remerging in the 2004 hit series *Lost*. Fox handled the success much better the second time around as *Lost* proved to be a hit for its struggling network, ABC.

Born on July 14, 1966, in Crowheart, Wyoming, Fox was the middle of three sons born to Francis and Loretta Fox. He grew up on the family ranch which was run by his father. Until the fifth grade, Fox went to school in a one-room schoolhouse where his mother was the teacher. Another public school he attended was populated primarily by Native American students. At Wind River High School, Fox was an athlete who played football, basketball, and track. Fox considered becoming a farmer, though his father thought he should move east.

Taking his father's advice, Fox went to the East Coast after graduating from high school. In 1984, he moved to Deerfield, Massachusetts, to take a year of college prep courses at Deerfield Academy. The following year, Fox entered Columbia University in New York City on a football scholarship. At Columbia, he studied economics with the goal of becoming a stockbroker on Wall Street. Until the last semester of college, Fox planned on going into business, until he realized it would not be right for him. Fox graduated from Columbia with his B.A. in 1989.

While a college student, Fox had dabbled in modeling. His girlfriend's mother was the owner of a modeling agency and she got him started in the business. He also was represented by the Ford Modeling Agency. Modeling soon led to appearances in a few commercials for Fox, one of which was a large role in a Midas advertisement. By the time he was 24 years old, Fox decided he wanted to try acting as a profession. While his parents were not particularly happy with his career choice, they supported him nonetheless.

To help launch his career, Fox studied acting in New York City. He was a student at the Atlantic Theater Company and The School for Film and Television, both located in New York City. Of his choice to be an actor, he told the *Sunday Mail*, "Something inside me kept pushing. But it was strange for me because I'm a shy person and getting up in front of people at acting class was painful.... I hated it. Some people are struck by that bolt of lightning that tells them: 'Hey, this is for me.' But my life had seemed more a series of crossroads and deciding which turn to take. But for all the early pain, I love the business."

The genre where Fox spent most of his acting career was television, where it began. One of his first roles on a television program was in a guest spot on the NBC hit situation comedy *Wings* in 1992. That same year, Fox was cast in his first role a television series. He played Danny Foley on the CBS drama *Freshman Dorm*. The series focused on first-year students living in a dormitory at a college which was located in California. However, the series was very short-lived: CBS canceled *Freshman Dorm* after airing only six episodes.

As Fox's career began taking off, his personal life was also undergoing a transformation. In 1992, he married his long-time girlfriend, Margherita Ronchi, a native of Italy. The couple met while Fox was a student at Columbia. The couple later had two children, Kyle Allison and Byron.

After the demise of *Freshman Dorm*, Fox acted in several projects. In 1993, he made his film debut with *My Boyfriend's Back*, a comedy that was targeted at teens with an unusual premise. The story focused on a dead high school student who comes back to life to live his one wish of dating a prom queen. Also in 1993, Fox appeared in a *CBS Schoolbreak Special* entitled *If I Die Before I Wake*. This child-targeted special focused on a high school track team who lose their lives in an airplane crash.

The big break of Fox's acting career came in 1994 when he was cast in the FOX network's dramatic series *Party of Five*. Fox played Charlie Salinger, the eldest of five siblings who is forced to leave behind his own single, developing life as a carpenter when his parents suddenly die. Fox's Charlie has to raise his younger siblings in their parents' home in San Francisco. While Charlie became their guardian, it was a role he only gradually grew into over the course of the series. *Party of Five* explored familial and love relationships among the main characters, which became stronger with each episode.

Commenting on his character, Fox told Harriet Winslow of the *Washington Post*, "That's what I love about Charlie so much, that he's human. His heart is in the right place. He's really a sensitive, good-hearted human being. But he just doesn't think about the consequences of his actions."

While *Party of Five* received critical praise and was a cult hit from the beginning, it was almost cancelled after its first season due to poor ratings. At the end of the 1994-95 television season *Party of Five* was ranked 99th out of 103 shows. Despite this situation, the network renewed the show, primarily because of the support its fans showed. After the renewal, FOX became very supportive of the show, which started to do better with certain audiences. *Party of Five* showed improved ratings over the years. During its six-year run, many issues were covered on the show, often in dramatic fashion. In addition to teen pregnancy, alcoholism, and infidelity, Fox's character ran away from his wedding to the nanny hired to care for his youngest brother and developed Hodgkin's disease in the third season. Charlie later married Kirsten, the nanny, and became a father. Fox found the challenges of playing a cancer patient exciting. He told Alan Pergament of the *Buffalo News*, "Any actor is going to be really excited about an opportunity to play this type of story line. There's a lot of different layers. You get to show a lot of colors. It's an incredibly emotional thing to go through. It's meaty material, and it's been very, very challenging."

While *Party of Five* became a success and drew many devoted fans, Fox avoided many public appearances because of the attention brought to him by the show. He chose not to lead a high-profile Hollywood life. Fox did not even want to do cast events. He spent most of his time with his wife and family, and was unable to trust many people, except his cast mates and others who worked on the show. Fox told *People*, "I fought fame for a long time. People think you are just like that character, and they make judgments about you."

Fox's acting abilities also garnered him more attention. Though he was becoming a more high-profile actor because of the success of *Party of Five*, Fox turned down the many film offers that came his way. The only role of prominence that he took while working on *Party of Five* was an appearance in a television movie for CBS called *Behind the Mask* in 1999. Based on a real story, the role was challenging for Fox. His character, James "Wolfman" Jones, was a mentally challenged man who saves a doctor's life after a heart attack. *Behind the Mask* co-starred Donald Sutherland as the doctor who gets help for Jones after the incident. In turn, Jones helps the doctor reassess his priorities in life. Ann Hodges, writing in the *Houston Chronicle*, commented, "Watching the relationship between James and the doctor grow is quite moving in the talented hands of Sutherland and Fox."

Another television project that Fox was involved in during this time period had special meaning to him. He served as host and narrator of a nature special titled *Survival of the Yellowstone Wolves*. His father's ranch was located in the area and he also appeared in the documentary. *Survival of the Yellowstone Wolves* looks at the program to reintroduce wolves to the area years after they were hunted to the point of extinction. While some residents support this return, others fear that their reintroduction could lead to problems with their livestock being attacked and killed.

After *Party of Five* ended its run in 2000, Fox was sorry to see the show end, but knew that it was time. He did not do much television acting for the next two years. Instead, he became a member of a repertory company based in Los Angeles. Fox did everything he could to distance himself from *Party of Five* and Charlie Salinger. Fox told Penelope Cross of the *Herald Sun,* "It was an intentional move to let people forget about me in that show. I wanted to come back doing something very different."

It was not until 2002 that Fox acted again on television. In UPN's *Haunted*, Fox played a private detective who could communicate with the deceased. While the show had the approval of a number of critics, it could not draw fans. *Haunted* was canceled after only a few episodes.

Two years later, Fox found himself on another hit television show. He played one of the many leads on the dramatic adventure series *Lost*, which aired on ABC beginning in 2004. Fox played a surgeon named Jack Shephard. Shephard was one of the 48 characters who survive a plane crash on a remote island. While Fox's character emerged as a hero, the first season's episodes featured strange occurrences and many twists and turns. Fox's character takes charge, helping those who needed to be rescued.

Critics found *Lost* to be an original show, and it found an audience as well. Though ABC was initially unsure if the show would catch on, *Lost* was the second-highest rated new show on television in the 2004-05 television season. The show went on to win the Emmy Award for Outstanding Drama Series in 2005. This time around, Fox enjoyed the fame that comes with a hit show. He was much more comfortable with the attention from fans and the paparazzi. Fox told *People*, "I'm in a really great place now. I've been doing this for 15 years, and I feel like I'm better at it than I've ever been."

Sources

Books

Celebrity Biographies, Baseline II, 2005.

Periodicals

Boston Herald, November 20, 1994, p. 11.
Broadcasting & Cable, October 11, 2004, p. 44.
Buffalo News (Buffalo, NY), November 3, 1996, p. 26TV; January 21, 1998, p. 7D; February 28, 1999, p. 14TV.
Chicago Sun-Times, November 19, 1997, p. 63.
Herald Sun (Melbourne, Australia), February 16, 2005, p. H3.
Houston Chronicle, February 27, 1999, p. 7.
People, August 28, 1995, p. 87; May 6, 1996, p. 78; November 8, 2004, pp. 85-86; November 29, 2004, p. 158.
San Diego Union-Tribune, May 3, 2000, p. E9.
Seattle Times, March 4, 1996, p. F1.
Sunday Mail (Australia), January 7, 1996.
Tampa Tribune (Tampa, FL), December 10, 1995, p. 30.
Times-Picayune (New Orleans, LA), January 15, 1998, p. E1.
USA Today, October 18, 1995, p. 3D.
Washington Post, October 30, 1994, p. Y7; September 27, 1995, p. B1.

—*A. Petruso*

Ian Ginsberg

Pharmacist and entrepreneur

Born c. 1962; son of a pharmacist, Jerry. *Education:* Earned pharmacy degree from Long Island University, 1985.

Addresses: *Office*—Bigelow Chemists, 414 Sixth Ave., New York, NY 10011.

Career

Pharmacist and buyer with Bigelow Chemists since 1985.

Sidelights

Ian Ginsberg became the third generation of his family to work at the family pharmacy, Bigelow Chemists, a historic landmark in New York City that dates back to 1838. Ginsberg brought the business into the twenty-first century by introducing its personal-care products to a wider audience, and they quickly emerged as cult favorites to rival another venerable New York City pharmacy with a comparable line, Kiehl's. In 2005, Ginsberg's company signed on with Bath & Body Works to sell its vintage-recipe balms, lotions, and other skin-care products at hundreds of stores belonging to the retail chain. "We couldn't play the chain-discounter game," he explained to *Crain's New York Business* journalist Laurie Joan Aron about the direction the business took once he came on board. "I figured we should just be ourselves."

Born in the early 1960s, Ginsberg was musically inclined and had once hoped to pursue that as a career, but satisfied his parents by enrolling in phar-macy school. His father, Jerry, had worked at Bigelow Chemists since graduating with his pharmacy degree back in 1952. Jerry's father, William, was also a pharmacist who bought the Greenwich Village business, then called C.O. Bigelow & Co., back in 1939. The name dated back to another pharmacist, Clarence Otis Bigelow, who owned the business from 1880 to 1922. The store, located at 414 Sixth Avenue, was even older than that, however. Galen Hunter, a pharmacist from Vermont, opened the first pharmacy at the site in 1838 as the Village Apothecary Shop, and ran it himself until 1863. George L. Hooper ran it after that before selling it to Bigelow in 1902.

Long known for its personalized customer service, Bigelow Chemists was a Manhattan fixture with a devoted customer base. Over the years, it had amassed a long list of famous customers. Mark Twain was one, and company legend claimed that when Thomas Edison burned his finger on a new invention he was working on called the light bulb, he hurried over to Bigelow's for a salve. In the mid-twentieth century, the pharmacy had a soda counter that sold fountain drinks and ice cream treats, a commonplace fixture in many drug stores of the era, and Ginsberg's first job was as its dishwasher there when he was a teenager. The counter, which dated from 1902, was removed in a 1984 remodeling of the building, and still had its original gas lamps until the renovation.

After graduating from the pharmacy college of Long Island University in 1985, Ginsberg joined the business full time. He eventually became its buyer, searching for the overseas personal-care products his customers requested, such as Phyto shampoo from France, Italian toothpaste, and Chidoriya's Gold soap from Japan. He also ventured into the company archives and came up with new products. These were modern reformulations of old skin-care remedies from the nineteenth century. Like Kiehl's, another vintage Greenwich Village pharmacy with a line of personal-care products, Bigelow's items became a favorite of magazine editors and fashion-industry insiders.

The new direction was necessary for Ginsberg, he said, along with his business partner, Joel Eichel, after they took over the business from his father, Jerry. "The big change for us happened in the 1980's, when all the chain pharmacies started coming," he said in an interview with SmartBiz.com, a Web publication. "We freaked out. But then we said to ourselves, we can't play that game—we'll never win, and it's not our game." Under his guidance, Bigelow Chemists launched a catalog operation in the mid-1990s, which enabled it to reach a larger audience. Ginsberg also hired a makeup artist to create a makeup line called Alchemy, launched in 1998, and even opened a second store, an in-house boutique at Jeffrey New York, an upscale clothing retailer. By the end of the decade, Bigelow Chemists products were available in more than 200 specialty stores across the United States, and had sales estimated at sales of $20 million in 2000.

In 2005, Ginsberg and Eichel struck a deal with Bath & Body Works, a major mall retailer with more than 1,500 stores, to sell their specialty wares under the vintage brand name of C.O. Bigelow & Co. Packaged in glass bottles with a retro feel, the line includes favorites such as Rose Wonder Cold Cream and 1838 Herbal Balm, scented with calendula, clover, and ginger. The Bath & Body Works deal also included a few new freestanding Bigelow stores, which totaled seven by the end of 2005.

Legendary in Manhattan for its personalized customer service, the original Bigelow Chemists still boasts messenger deliveries for prescriptions, house accounts, and even flavors the occasional pet medicine for its devotees. Famous names still shop there, including Greenwich Village denizens Sarah Jessica Parker and Robert De Niro. Ginsberg's business still has its original molded ceilings and oak cabinets from 1902, features found in none of the CVS, Rite-Aid, or Duane Reade stores chain drugstores that are a ubiquitous Manhattan presence. "I love chains," Ginsberg said in the interview with SmartBiz.com. "What they do and what I do is completely different. I love to go into the big chain pharmacy near my house, because every time I go in, I have a horrible experience, and I walk out with a smile on my face knowing my business has at least another ten years in it."

Sources

Periodicals

Crain's New York Business, October 8, 2001, p. 21.
Drug Topics, July 18, 1988, p. 66.
Record (Bergen County, NJ), November 2, 2005, p. B1.
Vogue, March 2005, p. 450.
WWD, July 30, 1999, p. 11.

Online

"Ian Ginsberg, Bigelow Chemists," *SmartBiz*, http://www.smartbiz.com/article/articleprint/394/-1/1 (April 23, 2006).

—*Carol Brennan*

Temple Grandin

Reproduced by permission of Future Horizons Inc.

Scientist, inventor, and author

Born August 29, 1947, in Boston, MA; daughter of Richard Grandin (a real estate agent) and Eustacia Cutler (a writer, singer, and actress; maiden name, Purves). *Education:* Franklin Pierce College, B.A. (with honors), 1970; Arizona State University, M.S., 1975; University of Illinois—Urbana, Ph.D., 1989.

Addresses: *Office*—Department of Animal Science, Colorado State University, Fort Collins, CO 80523.

Career

Livestock editor, *Arizona Farmer Ranchman*, Phoenix, AZ, 1973-78; equipment designer, Corral Industries, Phoenix, 1974-75; founder and consultant, Grandin Livestock Handling Systems, 1975—; chair of handling committee, Livestock Conservation Institute, Madison, WI, 1976-95; Colorado State University, Fort Collins, began as lecturer, became associate professor of animal science, 1990—; animal welfare committee, American Meat Institute, 1991—.

Member: American Society of Animal Science, American Society of Agricultural Engineers, American Society of Agricultural Consultants, American Registry of Professional Animal Scientists, National Institute of Animal Agriculture.

Awards: Recipient of numerous special education, livestock industry, and animal-welfare group awards, including: Meritorious Service, Livestock Conservation Institute, 1984; Trammel Crow Award, Autism Society of America, 1989; Industry Innovator's Award, *Meat Marketing and Technology* magazine, 1994; Industry Advancement Award, American Meat Institute, 1995; Animal Management Award, American Society of Animal Science, 1995; Harry Rowsell Award, Scientists' Center for Animal Welfare, 1995; Respect for animals, their nature and welfare award, Animal Welfare Foundation of Canada, 1995; Forbes Award, National Meat Association, 1998; Geraldine R. Dodge Foundation Award for humane ethics in action, Purdue University, 1998; Woman of the Year in service to agriculture, *Progressive Farmer* magazine, 1999; Humane Award, American Veterinary Medical Association, 1999; Animal Welfare Award, Animal Transportation Association, 1999; Founders Award, American Society for the Prevention of Cruelty to Animals, 1999; Joseph Wood Krutch Medal, Humane Society of the United States, 2001; Richard L. Knowlton Award for Innovation, *Meat Marketing and Technology* magazine, 2001; Richard L. Knowlton Award for Innovation, *Meat Marketing and Technology* magazine, 2002; Animal Welfare Award, Royal Society for the Prevention of Cruelty in Animals, 2002; University of Illinois Alumni Illini Comeback Award, 2002; President's Award, National Institute of Animal Agriculture, 2004.

Sidelights

Animal behavioral scientist Temple Grandin has devoted her career to improving conditions at the large processing plants that slaughter some of the 40 billion pounds of cattle and pigs for human consumption every year in the United States. She is a strong advocate for more humane livestock handling, and has designed numerous innovations at such facilities that help to reduce stress in the animals during their final minutes. Grandin's mission is deeply connected to her autism, and she credits this developmental brain disorder for her success as a scientist. Once she recognized that animals and autistic people share certain traits, such as a reliance on visual clues to navigate their environment, she began to rethink how livestock are handled in the beef and pork industry. Since the early 1990s, a large number of U.S slaughterhouses have implemented her designs and innovations, and comply with the humane-handling guidelines she authored for the American Meat Institute.

Grandin was born in 1947 in Boston, Massachusetts. Her father was a real estate agent, and her mother was a writer, singer, and actress who devoted her time to improving Grandin's life once she was a diagnosed with autism as a toddler. Autism is a developmental brain disorder, and its origins are the subject of tremendous scientific debate. Autism affects the areas of the brain that direct abstract thought, language, and social interaction, and Grandin displayed the classic symptoms of the condition in her earliest years—she spoke little, did not like to be held or touched, and was prone to dissolve into raging temper tantrums when provoked. In the early 1950s, however, autistic children were sometimes incorrectly judged to be developmentally disabled, and the medical profession often recommended institutionalization. Grandin's parents were told that their daughter was brain-damaged, and suggested a long-term care facility for her.

Grandin's mother instead took her to a neurologist, who proposed a course of speech therapy. She was duly enrolled in a program, and at home her mother read to her constantly. The family was also able to afford a caregiver whose job it was to play with Grandin and keep her from retreating into a corner, as autistic children prefer. Grandin's mother also sought out private schools with sympathetic staff who were willing to work with her daughter's special needs. Grandin credits this early intervention with pulling her out of the isolationist shell of autism and laying a path toward her professional success later in life.

As she grew older, Grandin became fascinated by rotating objects of any sort; such fixations are com-

mon in autism and another related condition, Asperger syndrome. She became incredibly stressed by anything that rotated or made a whirring noise, but learned that doors seemed to soothe her. Beset by panic attacks because of these fears, Grandin fled to her aunt's cattle ranch out West one summer during her teens.

One day at the ranch, Grandin saw a squeeze chute that ranchers commonly used to immobilize a cow so that it could be vaccinated or branded. The chute absolutely fascinated her, and her aunt agreed to let her try it out—and Grandin loved its soothing effect on her nerves. Back at home, she built her own squeeze chute in her bedroom, and an advanced version of that would go on to be used in scores of schools and treatment centers for autistic children in the years to come.

The summer on the ranch was significant for another revelation for Grandin: she began to sense that animals and autistic persons shared a significant trait: both relied on visual clues in order to navigate their world. For example, a squirrel will hide food in dozens of different places for the coming cold snap, but always knows where the acorns and corn cobs are stashed. Or an ant, passing by a landmark, will turn around and view it from the other side; Grandin says she does this too, while driving on her return trip. Furthermore, like autistic people, non-domesticated animals retreat from human touch.

Grandin entered Franklin Pierce College in New Hampshire, and graduated with honors in 1970. Though medical professionals discouraged her from using the homemade squeeze chute, one of her teachers suggested instead that she try to learn why it worked for her by studying science. She entered graduate school in animal science at Arizona State University, and began working in the cattle industry as well. She served as the livestock editor of the *Arizona Farmer Ranchman* for five years, and saw firsthand the methods used to slaughter cattle in the major meat-processing plants. She recognized that cattle, like some autistic people, exhibited signs of tremendous stress and anxiety when confronted by certain visual or audio clues.

Grandin began to think about reducing that unease by redesigning the chute which led the animals to their death. Her first success came when Corral Industries in Phoenix hired her to design some equipment for its plants, but Grandin recognized that though her autism was classified as the "high-functioning" kind, she did not have good interpersonal skills. Her communication with others was often blunt, and as a result she sometimes found herself alienated from co-workers. Grandin decided that working on her own, in temporary assignments, was probably preferable to a standard job where relationships developed over time, and so in 1975, the year she earned her master's degree, she founded her own company, Grandin Livestock Handling Systems.

Over the next two decades, Grandin became an expert in animal handling in slaughterhouses and one of the most respected names in her field. The results of the research studies she conducted were published in various academic journals and industry trade publications, and in 1989 she was granted her doctorate in animal science from the University of Illinois. By the mid-1990s, the fast-food industry began to pay attention to her work, thanks to a libel case that wound through the British court system. In that suit, associates of the Greenpeace environmental group wrote and distributed a leaflet about McDonald's, the fast-food giant, claiming that the practices at the slaughterhouses that worked under contract to McDonald's amounted to animal cruelty.

McDonald's, Burger King, and companies like ConAgra that sell meat to consumers via supermarket counters have perfected large-scale animal processing. These companies, or ones that work under contract to them, breed, feed, and slaughter cattle on vast rural facilities known as animal feeding operations, or APOs. Beef cattle are slaughtered between 14 to 16 months of age, and the process involves a shot to their foreheads with a stun gun, which renders them unconscious. The next step involves hoisting the animal up by one of its rear legs, and then its throat is slit on what is known as the bleed rail. If the stunning and slitting has been done properly, the animal dies quickly, and then moves on to other processing stations.

The McDonald's trial in Britain was a long and complicated legal proceeding, but one judge did agree that some of the accusations were founded, and that inhumane treatment sometimes occurred in the slaughterhouse. McDonald's hired Grandin as a consultant to improve conditions and avoid a wider public-relations debacle, and she first visited one of the company's APOs with several of the company executives. "The day I went to a cow slaughter plant," she recounted in an interview with the *Guardian*'s Dan Glaister, "there was an emaciated half-dead skinny cow. They watched that walk up a ramp and right into their product. They were not happy."

One of the most significant innovations that Grandin devised was a chute that led cattle through the slaughterhouse. Standard chutes were built in a straight line, and the cattle could usually see what lay ahead. Grandin knew that if a cow saw something unexpected ahead of them, they froze in their tracks. She designed a circular chute with high walls to remedy this. Though her ideas and suggestions were initially greeted with skepticism in the beef industry, the owners of cattle plants quickly realized that thanks to Grandin's design the cattle hesitated less, and therefore plant efficiency improved. Grandin redesigned other elements in slaughterhouses, based on other findings from her research: cattle resist being led from bright sunlight into a darkened room, for example, do not like the color yellow, and are upset by clanking metal sounds.

Grandin's innovations were backed up by concrete results. She wrote about PSE, a classification of pork which stands for "pale, soft, and exudative," or oozing. The condition, deemed unfavorable for meat quality, was tied to high levels of stress in pigs. Grandin urged plants to house hogs in less crowded conditions, and to keep them cool, even hosing them down if necessary, before slaughter. When her recommendations were implemented at a plant, PSE levels were reduced. She had the same results with cattle, suggesting improvements that led to a reduction in what the industry calls "dark-cutting beef." This is tied to reduced levels of glycogen in the muscles, which affects the pH balance of the meat.

McDonald's and other fast-food corporations, which are the largest processors of beef in the United States, began implementing Grandin's designs in the plants used by the companies. She has also written guidelines for the American Meat Institute, an industry group, and has devised an auditing system that rates how well a plant is complying with the Humane Slaughter Act, the federal guidelines for non-kosher meat-processing facilities in the United States. Her guidelines measure the number of animals that are still moving or making noises on the bleed rail, when they should theoretically have been stunned into unconsciousness, as well as how well the plant handles "downers," or animals that are too weak or injured to walk on their own.

Grandin wrote about her work in the 2005 book *Animals in Translation: Using the Mysteries of Autism to Decode Animal Behavior*, which she dictated to her co-author by telephone. In it, she concedes that while many animal welfare activists avoid eating meat entirely, livestock animals were essentially bred by humans to serve a purpose, and that humans should recognize their caretaking role and respond accordingly. "We owe them a decent life and a decent death, and their lives should be as low-stress as possible," she writes. "That's my job. I wish animals could have more than just a low-stress life and a quick, painless death. I wish animals could have a good life, too, with something useful to do. People were animals, too, once, and when we turned into human beings we gave something up. Being close to animals brings some of it back."

Grandin lives in Colorado and is an associate professor of animal science at at Colorado State University in Fort Collins. She is also the author of a 1986 autobiography, *Emergence: Labeled Autistic*, reissued ten years later when Grandin was becoming increasingly prominent in her field, as well as *Thinking in Pictures and Other Reports from My Life with Autism*. Eminent neurologist and author Oliver Sacks wrote the foreword to this last work, and Sacks also devoted an entire book of his own to Grandin's achievements, *An Anthropologist on Mars*.

Grandin wrote, with the help of co-author Kate Duffy, the 2004 book *Developing Talents: Careers for Individuals with Asperger Syndrome and High-Functioning Autism*. She also co-authored a book on social rules with Sean Barron titled *Unwritten Rules of Social Relationships* in 2005. She lectures frequently on the topic of autism, strongly urging parents and educators of autistic and Asperger-syndrome children to abide by some important rules—avoiding television and video games as a form of entertainment, for example—and encouraging the development of computer skills early on as a means of communication. Above all, she urges the non-afflicted to view the condition in a different light. "We've got to have a lot more emphasis on the talent," she told reporter Anne Williams of the Eugene, Oregon, *Register-Guard*, "and not so much emphasis on the disability."

Selected writings

(With Margaret M. Scariano) *Emergence: Labeled Autistic* (autobiography), Arena Press (Novato, CA), 1986; Warner Books (New York City), 1996.

Thinking in Pictures and Other Reports from My Life with Autism (autobiography), foreword by Oliver Sacks, Doubleday (New York City), 1995.

(With Kate Duffy) *Developing Talents: Careers for Individuals with Asperger Syndrome and High-Functioning Autism*, Autism Asperger (Shawnee Mission, KS), 2004.

(With Catherine Johnson) *Animals in Translation: Using the Mysteries of Autism to Decode Animal Behavior*, Scribner (New York City), 2005.

(With Sean Barron) *Unwritten Rules of Social Relationships*, Future Horizons, 2005.

Sources

Books

(With Catherine Johnson) *Animals in Translation: Using the Mysteries of Autism to Decode Animal Behavior*, Scribner (New York City), 2005.

Periodicals

Guardian (London, England), June 2, 2005, p. 4.
People, January 9, 1995, p. 42.
Register-Guard (Eugene, OR), October 12, 2003, p. C1.
Star Tribune (Minneapolis, MN), November 10, 1996, p. 1E.

Online

Dr. Temple Grandin's Web Page, http://www.grandin.com (August 18, 2005).
Dr. Temple Grandin, http://www.templegrandin.com (August 31, 2005).

—*Carol Brennan*

Brian Grazer

AP Images

Film producer

Born Brian Thomas Grazer, July 12, 1951, in Los Angeles, CA; married Corki Corman (divorced); married Gigi Levangie, 1997 (separated, April, 2006); children: Sage (daughter; from first marriage), Riley (son; from first marriage), Thomas, Patrick (from second marriage). *Education:* Attended the University of Southern California; studied law, early 1980s.

Addresses: *Home*—Pacific Palisades, CA. *Office*—Imagine Films Entertainment Inc., 9465 Wilshire Blvd., 7th Fl., Beverly Hills, CA 90212.

Career

Affiliated with Edgar J. Scherick-Daniel Blatt Co., late 1970s; intern in Warner Brothers' legal department, early 1980s; talent agent and independent film and television producer; co-chief executive with filmmaker Ron Howard, Imagine Films Entertainment Inc. (independent movie and television production company), 1986—. Producer of films, including: *Night Shift,* 1982; *Splash,* 1984; *Real Genius,* 1985; *Spies Like Us* (co-producer), 1985; *Armed and Dangerous* (co-producer), 1986; *The 'Burbs,* 1989; *Parenthood,* 1989; *Cry-Baby* (co-producer), 1990; *Kindergarten Cop,* 1990; *The Doors,* 1991; *Far and Away* (with Ron Howard), 1992; *For Love or Money,* 1993; *Apollo 13,* 1995; *The Nutty Professor,* 1996; *Liar Liar,* 1997; *Psycho,* 1998; *Life,* 1999; *How the Grinch Stole Christmas,* 2000; *A Beautiful Mind,* 2001; *8 Mile,* 2002; *The Cat in the Hat,* 2003; *Friday Night Lights,* 2004; *Cinderella Man,* 2005; *The Da Vinci Code,* 2006. Executive producer for television series, including: *Felicity,* 1998; *Sports Night,* 2000; *24,* 2001—; *Arrested Development,* 2003-06.

Awards: Academy Award for best motion picture of the year (with Ron Howard), Academy of Motion Picture Arts and Sciences, for *A Beautiful Mind,* 2001.

Sidelights

Brian Grazer is a modern-day Hollywood legend. A film producer and occasional screenwriter whose projects have racked up more than three dozen Academy Awards, he is one of a just a handful of his producer-peers to be honored with his own star on the Hollywood Walk of Fame. Grazer has spent much of his career working with director Ron Howard, beginning with their 1984 Tom Hanks mermaid romance, *Splash.* More than two decades later, the Grazer-Howard-Hanks alliance was still strong, with their 2006 *Da Vinci Code* one of the top-grossing films of the year. "Basically, our governing belief is that if you do something well, you make money," Grazer told Jim Carrey in *Interview* magazine in 2003. "And that's worked for us for 20 years."

Born in 1951, Grazer grew up in the San Fernando Valley area near Los Angeles. His father was a criminal defense attorney, but Grazer claimed he found himself disastrously out of his element when he started classes at the University of Southern California (USC). Taking a job as a short-order cook, he saved up enough money to buy himself a Porsche. "USC was filled with elitists, richies who would go skiing every weekend," he recalled in an interview with Cal Fussman for *Esquire.* "So I pretended like I was part of that world—to be accepted. No one knew the Porsche came from cleaning out the fry bin at the end of a shift at Howard Johnson's."

Grazer began his career in the entertainment industry in television. He joined the production company of Edgar J. Scherick, who had a long list of successful credits that ended with the 2004 remake of *The Stepford Wives* two years after his death. Grazer's first two projects at the Scherick office were a made-for-TV movie from 1978, *Thou Shalt Not Commit Adultery,* and a short-lived NBC series called *Zuma Beach* with Suzanne Somers. He decided to enroll in law school, and landed an internship with the legal department of Warner Brothers, the movie studio. True to form, Grazer was assigned his own cubicle, but happened upon an empty vice-president's office, and moved into that instead. When he dropped out of law school, he lost the internship.

Grazer spent some of the early 1980s as a script reader and talent agent. He was introduced to Howard, a former child actor best known at the time as the star of the hit ABC sitcom *Happy Days,* when Howard was just switching gears into directing television movies. Years later, when they spoke with Carrey for the *Interview* article, Howard recounted that fateful first meeting. "One day I was waiting to go into this executive's office—her name was Deanne Barkley—and Brian walks in, and Deanne says, 'You guys are going to wind up running the business, so you might as well shake hands,'" Howard said. The actor actually remembered Grazer from his own stint at USC, recalling him as the guy with the Porsche.

Grazer and Howard teamed up to make *Night Shift,* a 1982 comedy that starred Howard's *Happy Days* co-star, Henry Winkler. Grazer's first screenplay, and the first box-office smash directed by Howard, was 1984's *Splash.* Though other screenwriters finessed the idea, he was credited with the story idea about a hapless young executive, played by Tom Hanks, who falls in love with a mermaid (Daryl Hannah) who transforms into a human once she reaches land. The inspiration, Grazer said years later, came when he was driving along California's famous Pacific Coast Highway one day in the mid-1970s and feeling dejected about his dating prospects. Stuck in a romantic losing streak, he thought that all the women he knew "had so many prereq-

uisites," he told Leah Rozen in *People.* "You had to have all these things, and I got kind of discouraged. So I'm driving along and I think, 'I have to meet somebody real pure, somebody from a whole other world. Like a mermaid.'"

Splash was a major box-office hit the weekend it opened in March of 1984, and Hanks would later credit Grazer and Howard for launching his movie career. Even the name of Hannah's character, who calls herself "Madison" after the famous Manhattan avenue, became one of the most popular choices for baby-girl names over the next few years. The film also relaunched Walt Disney Productions as a major Hollywood player. The once-powerful kids' flicks-and-cartoons studio had fallen into financial disarray by the early 1980s, but its newly formed Touchstone Pictures scored its first hit with *Splash,* and went on to make dozens of other top-grossing films over the next 20 years.

As did Grazer and Howard, especially after they formed their own production company, Imagine Films Entertainment, in 1986. Grazer went on to serve as executive producer or producer for a long list of hit movies, some directed by Howard, that included *Cry-Baby, Kindergarten Cop, The Doors, Apollo 13, The Nutty Professor, Liar Liar,* and *How the Grinch Stole Christmas.* In 1998, he earned a double set of honors that attested to his fame: he was given his own star on the Hollywood Walk of Fame, and made a cameo appearance on the animated series *The Simpsons.*

By the turn of the new century, Grazer was one of Hollywood's most influential executives, and had even gained a reputation for being able to bring some notoriously un-cinematic stories to the big screen. This skill was best exemplified by the 2001 drama *A Beautiful Mind,* based on the real-life story of John Nash, a brilliant, Nobel Prize-winning mathematician at Princeton University in the 1950s whose career was derailed by schizophrenia. The film version starred Russell Crowe, and won the Academy Award for Best Picture as well as a first for Howard as Best Director. It was Grazer's first Oscar, though he had been nominated for the *Splash* screenplay and again in the Best Picture category for *Apollo 13,* the 1995 astronaut drama that starred Hanks and scored a number of Academy Award nominations.

Grazer was also instrumental in bringing the story of rapper Eminem to the big screen in 2002's *8 Mile,* though most studios were wary about musical biopics that starred inexperienced actors playing themselves. Grazer's career as a producer has had a few duds, too. A 1993 Michael J. Fox romantic comedy, *For Love or Money,* was one, and critics were scathing in their reviews of the Dr. Seuss-inspired kids' flick, *The Cat in the Hat,* in 2003. But Grazer was confident in his abilities to find the right projects and assemble a winning team to make a film audiences would remember, and the occasional miss did not deter him. "The ideal qualities of a producer," he told Anthony D'Alessandro in *Daily Variety,* "is someone with an unrelenting vision, someone who is completely impervious, and who doesn't take rejection personally."

Grazer is still involved in television projects. He has served as executive producer for *Felicity, Sports Night, 24,* and *Arrested Development.* It was the top-rated Kiefer Sutherland action series, *24,* that led him to his next major big-screen blockbuster. After reading Dan Brown's 2003 best-selling novel *The Da Vinci Code,* he inquired about buying the rights, thinking he might use it for a new storyline on *24.* He was outbid, but the winner was Sony Pictures, which then hired him and Howard to make the film. This was a notable departure from the way Grazer and Howard's Imagine Entertainment company usually operated, which was to develop their own projects and then shop them around to the studios.

The Da Vinci Code was released in May of 2006, and grossed $29 million in box-office sales on its opening day alone. Directed by Howard, it starred Hanks in the lead role of a sleuth investigating what hinted at a centuries-old conspiracy inside the Roman Catholic church. It was one of the most highly anticipated films of the year, but was not without controversy. Officials of the Vatican, the administrative center of the Roman Catholic church, voiced their objections; two authors unsuccessfully sued Brown in a British court for plagiarism; and Grazer and Howard even encountered some pressure from French President Jacques Chirac when they were invited to meet the leader. "We thought it was going to be a five-minute thing, like a trip to the Oval Office—a photo and a handshake," Grazer told *Newsweek*'s Devin Gordon, but instead they stayed for nearly an hour, and Chirac suggested to them that in return for securing the rights to film inside the Louvre Museum—a key plot point, but one of France's most revered national landmarks—they might think about casting the actor-friend of his daughter in the female lead. The filmmakers, however, had already signed French star Audrey Tautou for the role.

Post-*Da Vinci Code* projects for Grazer include *The Serpent and the Eagle,* a historical epic chronicling the Spanish conquest of Mexico; *American Gangster,* a tale of drug smuggling; and *The Incredible Shrinking Man,* directed by Keenan Ivory Wayans. One of Hollywood's more colorful personalities, Grazer favors Eighties-era skinny ties with his suits, owns a palatial home in Pacific Palisades that once belonged to the actor Gregory Peck, and surfs near his two other homes in Malibu and Hawaii. On land, he typically puts enough product in his hair to make it stand straight up, which became his trademark look by the late 1990s. The idea came from his daughter one day, as he told Fussman in *Esquire,* but once he left the house he was intrigued by the reaction it got. "People either liked it—thought it was courageous—or else they thought, Who ... do you think you are? So I left it up like this to quickly discern the truth about people I meet." He has four children from two marriages, and his second wife, Gigi Levangie, is another Tinseltown iconoclast. She has one screenwriting credit, for the 1998 Julia Roberts-Susan Sarandon film *Stepmom,* which she reportedly based on her own experiences as Grazer's new wife.

Grazer's wife has also written a string of novels that satirize Hollywood, including 2005's *The Starter Wife.* Its story centers around the wife of studio executive who has been "Cruised," which is a term that Grazer allegedly coined for a woman whose husband files for divorce just before the ten-year mark that, under California law, grants the wife an equitable share of the couple's property and assets. Grazer used it when referring to the highly publicized divorce between stars Tom Cruise and Nicole Kidman that occurred just before their tenth anniversary. In an odd twist, Grazer filed for separation in April of 2006, after eight years and seven months of marriage to Levangie.

Sources

Daily Variety, January 19, 2003, p. 16.
Esquire, January 2006, p. 90.
Interview, December 2001, 84; October 2003, p. 68.
Newsweek, December 26, 2005, p. 94.
People, April 9, 1984, p. 32.
Variety, July 12, 2004, p. 1.
W, February 2004, p. 118.

—*Carol Brennan*

Ismail Omar Guelleh

Patrick Kovarik/AFP/Getty Images

President of Djibouti

Born November 27, 1947, in Ethiopia; son of Omar Guelleh and Moumina Rirache; married; children: four.

Addresses: *Office*—Office of the President, La Presidence BP 6, Djibouti, Republic of Djibouti.

Career

Began career as a civil servant with the French colonial administration of Djibouti, 1968, and rose to become a police inspector by 1970; worked as an independence activist for *Lingue Populaire Africaine pour l'independence* (LPAI), a pro-independence political group, after 1975; launched pro-independence newspaper, *Djibouti Today*, and served as a foreign delegate representing the LPAI cause until 1977; served as chief of staff to President Hassan Gouled Aptidon, c. 1977-99; elected president of Djibouti, 1999; reelected, 2005.

Sidelights

Ismail Omar Guelleh serves as president of the Republic of Djibouti, the small East African nation strategically located just across the Arabian Peninsula. First elected to office in 1999, Guelleh rules over a nation troubled by longstanding ethnic hostilities between his own people, the Issa, and the minority Afar group. The internal troubles have led to political strife, which eventually resulted in the two main opposition groups boycotting the 2005 presidential election. Guelleh was reelected to another six-year term in that contest, but he was the sole candidate in the election.

Born in 1947, Guelleh originally hails from Dire-Dawa, a city in Ethiopia. He was born into the Mamassans clan of the Issa, who are also known as Somali and are an indigenous group of the Horn of Africa, as the area surrounding Djibouti is called. Djibouti is a tiny, predominantly Muslim nation carved out of territory once known as French Somaliland. It shares borders with Eritrea in the north, Ethiopia on the south and west, and Somalia on the southeast. It was known as the French Territory of Afars and the Issas until it gained formal independence in 1977.

In his youth, Guelleh attended a traditional Islamic school, and entered the civil service in 1968, when it was still under French colonial administration. He rose to the position of police inspector, but quit in 1975 to join the independence movement. Djibouti's push for self-rule was organized around the *Lingue Populaire Africaine pour l'independence* (African People's League for Independence, or LPAI), which was headed by his uncle, Hassan Gouled Aptidon. Guelleh worked for the LPAI, ran his own pro-independence newspaper, and even traveled abroad to advocate for Djibouti's independence. When that occurred, Aptidon became president, and Guelleh served as his chief of staff for the next 22 years. He also had special responsibility for overseeing the domestic-security forces.

By 1979, LPAI had evolved into a political party, the *Rassemblement Populaire pour le Progrès* (Peoples' Rally for Progress, or RPP), and Guelleh held positions within the party as well as his other posts in the government. But the earliest years of independence in Djibouti were marked by hostilities, with the majority Issa gravitating toward the RPP, which dominated the country. Though some Afar were named to cabinet positions in Aptidon's first government, disenchantment and longstanding rivalries escalated, and civil war broke out in 1981. Behind the strife was the rebel group, *Front Pour la Restauration de l'Unite et de la Democratie* (Front for the Restoration of Unity and Democracy, or FRUD), which was largely Afar in makeup. Aptidon outlawed all political parties, but international pressure forced multiparty elections in 1993, and Aptidon was reelected president with 75 percent of the vote.

Guelleh took on an increasing list of duties for his uncle, who was 81 years old when he won reelection again in 1997, as the president's health declined. He was named his successor when Aptidon formally stepped down in 1999, and Guelleh bested opponent Idris Moussa Ahmed in a presidential election called that year. The opposition groups claimed vote fraud had occurred, however. A year later, Guelleh fired the head of the Djibouti national police force, Yacin Yabeh, who later led an attempted coup that was quelled by Guelleh's security forces. In 2001, the attacks on the World Trade Center and the Pentagon reawakened U.S. interest in Djibouti, and U.S. Special Forces troops were deployed there. The country lies about 13 miles distant from Yemen, an Arabian Peninsula nation believed to harbor operatives of Al Qaeda, the militant Islamic group that claimed responsibility for the 9/11 attacks.

Despite the rather warm relations between Djibouti and the United States, Guelleh publicly opposed the U.S.-led invasion of Iraq in March of 2003. His country is the beneficiary of large aid packages from the United States and other countries, and retains strong ties with France, which oversees the largest deployment of French troops anywhere on the African continent. The foreign aid is sorely needed: Djibouti has an average per-capita income of $1,200; an infant mortality rate higher than Rwanda, one of Africa's poorest nations; and a life expectancy rate of just 51 years for men and 53 years for women. The unemployment rate hovers near 50 percent, and many of the country's 721,000 citizens live in desperately poor conditions.

Guelleh's government has been criticized by human-rights groups because of his regime's determination to maintain political stability. Members of his family's Mamassans clan hold positions of power in the cabinet and government, the RPP remains the dominant political force, and there have been charges that opposition groups, such as FRUD and the Union of Democratic Alliance (UAD), are unable to operate freely. FRUD has called upon other nations, especially the United States and France, to back a more aggressive transition toward democracy in the country. To his credit, Guelleh has made some efforts to lessen tensions with the Afar minority, but the potentially troubling situation was not diminished in the election of 2005. He ran on campaign promises to reduce poverty and increase women's rights and roles in the country, but the UAD called for a boycott of the election, and FRUD subsequently issued a statement of support for the boycott.

Guelleh, who is commonly referred to in Djibouti by his initials, "IOG," dismissed claims that his government had harassed its political challengers. "I accuse the opposition of not having the courage to give voters the right to choose between several candidates," Guelleh told the French newspaper *Le Figaro*, according to a BBC News report; the same account noted that opposition banners against Guelleh and the election read "We would rather die standing than follow on our knees." Two days before the April of 2005 election, government troops fired tear gas on protesters in Djibouti City, the capital. Guelleh was the only candidate on the ballot, and not surprisingly took 100 percent of the vote. He asserted afterward that he would not run for a third term in 2011.

Sources

Books

Worldmark Encyclopedia of the Nations: World Leaders, Gale, 2003.

Periodicals

Africa News Service, September 28, 2000; January 16, 2002; December 9, 2004; March 30, 2005.
Asia Africa Intelligence Wire, March 24, 2003; January 24, 2005; March 24, 2005.
Europe Intelligence Wire, January 11, 2003.

Online

"Djibouti leader wins one-man poll," BBC News, http://news.bbc.co.uk/2/hi/africa/4421515.stm (October 21, 2005).

"U.S. Department of State Country Report on Human Rights Practices 2004—Djibouti," United Nations High Commissioner for Refugees, http://www.unhcr.ch/cgi-bin/texis/vtx/print?tbl=RSDCOI&id=4226d96a11 (October 24, 2005).

—Carol Brennan

Paul Haggis

Screenwriter and television writer

Born Paul Edward Haggis, March 10, 1953, in London, ON; son of Edward H. (a road-construction company executive) and Mary Yvonne (Metcalf) Haggis; married Diane Christine Gattas, April 9, 1977 (divorced, 1994); married Deborah Rennard (an actress and singer), June 21, 1997; children: three daughters (from first marriage), one son (from second marriage). *Education:* Studied cinematography at Fanshawe College.

Addresses: *Agent*—Becsey/Wisdom/Kalajian, 9200 Sunset Blvd., Ste. 820, Los Angeles, CA 90069.

Career

Television writer for shows, including: *Diff'rent Strokes*, NBC; *One Day at a Time*, CBS; *The Facts of Life* NBC, 1984-86; *thirtysomething*, ABC, 1987-91; *City*, 1990; *L.A. Law*, NBC, 1994; *Walker, Texas Ranger* (also creator), CBS, 1993-2001; *Due South*, 1994; *EZ Streets*, CBS, 1996-97; *Michael Hayes* (also creator), CBS, 1997; *Family Law*, CBS, 1999-2001. Author of screenplays, including: *Million Dollar Baby*, 2004; *Crash* (also director and producer), 2005; *Flags of Our Fathers*, 2006; *Honeymoon with Harry*, 2006; *Casino Royale*, 2006.

Awards: Emmy Award for outstanding drama series, Academy of Television Arts and Sciences, for *thirtysomething*, 1988; Emmy Award for outstanding writing in a dramatic series, Academy of Television Arts and Sciences, for *thirtysomething*, 1988; program of the year, Television Critics Association, for *EZ Streets*, 1997; Academy Award for best motion

David Livingston/Getty Images

picture of the year (with Cathy Schulman), Academy of Motion Picture Arts and Sciences, for *Crash*, 2006; Academy Award for best writing, screenplay written directly for the screen (with Robert Moresco), Academy of Motion Picture Arts and Sciences, for *Crash*, 2006.

Sidelights

Paul Haggis, a relatively unknown Hollywood writer who had spent much of his career in television, made Academy Award history in 2006 when he became the first person to write two consecutive Academy Award-winners for Best Picture. His first screenplay was the 2004 Clint Eastwood-Hilary Swank drama *Million Dollar Baby*, which won an Oscar, and his next project, *Crash*, took the best picture honor as well as best screenplay at the 2006 Academy Awards. The inspiration for *Crash* and its interwoven tales of racial intolerance in Los Angeles came from Haggis' own brush with crime in the early 1990s, when he and his first wife were carjacked. "I wanted to look at my fears, my intolerances, not those bad people over there—yet I needed to be far enough away to see what most affluent people in L.A. will tell you doesn't really exist," he told Richard Corliss in an interview that appeared in the Canadian edition of *Time*.

Haggis has admitted that he was a heavy television watcher as a kid. Born in 1953 in London, Ontario, he spent his high-school summers working for his father's road-construction company, and wrote plays in his spare time. His father also owned a local theater, and the venue staged Haggis' earliest works. These included some notable bombs, such as an adaptation of *The Chronicles of Narnia* and a comedy-review called *Oh! Canada.* Eager to explore a more glamorous world, he headed to England for a time, and spent an impoverished year in London before returning to its namesake, his hometown, back in Ontario.

After studying cinematography at Fanshawe College, Haggis was again ready to leave Ontario. Though he was now married with a young family, he decided to move the household to Los Angeles in 1979, with the encouragement and financial support of his father. It took some years for him to break into the entertainment business, and he made ends meet by taking jobs that included furniture mover and department-store photographer. After taking some classes in the craft, he managed to land a screenwriting job back home, for a Canadian Broadcasting Company (CBC) sitcom pilot. Though the job failed to bring in any new work, he had made some friends in the industry by then, and one was a writer for a top-rated NBC sitcom called *Diff'rent Strokes.* When the friend experienced trouble finishing a script at the last minute, Haggis helped him finish it, and accepted a trade of a secondhand chair for his own living room. The same piece of furniture, reupholstered, still sat in Haggis' home years later, as a reminder of his early struggles.

Diff'rent Strokes was produced by Emmy Award-winning Norman Lear, who learned of Haggis' work and hired him as one of the show's team of writers. Lear also gave him a second job on another sitcom, *One Day at a Time.* That led to another assignment, this one on the boarding-school-set NBC sitcom *The Facts of Life.* When he made a suggestion that what the show needed was to actually be funny, instead of earnest, he was promptly fired.

Haggis fared better when he was hired for a new ABC drama about two middle-class American couples, *thirtysomething.* The show debuted in the 1987 fall line-up, and focused on the marital and career woes of the quartet and their relatives and friends. Equally loathed and loved by critics and the general public alike, the series nevertheless gained a cult following and won Haggis his first Emmy Awards during the first season, the first shared with executive producers Edward Zwick and Marshall Herskovitz for outstanding drama series, and the second with Herskovitz for outstanding writing in a drama series.

Haggis's career in television seemed to be well underway, but the next decade was marked by a long list of cancelled shows for him. These included *City,* a CBS series starring Valerie Harper that never made it past the first season; *Due South,* a joint venture with a Canadian network that centered around a Royal Canadian Mounted Police officer working the streets of Chicago; and *EZ Streets,* a gritty police drama that *People* called "an instant classic" in a review whose writer named Haggis the "new TV genius on the block."

EZ Streets starred Ken Olin, who played the likable advertising executive on *thirtysomething,* as a disgraced cop working undercover in his old neighborhood to root out underworld crime. The *New York Times* later described it as the forerunner to the hit HBO drama *The Sopranos,* and it even won Haggis an award from the Television Critics Association for program of the year in 1997. Reviewing it for the *San Francisco Chronicle,* John Carman asserted that Haggis' series "evokes a dream state with its languid depiction of a bleak urban landscape.... As a crime series with special resonance, *EZ Streets* is right up there with *NYPD Blue* and *Homicide: Life on the Streets.* With luck, it could become the richest of that select bunch, and finally propel Paul Haggis to the front lines of TV's thin creative legion."

The show was cancelled after just one season, however, as was another crime drama Haggis created, *Michael Hayes,* by CBS. As the millennium approached, and his fiftieth birthday neared, Haggis experienced a career crisis of sorts. "I got very tired of doing television," he told *Time*'s Coeli Carr. "It was sort of eating a hole in my soul." After reading a collection of stories about boxing called *Rope Burns: Stories from the Corner,* he decided to option the book, which necessitated taking out a second mortgage on the Santa Monica home he shared with his second wife, Deborah Rennard.

Haggis was particularly interested in author F.X. Toole's tale of a female boxer and her steely hearted manager, and this story evolved into Haggis' first feature film, *Million Dollar Baby,* which won the Oscar for Best Picture of 2004. The movie was made thanks to the support of Hollywood heavyweight Clint Eastwood, who liked Haggis' screenplay so much that he signed on to produce, direct, and star in it. Eastwood also won the Academy Award for Best Director, and his co-star Hilary Swank won in the Best Actress category. Haggis was nominated as well, for Best Adapted Screenplay.

Haggis' next project came from a script he had written a few years earlier with his friend, Bobby Moresco, which was partly inspired by the 1992 Los

Angeles riots. A year before that, Haggis and his first wife had been carjacked. "We pulled over to get a movie at Blockbuster," he recounted for *Denver Post* journalist Steven Rosen, "and when we came out two guys with guns said, 'We'll take your car.' I said, 'Absolutely, you will.' We never found the car, and the people were never identified." Happy to have escaped unharmed, Haggis changed the locks on his house later that night, and tried to put the incident behind him. But as he told Carr in the *Time* interview, it bothered him for years. "I really wondered who they were," he said. "I felt driven to write about them from their point of view." One night, after waking up at 2 a.m., he hammered out an outline of the screenplay that would become *Crash* in just eight hours.

The *Crash* screenplay made the rounds in Hollywood and, once again, lured some influential names. Don Cheadle, Matt Dillon, Chris "Ludacris" Bridges, Larenz Tate, Sandra Bullock, Brendan Fraser, Thandie Newton, and Ryan Phillippe all agreed to work for scale, or the minimum fee their Screen Actors Guild union membership guaranteed, in order to help Haggis complete the project on a budget of just $6.5 million. Cheadle and Haggis were part of the team of producers, which numbered 14 in all, and the picture also marked Haggis' directorial debut for the big screen. The story begins with the murder of a young African-American man, and follows a series of interwoven subplots from there that touch upon the racial tensions harbored by the contemporary Los Angeles characters.

Haggis made *Crash* over several months between 2003 and 2004, and suffered a mild heart attack midway through, which forced him to halt shooting for two weeks. When his doctor seemed reluctant to let him return to work, warning him that further stress could worsen his health issues, Haggis replied, "'I totally understand,'" he recalled in the interview with Carr for *Time*. "'So how much stress do you think it'll be for me to be sitting at home while, say, another director finishes my film?'" Haggis returned to the set, but a nurse also tagged along every day to keep an eye on his vital signs.

Crash premiered at the Toronto International Film Festival in 2004, and was picked up by Lion's Gate, an independent distributor. Released in May of 2005, just a few months after *Million Dollar Baby* swept the Oscars, Haggis' directorial debut was a controversial movie, with critics either panning it altogether as liberal-guilt-driven dreck or heralding it as one of the best pictures of year. "The stunning, must-see drama *Crash* is proof that words have not lost the ability to shock in our anesthetized society," declared *Entertainment Weekly* critic Lisa Schwarzbaum. "White folks, black folks, Hispanics, and Asians—nobody gets by in this amazingly tough, at times unexpectedly funny, and always humane movie without getting dented."

David Denby, film critic for the *New Yorker,* also delivered praise in superlative terms. "Apart from a few brave scenes in Spike Lee's work, *Crash* is the first movie I know of to acknowledge not only that the intolerant are also human but, further, that something like white fear of black street crime, or black fear of white cops, isn't always irrational," Denby asserted. As for the wrap-up of the multiple storylines, which seemed a bit forced to others, Denby noted this may "strike some viewers as overwrought. But hasn't Haggis earned the tears? He has laid the groundwork for emotional release by writing some of the toughest talk ever heard in American movies. Some things may be better left unsaid, but the exuberant frankness of this movie burns through embarrassment and chagrin and produces its own kind of exhilaration."

Crash gave Haggis the chance to step up to the podium and collect his first Academy Award himself. In fact, he won two that night in 2006: one with producer Cathy Schulman for Best Motion Picture of the Year, and another with Moresco for Best Screenplay Written Directly for the Screen. By then, Haggis was already immersed in his next projects, a screenplay for a World War II tale to be directed by Eastwood, *Flags of Our Fathers,* and another the adaptation of *Casino Royale,* one of the first tales in Ian Fleming's James Bond series. Both were slated for 2006 release.

After reaching the pinnacle of success in Hollywood, Haggis did admit that he wrote *Crash* to atone in part for his earlier work, particularly *Walker, Texas Ranger,* a Chuck Norris action series he created that ran from 1993 to 2001 on CBS and then lived on via syndicated reruns. It proved to be his longest-running television series, after scores of failed pilots and cancelled shows. "I had to do something to erase that," he told Joshua Rich in *Entertainment Weekly.* "I wanted to find something that scared me. I had written too many things that didn't ask questions about who I am."

Sources

Denver Post, May 22, 2005, p. F1.
Entertainment Weekly, May 13, 2005, p. 65; May 20, 2005, p. 38.
Newsweek, February 6, 2006, p. 58.

New Yorker, May 2, 2005, p. 110.
People, October 28, 1996, p. 20.
San Francisco Chronicle, October 25, 1996, p. C1.
Time, April 3, 2006, p. A14.
Time Canada, March 6, 2006, p. 50.

—Carol Brennan

Tarja Halonen

© *Suomen Kuvapalveluoy/Corbis Sygma*

President of Finland

Born Tarja Kaarina Halonen, December 24, 1943, in Helsinki, Finland; daughter of Vieno Olavi and Lyyli Elina Loimola Halonen; married Pentti Arajärvi (an attorney), August, 2000; children: (with Kari Pekkonen) Anna. *Education:* Earned master of laws degree from the University of Helsinki, 1968.

Addresses: *Home*—Helsinki, Finland. *Office*—Office of the President of the Republic of Finland, Mariankatu 2, 00170 Helsinki, Finland.

Career

Social affairs and general secretary, National Union of Finnish Students, 1969-70; attorney, Central Organization of Finnish Trade Unions, 1970-74, 1975-79; joined the Social Democratic Party (SDP) of Finland, 1971; parliamentary secretary to Prime Minister Kalevi Sorsa, 1974-75; elected to the Helsinki City Council, 1977, and served until 1996; SDP member of parliament, 1979-2000; minister of social affairs and health, 1987-90; minister of Nordic cooperation, 1989-91; minister of justice, 1990-91; foreign affairs minister, 1995-2000; elected president of Finland, 2000; reelected, 2006.

Sidelights

Voters in Finland elected Tarja Halonen as their country's first female president in 2000, but her re-election campaign six years later received some unusual media attention outside of Scandinavia. In the fall of 2005, American television personality Conan O'Brien turned the resemblance between him-

self and Halonen into a recurring gag on his nightly NBC show. O'Brien even traveled to Finland a month after Halonen's narrow victory at the polls to meet the left-leaning Social Democrat in person. Asked by *Newsweek*'s Nicki Gostin if he felt he had any influence on the election, O'Brien joked, "I either helped her to win or almost caused her to lose."

Halonen was born on Christmas Eve of 1943 in Helsinki, Finland's capital city. Her parents named her "Tarja" a Russian variant of Darius, the ancient Persian leader. The name was not on the official list of girls' names at the time, and was an even more unusual choice given the fact that at the time of her birth, Finland was at war with the Soviet Union in the latest of a history of skirmishes with its powerful neighbor to the East. The Halonens lived in Kallio, a part of the city that had traditionally been home to factory workers and their families since the late nineteenth century.

Like many of her postwar generation, Halonen was active in a number of leftist political movements during her time as a student at the University of Helsinki. She continued her involvement with such organizations after she earned a master of laws degree in 1968, and took a job with the National Union of Finnish Students as its social affairs and general secretary. In 1970, she was hired by the Central Organization of Finnish Trade Unions as an attorney, and formally joined the Social Democratic Party (SDP; in Finnish *Suomen Sosialidemokraattinen Puolue*), Finland's most powerful political entity, a year later.

In 1974, Prime Minister Kalevi Sorsa appointed Halonen to the post of parliamentary secretary, which she held for one year before returning to her job as a labor attorney. In 1977, she won a seat on the Helsinki City Council, and would serve five terms in all. Two years later, she was elected to the *Eduskunta*, Finland's unicameral parliament. Her first cabinet post came when Harri Holkeri, the new prime minister, appointed her to serve as minister of social affairs and health in 1987. From 1989 to 1991 she held the post of minister of Nordic cooperation, and was Finland's justice minister between 1990 and 1991. After 1995 elections, which returned SDP to power, new prime minister Paavo Lipponen named her to serve as minister for foreign affairs. She earned high marks during her five years on the job, particularly for standing firm against a proposed membership in the North Atlantic Treaty Organization (NATO), a collective defense unit created in the aftermath of World War II.

In 1999, Halonen announced her intention to run for the presidency in the coming year's elections. Participation by Finnish women in government, even at the parliamentary level, dated back to 1907, a year after Finland became the first European country to grant women the right to vote. By the 1990s, the country boasted some of the most impressive statistics in the world for the number of women holding elected office or appointed government posts. The first female candidate for Finland's presidency was Helvi Sipila in 1982, and 12 years later the country's then-minister for defense, Elisabeth Rehn, narrowly lost to Martti Ahtisaari, whom Halonen would succeed.

In the 2000 contest, Halonen was one of four women on the ballot for president, but her main foe was a fifth candidate, former prime minister and head of the Centre Party, Esko Aho. Because that party drew much of its support from outside Finland's cities, Aho courted votes from more conservative rural Finns by highlighting the differences between himself and Halonen. She was a single parent who had never married the father of her daughter, Anna, was estranged from the Lutheran church, and had once headed Finland's leading gay-rights organization in the 1980s. In the January 16 voting, neither Halonen nor Aho won the necessary majority, and a run-off election took place on February 6 in which Halonen squeaked by with 51.6 percent of the vote. She was sworn in as Finland's first female president on March 1, 2000.

Changes in Finland's constitution had recently reduced the powers of the president, relegating them to the domestic sphere, but Halonen remained commander-in-chief for the country's military forces, and voiced her opinion on foreign affairs when she deemed it necessary. She became known for frankness as well as for a rather down-to-earth personality, which resonated deeply with the characteristically sensible Finns. Her official Web page featured photographs of her two cats, Rontii and Miska, and when she was dubbed "Moominmamma" by the Swedish press—after a motherly cartoon character—the nickname took hold in Finland. A few months after taking office, she wed her longtime partner, attorney Pentti Arajärvi, in a private ceremony.

Halonen ran for reelection in January of 2006, and won a second six-year term after another run-off, this time against National Coalition Party candidate Sauli Niinistö. Again, it was a close election, with Halonen besting Niinistö in the January 9 contest by just three percentage points. Her campaign attracted an unusually high degree of international press attention thanks to Halonen's frequent mentions on *Late Night with Conan O'Brien*, which airs on one of Finland's cable-television channels. The jokes began in October of 2005, after the red-headed host was told that he resembled Halonen. "We decided to do a split screen and I've never gotten a laugh like that," O'Brien told Gostin in the *Newsweek* interview.

As election day in Finland neared, O'Brien endorsed Halonen's bid for a second term and even produced mock political ads that skewered Niinistö and her other opponents. A few weeks after her election victory, O'Brien traveled to Finland, where Halonen presented him with an award for most entertaining television personality of the year, based on a public poll conducted by the country's equivalent of *TV Guide*. A crowd of 2,000 Finnish fans greeted him at the Helsinki airport when he arrived for his five-day visit, with one holding a banner that read, according to the *New York Times*, "Tarja is our president but Conan is our king."

Sources

Financial Times, July 10, 2000, p. 2.
Independent (London, England), February 8, 2000, p. 15.

Nation, April 10, 2000, p. 20.
Newsweek, March 13, 2006, p. 71.
New York Times, February 13, 2006.
Presidents & Prime Ministers, May 2000, p. 16.

Scotsman (Edinburgh, Scotland), May 13, 2004, p. 14.

—*Carol Brennan*

Mariska Hargitay

Francis Specker/Landov

Actress

Born Mariska Magdolina Hargitay, January 23, 1964, in Los Angeles, CA; daughter of Mickey Hargitay (a bodybuilder) and Jayne Mansfield (an actress); married Peter Hermann (an actor), August 28, 2004. *Education:* Studied theater at the University of California—Los Angeles.

Addresses: *Contact*—c/o Law & Order: Special Victims Unit, National Broadcasting Co. (NBC), 30 Rockefeller Plaza, New York, NY 10112.

Career

Actress on television, including: *Falcon Crest,* 1984, 1988; *Downtown,* 1986-87; *Finish Line* (movie), 1989; *Tequila & Bonetti,* 1992; *Blind Side* (movie), 1993; *Can't Hurry Love,* 1995; *The Single Guy,* 1996; *ER,* 1997-98; *Prince Street,* 1997; *Night Sins* (movie), 1997; *Law & Order: Special Victims Unit,* 1999—; *Plain Truth* (movie), 2004. Film appearances include: *Ghoulies,* 1985; *Jocks,* 1987; *Mr. Universe,* 1988; *The Perfect Weapon,* 1991; *Bank Robber,* 1993; *Leaving Las Vegas,* 1995; *Lake Placid,* 1999; *Perfume,* 2001. Won Miss Beverly Hills 1982 pageant.

Awards: Golden Globe award for best performance by an actress in a television series, Hollywood Foreign Press Association, for *Law & Order: Special Victims Unit,* 2005.

Sidelights

Despite a pedigree that stretches back to Hollywood's golden era, Mariska Hargitay had difficulty finding work in film and on television actor before her star turn in the popular NBC series *Law & Order: Special Victims Unit.* Her portrayal of tough, seen-it-all sex-crimes investigator Olivia Benson on that show even won her a Golden Globe award in 2005. It marked the first time that *Law & Order: SVU* had won the Hollywood Foreign Press Association honor, and it was a first for Hargitay, too—though her late screen-siren mother, Jayne Mansfield, had been a co-recipient of the "Most Promising Newcomer" Golden Globe back in 1957. A decade later, Hargitay's mother died in a horrific automobile crash that left her three-year-old daughter and Hargitay's two brothers relatively unscathed. "I just always felt robbed," she told Kate Coyne in a *Good Housekeeping* interview. "Everyone else in the world had such strong feelings about this woman that I should have known the best. But I never got to know her at all."

Hargitay was born in Los Angeles in 1964, the third child and first daughter of Mansfield and Mickey Hargitay, a Hungarian-born professional figure skater-turned-bodybuilder who won the 1955 Mr. Universe title. With her platinum hair and famous curves, Mansfield could be best described as the Pamela Anderson of her era. The films she made were sub-par, but she was rarely out of the gossip columns or missing from a newsstand's row of magazine covers. She successfully carried off a "dumb blonde" image, but spoke several languages and had an impressively high I.Q., or intelligence quotient. Hargitay's father was Mansfield's second husband, and reportedly the love of her life; at their Beverly Hills home, Hargitay had "I Love You Jayne" tiled at the bottom of a heart-shaped swimming pool.

The marriage faltered, however, and Mansfield married a movie director, with whom she had a son. She later took up with the Los Angeles attorney who had handled her divorce, and she was with him, Hargitay, and Hargitay's two older brothers in a Buick traveling in the pre-dawn hours from the Gus Stevens Supper Club in Biloxi, Mississippi, to a scheduled radio interview in New Orleans on June 29, 1967, when the limousine plowed into the back of a trailer truck. Hargitay and her brothers suffered just minor injuries, and she remembers nothing of the crash or its immediate aftermath. An enduring legend about the accident was that both her mother and Sam Brody, the boyfriend, were decapitated, but this came from witnesses seeing one of Mansfield's blond wigs on the dashboard. The reality was bad enough: Hargitay's mother's skull was crushed. Hargitay was three years old at the time, and has a zigzag-shaped scar on her head from the accident. Deeper scars were equally hard to find, however. "Sometimes I can't believe I'm not a drug addict or an alcoholic," she told Coyne in the *Good Housekeeping* interview. "I would lapse into catastrophic thinking a lot, where I was just convinced that the worst thing would happen. But I worked hard to stop those patterns, because I realized, If you think something's going to end badly, sweetheart, it will."

Hargitay went to live with her father, who had remarried by then, and grew up in Beverly Hills. Sometimes she spent her summer breaks with her maternal grandparents in Colorado, but other times she was shipped to Hungary to visit her father's family there. It was a Communist bloc country at the time, and offered a drastically different view of life from her Beverly Hills environment. Back at Marymount High School, a Roman Catholic girls' school, Hargitay was a top swimmer and elected senior-class president. Until she was cast in a school play, she had little interest in acting, but was surprised to discover that she loved it. After winning the Miss Beverly Hills 1982 beauty pageant, she studied theater at the University of California at Los Angeles, and made her television debut in an episode of *Falcon Crest* in 1984. She also worked part-time in less-glamorous fields to pay for the UCLA apartment she shared with three other students, holding down jobs as a waitress and in a clothing store. In a 1985 *People* interview that was

one of the first instances of media exposure for her, she told writer Debra Zahn, "I'm proud to work. I just know too many spoiled rich kids who are full degenerate losers."

Hargitay made her feature-film debut that same year in *Ghoulies,* and eventually left UCLA before completing her degree. She did admit that she seemed to have had a delayed reaction to her mother's death, around the age of 22, when she sunk into a deep depression and cried constantly. After that, she vowed to stop speaking about her late mother in the press, and concentrated on her own career instead. She had a difficult time finding work for several years, however. There was a short-lived CBS series in 1986, *Downtown,* about a Los Angeles halfway house for ex-convicts and which also featured a young Blair Underwood, and then the movie *Jocks* a year later, a typical teen flick of the era about a losing college tennis team. Hargitay returned to *Falcon Crest* in 1988 for a recurring role, but could not land any film work for three years. "When I was younger, I used to deliberately avoid sexy roles, and even lost a part once when I refused to dye my hair blonde," she confessed to Sue Corrigan for the British newspaper *Mail on Sunday.* "The producer sacked me, but I wanted to stay away from sexual roles. I shied away because of my mother. I played lots of tomboys wearing flannel shirts and boots."

Hargitay's career continued to sputter through the 1990s. There was another quickly cancelled television series, *Tequila & Bonetti,* which starred Jack Scalia as a transplanted New York City cop and a French mastiff as his partner in crime-fighting; Hargitay played his new Los Angeles Police Department colleague, but obviously it was a secondary role to the voice-over thoughts of Tequila, the dog. Critics were merciless in their derision, and the show lasted just six episodes. Hargitay also made some television movies, including *Blind Side* and *Night Sins,* and had a brief walk-on in the 1995 Nicolas Cage film *Leaving Las Vegas* as a prostitute. Steadier work came when she was hired for the hit hospital drama *ER* as Cynthia Hooper, the meek desk clerk who has a crush on Anthony Edwards's character during the show's 1997-98 season.

Hargitay occasionally considered giving up the endless rounds of auditions and meetings. Her father was proved unflagging in his encouragement, however. "When I wanted to quit, my dad was the one who said, 'No, you don't. Get back out there and just do it better. Work harder,'" she told *Good Housekeeping*'s Coyne. Finally, in 1999, she was cast in *Law & Order: Special Victims Unit,* a spin-off from the immensely successful *Law & Order* show, on the air since 1990. Set in a hard-bitten New York City world of cops, crime, and the court system, the *Law & Order* franchise was the creation of hit-making producer Dick Wolf, and quickly scored with viewers and critics alike. *SVU* was the first *Law & Order* spin-off.

Hargitay was cast as Olivia Benson, a New York City detective who investigates sex crimes. Topics such as torture and pedophilia regularly drove the *SVU* story lines, which quickly became known as the "racy" *Law & Order*. Her co-star was Christopher Meloni, best known for his role as Chris Keller in the HBO prison drama *Oz*. In later seasons story lines revealed that some of Detective Benson's fierce attitude stemmed from the fact that she herself was the product of a sexual assault. The show scored consistently high ratings, even outperforming the original *Law & Order* at times. "The subject matter is compelling, and the chemistry between the leads even more so," noted Allison Hope Weiner in *Entertainment Weekly*. "The soulful, brooding Meloni looks like he kept enough of his *Oz* persona to rough up anyone who looks at him cockeyed, and nothing in Hargitay's resume prepared viewers for the fact that Jayne Mansfield's daughter can engage in some serious, sassy butt-kicking."

In 2005, Hargitay even won a rare Golden Globe award for best performance by an actress in a television series from the Hollywood Foreign Press Association. The honor was a first for *Law & Order: SVU*, which had never even been nominated for a Golden Globe at all in seven seasons—though the parent series had been nominated several times and then failed to win. Hargitay belongs to the cast of one of the most successful television series in history, with a total of four *Law & Order* shows generating about $1 billion a year. Not surprisingly, the gritty crime drama is popular around the world, too, and Hargitay's face is seen by viewers in 200 countries.

Hargitay rarely ventures into feature films any more, with an arduous *SVU* taping schedule making other commitments all but impossible. Her last two big-screen roles were in *Lake Placid* in 1999 and *Perfume* two years later. Viewers seemed to identify so strongly with her portrayal of Olivia Benson that Hargitay even receives letters from victims of sexual abuse or assault; their harrowing real-life stories haunt her worse than any script, and so Hargitay decided to train and volunteer as a rape crisis counselor. She also established the Joyful Heart Foundation to provide recovery help for victims of sexual abuse.

Since taking the *SVU* job, Hargitay has made New York City her home. She headed west, however, for her 2004 wedding to actor Peter Hermann in Santa Barbara, California. They met on the set of *SVU*, and Hargitay recalled that she had been instantly smitten, and said on their first real date that "I just about passed out when I saw him," she told *InStyle* journalist Sarah Stebbins. "I thought, That's my husband." She turned 41 a few months later, the same month she won the Golden Globe, and hopes to become a mother. She no longer harbors a fear that she will die young, as she for many years before she turned 34—the age her mother was when she died. She did, however, endure a motorcycle accident that same year, but emerged from it with nothing more than a sprained ankle. "That's when I told myself, You're not going to die; you're not your mother," she explained to James Servin in another *InStyle* interview. "That's when my whole life changed."

Sources

Entertainment Weekly, March 4, 2005, p. 26.
Good Housekeeping, October 2004, p. 162.
InStyle, June 1, 2000, p. 374; January 4, 2005, p. 318.
Mail on Sunday (London, England), December 19, 1999, p. 6; April 3, 2005, p. 25.
Parade, February 13, 2005, p. 16.
People, March 4, 1985, p. 59; April 6, 1992, p. 105.
Virginian Pilot, March 22, 2002, p. E1.

—*Carol Brennan*

Carey Hart

Motocross athlete and business owner

Born July 17, 1975, in Las Vegas, NV; son of Tom Hart (a construction company owner); married Pink (aka Alecia Moore; a singer), January 7, 2006.

Addresses: *Office*—Hart & Huntington Tattoo Company, Palms Casino, 4321 W. Flamingo Rd., Las Vegas, NV 89103.

Career

Began competing in motocross races, 1981; turned professional, c. 1993; competed in supercross races, c. 1993-96; began competing in freestyle motocross, c. 1996; completed first "Hart Breaker" at the Gravity Games, 2000; played bass with band Pennywise during the Warped Tour, 2001; won silver in the Big Air Discipline of Motocross, Summer X Games, 2002; won gold medal at the Australian X Games, 2002; opened Hart & Huntington Tattoo Company, Las Vegas, NV, 2004; appeared on reality show *The Surreal Life*, VH1, 2005; starred on reality show *Inked*, A&E, 2005—. Film appearances include: *Crusty Demons of Dirt, Vol. 3*, 2001; *Ultimate X: The Movie*, 2002; *xXx*, 2002; *Flipped Out*, 2003; *Charlie's Angels: Full Throttle*, 2003.

Sidelights

Though Carey Hart's career began as a motocross racer, a 2004 injury led him to expand his activities. He owns a tattoo parlor in his home town of Las Vegas, Nevada, and had featured roles in two reality shows in 2005. Hart also married long-time, on-again, off-again girlfriend, pop singer Pink, in

WENN/Landov

early 2006, as he prepared to return to his sport. Hart had been an freestyle motocross athlete of note as the inventor of a trick known as the "Hart Breaker"—a back flip on a 250cc (full-sized) motorcycle. He also invented the "Hart Attack"—a handstand on the motorcycle done in midair. Hart has broken at least 20 bones throughout his years as a motocross athlete. He told Scott Hoffman of *Dirt Rider*, "Every time I ride I get scared. Every time I hit a jump the first time I'm scared. Fear is definitely what keeps me doing it but it also slows me down."

Hart was born in 1975 in Las Vegas, where he was raised by his single father, Tom Hart, who owned a construction company, for much of his life. His parents divorced when he was young. Hart was given his first motocross bike when he was only four years old, a present from his father who rode motorcycles for fun. As Hart began riding dirt bikes, he also began competing in local races. When he was 18 years old, Hart turned pro as a motocross rider. He competed in supercross racing (motorcycle racing) for a significant amount of time, but did not find the experience satisfying. Hart told Hoffman of *Dirt Rider*, "I rode supercross for three seasons and really wasn't getting a whole lot out of racing. I did pretty decent my last season riding but nobody wanted to give me any help, so it was either change things up or quit altogether."

Since racing motorcycles to win was not enough for him, Hart decided to try something different. When he was 23 years old, Hart changed his focus to become a freestyle motocross rider, an emerging sport in which tricks and jumps are done on a motocross bike over a course in an allotted amount of time, usually two or three minutes. The dirt course has ramps and jumps, and is usually 275 feet by 185 feet. Judges award points for what the athletes accomplish on the course in competitions.

Within a short amount of time, Hart became the recognized leader of freestyle motocross. He first showed off moves on the Warped Tour—a summer touring extravaganza focusing on music and alternative entertainment—which led to the expansion of the sport and Hart's career in the late 1990s and early 2000s. Hart soon had sponsors and was earning hundreds of thousands of dollars each year in endorsements. Hart also competed in the premier sporting events like the Gravity Games and the X Games which featured freestyle motocross events. One significant moment came in the 2000 Gravity Games, held in Providence, Rhode Island. Hart made history when he became the first rider to complete a back flip on a full-sized motocross motorcycle in competition, the so-called "Hart Breaker." Hart had tried it at the 2000 X Games, but failed in that attempt. Completing the Hart Breaker made Hart a world-wide star and household name, but also left him in pain; Hart had compressed vertebra in his back and pulled ligaments. These injuries were caused by the fact that he landed on his back quite hard when he completed the move for the first time in competition. Hart told Stephen Sherill of the *New York Times*, "I was just ecstatic that I didn't kill myself."

When Hart tried to pull off the Hart Breaker again at the 2001 X Games, he was unable to complete the maneuver because he lost control of his bike. The attempt left Carey with broken foot bones, broken ribs, and a tailbone that was bruised. While recovering from these injuries, he found other activities to fill the time. During the Warped Tour in 2001, for example, he played bass with Pennywise, a band that performed during part of the tour. Returning to competition in 2002, he finished second in the Big Air Discipline of Motocross at the Summer X Games, where he completed a Hart Breaker. That year, he won a gold medal at the Australian X Games as well.

In the early 2000s, Hart also began appearing in videos and films. Most of his filmed appearances were on freestyle motocross tapes like *Crusty De-* *mons of Dirt, Vol. 3* in 2001, *Ultimate X: The Movie* in 2002, and *Flipped Out* in 2003. Hart filmed a music video with Kid Rock in 2002, the same year he moved into feature films with a cameo in the action film *xXx*. Hart also appeared as himself in 2003's *Charlie's Angels: Full Throttle*, the sequel to the hit movie.

After sustaining injuries which required extensive rest in 2004, Hart again found non-motocross activities to fill his time. In 2005, he joined the cast of season five of the VH1 reality show, *The Surreal Life*. The show mixes a variety of has-been and minor celebrities together in a house in Los Angeles. They are taped while completing tasks which sometimes highlight tensions between them. Hart shared the home with actor Bronson Pinchot, former supermodel Janice Dickinson, *Apprentice* competitor Omarosa Manigault Stallworth, and disgraced baseball player Jose Conseco. Hart was considered relatively normal on the show.

That same year, Hart was part of another reality show called *Inked* which aired on A&E. This show centered on the tattoo parlor Hart opened with nightclub promoter John Huntington in 2004, Hart & Huntington Tattoo Company in the Palms Casino in Las Vegas. *Inked* featured Hart dealing with his staff and clients, including his co-owner Thomas Pendleton, a tattoo artist. Hart was covered in tattoos himself, having gotten his first tattoo at the age of 17.

During his time off, Hart also married his girlfriend of several years, Pink, whom he met at the 2001 X Games. They were wed early in 2006 in an elaborate wedding in Costa Rica. He also prepared to return to competition with new sponsors like Jones Soda. Damage to his body was not going to prevent Hart from pursuing his sport. He told Bob Leddy of the *Providence Journal-Bulletin*, "There's no way an injury's going to keep me from doing it [competing]. I've got to stick with it. It's something you've got to deal with. You put it aside and go for it."

Sources

Periodicals

Chicago Sun-Times, December 18, 2002, p. 149.
Dirt Rider, September 2000, p. 88; October 2000, p. 18.
Las Vegas Review-Journal (Las Vegas, NV), November 10, 2000, p. 8C.
New York Times, April 8, 2001, sec. 6, p. 76.

People, November 28, 2005, p. 198; January 23, 2006, p. 78.

Providence Journal-Bulletin (Providence, RI), August 27, 1999, p. 4D.

Rocky Mountain News (Denver, CO), November 7, 2002, p. 4D.

Online

"Carey Hart Chat Transcript," EXPN.com, http://expn.go.com/xgames/sxg/viii/s/020808_hartchat.html (May 1, 2006).

"Carey Hart," EXPN.com, http://expn.go.com/athletes/bio/HART_CAREY.html (May 1, 2006).

"Carey Hart," Internet Movie Database, http://www.imdb.com/name/nm1144474/ (May 1, 2006).

"Carey Hart," Jones Soda Co., http://www.jonessoda.com/files_new/carey_hart.html (May 2, 2006).

"Inked: About the Show," A&E TV, http://www.aetv.com/inked/inked_about.jsp (May 2, 2006).

"Inked: Carey Hart," A&E TV, http://www.aetv.com/inked/inked_cast_and_crew.jsp?index=0&type=actor (May 2, 2006).

"Motocross: Carey Hart," Kidzworld.com, http://www.kidzworld.com/site/p2319.htm (May 1, 2006).

"The Surreal Life 5: Characters," VH1.com, http://www.vh1.com/shows/dyn/the_surreal_life_5/series_characters.jhtml (May 1, 2006).

—A. Petruso

Reed Hastings

Reuters/Fred Prouser/Landov

President, Chief Executive Officer, and Board Chair of Netflix

Born Wilmot Reed Hastings Jr., c. 1961; married; children: two. *Education:* Earned undergraduate degree in mathematics from Bowdoin College, 1983; earned master's degrees from Stanford University, in computer science, 1988, and in education.

Addresses: *Office*—970 University Ave., Los Gatos, CA 95032.

Career

Served in the Peace Corps in Swaziland, 1983-86; worked as a software developer, c. 1988-90; founded Pure Atria Software, 1990, and sold it to Rational Software, 1997; director of TechNet, a political lobbying group; president of the California State Board of Education, 2001-05; founded Netflix, Inc., 1998, and serves as president, chief executive officer, and board chair.

Sidelights

Reed Hastings founded the phenomenally successful DVD-rental company, Netflix, but the Web-based mail-order service was not his first entrepreneurial venture. Hastings was already wealthy from the software company he founded and sold in the dot-com boom of the 1990s. His own experience with an exorbitant late-rental fee from his local video store led him to launch Netflix in 1998. "Netflix is a powerful idea," wrote Stacey Grenrock Woods in *Esquire*, "one that combines old-timey mail, newfangled Internet, freedom of choice, and our God-given right to be lazy."

Hastings was born in the early 1960s and grew up in Washington, D.C., and the Boston area. His father was an attorney for the U.S. Department of Health, Education, and Welfare. After graduating from a private school in Cambridge, Massachusetts, Hastings went on to Bowdoin College in Maine, where he studied mathematics. He earned his degree in 1983 and immediately joined the Peace Corps, a U.S.-administered organization that sends trained volunteers to struggling parts of the non-industrialized world. Hastings spent three years teaching math to students in Swaziland, and then returned to California to earn a graduate degree in computer science from Stanford University.

Hastings became a software developer, and in 1990 started his own company, Pure Atria Software, which he then sold several years later to a larger software firm for a sum in the neighborhood of $750 million. When *USA Today* did a feature story on the growing number of instant millionaires in the Silicon Valley area of northern California, one of the photographs that ran with it showed Hastings and his Porsche sports car with the caption, "boom! you are rich!" Over the next few years, Hastings became active in educational philanthropy, working to increase the number of charter schools in the state and advocating stronger math and science curricula in all schools. Teaming with a well-known Silicon

Valley venture capitalist, John Doerr, Hastings successfully organized a drive to get a new proposal on the California ballot, called Proposition 39, in 2000, which decreased the minimum number of votes needed for school millage elections to pass. During this period Hastings even returned to school himself, earning a graduate degree in education from Stanford University.

Hastings came up with the idea for Netflix in 1997, when he had to pay $40 in late fees for a copy of *Apollo 13*. At the time, the bulky videocassette format was the standard still, but a smaller, cheaper, CD-based digital movie format, the DVD, had recently come onto the market; within a few years, affordable DVD players for the home would flood the consumer electronics market. Hastings thought that a company that sent out the lightweight DVDs to subscription customers by mail, and without a time limit to return them, might be a better alternative to the video store and its onerous return policies. He and a co-founder, Marc Randolph, set up Netflix in 1998, and began offering subscriptions a year later. Subscribers paid a $20 monthly fee, and in return, could have unlimited DVD rentals. Their selections were made from the company website, www.netflix.com, and a subscriber could take up to three movies at a time. Returning them was simple: a postage-paid envelope arrived with each rental, and every time one was returned, the subscriber's next choice was sent out.

Netflix struck deals with all the major Hollywood studios to provide newly released DVDs, and began amassing an inventory of DVDs which were stockpiled in their warehouse/distribution centers across the United States. In 2000, the company entered into an arrangement with electronics retailer Best Buy, which agreed to place Netflix stickers on boxes of new DVD players it sold; in return, a Netflix subscriber had the option to purchase a movie they had liked on the Netflix website via a "buy" button that took them directly to the Best Buy retail site.

Hastings was determined to grow his company carefully, and his prudence attracted the attention of Wall Street. In May of 2002, Netflix became a publicly traded company with an initial public offering (IPO) of stock. The company had 600,000 subscribers by then, but hit the one-million mark less than a year later. There was a 50 percent increase in subscribers for 2004, to 1.5 million, and by September of 2005 there were 3.5 million Netflix devotees. But perhaps the most telling sign of Netflix's success was the copycat-factor: both Blockbuster and Wal-Mart copied the DVD-by-mail concept. The ubiquitous rental chain had once dismissed Netflix as an insignificant competitor. "Blockbuster said, 'Well, they'll never get to 100,000 [customers].'" Hastings told *Video Business* writer Laura Dunphy. "Then they estimated our total market at a million. Now that we've passed a million, they've estimated our total market at three million." In the end, Wal-Mart eventually gave up, and even sold off the remainder of its venture to Netflix.

Future plans for Netflix have been debated in the business press almost since its inception. Might it become the primary provider, some day, of online, on-demand content? "We're starting to invest now," in the online content realm, Hastings told *Newsweek International* writers Karen Breslau and Daniel McGinn in 2003, "even though there's no real market for it today, so that when it comes, we're ready. [But] DVD will last as long as the gasoline engine, newspaper—any of your 'obsolete' in the very long term industries."

In 2004, Hastings's company announced a deal with TiVo, the digital recording service, but details about what they were planning remained somewhat murky. The basic premise of Netflix was going to be the cornerstone of the company for some time, the chief executive officer told *Newsweek*'s Brad Stone. "The U.S. mail, with its 800,000 employees delivering to 100 million homes six days a week, is the ultimate digital distribution network," Hastings asserted.

Hastings remained active in education issues, and between 2001 and 2005 served as president of the California State Board of Education. He is the father of two children, and admits that he still visits the old-school DVD rental stores when they are eager to see a new movie, and want it that same day.

Sources

Business 2.0, March 2005, p. 36.
Esquire, December 2003, p. 193.
Fortune, June 13, 2005, p. 34.
Newsweek, March 17, 2003, pp. E10-11.
Newsweek International, September 26, 2005, p. 56.
New York Times, June 3, 2002, p. C4.
Time International, July 19, 2004, p. 61.
Video Business, April 28, 2003, p. 13.

—*Carol Brennan*

Lene Vestergaard Hau

Physicist

Born November 13, 1959, in Vejle, Denmark. *Education:* Received B.S. and M.S. degrees from the University of Aarhus, and Ph.D., 1991.

Addresses: *Office*—Rowland Institute for Science, 100 Edwin H. Land Blvd., Cambridge, MA 02142.

Career

Postdoctoral fellow in physics, Harvard University, 1989-91; scientific staff member, Rowland Institute for Science, 1991—; Gordon McKay professor of applied physics and professor of physics, Harvard University, 1999—.

Awards: MacArthur Fellowship, John D. and Catherine T. MacArthur Foundation, 2001-06.

Sidelights

Danish physicist Lene Vestergaard Hau entered the annals of science history in 2001 when she and her team of researchers at Harvard University became the first to physically halt the speed of light. Later that year, Hau was awarded one of the MacArthur Foundation "genius" grants for her accomplishment. For a researcher whose proposal was once rejected for funding by the National Science Foundation because she had little practical experience in the experiments she was planning, the $500,000 MacArthur prize money was a welcome windfall. "If I discover a totally new area of research that I want to work in," she remarked to *Harvard*

Gazette writer William J. Cromie, "the fellowship gives me the funds to pursue it without being told that it's not my field."

Born in Vejle, Denmark, in 1959, Hau spent her college career at the University of Aarhus in her native country. She earned both undergraduate and master's degrees before moving to Cambridge, Massachusetts, to become a postdoctoral fellow in physics at Harvard University in 1989. The University of Aarhus would award her a Ph.D. two years later. Hau's area of interest was theoretical physics, but in Cambridge she became fascinated by the more experimental realm of physics. When the Rowland Institute for Science, which was affiliated with Harvard, hired her as a scientific staff member in 1991, she began to pursue her experimental work in earnest.

The Rowland Institute was founded in 1980 with a grant from Edwin H. Land, the inventor of Polaroid photography. Land wanted to create a working laboratory for experimental science research in the fields of physics, chemistry, and biology. Hau was particularly intrigued by what is known as the Bose-Einstein condensate. This was named for Albert Einstein, who first theorized it, and an Indian physicist, Satyendra Nath Bose, who correctly mapped out the theory. As *Smithsonian* writer John P. Wiley Jr. explained, "When you cool the right stuff down to a temperature of a few hundred billionths of a degree above absolute zero, strange things happen. The motion that animates every atom (in the macro world, we feel that motion as heat) nearly stops.... This is the world of quantum mechanics, where classic physics no longer applies." Wiley continued,

"The space in which each atom can be found spreads out farther and farther, overlapping with all the others. The atoms lose their identities," and the cloud of them that forms is known in science as the Bose-Einstein condensate.

The first hint that Hau was working on a possible breakthrough in stopping the speed of light came in a 1999 issue of the journal *Nature*, when she described a successful experiment she conducted the year before. Scientists know that light travels through space at 186,285 miles a second, a definition confirmed in 1926 by scientist Albert A. Michelson, the first American to win the Nobel Prize in his field. Scientists also knew that light could be slowed a bit if it encountered something transparent, like glass, which will refract the beam into the bent rays that the human eye sees as spectra, or the diffusion of color. By the same principle, Hau thought that the Bose-Einstein condensate could also be deployed in slowing the speed of light, because it has an unusually high refractive index.

In that 1998 project, Hau and her team managed to slow a beam of light down to just 38 miles an hour by shining it through a chamber filled with supercooled sodium gas. They used a laser beam and spent one long 27-hour stint trying to achieve the intended result. Hau described the elation she and her fellow researchers experienced in an interview with Marisa Cohen in *More*. "When you realize that this is the first time in history anybody has seen light go this slow," she enthused, "it's such an amazing moment, it's worth all the effort."

In 1999, Hau was appointed the Gordon McKay Professor of Applied Physics and Professor of Physics at Harvard. She was also given her own facility, known as the Hau Lab. There, she continued her experiments with slowing the speed of light even further, and had another breakthrough early in 2001, when she and the researchers actually stopped the beam of light completely. Another team of scientists, Ronald L. Walsworth and Mikhail D. Lukin of the Harvard-Smithsonian Center for Astrophysics, also announced the identical result, but noted that their own experiments had been based on Hau's initial findings published back in 1999. The Walsworth-Lukin group had not used sodium gas, but rather rubidium, an alkaline metal element.

New York Times science writer James Glanz explained the significance of both teams' work. "The achievement is a landmark feat that, by reining in nature's swiftest and most ethereal form of energy for the first time, could help realize what are now theoretical concepts for vastly increasing the speed of computers and the security of communications," Glanz wrote. "Quantum computers could crank through certain operations vastly faster than existing machines; quantum communications could never be eavesdropped upon. For both these systems, light is needed to form large networks of computers. But those connections are difficult without temporary storage of light, a problem that the new work could help solve."

Hau was given one of the most sought-after honors in the world when the John D. and Catherine T. MacArthur Foundation named her as one of its newest "genius grant" recipients later in 2001. Formally known as a MacArthur Fellowship, there is no application process for the grant, and an anonymous committee decides who will receive the generous half-million-dollar stipend, which is parceled out in fifths over a five-year period. The winners, drawn from the arts and sciences, can spend the amount in any way they choose. Like nearly all the MacArthur genius-grant awardees, Hau first learned that she was under consideration when the surprise telephone call came to inform her that she had won. "I was totally stunned," she admitted to Cromie in the *Harvard Gazette*. "I didn't have a clue."

Sources

Harvard Gazette, October 25, 2001.
More, June 2005, p. 87.
New York Times, January 18, 2001, p. A1.
Smithsonian, June 1999, p. 26.

—*Carol Brennan*

Sally Hershberger

Evan Kafka/Liaison/Getty Images

Hair stylist and salon owner

Born c. 1961, in Wichita, KS; daughter of an oil-company executive.

Addresses: *Home*—Los Angeles, CA, and New York, NY. *Office*—Sally Hershberger Downtown, 423 W. 14th St., New York, NY 10014.

Career

Hairstylist in the salon of Arthur Johns, Los Angeles, early 1980s; stylist for magazine editorial shoots with photographers such as Herb Ritts; portrait photographer for *Vanity Fair* and other magazines, early 1990s; executive style director for John Frieda salons; opened Sally Hershberger at John Frieda salon, Los Angeles, March, 2000, and Sally Hershberger Downtown in New York City, July, 2003; launched Sally Hershberger FacePlace skincare line, 2005; launched Shagg Downtown, a clothing line, 2005.

Sidelights

Sally Hershberger built her hair-salon empire upon the widely copied shag cut that she gave film star Meg Ryan in the 1990s. Hershberger is one of a handful of hairstylists who have earned a measure of celebrity over the years, but among those select ranks she is the first woman to achieve such success. With salons in both Los Angeles and New York City, Hershberger cuts the heads of a long list of famous clients, but is perhaps best known among the public for elevating the price of a haircut at her digs to a stratospheric $600. "People pay that much all day long for purses and shoes," she told the *New York Post* about the price. "You wear your hair 24 hours a day and people look at it more."

Born in the early 1960s, Hershberger spent her earliest years in Wichita, Kansas. Her father had earned a small fortune from his oil-exploration business, and was friendly with Republican Party heavy-hitters such as former president Gerald Ford and Kansas senator Bob Dole. Her parents divorced when she was a toddler, and Hershberger moved to Los Angeles with her mother and two brothers. "I was a bad girl," she told Erika Kinetz in the *New York Times*. "I always thought I was going to get all this money. Then my dad lost it all, when oil crashed, you know." The same journalist noted, however, that Hershberger's father had run into financial and legal difficulties that ended with a five-year, four-month stint in prison. Compounding her family troubles were the deaths of Hershberger's two brothers, one from a drug overdose and the other in a car accident.

Hershberger experimented on her own hair as a teen, but her decision to become a hairdresser happened almost by accident, as she told Lisa Armstrong in the *Times* of London. "It was never a passion," she explained. "It was more like, you're 18, you can't hang out any more. Go get a job." By the early 1980s, she was working at the Sunset Boulevard salon of Arthur Johns, a stylist for pop singer Olivia Newton-John. When Johns fell ill, Hershberger was tapped to replace him on Newton-John's tour for her hit *Let's Get Physical* LP in 1982. Thanks to that job, Hershberger was introduced to fashion photographer Herb Ritts, who liked her work enough to hire her for his magazine editorial work.

Hershberger went on to work with a number of esteemed fashion photographers, and eventually ventured into photography herself. Her portraits of celebrities appeared on the pages of *Vogue* and *Vanity Fair*, while she continued to cut hair in Los Angeles. It was her snips on the famous blonde head of Meg Ryan that launched Hershberger as an emerging new stylist; Hershberger gave Ryan a choppy shag that was actually the emblematic coif for stylish West-Coast lesbians, and after it debuted on Ryan in the 1995 romantic comedy *French Kiss*, Ryan's look became the second-most widely copied cut of the decade following Jennifer Aniston's "Rachel" coif, named after Aniston's character on the NBC sitcom *Friends*.

Other big names who considered Hershberger the go-to person for a new style included Michelle Pfeiffer and Tom Cruise, and she even styled Hillary Rodham Clinton when the First Lady appeared on the cover of *Vogue*. She also began working with British-born hairdresser John Frieda, which came about thanks to a 1990 trip to India. "I went there to get a blessing for my new career in photography," she recalled in the London *Times* interview with Armstrong. "But [her yoga guru] kept talking about John Frieda. I'd never heard of him—he hadn't launched his products then. And then she introduced us."

Hershberger worked with Frieda in developing his Sheer Blonde and Beach Blonde lines, which became some of the best-selling hair care products on the market when they were launched in the late 1990s. Her first eponymous salon, Sally Hershberger at John Frieda, opened in March of 2000 on Melrose Avenue in Los Angeles. The space included an indoor pool and even a waterwall, and she followed it three years later with a second location in New York City's trendy Meatpacking District. It was here that Hershberger introduced her $600 haircut, an amount that surpassed what the top Manhattan hairdressers—Frederic Fekkai and John Barrett among them—were charging at the time by at least $100. Part of Hershberger's decision to set her rate so high was to allow her to stay in the salon, which she preferred, rather than on location doing editorial or film-set work, which could net her as much as $4,500 a day. "I love working in a salon," she enthused to *W* writer Patricia Reynoso. "There's a certain freedom there that you can't get from a shoot. There's no one telling me what to do."

In 2005, Hershberger launched a line of skin-care products, as well as Shagg Downtown, a line of T-shirts and jeans similar to her classic workwear. She was also in the process of writing her own style bible, tentatively titled *Shagg*, thanks to a contract with Regan Books. Somewhat of a cult figure as an epitome of casual L.A. chic, Hershberger was rumored to have been the inspiration for the hairstylist character Shane on the hit Showtime series *The L Word* about a group of Los Angeles lesbians. The show's creator and executive producer, Ilene Chaiken, was a longtime friend of hers, but Chaiken claimed there was no truth to the rumor. Hershberger also dismissed the idea, noting that the Shane character was "not successful and she's kind of a wreck," she told the *New York Times*'s Kinetz. "Here's the bottom line: When there's going to be a show, it will be mine."

Sources

New York Post, November 10, 2003, p. 33.
New York Times, March 19, 2000, p. ST 1; September 25, 2005, p. ST1.
Times (London, England), February 7, 2000, p. 36.
W, July 2003, p. 50.

—*Carol Brennan*

J. Edward Hill

Courtesy of American Medical Association

Physician and educator

Born February 2, 1938, in Omaha, NE; married Jean Ware, November, 1963; children: two daughters. *Education:* University of Mississippi, B.S.; M.D., 1964.

Addresses: *Home*—Tupelo, MS. *Office*—American Medical Association, 515 N. State St., Chicago, IL 60610-4325.

Career

Began career as intern at the naval hospital in Charleston, South Carolina, 1964-65; served as General Medical Officer aboard the *USS Frontier* and at the Bremerton Naval Station near Seattle, Washington, 1964-68; private practice in Hammonville, Mississippi, 1968-1995; medical director, Maternal Child Health Program at Mississippi's South Washington County Hospital, 1970-84; president, Mississippi Affiliate of the American Heart Association, 1987-88; president, Mississippi State Medical Association, 1989-90; member, American Medical Association (AMA) Council on Legislation, 1990-99; director, Family Practice Residency Program at the North Mississippi Medical Center, Tupelo, Mississippi, 1995-2001; member, AMA Board of Trustees, 1996; returned to private practice, 2001; chairman, AMA Board of Trustees, 2002-03; president, AMA, 2005—.

Member: American Medical Association; Mississippi State Medical Association; Mississippi Academy of Family Physicians; American Academy of Family Physicians; Southern Medical Association; Ole Miss Alumni Association.

Awards: Runner-up, *Good Housekeeping* Family Doctor of the Year Award, 1977; John B. Howell Award for Mississippi Family Doctor of the Year, 1991; University of Mississippi Alumni Hall of Fame Distinguished Alumni Award, 2002.

Sidelights

In 1968, J. Edward Hill began practicing medicine in the impoverished rural Mississippi Delta, using his family station wagon as an ambulance. During the next quarter of a century, he made a difference in the lives of those rural Mississippians, establishing a maternal child health program that cut the area's soaring fetal mortality rate. Now, as president of the American Medical Association (AMA), Hill has broadened his focus and is hoping to make a difference in the lives of every U.S. citizen. During his tenure as leader of the 250,000-member AMA, the nation's most influential medical organization, Hill hopes to address the issue of uninsured Americans and develop a comprehensive health-education program for the nation's schools.

Hill was born on February 2, 1938, in Omaha, Nebraska, the son of Depression-era parents. When he was four, the family relocated to Vicksburg, Mississippi, where his engineer father worked on Mississippi River projects with the Army Corps of Engineers. Growing up in the South marked Hill in some ways. "It was a very segregated South and I am sure that this evil, aberrant, and wrong social structure had a strong influence on me," Hill told Lynne Jeter of the *Mississippi Medical News.* "However, I had parents that abhorred bigotry, and their influence was significant." In fact, Hill later returned to the South to practice medicine.

In high school, Hill played the flute and piccolo and sang in a quartet. He was student body president and voted Most Likely to Succeed. Influenced by his father, Hill decided to study civil engineering at the University of Mississippi. He changed his plans, however, after several visits home with his roommate, who came from a family of doctors. After earning his undergraduate degree in chemistry, Hill was accepted into the University of Mississippi's medical school. By the early 1960s Hill was in love and wanted to marry Jean Ware, who was studying to be an X-ray technician. He needed money, so he joined the Navy, which helped pay for his tuition and books. He married Ware in 1963 and in 1964 earned his medical degree.

Hill spent the next four years in the U.S. Navy, completing an internship at the naval hospital in Charleston, South Carolina, then serving aboard the Naval destroyer the *USS Frontier* and at the Bremerton Naval Station near Seattle, Washington. At Bremerton, Hill perfected his surgical skills caring for wounded Vietnam soldiers. "Casualties would be flown over the Pole to us, so we got them 36 hours after injury," Hill told CNN.com's Peggy Peck. The heavy, yet disparate, workload prepared Hill for the challenges of providing rural health care.

After being discharged, Hill returned to Mississippi with his wife and two daughters, settling in Hammonville. Hill, along with two medical school classmates, took over the clinic of a retiring doctor and began caring for some of the state's poorest residents. "At that time, the Delta was what I'd describe as third world," Hill told the *Mississippi Business Journal*'s Lynne Jeter, "and we wanted to see if we could make a difference." The clinic, the only one for miles, had to stay open 24 hours a day. The work was grueling. Hill sewed up wounds, delivered babies, set broken bones, performed minor surgery, and also provided routine medical care for mumps, measles, diabetes, and high blood pressure. Hill's partners soon burned out and left.

Hill's passion for medicine was ignited on July 20, 1969, when he was called to check on a local farmer's wife who had, with the help of a farmhand, delivered a baby a few days before and was still bleeding. Hill drove to the ramshackle farmhouse and found the woman in shock. She was too weak to move so Hill drove back to his clinic, typed her blood and returned with two units. That evening when Hill turned on the television and learned that Neil Armstrong had walked on the moon, he felt grief-stricken. "I couldn't sleep that night or for several nights after that," he told CNN.com's Peck, "because I couldn't get over the fact that a woman in Mississippi almost bled to death because she didn't have basic medical care the same day that Neil Armstrong walked on" the moon.

Hill decided to do something. He organized a maternal child health program to provide comprehensive prenatal care and persuaded the county to build a 42-bed hospital for his use, which he staffed with nurse-midwives and nurses aides. For patients, mandatory home health visits lasted two years after birth. Within a few years, the county's fetal mortality rate—once the highest in the nation—dropped to below the national average. This was Hill's "proudest accomplishment," he told Peck.

In 1995, Hill became director of the North Mississippi Medical Center's Family Practice Residency Program. The facility, in Tupelo, was one of the nation's largest rural medical-care centers, serving patients from 22 Mississippi counties and three Alabama counties. Hill stepped down as director in 2001 but remained on the faculty and continued in private practice.

On June 21, 2005, Hill became the AMA's 160th president and has ambitious plans for the organization. He believes the AMA should look past its own advocacy agenda and address public health issues. Specifically, Hill believes the AMA should work to curb issues such as obesity, teen pregnancy, sexually transmitted diseases, and violence, which cost hundreds of millions of dollars in medical expenses. Hill's other concern is the 44 million uninsured Americans. "A lack of insurance coverage in the richest country in the world is a national disgrace," he told Jeter in the *Mississippi Business Journal*. "It's an economic problem, but it's also a public health problem, and I think we need to become champions for those people without coverage."

To remedy this problem, Hill proposes a refundable tax credit to help people afford insurance. He envisions a tax credit available even to those who do not pay income tax. Some people might receive the credit in advance in the form of a voucher that could be used to pay premiums. Before making a final recommendation to Congress, Hill has been discussing the idea with industry leaders.

Another focus of Hill's tenure will be the development of a comprehensive health-education plan for schools to drive down long-term medical costs. "I'm not talking about sex education, I'm talking about health education," Hill told CNN.com. "Education that will help kids make the right choices about everything from diet and exercise to seat belts in cars and helmets for bike riders. That includes making the right decisions about sex, but it is much more than that."

Sources

Periodicals

Executive Speeches, October/November 2005, p. 1.
Mississippi Business Journal, July 12, 2004, p. B12.
Southern Medical Journal, October 1995, p. S2.

Online

"J. Edward Hill, MD," American Medical Association, http://www.ama-assn.org/ama/pub/category/print/1891.html (October 4, 2005).

"Medical Evolution: AMA President-Elect Initially Just Sought Steady Work," CNN.com, http://www.cnn.com/2005/HEALTH/06/14/profile.ama.hill/index.html (November 14, 2005).

"Physician Spotlight: Dr. J. Edward Hill," *Mississippi Medical News*, http://host1.bondware.com/~mississippi/news.php?viewStoryPrinter=219 (November 14, 2005).

—*Lisa Frick*

Philip Seymour Hoffman

Actor

B orn July 23, 1967, in Fairport, NY; companion of Mimi O'Donnell (a costume designer); children: Cooper (with O'Donnell). *Education:* New York University, B.F.A., 1989.

Addresses: *Agent*—Paradigm, 10100 Santa Monica Blvd., 25th Flr., Los Angeles, CA 90067. *Home*—New York, NY.

Career

A ctor in films, including: *Triple Bogey on a Par Five Hole,* 1991; *Szuler,* 1992; *Scent of a Woman,* 1992; *Leap of Faith,* 1992; *My Boyfriend's Back,* 1993; *Sliver,* 1993; *When a Man Loves a Woman,* 1994; *Twister,* 1996; *Hard Eight,* 1996; *Boogie Nights,* 1997; *The Big Lebowski,* 1998; *Happiness,* 1998; *The Talented Mr. Ripley,* 1999; *Magnolia,* 1999; *Flawless,* 1999; *Almost Famous,* 2000; *State and Main,* 2000; *Love Liza,* 2002; *Punch-Drunk Love,* 2002; *25th Hour,* 2002; *Owning Mahowny,* 2003; *Cold Mountain,* 2003; *Along Came Polly,* 2004; *Strangers with Candy,* 2005; *Capote,* 2005; *Mission: Impossible III,* 2006. Television appearances include: *Law & Order,* 1990; *The Yearling,* 1994; *Empire Falls,* 2005. Stage appearances include: *Food and Shelter,* Vineyard 15th Street Theatre, New York City, 1991; *The Merchant of Venice,* Goodman Theatre, Chicago, IL, 1994-95; *Defying Gravity,* American Place Theatre, New York City, 1997-98; *True West,* Circle in the Square Theatre, New York City, 2000; *Long Days Journey into Night,* Broadway production, 2003. Also co-artistic director of the LAByrinth Theater Company, New York City, and director of productions for it, including: *Jesus Hopped the A Train,* 2000; *Our Lady of 121st Street,* 2003.

Frank Micelotta/Getty Images

Awards: Golden Globe award for best performance by a male actor in a film, Hollywood Foreign Press Association, for *Capote,* 2006; Screen Actors Guild award for best performance by a male actor in a film, for *Capote,* 2006; Academy Award for best actor, Academy of Motion Picture Arts and Sciences, for *Capote,* 2006.

Sidelights

A fter spending more than a decade as a character actor best known for his scene-stealing secondary roles, Philip Seymour Hoffman appeared as the lead in *Capote* in 2005. His portrayal of Truman Capote—a gifted but controversial writer as well as one of the few openly gay celebrities in his day— won him critical acclaim as well as an Academy Award for Best Actor. The film chronicled the story behind *In Cold Blood,* a 1966 nonfiction crime thriller that would become Capote's most enduring work. "Hoffman, in his sublime, must-see feat of a performance, plays that famous foppish lilt like a hypnotist's instrument," asserted *Entertainment Weekly* critic Owen Gleiberman, "getting you to forget, in 30 seconds, that you're seeing an impersonation. He makes Capote a mesmerizing raconteur who gets people to trust him by nudging his fragility and genius into the center of every encounter."

Born in 1967, Hoffman grew up near Rochester, New York. His father worked for one of the area's biggest employers, Xerox, and his mother was an attorney and civil rights activist who later became a family-court judge. By his teen years, Hoffman's parents had divorced, and he was a year-round athlete who played football and baseball, and also put his solid, somewhat stocky frame to use on the high-school wrestling team. A neck injury from that sport ended his athletic career. He joined his school's drama club almost entirely by accident, when a young woman whom he liked walked past him in school, and he asked her, "'Where you going?' And she goes, 'I'm going to audition for a play.'" Hoffman recalled in an interview with Steve Kroft for the CBS newsmagazine *60 Minutes.* "And I turned around. And I followed her in.... And then all of a sudden it's not about the crush. All of a sudden you realize you like doing theater."

Hoffman became so involved in his new hobby that he went away to acting camp. At the New York State Summer School of the Arts in 1984, he met two fellow thespians who would become lifelong friends, Dan Futterman and Bennett Miller. Futterman later wrote the *Capote* screenplay, which Miller would direct. All three went on to New York University together, enrolling in its Tisch School of the Arts. After graduating with a B.F.A. in drama, Hoffman began appearing in Off-Broadway plays. He made his television debut in a 1990 episode of *Law & Order* and appeared in his first big-screen role, *Triple Bogey on a Par Five Hole,* a year later.

Hoffman spent the next five years appearing in a slew of movies, but almost always in supporting or minor roles. These include a nasty prep-schooler in *Scent of a Woman,* and as the post-recovery pal Meg Ryan's character befriends in *When a Man Loves a Woman.* His career fortunes began to change around 1996, when he appeared in the big-budget Hollywood action-pic *Twister,* and then in *Hard Eight,* one of the first feature films by writer-director Paul Thomas Anderson.

When Anderson was writing his next project, an epic overview of the Southern California pornography industry set in the 1970s, he wrote a part specifically with Hoffman in mind for it. *Boogie Nights* was one of the most talked-about movies of 1997, and among the sprawling cast several of its smaller roles—Hoffman's as well as those of Heather Graham and Alfred Molina—proved to be terrific, exceptional parts. Hoffman was Scotty, a chubby, tank-top-wearing sound technician for porn films who harbors an unrequited crush on the movie's lead, played by Mark Wahlberg.

A year later, Hoffman earned further kudos for his role as the reclusive obscene-phone-caller Allen in Todd Solondz's *Happiness.* He continued to work with outside-the-Hollywood-mainstream filmmakers like Anderson and Solondz, but also began to win roles in more conventional projects, too. He was the malevolent friend of Jude Law in *The Talented Mr. Ripley,* and was one of the two leads in *Flawless,* a 1999 film directed by Joel Schumacher, known for his big-budget Hollywood films like *A Time To Kill.* In it, Hoffman played Rusty, an oversized drag queen, who befriends and helps his conservative, somewhat rigidly macho neighbor (Robert DeNiro) recover from a stroke through singing lessons. *Flawless* was trounced by critics, but most gave Hoffman high marks for excelling in a somewhat daring job for any actor to tackle.

Hoffman appeared in *Magnolia,* another film from Anderson, and in *Almost Famous,* the 2000 Cameron Crowe period piece about a teenaged rock journalist in the 1970s. Hoffman was cast in a cameo of sorts, as the real-life Lester Bangs, the legendary music writer sometimes credited with coining the term punk rock. In the film, Bangs mentors the younger writer over the phone with his characteristic wry humor. Hoffman displayed his talent for effortlessly segueing between unusual roles that same year when he made his Broadway debut in a revival of Sam Shepard's *True West.* His co-star was John C. Reilly, a fellow actor out of Paul Thomas Anderson's informal ensemble. For the two lead roles of a pair of brothers, the actors actually switched parts every few days to keep things fresh. The production won enthusiastic reviews from critics and even set box-office records at its home, Circle in the Square Theatre.

Hoffman went on to appear in his first big-screen romantic lead role, as the screenwriter in *State and Main,* a David Mamet film, and in his first genuinely starring role in *Love Liza.* The 2002 film was written by Hoffman's brother Gordy, and featured Hoffman as a grief-stricken, gasoline-huffing widower still trying to come to terms with his wife's suicide. Todd McCarthy, reviewing the movie for *Daily Variety,* noted that Hoffman was rather nondescript-looking, but "as he almost always has in his numerous impressive character turns, the actor here displays a live-wire personality that makes him a magnetic figure even when portraying a state of thoroughgoing misery."

Hoffman seemed to gravitate toward characters who were either unlikable or a bit pathetic. He was the underworld mastermind who torments Adam Sandler in *Punch-Drunk Love,* another Anderson film, and then the nebbish English teacher in Spike Lee's *25th Hour,* another 2002 release. He played a compulsive gambler in *Owning Mahowny,* showed up briefly as a disgraced preacher in *Cold Mountain,* and proved his comic chops next to Ben Stiller in *Along Came Polly.* Other pre-*Capote* credits include the HBO mini-series *Empire Falls,* which garnered him an Emmy nomination.

Capote took several years to bring to the screen. Futterman, Hoffman's longtime friend, had written the screenplay in between acting jobs on *Will & Grace* and *Judging Amy,* and Hoffman agreed to star in it and serve as executive producer; the other member of their summer-camp trio, Miller, would direct. It was an impressive task for all—Miller's sole directing job before this had been for a 1998 documentary, and Futterman had no other screenwriting credits. Hoffman's reputation helped them get meetings with studio executives, but even he had his doubts about the project—especially when he began studying footage of Capote, who died in 1984. The Alabama-raised writer was a notoriously flamboyant character, and known for delivering scathing verbal bon mots with a pronounced lisp. Even Hoffman's natural voice was several octaves lower than Capote's, and once he began watching the talk-show clips from the 1960s and '70s, "I thought, 'Oh. My. God. There's no way I'm going to do that,'" he told Richard Corliss in *Time.* "I thought, 'If we never get the money, we'll all be off the hook.'"

Financial backing for the project was forthcoming, however, and the cast spent the summer of 2004 shooting in Winnipeg, Manitoba, a stand-in for the rural Kansas community where Capote researched *In Cold Blood.* By the time Capote showed up in Holcomb, Kansas, in 1959 on assignment for the *New Yorker,* he had enjoyed a decade's worth of New York literary fame. He was drawn to the story of a brutal family slaying that had rocked the quiet farm community, and morbidly fascinated by the two misfits who had been arrested for it. *Capote* chronicles the arduous six-year process it took to write what became *In Cold Blood,* which broke new literary ground as a much-copied merging of nonfiction reporting with a novelist's approach to prose.

Hoffman stayed in character during the entire five-week shoot, which resulted in what critics immediately described as an Oscar-worthy performance. "Hoffman starts with the physical and works inward to the soul," noted David Denby, the *New Yorker's* film critic. "He's only a few years older than Capote was when he went to Kansas, but his thicker features seem to forecast the coarsening of face and body and the spreading spiritual rot that afflicted the writer in the years after the book came out." The *Advocate,* a newsmagazine devoted to gay and lesbian issues, also commended Hoffman for a nuanced portrait of an imperfect human who nevertheless possessed an immense talent. "Capote could easily be portrayed as a vain, silly figure—played for laughs, as gay men, especially 'sissies,' so often are," its reviewer asserted. "But Hoffman exhibits the keen intelligence and seductive empathy that helped this exotic creature win the trust of informants."

Nearly every review had unstinting praise for some aspect of *Capote,* which garnered an Academy Award for Hoffman as well as nominations for Miller and Futterman. Critiquing it in the *New York Times,* A.O. Scott ventured that the process of writing *In Cold Blood* is a large part of the plot, and that in the end the biopic serves as "the story of a writer's vexed, all-consuming relationship with his work, and therefore with himself. This makes for better drama than you might expect. Capote's human connections are, for the most part, secondary and instrumental, which makes Philip Seymour Hoffman's performance all the more remarkable, since he must connect with the audience without piercing the membrane of his character's narcissism."

Even Hoffman's co-star, Catherine Keener as the writer Harper Lee, was nominated for an Oscar for her part. Hoffman tried to distance himself from the media-fueled frenzy of what had become the annual Oscar race. His next film role was a somewhat drastic departure from *Capote,* but *Mission: Impossible III* did return him to the screen with Tom Cruise, his co-star in one of *Magnolia*'s vignettes. When not on location, Hoffman lives in Greenwich Village, and has a toddler son with his partner Mimi O'Donnell, a costume designer. Guarding his privacy, Hoffman rarely talks about his family or his past, but he did reveal a prior drinking and drug problem to Kroft in the *60 Minutes* interview. He still revisits his theater roots occasionally, taking on acting or directing jobs for the LAByrinth Theater Company. "If you can go to the theatre, and you're in a room with a bunch of other people, and what's happening in front of you is not happening. But you actually believe it is. If I can do that, I've done my job," he explained to Kroft. "And that's the thing—that is a drug.... That's something you get addicted to."

Sources

Periodicals

Advocate, October 11, 2005, p. 100.
Daily Variety, January 23, 2002, p. 10.

Entertainment Weekly, October 16, 1998, p. 57; November 19, 1999, p. 62; October 7, 2005, p. 30, p. 49.

Independent (London, England), November 17, 2000, p. 11; May 15, 2002, p. 16.

New Yorker, October 10, 2005, p. 94.

New York Times, March 28, 2000, p. B1; September 27, 2005, p. E1.

Time, October 3, 2005, p. 74.

Online

"Philip Seymour Hoffman Gets Candid," CBSNews. com, http://www.cbsnews.com/stories/2006/ 02/16/60minutes/main1323924.shtml (February 20, 2006).

—Carol Brennan

Joel Hollander

AP Images

Chair and Chief Executive Officer of CBS Radio

Born c. 1956, in New York, NY; married Susan; children: two. *Education:* Earned degree in broadcasting from Indiana State University, c. 1978.

Addresses: *Office*—CBS Radio, 1515 Broadway, New York, NY 10036.

Career

Began career at radio station in Daytona, FL, c. 1978; held advertising-sales positions at several New York City-area radio stations after 1980; WFAN-AM, sales manager, 1987-91, and general manager, 1991-98; chief executive officer, Westwood One, 1998-2003; named president and chief operating officer, Infinity Broadcasting, June, 2003; chair and chief executive officer, January, 2005— (renamed CBS Radio, December, 2005).

Sidelights

Joel Hollander has spent his entire career in radio, and in 2005 reached the pinnacle of the profession when he was named chief executive officer and board chair of Infinity Broadcasting. He succeeded the legendary Mel Karmazin, who had built Infinity into a powerhouse with 180 stations, many of which dominate their local markets in ratings and advertising revenue. Later in 2005, in a nod to some corporate reshuffling, Hollander's company became CBS Radio.

Born in the mid-1950s, Hollander grew up in the New York City borough of the Bronx, the son of a formalwear store manager. He planned to study

sports medicine when he enrolled at Indiana State University, but switched to broadcasting. His roommate, future Olympic gymnast Kurt Thomas, knew someone at a radio station in Daytona, Florida, and that became Hollander's first post-college job. At the station, he produced shows, wrote copy, and even sold ads. "It was small, so I learned how to do everything," Hollander recalled in an interview with Robin Kamen for *Crain's New York Business.*

Hollander excelled in advertising sales, and worked for several New York City-area stations after returning to his hometown in 1980. In 1987, he joined a turnaround team at Emmis Broadcasting, which was in the process of changing over a Queens-based country music station to a 24-hour-a-day all-sports format. The concept was a new one at the time, and industry analysts were initially wary, but WFAN-AM emerged as a terrific success after it went on the air in August of 1987. Within a few years, its all-sports format was being replicated in other radio markets across the United States.

Hollander served as sales manager of WFAN, and when the station was sold to Karmazin's Infinity Broadcasting in 1991, he was made its general manager. Just over a decade after going on the air, WFAN was grossing $55 million annually, which made it the most successful radio property in the United States. In 1998, Karmazin promoted Hollander once again, this time to become chief executive of Westwood One, which was part of the CBS Radio group. (CBS Radio and Infinity Broadcasting merged in 1997, and operated under the Infinity name until 2005). Westwood One was a company that provided programming, such as college football games and nationally syndicated talk-show programs, to radio stations around the country.

Westwood One was not doing very well at the time, but Hollander managed to turn it into a major industry force in just a few short years. He helped develop programs for political pundits Bill O'Reilly and Laura Ingraham, oversaw the acquisition of Metro Networks, and increased its automated music format services, which beam content to stations via satellite. Karmazin, impressed once again by Hollander's talents, elevated him to president and chief operating officer of Infinity Broadcasting in June of 2003.

Infinity was the second-largest radio group in the United States when Hollander came on board. Its biggest revenue stream came from controversial "shock jock" Howard Stern, whose show went out in syndication to 27 stations across the United States. Stern and his vulgar jokes, industry analysts theorized, brought in an estimated $100 million a year in ad revenues for Infinity. But in the fall of 2004, Stern announced he was leaving terrestrial radio when his current contract expired, and was signing with Sirius Satellite Radio. The move—by one of the highest paid radio personalities in the country—was considered a turning point for satellite radio and, some said, the beginning of the end for terrestrial radio.

Hollander became responsible for dispelling those concerns when he became chair and chief executive officer of Infinity in January of 2005. The company was still on solid ground, he told *Forbes.com* writer Dorothy Pomerantz at the end of the year, not long after Stern's last day with Infinity. "When you're replacing someone who's been on the air for 20 years, it takes some time," he explained. "Will it take 24 months? I don't think so. We live in a society where people want quick answers, whether it's Wall Street or sports or politics. You have to be patient."

Stern's defection was only one part of the problem at Infinity, however. Over the past five years, radio had undergone a period of major consolidation. Nearly every station was owned by one of the big players, such as Infinity or its nearest rival, Clear Channel, and while radio had grown into a $21 billion-a-year industry and pleased Wall Street investors with its enormous profit margins, listeners were straying. Music formats had become too homogenized, some asserted, and the reliance on automated formats meant that many stations lost their local identity.

Hollander's solution to keep listeners from jumping to satellite radio was a multi-pronged approach. He introduced a new format in several top markets, which featured a much more extensive musical playlist, and okayed the development of Visual Radio, which could send content to cell-phone users. The company, which jettisoned the "Infinity" moniker and reverted back to CBS Radio name in December of 2005, also made radio history by launching the first podcasting radio station in the country. Listeners of KYOURadio in San Francisco can submit their own podcasts for broadcast. The term refers to individually created playlists of multimedia files, which can be played back over a computer or downloaded into mobile devices.

Hollander was also bullish on the possibilities promised by high-definition radio, which would gave broadcasters additional bandwidth for extra, specially targeted programming. "If you build the content and it's good, people listen," he told Phil Rosenthal in the *Chicago Tribune* about his company's commitment to the millions of remaining terrestrial radio listeners. "It's like *Field of Dreams*, if you build it and it's good, they come. If you build it and it's not good, they don't come."

Hollander is married and has two children. He and wife Susan's four-month-old daughter, Carly Jenna, died of sudden infant death syndrome (SIDS) in 1993. The Hollanders established the CJ Foundation for SIDS in her honor, which raises awareness of SIDS, which is sometimes called crib death. The Foundation holds an annual radiothon, hosted by Hollander's longtime radio colleague Don Imus, and provides grants for SIDS researchers.

Sources

Periodicals

Chicago Tribune, October 19, 2005.
Crain's New York Business, November 30, 1998, p. 19.
MediaWeek, May 2, 2005, p. 22.
New York Times, May 16, 2003, p. C4.
Time, March 13, 2006, p. A6.

Online

"No Stern? No Problem," *Forbes.com*, http://www.
forbes.com/business/forbes/2005/1212/058.
html (April 23, 2006).

—*Carol Brennan*

Chad Holliday

Mike Fuentes/Bloomberg News/Landov

Chair and Chief Executive Officer of DuPont

Born Charles O. Holliday, Jr., in 1948, in Nashville, TN; married; children: two sons. *Education:* Earned degree in industrial engineering from the University of Tennessee, 1970.

Addresses: *Office*—DuPont, 1007 Market St., Wilmington, DE 19898.

Career

Began career with DuPont as a summer intern, then hired as an engineer at a plastics factory in Old Hickory, TN, 1970; business analyst in the fibers division after 1974; held various manufacturing management positions until 1984; became a corporate plans manager, 1984; global business director for Nomex, 1986, and Kevlar, 1987; director of marketing for the pigments and chemicals division, 1988-90; began as vice president, became president, for DuPont's Asia Pacific operations, 1990-97; named company director, 1997; chief executive officer, 1998—; chair, 1999—.

Sidelights

As chief executive officer of DuPont since 1998, Chad Holliday has taken on a tough challenge: to steer the immense, global chemical manufacturer away from its reliance on nonrenewable source materials. The number-three chemical company in the United States, DuPont makes everything from Stainmaster carpet protection to Kevlar bulletproof vests, and many of the company's most successful patents

have been based on petroleum derivatives. Holliday has renewed the company's commitment to innovation, but told research chemists to focus on coming up with products made from plants instead. "We're a science company, we always have been," *Forbes* writer Chana R. Schoenberger quoted him as saying.

Born in 1948 in Nashville, Tennessee, Holliday captained the football team at Overton High School and planned to start his career with the industrial equipment distribution company his father owned once he finished college. Though his high school guidance counselor discouraged his plan to earn an industrial engineering degree at the University of Tennessee (UT), he went ahead anyway, but his father wound up selling the company a few months before he graduated. His first contact with DuPont came during one of his summers off from college, when he landed a short-term internship. When he graduated from UT in 1970, he was hired full-time as an engineer at DuPont's Old Hickory, Tennessee, plastics factory.

The plant was one of dozens around the world that bore the DuPont name. The company had been founded in Delaware back in 1802 as a gunpowder mill, and branched out during the late nineteenth and early twentieth centuries as manufacturer of an array of industrial chemicals. In 1930, chemists at the company made the breakthrough that resulted in nylon, and a few years later discovered Teflon, the most slippery substance known to exist. Over the next several decades, DuPont trademarked an array of synthetic fibers, including Lycra, Spandex, Tyvek, and Kevlar, that were used in hundreds of consumer products and industrial applications.

In 1974, Holliday moved over to DuPont's fibers division as a business analyst, and for the next few years held a series of managerial jobs inside the division's manufacturing plants. He became a corporate plans manager in 1984, and then global business director for its fire-retardant Nomex products in 1986. After holding the same title with DuPont's Kevlar division, in 1988 Holliday was promoted to director of marketing for the pigments and chemicals division. He spent the better part of the 1990s as a vice president and then president of Dupont's Asia Pacific operations, an experience he has said forced him to reevaluate the American versus the Asian approach to doing business on a global scale.

Named a company director in 1997, Holliday was chosen as DuPont's newest chief executive officer in 1998, and elevated to board chair a year later. His advance came at a tough time for the company, as it struggled to remain a world market leader. DuPont was once a blue-chip stock to own, but it had consistently failed to meet its own earnings expectations, and Wall Street analysts downgraded its rating. Holliday believed that the company needed to branch out into biotechnology in order to improve the bottom line. It sold off Conoco, an oil and gas company it owned, and then paid more than $7 billion for a biotech seed property; a few years later, when the plant company's promise failed to pan out, DuPont was forced to write off half that amount, which made investors irate. It also bought Pharma, a drug manufacturer, and hoped to build it into an industry leader, but Holliday was forced to make the decision to sell that, too, in 2001.

After a company reorganization in 2002, Holliday approved increased funding for new research efforts. Chemists at its famed Experimental Station began looking into new plant-based, not petroleum-based, formulations with consumer potential. One of these was a new fiber, Sorona, made from corn. In 2006, DuPont opened a much-heralded new manufacturing plant in Tennessee that would produce carpet fiber made from Sorona. Holliday also set a company goal: by 2010, 25 percent of DuPont products would be made from non-petrochemical sources. This goal commits the company to a future based on carbohydrates, which grow and are renewable, not hydrocarbons, which must be extracted from the Earth and are a finite resource. Engineers at the "Ex" Station, as it is known, are also working to improve fuel-cell technology and make thinner, brighter flat-panel displays for cell phones and other consumer electronics.

Some of Holliday's vision is less idealistic than simply practical—oil prices have fluctuated wildly since the start of the twenty-first century, and less reliance on oil means more easily controllable manufacturing costs. "Ten years ago it didn't seem logical to go after insect-resistant crops, either," he told Claudia H. Deutsch in the New York Times in 2006. "We're not betting the company on bio-based materials, but we do think they have the potential to have the same impact on us that long-chain polymers [the chemical compound that gave DuPont its breakthrough in nylon in the 1930s] once did."

Holliday is the co-author of Walking the Talk: The Business Case for Sustainable Development, which was published in 2002. He has also served a stint as chair of the World Business Council for Sustainable Development. Married with two sons, he is reportedly at his desk by 6:30 every morning, and is known to answer his own phone. Overseeing a company that posted 2005 revenues of $26.6 billion, and has some 60,000 employees around the world, is only one part of the challenges he faces daily. DuPont's future as the No. 3 chemical producer in the United States, behind Dow and ExxonMobil, is at stake for him. "The country has to protect its ability to innovate and grow," he told Time's Eric Roston. "If the U.S. doesn't get its act together, DuPont is going to go to the countries that do… And although we'd much rather be here—we're based here, it's our home—we have an obligation to our employees and shareholders to bring value where we can."

Selected writings

Walking the Talk: The Business Case for Sustainable Development, Berrett-Koehler Publishers, 2002.

Sources

Periodicals

Forbes, February 3, 2003, pp. 54-60.
Journal of Corporate Citizenship, Winter 2002, p. 123.
New York Times, February 28, 2006, p. C1.
Time, December 19, 2005, p. A34.

Online

"DuPont CEO Chad Holliday, Jr. Speaks to Overton Seniors," John Overton High School, http://www.overtonhighschool.com/content.asp?CID=88809 (April 24, 2006).

—Carol Brennan

Alan Hollinghurst

© Colin McPherson/Corbis

Author

Born May 26, 1954, in Stroud, Gloucestershire, England. *Education:* Magdalen College, Oxford University, B.A., 1975, M.Litt. 1979.

Addresses: *Office*—c/o Bloomsbury USA, 175 Fifth Ave., Ste. 300, New York, NY 10010.

Career

Lecturer in English at Magdalen College, 1977-78, Somerville College, 1979-80, and Corpus Christi College, 1981, all Oxford University; lecturer in English, University of London, 1982; *Times Literary Supplement,* assistant editor, 1982-90, poetry editor, 1990-95; visiting professor of writing, Princeton University, fall 2004. Author, c. 1970—.

Awards: Newdigate Prize for English Verse, Oxford University, 1975; Man Booker Prize for Fiction for *The Line of Beauty,* 2004.

Sidelights

British novelist Alan Hollinghurst won the prestigious Man Booker Prize for Fiction in 2004 for his fourth novel, *The Line of Beauty.* Called the first piece of gay fiction ever to win the honor, the story was also "a sprawling and haunting elegy to the 1980s," wrote *Entertainment Weekly* critic Jennifer Reese. Hollinghurst started his writing career as a poet, but once he began writing fiction his carefully crafted prose earned scores of exceptional reviews, despite the occasional lurid passage describing a sexual encounter. Most literary critics deemed his mastery of the English language—not the plot pacing or characters—the real star of his fiction. "Part of the pleasure of Hollinghurst's writing," remarked the London *Observer*'s Geraldine Bedell, "lies in the tension between the impeccably modulated prose and the pleasurably filthy things people get up to."

Born in 1954, Hollinghurst grew up an only child in the Cirencester area of south-central England, near the picturesque Cotswold Hills. His father was a bank manager who passed on his devotion to classical music to his son. After earning his degree from Magdalen College at Oxford University in 1975, Hollinghurst went on to graduate work there, and was granted an advanced degree in literature four years later. During his undergraduate career, he won the prestigious Newdigate Prize for poetry, an Oxford honor dating back to 1806 and one whose past winners have included Oscar Wilde and John Ruskin. His first career posts came at Oxford as well, first as a lecturer in English at Magdalen College; he later taught at Somerville and Corpus Christi colleges as well. He moved to London in the early 1980s to take a job as a lecturer in English at the University of London, but was soon hired by the eminent *Times Literary Supplement* as an assistant editor.

While reviewing dozens of titles for the *Times Literary Supplement,* Hollinghurst continued to write verse on the side, and a collection of verse, *Confidential Chats with Boys,* appeared in 1982. When he landed a contract with the Faber publishing house in 1985 for another book of verse, however, he began to suffer from writer's block, and turned to fiction instead. A friend from his Oxford days, Andrew Motion—the future Poet Laureate of Britain—was then serving as the editorial director at Chatto & Windus, another esteemed London publishing house, and bought Hollinghurst's first novel.

That debut, *The Swimming-Pool Library,* caused a stir when it appeared in 1988, partly due to its frank sexual content. Set in London during the summer of 1983, the story centered around 25-year-old Will Beckwith, an aspiring writer who is also struggling with his sexual orientation. Though financially supported by a wealthy grandfather, Beckwith takes a ghostwriting job for a much-older gay man, Lord Charles Nantwich, to pen his memoirs. Will is stunned to learn that his retired grandfather, who had been a well-known public prosecutor, once had Nantwich arrested on spurious charges of what was then called "male vice," in a long-ago era when homosexual acts were subject to criminal prosecution. Yet in Beckwith's own time, gay men are still the target of some harassment, as he realizes when a friend is arrested on similar charges.

The Swimming-Pool Library was set in the early 1980s, just before acquired-immune deficiency syndrome (AIDS) began to sweep through the gay community. A hedonist atmosphere threads through the novel, as Will delves further into London's secretive gay male subculture, but so too does a countervailing influence: that of Thatcherism, the catchword for a new political era led by Britain's first female prime minister, Margaret Thatcher. Elected in 1979, Thatcher and her Conservative Party colleagues ushered in an era of dramatic change in Britain. With tax cuts and policies that favored entrepreneurship at the expense of the working poor, Thatcher's policies roiled Britain, but also helped create a new middle class. *The Swimming-Pool Library* ends with her Conservative Party's 1983 landslide re-election.

Reviews for Hollinghurst's debut novel were enthusiastic, with Edmund White of the *Sunday Times* commending Hollinghurst's style, calling it "writing [that] is enviably supple and sonorously scored. This is not experimental writing. It is, on the contrary, classic English prose—capacious, sociable, extraordinarily efficient." White also asserted it was "surely the best book about gay life yet written by

an English author. How exhilarating to have such a summery book appear during this winter of deepest discontent." White may have been alluding to Clause 28, a controversial anti-gay amendment of the 1988 Local Government Act. Its wording prohibited government funding for any community program or initiative that was deemed to intentionally promote same-sex relationships. As Hollinghurst told Charles Kaiser of the *Advocate* many years later, *The Swimming-Pool Library* "was held up as an example of the kind of book that you might no longer be able to buy for a public library" because of Clause 28, which ultimately proved unenforceable.

Several years passed before Hollinghurst produced his second novel. In the interim, he served as the poetry editor at the *Times Literary Supplement.* Finally, in 1994 Chatto & Windus issued *A Folding Star.* Again, it featured a gay male protagonist who is somewhat conflicted about his sexual identity. Edward Manners seems to have a drinking problem and a penchant for furtive, anonymous sex in semi-public facilities, both of which he brings with him to Belgium when he takes a job as a teacher of English as a second language.

Edward has already fallen in love with one of his teenage students, Luc, from a photograph he was sent previously, and his crush is the focus of *A Folding Star*'s story; a secondary plotline concerns the restoration of a well-known work of art by the father of another one of Edward's pupils. The novel is set in the latter half of the 1980s, and this time the specter of AIDS appears in full—Edward returns to England briefly for a funeral, and at other points mentions certain pharmaceutical drugs that stave off the disease's progress. The *Sunday Times*'s reviewer, Lucy Hughes-Hallett, found Hollinghurst's second novel somewhat weakly plotted, but noted that "the strength of this novel lies not in its events but in the narrative that contains them. Hollinghurst is agile enough to be able to write equally vividly about the gradations of colour in a cloudy sky and about the feel of someone else's tongue in one's mouth."

A Folding Star was shortlisted for the 1994 Man Booker Prize, but two of the judges—a panel of four men and a female rabbi—were reportedly uneasy with the frankly chronicled sex scenes in Hollinghurst's story. The Booker Prize, as it is more commonly known, is considered one of the world's most prestigious literary honors, and has been awarded annually since 1968 to the best English-language novel written by a writer from one of the British Commonwealth countries or the Republic of Ireland, South Africa, or Pakistan. Past winners have included V.S. Naipaul, Iris Murdoch, Salman Rushdie, Michael Ondaatje, Ian McEwan, and Margaret Atwood.

In 1995, Hollinghurst was finally able to devote himself full time to writing after he left the *Times Literary Supplement*. He next produced *The Spell* in 1998, which was shortlisted for another leading British honor, the *Guardian* fiction prize. This time, Hollinghurst introduces a quartet of gay men, led by Alex, an opera-loving civil servant nearing middle age who heads to the countryside for a weekend vacation with his former lover, Justin. But Alex falls for Danny, the 22-year-old son of Justin's new partner. Back in London, Alex falls into a club-hopping, drug-ingesting nightlife habit with Danny as his guide. Critiquing *The Spell* for the *Independent Sunday*, Mark Bostridge made reference to the title in his assertion that "the spell cast by the countryside during one long hot summer, and Hollinghurst's evocation of it, has produced some of his most exquisite, elegant and deeply felt prose. But at the same time he manages to hold in the balance the humour of the situations in which his characters find themselves, and the pain and miserable vulnerability of their emotional predicaments."

Hollinghurst writes less than 500 words a day, and so six years passed before he produced his fourth novel, *The Line of Beauty*, which won the Booker Prize for 2004. In a way, the story picks up where Hollinghurst's debut concluded, at the 1983 reelection of Margaret Thatcher, and the prime minister is mentioned frequently in the text. Often referred to as the "PM" or simply "the Lady," Thatcher even makes a cameo appearance in the story. This time, the drama centers around Nick Guest, a proverbial fish out of water who takes up residence at the posh home of a friend from his Oxford college days, Toby Fedden, with whom he is secretly in love. The son of an antiques dealer, Nick is dazzled by the Fedden household in the ritzy London area of Notting Hill. Toby's father, Gerald, has just been elected to the House of Commons as part of the 1983 Conservative (Tory) Party landslide.

In London, Nick finally begins experimenting with same-sex partners after he places a personal ad. His first lover is a working-class black man, a civil servant, and the experience transforms him. The next section of the narrative shifts to 1986, with Nick now conducting a furtive, cocaine-fueled romance with the son of a Lebanese supermarket millionaire. Other characters include Toby's mentally unstable sister, Catherine, and the Fedden mother, Rachel, "a marvelously nuanced portrait of velvety graciousness lined with steel," remarked Anthony Quinn in the *New York Times Book Review*. Quinn commended Hollinghurst for creating female characters that were more fully drawn than in his earlier works.

Thatcher's cameo comes during the Feddens' wedding-anniversary soiree whose preparations including painting the front-entrance door exactly the right shade of Tory blue. During the party, Nick stuns the worshipful Conservative acolytes surrounding the prime minister by asking her to dance. After their spin, he then steals away with Wani, his playboy boyfriend, for three-way sex in the bathroom with a member of the catering staff. Wani starts bleeding from the nose, and the plot shifts precipitously at this point. Nick learns that Leo, his first lover, is ill with AIDS, and then Wani succumbs, too. The final third of the story is anchored by the stock market crash in October of 1987, and the Feddens' fortunes begin a rapid decline when Gerald becomes embroiled in a politically disastrous scandal. It is in this final section, noted *New York Times* book reviewer Michiko Kakutani, that "Hollinghurst seems to really find his voice, exchanging the detached, faintly satiric tone of the earlier parts of the book for a more earnest, heartfelt one. In these final pages, as shadows of illness, loss, and scandal begin to fall over the characters' lives, *The Line of Beauty* becomes more than a well-observed portrait of a decade; it becomes an affecting work of art."

Hollinghurst's Booker Prize win in October of 2004 was an honor as well as a lucrative gift to any writer, with its $89,000 prize purse, but the British press did seem eager to point out that it was the first win by a "gay" novel. Some of the less reputable tabloids ran titillating headlines the next day that included "Man's Gay Day" and "Top Man!" Other newspaper reports noted that the head of the judging panel was Chris Smith, the first openly gay man ever elected to Britain's House of Commons. Hollinghurst was relatively untroubled by the tag, as he told Stephen Moss in a *Guardian* interview. "I only chafe at the 'gay writer' tag if it's thought to be what is most or only interesting about what I'm writing," he asserted. "I want it to be part of the foundation of the books, which are actually about all sorts of other things as well—history, class, culture. There's all sorts of stuff going on. It's not just, as you would think if you read the headlines in the newspapers, about gay sex."

Selected writings

Confidential Chats with Boys (poetry), Sycamore Press (Oxford, England), 1982.

The Swimming-Pool Library (novel), Chatto & Windus (London, England), 1988; Vintage (New York City), 1989.

A Folding Star (novel), Chatto & Windus, 1994; Pantheon (New York City), 1994.

The Spell (novel), Chatto & Windus, 1998; Viking (New York City), 1999.

The Line of Beauty (novel), Bloomsbury, 2004.

Sources

Books

Contemporary Novelists, seventh ed., St. James Press, 2001.

Periodicals

Advocate, December 7, 2004, p. 73; January 18, 2005, p. 72.
Bookseller, February 13, 2004, p. 30.
Entertainment Weekly, October 22, 2004, p. 98.

Guardian (London, England), June 22, 1998; October 21, 2004, p. 8; October 25, 2004, p. 16, p. 18.
Independent (London, England), April 16, 2004, p. 23.
Independent Sunday (London, England), July 5, 1998, p. 28.
New Statesman, June 10, 1994, p. 37; April 12, 2004, p. 54.
New York Observer, December 13, 2004, p. 1.
New York Times, November 23, 2004, p. E1.
New York Times Book Review, October 31, 2004, p. 19.
Observer (London, England), October 17, 2004, p. 27.
Publishers Weekly, March 8, 1999, p. 48.
Sunday Times (London, England), February 21, 1988; May 22, 1994, p. 13.

—*Carol Brennan*

Felicity Huffman

WENN/Landov

Actress

Born December 9, 1962, in Bedford, NY; married William H. Macy (an actor, writer, and producer), September 6, 1997; children: Sofia Grace, Georgia Grace. *Education:* Attended Royal Academy of Drama Arts, London, England; New York University, Tisch School of the Arts, B.F.A., 1988.

Addresses: *Office*—c/o Desperate Housewives, American Broadcasting Co. (ABC), Inc., 500 S. Buena Vista St., Burbank, CA 91521.

Career

Actress on stage, including: *Boys' Life,* 1988; *Speed-the-Plow,* 1988. Television appearances include: *A Home Run for Love,* 1978; *Lip Service,* 1988; *Golden Years* (movie), 1991; *The Water Engine* (movie), 1992; *Quicksand: No Escape* (movie), 1992; *The X Files,* 1993; *The Heart of Justice* (movie), 1993; *Law & Order,* 1997; *The Underworld* (movie), 1997; *Sports Night,* 1998-2000; *A Slight Case of Murder* (movie), 1999; *Snap Decision* (movie), 2001; *Path to War* (movie), 2002; *Out of Order* (miniseries), 2003; *Frasier,* 2003; *Reversible Errors* (movie), 2004; *Desperate Housewives,* 2004—. Film appearances include: *Things Change,* 1988; *Reversal of Fortune,* 1990; *Hackers,* 1995; *The Spanish Prisoner,* 1997; *Magnolia,* 1999; *House Hunting,* 2003; *Raising Helen,* 2004; *Christmas with the Kranks,* 2004; *Transamerica,* 2005; *Choose Your Own Adventure: The Abominable Snowman,* 2005.

Awards: Emmy Award for best lead actress (comedy), National Academy of Television Arts and Sciences, for *Desperate Housewives,* 2005; Golden Globe Award for best actress in a leading role—drama, Hollywood Foreign Press Association, for *Transamerica,* 2006.

Sidelights

Veteran actor Felicity Huffman toiled on the sidelines for nearly two decades before winning a highly coveted Emmy Award in 2005 for *Desperate Housewives,* one of the top-rated television series of the 2004-05 season. Lynette Scavo, Huffman's character, is a stay-at-home mother consistently overwhelmed by her duties as cook, chauffeur, housekeeper, and general supervisor of a six-member household. "People pay lip service to stay-at-home moms, but it's not really respected," Huffman told *Newsweek* writers Marc Peyser and David J. Jefferson in a cover story about the *Desperate Housewives* phenomenon. "You say you're a stay-at-home mom and you can see the life force drain out of people. They're already bored with you."

Huffman was born in 1962 in New York state, but grew up in Woody Creek, Colorado. Her childhood nickname was "Flicka," after a popular horse movie from 1943, *My Friend Flicka;* the word was also Swedish for "girl." She was the last of eight children, and one of seven daughters. Though she grew up in a traditional and somewhat strict Roman Catholic family, she later recalled that as the youngest child she often got a pass on the rules. "My sisters broke my mother in," she told *Atlanta Journal-Constitution* writer Frazier Moore. "By the time I came along, it was like, 'What time will you be home? Oh, never mind.'"

Huffman's interest in acting was spurred by a movie-theater outing to see Italian director Franco Zeffirelli's 1968 film adaptation of *Romeo and Juliet*, which won several industry honors that year, including the Academy Award for cinematography. "I was way too young, and I had my eyes covered part of the time," Huffman recalled in an interview with the *Houston Chronicle*'s Luaine Lee. "One of my sisters sat behind me and covered my eyes at particular ardent points. I just fell in love with that story: 'Oh, I want to act, I want to act.'"

Thankfully, Huffman's family was supportive of her ambition, and she went off to acting camp every summer, and for high school even attended the Interlochen Arts Academy in northern Michigan, a boarding school whose alumni have included Tom Hulce (*Amadeus*) and the pop singer Jewel. During this time she also made her television debut, as Flicka Huffman, in a 1978 television movie called *A Home Run for Love*. "I didn't know what I was doing," Huffman confessed to Jenelle Riley in *Back Stage West*. "The first shot I was shaking so hard they had to keep stopping. I can't remember what it was about, even."

After graduating from Interlochen in 1981, Huffman studied at London's Royal Academy of Drama Arts and began a lengthy stint at New York University's Tisch School of the Arts. Though she did not earn her drama degree until 1988, she was active in the New York City theater scene, and by 1984 was working with the Atlantic Theater Company, which grew out of some workshops that Pulitzer Prize-winning playwright David Mamet had started with members of the NYU drama program. It was there that Huffman met her future husband, the Atlantic company's co-founder, William H. Macy.

The same year that Huffman earned her NYU degree, she made her Broadway debut in a highly publicized production of a new play from Mamet, *Speed-the-Plow*. Huffman replaced one of the original three leads, pop singer Madonna. Despite such an auspicious start, Huffman had a difficult time finding and even keeping work. "Basically, I got fired off of the play *Jake's Women*," she recounted to Moore in the *Atlanta Journal-Constitution*, referring to a notorious 1990 flop by playwright Neil Simon. "And then I did an ABC pilot with Ed Asner that was going to be a big deal and was called *Thunder Alley*, and I got fired from that." She had a brief role in the 1990 movie *Reversal of Fortune*, about the Claus von Bulow murder case, and was cast in a first-season episode of *The X Files*. She also appeared in a few made-for-television movies, including Stephen King's *Golden Years* and *Quicksand: No Escape*.

Huffman did not begin dating Macy until 1994, about ten years after they first met, when they reconnected at a London funeral of a mutual friend. They wed in 1997, and a few months after the wedding she appeared in the Mamet film *The Spanish Prisoner*. By then she had left New York City to be with Macy in Los Angeles, where his career was boosted by impressive performances in *Fargo* and *Boogie Nights*. Huffman, however, was ready to move on. "I decided to give up and go to Marinello School of Beauty. I actually got an application," she told *Entertainment Weekly*, but her career in cosmetology was thwarted when she was cast in *Sports Night*, a new series on ABC created by Aaron Sorkin of *West Wing* fame. Huffman won one of the leads, Dana Whitaker, a television producer at an ESPN-like cable network that served as *Sports Night*'s fictional setting.

Critics loved *Sports Night*, with Ray Richmond in *Variety* calling it "the most entertaining new comedy in primetime this fall"; Richmond also complimented a cast that included "a scene-stealing turn from Felicity Huffman, who has the look of a breakout star." *Entertainment Weekly* delivered a similarly laudatory tribute, asserting that "the series' strength is its speed-racer pace.... Characters tear through rooms spitting out staccato bursts of dialogue at each other. This machine-gun banter is expertly handled by the crack ensemble, especially Felicity Huffman (a veteran of David Mamet's verbal wars) as an interference-running producer."

Sports Night lasted just two seasons before the network cancelled it. Huffman took some time off, after the births of each of her daughters (Sofia in 2000, and Georgia in 2002), but landed an interesting, five-part miniseries for Showtime that aired in mid-2003 and allowed her to work with her husband once again. In *Out of Order*, she and Eric Stoltz were cast as moderately affluent Hollywood power-couple Lorna and Mark. Their future in screenwriting, however, appears to be succumbing to Lorna's depression; she behaves erratically, and Mark begins having an affair. Macy had a supporting role as one of their friends, an out-of-work producer. "Huffman's performance captures Lorna's agony and terror, her fear that she's 'going to fall into a black hole and never come out,'" noted the *New Yorker*'s television critic Nancy Franklin, "and also the aspects of depression that can be so frustrating for those outside it—the unreliability and the excuses that make it hard to tell whether the sufferer is dying inside or getting away with murder."

Later in 2003, Huffman had a recurring role as a Suze-Orman-styled financial expert at *Frasier*'s radio station on the NBC sitcom, and the following year had a supporting role in *Raising Helen*, the Kate Hudson comedy. Few expected her next job to become the breakout success of ABC's 2004 fall line-up that it did, but *Desperate Housewives* began pulling in viewers from its debut, and the numbers grew exponentially as the Monday-morning buzz surrounding it and critical acclaim increased; midway through the first season, 25 million viewers were tuning in every Sunday night. The pilot episode had been rejected by NBC, CBS, Fox, HBO, Showtime and even Lifetime, and the hourlong drama/comedy, noted Peyser and Jefferson in *Newsweek*, "is what network television isn't supposed to be. It's a soap opera in an era when procedural shows like *CSI* and its clones rule. It's on ABC, a network that hasn't launched a hit show since the fall of the Berlin wall. (That's only a slight exaggeration.)"

Huffman was cast as Lynette Scavo, one of a quartet of housewives on *Desperate Housewives*' Wisteria Lane. The campy drama revolved around several subplots, but was loosely tied together over the mystery surrounding the death of a fifth housewife, Mary Alice, who provides a narrative voice-over. Huffman's Lynette is a former high-powered corporate executive who had four children, including a set of twins, in six years, and quit her job to become a stay-at-home mom. The new workload is far worse than anything she ever encountered in the business world, and Lynette struggles to maintain her sanity. Compounding her dilemma are her exceedingly rambunctious twin boys, and her secret addiction to their attention-deficit-disorder medication.

On Wisteria Lane, Lynette's similarly desperate neighbors include Susan (Teri Hatcher), a divorced single mother; Marcia Cross as Bree, a perfectionist housewife; and risk-taking Gabrielle (Eva Longoria), who is having a torrid affair with the high-school student who mows the lawn. Edie, the local real-estate agent played by Nicollette Sheridan, rounds out the cast as Wisteria Lane's resident busybody. Writing about the series' success in the *New York Times*, Virginia Heffernan compared it to short stories of mid-century American fiction writer John Cheever, which gleefully punctured the facade of middle-class suburban life. "Much of what makes suburbia function in Cheever's stories are the lawns, fences, driveways, and other visible means of separating one life from another," wrote Heffernan. "On Wisteria Lane, where the desperate housewives live, inhabitants keep hedges high, cultivating—in contrast to other shows about girlfriends—great ignorance about one another."

By turns dramatic and comic, *Desperate Housewives* seemed to strike a nerve with viewers, and it was one of the top-rated shows of the 2004-05 season, even inspiring its own hour on Oprah Winfrey's show with real-life counterparts for the characters. "There's more than a kernel of truth in all of them, and I think that's part of the show's success," Huffman reflected in an interview with Bari Nan Cohen for *Redbook*. As a working actor who once hoped to have several children, Huffman could relate to Lynette's predicament and perpetually frazzled nerves. Prior to becoming a mother, she told Cohen, "no one ever pulled me aside and told me—and I'm not saying this is everyone's experience, at all—'It can be really hard, you can lose your mind.'"

As the debut of its second season neared, Huffman took home an Emmy Award for Outstanding Lead Actress in a Comedy Series, beating out fellow cast members Cross and Hatcher in the category. The shooting schedule for *Desperate Housewives* allowed Huffman to take on other projects, such as the feature film *Transamerica*, which opened in theaters in December of 2005. Produced by Macy, the story revolved around the sex-change operation Huffman's character undergoes. In 2006, Huffman won a Golden Globe for her role in that film. She also appeared in *Choose Your Own Adventure: The Abominable Snowman*, a unique interactive movie that once more gave her a chance to work with her husband.

Another family member of Huffman's is still her biggest fan. Her mother, she told Lee in the *Houston Chronicle*, comes to see "every one of my plays. She's now 80.... And she actually comes to previews and helps me out. She's got a really good eye."

Sources

Atlanta Journal-Constitution, March 9, 1999, p. E4.
Back Stage West, November 28, 2002, p. 1.
Entertainment Weekly, October 2, 1998, p. 58; July 25, 2003, p. 19; June 24/July 1, 2005, p. 46.
Houston Chronicle, May 28, 2003, p. 6.
Newsweek, November 29, 2004, p. 48.

Newsweek International, January 17, 2005, p. 50.
New Yorker, June 16, 2003, p. 198.
New York Times, March 1, 1988; November 28, 2004.
People, May 16, 2005, p. 32.

Redbook, May 2005, p. 110.
Variety, September 21, 1998, p. 44.

—*Carol Brennan*

Bob Iger

Chief Executive Officer of the Walt Disney Company

Born Robert A. Iger, February 10, 1951, in Ocean-side, NY; son of Arthur (a professor and business executive) and Mimi (a teaching assistant) Iger; married first wife (divorced); married Willow Bay (a television journalist and model), October 7, 1995; children: Katie, Amanda (from first marriage), Robert Maxwell, Will (from second marriage). *Education:* Ithaca College, undergraduate degree (magna cum laude).

Addresses: *Office*—c/o The Walt Disney Company, 500 S. Buena Vista St., Burbank, CA 91521-0001.

Career

Television news weatherman, Ithaca, NY; ABC, studio supervisor, New York, NY, 1974-76; ABC Sports, management positions, 1976-84, then vice president in charge of program planning and development, 1985-87, vice president of programming, 1987-88; executive vice president, ABC, 1988-89; president and chief operating officer, ABC Entertainment, 1989-93; president, ABC Television Network Group, 1993-94; president and chief operating officer, ABC, 1994-99; chair, ABC Group, 1999; president, Walt Disney International, 1999-2005; Walt Disney Company, president and chief operating officer, 2000-04, chief executive officer, 2005—.

Member: American Film Institute Board, trustee; Museum of Television and Radio, trustee; Ithaca College, trustee; Lincoln Center for the Performing Arts, member of board.

© *Reuters/Corbis*

Sidelights

After spending nearly the whole of his career with ABC and the company that later bought the network, the Walt Disney Company, Bob Iger was named the chief executive officer (CEO) of Walt Disney Company in 2005. Known for his even keeled demeanor and nose-to-the-grindstone work mentality, Iger was not always the first choice to replace longtime Disney head Michael Eisner. Nonetheless, when he was selected, George J. Mitchell, chair of Disney's board, was quoted by Business Wire as saying, "Bob is an experienced, talented and visionary leader who has made crucial and substantial contributions toward Disney's strong performance."

Born on February 10, 1951, Iger grew up in New York. By the time he was ten years old, Iger knew he wanted to work in television. His original goal was to be a television news correspondent. As a student at Ithaca College, he continued to pursue this goal. Iger hoped to work for CBS News one day. After graduating from Ithaca College, Iger began his professional career in Ithaca, New York. There, he did get to work in front of the camera for a local news station, but not in the way he originally planned: He was a television weatherman.

In 1974, Iger switched gears. He moved to New York City where he was hired by ABC as a studio supervisor. In this position, he was able to work on a number of programs, including game shows. He was also part of the production of a special starring legendary singer/actor Frank Sinatra. Two years later, in 1976, Iger joined ABC Sports, where he held management and executive positions for 12 years. By the 1980s, Iger was involved in programming for ABC Sports. In 1985, he was named vice president in charge of program planning and development. Iger worked on scheduling for ABC Sports as well as the acquisition of rights. Promoted in 1987, he became the vice president of programming. In this executive position, he was in charge of scheduling all of ABC Sports' programming. Iger was in charge of acquiring programming as well. In addition, he acted as the manager and director for ABC's key sports show, *Wide World of Sports.*

Iger's success at ABC Sports drew the attention of the heads of the network. In 1988, Iger left ABC Sports to work for the parent network, ABC. That year, he was named an executive vice president at the network. Iger was soon promoted again; in 1989, he named president and chief operating officer of ABC Entertainment. Four years later, he was named president of the ABC Television Network Group. In 1994, he received yet another promotion, when he was selected to be the president and chief operating officer of ABC.

In these positions, one of Iger's primary concerns was programming, especially in the early 1990s. He was heavily involved in the obtaining of programming and rights acquisition. He helped put programs on the air that made ABC the number-two network in the 1993-94 television season; ABC went on to become number one in 1994-95. Iger helped get hit situation comedies like *Home Improvement, Doogie Howser, M.D.,* and *Family Matters* on the air. He also had a hand in airing long-running dramas such as *NYPD Blue* and hits such *America's Funniest Home Videos.* However, Iger was quick to cancel shows with low ratings, like dramas *Twin Peaks, thirtysomething,* and *China Beach,* even though they had a loyal fan base.

Iger remained with ABC after the 1996 merger of the network and its parent company, Capital Cities, with Disney. In addition to helping the merger to be competed successfully, he continued to play a key role in programming the network. He and other executives found success with the hit prime time game show *Who Wants to Be a Millionaire* in 1999 and 2000, pushing it almost daily on the network's audiences. However, when ratings fell after the fad faded, the network did not have many new programs ready to take the game show's place and ratings for the network as a whole fell dramatically for several years. ABC also lost hundreds of millions of dollars per year and fell to the bottom of the ratings barrel for networks by 2002. Iger admitted he did not handle the situation well. He told Patricia Sellers of *Fortune,* "I think for the first time in my career, I let myself get sucked into the vortex of thinking 'Oh, my God, we're in third place ... fourth place ... we need action, action, action!'"

Despite these problems, Iger was given new posts at both ABC and Disney. In 1999, he became chair of the ABC Group. As head of the ABC Group, Iger was in charge of overall operations. Around the same time, he became president of Walt Disney International. He managed Disney's interests abroad, including the creation and organization of an internal operations structure. He also was in charge of coordinating products and services for international audiences. One area that Iger was especially concerned with was developing more Disney theme parks in other countries. He also wanted to increase international markets significantly.

In 2000, Iger stepped away from direct involvement with ABC when he was named Disney's president and chief operating officer (COO). He also joined Disney's board of directors. In addition, he became a member of Disney's executive management committee. As president and COO, Iger was in charge of the company's day-to-day operations. He still played a role at ABC. He helped ABC revive, though it was number three in 2003, but things got better in 2004 and 2005. At Disney, Iger emphasized technology. He also remained in charge of international operations. Iger was concerned with pirating even as he was looking to open up new theme parks and markets for Disney and its products in Asia.

As president and COO, Iger worked closely with Eisner, the long-time CEO of Disney, on many issues. The pair had a relatively a close relationship, despite Eisner's reputation as being difficult to work with. Eisner was notorious for holding grudges and forcing out creative employees who might have been good for the company had they stayed. Iger's position had been held by a number of people in the recent past, such as Michael Ovitz who later filed suit against the company. Iger did not seek out the limelight when he held the position, which might have contributed to his success in the post.

When Eisner announced in 2004 he planned to retire two years later, Iger was anointed his successor. Eisner ended up stepping down a year earlier than he originally planned and Iger was promoted to CEO in his place in 2005. This promotion was not without controversy. The move up for Iger was generally seen as a positive for Disney by industry analysts and supported by a majority of shareholders. However, Walt Disney's nephew, Roy Disney, did not initially support the promotion of Iger. Roy Disney went as far as to file a lawsuit related to Iger being named Eisner's successor. Roy Disney and Iger eventually made their peace, with Disney taking on a contract to act as a consultant to the company.

Iger was also criticized in a book about the inner workings of Disney called *DisneyWar,* written by journalist James Stewart. In the book, the author alleges that Iger did not have the best assessment skills for the moves he made at ABC. Stewart also accuses Iger of trying to please Eisner too much. In contrast, Marc Gunther of *Fortune* wrote, "The ultimate supporting-cast member—loyal, diligent, patient, and handsome to boot—Iger never stole the spotlight from Disney's longtime leading man, Michael Eisner. With Eisner's support, Iger courted directors, charmed investors, and became chief executive officer by default when every one of his rivals dropped out." Iger had no real competition for the job. Only an executive at eBay, Meg Whitman, had interviewed by the board of directors.

When Iger took charge of Disney, he began running an entertainment conglomerate that was worth about $57 billion. Disney had networks on cable and network, theme parks, and several movie studios. The company was not just concerned with entertainment, but also had a whole division devoted to producing and selling consumer products. The company as a whole had been slumping for some time, but had recently seen signs of improvement.

One project that Iger had been closely involved for some time was the creation of a Disney theme park in Hong Kong which was scheduled to open in fall 2005; the park cost about $3.6 billion to build. Iger firmly believed that Disney should continue to expand into Asia, despite expected short-term losses. He especially saw China and India as two markets where Disney must expand. He showed his interest by personally traveling to China four times in 2004 on business. China remained a priority for Iger as he took over as CEO, despite the many problems and restrictions that came with dealing with the Chinese government and media in that country. By 2005, Disney already had some presence in programming in China by providing some cartoon content for television networks, a little international sports programming under the ESPN name, and a

magazine of comics aimed at children. Iger hoped foreign markets as a whole to be at least 50 percent of Disney's profits by 2010.

Other Disney units doing well included its sports network, ESPN, as well as ABC. The latter network had high ratings for new hit dramas like *Desperate Housewives* and *Lost.* The latter was a show which Iger allegedly did not think would work when it was initially brought to the network, but he was proven wrong. However, Iger also fired the programmers for ABC, Lloyd Braun and Susan Lyne, who pushed for these shows to be on the air. Some observers wondered if Iger would be able to put the right creative talent in place.

Iger also faced other challenges including helping revive ABC Family, a cable network that had been struggling in the ratings. He also needed to work on renewing a contract with Pixar, the company that produced animated features such as *Monsters* and *The Incredibles.* Disney had distributed Pixar's films for a number of years, but the two companies could not come to terms on renewing that deal when Eisner had been charge. The relationship had been profitable for both parties, but Pixar was not happy with the agreement.

Iger wanted to increase Disney's profitability in other ways as well. He had a goal of increasing the number of video games offered by Disney, perhaps by acquiring another company that already produced such titles. He also wanted to emphasize technology via branding. For example, Iger wanted to use the successful names like ESPN and Disney on phones. In addition, he wanted to offer more high tech options along the lines of ESPN being offered in high definition. Iger wanted it to be possible to get Disney's content to anyone using any type of device at any time.

As CEO, Iger was especially concerned with the inner workings of Disney. Corporate culture under Eisner had been trying for many employees. Iger made some immediate moves to improve the morale of Disney's executives. One such action was to dissolve the strategic planning department. Executives were not fond of the department which was seen as a means by which Eisner used to micromanage Disney as a whole.

Though Iger was not as big of a personality as Eisner, he worked hard. He rose daily at 4:30 A.M. and was at the office within two hours. Calling him "a more traditional businessman" than Eisner, Nell Minow, the editor of *Corporate Library,* told Frank Ahrens of the *Washington Post*, "He's not as glitzy and showbizzy. He projects a lot of sincerity and has that rare CEO quality—humility."

Sources

Books

Celebrity Biographies, Baseline II, 2005.
Standard & Poor's Register of Directors and Executives, McGraw-Hill, 2005.

Periodicals

Business Wire, March 13, 2005.
Fortune, March 7, 2005, p. 23; April 4, 2005, p. 76; April 18, 2005, p. 170.
Los Angeles Times, March 14, 2005, p. C1; July 9, 2005, p. A1.
New York Times, March 14, 2005, p. C2.
Time, July 18, 2005, p. 52.
Washington Post, March 15, 2005, p. E1.

Online

"Disney Names New Boss," E! Online, http://www.eonline.com/News/Items/0,1,16122,00.html?tnews (March 15, 2005).
"Iger named next Disney boss," CNN Money, http://money.cnn.com/2005/03/13/news/newsmakers/disney.reut/index.htm (March 14, 2005).
"The Keys to the Magic Kingdom," CNN.com, http://www.cnn.com/SPECIALS/2003/global.influential/stories/iger/ (August 8, 2005).
"Robert A. Iger Executive Biography," The Walt Disney Company, http://corporate.disney.go.com/corporate/bios/robert_iger.html (August 8, 2005).

—*A. Petruso*

Jimmy Iovine

© Axel Koester/Corbis

Music producer

Born March 11, 1953, in Brooklyn, NY; son of Jimmy Iovine, Sr. (a longshoreman); married; children: one son, one daughter.

Addresses: *Office*—Interscope Records, 2220 Colorado Ave., Santa Monica, CA 90404. *Website*—http://www.interscope.com.

Career

Began as recording engineer at the Record Plant, New York, 1973; produced first album for Flame, 1977; worked as producer, 1977-1990; musical director and supervisor for the film *Sixteen Candles*, 1984; co-founded Interscope Records, 1990; formed Farm Club label, 1999; became sole chairman of Interscope, 2001; served as producer for the film *8 Mile*, 2002; served as executive producer for the television show *Interscope Presents: The Next Episode*, 2003; became chairman of Interscope Geffen A&M Records, c. 2003.

Sidelights

Jimmy Iovine, who rose to lead the powerful Interscope Geffen A&M recording label, began his career in the music industry during the early 1970s. He has worked as an engineer, producer, and record company executive, partnering with a group of diverse artists ranging from John Lennon and Stevie Nicks to Nine Inch Nails and Eminem. During his extensive career, he has also added film and television credits to his repertoire.

A native of Brooklyn, New York, Iovine grew up in an Italian-American family. His father, Jimmy Iovine Sr., was a longshoreman who passed away in 1985. Throughout his son's life, the elder Iovine was a strong influence and a major supporter of any endeavor the younger Iovine attempted. When Iovine played baseball during his childhood, his father was the team's coach. When he decided to join a band, his father stepped in as the group's manager. And when Iovine decided to embark on a career in the music business, his father was his biggest fan.

Iovine's entrance into the music business was a job as a recording engineer at the Record Plant recording studio in New York in 1973. From the beginning he worked with influential artists, including John Lennon. In 1975, Iovine served as the engineer for the recording of Bruce Springsteen's *Born to Run* album. After working as an engineer for several years, Iovine got his first break as a producer in 1977 with a New Jersey band called Flame.

The following year, Iovine's studio career took off when he produced *Easter* for Patti Smith, an album which included the Top 40 hit single "Because the Night." The album's exposure led to a high demand for Iovine's work. Over the next few years, he produced three albums for rocker Tom Petty: 1979's

Damn the Torpedoes, 1981's *Hard Promises,* and 1982's *Long After Dark.*

In 1981, Iovine formed a personal and professional partnership with vocalist Stevie Nicks when he produced her first solo album, *Bella Donna,* which included a single she performed with Petty, "Stop Draggin' My Heart Around." *Bella Donna* soon reached the top spot on the *Billboard* magazine album sales chart, and when the time came in 1983 to return to the studio to record her next effort, *The Wild Heart,* Nicks turned to Iovine. That same year, he produced U2's live recording *Under a Blood Red Sky.* By 1984, Iovine had established himself as a hit producer, and he had expanded his activities to include musical direction and supervision for the popular film *Sixteen Candles.*

The following year, he and Nicks returned to the studio to work on *Rock a Little,* but their personal and professional partnership ended before the album was complete. Nicks' drug addiction had started to interfere with her performance, and Iovine was helpless to change the course of things. Despite the setback in his personal life, his career did not miss a beat. Over the next five years, he produced the first album by the band Lone Justice, the *Once Upon a Time* album for Simple Minds, the Pretenders' *Get Close,* Patti Smith's *Dream of Life,* and U2's *Rattle and Hum.*

In 1990, Iovine partnered with Ted Field, an heir to the Marshall Field's retailing fortune, to form Interscope Records. Field and Iovine contracted with Atlantic Records, a division of the giant Time Warner conglomerate, for distribution in a $30 million joint venture. The label came out almost immediately with its first hit single, Gerardo's "Rico Suave," which was followed by hits from Marky Mark & the Funky Bunch and Primus—all in its first year of operation.

But Iovine and Field did not stop there. They decided to make a bold move into the world of hip-hop by investing a few million dollars to distribute the albums from Death Row Records, a label formed by Dr. Dre and Suge Knight. "For the time during the late 1980s and early 1990s, outside of one or two rock bands, hip-hop was the most potent message and the most true message that was being delivered in this country," Iovine told the Public Broadcasting System's *Frontline* program.

Backed by Interscope's distribution muscle, Death Row released a number of multiplatinum-selling albums from artists such as Dr. Dre, Tupac Shakur,

and Snoop Dogg. Robert Greenblatt, president of entertainment for Showtime cable television, later told Allhiphop.com that "Jimmy Iovine is the undisputed czar of hip-hop."

Despite the success of their hip-hop artists, Interscope did not focus solely on one genre of music. Their roster included R&B and pop acts, such as Blackstreet, and alternative rock bands, including Bush, Helmet, and Nine Inch Nails. Iovine relentlessly pursued a deal with Nine Inch Nails that took more than a year to seal. The group, led by Trent Reznor, had expressed its displeasure with their label, TVT Records, and wanted to move to another company. However, Steve Gottlieb, head of TVT Records, did not want to let them go. So Iovine called him every single day for an entire year until Gottlieb finally agreed to form a joint venture with Interscope for Nine Inch Nails.

"Jimmy has this gift to get things from his friends that further his career goals without making you feel that you've been used," Danny Goldberg, then chairman of Warner Bros. Records, explained to Patrick Goldstein in the *New York Times Magazine.* "It's a real art because Jimmy can do these things without making anyone unhappy." Once Iovine had Nine Inch Nails on Interscope's roster, Iovine made a deal with Reznor and his manager John Malm to form their own record label, Nothing Records, which led to the addition of shock rocker Marilyn Manson to the label's roster.

In 1995, Interscope Records began receiving criticism centering on the gangsta-rap artists in the Death Row lineup. Critics began exerting pressure on Atlantic Records' parent company Time Warner, and Atlantic elected to sell its stake of the label back to Field and Iovine, who refused to cave to the demands. "Unlike any other record executive, Jimmy will say, 'Go ahead and do it,'" Dr. Dre told Goldstein. "'We'll deal with the consquences later.'" Iovine would not ask the Death Row artists to compromise because to do so would have gone against the original mission of Interscope Records. "Our charter was to make deals with people that we really respect and give them complete and absolute control over their lives," Iovine explained to Alec Foege of the *New York Times.* "We felt that if we did that, we would bat really high." The following year, Interscope formed a distribution partnership with the MCA label.

Always looking toward new innovations, Iovine formed another partnership, this time with Doug Morris, chairman and CEO for Universal Music

Group, on November 9, 1999. The duo started a new record label that would attempt to take advantage of both the Internet and cable television media. The initiative, called Farm Club, began with a Web site to which musicians could submit their songs. From there, music fans and industry executives would submit their feedback on the music. Select artists were showcased on a television show that aired on the USA Network. However, the idea did not take off, and by 2001, Farm Club had shut down.

Despite the demise of Farm Club, Iovine's career did not slow down. In February of 2001, Field left Interscope Records to start his own label and to pursue his film career, and Iovine became chairman of the label. In 2002, Iovine added to his film credits as producer of *8 Mile*, which starred Interscope artist Eminem. The following year, he served as executive producer for the cable television show *Interscope Presents: The Next Episode*, a Showtime cable television reality show about rappers competing to be the top MC; the show created a situation similar to that depicted in the film *8 Mile*. "This show allows young hip-hop artists to compete in a way that is most true to the art form, and through that get a real opportunity," Iovine explained to MusicRemedy.com.

By this time, Iovine had expanded his responsibilities, becoming chairman of Interscope Geffen A&M Records, but despite the added responsibility, he had not lost sight of his original mission. "I always try to go where the excitement is, where the best music is," Iovine told PBS's *Frontline*. "I don't care what kind of music it is. I go with the best artist we can find."

Selected discography

As producer

(Flame) *Flame*, Warner Bros., 1977.
(Patti Smith) *Easter*, Arista, 1978.
(Tom Petty) *Damn the Torpedoes*, MCA, 1979.
(Dire Straits) *Making Movies*, Warner Bros., 1980.
(Tom Petty) *Hard Promises*, MCA, 1981.
(Stevie Nicks) *Bella Donna*, Mobile, 1981.

(Meat Loaf) *Dead Ringer*, Epic, 1981.
(Bob Seger) *The Distance*, Capitol, 1982.
(Tom Petty) *Long After Dark*, MCA, 1982.
(Stevie Nicks) *The Wild Heart*, Atlantic, 1983.
(U2) *Under a Blood Red Sky*, Island, 1983.
(Face to Face) *Face to Face*, Epic, 1984.
(Lone Justice) *Lone Justice*, Geffen, 1985.
(Simple Minds) *Once Upon a Time*, A&M, 1985.
(The Pretenders) *Get Close*, Sire, 1986.
(Patti Smith) *Dream of Life*, Arista, 1988.
(U2) *Rattle and Hum*, Island, 1988.

Sources

Periodicals

Fortune, July 7, 1997, p. 40.
New York Times, December 3, 1995; November 14, 2003.
New York Times Magazine, April 16, 1995, p. 24.

Online

"Celebrity Information: Jimmy Iovine," MSN Entertainment, http://entertainment.msn.com/celebs (April 7, 2006).
"Field Ankles Interscope to Sow Own Label," *Variety*, http://www.variety.com/article/VR111779 3206?categoryid=16&cs=1&query=jimmy+and+ iovine&display=jimmy+iovine (April 7, 2006).
"Interview: Jimmy Iovine," *Frontline*, http://www. pbs.org/wgbh/pages/frontline/shows/cool/ interviews/iovine.html (April 7, 2006).
"Jimmy and Doug's Farm Club Harnesses the Strength of the Internet, Cable Television, and the Universal Music Group to Create a Worldwide Record Label for the Digital Age," Universal Music, http://www.umusic.com/static/press/110 999.htm (April 7, 2006).
"Jimmy Iovine Biography," *RollingStone.com*, http://www.rollingstone.com (April 7, 2006).
"Rappers to be featured in new Showtime reality show," Allhiphop.com, http://www.allhiphop. com/hiphopnews/?ID=2210 (April 7, 2006).

—Sonya Shelton

John Irving

Simon Hollington/Photoshot/Landov

Author and screenwriter

Born John Wallace Blunt, Jr., March 2, 1942, in Exeter, NH; son of John, Sr. (an executive recruiter and writer) and Frances Blunt; stepson of Colin F. Irving (a teacher); married Shyla Leary (a painter and photographer), August 20, 1964 (divorced, 1981); married Janet Turnbull (a literary agent), 1987; children: Colin, Brendan (from first marriage), Everett (from second marriage). *Education:* University of New Hampshire, B.A. (cum laude), 1965; University of Iowa, MFA, 1967; also attended University of Pittsburgh, 1961-62, and Institute of European Studies, Vienna, Austria, 1963-64.

Addresses: *Office*—c/o Author Mail, Random House, 1745 Broadway, New York, NY 10019.

Career

English instructor, Mount Holyoke College, South Hadley, MA, 1967-72, later an assistant professor of English; published first novel, *Setting Free the Bears,* 1968; appeared in film adaptation of his novel, *The World According to Garp,* 1982; wrote first screenplay, *The Cider House Rules,* adapted from his own novel, 1999, and appeared in a cameo in the film; wrote film adaptation of his novel *A Widow for One Year* as *The Door in the Floor,* 2004. Taught at Windham College and the University of Iowa. Served as writer-in-residence, University of Iowa and Brandeis University, 1978-79; also worked as a wrestling coach.

Awards: National Books Award for Fiction (Paperback) for *The World According to Garp,* National Book Foundation, 1980; Academy Award for best adapted screenplay, Academy of Motion Picture Arts and Sciences, for *The Cider House Rules,* 1999; National Board of Review Award for best screenplay, National Board of Review of Motion Pictures, for *The Cider House Rules,* 1999; Golden Satellite Award for best motion picture screenplay (adaptation), International Press Academy, for *The Cider House Rules,* 1999; inductee, Wrestling Hall of Fame, National Wrestling Hall of Fame and Museum.

Sidelights

American novelist John Irving has sold millions of copies of his books around the world. They have been translated into at least 30 languages. A number of Irving's novels have been regarded as creative failures by reviewers, yet all but two have been best sellers. Critics often praise his use of language, though that element can get out of control. In his books, the plots are often complex, sometimes to the point of meandering, and feature many odd characters. Of the latter aspect, Irving told Dorman T. Shindler in *Book,* "The characters in my novels, from the very first one, are always on some quixotic effort of attempting to control something that is uncontrollable—some element of the world that is essentially random and out of control."

Irving did not fully know about his early life until he reached adulthood. He was born John Wallace Blunt, Jr., in 1942, in Exeter, New Hampshire. He was the son of John Blunt, Sr., and his wife, Frances, known as Frankie. His father was a soldier during World War II who ended his marriage two years after Irving was born. Though he requested visitation and wanted to get to know his son, Irving's mother would not allow him to ever see their son. Irving grew up knowing nothing about his biological father.

As a young child, Irving was raised by his mother and grandmother in his grandmother's home in Exeter. When he was about six years old, his mother married Colin F. Irving. Her new husband gave his name to his new wife's son. John Wallace Blunt, Jr., was now known as John Winslow Irving. Colin Irving was a history teacher at a well-known prep school, Phillips Exeter Academy.

Despite his dyslexia, Irving liked to read. Wrestling became another passion. He received his education at Phillips Exeter Academy where he was better at wrestling than at school because of his then-undiagnosed dyslexia. Irving also had a very religious upbringing which later played a role in some of his novels.

After graduating from prep school, Irving entered the University of Pittsburgh. He went there primarily because of the school's wrestling team, but only stayed for one year. Irving transferred to the University of New Hampshire and continued to wrestle. While a student there, he won a grant to study at the Institute of European Studies for year, 1963 to 1964. In 1964, Irving married his first wife, a painter and photographer named Shyla Leary, whom he met while studying abroad. Leary had become pregnant with the couple's first child, Colin. They later had a second son named Brendan.

Irving graduated cum laude from the University of New Hampshire in 1965 and then entered the prestigious MFA creative writing program at the University of Iowa. This program has produced a number of well-known novelists, including Kurt Vonnegut. When Irving graduated from Iowa, he took an academic position while he worked on his first novels. He also continued to wrestle competitively, a sport he participated in until he was 34 years old.

Irving spent the next five years teaching English at Mount Holyoke College in Massachusetts. He published his first novel, *Setting Free the Bears*, in 1968.

While the book received good reviews, it did not sell well. Irving wrote two more novels that also were ignored by the general public. *The Water-Method Man*, a farcical novel about sex, and *The 158-Pound Marriage*, were reviewed favorably by critics. Irving believed that his publisher, Random House, did not support the novels, and switched publishers.

Whether or not Irving was correct about Random House, his next novel was his breakthrough. In 1978, he published one of his best known books, *The World According to Garp*. This book made Irving famous and wealthy. After its publication, he left academia behind, except for stints as a writer in residence. *The World According to Garp* is a family saga about a single-mother nurse and her son, a wrestler named T.S. Garp. The novel is primarily set at Irving's alma mater, Phillips Exeter Academy. *The World According to Garp* was made into a film in 1982 that was a hit at the box office and featured a performance by actor Robin Williams as Garp. Irving himself had a cameo role as a wrestling referee.

The follow-up to *The World According to Garp* was not as embraced by critics. Titled *The Hotel New Hampshire*, this tragic comedy had several story lines including one about a brother who was in love with his sister. Despite the lack of critical support, *The Hotel New Hampshire* sold well.

That novel was published in 1981, a year in which much changed in Irving's life. He and his first wife divorced. Around the time of the divorce, his mother gave him a packet of information about his biological father. The packet included letters and newspaper articles about his heroism as a pilot during World War II. While this information satisfied some of the questions Irving had about his father, the novelist chose not to meet the man despite several opportunities over the years. Irving regarded the man who raised him, Colin Irving, as his father.

Though Irving's personal life was tumultuous for a time, he continued to write novels that had a wide following among readers. One book that was also better received by critics was *The Cider House Rules*. This novel focused on an orphanage in Maine run by a Dr. Larch, who also performed abortions on the side. Larch was assisted in his medical duties by a teenaged orphan named Homer, to whom Larch wants to teach the abortion procedure, but the boy is unwilling to learn. One character in the novel, an airman, was modeled on the information Irving learned about his father.

In 1987, Irving married his literary agent, Janet Turnbell. The couple had a son together, Everett. Turnbell is Canadian, so Irving and his family began spending part of every year in that country as well as living in his primary home in Vermont and a vacation home in Long Island, New York.

For his next novel, Irving again returned to Phillips Exeter Academy. Called *A Prayer for Owen Meany*, the book showed how much British author Charles Dickens influenced Irving's work. A sprawling book focused around a mythical story, the novel is narrated by John Wheelwright, a student at Exeter, whose life is greatly influenced by the title character, the diminutive Owen Meany. Meany is the son of granite quarrier and believes he is a tool of God. Wheelright undergoes a religious conversion because of Owen, though he later moves to Canada to dodge the draft for the Vietnam War. *A Prayer for Owen Meany* was very popular, becoming Irving's biggest seller after *The World According to Garp*. It also became a novel that was often read in literature classes in colleges and universities.

Irving went back to Random House starting with his next long novel, 1995's *A Son of the Circus*. Though a number of critics did not like the book, it still sold well. One theme in the novel was how when people inadvertently offend people through their actions they unknowingly reveal a truth about themselves. Irving uses this idea for comic effect as he focuses on the life of Dr. Daruwalla, an Indian-born physician who lives in Toronto, Canada, but does not feel at home in either place. The novel primarily takes place in India where the doctor works on a means to end dwarfism and also writes scripts for Bollywood mystery films.

Irving's 1998 novel, *A Widow for One Year*, was better received than his previous book. Critics noted that *A Widow for One Year* had much in common with *The World According to Garp* in terms of theme and structure. Driving this novel is Marion Cole, a mother whose two sons die in a car accident. Depressed, she leaves her husband and four-year-daughter behind and disappears for 37 years. She also has an affair with a 16-year-old boy named Eddie. Much of the novel focuses on the daughter Marion left behind as she grows, marries, has a child, and becomes a widow.

Over the years, Irving was not always happy with the way his novels were adapted for film. At this point in his career, he decided to take matters into his own hands. In 1999, he wrote an adaptation of his novel *The Cider House Rules*; the film won several awards. Irving chronicled the experience in his book *My Movie Business: A Memoir*. Six years later, he adapted *A Widow for One Year* for film. It was titled *The Door in the Floor* when it was released in 2004.

Though Irving found success as a screenwriter, his primary career remained writing novels. His next book, 2001's *The Fourth Hand*, was significantly shorter than most of his novels, only about 300 pages long, and much less complex and more lean in its execution. While critics were often dismissive, the book still sold extremely well. It was a number-one best seller within a week of its publication. The protagonist at the center of *The Fourth Hand* is a well-known television reporter named Patrick Wallingford. He attracts women and finds it hard to say no to their advances. His numerous affairs end his marriage, but after undergoing a change, he eventually finds true love. While *The Fourth Hand* was a more conventional novel, it still had many of Irving's signature peculiar moments and characters, such as a man who throws dog excrement at boaters on the Charles River. Wallingford himself loses his left hand to a lion and has hand transplant surgery. He falls in love with the hand donor's widow.

Irving's personal life was again changing in this time period. In December of 2001, Irving's half-brother, Chris Blunt, contacted him. Irving learned that he had two younger half brothers and a younger half sister from his biological father's other marriages. The novelist was also informed that his father had died about five years earlier. Irving became bonded to his new family members.

Even before *The Fourth Hand* was published, Irving was already at work on a novel, *Until I Find You*, that had a number of autobiographical elements to it. In the 820-page novel, Irving focuses on Jack Burns, an actor/screenwriter who learns about what he thinks is true about his somewhat tragic past from his rather difficult tattoo artist mother, Alice. One thing that Jack remembers was being sexually molested by an older women when he was only ten years old. Irving himself admitted that this happened to him as a child. When the novelist was eleven years old, he was repeatedly molested by an older woman for a year.

Jack is unsure about what really happened to him throughout his childhood and tries to find answers as he searches for his long-lost father, who he finds in the end. In interviews upon the book's publication, Irving admitted that the situation with his biological father had greatly influenced a number of his books much more than he realized or admitted to in the past. He initially wrote *Until I Find You* in first person, though he later changed it to a third person perspective before publication to make it more fictionalized for him and the reader.

Of the labor involved in writing his novels, Irving commented in the *New York Times*, "Being a writer is a strenuous marriage between careful observation and just as carefully imagining the truths you haven't had the opportunity to see. The rest is the necessary, strict toiling with the language; for me this means writing and rewriting the sentences until they sound as spontaneous as good conversation."

Selected writings

Novels

Setting Free the Bears, Random House (New York City), 1968.
The Water-Method Man, Random House, 1972.
The 158-Pound Marriage, Random House, 1974.
The World According to Garp, E. P. Dutton (New York City), 1978.
The Hotel New Hampshire, E. P. Dutton, 1981.
The Cider House Rules, Morrow (New York City), 1985.
A Prayer for Owen Meany, Morrow, 1989.
A Son of the Circus, Random House, 1995.
A Widow for One Year, Random House, 1998.
The Fourth Hand, Random House, 2001.
Until I Found You, Random House, 2005.

Collections

Trying to Save Piggy Sneed, Arcade Publishing (New York City), 1996.

Memoirs

My Movie Business: A Memoir, Random House, 1999.

Sources

Books

Celebrity Biographies, Baseline II, Inc., 2005.

Periodicals

Book, July 2001, p. 30.
Entertainment Weekly, July 15, 2005, pp. 75-76; July 22, 2005, pp. 40-46.
Independent (London, England), August 5, 2005.
Irish Times (Dublin, Ireland) July 14, 2001, p. 64.
Maclean's, September 5, 1994, p. 54; July 23, 2001, p. 41.
New York Times, August 22, 1982, sec. 7, p. 3; April 25, 1989, p. C13; April 28, 1998, p. E1.
People, July 30, 2001, p. 95; July 25, 2005, pp. 88-90.
Publishers Weekly, February 26, 1996, p. 24; July 16, 2001, p. 77.
Time, April 3, 1989, p. 80.
Weekly Standard, August 13, 2001, p. 35.

—A. Petruso

Jay-Z

WENN/Landov

Rap musician and record company executive

Born Shawn Corey Carter, December 4, 1970, in Brooklyn, NY; son of Adnis Reeves and Gloria Carter.

Addresses: *Record company*—Roc-A-Fella Records, 160 Varick St., 12th Fl., New York, NY 10013, website: http://www.rocafella.com.

Career

Record producer, 1994—. Released debut album, *Reasonable Doubt*, 1996; *In My Lifetime, Vol. 1*, 1997; released *Vol. 2: Hard Knock Life*, 1998; released *Vol. 3: The Life and Times of Shawn Carter*, 1999; established Rocawear clothing company, 1999; released *The Dynasty: Roc la Familia*, 2000; released *The Blueprint*, 2001; released *The Blueprint 2: The Gift & the Curse*, 2002; opened the 40/40 club in New York City, 2003; released *The Blueprint 2.1*, 2003; released *The Black Album*, 2003; retired from rap to focus on business ventures, 2004; feature film *Fade to Black* released in theaters, 2004; appointed president of Universal Music Group's Def Jam Recordings, 2004; partnered with French watchmaker Audemars Piguet to create a limited-edition watch, 2005; invested in Carol's Daughter hair, skin care, and home product line, 2005.

Awards: Grammy Award for best rap album, Recording Academy, for *Vol. 2: Hard Knock Life*, 1998; MTV Video Music Award for best rap video, for "Can I Get A...," 1999; *Source* Award for lyricist of the year, solo, 1999; *Billboard* Award for rap artist of the year, 1999; *Soul Train* Award, Sammy Davis Jr. Entertainer of the Year, 2001; BET Award for best male hip-hop artist, 2001; *Source* Award for best hip-hop artist, solo, 2001; *Soul Train* Award for album of the year, for *The Blueprint*, 2002; Grammy Award for Best R&B Song (with Beyonce Knowles), Recording Academy, for "Crazy in Love," 2003; Grammy Award for best rap/sung collaboration (with Beyonce Knowles), Recording Academy, for "Crazy in Love," 2003; ASCAP Golden Note Award, 2004; American Music Award for favorite male rap/hip-hop artist, 2004; Grammy Award for best rap solo performance, Recording Academy, for "99 Problems," 2005; *GQ* man of the year, 2005.

Sidelights

Jay-Z is all too familiar with the hard knock life. In his hit single "Hard Knock Life," Jay-Z samples the musical *Annie*'s signature song of the same name. "These kids sing about the hard knock life, things everyone in the ghetto feels coming up," Jay-Z said of the orphans in *Annie* in a *People* interview. "That's the ghetto anthem." The rap star grew up in a single-parent household in the Marcy Projects of Brooklyn, New York. Known for his honesty, Jay-Z has admitted in both his autobiographical lyrics and interviews that he sold drugs as a teenager. For Jay-Z, rap was his way out of the hard knock life. The money that came with a successful rap career took him out of the Brooklyn projects, and rap music gave him a means to express his feelings about knocks and blows he has taken.

The way, however, was not easy and Jay-Z encountered more hard knocks along the road. When he could not get a record deal, Jay-Z, along with two friends, formed his own record label. He also had run-ins with the law. The timing of Jay-Z's arrest in early December of 1999 for the stabbing of record executive Lance "Un" Rivera at a Times Square nightclub could not have been worse. His much-awaited album, *Volume 3: The Life and Times of S. Carter*, was due to be released right after Christmas and it was uncertain whether the negative publicity from this latest incident would hurt sales. However, for a man who grew up on the mean streets of Brooklyn this was just another one of the hard knocks that has formed his voice in rap.

Jay-Z was born Shawn Carter on December 4, 1970, in the borough of Brooklyn in New York, the youngest of four children. He grew up in the well-known Marcy Projects, where the J and Z subway trains run. His mother, Gloria Carter, worked as a clerk in an investment company. Jay-Z's father, Adnis Reeves, left when he was 12 years old. "To me, that was basically the end of our relationship," Jay-Z told *Vibe*. "That was when the hurt and then the healing began for me, from that day right there." Jay-Z's relationship with his father served as fodder for many of his songs, including the *Black Album*'s "Moment of Clarity," in which he forgave Reeves for abandoning his family. Jay-Z reconciled with his father in 2003, six months before his father passed away from a liver ailment.

When Jay-Z was first starting out in the rap world, he was introduced to Damon "Dame" Dash, who, by the time he was 19, had already gotten record deals for two acts. Dash soon became Jay-Z's manager and Dash's childhood friend, Kareem "Biggs" Burke, was then hired as Jay-Z's road manager. For two years, the three worked unsuccessfully to obtain a record deal. The trio then decided to form their own record company, Roc-A-Fella Records, in which they would all serve as partners. Jay-Z's role was that of marquee artist, Dash ran the company's day-to-day operations, and Burke, according to *Vibe*, served as "a barometer of the streets." After Roc-A-Fella secured a deal with Priority Records for the distribution of their albums, Jay-Z was ready to release his first record, *Reasonable Doubt*.

Jay-Z rose to fame with his 1996 gold-certified single, "Ain't No N-G-A (Like the One I Got)," a duet with Foxy Brown. The controversy started im-

mediately. The single's title was not the language that even the most daring disc jockeys wanted to play. According to Janine McAdams of *Billboard*, "For now, 'Ain't No N-G-A' has radio production rooms working overtime. None of the stations contacted for this story advocate the use of the n-word over the air, but their solutions are varied: Some edit the word out; others substitute 'brother' or 'player.'" Still, radio stations pointed out that, however reluctant they were to broadcast that and other offensive words, the public knew when it was cut out anyway. In some cases, the change altered the content enough to lose its intended impact and appeal.

Despite the hardcore quality of his first album, as Shawnee Smith of *Billboard*, noted, it was Jay-Z who also began to transform the hip-hop scene from its hardcore "gangsta rap" to something that bears a more refined style—that of "Armani suits, alligator boots, Rolex watches, expensive cars, broads, and Cristal." At the end of 1996, Havelock Nelson reflected on the year in rap for *Billboard*. Jay-Z, Nelson said, "masterfully reinvented himself after receiving battle scars from his previous rhyme life."

In addition to making music, Jay-Z was also interested in the corporate side of the business. Since 1994, Jay-Z had been producing records for other artists as chief of operations for the Roc-A-Fella label. The same handle he had for money in the drug business translated well into the music industry. He talked about his future at that time: "Although my album has already gone gold, it will be my last one. From this point, it's all about the business." Jay-Z did not retire from rap, however. Jay-Z told *Vibe* that he realized his music had a powerful effect on his fans. "There were cats coming up to me like, 'You must have been looking in my window or following my life….' It was emotional. Like big, rough hoodlum, hardrock, three-time jail bidders with scars and gold teeth just breaking down. It was something to look at, like, I must be going somewhere people been wanting someone to go for a while." So he returned to rap in 1997, with the album *In My Lifetime, Vol. 1*. In 1998 his best-selling *Vol. 2: Hard Knock Life* record won him a Grammy Award for Best Rap Album.

In 1999, Jay-Z headlined the Hard Knock Life Tour, which also featured DMX, Beanie Sigel, and others. Jay-Z used his stature as a hit-producing rap star to ensure that the rappers he wanted would be included on the tour. At the outset, there were fears that violence would break out on the tour. The tour concluded without incident, however, and was a resounding success.

A documentary crew joined the tour, filming the rappers as they performed, hung out backstage, and traveled in tour buses. The resulting film, *Backstage*, was released in September of 2000. Some reviewers lamented that the documentary did not provide a complete picture of Roc-A-Fella's place in the rap world. Although, Elvis Mitchell of the *Contra Costa Times* noted, hardcore fans are already familiar with the rivalries of the rap business. Mick LaSalle of the *San Francisco Chronicle* wrote, "The film makes no attempt to guide hip-hop novices. It just tosses the viewer into this musical experience, which will seem vital to some and depressing and repetitious to others."

In 1999, Jay-Z was preparing to release his fourth album. In the December 27, 1999, issue of *USA Today*, Steve Jones wrote that he noticed in a session he sat in on with Jay-Z and rapper Sigel, that Jay-Z never writes down a lyric. "I don't write songs," Jay-Z explained. "I just sit there and listen to the track, and I come up with the words. It's a gift. A gift from God." In the article Jay-Z also discussed his upcoming album, *Vol. 3: The Life and Times of Shawn Carter*. He talked about how his life had changed in the few short years of his success. "With five million records out there, there are all kinds of things that you have to deal with," he said. "Even though it's just been a year, people think that things change with you and start treating you differently. Street people start thinking that maybe you've gone soft. But I'm the same dude. That's why I did the song, 'Come and Get Me.' I'm still holding firm in my position."

In 1999, Jay-Z and Dash established Rocawear clothing company. By September of 2005, the company had grossed more than $500 million. That same year, Dash severed business ties with Jay-Z by selling back his stake in Rocawear for $22.5 million. Denying any hard feelings, Dash explained to UPI News-Track, "It was time for everybody to do their own thing."

In early December of 1999, Jay-Z was charged with first-degree assault and second-degree assault after Untertainment Records executive Lance "Un" Rivera was stabbed once in the stomach and once in the shoulder. According to *Newsweek*, Jay-Z suspected that Rivera had released bootleg copies of his fourth album, an act that would lead to the loss of millions of dollars in rightful profits. When the two came face to face at a record-release party for rapper Q-Tip held in a New York nightclub, eyewitnesses reported that there was an altercation between the two. In the commotion that followed, Rivera was stabbed. At his arraignment in early 2000, Jay-Z pleaded not guilty.

In the weeks between the stabbing incident in New York, and the release of his new album, Jon Caramanica talked about Jay-Z's difficult week in early December of 1999. "After the breakout success of last year's *Vol. 2: Hard Knock Life,* the expectations on Jay-Z were greater than ever," Caramanica wrote. "In fact, it's been speculated that the entire stabbing incident was part of some large marketing conspiracy to guarantee strong buzz and sales. In hip-hop, where crime is often flipped as a marketing tool, having your artist splashed across the cover of the *Daily News* may well work financial wonders, but that option seems absurd for a man in Jay's position. Still, the very existence of such a theory hints at an underlying belief that Jay, of all rappers, is too smart to go out like this. Business, never personal." Jay-Z commented in *Vibe* in December of 2000 on the fact that, one year after the stabbing incident, a trial date still had not been set. "I feel that if it was any other person," Jay-Z said, "it wouldn't still be dragging on this long." Yet he maintained a positive attitude. He told *Vibe*, "Everything happens for a reason. It's another learning experience for me."

Despite the mixed reviews of *Vol. 3: Life and Times of Shawn Carter* and his legal troubles, Jay-Z was still on top of his game. The album was an instant platinum success, emphasizing that he still had the power to be a number-one seller in the genre he helped to define. In 2000, Jay-Z released *The Dynasty: Roc la Familia*. He told *Vibe*, "I could make records as long as I have the desire to really dig deep and challenge myself to do it. I can do it for as long as I want." *Dynasty* featured a host of new producers, including Just Blaze and Kanye West, who would go on to produce some of Jay-Z's biggest hits. Jay-Z shared equal mic time with up-and-coming Roc-A-Fella artists on the album, including Memphis Bleek and Sigel. The album produced a few hits, including the huge success that was "I Just Wanna Love U (Give It To Me)."

Already in the public eye in 2001 with a chart-topping duet with R. Kelly, "Fiesta," Jay-Z dropped what would become an instant classic—*The Blueprint*—on September 18, 2001. Selling nearly a half million albums in less than a week, *The Blueprint* was universally praised by critics and loved by fans. The first track on the album, "Takeover," was a searing attack on New York rapper Nas (Nas would reply with his own track, "Ether," attacking Jay-Z in the following weeks), a five-minute narrative over a blistering, thumping sample of the Doors' "Five to One." But "Takeover," wrote *All Music Guide* critic Jason Birchmeier, was "just one song. There are 12 other songs on *The Blueprint*—and they're all stunning, to the point where the album almost seems flawless." Besides the battle track, the album also showcases Jay-Z's songwriting skills on tracks like "Song Cry" and "Heart of the City." Birchmeier concluded that *The Blueprint* is "a fully realized masterpiece."

In the months that followed, the battle with Nas heated up. In response to "Ether," Jay-Z delivered an exclusive freestyle to a New York radio station, "Super Ugly," that dug deep at Nas. Among concerns that the battle could result in tragedy (as was the case with the Notorious B.I.G. and Tupac Shakur in the 1990s), the battle slowly faded away. "Ultimately, Jay-Z and Nas have too much at stake for foolishness," wrote *Village Voice* contributor Selwyn Hinds, "and together they crafted a piece of hip-hop myth that will live for years to come."

Jay-Z recognized this in an MTV *Unplugged* session. Performing the track "Takeover," he referred to the act of the battle as "the truest essence of hip-hop," but one whose place was solely in recorded material. The MTV session, featuring the Roots as Jay-Z's backing band, was released in late 2001. Jay-Z was the first hip-hop artist to record an MTV *Unplugged* session, and Jay-Z's material translated to the format surprisingly well. "Hip-hop with live instrumentation has seldom sounded this good," wrote Hinds in the *Village Voice*.

The Blueprint 2: The Gift & the Curse, a double album with 25 tracks and numerous guest starts including Rakim, Dr. Dre, Lenny Kravitz, and Beyonce Knowles, followed within a year. The release was generally thought to be unfocused and too long; many reviewers agreed that if Jay-Z had edited the album down to a single disc, it would've been another classic. *All Music Guide* reviewer John Bush observed: "It's clear Jay-Z's in control even here, and though his raps can't compete with the concentrated burst on *The Blueprint*, there's at least as many great tracks on tap, if only listeners have enough time to find them." A few months later, Jay-Z released *The Blueprint 2.1*, featuring the best tracks from *The Blueprint 2* on a single CD.

Jay-Z began talking about retiring from the stage even before releasing *The Blueprint 2*. He told reporters that his next album, the follow-up to *The Blueprint 2*, would be his final official release. The original concept for the release was to make a prequel to *Reasonable Doubt*, with no guest stars and a different producer for each track. What resulted was *The Black Album*. Though somewhat removed from the original concept, Jay-Z often and rightfully referred to the release as his most introspective album. From the track "December 4th" (Jay-Z's birth-day), featuring spoken word interludes from his mother, to the bittersweet closing track "My First Song," Jay-Z used this turn in the studio to make an album that was at times hilarious and heart-breaking, and above all, honest. As he put it himself, "There's never been a n***a this good for this long, this hood or this pop, this hot for this long."

The Black Album was accompanied by an autobiography, *The Black Book;* a line of sneakers for Reebok, the S. Carter Collection; and a final sold-out show at New York's Madison Square Garden. Speaking to MTV's Sway, Jay-Z tried to explain why he planned to retire while still enormously popular. "I'm in the comfort zone as far as making music," he said. "I'm a young guy, and I still have to challenge myself in life. I have to step outside my comfort zone. That's just part of being alive."

A feature film, *Fade to Black,* arrived in theaters in late 2004. The documentary, shot during the recording of *The Black Album* and at Jay-Z's "farewell" show at Madison Square Garden, received a positive review from the *Chicago Tribune*: "Whether a legend was born (or retired) that night at the Garden remains to be seen, but even on film, it was one killer show."

His retirement was short-lived; Jay-Z soon collaborated with R. Kelly on a second album and embarked on an ill-fated tour with the controversial R&B star. Kelly was asked to leave the tour soon after it started; Jay-Z continued the tour with guest stars, billing the tour "Jay-Z and Friends". Jay-Z and Kelly traded lawsuits, each contending the other was to blame for sabotaging the tour.

Proving that again that he will never truly retire, at the end of 2004 Jay-Z accepted the position of president of Universal Music Group's Def Jam Recordings label, a position previously held by Lyor Cohen and Antonio "L.A." Reid. The three-year deal was to bring Jay-Z an estimated $8 to $10 million salary. According to *Entertainment Weekly*, it marked the first time a still-popular artist controlled a major label. Speaking to the *New York Times*, record executive Steve Stoute praised the decision to appoint Jay-Z president: "His opinion of music and his point of view on marketing is absolutely spot-on. I don't know who wouldn't want to work for him."

Selected discography

Reasonable Doubt, Roc-A-Fella, 1996.
In My Lifetime Vol. 1, Roc-A-Fella, 1997.
Vol. 2: Hard Knock Life, Roc-A-Fella, 1998.

Vol. 3: The Life and Times of Shawn Carter, Roc-A-Fella, 1999.

The Dynasty: Roc la Familia, Roc-A-Fella, 2000.

The Blueprint, Roc-A-Fella, 2001.

Unplugged (live), Roc-A-Fella, 2001.

The Blueprint 2: The Gift & the Curse, Roc-A-Fella, 2002.

(With R. Kelly) *The Best of Both Worlds,* Universal, 2002.

The Blueprint 2.1, Roc-A-Fella, 2003.

The Black Album, Roc-A-Fella, 2003.

(With R. Kelly) *Unfinished Business,* Def Jam, 2004.

(With Linkin Park) *Collision Course,* Warner Bros., 2004.

Sources

Periodicals

Billboard, June 29, 1996; November 23, 1996; December 28, 1996; September 17, 2005, p. 70.

Contra Costa Times (Walnut Creek, CA), September 7, 2000.

Daily News, April 20, 2005.

Entertainment Weekly, October 22, 2004.

Globe & Mail (Toronto, Canada), December 4, 2003.

Jet, September 27, 1999.

Los Angeles Times, December 27, 1999; December 31, 1999.

Newsweek, December 13, 1999.

New York Times, December 26, 1999; December 30, 1999; January 1, 2000; December 9, 2004.

People, April 5, 1999; October 25, 2004, pp. 75-76; January 17, 2005, p. 47.

Rolling Stone, October 14, 1999.

San Francisco Chronicle, September 6, 2000.

Teen People, June 16, 2002.

UPI NewsTrack, May 17, 2005; September 27, 2005.

USA Today, December 27, 1999; January 3, 2000.

Vibe, December 2000.

Village Voice, December 14, 1999; January 22, 2002; January 1, 2003.

Washington Post, December 14, 1999; January 2, 2000.

WWD, September 16, 2005, p. 20.

Online

"From A- to A," Slate Magazine, http://slate.msn.com/id/2091248 (April 4, 2004).

"Jay-Z," *All Music Guide,* http://www.allmusic.com (April 4, 2004).

"Jay-Z," Grammys.com, http://www.grammys.com/awards/search/index.aspx (October 6, 2005).

"Jay-Z: What More Can I Say?," MTV.com, http://www.mtv.com/bands/j/jay_z/news_feature_112103 (April 5, 2004).

Bobby Jindal

© Philip Gould/Corbis

Congressman

Born Piyush Jindal, June 10, 1971, in Baton Rouge, LA; married Supriya Jolly, 1997; children: Selia, Shaan. *Education:* Brown University, B.A.; Rhodes Scholar, Oxford University.

Addresses: *Office*—1205 Longworth House Office Building, Washington, DC 20515. *Website*—http://jindal.house.gov (congressional site). *Website*—http://www.bobbyjindal.com (campaign website).

Career

Intern to U.S. Rep. Jim McCrery; consultant, McKinsey & Co.; director of Louisiana health and hospitals department, 1996-98; executive director of the National Bipartisan Commission on the Future of Medicare, 1998-99; president of University of Louisiana system, 1999-2001; assistant secretary, U.S. Department of Health and Human Services, 2001-2003; Republican nominee for governor of Louisiana, 2003; elected to Congress, 2004; Congressman, 2005—.

Sidelights

Bobby Jindal, only the second Indian American to serve in the U.S. Congress, has a resume as impressive as some politicians in their 60s or 70s. Yet Jindal was only 33 when he became a congressman. By then, he had already run for governor of Louisiana and almost won, directed a system of universities in Louisiana, a huge department of state government, and a national commission made up mostly of U.S. senators and congresspeople, and

worked as an aide to President George W. Bush. Admirers attribute his success to his intelligence and a confidence that has converted many skeptics.

Jindal was born in 1971 in Baton Rouge, Louisiana, to parents who had just moved there from India to attend graduate school. They gave him the name Piyush, but when he was four, he told them he wanted to be called Bobby, after Bobby Brady in the television show *The Brady Bunch*. Though his parents are Hindu, Jindal converted to Christianity in high school. He attended Brown University, then went to England as a Rhodes Scholar for graduate work at Oxford University. He also worked as an intern for U.S. Rep. Jim McCrery and spent a year and a half with the consulting firm McKinsey and Co.

In 1996, at age 24, the new governor of Louisiana named Jindal the director of the state health and hospitals department. He got the job by calling McCrery. "In his spare time, Bobby Jindal told his old boss, he'd written a plan to salvage Louisiana's scandal-ridden Medicaid system," the *Washington Post*'s Amy Goldstein recounted. Jindal told McCrery he would like to be Louisiana's next secretary of health and hospitals, and he asked him to recommend him to the Republican candidate who was leading the race for governor. McCrery asked Jindal if he would consider an assistant secretary job, but Jindal said no. When a different Republican, Mike Foster, was elected governor of Louisiana, Jindal called again to ask McCrery to recommend him, and he agreed. Jindal was one of six people interviewed. As Foster admitted to the *Wall Street Journal*'s Emily Nelson, he was not looking forward to the interview, but within a half hour, Jindal had convinced him he was the best person for the job.

State legislators thought he would be totally ineffective. The job seemed impossible for anyone. The department, which took up 40 percent of the state budget, was running a deficit of $400 million. The federal government was investigating its administration of federal Medicaid funds. But within three years, Jindal had turned the department around, exposed millions of dollars of waste and fraud, and eliminated its massive deficit.

Jindal discovered that the state paid lump sums to hospitals at the beginning of a year based on how many Medicaid patients they estimated they would treat, but the state was rarely checking to see if they really treated that number. He discovered clinics that employed a dozen people but had no patients, even a clinic that bused in schoolchildren to receive candy instead of care. Few could argue with fighting abuses like that, though a representative of state pediatricians, Charles Vanchiere, told Goldstein of the *Washington Post* that some of Jindal's budget cuts hurt people relying on legitimate programs. "He did not have the life experiences to understand ... the effects of budgets on human misery," Vanchiere said.

Meanwhile, Jindal earned a reputation for honesty and frugality by buying a car instead of accepting a government vehicle, by talking in simple terms about politics in front of the legislature, and even, when he got married to Supriya Jolly (whom he knew from high school), asking ethics officials how he should handle wedding presents from people he might regulate, then including that advice in his wedding invitations.

After his success with the health and hospitals department, Jindal returned to Washington in 1998 to be the executive director of the National Bipartisan Commission on the Future of Medicare. The committee was mostly made up of senators, congressmen, health care experts, and others decades older than him. While two senators acted as the commission's chairmen, Jindal was responsible for its day-to-day operations. Ever since then, Jindal has con-

tinued to bounce back and forth between Louisiana and Washington. After running the Medicare commission, in 1999 Jindal was named president of the University of Louisiana system, which includes eight schools and 80,000 students. He held that job for two years. After George W. Bush became president, Jindal became an assistant secretary in the U.S. Department of Health and Human Services, which made him a senior health policy advisor to the president.

After that series of dazzling career moves, Jindal decided to add one more. In 2003, he ran for governor of Louisiana. He was not expected to do well in a state where white supremacist David Duke had been the Republican nominee for governor 12 years earlier. But Foster, the departing governor, endorsed him, and his intelligence, reputation for integrity, earnestness, religiosity and conservatism impressed voters. "That the sensation this political season in Louisiana is a dark-complexioned young policy wonk who neither hunts, fishes, drawls nor feeds from the public trough has astounded every political pro in the state," reported Lee Hockstader of the *Washington Post* in October of 2003, just before Jindal won one of the two spots in the primary.

Jindal's radio ads attacked abortion, gun control, and gay marriage while stressing his Catholicism. Meanwhile, on television, he pitched himself to moderates as a problem-solver. In speeches, he would impress audiences by rattling off several detailed plans on a variety of issues. He promised tax cuts to generate jobs. "We've created a climate in Louisiana that's hostile to business, to progress, to taxpayers," Jindal wrote in an op-ed piece in the *Wall Street Journal* just before the November election. "New Orleans was once the capital of the South, but 75 years of demagogues ranting in Technicolor ways about government being the answer to all our problems has taken a toll." He promised to eliminate Louisiana's unusual investment taxes, reform its tort system to lower the number of lawsuits, and ease regulations on businesses.

Jindal's Democratic opponent in the general election, Kathleen Babineaux Blanco, the lieutenant governor, criticized him as inexperienced. "The ship of state does not come with training wheels," Blanco said, as quoted by Hockstader in the *Washington Post*. She also claimed Jindal had thrown too many poor people out of Medicaid when he worked for the state. Also anti-abortion and anti-gun control, Blanco even showed off her hunting license during a debate with Jindal. But Jindal also defied typical partisan divisions by attracting more black voters than most Republicans. An endorsement from Ray

Nagin, the mayor of New Orleans and the most powerful black politician in Louisiana, helped. However, a tough anti-Jindal television ad ran just before the election; it criticized Jindal's actions as state health and hospitals director, but some of Jindal's defenders claimed its ominous warnings and dark photo of Jindal had racist undertones.

Though Jindal led in many polls before the election, Blanco beat him 52 to 48 percent. Within months of the election, Jindal announced that he would run for Congress, hoping to claim a seat that would open up thanks to the departure of a Republican congressman. Jindal fit the conservative bent of the district, which includes suburbs of New Orleans, including his home, Kenner, as well as a portion of New Orleans itself and rural areas separated from greater New Orleans by Lake Pontchartrain.

Jindal won the general election with 78 percent of the vote, making him the second Indian-American congressperson ever. Though he was only 33 when elected, the 23 freshman Republicans in Congress named Jindal their class president, and the House leadership named him an assistant whip. "He is one of the brightest people I've ever met. He's very attuned to listening to people, and what I call 're-conceptionalizing,'" Rep. Bill Thomas, chairman of the powerful House Ways and Means Committee, told writer Marilyn Werber Serafini of the *National Journal*. "A lot of people have experiences before they get to Congress, but rarely have they focused on particular policy areas like Bobby Jindal has, and also been in government at both the federal and state level."

Reporters found Jindal eager to talk about health care reform (built on individual choice, not government interference, he insisted), even though congressional leadership did not name him to a health care committee. With health care costs and the number of uninsured people rising, Jindal insisted that Republicans needed a positive vision of health care reform. "It has to be a proactive set of solutions that says, 'We're not in favor of a government-run system, but we do acknowledge gaps and challenges in the current system,'" he told Serafini of the *National Journal*.

Of course, his status as the only Indian-American congressman got him attention, too. News services in India often carried news about him. In July of 2005, Jindal and his wife were invited to a White House dinner with the prime minister of India. He also attracted notice for voting against the Central American Free Trade Agreement, which most Re-

publicans supported. (Sugar farmers in Louisiana felt the agreement would open U.S. markets to cheap sugar imports.)

When Hurricane Katrina hit the Gulf Coast on August 29, 2005, Jindal and his family were among the hundreds of thousands of people displaced. While he was returning from a trip abroad, his wife and children left their home in Kenner, joined the evacuation, and met up with Jindal at his parents' home in Baton Rouge. When New Orleans filled with floodwaters, killing hundreds of people, Jindal spoke to national news organizations about the crisis. Most of his constituents had either been driven from their homes or had water in them, he told CNN on September 1.

CNN anchor Soledad O'Brien asked Jindal why the government had not prepared better for a large hurricane hitting Louisiana. Jindal seemed ambivalent, saying he did not want to criticize state or federal efforts during rescue operations, but he also said warnings from Louisiana lawmakers had not been heeded. "In Congress, we've been fighting for years, saying if we don't restore our coasts, if we don't improve these levees, if we don't improve these pumps, we're going to pay a much more serious cost in federal disaster relief," he said. Asked about looting and other crimes taking place in the city, he called for zero tolerance of violence. A few days later, talking to Matthew Cooper in *Time*, he sounded more impatient about the federal response. "The bureaucracy needs to do more than one thing at a time," he said. "It's appropriate to save people with helicopters, but it can't be done to the exclusion of everything else." A week after the storm, Jindal told a reporter that he still did not know if his home had survived the flood.

Even though Jindal had only been a congressman for less than a year in the summer of 2005, political observers expected he had ambitions to go farther. He had more cash in his campaign fund ($1.2 million) than any other congressperson or senator from Louisiana. Much of it was said to be left over from his campaign for governor. Observers were already predicting that he would run in 2008 for the U.S. Senate seat held by Sen. Mary Landrieu.

Sources

Periodicals

AP Online, July 18, 2005.
Esquire, December 2003, p. 205.
Gannett News Service, July 19, 2005; July 28, 2005.

Hill, September 6, 2005.

National Journal, January 29, 2005, p. 294.

New York Times, January 30, 2004, p. A21.

Time, October 6, 2003, p. 18; September 12, 2005.

USA Weekend, January 2, 2005.

Wall Street Journal, January 30, 1998, p. A1; November 14, 2003, p. A12.

Washington Post, November 10, 1998, p. B1; October 4, 2003, p. A6; November 14, 2003, p. A9.

Weekly Standard, December 6, 2004.

Online

"Biography," U.S. Representative Bobby Jindal, http://jindal.house.gov (August 28, 2005).

Transcripts

American Morning, CNN, September 1, 2005.

—*Erick Trickey*

Jack Johnson

David Wimsett/Photoshot/Landov

Singer and songwriter

Born in May, 1975, in Oahu, HI; son of Jeff (a surf pro) and Patti Johnson; married Kim (a teacher); children: Moe. *Education:* Graduated from the University of California, Santa Barbara, c. 1997.

Addresses: *Home*—Oahu, HI. *Office*—c/o Moonshine Conspiracy Records, 2020 Union St., San Francisco, CA 94123.

Career

Filmed two surfing documentaries, *Thicker Than Water* and *The September Sessions,* late 1990s; first published song, "Rodeo Clowns," recorded with Garrett Dutton of G. Love and Special Sauce and appears on G. Love's 1999 album *Philadelphonic;* released *Brushfire Fairytales* on indie label Enjoy Records, 2001; toured with Ben Harper and the Innocent Criminals, 2001; signed distribution deal with Universal Records; toured as co-headlining act with Ben Harper, 2003; released CDs *On and On,* 2003, and *In Between Dreams,* 2005; established the Kokua Hawaii Foundation, a nonprofit environmental awareness group.

Sidelights

Singer-songwriter Jack Johnson reveled in some thoroughly unexpected success thanks to his debut record, *Brushfire Fairytales.* A collection of songs that the onetime pro surfer had merely played to entertain friends at beach campfires, the album reached the one-million sales mark in early 2003, less than two years after its release. Johnson's sec-

ond career was, he admitted, somewhat of a drastic departure from the competitive surf circuit. "Surfing, for me, isn't really about sharing," he replied when *Sports Illustrated* writer Josh Elliott asked him about the differences between his favorite sport and the music business. "It's about finding a good little spot, private and perfect. Surfing's too special to categorize. It's not a language, not communication. It's just complete, even when no one sees it. But my music feels incomplete if I'm not playing for somebody."

Johnson was born in 1975 on Oahu, the third largest island among the archipelago of Hawaii. His father, Jeff, was a well-known professional surfer and Johnson, like his two older brothers, Trent and Pete, spent his earliest years in and on the water. It was an idyllic childhood, he told Emma Hope in an interview that appeared in London's *Sunday Telegraph.* "My dad would take us out fishing or snorkelling every day, so we grew up in the ocean—it was our playground," he recalled. "We'd spend all our time outside. The house was just to sleep in. It was always too hot in my room."

Johnson learned to surf off Oahu's legendary North Shore, where surfers from around the globe gathered during the winter months. Its Banzai Pipeline, like other choice spots along the North Shore, was famous for the massive waves that rolled in from stormy North Pacific currents during the season. Johnson started surfing at the age of four, and emerged as a prodigy by his early teens. At the age of 14, he landed a sponsorship deal with Quicksilver, a surf-togs company, and competed on the professional circuit for a few years. In 1993, however, a near-disastrous wipeout left the 17-year-old Johnson with a broken nose and more than 100 stitches; he also lost a few teeth in the face-down collision with a reef.

During his recuperation, Johnson turned to music to pass the time. He had been playing guitar for about three years by then, and spent an increasing amount of hours practicing and playing for friends. A few months off also made him realize that the pro surf circuit was becoming distressingly commercialized, and so he opted to enter the University of California at Santa Barbara. It was not an easy transition, Johnson later admitted. "When I left for college, I watched my friends surf professionally, traveling all over the world, and it was tough," he told Elliott in the *Sports Illustrated* article. "I thought I'd made a mistake, choosing such a normal life."

Johnson began his college career as a math major, but switched to filmmaking. By 1998 he had graduated and was traveling extensively with his old surfing pals, and filming their exploits on the waves wherever they went. The footage he shot resulted in a documentary, *Thicker Than Water*. It follows Johnson and his friends on a global trek that stops at some of the top surfing spots. He followed it with *The September Sessions*, which features a few of Johnson's well-known friends taking a break from the competitive circuit for a few weeks to simply enjoy a few of their favorite surfing spots.

Johnson still played guitar, and began writing songs after he bought a Bob Dylan album on cassette during a surfing trip to Indonesia. He debuted his songs in the most low-key of settings, usually an audience of friends sitting around a beach campfire after a long day of surfing. He eventually made a four-track recording of what he considered his best work, and his surfer friends made copies for their friends on the circuit. The demo reached Garrett Dutton of G. Love and Special Sauce, an amateur surfer, who liked Johnson's "Rodeo Clowns" track, and invited him to record it for the *Philadelphonic* LP. That G. Love album was released in 1999, the same year as *Thicker Than Water*, and was the sole track to chart from it on the U.S. college-radio lists.

Johnson was introduced to J. P. Plunier, who managed singer-songwriter Ben Harper. Plunier put Johnson in touch with a drummer, Adam Topol, and bassist Merlo Podlewski, and sent them into the studio. *Brushfire Fairytales* was recorded in just seven days, and released on Enjoy Records. Plunier and a former Virgin Records executive had launched the label to issue the record, sensing that Johnson was wary of any deal with the majors, who were courting him nonetheless. During meetings, executives would ask, "Do you always have a shaved head? Would you be willing not to surf, not to make films and to tour instead?" as Johnson told Elliott in the *Sports Illustrated* interview. "Right there they'd shoot themselves in the foot. They had no idea what I was about at all."

Brushfire Fairytales was released in 2001, and Johnson toured as an opening act for Harper that year. Enthusiastic reviews followed for both the album and his performances. "With a supersoft vocal style and influences ranging from Jimmy Buffett and Cat Stevens to Ben Harper and De La Soul, Johnson has perfected the admittedly picayune art of contemporary beach music," asserted *Time* critic Josh Tyrangiel. Writing in *Sports Illustrated*, Elliott also compared Johnson's style to Buffett as well as a drastically different American icon, finding that *Brushfire Fairytales*'s "blend of folk and blues, its nods to [Jimi] Hendrix and Buffett, its mix of smoky vocals and playful guitar and hip-hop sensibility ... is as laid back as it is eclectic."

Steadily growing sales for *Brushfire Fairytales* prompted executives at Universal Records to offer a distribution deal for it. This helped sales pass the one-million mark, and Johnson's debut was certified platinum by the Recording Industry Association of America in early 2003. The achievement was doubly impressive given the fact that there had been virtually no marketing budget behind it, and the buzz around the record had mounted simply via word-of-mouth. There was talk that because the surfing crowd picked up on Johnson's music first, it moved effortlessly to a wider audience thanks to the cache of that first group. Johnson was skeptical about the idea that surfers were trendsetters responsible for the success of his music. "I don't know many real surfers who put a bunch of energy into trying to figure out what's coming next," he told Chris Mauro in *Surfer*. "That's the problem with labels sometimes, they have formulas for everything, always trying to figure out why things work and then duplicate them, but the bottom line is you can't formulate authenticity, timing, or luck."

Not surprisingly, Johnson still operated in the characteristically relaxed surfer mode despite his phenomenal success. "I can get stressed if there are too many shows in a row," he admitted to *Entertain-*

ment Weekly writer Carina Chocano. "I don't always feel like getting in front of people or entertaining a crowd. But once I get up, the energy from the crowd is always so good, I have fun." He returned to the studio to make his second record, *On and On,* but the studio was his brother's garage. Will Hermes reviewed it for *Entertainment Weekly* and gave it high marks. "There are signs of rhythmic sharpening," he noted, and commended some of the tracks that took a decidedly political stance, which he felt "show a man more culturally engaged than you'd suspect." Hermes also surveyed Johnson's place in his genre, and concluded that "while the vocal similarities to jam-band peers Harper and Dave Matthews are striking, Johnson's songs are, frankly, more instantly likable than theirs, more tuneful and less earnest."

Johnson remains based in Hawaii, where he lives with his wife, Kim, a math teacher he met at U.C.-Santa Barbara. In 2004, he began to hold benefit concerts to fund a charity he established, the Kokua Hawaii Foundation. Its goal is to promote the protection of the island state's fragile environment through educational efforts in the schools. Overdevelopment was one issue he felt strongly about, and had witnessed the long-reaching ramifications of resort-building on Oahu during his own lifetime. Where beachfront hotels cropped up, he noted, it seemed to tear apart the community, robbing Hawaiian teens of recreational activities, he told Hope in the *Sunday Telegraph.* The illegal drug known as crystal meth was a growing problem in the more populated areas of Hawaii, he pointed out. "Where there's access to surfing beaches, there's not really a drug problem," he asserted. "Kids that surf don't need any drugs."

Johnson's message of respecting the environment also came through on one of the songs that Johnson contributed to the soundtrack for *Curious George,* the 2006 film adaptation of the popular children's stories. "The Three R's" urged kids to become more environment-friendly consumers by re-using and recycling. "Sometimes it takes a big warning sign before people take notice, or you have to wait till it's all too far gone before they start worrying about it," he said in the *Sunday Telegraph* interview. "It seems to me that putting a little bit of energy into teaching kids can't hurt. You can't teach them too much—all you can do is put the seed into their minds. I try not to be too preachy about it."

Johnson released his third record, *In Between Dreams,* in March of 2005. A little more than a year later, it had sold more than two million copies. One single, "Good People," reached the Top 30 on the U.S.

modern-rock charts, and the album also did well in the United Kingdom. Still with Topol and Podlewski, Johnson continued to perform for sell-out crowds, including a two-night gig in New York City's Central Park in September of 2005. On a tour of England a few months later, adoring ticketholders greeted his performances with an enthusiasm that matched the ardor of his American fan base.

Known for appearing onstage in flip-flops or sometimes even barefoot, Johnson continues to divide his time between the demands of the Banzai Pipeline and those of his music career. He and his wife had become parents, to a son they named Moe. Johnson joked with Mauro in the *Surfer* article that people sometimes ask him about his three-pronged career and future direction, noting some say, "'You're so ambitious, is there anything else you want to tackle in life?' I just laugh because I've always considered myself more of a slacker than an ambitious person. In reality I wake up, surf, go shoot some film or play music for a couple hours, surf again, then at night play some more. It's just my lifestyle."

Selected discography

(Contributor) *Philadelphonic,* Sony, 1999.
(Contributor) *Loose Change* (soundtrack), Surf Dog, 2000.
(Contributor) *Out Cold* (soundtrack), RCA, 2001.
Brushfire Fairytales, Enjoy, 2001; reissued, Universal, 2002.
(Contributor) *The September Sessions* (soundtrack), Universal/Moonshine Conspiracy, 2002.
On and On, Universal/Moonshine Conspiracy, 2003.
In Between Dreams, Brushfire/Universal, 2005.
Sing-A-Longs and Lullabies for the Film Curious George, Brushfire/Island, 2006.

Sources

Books

Contemporary Musicians, vol. 45, Gale Group, 2004.

Periodicals

Entertainment Weekly, May 9, 2003, p. 74, p. L2T15.
New York Times, September 14, 2005, p. E1.
Sports Illustrated, May 27, 2002, p. A20.
Sunday Telegraph (London, England), April 2, 2006, p. 3.

Surfer, June 2003, p. 53.
Time, September 17, 2001, p. 100.

—*Carol Brennan*

Wendy Evans Joseph

Architect

Born c. 1955; daughter of Melvin and Fran Evans; first marriage ended in divorce; married Peter Joseph (a merchant banker; died c. 1998); married Jeffrey V. Ravetch (a scientist), October, 2001; children: Danielle, Nicholas (from second marriage). *Education:* Graduated summa cum laude from the University of Pennsylvania, 1977; earned architecture degree from Harvard University's Graduate School of Design.

Addresses: *Home*—New York, NY. *Office*—Wendy Evans Joseph Architecture, 500 Park Ave., New York, NY 10022-1606.

Career

Worked for a Cambridge, Massachusetts, architectural firm, c. 1977-78; with Pei Cobb Freed & Partners, c. 1981-93; founded own firm, Wendy Evans Joseph Architecture, New York City, 1993; president of the New York City chapter of the American Institute of Architects, 1999-2000.

Awards: Henry Adams medal, American Institute of Architects, for best student thesis while at Harvard University Graduate School of Design; Rome Prize, American Institute of Architects, c. 1983.

Sidelights

American architect Wendy Evans Joseph has built her professional reputation as a talented designer of museums and other public spaces. She and her eponymous New York City firm have also ventured into the hotel and restaurant sector, most notably with a renovation of a landmark Frank Lloyd Wright office tower in Bartlesville, Oklahoma.

Born in the mid-1950s, Evans Joseph completed her undergraduate education with top honors at the University of Pennsylvania in 1977. She graduated from the school with a major in design, but had originally begun her college career intending to study math and physics. One day, an architecture student happened to walk past her, and glanced at the notebook Evans Joseph had covered with her impressive sketches of the university's buildings, and encouraged her to rethink her chosen major.

After finishing at Penn, Evans Joseph worked for an architectural firm in Cambridge, Massachusetts, for a year before entering Harvard University's Graduate School of Design. Once again, she excelled at her studies, graduating first in her class and winning the coveted Henry Adams Medal from the American Institute of Architects (AIA) at her school for best senior thesis. Her winning proposal involved a design for the entrance to the Portland Museum of Art in Maine, and one of the judges had actually done the new addition, the Charles Shipman Payson Building, himself. That architect, Henry N. Cobb, was impressed enough to hire Evans Joseph for her first job out of Harvard, at Pei Cobb Freed & Partners, the New York City firm founded by Cobb and his more famous partner, the architect I.M. Pei.

Evans Joseph spent a dozen years with Pei Cobb Freed, seven of them as a senior associate. She was involved in one of the firm's most important projects, the U.S. Holocaust Memorial Museum in Washington, D.C., which opened to the public in 1993. That same year, she also struck out on her own and opened her own practice in New York City, Wendy Evans Joseph Architecture. By then she had wed for the second time, to merchant banker Peter Joseph, with whom she would have two children. But tragedy struck when her husband was diagnosed with cancer, and he died in 1998 at the age of 47.

Evans Joseph was immersed in caring for her ill husband in 1996 when she was contacted by Cathy Bonner, founder and president of a planned Women's Museum in Dallas, Texas. Bonner had just read an article about Evans Joseph's work, and wanted to meet with her about designing the museum building. Evans Joseph's firm had never taken on such a large-scale project to date; moreover, her personal family commitments were considerable at the time. But the Texas museum's board "hung in there until I got my life in order and could focus on their project," she told *Dallas Morning News* writer David Dillon. "They didn't even check references. They just had faith that I could figure things out."

The 70,000-square-foot Women's Museum opened in September of 2000, and in the interview that appeared in the *Dallas Morning News* with Dillon that same month, Evans Joseph conceded that not everything had been built as she originally hoped. "It was my first solo building," she noted. "I didn't have this big portfolio of work that enabled me to get my way. All I could do was say maybe this or that might work, and sometimes that wasn't enough." That same year, she was selected to design another museum, the National Jazz Museum in Harlem, the culturally rich historic center of African-American life in New York City.

With her firm's reputation on the rise, Evans Joseph won her first significant hospitality project, for Long Island's Greenporter Hotel and Spa, in the North Fork community of Greenport outside of New York City. Her task was to renovate a vintage 1950s-era motel, and it was a tough one. "Not only was the building old," she told Rachel Fishman in *Hospitality Design*, "it hadn't been built all that well in the first place." But Evans Joseph's renovation won a citation on that magazine's annual awards list of notable buildings in 2002.

Evans Joseph's next major commission was also for the hospitality industry, The Inn at Price Tower in Bartlesville, Oklahoma. The new facility was to be located inside a renowned Frank Lloyd Wright building, the Price Tower, a Bartlesville landmark that had fallen into disrepair. Wright was a legendary figure in the world of twentieth-century American architecture, and his 19-story Price Tower was a rare example of only two skyscrapers the master completed during his prolific career. Built in the mid-1950s for the H.C. Price Company, an oil firm, it was originally used as offices and living quarters for company executives. Wright was known for meticulously planning everything about a building, even down to its window treatments, and Evans Joseph borrowed some of those ideas, but adapted them by using contemporary materials. The Inn opened in mid-2002, and the restaurant and 21-room hotel helped provide the financial income for the next stage of the Price Tower renovation, the adjacent Price Tower Arts Center.

Evans Joseph is the past president of the New York chapter of the American Institute of Architects, and she also sits on the advisory boards of the Graduate School of Fine Arts at the University of Pennsylvania and for the Graduate School of Design at Harvard. She is also involved with the American Ballet Theater, a legacy of her second husband's generous support of that institution. She remarried in 2001, to molecular geneticist Jeff Ravetch, whom she met through her work. "I'm used to new clients, so I didn't notice when Jeff decided to 'get the girl' by having me design an observatory," she told *More* journalist Julia M. Klein. "He didn't wind up hiring an architect at all—he wound up marrying an architect, which is a lot cheaper."

Evans Joseph and Ravetch live in a Manhattan penthouse with their blended family of four children. They spend a month or two in Italy each summer, a legacy of her year in Italy when she won the AIA Rome Prize in the early 1980s.

Sources

Architecture, May 1999, p. 46; May 2000, p. 44; November 2002, p. 17.
BusinessWeek, November 3, 2003, p. 59.
Dallas Morning News, September 22, 2000.
Hospitality Design, November 2002, p. 72.
Interior Design, July 2003, p. 174.
Lodging Hospitality, July 1, 2003, p. 49.
More, December 2003/January 2004, p. 144.
New York Times, June 26, 1998; October 28, 2001; April 24, 2002; October 16, 2003.
Pennsylvania Gazette, November/December 2000.

—*Carol Brennan*

William Joyce

© Philip Gould/Corbis

Author, illustrator, and producer

Born William Edward Joyce, December 11, 1957, in Shreveport, LA; son of George Edward and Mary Katherine (Hargrove) Joyce; married Frances Elizabeth Baucum, December 28, 1985; children: Mary Katherine and Jackson Edward. *Education:* Southern Methodist University, Dallas, TX, B.A., 1981.

Addresses: *Home*—3302 Centenary Blvd., Shreveport, LA 71104. *Office*—c/o Harper Collins Publishers, 10 E. 53rd St., New York, NY 10022-5244.

Career

Began working as a children's book illustrator, 1981; author of children's books, 1985—; creative consultant, *Toy Story*, Disney, 1995; screenwriter, producer, and set designer, *Buddy*, 1997; developer of television specials for FOX Network, 1997—; visual effects consultant, *A Bug's Life*, Pixar, 1998; creator and executive producer, *Role Polie Olie*, Disney Channel, 1998—; executive producer, designer, story editor, *George Shrinks*, PBS, 2001—; producer and production designer, *Robots*, 2005.

Awards: Daytime Emmy Award for best production design, Academy of Television Arts and Sciences, for *Rolie Polie Olie*, 1999; named "Louisiana Legend" by Friends of Louisiana Public Broadcasting, 2003.

Sidelights

William Joyce has branched out from a successful career as a children's book author and illustrator to become the producer of the popular children's television shows *Rolie Polie Olie* and *George Shrinks*. In addition, he has contributed to the blockbuster movies *Toy Story, A Bug's Life,* and *Robots.* On both the page and screen, Joyce has become known for unique characters that appeal to kids and adults alike, as well as for a visual style that harkens back to earlier eras. His artwork has been collected by such grown-up celebrities as Robin Williams and Whoopi Goldberg.

Joyce was born in Shreveport, Louisiana, on December 11, 1957, to George and Mary Katherine Joyce. He demonstrated an early interest in his chosen field, entering a classroom contest for the best written and illustrated story in the fourth grade. While his classmates loved "Billy's Booger," the tale of a young boy who blows a green, globby superpower out of his nose, the teacher found the story offensive and sent young Joyce to the principal's office. Joyce had limited access to stories as a child, but thanks to a friendly librarian, he read many classics of children's literature, including *Peter Rabbit, Stuart Little,* A.A. Milne's Winnie the Pooh books, and Maurice Sendak's *Where the Wild Things Are.* "I didn't have many books as a kid," Joyce told CNN.com. "I lived in a small southern town and the only library was way out in the woods in an honest-to-God log cabin. Thankfully, however, there was a very courageous librarian who loved children's books. So I was able to, on occasional visits, see books that changed my life."

Joyce studied film at Southern Methodist University in Dallas, Texas, graduating with a B.A. in 1981. Upon graduation, he began working as a children's book illustrator, and in 1985 Harper published his first self-illustrated work, *George Shrinks*. The book tells the story of a boy who wakes up one day to find that he has shrunk. He devises clever maneuvers to accomplish his daily tasks, such as jumping into a goldfish bowl to feed his pet fish and riding on his brother's back to take out the trash. *George Shrinks* became a Public Broadcasting System (PBS) television series in 2001. Joyce introduced one of his most well-loved characters in his next book, *Dinosaur Bob and His Adventures with the Family Lazardo*, published in 1988. The book centers on a happy-go-lucky dinosaur who moves in with a human family. *Dinosaur Bob* was followed by 1990's *A Day with Wilbur Robinson*. A humorous look at the day in the life of an unusual family, Joyce based the book on events from his own childhood. Walt Disney Productions has optioned the book for a feature film. "It wasn't until I visited what were thought to be normal households as a child that I realized our family was different," Joyce observed in an interview for PBS' Reading Rockets website. "When I would go to a normal household where people sat around and ate dinner at the table and said grace and please and thank you, I thought that was curious and odd because at my house we were throwing food and there was opera playing and people were singing at the table. And there was so much pandemonium that quiet meals in the sitting position seemed very strange to me."

Joyce continued to publish books, including *Bently and Egg*, *Santa Calls*, and *The Leaf Men and the Brave Good Bugs*, a tender tale of memory and loss based on a story Joyce told his young daughter, Mary Katherine, after the death of a terminally ill friend. Joyce took his first foray into the world of film in 1995, when he served as creative consultant to the popular Pixar film *Toy Story*. Two years later he co-authored the screenplay to the Columbia Pictures live-action film *Buddy*, based on his book of the same name. In 1998, he worked on the special effects for the Pixar film *A Bug's Life* and, that same year, he began serving as executive producer of the animated television series, *Rolie Polie Olie*, for the Disney Channel. The concept for the show began as a book, Joyce explained to Reading Rockets. "It was about a planet of robots where everything is round," he recalled. "But I'd gotten tired of drawing circles. It was just boring me crazy. Circles are very precise and you really have to get it just right or it looks lumpy and bad and I'm really not much for preci-

sion. So I shelved it—until I got approached to do a television series." Through computer animation, Joyce could easily create precise circles without the tedium. He eventually finished the *Rolie Polie Olie* book as well; it was published in 1999.

George Shrinks, which is based on Joyce's 1985 book, premiered on PBS in 2001. Joyce serves as executive producer, designer, and story editor for the show. He returned to film in 2005 with *Robots*, produced by Blue Sky. Joyce served as producer and production designer, working mainly from his office in Shreveport and emailing drawings to director Chris Wedge. Reviewers were quick to praise the film's visual appeal, if not its pacing or plot. "*Robots* is one of the most visually impressive animated features ever made. In terms of design and execution, it's on par with *Pinocchio* and *Fantasia*," enthused Rudy Panucci and Melanie Larch of the *Charleston Gazette*. Writing for the *Denver Post*, Steven Rosen noted the vintage appeal of Joyce's designs, which were inspired by art deco and appliances and industrial objects from the 1930s and 1940s. "While kids may not notice, parents may think *Robots'* style is reminiscent of a 1940s-era gas station/diner on Route 66," Rosen observed. "Everything looks progressively new and exciting for its time—bright colors, bold graphics, lots of gauges and rivets, and a sense of industry on the march. The star robots in this film recall the gas pumps, auto parts, cash registers, jukeboxes, candy machines, toasters, and vacuum cleaners of Americana."

Although he says he enjoys all his projects, Joyce told the Baton Rouge *Advocate*'s Judy Bergeron that writing and illustrating books is his favorite job. "Doing books is like getting paid for recess. Nobody messes with you. It's great," he remarked. "TV shows are almost as good as recess. You have more people to play with, so sometimes there can be friction. Stakes are small enough for TV so that if it gets good ratings, they leave us alone. Movies cost more money. They're more frustrating, although 20th Century FOX has been great to us. They like everything we've done. That's rare." Joyce told CNN.com that technological advances have enhanced his work significantly. "We live in an age of technological wonders," he observed. "It is a thrilling time for a storyteller like me to be able to do my stories the way I want to do them in so many different media…. The technology is there and there are enough people in charge who are willing to trust that some backwater swamp rat like me might actually know what I am doing, and trust me enough to oversee a bunch of television shows. Pinch me so I will know this is true."

Selected writings

Author and illustrator

George Shrinks, Harper (New York City), 1985; special miniature edition, 1985.
Dinosaur Bob and His Adventures with the Family Lazardo, Harper, 1988.
A Day with Wilbur Robinson, HarperCollins (New York City), 1990.
Bently & Egg, HarperCollins, 1992.
Santa Calls, HarperCollins, 1993.
The Leaf Men and the Brave Good Bugs, HarperCollins, 1996.
Buddy, HarperCollins, 1997.
The World of William Joyce Scrapbook, HarperCollins, 1997.
Dinosaur Bob (board book), HarperCollins, 1998.
Life with Bob (board book), HarperCollins, 1998.
Baseball Bob (board book), HarperCollins, 1999.
Rolie Polie Olie, HarperCollins, 1999.
Snowie Rolie, HarperCollins, 2000.
Sleepy Time Olie, HarperCollins, 2001.
Rocket Up, Rolie, Disney, 2002.
Big Time Olie, Laura Geringer Books (New York City), 2002.

Illustrator

Catherine and James Gray, *Tammy and the Gigantic Fish*, Harper, 1983.
Marianna Mayer, *My First Book of Nursery Tales: Five Mother Goose Stories*, Random House (New York City), 1983.
Bethany Roberts, *Waiting-for-Spring Stories*, Harper, 1984.
Elizabeth Winthrop, *Shoes*, Harper, 1986.
Jan Wahl, *Humphrey's Bear*, Henry Holt & Company (New York City), 1987.

Joyce Maxner, *Nicholas Cricket*, Harper, 1989.
Stephen Manes, *Some of the Adventures of Rhode Island Red*, HarperCollins, 1990.

Screenwriter

(With Caroline Thompson) *Buddy* (screenplay), Columbia Pictures, 1997.

Sources

Books

Major Authors and Illustrators for Children and Young Adults, 2nd ed., 8 vols., Gale Group, 2002.

Periodicals

Advocate (Baton Rouge, LA), October 4, 1998, p. 30; March 30, 2003, p. 14.
Charleston Gazette (West Virginia), March 17, 2005, p. 16D.
Denver Post, March 15, 2005, p. F5.
Los Angeles Times, July 23, 1995, p. 10; March 11, 2005, p. E1.

Online

"Author William Joyce Talks about His Book, 'George Shrinks,'" CNN.com, http//www.cnn.com/chat/transcripts/2000/9/29/joyce/index.html (August 2, 2005).
"Reading Rockets Interview with William Joyce," Reading Rockets.org, http://www.readingrockets .org/transcrpts.php?ID=96 (August 2, 2005).

—Kristin Palm

Islam Karimov

Yuri Kadobnov/AFP/Getty Images

President of Uzbekistan

Born Islam Abdughanievich Karimov, January 30, 1938 in Samarkand, Uzbekistan; married Tatiana Akbarovna; children: two daughters. *Education:* Central Asian Politechnical Institute, mechanical engineering degree; Tashkent Institute of National Economy, doctorate in economics.

Addresses: *E-mail*—presidents_officepress-service.-uz. *Office*—Dom Pravitelstva, Tashkent 70000, Uzbekistan. *Website*—www.umid.uz/Main/Uzbekistan/President/president.html.

Career

Foreman at a farm machinery plant, c. 1960; engineer at an aircraft plant, 1961-66; worked at State Planning Committee of Uzbekistan, 1966-1983; appointed minister of finance of Uzbekistan, 1983; became chairman of the State Planning Committee and vice-chairman of Uzbekistan council of ministers, 1986; became first secretary of the Uzbekistan Communist Party's central committee, 1989; named president of Uzbekistan, 1990; declared Uzbekistan's independence from the Soviet Union, 1991; elected president of independent Uzbekistan, 1991; reelected president, 1995; reelected president, 2000.

Sidelights

Islam Karimov, a former Communist, became president of Uzbekistan in 1990, a year before his country became independent of the Soviet Union, and he has held on to the office ever since. His relations with Western countries have often been shaky,

because international observers have long complained that Uzbekistan has not held truly free elections since he became president and that his government often violates human rights. He became an ally of the United States in 2001, when that country went to war in Afghanistan and Uzbekistan's location north of Afghanistan became strategic. Karimov's cooperation with the war, including allowing the United States to set up a military base in Uzbekistan, led to U.S. President George W. Bush inviting him to visit the United States in 2002. Critics of the relationship complained that the United States was ignoring Uzbekistan's human rights record and turning prisoners over to Uzbekistan in spite of reports of torture in Uzbek prisons. When the American and British governments criticized Uzbekistan for a crackdown in May of 2005 that left many protesters dead, Karimov's government kicked the American base out of his country and sought to restore closer ties with Russia.

Karimov was born on January 30, 1938, in Samarkand, Uzbekistan, when his native country—in Central Asia, north of Afghanistan—was one of the 15 republics that made up the Soviet Union. His official biography says his father was an office worker, while a biography by Human Rights Watch says Karimov was raised in a Soviet orphanage. Karimov got an engineering degree at the Central Asian

Politechnical Institute and a doctorate in economics from the Tashkent Institute of National Economy. He worked for a while as a foreman at a farm machinery plant in Tashkent, the Uzbek capital, then, in 1961, became an engineer at a plant in Tashkent that made cargo planes. He went to work for the Uzbek government's State Planning Committee in 1966 and worked his way up to become its vice-chairman.

Karimov was appointed minister of finance for Uzbekistan in 1983, then moved up quickly through top government offices. In 1986, he became head of the planning committee and vice-chairman of the council of ministers. He became the republic's leader in June of 1989, when he was named first secretary of the Uzbekistan Communist Party Central Committee, and the Supreme Council of the Uzbek republic named him president in March of 1990.

While much of the Soviet Union underwent dramatic democratic change in 1991, Uzbekistan under Karimov did not. In August of 1991, when hardline Communists attempted a coup against Soviet leader Mikhail Gorbachev, Karimov at first supported the coup leaders. "We have always been supporters of firm order and discipline," he told the Uzbek parliament, according to Edward Gargan of the *New York Times.* "We have made order and discipline the basis of our policy. A leadership that abandons order and discipline can never return to power." During the coup in Moscow, Uzbek police and the KGB (Russian secret police) arrested and fined members of the Uzbek opposition party, Birlik. After the coup in Moscow collapsed, the Uzbek government changed course and denounced the coup leaders, and Karimov declared Uzbekistan to be an independent country. After an Uzbek court ruled that the arrests of the Birlik leaders were illegal, the opposition staged a large rally for reform in early September. Police broke it up, made arrests, deported journalists, closed Birlik's offices, and banned all independent newspapers.

Although the Uzbek Communist Party changed its name to the Popular Democratic Party of Uzbekistan that September, Karimov, according to Gargan of the *New York Times,* said he preferred the Chinese Communist model of government to democracy. "Maybe in other parts of the Soviet Union, the Baltics and Moscow, people can stand peacefully in a demonstration for hours," he said, but in Uzbekistan, "people quickly get excited" and "turn to violence." Karimov claimed 84 percent of the vote in the presidential election in November of 1991, which Human Rights Watch described as "seriously marred." In 1993, Muhammed Salih, who ran against Karimov in the election as a candidate of the Erk (Freedom) Party, and Abdurahman Pulatov, leader of Birlik and an organizer of the September of 1991 protest, left the country and went into exile.

Another *New York Times* reporter, Michael Specter, found little had changed when he visited Uzbekistan in April of 1995, a month after Karimov ran unopposed for reelection and received 99.6 percent of the vote. "Uzbekistan is a country locked deep in the Soviet past, where cars are constantly stopped and searched for no reason, and a cautious pedestrian's eyes are always focused on the ground," he wrote. "The only way to speak freely with someone here is to rendezvous on a park bench."

Quotes from Karimov were taught in all Uzbek schools, Specter reported. "He controls everything from the secret industrial production plans to the schedule for sweeping this sprawling capital's streets," Spector wrote. Karimov, Specter added, retained power "by locking up many of his opponents. Uzbeks and foreigners agree that his grip is absolute." A government spokesman told Specter that Uzbeks were not prepared for democracy and valued stability more. Specter wrote that the chaos and war that dominated Afghanistan, to the south, and Tajikistan, another former Soviet republic, to the east, helped explain the Uzbek desire for order. "We know that the President is not kind," an anonymous merchant told Specter. "But we can live well here if we are quiet. There is no war, no famine."

Karimov's insistence on state control of the economy kept him from having much success attracting investors from developed countries. In 2001, the International Monetary Fund (IMF) effectively closed its office in Tashkent to protest the Uzbek government's economic decisions. For instance, the government had never allowed the free exchange of the Uzbek currency, the som, leaving Western businesses holding profits they could not take out of the country or use to import equipment. "This is a complete corruption of the economy because there are so many ways of playing the exchange rates. Any system of this kind generates enormous profits for the select few who are favored by the government," the departing IMF representative, Christoph Rosenberg, told Steve LeVine of the *Wall Street Journal.*

Meanwhile, Uzbekistan's many Muslims found that the government was increasingly restricting their rights and even imprisoning them, after a brief period when their religion enjoyed more freedom in the early 1990s. In 1992, when the war began across the border in Tajikistan, the government banned an Islamic political party, and imams (religious leaders) at mosques were ordered to end every sermon with praise for Karimov. Many mosques were closed in 1998. "I agree some of my actions seem authoritarian," Karimov told Matthew Kaminski of the *Wall Street Journal,* but "it is necessary in order to avoid bloodshed," he claimed, citing Islamic fundamentalists as a danger.

The crackdown increased after several bombs exploded in Uzbek government offices in 1999, in what appeared to be an attempt to assassinate Karimov. The government blamed the armed Islamic Movement of Uzbekistan. But Muslims in Uzbekistan claimed that religious Muslims in general were targeted for arrest, especially members of the Hizb-ut-Tahrir, or the Party of Liberation, which Western diplomats described as non-violent.

About 4,000 Muslims were imprisoned in Uzbekistan from 1997 through 2000, human rights and religious groups estimated. The groups charged that government forces had beaten and pulled out the toenails of some prisoners. Prisoners in one Uzbek prison "have told their families that they are confined to their cells 23 hours a day and spend hours squatting, with their hands behind their heads," Douglas Frantz of the *New York Times* reported. "Whenever they move a limb, they are required to recite their thanks to President Karimov, their relatives say." The government denied torturing but defended its crackdown, saying it did not want religious extremists to impose a harsh fundamentalist government. Still, a report by the U.S. State Department in 2001 sharply criticized human rights violations by the Karimov regime.

But the United States' policy toward Uzbekistan changed sharply after the September 11, 2001, terrorist attacks, when the U.S. government determined they were the work of the terrorist organization Al Qaeda, which was based in Afghanistan, Uzbekistan's southern neighbor. Suddenly Uzbekistan was a strategic location to the United States. Bush singled out the Islamic Movement of Uzbekistan, which was based in Afghanistan, as a terrorist organization in his address to Congress after the terrorist attacks, a sign that the U.S. president was seeking an alliance with Karimov.

The United States quickly forged the new partnership, offering a strong hint that it would help Uzbekistan if it were ever attacked, while Karimov allowed the United States to set up a military base in his country for the invasion of Afghanistan in fall of 2001. Much of the Islamic Movement of Uzbekistan was destroyed during the invasion. U.S. Secretary of State Colin Powell thanked Karimov by visiting him toward the end of the war and delivering a letter from Bush inviting Karimov to Washington, D.C. However, Powell also had to strongly lobby Karimov to open the Friendship Bridge between Afghanistan and Uzbekistan to international relief workers who wanted to help Afghan war refugees; Karimov had closed the bridge years earlier when the Islamic fundamentalist Taliban movement had taken over Afghanistan.

Meanwhile, one of Karimov's exiled rivals was reminding the world that the president did not permit dissent. Muhammad Salih, Karimov's former opponent in the 1990 elections, was arrested during a visit to the Czech Republic on an Uzbek arrest warrant logged into the files of the international police organization Interpol. The Uzbek government had accused Salih of being involved in the 1999 bombings in Uzbekistan, even though Salih had left the country six years earlier. Human-rights organizations said the trial of Salih in abstenia was unfair and warned that they expected Salih to be tortured and killed if he were sent back to Uzbekistan. Salih spent weeks in a Czech jail, drawing comparisons to Czech President Vaclav Havel, who had once been imprisoned for his protests against his country's Communist regime.

After the Czechs released him, Salih wrote an opinion piece for the *New York Times,* warning that Uzbekistan was "drifting toward an anti-American stance, if one understands 'American' as implying democracy, human rights and the struggle against state-sponsored terror." Karimov, he noted, reversed a decision to give amnesty to hundreds of political prisoners after September 11, once he was assured of the United States' support. Karimov had been re-elected in 2000, Salih noted, in an election in which even Karimov's opponent said he would vote for Karimov, and his term had recently been extended from five years to almost eight.

In 2002, Karimov visited the United States, meeting with Bush, Powell, and other top American officials. The meeting solidified the two countries' strategic relationship. "The United States may remain in Uzbekistan as long as they think it is necessary; in other words, as long as it takes to finish disrupting the terrorist network," Karimov said, as quoted by Todd S. Purdum of the *New York Times.* The statement was a reminder that Karimov valued American help eliminating what was left of the Islamic Movement of Uzbekistan. Around the time of the visit, the United States tripled its foreign aid to

Uzbekistan. However, just before the visit, the U.S. State Department again criticized Uzbekistan for torture. "We do have problems with human rights," Purdum quoted Karimov as saying. "We're going to promote democratic development not because we want to get into the good books of the United States, but because it is in our interests," he pledged, but did not give details.

The United States faced increasing criticism for its alliance with Karimov. In 2005, a *New York Times* investigation reported that the U.S. government had flown dozens of detainees it suspected of terrorism to Uzbekistan to be interrogated, even though the U.S. State Department was criticizing the Uzbeks for torturing prisoners. U.S. officials denied that the country sent prisoners anywhere expecting them to be tortured.

A rift between Karimov and the West opened in May of 2005, when Uzbek government forces opened fire on crowds in the city of Andijan during an anti-government demonstration that followed an armed prison break. Karimov's government insisted that the clashes were part of an Islamic uprising; residents of the area said the prison break was meant to free Muslim businessmen convicted of false charges. The government eventually said 187 people were killed in the incident, while human rights groups said several hundred died, mostly unarmed civilians. The British government condemned the Uzbek military for what it called a clear abuse of human rights, and the U.S. government said it was deeply disturbed by the incident. The United States and other Western governments pressured Karimov to allow an independent investigation, but Karimov refused. Some U.S. senators argued that the Bush Administration should reevaluate its relationship with Karimov.

Karimov responded by ending his alliance with the United States and renewing ties with Russia. In June of 2005, Russian President Vladimir Putin invited Karimov to visit him, and the two men agreed to joint military exercises for their armies. By July, Uzbekistan, Russia, China and three other former Soviet republics in Central Asia demanded that the United States close its bases in the region. The Uzebek parliament then voted to cancel the American lease on the base within 180 days. In November of 2005, Uzbekistan and Russia signed a treaty that may lead to deployments of Russian troops in Uzbekistan.

At the beginning of 2006, Uzbekistan joined the Eurasian Economic Community, a group of former Soviet states led by Russia. Uzbekistan's government-owned oil and gas company also signed a deal with Gazprom, the Russian gas monopoly, to develop some natural gas fields in Uzbekistan and to let Gazprom control Uzbek gas exports—a significant step toward a closer alliance, since it came as Russia was using Gazprom as a carrot to reward its allies among the former Soviet republics while threatening to cut off supplies or raise prices for ex-Soviet republics such as Ukraine which had forged closer ties to the West. Karimov's term as president was scheduled to continue until December of 2007.

Sources

Periodicals

Guardian, May 16, 2005.
New York Times, September 18, 1991, p. A1; April 16, 1995; February 17, 1999, p. A3; October 29, 2000; October 13, 2001, p. A1; December 9, 2001; March 11, 2002, p. A21; March 14, 2002, p. A18; April 6, 2002, p. A10; May 23, 2005, p. A1; May 31, 2005, p. A1; June 9, 2005, p. A3; July 6, 2005, p. A3.
Wall Street Journal, September 8, 1998, p. 1; February 17, 1999, p. A18; March 27, 2001, p. A18; September 24, 2001, p. A19; November 21, 2001, p. A11; September 2, 2005, p. A13; November 15, 2005, p. A20; January 30, 2006, p. A1.

Online

"President of Uzbekistan: Islam Karimov," Uzbekistan, http://www.umid.uz/Main/Uzbekistan/President/president.html (February 26, 2006).
"Profile of President Islam Karimov," Human Rights Watch, http://www.hrw.org/press/2002/03/karimovprof.htm (February 26, 2006).

—*Erick Trickey*

Mel Karmazin

Laura Cavanaugh/UPI/Landov

Chief Executive Officer of Sirius Satellite Radio

Born Melvin Alan Karmazin, August 24, 1943, in New York, NY; married Sharon (a librarian and theatrical producer), 1971 (divorced, 1994); children: Dina, Craig. *Education:* Earned business administration degree from Pace College, 1967.

Addresses: *Office*—Sirius Satellite Radio, 1221 Avenue of the Americas, New York, NY 10020.

Career

Began career with Zlowe Co. as a typist, 1960, and became radio advertising buyer; advertising salesperson, WCBS-AM, 1967-70; advertising salesperson, Metromedia, 1970-75; general manager of WNEW-FM, 1975-81; president, Infinity Broadcasting, 1981-96; president, CBS Radio, 1996-2000; president and chief operating officer, Viacom, Inc., 2000-04; chief executive officer, Sirius Satellite Radio, 2004—.

Awards: Inducted into the Broadcasting Hall of Fame, 1996; recipient of the National Association of Broadcasters National Radio Award, 1997; inducted into the Radio Hall of Fame, 2003.

Sidelights

Mel Karmazin made Infinity Broadcasting one of the most profitable media companies in the United States in the 1990s. Known for his ruthless cost-cutting measures and talent for closing a deal,

Karmazin was a key player in the historic shake up of the radio industry during that decade. To the general public, he may perhaps be better known as the man who brought radio shock-jock Howard Stern to national prominence. After a stint as the number-two person at Viacom, the powerful entertainment conglomerate, Karmazin joined Stern at Sirius Satellite Radio in 2004. The move surprised many in the industry, for Karmazin had previously dismissed satellite radio, with its fee-for-service business model, as irrelevant to free, over-the-airwaves radio. Some industry analysts saw Karmazin's move as the first nail in the coffin for traditional radio, which had grown increasingly homogenized in its music playlists and riddled with commercial breaks—ironically, the after-effects of that corporate consolidation that Karmazin himself had helped to engineer. "Some call Karmazin an opportunist," noted Daren Fonda in a *Time* article about the career move, "or, more unkindly, a traitor to the old radio business—but nobody ever called him stupid."

Born in 1943, Karmazin grew up in the New York City borough of Queens, and more specifically in a public-housing project in Long Island City near the 59th Street Bridge. His father drove a taxi, and his mother worked in factory that made curtain rods. "My family had zero money," Karmazin recalled in an interview with Marc Gunther in *Fortune.* "We never had a vacation. We never had a car." In high school, a supportive teacher put Karmazin in contact with a Manhattan advertising agency called Zlowe, where the 16-year-old was hired as a typist. The firm's founder recognized the teenager's ambition, and encouraged him to get a college degree.

For several years Karmazin took night classes at Pace College while working full-time as an advertising sales associate at Zlowe. He had a tenacious, driven personality ideally suited to the job, and after earning his degree in business administration in 1967, he was hired by a New York City station, WCBS-AM Radio, as a salesperson. The job involved selling local businesses commercial air-time on the station, and it paid $17,500 plus commissions, a rather respectable salary at the time. Karmazin excelled in it, and soon began posting impressive sales numbers. He proved so talented at the job that the station was forced to adjust his commission rate when he quadrupled his base salary. His boss asserted that $70,000 was too much for a salesperson to be making. "That was the dumbest thing I'd ever heard in my life," Karmazin told Gunther in the *Fortune* interview. "I quit."

In 1970, Karmazin went to work for Metromedia, a broadcasting company that owned a number of small television stations as well as radio properties like WNEW-AM in New York City. Again, he displayed an uncanny knack for the job, and within five years was made general manager of WNEW-FM, Metromedia's New York City rock station. Karmazin soon made the station an immensely profitable one thanks to his cost-cutting and promotional strategies, and some of his compensation came in the form of stock shares of Metromedia. He later said that it was those shares that made him a millionaire when Metromedia was sold to media tycoon Rupert Murdoch in 1986 for his fledgling FOX Network.

By then Karmazin had jumped ship to Infinity Broadcasting, a relatively new radio group started by two former colleagues of his at Metromedia. He joined the company in 1981, not long after he had been passed over for the job of Metromedia's radio division head, when Infinity was about to double its radio-station holdings to six. He agreed to take the job only if the founding partners let him be in charge, and they agreed. He spent the next several years building it into one of the most powerful corporate entities in broadcasting, to be rivaled only by Clear Channel Communications. Infinity eventually expanded to 180 stations, and Karmazin proved

adept in acquiring what he commonly called "oceanfront properties," or large-market stations in cities like New York and Los Angeles. Though some of these stations were bought for record-setting price tags, Karmazin was a former advertising sales executive who knew that such media properties had comparable overhead costs to Infinity stations in smaller markets, but the advertising rates they commanded for air time were much higher.

One of the stations Karmazin acquired was a New York City disco station with the call letters of WKTU-FM. Infinity paid $15.5 million for it in the early 1980s, which set a record as highest price ever paid for single station at the time. Karmazin turned it into WXRK-FM, a rock station popularly known as "K-Rock," and in 1985 hired a somewhat controversial disc jockey named Howard Stern for its morning drive-time slot. Stern had recently been fired by another New York station for his vulgar on-air chatter, and Karmazin told Stern that it was okay if he kept his running commentary on issues of the day as well as various scatological topics, but barred him from ever mentioning Karmazin's name on the air unless he said something positive. WXRK began pulling in strong ratings numbers, and within a year Karmazin had decided to put Stern's morning show on the air in other radio markets. At the time, it was rare for a radio personality to have an audience outside of local market, but Stern's ribald humor began beating out the local competitor stations in cities like Los Angeles and Philadelphia.

Karmazin found that Stern was somewhat of a financial liability, with the Federal Communications Commission (FCC) officials regularly fining Infinity when Stern's show crossed the line into sexual or otherwise offensive content. Karmazin and the station regularly went to bat for Stern, challenging the FCC fines in lengthy legal battles, but eventually Infinity paid a lump sum of $1.7 million to settle the dispute. Karmazin had less trouble with Don Imus, another New York radio host whom he also turned into a nationally known media personality. Both Stern and Imus boosted Infinity's profile, and the company emerged as a solidly performing stock during the 1990s. Its share price climbed an average of 58 percent annually, and the company's profits were used to buy even more stations. Infinity's growth was due to new FCC ownership rules for radio and television stations, enacted as part of the Telecommunications Reform Act of 1996. The new rules rescinded the previous limit on how many stations one company could own, and even allowed for up to eight media properties in one city alone. The change made both Infinity and Clear Channel the leading players in the industry.

The Infinity radio group changed hands in 1996, when Westinghouse Electric Corporation, the parent company of CBS, bought it for $4.9 billion. Karmazin was named the head of CBS Radio, a prestigious and venerable network of stations. Long known in the industry as a ruthlessly budget-conscious executive, Karmazin brought that same management style to CBS Radio, and his tactics even included auditing the phone bills at radio stations and then excoriating the station managers for making too many personal calls. After three years of immense profits, Westinghouse, which had changed its name to the CBS Corporation, entered into a deal with Viacom, the entertainment giant that owned Paramount Pictures as well as MTV Networks. The merger, completed in 2000, made Viacom the second largest entertainment company in the world.

Viacom's immense growth had been largely the work of Sumner Redstone, who made his early fortune building multiplex cinemas in the 1970s. With the merger, Karmazin became president and chief operating officer under the terms of his three-year contract, but from the start media pundits and Wall Street analysts wondered if he and Redstone had some issues working together. Karmazin was known as an intensely involved manager, and though Redstone was not, the Viacom chair was reportedly displeased with the amount of control he had given over to Karmazin. When the contract was renewed for one year in late 2003, Karmazin indeed conceded some power, but he had also managed to protect himself from being fired outright by Redstone.

On the first day of June in 2004, Karmazin announced he was resigning for personal and professional reasons. Later that year, on November 18, Sirius Satellite Radio named him its new chief executive officer. The move followed the headline-making news of Howard Stern's departure from Infinity just six weeks earlier. Sirius was one of two satellite-radio companies gaining thousands of new listeners every month, along with XM. Satellite radio users had to buy a special receiver for their home, automobile, or personal stereo, and then pay a monthly fee for access. But satellite radio was dazzling in its variety: there were dozens of channels and formats, ranging from stations that pumped out 1970s disco hits to others that broadcast only unsigned bands; other stations featured Afro-pop or opera, and the service was rounded out by an array of talk and news-radio stations. Part of Stern's decision, he said, was that satellite radio was free from FCC interference over content. Karmazin was likely tired out by his battles with the government agency,

too, having endured a lengthy grilling before a Congressional committee over the Super Bowl XXXVIII halftime show in early 2004, thanks to a "wardrobe malfunction" on singer Janet Jackson's costume that exposed one of her breasts. The game, traditionally one of the most-watched television events of the year, aired on CBS but the halftime show was produced by MTV Networks, which was owned by Viacom.

Karmazin had once ridiculed satellite radio as anything but a threat to free, over-the-airwaves broadcast radio, but thanks to the consolidation of the U.S. radio market in which he had played such a key role during the 1990s, listeners had been tuning out in large numbers. Many voiced complaints that radio had become bland and overly corporate-monitored, with stations sticking to a shock-jock talk format or else a musical one restricted to a short playlist and endless commercials. Though Sirius, launched in 2002 a year after XM, was in second-place in the satellite-radio market, both companies were drawing thousands of new subscribers every month; by March of 2005, Sirius XM boasted 1.45 million subscribers, though that remained far behind XM's 3.77 million listeners.

Karmazin set out to change that with his characteristic vigor. One of the first major deals he scored was with domestic diva Martha Stewart, recently released from prison, for a 24-hour lifestyle channel on Sirius that was set to debut in late 2005; one of the channel's time slots would even feature the formidable homemaking tycoon taking calls from listeners. Karmazin also managed to grab the NASCAR stock-car racing deal from XM, and that was scheduled to move to Sirius in 2007. Competition between the two companies was fierce, Karmazin conceded, but satellite radio was the future, he believed. "I see a duopoly, like Coke and Pepsi," he told *Institutional Investor*'s Steven Brull. "It's a big market. Both companies will be financially very successful."

Karmazin is himself financially successful. His Sirius compensation package is estimated at $1.25 million annually, plus 30 million stock options in the company, and he was reportedly paid $35.4 million to walk away from Viacom. He reportedly never even cashed his Viacom paychecks, which were deposited instead into the bank account of his charitable foundation run by his daughter, Dina. Divorced from Sharon, a librarian turned Broadway producer, Karmazin is also the father of Craig, a budding radio mogul whose Good Karma Broadcasting owns a number of old-school, terrestrial-based radio stations.

Sources

Periodicals

Broadcasting & Cable, February 16, 2004, p. 8.
Crain's New York Business, November 24, 1997, p. 1.
Fortune, April 14, 1997, p. 110; April 16, 2001, p. 122.
Institutional Investor (International Edition), June 2005, p. 14.
Mediaweek, November 15, 1993, p. 22.

New York Times, January 27, 2003, p. C1.
Time, May 9, 2005, p. A6.

Online

"Karmazin's Exit: Old Plot, Same Ending," *Business Week Online,* http://www.businessweek.com/bwdaily/dnflash/jun2004/nf2004062_7946_db035.htm (August 4, 2005).

—Carol Brennan

Marian Keyes

© Colin McPherson/Corbis

Author

Born in September, 1963, in Limerick, Ireland; daughter of Ted and Mary (Cotter) Keyes; married Tony Baines (a computer analyst), December 29, 1995. *Education:* University College, Dublin, Ireland, BCL.

Addresses: *Contact*—c/o J. Lloyd, Curtis Brown, 28-29 Haymarket, London SW1Y 4SP United Kingdom. *Office*—c/o Penguin Publicity, 80 Strand, London WC2R 0RL United Kingdom.

Career

Worked as a waitress, London, England, beginning c. 1986; worked as an accounts clerk, London, England, through 1996; began writing short stories, 1993; published first novel, *Watermelon*, 1995; full-time writer, 1996—.

Awards: Irish Tatler Literary Award, 2001; Irish World Literary Award, 2002.

Sidelights

Popular "chick lit" author Marian Keyes is the writer of novels targeted at a female audience. Drawing on her own life's difficulties, she infuses her books with both humor and darker real-life situations such as drug addiction, depression, and miscarriages, but always writes a happy ending. Nearly all of her works are best sellers and most were translated into 30 languages. Keyes' books are more popular with readers than critics, selling more than

nine million copies by 2005. As a result of her success, she has become one of the wealthiest women in the British isles.

Born in Ireland in 1963, Keyes was raised in various cities in that country, including Cavan, Cork, Galway, and the Dublin suburb of Monkstown. Her family led a middle-class existence, and Keyes and her four younger siblings were raised in a stable, loving home. Despite her positive family situation, Keyes later stated that she felt insecure by the time she was a toddler and believed that she did not belong from an early age. Although she was an academic achiever at convent schools, Keyes was not secure at all in social situations and relationships, especially with men. By the time she was 14 years old, Keyes had begun drinking.

Keyes continued to do well as a student at University College in Dublin, where she studied law and accountancy. She earned a law degree, but was not secure enough to use it. She told Jennifer Falvey of the *Daily Telegraph*, "I always had this kind of ability to self-destruct and I never did anything to its completion and even though I was blessed with brains, I didn't have the confidence to use them properly." Already attracted to writing, Keyes applied to get a post-graduate degree in journalism, but was not accepted into a program. Instead, Keyes moved to London, England, in 1986 after completing college. She thought she was being rebellious and was attracted to living in the big city. Her first job was as a waitress in part because she could not see herself as anything else. She spent much of her free time drinking and going to parties.

After a few years, Keyes began using her degree when she worked as an accounts clerk in London. She continued to drink heavily and struggled greatly with her self-esteem. Though Keyes understood that she drank to fit in, she also knew her life was a mess and she longed to live in a more conventional manner. She began making errors at work and not taking care of herself as she regularly drank two bottles of wine a day. Keyes told Marian Pallister of the *Herald*, "It was killing me and I felt terribly lonely and a terrible failure. There are plenty of people who can live a free-spirited life, but I wasn't one of them."

Keyes reached rock bottom in January of 1994 when she attempted suicide by overdosing on pills, including antidepressants, sleeping pills, and painkillers, with a swig of alcohol. She called a friend who got her immediate help. Her parents then took her home to Ireland so she could get treatment at a rehabilitation clinic, Rutland, for three months. There, she admitted she was an alcoholic and got her life together. Keyes remained sober from that point forward.

After treatment, Keyes returned to London and began writing novels. Shortly before her suicide attempt, she had written a few short stories. While she did not initially intend to write a novel, she had decided to send her short stories to a publisher, Ireland's Poolbeg Press. In a letter she enclosed, she mentioned that she had begun work on a novel (one that did not yet exist). The publisher was impressed and asked to see some chapters of her novel so Keyes quickly composed four chapters of what became *Watermelon*.

Of the novel, Keyes told Pallister of the *Herald*, "It poured out, and I do feel it was already written in some locked room in my head, and all I had to do was turn the key." Published in 1995, *Watermelon* focused on Claire Webster, who is abandoned by her husband, James, just after she gives birth to their child. Claire takes her baby and returns to her family home in Dublin, meets another man, and considers her future. A hit in Ireland, Great Britain, and the United States, the book was written in an informal style that many readers found appealing.

Soon after the publication of *Watermelon*, Keyes' own life continued to improve. She married an Englishman, Tony Baines, on December 29, 1995. Keyes was able to quit her accounting job in 1996, and the couple moved to Ireland. They eventually settled in Dublin. While Keyes found it hard to write full time, she was able to turn the situation into a positive one.

Though she was worried that she could not duplicate the success of *Watermelon*, Keyes' second novel was even more popular than the first. A dark comedy set in London, *Lucy Sullivan Is Getting Married* was published in 1996. The title character is in her mid-twenties and has a very limited life. Lucy and three friends visit a fortune teller who makes several predictions, including that Lucy will be married within the year. Other predictions come true so Lucy believes in hers as well. Keyes uses this experience to examine the life of single women in London. The book also features Lucy's father, an alcoholic, who is partially based on Keyes herself. *Lucy Sullivan Is Getting Married* was later made into a 16-part television series.

The success of these two novels led to a bidding war between publishers over Keyes. She walked away with a very lucrative four-book deal from Penguin in the United Kingdom in 1996. Keyes proved her value with another successful book. *Rachel's Holiday* was a 700-page epic that mirrored Keyes' own experience as an alcoholic. The central character, Irish native Rachel Walsh, had been living the high life in New York City for about eight years. Suffering from low self-esteem, Walsh becomes addicted to cocaine and tranquilizers. Because of her addiction problems, her family takes her back to Ireland where she enters a well-known rehab clinic, the Cloisters. Though a dark story, the text was inflected with a dry sense of humor.

Keyes continued to explore women's problems in 1999's *Last Chance Saloon*. The book focused on three friends from childhood who are natives of Ireland and live in London and face many personal difficulties. The two women of the trio, Tara and Katherine, have difficulties finding boyfriends; Tara is overweight, while Katherine keeps men at arm's length. Fintan, a gay man, shows his friends that there is more to them than superficial concerns as he struggles with cancer. His dying wish helps them make the decision to change their lives.

By late 1990s, Keyes was becoming one of the best-known Irish authors and one of the wealthiest people in the British isles. Though her blockbuster status meant increased scrutiny, she continued to write and push herself. Over the years, the tone and setting of her books changed. Her novels focused more on the workplace and became more accessible to a wider audience of readers.

The first of Keyes's novels to focus on work was 2000's *Sushi for Beginners*. Set in the office of a new women's magazine in Dublin, the book explores the lives of three women employed there, an English editor and two Irish women, who are looking for happiness. Though they lead unhappy lives for different reasons, they all come to realize that they need to find contentment inside themselves, not from an outside source. *Sushi for Beginners* was a number-one best-seller on the *Sunday Times* list.

While Keyes was gaining fame for her novels, she was also contributing essays and columns to various publications. Many of the pieces were about her life, friendships, relationships, travel, living abroad, and many other topics. She published a collection of these non-fiction works, *Under the Duvet*, in 2001. One prominent piece in the book was about her alcoholism. Keyes donated her royalties from the book's sales in Ireland to a charity, Simon Community, an organization which benefited the homeless in the area.

Keyes took another chance with her next novel. *Angels*, published in 2002, was set in Los Angeles, California. The primary character was an Irish girl named Maggie, who was related to characters in previous novels by Keyes. Maggie was married to man named Gary for nine years, but has separated from him after she learns that he had an affair. She also loses her job and moves to Los Angeles to live with a friend, Emily, who works as a screenwriter. Maggie becomes her assistant and tries to be a "bad girl," experiencing many types of relationships. Over the course of the book, she comes to terms with her own problems and decides she might want to reconcile with her husband. Many critics found the book a funny, witty take on Los Angeles and the lives of her characters.

In an interview with Keyes upon the publication of *Angels*, Yvonne Nolan of *Publishers Weekly* noted, "Whilst in the wake of the success of *Bridget Jones' Diary*, many writers and critics have sought to dismiss chick-lit as froth, Keyes' fiction is so genuinely funny, sharply observed and winning as to make such reservations seem stuffy and wrongheaded."

Keyes made another creative leap with the novel *The Other Side of the Story*. The structure of this novel is different than her previous works. There are three stories about three women that are only slightly linked. All the stories are set in an inter-related publishing world. One main character is Jojo Harvey, an American literary agent working in London. She is in a frustrating relationship with a married man, and represents a writer named Lily. Lily's story focuses on her life as a best-selling author and a mother. Her child was fathered by Gemma's former boyfriend. Gemma has a story as well. She works as an event planner and is coping with a difficult family life. Her parents separate when her father leaves her mother for a younger woman. Gemma eventually triumphs with her own lucrative book contract and satisfying relationship. While *The Other Side of the Story* retained Keyes' trademark humor while dealing with the dark situations in her characters' lives, some critics found the relationship between the stories to be too loose for the novel to be effective as a whole.

Despite an occasional negative review, Keyes remains sure of her voice as a writer and keeps her ability in perspective. Keyes told Crawford Wayne of *Hobart Mercury*, "I don't know where this ability to write comes from so if disappears I don't know how to get it back.... I don't really worry too much about getting writer's block, because if I get it there's nothing I can do. All this is a bonus. Just being sober is enough."

Selected writings

Novels

Watermelon, Poolbeg Press (Dublin, Ireland), 1995.
Lucy Sullivan is Getting Married, Poolbeg Press, 1996.
Rachel's Holiday, Penguin (London, England), 1998.
Last Chance Saloon, Penguin, 1999.
Sushi for Beginners, Penguin, 2000.
Angels, Penguin, 2002.
The Other Side of the Story, Poolbeg Press, 2004.

Nonfiction

Under the Duvet: Shoes, Reviews, Having the Blues, Builders, Babies, Families, and Other Calamities, Michael Joseph (London, England), 2001.
Cracks in My Foundation: Bags, Trips, Make-Up Tips, Charity, Glory, and the Darker Side of the Story, Avon/HarperCollins (New York City), 2005.

Sources

Books

Debrett's People of Today, Debrett's Peerage Ltd. (London), 2004.

Periodicals

Booklist, June 1, 2001, p. 1845.
Daily Telegraph (Sydney, Australia), April 19, 1997, p. 105.
Dominion Post (Wellington, New Zealand), February 26, 2004, p. D3.
Europe, April 1998, p. 45.
Guardian (London, England), October 19, 2002, p. 26; June 19, 2004, p. 27.
Herald (Glasgow, Scotland), February 27, 1997, p. 17.
Herald Sun (Melbourne, Australia), January 27, 2001, p. W17.
Hobart Mercury (Australia), April 21, 1997.
Independent (London, England), June 4, 2004, pp. 20-21.
Kirkus Reviews, May 1, 2002, p. 600; March 15, 2004, p. 244.
Library Journal, June 15, 1998, p. 106; January 2004, p. 110.
More, May 2004, p. 32.

Observer, October 22, 2000, p. 3; May 23, 2004, p. 16.
Press (Christchurch, New Zealand), March 13, 2004, p. D12.
Publishers Weekly, April 13, 1998, p. 48; June 26, 2000, p. 50; June 3, 2002, p. 62; June 17, 2002, p. 37.
Scotsman (Scotland), February 13, 1998, p. 15.
Sunday Herald (Scotland), August 27, 2000, p. 2.
Sunday Mirror, May 24, 1998, pp. 14-15.

Online

"About Marian: Autobiography," MarianKeyes.com, http://www.mariankeyes.com/aboutMarian/profiles/autobiography.html (October 15, 2005).
"About Marian: Biography," MarianKeyes.com, http://www.mariankeyes.com/aboutMarian/profiles/biography.html (October 15, 2005).

—*A. Petruso*

Alicia Keys

© Mike Blake/Reuters/Corbis

Singer

Born Alicia Augello Cook, January 25, 1981, in New York, NY; daughter of Craig Cook (a flight attendant) and Terri Augello (a paralegal and actress). *Education:* Attended Columbia University, voice major.

Addresses: *Home*—Harlem, NY. *Record company*—J Records, 745 5th Ave., New York, NY 10151.

Career

Singer, songwriter, pianist, and producer. Released debut album *Songs In A Minor,* 2001; released *The Diary of Alicia Keys,* 2003; published book of poetry, 2004; released *Alicia Keys: MTV Unplugged,* 2005.

Awards: MTV Video Music Award for best new artist, for "Fallin'," 2001; Grammy Award for song of the year, Recording Academy, for "Fallin'," 2002; Grammy Award for best new artist, Recording Academy, 2002; Grammy Award for best female R&B vocal performance, Recording Academy, for "Fallin'," 2002; Grammy Award for best R&B song, Recording Academy, for "Fallin'," 2002; Grammy Award for best R&B album, Recording Academy, for *Songs in A Minor,* 2002; American Music Award for favorite new artist—pop or rock 'n roll music, 2002; American Music Award for favorite new artist soul/rhythm & blues music, 2002; NAACP Image Award for outstanding new artist, 2002; NAACP Image Award for outstanding female artist, 2002; MTV Video Music Award for best R&B video, for "If I Ain't Got You," 2004; American Music Award for favorite female artist soul/rhythm & blues music, 2004; NAACP Image Award for best female artist, 2004; NAACP Image Award for best song, 2005; NAACP Image Award for best music video, 2005; MTV Video Music Award for best R&B video, for "Karma," 2005; Grammy Award for best female R&B vocal performance, Recording Academy, for "If I Ain't Got You," 2005; Grammy Award for best R&B song, Recording Academy, for "You Don't Know My Name," 2005; Grammy Award for best R&B performance by a duo or group with vocals, Recording Academy, for "My Boo" (with Usher), 2005; Grammy Award for best R&B album, Recording Academy, for *The Diary of Alicia Keys,* 2005; Rhythm & Soul Award for songwriter of the year, American Society of Composers, Authors, and Publishers, 2005.

Sidelights

Innovative, dynamic, and drop-dead gorgeous are words that have been used to describe Alicia Keys. The talented singer and musician has been wowing audiences since her first album, *Songs In A Minor,* debuted. While some artists suffer a second album slump, Keys was poised to not only match her first album's success but also exceed it by leaps and bounds. In her short career span, she has also released a book of poems and her songs' lyrics. The book, titled *Tears For Water: Songbook of Poems & Lyrics*, was labeled as some of Keys' most private thoughts. Not one to get comfortable in any juncture, Keys was also scheduled to make her film debut in 2006.

Keys was born Alicia Augello Cook on January 25, 1981, in New York City. Her parents, Craig Cook and Terri Augello, did not stay together for long, and Keys was raised mostly by her mother. She grew up in Hell's Kitchen, a tough neighborhood in Manhattan. Though Keys is biracial, she considers herself black. However, she still loves both sides of her heritage, and it was a non-issue in her neighborhood since most of its inhabitants came from diverse backgrounds.

Life was tough for Keys. Her mother struggled to make a living as a paralegal and actress. The two lived in a tiny one-bedroom apartment. However, Keys' mother wanted her daughter to learn the piano. A friend of the family gave them an old upright, and Keys began taking lessons. Keys saw how much her mother struggled to make ends meet and begged her mother to let her quit, but Augello refused. At an early age, Keys learned to play classical music. She composed her first musical piece in tribute to her grandfather; at eleven years old, she wrote her first song. She told Toure of *Rolling Stone*, "I've had a deep love for music since I was four. Music came before everything, everything, everything. It just meant more than anything ever meant. I would risk everything for it. I'd mess around and get kicked out of school for it or kicked out of my Momma's house for it. There was nothing that was more important to me." Her influences included classical composer Wolfgang Amadeus Mozart, rock group Led Zeppelin, soul singer Nina Simone, and rapper Notorious B.I.G.

Keys entered the Professional Performance Arts School in Manhattan, majoring in voice. She saw a future as a singer, and quickly found a manager to help her get started right away. Manager Jeff Robinson began grooming Keys, helping her put together a demo, and placing her in showcases where people in the record industry could hear her. He also convinced her to join a girls' choir through the Police Athletic League in Harlem. Keys and Robinson decided that she did not need backup singers or a live band, just a piano and she would get a contract. Once the executives heard her sing, a bidding war

broke out. In the end, Keys signed with Columbia Records because they also included a baby grand piano in the contract; she was just 15.

In addition to signing with Columbia, Keys also graduated from high school two years early. She was the valedictorian as well. She was accepted at Columbia University, but only lasted four weeks. She told *Rolling Stone* it was too much handling class during the day with studio sessions at night. She also moved into her own apartment at 17.

But what was once Keys' biggest opportunity turned into her worst nightmare. Columbia Records had an idea of how they wanted to proceed with her career but she had differing ideas. Keys wanted to create music from the soul that touched the hearts of people; the record company wanted either another pop teen sensation like Britney Spears or beautiful balladeer like Mariah Carey. They brought in several big-name producers to help her write and produce the music for her debut album, but she battled with Columbia to allow her to write and produce her music herself. The company relented but they disapproved of the music she created. Columbia also wanted to give Keys an image makeover. Though she was already thin and a natural beauty, the company wanted her to lose weight, straighten her hair, and shorten her skirts. However, Keys refused to change from her jeans-and-braids style.

Because of all of the battles with record company, Keys never released an album for Columbia Records. Instead, she began talks with legendary record company mogul Clive Davis, who helped launch a number of superstars' careers, including Aretha Franklin, Bruce Springsteen, and Whitney Houston. Instead of looking at Keys as a commodity, Davis wanted to make her dreams come true. He bought out Keys' contract from Columbia, and brought her over to Arista Records. With creative control, Keys began putting together her debut album, *Songs In A Minor*. Davis told Toure in *Rolling Stone*, "I knew she was unique, I knew she was special, I knew she was a self-contained artist.... Few new artists can be showcased this way and blow people away...."

As she was adding the finishing touches to her debut, Davis was forced out of Arista, the company he founded, by parent company Bertlemann AG. As a result, Keys' album's release seemed unlikely. However, Davis created a new record label, J Records, and quickly signed Keys. In June of 2001, *Songs In A Minor* was released and it debuted at number one. The first single off of her new album was "Fallin'." The single was number one on the charts for six weeks as radio stations with differing formats played the tune nonstop. To help it along, both MTV and BET placed Keys' video in heavy rotation. "Fallin'," a song mixing an old 1970s soul music feel with today's hip-hop, is a song to which many can relate. With little use of sampling, many thought the song was fresh and different from what was usually offered to the masses. The song was so popular and so well-sung, that on shows like *American Idol* the song was banned because the judges thought others would ruin it.

Davis put Keys on a media blitz that included stops at both *The Oprah Winfrey Show* and *The Tonight Show With Jay Leno.* This was something that was never done for someone as green to the industry as Keys. She was also scheduled to talk with numerous reporters and broadcasters. The blitz paid off as Keys' album sales soared worldwide. Her second single, "A Woman's Worth" also made it to the top of the charts. In all her first album sold ten million copies worldwide. Keys performed on *America: A Tribute to Heroes*, a telethon to raise money for the victims of the terrorist attacks on September 11, 2001, that was broadcast globally and viewed by 90 million people.

The year following *Songs In A Minor*'s release was a major one for Keys. She was nominated for six Grammy awards, and won five: Song of the Year, Best New Artist, Best Female R&B Vocal Performance, Best R&B Song, and Best R&B Album. Only one other artist in the Grammys' history had ever won five awards, and that honor belonged to hiphop star Lauryn Hill in 1999. Keys also won awards from several other entities, including the NAACP Image Awards, the American Music Awards, and MTV Video Music Awards.

Keys toured heavily to promote her album. She first opened for R&B singer Maxwell, before headlining her own worldwide tour. She soon returned to the recording studio to began work on her second album. She also collaborated with rapper Eve on the single, "Gangsta Lovin'," in 2002.

In late 2003 *The Diary of Alicia Keys* was released. The album entered the charts at number one as more than 600,000 copies were sold the first week of release. The first single, "You Don't Know My Name," landed in the top ten. Her second single, "If I Ain't Got You," a soulful ballad, also did well.

A review of *The Diary of Alicia Keys* in America's Intelligence Wire reflected on her future, "Alicia Keys did a great job bringing us into her music world with her latest CD, and with her growth and refusal to compromise with weak trends, she will continue to bring originality to the music game."

Keys won numerous awards for her new album. She also joined The Ladies First tour with platinum sellers Beyonce Knowles and Missy Elliott. She did a duet with R&B singer Usher on the hugely popular song, "My Boo." The single garnered another Grammy win for the singer. In addition to the awards, Keys was also made an honorary member of the Alpha Kappa Alpha sorority in 2004. She also was nominated for several awards in 2005, and was named Songwriter of the Year by the American Society of Composers, Authors, and Publishers during their Rhythm & Soul Awards.

Keys wrote the majority of her songs on both of her albums, so it came as no surprise to anyone when she released a book of poems and her songs' lyrics, titled *Tears For Water: Songbook of Poems & Lyrics. Black Issues Book Review*'s Samantha Thornhill called the work "a curious amalgamation," and that while it was a fine first effort, "Keys' poetic voice just isn't developed enough yet to allow her true phosphorescence to shine."

In addition to releasing her book, Keys also helped two charities, From tha Ground Up, and Keep A Child Alive, an organization that helps children living with AIDS. She told Oprah Winfrey in an interview printed in *O, The Oprah Magazine*, "Everything I do stems from something personal, not just because it will look good on paper or be a tax write-off…. These possibilities give my life meaning, and they give me something other than the red carpet to look forward to."

In 2005 Keys was tapped to help MTV bring back its *Unplugged* series. She filmed her show, which included guest performers Common and Mos Def, in July of 2005. The program was scheduled to air in October of the same year. Her performance was recorded, and an album of the performance was released in the fall of 2005. In October of 2005, it was announced that Keys was going to appear in her first film, an action-comedy called *Smokin' Aces*, which was due for release in 2006. Keys was also scheduled to make another film appearance in an untitled Philippa Schuyler biopic. Schuyler was a child prodigy who toured the world playing classical music. Keys will portray the classically trained pianist and journalist, who died in a helicopter accident while covering the Vietnam War.

Despite her rapid rise to stardom, Keys is still the same girl she was before she became famous. As of 2005, she still had a apartment in Harlem as well as the same friends and boyfriend. For her 24th birthday, she chose to go glow-in-the-dark bowling with her friends, unlike other celebrities who spend millions to celebrate their birthdays.

Keys declared that she hoped her music would stay indescribable. She told Winfrey in *O, The Oprah Magazine*, "I want my music to be able to fit into any category. I want it to float wherever my heart goes. My music is heart music; giving it any other description is dangerous." It is no doubt that as long as Keys continues on her musical journey, her star will continue to rise.

Selected writings

Tears For Water: Songbook of Poems & Lyrics, G. P. Putnam's Sons, 2004.

Selected discography

Songs In A Minor, J Records, 2001.
The Diary of Alicia Keys, J Records, 2003.
Alicia Keys: MTV Unplugged, J Records, 2005.

Sources

Books

Contemporary Black Biography, vol. 32, Gale Group, 2002.
Notable Black American Women, book 3, Gale Group, 2002.

Periodicals

America's Intelligence Wire, January 2, 2004.
Asia Africa Intelligence Wire, September 27, 2004; February 2, 2005.
Billboard, July 9, 2005, p. 59.
Black Issues Book Review, March/April 2005, p. 24.
Jet, September 13, 2004, p. 22.
O, The Oprah Magazine, September 2004, p. 256.
People, October 17, 2005, pp. 93-94.
Rolling Stone, November 8, 2001.

—*Ashyia N. Henderson*

Marcia Kilgore

Entrepreneur and spa founder

Born October 16, 1968, in Outlook, Saskatchewan, Canada; daughter of Monty (a real estate agent) and Lorene Kilgore; married Thierry Boué (an executive); children: Louis. *Education:* Attended New York University, c. 1987-96, and the University of California at Los Angeles.

Addresses: *Home*—Brooklyn, NY. *Office*—BlissWorld, 75 Varick St., New York, NY 10013.

Career

Worked as a waitress, aerobics instructor, and gymnastics coach in Saskatoon, Saskatchewan, Canada as a teenager, mid-1980s; personal trainer in New York City, c. 1987-92; opened Let's Face It!, a skin-care treatment center, New York City, 1993; opened Bliss Spa, New York City, 1996; sold stake in Bliss to LVMH Moet Hennessy Louis Vuitton, 1999; introduced product line and expanded to locations in California and the United Kingdom.

Sidelights

Marcia Kilgore is the founder of the extraordinarily successful chain of spas known as Bliss. From its modest Manhattan beginnings, Bliss expanded over the years to include locations on two continents as well as mail-order and Internet businesses that retail the Bliss product lines. Both her services and the skin-care items have lured a cult following, and the Canadian-born Kilgore has also been credited with bringing the spa concept into the modern era. "Until Bliss, day spas approached

beauty as either quasi-medical alchemy," wrote *Time International*'s Christine Shea, "or a ritual for aging matrons, with decors to match."

Born in 1968, Kilgore was the last of three daughters in her family, and started life in a small farm town called Outlook, in the Canadian prairie province of Saskatchewan. The family eventually moved to Saskatchewan's largest city, Saskatoon, where Kilgore's father worked as a real estate agent, and then on to Edmonton and Calgary in the neighboring Alberta province. When their father died of cancer when Kilgore was 13, the girls moved with their mother back to Outlook before settling again in Saskatoon. Kilgore recalled this period as a time of grief and financial worries at home, as she told Jane O'Hara in an interview that appeared in *Maclean's.* "It was devastating. Mom had to work and took the attitude that she was going to hold things together, but I remember saying to her, 'Don't worry, I'll get a paper route, I'll help, I'll hold it together.' I really wanted to work to make my mom feel better."

Kilgore was focused and goal-oriented even in her teens. She earned top grades at her Saskatoon high school, played in its school band, was involved in sports, and held jobs that ranged from gymnastics coach to waitress. A stint as an aerobics instructor led to an interest in bodybuilding, and she went on to win her province's middleweight women's title. When she applied for a car loan at the age of 16, the loan officer glanced over the work history she had submitted, and decided to approve her for credit without the necessary guarantee signature from her mother.

Kilgore brought that same drive to New York City, where she joined her sister, a moderately successful model, in 1987. Her intent was to enroll at Columbia University, but when her tuition aid was delayed, she decided to get a job instead and take classes on a part-time basis. She had little trouble finding work as a personal trainer, and built up a clientele that included some moderately wealthy and well-connected names, such as the singer Paul Simon. A few years later, when all her clients seemed to be out of town for the summer, Kilgore decided to take a skincare course at Christine Valmy, a Manhattan cosmetology institute. It was a personal matter: her skin had been prone to breakouts since her teen years, and she wanted to learn how to fix it herself. Her complexion "made me so self-conscious," she told Rachel Cooke in a London *Daily Telegraph* interview. "It kinda haunted me through my teenage years."

At Valmy, Kilgore learned how to do facials and work with natural, plant-based remedies, and her skin improved. Others soon took notice, including her fitness clients, "so I began giving people facials at my apartment, and they just wouldn't go home," told Cooke. "I had to get an office." In June of 1993, she went from a one-room studio to a business she called Let's Face It!. By this time she had a small staff, and the client list also grew. As a facialist, Kilgore gained a reputation for being able to heal blemished skin, and soon there was a seven-month waiting list at the front desk.

Forced to expand once again, Kilgore opened Bliss Spa in New York City's SoHo neighborhood in July of 1996. That same year, *Vogue* magazine mentioned her and the business, which brought even more clients. Celebrities like Madonna, Calvin Klein, Cindy Crawford, Oprah Winfrey, and Jennifer Lopez were among the devotees of Kilgore's Triple Oxygen Facial and other Bliss-exclusive treatments. The company eventually lured a corporate suitor, too, in the form of luxury-goods conglomerate LVMH Moet Hennessy Louis Vuitton. In early 1999, LVMH bought a stake in Kilgore's company—an investment rumored to be around $30 million—but she remained in control as executive director. The access to capital, however, allowed her to enlarge the Bliss business with another Manhattan spa location.

Kilgore also launched a product line called Bliss-Labs, which featured her signature skin-care products as well as bath and body treatments, and this was followed by a cosmetics line. In late 2001, she opened BlissLondon, the company's first overseas venture. Bliss spas in Chicago, San Francisco, and Los Angeles followed, and thousands of potential new spa visitors were spread out across the United States, Canada, and the United Kingdom thanks to the popular "Blissout" mail-order catalog, which had more than ten million subscribers.

Kilgore still wrote most of the lighthearted copy for the catalog herself, but the growing list of executive-related duties left her little time for giving facials any more. Her husband, Thierry Boué, is a former Shiseido executive who helps manage the Bliss business. They live in a renovated Brooklyn building, in a 14th-floor spread with spectacular skyline views, and have a son named Louis.

Kilgore never managed to finish her college degree, after having taken part-time courses all the way up to the point her first Bliss venture opened its doors in 1996. Back then, she was surviving on just a few hours of sleep for weeks on end, and realized she was woefully unprepared for one of her final exams. At that point, she dropped out. "If I had to decide what to do all over again, I would make the same choices," she told *Marie Claire* about her stalled college degree. "I found by accident what I'm good at, and I'm glad I did."

Sources

Periodicals

Daily Telegraph (London, England), November 30, 2000, p. 25; July 2, 2002.
Global Cosmetic Industry, September 2003, p. 80.
Maclean's, February 14, 2000, p. 38.
Marie Claire, June 2005, p. 118.
New York Times, March 21, 1999.
Observer (London, England), November 19, 2000, p. 86.
People, September 22, 1997, p. 119.
Shop Etc., September 2004, p. 188.
Time International, April 21, 2003, p. 49.
W, December 2001, p. 146.

Online

"Have Taste, Will Travel—In Style," E! Online, http://www.eonline.com/Gossip/Fashion/TrendSpy/Archive2006/060218.html (February 22, 2006).

—Carol Brennan

Eugenia Kim

AP/Wide World Photos

Milliner

Born c. 1974 in Pennsylvania. *Education:* Earned psychology degree from Dartmouth College, 1996; attended Parsons School of Design, late 1990s.

Addresses: *Home*—New York, NY. *Office*—Eugenia Kim, 203 E. Fourth St., New York, NY 10009.

Career

Worked in publishing in New York City after 1996, and at *Allure* magazine; started her eponymous millinery firm, 1997; launched footwear line, 2004.

Awards: Council of Fashion Designers of America, Perry Ellis award for Accessories Design for footwear, 2004.

Sidelights

New York City hatmaker Eugenia Kim has a devoted clientele of discriminating fashionistas and celebrity trendsetters for her fanciful headgear. Constructed out of unusual materials and trimmed with materials that include beading, vintage satin, and lizard, Kim's works are made entirely by hand, as traditional millinery was once done. "My hats are graceful and elegant in shape," she told Nicole Phelps in *WWD*, "but quirky and over-the-top when it comes to color."

Kim grew up in Pennsylvania in a Korean-American family. Her parents were émigrés from Korea, and she was their first child. She excelled in science and math, and her parents hoped she would follow in her father's footsteps and become a doctor. She entered Dartmouth College in the early 1990s, where she earned a degree in psychology. After graduating in 1996, she settled in New York City to think about what she wanted to do next. She had not yet ruled out medical school, but took a job in the publishing industry while enrolling part-time at the Parsons School of Design. A millinery class decided her future career direction, though she admitted she had always loved hats. "I have no cheekbones, and I never learned to use eyeliner," she explained to *New York Times* fashion writer Ruth La Ferla, "A hat accents things that I don't have."

Kim learned more about the fashion world during a year-long stint at *Allure* magazine. The victim of a self-inflicted bad haircut, Kim decided to wear a cloche hat she had made for her Parsons class when she went out shopping in Soho—New York's trendy boutique area—to cover the mistake. She earned several compliments for the feather-embellished hat, including one from actress Parker Posey (a New York denizen known for her funky downtown style) and others from store owners. One of them asked to see the rest of her line, and so Kim went home and made a few other cloche hats in different colors, and wound up with a deal to sell them at Bond 07, a trendy store in Soho.

Kim also landed an order from leading fashion retailer Barneys New York, and with that decided to start her own business. "The timing was just right," she told Pilar Guzman in an interview with *Marie Claire*, "because nobody my age was really doing hats." Within a year, she had found a multi-floor space in the East Village that did triple-duty as her apartment, workshop, and retail store. Her parents, however, were not happy about her plans at first, as she told Guzman. "For the first six months, my parents absolutely didn't support me," she recalled in the *Marie Claire* interview.

But Kim's hats began to catch on with fashion-industry insiders, and were soon featured in the pages of *Elle, Lucky,* and *W* magazines. A growing list of wearers included Madonna, Gwen Stefani, Gwyneth Paltrow, Lauryn Hill, Britney Spears, Kirsten Dunst, and Christina Aguilera. Jennifer Lopez wore one of Kim's hats when she appeared onstage at the 2001 American Music Awards, and rapper Eve sported another style on the cover of her 2001 album *Scorpion*. Kim, however, was oblivious to all but the most well-known faces. "I never even recognize celebrities," she told *People*, "until I see their name on their credit card."

In 2004, Kim's company launched a footwear line that included rabbit-fur trimmed boots and other whimsical creations. The collection won her the Council of Fashion Designers of America Perry Ellis award for accessories design that year, a prestigious honor for an upstart company. Past winners include Kate Spade and Miranda Morrison and Kari Sigerson of Sigerson Morrison. Kim's line of hats and shoes are sold at such top retailers as Saks Fifth Avenue and Nordstrom, among the 120 stores around the world that carry them.

As a first-generation Korean American, Kim says that her heritage still plays a role in her work life. "I have mostly Japanese and Chinese staff members," she told Guzman in the *Marie Claire* interview, "because we all have the same work ethic and design aesthetic." She also said that certain personality traits have helped her in her career, once she found a way to channel her obsessive-compulsive disorder (OCD) and attention deficit disorder (ADD) effectively. "OCD feeds the micromanaging part of it, which you need when your business is small," she admitted in the *Marie Claire* article. "And my ADD lets me jump from one thing to the next when I can't focus on it anymore. I've learned to give in to it by playing to my strengths in the moment and switching when I get the urge."

Sources

Periodicals

Entertainment Weekly, April 13, 2001, p. 18.
Marie Claire, September 2002, p. 167.
New York Times, September 30, 2001, p. ST8.
People, June 21, 2004, p. 132.
WWD, April 27, 1998, p. 10S.

Online

"Bio," Welcome to Eugenia Kim, http://www.eugeniakim.com/lis/bio/html/index.html (August 24, 2005).

—*Carol Brennan*

Ruud Kleinpaste

Entomologist and television personality

Born in 1952 in Indonesia; immigrated to Holland, then New Zealand, 1978; married Julie (a teacher); children: Tristan, another son, two stepchildren. *Education:* Wageningen University, MSc (honours).

Addresses: *Agent*—Karen Kay Management Ltd., PO Box 446, Auckland 1, New Zealand; 2/25 Sale St., Freemans Bay, Auckland 1, New Zealand.

Career

Scientific advisor, Nature Conservation Council, Wellington, New Zealand, 1979; contract scientist, Mt. Albert Research Centre, New Zealand, 1979-81; contract scientist, New Zealand Forest Service, 1981-82; entomologist, Ministry of Agriculture and Fisheries, Auckland, New Zealand, 1983-96; began making radio appearances, 1987, including *Ruud's Awakening,* Newstalk ZB; began publishing articles and columns, 1988; freelance entomological consultant, 1992—. Television appearances include: *The Enduring Land* (special), TVNZ (New Zealand); 1990; *Early Bird Show,* TV3 (New Zealand), 1991, 1992; *Maggie's Garden Show,* 1992-2003; *What Now?,* 1994; *The Bughouse* (documentary), TV One (New Zealand), 2001; *The World's Biggest and Baddest Bugs* (special), Discovery Channel and Animal Planet, 2003-04; *Buggin' with Ruud,* Animal Planet, 2005—; *New Zealand Today Show.*

Sidelights

After years of working as a scientist in New Zealand, Ruud Kleinpaste transitioned into a media career and became known as "The Bug Man" for his expertise in entomology (the study of insects). He worked in radio, print, and television, sharing his belief that people should appreciate and save bugs, not kill them.

Kleinpaste (pronounced KLINE-pahss-tuh) was born in Jakarta, Indonesia, to parents who were natives of the Netherlands. By the time he was a toddler, his family had moved to Holland when Dutch citizens were forced to leave Indonesia. There, Kleinpaste received the bulk of his education. He was interested in natural history as a child, and spent much time in the field studying birds.

In college, Kleinpaste studied forestry-related subjects. He earned his degree in silviculture (the study, cultivation, and management of trees in the forest), animal ecology, and conservation. While a student, Kleinpaste became interested in entomology through the father of a college friend who worked in that field. Kleinpaste learned much about insects from him.

While a college student, Kleinpaste had been traveling throughout Europe and other countries in the world. He decided he did not want to live in Europe because of the harshness of the climate. In the late 1970s, after a brief stint in Sri Lanka, Kleinpaste moved to New Zealand.

Kleinpaste worked briefly in a timber mill, then spent the next few decades in scientific posts in New Zealand. His first post was in Wellington, New Zealand, for the Nature Conservation Council, where he served as a scientific advisor. Later he worked for Mt. Albert Research Centre. A very educational experience came when Kleinpaste worked for the New Zealand Forest Service for 18 months. During that time, Kleinpaste conducted a study in the Waitangi State Forest on the brown kiwi's ecology. He studied the bird's diet, among other things.

His interest in entomology was increasing and he soon was able to make it his primary career. By 1983, he was hired as an entomologist with the Ministry of Agriculture and Fisheries in Auckland, New Zealand. Through 1996, Kleinpaste worked at a plant health diagnostic station on various projects, from identifying pests to issues related to biosecurity. He eventually resigned because his burgeoning media career was taking up too much of his time.

Kleinpaste's second career began in radio in New Zealand in 1987. He had a show called *Ruud's Awakening* which ran in some form for at least 17 years. The show was only an hour at first, but later expanded to three hours. During the show, he answered his listeners' questions about bugs.

A year after his radio show began, Kleinpaste expanded to the written word. He began publishing pieces in magazines and newspapers, primarily in New Zealand. Some works were columns, while others were articles. He regularly offered advice to gardeners in his pieces. Kleinpaste also published his first book in 1997, *Scratching for a Living*. This book was a humorous, but factual, look at many bugs and their purposes. He continued to write while his career expanded into television. He published his second book in 2005, *Backyard Battlefield*, which was also about insects.

By 1990, Kleinpaste was working in television, again beginning in New Zealand. He made guest appearances on and created segments for talk shows, children's shows, and morning shows. Kleinpaste regularly appeared on the children's program, *What Now?*, for some time. He also had a long-running stint on *Maggie's Garden Show* from 1992 to 2003. Entomology was not his only topic in such appearances. He also spoke about related natural history. In 1990, for example, he served as a presenter of *The Enduring Land*, a documentary about the history of New Zealand's agriculture.

In the early 2000s, Kleinpaste made the leap to an international audience, though he still appeared on television in New Zealand. In 2001, he had a documentary on New Zealand television called *The Bughouse* which showed many different types of bugs up close and personal in their world through detailed camerawork. Kleinpaste told Frances Grant of the *New Zealand Herald*, "I think the documentary is saying that we think we are the cleverest animal species in this world, being the most advanced predator on the earth, sea and air. But we have nothing on the insects. They are the big force in this world."

Two years later, Kleinpaste made another bug documentary, this time for Animal Planet and the Discovery Channel in the United States. Called *The World's Biggest and Baddest Bugs*, it served as a pilot for a series which began airing on Animal Planet in 2005. The series was called *Buggin' with Ruud*. Reviewing the show, Joanne Weintraub wrote in the *Milwaukee Sentinel*, "The point in almost all of Kleinpaste's stunts and stories is the same: We have no way of living without insects, so we should learn to live with them and like it."

Buggin' with Ruud was filmed around the world, including segments taped in the United States and Australia. The program showed Kleinpaste interacting with many types of bugs. He wanted to show how interesting bugs were, what purpose they served, debunk myths, and compare what insects do to human activities. Kleinpaste participated in some stunts that drew comparisons to another Animal Planet star, Australian Steve Irwin the *Crocodile Hunter*. In one segment, Kleinpaste was inadvertently stung by killer bees 30 times due to a wardrobe error, when he had 50,000 of the bees on his face. Another segment focused on bug wranglers who make bugs look good in Hollywood movies.

Kleinpaste has made a career of explaining how important bugs are in the world through his many educational ventures. He told Kate O'Hare of Zap2it.com, "I'd done some research and come to the conclusion that the world as we know it is run by insects, not the dollar, not the stock market, not the white mice, according to Douglas Adams in *Hitchhiker's Guide to the Galaxy*, but by bugs."

Selected writings

Scratching for a Living, Random House, 1997.
Backyard Battlefield, Random House, 2005.

Sources

Periodicals

Associated Press, July 22, 2005.
Dominion Post (Wellington, New Zealand), June 4, 2005, p. 5.
Evening Post (Wellington, New Zealand), March 12, 1998, p. 18.
Knight Ridder/Tribune News Service, June 20, 2005.

Milwaukee Journal Sentinel (Milwaukee, WI), June 14, 2005, p. E1.

New York Times, June 15, 2005, p. E7.

New Zealand Herald, August 13, 2001.

PR Newswire U.S., January 13, 2005.

Southland Times (New Zealand), December 2, 1997, p. 12; October 1, 2004, p. 5.

Washington Post, June 15, 2005, p. C15.

Online

"Animal Planet's 'Bug Man' Suffers For Science," Zap2it.com, http://www.zap2it.com (October 15, 2005).

"Biography," Karen Kay Management, http://www.actors.co.nz/viewbio.asp?id=172 (October 15, 2005).

"Ruud Kleinpaste—The Bugman," TV One, http://tvnz.co.nz/view/page/410940/467959 (October 15, 2005).

"Trustee—Ruud Kleinpaste," Project Crimson, http://www.projectcrimson.org.nz/WSMApage/0,1567,16273-0-article-32705,00.html (October 15, 2005).

—A. Petruso

Heidi Klum

Kevin Winter/Getty Images

Model and television show host

Born June 1, 1973, in Bergisch-Gladbach, Germany; daughter of Gunther (a cosmetics company executive) and Erna (a hairdresser) Klum; married Ric Pipino (a hairdresser), 1997 (divorced, c. 2002); married Seal (a British pop star), May 10, 2005; children: Leni (with Italian businessman Flavio Briatore), Henry Gunther Ademola Dashtu Samuel (with Seal).

Addresses: *Agent*—William Morris Agency, One William Morris Place, Beverly Hills, CA 90212. *Contact*—IMG Models, 304 Park Ave. S., Penthouse N., New York, NY 10010. *Home*—Los Angeles; London; New York. *Publicist*—Full Picture, 8899 Beverly Blvd., Ste. 412, West Hollywood, CA 90048.

Career

Won German national modeling contest in her late teens; did catalog work for J.C. Penney, Chadwick's and Newport News, early 1990s; runway model for Victoria's Secret, 1990s—; landed on cover of the *Sports Illustrated* swimsuit edition, 1998; appeared on cover of *Vogue, Marie Claire, Arena, Elle, GQ,* and other prominent fashion magazines, late 1990s—; made television guest appearance debut on *Spin City*, 1998; made film debut in *Zoolander*, 2001; host of television reality show, *Project Runway*, 2004—.

Awards: Named one of *People* magazine's "50 Most Beautiful People," 2001.

Sidelights

Most supermodels begin to fade away in their 30s, but German knockout Heidi Klum was just getting started. With an entrepreneurial eye, Klum used her cover girl status to make a brand name of herself and has successfully launched her own fragrance, clothing, and jewelry lines, as well as a footwear line through Birkenstock. In 2004, Klum's fashion-driven reality television show, *Project Runway*, hit the air and secured an Emmy nomination, ensuring Klum will not disappear from the limelight anytime soon.

The youngest of two children, Klum (pronounced Kloom) was born on June 1, 1973, in Bergisch-Gladbach, Germany. Klum's mother, Erna, worked as a hairdresser, while her father, Gunther, was an executive with a large German cosmetics company. Kloom watched her father work hard to achieve success in his career, and she adopted a similar style. "My father was always early out of the house and coming home late," Klum recalled in an interview with Sara Vilkomerson, which was published in the *Ottawa Citizen*. "I saw that in order to make money—we didn't have a lot, but we did do things like go on holiday—I understood it was because my father worked so hard."

As a teenager, Klum became interested in fashion and at 18 she was accepted into a design school in Dusseldorf, Germany. Klum never considered modeling until one day, while thumbing through a magazine with a friend, she noticed an advertisement for a modeling contest sponsored by *Petra* magazine and a New York modeling agency. At the urging of her friend, Klum decided to enter the contest and the two sent off some Polaroids. Five months later, contest officials notified Klum that she had made the first-round cut in the national contest. In the end, Klum stood out above the field of 30,000 entrants and won the title of "Ms. Model 1992."

Winning the contest garnered Klum instant notoriety and the chance to sign with a modeling agency, which sent her to Paris and Milan, though her career failed to ignite. Standing five-feet-nine-inches tall and with a curvy frame, Klum did not fit in with the angular, waif-like models that were popular in the early 1990s. Agency staffers kept tabs on her body measurements and suggested she lose weight. Frustrated, Klum asked to be relocated and ended up in the United States, where she picked up catalog work for J.C. Penney, Chadwick's and Newport News. Klum, however, yearned to appear on the runway so she switched agencies and told her new agency she wanted to try for a spot with the lingerie company Victoria's Secret. The agency did not think it was a good fit and initially refused, but Klum would not give up. "You can't wait for things to come to you, especially in this business," Klum told the *Ottawa Citizen*'s Vilkomerson.

Victoria's Secret hired Klum and she made a splash strutting down the runways wearing jewel-studded bras. This work led to a 1997 appearance on *Late Show with David Letterman*, where she surprised the audience with her yodeling. Afterward, *Sports Illustrated* swimsuit edition editor Elaine D'Farley received a copy of the show. Although D'Farley knew that Klum lacked the portfolio and experience of the models *Sports Illustrated* typically used, she decided to take a chance on Klum. Viewing the tape, D'Farley caught a glimpse of Klum's alluring charm, which she figured would translate well into photographs. Not only did Klum get invited to the shoot, the green-eyed blonde ended up on the cover of the 1998 swimsuit edition and quickly became one of the profession's top-earning models. She ended up on the covers of *Vogue, Marie Claire, Arena, Elle* and *GQ*.

In 1997 Klum married celebrity hairdresser Ric Pipino, who was 18 years her senior. The marriage lasted five years. After her divorce, Klum dated Italy's Renault Formula One race team boss Flavio Briatore. After they split, Klum gave birth to their daughter, Leni, in May of 2004. Klum later married British singer-songwriter Seal and they welcomed the birth of their son, Henry Gunther Ademola Dashtu Samuel, on September 12, 2005.

Klum believes this relationship will endure. "Seal and I are a great couple because we're very attracted to each other," Klum told Cindy Pearlman in the *Chicago Sun-Times*. "We compliment each other. I'm Speedy Gonzales. I do a million things at once. Seal likes to focus. He puts everything into talking to the baby or brushing Leni's hair.... This man takes his time to love. I love that about him."

Though Klum still models, she has other interests. She has her own line of perfume and swimsuits and a line of jewelry for Mouawad, which raked in millions its first year. Klum also designed a line of Birkenstocks made from frayed denim, pony hair, and jewels, hoping the "punk" shoes would appeal to a broader audience. Unlike many celebrities, Klum will not endorse a product unless she has been involved in its development. "I need to have complete control over how something is going to look if my name is going to be attached to it," she told the *Daily Telegraph*'s Bryony Gordon.

Klum's popularity earned her appearances on episodes of *Spin City* and *Sex in the City*. She also made it to the big screen, with small roles in 2001's *Zoolander* and *Blow Dry*, as well as 2004's *Ella Enchanted*. It was on television, however, as host of *Project Runway*, that Klum really hit her screen stride. The highly popular reality television show debuted on Bravo in December of 2004, earning an Emmy nomination as well as second-season renewal.

The show features up-and-coming fashion designers competing for money—and recognition—to help launch their own lines. Host Klum puts the contestants through the paces in what can only be described as a fashion design boot camp. One of Klum's favorite exploits is the "clothes off your back" challenge, where contestants are asked to make a new outfit from whatever they are wearing at the moment.

Klum also published a book, *Heidi Klum's Body of Knowledge: 8 Rules of Model Behavior (to Help You Take Off on the Runway of Life)*. One message Klum drives home in the book is that people should never give up on their dreams. Speaking to *Redbook*'s Jennifer Graham, Klum related the story of how her modeling agency told her she would never do magazines but she refused to listen. "My book's message is about trying different things and not being afraid of getting pushed back sometimes. It's about being creative to get ahead."

Selected writings

(With Alexandra Postman) *Heidi Klum's Body of Knowledge: 8 Rules of Model Behavior (to Help You Take Off on the Runway of Life)*, Crown, 2004.

Sources

Chicago Sun-Times, November 27, 2005, p. 2.

Daily News (New York), December 7, 2005, p. 103.

Daily Telegraph (London, England), February 6, 2003, p. 19.

Ottawa Citizen, March 12, 2005, p. I7.

People, May 14, 2001, p. 140.

Redbook, February 2005, p. 90.

—Lisa Frick

Elizabeth Kostova

Reuters/Landov

Author

Born Elizabeth Johnson in 1964 in New London, CT; daughter of David (a professor of urban planning) and Eleanor (a university employee) Johnson; married Gyorgi Kostov (a computer systems administrator), 1990. *Education:* Yale University, B.A., 1988; did post-graduate work in Slavonic music; University of Michigan, M.F.A.

Addresses: *Agent*—Amy Williams, Collins McCormick, 30 Bond St., New York, NY 10012. *Home*—Ann Arbor, MI. *Office*—Author Mail, Little, Brown and Co., 1271 Avenue of the Americas, New York, NY 10020.

Career

Worked as a writing teacher, and landscaper; writing teacher, University of Michigan; author, 1995—.

Sidelights

Elizabeth Kostova's vampire-lore bestseller, *The Historian,* earned a fair share of publishing-world attention and media buzz even before it appeared in bookstores in the summer of 2005. Kostova's eerie, elegant, and intricately plotted tale takes its reader on a journey across Europe's capitals and delves deep into folklore and the historical record, and for it she earned a stunning $2 million advance when the manuscript was accepted—an enormous sum for a first-time novelist. She was pleasantly surprised by the bidding war that ensued among publishing houses, as she told *Guardian* interviewer Gary Younge. "I thought maybe in six months," she admitted, "someone would write back and say, 'Sorry, but this is such a strange book we don't know how we would market it but good luck in sending it somewhere else.'"

Kostova was born in Connecticut but lived in various college towns and spent time in Europe during her formative years, thanks to her father's academic career. She graduated from Yale University in 1988, and began post-graduate work in Slavonic music, which took her to Bulgaria just days after its long-time Communist dictatorship fell in 1989. There she met her future husband, Gyorgi Kostov, who became one of the first hundred citizens to be granted a passport to travel abroad in Bulgaria's first days of democratic freedom. They wed in 1990, and settled in the Philadelphia area. There, Kostova held a series of jobs, which included landscaping and teaching business writing.

During this period of her life, Kostova and her husband took a hike through the Appalachians, which made her recall the stories her father used to tell her during their own trips when she was a youngster. They were often creepy vampire tales, steeped in Old-World lore, and as Kostova recalled in an interview with Anne Sanow of *Publishers Weekly,* "I thought: what if the daughter realizes that Dracula is somehow listening? I think every novel has its moment of genesis, and that was it for me." On that same hike, Kostova wrote down seven pages of notes for a possible novel, and spent the next ten years working on her book.

The Historian begins in 1972, and is narrated by the quiet, studious 16-year-old daughter of an esteemed diplomat. Her mother died when she was young, and she and her father are now living in Amsterdam. One day, she discovers an odd book and packet of letters tucked away in his study; the book is blank except for a center spread that depicts a dragon, and the letters dated back to 1930 and hinted of a tantalizing mystery. "I feel sorrow at bequeathing to another human being my own, perhaps unbelievable, experience of evil," one of the letters reads. They appear to be from her father's graduate-school days at Oxford University, and when she summons up the courage to ask him about the story, he reluctantly begins to share the tale.

The mystery of *The Historian* reaches back to the graduate-school advisor of the narrator's father—a man who, her father relates, one day vanished entirely, leaving only bloodstains on the ceiling—and also to her Romanian-born mother. It also stretches back even further to Vlad III Dracul, an actual prince of Wallachia who lived from 1431 to 1476. A ruthless tyrant, Vlad was later dubbed *Vlad Tepes* ("Vlad the Impaler") after his death because of his favorite method of dealing with his hostile Bulgarian and Turkish neighbors—impaling entire villages on stakes, a practice already common to the area during that time and place. Vlad was the inspiration for the bloodthirsty immortal count created by Bram Stoker in the 1897 novel *Dracula*, a monster who feeds off human blood, which was the basis for a number of 1930s-era horror movies that starred Bela Lugosi.

Kostova's plot wends its way back to the story of Vlad and his descendants, to whom the narrator may possibly be linked by birth. "No one knows what happened to his body after his death," Kostova pointed out to Julie Wheelwright in an interview that appeared in the London daily, the *Independent*. "It's a question that's been examined by archaeologists and historians for centuries, so I took this as the starting point of my speculation." In a *Newsweek* review of the novel, Malcolm Jones found that "Kostova's vampire is no campy [Bela] Lugosi knockoff but a blend of the cunning, powerful count who debuts in Bram Stoker's 1897 classic novel and the actual Dracula, Vlad the Impaler.... Blending his-

tory and myth, Kostova has fashioned a version so fresh that when a stake is finally driven through a heart, it inspires the tragic shock of something happening for the very first time."

Kostova was the beneficiary of an immense advance from the Little, Brown publishing house for *The Historian*. Prior to publication, her book earned comparisons to Dan Brown's 2003 bestseller *The DaVinci Code* as the next blockbuster historical thriller for its well-crafted tale of an American caught up in a centuries-old mystery. But Kostova's debut went on to outsell *The DaVinci Code*'s first-day sales, and became the first debut novel to appear on the No. 1 spot on the *New York Times* best-seller list the same week it was published.

By then, Kostova had settled in Ann Arbor, Michigan, with her husband, and earned a master's degree in fine arts from the University of Michigan. Some of the proceeds from her $2-million advance check were used to buy a house, and some went back to Gyorgi's mother's house in Bulgaria for the installation of a hot-water heater. The film rights for *The Historian* were sold to Sony Pictures, which netted her another tidy sum, but Kostova conceded in some interviews that she found the subject of her newfound success a somewhat thorny one to discuss. "I do find it tiresome that people are more interested in the money than in the book," she told Younge in the *Guardian* interview, "because I didn't write it angling for an advance. But I think it's a natural interest: it's just so unusual to get that kind of money for a first book.... It's just such a freaky thing to have happened."

Selected writings

The Historian, Little, Brown (New York City), 2005.

Sources

Books

Kostova, Elizabeth, *The Historian*, Little, Brown (New York City), 2005.

Periodicals

Entertainment Weekly, May 27, 2005, p. 103; June 24, 2005, p. 166.
Guardian (London, England), July 18, 2005, p. 4.

Independent (London, England), August 5, 2005, p. 20.

Newsweek, June 13, 2005, p. 74.

New York Times, July 10, 2005, p. 16.

Publishers Weekly, April 11, 2005, p. 32; May 23, 2005, p. 10; July 11, 2005, p. 5.

Times (London, England), July 16, 2005, p. 7.

—*Carol Brennan*

Diane Lane

Actress

Born January 22, 1965, in New York, NY; daughter of Burt Lane (an acting coach) and Colleen Farrington (a cabaret singer); married Christopher Lambert (an actor), October, 1988 (divorced, March, 1994); married Josh Brolin (an actor), August 15, 2004; children: Eleanor Jasmine (from first marriage). *Education:* Attended University of California, Los Angeles, 2000.

Addresses: *Agent*—Endeavor Talent Agency, 9701 Wilshire Blvd., tenth fl., Beverly Hills, CA 90212.

Career

Actress in films, including: *A Little Romance*, 1979; *Touched by Love*, 1980; *Ladies and Gentlemen, the Fabulous Stains*, 1981; *Six Pack*, 1982; *The Outsiders*, 1983; *Rumble Fish*, 1983; *Streets of Fire*, 1984; *The Cotton Club*, 1984; *The Big Town*, 1987; *Lady Beware*, 1987; *Love Dream*, 1989; *Vital Signs*, 1990; *Knight Moves*, 1992; *My New Gun*, 1992; *Chaplin*, 1992; *Indian Summer*, 1993; *Judge Dredd*, 1995; *Wild Bill*, 1995; *Jack*, 1996; *Mad Dog Time*, 1996; *Murder at 1600*, 1997; *Gunshy*, 1998; *A Walk on the Moon*, 1999; *The Perfect Storm*, 2000; *My Dog Skip*, 2000; *Hard Ball*, 2001; *The Glass House*, 2001; *Unfaithful*, 2002; *Under the Tuscan Sun*, 2003; *Fierce People*, 2005; *Must Love Dogs*, 2005. Television appearances include: *Summer* (movie), 1981; *Child Bride of Short Creek* (movie), NBC, 1981; *Miss All-American Beauty* (movie), CBS, 1982; *Lonesome Dove* (miniseries), 1989; *Descending Angel*, 1990; *Oldest Living Confederate Widow Tells All* (miniseries), CBS, 1994; *A Streetcar Named Desire* (movie), CBS, 1995; *Grace & Glorie* (movie), 1998; *The Virginian*, TNT, 2000. Stage appearances include: *Medea*, La Mama, New York City, 1971; *Runaways*, New York Shakespeare Festival and Broadway production, 1977-78.

Paul Hawthorne/Getty Images

Awards: New York Film Critics' Circle Award for best actress, for *Unfaithful*, 2002; National Society of Film Critics Award for best actress, for *Unfaithful*, 2002; ShoWest Female Star of the Year, 2003.

Sidelights

American actress Diane Lane has been acting since she was a small child and was a star by the time she hit her early teens. Though her transition into adult roles was a bit difficult, she built a solid career appearing primarily in films, with occasional appearances in television movies and miniseries. By the early 2000s, Lane had returned to prominence in a series of successful films, including an Academy Award-nominated performance in 2002's *Unfaithful.*

Lane is the daughter of Burt Lane, an acting coach and cab driver, and his wife, Colleen Farrington. The marriage did not last as the couple divorced only a few weeks after their daughter was born. Farrington had primary custody of Lane until she was about six years old. At that time, Farrington left New York City and returned to her native Georgia, so Lane was primarily raised by her father, and grew up living in residential hotels in New York City.

Lane's acting career began soon after she started living with her father. After spotting an ad for a theater troupe looking for a young girl for a role, he took his daughter to the audition and she won the part. Burt Lane then acted as his daughter's manager for many years. In 1971, she appeared in a La Mama production of *Medea,* which was performed in Greek. Lane eventually became a member of the La Mama Repertory Troupe and traveled abroad each summer to appear in productions with the company.

In addition to such summer ventures, Lane continued to appear on stage and work on her acting skills in New York. She believed acting was a form of child care for her father. She told Jamie Diamond of the *New York Times,* "You can get into trouble on the streets of New York. So I'd go right from school to the La Mama workshop. We'd do exercises where we'd pretend to be animals." Lane's stage career was winding down by the late 1970s. One of her last roles of significance in the theater came in 1977 when she played a young prostitute in *Runaways.* The production was nominated for Tony Awards.

When she became a teenager, Lane wanted to be a model. However, she gave up this dream when Eileen Ford of the famous Ford Modeling Agency informed her that her neck was not long enough for modeling. Instead, Lane focused her attention on film roles. Her first film role came in 1979's *A Little Romance.* Lane played a young American girl on vacation in Europe with her parents who falls in love with a French youth. She runs away with the help of a petty criminal played by Laurence Olivier. Lane received rave reviews for her performance and strong acting skills. That same year, she appeared on the cover of *Time* magazine, which touted her as a rising Hollywood star.

Despite her growing success, her family life was problematic. Lane still lived with her mother on occasion, but Farrington was not always capable of mothering and also made several poor business decisions on her daughter's behalf. After running away with a boyfriend to California when she was 15 years old, Lane returned and would not live with her father. Instead she lived with friends, paid rent, and continued working. In 1981, she entered high school after taking correspondence courses for several years. Her mother found her and forced Lane to come to Georgia with her to talk. This event led to court action by her father. Within a few months Lane had returned to her life in New York, though she later reconciled with mother and even bought a house in Georgia when she was a teenager.

Lane's acting career continued to prosper in the early 1980s. She appeared in several television movies of note as well as a few films directed by Francis Ford Coppola. The television movies featured Lane playing young roles and doing well in them. She played a pageant contestant in *Miss All-American Beauty,* for example. More prominent were the teen-oriented films directed by Coppola. She had the female lead in both *The Outsiders* and *Rumble Fish,* and was already better known than her male co-stars.

The third film Lane appeared in that was directed by Coppola was *The Cotton Club.* It was a complete failure at the box office and with reviewers. Critics believed that Lane was miscast. Though only 18 years old, she played the girlfriend of a gangster, played by Richard Gere. Her character eventually has an affair with a musician. One point that critics harped on was her lack of on-screen chemistry with Gere.

After the disappointment of *The Cotton Club,* Lane stopped acting for a couple of years. She was already a millionaire several times over. She spent time on tour with a rock musician boyfriend and worked in her garden. Lane also pondered her future as an actress. She felt pushed into the career by her father and was unsure if she wanted it for herself. Eventually, Lane decided that she did and worked to rebuild it.

The late 1980s and early 1990s were tough for Lane. Though she worked on a fairly steady basis, her choice in roles was not always great. Lane even turned down parts in what became hit films. For example, Lane was offered the mermaid role, played by Daryl Hannah, in *Splash.* Lane chose instead to play a singer in the bust *Streets of Fire.* Roles in films like *Lady Beware* also did not show Lane at her best. Despite these problems, her personal life was improving. She married actor Christopher Lambert in October of 1988. The couple had a daughter, Eleanor, before divorcing in 1994.

Lane did make a few acting good choices in this time period as well. Only a few were in films. She had a small role in the 1992 Robert Downey Jr. vehicle, *Chaplin,* as actress Paulette Goddard. A lead role in the indie comedy *My New Gun* was well-received, though the film was only a minor hit.

More high profile, career-building roles came on television. In 1989, she played a prostitute named Lorena Wood in the miniseries *Lonesome Dove,* which was based on a novel by Larry McMurtry. This role was seen as a comeback for the young actress. Lane earned an Emmy Award nomination for her portrayal of Wood. In another miniseries, *Oldest*

Living Confederate Widow Tells All, she played the young version of the title character, Lucy Marsden. The teenaged Marsden marries a much older man, who served in the Confederate Army. Another role of significance for Lane was *A Streetcar Named Desire.* She played Stella in the television version of the Tennessee Williams stage play.

Lane's film career continued to struggle in the mid- to late 1990s, but her film roles were in higher profile productions. She appeared in the 1995 action-adventure flop, *Judge Dredd,* which starred Sylvester Stallone. Lane later admitted taking the role was not a great move. She told Jamie Portman of the *Ottawa Citizen,* "My agents absolutely filibustered me into doing that movie. They told me it would give me high visibility and improve my 'foreign stock.' I said to them: 'Look at Stallone's last eight movies. What did they do for any of the women he worked with in those?'" She later fired her agents.

Some of her roles were in better films. Lane appeared in another Francis Ford Coppola film, *Jack,* which was a minor hit. She played the mother of the title character, a young boy with a disease that ages him rapidly, played by Robin Williams. She also had a role in *Murder at 1600* as a security agent in the White House.

Lane finally had a breakout role in 1999's *A Walk on the Moon.* She played Pearl Kantrowitz, a somewhat repressed, world-weary Jewish housewife who has never really lived on her own or for herself. She has an affair with a salesman, Walker Jerome, played by Viggo Mortensen, while on vacation with her family in the Catskills. She leaves her family to go to Woodstock with him. Lane received great reviews for the role. In a review of the film in *Time,* Richard Corliss wrote, "She locates Pearl's yearning in vagrant sighs and in sidelong glances at the big world exploding, outside her small one, into sex, drugs and external adolscence." Lane's career in films was rejuvenated.

Lane had roles of more significance in the early 2000s. One high profile role was in the drama *The Perfect Storm* in 2000. She played Christina Cotter, the girlfriend of one of the men caught at sea in a fishing boat in a deadly storm. That same year, she had a small role in *My Dog Skip,* a high quality children's movie set during World War II. She played the mother of the main character, a boy who acquired the dog.

Lane's career took another step forward with her appearance in 2002's *Unfaithful,* which was directed by Adrian Lyne. She played the lead role in the erotic drama. Her character, Connie Sumner, is a rich woman with a good life at home and a family. One day for no particular reason, she starts what becomes an all-consuming affair with a younger Frenchman, Paul Martel, played by Olivier Martinez. Lane's deft portrayal of Sumner won critical raves and took her to leading lady status. She also was nominated for several prominent awards, including an Academy Award, a Golden Globe, and a Screen Actors Guild Award.

She landed the lead in 2003's *Under the Tuscan Sun.* The movie was a small hit. Lane played a writer whose husband has had an affair. While they are divorcing, Lane goes on vacation in Italy, decides to buy a home in Tuscany, renovates it, and falls in love with a local. The film was based on the nonfiction book by Frances Mayes.

Though Lane's career was again reaching a high point, she was not afraid to play hardball on the business side if necessary. She sued Intermedia Film Equities USA for several million dollars in 2003 when the company signed her to a deal to star in a film entitled *Me Again,* which was never made. Lane's case stipulated that her contract was to pay her whether or not the film was made. The matter was later settled out of court.

Lane's personal life also blossomed. She had been a single mother to her daughter for nearly a decade when she married for a second time. She had known actor Josh Brolin for years and after two years of dating, married him in August of 2004. Around the same time, she filmed a somewhat successful romantic comedy, *Must Love Dogs.* In the film, which was released in 2005, Lane played a recently divorced teacher, Sarah Nolan, who is looking for a husband via internet dates, many of which turn out badly. The film co-starred John Cusack, who eventually turns out to be the right man for her character.

Lane planned to continue to challenge herself with future film roles. She told Bob Thompson of the *Toronto Sun,* "My mind is always on autoscan for what's different, fun and innovative. As long as I'm drawing breath in this business, I've got to have creative fantasies in my head."

Sources

Books

Celebrity Biographies, Baseline II, Inc., 2005.

Periodicals

Chicago Sun-Times, July 24, 2005, p. 10.
Entertainment Weekly, May 24, 2002, pp. 52-55.
Houston Chronicle, September 28, 2003, p. 8.
InStyle, February 1, 2000, p. 240.
Los Angeles Times, July 28, 2005, p. E6.
Newsweek, May 13, 2002, p. 64.
New York Times, February 21, 1993, sec. 2, p. 17.
Ottawa Citizen (Ottawa, Ontario, Canada) April 19, 1997, p. E16.
People, February 13, 1989, p. 77; May 2, 1994, p. 15; August 8, 2005, p. 31; August 15, 2005, p. 71.
San Diego Union-Tribune, May 4, 2002, p. E7.
San Francisco Chronicle, September 21, 2003, p. O1.
Time, April 12, 1999, p. 90.

Toronto Sun, April 11, 1999, p. S3; March 6, 2000, p. 34.
Washington Post, September 25, 2003, p. C1.

Online

"Diane Lane," Internet Movie Database, http://www.imdb.com/name/nm0000178/ (October 15, 2005).
"Diane Lane Profile," Celebritywonder.com, http://www.celebritywonder.com/html/dianelane.html (October 15, 2005).

—A. Petruso

Heath Ledger

Actor

Born Heathcliff Andrew Ledger, April 4, 1979, in Perth, Western Australia, Australia; son of Kim Ledger (an engineer and auto racer) and Sally Bell (a teacher); stepson of Roger Bell; companion of Michelle Williams (an actress); children: Matilda (with Williams).

Addresses: *Home*—Brooklyn, NY. *Contact*—c/o Bloom, Hergott, Cook, Diemer & Klein, 150 South Rodeo Dr., 3rd Fr., Beverly Hills, CA 90212.

Career

Actor in films, including: *Blackrock*, 1997; *Paws*, 1997; *10 Things I Hate About You*, 1999; *Two Hands*, 1999; *The Patriot*, 2000; *A Knight's Tale*, 2001; *Monster's Ball*, 2001; *The Four Feathers*, 2002; *Ned Kelly*, 2003; *The Order*, 2003; *Candy*, 2005; *Lords of Dogtown*, 2005; *The Brothers Grimm*, 2005; *Brokeback Mountain*, 2005; *Casanova*, 2005. Television appearances include: *Ship to Shore*, 1993; *Sweat*, 1996; *Roar*, FOX, 1997; *Home and Away*, 1997; *Bush Patrol*; *Corrigan*. Stage appearances include: *Peter Pan*; *The Name of the Father*; *Bugsy Malone*.

Awards: Blockbuster Entertainment Award for favorite male newcomer, for *The Patriot*, 2001; ShoWest Award for male star of tomorrow, ShoWest Convention, 2001; New York Film Critics Circle Award for best actor, for *Brokeback Mountain*, 2005; San Francisco Film Critics Critics Circle Award for best actor, for *Brokeback Mountain*, 2005.

© *Arnd Wiegmann/Reuters/Corbis*

Sidelights

After beginning his career in television, Australian actor Heath Ledger became an international film star in the late 1990s and early 2000s. He first gained notice in the teen take on William Shakespeare's *The Taming of the Shrew*, 1999's *10 Things I Hate About You*, and as Mel Gibson's son in the 2000 historical drama *The Patriot*. Ledger went on to appear in consistently challenging and engaging, though not always critically successful, films. Ledger's career reached new heights in 2005 when he played a sexually conflicted cowboy in the controversial, critically acclaimed western love story, *Brokeback Mountain*.

Born in Australia in 1979, Ledger's was named after the main male character in his mother's favorite book, *Wuthering Heights*. (Ledger's older sister, Katherine, was also named after a character in the book.) Growing up in a suburb of Perth called Subiaco, Ledger was not particularly focused on academics at Guildford Grammar School. He became a state junior chess champion at the age of ten, around the same time his parents divorced. Sports were a particular interest of his, including hockey, cricket, and racing go-karts.

Around 1991, Ledger first became interested in acting. Though he had appeared as a donkey in a Christmas play as a child, it was not until his sister, Katherine, got him involved with her amateur theater group that he caught the bug. When he was 12 years old, he played the title role in a production of *Peter Pan* in Perth. By the time he was 13, Ledger's hockey coach made him choose between acting and hockey—he chose acting. Ledger's work in this time period focused on the stage, appearing in amateur productions of Shakespeare's plays, as well as productions such as *Bugsy Malone* and *The Name of the Father*. Ledger honed his craft by attending acting workshops and dance classes.

By the time Ledger was in his teens, he moved into roles in television. He dropped out of school after the tenth grade, focusing on his acting career. In addition to guest spots in Australian television series such as *Ship to Shore* and *Corrigan*, Ledger had his first starring role in a drama on Australian television: *Sweat*. The show was set at the Institute of Sport, an academy where elite young athletes trained. Ledger played Snowy Bowles, a homosexual cyclist.

Though Ledger had found some success, he was still unsure if he wanted to act and if he was really good at it. Looking at his performances, Ledger saw how much he had to learn. He told Kate de Brito of the *Daily Telegraph*, "*Sweat* was my first recurring gig in front of the camera and basically I had no idea what I was doing. I can remember watching the rushes and thinking 'Oh God.' I didn't know what the camera was doing, I didn't know what I was looking like on the other side. There were so many little technicalities of acting I didn't know." Ledger decided to persevere and worked hard to improve his acting skills.

While still working in his native country, Ledger was given a chance to audition for an American television show that was going to film in Queensland, Australia. He flew to Los Angeles over a weekend and gave what both he and the show's creator, former teen idol Shaun Cassidy, considered a poor audition. Despite this flub, Ledger was cast in the title role of the show, called *Roar*. In the adventure series set in Celtic Ireland in about 400 A.D., Ledger played Conor, a newly crowned Celtic prince trying to bring his people together in the wake of his family's murder. Conor also had to fight his enemies, the Romans, led by Queen Diana. Though critics often compared the show to the hit Mel Gibson movie *Braveheart* and found Ledger still raw as an actor, *Roar* also demonstrated his expanding range.

Roar became a cult hit but it only lasted a season on FOX in 1997. After the show's end, Ledger moved to Los Angeles to pursue his acting career, where he primarily focused on films. He had already appeared in a few films, including his debut in *Blackrock* in 1997, but the parts were small. Ledger had a much bigger role in his first major Hollywood release, *10 Things I Hate About You*, a high school version of Shakespeare's *Taming of the Shrew*. In the film, Ledger played Patrick Verona, who is a bit mysterious and loner, with the actor's accent kept intact. Patrick is convinced to win over the reluctant, man-repulsing Kat, played by Julia Stiles, so that her younger sister, Bianca, may begin dating a fellow student, Joey Donner. (Kat and Bianca's father has a rule that Bianca cannot date until her older sister has a boyfriend.) *10 Things I Hate About You* proved to be a success at the box office in the United States and abroad, and making Ledger an "it" boy of the moment.

While Ledger's primary homebase remained in California, he also appeared in some films shot in Australia. In the 1999 black comedy *Two Hands*, Ledger played Jimmy, who inadvertently becomes involved in organized crime in Sydney, Australia. While doing an errand for Pando, a crime boss played by Bryan Brown, Jimmy loses the money he is entrusted with delivering, and must repay it. *Two Hands* was screened at the Sundance Film Festival and led to an American Film Institute award nomination for best actor for Ledger.

Ledger's Jimmy was a tougher role than the parts he was offered in the United States. In that country, many scripts that were sent to him were teen films but Ledger refused to be typecast. He wanted more substantive roles and auditioned while living on his savings. At times, he came close to considering returning home to Australia. Ledger received a huge break when he was cast as Gabriel Martin in the $100 million epic *The Patriot*. Set during the American Revolutionary War, Ledger's character, Gabriel, is the son of pacifist, played by Mel Gibson. Gabriel joins the army and is captured by the enemy. Ledger found he had much in common with Gibson, who spent much of his life in Australia as well. Ledger was often compared to Gibson in the press and seen as his successor in Hollywood. Reviews praised Ledger's work in the film, which made him a bona fide star.

Ledger continued to appear in solid Hollywood films like 2001's *A Knight's Tale*, set in fourteenth century Europe. Ledger had the lead in the summertime smash comedy about knights, their jousts, and class conflicts with a jovial tinge. He played

William Thatcher, a poor knight's squire who fulfills his long-time goal to become a knight himself by pretending to be a nobleman named Ulrich von Lichtenstein. That same year, Ledger had a small, but pivotal, role in the intense drama, *Monster's Ball*. He played Sonny Grotowski, the tormented son of a prison guard who kills himself because he cannot be loved by his father.

Most of Ledger's Hollywood output did not have this weight, though the actor did vary his roles. A much heralded remake of the 1939 film *The Four Feathers* was a box-office failure. In the war adventure flick, he played Harry Feversham, a British army officer in the late nineteenth century. Feversham is so afraid of combat that he quits before his group is to leave for a conflict in the Sudan. Feversham later changes his mind, disguises himself as an Arab, and helps his friends. Also released without much notice was one of his first serious adult roles in *The Order* (also known as *The Sin Eater*). In this film, Ledger played Father Alex Bernier, a rebel priest. Bernier must deal with a secret order working within the church.

While Ledger continued to take on interesting roles, a number of these films failed to impress critics or sell tickets. He went back to his Australian roots by playing the title role in *Ned Kelly*, about a well-known nineteenth century, Irish-born Australian. Kelly was put in prison unjustly and later attacked the Australian government. *The Brothers Grimm*, directed by former Monty Python member Terry Gilliam, received many negative reviews, but had some box office success. The fantasy adventure film played on the name of the famous fairy-tale authors. It features Ledger as Jacob Grimm to co-star Matt Damon's Will. The pair played con men in eighteenth century Germany who visit small villages and claim to get rid of curses and demons. Their con is compromised when they get drawn into a real fight in one village, where young girls have been disappearing.

In the summer of 2005, Ledger appeared in a box office bomb, *Lords of Dogtown*. Based on the true story of the Z-Boys, legendary skateboarders in the 1970s who played an influential role in the development of that sport as well as extreme sports in general, Ledger had a supporting role as surfing/skateboard guru Skip Engblom. Engblom owned the Zephyr Surf Shop and was the founder of the Z-Boys team. Later in the year, Ledger had leading roles in two films which proved his mettle as an actor. In *Casanova*, he played the title role, a fictionalized, breezy comedy based on the legendary lover. The film was a modest art house hit.

Casanova was filmed over several months in Venice, Italy, immediately after completion of what proved to be his most acclaimed role in *Brokeback Mountain*. Based on a short story by E. Annie Proulx and directed by Ang Lee, the film tells the story of Ennis del Mar, a Wyoming-based ranch hand, who becomes romantically involved with Jack Twist (played by Jake Gyllenhaal), a rodeo rider. The pair begin their affair in 1963, and the film tells the story of how their forbidden love grows over the years, as they meet and marry women, have families, but always return to each other.

While the gay theme proved controversial, Ledger was roundly applauded for his subtle performance of Ennis. Reviewing the film in the *Los Angeles Times*, Kenneth Turan called Ledger "breathtaking" and noted that "Ledger brings this film alive by going so deeply into his character you wonder if he'll be able to come back. Aside from his small but strong part in *Monster's Ball*, nothing in the Australian-born Ledger's previous credits prepares us for the power and authenticity of his work here as a laconic, interior man of the West, a performance so persuasive that *Brokeback Mountain* could not have succeeded without it. Ennis' pain, his rage, his sense of longing and loss are real for the actor, and that makes them unforgettable for everyone else." In addition to such critical raves, Ledger was also nominated for major acting awards, including a Golden Globe and an Academy Award.

Brokeback Mountain changed Ledger's life in other ways as well. He became involved with the actress who played his film wife, Michelle Williams. While Ledger had dated a number of actresses in the past, including Heather Graham and Naomi Watts, his relationship with Williams became serious. The couple had a daughter, Matilda, at the end of 2005. Ledger's new family became a priority and as he had repeatedly said over the years, if he wanted to do something else, he could easily leave acting behind. Despite Ledger's detachment, the director of *The Four Feathers*, Shekhar Kapur, believed Ledger's talent was special. He told Alona Wartofsky of the *Washington Post*, "To be a great actor, what you have other than talent is honesty, and you cannot be afraid of exposing yourself. Heath Ledger ... is honest and he's not afraid to reveal himself—and that makes him a great actor."

Sources

Books

Celebrity Biographies, BASELINE II, Inc., 2005.

Periodicals

Atlanta Journal-Constitution, September 20, 2002, p. 1P; June 3, 2005, p. 3H.

Buffalo News (Buffalo, NY), July 13, 1997, p. 24TV.

Daily Telegraph (London, England), September 5, 2005, p. 19.

Daily Telegraph (Sydney, Australia), June 17, 1999, p. T8; July 20, 2000, p. T1.

Gazette (Montreal, Quebec, Canada), May 6, 2001, p. A12.

Los Angeles Times, November 20, 2005, p. E1; December 9, 2005, p. E1.

Newsweek, July 10, 2000, p. 62; May 14, 2001, p. 57; November 21, 2005, p. 68; December 9, 2005, p. E1.

New Zealand Herald, August 5, 2000.

People, July 24, 2000, p. 63.

St. Louis Post-Dispatch, July 12, 1997, p. 37.

Sunday Mail (Queensland, Australia), August 21, 2005, p. 7.

Sunday Telegraph (Sydney, Australia), June 20, 1999, p. 193; June 11, 2000, p. 1.

Washington Post, September 8, 2002, p. G1.

Online

"Heath Ledger," Internet Movie Database, http://www.imdb.com/name/nm0005132/ (January 24, 2006).

—A. Petruso

Jason Lee

Actor

Born April 25, 1970, in Orange, CA; son of Greg (a car dealership manager) and Carol (a homemaker) Lee; married Carmen Llywellyn (an actress and photographer), 1995 (divorced, 2001); children: Pilot Inspektor Riesgraf-Lee (son; with Beth Riesgraf).

Addresses: *Home*—Los Angeles, CA. *Office*—c/o National Broadcasting Corp. (NBC), 30 Rockefeller Plaza, New York, NY 10112.

Career

Actor in films, including: *Mi vida loca—My Crazy Life*, 1993; *Mallrats*, 1995; *Chasing Amy*, 1997; *Enemy of the State*, 1998; *Kissing a Fool*, 1998; *Dogma*, 1999; *Mumford*, 1999; *Almost Famous*, 2000; *Vanilla Sky*, 2001; *Jay and Silent Bob Strike Back*, 2001; *Heartbreakers*, 2001; *Stealing Harvard*, 2002; *Dreamcatcher*, 2003; *A Guy Thing*, 2003; *Jersey Girl*, 2004; *The Incredibles* (voice), 2004; *The Ballad of Jack and Rose*, 2005; *Drop Dead Sexy*, 2005; *Monster House* (voice), 2006; *Clerks II*, 2006. Television appearances include: *Weapons of Mass Distraction*, HBO, 1997; *Perversions of Science*, HBO, 1997; *My Name Is Earl*, NBC, 2005—. Professional skateboarder, c. 1988-96; founder of Stereo Manufacturing (a skateboard company).

Sidelights

Jason Lee stars in the NBC sitcom *My Name Is Earl*, the surprise comedy hit of the 2005-06 television season. Retired from his career as a professional skateboarder, Lee was initially reluctant to take the

© Fred Prouser/Reuters/Corbis

small-screen job when it was offered to him, having carved out a solid niche as a film actor with memorable roles in such movies as *Mallrats* and *Vanilla Sky*. His "Earl"—a harebrained habitual offender determined to reform—scored well with audiences and critics alike, with *Time*'s James Poniewozik asserting that "Lee plays the lead with a dazed, beatific air, like a man who's just been hit with a frying pan but realizes he probably deserved it."

Born in 1970 in Orange, California, Lee and his older brother remained with their homemaker mother, Carol, after their parents' divorce. A hyperactive child, Lee began skateboarding when his mother bought him a board with the hopes that he could use it to burn off some of his excess energy. Hooked instantly, Lee spent most of his free hours perfecting his craft, and eventually dropped out of Ocean View High School in Huntington Beach to turn pro. "My mom was a little upset about it," he admitted to *People*'s Michelle Tauber.

The choice proved a lucrative one, however. Lee's skateboarding talents netted him an endorsement deal with Airwalk for his own shoe, and he eventually formed a company with a friend that sold clothes and gear to other skateboard enthusiasts. He was active on the professional circuit for the better part of a decade, and his signature move was the 360 flip, which involved spinning the board underfoot into a full mid-air turn. Indie-rock video director Spike Jonze cast him in the video for "100 percent," a song by New York City alt-rockers Sonic Youth. That led to an introduction to Allison Anders, who gave Lee a small part in her 1993 film, *Mi vida loca—My Crazy Life.* He played a teenage drug customer, standing next to Jonze. "What you see onscreen is me being nervous," Lee joked when filmmaker Kevin Smith spoke with him for *Interview.* "All I had done before that was a music video."

The experience was thrilling for Lee despite his jitters. As he later recalled in an interview with Robert Abele for *In Style,* "I was thinking, Wow, this is what it's like to be in a movie. I'm in a scene right now, and I can see the camera. This is how it must feel for Robert De Niro!" Again, he was instantly hooked and began auditioning for television parts, but his efforts amounted to nil until he began dating a woman whose brother was the actor Giovanni Ribisi. The Ribisis' mother, in turn, was a talent manager who helped Lee land his first real part, a lead in the 1995 Kevin Smith comedy *Mallrats.* Lee was cast as Brodie Bruce in this second effort from Smith, who had scored box-office success a year earlier with *Clerks.* In *Mallrats,* Lee played one half of a dejected pair who head to the mall to take their mind off their respective girlfriend problems. Ken Tucker, reviewing the comedy for *Entertainment Weekly,* singled out Lee's performance as "an impressively charming acting debut."

Lee formally retired from the pro skateboarding circuit in 1996. His next project was in another film by Smith, *Chasing Amy,* in which he played Banky Edwards, best friend to Ben Affleck's Holden McNeil. The pals' comic-book authorship success and friendship is threatened thanks to Holden's crush on Joey Lauren Adams's character, who may or may not be gay. Janet Maslin, reviewing the 1997 release for the *New York Times,* noted that "Lee ... was the best thing in 'Mallrats' and is again darkly funny here."

Lee ventured briefly into television that same year with an HBO movie, *Weapons of Mass Distraction,* and also appeared in one episode of a *Twilight Zone*-ish series, also on HBO, called *Perversions of Science.* He broke into major-budget Hollywood flicks with a supporting role in the 1998 action thriller *Enemy of the State,* but continued to work with Smith in such fare as *Dogma,* in which he played a demon. Noted director Lawrence Kasdan cast him in *Mumford,* which seemed to mark his last appearance on film on a skateboard. He played Skip Skiperton, an eccentric software tycoon, in the little-seen comedy.

Many more would see Lee in his next picture, the 1970s rock-star epic *Almost Famous.* Filmmaker Cameron Crowe chose him to play Jeff Bebe, lead singer for the rock band called Stillwater whose on-the-road antics drive the storyline of the film. Of his fellow on-screen bandmates, Lee was the only one who actually had some solid musical experience, having played guitar for a decade by then. He later said he modeled his stage persona after British rocker Paul Rodgers of Free and Bad Company. Crowe also chose Lee to play the pivotal role of Brian Shelby, best friend of Tom Cruise's character, in the much-maligned *Vanilla Sky.*

When *Vanilla Sky*'s shooting schedule permitted, Lee helped out his friend Smith by taking on two roles in *Jay and Silent Bob Strike Back,* reprising both the Brodie Bruce and Banky Edwards characters. He went on to appear in *Heartbreakers,* his third film of 2001, and with Tom Green and Megan Mullally in *Stealing Harvard* the following year. Kasdan offered him a choice role in his alien thriller, *Dreamcatcher,* in 2003, which was released the same year as *A Guy Thing,* a romantic comedy that paired Lee with Julia Stiles and Selma Blair. In the latter film, he played a soon-to-be groom desperate to avoid any semblance of impropriety after he wakes up from his bachelor party with an unknown woman (Stiles) in his bed. "Most of the meager charms of the chaotic romantic farce," wrote *New York Times* critic Stephen Holden, "spring from the deft comic contortions of Hollywood's ultimate nerdy sidekick, Jason Lee. As Paul Morse, a Seattle ad salesman about to marry his boss's daughter, Karen (Selma Blair), this 32-year-old actor expands from the blandly goofy Keanu-manqué he often plays into a variation on the comic leading man Ben Stiller has made into a specialty."

Lee had a small role in *Jersey Girl,* Smith's next studio project, and was the voice of Buddy Pine in the animated feature *The Incredibles.* He had a supporting role in *The Ballad of Jack and Rose* in 2005 and a starring one in a kidnapping caper, *Drop Dead Sexy,* which was also released that year. When his agent handed over a script for a new television pilot whose creators hoped to snag him for the lead, Lee read it with some reluctance, having vowed to stay away from television roles. He was surprised to find that the script for *My Name Is Earl* "read like a short film," he told Dan Snierson of *Entertainment Weekly.* "It felt like its own world. That's what made it difficult. I went through a bit of hell making my decision. I would say maybe. Then no. Then yes. Then no. Then maybe. I really put them through the wringer."

Lee eventually agreed—on paper, and with ink—to play the harmlessly sociopathic trailer-park-dweller Earl Hickey in the wickedly funny NBC sitcom that debuted in September of 2005. The show's premise centers around Earl's revelation that bad deeds come back to haunt a person: he lived a life of petty crime and dishonest deeds, then won $100,000 in the lottery but lost the ticket. Struck by a car, he hears MTV personality Carson Daly talk about karma from his hospital bed, and decides he needs to make amends for all his past transgressions, which total 258 in all. His attempts to reverse his karma are aided or thwarted by his dense brother, Randy (Ethan Suplee, who had a small role in *Mallrats*).

My Name Is Earl scored impressive ratings during its first season, especially among viewers in their twenties, who had previously demonstrated a penchant for choosing reality shows over sitcoms. Critics liked it, too, and many even called it the best new sitcom of the network season. "Lee brings such a goofy, dimwitted earnestness to the role that it's hard not to smile at him, what with his hair perpetually disheveled and one eyebrow askew," asserted Brian Lowry in *Daily Variety*. Lowry went on to note that *My Name Is Earl* was "blessed less with belly laughs than an amusingly wry tone," and liked the way it "disarmingly focuses on an underclass that seldom gets much attention in the neatly manicured world of primetime."

Time's Poniewozik made a film comparison that was echoed by other reviewers when he wrote that Lee's show "has the deadpan, off-kilter feel of a Coen brothers movie (specifically, *Raising Arizona*).... There's something sweet and innocent about his inept quest for purity." There were a few dissenters on the merits of *Earl*, however, with *New Yorker* critic Nancy Franklin one of them. "Over all, the show is charmless and patronizing, and as refreshing as dust," Franklin wrote, but praised Lee as "an amazingly charismatic actor who can charm the blue off your jeans. Lee manages to make selfishness and monomania seem like delightful qualities."

Lee makes his home in Los Angeles, where he plays in a band with friends called Chiaroscuro, collects art, dabbles in automotive racing and photography, and lives with photographer Beth Riesgraf. The pair became parents to a son, whom they named Pilot Inspektor Riesgraf-Lee, in 2003, which is nearly always invoked in media reports about celebrities who give their offspring unusual names. Lee has said that the name came partly in homage to Peter Sellers' famous Inspector Clouseau character from the 1970s-era *Pink Panther* films, and partly from a song by a band he liked, Grandaddy, titled *He's Simple, He's Dumb, He's the Pilot.*

Lee's next projects were *Monster House,* an animated thriller with an all-star cast that included Nick Cannon and Maggie Gyllenhaal, as well as a sequel to *Clerks.* His somewhat-famous young son would probably be old enough in 2007 to sit through Lee's next project, the animated feature *Underdog,* based on the 1960s cartoon series about a crime-fighting superhero canine. Though Lee may have regretted leaving high school early, he had no qualms about leaving the highly competitive world of pro skateboarding. "Skateboarding is its own world, a much smaller world, but you've got to stay up to date like everyone else," he told *St. Petersburg Times* writer Steve Persall. "People kind of start looking down on you if you aren't. The great thing about acting is that, when I'm not acting, I can do whatever I want to do. With skating, you've got to constantly be practicing, surrounded constantly by that world."

Sources

Daily Variety, September 20, 2005, p. 4.
Entertainment Weekly, November 3, 1995, p. 44; September 9, 2005, p. 66; January 20, 2006, p. 36.
Guardian (London, England) December 1, 2001, p. 15.
In Style, September 1, 2000, p. 511.
Interview, October 2002, p. 100.
Los Angeles Magazine, November 2002, p. 29.
New Yorker, November 7, 2005, p. 146.
New York Times, April 4, 1997; January 17, 2003.
People, April 7, 2003, p. 177.
St. Petersburg Times (St. Petersburg, FL), September 22, 2000, p. 1D.
Time, April 7, 1997, p. 76; September 19, 2005, p. 67.
Variety, September 20, 1999, p. 82.

—Carol Brennan

Nanette Lepore

© Zack Seckler/Corbis

Fashion designer

Born c. 1964, in Youngstown, OH; married Robert Savage (a company president); children: Violet. *Education:* Earned undergraduate degree from Youngstown University, and degree from the Fashion Institute of Technology.

Addresses: *Home*—New York, NY. *Office*—423 Broome St., New York, NY 10013.

Career

Began career as co-designer of Robespierre, a clothing line and store in New York City, 1987; sole designer for Robespierre after 1989, and under her own name after 1996; launched fragrance and footwear lines, 2006.

Sidelights

Nanette Lepore's lighthearted, feminine dresses, blouses, and accessories are worn by some of Hollywood's biggest names. In business since the late 1980s, the Ohio-born designer struggled for a number of years to keep her small company financially solvent. In the highly competitive world of fashion, her longevity and success are the exception, not the rule. "I never had big plans, and when I think back on it, I'm amazed it worked," *New York* magazine quoted her as saying. "Most of it is because I'm really, really stubborn."

Born around 1964 in Youngstown, Ohio, Lepore was one of four children in a family headed by her free-spirited, Midwestern-bohemian parents. Her father was an artist and college professor, while her kindergarten-teacher mother was known for her *au courant* outfits. Every summer, the Lepores took their children on road trips out West, often taking the longer, legendary Route 66 instead of the newer highways. After earning her undergraduate degree from Youngstown University, Lepore moved to New York City when she was accepted at the prestigious Fashion Institute of Technology (FIT). "There's a weird drive when you come out of a place like Youngstown," she told Marshall Hood in *Columbus Dispatch* interview. "It pushes you harder. You feel like the odds are stacked against you."

While working at a designer clothing boutique called Carol Rollo Riding High, Lepore met Mary Ann Vassilakos, and the two women decided to launch their own line. By this time Lepore was married to Robert Savage, a painter, who provided the necessary encouragement for her to strike out on her own after earning her FIT degree. "I was traipsing through the garment district trying to get a job and my husband kept urging me to open my own business," she told a writer for *WWD*. "I hated the garment district. And after one too many disappointments, I approached Mary Ann with the idea of a collection."

The pair called their new line Robespierre, after a notorious figure in the French Revolution, and in August of 1987 they opened a small retail space in New York City's East Village, which was a rough neighborhood at the time and known for its illicit-drug trade. "The rent was $500," Lepore admitted in the *Columbus Dispatch* article. "It was not an ideal location." The 400-square-foot store featured designs by Lepore and Vassilakos that were essentially vintage looks updated for the punk-rock crowd, such as pompom skirts and smoking jackets. Within a year, Lepore and her partner decided to close the store and concentrate on their wholesale business instead, which seemed promising after posh clothing retailer Barneys New York placed an order. More than 50 other stores across the United States were also interested in carrying Robespierre, but Lepore's second collection did not fare as well, and the business tanked. She had financed the manufacturing costs with the help of a loan from her parents. "My father mortgaged the house, and I lost it," she told Hood in the *Columbus Dispatch*. "Within three years ... [the money] was gone. I had to work five years to get it back."

By the mid-1990s, Lepore was on her own, and staying afloat by putting out eminently wearable, feminine items that were priced in the moderate bridge sportswear category. She opened a new space in Manhattan in 1996, and dropped the Robespierre moniker in favor of her own name on the label. After adding a dress line, she began showing her fall/winter and spring/summer collections during New York Fashion Week, the twice-yearly event held in Bryant Park in which designers present their newest wares to store buyers and the press. It was a major expense, but by 2000 her SoHo boutique was doing well enough to help defray the staging costs. "You definitely benefit from doing the shows," she told *WWD*'s Lauren DeCarlo. "It pushes you to experiment with more newness; otherwise, you get comfortable. The shows help you push the envelope. It's crazy, and I complain about it for three months, but it's worth it in the end."

By 2003, Lepore had also opened a retail space in Los Angeles, and entertainment-industry insiders began to clamor for her clothes to use on screen. She dressed Reese Witherspoon in the 2003 comedy *Legally Blonde 2*, and Lepore's designs also appeared regularly on Sarah Jessica Parker on the hit HBO series *Sex and the City*. One outfit not listed on the series' fashion-credits page was the rainbow-hued dress that Parker's Carrie Bradshaw wore when she fell into the water at a lakefront eatery in New York City's Central Park. There was a rush of viewer interest in it, but it was a one-off, Lepore told the *New York Post*. "It was so sad, because everyone on the planet wanted that dress," she lamented. "But we couldn't make it because the fabric was printed really crooked, and we couldn't find a manufacturer."

Lepore's business had grown steadily over the decade. With items priced from $45 to $400 at retail, her company managed to do a respectable $63 million in estimated sales for 2005. In 2006, she launched fragrance and footwear lines, and had stores in Boston, London, Las Vegas, and even Tokyo. Her husband serves as president of her company, while her Ohio family are still her most enthusiastic supporters. "I couldn't be more proud of Nanette," her mother, Jeannie, told Cleveland *Plain Dealer* fashion columnist Kim Crow while visiting backstage at Lepore's Spring 2006 collection. "I never put it together at the time, but she was always taking cutouts and making clothes for her paper dolls. I never guessed it would lead to this." In turn, Lepore credits much of her success to her family, which includes her sister, Michelle Hagan, the wife of Youngstown's mayor. "I have to be able to stare in the mirror and know it's going to be great," she told Crow about her creative process. "I always think about how it's going to look on my family, my friends, not just the models."

Sources

Periodicals

Columbus Dispatch (Columbus, OH), September 21, 2003, p. 1B.
New York Post, March 2, 2003, p. 47.
Plain Dealer (Cleveland, OH), September 15, 2005, p. F2.
WWD, November 16, 1988, p. 8; September 4, 1996, p. 10; November 3, 2005, p. 12.

Online

"Nanette Lepore," *New York*, http://www.newyorkmetro.com/fashion/fashionshows/designers/bios/lepore/ (April 23, 2006).
Nanette Lepore Website, http://nanettelepore.com (April 23, 2006).

—*Carol Brennan*

Beth Lisick

Author and journalist

Born c. 1969; married Eli Crews (a musician and music producer); children: Gus. *Education:* Earned degree in American studies from the University of California—Santa Cruz, 1991.

Addresses: *Office*—c/o HarperCollins, 10 E. 53rd St., New York, NY 10022.

Career

Assistant to the publisher of the *Bay Guardian,* early 1990s; also worked in operations at SFGate, the online news site of the *San Francisco Chronicle,* c. 1995; writer of the "Buzz Town" column for www.sfgate.com after 1997; first book, *Monkey Girl,* published by Manic D Press, 1997; poet, spoken-word, and founder of The Beth Lisick Ordeal, a music-and-poetry ensemble, which released their first album, *Pass,* on the Dunord Recording label, 1999; collaborates with Tara Jepsen on stage and film; co-founder of the Porchlight storytelling series with Arline Klatte, c. 2002; signed to book deal by Regan Books, for the 2005 memoir *Everyone into the Pool: True Tales.*

Sidelights

San Francisco-area comedian, writer, and musician Beth Lisick is the author of *Everyone into the Pool: True Tales,* a collection of entertaining essays that chronicle her life to date as a poet, band frontwoman, and mother. Throughout the chapters, Lisick's counterculture attitude and penchant for wisecracks echo her stage performances as well as the nightlife column she once authored for a Bay Area newspaper. "I tried to write a book of funny stories without resorting to things typically associated with women," she explained to Reyhan Harmanci in the *San Francisco Chronicle,* "like 'men' or 'shopping.'"

In the mid- to late 1980s, when Lisick was at Saratoga High School in California's Santa Clara Valley, she was both a track champion and her school's homecoming queen. After graduating from the University of California's Santa Cruz campus in 1991 with a major in American studies, Lisick moved to San Francisco and drifted through a series of low-wage jobs. "For a long time, I thought I wanted to be a pastry chef," she recalled in the *San Francisco Chronicle* interview. "Talk about bad hours and bad pay!" She discovered her true calling one night when she took the stage at a San Jose venue for open-mike night. As she told Harmanci, "I learned something really important after that first time—that I'm not afraid of public speaking."

By 1997, Lisick had had her first book published locally—a collection of poetry and prose titled *Monkey Girl*—and was writing a nightlife column for the website of the *San Francisco Chronicle.* She also founded a band, The Beth Lisick Ordeal, which featured her poetry backed by Beatnik-style instrumentation. Her act won a slot on the 1998 Lilith Fair, the national tour showcasing female musicians, and a year later they released an album, *Pass,* on a San Francisco record label.

Much of Lisick's poetry and storytelling revolved around her rather mundane childhood in Saratoga, the daughter of two parents who were transplanted Midwesterners to northern California, but missed out entirely on the hippie era. "At open-mike bars, everyone was denying their past like it wasn't cool," she told *Las Vegas Sun* journalist Kristen Peterson. "They're acting like they were raised in the Chelsea Hotel. I loved growing up in the suburbs."

In 2001, Lisick's second book, *This Too Can Be Yours*, was published, and around this same time she had a child, a son named Gus, with her husband, a musician and music producer. She landed a book deal after an appearance at a 2002 event called Litquake, when a literary agent in the audience was impressed by her reading of a selection from *This Too Can Be Yours*. Signed to Regan Books, an imprint of HarperCollins known for its nonfiction bestsellers, Lisick produced *Everyone into the Pool: True Tales*, a collection of stories from her life. She revisits her suburban high school life, reveals incidents of sexual experimentation, and chronicles her experiences inside San Francisco's thriving alternative culture, which included a stint as a squatter, or illegal resident of a dwelling unzoned for residential use.

As Lisick writes in the introduction, she had a pleasant-enough childhood and family, and "it seemed as if I was on my way to becoming a highly functioning member of society or at least someone who wouldn't end up living the way I did. I'm talking about the illegal warehouse spaces, the ten-year lapse without seeing a doctor or dentist, driving cars held together by Bondo, crashing on floors across the United States and Europe while touring with my 'poetry.' Now, at age 35, my yearly income hovers right near the poverty line."

Everyone into the Pool earned good reviews, and prompted comparisons to humorist David Sedaris from some critics. "Lisick's self-effacing voice keeps the book moving at a brisk pace," noted *People* book reviewer Jonathan Durbin, while Jennifer Reese, writing in *Entertainment Weekly*, described Lisick's writing style as "both offbeat and upbeat, wised-up yet curiously wholesome."

Lisick has continued to collaborate with others, including Arline Klatte, with whom she founded the Porchlight storytelling series in the Bay Area. She also works with friend Tara Jepsen on film projects, some of them involving an act they call "Mitzi and Carol." She also performs occasionally with her husband, Eli Crews, as The Loins. Their stage shows involve dancing and singing to pre-recorded music tracks. "It's sweaty couples-therapy rock," Lisick told Lessley Anderson in the *New York Times*. "We're working out our relationship issues through a series of dance moves."

Lisick's next book project involves meeting do-it-yourself experts from across the United States, such as a Wiccan in Indiana and a table-tennis champ in Wisconsin. She and Crews live in a Bay Area community best described as in transition. "We live basically on the Berkeley-Oakland border," Lisick told *Portland Tribune* writer Eric Bartels, but noted that their neighborhood was not the ideal place to raise a three-year-old. "I'm ready to be able to live decently. It's so gnarly in our neighborhood; he's just being shuttled in and out of the house—no hanging out in the street. It's just these crazy kids running around barefoot and lighting firecrackers off their parents' lit cigarettes."

Lisick does not refrain from taking the occasional odd job for extra cash. She appeared in a series of television commercials for a Bay Area check-cashing chain, and as late as 2002 helped out a friend's food-delivery company by appearing in a public-relations stunt that involved impersonating a piece of fruit. "I realized as soon as I put on the foam banana suit that I wasn't really embarrassed about it," she recalled with her characteristic wit in the interview with Harmanci for the *San Francisco Chronicle*, "but I felt bad for other people seeing me, a thirtysomething mother in a foam banana suit, who felt bad."

Selected writings

Monkey Girl (poetry and prose), Manic D Press, (San Francisco, CA), 1997.
This Too Can Be Yours (short stories), Manic D Press, 2001.
Everyone into the Pool: True Tales (memoir), Regan Books/HarperCollins (New York City), 2005.

Sources

Periodicals

Entertainment Weekly, July 8, 2005, p. 75.
Las Vegas Sun, July 21, 2005.
Library Journal, June 1, 2005, p. 128.
New York Times, August 28, 2005, p. ST4.
People, July 18, 2005, p. 49.
Portland Tribune, August 26, 2005.
San Francisco Chronicle, January 21, 1999, p. D1; November 4, 2001, p. 1; July 12, 2005, p. E1.

Online

Beth Lisick Website, http://www.bethlisick.com/ (October 12, 2005).
Excerpt from *Everyone into the Pool: True Tales*, Amazon.com, http://www.amazon.com (October 12, 2005).

—Carol Brennan

Benilde Little

Author

Born c. 1959, in Newark, NJ; married Cliff Virgin; children: Baldwin, Ford. *Education:* Howard University, B.A.; attended graduate school at Northwestern University.

Addresses: *Publisher*—Simon & Schuster, Inc., 1230 Avenue of the Americas, New York, NY 10020. *Website*—http://www.benildelittle.com.

Career

Reporter for the *Cleveland Plain Dealer, Newark Star-Ledger,* and *People*; senior editor for *Essence*; author of novels, including *Good Hair,* 1996, *The Itch,* 1998, *Acting Out,* 2003, and *Who Does She Think She Is?,* 2005.

Awards: Ten best books of 1996, *Los Angeles Times,* for *Good Hair*; best new author, Go On Girl Book Club.

Sidelights

Benilde Little, a former journalist, achieved success as a novelist with her sharp observations of class distinctions among African Americans. When her first novel, *Good Hair,* was published in 1996, critics described her as part of a literary wave of black female novelists forsaking tales of slavery and poverty to write about the black middle class and upper class. When that same wave of writers began to be pigeonholed as "black chick lit" in the 2000s,

Little, in her mid-40s, expanded her range, combining the usual "chick lit" preoccupation with men and dating with a portrayal of generational differences in African-American families.

Little was born and raised in Newark, New Jersey. Her parents were an auto worker and a nurse's aide, placing the family on the cusp between the working class and the middle class, but her parents tried hard to elevate their children into middle-class life through education and a stable home. In one interview, Little described watching her Newark neighborhood change as white families left and poorer black families moved in. The new kids at her school, less well-off than her, disdained her middle-class wardrobe and home.

That made Little conscious from an early age of how class differences can divide African Americans, an idea that was cemented in her mind when she attended the historically black Howard University, which has long educated much of America's black elite. Fellow students would ask her what her father and grandfather did for a living or what car her father drove. "I don't come from a really rich background or anything," she told Etelka Lehoczky of the *Chicago Tribune.* "I went to college and saw people who had a lot of stuff, and was kind of like, 'Oh, my God.' I thought we were privileged, and then I got to college and it was like, 'No, we're not.'"

Little attended graduate school at Northwestern University and worked as a newspaper reporter for the *Cleveland Plain Dealer* and *Newark Star-Ledger.*

She also reported for *People*, then became an editor for the black women's magazine *Essence*. Meanwhile, she wanted to write a novel. But, in the late 1980s, she was told that she had to write about slavery or the ghetto to succeed as a black female writer. Fortunately for her, she ignored that advice. But she kept her work on her first novel secret from her colleagues at *Essence*.

At the magazine, she had the job of editing book reviews, and advance copies of books without the slick covers constantly came across her desk. "That was really the key," she told Lehoczky in the *Chicago Tribune*. "At *People*, I did a lot of author interviews, but I'd see the finished book, and I'd [think] 'Wow, this person's a genius. I can't do this,'" she says. "But when I was looking at manuscripts, it was like, 'Hey, I can do this. I can do this.' It was like the little engine that could."

Good Hair, Little's first novel, published in 1996, told the story of a newspaper reporter from a working-class background (not too different from Little herself) and her romance with a Harvard-educated doctor, exploring the class differences between African Americans along the way. Reviews were good to fair, and the subject matter generated a lot of buzz. Andrea M. Wren, writing for the *Washington Post*, gave the book a mixed review, complaining that the main character was not as self-aware as she claimed to be and that some parts of the plot were predictable, but called it a "respectable novel about male-female relationships and the black bourgeoisie." A *Los Angeles Times* writer celebrated the seeming novelty that *Good Hair* was a black comedy of manners, that is, a study of upper-class habits and preoccupations. That aspect of the book seemed to come directly from Little's own experiences. Dwight Garner, a writer for Salon.com, was struck by a scene near the beginning of the novel: a party in Manhattan full of black professionals who are not actually having a good time because they are engaged in a sort of game Little calls "Negro Geography." She defines it as a series of tests of social status through questions such as where someone went to school, who they knew, and what they did for a living. Many black professionals, Little explains, try to distance themselves from white people's stereotypes of lower-class blacks.

One of the male characters in *Good Hair* even classified black women into three categories, Garner explained, quoting the book: the "commoner," or "women with names like LaQwanda, who wore lycra regardless of dress size"; the BAP, or black princesses, well-off and well-educated; and Afrotiques,

or "righteous womanist sisters with natural hair and clothes made from natural fabric." Also, some of the Negro Geography tests are about looks, Little explains in the book, including shades of skin color and hair styles. Even the title of the book is a reference to such distinctions: "good hair," to snobs in black professional circles, is straight or wavy, not too kinky.

Critics heralded Little as part of a new generation of African-American female writers, flourishing after the success of Terry McMillan and her 1992 novel *Waiting to Exhale*. These writers, critics such as Salon.com's Garner said, create simple, snappy stories about middle-class black women, in contrast with older, more political writers of weighty literary novels, such as Toni Morrison and Alice Walker. Garner declared that fans of the two camps were playing their own version of Negro Geography, feuding over status.

The Itch, Little's second novel, followed two women as they try to start a movie production company and suffer through bad luck with the opposite sex. Again, the new novel examined, as *Washington Post* profiler Pamela Newkirk put it, the ways "successful blacks straddle two worlds and the price they pay to achieve the American Dream." Newkirk's profile took great interest in Little's ideas about class divides and the author's own status markers, noting that Little owned mink coats and expensive jewelry, yet her home in a suburb of New York City was full of simple, unpretentious decor.

It took five years for Little to publish her third novel, an absence she addressed on her website. Helping out at her daughter's cooperative school, finding a new house, and getting pregnant with her second child and being a full-time mother through his first year all distracted her from writing, she said. The book, 2003's *Acting Out*, begins with the breakup of protagonist Ina's marriage. Until her husband leaves her for another woman, Ina has lived as a housewife, giving up her youthful ambitions for upper-class comfort. On her website, Little shied away (as most authors do) from saying her fiction was autobiographical, but she said her new book drew from the experiences of other women living in the suburbs: "I watch, listen to stay-at-home moms who used to be investment bankers, lawyers, doctors, professors, you name it, and the frustrations they feel and the mothers who also work outside the home and the tension between the two groups of mothers," she wrote. "I observed women who seem to have it all, married to men who can provide the kind of lifestyle where money really isn't a problem and how that can be its own problem."

Acting Out questioned bourgeois materialism. "*House Beautiful* homes, shopping as an Olympic sport and social busyness were all distractions to keep the ennui at bay, to keep conversations with that real self away, the one who you were before you got hurt, lost first prize, discovered you didn't have the energy to fight for who you really wanted to become," Little wrote in *Acting Out*, as quoted in the *Chicago Tribune*. She told the *Chicago Tribune*'s Lehoczky that she thought materialism and consumerism hurt black people—which surprised the journalist since Little's novels often describe material trappings. "This rampant materialism is a real issue for oppressed people," Little told Lehoczky. "It's an American problem, and then it's magnified by people who come out of oppression. I'm not saying there's anything wrong with [material] things; I'm just saying that you can't define yourself like that."

That idea struck reviewer Marta Salij of the *Detroit Free Press* as too obvious. Salij was not impressed with *Acting Out*, complaining that Little did not have much new to say about the suburban lifestyle. In the book, Ina claims she feels stifled and misses her free-spirited life from the past, but Salij saw little evidence of actual creative inspiration in Ina. "I think Ina just likes to whine," Salij wrote. "I'm not sure Little knows how silly Ina is. She's written the book in Ina's voice, which suggests she thinks Ina's insights are profound or at least worth hearing." Monica Harris of *Essence*, more willing to believe Little was writing out of wisdom, asked Little why her novels end on bittersweet notes. "In order to have real insight, we have to be honest," Little told her. "Relationships change. They go through cycles and phases; they get boring. It's a bit unsettling to realize this, but perfection doesn't exist."

By 2005, when her fourth novel, *Who Does She Think She Is?*, came out, reviewers were still lumping Little in with other black female writers, though now with a new angle: Little, 46 years old in 2005, was breaking new ground by describing middle-aged maturity among black professionals. "Often considered the midwives of black chick lit, these writers are all baby boomers who paved the way more than a decade ago for popular fiction featuring a world of black characters," wrote Felicia R. Lee of the *New York Times*, referring to Little, McMillan, and novelist Connie Briscoe. "Now the writers (and many of

those characters) have grown up—they got the man, had the kids, and moved to the suburbs—but they are still pioneers." Little agreed. "We're really the only place you're going to see black women of a certain age and a certain sort of history," she told Lee.

Who Does She Think She Is? is told in three voices. The 26-year-old protagonist, Aisha, is caught between two men, her white fiancé and a dashing black gentleman she meets at her engagement party. Meanwhile, her mother and grandmother reexamine their life choices when confronted by Aisha's dilemma. "Little strikes a nice balance between heartfelt intergenerational saga and sexy love story," *Publishers Weekly* wrote. Little explained she mixed the love story with the family story to explore more serious themes than some of her younger peers. "The black chick-lit books that I've read, it's all about 'gotta find a man' and that's it," she told Lee of the *New York Times*. "These characters just spring up, they don't have a background, they don't have parents, they don't have brothers and sisters and concerns." The novel also touched on the effect that growing up with their fathers absent can have on women, an issue Little was exposed to while working on articles for *Essence*. "I found out how big the 'daddy hunger' issue is for black women," she told Paula L. Woods of the *Los Angeles Times*. "I grew up with my dad in the house, so I took it for granted even though I knew people in my neighborhood … who didn't have their dads. I'd meet or read about all these really together women, at least on the surface, and their [sense of incompleteness] was generally due to lack of a daddy presence."

Little told *Essence* writer Kyle Smith that her goal in writing is not to keep covering the same ground. "Recently a woman asked me, 'Why don't you write another *Good Hair*?' As a writer, I'm bored with those characters now. I'd like to change the focus of what I'm doing. I'm working to that end and writing nonfiction. It may surprise some of my readers, but I'd like to write about topics like the impact of poverty on our community. And I hate to sound flip about that because it's not flip. I do have other stories I need to tell."

Selected writings

Novels

Good Hair, Simon and Schuster, 1996.
The Itch, Simon and Schuster, 1998.
Acting Out, Free Press, 2003.
Who Does She Think She Is?, Free Press, 2005.

Sources

Periodicals

Buffalo News, March 5, 1997, p. C1.

Chicago Tribune, February 26, 2003, p. 3 (Woman News section).

Detroit Free Press, January 29, 2003, p. 1D.

Essence, July 1998, p. 66; February 2003, p. 96; June 2005, p. 107.

Los Angeles Times, December 29, 1996, p. 6; July 9, 2005, p. E1.

New York Times, June 27, 2005, p. E1.

Publishers Weekly, April 11, 2005, p. 34.

Washington Post, November 14, 1996, p. B2; December 1, 1998, p. C1.

Online

"Bio," *Essence,* http://www.essence.com/essence/summit/bio_b_little.html (November 20, 2005).

"Q & A," Benilde Little, http://www.benildelittle.com/qa.html (November 25, 2005).

"Sistahood Is Lucrative," Salon.com, http://www.salon.com/weekly/blacklit960923.html (November 20, 2005).

—Erick Trickey

Christian Louboutin

Eleanor Bentall/Bloomberg News/Landov

Shoe designer

Born in 1963 in Paris, France; son of Roger (a cabinetmaker) and Irene (a homemaker) Louboutin; partner of Louis Benech (a landscape architect) since 1997. *Education:* Attended the Academie Roederer, late 1970s.

Addresses: *Office*—Christian Louboutin, 941 Madison Ave., New York, NY 10021.

Career

Began career with shoe designer Charles Jourdan, c. 1982; apprentice to shoe designer Roger Vivier; freelance shoe designer for Chanel, Yves Saint Laurent, Maud Frizon, and other fashion designers and shoe companies; launched own line, 1989; opened first store in Paris, 1991; opened New York City store, 1993; launched handbag line, 2003.

Sidelights

Shoe designer Christian Louboutin creates luxury footwear for women known for their distinctive materials and delicate embellishments. Long a favorite of some of the world's most stylish women, Louboutin's shoes are instantly recognizable to fashion cognoscenti for their trademark lipstick-red soles. The Paris-based designer sells his perilously high heels—and the occasional flat—at his eponymous boutiques in Paris, London, New York, and even Moscow, as well as at top American retailers like Neiman Marcus.

Born in 1963, Louboutin grew up in Paris as the only son of a cabinetmaker. His three sisters, he has said, played a crucial role in helping him develop an appreciation for fashion and femininity, but his fascination with shoes was directly related to a 1976 visit to a Paris museum near his home, the Musee des Arts Africains et Oceaniens on the Avenue Daumesnil. Its collection of sculpture and handiwork from Mali, Ivory Coast, and Australasia was housed in a building from the 1930s that featured priceless mosaic and parquet floors. Louboutin recalled that there was a pictograph sign barring visitors from wearing spike-heel shoes—by then merely a vintage fashion memory from the 1950s—which could damage the floor surfaces. "I had never seen these kind of shoes in the '70s," he recalled in an interview with Katherine Weisman in *Footwear News.* "How could someone make a [drawing] of a shoe that no longer existed to tell people not to wear them? I became obsessed."

Louboutin began sketching shoes in his early teens, and found himself increasingly drawn into the world of fashion at the expense of his studies. He was expelled from four schools, but "I didn't care, because I felt so different from my peers," he told Natasha Fraser-Cavassoni in *Harper's Bazaar.* "I discovered Cher on television, and no one knew who she was, and I thought, I come from another culture—mine is Cher." He went through a punk-rock phase, and appeared in a few films, one of them a 1979 cult classic, *Race d'ep,* which played to

English-language audiences under the title, *The Homosexual Century.*

Louboutin had some formal training at the Academie Roederer, where he studied drawing and the decorative arts. Increasingly intrigued by world cultures, he had already run away to see Egypt while still in his teens, and also traveled through India for a year. Back in Paris in 1981, he assembled a design portfolio of his most elaborate high heels, and showed it to some of the city's top couture houses. His efforts landed him a job with Charles Jourdan, the legendary shoe designer, and then he met Roger Vivier, another well-known shoe designer who had worked with Christian Dior in the 1950s. Louboutin had known of Vivier's work since his teens, for Vivier was said to have invented that famous spike (or stiletto) heel whose image so intrigued him at the Avenue Daumesnil museum. Named for a type of slim knife, the stiletto heel was a high shoe with a tapered, narrow heel that resembled the namesake knife blade. Vivier liked Louboutin's work, and offered him an apprenticeship. "Vivier taught me that the most important part of the shoe is the body and the heel," Louboutin told Dana Thomas in *Newsweek International.* "Like good bone structure, if you get that right, the rest is makeup."

During the rest of the 1980s, Louboutin was a freelance shoe designer, creating heels for the collections of Chanel and Yves Saint Laurent, as well as Maud Frizon, another shoe designer with immense name-brand cache in the 1980s. He launched his own company, with the help of two financial backers, and in November of 1991 opened a Paris shoe boutique under his own name. One of his first famous customers was Princess Caroline of Monaco, who enthused over his shoes one day when a fashion journalist happened to be in the store as well. The resulting press helped boost Louboutin's profile immensely, and such well-known fashionistas as Diane Von Furstenburg and Catherine Deneuve became devoted clients. Later devotees of his stiletto heels included Madonna, Gwyneth Paltrow, Jennifer Lopez, and Sarah Jessica Parker, who wore Louboutins on her wedding day.

Louboutin first attracted the attention of fashion-lovers outside of Paris with his "inseparables," a footwear-industry term for a single design or word that runs from the vamp of one shoe to the other; his quirky "LO" "VE" shoes were a highly coveted item for a time in the early 1990s on both sides of the Atlantic. He opened a New York City store in 1993, and heeded Russian women's demand for his shoes by opening a Moscow outpost in 2002. For the autumn 2003 season, he introduced his first line of handbags.

Louboutin's stores feature his latest shoe collections, all of which are made in Italy with the characteristic red soles. He began using the color for the bottom of the shoes one day as he watched his assistant was painting her nails with the color and thought it was immensely flirtatious. More general inspiration, he told Jennifer Tung in *Harper's Bazaar,* comes from extensive travel. "I like to go to countries that are almost forbidden, like Syria or Uzbekistan. It's like traveling in the 19th century: There's no one around, and you discover things." Back at his studio, he uses the colors and textiles he saw to create another line of elaborate, well-crafted shoes.

Louboutin and his partner, landscape architect Louis Benech, spend time at a vacation home in Luxor, Egypt, that has been featured in both *Vogue* and *Harper's Bazaar* for its unique architecture and delightful, treasure-filled interior. Louboutin invites his famous friends to visit, and takes them on cruises down the Nile in a traditional flat-bottomed boat he commissioned. He leads a suitably madcap life elsewhere: when Elisa Anniss, a writer for *Footwear News,* asked him about his passions outside of fashion, he replied, "Flying trapeze. I took it up after seeing the movie *Wings of Desire,* but I had to stop because the circus where I did it went bankrupt. I am also interested in showgirls and music halls." As he told Tung in the *Harper's Bazaar* interview, he draws his creative inspirations from these and other wide-ranging sources. "The last thing that would ever influence me is fashion," he declared. "In fashion, things get dated extremely quickly."

Sources

Footwear News, June 1, 1992, p. S8; December 9, 2002, p. 50.
Harper's Bazaar, December 1999, p. 104; April 2001, p. 226.
Newsweek International, February 24, 2003, p. 48.
People, February 10, 2003, pp. 87-88.
Vogue, June 2004, p. 206.

—*Carol Brennan*

Richard Louv

Photo by Robert Burroughs. Courtesy of Richard Louv.

Author, columnist and speaker

Born in February of 1949 in New York, NY; married Kathy Frederick (a nurse practitioner), c. 1979; children: Jason, Matthew. *Education:* Graduate of the William Allen White School of Journalism at the University of Kansas.

Addresses: *Home*—San Diego, CA. *Office*—*San Diego Union Tribune,* P.O. Box 120191, San Diego, CA 92112-0191.

Career

Intern, Arkansas City, KS, newspaper, 1968; reporter and columnist, *San Diego Union-Tribune,* 1980s—. Also works as visiting scholar at the Heller School for Social Policy and Management at Brandeis University.

Member: Advisor to the Ford Foundation's Leadership for a Changing World award program and the Scientific Council on the Developing Child.

Awards: Has been honored with awards from the International Reading Association, the National Association of Social Workers, Inc., the San Diego Academy of Psychologists and the California Association for the Education of Young Children.

Sidelights

Newspaper columnist and author Richard Louv created a stir in 2005 when he coined the term nature-deficit disorder, which he described as a childhood severed from nature. In his 2005 book *Last Child in the Woods,* Louv argues that the disconnect between nature and today's wired generation of children has negative consequences for both the minds and bodies of these youth. The *New York Times* referred to Louv's book as "an inch-thick caution against raising the fully automated child." Mostly, Louv hoped the book would get parents, schools, and communities thinking about the society they are creating.

"I don't declare I've discovered a new world here," Louv told Kevin O'Connor of the *Rutland Herald,* "and I'm also cautious that this research is limited and new. But I expect a lot of people to start looking at this. When parents and educators begin to think of this as a physical, emotional, and mental health issue, suddenly it makes all the sense in the world to take our kids outside."

Louv was born in February of 1949, in the borough of Brooklyn in New York City, but grew up in the Kansas City area, alongside his brother, Mike. Louv's mother worked as a freelance greeting-card artist, initially getting her start with Kansas City-based Hallmark Cards. As a child, Louv spent many hours standing next to his mom's art table watching her work. When he got bored, he picked her discarded blotter paper off the floor and drew his own artwork.

In the mid- to late 1950s, Louv attended Southwood Elementary in Raytown, Missouri, but in 1960, the family moved across the state line to Kansas. As a child Louv enjoyed exploring the woods and fields that surrounded his suburban neighborhood. "I spent most of my waking hours in those woods, digging and exploring," Louv told the *Wichita Eagle*'s Suzanne Perez Tobias. "They were my woods. I owned them. Those woods were in my heart, and they're as real to me today as anything else." He also spent a lot of time at his grandmother's home in Independence, Missouri—a home just down the street from U.S. President Harry and Bess Truman's house.

Louv spent the summer of 1968 as an intern at the local paper in Arkansas City, Kansas, and graduated from the William Allen White School of Journalism at the University of Kansas in Lawrence. By 1981 he was a reporter at the *San Diego Union-Tribune* writing about long-range social and political trends. Along the way he earned a reputation as a capable and competent columnist. His favorite topics included family, nature, and community. His columns became so popular and poignant that they were snatched up by other papers and have appeared in the *Chicago Tribune, Christian Science Monitor, Philadelphia Inquirer, San Francisco Chronicle, Baltimore Sun, Detroit News* and many more.

In the 1980s, Louv decided to broaden his audience base and delve into his topics in a deeper and lengthier way by writing a book. He published *America II: The Book that Captures Americans in the Act of Creating the Future,* in 1983. The book examines the advantages and disadvantages of living in the post-industrialist economy of the United States. Louv filled the book with first-person interviews and statistics aimed at examining the demographic shifts associated with the changing economy.

Louv followed with *Childhood's Future: Listening to the American Family—New Hope for the Next Generation.* Published in 1990, *Childhood's Future* is a retrospective on family life. To produce this book, Louv spent three years journeying around the United States listening to parents and children talk about the experiences of their lives. He noticed a trend—one after another, parents lamented the lack of time spent together as a family and the lack of connection with each other.

The idea for the book was sparked by Louv himself wondering about the ways in which society had changed since his Baby Boomer upbringing. He realized that children were spending more time in structured day care and extracurricular activities than ever before and he wondered how the change was affecting society. "They are the first day-care generation, the first post-sexual-revolution generation, the first generation to grow up in the electronic bubble, the first for whom nature is often an abstraction rather than a reality," he told the *Kansas City Star*'s Karen Uhlenhuth.

While Louv called the changes a crisis, he also offered amenities and hoped to touch off a family liberation movement. In the book, Louv argues that the lack of connection families feel is due to the American industrial machine. He said the problem could be fixed if employers offered parents more flexible work hours. He proposes a "Family Ties Bill" that would force employers to give parents a few hours off each month to visit and help at their child's day care. Louv believes childless workers should get the same time off to visit elderly parents or do volunteer work with children or senior citizens.

After Louv discussed his Family Ties Bill in a *San Diego Union-Tribune* column, the paper received "an avalanche" of replies both for and against such a measure, he told Uhlenhuth in the *Kansas City Star.* Louv's idea, however, spurred the regional manager of Southland Corp., owner of 7-Eleven, to put the plan into place in Southern California. The book generated national debate on the topic and was excerpted for a *New York Times Magazine* cover story. In addition, Bill Moyers produced a PBS special around the topic. The book also helped kick off a speaking career for Louv.

In the 1990s Louv published more books on social and family issues, including *FatherLove: What We Need, What We Seek, What We Must Create; 101 Things You Can Do for Our Children's Future,* and *The Web of Life: Weaving the Values that Sustain Us.* The latter book is a collection of essays and short stories culled from his columns that drive home the need for people to create a "web of life" with strands to family, nature, and community.

Louv switched gears a bit for his next book, 2000's *Fly-Fishing for Sharks: An American Journey.* To write this book, Louv spent two years traveling to various United States fishing spots asking anglers why they love to fish. The book, however, turned out to be about much more than fishing. Speaking to anglers, Louv discovered an America anyone could love. The *Star Tribune* noted that the book "tells as much about modern life as it does about angling.... a unique and upbeat glimpse of the American psyche."

The idea for the book was not Louv's. "I was going over some new book ideas with my agent," Louv recalled in an interview with PBS's Margaret Warner. "I had written five books prior to that, and I said, 'You know, all I have here are depressing social issues again, and every time I think of writing another book about a depressing social issue, I get a headache.'" Louv's agent asked him if he ever thought of writing a book about fishing because whenever he discussed the topic, he seemed happy. And so the idea was born.

Examining the United States through the lens of fishing helped Louv see an entirely different country than the one he had discovered in his previous books. Louv found that the United States was filled with generous, passionate people. As he told PBS's Warner, "I mean, really the truth about America isn't in the headlines. It's in the small details. It's in the folks you meet.... It's in the stories that people tell about their lives, and about America."

In 2005, Louv sparked more debate when he published *Last Child in the Woods: Saving Our Children from Nature-Deficit Disorder*. The idea for the book was sparked during an interview with a fourth-grader years before who told Louv that he preferred to play indoors because that is where all the electrical outlets are located.

In the 310-page book, Louv discusses how computers, television, and video games keep children inside. In addition, he notes that many parents have irrational fears that danger—or abductors—lurk at every corner, so they keep their kids inside. Parents also fear the West Nile virus and Lyme disease, causing them to discourage outside play. Louv noted that by the 1990s, the area children were allowed to roam in their neighborhoods had shrunk to one-ninth the size it had been in the 1970s. Using studies and anecdotes, Louv builds his case suggesting nature-deficit disorder is a real phenomenon. He cites countless studies that show unstructured playtime in the woods or on the beach helps kids become healthy, creative adults, and can also help kids who suffer from depression, attention deficit and hyperactivity disorder (ADHD), and obesity.

Louv's examples are compelling. For instance, he cites a University of Illinois study that found that concentration among ADHD kids improved when they completed activities in nature, as opposed to an urban setting. He also cites studies conducted in Scandinavia that examined the play value of those who frolicked on natural playgrounds with trees and bumpy terrains versus those who played on level asphalt playgrounds, such as those found in the United States. "They found that play was much more creative on the uneven, more natural surfaces," Louv told the *Sacramento Bee*'s David Barton, "and what was more surprising was that they were also more cooperative." He also cites studies that show being in nature reduces stress and stimulates creativity. In addition, he discusses a British study that found eight-year-olds could easily identify Pokemon characters but struggled with otter, beetle, and oak tree. Louv suggests this disconnect does not bode well for the future of the environment.

Louv further drives his point home by including compelling anecdotes. According to the *Rutland Herald*, in one chapter, Louv relays an interview he conducted with a camp counselor who recalled the night she showed a nine-year-old city girl the stars. The girl's first reaction was to gasp and grab for her counselor. "She had never seen the stars before. That night, I saw the power of nature on a child. She was a changed person. From that moment on, she saw everything, the camouflaged lizard that everyone else skipped by. She used her senses. She was awake." Louv believes that children who spend a lot of time focusing narrowly on a single thing—like a computer screen—miss out on activating all of their senses, such as seeing, hearing, touching, and tasting, which are simultaneously engaged while in nature.

Louv, however, does not see electronics as the enemy; he just believes game time should be balanced with nature time. As he told the *Sacramento Bee*'s Barton, "I didn't ban computer games for my kids. But I don't think it's easy to have a sense of wonder when you're playing *Grand Theft Auto*. You need to offer your kids something more. You need to offer them that sense of wonder." Louv hopes the book spurs parents to take their kids outside so they can connect with nature. He also hopes schools, which have been cutting recess time, realize the value of unstructured play.

Louv's interest in child and family issues was sparked by his two sons, Jason and Matthew. As a journalist, Louv had a flexible schedule and was able to work at home with his children beside him; at other times, he chose a cooperative day-care center and spent time there each month. Also, Louv and his nurse-practitioner wife, Kathy, provided the children with opportunities to commune with nature. Speaking to *People*'s Howard Breuer, Louv recalled a camping trip with his younger son to Kodiak Island, Alaska. "A bear looked like it was charging us, but instead it dove in the water, where we had just been fishing. Matthew will never forget that. That lasts forever."

Selected writings

America II: The Book that Captures Americans in the Act of Creating the Future, Penguin, 1983.

Childhood's Future: Listening to the American Family—New Hope for the Next Generation, Houghton Mifflin, 1990.

FatherLove: What We Need, What We Seek, What We Must Create, Pocket Books, 1994.

101 Things You Can Do for Our Children's Future, Anchor, 1994.

The Web of Life: Weaving the Values that Sustain Us, Conari Press, 1996.

Fly-Fishing for Sharks: An American Journey, Simon & Schuster, 2000.

Last Child in the Woods: Saving Our Children from Nature-Deficit Disorder, Algonquin Books, 2005.

Sources

Books

Louv, Richard, *Childhood's Future: Listening to the American Family—New Hope for the Next Generation*, Houghton Mifflin, 1990.

Louv, Richard, *The Web of Life: Weaving the Values that Sustain Us*, Conari Press, 1996.

Periodicals

Kansas City Star, March 12, 1991, p. E1.
New York Times, April 28, 2005.
People, June 13, 2005, pp. 147-48.
Sacramento Bee, July 21, 2005, p. E1.
Wichita Eagle, August 25, 2005, p. 1C.

Online

"About Richard Louv," Future's Edge, http://www.thefuturesedge.com/RichardLouvBio.html (September 26, 2005).

"A Conversation with Richard Louv," Public Broadcasting System, http://www.pbs.org.newshour/gergen/july-dec00/louv_7-4.html (October 3, 2005).

"Fly Fishing for Sharks" *Star Tribune* (Minneapolis/St. Paul, MN), http://www.startribune.com/384/story/31272.html (November 20, 2005).

"Nature Deficit? Book aims to unplug our kids from new 'disorder,'" *Rutland Herald* (Rutland, VT), http://www.rutlandherald.com/apps/pbcs.dll/article?AID=/20050501/NEWS/505010352/1031 (November 20, 2005).

"Richard Louv," Citistates Group, http://www.citistates.com/assocspeakers/r_louv.html (October 3, 2005).

—*Lisa Frick*

Alexander Lukashenko

© Reuters/Corbis

President of Belarus

Born August 30, 1954, in Kopys, Vitebsk, Belarus. *Education:* Earned degrees from the Mogilev Teaching Institute, 1975, and Belarusian Agricultural Academy, 1985.

Addresses: *Office*—c/o Embassy of Belarus, 1619 New Hampshire Ave. NW, Washington, DC 20009.

Career

Served in the Border Guards, 1975-77, and Soviet Army, 1980-82; Komsomol chapter leader, 1977-78; deputy chair of a collective farm, 1982-85; director of a state farm and construction materials plant, 1985-90; elected deputy to the Supreme Soviet of the Republic of Belarus, 1990; manager of a state farm, c. 1991-93; elected chair of an anti-corruption committee in the Belarusian parliament, 1993; elected president of Belarus, 1994; re-elected, 2001 and 2006.

Sidelights

In 1994, voters in the former Soviet republic of Belarus elected Alexander Lukashenko to the presidency in the country's first democratic elections. They were also apparently the last, for Lukashenko moved quickly during his first term to restrict political dissent and enlarge the powers of his office. Re-elected twice by suspiciously wide margins, the former farm manager has been accused of ruthlessly silencing his political opponents, some of whom have vanished entirely. His Belarus, a nation of 10.4 million, is often deemed the last outpost of Soviet-style authoritarian rule, and Lukashenko is referred to in the West as Europe's last remaining dictator.

Born in 1954, Lukashenko grew up in a single-parent household headed by his mother. He came from a village called Kopys in the rural Vitebsk province of what was then known as the Byelorussian Soviet Socialist Republic. The Belarus people were eastern Slavs, and inhabited a region located somewhat unfortunately between more powerful states; over the centuries they had been ruled by their Lithuanian and Polish neighbors, before becoming part of Imperial Russia in the 1790s. Belarus enjoyed a brief period of independence following World War I, but was subsumed into the Soviet Union in 1919. Purges ordered by Soviet leader Josef Stalin in the late 1930s decimated its intelligentsia in Minsk, the capital, which was followed by Nazi German occupation during World War II. As a result of both, Belarus—the contemporary transliteration of a term usually referred to in English as "white Russian"—suffered heavy population losses estimated at a third in just a decade's time.

Lukashenko grew up under Soviet communism, and joined the local chapter of Komsomol, the youth wing of the Communist Party of the Soviet Union

(CPSU), when he was a student at the Mogilev Teaching Institute. After graduating in 1975, he served two years as a border guard, and returned to Mogilev to head the Komsomol chapter. He spent another two years in the Soviet Army, and upon his discharge in 1982 was given a post as deputy chair of a collective farm. These were the mass agricultural outfits in which farmers worked under the communist system, which had abolished private property. After further study at the Belarusian Agricultural Academy, Lukashenko was named director of a state farm and construction materials plant in the Shklov district in 1985.

Lukashenko entered the political arena in 1990 when he was elected a deputy to the Supreme Soviet of the Republic of Belarus. Earlier that year, the country had declared its independence from the Soviet Union, joining the Soviet republics of Lithuania, Latvia, and Estonia as part of the first wave of breakaway states that by the end of 1991 resulted in the formal dissolution of the Soviet Union. Initially one of the reformers who supported Soviet leader Mikhail Gorbachev, Lukashenko sided with CPSU hardliners who attempted to wrest control of the Soviet state from Gorbachev in August of 1991. The Moscow coup failed, Gorbachev resigned, and the Commonwealth of Independent States (CIS) was formed in its place as an alliance of eleven former republics. Lukashenko voted against ratification of the agreement that made Belarus part of the CIS in December of 1991.

Lukashenko returned for a time to managing a state farm, but re-entered politics and rose to chair an anti-corruption committee in the Belarusian parliament in 1993. He gained widespread attention for his accusations that many of the former Communist elite, who still wielded political power, were enriching themselves by pocketing state funds. In 1994, voters in Belarus approved a new constitution, and the country's first-ever democratic elections were held in July. Lukashenko was one of six candidates, and was the surprise finisher over Vyacheslav Kebich, the current prime minister.

Lukashenko ran as an independent, promising to root out the high-level corruption that was exacerbating the country's serious economic troubles, which had started with the collapse of the Soviet system. He also vowed to avoid privatization—the selling-off of formerly state-owned industries to private investors—that had taken hold throughout much of the former Soviet Union. Privatization had created a new ruling class, the oligarchs, but adversely affected the average citizen, who was suddenly forced to pay market price for goods and services that were once generously subsidized by the state.

In the July of 1994 elections, Lukashenko won 45 percent of the vote, against Kebich's 15 percent, and then bested him in a run-off election with 80 percent of the vote. One of his first presidential acts was to double the minimum wage, and he also re-instituted Soviet-era state price controls. He earned the scorn of the international community by refusing to enact any free-market reforms at all, and in 1995 both the World Bank and International Monetary Fund suspended lending to the country because of its defiance on the matter. As its free-market-friendly neighbors began to prosper, domestic opposition to Lukashenko's economic policies mounted, and he began to consolidate his political power.

In the summer of 1996, Lukashenko was the target of an impeachment attempt, which he managed to avoid by calling in high-ranking Russian officials to mediate. That November, a referendum was held on the matter of granting him increased presidential powers, including the extension of his term from four years to six. After a "vote yes" campaign carried out in the state-controlled media, and a campaign of harassment carried out against the opposition, the referendum passed by 70 percent.

In retaliation for the impeachment attempt, Lukashenko dissolved parliament, and set up his own handpicked legislature. The prime minister resigned in protest, as did several judges on the constitutional court, and Lukashenko continued his crackdown on his political opponents by closing independent newspapers and granting increased powers of surveillance and detention to the Belarusian secret police, which was a remnant of the Soviet-era force and even retained the dreaded acronym KGB (*Komitet Gosudarstvennoy Bezopasnosti*, or State Security Committee).

By 1999 Lukashenko's authoritarian regime was firmly entrenched. In May of that year, a former Minister of Internal Affairs who had opposed Lukashenko, Yuri Zakharenko, was last seen being hustled into a car by men while out for a walk in his neighborhood. Four months later, another outspoken critic of Lukashenko's, Viktor Gonchar—formerly the deputy speaker in the parliament dissolved by Lukashenko in 1996—disappeared along with the financial backer of his new political party when they visited the *banya*, or ritual baths, in Minsk. The Belarusian KGB were widely suspected of foul play in both incidents.

Belarus and Russia signed a 1999 agreement that some predicted was a blueprint for an eventual merger, but Lukashenko found himself drastically outmatched by another hardliner, new Russian president Vladimir Putin. International political observers wonder if Putin—a former KGB man—provides some behind-the-scenes support for Lukashenko's authoritarian regime, especially after Belarus became the last buffer state between Russia and the European Union when Poland, Lithuania, and Latvia became EU member nations in 2004.

Lukashenko earned a somewhat dubious moniker after October of 2000, when Serbian tyrant Slobodan Milosevic was ousted, and Lukashenko inherited the title of "Europe's last dictator" in the press. In September of 2001 he was reelected to a second term by a predictably wide margin, beating his main challenger, labor leader Vladimir Goncharik, with 75 percent of the vote. The European Union and United States termed the election invalid, and Lukashenko has responded in strong terms denouncing foreign powers he claims wish to subvert democracy in Belarus. His hostility toward the West has also taken other forms: Belarus has been suspected of selling arms to Iran, Sudan, and Saddam Hussein's Iraq, and around the time of the U.S.-led invasion of Iraq in 2003, reportedly issued emergency Belarusian passports to high-ranking officials in Hussein's regime when they were forced to flee.

In October of 2004, voters in Belarus approved another referendum ballot, this one eliminating presidential term limits entirely, which had been restricted to two in the 1994 constitution. That same day, parliamentary elections were held, and the pro-Lukashenko candidates won all available seats after opposition candidates were disqualified on technicalities. Lukashenko's rubber-stamp parliament approved a measure in 2005 that specified a jail term of three to five years for criticizing the president or organizing an anti-government protest. There was also a repeal of a provision that allowed the police and security services to disobey an order deemed unlawful, such as firing on protesters.

Lukashenko presides over a nation that journalists describe as a bizarre, Soviet Communist-era theme park. The international airport in Minsk is sparsely lit to conserve energy, there is almost no advertising—instead government propaganda posters tout the regime's successes—and no foreign goods in stores. Allegedly Lukashenko is a keen athlete, and sometimes shuts down entire city blocks in Minsk for in-line skating competitions, which he always wins. "An authoritarian ruling style is characteristic of me, and I have always admitted it," he told Belarusian radio in 2003, according to *Guardian* journalist Nick Paton Walsh. "Why? We could spend hours talking about this. You need to control the country and the main thing is not to ruin people's lives."

Western visitors also describe a climate of fear in Belarus, where anti-Lukashenko activists are fanatically cautious about speaking to journalists, and assert that the KGB handily intercepts cell-phone text messages. Events in neighboring Ukraine in late 2004 and early 2005—in which mass protests in Kiev dislodged an authoritarian incumbent suspected of election fraud and foul play against his pro-democracy opponent, Viktor Yushchenko—seemed to spark hope that what had been dubbed Ukraine's Orange Revolution might be repeated in Belarus. As the next presidential election loomed, however, Lukashenko warned against challenges to his rule in strong terms. "Any attempt to destabilize the situation will be met with drastic action," he said on Belarus television in January of 2006, according to Steven Lee Myers in the *New York Times Magazine*. "We will wring the necks of those who are actually doing it and those who are instigating these acts."

Not surprisingly, Lukashenko won his third presidential term on March 19, 2006, with 84 percent of the vote. His opponent, Alexander Milinkevich, polled just two percent, according to official results. There were protests, however, that numbered some 10,000 in Minsk alone, and a week later there was another wave of anti-government demonstrators who gathered, but they were blocked by riot police. Lukashenko was last seen in public a day later, and then vanished on the eve of a scheduled visit to Moscow. His inauguration was even postponed, and rumors flew that the usually indomitable and apparently physically robust president was either suffering from depression or some unknown health issue. He resurfaced and was sworn in on April 8.

In June of 2006, the European Union froze Lukashenko's assets, along with those of other top government officials, and issued a ban on travel visas for the president and other high-ranking cronies of his. Americans were forbidden from conducting any kind of business with Lukashenko. U.S. Secretary of State Condoleezza Rice has named Belarus as one of the last "outposts of tyranny" on the planet, along with Cuba, Myanmar, North Korea, Iran, and Zimbabwe. Just before the 2006 election, Lukashenko responded to Rice, the European Union, and the entirety of his foreign and domestic critics with characteristic bombast. "I've been hearing these accusations for over ten years and we got used to it," a report from BBC News quoted him as saying. "We are not going to answer them. I want to come from the premise that the elections in Belarus are held for ourselves. I am sure that it is the Belarus people who are the masters in our state."

Sources

Periodicals

Contemporary Review, January 2002, p. 22.
Financial Times, May 15, 2006, p. 6.
Foreign Policy, November-December 2003, p. 35; November-December 2005, p. 81.
Guardian (London, England), March 2, 2006, p. 12.
Independent (London, England), October 16, 2004.

New York Times Magazine, February 26, 2006, p. 48.
Times (London, England), April 3, 2006, p. 33.

Online

"Profile: Alexander Lukashenko," BBC News, http://news.bbc.co.uk/2/hi/europe/3882843.stm (June 18, 2006).

—*Carol Brennan*

Pony Ma

Chief Executive Officer of Tencent Holdings

Born Ma Huateng, c. 1971, in Hainan, China. *Education:* Shenzhen University, B.S., 1993.

Addresses: *Office*—Floor 5-10, FIYTA Hi-tech Building, Gaoxinnanyi Ave., Southern District of Hi-tech Park, Shenzhen, 518057 China.

Career

Executive, China Motion Telecom Development, Ltd., China, 1993-98; executive, Shenzhen Runxun Communications Co., Ltd., China; cofounder of Tencent Holdings, Ltd., China, 1998, then president, chairman of the board, chief executive officer, and other executive positions.

Awards: Named a Global Business Influential by *Time,* 2004; named one of the top ten Economic Influentials—Innovation by China Central Television.

Sidelights

Pony Ma is the founder, president, chief executive officer, and executive board member of Tencent Holdings, Ltd., one of the most important telecommunications companies in China. Tencent, with its well-known penguin icon, controls China's largest instant messaging (IM) service and has expanded to other mobile telephone and internet services. Ma's interest in Tencent has made him quite wealthy, and he is regarded as one of China's most desirable bachelors.

Born around 1971, on the island of Hainan, China, Ma uses the nickname "Pony" which is derived from the English translation of his family name, which is "horse." When he was a teenager, he moved to Shenzhen. In 1993, he graduated from Shenzhen University, earning his B.S. in software engineering. After graduation, Ma became employed by China Motion Telecom Development, Ltd. He worked in the Internet paging system development, in charge of research and development. This company supplied such systems to the Chinese government. He also worked for Shenzhen Runxun Communications Co., Ltd., where he also worked in the research and development area. He oversaw Internet calling systems.

Ma also had a personal interest in the developing Internet and surfed the Web at home. He soon came to the conclusion that China was ready for its own IM service. To that end, he and four friends founded Tencent in 1998. They began the company with only $120,000, primarily garnered from money earned while playing the stock market. The first years of the company were difficult. Ma had to wear many hats in the first year, from janitor to website designer, as the company lacked experienced employees and financial health. The company's early offerings included e-mail and internet paging services.

Within a few years, Tencent added more employees and Ma began focusing on strategic planning, positioning, and management of the company. He was eventually named chief executive officer, executive board member, and chairman of the board. By 1999, Tencent launched the product that would bring it much success and wealth. After initially focusing on a text messaging product, it offered its instant messaging service, originally called OICQ, but later known as QQ. Initially, OICQ was only one of many IM services in China and did not have a big market share.

Ma changed the fortune of his company when OICQ began being offered as a free download. The free download attracted many young users. Demand grew high, with as many as five million users added in one year. This success created problems for Ma and his young company. Because Tencent could not afford the servers or server space needed to service all these customers, Ma tried to sell OICQ, but no deal could be reached. American venture capitalists eventually invested a couple million American dollars to keep Tencent afloat. At that time, OICQ became QQ.

To continue Ma's company's success, QQ users were offered more value-added services each year, such as QQ membership, ring tones, and other services for cellular telephones, as well as the ability to customize some products. Ma also signed deals to work with a number of internet technology companies around the world. By 2004, Tencent was the largest IM service in China. About 335 million Chinese, or 74 percent of the market, used Tencent's services. Ma himself was worth $190 million in 2004. He was named a Global Business Influential by *Time* magazine as well as one of the top ten Economic Influentials in Innovation by Beijing, China's China Central Television.

In June of 2004, Tencent had its initial public offering (IPO) in the Hong Kong Stock Exchange. It was successful and within a few months, the stock prices had risen nearly 60 percent. Profits rose more than 40 percent from the beginning of 2004. Ma said the company went public in part to have the funds to purchase companies to help enhance the QQ IM service. Ma did not let Tencent rest on its laurels, but continued to expand around its core IM business. He hoped to buy firms working in new areas like wireless technologies to help Tencent retain its position as the number-one company in China. Such acquisitions were intended to keep Tencent competitive in the face of ever increasing foreign competition. Microsoft and Yahoo! both were competing for the same market in China. While Tencent was doing well, it was already facing eroding profit margins as the cost of development and marketing continued to rise.

In 2004, Ma announced that different kinds of games, created within Tencent, would be added regularly to Tencent's services, to keep the customers' interest. This strategy paid off by attracting more than one million online gamers in China, making it the largest such service in that country. Tencent also began offering the first licensed radio broadcasts over the Internet in China. However, IM remained the most significant Tencent service. By early 2005, Tencent was the most popular IM service in Asia with 150-160 million active users. Because other companies offered free IM, like Microsoft, Ma looked for new ways to make that service profitable. One way was with the development of new paying services such as an IM product solely for businesses in China called RTX (Real Time Xchange System), launched in 2005. RTX was soon used by 85,000 companies in China. Tencent also added profits by licensing the QQ brand name to another Chinese company, Guangzhou Donglihang, to produce products like toys with the QQ name.

Ma's next move was to add e-commerce, primarily consumer to consumer sites like auction sites for the registered members of its IM service as well as through its website. His goal was to make Tencent's services the focus of its users' Internet life, as many of its subscribers were under 30 years of age. Mary Meeker, an analyst at Morgan Stanley, believed Tencent was quite successful in this arena. She told Bruce Einhorn of *BusinessWeek Online*, "If you look at instant messaging and the ability to enhance services and generate revenue from them, Tencent is probably the leader in the world." Ma continued on this path by signing a partnership deal with Google. Despite the deal, Ma did not intend to sell out to a foreign company, but continued to add more gaming, community searches, and advertising to retain its customers and add new ones.

By August of 2005, Tencent had more than 438 million registered users and 173 million active users. Revenues continued to grow. Ma wanted to further expand Tencent and keep its position as the leading IM service in China. Making partnership deals with other companies, like Google, were ideal. Ma told Liu Ke of *China Today*, "Concentration does not mean stubbornly sticking to your own ideas. When we see an opportunity, we grasp it. To succeed in this game, you need an acute sense of business and the markets. We view our challenges not as more pressure, but as roads to success."

Sources

Periodicals

AFX—Asia, August 24, 2005.
Alestron, October 20, 2005.

Asia Africa Intelligence Wire, November 26, 2004; July 14, 2005; August 25, 2005.

China Today, March 2005, pp. 56-58.

SinoCast China IT Watch, August 30, 2005; September 22, 2005.

South China Morning Post, June 7, 2004, p. 1; December 1, 2005.

Online

"China's Internet players step up to battle U.S. giants," Investors.com, http://www.investors.com/breakingnews.asp?journalid=28799353&brk=1 (February 12, 2006).

"China: Tencent Holdings: March of the penguin," *BusinessWeek Online,* http://www.businessweek.com/print/magazine/content/05_46/b3959421.htm?chan=gl (February 12, 2006).

"Distinguished Guests of 2005 China Internet Summit at West Lake," Alibaba.com, http://www.alibaba.com/trade/servlet/page/static/campaign/westlake_speakers (February 12, 2006).

"Ma Huateng, Chief Executive Officer," Tencent, http://www.tencent.com/about/manage_e.shtml (February 11, 2006).

"Pony Ma, Tencent Holdings," CNN.com, http://www.cnn.com/SPECIALS/2004/global.influentials/stories/ma (February 11, 2006).

"Tencent CEO Pony Ma named '2004 Economic Influentials—Innovation' by CCTV," Tencent, http://www.tencent.com/about/mo_dt_e.shtml?/about/2004/20041229_e.shtml (February 11, 2006).

"U.S. Web Giants Target China," *BusinessWeek Online,* http://www.businessweek.com/print/magazine/content/05_24/b3937058.htm?chan=gl (February 12, 2006).

—*A. Petruso*

Seth MacFarlane

AP/Wide World Photos

Television series creator and animator

Born October 26, 1973, in Kent, CT. *Education:* Earned degree from Rhode Island School of Design, 1995.

Addresses: *Office*—c/o FOX Entertainment Group, 1211 Avenue of the Americas, New York, NY 10036.

Career

Animator for Hanna-Barbera Studios after 1995; his short animated feature *Larry and Steve* was shown on the Cartoon Network's *World Premiere Toons,* 1996; first series, *Family Guy,* ran for three seasons on FOX, 1999-2002, and was renewed by the network for the spring 2005 season; a second series, *American Dad,* debuted on FOX in January, 2005.

Awards: Emmy Award for outstanding voice-over performance, Academy of Television Arts and Sciences, for voice of Stewie on *Family Guy,* 2000.

Sidelights

Seth MacFarlane is the creator of FOX TV's animated series *Family Guy.* Barely out of college when the network handed him his own show, MacFarlane delivered a series known for its tasteless humor and amusingly witty talking dog. *Family Guy* lasted just three seasons before network executives pulled the plug on the series in 2002, but over the next few years it developed a cult following in cable reruns, and FOX took the historic step of bringing it

back for another prime-time run—it is said to be the first show in television history to be resurrected by the same network that cancelled it in the first place. MacFarlane never imagined that *Family Guy* would return, as he told Josh Wolk in *Entertainment Weekly.* "There was no precedent for it," he remarked. "It would require a network to say, 'We've made a mistake.'"

Born in October of 1973, MacFarlane grew up in Kent, Connecticut, a town in Litchfield County whose most notable residents are former U.S. National Security Advisor Henry Kissinger and the Kent School, a co-educational boarding school founded in 1906. MacFarlane's mother worked at the school, and he himself graduated with its 1991 class. He went on to the Rhode Island School of Design in Providence, where he studied animation. MacFarlane's choice of career had been decided for him at the age of 14, when he saw his first episode of *The Simpsons,* the immensely popular FOX Network animated series about a working-class family. He had already made some of his first sci-fi-themed films with the help of an eight-millimeter movie camera his parents had bought for him.

The Rhode Island School of Design, known informally as RISD ("ris-dee") is considered one of the top art schools in the United States. MacFarlane's

1995 degree from it helped him land him a job on the West Coast at Hanna-Barbera Productions, the famed animation studio in West Hollywood, California. Hanna-Barbera, the creator of such perennial cartoon favorites as Yogi Bear and the Flintstones, became the Cartoon Network Studios not long after MacFarlane joined the team. He worked on the series *Johnny Bravo* and *Dexter's Laboratory.*

MacFarlane also wrote his own stories, and honed his comic skills as a stand-up comic for a time. At RISD, he had made a well-received student film called *The Life of Larry,* the story of a hapless bumbler who became the forerunner of the dad on *Family Guy.* A sequel he made to it, *Larry and Steve,* featured Larry's improbably brilliant talking-dog companion, and made it onto the Cartoon Network's showcase *World Premiere Toons* in 1996. Executives at the FOX Network liked what they saw and asked MacFarlane to do some short animated bits for their *MAD TV* series. From there, FOX signed him to a $2.5 million-a-year production deal in May of 1998 to create his own series based on the Larry and Steve characters.

The result was *Family Guy,* and the animated series debuted on the FOX Network on January 31, 1999, right after the Super Bowl game. The storylines revolved around the household of Peter Griffin, a toy-factory worker in Rhode Island, and his wife and three children, who included a genius toddler, Baby Stewie. Rounding out the cast was Brian, the Griffins' martini-drinking, quip-delivering dog. FOX put the show on the air for its first regular season, beginning in April of 1999, in a terrific Sunday-night slot—after *The Simpsons* and before *The X-Files.*

FOX launched *Family Guy* with a generous publicity blitz, and much was made of the boy-genius aura surrounding MacFarlane, its creator, who was just 25 years old at the time. In viewing the show, however, critics were puzzled by the mix of high and low humor, with *Entertainment Weekly's* Ken Tucker describing it as *"The Simpsons* as conceived by a singularly sophomoric mind that lacks any reference point beyond other TV shows." Tucker also mentioned the massive FOX marketing push surrounding the *Family Guy's* debut, and predicted that this was "shaping up to be the hollowest hype of the year." In *Newsweek,* critic Kendall Hamilton also mentioned its "golden launch" and remarked that FOX executives seemed assured in their conviction that *Family Guy* would be the next *Simpsons.* "If it isn't, it won't be because *Family Guy* compares unfavorably with other clever cartoons plying the airwaves," Hamilton noted. "It'll be because it's not measurably better."

Despite the jibes, and an audience that seemed to dwindle weekly, MacFarlane's *Family Guy* caught on with a number of viewers who remained devoted to the series. FOX moved the show several times, however—a surefire strategy to lose an audience. For its second season, it was put in a time slot that forced it to compete for viewers with wrestling night on the rival United Paramount Network (UPN). Less than a month later, MacFarlane's series was put on hiatus, but returned with new episodes in March of 2000. This time, network executives placed it up against the hit ABC series *Who Wants to Be a Millionaire?* on the prime-time Tuesday line-up.

MacFarlane, who was intensely involved in the writing and production of show, also did three of its voices: Peter, Baby Stewie, and Brian the dog. He won an Emmy in August of 2000 for that work, but by then FOX was thinking of canceling the show altogether. He had even had to let some of his staff go, but *Family Guy* was renewed for a third season, helped by the fact that FOX's new president, Gail Berman, liked the show. "We got a call from the network at one point telling us that it was the single largest fan push for a show that FOX had seen in the history of the network, including *Party of Five,"* MacFarlane recalled in an interview with Terri Roberts for *Ross Reports Television & Film.* Berman greenlighted another 13 episodes for the 2001 season, but the finished product went up against the CBS hit reality series *Survivor* on Thursday nights, as well as NBC's longtime first-place ratings-war winner, *Friends.* Bested by tough competition, the *Family Guy* was finally cancelled. Its last episode aired in February of 2002. MacFarlane was not technically out of a job at that point, since his contract with FOX gave him permission to create another series.

There was a still a devoted *Family Guy* fan base, and some of the more ardent champions petitioned FOX to release all three seasons on DVD. Hoping to recoup some of the production costs (declining ratings for a show means that the network must reduce its rates for commercial air time during the episodes), they agreed, and struck a deal with the Cartoon Network—a cable channel also in the FOX corporate family—to take the show and add it to its weeknight schedule in return for some free promotional spots trumpeting the April of 2003 DVD release.

Family Guy became part of the Cartoon Network's "Adult Swim" lineup of animated series, including *Futurama,* which was aimed at 18- to 34-year-old male viewers. The 50 episodes of MacFarlane's defunct series began to score impressive ratings, and in some markets it even beat out Jay Leno's *Tonight Show* and *Late Show with David Letterman.*

The *Family Guy* DVD release was also an unexpected success. When the first 28 episodes were released in the spring of 2003, they quickly sold a million copies, and *Family Guy* became the number-two best-selling television show on DVD ever, following first-place finisher, comedian Dave Chappelle's first season collection of *Chappelle's Show*. MacFarlane, meanwhile, had been working on his next series, and had wrapped it up when FOX called him in for a meeting. He knew his new animated show, *American Dad,* was going to make its debut soon, but was stunned when the president of 20th Century FOX television production, Gary Newman, asked MacFarlane if he would be interested in resurrecting *Family Guy* as well. "It was like when you ask out a girl and she says yes and you try not to look too excited," MacFarlane recalled about that meeting in an interview with Devin Gordon for *Newsweek.* "I'm sitting there, trying to seem professional, and all I'm thinking is, 'My God, how did this happen?'"

To make up for lost time, and to soothe fears about MacFarlane having to rehire a staff he had once had to fire, FOX asked for 35 episodes, instead of the usual 22 per-season deal. They also sweetened the pot with plans for a book, *Stewie's Guide to World Domination,* and asked for an 80-minute original *Family Guy* DVD movie. The fourth season began airing on FOX in the spring of 2005, and in its first episode MacFarlane even managed to write in a sly dig at the network with a mention of a long legacy of canceled FOX shows, among them *Titus, That '80s Show, Girlsclub, Cracking Up,* and *Normal, Ohio.*

MacFarlane's other animated series, *American Dad,* debuted in January of 2005. It featured some strong political comedy thanks to the title character, Stan Smith. Stan is a Central Intelligence Agency employee, right-wing Republican, and fully formed conspiracy theorist. Some of the political humor had its origins in MacFarlane's near-death experience: in September of 2001, he gave a speech at his alma mater, and was scheduled to fly back to Los Angeles out of nearby Logan Airport in Boston. He missed his plane, and that American Airlines flight was the plane that hit the north tower of the World Trade Center on the morning of September 11.

American Dad is firmly rooted in the "zany-family" sitcom tradition, with the intensely patriotic Stan presiding over a brood that includes his dimwitted wife Francine, liberal teenage daughter Hayley, nerdy son Steve, and Roger, an alien that Stan has rescued from the mythic Area 51, where conspiracy theorists believe the U.S. government has secreted evidence of extraterrestrial landings. The resident alien is clearly a violation of Stan's workplace security protocols, as is the family's other "pet," a German-speaking goldfish named Klaus. Klaus is a failed Central Intelligence Agency experiment, and is desperately in love with Francine. MacFarlane's sister, Rachael, provides the voice for Hayley, and MacFarlane does the voices for Stan and Roger.

Besides having his first series cancelled, though later renewed, the only other setback in MacFarlane's career was an odd boycott campaign that rolled out in mid-1999 during the first season of *Family Guy.* The campaign was instigated by his former headmaster at the Kent School, Father Richardson Schell, who urged advertisers to boycott the show because of its racy and often politically incorrect humor. The crusade died out when the media linked Schell's discontent to the fact that the fictional family name, Griffin, was also the last name of the longtime school secretary, though MacFarlane assured everyone that the coincidence was purely accidental.

Roberts, who interviewed MacFarlane for *Ross Reports Television & Film,* asked him if he ever anticipated that his career would turn out so well, when so many animators toil in obscurity for years. "I did," he admitted somewhat candidly, "but it was only out of naïveté. It wasn't like I had an overblown idea of self-worth, it was more that I didn't realize how difficult it was. I saw what happened with *The Simpsons* and thought, 'Gosh, how hard can that be?' Obviously, very hard. They made it look very easy, but it was very difficult. But it's been worth all the time it's taken."

Sources

Broadcasting & Cable, June 21, 2004, p. 12.
Daily Variety, February 4, 2005, p. 10.
Entertainment Weekly, January 8, 1999, p. 39; April 9, 1999, p. 52; April 22, 2005, pp. 36-39.
Newsweek, April 12, 1999, p. 73; April 4, 2005, p. 50.
New York Observer, June 19, 2000, p. 22.
New York Times, September 3, 2000, p. 59.
Ross Reports Television & Film, November 2004, p. 5.
Variety, August 21, 2000, p. 12.

—Carol Brennan

John J. Mack

Chief Executive Officer of Morgan Stanley

Bloomberg News/Landov

Born November 17, 1944, in Mooresville, NC; son of Charles (a wholesale grocery business owner) and Alice Azouri Mack; married Christy Rose; children: John, Stephen, Jenna. *Education:* Duke University, B.A., 1968.

Addresses: *Office*—Morgan Stanley, 1585 Broadway, New York, NY 10036.

Career

Worked for two brokerage firms, including one in North Carolina and Smith Barney, before joining Morgan Stanley, New York, NY; began career at Morgan Stanley in sales in the fixed-income division, 1972; became managing director, 1979; named head of taxable fixed-income division, 1985-92, then chairman of operations committee, 1992-93, president, 1993-97; after merger with Dean Witter, Discover & Company, was president and chief operating officer of Morgan Stanley Dean Witter, 1997-2001; resigned from newly re-christened Morgan Stanley, 2001; joined Credit Suisse First Boston as chief executive officer, and Credit Suisse Group as vice chairman, 2001; promoted to co-chief executive officer of Credit Suisse Group, 2002; left Credit Suisse Group, 2004; served as chairman of Pequot Capital, a hedge fund, 2004-05; returned to Morgan Stanley as chief executive officer and chairman of the board, 2005.

Sidelights

Several years after leading Morgan Stanley as president and chief operating officer and being forced out in a power struggle, John J. Mack was hired as its chief executive officer and chairman of the board. Mack had worked his way to the top of Morgan Stanley from a sales position. After leaving the company, Mack held executive positions at Credit Suisse before being asked to return to Morgan Stanley. In a *New York Times* article, David Barboza wrote of Mack, "He is a dynamic, decisive leader, a manager who clearly knows where he wants to go, and insists on action and on executing orders—a style that once earned him the nickname 'Mack the Knife.'"

Mack was born and raised in Mooresville, North Carolina, with his five older brothers. His father, Charles, was of Lebanese descent and ran his own wholesale grocery business. Football was a passion of young Mack's life. His success on the gridiron led to a football scholarship at Duke University, where he played line backer. Mack already had good business sense, selling snacks to fellow students out of his own dorm room store. He graduated from Duke University in 1968 with B.A. in history.

After graduation, Mack immediately began working with brokerage firms. His first job was for a small company in North Carolina, before joining Smith Barney. Mack was hired at Morgan Stanley in 1972, working as a salesman in the fixed-income division. Seven years later, he was named managing director of that division. In 1985, Mack became the head of the taxable fixed-income division, which included bonds. He spent the next seven years in that position, where he developed a reputation as a harsh cost cutter. Mack faced a tough challenge in 1992 when a number of bond traders left the company together and became employed by a competitor. He rallied those traders who remained with Morgan Stanley.

In 1992, Mack moved on to a new department, serving as the chairman of the operations committee. In this position, he was in charge of coordinating the daily affairs of certain parts of the company. His goal was to better coordinate communications between clients and various divisions in the company as Morgan Stanley continued to expand globally. In this position, Mack also had other responsibilities, including some management of personnel, controlling of expenses, and coordinating of operations. In the spring of 1993, he was named president of the Morgan Stanley Group and put in charge of the Investment Banking Division.

When retail brokerage firm Dean Witter, Discover & Company, bought Morgan Stanley for $10 billion, Mack took on new challenges in the newly merged company, now known as Morgan Stanley Dean Witter. Mack was already being groomed to become chief executive officer of Morgan Stanley before the merger took place. After the merger, Mack was named president and chief operating officer and did well. However, he still wanted the top job at Morgan Stanley Dean Witter. This desire eventually resulted in a power struggle with the company's chief executive officer and board chairman, Philip J. Purcell, who had been the head of Dean Witter before the merger. Purcell retained the control and had no plans to retire, though Mack's divisions did exceptionally well in producing a vast majority of the firm's revenues by 2001.

Mack could not convince the board of Morgan Stanley Dean Witter to change their mind. The power struggle came to an end when Mack suddenly left the company, by then again known as Morgan Stanley, early in 2001. During the few months Mack was unemployed, he played golf daily and went through some difficult times. However, Mack soon found a new job. He was hired as chief executive officer of Credit Suisse First Boston (CSFB), a troubled investment banking firm. At the same time, he was named vice chairman of its parent company, the Credit Suisse Group. Like Morgan Stanley, Credit Suisse First Boston was the product of a recent merger of parts of Credit Suisse Group, a large Swiss bank, and First Boston, another banking firm. The merger was not gelling and there had recently been a scandal involving the man Mack replaced, Allen D. Wheat, concerning First Boston stock sales and initial public offerings in the late 1990s.

When Mack was hired, some observers were unsure about Mack's leadership because he had never run a whole company before and faced many difficult management issues at CSFB. He ran half of the newly reorganized company, and was in charge of investment banking, trading, and asset managements. (The other half was the financial services unit.) Critics were also concerned that while Mack served as CEO of Credit Suisse First Boston, he had to retain several million shares of Morgan Stanley stock worth hundreds of millions of dollars. Mack was one of the largest shareholders of Morgan Stanley because he was restricted from selling his shares. Credit Suisse First Boston was a major competitor of Morgan Stanley.

At CSFB, Mack wanted to improve morale among employees, increase teamwork, make it the largest investment bank in the world, and re-define the company's vision as well as reduce costs. Within a year, Mack reorganized and reduced the size of the company and convinced key employees to restructure their pay arrangement to be more in line with other Wall Street companies so CSFB could grow again. He also dealt with looming legal issues from the previous regime by agreeing to pay hefty fines to settle charges related to problematic stock sales. Mack made another deal over charges that CSFB tried to run the Treasury bond market. He paid out a total of $130 million in fines, but did not admit to any wrongdoing on the part of CSFB, and avoided fraud charges. Mack emphasized the importance of acting ethically on every level, an ongoing problem at the company. He was able to quickly return CSFB to profitability, primarily through cost-cutting.

In the fall of 2002, Mack was named the co-chief executive officer of the Credit Suisse Group, with Oswald J. Grubel, who led the financial services unit of the company. They replaced Lukas Muhlemann, the CEO of Credit Suisse Group. While assuming additional duties, Mack remained in charge of CSFB and hoped to better integrate it into the Credit Suisse Group. He continued to face new CSFB-related legal problems with federal regulators. The government believed that the company's analysts had given out misinformation to land investment banking deals. Some CSFB bankers were also believed to use initial public offering shares to gain the attention of clients. Mack was not happy about the new charges as he believed that firms should be ethical, well-managed, and take care of clients before making money. He continued to overhaul CSFB in this area by establishing a strict code of conduct and company procedures for dealing with clients. Legal challenges continued in 2003 when one of CSFB's leading bankers in the 1990s, Frank P. Quattrone, was arrested. Quattrone had been a significant part of many of the previous federal investigations into CSFB's practices.

Though CSFB had earnings of $1.7 billion in 2003, after losing $1.3 billion in 2002, and continued to post profits in 2004, the company's legal problems seemed never ending. CSFB had to pay more fines to the U.S. government. Moreover, Mack had to spent less time with CSFB and more time with the parent company, Credit Suisse, at its headquarters in Zurich, Switzerland. Mack's presence was needed at Credit Suisse to develop strategies to deal with a number of complex issues in the company. There was also talk that Credit Suisse as a whole might be for sale since the company still faced money problems. Mack believed the best way to improve Credit Suisse and take it to the next level was by merger, but the Credit Suisse board members did not want to take this route. Mack was also under pressure to move to Zurich, a move he did not want to make. Early in the summer of 2004, Mack decided not to renew his contract with the company, which expired in July of 2004.

Mack soon joined a smaller hedge fund, Pequot Capital, as chief executive officer. As Mack was getting settled in his new job, Morgan Stanley was struggling financially and in the market for a new CEO. Though Morgan Stanley's board was initially reluctant to even consider asking Mack back and even publicly stated at one point that he was not a candidate, speculation spread inside and outside the company that Mack was to be named CEO. Mack was offered the job, succeeding Purcell, the man he tried to replace in 2001. Purcell had been forced out by an internal revolt of traders and bankers. Mack was seen as someone who understood the company's problems and it was believed that he could bring the firm together better than anyone else. Many directors wanted Mack, but he wanted to make sure the board was composed of members that supported him, since all but one had been selected by Purcell. However, even some of these members supported Mack's return. Mack and Morgan Stanley finally came to an agreement in June of 2005, with Mack signing a five-year contract paying him about $25 million per year, at least for the first 18 months.

Mack again faced many challenges as the new Morgan Stanley CEO. He wanted certain executives who had left after a shakeup several months earlier to return. This move meant that some current executives would leave or, at the very least, be antagonized. Mack also had to deal with morale problems, dropping stock prices, and profits that were not expected to be strong in the short term. In addition, he had to answer strategic questions, including what to do with the credit card unit (the company owned the Discover Card) and retail brokerage units, which were not making as much money as the rest of the company. And, as at CSFB, he faced a few regulatory questions because of a lack of certain documentations. Morgan Stanley was also ordered to pay out millions in damages to a financier because of a lawsuit.

When Mack took over Morgan Stanley, many top executives stepped down, but he was able to bring aboard significant personnel. Mack's first big hire was an outsider, James P. Gorman, to head the individual investor group. Observers believed that this hire showed Mack was committed to turning the company around. Mack also looked to acquire a hedge fund and put the right people in place to ensure Morgan Stanley returned to profitability and a leading position in the marketplace.

Though Mack was known for his toughness and being physically imposing, he also had a reputation for being an executive who was compassionate and cared deeply about his employees. Many noted his ability to listen and relate to others. Describing this aspect of his professional personality, Barboza in the *New York Times* called Mack "a dedicated, passionate leader who insists on accountability and loathes incompetence."

Sources

Books

Standard & Poor's Register of Directors and Executives, McGraw-Hill, 2006.

Periodicals

BusinessWeek, February 12, 2001, p. 84; July 30, 2001, p. 76; September 23, 2002, p. 90.
BusinessWeek Online, June 25, 2004.

Business Wire, January 24, 2001.

New York Times, March 3, 1993, p. D4; February 6, 1997, p. D7; July 13, 2001, p. C1; January 27, 2002, sec. 3, p. 1; September 20, 2002, p. W1; April 25, 2003, p. C1; June 23, 2005, p. C1; June 28, 2005, p. C1; June 30, 2005, p. A1; July 1, 2005, p. C1, p. C8; July 6, 2005, p. C1; August 17, 2005, p. C1; November 24, 2005, p. C1; January 12, 2006, p. C1; January 21, 2006, p. C1.

—A. Petruso

Chris Madden

Interior designer, television host, and author

Born Annchristine Casson, June 1, 1948, in Rockville Centre, NY; married Kevin Madden (a publisher), 1974; children: Patrick, Nick. *Education:* Attended Fashion Institute of Technology.

Addresses: *Office*—Chris Madden, Inc., 181 Westchester Ave., Ste. 408, Port Chester, NY 10573.

Career

Photo assistant, *Sports Illustrated*; public relations employee, Simon and Schuster, Inc.; public relations director, Farrar, Straus & Giroux; launched own public relations firm, 1976; founded of Chris Madden, Inc., 1995; design correspondent for *The Oprah Winfrey Show* and appeared on *Today* and *Good Morning America*, 1990s; host of *Interiors by Design*, Home and Garden Television, 1995-2003; designer and spokesperson for Bassett, 1998-2004; designer and spokesperson for Mohawk, beginning in 2001; designer and spokesperson for J.C. Penney, 2004—; debuted magazine, *At Home with Chris Madden*, 2005; author of syndicated newspaper column and numerous cookbooks and books on interior design.

Sidelights

Even though she owns her own self-titled company, designs and licenses her name to housewares, hosted her own television show, and recently launched a magazine, Chris Madden discourages comparisons with fellow interior designer and media maven Martha Stewart. While Stewart is known for the detailed, labor-intensive projects highlighted on her television show and in her magazine, Madden stresses simplicity. "I have done it my way for three decades," Madden told the *Chicago Tribune's* Pamela Sherrod in 2004. "It's great [Stewart] paved the way for all of us. She made it easier for women's voices to be heard in the design arena. She opened the doors for us to love our homes.... But I do it my way."

The oldest daughter among the eleven children of a corporate executive and a homemaker, Madden was born Annchristine Casson in Rockville Centre, New York, in 1948. Her mother taught Madden and her siblings to sew, and she also cut the children's hair, upholstered furniture, and excelled in the kitchen. "She really was Martha Stewart before Martha Stewart," Madden told Jura Koncius of the *Washington Post*. As a child, Madden published a neighborhood newspaper, designed costumes for school plays, and demonstrated an early flair for design. "I used to give Mom advice on what to do with the house. I even picked out a sofa for the living room. It has just always been a passion of mine," Madden told Elizabeth Hlotyak of the *Westchester County Business Journal*. She also modeled until the age of 16. Madden's design sense earned her a scholarship to the Fashion Institute of Technology in New York City, although she left before graduating. Her early work experience included a stint as a photography assistant at *Sports Illustrated*, as well as a public relations position at the publishing house Simon and Schuster, Inc. She went on to become public relations director at publishing company Farrar, Straus & Giroux. She met Kevin Madden, a publisher, during a company softball game in the early 1970s and the pair were married in 1974. They have two sons, Patrick and Nick.

Madden launched her own public relations firm in 1976 and began writing cookbooks as well as books on home decorating and interior design. She came to be recognized as an important voice in the interior design field with the publication of her 1988 book *Interior Visions: Great American Designers and the Showcase House.* In 1995, Home and Garden Television (HGTV) tapped Madden to become one of the network's four original hosts. Her program, *Interiors by Design,* ran for eight years. Also in 1995, Madden launched her own company, Chris Madden, Inc. Her husband joined her as chief executive officer. During the 1990s, Madden also became the design correspondent for *The Oprah Winfrey Show* and appeared on *Today* and *Good Morning America.* She designed rooms for Winfrey, talk show host Katie Couric, and author Toni Morrison.

Madden achieved increased visibility with the 1997 publication of *A Room of Her Own: Women's Personal Spaces,* a look inside the cherished rooms of 38 women, including Winfrey and other celebrities. Madden conceived of the book, which sold 100,000 copies, after creating her own private space following the death of her younger sister. "I realized that I didn't have a place to mourn her. So I had this little tiny bedroom on the second floor that I decided to make into my personal sanctuary," she told the *Westchester County Business Journal*'s Hlotyak.

Madden's commitment to design became even more steadfast after a 1998 near-drowning accident during a whitewater rafting trip with her family in Colorado. "Within seconds of being pulled out of the water my priorities shifted," she revealed to Ryan Underwood in *Inc.* "I counted on two fingers what I wanted for my life: to be with my family and follow my vision for design." That same year, Madden leveraged a request to serve as a spokesperson for Bassett Furniture Company into a design partnership. She spent two years perfecting the products, and the 70-item Chris Madden furniture line debuted in 2000. The line made $100 million its first two years. Madden and Bassett parted ways in 2004 when Madden launched a line of housewares and furniture for J.C. Penney called the Chris Madden Home Collection. By the following year, the collection had grown to 2,000 pieces and was projected to represent 75 percent of all furniture sold by the chain, far exceeding the company's expectations. Also in 2004, Clarkson Potter published Madden's *Haven: Finding the Keys to Your Personal Decorating Style.* Madden told *USA Today*'s Olivia Barker the same year that the need to create sanctuary at home was especially necessary in contemporary society. "Now more than ever, people need their homes to be havens, because of everything that's gone on in the world," she explained.

In May of 2005, Madden debuted *At Home with Chris Madden,* an interior design magazine published by Hachette Filipacchi Media U.S. Geared toward women, the magazine set out to focus on simple design and the creation of comfortable personal spaces. "Your home should be a nurturing haven for everyone, starting with yourself," Madden told the *Washington Post*'s Koncius. "I'm not looking to add any more obligations to women's lives. But I'm trying to help consumers not to be overwhelmed by all the choices out there." Coming on the heels of a jail sentence for competitor Stewart, who was convicted of insider trading, many in the media hailed Madden as Stewart's replacement in the public eye. Madden explained to Koncius, "Martha and I had many similarities: the same book publisher, the TV shows and newspaper columns. Even the fact that we were both blondes. But it made me cranky that the media saw me as an overnight sensation. I've been in the trenches designing, writing, photographing, and speaking." Madden, whose company made $2.5 million in 2004, observed in her interview with *Inc.*'s Underwood that her range of professional experience has contributed to her success. "Everything I did, from learning how to photograph a Mets game to learning about a piece of fabric, added to the big picture," she said. Even though she has suffered daily pain since her rafting accident, Madden remains thoroughly involved in her growing company, easing her condition with regular yoga. "[Y]ou have to be a control freak to do this, and I don't think that's a bad thing to say," she told *Fortune*'s Julie Rose. "If I have control, I can be creative."

Selected writings

(Co-author) *The Compleat Lemon Cookbook,* Holt, Rinehart and Winston, 1979.

The Summer House Cookbook, illustrated by Jody Newman, Harcourt (New York, NY), 1979.

(With others) *The Photographed Cat,* Doubleday (New York, NY), 1980.

(With others) *Manhattan,* Harry Abrams (New York, NY), 1981.

Baby's First Helpings: Super-Healthy Meals for Super-Healthy Kids, Mary Ellen Family Books (Garden City, NY), 1983.

Interior Visions: Great American Designers and the Showcase House, Stewart, Tabori & Chang (New York, NY), 1988.

Rooms with a View: Two Decades of Outstanding American Interior Design from Kips Bay Decorator Show Houses, PBC International (Glen Cove, NY), 1992.

Kitchens, photographs by Michael Mundy and John Vaughan, Clarkson Potter (New York, NY), 1993.

Bathrooms, photographs by John Vaughan, Clarkson Potter (New York, NY), 1996.

A Room of Her Own: Women's Personal Spaces, photographs by Jennifer Levy, Clarkson Potter, 1997.

Chris Madden's Guide to Personalizing Your Home: Simple, Beautiful Ideas for Every Room, Clarkson Potter, 1997.

Getaways: Carefree Retreats for All Seasons, photographs by Jennifer Levy and Nancy Hill, Clarkson Potter, 2000.

Bedrooms: Creating the Stylish, Comfortable Room of Your Dreams, photographs by Nancy E. Hill, Clarkson Potter, 2001.

Chris Casson Madden's New American Living Rooms, Clarkson Potter, 2003.

Haven: Finding the Keys to Your Personal Decorating Style, photographs by Nancy E. Hill, Clarkson Potter, 2004.

Sources

Periodicals

Chicago Tribune, June 3, 2004, p. 16.
Fortune, October 28, 2002, p. F192.
Home Accents Today, October 1, 2001.
Inc., February 1, 2005, p. 54.
USA Today, September 24, 2004. p. D7.
Washington Post, March 3, 2005, p. H1.
Westchester County Business Journal, March 24, 2003, p. 28.

Online

Contemporary Authors Online, Thomson Gale, 2005.

—*Kristin Palm*

Joe Manchin

AP Images

Governor of West Virginia

Born Joseph Manchin III, August 24, 1947, in Farmington, WV; married Gayle Conelly, c. 1968; children: Heather, Joseph IV, Brooke. *Education:* West Virginia University, B.S., 1970.

Addresses: *Office*—1900 Kanawha Blvd. East, Charleston, WV 25305.

Career

Owner of a carpet store in Marion County, WV, 1980s; elected to West Virginia's House of Delegates, 1982, and to the state senate, 1987 and 1992; elected West Virginia secretary of state, 2000, and governor, 2004. Vice chair, Democratic Governors Association.

Sidelights

Tragedy elevated West Virginia governor Joe Manchin to national prominence in early 2006, when an explosion at his state's Sago Mine trapped several workers underground. As the first day stretched into a second, and rescue teams worked to free the men, Manchin was a frequent presence on national news coverage of the event. The first-term Democrat was commended for his handling of his state's worst mining accident in 37 years, and afterward he promised the coal-mining industry that it would face tougher safety regulations to prevent future casualties.

Manchin was born in 1947 in Farmington, West Virginia, a small town in the northern part of the state. His father's side of the family would produce other future politicians, including Manchin's uncle, a longtime state lawmaker who served as West Virginia treasurer in the 1980s, and a cousin who served in the state senate. Manchin's father owned a furniture store, and his mother was a former basketball prodigy who encouraged her son's athletic pursuits. In high school, he lettered in four sports (baseball, football, basketball, and track), and though several colleges expressed interest in him, he accepted a football scholarship from West Virginia University in Morgantown.

Manchin's stint as a WVU Mountaineer ended with a knee injury. He graduated in 1970 with a degree in business administration, and entered the family business. After running his own carpet store in Marion County for a number of years, he entered politics in 1982 when he ran for a seat in the lower house of the West Virginia legislature, the House of Delegates. Elected to a two-year term, he went on to win a seat in the West Virginia state senate in 1987. In 1992 he won a second five-year term; four years later he made his first run for the governor's office, but lost in the primary race.

In 2000, West Virginia voters elected Manchin their next secretary of state by a large margin. He ran again for governor in 2004, and this time won the primary and then pulled an impressive number of votes in the election. A moderate Democrat, Manchin sought to balance the interests of the state's business community with those of citizens who favored increased spending on essential services such as health and education. For more than a century West Virginia's economy had been heavily dependent on coal mining, and the state was the number-two producer of the energy source in the country. However, it was also among the bottom three nationwide in per-capita income. The site of violent labor-union clashes earlier in the twentieth century, West Virginia's coal-mining communities remained closely linked to the corporations which owned the majority of the state's 544 active mines.

Manchin was sworn in as governor on January 17, 2005. One of his first acts was to meet with both chambers of the state legislature in a special session to overhaul the state's workers' compensation system. Because of the unusually high number of occupational health risks associated with coal mining, West Virginia's agency that investigated claims of job injury and provided benefits to permanently disabled workers was overextended, and required some repair. Later that year Manchin clashed with one of the state's most powerful corporate executives, Don Blankenship, who filed suit against Manchin in July. Blankenship was president of Massey Energy, the fourth-largest U.S. coal producer, and had donated heavily to the political campaigns of pro-business candidates. He contributed to a bitter 2004 contest that ended with the ouster of a West Virginia Supreme Court of Appeals justice with a long and distinguished career as a labor-union supporter. In his suit against Manchin, Blankenship claimed that permit approvals for his businesses had been revoked as a form of retaliation for his campaign financing.

Manchin's toughest challenge came just before his one-year anniversary as governor. On January 2, 2006, he received word that there had been an explosion at the Sago Mine in Tallmansville, and several miners were trapped underground. Manchin was out of state at the time, in Atlanta, Georgia, to attend that day's Sugar Bowl, a college-football contest in which his alma mater was competing. He returned to West Virginia immediately, and met with rescue-team personnel as well as the families of the trapped miners, who had gathered near the mine entrance. He also sat for interviews with all the major news outlets, who had descended upon Tallmansville to cover the story. At the end of the second day, word circulated that 12 men had been found alive, but by the time the morning-news broadcasts went on the air the next day, the rumor

had been discounted, and Americans learned that only one miner, the youngest of the missing 13, had survived.

Manchin had appeared on media reports of the initially hopeful news, but was later criticized for speaking publicly before the outcome had been officially confirmed. Some of his candor was related to his own experience with mining disasters: in 1968, an explosion at a mine in his hometown of Farmington resulted in the loss of 78 lives, with his uncle and several friends from high school among the dead. The governor nevertheless won praise for spending hours with the grieving families, and for pledging to launch a full inquiry into the disaster.

A few weeks later, both West Virginia state legislatures voted to enact stricter mine safety rules. One of the bill's provisions required companies to provide wireless tracking devices for mine workers so that in the event of another emergency they could be more easily located by rescue personnel. The new laws also required mines to install reserve oxygen-supply stations underground; miners carry oxygen with them, but the canisters provide only an hour or so of air. It took more than forty hours for Sago teams to locate the trapped miners. Manchin also traveled to Washington, and urged Congress to pass stricter federal mine-safety rules.

West Virginia law limits Manchin to two terms as governor. Even before his impressive response to the Sago Mine disaster, political soothsayers predicted he might some day move on to the national stage. His name regularly came up in lists of future vice-presidential candidates for a 2008 or 2012 Democratic Party ticket. Manchin claimed to have little ambition to move beyond his beloved home state. "The only job that I'm interested in is what I do now," the *Houston Chronicle* quoted him as saying. "This is the greatest job in the world."

Sources

Periodicals

Dominion Post (Morgantown, WV), January 2, 2006.
Houston Chronicle, January 29, 2006, p. 6.
New York Times, February 2, 2006, p. A15.
USA Today, January 5, 2006, p. 4A.

Online

"Governor Promises to Make Mines Safer," CNN.com, http://www.cnn.com/2006/US/01/22/mine.fire.ap/index.html (January 23, 2006).

—*Carol Brennan*

Mary Ellen Mark

© Christopher Felver/Corbis

Photographer

Born March 20, 1940, in Philadelphia, PA; married Martin Bell (a documentary filmmaker). *Education:* University of Pennsylvania, Philadelphia, B.A., 1962; Annenberg School of Communications, University of Pennsylvania, M.A., 1964.

Addresses: *Agent*—Lee Gross Associates, 366 Madison Ave., New York, NY 10017. *Office*—143 Prince St., New York, NY 10012. *Website*—http://www.-maryellenmark.com.

Career

Traveled to Turkey on a Fulbright scholarship to take photographs; established New York City photography studio, 1966; with Magnum Photos (an agency), 1976-81.

Awards: United States Information Agency Grant, 1975; National Endowment for the Arts photography fellowship, 1977, 1979; Creative Arts Service Grant, New York, 1977; Page One award for excellence in journalism, Newspaper Guild of New York, 1980; feature picture story award, Pictures of the Year Competition, University of Missouri, Columbia, 1981; first prize, Robert F. Kennedy Journalism Awards, 1981, 1984; Leica Medal of Excellence, 1982; Canon photo essayist award, New York, 1983; Philippe Halsman Photojournalism Award, New York, 1986; photographer of the year award, The Friends of Photography, 1987; 67th Annual Exhibition Distinctive Merit Award, Art Directors Club, 1988; Creative Arts Awards Citation For Photography, Brandeis University, 1988; World Press award for out-standing body of work throughout the years, 1988; George W. Polk Award for photojournalism, 1988; distinguished photographer's award, Women In Photography, 1988; Art Directors Club Award, 1989; World Hunger Media Award for best photojournalism, 1989; pictures of the year award for magazine portrait/personality, *Fortune* Magazine, 1990; Victor Hasselblad Cover Award, 1992; Award of Distinctive Merit, Society of Publication Designers, 1992; Award of Excellence, Society of Newspaper Design, 1992; Award of Excellence, Communication Arts Photography Annual, 1993; Front Page Award, Newswomen's Club of New York, 1993; American Photography Competition, Certificate of Excellence, 1993; Golden Light Award for photographic book of the year, 1993; Professional Photographer of the Year Award, Photographic Manufacturers & Distributors Assoc., 1994; Matrix Award for film/photography, Hearst Magazine and New York Women in Communications, Inc., 1994; Dr. Erich Salomon Preis Award, The Deutsche Gesellschaft fur Photographie, 1994; Certificate of Excellence, American Photography Competition, 1994, 1995; pictures of the year, 1st place magazine division and 3rd place magazine division, *Freelance/Life Magazine*, 1995; Certificate of Appreciation in generously supporting the Art in Embassies Program, United States Department of State, 1996; Master Series Award, School of Visual Arts, 1996; Infinity Award, International

Center of Photography, 1997; Merit Award for design feature story, Society of Publication Designers, 1997; Award of Excellence (editorial category), Communication Arts Photography Annual, 1998; Merit Award, Art Directors Club, 1998; Silver Award, Art Directors Club, 1998; Gold Medal Award for design entire issue, Society of Publication Designers, 1998; Award of Excellence (editorial category), Communication Arts Photography Annual, 1999; Leadership Award, International Photographic Council, 1999; Award for Excellence in photojournalism, Photographic Administrators Incorporated, 1999; Merrill Panitt Citizenship Award, Annenberg School for Communication, University of Pennsylvania, 2000; Cornell Capa award for distinguished achievement, International Center of Photography, 2001; Lucie Award for Documentary Photography, 2003; first prize in the arts, World Press Photo Awards, 2004.

Sidelights

Mary Ellen Mark's stark, black and white portraits have earned her a reputation as one of America's most incisive and gifted photographers. Her images manage to deftly capture the portrait sitter's dignity and vulnerability, a delicate task given the fact that her preferred subjects are often the homeless, the loveless, or the reasonless. In 2005, four decades of Mark's work was showcased in *Mary Ellen Mark: Exposure*, which also incorporated her text notes relating the stories behind the photographs. The 134 images, noted a review in *O, The Oprah Magazine*, "reveal the beauty behind grim reality."

Born in 1940, Mark grew up in Philadelphia, and owned her first camera, a Kodak Brownie, as a youngster. She studied painting and art history at the University of Pennsylvania, but chose photography when she enrolled in graduate school at the Annenberg School of Communications, which was part of the University of Pennsylvania, because she found she did not like being confined to the studio. After earning a master's degree, she won a Fulbright scholarship that allowed her to travel to Turkey to take photographs. She roamed extensively throughout Europe and the Middle East after that, building up a portfolio of work, and returned to the United States and settled in New York City in 1966.

Mark first won attention with a photo-essay that appeared in *Look* magazine, a renowned photojournalism periodical, about heroin addicts in London, England. She landed other magazine assignments over the next few years, and also worked on film sets as a still photographer. Her screen-industry credits include 1971's *Carnal Knowledge* and *One Flew*

Over the Cuckoo's Nest four years later, both of which starred Jack Nicholson. The latter film, about a fictional group of patients in a psychiatric hospital and based on writer Ken Kesey's work in a Veterans' Administration hospital, won five Academy Awards in 1976. Mark's involvement in the project prompted her to request permission to live inside the facility where the movie was actually filmed, a state psychiatric hospital in Oregon. Her images of the women she befriended during her two months there—some of them locked away because they had been deemed a danger to themselves or to others—appeared in the book *Ward 81*, published in 1979. This was also the title of a traveling exhibition that further boosted Mark's reputation as a trenchant chronicler of the dispossessed.

Mark has long been fascinated by India, and made several trips there to photograph its various subcultures. Her images of prostitutes in Mumbai, *Falkland Road*, appeared in book form in 1981, and she also spent time with the Roman Catholic humanitarian worker Mother Teresa in her Calcutta mission. Mark gained further renown for her series on Indian circuses, and the best images culled from all of these trips were included in *Exposure*, the 2005 retrospective volume.

Often, Mark's most gripping photographs show the exceedingly vulnerable—the underage—and her talent for capturing this is best exemplified by the series *Streetwise*. An assignment for *Life* magazine she did in 1983, Mark spent time with runaways and street kids in Seattle, Washington, and captured the desperate circumstances of their young lives with a heart-rending frankness. The photographs became the basis of a documentary film of the same name a year later, made by her husband Martin Bell, which was nominated for an Academy Award.

The movie poster for *Streetwise* used what has become one of Mark's most famous photographs, a portrait of Erin, a young teenage prostitute who went by the street name of Tiny. Her arms are crossed, she sports a black pillbox hat with a veil, black gloves, and a sleeveless black dress, and her mouth is set in a grim line. Mark returned to Erin's life over the years to update her portrait, and the subsequent images show a woman who seemed to have skidded from adolescence directly into middle age. Mark recounted some of Erin's hardships in *Exposure*, including substance abuse problems and becoming mother to nine children by five different fathers. "She has changed physically a lot," Mark told James Bone in a *Times* of London interview, "but I still find her in her own way beautiful.... It's not beauty in the conventional sense. It's just this look of someone where everything is right out there. You can just feel what she feels."

Mark's other subjects include a Los Angeles homeless family, the Damms, whom she first shot when they were living in their car in 1987. She returned five years later to their "home," an abandoned rural property on which they were living illegally. One image from the later series shows their daughter, Crissy, wedged between both parents in bed. "At the center of the picture is the face of a girl literally hemmed in by a world she seems appalled to have realized is hers," wrote *Time's* Richard Lacayo. "She gazes upward from the debris with an expression somewhere between foreboding and resignation."

Other images from Mark's lens have been immortalized in books such as 1999's *American Odyssey*, and *Twins*, published in 2003. The photographs from the latter volume were culled from her recurring visits to the annual Twins Days Festival in Twinsburg, Ohio. Mark has also been honored with several museum shows over the years, including a retrospective at Manchester Art Gallery in England in 2004. Sometimes considered a social-conscience or "concerned" photographer, Mark finds these kinds of labels as restricting as the painting studio she left behind long ago. "I think concerned photographers are those that go off to war and photograph the plight of people," she said in the *Times* of London interview with Bone. "I don't do that. I'm much more of a coward—always have been. I'm for the underdog. I certainly feel that it's a land of unequal opportunity. I'm interested in having people feel for the people I photograph. It's an unfair world."

Selected writings

Passport, Lustrum Press, 1974.
Ward 81, with text by Karen Folger Jacobs, Fireside Books (New York, NY), 1979.
Falkland Road, Alfred A. Knopf, 1981.
Mother Teresa's Missions of Charity in Calcutta, The Friends of Photography, 1985.
Streetwise: Photographs by Mary Ellen Mark, University of Pennsylvania Press (Philadelphia, PA), 1988; Aperture, 1992.

The Photo Essay: Photography by Mary Ellen Mark, Smithsonian Institution Press, 1990.
Mary Ellen Mark: Twenty Five Years, Bullfinch Press (in conjunction with George Eastman House/Kodak), 1991.
Indian Circus, Chronicle Books (San Francisco, CA), 1993.
A Cry For Help: Stories of Homelessness and Hope, Simon and Schuster, 1996.
Portraits, Smithsonian Institution Press (Washington, DC), 1997.
American Odyssey: 1963-1999, Aperture (New York, NY), 1999.
Mary Ellen Mark: 55, Phaidon (London, England), 2001.
Twins, Aperture, 2003.
Mary Ellen Mark: Exposure, Phaidon Press (New York, NY), 2005.

Sources

Books

Contemporary Photographers, third ed., St. James Press, 1996.

Periodicals

Independent (London, England), November 6, 1999, p. 37.
Life, February 1991, p. 2.
National Review, June 28, 1985, p. 45.
O, The Oprah Magazine, July 2005, p. 121.
Petersen's Photographic, August 2000, p. 36.
Photo Marketing, January 2002, p. 61.
Publishers Weekly, October 6, 2003, p. 78.
Time, May 29, 2000, p. 79.
Times (London, England), June 19, 2004, p. 31.
Variety, May 16, 2005, p. S18.

—*Carol Brennan*

Judy McGrath

Bloomberg News/Landov

Chair and Chief Executive Officer of MTV Networks Group

Born in 1953; married Michael Corbett (a systems analyst); children: Anna Maeve. *Education:* Cedar Crest College, B.A. (English).

Addresses: *Office*—c/o Viacom, 1515 Broadway, New York, NY 10036.

Career

Had first job in radio; worked at Conde Nast publications as a copy chief for *Glamour* and senior writer for *Mademoiselle*; MTV, copywriter, 1981, then editorial director, creative director and senior vice president, then executive director, 1991-94, president, 1994-2002, and international creative director; executive producer, *Joe's Apartment* (film), 1996; MTV Networks Music Group, president and international creative director, 2002-03; MTV Networks Group, president, 2003-04, chair and chief executive officer, 2004—.

Member: Board, New York City Ballet; board, McCarton School; board, Rock the Vote; advisory board, LifeBeat.

Awards: Woman of the Year award, *Glamour,* 2004; Woman of the Year award, Women in Cable & Telecommunications, 2004.

Sidelights

Judy McGrath has put her stamp on MTV since the cable network's founding. After holding a few other jobs in media, she joined the network shortly after it went on the air in 1981. McGrath began as a writer, but moved her way up the executive ranks to become the network's president in 1994. She helped form the network as it evolved, and played a key role in the move from airing music videos to more original programming. Her success with MTV led to her move up to become the head of MTV Networks and other channels for Viacom, MTV's parent company.

Born in 1953, McGrath was raised in Scranton, Pennsylvania. Her father worked as a social worker. He also had a love of music that he passed on to his daughter. Her mother worked as a teacher who inspired her daughter to persevere. After graduating from high school, McGrath attended Cedar Crest College in Allentown, Pennsylvania, where she studied English.

After graduating from college with her B.A., McGrath began her professional career in radio. She then moved to the print world. She worked at

Conde Nast publications, the parent company of many leading magazines. McGrath was the copy chief of the women's magazine *Glamour*. She was also a senior writer for the young woman's periodical *Mademoiselle*. McGrath left Conde Nast because she wanted to write for music magazine *Rolling Stone*. Instead, McGrath found herself in the music business in an entirely different way.

In 1981, McGrath joined MTV soon after the cable channel hit the airwaves. Her first job at the network was as a copy writer for on-air promotions. She composed the on-air prompts that aired between the music videos which dominated the early programming at the channel. In addition, McGrath had a hand in creating the animated network IDs that aired constantly on MTV.

When McGrath began at MTV, she did not intend to stay for long. She hoped her experience at MTV would lead to that coveted job at *Rolling Stone*. At the time, she and others were also unsure if MTV would take off or even last very long. Instead, McGrath spent most of the rest of her career at the network, playing a key role in the development of MTV as a brand. One of her early ways of gaining attention for MTV was its on-air contests. She came up with unique contests such as Devo Goes Hawaiian and One Night Stand with Journey.

From the beginning, McGrath and others took a unique point of view about what kind of channel MTV would be, provided it survived. She told Louis Chunovic of *Broadcasting & Cable*, "We thought of it as a promise, and we very much wanted MTV to be meaningful despite the changing nature of pop music or the personalities who might come and go. It was not going to be static and marry one generation and grow old with it.... Our goal was to be the non-network network."

Within a few years, McGrath was promoted within the network. She first became the editorial director of MTV. She was later promoted to senior vice president and creative director. Early on, she was already pushing the network to change, to continue to be different so that it would hold onto its audience. McGrath tried different shows. Some of these shows were centered around a certain type of music. Other shows were more traditional in format. In 1989, she told Michael Freitag of the *New York Times*, "MTV will continue to feed off culture and to feed into it. But if I could predict exactly where it's going, I wouldn't be working here anymore; you have to be open-minded and make it up as you go along."

In 1991, McGrath became the network's co-executive director, with Sara Levinson. While Levinson took charge of the business side of the operation, McGrath headed MTV's network operations. She oversaw programming, what music videos would air, production of other on-air segments, promotion, production, and development. McGrath had a big say in what videos aired on the network, making her a very powerful person in the music industry. In 1994, she became president, taking charge of the overall strategic direction and all revenue and spending for MTV.

McGrath remained concerned with maintaining MTV's youth appeal. One area of concern for her was the VJs (video jockeys, or the hosts and hostesses that appeared on the network introducing the videos, interviewing musicians, and serving as the face of the network). In the 1990s, McGrath continued to push broadcasting more shows instead of videos, as well as taking more chances with on-air programming. In 1992, for example, the network became more involved with the presidential election and voting, with the advent of the "Choose or Lose" election coverage.

As the 1990s progressed, McGrath played a primary role in MTV's move further and further away from music videos to a variety of original programs. The network experimented with dance shows like *The Grind*, a dating show called *Singled Out*, and animated shows like *Beavis and Butt-head*. Such shows attracted solid viewership, at least for a time. MTV also took chances on re-running network shows with youth appeal like *My So-Called Life*.

One of the most popular and enduring original programs McGrath had a hand in putting on MTV was its documentary/reality show called *The Real World*. McGrath served as the executive at MTV in charge of *The Real World* for many years. Unlike most of MTV's programming, this show has stayed on the air from the 1990s to the early 2000s. One reason for the show's longevity was its format. Each year the show followed around a different college-aged cast living in a different city, primarily in the United States.

A precursor to the reality shows which became popular staples on other networks in the early 2000s, *The Real World* surprised McGrath with its longevity. McGrath told Lynda Richardson of the *New York Times*, "I didn't think *The Real World* would last as long as it has but it seems kind of evergreen. Usually you think when the world gets onto something, we have to get off."

There were other types of programming on MTV that had a long shelf life as well. McGrath led MTV to branch out into its own awards ceremonies, beginning with the MTV Video Music Awards. This annual awards show honors the best music videos of the year. An afternoon video count down show, *Total Request Live* or *TRL*, airs live from New York City most week days. Some of the shows that McGrath put on the air were flops. A program featuring sock puppets, *Sifl and Olly*, as well as *The Jon Stewart Show* were both short lived.

Later in the 1990s, McGrath moved MTV into the feature film business. She served as executive producer of 1996's *Joe's Apartment*. MTV later branded other films such as *Save the Last Dance* and *Election*.

During her tenure running MTV, the network had high ratings. However, ratings fell in 1997 and McGrath adjusted. By this time, she sensed that MTV had emphasized original programming too much to the detriment of the music and music videos which had been so important to the network. She re-focused on the music, sparking an increase in the ratings. McGrath was known for having a sense of what the audience wanted. She told Lawrie Mifflin of the *New York Times*, "In our business, there's nothing worse than missing a moment."

By the early 2000s, McGrath continued to have a hand in the programming of MTV. Original programming continued to be important. She helped develop new hit shows like *The Osbournes*, a reality show featuring heavy metal star Ozzy Osbourne and his family, and *Punk'd*, a prank show created by actor Ashton Kutcher. McGrath also took on new responsibilities, adding international creative director to her titles. She was put in charge of MTV's international networks.

In 2002, McGrath was given a promotion. She was named president of the MTV Networks Music Group. This meant that she was in charge of the whole MTV family of networks, which included MTV, MTV2, VH1, and CMT (Country Music Television). In addition, she was in charge of music-related Internet businesses, digital music brands, and all other ancillary businesses. McGrath also became the International Creative Director for VH1 and CMT as these brands also aired around the world in different forms.

After a company reorganization in 2003, McGrath became the MTV Networks Group president. In this capacity, she was in charge of MTV, MTV2, VH1, CMT, and Comedy Central, a comedy cable network. In whatever position she held, McGrath was lauded for her creativity and success. From 2002 to 2004, she took a particular interest in the programming of VH1, another music video network, which had viewership problems for many years. The programming choices she made, including the addition of much more original programming and fewer videos, led to a significant increase in viewership for VH1.

In 2004, McGrath was promoted again. She was named the chair and chief executive officer of MTV Networks. She was put in charge a number of networks owned by Viacom, including LOGO, Comedy Central, TV Land, Nickelodeon, Noggin, The N, all the MTV Networks, MTV Networks Digital Suite, MTV International Networks, Nick at Night, and Spike TV. She was charged with helping these channels to continue to evolve and grow. This position was quite powerful. As a CNN correspondent wrote, "Known for her originality and creativity, she influences programming that reaches 400 million viewers of more than 100 channels broadcast in 164 countries and 18 languages."

McGrath wanted to bring her own touch to her role, though she knew she was facing new challenges. She was still very concerned with MTV, and wanted to continue to expand the MTV brand in particular. In 2004, she announced the launch of the African-based MTV Base, the 100th channel launched by MTV around the world. McGrath also had to deal with controversy. MTV produced the Super Bowl halftime show featuring singer Janet Jackson. During her performance with Justin Timberlake, Jackson experienced what was later termed a "wardrobe malfunction," where one of her breasts was exposed. This incident led to a lot of criticism in the media and crackdowns by the Federal Communications Commission. In February of 2005, Viacom launched LOGO, the first gay and lesbian-targeted network. This move was also expected to attract criticism. McGrath continued to be innovative and take advantage of her networks' success. In 2004, for example, she considered expanding the Comedy Central name to international channels the company already owned.

In 2004, McGrath's success was honored when she was named one of *Glamour's* women of the year. She was strong in her job and close to the culture and people to which her networks had to appeal. Capitol Records president Andrew Slater told Bill Carter of the *New York Times* that McGrath "never comes off as a person from the cold and mathematical side of the business. She understand the culture and music and fashion and style and how they blend together, and that's reflected in the channel she runs."

Sources

Books

Celebrity Biographies, Baseline II, 2005.

Periodicals

Adweek, November 15, 2004.
Billboard, November 6, 1993, p. 16.
Broadcasting & Cable, November 17, 1997, p. 70; June 21, 2004, p. 2.
Entertainment Weekly, October 22, 2004, pp. 46-48.
Financial Times (London, England), December 7, 2004, p. 12.
Multichannel News, July 18, 1994, p. 2; November 1, 2004, p. 4A; December 13, 2004, p. 4.

New York Times, April 9, 1989, sec. 1, pt. 2, p. 38; August 31, 1998, p. D5; June 11, 2003, p. B3; July 26, 2004, p. E1.
PR Newswire, March 15, 2002; May 29, 2003; July 20, 2004.
Realscreen, November 1, 2004, p. 35.

Online

"McGrath transforms television," CNN.com, http://www.cnn.com/SPECIALS/2004/global.influentials/stories/mcgrath.profile/ (August 8, 2005).
"Senior Management," Viacom, http://www.viacom.com/management.jhtml (August 8, 2005).

—A. Petruso

Julian McMahon

AP/Wide World Photos

Actor

Born Julian Dana William McMahon, July 27, 1968, in Sydney, Australia; son of Sir William (prime minister) and Lady Sonia McMahon; married Dannii Minogue (a singer and actress), January 2, 1994 (divorced, 1995); married Brooke Burns (an actress), December 22, 1999 (divorced, 2001); children: Madison (from second marriage). *Education:* Attended University of Sydney, studied law.

Addresses: *Agent*—Agency for the Performing Arts, 9200 Sunset Blvd., Ste. 900, Los Angeles, CA 90069. *Home*—Hollywood Hills, CA. *Management*—Louise Spinner Ward, Talent Entertainment Group, 9111 Wilshire Blvd., Beverly Hills, CA 90210.

Career

Actor on television, including: *The Power, the Passion,* 1989; *Home and Away,* 1990-91; *Another World,* 1992-94; *The Profiler,* 1996-2000; *Will & Grace,* 1998; *Charmed,* 2000-03, 2005; *Another Day* (movie), 2001; *Nip/Tuck,* 2003—. Film appearances include: *Wet and Wild Summer!,* 1992; *Magenta,* 1996; *In Quiet Night,* 1998; *Chasing Sleep,* 2000; *Fantastic Four,* 2005. Executive producer of film *Meet Market,* 2004. Stage appearances include: *Home and Away,* England; *Love Letters,* Sydney, Melbourne, Australia. Model, c. 1987-89.

Sidelights

The epitome of the phrase tall, dark, and handsome, Julian McMahon began his career as a model in his native Australia, and later began his

acting career in a couple of Australian soap operas, before coming to the attention of American audiences through his stint on the daytime serial *Another World.* Within months of his first appearance, fan clubs sprouted around the county. He later won a supporting role on the hit show, *The Profiler.* McMahon's breakthrough role was on the WB's *Charmed.* His popularity grew when he took on the role of Dr. Christian Troy on the F/X Channel show, *Nip/Tuck.* He also had a starring role in the 2005 hit film *Fantastic Four.*

McMahon (pronounced Mc-Man) was born on July 27, 1968, in Sydney, Australia. His father, Sir William McMahon, was prime minister of Australia in the early 1970s. His mother, Lady Sonia, was an attaché to fashion mogul Yves St. Laurent. Adding to the family were his older sister, Melinda, and his younger sister, Debbie. Though his parents were leading society figures, and McMahon and his sisters led a privileged life, his parents still insisted on the children having chores to do. In addition to cleaning his room, he also rode the bus to his private school, and, as he told Tom Gliatto of *People,* "I had a paper route at nine. I took the trash out...."

McMahon went through a rebellious stage during his teen years, clashing with his parents on many things. Influenced by various bands including the

Cure and Kiss, he once asked his parents if he could add a slit in his tongue like a snake's. He attended the University of Sydney for a year, but he told *In-Style*'s Ellen Lieberman that "It was too much studying and too intense." He was offered a modeling campaign, and soon worked with various designers and ad campaigns, including Calvin Klein, Coca-Cola, and Levi's. He also traveled the world, getting modeling jobs in Rome, Milan, Italy, and Los Angeles. His decision to drop out of college caused a rift with his parents, but they were able to reconcile before his father died in 1988.

McMahon's high visibility as a model led to a Levi's commercial that showed him pulling on a pair of jeans. Industry types took notice. Because of the commercial, he was given the opportunity to play a medical student on *The Power, the Passion*, a soap opera that aired in Australia in 1989. With his interest in modeling waning, McMahon jumped at the chance. He explained his reasons for turning to modeling and then acting in an interview with Paul Fischer at Dark Horizons.com: "It was almost an escapist kind of attitude that I had of getting away from stuff that I didn't feel like I wanted to do, then after [acting] for a number of years I developed such a passion for it that it actually became something I realized I wanted to continue doing and hopefully do for as long as I could." He later joined the serial, *Home and Away*, that also showcased rising stars Heath Ledger and Guy Pearce.

While on the show, McMahon began dating singer and fellow soap star Dannii Minogue, younger sister of pop sensation Kylie Minogue. Their relationship deepened, and because of his family lines and her star status, the two were hounded by the press. They were married as helicopters flew around capturing the event on film.

McMahon also performed in the musical stage production of *Home And Away* in London, England. He was a hit, and again, the couple was chased by the press and adoring fans. In addition to doing *Home And Away* on stage, McMahon also appeared in the Australian production of the play *Love Letters*, both in Sydney and Melbourne. He made his big-screen debut in *Wet and Wild Summer!*.

McMahon decided to move to the United States to further his acting career. His wife, who was building her singing career, stayed in London. Despite his looks and his resume, McMahon could not find work, mainly because of his accent. He studied with an accent coach and soon won a role on the soap *Another World*, portraying sexy gardener Ian Rain.

Within months of his introduction on the show, though not on the same level as his time on the Australian soap operas, fan clubs devoted to him sprang up around the country. However, on the personal front, his bi-continental marriage was on the rocks. He and Dannii grew apart and divorced.

With this increased exposure on the soap opera, McMahon landed a role as an FBI agent on NBC's drama *The Profiler*. Although it received critical acclaim, the show was cancelled in 2000. McMahon kept working, picking up bit parts in various films including *Magenta, In Quiet Night,* and *Chasing Sleep.* He also guest-starred on the NBC sitcom *Will & Grace.* In 2000 McMahon won a recurring part on the WB's hit show, *Charmed.* He played Cole Turner, a demon who falls in love and marries Phoebe Halliwell, one of three sister witches, played by Alyssa Milano. McMahon stayed with the show for two and a half seasons, through the 100th episode of the series when his character was vanquished by the witches.

Throughout this period, McMahon also met and married actress Brooke Burns, who starred on the syndicated show, *Baywatch,* and on the short-lived reality game show, *Dog Eat Dog.* The couple soon had a daughter, Madison. They later divorced, but remained on good terms. McMahon spoke of his personal life to *InStyle*'s Lieberman, "I love being a dad. I love the fact that I'm going to go home today and my kid … is going to jump into the pool with me…. Brooke and I see a lot of each other. There's no animosity. It's beautiful."

In 2000 McMahon campaigned for a role on the new drama show, *Nip/Tuck,* which aired on the F/X Channel. He told England's *Birmingham Post*, "I think it's one of those things where it hasn't been done before…. I think it's an extremely well-written show…." *Nip/Tuck,* created by former *Entertainment Weekly* journalist Ryan Murphy, follows the lives of two Miami-based plastic surgeons as they change people's lives while their own lives stay in a constant state of turmoil. McMahon joined the cast as the hedonistic and amoral Dr. Christian Troy. His character sleeps around, and is deceitful and very narcissistic. While McMahon may be nothing like his character, he told Fischer on DarkHorizons.com, "I can relate to him because I can identify with the kinds of journeys that he went through. I always felt like Christian made many mistakes in life and had to kind of figure out how to get the best out of them and I feel like I've had a similar kind of past."

From the beginning, the show was a hit among viewers. *Entertainment Weekly's* Ken Tucker described *Nip/Tuck* as "a great soap opera disguised as very good prime-time trash." While many critics of the show decried its glamorization of plastic surgery, as well as its extremely graphic surgery scenes, more and more viewers tuned in each week. Thanks to the show, McMahon has people clamoring to get his attention, and many think of him as the doctor he portrays. He told Denise Martin of *Daily Variety,* "I've had people run up and hug me and scream at me and ask for boob jobs and butt jobs. It's really quite overwhelming, which is great, because you know you've struck a place in people."

As a result of its growing popularity, *Nip/Tuck* won a Golden Globe for Best Drama Series in 2005. McMahon was nominated for a Golden Globe for his portrayal of Dr. Troy, but lost to Ian McShane, who starred on HBO's *Deadwood.* The nomination came as a shock to McMahon, but he told Brad Pomerance of *TelevisionWeek,* "These awards can mean so much to people by elevating their status. And I like the fact that newcomers can break through. It's wonderful."

Nip/Tuck's shooting schedule allowed McMahon the chance to take on the role of Dr. Victor Von Doom in the 20th Century Fox release of *Fantastic Four,* based on the comic book of the same name. The film also costarred Michael Chiklis, Jessica Alba, Ioan Gruffudd, and Chris Evans. This was McMahon's second portrayal of a person people either loved to hate or begrudgingly loved. He told *InStyle's* Lieberman, "When you play bad guys, you need to ingratiate yourself with the audience." He relished playing the role because, as he told Fischer at Dark Horizons.com, "To me it was just taking on a great character, having been a comic book and cartoon fan of the *Fantastic Four,* knowing about Victor Von Doom since I was a five- or six-year-old kid, so it was kind of more about taking on that kind of responsibility then it was taking on a villain."

Fantastic Four opened with favorable reviews, though many diehard fans of the comic would have seen the film anyway. It was a major hit, opening at number one in its first weekend. Since its opening the movie has grossed more than $150 million in the United States alone. The film also did well overseas.

In his personal time, McMahon enjoys collecting classic books, watching rugby matches, and tuning into the Discovery Channel to watch programs on FBI crimes. He also likes cooking and has prepared both American cuisine, such as pot roast as well as exotic gourmet meals. He also like to play all types of sports. In addition to spending time with his daughter, McMahon also enjoys playing with his two dogs that he rescued while taping *The Profiler.*

Unlike his characters, McMahon is considered by many to be a nice guy. His cast mate on *Nip/Tuck,* Joely Richardson, described him to *People's* Gliatto: "He's very loud—a big joker." In the same article, series creator Murphy stated, "Julian is like a nerdy 12 year old. He's always in his trailer playing video games. Julian's not a ladies' man at all." Actress Amy Carlson, who appeared on *Another World* with McMahon, told Gliatto, "Julian is chivalrous, has wonderful etiquette and style in his soul. You can tell he was raised proper." McMahon has not allowed his celebrity to go to his head. His only splurges have been a Mercedes Benz 560 SEL and a housekeeper.

McMahon also found time to return to *Charmed* to appear in its 150th episode. He will play the lead in his next film, *Prisoner,* which was in post-production in September of 2005. His fans also wait for the start of *Nip/Tuck's* third season. Though his dropping out of school caused a rift, McMahon's greatest fan is his mother. With his uncanny ability to choose great roles as well as the talent and looks to keep McMahon in the spotlight, many would challenge his mother's position as his biggest fan.

Sources

Books

Contemporary Theatre, Film and Television, vol. 42, Gale Group, 2002.

Periodicals

Birmingham Post (England), January 7, 2004, p. 14.
Daily Variety, June 11, 2004, p. A10; May 12, 2005, p. 3.
Entertainment Weekly, June 18, 2004, p. 38; June 25, 2004, p. 149; July 15, 2005, p. 14.
InStyle, August 1, 2005, p. 145.
People, December 15, 1997, p. 151; October 13, 2003, p. 87.
TelevisionWeek, January 10, 2005, p. S7.
Washington Times, January 26, 2005, p. B6.

Online

"Exclusive Interview: Julian McMahon," Dark Horizons, http://www.darkhorizons.com/news05/fantastic1.php (August 29, 2005).

—*Ashyia N. Henderson*

Larry McMurtry

Kevin Winter/Getty Images

Author

Born Larry Jeff McMurtry, June 3, 1936, in Wichita Falls, TX; son of William Jefferson (a rancher) and Hazel Ruth McMurtry; married Josephine Ballard, July 15, 1959 (divorced, August, 1966); children: James Lawrence (a singer). *Education:* University of North Texas, B.A., 1958; Rice University, M.A., 1960; also attended Rice, c. 1954-55, and Stanford University, 1960-61.

Addresses: *Home*—P.O. Box 552, Archer City, TX 76531. *Office*—Booked Up, Inc., 2509 North Campbell Ave., No. 95, Tucson, AZ 85719.

Career

Worked as a bookstore manager in Houston, TX, c. 1958-60; wrote freelance book reviews for the *Houston Post* and freelance pieces for other publications, c. 1960s; taught at Texas Christian University, Fort Worth, Texas, 1961-62; published first novel, *Horseman, Pass By*, 1961; taught English and creative writing at Rice University, 1963-64, 1965-69; published novel *The Last Picture Show*, 1966; taught at George Mason University, Fairfax, VA, 1969-70; taught at American University, Washington, D.C., 1970-71; opened first book store, Booked Up Book Store, Washington, D.C., 1970; co-wrote screenplay with director Peter Bogdanovich for film version of the book *The Last Picture Show*, 1971; published critically acclaimed novel *Terms of Endearment*, 1975; opened up bookstore Blue Pig (later known as Booked Up Book Store), Archer City, TX, 1987; wrote script for *The Murder of Mary Phagan*, NBC, 1988; head of PEN American Center, New York City, 1989-91; wrote first original teleplay, *Montana*, TNT, 1990;

executive producer and co-writer of script for *Streets of Laredo* CBS, 1995; co-wrote script for *Dead Man's Walk*, ABC, 1996; optioned and wrote film script for E. Annie Proulx short story "Brokeback Mountain" with Diana Ossana, c. late 1990s; began "The Berrybender Narratives" series, 2002; *Brokeback Mountain* film released, 2005.

Awards: Wallage Stegner fellowship, 1960-61; Jesse H. Jones Award, Texas Institute of Letters, for *Horseman, Pass By*, 1962; Guggenheim fellowship, 1964; New York Film Critics Circle Award (with Peter Bogdanovich) for best screenwriting, for *The Last Picture Show*, 1971; British Film Academy Award (with Peter Bogdanovich) for best screenplay, for *The Last Picture Show*, 1972; Academy Award for best screenplay based on material from another medium (with Peter Bogdanovich), Academy of Motion Picture Arts and Sciences, for *The Last Picture Show*, 1972; Barbara McCombs/Lon Tinkle Award for continuing excellence in Texas letters, Texas Institute of Letters, 1986; Pulitzer Prize in Fiction for *Lonesome Dove*, 1986; Spur Award, Western Writers of America, for *Lonesome Dove*, 1986; Texas Literary Award, Southwestern Booksellers Association, for *Lonesome Dove*, 1986; Robert Kirsch Award, *Los Angeles Times*, for body of work, 2003; Academy Award for best adapted screenplay (with Diana Ossana), Academy of Motion Pictures Arts and Sciences, *Brokeback Mountain*, 2006.

Sidelights

Texas author Larry McMurtry is best known as a writer of western novels, many of which are set in the Old West, including the Pulitzer Prize-winning *Lonesome Dove*. Some of his novels focus on life in small town Texas, like *The Last Picture Show*, while others focus on relationships, such as *Terms of Endearment*. McMurtry also adapted several of his books into films and television productions, wrote other original scripts, and occasionally adapted other authors' work. In 2006, he won an Academy Award with long-time writing partner Diana Ossana, for their adaptation of a short story by E. Annie Proulx into the hit film *Brokeback Mountain*. In addition to writing, McMurtry also devotes much of his time to the bookstores he owns and operates in three locations in the United States.

Born in 1936 in Wichita Falls, Texas, McMurtry was raised on the family's cattle ranch in Archer City, Texas, living with his grandparents some of the time. He was the oldest of four children of William and Hazel McMurtry. Though he worked on his father's ranch until his early twenties, McMurtry liked reading better than ranching from an early age. He was an honor student, writer, and popular athlete at Archer City High School. After graduating in 1954, McMurtry spent a year at Rice University, then completed his undergraduate degree at University of North Texas (later known as North Texas State University). McMurtry earned his B.A. in English in 1958.

After McMurtry graduated, he moved to Houston, where he worked as a bookstore manager while earning his M.A. from Rice. He then went to Stanford University from 1960 to 1961 on the Wallage Stegner Fellowship in fiction. When his fellowship was complete, McMurtry returned to Texas. He wrote freelance book reviews for the *Houston Post* and other freelance pieces, and began working on his own fiction while holding down several teaching positions. He taught at Texas Christian University in Fort Worth, Texas, from 1961 to 1962, before returning to Rice, where he taught English and creative writing from 1963 to 1964, and again from 1965 to 1969. From 1964 to 1965, McMurtry focused on fiction writing as the holder of the Guggenheim Fellowship in creative writing. McMurtry was also married in this time period to Josephine Ballard. The couple had a son together, James, whom McMurtry raised alone after the couple divorced in 1966.

While a student and educator in the early 1960s, McMurtry was writing what became his first novel, *Horseman, Pass By,* published in 1961. Set in the late 1950s, the novel was told from the point of view of 17-year-old Lonnie Bannon who lived on his grandfather's ranch. His grandfather is willing to ruin his own herd of cattle and financial well-being to help a neighbor with cattle infected with hoof-and-mouth disease. The grandfather is in conflict with his stepson, Hud, who wants to make money by selling the cattle. *Horseman, Pass By* explores such generational clashes as a metaphor for the tension between past and present. The book was generally well-received, though it took several years to find a following. *Horseman, Pass By* was later adapted into a hit Hollywood film, 1963's *Hud,* starring Paul Newman. McMurtry's next novel, *Leaving Cheyenne,* published in 1963, also looked at ranching life, focusing on a love triangle between a rancher, a cowboy, and a woman who loved them both. This novel was also adapted into a film, 1974's *Lovin' Molly.*

In 1966, McMurtry published one of his best-known books, *The Last Picture Show.* A reflection of the author's teen years in a small town in Texas, the novel established his career as a serious novelist. The story focuses on three adolescents growing up the dying Texas town of Thalia (a stand-in for Archer City), as they deal with the transition to adulthood in the midst of the emptiness of life and lack of potential in such towns. *The Last Picture Show* was controversial for its open discussion of sexuality and the sexual habits of teenagers, and the residents of Archer City perceived the novel as a negative portrayal of their community. In 1971, McMurtry cowrote the screenplay for a film version of the novel with the film's director, Peter Bogdanovich. The screenplay won several awards and the film was a success.

By this time, McMurtry had been away from Texas for several years. In 1969, he left Texas to take a teaching job at George Mason University in Fairfax, Virginia. McMurtry then taught at American University in Washington, D.C., from 1970 to 1971. In 1970, he opened a book store with friends called Booked Up Book Store in Washington, D.C. The store primarily sold rare and used books. McMurtry later added locations in Archer City, Texas, and Tucson, Arizona. He opened the Archer City location with his sister, Sue Deen, in 1987 under the name the Blue Pig. It was later renamed the Booked Up Book Store as well.

As his life changed, the focus of McMurtry's novels also evolved. The author became more concerned with urban settings for a time. Beginning in 1970, he published a series of novels related by their use of the same characters and an exploration of the human condition. The first novel, *Moving On*, focuses on a young married affluent couple, Pete and Patsy Carpenter, who are trying to find purpose in their lives. McMurtry's next novel, 1972's *All My Friends Are Going to Be Strangers*, concerns a character introduced in *Moving On*: Danny Deck. More autobiographical for McMurtry, the story focuses on Deck, a first-time novelist who finds himself rich and famous after his book becomes a film. However, he loses his family and himself in the process.

In 1975, McMurtry published *Terms of Endearment*, another one of his best-known and most critically acclaimed books. A primary character, Emma Horton, was introduced in *Moving On*, and the novel also uses characters from McMurtry's previous two novels. This book focuses on Emma and her relationship with her mother, Aurora Greenway, both women's relationships with men, and Emma's death from cancer. McMurtry told Mary Kaye Schilling of *Entertainment Weekly*, "Emma is probably my favorite character. I envied her generosity and courage—things I always look for in women." In 1983, *Terms of Endearment* was adapted into a Hollywood film, which won several Academy Awards. McMurtry ended the series of related novels with a sequel to *Terms of Endearment, Evening Star*.

While McMurtry's next two novels were not as successful with critics or audiences, the author also enjoyed the character Harmony, an aging Las Vegas show girl who leads a complex life in her relationships with her children. The first Harmony book, *The Desert Rose*, was written in three weeks. His next major novel, 1985's *Lonesome Dove*, was one of his best-known works and the winner of the Pulitzer Prize for fiction in 1986. Set in 1876, the story focused on two aging Texas Rangers, Augustus McCrae and Woodrow F. Call, as they lead a cattle drive to Montana. McMurtry explores how hard life really was in the West during this time period, breaking many commonly believed myths. In 1989, the novel was adapted by another writer, Bill Wittliff, for television and became a hit miniseries on CBS. Because of the success of the miniseries, CBS produced another miniseries, 1993's *Return to Lonesome Dove*, based on the characters in the original.

In the late 1980s and early 1990s, McMurtry continued to produce novels about the Old West, while also adding more television and film credits. His 1988 novel *Anything for Billy* follows a nineteenth-century dime novelist, Ben Sippy, who goes west to find out how the real West is compared to what he has been writing. Sippy eventually joins forces with the man who became Billy the Kid, who was not as great as the myth that Sippy created for him. In 1990's *Buffalo Girls*, McMurtry focuses on mythical western figures like Calamity Jane, Wild Bill HIckock, Buffalo Bill Cody, and Sitting Bull as they reach the end of their lives. In this period, McMurtry also wrote the story for the 1988 NBC television movie *The Murder of Mary Phagan*. In 1990, he wrote his first original teleplay for the TNT drama *Montana.*

McMurtry again returned to characters he had created in earlier novels on several occasions. In 1987, he published his sequel to *The Last Picture Show*, entitled *Texasville*. Taking place several decades after the original novel, the characters in *Texasville* are losing the money they accumulated in the oil boom and use sex to fill their empty lives. Three years later, McMurtry and Bogdanovich wrote the script for the film version of *Texasville*. Though many of the original actors returned, the film did not do nearly as well as the original. McMurtry completed the trilogy with the 1999 novel *Duane's Depressed*. This novel focused on the characters as they reached their sixties, including the title character who changes his life to find himself.

McMurtry's life was also changing in the late 1980s and early 1990s. In 1989, he was named the head of PEN American Center, a prestigious literary organization based in New York City. McMurtry was the first person from outside of New York to be named president since the 1920s. In late 1980s, he bought a house in Archer City, Texas. and by the 1990s, he made it his primary residence. McMurtry also suffered from ill health. He had to have quadruple-bypass surgery in December of 1991 after hitting a cow with his car and suffering a heart attack. His recovery was difficult, especially mentally, and the author was depressed for a time. Though McMurtry continued to write, often with his friend, Diana Ossana, as a collaborator, he began to focus on his bookstores more and brought most of his stock to his Archer City store.

While McMurtry continued to write original novels and scripts, he also wrote a sequel and two prequels to *Lonesome Dove*. First came 1994's *Streets of Laredo*, which explored what happened to the characters after the end of *Lonesome Dove*. The novel focused on what happened in Call's life after his friend died. The prequels, 1995's *The Dead Man's Walk* and 1997's *Comanche Moon*, looked at the lives of the two rangers in their younger days. Two of these books were also adapted for television. McMurtry served as executive producer of the 1995 adaptation of *Streets of Laredo* for CBS and was the cowriter of the script with Diana Ossana. He also co-wrote the television version of *Dead Man's Walk* with Ossana, which aired on ABC in 1996.

While McMurtry began a new novel series in the early 2000s that was set in the West of the 1830s, the "Berrybender Narratives," he also spent much of his time working in his book store in Archer City. By the 2000s, it was the largest used and rare bookstore in Texas. Yet more acclaim for his work came his way. McMurtry and Ossana came into the spotlight with their adaptation of Proulx's 1997 short story "Brokeback Mountain." The pair had optioned the story themselves and wrote a script soon after. It took eight years to get the film made, primarily because of its content and the difficulty in finding the right cast. The story is about two male cowboys who fall in love with each other while tending sheep one summer and the effect of their lifetime of stolen time together. When the film was finally made and released in 2005, it was controversial but critically acclaimed. The script by McMurtry and Ossana won the Academy Award for Best Adapted Screenplay in 2006. McMurtry did not focus on such accolades, preferring to spend most of his time writing and working in his bookstore. Of McMurtry and his temperament, director James L. Brooks told Schilling of *Entertainment Weekly*, "There's no froufrou with McMurtry. He's blunt. He doesn't waste time. But there's something very noble behind the impatience."

Selected writings

Novels

Horseman, Pass By, Harper (New York City), 1961.
Leaving Cheyenne, Harper (New York City), 1963.
The Last Picture Show, Dial Press (New York City), 1966.
Moving On, Simon & Schuster (New York City), 1970.
All My Friends Are Going to Be Strangers, Simon & Schuster, 1972.
Terms of Endearment, Simon & Schuster, 1975.
Somebody's Darling, Simon & Schuster, 1978.
Cadillac Jack, Simon & Schuster, 1982.
The Desert Rose, Simon & Schuster, 1983.
Lonesome Dove, Simon & Schuster, 1985.
Texasville, Simon & Schuster, 1987.
Anything for Billy, Simon & Schuster, 1988.
Some Can Whistle, Simon & Schuster, 1989.
Buffalo Girls, Simon & Schuster, 1990.
Evening Star, Simon & Schuster, 1992.
(With Diana Ossana) *Pretty Boy Floyd*, Simon & Schuster, 1994.
Streets of Laredo, Simon & Schuster, 1994.
The Dead Man's Walk, Simon & Schuster, 1995.
The Late Child, Simon & Schuster, 1995.

(With Diana Ossana) *Zeke and Ned*, Simon & Schuster, 1997.
Comanche Moon, Simon & Schuster, 1997.
Duane's Depressed, Simon & Schuster, 1999.
Sin Killer: The Berrybender Narratives, Book 1, Simon & Schuster, 2002.
The Wandering Hill: The Berrybender Narratives, Book 2, Simon & Schuster, 2003.
By Sorrow's River: The Berrybender Narratives, Book 3, Simon & Schuster, 2003.
Folly and Glory: The Berrybender Narratives, Book 4, Simon & Schuster, 2004.
Loop Group, Simon & Schuster, 2004.
Telegraph Days, Simon & Schuster, 2006.

Biographies

Crazy Horse, Viking (New York City), 1999.

Memoirs

Walter Benjamin at the Dairy Queen: Reflections at Sixty and Beyond, Simon & Schuster, 1999.
Roads, Driving America's Greatest Highways, Simon & Schuster, 2000.
Paradise, Simon & Schuster, 2001.

Sources

Books

Celebrity Biographies, Baseline II, Inc., 2005.
Contemporary Novelists, 7th ed., St. James Press (Detroit, MI), 2001, pp. 690-92.
Major 21st-Century Writers, vol. 4, Thomson Gale (Detroit, MI), 2005.
Scribner Encyclopedia of American Lives, Thematic Series: The 1960s, vol. 2, Charles Scribner's Sons (New York City), 2003, pp. 25-27.
St. James Encyclopedia of Popular Culture, vol. 3, St. James Press (Detroit, MI), 2000, pp. 330-31.

Periodicals

Entertainment Weekly, November 28, 2003, pp. 83-88, p. 91.
Hollywood Reporter, March 6, 2006, p. 45.
Los Angeles Times, December 13, 2005, p. E1.
Texas Monthly, December 1997, p. 110.
Washington Post, April 6, 1999, p. C1.

—*A. Petruso*

W. James McNerney

Chief Executive Officer of Boeing

General Electric/Newsmakers/Getty Images

Born Walter James McNerney, Jr., August 22, 1949, in Providence, RI; son of Walter James Mc-Nerney, Sr. (a professor and executive); married first wife (divorced); married Haity; children: two from first marriage, three from second marriage. *Education:* Yale University, B.A., 1971; Harvard University, M.B.A., 1975.

Addresses: *Office*—Boeing Corporate Offices, 100 North Riverside, Chicago, IL 60606.

Career

Worked at Procter & Gamble as a brand manager, 1975-78; worked at McKinsey & Co., Inc., Chicago, IL, and Germany, 1978-82; joined General Electric (GE), 1982, working in the Information Services Group and Mobile Communications; held successive executive positions at General Electric, including vice president/senior vice president of GE Information Services, 1982-86, general manager of GE Mobile Communications, 1986-88, president of GE Information Services, 1988-89, executive vice president of GE Capital, 1989-91, president and chief executive officer of GE Electrical Distribution and Control, 1991-92, president of GE Asia-Pacific, 1992-95, president and chief executive officer of GE Lighting, 1995-97; president and chief executive officer of GE Aircraft Engines, 1997-2000; left GE in 2000 for 3M, St. Paul, MN, becoming chief executive officer and chairman of the board, 2001; joined the board of the Boeing Company, Chicago, IL, 2001; left 3M to join Boeing Company as president, chief executive officer, and chairman, 2005.

Awards: Named Chief Executive Officer of the Year, *Industry Week*, 2004; named one of the best managers of 2003 by *BusinessWeek*, 2004.

Sidelights

Business executive W. James McNerney spent many years at General Electric (GE), before serving as chief executive officer (CEO) and chairman of the board first at 3M and then Boeing. He took the job at 3M after being passed over for the chairman of the board position at GE. While McNerney reorganized 3M and increased the company's profitability, he decided to take an offer from Boeing, a company best known as the manufacturer of aviation technology. McNerney hoped to have the same success at Boeing that he had at 3M.

McNerney was born in 1949 in Providence, Rhode Island. He and his four younger siblings were raised in Ann Arbor, Michigan, Pennsylvania, and Chicago, Illinois. His father, Walter McNerney, Sr., was a professor of health policy as well as a president of Blue Cross and Blue Shield Association. After graduating from Chicago's New Trier Township High School, McNerney entered Yale University, where he played baseball with future president

George W. Bush. He earned his B.A. in American Studies from Yale in 1971. He then spent some time teaching sailing on Lake Michigan, working on a ranch in Colorado, and holding an insurance position in London, England. McNerney later returned to the classroom, earning his M.B.A. from Harvard University in 1975.

With M.B.A. in hand, McNerney began his professional career at Procter & Gamble. He spent two-and-a-half years as a brand manager, in charge of several consumer products including Coast soap, Bounce fabric softener sheets, and Downy liquid fabric softener. In 1978, McNerney joined the consulting firm McKinsey & Co., Inc., in Chicago, Illinois, as a senior manager. He spent the next few years taking care of high technology interests for international markets, primarily from the company's offices in Germany.

McNerney joined GE in 1982 as vice president of GE Information Services, a supplier of network computer services. He was promoted to senior vice president then moved to another position in GE in 1986. McNerney was next named the manager of GE Mobile Communications business. In 1988, he returned to Information Services as president. A year later, McNerney moved again, this time to become executive vice president of GE Capital, the company's financial services unit and one of the largest such companies in the world. He built business relationships with retailers, operators of rail cars, and auto fleets for GE Capital, as well as acted as supervisor of the Genstar Container business.

In 1991, McNerney was promoted to president and chief executive officer of GE Electrical Distribution and Control, a business worth $1.7 billion. In this position, he dealt with a number of different kind of products, including industrial equipment like circuit breakers, switches, and transformers. McNerney then moved into several more executive positions, gaining more experience in the variety of businesses run by GE. In 1992, he was named president of GE Asia-Pacific. McNerney spent the next three years based in Hong Kong. He returned to the United States in 1995 when he was selected to be the president and CEO of GE Lighting, based in Cleveland, Ohio. He did well in this post, seeking out new markets for the high-tech lamps and light bulbs produced by this division.

McNerney's last position at GE began in 1997 when he was named president and CEO of GE Aircraft Engines. This division, based in Cincinnati, Ohio, made engines for commercial and military planes.

Under his leadership, the division became number one in the aerospace industry, replacing former number one Pratt & Whitney. It landed big contracts and handled important customers, including a deal with Boeing to provide the GE90 engine for its 777 jet. McNerney also greatly increased the sales and profitability of this division. In 1999, annual sales reached nearly $11 billion, up from $6.3 billion in 1996. Profits in the same time period increased from $1.2 billion to $2.1 billion. McNerney made GE Aircraft Engines one of the best performing units at GE, producing the second-most profits in GE.

By the time McNerney was moved to GE Aircraft Engines, observers believed that he was being groomed to take over as chairman of GE. After two decades at helm, legendary chairman John F. Welch announced his intention to retire in 2000, with the actual event occurring in 2001. McNerney seemed like an ideal candidate to replace Welch because of his vast experience in the company and because the company wanted to promote someone from a manufacturing or equipment business in GE. McNerney was already being pursued by other companies for executive positions. He even had an offer to become the chief operating officer at Microsoft, but turned it down. McNerney wanted to remain at GE, though there were concerns about his age and charisma as a potential candidate to replace Welch. However, McNarney had two competitors for the job, Robert L. Nardelli and Jeffrey R. Immelt. McNerney decided to leave GE in late 2000 when it became clear he would not be chosen to replace Welch. Instead, Immelt was named GE's new CEO.

McNerney had been heavily recruited by other companies by this time. Though he had a similar offer from Lucent, McNerney decided to leave GE for 3M (or Minnesota Mining and Manufacturing Co.) as chief executive officer and chairman of the board. McNerney's position began January 1, 2001, replacing L.D. "Desi" DeSimone who was being forced into mandatory retirement at the age of 65. 3M was a $20 billion technology company which produced a variety of consumer products, office supplies, health care products, safety products, electronics, telecommunications, and industrial products. Some of its more well-known goods included Post-It Notes, Scotch Tape, Scotchguard, and Thinsulate. 3M had customers in 200 countries, with operations in 60 of them.

The hiring of McNerney by 3M was considered an unusual move. It marked the first time in the company's history that an outsider was selected to run 3M. However, it was believed that one reason he was brought aboard was that he fit into the corporate culture at 3M, with a pleasant though determined personality. McNerney was also expected to bring some of GE's success-driven corporate culture to 3M. The companies were similar in that they were both quite large and did business in a number of different areas. Of McNerney, outgoing CEO DeSimone told Josh L. Dickey of the Associated Press State & Local Wire, "He understands the diverse business circumstances here, he has worked internationally, and he has a personal style that will fit very, very well with 3M. I don't see the hurdles you might expect [for a newcomer]."

While 3M was performing well financially when McNerney was hired, he was expected to help the company get the most value out of its products and assets by improving productivity. He wanted to get either get rid of or fix any product lines that were underproducing and control costs across the board. McNerney intended to make 3M's products number one or number two in their markets, eliminate unnecessary management layers, and demand more accountability among its employees. Wall Street believed in McNerney as a leader. Upon his announcement that he intended to act aggressively as CEO, stock prices jumped more than eleven dollars in one day alone.

McNerney had a rough first couple of years at 3M in part because of the poor world economy in 2001 and 2002, as well as the negative effects on business caused by the terrorist attacks on the United States on September 11, 2001. Though sales and revenues were down in 2001, especially in 3M's telecommunication business, McNerney helped control profit loss by cutting costs. He eliminated about 6,500 jobs, limited budgets for office supplies and travel, cut inventories, and limited accounts receivable. By the end of 2001, values of shares had climbed nearly 20 percent since the announcement that he had been hired. McNerney wanted to improve the culture at 3M and did so by adding a leadership development center.

One area of particular concern for some 3M employees was its research and development (R&D) budget. While McNerney left the billion dollar budget in place, he added some uniform performance standards and centralized some operations. Previously, scientists and other researchers were given free rein as they developed new ideas for goods. Such a loose atmosphere had resulted in the development of many successful products for 3M. McNerney wanted R&D to remain innovative, but only focus on products that truly had the potential to make it on the market. He also wanted products to reach the market faster, and for the scientists to think more like consumers as they came up with their new ideas. Many 3M employees generally embraced McNerney's vision as well as the end result. As McNerney told John S. McClenahen of *Industry Week*, "Retaining our culture of innovation—and, in fact, nurturing it—is a big part of what I am trying to get done with my team here [at 3M]. And that directly supports the organic growth [of the company]."

McNerney's reorganization of 3M paid off. While 3M faced many economic difficulties during his tenure, he had the support of Wall Street analysts who believed that the company, which had always been profitable would continue to be so. Noting the many successes of the health-care arm of the company, he wanted to add more treatments and other products to its line of pharmaceuticals, as well as grow the display and graphics division. McNerney hoped to expand 3M by acquisition, but only if the right business became available. In 2003, for example, he bought the precision lens business of Corning for $680 million. In 2004, 3M posted record sales of $4 billion and profits of $3 billion. McNerney was named one of the best managers of 2003 by *BusinessWeek* and CEO of the year by *Industry Week* in 2004.

In addition to running 3M, McNerney served on the board of directors for several companies. He joined Boeing's board in 2001. The $52 billion company produced commercial and military airplanes and jets as well as defense systems, electronic systems, missiles, satellites, information systems, and communications systems. By 2004, Boeing was considering McNerney as a potential CEO. McNerney was offered the job twice, but told the company he was not interested in leaving 3M. However, in the spring of 2005, McNerney had a sudden change of heart. He told Jeff Bailey of the *New York Times*, "I realized that the job was about to go away, and I realized I did want it, and that 3M could live without me." McNerney left 3M and joined Boeing as its president, CEO, and chairman of the board in July of 2005.

The job McNerney faced at Boeing was similar to that of 3M's in the beginning. The company was already profitable. In addition, it was generally on the right financial and strategic path in McNerney's opinion. McNerney had to fix the bureaucracy and a lingering negative corporate culture. The last CEO, Harry Stoneciper, had been forced out because of ethical questions, which also had to be addressed. In addition, Boeing had acquired three companies between 1996 and 2000 which had yet to be fully integrated.

The move to Boeing also allowed McNerney to return to one of his childhood homes: Chicago. He did not plan to leave Boeing before retirement, telling Dominic Gates of the *Seattle Times,* "I certainly view this as my last job." Regarding McNerney's hiring as Boeing's leader, outgoing Boeing chairman Lewis Platt told Stanley Holmes of *BusinessWeek Online,* "Jim met all the board's criteria. He is, in the unanimous judgment of our board members, the ideal person to lead Boeing. Jim wins respect for his integrity, ethical leadership, and personal business style wherever he goes."

Sources

Periodicals

Aerospace Daily & Defense Report, July 1, 2005, p. 5.
Associated Press, August 1, 1997; June 29, 2005.
Associated Press State & Local Wire, December 5, 2000; June 30, 2005.
Aviation Week & Space Technology, July 4, 2005, p. 22.
Business Courier Serving Cincinnati-Northern Kentucky, February 17, 2000, p. 3.
BusinessWeek, October 2, 2000, p. 134; December 18, 2000, p. 214; January 21, 2002, p. 50; January 12, 2004, p. 61; July 18, 2005, p. 44.
BusinessWeek Online, November 13, 2002; July 1, 2005.
CityBusiness (Minneapolis, MN), December 8, 2000, p. 8.
Crain's Chicago Business, July 4, 2005, p. 1.
Forbes, February 17, 2003, pp. 64-65.
Fortune, August 12, 2002, p. 127.
Industry Week, January 2004, p. 37.
New York Times, December 27, 1991, p. D3; July 1, 2005, p. C3.
PR Newswire, December 5, 2000; May 8, 2001.
St. Louis Post-Dispatch (St. Louis, MO), July 1, 2005, p. A1.
Seattle Times (Seattle, WA), July 1, 2005.
Star Tribune (Minneapolis, MN), December 5, 2000, p. 1A, p. 1D; December 6, 2000, p. 1A; December 7, 2000, p. 1D; December 19, 2001, p. 1D; May 12, 2004, p. 1D; July 1, 2005, p. 1D.

Online

"W. James McNerney, Jr., " Boeing, http://www.boeing.com/companyoffices/aboutus/execprofiles/mcnerney.html (February 12, 2006).

—A. Petruso

S. Epatha Merkerson

AP Images

Actress

Born Sharon Epatha Merkerson, November 28, 1952, in Saginaw, MI; daughter of Ann (a postal worker); married Toussaint L. Jones Jr. (a social worker), March, 1994 (divorced). *Education:* Wayne State University, B.F.A., 1975.

Addresses: *Agent*—David Nesmith, PMK/HBH Public Relations, 650 5th Avenue, 33rd Fl., New York, NY 10019.

Career

Member of a children's theater company in Albany, NY, c. 1975-78; moved to New York City and began appearing in Off-Broadway productions. Actress in films, including: *She's Gotta Have It*, 1986; *Jacob's Ladder*, 1990; *Navy Seals*, 1990; *Terminator 2: Judgment Day*, 1991; *Random Hearts*, 1999; *The Rising Place*, 2001; *Radio*, 2003; *Jersey Girl*, 2004; *Black Snake Moan*, 2006. Television appearances include: *Pee-wee's Playhouse*, CBS, 1986-91; *Elysian Fields* (movie), 1989; *Equal Justice* (movie), 1990; *Mann & Machine*, NBC, 1992; *It's Nothing Personal* (movie), 1993; *Law & Order*, NBC, 1993—; *A Place for Annie* (movie), 1994; *A Mother's Prayer* (movie), 1995; *Breaking Through* (movie), 1996; *An Unexpected Life* (movie), 1998; *A Girl Thing* (miniseries), 2001; *Lackawanna Blues* (movie), 2005. Stage appearances include: *The Piano Lesson*, Walter Kerr Theatre, 1990-91; *The Old Settler*, Studio Theatre, Washington, D.C., 1999; *Birdie Blue*, Second Stage Theatre, New York City, 2005.

Awards: Obie Award for performance, *Village Voice*, for *I'm Not Stupid*, 1991-92; Helen Hayes Award for outstanding lead actress (resident play), Washing-

ton Theatre Awards Society, for *The Old Settler*, 1999; Emmy Award for outstanding lead actress in a miniseries or a movie, Academy of Television Arts and Sciences, for *Lackawanna Blues*, 2005; Obie Award for performance, *Village Voice*, for *Birdie Blue*, Second Stage Theatre, 2005; Golden Globe award for best performance by an actress in a mini-series or a motion picture made for television, Hollywood Foreign Press Association, for *Lackawanna Blues*, 2006; Screen Actors Guild award for outstanding performance by a female actor in a television movie or miniseries, for *Lackawanna Blues*, 2006.

Sidelights

S. Epatha Merkerson is known to millions of television viewers as Lieutenant Anita Van Buren on the hit NBC series *Law & Order*. Merkerson has been a staple of the show since 1993, three years after its launch, and more than a dozen years later her name became the answer to a trivia question: she is the longest-serving African-American actor on a prime-time drama series. In 2005, she won both an Emmy and a Golden Globe award for her work in the well-received HBO film, *Lackawanna Blues*.

Merkerson avoids divulging what the initial "S" stands for, but some sources note that her given name is Sharon; the name she uses professionally is pronounced "ee-PAY-thuh." She was born on November 28, 1952, in Saginaw, Michigan, but grew up in Detroit as one of five children raised by her divorced mother, Ann, a postal worker. At a time when the racial demographics of the city were rapidly shifting, the Merkersons moved to a predominantly white neighborhood in Detroit. Their address was the first black-owned house on the street, which prompted a flurry of "For Sale" signs, she recalled, and tensions flared elsewhere in the city into race riots that lasted for days the summer when she was 14. The city's police force was largely white, and Merkerson experienced firsthand how harrowing a routine traffic stop could become. "My older brother, Zephry, and I were out driving, and the police were looking for someone driving a car like his," she recalled in an interview with Galina Espinoza for *People*. "One of them pointed a gun at the back of my head."

Merkerson's home life provided her with the impetus to succeed in life. "When I was a kid going to high school, it was ninety percent white," she told *Black Issues Book Review* writer Sharon D. Johnson. "I remember sitting at the kitchen table and [my mother] telling me, 'Don't you let a soul in this school tell you that you can't do anything that you want to do. No one can take your education from you. If they say you can't do it, prove them to be the liar.'" Further inspiration to excel came from the cultural events she regularly attended with her family, most memorably the dancer Judith Jamison performing with Alvin Ailey's acclaimed dance company. Jamison's stage presence moved Merkerson so deeply that she decided to major in dance when she entered college.

At Wayne State University in her hometown, Merkerson eventually switched over to the drama department. She found herself the sole African-American student in the program, and though she asserted she received a solid training for the stage, "because I was the only black student in the department, I didn't work on the main stage," she said in an interview with Simi Horwitz for *Back Stage*. "I worked in master classes, the studio theatre, and at recitals, but never the main stage. I learned racial typecasting in college. But as a result, I was prepared when I came to New York, knowing I would be typecast as an African American and generally not expecting much."

Merkerson did not immediately head for Manhattan once she earned her Wayne State degree in 1975, but instead took a job in Albany, New York, with a children's theater company. She arrived in New York City in 1978, and worked in Off-Broadway pro-

ductions for a number of years. Her first screen credit came when a young filmmaker, Spike Lee, cast her in his breakthrough 1986 film, *She's Gotta Have It*, as Doctor Jamison. Later that year she also found a regular gig as Reba the mail carrier on Paul Reubens' CBS children's series *Pee-wee's Playhouse*. The show, which had nearly as many adult fans as younger ones, won three Daytime Emmy Awards for its first season. Both Natasha Lyonne (*American Pie*) and Laurence Fishburne (*The Matrix*) were fellow cast members on the series.

Pee-wee's Playhouse ran until 1991, and the job helped Merkerson secure steady work in film and television over the course of its run. She appeared in the made-for-TV films *Elysian Fields* and *Equal Justice*, and in two feature films from 1990, *Navy Seals* and *Jacob's Ladder*. She also continued to take theater work, most notably in the original Broadway production of playwright August Wilson's Pulitzer Prize-winning drama *The Piano Lesson* in 1990. Her portrayal of Berniece, a woman fighting to preserve her family's most prized possession, was nominated for a Tony Award. In 1991, she appeared in the Hollywood action thriller *Terminator 2: Judgment Day* as Tarissa Dyon.

In 1992, legendary television producer Dick Wolf hired Merkerson for his new cop series, *Mann & Machine*, and though the show was cancelled after its first season, Wolf called her a year later when network executives strongly suggested that he needed to diversify the cast of *Law & Order*. The gritty, well-written police procedural was set in New York City and had lured a large viewership since its inception in 1990. Wolf cast Merkerson in the part of the humorless Lieutenant Anita Van Buren without even asking her to audition, so convinced was he that she was ideal for the part.

Merkerson occasionally provided input on certain plotlines in rehearsals for *Law & Order* episodes. For example, she objected to a premise in which a black man, passing for white, has a baby with his wife, who is white, and the infant is born much darker than either parent. This was genetically impossible, and a few African-American viewers were irate. "We try to do shows that are correct," Merkerson told the *St. Louis Post-Dispatch* a few seasons into her run, after recounting that episode's controversy and the letters she received from viewers. "Not politically correct, not artistically correct, but correct in reality. It's the minutiae, those little things that present themselves in our culture that I've spent my career fighting for."

Law & Order's shooting schedule allowed Merkerson to remain active in film and theater. In 1999, she won the Helen Hayes Award for her lead role in

The Old Settler, a play about Harlem in the 1940s staged at the Studio Theatre in Washington, D.C. She also appeared in the 1999 Harrison Ford thriller *Random Hearts,* the Cuba Gooding Jr. feel-good sports tale *Radio,* and the Ben Affleck-Jennifer Lopez romantic comedy *Jersey Girl* in 2004, and in several more made-for-television movies. Despite her lengthy resume, she was most often recognized as Lieutenant Van Buren. Real-life New York City cops, in particular, were among her most ardent fans, and as she told Horwitz in the *Back Stage* interview, they often call out "Loo," short for lieutenant, to her. "Not too long ago, several cops who saw me go into a store waited for me to come out," she also recounted to Horwitz. "They had just arrested some guys and put them in the police van, but the cops weren't going anywhere. They wanted the chance to say hello to me."

Veteran Broadway director George C. Wolfe (*Bring In 'Da Noise, Bring in 'Da Funk,*) cast Merkerson in a highly coveted lead role for his 2005 HBO Films project, *Lackawanna Blues.* Based on a one-person play by Ruben Santiago-Hudson, the movie was set in an all-black suburb of Buffalo, New York, during the 1950s, and featured a stellar cast, including Jimmy Smits, Macy Gray, Jeffrey Wright, Mos Def, and Rosie Perez. Merkerson played Rachel "Nanny" Crosby, the woman who became a parental figure for young Santiago-Hudson as the proprietor of a boardinghouse. "It's not just about a young boy and the woman who raised him," Merkerson explained in an interview with Les Spindle for *Back Stage East.* "It's also about a period of time when this could happen. All of these people would be in this home because of what was going on in the larger world. It shows what people had to do to make it through their lives at that time and how they needed to support each other."

The pre-civil rights black community depicted in *Lackawanna Blues* was not unlike the world Merkerson knew in her earliest years in Detroit. "All elements were in the neighborhood, but there were checks and balances," she recalled when discussing the *Lackawanna* milieu with *Chicago Tribune* writer Michael Kilian. "You know, 'That's Dr. Jones' house. You don't make a lot of noise there.'"

Merkerson collected an Emmy Award for Outstanding Lead Actress in a Miniseries or a Movie as well as a Golden Globe and a Screen Actors Guild award for *Lackawanna Blues.* When she accepted the last award, she mentioned her divorce lawyer in the speech. She had married a social worker in 1994, and commuted to and from New York City from the Maryland home they shared for a number of years, but the marriage ended. As she told *Entertainment Weekly* writer Alynda Wheat, her professional success provided some solace after a tough year. "That was another reason [the award] was so exciting," she admitted. "It was happening at a time when someone was trying to take my spirit."

Merkerson still appears on stage, and won her second Obie Award from the *Village Voice* for her turn in *Birdie Blue,* which ran at the Second Stage Theatre in the summer of 2005. She also makes time to work with the Campaign for Tobacco-Free Kids, an anti-smoking organization. She gave up the habit herself after losing two friends to lung cancer. In 2006, she was slated to appear in *Black Snake Moan,* an interracial drama starring Samuel L. Jackson, Christina Ricci, and Justin Timberlake. She also began her fourteenth season on *Law & Order,* which was edging toward a record as the longest running drama series on television. Among its lengthy roster of cast members over the years, she was now the veteran. Despite her longevity in the role, Merkerson claims she never tires of the job. "The thing about Lt. Van Buren is that there are certain things she's going to do and you'll be guaranteed them every week," she told Kilian in the *Chicago Tribune.* "That's why people like [her].... What makes it fresh for me is that we have these new stories every week. It would be different if it were a serial."

Merkerson's real ambition, however, was to produce. When the interview in *Black Issues Book Review* appeared in early 2006, she had recently acquired the rights to a 2004 novel by Diane McKinney-Whetstone, *Leaving Cecil Street,* that had won several literary accolades. Merkerson was moved by the stories, which were set in a Philadelphia neighborhood in the 1960s that reminded her of her own Motown upbringing. She viewed her investment in the project as a way to bring more stories about African-American life to the screen. "We never, ever are lacking talent in front of the camera," she told Johnson for the journal. "What we are lacking are the people behind the scenes who are the decision makers. That's why I want to produce."

Sources

Back Stage, July 7, 2005, p. 7.
Back Stage East, December 15, 2005, p. 46A.
Black Issues Book Review, March/April 2006, p. 12.
Boston Herald, November 27, 2005, p. 57.
Chicago Tribune, February 11, 2005.
Entertainment Weekly, March 10, 2006, p. 32.
Jet, February 14, 2005, p. 52.
People, August 13, 2001, p. 93.
Record (Bergen Co., NJ), February 6, 2006, p. E1.

St. Louis Post-Dispatch, June 10, 1998, p. E8.
Time, January 30, 1989, p. 69.
Variety, June 27, 2005, p. 72.

—*Carol Brennan*

Nancy Meyers

Lucy Nicholson/Reuters/Landov

Screenwriter, director, and producer

Born Nancy Jane Meyers, December 8, 1949, in Philadelphia, PA; daughter of Irving (a businessman) and Patricia (an interior designer; maiden name, Lemisch) Meyers; married Charles Shyer (a screenwriter, producer, and director), July 28, 1995 (divorced); children: Annie, Hallie. *Religion:* Jewish. *Education:* American University, B.A. (journ- alism), 1971.

Addresses: *Contact*—Sony Pictures Entertainment, 10202 W. Washington Blvd., Culver City, CA 90232. *Home*—Los Angeles, CA.

Career

Screenwriter for film and television, including: *Private Benjamin*, 1980; *Private Benjamin* (television series), CBS, 1981; *Irreconcilable Differences*, 1984; *Protocol*, 1984; *Baby Boom*, 1987; *Baby Boom* (television series), 1988; *Father of the Bride*, 1991; *Once Upon a Crime*, 1992; *I Love Trouble*, 1994; *Father of the Bride Part II*, 1995; *The Parent Trap*, 1998; *Something's Gotta Give*, 2003. Director of films, including: *The Parent Trap*, 1998; *What Women Want*, 2000; *Something's Gotta Give*, 2003. Producer credits include: *Private Benjamin*, 1980; *Baby Boom*, 1987; *Father of the Bride*, 1991; *I Love Trouble*, 1994; *Father of the Bride Part II*, 1995; *What Women Want*, 2000; *Something's Gotta Give*, 2003. Also was a production assistant for *The Price is Right*, 1972-74; became a story editor for producer Ray Stark, 1974; launched cheesecake business and worked on scripts, c. 1975-76; began writing with Charles Shyer, c. 1976.

Member: American Society of Composers, Authors, and Publishers; Academy of Motion Picture Arts and Sciences; Writers Guild of America.

Awards: Writers Guild of America award for best comedy written directly for the screen, for *Private Benjamin*, 1981; ShoWest Director of the Year for *Something's Gotta Give*, 2004.

Sidelights

For more than two decades writer/director Nancy Meyers has been at the forefront of those women seeking to break through the "celluloid ceiling." As of the mid-2000s, just five percent of all films were directed by women, with Meyers leading the fray. On her own, or with former husband Charles Shyer, Meyers has written more than ten motion pictures, was nominated for an Academy Award for co-writing 1980's *Private Benjamin,* and was named the 2004 ShoWest Director of the Year for *Something's Gotta Give,* which proved that romantic comedies, done right, are viable blockbusters. In addition, Meyers directed 2000's *What Women Want,* which earned $183 million domestically to become the highest-grossing, female-directed film to date.

While there is no doubting Meyers' directing ability, her passion lies in writing. "Directing is really a way of protecting the writing," she told Sheri Linden of the *Hollywood Reporter.* "The reason I direct movies is so that what I've written can get on the screen. I don't feel driven to direct; I feel driven to write. And then, because I write, I'm driven to direct."

A native Philadelphian, Meyers was born into the Jewish family of Irving and Patricia Meyers in 1949. Her father was an executive with a voting machine manufacturer, while her mother worked in interior design. In 1967 Meyers graduated from Lower Merion High School in Lower Merion, Pennsylvania, and headed to American University in Washington, D.C., earning her journalism degree in 1971. She found employment at WHYY, a Philadelphia-based public television station.

In 1972 Meyers moved to Los Angeles and became a production assistant for the long-running daytime television game show *The Price is Right*. Working as a gofer for producers Mark Goodson and Bill Todman taught Meyers plenty about production. She left after about two years to become a story editor for producer Ray Stark, which put her in the company of fellow screenwriter hopefuls.

Soon, the desire to write overwhelmed Meyers. She quit her steady job so she would have more time to bang out scripts. To earn money Meyers launched a cheesecake-baking business and sold her sweets to area restaurants. Meyers lived in a tiny Beverly Hills apartment and quickly outgrew her oven. "I'd pay the gas bill for my neighbors so I could use their ovens," she recalled to *InStyle*'s Jamie Diamond.

In the mid-1970s fellow writer Harvey Miller introduced Meyers to his best friend, Charles Shyer. By 1976 Meyers and Shyer were dating and eventually began writing together. Their first effort was 1980's *Private Benjamin*. The premise for the script came from Meyers. Speaking to the *Hollywood Reporter*, Meyers recalled the moment the film idea came to her. "I remember driving on the Ventura Freeway when I was about 27, to run an errand, when I thought, 'What if a girl joined the Army to escape her problems?'"

Meyers, Shyer, and Miller collaborated on the script, which featured Goldie Hawn as a pampered princess who joins the army after her husband dies. The flick, lacking a male lead, was cutting-edge for the time and became one of the most profitable movies Hawn ever made, proving a woman could carry a film to box office success. The screenwriting trio garnered an Academy Award nomination for best writing.

Meyer and Shyer continued writing together and churned out 1984's *Irreconcilable Differences* and 1987's *Baby Boom*, as well as the *Father of the Bride* movies of the 1990s. They also had two daughters, both born in the 1980s. They finally married in 1995 but separated a few years later and severed their professional ties as well.

In 1998, Meyers made her directing debut with *The Parent Trap*, a remake of the 1961 Disney classic about twins who discover each other's existence at a summer camp, then vow to reunite their divorced parents. Widespread success came with her second directorial effort, 2000's *What Women Want*. The romantic comedy featured Helen Hunt opposite Mel Gibson who played a male chauvinist who gains the ability to read women's minds. The movie, raking in $183 million at the U.S. box office, made Meyers one of the few female directors to crack the $100 million mark. Worldwide sales hit $375 million.

In the meantime, Meyers stayed busy writing her first solo script, which became 2003's *Something's Gotta Give*. While working on the screenplay, Meyers found many skeptics who doubted the drawing power of a movie featuring a middle-aged love affair.

Over lunch one day, Meyers pitched the movie to actress Diane Keaton. "I just sat there and ate the meal and thought, 'Good luck,'" Keaton recalled to the *Dominion Post*. In the end, Keaton agreed to play the lead female role opposite Jack Nicholson, who played Harry Sanborn, a 60-something playboy who always dates women at least half his age. Instead, he falls for the more age-appropriate Erica Barry, the mother of his latest love interest. Barry, played by Keaton, is an uptight divorced playwright who feels most comfortable in turtlenecks, symbolic of the layers of protection she has swaddled around herself.

The highly nuanced comedy struck a chord with baby boomers, easily surpassing the $100 million mark domestically. In its first weeks out, box office sales topped what was thought would be bigger films, like *Cold Mountain* and *Master and Commander*.

Meyers, a keen observer of the human condition, does not deny that the film hits close to home. Divorced at 48, Meyers has experienced life as an aging dater. Erica Barry could very well be Meyers. "It's a real story I'm telling about what it's like to be her age and single," Meyers told the *New York*

Times' Nancy Griffin. "To have been married for a long time and to be without that, and the shell she shrinks inside of."

Both Nicholson and Keaton earned Golden Globe nominations for their performances, with Keaton winning the award. Nicholson credited Meyers for driving him to such a great performance. He called Meyers a "grinder," who forced him to work through scenes over and over. "She knows what she wants and she's not afraid to get bloody to get it," Nicholson recalled to the *New York Times'* Griffin. Prior to the Meyers film, Nicholson had appeared in more than 75 movies, but this was the first time he could recall a woman directed him.

Not one to rest on her laurels, Meyers was busy on another script within about a year of the film's release. Tentatively titled *Holiday*, the film, about two women with men troubles who befriend each other, was set for release in 2006. For Meyers' fans, the movie would not come soon enough.

Sources

Periodicals

Dominion Post (Wellington, New Zealand), January 7, 2004, p. 7.
Hollywood Reporter, March 23, 2004, p. 25, p. 31.
InStyle, April 15, 2004, p. 158.
New York Times, December 10, 2000, sec. 2, p. 15; December 14, 2003, Arts & Leisure, p. 15.

Online

"Nancy Meyers," American University School of Communication Alumni, http://www.socalumni.american.edu/waves.cfm?pageid=23 (July 27, 2005)
"Nancy Meyers," Internet Movie Database, http://www.imdb.com/name/nm0583600/ (August 4, 2005).

—Lisa Frick

Benjamin Millepied

AP Images

Dancer and choreographer

Born c. 1977, in Bordeaux, France; son of a decathlete and a dance teacher. *Education:* Trained at the School of American Ballet, New York City, 1993-95.

Addresses: *Office*—c/o New York City Ballet, 20 Lincoln Center Plaza, New York, NY 10023-6965.

Career

New York City Ballet, corps de ballet dancer, 1995-98, soloist, 1998-2002, principal dancer, 2002—.

Sidelights

Benjamin Millepied is a principal dancer with the New York City Ballet, one of the top dance companies in the world. The French-born Millepied, whose name means "thousand-footed" in his native tongue, has earned impressive accolades since beginning his professional career in 1995. Anna Kisselgoff, a *New York Times* critic, described him as "a standout in his explosive energy, dazzling speed, and astonishing high leaps."

Born in the mid- to late 1970s, Millepied seemed blessed with a gifted genetic legacy from the start as the son of a dance teacher and a father who was a decathlete. The family left their native Bordeaux, France, for Dakar, Senegal, when Millepied was still quite young when his father took a job training Senegalese track and field athletes. Millepied's ear-

liest talents seemed to be musical, however. "We lived next to this really famous family of drummers, so I played the drums seriously until I was 12 or 13," he told *Vogue* writer Gia Kourlas.

The family returned to Bordeaux when Millepied was five, and three years later he began taking dance classes under his mother's tutelage. A videocassette copy of the 1985 feature film *White Nights*, which starred Russian émigré ballet star Mikhail Baryshnikov, positively entranced a young Millepied, and he set his sights on following Baryshnikov's career path. He went on to study at the Bordeaux Opera House before winning a place at the Conservatoire National in Lyon, France, at the age of 13. Initially, he was placed in its modern dance division, but successfully argued to be reassigned to the ballet classes.

Millepied came to the United States in 1992 to take classes in the summer program of the School of American Ballet (SAB), the official school of the New York City Ballet (NYCB). The company was founded in 1948 by George Balanchine, one of the most renowned ballet masters and choreographers of the twentieth century, and the equally eminent Lincoln Kirstein. A long roster of well-known performers had spent the better part of their careers with the

NYCB, including Baryshnikov, Suzanne Farrell, Darci Kistler, and Peter Martins.

Millepied returned to SAB in 1993 as a full-time student after winning a scholarship from the French government. A year later, he won a prestigious international scholarship competition for young dancers, the Prix de Lausanne. Jerome Robbins, a legendary figure in American ballet and the NYCB ballet master during these years, cast a young Millepied in a highly coveted role that same year in the premiere of Robbins' *Two- and Three-Part Inventions.* "As a student, he already had an air of calm authority that suggested a coiled spring," wrote Harris Green in *Dance* magazine of Millepied a few years later.

In 1995, his SAB training over, Millepied was invited to join the NYCB's corps de ballet. Though his artistic excellence was already gaining attention, some critics noted that his technical proficiency lacked finesse. "His feet were not always pointed and his legs were never quite turned out enough to make him a model of classical style," remembered Kisselgoff in the *New York Times.* Over the next three years, however, Millepied's physical prowess improved, and he was cast in a number of plum male-dancer roles. These included Oberon in *A Midsummer Night's Dream* and as the Faun in Robbins' *The Four Seasons,* in which one of Millepied's leaps set a new elevation record at the NYCB.

Millepied became an NYCB soloist in 1998, the same year that *Dance* magazine named him one of the five new male dancers to watch, along with Christopher Wheeldon, Sebastien Marcovici, Edward Liang, and James Fayette. By the spring of 2002, Millepied advanced to the category of principal dancer with the NYCB, and also began exploring his interest in choreography. He participated in City Ballet's New York Choreographic Institute that year and the following, and also organized a small touring company made up of 17 NYCB dancers, called Danse Concertantes, that performed in London at Sadler's Wells Theater. The troupe returned to England in the fall of 2004, this time with a new work that Millepied had choreographed, *Circular Motion.* The evening's performance was reviewed by David Dougill in the London *Sunday Times,* and Dougill termed Millepied's newest work as "a brisk set of dances for four excellent men, a kind of friendly contest that conveyed personalities as well as technique."

In 2005, Millepied began a project with his hero, Baryshnikov, that featured vintage footage of the star along with live performance. Other works that Millepied had choreographed had their premieres at NYCB events. He was still a popular performer with the company during its regular season, noted Kisselgoff. "A thinking man's dancer," she noted in the *New York Times,* "Millepied shows a very different side in romantically tinged ballets. In works like Christopher Wheeldon's *Carousel (A Dance)* the intensity of his matinee-idol presence comes into full play."

By early 2006, Danse Concertantes was performing under the name Benjamin Millepied & Company. *Village Voice* dance critic Deborah Jowitt wrote about one of its engagements at the Joyce Theater in March of 2006, and called the pickup company "a dream team of terrific dancers." She noted that Millepied choreographed some of the works performed that evening, and appeared in two of them himself, including a duet with Gillian Murphy, *Closer.* Jowitt commended both his performance and the choreography, noting that its steps appeared "fluid, easy, understated even when difficult. Both dancers wear soft slippers, and their solos are full of little springy steps and easily spun out turns. Their shoulders, twisting and shrugging subtly, give a lightly temperamental edge to the steps. These are two handsome, extraordinarily gifted dancers, and Millepied has created some imaginative but never strained partnering."

Millepied lives with his girlfriend, Danish-born NYCB ballerina Saskia Beskow, in New York's trendy East Village neighborhood. He could not imagine living anywhere other than New York, he asserted in the interview with *Vogue.* "This is the place where Balanchine and Jerry made their ballets," he told Kourlas. "This is the place where there are people who really *get* the kind of work that I believe in."

Sources

Dance, November 1998, p. 70.

New York Times, January 10, 2001, p. B5; April 5, 2005, p. E1.

Sunday Times (London, England), October 24, 2004, p. 34.

Village Voice, March 17, 2006.

Vogue, April 2005, p. 234.

—Carol Brennan

Denise Mina

© Colin McPherson/Corbis/Sygma

Author

Born in 1966, in East Kilbride, Lanarkshire, Scotland; children: Fergus (with partner, Steve [a forensic psychologist]). *Education:* Received law degree from Glasgow University; graduate student at Strathclyde University.

Addresses: *Agent*—The Sayle Literary Agency, Bickerton House, 25-27 Bickerton Rd., London N19 5JT England.

Career

Worked in a meat factory, and as a bartender, cook, and auxiliary nurse in a nursing home; later became university tutor in criminology and criminal law; first novel, *Garnethill: A Novel of Crime,* published in Britain, 1998.

Awards: John Creasey Memorial Dagger for best first crime novel, Crime Writers' Association, for *Garnethill: A Novel of Crime,* 1998; Macallan Short Story Dagger, Crime Writers' Association, for "Helena and the Babies," 1998.

Sidelights

Crime-fiction writer Denise Mina has attracted a devoted following for her gritty, well-plotted novels whose secondary character is the urban underbelly of her native Glasgow. Mina belongs to a new genre of crime writers known as the "tartan noir" set for their unflinching fictional images of a more malevolent Scottish character. "Mina's books portray a city she loves—a real, tangible Glasgow—in its patter and its rainy skies, and in the deprivation and ruthlessness of its dark side," wrote *Scotsman* journalist Susan Mansfield.

Mina was born in 1966 in East Kilbride, a town in the Lanarkshire district not far from Glasgow. The family relocated several times around Europe when she was a child because of her father's job as an oil engineer. It was also a Roman Catholic clan, and Mina attended convent schools for girls until the age of 16, when she struck out on her own. She worked as a bartender, cook, meat factory employee, and as an auxiliary nurse in a nursing home before deciding to enter college when she was in her early twenties. She studied law at Glasgow University, but never practiced after earning her degree; instead she taught law and criminology courses, and entered Strathclyde University with the goal of a Ph.D. Mina was especially interested in the prevalence of mental-illness diagnoses in female criminal offenders, but her research into false-memory syndrome began to weigh heavily on her, and she decided to take a break by writing some fiction.

Mina sent 80 pages of what she had written to an agent, who then asked to see the rest of it. She took three months off from her job, and wrote what became her first novel, *Garnethill: A Novel of Crime.* Published in Britain in 1998 and in the United States within a year, it became a U.K. bestseller and won Mina the John Creasey Memorial Dagger for best first crime novel from the Crime Writers' Association. *Garnethill*'s story is set in Glasgow, where Mina had spent the majority of her adult years, and centers on amateur sleuth Maureen O'Donnell, who as adult realizes she was the victim of sexual abuse as a child. The perpetrator was her own father, but he vanished long ago. Maureen's brother, Liam, a drug dealer, is supportive of her, but her mother and sisters treat her allegations of abuse as lies. When the novel begins, Maureen has just been released after three years in a psychiatric treatment facility, where she had become romantically involved with Douglas Brady, one of her doctors. She wakes one morning to find his murdered body in her living room, and sets out to prove she was not his killer, though all clues seem to point to her.

Mina's next novel, *Exile*, also featured the down-to-earth and likable Maureen. In this story, she becomes involved in a domestic abuse shelter for women, suspects she is being stalked by Dr. Brady's killer, and tries to solve the murder of a woman from the shelter—though Jimmy, the dead woman's boyfriend, seems to be the prime suspect, and he is also the cousin of her close pal, Leslie. In Mina's third novel, *Resolution*, psychologist Angus Farrell is finally set to go on trial for Douglas Brady's murder, and once again Maureen fears for her safety because of her incriminating testimony. Compounding her problems are the return of the long-lost O'Donnell father, and the death of a poor, nearly illiterate older woman Maureen knew from the flea market that seems tied to the Glasgow underworld.

Sanctum was Mina's first novel not to feature the intrepid Maureen. The book was published in the United States under the title *Deception* in 2004, and centers on the appeal case for Susie Harriot, a forensic psychiatrist convicted for the murder of one of her patients. The story is told through Susie's husband, Lachlan, who is trying to solve the case by combing through Susie's files, and he learns that his wife may not have been what she seemed—then Lachlan's own character is called into question as the novel unfolds. A book reviewer for *People*, Ellen Shapiro, praised *Deception* as a story that successfully blends "unnerving suspense with the uncommon pleasure of being inside Lachlan's unreliable, charmingly vain, and appallingly funny head."

Hollywood actor Brad Pitt read *Deception* and liked it so much that phone calls were made to Mina's publisher about acquiring the story rights, but it had already been sold for a planned British Broadcasting Corporation movie. Mina's next novel earned comparisons to *Mystic River*, the 2003 film based on Boston crime writer Dennis Lehane's tale of an insular, working-class neighborhood and a horrific crime. *The Field of Blood*, published in Britain in 2005, featured a new fictional female sleuth, the young Glasgow journalist Patricia (Paddy) Meehan. The story is set in the city in the early 1980s, and centers upon a terrible crime: the murder of a toddler by two older boys. One of the juvenile suspects is the cousin of Paddy's fiancé, Sean, and Paddy tries to untangle the threads that brought the two boys to commit such a deed.

The Field of Blood attracted a fair share of attention for Mina, though her novels regularly appear on the U.K. bestseller lists, because of its similarities to a real case in Merseyside, England, in 1993, when store security cameras captured footage of two older boys leading a toddler out of a shopping center; the youngster was later found beaten to death and run over by a train. She finished the draft for the book just days before she gave birth to a son, Fergus, and lives with her partner, Steve, a forensic psychiatrist, in the West End area of Glasgow. Under contract for several more Paddy Meehan stories, Mina asserts that becoming a parent has not quelled her penchant for writing about the darker side of her city, nor her ability to chronicle it in gritty prose. "I was told everything would change when I had a baby," she joked in the interview with the *Scotsman*'s Mansfield. "That I wouldn't want to watch the news anymore, I wouldn't be interested in stuff like this, I wouldn't like violent films—and none of that has happened."

Selected writings

Garnethill: A Novel of Crime, Bantam (London, England), 1998; Carroll & Graf (New York City), 1999.
Exile, Bantam, 2000; Carroll & Graf, 2001.
Resolution, Bantam, 2001; Carroll & Graf, 2002.
Sanctum, Bantam, 2002; published in the United States as *Deception*, Little, Brown (Boston, MA), 2004.
The Field of Blood, Little, Brown, 2005.

Sources

Periodicals

Daily Mail (London, England), April 5, 2005, p. 15.
Daily Record (Glasgow, Scotland), March 1, 2005, p. 18.
New York Times, September 9, 2002, p. B1.
People, August 23, 2004, p. 49.

Publishers Weekly, March 1, 1999, p. 63; January 1, 2001, p. 70; April 29, 2002, p. 45; July 26, 2004, p. 39; May 9, 2005, p. 40.

Scotsman (Edinburgh, Scotland) April 14, 2005, p. 36.

Online

"Biography," Denise Mina Website, http://www.denisemina.co.uk/contents/bio.htm (August 23, 2005).

—*Carol Brennan*

Hayao Miyazaki

© Nicolas Guerin/Azimuts Production/Corbis

Animator, director, and screenwriter

Born January 5, 1941, in Tokyo, Japan; son of Katsuji Miyazaki (an aeronautical engineer); married Akemi Ota (an animator); children: two sons. *Education:* Gakushuin University, degree in political science and economics, 1963.

Addresses: *Office*—Studio Ghibli, 1-4-25 Kajino-cho, Koganei-shi 184, Japan.

Career

In-betweener, Toei-Cine, 1963-71; animator, A-Pro studio, 1971-73; Zuiyo Pictures, 1973-84; co-founder, Studio Ghibli, 1984—. Director and animator of films, including: *The Castle of Cagliostro*, 1979; *Nausicaa of the Valley of the Winds*, 1984; *Sherlock Hound, the Detective*, 1984; *Castle in the Sky*, 1986; *My Neighbor Totoro*, 1988; *Kiki's Delivery Service*, 1989; *Crimson Pig*, 1992; *On Your Mark*, 1995; *Princess Mononoke*, 1997; *Spirited Away*, 2001; *Howl's Moving Castle*, 2004. Writer of screenplays, including: *Panda! Go Panda!*, 1973; *Panda and Child: Rainy Day Circus*, 1973; *Future Boy Conan* (also director), 1978; *The Castle of Cagliostro*, 1979; *Warriors of the Wind*, 1984; *Castle in the Sky*, 1986; *My Neighbor Totoro*, 1988; *Kiki's Delivery Service*, 1989; *Crimson Pig*, 1992; *On Your Mark*, 1995; *Whisper of the Heart*, 1995; *Princess Mononoke*, 1997; *Spirited Away*, 2001; *Howl's Moving Castle*, 2004.

Awards: Mainichi Film Concours, Ofuji Noburo Award, 1980, for *The Castle of Cagliostro*; Academy Award for best animated feature, Academy of Motion Picture Arts and Sciences, for *Spirited Away*, 2002; Mainichi Film Concours, best animated film, for *Spirited Away*, 2002; Blue Ribbon award for best film, for *Spirited Away*, 2002; best narrative feature, San Francisco International Film Festival, for *Spirited Away*, 2002; Annie Award for outstanding directing in an animated feature production, for *Spirited Away*, 2002; Annie Award for outstanding writing in an animated feature production, for *Spirited Away*, 2002; Silver Scream Award, Amsterdam Fantastic Film Festival, for *Spirited Away*, 2003; Golden Berlin Bear, Berlin International Film Festival, 2002; Lifetime Achievement Award, Awards of the Japanese Academy, 2002; best feature film, Catalonian International Film Festival, Sitges, Spain, for *Howl's Moving Castle*, 2004; Career Golden Lion, Venice Film Festival, 2005.

Sidelights

Hayao Miyazaki has become one of the forerunners of Japanese animation. Fellow animator Stan Lee, writing for *Time* magazine, said of him, "In the field of theatrical animation, where talent abounds and everyone has his or her own style, the art and creativity of Hayao Miyazaki are unrivaled. For decades, he has arguably been Japan's leading cult figure to fans of manga (comic books) and anime (animated films)—in a nation where those art forms are held in the highest regard." Miyazaki first became famous in his own country, but his animated films are such works of art that they cross all international barriers, and he has become a sensation around the world. He is known primarily for his films *Princess Mononoke, Spirited Away,* and most recently *Howl's Moving Castle.* David Ansen of *Newsweek* said of the animator, "Hayao Miyazaki seems to be one of those artists (and there aren't many) who just can't fail to make magic."

Miyazaki was born on January 5, 1941, in Tokyo, Japan to Katsuji Miyazaki, an aeronautical engineer and his wife. His father's career became an interest of Miyazaki's when he was young and continued into his adulthood. In fact, his later animated films showed this love of aeronautics with his carefully designed and drawn aircrafts zipping through the wilderness. Miyazaki's father worked at the family business, the Miyazaki Airplane, and since young Miyazaki was born during World War II, the war had quite an effect on him, especially since his family's company built fighter airplanes. His family was evacuated from Tokyo in 1944 and were unable to return until 1947. It was shortly after that that Miyazaki's mother discovered she had spinal tuberculosis, something that kept her in bed for eight years. During those years she had a strong influence over Miyazaki, as did his school, which was a copy of American schools and hence lent a Western influence to his upbringing. By the time he reached high school, Miyazaki—who had shown an early aptitude for art—was determined to become an artist of some sort. He was especially interested in Manga, the Japanese comic book art, which was forming at the time. Anime, the Japanese animated film style, was arising at the same time.

Although he was interested in drawing, he was also practical, so when he entered Gakushuin University, Miyazaki studied political science and economics, with a plan to help Japan reestablish its economy and recover from the war. His interest in children's stories flourished in college too, as he became part of a children's literature research society that exposed him to fables and tales from around the world. He graduated in 1963, but instead of going into politics or academics, he joined an animation studio, Toei-Cine, taking on the role of in-betweener, a position that is responsible for adding in the drawings that go between the main ones to make the action scenes complete. He fell in love with the work and never once considered turning back to go into industry or politics.

Instead, in 1971, he moved to another studio, A-Pro studio, following fellow animator and friend Isao Takahata whom he had met at Toei-Cine. Two years later the pair moved to Zuiyo Pictures where Miyazaki's talents, cleaned up and perfected over the years, were soon widely recognized. The first film he worked on as both writer and animator was the short *Panda! Go Panda!*. He followed it the next year with *Panda and Child: Rainy Day Circus.* He directed his first series in 1978, *Future Boy Conan.* Miyazaki's big break came, however, in 1979 when Tokyo Movie Shinsha hired him to direct a movie adaptation of the popular comic book *Lupin III,* which became 1979's *The Castle of Cagliostro.*

This film left Miyazaki with a desire to do different movies, ones that would express not what animation had become, but rather what he could make it. So, in 1984 Miyazaki, longing for a greater freedom in animation, started his own business, Studio Ghibli, with his longtime friend Takahata. The studio was a place where the two enjoyed creating their own pieces, often controversial and pushing the boundaries of traditional animation. Their first movies, *Castle in the Sky, My Neighbor Totoro,* and *Kiki's Delivery Service* were all successes, as have all his films since. It was having his own company that gave Miyazaki the ability to do the animation that was outside the norm and that eventually led to his being recognized as a master of the art. Miyazaki is not just unusual for the content of his films, but also for the way he goes about making them. According to *Time*'s Lee, Miyazaki often begins "constructing a film without a full script," letting the drawings lead the story. Miyazaki usually has no idea who the main characters are when he starts or what they will eventually end up doing. He has said, according to Lee, that working in this way ensures that he keeps his interest in the project as it progresses and helps give the end product a feeling of spontaneity.

In 1984 Miyazaki released *Nausicaa of the Valley of Wind,* his first major foray into changing the status quo of animation filmmaking. In the film he did away with the trendy metallic look that was prevalent in Japanese anime at the time for a more naturalistic approach, including forests dripping with fungus. The story is about a special teenage princess who lives in a small valley in a futuristically dark and empty post-apocalyptic Earth. A Poisonous forest threatens to kill off the remaining inhabitants of earth and she decides to participate in a war between neighboring kingdoms for the survival of her people. However, she soon finds that she is a pacifist and is much more interested in exploring the forest than in fighting, and from there the adventures really begin. Steve Raiteri in the *Library*

Journal said of the film, "Highly recommended for teens and adults alike, this tremendous series belongs in every library."

It was Miyazaki's 1997 animated film *Princess Mononoke* that brought the director to the eyes of mainstream audiences across the globe. Before the release of this film Miyazaki was known outside his country only in niche markets of people who had a great interest in Japanese anime. *Princess Mononoke* was released in the United States by Disney, although it was done through their more artistic branch, Miramax. *Princess Mononoke* is about a medieval prince and his quest through a mythical forest. It is while he is on his quest that he meets the girl for which the film is named. *People*'s Tom Gliatto said of the film, "The convoluted, violent story, which begins when the prince slays the demon and incurs a curse that can be lifted (if at all) only by journeying to the monster's homeland, makes this unsuitable fare for kids.... But the animation—from elaborate (the supernatural creatures) to simple (a rain shower)—is superb." *Entertainment Weekly*'s Ty Burr wrote, "A windswept pinnacle of its art, *Princess Mononoke* has the effect of making the average Disney film look like just another toy story." Leonard Klady in *Variety* magazine called it "a rich cartoon fable of bygone gods locking horns with man and with industry." It became the highest-grossing film in Japan ever.

Then Miyazaki made 2001's *Spirited Away*, which took over *Princess Mononoke*'s record as Japan's largest money-making film of all time. It is about a young girl, Chihiro, who when driving home with her parents one day is swept into a parallel world when her parents take a wrong turn. The new world is inhabited by a whole slew of gods, ghouls, and goblins, and Chihiro, a rather spoiled brat at the beginning of the story, is forced to deal with situations that most adults would not be able to handle. In fact Chihiro's parents are soon turned into pigs for turning their noses up at food offered them, and Chihiro alone is put to work serving the gods. The world is morally ambiguous and there is no straightforward battle between good and evil. In the end Chihiro manages to save her parents and escape, but the evil is not changed as much as she is. She changes from a spoiled brat into a brave, self-reliant girl who turns her back on a world of materialism and semi-evil. Steve Vineburg in the *Christian Century* said of the film, "The world Hayao Miyazaki conjures up in the Japanese animated feature *Spirited Away* is so exotic and in a state of such constant metamorphosis that you may have the impression, as you stagger out of the theater, that you've watched the entire movie with your mouth open.

Spirited Away runs close to two hours, and there isn't a banal image in it."

In 2003, *Castle in the Sky: Volumes 1-4*, an adaptation of his 1986 film, was published. The storyline follows Princess Sheeta, who is in exile, and her friend, Pazu, an orphan who is an inventing genius. They go on an adventure to save a magic levitation stone and in the process are chased by a whole litany of soldiers and pirates. *Publishers Weekly* said of this book version of the film, which included stills directly from the movie, "Miyazaki's production design is gorgeous, and the full-color reproduction is nicely authentic—anime buffs will drool over the floating city, cleverly retro-looking airships, half-rusted giant robot soldiers, lush landscapes and sensitively handled lighting in every scene."

Then in 2004 Miyazaki made *Howl's Moving Castle*. Rather than his usual way of making films, Miyazaki based this one on the book by British author Diana Wynne Jones. He had read the book and was really taken with the storyline and underlining moral message and decided it would make a great film. It was not as popular as some of his others for the simple reason that some people did not understand the film. In an interview with Devin Gordon for *Newsweek* magazine, Miyazaki said, "A lot of people say they don't understand the film, and what that means is just that they have a set definition of how a story is supposed to be told. When the story betrays their anticipations, then they complain." The film is about a young girl, Sophie, who is rescued by the wizard Howl one day when she is being hit on by some soldiers. The evil Witch of the Waste hears of the event and jealous, turns Sophie into an old woman. Sophie runs from her village and manages to find a hiding place in Howl's famous moving castle—a castle that actually moves around on bird feet. Furious at the evil witch's spell, Sophie discovers a strength inside herself she would never have discovered otherwise and soon has taken control of things, including helping Howl go into battle for the King. Howl himself does not recognize Sophie, although she falls more and more in love with him as she gets to know the wizard. The whole story, Miyazaki felt, was an interesting look at age and how humans do or do not let it affect them. Richard Corliss of *Time* magazine said, "*Howl's Moving Castle* ... is the perfect e-ticket for a flight of fancy into a world far more gorgeous than our own. The film doesn't halve itself to appeal to two generations. At its best, it turns all moviegoers into innocent kids, slack-jawed with wonder."

Miyazaki is married to Akemi Ota, a fellow animator. They have two sons. As of 2005 Miyazaki was busy at work animating his next film.

Sources

Books

Authors and Artists for Young Adults, vol. 37, Gale Group, 2000.
Contemporary Theatre, Film, and Television, vol. 35, Gale Group, 2001.

Periodicals

American Prospect, October 21, 2002, p. 32.
Christian Century, October 9, 2002, p. 64; August 23, 2005, p. 36.
Economist, February 23, 2002.
Entertainment Weekly, November 5, 1999, p. 50; September 27, 2002, p. 57; October 4, 2002, p. 128; April 18, 2003, p. 53; March 11, 2005, p. 110; June 24, 2005, p. 142.

Library Journal, July 2004, p. 62.
Newsweek, June 20, 2005, p. 62.
People, November 8, 1999, p. 41; June 27, 2005, p. 32; July 18, 2005, p. 29.
Publishers Weekly, May 12, 2003, p. 46; September 8, 2003, p. 58.
School Library Journal, December 2003, p. 89; May 2005, p. 163.
Time, September 30, 2002, p. 88; April 18, 2005, p. 123; June 13, 2005, p. 53.
U.S. News & World Report, October 25, 1999, p. 70.
Variety, August 4, 1997, p. 9; February 2, 1998, p. 28; November 1, 1999, p. 88; February 25, 2002, p. 72; April 15, 2002, p. 4; September 13, 2004, p. 46; December 20, 2004, p. 21; February 21, 2005, p. 2; March 7, 2005, p. 52; August 29, 2005, p. 21.

—*Catherine Victoria Donaldson*

Kathryn Morris

Francis Specker/Landov

Actress

Born January 29, 1969, in Cincinnati, OH; daughter of Stanley (a Bible scholar) and Joyce (an insurance agent) Morris. *Education:* Attended Temple University, early 1990s.

Addresses: *Office*—c/o Columbia Broadcasting System (CBS), 51 W. 52nd St., New York, NY 10019.

Career

Actress on television, including: *Long Road Home* (movie), 1991; *Oldest Living Confederate Widow Tells All* (movie), 1994; *A Friend to Die For* (movie), 1994; *Family Values* (movie), 1995; *Pensacola: Wings of Gold,* CBS, 1998; *Inherit the Wind* (movie), 1999; *Hell Swarm* (movie), 2000; *And Never Let Her Go* (movie), 2001; *Cold Case,* CBS, 2003—. Also appeared in episodes of *Murder, She Wrote, Poltergeist: The Legacy, Xena: Warrior Princess, Providence,* and *The Mind of the Married Man.* Film appearances include: *Cool as Ice,* 1991; *Sleepstalker,* 1995; *As Good as It Gets,* 1997; *Deterrence,* 1999; *Screenplay,* 1999; *The Contender,* 2000; *Role of a Lifetime,* 2001; *Minority Report,* 2002; *Hostage,* 2002; *Paycheck,* 2003; *Mindhunters,* 2004;

Sidelights

After years of small film roles and made-for-television movies, Kathryn Morris found herself one of prime time's newest stars in 2003 as Detective Lilly Rush on the CBS drama *Cold Case.* In it, Morris played a dedicated Philadelphia cop with an uncanny ability to solve the city's most challenging murders from the "Unsolved" file cabinet, and her character seemed to strike an emotional nerve with viewers. "I've had so many people come up and just share how it's so nice to see a woman in a man's world.... It's not just about being a cop," *Detroit Free Press* television critic Mike Duffy quoted her as saying. "It's almost like I've become a spokesperson for the single working woman. I find that very interesting and very challenging."

Born in 1969 in Cincinnati, Ohio, Morris grew up in Connecticut as the youngest of three children in the family. Her father, Stanley, was divorced from her insurance-agent mother, Joyce, the year Morris turned six. She and her siblings lived with their father, a Bible scholar who formed a family gospel act they dubbed Morris Code. They sang at church functions and weddings, eventually even touring the country. Active in theater during her high school years, Morris enrolled in a small Christian college after graduation, and later transferred to Temple University in Philadelphia. When a faculty strike at the school delayed the start of her senior year, she headed to Hollywood. "I took a Greyhound bus with two suitcases and $60 all the way to California," she recalled in an interview with *Philadelphia Inquirer* writer David Hiltbrand.

On her way to her first professional job one day in 1990, Morris was the victim of a hit-and-run automobile accident, and though she had whiplash from the impact, she showed up to dance in the Japanese music video anyway. The next decade was a struggle to break into the business, however, and for a time she made ends meet by working on a cruise ship as a dancing waitress. Her first television role was in a made-for-television movie, *Long Road Home,* in 1991, a story about farmers during the Dust Bowl environmental crisis of the 1930s. Her feature film-debut came that same year in *Cool as Ice,* a teen-angst drama that starred rapper Vanilla Ice.

Morris appeared in several television-series pilots that were never picked up for a full season. After a slew of made-for-TV movies, she landed a recurring role on the CBS series *Pensacola: Wings of Gold,* as Lieutenant Annalisa "Stinger" Lindstrom for several months in 1998. A year later, she appeared as the villainous Najara on the cult-favorite series *Xena: Warrior Princess.* Her breakout role came in the 2000 feature film, *The Contender,* as a special agent involved in a political scandal involving Joan Allen's character, the U.S. vice presidential nominee. "Morris makes a big impression as an FBI investigator," asserted *San Francisco Chronicle* critic Bob Graham in his review of the film. "She may appear ingenuous, but her interviewing technique is sharklike."

Morris went on to a part in the 2001 Steven Spielberg sci-fi thriller *Artificial Intelligence: AI,* but her scenes were edited out of the final cut. "I felt if I got hit by a bus," Morris told *People* about learning of the excision, but refused to consider it a career setback. "I was okay with it because I got to work with Steven Spielberg," she concluded. Spielberg felt so bad about leaving her scenes out that he cast her in his next film, *Minority Report,* with Tom Cruise.

It was her work in *The Contender* that led to Morris's greatest career triumph: producers of a new crime drama, *Cold Case,* chose her for the lead role of Lilly Rush based on her appearance in the film. As series creator Meredith Stiehm told Jill Feiwell in *Daily Variety,* "We knew she was the one before there was ever a meeting. Six executives, including myself, watched a tape of her in *The Contender,* and she played that character exactly the way we envisioned Rush would be—cunning and direct."

Cold Case debuted on the CBS network's prime-time schedule in the fall of 2003. Morris' character was a Philadelphia cop with a reputation for being able to

solve long-dormant cases. As the lone female detective on the Philadelphia homicide squad, Rush works with partner Scotty Valens (Danny Pino) and other colleagues to solve difficult cases in which the trail of clues had led nowhere for the original investigating cops. The episodes feature flashback storylines to the date of the crime, such as the murder of a college athlete back in the 1960s that Rush suspects was a gay hate crime.

Despite being given somewhat of a graveyard slot on Sunday nights, *Cold Case* scored impressive ratings in its first season, which tallied into the highest ratings for any new drama for the 2003-04 television year. It even did well during its second season, pulling nearly 17 million viewers weekly, though ABC's *Desperate Housewives* quickly emerged as the time slot's ratings winner. Morris' intuitive crime-solver earned praise from critics, and the actress enjoyed playing her. The character became known for her somewhat unkempt hair, but as Morris explained to Hiltbrand in the *Philadelphia Inquirer,* it was all part of the character. "She's a woman who eats real food and doesn't have a $500 hair-color job," Morris said. "Sometimes her roots are showing and sometimes her outfit isn't completely together. That's a character that has been missing from television."

Morris was slated to appear in *Resurrecting the Champ,* a 2007 boxing drama with Samuel L. Jackson and Josh Hartnett and directed by Rod Lurie, who also helmed *The Contender.* Her primary job remained *Cold Case,* however, and she learned rather quickly how well-liked the show was, as she told the *Philadelphia Inquirer.* During the first season, she went to New York City as the holidays neared. "I was thinking, 'I'll take a break. No one knows about my show,'" she told Hiltbrand. "I was trying to do this last-minute Christmas shopping frenzy, but everyone wanted to come up and talk about Lilly Rush."

Sources

Daily Variety, June 11, 2004, p. A14.
Detroit Free Press, August 27, 2004.
People, November 10, 2003, p. 104.
Philadelphia Inquirer, January 29, 2004.
San Francisco Chronicle, October 13, 2000.

—*Carol Brennan*

Rob Morrow

Actor

Born Robert Alan Morrow, September 21, 1962, in New Rochelle, NY; son of Murray (an industrial lighting manufacturer) and Diane Francis (a dental hygienist; maiden name, Markowitz) Morrow; married Debbon Ayer (an actress), 1998; children: Tu Simone Ayer Morrow.

Addresses: *Agent*—William Morris Agency, 151 South El Camino Dr., Beverly Hills, CA 90212. *Home*—New York, NY, and Santa Monica, CA.

Career

Actor on television, including: *Saturday Night Live* (uncredited), NBC, 1980; *Fame*, 1985; *Tattingers*, NBC, 1988-89; *Northern Exposure*, CBS, 1990-95; *The Day Lincoln Was Shot* (movie), TNT, 1998; *Magic* (movie), 1998; *Elements* (movie), 1998; *The Thin Blue Lie* (movie), Showtime, 2000; *Jenifer* (movie), CBS, 2001; *Street Time*, Showtime, 2002; *Numb3rs*, CBS, 2005—. Film appearances include: *Private Resort*, 1985; *Quiz Show*, 1994; *Last Dance*, 1996; *Into My Heart*, 1998; *Maze* (also director, producer, and author of screenplay), 2000; *The Guru*, 2002; *The Emperor's Club*, 2002; *Going Shopping*, 2004. Director of television episodes, including: *Oz*, HBO, 2002; *Street Time*, Showtime, 2002; *Joan of Arcadia*, CBS, 2004. Assistant to the director for the Los Angeles production of *Dreamgirls*, 1983. Stage appearances include: *Escape from Riverdale*, Jewish Repertory Theatre, New York, 1984; *I, Shaw*, Jewish Repertory Theatre, 1986; *The Return of Pinocchio*, 47th Street Theatre, New York, 1986; *The Chosen*, Second Avenue Theatre, New York, 1987-88; *The Exonerated*, 45 Bleecker, New York, 2002.

© Lisa O'Connor/ZUMA/Corbis

Sidelights

Rob Morrow has struggled for much of his career to break free of typecasting as the quintessential "nice Jewish boy," a role best exemplified by his highly successful stint as Dr. Joel Fleishman on the acclaimed CBS series *Northern Exposure* in the early 1990s. After a number of other career detours, including portrayals of an ex-con and a Tourette's syndrome sufferer, Morrow scored another hit show with *Numb3rs* in 2005. In it, he plays a clever criminal detective whose toughest cases are solved with the help of his even brainier younger brother, a math genius. The hourlong crime drama presented a welcome change of pace for the veteran actor. "I'm not a gun guy, but I'm really into this," he enthused to *Philadelphia Inquirer* journalist David Hiltbrand. "We get some cool weapons. I love the action scenes."

Morrow was born in 1962 in New Rochelle, New York, a suburb of New York City. His father was an industrial lighting manufacturer, and his mother worked as a dental hygienist. They divorced when he was nine, and the situation troubled him over the next few years. "I started cutting school," he told Mike Lipton in *People*, "and I'd get caught in petty, stupid things—I stole a baseball glove once." His delinquency worsened during his sophomore year at Edgemont High School in nearby Scarsdale, when he was caught stealing some team uniforms, and was expelled for it.

Morrow settled on his future career almost by accident. Coming out of a movie theater after seeing the 1950s-set musical *Grease*, the box-office hit of the summer of 1978, Morrow casually remarked to his friend, "'You know, I'm going to be an actor,' as if I had been planning it all my life," he recalled in the *Philadelphia Inquirer* interview with Hiltbrand. "I'd never even thought about it before. He said, 'I didn't know that.' I was like, 'Oh, yeah.'"

Morrow managed to finish his high-school education, and at the age of 18 a friend helped him land his first professional job, which was an uncredited one but nevertheless impressive—he appeared in a 1980 *Saturday Night Live* skit. Over the next few years, Morrow subjected himself to countless auditions while struggling to make ends meet in New York City by waiting tables and working odd jobs. He landed a steadier behind-the-scenes position as an assistant for the Los Angeles production of *Dreamgirls*, the hit Broadway musical, and made a somewhat auspicious film debut in a 1985 teen comedy, *Private Resort*, in which he co-starred alongside a then-unknown Johnny Depp.

After that, Morrow had an impressive run in some off-Broadway productions in New York City, including *I, Shaw* at the Jewish Repertory Theatre and in *The Chosen*, a 1987 musical adaptation of the Chaim Potok novel set in Brooklyn's Orthodox Jewish community in the 1940s. By this point he was active in a theater group he co-founded, Naked Angels, whose other founding members included Marisa Tomei, Fisher Stevens, Gina Gershon, and Annabella Sciorra. The stage work helped him land his first regular television role in *Tattingers*, an NBC sitcom set in a Manhattan restaurant. Unfortunately, the series was cancelled after its brief 1988-89 run.

Morrow's big break came, somewhat characteristically, almost by accident. He was cast in the starring role for a summer replacement series on CBS, *Northern Exposure*. The show debuted in July of 1990, and began to draw impressive ratings over the next few weeks. The network immediately ordered more episodes, and Morrow suddenly found himself a household name thanks to his portrayal of Dr. Joel Fleischman, a recent medical school graduate who moves to a remote town in Alaska. The character is a lifelong New Yorker who made it

through medical school with the help of a scholarship from the state of Alaska, and in return must spend the first four years of his career in the doctor-scarce state. Thinking he will be sent to one of Alaska's cities, Morrow's Fleischman is instead assigned to Cicely, population 500, and shown his living quarters, a log cabin. In the pilot episode, the hour-long comedy displayed the quirky humor that would make it a favorite of viewers and critics alike, including the scene when Maurice (Barry Corbin), the former astronaut who owns most of town, tells Fleischman that he and the rest of Cicely are "delighted to have a Jew doctor from New York—you guys have an outstanding reputation."

Morrow's young doctor served as the comic foil for Cicely's eccentric residents on *Northern Exposure*. Over the next few seasons, Fleischman endured an off-again, on-again romance with Maggie, a bush pilot played by Janine Turner, and took and gave counsel to Cicely's radio DJ, Chris Stevens, played by future *Sex & the City* heartthrob John Corbett. The show scored several Emmy Award nominations, including one for Morrow as best lead actor in 1992, and opened up new career directions for him. Producer Robert Redford liked his *Northern Exposure* performance so much that he cast him in *Quiz Show*, a 1994 movie based on an actual television game-show scandal back in the 1950s.

In *Quiz Show*, Morrow played Richard Goodwin, the congressional investigator probing the behind-the-scenes story of *Twenty-One*, a popular quiz show rumored to be a sham. The double-dealing involved Charles Van Doren (Ralph Fiennes), whose father was a well-known American poet, and the actual whistleblower was another contestant on the show, Herbert Stempel (John Turturro). "Morrow faces a difficult job," asserted *New York Times* critic Janet Maslin, "since the film ascribes too much crusading nobility to Mr. Goodwin, and since Mr. Redford's own acting career has helped make the heroics of the lone investigator look so familiar. But the performance is vigorous, and when the film sets Goodwin between Stempel and Van Doren, it touches currents of anti-Semitism, self-deception and golden-boy quicksand that once again lift it out of the ordinary."

Morrow appeared in fewer episodes of *Northern Exposure* during its final season, which was explained by his move to an even remoter community of Native Americans, and then finally the release of his contractual obligation to the state of Alaska. The series ended in 1995, and Morrow began to take on more film roles over the next few years. He landed the lead in *Last Dance*, a 1996 drama from acclaimed director Bruce Beresford, about a rascally lawyer who attempts to save a death-row inmate played by Sharon Stone. Plagued by comparisons to *Dead Man Walking,* an Oscar-nominated film of the previous year, *Last Dance* failed to do well at the box office or with critics.

Determined to bring his own projects to the screen, Morrow teamed with several other Naked Angel friends to make *Maze,* a 2000 film that also marked his feature-length directorial debut. He also took the title role as Lyle Maze, a sculptor afflicted with Tourette's syndrome, the neurological disease that causes its sufferers to twitch, make odd noises or grunts, and sometimes even swear uncontrollably. Morrow co-wrote the screenplay with another Naked Angel founding member, Bradley White, and cast his friend Craig Sheffer (*One Tree Hill*) as one of the leads. Laura Linney, who also had Naked Angel ties, played the woman whose love the two men vie for. The tormented Lyle believes he can never achieve a real relationship because of his disorder, and he based the character, as he told *Denver Post* journalist Diane Eicher, on a Canadian artist he had seen in a documentary film about Tourette's sufferers. "He was a sweet, charming guy, but he had reconciled himself to a life without love," Morrow recalled.

Maze earned a mixed review from *New York Times* critic Elvis Mitchell, who noted that "though Mr. Morrow places an almost ridiculous number of obstacles in his path—the difficulty of directing and starring in a picture being the biggest—he comes through with a notable performance, deftly using the attention-getting device of an affliction that leaves him twitching and explosive." Taking on the multiple jobs of writer, actor, and director in this project presented less of a challenge for Morrow than assumed, however. He was well-trained from his Naked Angels days, he explained to Leslie Blake in *Back Stage.* "We'd double dare each other into doing stuff," he said. "No doubt I gained a lot of confidence and it made me feel comfortable because the stakes weren't that high. And now that the stakes are higher, I can take care of myself."

Morrow went on to appear in supporting roles for a number of other Hollywood films, including *The Guru* and *The Emperor's Club* in 2002, and writer-director Henry Jaglom's *Going Shopping* in 2004. There was also a two-season series for the Showtime cable channel, *Street Time,* in which Morrow played a man recently released from prison who is struggling to return to a normal life. "While Morrow isn't particularly convincing as a baddie who could survive the state penitentiary," declared Michael Speier in a *Daily Variety* review, "he eventually evolves into someone mired in moral dilemmas and one-way streets."

Morrow returned to the CBS prime-time line-up when he was cast as one of the leads in *Numb3rs,* which debuted in January of 2005. He played Don Eppes, an agent with the Los Angeles division of the Federal Bureau of Investigation (FBI) whose math-whiz younger brother Charlie (David Krumholtz, the elf in both *Santa Clause* comedies) steps in to help him solve some of the Bureau's knottier Southern California cases. The series had a rather impressive pedigree for television: its executive producers were filmmaker-brothers Ridley and Tony Scott, and the scripts were vetted by a team at the prestigious California Institute of Technology in Pasadena for accuracy. *Newsweek* writer Devin Gordon called the show "a gripping hour of TV, with unexpected shades of character, crisp acting and enough gee-wizardry to excite anyone with even a quark of scientific curiosity." Reviewing it for *Variety,* Brian Lowry ventured that "at first glance, Morrow seems a trifle miscast as the FBI agent, but he's effective enough so long as the series stays on a relatively cerebral (as opposed to busting-down-doors) plane."

Morrow has broadened his experience behind the camera as a director of episodes for *Numb3rs, Street Time,* the HBO series *Oz,* and *Joan of Arcadia.* Married since 1998 to Debbon Ayer, an actress, he was instrumental in the decision to carry on the pun of his wife's name when it came time to label their newborn daughter, settling upon Tu Simone Ayer Morrow. Becoming a parent changed his life, the once-troubled teen told Lipton in *People.* "It's freed me up in a certain way," reflected Morrow. "Now nothing matters really except that. And I know that it doesn't matter even if, you know, I have to go work at Burger King. I'll do it. It's someone that you put your life on the line for."

Sources

Books

Contemporary Theatre, Film, and Television, vol. 59, Thomson Gale, 2005.

Periodicals

Back Stage, November 9, 2001, p. 28.
Daily News (Los Angeles, CA), May 2, 1996, p. L3.
Daily Variety, June 21, 2002, p. 6.

Denver Post, April 2, 2001, p. E3.

Entertainment Weekly, April 14, 1995, p. 70; January 28, 2005, p. 52.

New Republic, May 20, 1996, p. 26.

Newsweek, January 24, 2005, p. 64.

New York Times, July 12, 1990; September 14, 1994; November 9, 2001.

People, July 8, 1991, p. 73; October 10, 1994, p. 120; April 18, 2005, pp. 95-96.

Philadelphia Inquirer, February 16, 2005.

Time, May 20, 1991, p. 64.

Variety, January 17, 2005, p. 34.

—Carol Brennan

Kim Mulkey-Robertson

John Gress/Reuters/Landov

Head coach for the Baylor University women's basketball team

Born Kim Mulkey, May 17, 1962, in Hammond, LA; daughter of Les and Dru (a medical assistant) Mulkey; married Randy Robertson (a public relations firm owner), 1987; children: Mackenzie, Kramer. *Education:* Louisiana Tech University, bachelor's degree (summa cum laude), 1984.

Addresses: *Office*—c/o Baylor Athletic Department, 150 Bear Run, Waco, TX 76711.

Career

Basketball player, Louisiana Tech University, 1980-84; played for South team at Olympic Festival, Syracuse, NY, 1981; member of USA Basketball Select Team, 1982; member of U.S. women's basketball team, Pan Am Games, 1983; member of U.S. Olympic women's basketball team, 1984; assistant coach, Louisiana Tech, 1985-96, then associate head coach, 1996-2000; head coach, Baylor University, 2000—.

Awards: Gold medal winner (women's basketball, South team), Olympic Festival, Syracuse, NY, 1981; Academic All-American, 1983, 1984; gold medal winner (women's basketball), Pan Am Games, 1983; NCAA Postgraduate Scholarship winner, 1984; James Corbett Award for Louisiana's College Athlete of the Year, 1984; Frances Pomeroy Naismith Small Player of the Year, 1984; gold medal winner (women's basketball), Summer Olympic Games, 1984; inducted into National High School of Fame, 1985; inducted into Louisiana High School Hall of Fame, 1986; inducted into Louisiana Sports Writer Hall of Fame, 1990; inducted into Louisiana Tech Athletics Hall of Fame, 1992; inducted into Women's Basketball Hall of Fame, 2000; National Coach of the Year Award, *Real Sport Magazine,* 2001; named Big 12 Coach of the Year, *Dallas Morning News,* 2001; named Big 12 Coach of the Year, *Waco Tribune-Herald,* 2001; Senior College Coach of the Year Award, Texas Association of Basketball Coaches, 2002; inducted into CoSIDA Academic All-America Hall of Fame, 2003; named Big 12 Coach of the Year, Big 12 Athletic Conference, 2005; Winged Foot Award, National Athletic Club, 2005.

Sidelights

A naturally talented athlete, Kim Mulkey-Robertson found success as both a player and a coach. Mulkey-Robertson focused on the sport of basketball by the time she was in high school. A state champion on the high school level, Mulkey-Robertson came into the national spotlight as a college player at Louisiana Tech. She began her coaching career at Louisiana Tech as well. Though expected to become the head coach at her alma mater, a contract disagreement led to her assuming head duties at Baylor University. Within five years, she turned around that school's struggling program and coached her team to the NCAA women's national championship in 2005. With that win, she became the first woman to win the NCAA tournament as both a coach and player.

Born on May 17, 1962, in Hammond, Louisiana, Mulkey-Robertson was raised in rural Tickfaw, Louisiana, with her younger sister, Tammy. Both girls were active in sports from an early age. Their father, Les, taught them several sports. Mulkey-Robertson particularly took to competition, primarily in baseball and basketball. She and her sister played Little League because there was no softball program for girls.

As a child, Mulkey-Robertson focused much of her attention on baseball. By the time she was 12 years old, she was considered the best baseball player in her area, better than all the boys. When the local Little League held its draft, she was selected first as a 12 year old. She played well and made a regional all-star team. Mulkey-Robertson garnered media attention at the game, which was played in another municipality, because she was told by the local commissioner that she was not allowed to participate in the game because of her gender. To protect her interests, her father obtained a restraining order so the game could not be played. However, Mulkey-Robertson decided that the game should go on and did not want the order enforced. She supported her team by cheering for them near the dugout. Her team won and dedicated the victory to her. Mulkey-Robertson never had to face this problem again when she moved up to the Pony League for older players.

In addition to her athletic skills, Mulkey-Robertson was also an outstanding student who never missed a day of school. This academic success continued when she entered Hammond High School. By the time she began high school, Mulkey-Robertson stopped playing baseball and focused on basketball. She dominated the girls' basketball program for the whole of her high school career, 1976 to 1980. In addition to being a four-year letter winner, Mulkey-Robertson was a four-year starter. Her team also won the state championship four straight times. Mulkey-Robertson averaged 38 points per game and set a high scoring record. She also set a national scoring record by netting 4,075 points over the course of her high school career. Mulkey-Robertson was not only a great athlete; she maintained a 4.0 grade point average and was the valedictorian of her class.

After high school, Mulkey-Robertson entered Louisiana Tech because it had the best women's basketball program in the state at the time. She was re-cruited by other schools, including the future powerhouse Louisiana State University, as well. As in high school, Mulkey-Robertson played all four years for the Lady Techsters and was a four-year letter winner. Though she only stood 5'4", Mulkey-Robertson did not play like women were expected to, but with a brashness. A great passer, she was able to pass the ball behind her back, between her legs and sometimes between opponents. Her play, as well as her blonde French braids, earned Mulkey-Robertson national attention.

In sum, the team's record during the four years that Mulkey-Robertson played was 130 wins and only six losses. She won several awards as a senior, including the first Frances Pomeroy Naismith Award in 1984. This award was given to the best basketball player in the nation under the height of 5'7". Mulkey-Robertson also earned her bachelor's degree in 1984, and won the NCAA Postgraduate Scholarship. As Bill Campbell wrote in the *Times-Picayune,* "When she was 21 years old, Mulkey was a darling of the women's basketball world—the tiny point guard in the pigtails who set national high school scoring records before leading her college team to national championships and her country to Olympic gold."

While Mulkey-Robertson was a college student-athlete, she also participated in several international competitions and won regularly. In 1981, she won a gold medal with the South Team, while playing at the Olympic Festival held in Syracuse, New York. The following year, Mulkey-Robertson was a member of the USA Basketball select team. In 1983, she played on the American team which won gold at the Pan Am Games, which were held in Caracus, Venezuela. At the 1984 Summer Olympics, which were held in Los Angeles, California, Mulkey-Robertson played on the U.S. women's basketball team, which also won gold.

After the Olympics, Mulkey-Robertson returned to Louisiana Tech to begin graduate school. She was studying business and did not intend to become a coach. However, during class one day, she was taken out of a class by escort to meet with the university's president on the matter. The president asked her to work with Leon Barmore, who was hired to be the Lady Techsters' head coach in 1985.

Mulkey-Robertson served as an assistant coach for Louisiana Tech's women's basketball team from 1985 to 1996. In 1996, she was promoted to associate head coach. During her coaching run at Louisiana Tech, the team's record was impressive. The

Lady Techsters had a record of 430 wins and 68 losses. Seven times, the team made it to the Final Four in the NCAA tournament. Louisiana Tech won only one NCAA title, in 1988. They lost in the championship game three times: in 1987, 1994, and 1998.

During this time, Mulkey-Roberton's personal life was also transformed. She married Randy Robertson in 1987. Like his wife, Robertson had been an athlete at Louisiana Tech, playing for the football team as a quarterback. He was the owner of a public relations firm. The couple had two children, Mackenzie and Kramer. Mulkey-Robertson brought her kids with her when she had to travel as long as it did not have to interfere with their attendance at school.

Mulkey-Robertson thought she and her family would be at Louisiana Tech for life. Barmore had selected her to be his successor as head coach when he chose to retire. In 2000, when Barmore retired, the school offered Mulkey-Robertson a four-year contract. She was offended by that offer. She wanted a five-year deal, which she believed was standard among coaches. Mulkey-Robertson told Kathleen Nelson of the *St. Louis Post-Dispatch*, "I felt I deserved loyalty. If I had been given a five-year offer, I would have stayed. Thank God for unanswered prayers. Baylor was the school that called."

Other schools had made offers to her while she worked at Louisiana Tech. Schools such as Texas A&M, Missouri, South Carolina, and Oklahoma had shown interest. Mulkey-Robertson instead signed on to be head coach of a program without the same prestige of Louisiana Tech nor a reputation for winning. On April 4, 2000, she was named head coach of Baylor University in Waco, Texas, with the five-year deal she wanted. The contract allegedly was worth about one million dollars over the life of the contract. Mulkey-Robertson was only the fourth coach in the team's history.

Mulkey-Robertson slowly built the Baylor Lady Bears into winners. The season before she was hired, the team won only seven games. Her first order of business was recruiting players, which was tough in a state with several prestigious programs. This problem would plague her throughout the early days of her coaching career with Baylor, but she worked hard with the players she did get. These new players were not necessarily stars in the programs they came from, but Mulkey-Robertson worked with the athletes to make them winners. She also helped returning players to improve and think better of themselves as athletes. Mulkey-Robertson gave the team a new attitude, one that embraced winning.

In the first season in which she was head coach, Mulkey-Robertson turned the team around. The Lady Bears won 21 games that first season and were given an invitation to the NCAA tournament. Baylor, however, was knocked out of the tournament in the first round. They won a similar amount of games in 2001-02, and made it to the second round of the NCAA tournament in 2002. Mulkey-Robertson's team got better and better in 2003 through 2005. In 2003, the Lady Bears were not invited to the NCAA tournament; instead, they went to the WNIT (Women's National Invitational Tournament). They made the finals, but lost in the final round. In 2004, the Lady Bears returned to the NCAA tournament and made the round of 16.

While Mulkey-Robertson was building a worthwhile program at Baylor, she also had to deal with related negative public perception and misfortune. The men's basketball team at Baylor suffered a horrific tragedy in 2003 when one player, Carlton Dotson, was arrested for the murder of his teammate, Patrick Dennehy. In addition, it was revealed that head coach Dave Bliss had tried to hide the improper benefits given to Dennehy by spreading rumors that the deceased player had been a drug dealer. Bliss resigned, as did the school's athletic director Tom Stanton, and the Baylor name was dragged through the mud. The success of Mulkey-Robertson's team helped heal these wounds and improve the Baylor name. Mulkey-Robertson commented to Lori Riley of the *Hartford Courant*, "We're a positive in Waco. There's a lot of good there."

Mulkey-Robertson had her moment of triumph which helped overshadow these issues in 2005. Her Lady Bears, led by Sophia Young and Steffanie Blackmon, won the 2005 NCAA women's basketball tournament. They defeated Michigan State University in the championship game by the score of 84 to 62 at the RCA Dome in Indianapolis, Indiana, after posting a regular season record of 33 wins and three losses. The team had made it to the finals by defeating three number-one seeded teams along the way.

Through the 2004-05 season, the Lady Bears under Mulkey-Robertson had an impressive record, with 131 wins and 38 losses. After the success of the 2004-05 season, Mulkey-Robertson signed a six-year contract extension, which included an increase in salary, with Baylor. This deal would make her Baylor's coach through 2011.

With all her success at Baylor, her hometown had not forgotten her. Tickfaw named a street "Kim Mulkey Drive." Yet economic realities have not been lost on her and she rewards loyalty with loyalty. Joseph Sanchez of the *Denver Post* quoted Mulkey-Robertson as saying, "Louisiana Tech was my heart and soul for 19 years, and I'll always want to see Louisiana Tech do well. But times have changed. The bigger conferences are paying higher salaries; the teams in the bigger conferences are getting more exposure. It's just a different era."

Sources

Periodicals

Boston Globe, April 3, 2005, p. C13; April 6, 2005, p. F8.

Denver Post (Denver, CO), April 1, 2005, p. D10.

Hartford Courant (Hartford, CT), April 6, 2005, p. C1.

Houston Chronicle, April 5, 2000, p. 8; April 1, 2005, p. 10.

St. Louis Post-Dispatch (St. Louis, MO), April 3, 2005, p. C3.

San Antonio Express-News (San Antonio, TX), March 14, 2002, p. 9C.

Times-Picayune (New Orleans, LA), June 22, 1993, p. E1; April 3, 2005, p. 29; April 5, 2005, p. 4; April 6, 2005, p. 1.

USA Today, March 31, 2005, p. 3C.

Online

"Kim Mulkey-Robertson," Baylor University, http://baylorbears.collegesports.com/sports/w-baskbl/mtt/mulkey-robertson_kim00.html (August 8, 2005).

—*A. Petruso*

Yoshitomo Nara

Artist

Born December 5, 1959, in Hirosaki, Aomori Prefecture, Japan. *Education:* Studied at Musashino Art University, 1979-81; Aichi Prefectural University of Fine Arts and Music, Nagoya, Japan, B.F.A., 1985, M.F.A., 1987; graduated from Kunstakademie Düsseldorf (German State Academy of Arts), Düsseldorf, Germany, 1993.

Addresses: *Contact*—Hara Museum of Contemporary Art, 4-7-25 Kitashinagawa, Shinagawa-ku, Tokyo, Japan; 140-0001; Marianne Boesky Gallery, 535 W. 22nd St., New York, NY 10011; Blum & Poe, 2754 S. La Cienega Blvd., Los Angeles, CA 90034. *Home*—Tokyo, Japan. *Website*—http://www.happyhour.jp.

Career

Lived and worked as a professional artist and instructor in Köln, Germany, 1993-2000; visiting professor, University of California at Los Angeles, 1998; based out of studio in Tokyo, Japan, 2000—.

Awards: Award for Artist, Nagoya City, Japan, 1995.

Sidelights

Japanese artist Yoshitomo Nara specializes in flat, two-dimensional drawings depicting sulky, big-headed cartoonesque characters who are cunningly cute yet corrosive. His pictures, clearly full of angst, pack a warped visual punch that appeals to a broad range of viewers. During the 1990s, Nara burst onto the international art scene, showing his work at solo exhibitions across the globe, from Tokyo and Berlin to New York and Los Angeles. Within a few years he had achieved cult status for his work, which is admired by art critics and punk kids alike. Nearly every fan can afford a Nara piece to fit their budget. Fine art pieces can top $20,000, while Nara key chains cost just a few dollars.

Some critics have been at a loss to describe the Nara phenomenon. Most often they admit it is sometimes hard to take Nara's work seriously, but on the other hand, they acknowledge it is also hard to dismiss. Art critic Kristin Chambers, writing on the San Jose Museum of Art website, had this to say: "Exploring Nara's realm and its inhabitants can be as bewildering and delightful as taking one of Alice's trips through Wonderland." She went on to describe Nara's characters as "devilish, fairy-tale strange, and not afraid to embrace the experiences of anxiety, fear, and escape into fantasy that define human existence at any age."

Nara was born on December 5, 1959, in Hirosaki, a rural village in Northern Japan. Though he was the youngest of three boys, Nara's upbringing more closely resembled that of an only child because his brothers were so much older. In addition, Nara's parents kept busy work schedules, as did many adults in post-World War II Japan, an era of fast-paced economic development. Because his parents worked so much—and because he was so introverted and sensitive—Nara spent most of his time alone with his imagination, his pets, and the television for company. He liked to watch cartoons, particularly *Astro Boy, Gigantor,* and *Speed Racer.* He also amused himself by painting and drawing.

There were other children to play with, but Nara was not outgoing and struggled to fit in. He recalled being so sensitive that when a group of boys stormed off to smash an anthill, he could not join them. While Nara has acknowledged that his lonely childhood influences his art, he said that he did not realize he was lonely when he was young. "When you are a kid, you are too young to know you are lonely, sad, and upset," he told *ARTnews'* Kay Itoi. "Now I know I was."

During high school Nara took a nude-sketching class and realized that drawing was a natural outlet for his fertile imagination. He finally found a way to express all that he held inside. Speaking to the Tokyo-based *Asahi Shimbun* newspaper, Nara described his awakening this way: "It was just copying what I saw on the paper by drawing lines. Everyone does the same thing, but I found my originality there."

From 1979 to 1981, Nara took art classes at the Musashino Art University. Next, he studied at the Aichi Prefectural University of Fine Arts and Music in Nagoya, Japan, earning his bachelor of fine arts in 1985 and his master of fine arts in 1987. Then it was off to Düsseldorf, Germany, to study at the Kunstakademie Düsseldorf, also known as the German State Academy of Arts. After graduating in 1993, Nara stayed in Germany, setting up a studio in Köln. That same year he received a small amount of exposure after drawing promotional poster art for the Swedish film *Letta Leaves Home.*

During the years he spent in Köln, Nara refined his skills and began exploring his own vision of art by plumbing the depths of his subconscious. His first sulky-girl portraits materialized during this time. Nara said that his artwork comes through him and reflects his accumulated past. "When I make the drawings, I don't think of it," he told *Asahi Shimbun.* "My brush just moves unconsciously."

After completing his art training Nara resisted taking his portfolio around to galleries or entering contests because he still felt tentative about the vocation. "All through university I was never sure that I wanted to be an artist by profession," Nara remarked in an article printed in the *Japanese Art Scene Monitor.* "I went to art school because I could draw. It was when I was teaching art ... and I was telling all the students that '*this* is how artists should be,' and so on, it occurred to me that one could draw as a way of finding oneself." Following this realization, Nara made a long-term commitment to the profession.

Nara's first big break came in the late 1990s when he joined Japanese cult novelist Banana Yoshimoto on a book project. Around this time Nara also created the CD jacket artwork for The Star Club, a Japanese punk band, as well as for Japanese girl band Shonen Knife. These projects exposed Nara's work to a broader audience. He continued teaching and in 1998 worked as a visiting professor at the University of California at Los Angeles.

In 2000 Nara packed up his studio in Köln and returned to Japan, setting up shop in a two-story Tokyo warehouse. Though the place was cold in the winter and hot in the summer, the high ceilings and open floor plan made it an ideal workplace. In the early 2000s, photographer Mie Morimoto spent six months with Nara and produced a documentary book titled, *Birth and Present: A Studio Portrait of Yoshitomo Nara.* In the book, Morimoto made notations about Nara's lifestyle. She said Nara uses the second floor of the building for working and living space. The first floor is for storage and also has a kitchen; however, Morimoto said that Nara generally ate dinner at his assistant's neighboring home or at local fast-food restaurants; rarely did he cook his own meal.

Morimoto also described Nara's unflinching ability to press on with work. "He plays deafeningly loud punk rock as he works through the night and sleeps whenever he chooses to. In his daily routine, life and work have become one." She also noted that when Nara is preparing for an exhibition, he works without ceasing. As soon as he finishes one piece, he is on to the next and seems irritated at the time lost priming a canvas.

Over the years Nara has developed his own distinctive style. Common motifs include children who have fallen into water, or into a hole. Animals, particularly Snoopy-like dogs, also populate his work. His children are typically bulbous-headed with crescent eyes and cynical grins. His work shows a heavy influence from a childhood spent watching 1960s-era cartoons in that his characters are simplistic and rounded like the early animations found in *Speed Racer* as opposed to the more contemporary anime, where characters are detailed and angular.

Some of Nara's characters smoke cigarettes or wield tiny knives. Steam emerges from their heads and expletives—written in either German, English, or Japanese—are common. Writing in *Metro*, art critic Sharon Mizota described the artist's oeuvre this way: "Nara's children, with their oversized heads, milk-saucer eyes and blunt, pawlike limbs, look infantile and defenseless, but far from innocent. They sneak sidelong glances and grimace knowingly, hinting at some secret transgression or imagined subversion." Mizota continued her description by saying, "Their faces, at first placid and cute, betray an indignant, yet impotent anger." The pieces, however, do not just show the angry side of human nature. They exude a clear understanding of the duality of being—Nara's children are both sweet and sour, happy and sad, generous and mean, all at the same time.

A recurring character in Nara's work is a girl called Ramona, named in honor of the New York punk band the Ramones. Rebellion can almost be seen percolating inside her. The punk movement has always played an important role in Nara's life. Not only does he listen to punk music while he works, he also got his start doing cover art for punk bands, which are typically adored by disaffected youth. In the same way that punk bands use their music to convey their displeasure with the status quo, Nara uses his characters to send the same message. At several shows he includes an installation titled *My Drawing Room,* which resembles his workspace at home, complete with personal belongings and sketches he keeps in his work area. The display even features a replica of his desk with a note written in German which translates to: "For always I want to be a punk, for always I want to punk, because there still is something I must do."

Nara's other influences include Renaissance painting, Japanese pop culture, and minimalism. He also likes the music of The Star Club and Neil Young and takes song titles from favorite bands as an inspiration for his own titles. Nara has titled works *I just want to be a cosmic cowboy* and *My 13th Sad Day.* Other pieces include *Melting Moon/Moon Children,* which features an assortment of vacant-faced, three-dimensional baby heads sitting atop a large, white plate. The angle of each head is different, each portraying a distinct phase of the moon. Another piece is called *Slash With a Knife.* In this one, an overly wide-eyed child, complete with miniature knife, snickers at viewers, leaving them to wonder if the child is about to make a nasty remark. While many of Nara's pieces convey anger and sorrow, he also tackles the emotion of hope. *Sprout the Ambassador* is one such piece. This Nara child is shown offering green sprouts, representing hope, in each hand.

Besides oil and acrylic paintings, Nara crafts installations that take up whole rooms. He makes the figures for these pieces out of fiber-reinforced plastic. One example is 1994's *Hula Hula Garden.* This piece features three kid-sized dolls, lying face down on the floor looking at children's books. The floor is littered with small, plastic flowers. The walls are bedecked with animal-child heads mounted like hunting trophies. They feature names like *Upset Kitty, Puffy Girl* and *Grinning Little Bunny.* Nara usually installs this piece in a closed room, forcing viewers to look through low, tiny windows, thus evoking a sense of those childhood worlds adults cannot enter.

In 2004 and 2005 a Nara retrospective titled *Yoshitomo Nara: Nothing Ever Happens,* toured the United States, making stops at several venues, including the San Jose Museum of Art in California, the Contemporary Art Museum in St. Louis, the Institute of Contemporary Art at the University of Pennsylvania, and the Contemporary Museum in Honolulu, Hawaii. It contained pieces Nara created between 1997 and 2004, many of which had never been on display. The show featured Nara's sulky kids on huge, nearly six-foot plates, as well as drawings and large-scale sculptural relief.

Because Nara has found a way to straddle the line between fine art and illustrator, he has earned a legion of fans from serious art collectors to punk youth. His art is accessible, with his characters appearing on gallery and museum walls, as well as on T-shirts, key chains, CD cases, ashtrays, and clocks. Nara's cult status became evident when television characters on *Dawson's Creek* and *Buffy the Vampire Slayer* appeared in Nara T-shirts.

Despite his raging success, Nara still feels like a lonely kid sometimes and finds it hard to work. When he hits such lows, he reads positive exhibition comments until he feels well enough to go back to work. For inspiration, Nara also keeps little notes tacked to his studio walls with messages such as "It's only drawing but I like it!." To remember to work freely and without pressure, just for the joy of it, Nara keeps these words posted: "Never forget your beginner's spirit." It is a state of mind he tries to dwell in daily as he works.

Selected solo exhibitions

It's a Little Wonderful House, Love Collection Gallery, Nagoya, Japan, 1984.
Wonder Room, Gallery Space to Space, Nagoya, Japan, 1984.
Recent Works, Gallery Space to Space, Nagoya, Japan, 1985.
Goethe Institut, Düsseldorf, Germany, 1988.
Innocent Being, Galerie Humanite, Nagoya and Tokyo, Japan, 1988.

Irrlichtteater, Stuttgart, Germany, 1989.

Galerie d'Eendt, Amsterdam, 1990, 1991.

Cogitationes cordium, Galerie Humanite, Nagoya, Japan, 1991.

Harmlos, Galerie im Kinderspielhaus, Düsseldorf, Germany, 1991.

Drawings, Galerie d'Eendt, Amsterdam, Netherlands, 1992.

Loft Gallery, Deventer, The Netherlands, 1992.

Galerie Johnen & Schöttle, Köln, Germany, 1993.

Hula Hula Garden, Galerie d'Eendt, Amsterdam, Netherlands, 1994.

Project for Gunma, Gunma Prefectural Museum of Modern Art, Takasaki, Japan, 1998.

Pacific Babies, Blum & Poe, Santa Monica, CA, 1998.

Cup Kids, Museum of Contemporary Art, Nagoya, Japan, 1998.

Empty Surprise, Artium, Fukuoka, Japan, 1999.

Lonesome Puppy, Tomio Koyama Gallery, Tokyo, Japan, 1999.

Galerie Johnen & Schöttle, Köln, Germany, 1999.

Sleepless Night, Galerie Michael Zink, Regensburg, Germany, 1999.

Drawing Days, Hakutosha, Nagoya, Japan, 1999.

Lonesome Puppy, Hakutosha, Nagoya, Japan, 1999.

Screen Memory, Tomio Koyama Gallery, Tokyo, Japan, 1999.

Pacific Babies, Blum & Poe, Santa Monica, CA, 1999.

Tomio Koyama Gallery, Tokyo, Japan, 1999.

Happy Hour, Hakutosha, Nagoya, Japan, 1999.

Done Did, Parco Gallery, Nagoya, Japan, 1999.

Pave Your Dreams, Marianne Boesky Gallery, New York, NY, 1999.

Projektraum Berlin, Berlin, Germany, 1999.

Blum & Poe, Santa Monica, CA, 2000.

Walk On, Museum of Contemporary Art, Chicago, IL, 2000.

Empty Fortress, Galerie Johnen & Schöttle, Köln, Germany, 2000.

Lullaby Supermarket, Santa Monica Museum of Art, Santa Monica, CA, 2000.

Stephen Friedman Gallery, London, England, 2000.

I Don't Mind if You Forget Me, Yokohama Museum of Art, Japan, 2001.

Centre National de l'estampe et de l'arte imprimè, Chatou, France, 2002.

Cleveland Center for Contemporary Art, Cleveland, OH, 2003.

Yoshitomo Nara: From the Depth of my Drawer, Hara Museum of Contemporary Art, Tokyo, Japan, 2004.

Yoshitomo Nara: Nothing Ever Happens (traveling exhibition in United States), Institute of Contemporary Art at the University of Pennsylvania; San Jose Museum of Art, San Jose, CA; Contemporary Art Museum, St. Louis, MO, all 2004.

Johnen & Schöttle, Köln, Germany, 2004.

Blum & Poe, Los Angeles, 2004.

Yoshitomo Nara: Nothing Ever Happens, The Contemporary Museum, Honolulu, HI, 2005.

Gallery Zink and Gegner, Munich, Germany, 2005.

Selected group exhibitions

Two Person Show, Gallery Denega, Hirosaki, 1984.

Paranoia, Westbeth Gallery, Nagoya, Japan, 1984.

Five Person's Musical Band, Love Collection Gallery, Nagoya, Japan, 1985.

Sense of Vision and Touch, Westbeth Gallery, Nagoya, Japan, 1985.

Present '86, Gallery NAF, Nagoya, Japan, 1986.

Each Person's Expression of Space, Gifu Prefectural Art Museum, Japan, 1986.

New Artists in Nagoya, Westbeth Gallery, Nagoya, Japan, 1987.

Feeling House, Mie Prefectural Art Museum, Japan, 1988.

Mensch und Technik, Nixdorf A.G., Düsseldorf, Germany, 1989.

Acqua Strana, Galerie Ulla Sommers, Düsseldorf, Germany, 1990.

Brille, Galerie Pentagon, Köln, Germany, 1990.

Pack, SA-IN Gallery, Pusan, Korea, 1991.

4th Nagoya Contemporary Art Fair, Nagoya, Japan, 1991.

Tijdeljk Asiel, Arti et Amicitiae, Amsterdam, Netherlands, 1992.

In Situ, Theateraan het Vrijthof, Maastricht, Belgium, 1993.

Harvest '93, Haus Bockforf, Kempen, Germany, 1993.

Animals, Galerie Tanya Rumpff, Haarlem, Netherlands, 1993.

Partners, Galerie d'Eendt, Amsterdam, Netherlands, 1993.

Art Against AIDS, Art Cologne, Köln, Germany, 1994.

Harvest Kempen-Nagoya, Hakutosha, Japan, 1994.

Harvest '94, Haus Bockdorf, Kempen, Germany, 1994.

My Room is Your Room, 7th Nagoya Contemporary Art Fair, Nagoya, Japan, 1994.

Gunma Biennale, Gunma Prefectural Museum of Modern Art, Japan, 1995.

Osaka Contemporary Art Center, Japan, 1995.

Takeoffs, Guggenheim Gallery, Chapman University, Orange, CA, 1995.

The Future of Paintings, 1995, Osaka Contemporary Art Center, Osaka, Japan, 1995.

Düsseldorf-andere Ort, Orangerie Schlos Brake, Lemgo, Germany, 1995.

POSITIV, Museum am Ostwall, Dortmund, Germany, 1995.

Book and Weight, Gallery Kuranuki, Osaki, Japan, 1995.

That Figures, Galerie d'Eendt, Amsterdam, 1995.

Art x = , SAM Museum, Osaka, Japan, 1995.

Endless Happiness, SCAI The Bathhouse, Tokyo, Japan, 1995.

Drawing Chat, Shinanobashi Gallery, Mie Prefectural Art Museum, Osaka, Japan, 1995.

Gallery d'Eendt, Amsterdam, Netherlands, 1995.

Galerie & Ediciones Ginkgo, Madrid, Spain, 1997.

Drawing Show, Galerie d'Eendt, Amsterdam, Netherlands, 1997.

Japanese Contemporary Art Exhibition, National Museum of Contemporary Art, Seoul, Korea, 1997.

Dream of Existence, Municipal Museum of Art, Budapest, Hungary, 1997.

Tendance, Abbaye Saint-Andre Centre d'art Contemporain, Meymac, France, 1999.

Yoshitomo Nara and Hiroshi Sugito, Gallery Hakutosha, Nagoya, Japan, 1999.

Vergiss den Ball und spiel weiter, Nuremberg Kunsthalle, Nuremberg, Germany, 1999.

Almost Warm & Fuzzy: Childhood and Contemporary Art, Des Moines Art Center, Des Moines, IA, 1999.

Spellbound, Karyn Lovegrove Gallery, Los Angeles, CA, 1999.

Viewing Path, Saarbrucken Staatgalerie, Saarbrucken, Germany, 2000.

Continental Shift, Ludwig Forum, Aachen, Germany, 2000.

Dark Mirror from Japan, De Appel, Netherlands, 2000.

Presumed Innocent, Cape Musée d'art Contemporain, Bordeaux, France, 2000.

Super Flat, Parco Gallery, Tokyo, 2000.

Drawings 2000, Barbara Gladstone Gallery, New York, NY, 2000.

Marianne Boesky Gallery, New York, NY, 2000.

Super Flat, The MOCA Gallery at the Pacific Design Center, West Hollywood, CA, 2000.

My Reality: Contemporary Art and the Culture of Japanese Animation, Des Moines Art Center, Des Moines, IA, 2001.

Almost Warm & Fuzzy: Childhood and Contemporary Art, PS 1 Contemporary Art Center, Long Island, NY, 2001.

Painting at the Edge of the World, Walker Art Center, Minneapolis, MN, 2001.

Murakami/Nara, Tomio Koyama Gallery, Tokyo, Japan, 2001.

Galleri Nicolai Wallner, Copenhagen, Denmark, 2005.

Staatsgalerie Stuttgart, Stuttgart, Germany, 2005.

James Hyman Fine Art, London, 2005.

Yoshitomo Nara + graf "A to Z," Yoshii Brick Brew House, Hirosaki, Japan, 2006.

Sources

Books

Wada, Kyoko, editor, *Birth and Present: A Studio Portrait of Yoshitomo Nara,* Gingko Press, 2003.

Periodicals

ARTnews, May 1998, p. 153.

Asahi Shimbun (Tokyo, Japan), February 25, 2002.

Daily Yomiuri and the Yomiuri Shimbun (Tokyo, Japan), September 30, 2004.

St. Louis Post-Dispatch, December 2, 2004.

Online

"Little Triggers," *Metro,* http://www.metroactive.com/papers/metro/07.21.04/nara-0430.html (September 21, 2005).

"Yoshitomo Nara: From The Depth of My Drawer," *Metropolis Tokyo,* http://metropolis.japantoday.com/tokyo/547/art.asp (September 21, 2005).

"Yoshitomo Nara," Marianne Boesky Gallery, http://www.marianneboeskygallery.com/artist/yoshitomonara/index.html# (September 21, 2005).

"Yoshitomo Nara: Nothing Ever Happens," San Jose Museum of Art, http://www.sjmusart.org/content/exhibitions/upcoming/exhibition_info.phtml?itemID =147 (September 21, 2005).

"Yoshitomo Nara Reveals the Secret of Youth," *Japanese Art Scene Monitor,* http://www.jasm.australia .or.jp/jasm0109.pdf (September 21, 2005).

—*Lisa Frick*

Nursultan Nazarbayev

Reuters/Landov

President of Kazakhstan

Born Nursultan Abishevich Nazarbayev, in July, 1940, in Kazakhstan; married Sara Alpysovna; children: Dariga, Dinara, Aliya. *Education:* Earned degree in metallurgy, 1967.

Addresses: *Office*—Office of the President, Government of the Republic of Kazakhstan, Krasnyy Yar, Astana, Kazakhstan.

Career

Began career as a laborer at the Temirtau steelworks, Kazakhstan, c. late 1950s; joined Communist Party of Kazakhstan, early 1960s; worked as a technician and later an economist at a metalworks facility in Karaganda, Kazakhstan, after 1967; secretary for the Karaganda committee of the Communist Party, 1973-77, and of the Karaganda Regional Committee, 1977-79; Kazakh Communist Party (KCP), secretary of the Central Committee, 1979-84; chair, Kazakh Council of Ministers, 1984-89; appointed head of the KCP by Mikhail Gorbachev, 1989, and elected presidium chair of the Kazakh Supreme Soviet; named president of Kazakhstan by the legislature, April, 1990; resigned from the KCP, 1991; formed Socialist Party of Kazakhstan; elected Kazakhstan president by popular vote, 1991; presidency extended to the year 2000 by a 1995 referendum vote; re-elected, 1999 and 2005.

Sidelights

Nursultan Nazarbayev has ruled the Central Asian nation of Kazakhstan since the dissolution of the Soviet Union in 1991. A rare post-Soviet leader who has managed to maintain his leadership despite the immense political and economic turmoil of the intervening years, Nazarbayev is alternately described in the Western media as either a despot or a politically astute leader whose policies have helped his nation—the ninth largest in the world—prosper and remain at peace. Though Nazarbayev has engaged in some questionable maneuvers to ensure his grip on the presidency, he appears to be a well-liked leader among Kazakhs, and his country is poised to become one of the world's leading oil exporters by the year 2015.

Born Nursultan Abishevich Nazarbayev in 1940, the future president grew up in a village near Kazakhstan's border with Kyrgyzstan in the southeast. He came from a family of shepherds, a common line of work in the area and a historic legacy of the Kazakh people. A nomadic people descended from Turkic and Mongol invaders who conquered the steppes in medieval times, the Kazakhs emerged as a nation around the fifteenth century. A series of invasions in the nineteenth century brought the Kazakh republic under imperial Russian rule, along with much of the rest of Central Asia.

By the time Nazarbayev was born, Kazakhstan was officially known as the Kazakh Autonomous Soviet Socialist Republic, and was ruled by Moscow with an iron hand. The tribal Kazakhs had strongly re-sisted Russian domination over the years, and suffered heavy population losses in the decade before Nazarbayev's birth when they balked at the forced collectivization of their farm and pastoral lands. The area was industrialized, too, and it was at the massive Temirtau steelworks complex that Nazarbayev began his working life while still in his teens. He was an iron caster, and his long workday inside the overheated blast furnaces required him to drink salt water in order to maintain his body temperature.

Nazarbayev joined the Communist Party in the early 1960s, while studying toward a degree in metallurgy. Party membership was obligatory during the Soviet era for anyone who hoped for professional advancement in their careers, and after Nazarbayev graduated in 1967 he went to work at a metalworks facility in Karaganda, a large industrial city in the north of Kazakhstan. He began as a technician, and later became an economist. He was active in the Komsomol, the youth organization of the Communist Party, and became the local secretary of Karaganda's Communist Party committee in 1973. Four years later, he advanced to the post of secretary of the Karaganda Regional Committee of the Kazakh Communist Party (KCP).

After a stint as secretary of the KCP Central Committee from 1979 to 1984, Nazarbayev was appointed chair of the Kazakh Council of Ministers. He held this post until 1989, when Soviet leader Mikhail Gorbachev named him the new head of the KCP. His local party colleagues also elected him chair of the presidium of the Kazakh Supreme Soviet. But the Soviet Union was quickly disintegrating into political turmoil thanks to the fall of the Berlin Wall in 1989 and the declarations of independence made by the Soviet satellite states of Eastern Europe. In Kazakhstan, there had long been deep discontent with Moscow, most recently in clashes that occurred in the winter of 1986, when Soviet troops used force against protesters on the streets of Almaty, the capital.

In April of 1990, a newly convened Kazakh national legislature selected Nazarbayev to serve as president, and six months later declared its sovereignty as a republic within the Soviet Union. This was different than declaring independence, for some in the country—Nazarbayev among them—believed it would be better to ally with the powerful Soviet bloc than against it. This was crucial to the stability of Kazakhstan's economy, because at the time, nearly all of its exports went to Soviet-controlled lands.

The break with Soviet-style communism, however, was completed within a year, with Nazarbayev formally resigning his membership after hardliners within the party made an unsuccessful coup against Gorbachev. "Don't ask what we're building in Kazakhstan, communism or capitalism," he told journalist Robin Knight for a September of 1991 article in *U.S. News & World Report*. "I'm tired of this tedious question. We have believed in myths for too long. We now want to fling the doors wide open."

A few months later, in the wake of the dissolution of the Soviet Union, Kazakhstan declared its independence. It joined the newly formed Commonwealth of Independent States (CIS) with Russia, Ukraine, Georgia, and seven other former Soviet republics, and elections were held that same month, in December of 1991 Nazarbayev ran unopposed, and was elected president. He continued to maintain a cordial alliance with Moscow, but at the same time, courted favor with the West by dismantling the nuclear test facilities located in Kazakhstan.

The year 1995 marked a turning point in Nazarbayev's political career. Results from legislative elections were declared invalid by the Kazakh Constitutional Court, and the country's parliament was ordered dissolved until new elections could be held. Nazarbayev approved the dissolution, partly because he was unhappy with the body's lack of support for his policies. He assumed legislative powers himself, also known as rule by decree. A new constitution was approved by referendum, but vote fraud was rumored to have occurred. The new constitution gave him additional powers, and another referendum that year approved a measure to extend his presidency until the year 2000.

Such political tactics caused some international political analysts to question whether democracy had taken hold in the country, but Nazarbayev courted favor with both Russia and the West. He allowed international oil companies, for example, into the rich oil fields in Tengiz and Kashagan. The Kashagan deposits, discovered in 1979, comprise the second largest oil field in the world, and also contain vast natural gas reserves. ChevronTexaco, ExxonMobil, and government-owned entities of Russia and Kazakhstan are partners in developing the Tengiz field, which is expected to reach full capacity of 700,000 barrels a day by 2010. Construction of a massive pipeline route to take the oil to the West, via a longer Caspian Sea route instead of through Iran, also began.

Nazarbayev called the next presidential election a year early, in January of 1999, and this time the fairness of the ballot was undisputed: his daughter,

Dariga, was his nominal opponent, but her slogan was, roughly translated, "there is no alternative to the current president." She also controlled the state-run news agency. Nazarbayev's most credible opponent, the former prime minister Akezhan Kazhegeldin, was declared ineligible to run because of a political meeting he attended. Candidates also needed to post a $30,000 deposit to register for a place on the ballot, an amount that would be forfeited if they lost. To the surprise of few, Nazarbayev won another seven-year term with 78 percent of the vote. The Communist Party candidate, Serikbolsyn Abdildin, finished in second place with a little more than 13 percent.

Thanks to the country's oil wealth, Kazakhstan became the first of the 15 former Soviet republics to repay its debt to the International Monetary Fund. Its economy grew nine percent in 2004 and 2005, and petroleum-industry analysts predicted that the country will enter the list of the world's top ten oil exporting nations by 2015. Nazarbayev funneled some of that new wealth into a new capital, called Astana, which featured nationalist paeans to Kazakh history and to his leadership, too. The heavily restricted Kazakh press, meanwhile, reported little on the 2005 indictment in U.S. federal court in New York City of James Giffen, a U.S. citizen who had worked as a consultant to the Kazakh oil ministry. Giffen was charged with handing out some $84 million in cash payments to Nazarbayev and two other top officials, including the former prime minister, when the contracts with Chevron and Exxon for oil rights in the country were in negotiation. Nazarbayev's political enemies claim he has secreted his windfall away in private Swiss bank accounts.

Kazakhstan's next presidential elections were scheduled for December 4, 2005. Again, human-rights groups charged Nazarbayev's regime with engaging in underhanded tactics to silence genuine political discourse, a claim that took a sinister turn when his main adversary, a former government minister named Zamanbek Nurkadilov who had promised to speak publicly about government corruption, was found shot to death three weeks before the election. Nazarbayev won the election with more than 90 percent of the vote, and was sworn into office on January 11, 2006.

Despite his authoritarian ways, Nazarbayev is tolerated and even respected by many citizens, according to Western journalists, who also report that there are visible signs of the country's newfound prosperity, especially in the main urban centers. Nazarbayev's youngest daughter, Aliya N. Nazarbayeva, constructed a grand spa in Almaty, the former capital and largest city, that was modeled on Egypt's famed temple of Luxor. When it opened for business in March of 2005, an annual family membership could be bought for a sum of *tenge*, Kazakhstan's unit of currency, that approached $8,000, about twice what an average worker takes home annually. Her sister, Dariga, left the media business to form a political party, Asar ("All Together") and was elected to parliament in 2004.

Dariga Nazarbayev was widely quoted in the Western media for speaking out against the official reaction to British-born comic Sacha Baron Cohen around the same time of the 2005 election. Cohen stars in an HBO sketch-comedy series, *Da Ali G Show*, in multiple roles. One of his characters is a fictional journalist from Kazakhstan, Borat Sagdiyev. On his reporting travels across the United States, Borat makes jokes about his homeland, often citing the rampant drunkenness and polygamous nature of its men, and occasionally mentioning the Kazakh national beverage, which he claims is fermented horse urine. The most popular drink in the country is actually kumys, made from fermented horse milk, which was first made in the thirteenth century and survives as a legacy of the formerly nomadic Kazakh lifestyle.

Borat's lewd blunders and racist remarks may serve, unfortunately, as the only image many Americans and Britons have of the Kazakh people, but Borat was beamed worldwide in November of 2005 when Cohen hosted the MTV Europe Music Awards in character as Borat. A spokesperson for the Kazakh Foreign Ministry objected to Cohen's character, asserting that the jibes were actually the work of anti-Kazakh elements, and even hinted that legal action might be forthcoming. In response, Cohen set up a website, borat.kz, which was blocked by the government agency that governs Internet domain usage in Kazakhstan. Dariga Nazarbayev voiced her dismay over the move, commenting that the borat.kz site "damaged our image much less than its closure, which was covered by all global news agencies," she was quoted as saying by the Canadian Broadcasting Company. "We should not be afraid of humour and we shouldn't try to control everything, I think."

Dariga Nazarbayev is considered one of the two possible successors to her father, the other being her cousin, Kairat Satybaldy, an executive with the state-run oil company, KazMunaiGaz. Others hope that Kazakhstan will successfully—and peacefully—transition into a genuine democracy. One of Nazarbayev's critics is U.S. Senator John McCain, who told Paul Starobin in the *Atlantic Monthly* that the United States "cannot support despotic governments and expect over time not to pay a heavy price."

Sources

Periodicals

Atlantic Monthly, December 2005, p. 98.
Christian Science Monitor, November 30, 2005, p. 20.
New York Times, December 23, 2005, p. C1.
Sunday Times (London, England), December 16, 1990.
Times (London, England), December 2, 2005, p. 2.

U.S. News & World Report, September 23, 1991, p. 45.

Online

"Daughter of Kazakhstan's President Defends Borat," CBC.com, http://www.cbc.ca/story/arts/national/2006/04/21/borat-kazakhstan-d efence.html?ref=rss (May 14, 2006).

—*Carol Brennan*

Angela Nissel

Photo by Ray Garcia. Courtesy of Angela Nissel.

Author and television writer

Born in 1974 in Philadelphia, PA; daughter of Jack and Gwen (a nurse) Nissel. *Education:* University of Pennsylvania, B.A., 1998.

Addresses: *Office*—c/o Author Mail, Random House, Villard Books, 299 Park Ave., New York, NY 10171.

Career

Began writing online journal while a college student, c. 1997; temporary receptionist in a law office and at the Internal Revenue Service; cofounder and site manager, Okayplayer.com, 1999; published book based on online journal entries, *The Broke Diaries: The Completely True & Hilarious Misadventures of a Good Girl Gone Broke*, 2001; *Scrubs*, television series staff writer, 2002—, story editor, 2004, consulting producer, c. 2006—; published second book, *Mixed: My Life in Black and White*, 2006.

Awards: Best New Website Award, Online Hip-Hop Awards, for Okayplayer.com, 2001.

Sidelights

Ahumorous online journal Angela Nissel wrote while an underfunded college student at the University of Pennsylvania launched her career as a writer. After a publisher approached her about turning the journal into a book two years after it was originally written, Nissel moved to Los Angeles and became a writer for the NBC television series *Scrubs*.

She later published a second book about her experiences as a person of mixed race, *Mixed: My Life in Black and White*.

Nissel was born in 1974 in Philadelphia, Pennsylvania, the daughter of Jack Nissel, a white man, and his wife, Gwen, a black woman and former militant member of the Black Panthers. Nissel's father left the family when she was eight years old and was not involved in her upbringing nor that of her younger brother. Gwen Nissel raised her children as a single mother on a nurse's salary in the southwestern part of the city. Nissel attended Catholic schools, and graduated from the Baldwin School.

In 1992, Nissel entered the University of Pennsylvania, where she studied medical anthropology. Her college years involved some difficulties. During her first year of college, she suffered from depression and had a brief stay in the psych ward. She later took semesters off on occasion to gather the funds to pay for school. By the time she reached her senior year, 1997-98, Nissel's financial difficulties seemed to crest.

During the summer of 1997, she returned to Philadelphia after doing an unpaid internship on the news program *Dateline NBC*. On her door was an eviction notice; she had used all the money she had to complete the internship. Nissel needed to do something for free to entertain herself while she finished school. She learned HTML by skipping class and going to the library, and used her new skills to write an online journal about being a starving college student. Nissel told Elizabeth Jones of the *Lantern* in an article published on the University Wire, "It seemed normal when I started writing them on the web, but the more I wrote the crazier things went."

Nissel wrote about what she did to make money, eat cheaply, and get free food and books, including some odd dates, stealing a textbook from a teaching assistant's office, and difficult banking situations. She also talked about her jobs as a babysitter, telemarketer, and her work-study positions. Nissel told Andrea Dingman of the *Daily Bruin* in an article published on the University Wire, "At first I was just writing it for myself, just a sane way to keep perspective on things and make myself laugh." But she came to realize that an audience was there.

Nissel graduated from University of Pennsylvania in 1998 and stopped writing in the journal a few months later. She began working as a temporary receptionist in a law office and at the Internal Revenue Service. In 1999, she co-founded her own website/web-based community, Okayplayer.com. The business created and managed websites for hip-hop and soul musicians like ?uestlove, whom Nissel had met years earlier when they both worked at a telemarketing firm when she was in high school. Nissel designed websites and served as site manager for the business. Okayplayer.com received 300,000 hits per day.

That same year, Nissel was approached by Villard Books about publishing her online journal. Skeptical at first, she finally agreed to a deal and spent two years preparing the journal for publication. After the book was published in 2001, she left her partner in charge of Okayplayer.com and focused on writing full time.

The compilation of journal entries was published as *The Broke Diaries: The Completely True & Hilarious Misadventures of a Good Girl Gone Broke.* In the edited version, Nissel discussed how to live cheaply like a college student does on a limited budget. Ramen noodles, she emphasizes, are a dietary staple. Nissel also describes some of the difficult situations her financial status got her in. Yet, throughout the text, she remains hopeful because she knows her poverty is only temporary because of her forthcoming degree. Many critics found the book poignant and funny. Reviewing *The Broke Diaries* in *USA Today*, Tara McKelvey wrote, "What makes Nissel's book shine is her unsentimental prose and wicked sense of humor."

Around the time *The Broke Diaries* was published, Nissel moved to Los Angeles to pursue writing. Initially, her goal was to turn the book into a screenplay or television series. While pursuing this ambition, Nissel began writing on a freelance basis for magazines. Through the sale of some of her personal items for cash on eBay, she met a television executive who helped her find an agent. The agent sent her book around and Nissel was given her choice of television shows for which to write.

Nissel decided to join the staff of *Scrubs*, a medical-based situation comedy which allowed her to use her college degree. She joined the writing staff of the NBC cult hit in 2002. By 2004, she was story editor on the show, and was later named consulting producer. Nissel penned several episodes, which aired in 2002, 2004, and 2006. While writing for *Scrubs*, Nissel worked on her second book, a memoir of growing up a biracial child in Philadelphia. She describes how she dealt with the questions and situations raised because she was of mixed race. *Mixed: My Life in Black and White* was published in 2006. Critics lauded the book and its author for her amusing take on sometimes-difficult life situations.

Nissel also continued to pursue getting *The Broke Diaries* as well as *Mixed* adapted for a visual media. Originally, *The Broke Diaries* was to be a feature film with the script co-written by Nissel and Aaron McGruder, the cartoonist responsible for *The Boondocks* comic strip. However, this project did not pan out.

Later, actress Halle Berry optioned both books. She intended to turn *The Broke Diaries* into an HBO film, but was also considering combining both books for a situation comedy pilot on HBO. Nissel was working on the HBO project, and decided not to write another book at least until the end of the run of *Scrubs*. She wanted her voice heard on television. Nissel told DeBorah B. Pryor of EURweb.com, "Books are my passion but I know how many people you can reach through TV; and being in there and being the only black writer in the room I know how powerful it is when I say 'no' to doing certain things. I want to be the person who can say 'yes' to doing certain things; getting shows on the air that I can look at and be proud of as a black woman."

Selected writings

The Broke Diaries: The Completely True & Hilarious Misadventures of a Good Girl Gone Broke, Villard Books (New York City), 2001.

Mixed: My Life in Black and White, Villard Books (New York City), 2006.

Sources

Books

Who's Who Among African Americans, 18th ed., Thomson Gale (Detroit, MI), 2005, p. 932.

Periodicals

Essence, April 2006, p. 72.

PR Newswire, February 12, 2003.

Publishers Weekly, January 30, 2006, p. 57.

Sunday News (Lancaster, PA), August 5, 2001, p. P5.

Toronto Sun, April 13, 2001, p. E23.

University Wire, April 16, 2001; May 9, 2001; June 28, 2001.

USA Today, April 12, 2001, p. 7D.

Online

"Angela Nissel," Internet Movie Database, http://www.imdb.com/name/nm1238485/ (May 1, 2006).

"Angela Nissel," Random House, http://www.randomhouse.com/author/results.pperl?authorid=22222 (May 1, 2006).

"Angela Nissel: Write On, Pts. 1 and 2," AllHipHop.com, http://www.allhiphop.com/Alternatives/?ID=300, http://www.allhiphop.com/Alternatives/?ID=297 (May 1, 2006).

"Hair Peace," Oprah.com, http://www.oprah.com/health/beauty/beauty_200604_flaws_350_105.jhtml (May 1, 2006).

"Memoir: *Mixed,* but Mixed Up No More," NPR.com, http://www.npr.org/templates/story/story.php?storyid=5306614 (May 1, 2006).

"*Mixed: My Life in Black and White*: Angela Nissel's new book reveals the drama of growing up Biracial," EURweb.com, http://www.eurweb.com/printable.cfm?id=25703 (May 1, 2006).

"The Official Bio," http://www.angelanissel.com/ (May 1, 2006).

"Poor Little Poor Girl," PhiladelphiaCitypaper.net, http://citypaper.net/articles/041201/ae.books.shtml (May 1, 2006).

—*A. Petruso*

Bob Nixon

Environmentalist and filmmaker

Born Robert Henry Nixon, c. 1954; son of Robert H.A. (an auto executive) and Agnes (a television show creator; maiden name, Eckhardt) Nixon; married Sarah Thorsby Guinan (a director of a film production company), October 29, 1994; children: Bobby, Maggie, Jack.

Addresses: *Office*—Earth Conservation Corps, First Street & Potomac Ave. SE, Washington, D.C. 20003. *Website*—http://www.ecc1.org.

Career

Produced ABC-TV's *American Sportsman* series, 1970s. Produced first film, *Gorillas in the Mist*, 1988. Producer and director of films, including: *Sea Turtles: Ancient Nomads*, 1988; *Amazon Diary*, 1989; *America the Beautiful*, 1990; *The Last Rivermen*, 1992; *Endangered Species*, 2004. Began hands-on environmental work, taking over leadership of the Earth Conservation Corps, 1992; chairman, Earth Conservation Corps, 2004—.

Awards: Harvard Foundation Award, 2001; Chesapeake Bay Foundation Environmental Educator of the Year, 2001; Saks Fifth Avenue and *Washington Life* magazine's Men and Women of Substance and Style Awards, 2004.

Sidelights

A self-taught environmentalist, Bob Nixon spent more than 15 years behind the camera lens producing films and television programs depicting some of the earth's most endangered ecosystems and species. In 1992, he stepped out from behind the camera, taking the reins of the Earth Conservation Corps (ECC), a nonprofit organization that teaches disadvantaged youth job skills by putting them to work cleaning up the environment. Since then, ECC members have attempted to restore the natural balance of the heavily polluted Anacostia River, which runs through the nation's capital. Nixon intended to spend a year on the project, but more than a dozen years later he remains the group's impassioned leader. "I came here because I thought, you know, point out the problem, and the cavalry would arrive and I'd go back to making feature films," he told CBS News correspondent Ed Bradley. "I'm still waiting for the cavalry, you know?"

Nixon was born around 1954. His father, Robert, was an executive with Chrysler and his mother, Agnes, created the famed daytime drama *All My Children*. Raised in a Philadelphia suburb, Nixon took an early interest in nature. He struggled through school—graduating next to last in his high school class—and believes he is dyslexic. Nixon aspired to be a wildlife photographer and relocated to England to study falconry, which is the ancient art of training raptors to hunt game. Afterward, he trained birds for film and television appearances. Through this work Nixon made connections in the entertainment industry and by 1976 was producing programming for ABC-TV's *American Sportsman* series.

In 1979, Nixon traveled to Rwanda to produce a documentary about famed zoologist Dian Fossey. Nixon asked the gorilla activist if he could make a movie about her life. Fossey told him yes, so long as he dedicated one year of his life to an environmental project. Fossey was murdered in 1985 and Nixon told her story in the 1988 feature film *Gorillas in the Mist*. Nixon co-produced the movie, which starred Sigourney Weaver. He also directed 1989's *Amazon Diary*, which earned an Academy Award nomination for best live-action short film.

Nixon's film career was budding in the early 1990s when he heard about the garbage-choked Anacostia River, which runs through Washington, D.C. Nixon decided that cleaning up the river would be his environmental project in honor of Fossey. Nixon left his sunny Malibu, California, home for Washington, D.C., and secured a $50,000 grant from the Coors Foundation. Next, he persuaded some young adults from an area housing project to help him haul thousands of tires from the foul-smelling water.

When Nixon arrived in 1992, the river's banks were so trash-filled that the water was not even visible from the shoreline in places. There was also a sewage problem. Following heavy rains, raw sewage flooded the river because the drainage channel—carrying both sewage and storm drainage to the wastewater treatment plant—would overflow. Nixon soon discovered that the river was not the only thing endangered. The area's youth faced a grim future, too. In the Anacostia district of Washington, D.C., unemployment runs rampant and nearly 40 percent of the residents live below the poverty line. Lacking opportunity, many youths turn to drug peddling. "Anacostia's always been a haven for the poorest people," Anacostia native David Smith told CBS News. "This is where they dump their trash and dump the people, who I guess the city didn't want to see." The neighborhood is one of the nation's most troubled. Half of Washington's annual 200-plus murders take place there.

Under Nixon's leadership, the ECC program has become so popular that there is a waiting list. About 20 new members are brought aboard each year. Many are high school dropouts with criminal records. The program is simple—the youth agree to spend 1,700 hours working on the murky Anacostia River. In return, they get a nominal bi-weekly stipend and a college scholarship through the federal AmeriCorps program. The ECC program also provides the youth with structure, discipline, and job skills, thus helping to improve their lives as well as that of their community.

One of the ECC's success stories is LaShauntya Moore (sometimes spelled LaShauntaye), who was raised in public housing by a crack-addicted mother.

By 20, Moore had two children, was pregnant, and living in a homeless shelter. A relative told her about the program and she joined. By the time Moore turned 25, she was the ECC's program director, was married, had earned her GED and was planning to use her AmeriCorps money for college. "I needed something stable to give me skills to get a good job," she told *People*. "Bob believed in me when no one else did." While many corps members have gone on to brighter futures, several became victims of the neighborhoods they were trying to escape. Between 1992 and 2005, nine corps members were murdered.

Nixon is the kind of leader who does more than offer direction; he works right alongside the corps members. *Washington Business Journal* writer Sean Madigan described Nixon as a man with "a compact frame, dusty blond hair, and the rugged features of someone who doesn't spend much time behind a desk." In the years since Nixon took over the ECC, he and the corps members have shoveled tons of garbage, replanted the river's banks with trees, hedges, and wild grasses; removed invasive plants, and built a stone riverwalk trail. The innovative walkway filters contaminates out of the rainwater before it pours into the river. In the mid-1990s, the group reintroduced the bald eagle to the area, building nests and feeding eaglets fish with a rope and pulley system. Pollution had forced the bird out of the area in the 1940s.

The ECC also runs a sister program, called the Salmon Corps, in the Pacific Northwest. This program employs Native American youth to restore salmon habitats along the Columbia River basin. While some onlookers have been surprised at Nixon's accomplishments, like getting former gang members to baby-sit eagle nests, Nixon finds no mystery in the success. "If you give nature half a chance, it's going to come back," he told *People*'s Richard Jerome. "And if you give a young person half a chance, some great things can happen." Despite his environmental endeavor, Nixon has not completely given up filmmaking. In 2004, the ECC released *Endangered Species*, a documentary about the corps members and their struggles for success and survival while growing up among the industrial decay and poverty of Anacostia.

Sources

Periodicals

People, August 11, 1997, p. 117; August 1, 2005, p. 78.
Washington Post, October 30, 2004, p. B9.

Online

"A Bird's-Eye View," *Washington Business Journal,* http://washington.bizjournals.com/washington/stories/2004/05/03/story8.html (April 17, 2006).

"Board of Directors: Robert H. Nixon," Earth Conservation Corps, http://www.ecc1.org/boardmembers/nixon_robert.html (April 17, 2006).

"Bob Nixon," *Washington Life,* http://www.washingtonlife.com/issues/2004-04/substancestyle/nixon.html (April 17, 2006).

"Saving Their Community," CBS News, http://www.cbsnews.com/stories/2005/04/21/60minutes (April 17, 2006).

—Lisa Frick

Christopher Nolan

MJ Kim/Getty Images

Director, screenwriter, and producer

Born Christopher Johnathan James Nolan, July 30, 1970, in London, England; married Emma Thomas (a producer); children: Flora. *Education:* Attended University College, London, England.

Addresses: *Agent*—c/o The Gersh Agency, 232 N. Canon Dr., Beverly Hills, CA 90210.

Career

Filmmaker of *Tarantella* (short), PBS, 1989; filmmaker of *Larceny* (short), 1996; director and screenwriter of *Doodlebug* (short), 1997; director, screenwriter, producer, cinematographer, and editor of *Following,* 1998; director and screenwriter of *Memento,* 2000; director of *Insomnia,* 2002; director and screenwriter of *Batman Begins,* 2005. Also shot corporate training videos, c. late 1980s.

Awards: Best Director Award, Newport International Film Festival, for *Following,* 1999; Tiger Award, Rotterdam International Film Festival, for *Following,* 1999; Black & White Award, Slamdance International Film Festival, for *Following,* 1999; Silver Hitchcock Award, Dinard British Film Festival, for *Following,* 1999; CinéLive Award, Critics Award, and Jury Special Prize, Deauville Film Festival, for *Memento,* 2000; Prize of the Catalan Screenwriter's Critic and Writer's Association, Catalonian International Film Festival, for *Memento,* 2000; ALFS Award for British screenwriter of the year, London Critics Circle, for *Memento,* 2001; Los Angeles Film Critics Association Award for best screenplay, for *Memento,* 2001; Waldo Salt Screenwriting Award (with Jonathan Nolan), Sundance Film Festival, for *Memento,* 2001; Toronto Film Critics Association Award for best screenplay, for *Memento,* 2001; Boston Society of Film Critics Award for best screenplay, for *Memento,* 2002; American Film Institute Award for screenwriter of the year, for *Memento,* 2002; Bram Stoker Award for screenplay (with Jonathan Nolan), for *Memento,* 2002; Broadcast Film Critics Association Award for best screenplay, for *Memento,* 2002; Chicago Film Critics Association Award for best screenplay, for *Memento,* 2002; Russell Smith Award, Dallas-Fort Worth Film Critics Association, for *Memento,* 2002; Edgar Allan Poe Award for best motion picture, for *Memento,* 2002; Florida Film Critics Circle Award for best screenplay, for *Memento,* 2002; Independent Spirit Awards, best director and best screenplay, for *Memento,* 2002; Sierra Award for best screenplay, Las Vegas Film Critics Society, for *Memento,* 2002; MTV Movie Award for best new filmmaker, for *Memento,* 2002; ALFS Award for British director of the year, London Critics Circle, for *Insomnia,* 2003; Visionary Award, Palm Springs International Film Festival, 2003.

Sidelights

A filmmaker since his childhood, Christopher Nolan moved from working on training videos and making his own film shorts to creating critically acclaimed features. The first, *Following*, uses an altered chronology to tell the story and served as Nolan's calling card to Hollywood. Nolan had an independent smash hit with *Memento*, which told its story backward. After directing a film entitled *Insomnia*, Nolan successfully revived the "Batman" franchise with his own take on the saga in *Batman Begins*.

Born in the early 1970s in England, Nolan was one of three sons of a British father, who owned an advertising business, and an American mother, a flight attendant for United Airlines. Though the family primarily made their home in England, they lived in Chicago for three years, beginning when Nolan was around eight years old. His father owned a Super 8mm camera with which Nolan began making movies. Nolan did so with his older brother, Matthew, who later became an author. Some of their works featured action figures in war settings, though they also created science fiction. After this point, Nolan told Jamie Portman of the *Ottawa Citizen*, "I never really stopped. I just carried on in whatever form was available to me at the time in making films, and they've just become bigger and longer." By the time Nolan was eleven or 12, he knew he wanted to be a film director.

When Nolan was an undergraduate student, he studied English literature at University College in London, England. Though he was not a film student, he did join a film society. He made sophisticated short films from the late 1980s through the mid- to late 1990s. One of his shorts was *Tarantella*, which aired on television in the United States in 1989. *Larceny*, another short, was shown at the Cambridge Film Festival in 1996. Nolan had a day job shooting training videos for corporations, and used a significant amount of his income on film stock and processing for his shorts.

In 1998, Nolan released his first feature-length film, the noir-influenced thriller *Following*. In addition to directing the movie, he also served as writer, producer, editor, and cinematographer. Because everyone involved, including the actors, still had day jobs, it was shot on weekends over 14 months primarily at Nolan's parent's home. The story in *Following* focuses on a writer named Bill suffering from a difficult case of writer's block. Bill starts to follow random people he does not know, hoping it will improve, and shows his voyeuristic tendencies. Someone he follows, Cobb, catches on and connects with the writer. Cobb is a thief who draws Bill into committing several crimes with him, primarily petty thefts.

The deceptions are complicated by the shifting time perspectives Nolan incorporated into the final film. Nolan edited the film so that the beginning, middle, and end all run at the same time. Janet Maslin in the *New York Times* quoted Nolan as saying, "I decided to structure my story in such a way as to emphasize the audience's incomplete understanding of each new scene as it is first presented." The final version was only about 70 minutes long, and cost about £7000 (about $6,000 in U.S. dollars) to make. *Following* was a critical favorite when it was shown in England. Yet Nolan had no real offers from British film companies.

Nolan had more luck showing *Following* at numerous film festivals in the United States. Nolan had moved to America after completing the film, in part because his future wife, producer Emma Thomas, had taken a job in Los Angeles. The film festival circuit led to a deal to make his next film, *Memento*. Nolan came up with the idea for the film while driving across the United States with his younger brother, Jonathan, to join Thomas in California. Jonathan Nolan told his brother about an idea he was working on about a revenge-seeking man with memory loss and how he keeps the information he needs. The brothers agreed to each write the story in their own medium. Nolan developed a script around the idea, while Jonathan Nolan completed a short story, which was published in *Esquire* in March of 2001.

Like *Following*, *Memento* was a noir-influenced story that also played with chronology. In this case, the story is told backwards, in part, to give viewers a sense of disconcertment similar to what the memory-challenged protagonist feels. In addition, *Memento* also had a much bigger budget, between $5 and $10 million, but was still shot in 25 days, primarily in run-down motels in Burbank, California.

Memento focuses on Leonard Shelby, played by Australian actor Guy Pearce, who is suffering from anterograde amnesia. The amnesia comes as a result of being bashed in the head by the same man who sexually assaults and kills Shelby's wife. In Shelby's case, this kind of memory loss means that though he does remember his life up until the incident, he cannot remember anything beyond about 15 minutes at a time. Shelby had been employed as an insurance investigator, and uses his skills to find who murdered his wife and hurt him. Because of his amnesia, Shelby goes to extremes to retain knowledge, including Polaroid pictures and tattooing information on his body. There are other characters Shelby meets along the way, such as femme fatale Natalie (played by Carrie-Ann Moss) and Shelby's shifty friend Teddy (played by Joe Pantoliano), but Shelby is unsure if he can trust or believe them in any way. Set in Los Angeles, the film begins with Shelby killing the man he believes committed the crime.

The three years Nolan spent creating *Memento* were well-spent. It was a critical favorite and was nominated for numerous awards. Critics were especially appreciative of how challenging it was to audiences, a goal that Nolan had set for himself. He told James Mottram of the *Independent*: "One of the things I was interested in trying to do with this kind of revenge story is create an unsettling experience. It seems to me that too often in films, things that should be disturbing aren't. I was interested in reclaiming some of these concepts, such as revenge, and making the audience look at them in a slightly different way than they might with other movies where the revenge element is simply an excuse to view the main character going off and killing someone." Reviewing the film in *Newsweek*, Jeff Giles picked up on this aspect, noting "Nolan's film demands intense concentration. It's an exhausting, exhilarating movie that reminds us how passive we've become as moviegoers."

There was some controversy after the general release of *Memento*. Nolan earned Golden Globe and Academy Award nominations for best screenplay. The Academy Award was specifically for best original screenplay, not adapted screenplay, though it was based on the idea behind Jonathan Nolan's short story. However, because the story had not been published at the time the script was written, the Academy considered the script original. Also contentious, at least for some viewers, was the several possible interpretations of the film and the events that drive its plot. Nolan wanted the film to be somewhat ambiguous. He told Laura Winters of the *New York Times*, "I wanted people watching *Memento* to become aware of the inadequacies of their own memory, and of the way that a lot of memory is interpretation, rather than strict recording. That's why it was important to me that the film be able to sustain several different interpretations."

After *Memento*, Nolan found more doors open in Hollywood. For his next project, he decided to wanted to direct a remake of a 1997 Norwegian film called *Insomnia*. In the Americanized version of the thriller, the story focuses on a veteran Los Angeles police detective Will Dormer, played by Al Pacino, whose secrets are physically and psychologically weighing on him. Already bothered by an ongoing investigation by Internal Affairs in Los Angeles, Dormer and his partner, Hap Eckhart (played by Martin Donovan) have traveled to Alaska during the summer time when the sun never sets to help an old friend, the local police chief, on a murder case. In Alaska, Dormer seemingly accidentally kills Eckhart, and hides the body. Dormer's intent is unclear; however, Eckhart was under pressure by Internal Affairs to reveal what he knows about Dor-

mer. Dormer continues to help the local chief with his investigation into the murder of a young girl. He believes that crime fiction author Walter Finch (played by Robin Williams) committed the crime. Finch turns the tables on Dormer, as he knows the detective's secret as well. Though *Insomnia* received mixed reviews, the film made $67 million in the United States alone, while the budget to make it was only $50 million.

In 2005, Nolan continued to move toward mainstream success, albeit on his terms. *Insomnia* had been produced by Warner Brothers. The studio then hired him for another project: reviving the Batman franchise. Since the last movie about the comic book hero was a critical and box office failure, the studio had been looking for someone with a new take. Nolan went back to the original source, the comic books and graphic novels, to devise the plot, feel, and focus of *Batman Begins* and rethink the franchise as a whole. Featuring Christian Bale as Bruce Wayne/Batman, Michael Caine as his loyal butler/assistant Alfred, and Katie Holmes as Rachel Dodson, a local district attorney and Wayne's love interest, Nolan answered fundamental questions about Batman that other films glossed over or ignored all together. Viewers saw what motivated Wayne to need an alter ego, primarily the outfall from seeing his parents gunned down in front of him in a Gotham City alley as a small child. They also learned how he reached the point of creating Batman, how he obtained all the necessary gadgets like the Bat suit and Batmobile, and more about the inner workings of Wayne Enterprises, the family business. Nolan also ensured that the film was as visually interesting as possible.

Though Nolan had the biggest budget of his career with *Batman Begins*, $150 million, he approached its creation the same way as his previous films. He told Andrew Pulver of the *Guardian*, "I made *Batman* the way I made every other film, and I've done it to my own satisfaction—because the film, truly, is exactly the way I wanted it to be. You're not often going to hear that from someone who's made a film this big." Reviewers generally responded with enthusiasm. Critiquing the film in the *New York Times*, Manohla Dargis wrote, "What makes this *Batman* so enjoyable is how Mr. Nolan balances the story's dark elements with its light, and arranges the familiar genre elements in new, unforeseen ways." In the same review, Dargis also noted, "What Mr. Nolan gets, and gets better than any other previous director, is that without Bruce Wayne, Batman is just a rich wacko with illusions of grandeur and a terrific pair of support hose."

While Nolan was not committed to make subsequent Batman films, he already had other films in preproduction. Nolan is writing, producing, and directing *The Prestige,* an adaptation of the novel by Christopher Priest. He was also scheduled to direct a film called *The Exec,* based on a comic by Doug Miers. Both were set for release in 2006. Of his career, he told Dixie Reid of the *Sacramento Bee,* "As an independent filmmaker, I've been in a position where I'm making a film no one will want to see. No one will care if I finish it. So you have to develop your own motivation, your own reasons for doing what you do. You have to be making a film simply because it needs to be made. I've had years of working that way, and it sort of frees you up to approach filmmaking from a very interior position. You're not looking for approval. When you do something you love, you don't question it."

Sources

Books

Celebrity Biographies, Baseline II, Inc., 2005.

Periodicals

Daily Telegraph (London, England), August 10, 2002, p. O1.
Guardian (London, England), June 15, 2005, p. 12.
Herald (Glasgow, Scotland), June 11, 2005, p. 8.
Independent (London, England), October 15, 2000, p. 2.
Newsweek, March 19, 2001, p. 60; June 21, 2004, p. 64.
New York Times, April 2, 1999, p. E24; February 25, 2001, sec. 2, p. 23; May 24, 2002, p. E1; June 15, 2005, p. E1.
Observer (London, England), October 15, 2000, p. 8.
Ottawa Citizen (Ottawa, Ontario, Canada), May 23, 2002, p. E1.
Sacramento Bee, May 23, 2002, p. E1.
San Francisco Chronicle, March 25, 2001, p. 48.
Time, June 3, 2002, p. 69.

Online

"Christopher Nolan," Internet Movie Database, http://www.imdb.com/name/nm0634240/ (January 24, 2006).

—*A. Petruso*

Olufunmilayo Olopade

AP Images

Physician, oncologist and geneticist

Born c. 1957 in Nigeria; married Christopher Sola Olopade (a physician); children: two daughters, one son. *Religion:* Episcopalian. *Education:* University of Ibadan, Nigeria, MD, 1980.

Addresses: *Home*—Chicago, IL. *Office*—University of Chicago Hospitals, 5841 S. Maryland Ave., MC 2115, Chicago, IL 60637.

Career

Medical officer, Nigerian Navy Hospital, c. 1980; internal medicine intern, Cook County Hospital, Chicago, IL, 1983-84; internal medicine resident, Cook County Hospital, 1984-86; chief resident, Cook County Hospital, 1986-87; post-doctoral fellow in hematology/oncology, University of Chicago, 1987-91; assistant professor of hematology/oncology, Pritzker School of Medicine, University of Chicago, 1991-2002; director, Cancer Risk Clinic, University of Chicago Hospitals, c. 1992—; associate professor of medicine, University of Chicago, 2002; professor of medicine and human genetics, University of Chicago, early 2000s—.

Member: American Association for Cancer Research; American Association for the Advancement of Science; American College of Physicians; American Society for Preventative Oncology; American Society of Breast Disease; American Society of Clinical Oncology; American Society of Hematology; Association of American Professors; Nigerian Medical Association; African Organization for Research and Training in Cancer; American Society for Clinical Investigation; Association of American Physicians; board, Young Survival Coalition; board, Inflamma-

tory Breast Cancer Research Foundation; board, Y-Me National Breast Cancer Organization.

Awards: Nigerian Federal Government Merit Award, 1975; Nigerian Medical Association Award for Excellence in Pediatrics, 1978; Nigerian Medical Association Award for Excellence in Medicine, 1980; University of Ibadan College of Medicine Faculty Prize, 1980; University of Ibadan College of Medicine departmental prizes in pediatrics, medicine, and surgery, 1980; University of Ibadan Sir Samuel Manuwa Gold Medal for Excellence in the Clinical Sciences, 1980; Association for Brain Tumor Research/Ellen Ruth Lebow Fellowship, 1990; American Society for Clinical Oncology Young Investigator Award, 1991; James S. McDonnell Foundation Scholar Award, 1992; Doris Duke Distinguished Clinical Scientist Award, 2000; Phenomenal Woman Award for work within the African-American community, 2003; Access Community Network's Heroes in Healthcare Award, 2005; MacArthur Fellow, 2005.

Sidelights

During the 1990s, cancer specialist Olufunmilayo Olopade became perplexed when she realized that breast cancer tended to hit women of African descent earlier—and harder—than their United States and European counterparts. Since then, Olopade has dedicated her career to finding out why in hopes of discovering a cure. Along the way, Olopade has made many groundbreaking discoveries about the disease and in 2005 was awarded a $500,000 MacArthur Foundation "genius grant" to continue her research. Speaking to Kelli Whitlock Burton of *Medicine on the Midway*, Olopade discussed her drive to find out more about the disease. "Part of our work as scientists is not only to study biology and science, but also to engage society. If we can't translate our research to help people, then why are we doing the work?"

The fifth of six children, Olufunmilayo Falusi Olopade was born around 1957 in Nigeria. The future physician-scientist, known to friends as Funmi (pronounced FOON-me), was the daughter of an Anglican minister. Doctors were scarce in the Nigerian villages where Olopade was raised so her parents decided that one of their children should become a doctor; Olopade was the first to express any interest. After earning her medical degree in 1980 from Nigeria's University of Ibadan, Olopade worked as a medical officer at the Nigerian Navy Hospital in Lagos to fulfill her country's requirement that university-educated young adults put in a year's service with the National Youth Service Corps.

Olopade then relocated to the United States to complete an internship and residency at Chicago's Cook County Hospital, where she ended up chief resident in 1986. Olopade left the hospital in 1987 to study hematology and oncology as a post-doctoral fellow at the University of Chicago. Meanwhile, a military coup had overthrown the Nigerian government, so she decided to stay in the United States. In 1991, she joined the University of Chicago faculty as an assistant professor in hematology and oncology.

Olopade's interest in cancer led her to push for the 1992 formation of the Cancer Risk Clinic at the University of Chicago, which she now oversees. The clinic specializes in treating high-risk cancer patients and also conducts studies on the disease, paying close attention to genetics. While working at the clinic, Olopade realized that the African-American women she treated for breast cancer seemed much younger than other sufferers of the disease.

Olopade did not realize how peculiar the situation was until 1997 when she went back to Nigeria for a niece's wedding. While there she visited a breast cancer clinic and as she walked through the waiting room it hit her—the women were all so young, just

in their 20s, 30s and 40s. Just like in her Chicago clinic, breast cancer in Nigeria was a young woman's disease, whereas the typical Caucasian woman with breast cancer gets the disease after menopause when she is in her 50s or 60s.

Olopade wondered if there was a genetic reason for this anomaly. In other words, perhaps there was something about a woman's African ancestry that induced breast cancer at a younger age. In addition, Olopade wondered why African-American women with breast cancer had a higher mortality rate despite a lower incidence of the disease. Fighting the disease also turned personal. Olopade had a cousin in her mid-thirties die of the disease after Nigerian doctors misdiagnosed a breast tumor as a boil.

Intent on finding out more, Olopade, in 2000, launched a small study of Nigerian breast cancer patients. After studying tissue samples from her Chicago patients and the Nigerian patients, Olopade realized that mutations in two genes—BRCA1 and BRCA2—occurred in the patients with early-onset breast cancer. At this point, Olopade wanted to know more about the genetics of breast cancer, so she gained approval for a larger study through the university's Center for Interdisciplinary Health Disparities Research, which secured a $9.7 million grant from the National Institutes of Health. This ongoing study, which began in 2003, has looked at cancer patients in Nigeria and Senegal. Research results have yielded new, innovative approaches to treating breast cancer in this population. Olopade is one of four principal investigators involved in the study.

Early on, the study found that breast-cancer tumors in African women develop from basal-like cells, whereas women of European ancestry develop breast tumors from milk-duct cells. The biggest find, however, was the discovery that nearly 80 percent of African breast tumors are estrogen-receptor (ER) negative compared to 20 percent of Caucasian breast cancer tumors. This meant that hormone therapy, often used to treat breast cancer, would not work in the African population. "Tumors that are estrogen-receptor positive depend on estrogen to grow," Olopade told *Medicine on the Midway*'s Whitlock Burton, explaining that many doctors treat breast cancer with estrogen-blocking drugs. "The estrogen-receptor-negative tumors are estrogen independent. To kill them you have to use chemotherapy, which has all the side effects and may not always work."

These discoveries have led Olopade to rethink prevention and treatment strategies for women of African descent. She has been vocal in urging women in this risk group to start screenings at a younger age. Despite the advances, Olopade is still wrestling with one big question—how should doctors treat this more aggressive, ER negative form of breast cancer? To help find proper treatment, Olopade has been working with doctors in Nigeria to establish a clinical trial of chemotherapy tablets called Herceptin and Xeloda. Her goal is to improve mortality for African women. In the United States, the five-year survival rate for breast cancer is 85 percent, but it hovers at just 10 percent in Nigeria. Olopade believes more research is needed. "Breast cancer isn't one single disease," she told *Essence*'s Kimberly L. Allers. "It affects women of different populations in different ways."

In 2005, the John D. and Catherine T. MacArthur Foundation, one of the United States' largest private philanthropic foundations, awarded Olopade a $500,000 grant to continue her research. The MacArthur grants are given to people who show exceptional promise in making a difference in the world. The awards are unique in that a person cannot apply; the foundation simply selects winners. "I was shocked," Olopade told the *Chicago Sun-Times*' Jim Ritter. "I didn't know that anyone was paying attention to my work."

Along the way, Olopade married fellow physician Christopher Sola Olopade, whose specialty is treating asthma and sleep disorders. They have two daughters and a son. They live in the Hyde Park-Kenwood neighborhood near the University of Chicago.

Sources

Periodicals

Chicago Sun-Times, September 20, 2005, p. 22.
Essence, January 2006, p. 90.

Online

"AORTIC Member Wins Prestigious MacArthur Fellowship—Also Known as the 'Genius Grant,'" AORTIC (African Organization for Research and Training in Cancer) News, http://africa.aortic.org/AORTIC_News_issue_4.pdf (February 1, 2006).

"Conference Promotes Breast and Cervical Cancer Awareness in Nigeria," University of Chicago Hospitals, http://www.uchospitals.edu/news/2004/20040514-nigeria.html (February 28, 2006).

"The Face of Breast Cancer," *Medicine on the Midway*, http://www.uchospitals.edu/pdf/uch_009154.pdf (February 1, 2006).

"Olufunmilayo Olopade, MD, FACP," University of Chicago Hospitals, http://www.uchospitals.edu/physicians/olufunmilayo-olopade.html (February 1, 2006).

"University of Chicago Cancer Specialist Receives 2005 MacArthur Foundation 'Genius Grant,'" University of Chicago Hospitals, http://www.uchospitals.edu/news/2005/20050920-geniusgrant.html (February 28, 2006).

—Lisa Frick

Joel Osteen

WENN/Landov

Minister and author

Born Joel Scott Osteen, March 5, 1963, in Houston, Texas; son of John (a minister) and Dodie (a church official; maiden name, Pilgrim) Osteen; married Victoria Iloff, 1987; children: Jonathan; Alexandra. *Education:* Attended Oral Roberts University, c. 1981-82.

Addresses: *Home*—Houston, TX. *Office*—Joel Osteen Ministries, P.O. Box 4600, Houston, TX 77210.

Career

Produced and directed broadcasts for Lakewood Church, 1982-99; became senior pastor of Lakewood Church, 1999; host of the *Joel Osteen* show.

Sidelights

By October of 2005, Joel Osteen's *Your Best Life Now: 7 Steps to Living at Your Full Potential* had spent a full year on the *New York Times* list of best-selling hardcover advice books. Osteen heads what has been called the largest church congregation in the United States, the 30,000-member Lakewood Church of Houston, Texas. Osteen's book is a distillation of his message from the pulpit, encouraging personal fulfillment through prayer and positive thinking. "With a blend of Christian morality and motivational cheerleading—and a blinding grin that has earned him the nickname Smiling Preacher—he's forged a connection with a racially mixed, economically diverse following that unites CEOs and former addicts," wrote *People*'s Susan Schindehette of Osteen's appeal.

Osteen's father, John, founded Lakewood Church back in 1959. The son of a Texas cotton farmer, John Osteen was a Southern Baptist minister before his faith took on a more charismatic turn in the late 1950s. He founded his own nondenominational church in a predominantly African-American neighborhood in Houston, and over the next four decades shepherded it into a dynamic, thriving congregation. The senior Osteen's feel-good message, in which he exhorted churchgoers to have deep faith, and the blessings of the material world—good health, prosperity, and a solid family unit—would be theirs, caught on with Houstonians, and the church had grown to 5,000 members by 1979.

Osteen, born in 1963, was one of six children in their own family unit, which included one son from his father's first marriage. He did not seem to initially inherit his father's zeal and ease before crowds, for at his suburban Houston high school Osteen was shy and did not even attend his senior prom, though he excelled in sports. He went on to Oral Roberts University in Oklahoma, the largest Christian charismatic university in the world, but returned home after a year and suggested to his parents that he set up a television ministry for Lakewood Church. His father, however, was wary of the growing number of televangelists on the air at the time—ministers like Jim Bakker and Jimmy Swaggart, who used the electronic medium to solicit donations—and okayed the new venture only with the stipulation that Lakewood would never use its media pulpit to appeal for contributions.

For the next 15 years Osteen directed and produced the weekly Sunday service at Lakewood, which aired on a local Houston station, and later on the Family Channel, a cable network. He traveled with his father, even as far as India, to assist in the church's missionary and outreach work, but scrupulously avoided a more active role. Occasionally, his father asked if he would like to deliver a sermon or speak during the church services—his mother Dodie and sister Lisa regularly did so—but he declined the invitation. But by early 1999, John Osteen's health was deteriorating, and he felt increasingly taxed by heart and kidney problems one week. He asked his son to deliver the Sunday sermon, and Osteen once again refused—but then called back a few minutes later and told his father that he would do it.

Nervous and wearing a pair of his father's shoes for emotional support, Osteen spoke that day before a crowd of 6,000, and the churchgoers responded well to his easygoing, affable style. Eleven days later, his father died of a heart attack, and Osteen was named to succeed him as pastor of the church. Lakewood's attendance numbers began to grow almost immediately, thanks to Osteen's blend of his father's self-improvement-through-faith message, tempered with anecdotes from his life and times. In one early sermon, he discussed the hardships of modern marriage, and urged wives to consider lingerie as a way to strengthen their unions. Lakewood also began using more music in the services, and congregants were encouraged to let the spirit move them if they so chose when the country-gospel ensemble began playing.

Among traditional Protestant faiths, Osteen's sermons were more inspirational—urging churchgoers to have faith that a higher power was in charge—than hectoring them about their possible shortcomings as Christians. He rarely discussed biblical scripture at any length, as standard sermons did. "We need doctrine, but I think the average person is not looking for doctrine," Osteen explained in an interview with William Martin for *Texas Monthly*. "They are looking to ask, 'How do I let go of the past?' 'How do I have a better marriage?'"

Over the next five years, Osteen's church swelled exponentially in number, outgrowing the large facility his father had built back in 1987. Perhaps even more impressive was the diversity of its congrega-

tion, which drew from various socio-economic backgrounds and races. Some of the popularity stemmed from the connection it offered—though it was large in number, the church ran various smaller groups and ministries in which its members could interact. There were ministries for teens, singles, and seniors, and support groups for various problems, including marital infidelity. It even offered free financial counseling services.

Osteen's Sunday sermons were broadcast weekly on religious channels such as TBN, and showed up on cable channels that included ABC Family, USA, and BET. Osteen also had his own show, *Joel Osteen*, and began touring U.S. cities in one-night speaking engagements that drew fans to arenas. Asked about why his message and ideas seemed to resonate with his Houston congregation and ardent cross-country television audience, he theorized that his pastoral mission struck a chord with the average American. "There's so much negativity pulling people down," he told Carolyn Kleiner Butler in *U.S. News & World Report*, "that I think they respond when you say, 'You know what: God's not mad at you; He's on your side, He's got a good plan for your life, and when we obey what He wants us to do, we're going to prosper.'"

Osteen's appealing message led to the book, *Your Best Life Now: 7 Steps to Living at Your Full Potential*, which was published by Warner Faith—a subsidiary of the immense Time-Warner media empire—in October of 2004. It rapidly advanced up the *New York Times* best-seller list in November, and earned the impressive distinction of becoming the fastest-selling nonfiction book in publishing history. At one point, it even outpaced sales of his nearest competitor, Rick Warren, a pastor from Lake Forest, California, whose 2002 book, *The Purpose-Driven Life*, also racked up extraordinary sales figures. Osteen's book, like Warren's, was usually slotted into the self-help section of bookstores. Butler, of *U.S. News & World Report*, asked Osteen if he objected to being put alongside pop-psychology tomes rather than among more contemplative religious writings. "I wouldn't have necessarily put it in that category by choice," he responded, "but it doesn't bother me because it does, it's there to help you live a better life, to live by God's principles, so it doesn't bother me at all."

In 2005, Osteen's Lakewood Church moved into a new local meeting-house, the Compaq Center, which was the former home arena of the Houston Rockets. His organization negotiated a rather tough sale with municipal authorities, beating out an affluent real-estate developer determined to build on the site, and then went on to spend more than $90 million to renovate it into a 16,000-seat church.

Those funds came from the well-managed operation that Osteen oversees, in which family members and trusted cohorts play leading roles. Even Osteen's brother, a surgeon, gave up his practice and works for Lakewood Church. Their mother, Dodie, still speaks at every Sunday service, and Osteen is nearly always seen with his wife, Victoria, by his side, a statuesque blond with similarly telegenic good looks. The two married in 1987, two years after Osteen met her when he stopped by the jewelry store her father owned. Their two young children, Alexandra and Jonathan, also take an active role in Sunday services.

Lakewood Church belongs to a growing category dubbed the megachurch—Protestant, usually evangelical or charismatic religious groups with 2,000-plus members. At 30,000 members, Osteen's is the largest of this new breed of the American religious experience, and likely the most lucrative, too. Its annual revenues are estimated at $60 million, but concrete numbers are not readily disclosed, since it is technically a family run church. Under U.S. law, churches are tax-exempt, but still have to submit some data to the Internal Revenue Service (IRS). Family-run churches like Lakewood, however, are excused from such scrutiny.

Osteen lives in the posh Tanglewood section of Houston, a prosperous outcome that owes much to his former second career before he took over his father's church, in which he bought and renovated rental properties. At Lakewood, much of his work week is spent writing and practicing his Sunday sermon, while other Lakewood ministers handle the bulk of the other pastoral duties—weddings, funerals, and other engagements. He is sometimes termed the likely successor to the Reverend Billy Graham, whose successful ministry—one of the first to use television—made him a figure of immense renown and respect in the United States and abroad.

Osteen is hesitant to involve himself in politics, and avoids taking a stance on issues like gay marriage and reproductive rights. He did run into trouble after a June of 2005 appearance on CNN's *Larry King Live* to promote *Your Best Life Now.* King asked Osteen about his thoughts on other faiths that do not consider Christ as the savior, particularly Judaism and Islam, and did he think that those believers would reach heaven. Osteen responded considerately, noting that he had traveled to India with his father, and met many different people who impressed him with their faith. As Martin related in the *Texas Monthly* article, that "humane, large-spirited response—quite similar to comments Billy Graham has made on occasion—apparently brought a flood of critical calls, letters, and e-mails to the Lakewood office, prompting Joel to issue an abject apology on his Web site, asserting that he believes 'Jesus Christ is the only way to heaven.'"

Despite his popularity, Osteen is sometimes criticized by mainstream Protestant scholars for not condemning materialism more ardently, and perhaps even encouraging it. "Osteen is an easy theological target," asserted Jason Byassee in *Christian Century.* "He merits attention mostly as an unreflective exemplar of temptations all ministers face—to translate the charged political and theological language of the scriptures into a vague religiosity, or into more easily digestible categories of self-help and self-improvement." Byassee discussed Osteen's place in a nondenominational group of American churches sometimes called "Word of Faith," but harsher critics call it Christianity Lite. Osteen defended his sermons and writings against the charges of an over-emphasis on the material world, telling Martin in the *Texas Monthly* interview, "I never knew it was such a bad thing to be a Word of Faith preacher, but I never preach that whatever you say, you can get—'I want five Cadillacs.' 'I'm going to be the president of this company.' I never believed that kind of stuff."

Even Byassee conceded that Osteen's message was not that drastically at odds with the underpinning philosophies of Western civilization itself. "In some ways Osteen echoes an ancient and venerable Christian tradition that borrows from Aristotle," the *Christian Century* writer noted, "in calling itself 'eudaemonistic.' That is, Christianity offers the happiest life possible." It was an idea that Osteen regularly expounded in his Sunday sermons, and in his increasingly frequent media interviews. "Prosperity is not just money," he reminded Martin in the *Texas Monthly* article. "It's a healthy relationship with your wife, with your kids; it's a healthy body. We need to get away from the dollar sign on prosperity."

Selected writings

Your Best Life Now: 7 Steps to Living at Your Full Potential, Warner Faith (New York City), 2004.

Sources

BusinessWeek, May 23, 2005, p. 78.
Christian Century, July 12, 2005, p. 20.
Christianity Today, April 2005, p. 103.
People, June 6, 2005, pp. 123-24.
Texas Monthly, August 2005, p. 106.
U.S. News & World Report, October 3, 2005, p. 57.

—*Carol Brennan*

Dawn Ostroff

Cliff Lipson/UPN/Landov

Entertainment President of the CW Network

Born in 1960, in Brooklyn, NY; married Mark; children: two.

Addresses: *Home*—Los Angeles, CA. *Office*—United Paramount Network, 11800 Wilshire Blvd., Los Angeles, CA 90025.

Career

Intern at radio and television stations in Miami, FL, mid-1970s; reporter and anchor for WINZ, a Miami radio station; secretary, 20th Century-Fox, early 1980s; associate with Kushner Locke, a production company, mid- to late 1980s, and with Michael Jacobs Productions, early 1990s; senior vice president of creative affairs, FOX Television; executive vice president for programming and production, Lifetime Television, 1996-2002; president of entertainment, United Paramount Network, 2002-05, president, 2005-06; entertainment president, the CW network, 2006—.

Sidelights

Television executive Dawn Ostroff joined the growing ranks of women who hold influential positions within the broadcast industry in January of 2006, when it was announced that she would become president for entertainment of the planned merger of two networks, her own United Paramount Network (UPN) and Warner Brothers (WB). A longtime protégé of CBS president Les Moonves, Ostroff was promoted to president of UPN in 2005 after fixing its struggling prime-time line-up. Before that, she was responsible for helping vault the Lifetime channel from sixth place to number one in the cable-ratings race.

Born in Brooklyn, New York, in 1960, Ostroff began her career in the entertainment industry while still in her teens. As a high-schooler in Miami, Florida, she talked her way into her first job, as she told *Jewish Journal of Greater Los Angeles* writer Soriya Daniels. "I was already very interested in the media and wound up answering request lines at a local station in Miami. Then I ended up interning at a lot of different TV stations down there." At the age of 18, while interning at a Miami radio station, she convinced her bosses to put her on the air. This was at WINZ, an all-news station. "I worked weekends at the radio station as a reporter and an anchor and I worked the weekdays as an intern at the local CBS television affiliate," she explained to Daniels, but she eventually realized that hard news was not for her. "At 18, I had seen more tragedy, death and despair that most people see in a lifetime," she said in the *Jewish Journal* interview. "I decided that there might be a happier way for me to earn a living."

Ostroff graduated from college at 19, and moved to Los Angeles two years later. Her first job in Hollywood was as a secretary at 20th Century-Fox, and she went on to a job with Kushner Locke, a production company. After seven years there, she was hired to serve as president of Michael Jacobs Productions, the company that created *Boy Meets World*, a kids' show that had a successful run on ABC from 1993 to 2000. She returned to 20th Century-Fox, this time as a development executive for its FOX network. She helped turn one of its film-studio properties, a 1992 B-movie called *Buffy the Vampire Slayer*, into a seven-season-long television series that accrued a devoted cult following.

In October of 1996, Ostroff joined Lifetime Television as executive vice president for programming and production. The cable network, aimed at female viewers, was lagging at the No. 6 spot in the non-broadcast ratings, but Ostroff worked to launch several original series, including *Strong Medicine* and *Any Day Now*, that helped it advance to first place a few years later. She also gained a reputation for being able to lure creative writers, producers, and directors to Lifetime, which had earned some industry derision for its melodramatic movies featuring beleaguered female characters.

Ostroff's good track record at Lifetime caught the attention of Les Moonves, the president of CBS. The two actually knew one another from their stints at 20th Century-Fox, back when Moonves headed its television movies and miniseries division. "She was the secretary who read everything," Moonves recalled of Ostroff in an interview with Leslie Ryan for *Electronic Media*. "She wanted to know about the business. She wanted to know about every piece of material and every writer, and she was clearly very bright." In February of 2002, Moonves hired Ostroff to become the president of entertainment at UPN, which was the television arm of Paramount Studios. Paramount's parent company was Viacom, which was a CBS property.

UPN was a relatively new network compared to CBS Television, on the air only since January of 1995. Seven years down the road, the network was struggling along, best known as the home of the contemporary *Star Trek* franchise. Critics claimed UPN had no identity as a network, and simply foisted a slew of new sitcoms and dramas every season that targeted widely varying groups of viewers. Ostroff set about changing that, by retooling the programming on a night-by-night basis over the next few years. She succeeded in part by bringing more African-American and Hispanic-focused programming to the network, which she felt was crucial in luring loyal viewers. "We believe that as our country is multicultural, that's what we want this network to reflect," she told Ryan in *Electronic Media*. "And that's what we feel is not really reflected on television."

Ostroff also greenlighted a few new shows which scored quite well in the ratings, including *America's Next Top Model*, or ones that were a hit with critics, such as the teen-detective series *Veronica Mars*. In February of 2005, Ostroff was promoted to president of UPN, making her one of a new generation of female television executives, among them Gail Berman, president of FOX Television; Susan Lyne, president of ABC Entertainment; and Nancy Tellem, a top CBS and Paramount executive.

In January of 2006, UPN announced it would merge with another relatively new network, the WB. The new property would be named the CW, a nod to parent companies CBS and the Warner entertainment empire, and Ostroff was handed the task of programming its new line-up when she was named the CW's president for entertainment. This gave her final say over the entire fall 2006 prime-time lineup.

Ostroff rises at 4 a.m. daily to begin her workday at her home office, which lets her spend time in the morning with her two young children. Typically, her work day does not end until after 7 p.m., and her husband spends half the month in New York City for his job. After exiting the world of broadcast journalism so many years ago, Ostroff remains convinced she made the right career decision. "I can't really say that there's too many days when I wake up and say, 'Ugh, I've got to go to work,' like I felt about school," she told Daniels in the *Jewish Journal* article. "I'm excited every day and I've been doing it forever."

Sources

Periodicals

Broadcasting & Cable, January 30, 2006, p. 6.
Crain's New York Business, November 11, 1999, p. 37.
Electronic Media, January 20, 2003, p. 54.
MediaWeek, April 12, 2004, p. 30.
TelevisionWeek, January 31, 2005, p. 10.
Variety, January 13, 1997, p. 73.

Online

"Balance Paramount to UPN Head Ostroff," *Jewish Journal of Greater Los Angeles*, http://www.jewishjournal.com/home/preview.php?id=12456 (April 24, 2006).

—Carol Brennan

Clive Owen

WENN/Landov

Actor

Born October 3, 1964, in Keresley, Warwickshire, Coventry, England; married Sarah-Jane Fenton (an actress), 1995; children: Hannah, Eve. *Education:* Earned degree from the Royal Academy of Dramatic Art, 1988.

Addresses: *Agent*—Creative Artists Agency, Inc., 9830 Wilshire Blvd., Beverly Hills, CA 90212-1825.

Career

Actor in films, including: *Vroom*, 1988; *Close My Eyes*, 1991; *Century*, 1993; *The Rich Man's Wife*, 1996; *Bent*, 1997; *The Echo*, 1998; *Croupier*, 1998; *Split Second*, 1999; *Greenfingers*, 2000; *Gosford Park*, 2001; *The Bourne Identity*, 2002; *I'll Sleep When I'm Dead*, 2003; *Beyond Borders*, 2003; *Closer*, 2004; *King Arthur*, 2004; *Sin City*, 2005; *Derailed*, 2005; *Inside Man*, 2006; *The Children of Men*, 2006; *Elizabeth: The Golden Age*, 2006; *Sin City 2*, 2006; *Shoot 'Em Up*, 2006. Also appeared in a series of short films for BMW as "The Driver," 2001-02. Television appearances include: *Boon*, 1988; *Capital City*, 1989; *Chancer*, 1990; *Class of '61* (movie), 1993; *Century* (movie), 1993; *The Return of the Native* (movie), 1994; *Sharman*, 1996; *Second Sight* (movie), 1999; *Second Sight: Hide and Seek* (movie), 2000; *Second Sight: Kingdom of the Blind* (movie), 2000; *Second Sight: Parasomnia* (movie), 2000. Stage appearances include: *Romeo and Juliet*, c. 1988; *Closer*, 1997; *Design for Living*, 2000; *A Day in the Death of Joe Egg*, 2001.

Awards: Golden Globe award for best performance by an actor in a supporting role, Hollywood Foreign Press Association, for *Closer*, 2004.

Sidelights

After nearly two decades of film work, British actor Clive Owen finally attained a more international level of stardom thanks to a string of—quite literally—killer roles. Darkly handsome and adept at emitting a deadly cool demeanor, Owen seems to have become Hollywood's go-to guy for villain-casting, and there has sometimes been rumors that he would become the next actor to take on the classic James Bond role. Owen instead segued into more diverse acting jobs, such as a 2005 pairing with Jennifer Aniston as two adulterous business executives hoping to evade their blackmailer in *Derailed*, and opposite Cate Blanchett's Queen Elizabeth I as Sir Walter Raleigh in the period drama *Elizabeth: The Golden Age*, slated for 2006. "It's whether you're nurturing or protecting an image, that's the key," he asserted to Chris Jones in an interview for *Esquire*. "And I'm not. I'll deliberately mess it up.... I'm just a working actor. I always want my options to be open. I always want to do something different."

Born in 1964, Owen grew up in the Coventry area of England's Midlands. He was the fourth of five sons in the family, but his father, a country and western singer, left when he was three, and Owen only met him once, as an adult. His mother remarried, and their household was a conventional, working-class British one of the era. Owen's interest in the performing arts was sparked when he was cast as the Artful Dodger in the musical *Oliver!* at the age of 12; from there, he joined a Coventry Theatre youth group and stayed with it through his teens.

At Coventry's Binley Park Comprehensive school, Owen earned good grades, but seemed to lose interest in academics as his desire to perform grew. He nearly flunked out at one point, and a sympathetic teacher helped him strike a deal that would allow him to retake some necessary exams while studying toward the further tests he needed to qualify for university admission. Recognizing where his interests lay, the teacher also suggested he think about applying to drama school rather than a university. "But I was a very prickly kid," Owen recalled in a *Times* of London interview with Alan Jackson. "I genuinely believed it was something you couldn't be taught, and gave her my little speech to that effect. It ended, 'And even if I were to want to go, there's only one, isn't there?'" He named the prestigious Royal Academy of Dramatic Art (RADA) in London, a school whose alumni roster includes John Gielgud, Harold Pinter, and Kenneth Branagh. Entrance is limited to a select few, and in 2005 the tuition and fees were more than $20,000 a year. His teacher dismissed the idea, reminding Owen that he came from a working-class background, and suggested a smaller London school for drama instead. But Owen managed to win the necessary interview for consideration, and his teacher bought him the train ticket.

In the interim, personal issues caused the hotheaded Owen to leave home and drop out of school altogether. When he learned that he had been accepted at RADA, he announced that he would not go. For the next two years, he survived on unemployment benefits, appeared in a few local plays, and earned extra cash as a pool hustler. Finally, he reapplied to RADA, and was granted admission. He was there at the same time as Ralph Fiennes and Jane Horrocks, two Britons who went on to enjoy notable careers, and excelled at the school. Just before he graduated in 1988, he was involved with a workshop for a new play, and when one of the stars—Gary Oldman—fell ill once the play was running at the Royal Court Theatre, Owen was asked to step in for Oldman at the last minute. His stint lasted a week, and won praise from drama critics as well as calls from agents eager to sign him.

Owen made his film debut in a 1988 movie called *Vroom*. Its novice director, Beeban Kidron, would later go on to direct the second Bridget Jones movie,

The Edge of Reason. Owen then won a plum role in a new British television series called *Chancer*. It ran for just one season, but was a tremendous hit with critics and viewers alike. After playing a shady yet somewhat magnetic car dealer, Owen suddenly found himself a regular target of the notoriously overeager British tabloids. Still young and of a somewhat impetuous mind, he reacted to the intrusive speculation about his personal life rather badly, and gave quotes that made him appear arrogant.

After *Chancer* ended, Owen took a daring role in a film by British playwright Stephen Poliakoff, *Close My Eyes*. The 1991 drama co-starred Saskia Reeves as his sister, and the two become involved in a torrid affair that threatens her marriage. In a *New York Times* review, film critic Stephen Holden found that their "love scenes, and later their fight scenes, have a visceral energy that seems so spontaneous there are moments when one feels almost embarrassed to be caught watching."

Owen spent the next few years doing some forgotten British films before heading to Hollywood, where he was cast as Halle Berry's lover in *The Rich Man's Wife*, a 1996 film. It earned terrible reviews, and Owen returned to England to take on yet another somewhat daring leading role as a gay man in a Nazi concentration camp in the film version of an acclaimed stage play, *Bent*. But his career took an unusual turn with *Croupier*, a little-seen 1998 British film that suddenly began gathering terrific buzz in Hollywood when it was released in the United States in the spring of 2000.

In *Croupier*, Owen played a dejected writer who returns to his former job as croupier at an underground London casino, and becomes involved in a deadly web of blackmail and murder. There was even some talk of an Academy Award nomination for him in the Best Actor category, but it turned out the film was ineligible because it had aired once on Dutch television. "Owen conveys a sharp, cynical intelligence that rolls off the screen in waves whenever he widens his glittering blue eyes," noted Holden in the *New York Times*—though Owen's eyes are actually green—and compared him to several other current Hollywood leading men, but asserted "the actor he most strongly recalls is the young Michael Caine, who purveyed a similarly offbeat blend of iciness and affability" back in the 1960s. Interestingly, *Croupier* was also a surprise hit for its veteran director, Mike Hodges, whose last solid box-office hit had been *Get Carter* back in 1971, with Caine in the title role.

Hollywood seemed once again interested in Owen, and he returned for the obligatory rounds of meal-meetings with studio executives and producers. A few years earlier, the same experience had been soul-crushing. "The minute they'd go, 'Well, hey! Clive Owen!' I'd know they knew nothing about me," he recalled in the *Times* of London interview with Jackson. "When they'd say, 'So you do a lot of theatre!' I'd know they hadn't seen a single thing I'd done." But after the Hodges movie, his status suddenly improved. "My history in Hollywood begins with *Croupier*," he told Lynn Hirschberg in a *New York Times Magazine* profile. "Before that, they hadn't built a radar strong enough to detect me. That movie changed my career."

Solid Hollywood roles were still slow in coming, and so Owen returned to the small screen in Britain with a quartet of *Second Sight* films, four gripping crime dramas about a detective who is losing his eyesight. He also appeared in *Greenfingers* in 2000, as a prison inmate who takes part in a national gardening competition, which was based on a true story. Beginning in 2001, Owen also starred in a series of well-crafted short films commissioned by German luxury automaker BMW under the group title *The Hire*. Each of the eight films was directed by a different star director—Guy Ritchie, Tony Scott, and John Woo were among them—and featured Owen as the anonymous "Driver" of a BMW spiriting away or otherwise aiding an imperiled passenger. Ritchie's wife, the pop star Madonna, was Owen's co-star in one of the shorts, titled *Star*.

Owen, reportedly, was the first cast member chosen by director Robert Altman for his star-studded film-*Gosford Park*, which was released in 2001. Owen played a servant at a lavish English country house that is hosting a long weekend of esteemed guests in the 1930s. In the 2002 thriller *The Bourne Identity*, he had a scant few lines of dialogue but maintained a gripping screen presence as an assassin sent to kill Matt Damon's Bourne. Critics singled out his brief role in that film, but wrote more scathingly of his lead in a 2003 drama, *Beyond Borders*. This movie co-starred him with Angelina Jolie as a humanitarian-aid physician, and was given a sound drubbing by most critics for its preposterous plot and tinny dialogue. A title role in the epic, $100 million *King Arthur* also failed to win over audiences; again, reviewers faulted this film on several fronts, but lastly for Owen's portrayal of Arthur.

Critics were more forgiving for Owen's part in *Closer*, a 2004 film that also starred Jude Law, Julia Roberts, and Natalie Portman, and was directed by Mike Nichols. The project was taken from a play by Patrick Marber, and Owen had been in its original cast when it debuted at London's National Theatre in 1997, though as the other male lead in the adultery-fueled drama. In the film version, he played Larry, the dermatologist who woos Anna, Julia Roberts' character, and does memorable verbal battle with Dan, Jude Law's character, in one of the final scenes. "Owen is stupendous as Larry," asserted *Entertainment Weekly* reviewer Lisa Schwarzbaum. "Tearing into Larry's viciousness, his competitiveness, his basest, most sex-driven animal self … is the throbbing motor with which *Closer* surges ahead; he's a galvanizing force."

Closer won Owen his first Golden Globe award for Best Performance by an Actor in a Supporting Role in a Motion Picture, and he was also nominated for an Academy Award for it as well. He went on to appear in a comic-book adaptation, *Sin City*, in 2005, with another all-star line-up of Hollywood talent. Subsequent film projects on the deck for Owen included a sequel to *Sin City* as well as a long-awaited screen adaptation of the P.D. James novel *The Children of Men*, slated for 2006 release. The film is set in a future where human reproduction has stopped, and the youngest person on Earth, an 18-year-old, has just died. Julianne Moore's character suddenly conceives, and Owen is the bodyguard sent to protect her. He was also set to star opposite Denzel Washington in Spike Lee's bank-heist drama *Inside Man*, also set for a 2006 release.

Known as a rogue and a killer on-screen, Owen leads a quiet family life with wife Sarah-Jane Fenton, whom he met while playing Romeo to her Juliet in a London stage production in the late 1980s. Married since 1995, they have two daughters, Hannah and Eve. The girls, he has noted, are far too young still to see any of their father's movies, and the often preternaturally calm villains he usually plays in them. "The idea of goodies and baddies has always fascinated me," he reflected in the interview with Jones in *Esquire*, "and what people consider to be a goodie or a baddie, because I've never seen any of my characters as baddies…. In reality, we're all made up of both. And it's much more interesting for me to play a character who has conflict, who's grappling with something, who isn't perfect."

Sources

Entertainment Weekly, December 10, 2004, p. 63.
Esquire, March 2005, p. 132.
Guardian (London, England), August 26, 1999, p. 17; June 9, 2000, p. 7.
New York Times, February 21, 1992; April 21, 2000.
New York Times Magazine, September 19, 2004, p. 172.
Observer (London, England), July 11, 2004, p. 14.
People, November 10, 2003, p. 137.
Times (London, England), January 13, 2001, p. 14.

—*Carol Brennan*

Gary Parsons

Chairman of XM Satellite Radio

Born Gary M. Parsons, c. 1950, in Columbia, SC; married Kathy (an ad agency owner); children: Kenneth, Michael. *Education:* Graduated from Clemson University, bachelor's degree (engineering); University of South Carolina, M.B.A., 1978.

Addresses: *Home*—Potomac, Virginia. *Office*—1500 Eckington Place NE, Washington, DC 20002. *Website*—http://www.xmradio.com.

Career

Began career as a radio disc jockey in high school, c. 1960s; engineer, BellSouth Corp., 1970s; joined Telecom*USA, 1984; stayed on after Telecom*USA was purchased by MCI and worked his way up to executive vice president of MCI Communications and chief executive officer of MCImetro Inc., 1990-96; joined American Mobile Satellite Corp., chairman and CEO, 1996-2000 and stayed on as president and CEO when American Mobile changed its name to Motient Corp., 2000-02; founded XM Satellite Radio, serving as chairman and CEO, 1997; stepped down as CEO and remained chairman, XM Satellite Radio, 1998—.

Awards: *Washington Business Journal*'s Entrepreneur of the Year—Technology (shared with Hugh Panero), 2003.

Sidelights

Growing the cutting-edge companies of tomorrow is a risky business, but Gary Parsons savors the challenge. Parsons is founder and chairman of XM Satellite Radio, which provides more than 150 crystal-clear digital stations to subscribers coast-to-coast. Parsons, who believes his product will become the next-generation car radio, has been at the forefront of developing the technology. Growing the business, however, has been slow. Traditional radio is free—XM subscribers pay a $12.95 monthly fee plus an upfront cost to buy a receiver. As such, XM has trouble persuading people to sign on. "You can't just hear about it," Parsons told Paul Dykewicz of *Satellite News*. "You have to hear it. Then it sells itself."

XM sells itself by offering an unparalleled, staggering array of programming. From its home base in Washington, D.C., XM's disc jockeys and programmers pump out 67 commercial-free music channels featuring all musical genres. There are also dozens of news channels produced with partners such as ABC News, FOX News, MSNBC, and the CNN Financial Network. Traffic and weather reports are also part of the mix.

A middle child, Parsons was born and raised in Columbia, South Carolina. His mother was a homemaker and his father was an executive with a fishing rod company. As a teenager, Parsons began working in radio. During high school he covered the 6 p.m. to midnight shift at the Newberry, South Carolina-based WKDK-AM. He had his own show, called "Gary Parsons' Night Flight," which focused on contemporary music. This early work in radio sparked a lifelong passion for music and technology, which he later fused into a career.

After earning an engineering degree from Clemson University, Parsons spent a few years at BellSouth Corp., then entered the MBA program at the University of South Carolina, graduating in 1978. In

1984, Parsons joined Telecom*USA, a long-distance startup later acquired by MCI. He stayed on at MCI and worked his way up to executive vice president of MCI Communications and chief executive officer of MCI subsidiary MCImetro Inc. He was courted by American Mobile Satellite Corp. and joined the company in 1996 as chairman and CEO.

At the time American Mobile, a data-services provider, was developing wireless communications—via satellite technology—for truckers, the Red Cross, and government entities. While working there, Parsons came to believe that satellite telecommunications technology could have broader applications beyond the customer base American Mobile targeted. Inspired by his wife, Kathy, who had established her own ad agency years before, Parsons founded XM Satellite Radio in 1997 and within a year, had procured an FCC license.

Getting the license, however, was the easy part. Establishing a satellite radio company is highly capital intensive and requires mass infrastructure. Parsons' initial efforts involved attracting investors. Before even going on the air, XM spent more than $1.2 billion to launch its two satellites, turn an abandoned factory into a headquarters with 80 recording studios, and erect nearly 1,000 earth-based repeaters to rebroadcast the signals. XM's satellites are named "Rock" and "Roll." Parsons' people skills and passion for the business helped him round up enough investors to get the company rolling. In 1999, General Motors invested $100 million. Hugh Panero, XM's CEO since 1998, is amazed by Parsons' negotiating skills and ability to get others on board with his ideas. "He lets nothing faze him," Panero told Theda Wrede of the *Carolinian*. "He's a financial wizard, but no one ever leaves the table feeling as though he has lost something. He's a man who thrives on challenge."

Parsons stayed on at American Mobile, which in 2000 changed its name to Motient Corp.; he left in 2002. Meanwhile, XM launched its service in September of 2001 and initially, the future looked promising. By 2003, XM had 600,000 subscribers and eventually secured its first one million customers at a faster rate than any other new entertainment technology ever did, including CDs, the Internet, and videos. But after the initial enthusiasm, growth slowed. XM has several competitors, including New York-based Sirius Satellite Radio, which launched a few months after XM. In addition, XM faces competition from traditional land-based radio stations, which are free to listeners but are frequently interrupted by commercial breaks. Parsons believes this is XM's greatest strength—its music channels are commercial free, although a few other channels carry limited advertising.

Another advantage to XM Satellite Radio is that it will not fade away—subscribers can drive from Seattle to New York and never lose their favorite station. XM offers another benefit for music fans in that when a song plays, the title and artist are displayed on the receiver's output screen ensuring listeners will never be left to wonder about the name of a catchy new song they hear.

Since its inception, XM has suffered from cash-flow problems and has operated in the red, making Wall Street investors and stockholders leery. Also, some venture capitalists have been slow to get onboard, remembering the dot.com bust. Parsons has done a lot of financial wrangling to keep the company afloat, but the ride has been rocky. In 2000, XM's stock stood at about $46 a share, but plunged to less than $2 in 2003 when it looked as if XM might run out of money.

In order to turn a profit, XM needs to increase its subscriber base to improve monthly cash flow. XM had five million customers in the fall of 2005 and was projected to hit the 8.2 million mark in 2006. Merrill Lynch analyst Laraine Mancini sees a positive future for XM. She predicted that 2006 sales would rise 64 percent. "Satellite radio is a viable-model business," Mancini told Leon Lazaroff in the *Chicago Tribune*. "Compared to the rest of the industry, it's one of the few growth stories in broadcasting."

XM is expecting the market to take off. As of 2006, General Motors, Honda, Toyota, Hyundai, and Nissan offered the satellite systems in their cars; it comes standard on some models. In addition, the price of the palm-sized receivers has dropped. Customers can buy them at retailers such as Circuit City for about $50 to $300, depending on features. Many units are portable and can be used in the car or the home.

Parsons believes XM will have 20 million customers by the end of the decade. Looking toward the future, he envisions XM entering the worldwide market and in 2005 steered XM to buy a stake of WorldSpace, which provides satellite radio in Asia and Europe.

Sources

Periodicals

Aviation Week & Space Technology, August 1, 2005, p. 26.
BusinessWeek, July 7, 2003, pp. 90-92.
Chicago Tribune, October 2, 2005, p. 8.

Internet Week, September 27, 2005.
Satellite News, October 1, 2001, p. 1.
Washington Post, August 16, 2004, p. E1.

Online

"Fast Facts," XM Satellite Radio, http://www.xm
     radio.com/corporate_info/fast_facts.html (No-
     vember 19, 2005).
"Sound Management," *Carolinian,* http://www.sc.
     edu/carolinian/features/fea_04dec_02.html (No-
     vember 19, 2005).

—Lisa Frick

Tyler Perry

Francis Specker/UPI/Landov

Playwright and actor

Born Emmitt Perry, Jr., September 13, 1969, in New Orleans, LA; son of Emmitt Perry Sr.

Addresses: *Office*—Atlanta, GA. *Website*—http://www.tylerperry.com.

Career

Writer and actor, 1998—; adapted, produced, and directed *Madea's Family Reunion,* 2002, and *Madea's Class Reunion,* 2003. Adapted and produced film *Diary of a Mad Black Woman,* 2005.

Sidelights

Called "a playwright with a Midas touch for an uninhibited urban comedy," by the *New York Times'* Marcia A. Cole, Tyler Perry came to the attention of critics across the United States when his play *Diary of a Mad Black Woman* was made into a popular movie. Perry had become a playwright when all odds were against him. He raised himself above an abusive past and followed his dreams with unswerving determination. By 2005 he was a millionaire and a much sought-after writer, actor, director, and producer.

Perry was born in New Orleans, Louisiana, on September 13, 1969. He was a middle child, with two older sisters and a younger brother. According to Margena A. Christian in *Jet,* "He says that he endured years of abuse as a child by his father 'whose answer to everything was to beat it out of you.'

Perry says he would 'go places in his mind' following beatings." At one point, unable to take it anymore Perry attempted to kill himself, slashing his wrists in an action that he has called a cry for attention. "I was pretty young and totally frustrated," he told Christian. After the incident he happened to be watching *The Oprah Winfrey Show* and heard about how sometimes troubles in life could be worked through if you wrote them down—a form of release that could be very cathartic and therapeutic. Perry gave it a try and discovered that he not only liked it, but that he was good at it, too. His first writings were in the form of letters to himself. Through them he came to terms with his childhood and even brought himself to the point where he could forgive his father for all the anguish he caused Perry's family. Perry was quoted by Zondra Hughes in *Ebony* as having said, "The things that I went through as a kid were horrendous. And I carried that into my adult life. I didn't have a catharsis for my childhood pain, most of us don't, and until I learned how to forgive those people and let it go, I was unhappy." With a newfound skill and a more positive attitude, Perry was ready to take on his future.

He wrote the musical *I Know I've Been Changed* based on those letters he had written in his journal to himself. According to the Tyler Perry website, "Because of having put all of his eggs in one basket, Tyler would eventually find himself homeless on one or more occasions over the following six years." Through it all, however, Perry kept up his spirits through his faith and his seemingly endless belief that things would turn out all right in the end. At one point he had saved up $12,000 and rented a theatre to put on his show. It took a lot of courage to put everything he had into a play that was not guaranteed to be successful, but Perry had a dream and he figured if he was going to succeed at it, he would have to give the endeavor his all. Unfortunately the gamble did not pay off, and *I Know I've Been Changed* failed horribly. Only 30 people showed up the first weekend to see the play. But Perry was not ready to give up yet. For six years he took on a slew of odd jobs in order to keep the show running, while sometimes living on the street because he could not afford to pay rent.

The play, however, despite all the effort Perry put behind it, continued to do poorly. He was just starting to think about quitting and giving the whole writing career up when he decided to do one last show so that he could say that he had really given it a try. The play opened at the House of Blues in Atlanta, Georgia, in the summer of 1998 and sold out eight times in a row. Two weeks later, the play moved to the Fox Theater in the same city where it also continued to sell out—this time selling out a much larger arena, since the Fox featured around 4,000 seats. Perry was flabbergasted. And that was not the end of the show's success. *I Know I've Been Changed* went on to gross several million dollars. It also brought the world of African-American theater into a more favorable light with theatre goers and critics alike. Once known by the rather derogatory term "Chitlin Circuit," African-American theater started to be called "urban theater," something that Perry and his play had a lot to do with.

Perry began receiving messages from many fans of the play who wrote that his show had changed their lives, encouraged them to confront problems with their past and other members of their family, and helped with the healing process. The play went on tour for the 1998-1999 season to cities like Washington D.C., New York, Chicago, Philadelphia, Miami, and Dallas. In all locations the show played to sell-out crowds. Perry was becoming a household name in African-American communities across the country.

The success of Perry's first play opened the doors to a whole new world that Perry was eager to enter. Bishop T. D. Jakes came to one of the shows in Dallas and immediately afterward invited Perry to become involved in the play *Woman, Thou Art Loosed,*

a project Jakes had been working on and looking to find someone to help with. Perry agreed to do so as long as he was allowed to rewrite the play, produce it, and direct it, not for arrogant reasons but because he had learned to work that way. Jakes gave him his go ahead; when the show opened in 1999 it met with great success. It made more than $5 million in just five months.

In 2000 Perry opened the play *I Can Do Bad All By Myself.* By this time Perry's name on a play guaranteed that it would sell well within certain markets and this play opened to rave reviews and sold-out shows in New York, Washington D.C., Memphis, Chicago, Atlanta, and New Orleans. Perry played one of the roles, a character named Madea Simmons, himself. Madea was a 68-year-old grandmother with a smart aleck mouth and a larger-than-life personality who audiences found hilarious. In 2001 Perry was nominated for the Helen Hayes Award for Outstanding Lead Actor for this role.

He next worked on another musical with Jakes which was called *Behind Closed Doors.* It was the first Broadway gospel show of its kind, and it met with success equal to *Woman, Thou Art Loosed.* Perry was nominated for an NAACP Theatre Award for his production of the musical.

He next worked on the play *Diary of a Mad Black Woman,* which opened in New Orleans to a full house in January of 2001. One thing that was different about this production was that the ending to the play changed; how it ended depended on the night it was seen. It was an interesting idea and one that audiences loved. The play was about Helen whose husband kicked her out of their house right before their 18th wedding anniversary so that his longtime mistress and their child could move in. The Madea character was in this play, too, and again Perry took on the role for the play.

In 2002, with audiences clamoring to see more of the character Madea, Perry wrote the play *Madea's Family Reunion* in which Perry again took on the role and toured all over the country. The character and her plays were so popular that in 2003 Perry wrote *Madea's Class Reunion.*

It was in 2005, however, that Perry got his foot in the door in Hollywood. Perry's script to *Diary of a Mad Black Woman* was purchased for a film which was released in February of that year. Called "a mix of broad comedy, soapy drama, social commentary, and earnest spiritualism" by *Entertainment Weekly*'s Gregory Kirschling, the movie was a hit. It earned

$22 million in the United States and Canada in its opening weekend. At the box office, the movie even beat such films as the Will Smith romantic comedy *Hitch* and the horror film *Cursed,* both of which analysts had thought would sweep the market. The movie moved Perry from a well-known figure in the African-American community to a playwright known by all ethnicities.

Also in 2005 Perry opened a new play: *A Jazz Man's Blues.* The play is the story of a male jazz singer who falls in love with a woman who wants a better life than the musician can give her. It was set in New Orleans in 1947.

Because of the demand to see more of Madea, in 2005 publishers vied to have Perry write a book from Madea's perspective. The proposed book would offer comic advice to African-American women. It was scheduled for publication in 2006 and be titled *Don't Make a Black Woman Take Off Her Earrings: Madea's Uninhibited Commentaries on Love and Life.*

When asked why Perry's works have been so successful, the playwright always puts it down to an non-traditional approach to storytelling. "I was never interested in learning the 'traditional' way to put together a play because I felt that would take away from the realness found in urban theaters…. People who understand the formalities of theater are caught off guard by my plays because they break all the rules," he told the *New York Times'* Cole. Whatever the case may be, Perry definitely knows how to connect with his audience; they love his honesty and humor.

With all the success of his plays and movies it is needless to say that Perry is no longer homeless. He had a house built in Georgia that would show to the world that anything was possible if you only dreamed big enough, stuck to it, and had faith that God would provide. "I wanted this house to be vast. I wanted to make a statement, not in any grand or boastful way, but to let people know what God can do when you believe. I don't care how low you go, there's an opposite of low, and as low as I went I wanted to go that much higher. And if there was an opposite of homelessness, I wanted to find it," Perry told *Ebony's* Hughes.

As of March of 2005, Perry's plays had grossed more than $75 million in tickets and DVD sales. The Internet Movie Database quoted Perry as having said,

"I know my audience, and they're not people that the studios know anything about." If sales are any indication, this statement would seem to be true. And equally true is that audiences across the country are waiting to see what Perry will do next.

Selected writings

Plays

I Know I've Been Changed, 1998.
Woman Thou Art Loosed, 1999.
Diary of a Mad Black Woman, 2001.
Madea's Family Reunion, 2002.
Madea's Class Reunion, 2003.
A Jazz Man's Blues, 2005.
Also wrote *Madea Goes to Jail, I Can Do Bad All By Myself, Why Did I Get Married, Behind Closed Doors,* and *Meet The Browns.*

Sources

Books

Who's Who Among African Americans, 18th ed., Gale, 2005.

Periodicals

Black Enterprise, March 2001, p. 113.
Buffalo News (New York), March 6, 2005, p. G1.
Ebony, January 2004, p. 86.
Entertainment Weekly, March 11, 2005, p. 12; April 29, 2005, p. 152; June 24, 2005, p. 149.
Jet, December 1, 2003, p. 60.
New York Times, May 5, 2003, p. E3.
People, August 9, 2004, pp. 101-02.
Publishers Weekly, March 21, 2005, p. 12.
Star-Ledger (Newark, NJ), March 9, 2005, p. 32.
Variety, February 28, 2005, p. 56; April 18, 2005, p. 2.

Online

"Tyler Perry," Internet Movie Database, http://www.imdb.com (September 10, 2005).
Tyler Perry Online, http://www.tylerperry.com (September 10, 2005).

—*Catherine Victoria Donaldson*

Barry Prevor and Steven Shore

Owners of Steve & Barry's University Sportswear

Born Barry Prevor, c. 1963. Born Steven Shore, c. 1963. *Education:* Prevor: University of Pennsylvania, Wharton School of Business, business degree. Shore: Tulane University, business.

Addresses: *Office*—Steve & Barry's University Sportswear, 12 Harbour Park Dr., Port Washington, NY 11050.

Career

Began partnership selling T-shirts at flea market, c. 1970-84; co-CEOs, Steve & Barry's University Sportswear Inc, 1980s—; co-CEOs, 4004 Inc., 1980s—; opened first store, Philadelphia, 1985; expanded to more than 100 stores by 2005.

Sidelights

Barry Prevor and Steven Shore and are trying to revolutionize the clothing retail business in the same way Home Depot changed home improvement and Starbucks turned selling coffee into a multi-million dollar business. The two co-chief executive officers of Steve & Barry's University Sportswear began selling T-shirts in New York flea markets before opening their first store in Philadelphia, Pennsylvania. Their plan of keeping overhead costs low by strategies ranging from purchasing cheap office furniture to using the U.S. tariff system to their advantage, has resulted in the company being able to sell merchandise for up to only $10.

Both Prevor and Shore grew up on Long Island, just 20 miles apart from one another. They met at at the age of 15 during a camp that aimed to bring together various kids from different communities. Prevor and Shore became best friends. Both had a mutual interest in business. With just $100 they became business partners. Prevor designed T-shirts and they sold them at local flea markets for $1 a piece.

Though both attended college, with Prevor enrolled in the Wharton School of Business at the University of Pennsylvania and Shore at Tulane University, they continued selling their wares at local flea markets. After graduation, the duo continued growing their business. Both were careful to reinvest their money in the business so they could continue to sell their T-shirts for a dollar.

In 1985 Prevor and Shore opened Steve & Barry's University Sportswear in Philadelphia. The majority of their merchandise was the University of Pennsylvania's clothing. Though they could not continue selling their wares for $1, the company did sell clothing at a price that constantly beat the university bookstore's prices.

Prevor and Shore continued to open stores around the country, usually near a college or university campus. The company continued to make a profit, thanks in part to their low prices, low overhead costs, using little advertising in favor of word-of-mouth, and shrewdly using the United States' Harmonized Tariff System to their advantage. Also, the company's clothing, though sold at rock bottom prices, was made with quality products that may be slightly off, thanks to Prevor's skillful tariff engineering. By having the majority of the clothes made in different countries, especially those that had lower tariffs like Jordan, Swaziland, and Madagascar; or by adding such things as more cotton or ramie in a garment or making sure that a jacket was lined with a waterproof coating, Steve & Barry's University Sportswear saved millions and promptly passed the savings on to their customers. In addition to tariff engineering, Shore and Prevor also allowed their distributors the flexibility to pack their wares tightly and hold off shipping until the cargo hold was at capacity. In a *Newsday* article posted at the Atlasphere website, Shore stated, "Our slogan can't be 'We won't screw you,' because that just can't be a slogan. But they [customers] know they can come to us and not be taken advantage of."

By 1998 Prevor and Shore had opened eight stores around the United States. Their stores in Michigan came to the attention of a Taubman Centers employee who thought their concept would work well at one of the malls in the area, Great Lakes Crossing. The companies began negotiating and soon Steve & Barry's University Sportswear had opened their first mall store. The company also expanded their lines to include everyday wear for men, women, and children. The merchandise's prices still remained at $10 or less.

After opening at Great Lakes Crossing, Shore and Prevor as well as Taubman Centers saw immediate success. Customers flocked to their store to purchase quality clothing that did not put a dent in their pocket. In an interview with Greta Guest of the *Detroit Free Press,* David Weinert, senior vice president of leasing at Taubman, said, "It is a fun store, it is an exciting store. I would call it throwaway fashion like H&M and Forever 21. Steve & Barry's brand is really patterned after them with a little Old Navy thrown in. Their opportunity is huge in this country." With an increase in traffic, the Taubman Centers found the mall packed on a regular basis, thanks in part to Steve & Barry's.

With this new development, Prevor and Shore saw a way to get their products to a larger consumer base that would increase their revenue. The company continued to expand by acquiring space in local malls in the Midwestern and Southern states. With many major retail and department stores closing across the country, mall landlords were looking for new retailers to anchor their floundering malls. Steve & Barry's focused on these locations where they could rent 50,000 to 150,000 square feet. They also negotiated strongly so they could keep the cost of rent down, but still renovated so each new store

would follow the same style as the others. With its bright blue and yellow colors, a fun atmosphere that included loud music and televisions broadcasting ESPN, and continued record-low prices, the company consistently turned a profit with each new store opening. The increase in foot traffic at the malls also resulted in profits for both the mall and other neighboring stores.

Prevor and Shore also continued to keep costs low by furnishing their headquarters with second-hand furniture, sleeping in their newly rented space instead of in hotels, and doing their own secretarial work. While other stores are merging, shrinking, or even going out of business, Steve & Barry's had expanded to almost 100 stores in 2005, with plans to reach 120 by the end of that year. The duo also planned to continue their expansion by opening 60 more stores in 2006. Their revenues have doubled since 2003, and according to Peter Lattman of *Forbes,* "their chain should earn an estimated $50 million pretax on $700 million in sales" in 2005.

Prevor and Shore have had much success; their only negative has been the closing of their Purdue store due to a failed negotiation with Purdue University. Steve & Barry's University Sportswear is a privately held company with no plans to go public. Prevor told Divya Watal of *U.S. News & World Report,* "we're certainly exploring all our options in terms of raising capital and expanding beyond 80 stores to the 800 or 8,000 stores that we believe the company has the potential to achieve." As Prevor and Shore continue to expand others have taken notice. Lois Huff, a senior vice president at market-research firm Retail Forward, told *U.S. News & World Report's* Watal, "Steve & Barry's is at the forefront of a trend in retailing—what's called extreme retailing.... They target the 'good enough' consumer." With their low prices and smart business acumen, Prevor and Shore are changing the way consumers shop.

Sources

"Cheapskates," *Forbes,* http://www.forbes.com/business/forbes/2005/0704/076.htm (October 7, 2005).

"Differing views force Steve & Barry's to close its doors," *Purdue Exponent,* http://www.purdueexponent.org/interface/bebop/showstory.php?date=2005/03/01&section=campus (October 7, 2005).

"Luring the 10-buck crowd," *U.S. News & World Report,* http://www.usnews.com/usnews/biztech/articles/050919/19eeretail.htm (October 7, 2005).

"More from Steve & Barry," *U.S. News & World Report,* http://www.usnews.com/usnews/biztech/articles/050910/10stevebarry.htm (October 7, 2005).

"Pinching pennies: Steve & Barry's use many methods to cut customer costs," *Southeast Missourian,* http://semissourian.com/story/1118780.html

"Retail Clothing Entrepreneur Steve Shore," The Atlasphere, http://www.theatlasphere.com/metablog/316.php (October 7, 2005).

"Steve and Barry's relocates, creating world's largest 'M' clothing outlet," *Michigan Daily Online,* http://www.pub.umich.edu/daily/1996/sep/09-19-96/arts/arts2.html (October 7, 2005).

"Steve & Barry's Retail Revolution: The price is right," *Detroit Free Press,* http://www.freep.com (October 7, 2005).

"Steve & Barry's Scores A Hit," *Retail Traffic,* http://retailtrafficmag.com/mag/retail_steve_barrys_scores/ (October 7, 2005).

—*Ashyia N. Henderson*

Deborah Pryce

© *Paul Morse/White House Photo/Reuters/Corbis*

Chairman of the House Republican Committee

Born Deborah D. Pryce; July 29, 1951, in Warren, Ohio; married Randy Walker (divorced, 2001); children: Caroline, Mia. *Education:* Ohio State University, B.A., 1973; Capital University Law School, J.D., 1976.

Addresses: *Office*—204 Cannon House Office Building, Washington, DC 20515. *Website*—www.house.gov/pryce.

Career

Administrative law judge for the Ohio Department of Insurance, 1976-78; held several jobs in Columbus (Ohio) City Attorney's Office, including first assistant city prosecutor, senior assistant city attorney, and assistant city manager, 1978-85; Franklin County (Ohio) Municipal Court judge, 1989, 1990 and 1992; elected to U.S. Congress, 1992; sworn in, 1993; became House Republican Conference Secretary, 1997; vice-chairman of the House Republican Conference, 2000; became House Republican Conference Chairman, 2002.

Awards: Inducted into the Ohio Women's Hall of Fame, 2001.

Sidelights

Congresswoman Deborah Pryce, chairman of the House Republican Committee, is, as Elizabeth Auster of the *Plain Dealer* in Cleveland wrote, "the most powerful Republican congresswoman in history." The former judge was elected to Congress in 1992, allied herself with Newt Gingrich as he led Republicans to a majority in the House of Representatives, and took her first leadership position in the House in 1997. Her personal life and her work as a lawmaker have sometimes been intimately related. A strong supporter of laws encouraging adoption, she has adopted two children herself. Her first daughter died in 1999 of cancer, and Pryce has become outspoken on cancer issues. After divorcing her husband, she adopted another daughter at the age of 50.

Pryce, born in 1951, grew up in Champion, a small town in northeast Ohio. She is the oldest of five children. Her parents were both pharmacists, and she spent some of her childhood helping out at their pharmacies. She got her undergraduate degree from Ohio State University and her law degree from Capital University Law School, both in Columbus, Ohio. After working as an administrative law judge for the state government, she spent several years working for the Columbus city attorney's office.

For most of her political career, Pryce has been known for being shy and not particularly aggressive. She has attributed her shyness in public to her mother, who used to make comments about women who were dressed too audaciously in church. Pryce first ran for a judgeship at the suggestion of her boss in the city attorney's office, joining the Franklin County municipal bench in 1989. The next year, she and her husband Randy Walker, a real estate developer, adopted a daughter, Caroline.

When a veteran Republican congressman from suburban Columbus retired in 1992, Pryce ran for his seat. She was unopposed in the Republican primary, but in the general election, in addition to facing a Democrat, she had to contend with an independent candidate who ran on an anti-abortion platform after finding out Pryce supported abortion rights. Pryce beat her two opponents with 44 percent of the vote.

Pryce was sworn in as a representative in 1993. She tried to get a seat on the House Judiciary Committee, thinking she was a natural choice since she used to be a judge. But she did not get the position because she supported abortion rights, and the chairman of the committee, Henry Hyde, was strongly anti-abortion. That year, Pryce, who was part of a wave of new female lawmakers elected in 1992, got 34 of her Republican colleagues to sign a petition protesting Rep. Fortney Stark's comment that Rep. Nancy Johnson, one of the Republican caucus' health-care experts, had learned about a health-care issue during "pillow talk" with her husband, a doctor. "When it's said in a public hearing to a woman, it denigrates all the women in the House and all the women in America. This is the kind of thing we just need to be vigilant about," Pryce told Kevin Merida of the *Washington Post.*

But Pryce was not an outsider for long. Two years later, when the Republicans took over Congress and Newt Gingrich became speaker of the house, Gingrich asked her to serve on a committee that looked at the rules and laws involved when control of the House transfers from one party to the other. Next, Gingrich put Pryce on the powerful Rules Committee. Pryce, in return, told the *New York Times* that she valued Gingrich's ability to listen to advice and suggestions.

In 1997, Pryce won her first leadership post in the House as secretary of its Republican conference. She was still famously ambivalent about being a public figure; former congresswoman Susan Molinari had to coax Pryce to run for the job. She ran for secretary in part because she felt the party leadership at the time needed to speak more to the party's "qui-

eter, hard-working tax-paying moderate middle," as she put it to Pat Griffith of the Toledo *Blade.* Pryce proudly called herself a moderate, especially on social issues, but she was conservative enough that she won the trust of the party's conservatives. She was loyal to Gingrich and the Contract With America, the platform he championed, and she beat an anti-Gingrich candidate for the secretary post. It was a time of chaos among House Republicans. Moderates in the House had tried and failed to remove Gingrich as speaker. So the first leadership meeting Pryce had to organize was dedicated to confronting the coup plotters; while doing so, she found that both Gingrich loyalists and moderates trusted her.

Pryce became known as a specialist on legislation about adoption, health, and crime. She was also known for getting representatives on different sides of divisive issues to compromise, a talent she had developed during her years as a judge. "She's very smooth," Rep. John Boehner, a fellow Ohio Republican, told Auster of the *Plain Dealer.* "She's always moving, always seeking higher ground, and she does it in a way that doesn't threaten people."

In 1998, Pryce's life turned tragic. Her eight-year-old daughter, Caroline, was diagnosed with a cancer called neuroblastoma that attacks the nerves. Pryce took a leave of absence from Congress for two months to care for her. Her condition seemed to improve after treatment, but in August of 1999 doctors discovered the cancer had spread to her spine; one month later, she died. In Caroline's honor, Pryce and her husband started a charity for childhood cancer patients, Hope Street Kids. Pryce also became a leading advocate in Congress for cancer patients and sponsored a bill for improving the end-of-life care of terminally ill children; at one point, when Caroline was near death, a hospice denied Pryce's request for more pain medication for her, and Pryce moved her daughter home and enrolled her in a home hospice program with different rules about dispensing drugs.

Two years after Caroline's death, Pryce announced that she and her husband were divorcing. Pryce later explained that the stress of Caroline's death hurt their marriage, and that she wanted to adopt again, while her husband, who was in his 50s, did not. "Randy just wasn't ready for another child," Pryce told the *Plain Dealer*'s Auster. "I came from a big, close, wonderful family and I just can't imagine going through life without that."

Pryce adopted a newborn daughter, Mia, becoming a single mom at age 50. Her job and her daughter have helped distract her from her grief, she told

Auster of the *Plain Dealer*. "If I didn't have this other stuff going on, I couldn't stand it. I'd have a lot more time to feel sorry for myself, and that wouldn't help the situation." One of her close friends and several members of her family watch the baby while Pryce is working. Mia is African American, so Pryce tries to make sure her daughter grows up with a knowledge of African-American culture, buying her children's books with black characters and taking her to a multicultural church in the Columbus area.

After more than a decade in Congress, Pryce is still generally considered socially moderate and conservative on foreign policy and economics. In 2003, for instance, she said she was in favor of war with Iraq and President George W. Bush's economic plan, was personally opposed to abortion but not willing to make it illegal, and in favor of stem cell research. She and other Republican congresswomen have worked to include more child-care funding in welfare reforms.

In 2000, Pryce moved up to the number-five position in House Republican leadership, vice-chairman of the House Republican Conference. In 2002, Pryce beat two men more conservative than her to become chairman of the conference, making her the fourth most powerful House Republican, one of the "Big Four" leaders who determine the House's agenda. She said she hoped to help the Republican Party speak to a broader audience and not be led only by conservative men. "If you talk about tax relief in terms of a mom trying to make ends meet and paying the grocery bills, it's a different message than just talking about it in terms of business and stocks and bonds and that type of thing," she told the *Plain Dealer*'s Auster. She often told fellow Republicans, during closed meetings, not to use language that might alienate female voters. Pryce also founded a political action committee, VIEW PAC, to help female Republican candidates.

Still, Pryce could fight with Democrats and stand by Republican leadership's decisions as well as any conservative. When asked if the leadership's attempt to pass a constitutional amendment banning flag-burning contradicted its pledge to focus on bills that affect people's everyday lives, she told Mike Allen of the *Washington Post*, "This is probably as relevant to people's lives now as any other time because of what's going on with Democrats putting everybody in the world before our soldiers and the American safety." She suggested that Democrats were overly worried about conditions in the U.S. military prison at Guantanamo Bay, Cuba. "And the flag has a place in that debate."

Pryce also became a crusader in the fight against the trafficking of women. She wrote a bill to fight sex trafficking, held congressional hearings on the subject and led a tour of congresspeople who went to southern and eastern Europe on a fact-finding mission about such crimes. She also arranged for surgery for a woman from Moldova who was severely injured while escaping from a forced-prostitution ring. "A nation that stands for the freedom and dignity of every human being cannot tolerate the degradation and exploitation of the innocent going on on our own soil," Pryce said, as quoted by Sabrina Eaton in the *Plain Dealer*. Congress passed Pryce's bill in 2005 and Bush signed it into law in January of 2006.

Around the same time, when some Republican moderates voted against Bush's budget-cutting package, which imposed new rules on welfare, Medicaid, and student loan recipients, and other Republicans questioned the prudence of a new round of tax cuts, Pryce stood up for both bills. "American taxpayers, and anyone concerned with the nation's long-term fiscal stability, have won a great victory today," she said when the budget cuts passed by two votes in February of 2006, as quoted by Jonathan Weisman of the *Washington Post*.

As 2005 ended, Democrats hoping to win Republican seats in Ohio's 2006 elections became optimistic that they could unseat Pryce. Though she had been considered unbeatable in past elections, she won in 2004 with only 60 percent of the vote. Because of Republican scandals in Washington and Ohio and many voters' disenchantment with the president and the Iraq war, many Democrats believed their challenger to Pryce, Mary Jo Kilroy, president of the Franklin County Board of Commissioners, could beat her. However, Pryce said she felt the tide would turn back toward Republicans by November, once statewide scandals receded and if progress were made in the Iraq war. "I think that things will change enough that Ohio won't be quite as fertile as the Democrats believe it is right now," she told Sheryl Gay Stolberg of the *New York Times*. Pryce dodged what would have been a serious setback to her career in February of 2006, when she held onto her leadership position after a brief period in which it appeared she might be challenged. Even if she retains her seat, Pryce's allies wonder how much higher she can rise in House Republican leadership, considering her support of abortion rights. She is unlikely to ever become speaker of the house, for instance. However, when asked about her future, Pryce did not rule out a run for another position, such as a statewide office.

Sources

Periodicals

Blade (Toledo, OH), October 12, 1997, p. F2.
Cincinnati Post, June 8, 2000, p. A3.
Dayton Daily News (Ohio), February 6, 2006, p. B1.
Good Housekeeping, September 2004, pp. 134-37.
Lancaster Eagle-Gazette (Ohio), September 19, 2003, p. A4.
New York Times, December 26, 1994; August 9, 1997; December 3, 2005, p. A16.
Plain Dealer (Cleveland), March 16, 2003, p. 8 (Sunday magazine); January 11, 2006, p. A9.

Washington Post, March 30, 1994, p. A1; April 29, 1998, p. A19; November 15, 2000, p. A5; June 22, 2005, p. A8; December 8, 2005, p. A1; February 2, 2006, p. A1.

Online

"Biography," United States House of Representatives, http://www.house.gov/pryce/biography.htm (February 25, 2006).
"Pryce, Deborah D.: Biographical Information," Biographical Directory of the United States Congress, http://bioguide.congress.gov/scripts/biodisplay.pl?index=P000555 (February 25, 2006).

—Erick Trickey

Anders Fogh Rasmussen

Jason Reed/Reuters/Landov

Prime Minister of Denmark

Born on January 26, 1953, in Ginnerup, Nørre Djurs, Denmark; son of Knud (a farmer) and Martha Rasmussen; married to Anne-Mette; children: three. *Education:* Earned degree in economics from the University of Århus, 1978.

Addresses: *Office*—Statsministeriet (Prime Minister's Office), Christiansborg, DK-1218 Copenhagen K, Denmark.

Career

Founder and chairman of the Young Liberals organization at Viborg Cathedral School, 1970-72; first elected to Folketing (legislative assembly of Denmark), 1978; served as minister for taxation, September, 1987-November, 1992; served as minister for economic affairs, December, 1990-November, 1992; leader of Denmark's Liberal Party, 2001—; became prime minister, November, 2001, elections, and formed coalition government; reelected February, 2005.

Sidelights

Anders Fogh Rasmussen, head of Denmark's Liberal Party, has served as prime minister since 2001. That year's election results marked the first time since the 1920s that Denmark's politically dominant leftist party, the Social Democrats, had been spurned by voters. As party leader, Rasmus-

sen became prime minister and formed a center-right coalition government with another party. In his first years in office, Rasmussen's government enacted several sweeping reforms, most aimed at curbing immigration and increasing free-market competition inside the Danish economy.

Rasmussen was born on January 26, 1953, in Ginnerup, a town in the Nørre Djurs coastal region of Denmark's Jutland peninsula. He grew up on one of the many small family farms that dotted the Århus county area, and emerged as a political leader while still in his teens. At the Viborg Cathedral School, he became one of the founders of the Young Liberals group, a youth group affiliated with Denmark's center-right Liberal Party. It was an era of widespread protest among his generation, but the Young Liberals were formed in reaction to the sweeping student movement in Western Europe that had taken a decidedly leftist tone. Denmark's Liberal Party—called *Venstre* ("left")—was actually less of a left-of-center group than the term "liberal" commonly denotes in North American political terminology. Generally known as a pro-business party, the Liberals called for less government regulation and lower taxes.

Rasmussen studied economics at the University of Århus, and became the national chairperson for the Young Liberals group in 1974. In 1978, the same year he earned his degree, he was elected to the *Folketing,* Denmark's national legislative body, on the Liberal Party ticket. Since the 1920s, the seats in the Folketing had been dominated by the Social Democrats, Denmark's traditional center-left party. Other competing factions included the Danish People's Party, the far-right group; the Conservative Party, the Socialist People's Party, and the Christian People's Party.

Rasmussen served several years in the Folketing, and became known for his economic expertise. He authored a number of books on the subject, including 1979's *Opgør med skattesystemet* ("Showdown with the Tax System") and *Fra Socialstat til Minimalsta* ("From Social State to Minimal State"), which was published in 1993. Denmark has one of the highest tax-per-person ratios in the world, but the taxes pay for a generous social-service net and its citizens enjoy one of the world's highest standards of living. In his writings and in his political speeches, Rasmussen argued that such a system fosters a dependency on the government, and quells initiative and free enterprise.

In 1987, Rasmussen was appointed to the important cabinet post of minister for taxation. Three years later, he was made minister for economic affairs for a two-year stint; after 1992, he held his seat in the Folketing while retaining various roles in the Liberal Party leadership, including party spokesperson. In 2001, the Prime Minister, Poul Nyrup Rasmussen—no relation—thought November would be a good time for his Social Democrat Party to capitalize on a wave of solidarity stemming from the terrorist attacks on the United States on September 11 of that year, and called for national elections that month. The poll results, however, brought a surprise, with the Social Democrats winning just 29 percent of the Folketing seats, and Rasmussen and the Liberal Party taking 31 percent. It marked the first time that the Social Democrats had been bested by another party since the 1920s. Another surprise was the votes cast for the far right Danish People's Party, which amounted to 12 percent of the tally. Its leader had made anti-Muslim statements that seemed to resonate with nervous Danes in the fearful post-9/11 climate, despite the country's reputation for tolerance. About six percent of Denmark are immigrants, and three percent of the total population list their faith as Muslim in what has historically been a country with a strong Lutheran tra- dition.

Since Rasmussen and his party did not win an outright majority in the Folketing, he formed a coalition government with the Conservatives, which had won nine percent of the vote. The new center-right government, led by Rasmussen, succeeded on most of the reforms it pledged to push forward during the campaign. There were new restrictions on immigration, for example, and in July of 2002 the government issued a decree that Denmark would only to accept refugees who could prove that they were victims of religious, political, or ethnic persecution. That resulted in a dramatic drop in number of those applying for asylum in Denmark, from 12,000 in 2001 down to just 3,000 in 2004.

Rasmussen supported U.S. president George W. Bush and his plans for the 2003 U.S.-led invasion of Iraq, unlike many Western European leaders. Denmark even sent a contingent of troops, but public support lessened considerably for Denmark's participation over the next two years. In February of 2005, Danes went to the polls again, and though Rasmussen's Liberal Party lost four seats, it maintained its lead in the Folketing and kept control of the government. The prime minister received a high number of personal votes, more than 61,000, which was said to be the most ever won by a Danish politician. His main rival was Mogens Lykketoft, head of Social Democrat Party. Rasmussen is known for his telegenic looks and ease before both the Folketing and television cameras, by contrast to the stodgier, bearded Lykketoft, who resigned from his party leadership after the 2005 election.

Rasmussen surprised many in the spring of 2005 on the 60-year anniversary of the end of World War II in Europe, when he issued a formal apology for Denmark's wartime collaboration with Nazi Germany. The country had been invaded by Nazi Germany, and initially refused to comply with orders to identify and round up its Jewish citizens. Some 7,000 Jews were rescued by a collaborative effort between Danish authorities, the resistance movement, and ordinary citizens, but about 450 were transported to Nazi extermination camps in Eastern Europe. Rasmussen specifically apologized for the government's cooperation in the extradition of those Jews, calling it "shameful" and "a stain on Denmark's otherwise good reputation" according to a BBC News report.

Rasmussen is married and has three children. Known for his healthy lifestyle, he runs every morning, which he claims clears his head for the day's work ahead.

Sources

Books

Worldmark Encyclopedia of the Nations: World Leaders, Gale, 2003.

Periodicals

Europe, December 2001, p. 25; June 2002, p. 26.
Independent (London, England), February 8, 2005, p. 20.
New York Times, November 22, 2001, p. A16.
Times (London, England), November 22, 2001, p. 19.

Online

"Anders Fogh Rasmussen," Folketingnet, http://www.folketinget.dk/BAGGRUND/Biografier_english/Anders_Fogh_Rasmussen.htm (August 23, 2005).
"Danish PM's collaboration apology," BBC News, http://news.bbc.co.uk/2/hi/europe/4515089.stm (August 23, 2005).
"Profile: Denmark's new prime minister," BBC News, http://news.bbc.co.uk/1/hi/world/europe/1669243.stm (August 23, 2005).

—*Carol Brennan*

Harry Reid

Roger L. Wollenberg/UPI/Landov

United States Senate Minority Leader

Born December 2, 1939, in Searchlight, NV; son of Harry Sr. (a gold miner) and Inez (a laundry worker) Reid; married Landra Gould, 1959; children: Lana, Rory, Leif, Josh, Key. *Religion:* Mormon. *Education:* Utah State University, B.A., 1961; George Washington University, J.D., 1964.

Addresses: *Office*—528 Hart Senate Office Building, Washington, DC 20510. *Website*—http://www.reid.senate.gov.

Career

Police officer at U.S. Capitol, c. 1961-63; city attorney, Henderson, NV, 1964-66; Nevada state assemblyman, 1969-1970; Nevada lieutenant governor, 1970-74; ran for U.S. Senate but lost, 1974; chairman of the Nevada Gaming Commission, 1977-81; attorney in private practice, 1981-83; congressman, 1983-87; U.S. senator, 1987—; Senate Democratic Whip, 1998-2004; Senate Minority Leader, 2005—.

Sidelights

When Harry Reid was elected to lead the U.S. Senate's Democrats in November of 2004, his party was struggling and needed new direction. The Democrats had just lost the presidential race to George W. Bush and seen their former Senate leader lose his re-election campaign. At first glance, Reid might not have seemed like the obvious choice to take over the job. He is blunt, sometimes shy, not a gifted speaker, and more conservative than most Democrats on some social issues. But Reid, a savvy

legislator skilled at making deals, quickly showed a willingness to joust with the president on core Democratic issues such as preserving Social Security. Also, Reid comes from Nevada, the sort of moderate-to-conservative swing state where Democrats need to win in order to make a national comeback. Most of all, for a party whose last two presidential candidates were criticized for not relating well to regular people, Reid is a humble leader with a tough, self-made life story.

Reid was born in 1939 in Searchlight, Nevada, a town so small that he had the same teacher for eight grades. His father, Harry Sr., was a gold miner with a limited education; his mother, Inez, did laundry, some of it from Searchlight's bordellos. Reid's home when he was growing up was made out of railroad ties. There was no indoor toilet or running water. In a town where most people had a nickname, sometimes a cruel one, Reid was known as "Pinky" (either for his pinkish skin tone or his reddish hair). There was no high school in Searchlight, so Reid hitchhiked every week to Henderson, 40 miles away, and spent the week with relatives there while he went to high school.

In Henderson, he became friends with Mike O'Callaghan, a high school teacher who taught him how to box and later became a key political ally. He also met his wife, Landra Gould. In 1959, when he was 20 and she was 19, they eloped. (Her parents had disapproved of their relationship because they were Jewish and he was not, but once the young couple called from Las Vegas with the news that they were married, the Goulds supported their daughter's decision.) Reid went to college in Utah, where he also boxed as an amateur middleweight. He and his wife converted to Mormonism while there (he was not raised in a religion), but they also observed Jewish holidays until the deaths of both of her parents.

After graduating from college in 1961, Reid moved to Washington, D.C. to attend George Washington University law school. Money was tight for him and his young family (his oldest son and only daughter were born in 1961 and 1962); he worked six days a week as a police officer at the U.S. Capitol. He returned to Henderson to practice law, and became the city government's attorney.

Reid was elected to the Nevada state assembly in 1968—beginning his term in 1969—where he criticized the telephone company for providing bad service, one of the issues that gave him a reputation as a consumer advocate. Two years later his friend O'Callaghan, who had also become successful in politics, decided to run for governor of Nevada and invited Reid, just 30 years old, to run for lieutenant governor; Reid accepted. O'Callaghan was considered unlikely to win, but he did and so did Reid. Four years later, Reid decided to run for U.S. Senate, but he ran a negative campaign and narrowly lost. "I was young and impulsive and attacked everybody," he told New Yorker writer Elsa Walsh. "Every day, we would get up and find out who we were going to attack that day."

O'Callaghan gave Reid a new, tougher job in 1977: he appointed him to head the Nevada Gaming Commission, which regulates the state's casinos. The commission was fighting to keep organized crime from taking over gambling in the state; Reid banned several mobsters from all of Nevada's casinos and closed some casinos entirely. When a man named Jack Gordon tried to bribe Reid with $12,000 to win approval of his gaming devices, Reid reported him to the FBI, which arranged a sting. They caught Gordon on tape about to hand Reid the money. Reid, furious that Gordon thought him corruptible, tried to choke Gordon until FBI agents stopped him. Two years later, Reid's wife discovered that the family car had been rigged with a bomb that failed to explode. Reid suspected Gordon of having the bomb planted, but no connection was ever proven.

After his term on the commission, Reid spent some more time as a lawyer in private practice, then ran for Congress in 1982. He won, taking office in 1983.

He moved up to the Senate four years later. His website touts his work in the Senate on prescription drug costs and health care funding, securing more funds for military bases in Nevada, protecting scenic areas of Nevada such as Lake Tahoe and Red Rock Canyon, and increasing federal funding for education.

Reid became the Senate's Democratic whip, the number-two leader, in 1998 (after winning a third term in the Senate by less than 500 votes). The job of the whip is to gather votes for the party's priorities, and it fit Reid's talents. He "had long been adept at the hand-holding and favor-brokering that lubricate so much Senate business," wrote the Washington Post's Mark Leibovich. "Some senators are known for their constituency work, some for their campaign skills, some for their media savvy." Reid, Leibovich wrote, "is a floor-and-cloakroom guy," meaning someone whose power comes from persuading colleagues behind the scenes.

In 2001, Reid played a major role in convincing James Jeffords, a senator from Vermont, to leave the Republican Party to become an independent, and vote with the Democats, briefly giving the Democrats a majority in the Senate. Reid also gained attention for single-handedly conducting an eight-hour filibuster in 2003—speaking on the Senate floor in order to keep the Senate's Republican majority from scheduling bills and advancing its agenda before its Thanksgiving recess.

Reid's chance to become leader of the Senate Democrats came with the 2004 election, when Sen. Tom Daschle, then minority leader, lost his campaign for re-election (while Reid won another term with 61 percent of the vote). Reid had earned a good reputation as the minority whip, and he had explored running for the top post earlier, when Daschle was considering a run for president. By the morning after the election, Reid had lined up the support he needed.

Senate Democrats chose Reid to lead them even though he has more conservative views than most of them on some social issues: he is against gun control, abortion, and gay marriage. Since Nevada often votes Republican (Bush won it, 50 to 48 percent, in 2004), Reid is said to be sensitive to fellow Democrats from Republican-leaning states when they feel the need to follow to the wishes of their constituents, not the party. That helped make Reid a good choice for minority leader, some observers argued, since some Democratic senators up for reelection in 2006 are also from states that supported Bush, and Democrats need to expand their appeal if they want to win the presidency in 2008.

Reid strikes many observers as an unlikely leader because he is not a gifted public speaker or particularly charismatic. "I know my limitations," he told Walsh of the *New Yorker*. "I haven't gotten where I am by my good looks, my athletic ability, my great brain, my oratorical skills." Walsh agreed: "He is sixty-five, a trim man with short, graying hair and slightly stooped shoulders, and not someone who appears likely to jump up and down screaming," she wrote. "In public presentations, Reid is sometimes barely audible. In his haste to finish a speech, he sometimes mangles the text, and he is not much liked by television—he suffers from a certain charisma gap."

But, Walsh noted, the fact that Reid does not try hard to impress the media makes his fellow senators trust him more. Reid, she added, has done better than other Senate leaders at keeping his party united (at least in his first several months as leader). "He is in constant contact with colleagues, and even reserves a pocket in his suit for their written requests," Walsh wrote. She also quoted Reid's chief of staff, Susan McCue, as saying that her boss is always watching for someone's vulnerabilities in order to "disarm, to endear, to threaten, but most of all to instill fear."

The *Washington Post*'s Mark Leibovich portrayed Reid as a rough, tough guy who would rather talk about fistfights and boxing matches from his youth than become more polished. Reid has worked with a media consultant, but he dismisses the therapy-like advice of certain consultants (who advise, for instance, that the Democrats need to seem like strong father figures, not weak ones). A session with a speech-making coach who tried to make him more conscious about hand motions and other non-verbal cues did not go well.

"I always would rather dance than fight, but I know how to fight," Reid told reporters, as quoted by the *Washington Post*'s Dan Morgan after he was officially elected minority leader in November of 2004. That seemed to summarize Reid's approach to dealing with Republicans: willing to attack them on some issues and compromise with them on others.

In the first few months of his leadership, Reid's blunt attacks on the president gained more attention than any deal-making. He has called President Bush a "loser," and "liar," and "King George." At one weekly news conference in May of 2005, he blamed the president for "a fictitious crisis on Social Security," "deficits that are absolutely unbelievable," "an intractable war in Iraq," "destroying public education," and leaving people "begging for prescription drugs," according to the *Washington Post*'s Dana

Milbank. "It's either his way or no way," Reid complained about Bush at an appearance at an elementary school in Las Vegas, according to Walsh in the *New Yorker*.

Some of Reid's problems with Bush involve his decision to support storing nuclear waste inside Yucca Mountain, Nevada, a plan Reid opposes. Bush appeared to oppose the plan in 2000, when running for president, but he approved it once he was president. Reid confronted Bush at an Oval Office meeting about the issue in early 2002 (at a time when most Democrats were being careful to support the president because of the September 11, 2001, terrorist attacks); that was the first time he called Bush a liar. Another dispute came up in April of 2005, when Reid claimed Bush told him he would stay out of a Senate debate over the use of the filibuster. Vice-President Dick Cheney soon declared that, as president of the Senate, he would vote to change the filibuster rule if a Senate vote on it ended in a tie, infuriating Reid.

In March of 2005, Reid also called Federal Reserve Chairman Alan Greenspan (whom many Democrats have exempted from partisan criticism) one of Washington's biggest "political hacks," according to Dan Balz of the *Washington Post*. Reid was angry that Greenspan had supported fellow Republican Bush's privatization plan for Social Security and had not opposed the president's deficit spending.

Republicans fought back. In February of 2005, the Republican National Committee (RNC) attacked the new minority leader as too partisan and brought up a 2003 *Los Angeles Times article* about how one of Reid's sons and his son-in-law had worked as lobbyists for groups seeking support from Reid. (After the article came out, Reid banned relatives from lobbying him.) Reid denounced the RNC's attack and the president on the Senate floor. But he had already received an invitation to a dinner at the White House that night, and he went anyway. When he arrived, the president assured Reid he had nothing to do with the attack. The material about Reid was later removed from the RNC's website, on orders from Bush strategist Karl Rove.

Sometimes, Reid's bluntness has even upset fellow Democrats. They were upset when he declared on the Senate floor that it would take a miracle for the Democrats to regain a majority in the Senate in 2006, and when he speculated that he could support outspoken conservative Supreme Court justice Antonin Scalia for chief justice. Reid also reportedly had an argument with Sen. John Kerry, the 2004 Democratic candidate for president, about how best to oppose Bush in early 2005. But most early reviews of Reid's tenure as the Senate Democrats' leader were positive. Joe Klein of *Time,* for instance, noted that Reid had successfully opposed Bush's privatization plan for Social Security and convinced moderate Republicans to ally with Democrats to pass a major budget bill with grants for education, Medicaid, and cities.

In August of 2005, Reid was briefly hospitalized in Las Vegas for what was alternately described as a small stroke and a transient ischemic attack, a neurological dysfunction sometimes considered a warning sign for a stroke. It did not slow him down for long. Within a week, he was making a public appearance in North Las Vegas, where, in another reference to his past as a boxer, he joked that he felt ready to go a couple of rounds with the reporters there.

Reid surprised some observers in September of 2005 by announcing that he would vote against John Roberts, whom Bush had nominated to be chief justice of the Supreme Court. Reid said the arguments of civil rights and women's groups had swayed him. Reid declared that he had too many unanswered questions about Roberts (who, like most Supreme Court nominees, had declined to discuss how he would rule on specific issues). He also noted that Roberts had not distanced himself from remarks in his legal writings from when he was a lawyer for the Reagan Administration that some considered insensitive. However, Reid also declared that Democratic senators should vote their consciences, and many of them quickly announced they would support Roberts. Observers speculated that, since Roberts seemed destined to win Senate confirmation, Reid was using his vote to send a signal that Bush should choose a moderate as his second Supreme Court nominee.

By mid-fall of 2005, Reid was facing several tests as a leader, including how he and other Democratic senators would react to Bush's second Supreme Court nomination, how the Democrats would respond to a dip in Bush's popularity due to the Iraq war and Hurricane Katrina relief efforts, and how his party would fare in the Senate races of 2006.

Reid still lives in Searchlight, Nevada, which now has two casinos and a population of about 600, up from about 200 when he was born. Reid's official Senate biography cites his ties to Searchlight to suggest that he is grounded in the strong "Nevada values" of "hard work, opportunity, and independence." Reid even wrote a book about his town, which was published in 1998 and titled *Searchlight: The Camp That Didn't Fail.*

Some Nevadans have questioned Reid's use of his Searchlight tales for political effect. Las Vegas political analyst Jon Ralston told the *Washington Post*'s Leibovich that Reid's "practiced, pale-faced-bumpkin-from-Searchlight act" masked a "ruthless" and "Machiavellian" politician. But most observers acknowledge Reid's tough-upbringing stories are legitimate. Reid's father, who suffered from alcoholism, depression, and several work-related injuries, including silicosis, a lung disease common in miners, committed suicide at the age of 58.

Reid and his wife lived in a double-wide trailer in Searchlight until about 2001, when they had a two-bedroom house built for them on 100 acres. The home is decorated in a Western mining theme, with a gate from an old Searchlight mine hanging on the wall; from the house, the remains of a mine where his father worked are visible.

"I'm the face of the Democratic Party today," he told cable news channel Las Vegas One, as quoted by the *Washington Post*'s Charles Babington. "I'm not too sure that we need a show horse at this stage. I think maybe a workhorse may be what the country needs."

Selected writings

Searchlight: The Camp That Didn't Fail, University of Nevada Press, 1998.

Sources

Periodicals

Knight-Ridder News Service, March 3, 2005.
New Yorker, August 8/15, 2005, pp. 42-49.
New York Times, November 14, 2004, p. A26; February 9, 2005, p. A16; August 20, 2005, p. A11; September 21, 2005.
Time, November 22, 2004, p. 60; March 28, 2005, p. 23.
Washington Post, June 7, 2001, p. A3; July 9, 2001, p. A15; March 3, 2002, p. B7; November 16, 2004, p. A3; November 17, 2004, p. A4; March 4, 2005, p. A6; March 6, 2005, p. A5; May 11, 2005, p. A4; July 17, 2005, p. D1; August 25, 2005, p. C3.

Online

"Senator Reid," US Senator Harry Reid for Nevada, http://reid.senate.gov/biography.cfm (August 28, 2005).

—*Erick Trickey*

Karl Rove

Jim Bourg/Reuters/Landov

Deputy chief of staff for U.S. President George W. Bush

Born December 25, 1950, in Denver, CO; married Valerie Wainwright, 1977 (divorced, 1979), married Darby Hickson, 1986; children: Andrew (from second marriage). *Education:* Attended the University of Utah, the University of Texas at Austin, and George Mason University.

Addresses: *Office*—The White House, 1600 Pennsylvania Ave. NW, Washington, DC, 20500.

Career

National executive director, College Republicans, 1971-72; chair, College Republicans, 1973-74; worked for the Republican National Committee, 1973; finance director, Virginia Republican Party, 1976; worked for campaigns of George H.W. Bush, George W. Bush, and Bill Clements, 1977; chief of staff for the governor of Texas, 1978-81; founded the direct-mail business Karl Rove & Co., 1981; adviser to George W. Bush's campaigns for governor, 1993-94 and 1998; adviser to Bush presidential campaign, 2000; senior political adviser to President George W. Bush, 2001-04; deputy chief of staff for President George W. Bush, 2005—.

Sidelights

Karl Rove, the foremost American political strategist of his time, has wielded unprecedented power since George W. Bush, whom Rove advises, became president of the United States. Unlike strategists who served other presidents, and focused only on helping them win elections and influence the public, Rove followed Bush to the White House, where he helped form much of the Bush Administration's domestic policy agenda. "Rove is the administration's indispensable man, the connective tissue between the policies and constituencies needed to win elections and govern," wrote John D. McKinnon of the *Wall Street Journal*. Rove receives extensive credit for Bush's political success; one book about Rove was entitled *Bush's Brain*.

Before reaching the national stage with Bush, Rove developed a cutthroat reputation by developing a winning strategy for Republicans to take over and dominate politics in Texas. According to the *Guardian*'s Julian Borger, one political consultant, Mark McKinnon, called Rove "the Bobby Fischer of politics" (a reference to the former chess champion), because "he not only sees the board, he sees about 20 moves ahead."

Rove was born in Denver, Colorado, in 1950. He became politically aware and a staunch Republican at a very early age. At the age of nine, he was such an outspoken fan of Richard Nixon's presidential campaign that he was beaten up by an older girl who preferred John F. Kennedy. His family moved to Salt Lake City, Utah, where Rove attended high school and became a champion debater, going to school in a coat and tie and scaring his debate opponents by bringing boxes of index cards to debates (they did not know the cards were blank). He was elected president of his student government and worked on a U.S. senator's reelection campaign as a class project.

In 1969, Rove went to the University of Utah, where he joined the College Republicans. Through the group, he went to Illinois to work on a U.S. Senate campaign. By 1971, he became the College Republicans' national executive director. He showed a talent for writing short, simple, effective political messages and became a specialist in creating political literature and direct mail. He also traveled across the country on weekends, teaching seminars on activism to college conservatives. Meanwhile, Rove's parents divorced, and Rove learned that the man who had raised him—Louis, a mineral geologist—was not his biological father. (He did not meet his birth father until decades later.)

Rove never finished college. He left school to run for chair of the College Republicans in 1973, with Lee Atwater (who went on to run George H.W. Bush's campaign for president in 1988) as his top assistant. The bitter campaign for the chairmanship ended in a disputed election, and George H.W. Bush, then the chairman of the Republican National Committee, was asked to resolve the dispute. Bush not only ruled in Rove's favor, but got Rove a job with the Republican National Committee and became a mentor to him. While running an errand for Bush in 1973, Rove met Bush's son, George W. Bush, and the two became friends.

The Virginia Republican Party hired Rove in 1976 as its finance director, and Rove quickly demonstrated his fund-raising talents, raising $400,000 by mail within a year. His friendship with the Bush family took him to Texas in 1977, where he helped raise money for the elder Bush, who was thinking about running for president. He also informally advised the younger Bush in his unsuccessful campaign for Congress, and helped Bill Clements with his successful run for governor. Clements then made Rove his chief of staff.

Meanwhile, Rove's personal life continued to be troubled. He married Valerie Wainwright, a friend of the Bush family, in 1977, but his job did not leave him much time for her, and she divorced him two years later. In 1981, his mother committed suicide. In 1986, he married Darby Hickson, a graphic designer who worked for his direct-mail business.

Rove had started the business, Karl Rove & Co., in 1981 to aid Republican candidates in Texas. At the time, Texas was a Democratic state, and his candidates usually lost. His former boss, Clements, lost the governor's office in 1982. But Rove correctly predicted that the politics of Texas were about to change thanks to the growth of conservative suburbs. He helped U.S. Senator Phil Gramm switch to the Republican Party in 1983 and win reelection in 1984. Soon after, Rove wrote key memos that outlined a path to victory for Texas Republicans and formed a blueprint for campaigns he advised later. According to Joshua Green of the *Atlantic Monthly*, one memo, citing the French emperor Napoleon, told Clements to combine a "well-reasoned and extremely circumspect" defense with a "rapid and audacious attack." Another memo advised Republicans to appeal to suburbanites with a platform of lower taxes and support for education and traditional values. The strategy helped Clements get elected governor again in 1986. Rove followed up that victory with a Republican takeover of the Texas Supreme Court in 1988 by using the issue of tort reform, having Republican candidates argue that the court's Democratic judges were awarding too much money to plaintiffs. By the early 1990s, Rove was extremely influential in determining which Republicans became candidates for statewide office.

In 1993, Rove convinced George W. Bush to run for governor of Texas to unseat popular Democratic incumbent Ann Richards. With Rove's advice, Bush campaigned on four issues meant to appeal to suburban voters: welfare reform, support of education, tort reform, and juvenile justice. Bush stuck relentlessly to his message throughout the 1994 campaign and won. Next, Rove helped Republicans take over the Texas state senate in 1996 and helped Bush win reelection by a large margin in 1998. Meanwhile, Rove was also advising candidates for judgeships in Alabama. Green's *Atlantic Monthly* profile of Rove attributed several dirty tricks to him or the campaigns he managed there. For instance, in 1996, Rove arranged for vicious fliers to be distributed attacking his own candidate for state supreme court, Harold See, correctly guessing that voters would blame See's opponent for the offensive attack and elect See.

As George W. Bush began to explore a run for president of the United States, Rove recruited experts to tutor Bush in issues he did not understand well and made sure that Bush met various important people in full view of reporters. In 1999, Bush announced he would run for president. By June of that year, with Rove's help, he had raised an intimidating $36 million, making him the front-runner for the Republican nomination. When the 2000 primaries began, Bush was almost upset by Sen. John McCain of Arizona, who beat Bush by 19 points in New Hampshire. But Bush (again, with Rove's help) recovered in South Carolina, attacking McCain aggressively on abortion and other issues. McCain also faced a dirty rumor campaign questioning his mental health and falsely claiming he fathered an illegitimate child, though the Bush campaign denied involvement. Bush beat McCain in South Carolina and went on to win the Republican nomination. During the general election, Rove encouraged Bush to stick to similar themes as those he used in Texas: education, faith-based initiatives, and a promise to be a "compassionate conservative." The election ended up very close, with Vice-President Al Gore leading in the popular vote but Bush winning the most electoral votes, and the presidency, after being declared the winner in the disputed state of Florida.

Bush named Rove a senior adviser, and Rove immediately began strategizing for the 2002 congressional elections and the 2004 presidential campaign. In January of 2001, he announced a plan called the 72-Hour Task Force, meant to organize grassroots efforts to get out the vote in the last three days of a campaign. Rove also developed a new political strategy, focused less on suburban swing voters and more on mobilizing core Republican supporters, including evangelical Christians, since Rove's statistics on the 2000 presidential election showed that four million evangelicals did not vote. To minimize dissent and mixed messages in the Bush Administration, Rove held weekly meetings with the chiefs of staff of all the departments in Bush's cabinet.

By mid-2002, Rove was stressing that after the attacks of September 11, 2001, the war on terror could be a powerful campaign issue for Republicans. Sure enough, Rove and many Republican candidates attacked Democrats for opposing Bush's plan for establishing a homeland security department. As the elections neared, Rove decided to have Bush campaign in person for candidates for Senate in close races in states such as Georgia and Minnesota. At the grassroots level, Republicans executed Rove's voter-turnout strategies. The plans worked. Republicans won big in the 2002 elections, winning back control of the U.S. Senate. *Time* named Rove its Person of the Week after the election, with writer Jessica Reaves calling him "one of the country's sharpest and most instinctive political minds."

Rove's influence as Bush's political adviser was vast. He reportedly met with the president daily whenever both were in Washington. *New Yorker* journalist Nicholas Lemann reported that Rove "appears to have supervisory authority over the Re-

publican National Committee, ... functions as a national personnel director for the Republican Party, hand-selecting candidates for governorships and seats in the Senate and House, ... closely supervises political fund-raising," had proteges installed in several Cabinet departments, and was playing an important role in forming Bush's domestic policy. James Carney and John F. Dickerson of *Time* agreed. "There are few decisions, from tax cuts to judicial nominations to human cloning, in which Rove is not directly involved," they wrote.

But Carney and Dickerson discounted the common view of Bush critics that Rove was the mastermind behind Bush. Instead, they argued, Bush's partnership with Rove reflected the president's view that politics and policy were closely linked. "Bush and Rove share a mutual irreverence, a deep conservatism, a belief in the individual and in America's moral superiority, a disdain for northeastern elitists, and a revulsion against the if-it-feels-good, do-it liberalism of the '60s and '70s," Kenneth T. Walsh of *U.S. News and World Report* wrote.

When Senator John Kerry of Massachusetts won the Democratic nomination in 2004, Rove devised a strategy to beat him: attacking him for his Senate votes on the war in Iraq by accusing him of changing his position, or "flip-flopping." By contrast, Rove told Walsh of *U.S. News and World Report*, during the war on terror, Americans "want to know the president is not going to get up in the morning and change his beliefs because of what he thinks is fad or fashion." Rove also successfully advocated for the Republican National Convention to be held in New York City, again believing that reminding voters of the 9-11 terror attacks would help Bush politically. In August and September of 2004, when an organization called the Swift Boat Veterans for Truth aired ads suggesting Kerry had lied about his Vietnam War record, the Kerry campaign blamed the Bush campaign for the ads by pointing to Rove's friendship with Bob Perry, a major donor to the Swift Boat veterans. But Rove and the Bush campaign denied any connection.

Bush beat Kerry in the 2004 election by winning the key states of Florida and Ohio. Bush called Rove "the architect" in his acceptance speech. "Everyone in the room knew what that meant," *Washington Post* reporter Mike Allen told the PBS documentary program *Frontline*. Rove "was the architect of the public policies that got them there, he was the architect of the campaign platform, he was the architect of the fund-raising strategy, he was the architect of the state-by-state strategy, he was the architect of the travel itinerary. His hand was in all of it."

In February of 2005, Bush promoted Rove to deputy chief of staff. He began devising a legislative strategy that he hoped would help create support for an enduring Republican majority, including appointing conservative judges and reforming and partially privatizing Social Security.

But by the summer of 2005, Rove was back in the news for reasons he had not engineered. Special counsel Patrick Fitzgerald was investigating whether Rove had committed a crime by leaking the identity of Central Intelligence Agency (CIA) agent Valerie Plame to reporters in 2003. Plame's husband, former U.S. ambassador Joseph Wilson, believed that Bush administration officials had plotted the leak to retaliate for Wilson's public debunking of part of the case for war in Iraq, and Wilson declared that he wanted to see Rove "frog-marched out of the White House in handcuffs," as quoted by Nancy Gibbs of *Time*. In 2005, reports in *Newsweek* and *Time* confirmed that Rove had told *Time* reporter Matthew Cooper that Plame worked for the CIA. Rove had long denied leaking Plame's name, but this turned out to be a technicality: he had described her to Cooper as Wilson's wife instead of using her name.

But on October 28, 2005, Fitzgerald announced only one indictment, that of I. Lewis Libby, chief of staff to vice-president Dick Cheney. The prosecutor informed Rove he remained in legal jeopardy, the *Wall Street Journal* reported, but Fitzgerald appeared to have considered indicting Rove on charges of perjury or false statements, then backed away. By mid-November, Rove began to emerge from the low-profile stance he had taken during the Plame affair. He gave a speech in Washington, and White House staff reported that he was running meetings again and trying to recruit candidates for the 2006 elections. But at the end of November, Fitzgerald called a second *Time* reporter, Viveca Novak, to testify before the grand jury, a sign that Rove was still under investigation, though one news report suggested Novak's knowledge might actually be key to Rove's defense against possible charges.

After the 2004 election, Rove declared that he would not be involved in any more presidential campaigns, but he retreated from the statement soon after. Even if he is never the dominant strategist for another presidential candidate, few observers expect his ambitions to end with Bush's presidency. That is why so many Democrats were hoping, in late 2005, to see the Plame affair end Rove's career. Rove's ultimate goal, wrote Lemann in the *New Yorker*, "is creating a Republican majority that would be as solid as, say, the Democratic coalition that Franklin Roosevelt created—a majority that would last for a generation and ... would wind up profoundly changing the relationship between citizen and state in this country."

Sources

Periodicals

Atlantic Monthly, November 2004.
Guardian (London, England), July 22, 2005.
New Yorker, May 12, 2003.
New York Times, August 23, 2004, p. A1; October 26, 2005, p. A1; October 29, 2005, p. A14; November 11, 2005, p. A19; November 28, 2005, p. A17.
Time, November 7, 2002; November 18, 2002, pp. 44-45; July 22, 2005, pp. 25-40.
U.S. News and World Report, September 6, 2004, p. 30.
Wall Street Journal, October 10, 2005, p. A4; October 28, 2005, p. A3.
Washington Post, November 29, 2005, p. A1.

Online

"Karl Rove—The Architect: Mastermind: Chronology," PBS.org, http://www.pbs.org/wgbh/pages/frontline/shows/architect/rove/cron.html (November 15, 2005).

—Erick Trickey

Marjane Satrapi

AP Images

Graphic novelist

Born in 1969 in Rasht, Iran; married, c. 1994. *Education:* Graduated from L'Ecole de Beaux-Arts, Tehran, Iran; studied at Arts Deco in Strasbourg, France.

Addresses: *Agent*—Steven Barclay Agency, 12 Western Ave., Petaluma, CA 94952. *Publisher*—Pantheon, 1745 Broadway, New York, NY 10019.

Career

First graphic novel, *Persepolis*, published in France, 2000; *Persepolis 2* published in the United States, 2004; *Embroideries* published in the United States, 2005.

Awards: Prix Alph'art Coup de Coeur (beginning comic artist award), Angouleme International Comics Festival, for *Persepolis*, 2001; Prix du Lion, Belgian Center for Comic Strips, for *Persepolis*, 2001; Prix France Info for best news comic strip, France Info, for *Persepolis*, 2002; Prix Alph'art for best script, Angouleme International Comics Festival, for *Persepolis Tome 2*, 2002; Fernando Buesa Blanco Peace Prize, Fernando Buesa Blanco Foundation, 2003; Prix d'Angouleme for best book of the year, Angouleme International Comics Festival, for *Chicken and Plums*, 2005.

Sidelights

By recounting her life story of growing up in Iran and emigrating to Europe, and by telling it in graphic-novel form, Marjane Satrapi has become an unusual ambassador for her native country. She has also become a spokeswoman for greater freedom there and a voice against war and for cross-cultural understanding. Her use of graphic novels to tell autobiographical stories with political facets to them makes her messages especially accessible and affecting while bringing serious attention to the graphic-novel form.

Born in 1969 in Rasht, Iran, Satrapi grew up in Iran's capital, Tehran. She was an only child of secular, Marxist parents. Iran's Islamic Revolution against the shah, the country's monarch, took place in 1979, the year Satrapi turned ten, and her child's-eye view of the changes in her country later became a focus of her first book. Her parents, who were against the regime of the shah, happily joined in the first protests that helped depose him, but the religious rule that followed turned out to be worse for them. An uncle of Satrapi's was imprisoned by the shah's regime, then executed by revolutionaries. Her mother, who was not religious, eventually felt compelled to wear Islamic garb to avoid attracting the attention of the religious police.

Satrapi studied at the Lycee Francais, the French high school in Tehran. Her parents, who had taught her to think freely and not believe the propaganda the government required the teachers to teach, became concerned when Satrapi began to openly question the teachers. They wanted their rebellious daughter to live in a freer society, so they sent her to Austria to study.

In Vienna, as she later recounted in her second book, Satrapi expected to live with a friend of her parents, but when the friend decided she did not want Satrapi with her any longer, she sent the young woman to live in a convent. She left, according to the book, when one of the nuns used ethnic slurs while yelling at her. She threw herself headlong into life as a western teenager, befriending punks and anarchists and throwing herself into romantic relationships and drug use. She found various temporary homes until, finally, she ended up homeless in wintertime and woke up in a hospital.

At 18, she moved back to Tehran, where she attended college and struggled to adjust to living behind a veil and under the watch of the religious police, which would sometimes raid and break up the parties where she and her friends would wear makeup and western clothes. After college, she moved to France, where she studied art in Strasbourg, then moved to Paris. Some of her friends there, who were part of a prominent artist's studio called the Atelier des Vosges, introduced her to graphic novelists, starting with Art Spiegelman, whose graphic novel *Maus* told the story of the Holocaust through the lives of a few Jewish survivors. She realized she could tell stories and make serious points the same way. "Images are a way of writing," she wrote on the Pantheon website. "When you have the talent to be able to write and to draw it seems a shame to choose one. I think it's better to do both." Graphic novels had some of the advantages of filmmaking as a way to tell stories, but without needing sponsors or actors, she added.

Inspired, Satrapi created a book of black-and-white comic strips about living in Tehran from ages six to 14. The book, *Persepolis: The Story of a Childhood* (named after a part of Iran known for its ruins) tells the story of her growing up, while also showing the Islamic Revolution and its effects on Iranians. Toward the end of the book, war breaks out between Iran and Iraq, and her mother puts tape on the windows of the family home, anticipating correctly that Iraqi bombs will fall nearby. The book also included moments of humor. "Tales of torture and war are offset by lighter scenes, like the 13-year-old Marjane trying to convince the morals police that her Michael Jackson button is really a button of Malcolm X, 'the leader of black Muslims in America,'" wrote Tara Bahrampour in the *New York Times*. Iranians, Satrapi explained, are used to using humor to stave off despair.

Satrapi said she hoped *Persepolis* would combat the negative images people had of her native country. When the Iranian Revolution broke out, most people in the West only saw images of the revolutionary leaders, which did not reflect the lives of ordinary Iranians, she said. "If people are given the chance to experience life in more than one country, they will hate a little less," she wrote on the Pantheon website. "That is why I wanted people in other countries to read *Persepolis*, to see that I grew up just like other children." She also said she hoped to find a way to get the book to young Iranians, perhaps through the Internet, so that more of them could learn the truth about what happened in their country in the early 1980s.

Persepolis was published in France in two volumes in 2000 and 2001. Critics picked up on the influence of Spiegelman and favorably compared Satrapi's work to his. The first volume won two of Europe's biggest awards for comic books and graphic novels, the Angouleme International Comics Festival's Coup de Coeur award (for a book by an author who has published three or fewer books) and the Prix du Lion from a comics association in Belgium. When it appeared in the United States in 2003, it earned an endorsement from leading American feminist Gloria Steinem. Edward Nawotka, writing in *People*, called *Persepolis* "one of the quirkiest, most entertaining memoirs in recent years." Dave Welch of Powells.com said it "expressed in deceptively simple black-and-white drawings the broken heart and crushed hope of a people." One slightly dissenting comment came from Joy Press, writing in the *Village Voice*, who found Satrapi's youthful, innocent voice powerful but complained that the book did not reach the emotional depth of *Maus* and that its summaries of Iranian history were cute but not insightful. "Satrapi keeps us at arm's length, so that we never feel fully involved in this girl's intellectual and moral transformation," Press wrote.

The sequel, *Persepolis 2: The Story of a Return*, was published in the United States in 2004. Nawotka of *People* declared it "the most original coming-of-age story from the Middle East yet." It told the story of Satrapi's years in Austria and her return to Iran at 18, showing Iran through the new eyes she had when she returned, not just struggling against life under a fundamentalist regime, but also facing the suffering the war with Iraq had caused. In the sequel, she and her college friends found small ways to rebel. In art class, they had to draw women in head-to-toe chadors, and when she was sketching a clothed male model, she was scolded for staring at him too much. In private, she and her friends dressed up, wore makeup, and dated, which gave them bad reputations among their more conservative classmates. Many Iranians react to the religious police's regulation of behavior by living double lives, she said. "You know in the school you have to behave in a way, and in your home another way," she told Noreen S. Ahmed-Ullah of the *Chicago Tribune.* "You get older, and then you have to behave in some way in the street and in some other way in your home. That makes you become an extremely multipersonality person."

The simple style of Satrapi's art helped make her books accessible. "Satrapi's bold black-and-white drawings manage to be both highly graphic and almost cute," wrote book reviewer Karen Sandstrom in the Cleveland *Plain Dealer.* "Dynamic and clean-lined, they tend to reflect the text more often than complement or build upon it, yet Satrapi can't be accused of being too literal. Especially in scenes that revolve around military action or the most political aspects of the story, the artwork evokes the rhythmic, repetitive imagery common to Jazz Age art in the West."

Satrapi, who lives in France, writes her books in French, and they are published in France first, then translated and released in other countries later. Because her first book was released in the United States in 2003, the year that country went to war in Iraq and two years after the September 11 terrorist attacks, her American book tours were politically charged. She was detained and interrogated when entering the United States and often criticized the war and U.S. President George W. Bush. In interviews and cartoon commentaries in American publications, Satrapi said Bush reminded her of the religious fundamentalists in power in Iran and questioned whether Bush was really opposed to the Iranian government because he wanted American access to Iran's oil, not because of its reported attempts to build nuclear weapons.

Yet Satrapi also expressed surprise and gratitude at how well American audiences received her. "I have myself been judged by the government of my country, so I would never judge people by their countries," she told Connie Ogle of the *Miami Herald.* "She has discovered that strong and sometimes uncomfortable political convictions delivered in word bubbles by round-eyed cartoon characters can be easier to swallow than words alone," commented Bahrampour, writing for the *Washington Post.* In 2005, Satrapi spoke at the West Point military academy in the United States, where *Persepolis* was required reading. She described the experience in a commentary published in the *New York Times* in comic strip form. She was afraid the cadets would react angrily to her speech, in which she said she was against the war in Iraq. ("Democracy is not a present you give to people by bombing them," she quoted herself as saying.) Instead, the cadets she spoke to after the speech were open-minded about her point of view; one called her story inspiring.

Satrapi also spoke out about politics in her new home, France. When the French government decided to ban Muslim girls from wearing veils in public school, in an attempt to keep the schools strictly secular, Satrapi wrote in the British newspaper the *Guardian* that even though she was very much opposed to the veil, she felt that forbidding girls from wearing veils was just as repressive as forcing them to wear them. As for her native country, Satrapi stopped visiting Iran after her first book was published, concerned that her criticism of the regime might make it unsafe for her there.

Satrapi followed up her autobiographical stories with the book *Embroideries,* published in the United States in 2005. It is a frank account of a long conversation in Tehran with her mother, aunt, and grandmother and their friends about men, love, and sex. Many reviewers commented on how the women's candid talk contrasted with Western assumptions that Iran must be a sexually repressed society. Though religious police try to regulate the romantic lives of single Iranians, *Embroideries* shows that women speak frankly behind closed doors, and married women especially show little embarrassment about talking about sexual matters.

Satrapi is married to a Swedish man. She has also authored the French children's books *Adjar* and *Le Soupir.* Her next book for adults, *Chicken with Plums,* about her great-uncle, a musician, who tells his life story in the last few days before he dies, was published in France in 2004 and was scheduled to be published in the United States in the fall of 2006. As 2006 began, according to her agent's website, she was working on adapting *Persepolis* into an animated film.

Selected writings

Sagesses et malices de la Perse (with I. Ouali and N. Motalg), Albin Michel, 2001.
Adjar, Nathan Jeunesse, 2002.
Persepolis: The Story of a Childhood, Pantheon, 2003 (published in France as *Persepolis Tome 1* and *Persepolis Tome 2* by L'Association, 2000 and 2001).
Persepolis 2: The Story of a Return, Pantheon, 2004 (published in France as *Persepolis Tome 3* and *Persepolis Tome 4* by L'Association, 2002 and 2003).
Le Soupir, Breal, 2004.

Embroideries, Pantheon, 2005 (published in France by L'Association, 2003).

Chicken with Plums, L'Association, 2004 (forthcoming in the United States from Pantheon, 2006).

Sources

Periodicals

Chicago Tribune, May 11, 2003; October 10, 2004, p. Q3; June 22, 2005.

Guardian, December 12, 2003.

Miami Herald, October 9, 2004, p. 1E.

New York Times, May 21, 2003, p. E1; May 28, 2005.

People, September 6, 2004, p. 53.

Plain Dealer (Cleveland, OH), August 29, 2004, p. J12.

San Francisco Chronicle, August 29, 2004, p. M1; October 2, 2004, p. E1.

Seattle Weekly, September 8, 2004.

Village Voice, May 2, 2003.

Washington Post, November 28, 2004, p. T4.

Online

"Author Biography," Pantheon Graphic Novels, http://www.randomhouse.com/pantheon/graphicnovels/satrapi.html (February 25, 2006).

"Authors: Marjane Satrapi," Random House, http://www.randomhouse.com/author/results.pperl?authored=43801 (February 25, 2006).

"Marjane Satrapi," Clair de Bulle, http://clairdebulle.com/Auteur3633b98ab5cc4ff7b3e63634f3160370.aspx (March 3, 2006).

"Marjane Satrapi: On Writing Persepolis," Pantheon Graphic Novels, http://www.randomhouse.com/pantheon/graphicnovels/satrapi2.html (February 25, 2006).

"Marjane Satrapi Returns," Powells.com, http://www.powells.com/authors/satrapi.html (February 25, 2006).

"Marjane Satrapi," Stephen Barclay Agency, http://www.barclayagency.com/satrapi.html (February 25, 2006).

—Erick Trickey

Kyra Sedgwick

Actress

© Lori Conn/ZUMA/Corbis

Born August 19, 1965, in New York, NY; married Kevin Bacon (an actor), September 3, 1988; children: Travis, Sosie. *Education:* Attended Sarah Lawrence College, New York, NY; attended University of Southern California, c. 1982-85.

Addresses: *Agent*—Endeavor Agency, 9601 Wilshire Blvd., tenth fl., Beverly Hills, CA 90212.

Career

Actress on television, including: *Another World,* 1982-83; *Cindy Eller: A Modern Fairy Tale* (movie), 1985; *Miami Vice,* 1985; *Amazing Stories* 1986; *The Wide Net* (movie), 1987; *The Man Who Broke 1,000 Chains* (movie), 1987; *Lemon Sky* (movie), 1988; *Women and Men: Stories of Seduction* (movie), 1990; *Women & Men 2: In Love There Are No Rules* (movie), 1991; *Miss Rose White* (movie), 1992; *Family Pictures* (movie), 1993; *Losing Chase* (movie), 1996; *Talk to Me,* 2000; *Door to Door* (movie), 2002; *Something the Lord Made* (movie), 2004; *The Closer,* 2005—. Film appearances include: *War and Love,* 1985; *Kansas,* 1988; *Born on the Fourth of July,* 1989; *Mr. & Mrs. Bridge,* 1990; *Singles,* 1992; *Something to Talk About,* 1995; *Murder in the First,* 1995; *Phenomenon,* 1996; *Montana,* 1998; *Labor Pains,* 2000; *What's Cooking?,* 2000; *Behind the Red Door,* 2002; *Just a Kiss,* 2002; *Personal Velocity,* 2002; *Secondhand Lions,* 2003; *Batman: Mystery of the Batwoman* (voice), 2003; *Cavedweller,* 2004; *The Woodsman,* 2004; *Loverboy,* 2005. Also executive producer of *Losing Chase,* 1996; *Talk to Me,* 2000; *Cavedweller,* 2004. Producer of *Loverboy,* 2005.

Sidelights

Kyra Sedgwick vaulted over an invisible show-business barrier in 2005 when she won rave reviews as *The Closer,* a superbly smooth police detective in a new series for the cable network TNT. Long known as an able supporting player and too-often typecast as a scrappy, foul-mouthed blonde, Sedgwick is also somewhat famous for being the spouse of Kevin Bacon in one of the entertainment world's more enduring marital unions. Prior to the TNT hit, Sedgwick had rarely carried a picture or series on her own, and had not always fared well when she did. Her new cop drama was a perfect fit, however. "I feel like I've fallen into a jar of honey," she told *Entertainment Weekly* writer Missy Schwartz. "I love this character. She's so rich, so flawed, so smart. I feel hugely attached to her."

Sedgwick bears the name of an esteemed New England family whose roots in America date back to the 1630s, and have included several prominent judges, politicians, and literary achievers over the generations. She shared a great-grandfather with Edie Sedgwick, a model and downtown New York art-scene denizen who appeared in the American edition of Vogue in August of 1965, the same month that Sedgwick was born. Her cousin was part of the crowd who hung out with pop artist Andy Warhol at his Factory loft and filmmaking space, but disappeared from the scene and died of a drug overdose in 1971 at the age of 28.

Sedgwick grew up in a drastically more sedate milieu, in New York City as the daughter of a venture capitalist and a mother who was a speech therapist but later became a family therapist. Drawn to the dramatic arts from an early age, she took acting classes and worked in summer-stock theater before landing her first professional role, on the NBC daytime drama *Another World* in 1982. After finishing at Friends School in Manhattan, she spent a semester at Sarah Lawrence College in the Bronx, and then headed west to take classes at the University of Southern California while trying to land work in Hollywood. Her somewhat unconventional beauty—an angular face, wide mouth, and cascading blond locks—made producers and directors wary about casting her. "I'd hear: 'Kyra gave the best reading, hands down' or 'Kyra really gives good meeting,'" she told Los Angeles *Daily News* writer Jan Hoffman, "And then comes, 'But we're looking for a different type.'"

Sedgwick's feature-film debut came in a little-seen 1985 movie about a young Jewish man in Warsaw, Poland, during World War II called *War and Love*. *New York Times* critic Vincent Canby slammed the film as "a series of awkwardly posed scenes" that failed to convey any dramatic tension or narrative pacing, but Canby did praise Sedgwick and her co-star, Sebastian Keneas. "Without any apparent support system, he does surprisingly well, as does Kyra Sedgwick, a pretty blond actress who looks like a teen-age Julie Christie," Canby wrote.

That same year, Sedgwick also appeared in an ABC Afterschool Special alongside Jennifer Grey, later of *Dirty Dancing* fame, titled *Cindy Eller: A Modern Fairy Tale*. After that, roles were scarce for her. She appeared in episodes of *Miami Vice* and *Amazing Stories* before landing a part in a Lanford Wilson play, *Lemon Sky*, filmed as part of the acclaimed Public Broadcasting Service's *American Playhouse* series. It was there, while filming in Cambridge, Massachusetts, in 1987 that Sedgwick met her future husband, Kevin Bacon. At the time, Bacon was one of a new breed of young Hollywood stars known for their box-office draw, and already had a long list of credits besides his 1984 hit *Footloose*. "I didn't think he had any interest in me at all," Sedgwick recalled in an interview with David Keeps for *Redbook*. "When we were rehearsing, he kept looking at me, and looking at me, and I thought, He thinks I'm terrible!"

The pair were wed ten months later, and a month after that, Sedgwick discovered she was expecting the first of their two children. She was just 23 years old, and was warned that her career now was essentially over. But over the next several years, she and Bacon shared parenting duties for son Travis, born in 1989, and daughter Sosie, who followed in 1992, and kept their home in New York City or Connecticut. Her husband also followed an iconoclastic career path, noted *W*'s Meredith Kahn, who noted that he "achieved pop-hunk status with *Footloose* in the Eighties and promptly threw it out the window, playing a string of murderers, bullies, crooked cops, and all-around creeps."

Sedgwick, meanwhile, shone in supporting or ensemble roles that included the antiwar protester girlfriend of Tom Cruise's disabled Vietnam War veteran in *Born on the Fourth of July* in 1989, and in *Singles,* a 1992 Cameron Crowe film about a group of Seattle twentysomethings. Her star seemed to rise a bit in the mid-1990s, when she was nominated for a Golden Globe award for best supporting actress as the spirited, profanity-spewing sister of Julia Roberts's character in *Something to Talk About*. She also played John Travolta's romantic interest in the 1996 film *Phenomenon*, and that same year she served as executive producer and co-star of *Losing Chase*. The latter project, in which Sedgwick played opposite British actor Helen Mirren, premiered at the Sundance Film Festival to good reviews, and later aired on the Showtime cable channel.

Solid, interesting parts were still scarce for Sedgwick, however, and she looked for interesting works to produce on her own, or became involved in the occasional joint project with Bacon. In 2000, ABC television executives offered her a sitcom, *Talk to Me,* which replaced the well-liked *Sports Night*. In it, Sedgwick played a New York City radio talk-show host, Janey Munro, who ventures back into the dating pool after a particularly rough breakup. "The script gives Sedgwick very little to work with and her forced, manic performance borders on career-killing role-playing," declared *Boston Herald* television critic Amy Amatangelo, who also noted that the star was also the sitcom's co-executive producer. "If she can't come up with better material for herself, what does that say about the state of sitcoms or about the projects that are being green-lighted by network executives," Amatangelo wondered. The slew of bad reviews, coupled with a loss of four million viewers from its debut in mid-April, caused ABC executives to pull the plug after just three weeks.

Sedgwick remained out of the public eye for much of 2001, but the following year saw the premiere of several new works, including the drama *Personal*

Velocity, directed by Rebecca Miller, daughter of playwright Arthur Miller, from a trio of short stories she had written. Sedgwick played Delia, another scrappy fighter who finally leaves an abusive husband. The work won the Grand Jury Prize for drama at the 2002 Sundance Film Festival. In 2003, she appeared in another acclaimed drama, *Secondhand Lions,* and a year later starred in *Cavedweller,* for which she also served as executive producer. The work was based on a novel by Dorothy Allison about a musician who tries to reunite with the daughters she left behind with an abusive husband (Aidan Quinn) years before.

Both Sedgwick and Bacon took a chance on *The Woodsman,* an independent film co-written and directed by a novice filmmaker, Nicole Kassell. Bacon starred as a pedophile recently released from prison after 12 years who takes a job at a lumber yard and begins a tentative romance with Sedgwick's hardbitten character, who seems to have her own somewhat shady past. She hesitated before taking the role opposite her husband, she told *W*'s Kahn. "I don't think that people are all that crazy about seeing actors work together over and over again," she noted, but felt the project was a worthwhile one. Bacon also directed her in *Loverboy,* a little-seen 2005 film about an overprotective parent.

After such a long string of supporting roles and sideline-sitting, Sedgwick was perhaps as surprised as anyone when she began to score laudatory reviews for her title role in *The Closer.* The TNT series debuted on a Monday night in mid-June of 2005, and set an all-time ratings record for basic cable television on its first outing. Some seven million viewers tuned in that night, the highest ever for a scripted series, though to be fair it also was hyped with a generous, $10 million marketing campaign prior to its debut.

Sedgwick's character, Deputy Police Chief Brenda Johnson, bears the nickname of the show's title for her superior interrogation skills and ability to elicit a confession from a suspect that will stick in court. Trained at the Central Intelligence Agency, Sedgwick's Johnson is a newcomer to the top job at a special-crimes unit inside the Los Angeles Police Department. The transplanted Southerner, with a Southern drawl that belies her nerves of steel, finds herself the boss of a few officers who had been hoping to land the job themselves, but makes her authority clear in the rather frank, profanity-laced manner which Sedgwick has managed to successfully pull off consistently throughout her career. Finally, noted *Entertainment Weekly* critic Gillian Flynn, "Sedgwick has a big, bouncy role finely tailored to her.... Johnson is a charming blend of don't-give-a-crap arrogance and a defensiveness that comes from succeeding in a deeply macho world."

The Closer also won praise from *New York Times* television critic Alessandra Stanley, who grouped it along with a new crop of crime shows on television featuring women in starring roles—among them NBC's *Medium* with Patricia Arquette and *Cold Case* on CBS. Stanley conceded that fictional female cops were nothing new on television, but asserted that predecessors like *Cagney and Lacey* from the 1980s already seemed relics of a bygone era. "Those women mirror the feminist ethos of the past—dedicated, seasoned, and tough," Stanley noted. "Now, the new female investigators are not just equal to their male peers; they are superior in a spooky, almost supernatural way."

Sedgwick remains based in New York City, where she and Bacon are the parents of teenagers. *The Closer* is filmed in Los Angeles, which requires her to be away from home for four months of every year. The couple is regularly seen around Manhattan leading improbably regular lives, and rarely give joint interviews or appear in magazines solely as a celebrity team. "It's nauseating for us to trade on our coupledom," Bacon told *W*'s Kahn in one of their rare joint interviews. "It's like, Kyra and Kevin's tips for fun during the holidays! It just makes you want to puke when you see it." They also appear with alarming infrequency in gossip columns, which Sedgwick claimed, in the same interview, is "a testament to how boring we are."

Sources

Advocate, November 21, 2000, p. 88.
Boston Herald, April 11, 2000, p. 46.
Daily News (Los Angeles, CA), July 10, 1996, p. L7.
Entertainment Weekly, November 15, 2002, p. 86; June 17, 2005, p. 68; July 8, 2005, p. 34.
InStyle, May 1, 2000, p. 313.
Interview, July 1996, p. 94.
New York Times, September 13, 1985, p. C6; April 11, 2000, p. B8; June 13, 2005, p. E9.
Redbook, November 2004, p. 130.
W, December 2004, p. 304.

—*Carol Brennan*

John Sentamu

EPA/Landov

Archbishop of York

Born June 10, 1949, in Kampala, Uganda; son of Rev. John (a preacher) and Ruth Walakira; married Margaret; children: Grace, Geoffrey. *Religion:* Anglican. *Education:* Makerere University, Kampala, LLB; attended Law Development Centre; Cambridge University, Selwyn College, MA, PhD.

Addresses: *Office*—Bishopthorpe Palace, Bishopthorpe, York YO23 2GE England.

Career

Barrister-at-law, legal assistant to Chief Justice, Diocesan Registrar, Advocate High Court, 1971-74; assistant chaplain, Selwyn College Cambridge, 1979; assistant curate, St. Andrew Ham Common and chaplain HM, Remand Centre Latchmere House, 1979-82; assistant curate, St. Paul Herne Hill, 1982-83; priest i/c, Holy Trinity and parish priest, St. Matthias Tulse Hill, 1983-84; vicar, Holy Trinity and St. Matthias Tulse Hill, 1984-96; priest i/c, St. Saviour Brixton, honorable canon, Southwark Cathedral, 1993-96; bishop of Stepney, 1996- 2002; advisor to Stephen Lawrence murder inquiry, 1997-99; chaired Damilola Taylor murder review, 2002-03; bishop of Birmingham, 2002-05; archbishop of York, 2005—.

Awards: Midlander of the Year, 2003; Freeman, City of London, 2000; honorary Doctorate, Open University; honorary Doctorate of Philosophy, University of Gloucester; honorary Doctorate of Divinity, University of Birmingham; fellowship UC, Christ Church Canterbury; fellowship, Queen Mary & Westfield College London; FRSA; honorary Doctor of Laws, Newman College of Higher Education in the West Midlands; part of exhibit, *Movers and Shakers—Faces of the Changing City,* 2005.

Sidelights

Known as "a visionary and able teacher," according to Sue Leeman of the *Washington Post*, the Right Reverend John Sentamu has made quite a name for himself in the Anglican Church and the international religious community in general. He raised himself from humble roots in Africa to become the first black archbishop in Britain. The *Washington Post*'s Leeman wrote, "In a statement, [Archbishop of Canterbury, Rowan] Williams said that Sentamu 'is someone who has always combined a passion for sharing the Gospel with a keen sense of the problems and challenges of our society, particularly where racism is concerned.'" Much was expected of the priest as he took the reins of archbishop at the end of 2005.

Born to Rev. John and Ruth Walakira on June 10, 1949, Sentamu grew up in Uganda near the capital city of Kampala. His family lived in a rather out-of-the-way village where his father was a priest, and

Sentamu himself was the sixth of 13 children. They were very poor. At his birth Sentamu weighed just four pounds and his family feared he would not survive, but with careful attention they managed to save the young child. He had a rather quiet, happy childhood, and then when he was old enough Sentamu attended Makerere University where he studied law. Upon graduation he was appointed judge in Uganda's high court. He was outspoken in his opinions against Ugandan dictator Idi Amin, and was eventually thrown into jail for his outpourings against him. While in prison, Sentamu was beaten by Amin's men and almost died, but was eventually released after he regained some semblance of health. He spent several months under house arrest in 1974 before finally leaving Uganda and settling in Britain. He decided to become a priest and was ordained five years after he arrived in the United Kingdom. He attended Cambridge University where he obtained his doctorate in theology.

He became very prominent in his chosen profession and soon was a respected and sought-after priest. He continued his outspoken protests against racism, unfairness, and violence. In fact, according to Leeman in the *Washington Post*, "In 1997, [Sentamu] became an adviser to an inquiry into the bungled police investigation of the 1993 killing of black teenager Stephen Lawrence. The inquiry concluded that London police were institutionally racist." Sentamu himself was a victim of racism during the trials. At one point he received a photograph of Lawrence's murdered body with the words "You are next" written underneath it in red. And that was not even the worst of what he was sent at the time. Sentamu gave the picture and other letters to the authorities, but as of 2005 no one had been charged for the crimes.

In 2002 Sentamu became the bishop of Birmingham, a position that gave him more power and a platform from which he was able to more effectively spread his messages of good will, fighting against racism and gun crime of any kind, and striving for peace. He supports women becoming bishops and has even said that he loves ordaining women, an event that many of his fellow priests think should not be allowed. He is a supporter of the Lambeth Resolution of 1998, which opposes gay priests and refuses to allow gay marriage in the church, but he dislikes the way some Anglicans discuss gay issues. He was quoted by Stephen Bates in the *Guardian* as having said, "Some of our disagreements are not Christian really.... It seems to suggest that all the great evils of the world are being perpetrated by gay and lesbian people, which I cannot believe to be the case. What is wrong in the world is that people are sinful and alienate themselves from God

and you do not have to be gay to do that. To suggest that to be gay equals evil, I find that quite unbelievable."

Sentamu has also shown himself to be avidly against war for any reason. Before the war in Iraq began, in fact, Sentamu organized and led a public protest in Birmingham against the war to coincide with a large demonstration that took place in London; thousands of people attended. During his reign as bishop, Sentamu was behind the publication of a book delving into a century of Christian worship in his diocese. The book, *Celebrating a Century of Christ—The Diocese of Birmingham 1905-2005,* was written by Canon Terry Slater. It looks at issues that have existed in the church for 100 years such as whether or not women should have a leading role in the ministry, something that Sentamu said had been argued for more than those 100 years. The book was well-received. There were many other things that made Sentamu's reign as bishop stand out and made people flock to him with pride.

Even with such successes and accolades under his belt, however, racist remarks and incidents were still addressed at the priest. In 2002, he was assaulted on his way home from St. Paul's Cathedral where he had been celebrating the Queen's golden jubilee. "A young man spat on me and said 'n***** go back'," Sentamu told Christopher Morgan and Jasper Gerard of the *Times*. "He then pushed me down an escalator. I had to go to hospital. I had just finished singing hymns and he realized where I had come from."

Despite protests of this sort, in October of 2005 at St. Mary-le-Bow church in London Sentamu was confirmed as Lord Archbishop of York, Primate of England and Metropolitan. It is the second highest position in the entire Anglican Church, second only to the prestigious position of Archbishop of Canterbury, who is in charge of the well-being of the entire world-wide Anglican Church. Sentamu took office on November 30, 2005, with department store Marks & Spencer providing a picnic lunch for the attendees. Some churchgoers were upset about this fact, though, because it seemed like free advertising for the company, something that traditional churchgoers found to be appalling in a confirmation ceremony. Sentamu, however, defended the Church of England's action, saying that he did not wish his ceremony to end with a fancy lunch for only a select few, but wanted to invite all the attendees to share in the joy. In that case, the lunch would have to be something small and Sentamu was happy that Marks & Spencer had volunteered to help sponsor the event. This promotion made Sentamu the first black Archbishop of the Church of England. Archbishops are appointed by the monarch of England under recommendation by the prime minister. Upon his acceptance of the position, Sentamu was quoted by Leeman in the *Washington Post* as having said, "It is important that the Church of England's voice is heard locally, nationally, and internationally, standing up for justice, bringing good news to the poor, healing to the brokenhearted, setting at liberty those who are oppressed, and proclaiming the death of Christ and his Resurrection."

Sentamu hopes to use the additional influence of his new position to take care of all those things. The *Birmingham Post* wrote, "Dr. Rowan Williams, [the Archbishop of Canterbury,] who led the service with six senior bishops, said the people of his diocese would be looking to Dr. Sentamu to 'engage with the great public issues of the day.'" Williams also expected Sentamu to not only be a true leader and defender of the faith, but to help put through changes that seem necessary in today's age. He told the *Birmingham Post*, "All of us are committed to that but we need people whose experience ... demonstrates this can be done, that it is possible to enthuse people of all kinds from all backgrounds, ethnic communities, or ages with the vision of the Kingdom."

As he prepared to leave the post of Bishop of Birmingham, the council members of the city got together and gave Sentamu, who is an avid fan of cricket, a signed cricket bat. According to the *Birmingham Evening Mail*, council leader Mike Whitby said, "The whole council wanted to do this as a thank you to the Bishop who has done so much to embrace all faiths during his time here. Since his time here he has embraced all religions and done much to unite our city." Not everyone felt so positively about Sentamu, however, and not all were happy about his promotion. As soon as his appointment was announced, Sentamu began receiving hate letters, many of them using vile, racist words and covered with excrement. Ruth Gledhill of the *Times* discussed this with Sentamu. "Asked if he felt angry about the hate letters, he said: 'Yes, particularly when they had human excrement in them. I don't want to have those sorts of things and I say, "Why do people do this?"'" The acts of racism were condemned by politicians across the United Kingdom. Sentamu himself declared that he would not let the racist few ruin his opinion of the whole, as he had found Britain to be one of the least racist countries he had ever encountered, one of the reasons he chose to settle there in the first place. Rather than yelling about the incidents, very appropriately Sentamu said that he had been praying for the perpetrators.

Sentamu has received many awards during his career, including an honorary degree of Doctor of Laws from Newman College of Higher Education in the West Midlands. The City of Birmingham put on a month and a half long show in September and October of 2005 to show hundreds of portraits of people who have made significant contributions to the city to help in its regeneration; Sentamu's portrait was included in the exhibit. The exhibit was called *Movers and Shakers—Faces of the Changing City.* Sentamu has also been asked to contribute to numerous books. In one of them, *Rejection, Resistance, and Resurrection,* he used the opportunity to speak out against racism in the Church, giving a forceful and honest account about how many black Anglicans feel like they exist only on the fringes of the Church and not as a central and integral part of it. He is married and has two children.

People across the Anglican Church are looking to Sentamu to lead the church toward changes that are necessary for its survival, and Sentamu himself is optimistic. He was quoted by Ian Herbert in the *Independent* as having said at his confirmation ceremony, "It is imperative that the Church regains her vision and confidence in mission, developing ways to reconnect imaginatively. We need ... to revitalize ourselves. We need a fresh vision. This has been true of all churches throughout history, that a time comes when there is an ebb and flow and at one particular point you are in a trough." It is believed that if anyone can help lead the Church out of that trough it is Sentamu, and Anglicans around the world watch to see how the Archbishop will rise to his new position.

Sources

Books

Debrett's People of Today, Debrett's Peerage Ltd., 2005.

Periodicals

Birmingham Evening Mail (England), August 26, 2005, p. 67; September 22, 2005, p. 13.
Birmingham Post, September 23, 2005, p. 2; October 4, 2005, p. 5; October 6, 2005, p. 3.
Daily Mail (London, England), October 10, 2005, p. 39; October 22, 2005, p. 19.
Daily Post (Liverpool, England), October 6, 2005, p. 2; October 25, 2005, p. 2.
Daily Telegraph (London, England), August 29, 2005; August 31, 2005; October 6, 2005, p. 3; October 22, 2005, p. 7.
Guardian, October 6, 2005, p. 9; October 10, 2005, p. 5; October 22, 2005, p. 8.
Independent (London, England), October 6, 2005, p. 20; October 22, 2005, p. 4.

Jet, July 4, 2005.

Sunday Times, October 9, 2005, p. 12; October 23, 2005, p. 3.

Times (London, England), October 8, 2005, p. 80; October 21, 2005, p. 83; October 22, 2005, p. 9.

Washington Post, June 18, 2005, p. B9.

Western Mail (Cardiff, Wales), October 6, 2005, p. 8; October 25, 2005, p. 4.

Online

"Backlash Against War," *Times,* http://www.times online.co.uk/newspaper/0..173-576015.00.html (November 24, 2005).

—*Catherine Victoria Donaldson*

Gyanendra Shah

Gopal Chitrakar/Reuters/Landov

King of Nepal

Born Gyanendra Bir Bikram Shah Dev, July 7, 1947, in Kathmandu, Nepal; son of Mahendra (a king) and Indra Rajya Laxmi Devi; married Komal Rajya Laxmi Devi, 1970; children: Paras (a son), one daughter. *Education:* Earned degree from Tribhuvan University, 1969.

Addresses: *Home*—Narayanhity Royal Palace, Kathmandu, Nepal. *Office*—c/o The Royal Nepalese Embassy, 2131 Leroy Place, NW Washington, DC 20008.

Career

Owner of a hotel, tea plantation, and cigarette factory; chair of the King Mahendra Trust for Nature Conservation, 1982-2001; became king of Nepal, June 4, 2001; also supreme commander of the Royal Nepalese Army.

Sidelights

Nepal's King Gyanendra came to the throne in 2001 after a notorious palace bloodbath that killed ten members of the royal family. An entrepreneur who had played little role in Nepali politics since the world's only Hindu kingdom became a parliamentary democracy in 1990, Gyanendra found himself next in line for the throne in the aftermath of the tragedy that robbed Nepal of its beloved King Birendra, his brother. In the years that followed, Gyanendra enacted tough measures to quell a vicious internal war that has pitted a communist insurgency against the Royal Nepalese Army (RNA).

"It's not a question of winning or not winning," Gyanendra told *Time International* correspondent Alex Perry in April of 2005. "No law-abiding citizen should feel pain. Those who do not abide by the law will feel pain."

The thirteenth king of Nepal was born Gyanendra Bir Bikram Shah Dev on July 7, 1947. His family, the Shahs, had ruled the remote kingdom since 1768, when their ancestor, a legendary warrior named Prithwi Narayan Shah, completed his conquest of several smaller kingdoms and a section of northern India, and then united the lands into a single entity called Nepal. Nestled in the Himalaya mountain range, the nation shares borders with China and India, and is the home of the world's highest peak, Mount Everest, as well as the ancient birthplace of Lord Gautam Buddha. In the eighteenth century, the kingdom was considered so impenetrable that the British East India Company chose to leave it be, despite having established lucrative trading posts—often by force—across much of the Indian subcontinent.

The 2001 bloodbath was not the first royal massacre in Nepal's history. The Shahs had been forced to cede a share of their power in 1846 after the infamous Kot Massacre; a competing dynasty, the

Ranas, then became hereditary prime ministers of the country. The Ranas claimed to be descended from royal blood, in this case from an princely Indian family of the 1300s. Over subsequent generations, the two families forged a cooperative truce and ties between the two were cemented by intermarriage.

Nepal was closed off to the rest of the world until a series of events in the early 1950s served to disrupt Shah rule. When Gyanendra was three years old, tensions between his family and the Ranas reached a crisis point yet again, thanks to a liberal democratic movement that arose in response to dissatisfaction with conservative Rana policies. Gyanendra's grandfather, King Tribhuvan, supported the people's wish for less authoritarian rule. Both Tribhuvan and the Shah monarchy had enjoyed British protection over the years, but when Britain pulled out of India in 1947 at that country's bid for independence, the Shahs were left to fend for themselves. The ensuing crisis forced the Shahs to flee to India in late 1950, and Gyanendra, the son of Crown Prince Mahendra, was left behind. Three years old at the time, he was second in line to the throne, and was briefly proclaimed king by the Ranas. Nepal erupted in mass protests over this, and international pressure forced the Ranas to allow the Shah family safe passage back into Nepal.

Gyanendra's grandfather Tribhuvan was restored to his throne in 1951. The Rana rule came to an end, some democratic reforms took place, and Tribhuvan opened Nepal's borders to the outside world. Tribhuvan died in 1955, and was succeeded by Gyanendra's father, Mahendra, as king. During these years, Gyanendra was sent to a British-run boarding school in Darjeeling, India, and after that went on to Tribhuvan University in Kathmandu, Nepal's capital. In 1970, a year after earning his degree, he wed Komal Rajya Laxmi Devi, daughter of a Rana military officer, and the couple became parents to a son and daughter. When Mahendra died in 1972, Gyanendra's older brother, Birendra, became king, and proved to be a popular, well-liked monarch in the years to come. Like his father, Birendra enjoyed absolute power, but would eventually heed the growing call for democratic reform.

Gyanendra served as an advisor to his brother for several years, though his main activities were business-related. He owned a hotel in Kathmandu, a cigarette factory, and a tea plantation. When Britain's Prince Charles visited Nepal in December of 1980, Gyanendra served as the unofficial royal host to the future King of England, who reportedly had come to Nepal in order to consider his future and the possibility of becoming engaged to the young woman he was dating, Lady Diana Spencer. Gyanendra took Charles on a royal trek near the peak of Machhapuchhre.

Gyanendra and his brother had a falling-out in 1990, when Birendra lifted a ban on Nepal's political opposition parties. Parliamentary democracy came to Nepal's 27 million citizens that same year, but the popularly elected governments were torn apart by internal disagreements, and rarely lasted more than a year. The standard of living remained the same—abysmal—for most Nepali as before the new political era, but corruption was said to be rampant among the newly created political elite, and resentment grew for the new mansions that sprang up around Kathmandu.

Kathmandu had been a tourist destination since the 1960s, as was Mount Everest, but the rest of Nepal remained dreadfully poor. Most villagers live without electricity or telephones, and some places were entirely inaccessible by road. The country's per-capita income was just $240, meaning that many Nepali subsisted on less than seventy cents a day. In such conditions a leftist insurgency easily gained ground, and a civil war began in 1996. The unrest was fomented by a Maoist group, the Communist Party of Nepal, who demanded a new elected assembly to draft a new constitution—one that would create a republic of Nepal and end the monarchy for good. The Maoists' guerrilla army, one of the last active ones in the world, grew to 10,000, and the RNA fought back fiercely.

Gyanendra and his family were not immune from accusations of misconduct, and his son, Paras, was one of the most disliked royals in Nepali history. In 2000, Paras was involved in a car accident that resulted in the death of a popular Nepali singer, and alcohol was reportedly a factor in the crash. Showing their displeasure with the leadership, some 500,000 Nepalis signed a petition urging Paras' prosecution, but members of the royal family are immune from prosecution unless the king gives permission, and Birendra did not.

Birendra's own son, the 29-year-old Crown Prince Dipendra, was also proving difficult. On the night of June 1, 2001, when the Shahs were gathered for a weekly family dinner gathering at Kathmandu's Narayanhity Royal Palace, Dipendra was reportedly drinking heavily. The prince was said to have been upset because of his mother's disapproval of his choice of wife, Devyani Rana. She came from the same Rana family who had once served as Nepal's prime ministers, but was from an immensely wealthy Indian branch of the family. She and the Crown Prince had been dating openly in Kathmandu, which was a daring breach of etiquette in Nepali royal society, where marriages are arranged by families and social interactions among young people are severely restricted.

On that June night, Dipendra left the table and stalked off to his quarters at the palace, and returned to the dining room dressed in combat fatigues and carrying a pistol, assault rifle, and submachine gun. He opened fire on his family, and then shot himself. The casualties included his father, King Birendra; his mother, Queen Aishwarya; his brother, Prince Nirajan; and his sister, Princess Shruti. Also killed were the king's other brother, who had renounced his claim to the throne; the king's cousin, Princess Jayanti; two other princesses, Shanti and Sharada, who were Birendra's sisters; and one of their husbands.

Gyanendra was not in attendance at the family gathering that evening, having gone to spend the weekend at another royal property in the resort town of Pokhara. His wife Komal, however, was present and caught in the line of fire; she lost a lung but survived. Their son Paras and his sister were there, however, and were unharmed after reportedly pleading with Dipendra for their lives. Dipendra shot himself shortly after killing his mother.

Notified of the emergency, Gyanendra was flown in by helicopter back to Kathmandu. As the Crown Prince, Dipendra was named king while he lay in a coma, with Gyanendra appointed to serve as his regent, but Dipendra never regained consciousness. Gyanendra quickly issued an official statement claiming that the massacre had been the result of an automatic weapon accidentally misfiring, which was greeted with widespread disbelief once the news of the palace massacre began to spread. When Dipendra died on June 4, Gyanendra was named king, and for the second time in his life crowds rioted in Kathmandu that night in response.

Some Nepalis believed that Gyanendra or Paras may have played a role in massacre, because the two were almost the only male royal family members to survive. A few months later, in a climate of deep unease, the Maoist insurgency intensified, and the countryside became a bloody battleground. International human-rights observers accused both sides of committing atrocities, with the rebel army torching entire villages and carrying out public executions of local officials; one politician was report-

edly skinned alive. The United Nations High Commissioner for Human Rights criticized the RNA for abuses that included the torture and murder of suspected Maoist guerrillas.

In October of 2002, Gyanendra dismissed Nepal's elected prime minister, Sher Bahadur Deuba, and named his own government. His decision provoked widespread anger that he had ignored the constitution, and popular sentiment against him deepened. He was forced to reappoint Deuba, but dismissed him once again in February of 2005. On that day, Deuba and other senior government officials were placed under house arrest, and mass arrests of journalists, dissidents, student protesters, and even human-rights workers took place throughout the country. Nepal's mobile phone networks and Internet traffic were closed down, and RNA soldiers were stationed at newspaper offices and television stations to ensure the press did not incite the people further. Gyanendra claimed that the Deuba government had failed to quell the Maoist insurgency, and had not arranged for new parliamentary elections as ordered. The Maoists, however, had promised a bloodbath if elections were announced.

Gyanendra appeared on television the next morning, telling the nation that he had declared a state of emergency. "Nepal's bitter experiences over the past few years tend to show that democracy and progress contradict one another," he asserted on the broadcast, according to Perry in *Time International.* "In pursuit of liberalism, we should never overlook an important aspect of our conduct, namely discipline." The clampdown embarrassed the governments of Britain, the United States, and India, which had provided military aid to the RNA for its struggle against the Maoists. The insurgency was considered a threat to neighboring countries, for if Nepal fell to the communist guerrillas, which some international observers believed was a strong possibility, the nearby kingdom of Bhutan between India and China might also fall, and the Nepali Maoists were known to have ties to left-wing guerrillas in India and could jointly establish a buffer zone with them, thus endangering India's democracy.

Gyanendra was formerly one of the country's most ardent conservationists, heading the King Mahendra Trust for Nature Conservation after 1982, and has published his own poetry. He promised to restore democracy in Nepal once the rebel war is subdued, and defended his suspension of the constitution in the interview with Perry in *Time International.* He asserted that he is merely acting on behalf of a beleaguered Nepali citizenry weary of the horrendous civil war. "The monarchy is not going to allow anyone to usurp the fundamental rights of the people," he said. The embattled king rarely leaves his palace because of the danger of assassination. "It is lonely," he told Perry. "I miss my brothers and sisters. I am a human being after all."

Sources

Periodicals

Global Agenda, February 4, 2005.
Independent (London, England), February 5, 2005, p. 42.
New Yorker, July 30, 2001, p. 42.
Time International (Asia Edition), February 2, 2004, p. 14; February 14, 2005, p. 26; April 25, 2005, p. 20, p. 25.

Online

"His Majesty King Gyanendra Bir Bikram Shah Dev," Official Site of the Royal Court of Nepal, http://www.nepalmonarchy.gov.np/index.php/king.htm (August 17, 2005).

—*Carol Brennan*

John Patrick Shanley

Evan Agostini/Getty Images

Playwright

Born October 13, 1950, in New York, NY; son of a meatpacker; married and divorced first wife; married Jayne Haynes (an actress; divorced); children: Nick, Frank. *Education:* New York University, B.S., 1977.

Addresses: *Agent*—Creative Artists Agency, 9830 Wilshire Blvd., Beverly Hills, CA 90212-1815.

Career

Career as off-Broadway playwright began in 1978 with *Saturday Night at the War;* a collection of one-act plays were staged in 1982 as *Welcome to the Moon;* made London theater debut with *Danny and the Deep Blue Sea,* 1984; first two screenplays, *Moonstruck* and *Five Corners,* both produced by Hollywood studios in 1987; made screen directing debut with *Joe Versus the Volcano,* 1990; made Broadway debut with *Doubt, a parable,* 2005. Also author of the teleplays *Danny i Roberta,* 1993, and *Live from Baghdad,* 2002.

Awards: Academy Award for best screenplay, Academy of Motion Picture Arts and Sciences, for *Moonstruck,* 1987; Writers Guild of America award for best screenplay written directly for the screen, for *Moonstruck*1987; Pulitzer Prize for drama, for *Doubt,* 2005; Lucille Lortel Award for best play, for *Doubt,* 2005; Outer Critics Circle Award for best Broadway play, for *Doubt,* 2005; Obie Award for *Doubt, Village Voice,* 2005; Drama Desk Award for best play, for *Doubt,* 2005; Antoinette Perry (Tony) award for best play, League of American Theaters and Producers and the American Theatre Wing, for *Doubt,* 2005.

Sidelights

John Patrick Shanley has written some two dozen off-Broadway plays since the 1970s, but New York theater critics were rarely kind in their assessments. That changed when he made an impressive Broadway debut in 2005 with *Doubt, a parable,* which went on to win the Pulitzer Prize in drama as well as the Best Play honors at the season-ending Tony Awards. "The play's not so much about the scandal itself, but the philosophical power in embracing doubt," he remarked in an interview with Everett Evans of the *Houston Chronicle.* "If I'm proselytizing at all, it's to say, 'Live with it, brother. Doubt is part of life.'" *Doubt* was not the first time Shanley seemed to hit one out of the ballpark, however: in 1987, his screenplay for *Moonstruck* won him an Academy Award.

Born in 1950, Shanley grew up the youngest of five children in an Irish-Catholic family whose home was in the Bronx neighborhood of East Tremont. His father, a meatpacker, was an Irish immigrant, while Shanley's mother was herself the daughter of Irish immigrants. The East Tremont streets were home to similar working-class Irish and Italian families. "It was extremely anti-intellectual and extremely racist and none of this fit me," the playwright revealed in an interview with Alex Witchel that appeared in the *New York Times Magazine.* He recalled being "in constant fistfights from the time I was six," though he asserted he rarely picked the fight himself. "People would look at me and become enraged at the sight of me," he explained. "I believe that the reason was they could see that I saw them."

Shanley spent the first eight years of his formal education at St. Anthony's, a Roman Catholic school run by the Sisters of Charity religious order. He went on the all-boys Cardinal Spellman High School, where he rebelled against the strict, no-nonsense priests who taught at the school. During his two years there, Shanley spent every single week in after-school detention, until he was asked to leave. Instead of a public high school in the Bronx, he opted to attend a private school in New Hampshire that was affiliated with the Catholic church.

At the Thomas Moore school, away from the Bronx, Shanley began to thrive. His teachers encouraged his writing talents, which started around the age of eleven, and as a teen he wrote reams of poetry. When he graduated, he went on to New York University, but left after a semester of poor grades. He enlisted in the Marine Corps which, somewhat perversely, he liked for its Catholic-school style of discipline. He returned to New York University after his Vietnam War service ended, and in 1977, the year he turned 27, graduated as the valedictorian of his class.

Shanley had already started writing plays by then. In his early twenties, he later recalled, "I tried the dialogue form, and it was instantaneous," he told *American Theatre*'s Robert Coe. " I wrote a full-length play the first time I ever wrote in dialogue, and it was produced a few weeks later." By the early 1980s, he had written a half-dozen works, and some of the one-act plays were staged together in a late 1982 production titled *Welcome to the Moon.* Its collective themes centered around love and the absence of it, and were filled with rather fanciful characters and props, such as a mermaid and a magical coat. Critics were less than kind. Frank Rich, later the *New York Times* op-ed columnist, was once the paper's theater critic, and reviewed *Welcome to the Moon* that year. Rich opened his critique with a line of dialogue, "It's a relief to say things, even if they are sophomoric," Rich quoted one of the characters as saying. "No doubt that's true for the person who's doing the talking," the critic quipped, "but what about those who have to listen? "

Shanley had somewhat better luck with *Danny and the Deep Blue Sea,* first produced in Waterford, Connecticut, in 1983. It went on to the New York stage the following year and then a London production as well that same year when it was included as part of the traveling arm of the Louisville Festival, a relatively new event at the time that showcased the best new American plays in the Kentucky city first. The play's action focused on two star-crossed lovers who meet in a seedy Bronx bar. John Turturro, who later went on to fame in films by Spike Lee and the Coen brothers, was the original Danny.

Shanley's rising star gave him access to a generous National Endowment for the Arts (NEA) grant, which freed him from the long series of jobs he usually held in order to make ends meet, including elevator operator, apartment painter, and bartender. When the NEA funds began running low, he thought that if he wrote a screenplay instead of a play, he might earn enough from selling it to Hollywood to get by for another year or so. He mined the familiar territory of the outer New York City boroughs and voluble Italian-American families for a script he originally titled "The Bride and the Beast." The title used instead, after a moderately well-known Hollywood director Norman Jewison filmed the story, was *Moonstruck.* It starred Cher as an Italian-American woman, widowed young, whose is engaged to be married again. When her fiancé visits Italy, she attempts to make peace on his behalf with his brother (Nicolas Cage), a baker with one wooden hand, and winds up falling in love with him instead. A strong supporting cast and interesting subplots centering around love and infidelity rounded out the work, which won Shanley the 1987 Academy Award for best screenplay.

Shanley had little success in Hollywood after that point, however. His next work was a 1989 thriller, *The January Man,* which starred Kevin Kline, Susan Sarandon, and Harvey Keitel. It earned terrible reviews, as did Shanley's next, *Joe Versus the Volcano,* which he directed as well. The film starred Tom Hanks as a man who learns he has a fatal brain tumor, and heads to a remote tropical island to throw himself into a volcanic crater. Despite the presence of big-name box-office draws such as Hanks and Meg Ryan, the movie tanked at the box office.

Shanley went on to write a few more Hollywood projects, such as the adaptation of a popular book from the 1970s based on a true story about an Uruguayan rugby team whose plane crashed in the Andes Mountains of South America in 1972. Ethan Hawke was one of the stars of the 1993 film version of *Alive,* but the most memorable feature of both the book and the movie may have been that the survivors resorted to cannibalism to stay alive. Shanley also wrote the screenplay for 1995's *Congo,* a reworking of a Michael Crichton bestseller about apes and genetic mutation.

Shanley was still active in the New York theater world during these years. His plays included *Italian American Reconciliation*, from 1988, and *Beggars in the House of Plenty*, which was first produced in New York in 1991 and featured the typically dysfunctional characters who had become the hallmark of Shanley's work. In it, a Bronx butcher terrorizes his meek wife and adult children, one of whom turns to writing as a solace after finding little satisfaction in starting fires. Two more plays, *Kissing Christine* and *Missing Marisa*, debuted at the Louisville Festival in the 1990s, but Shanley found a more permanent home for his work finally in 2001 when he became involved with New York's LAByrinth Theater Company. His first play to be staged there was *Where's My Money?*, a drama about several jaded New Yorkers whose adulterous lives intersect. It contains one of Shanley's most-quoted lines of dialogue, as one of the play's lawyer-characters asserts, "Monogamy is like a 40-watt bulb. It works, but it's not enough."

Shanley wrote a few more plays, including 2003's *Dirty Story*, set in a post-9/11 world and dramatizing the Israeli-Palestinian conflict through its main characters, and *Sailor's Song*, a romantic fairy tale set to the waltzes of nineteenth-century German composer Johann Strauss. "This is not Mr. Shanley at his best," remarked Charles Isherwood in a *New York Times* review, who found it "drenched in ponderous, explicit talk ... it has the soggy consistency of an overdressed salad. "

By contrast, *Doubt, a parable* earned outstanding praise from critics, as well as the most impressive honors for which a playwright could ever hope: the Pulitzer Prize for drama and the 2005 Tony Award for best play of the 2004-05 season. *Doubt* began its off-Broadway run in November of 2004, and went on to Broadway's Walter Kerr Theatre the following March. The story is set on familiar territory for Shanley: a Roman Catholic school in the Bronx in 1964. The original leads were Cherry Jones as the school principal Sister Aloysius (Mrs. Clack in M. Night Shyamalan's *The Village*), and Brian F. O'Byrne as Father Flynn, one of the parish priests whom the Sister suspects of molesting the school's first African-American student.

Again, Shanley's intense dialogue served to anchor the drama, while the conclusion failed to answer any of the questions the play raised. Writing in the *New York Times*, Ben Brantley claimed that as the play's author, "Shanley is on no one's side. It seems safe to say the playwright agrees with Father Flynn when he explains his preference for parables over reality: 'The truth makes for a bad sermon. It tends to be confusing and have no clear conclusion.' But *Doubt* presents each point of view with reasonableness and an eloquence that never seem out of sync with the characters' Bronx accents and ecumenical backgrounds."

Part of the reason that *Doubt* resonated with theater audiences was the timeliness of its subject matter, with new revelations of past sexual abuse by Roman Catholic priests—and the ensuing legal proceedings—a frequent media topic over the past two years. As Shanley said in the *American Theatre* interview with Coe, those news stories prompted him to think about the nuns who taught him during his formative years at St. Anthony's. "I realized later on when the Church scandals were breaking that the way a lot of these priests were getting busted had to be by nuns.... But the chain of command in the Catholic Church was such that they had to report it not to the police but to their superior within the Church, who then covered up for the guy. This had to create very powerful frustrations and moral dilemmas for these women."

Shanley was working on a screenplay for a movie called *Bread and Tulips*, and his next play, *Defiance*, was scheduled to premiere on February 28, 2006, in a production by the Manhattan Theater Club. He lives in New York City's Brooklyn Heights neighborhood, and is parent to two teenagers, whom he and his former wife adopted within months of each other and now share joint custody. He has undergone several surgeries for glaucoma, and lost some of his vision despite them. Uninterested in returning to Hollywood, he said in the *New York Times Magazine* profile that the lucrative screenwriting work he once did seemed to satisfy his desire for fame and fortune for good. "Money is like heroin, and I grew up in a neighborhood that was destroyed by heroin," he told Witchel. "I've watched addiction all my life. Celebrity is like heroin. And constant praise is like heroin. And, you know, no one can resist constant praise. I had to get out."

Selected writings

Plays

Saturday Night at the War, produced in New York, 1978.

George and the Dragon, produced in New York, 1979.

Danny and the Deep Blue Sea, produced in Waterford, Connecticut, 1983; New York, 1984; London, 1984.

Savage in Limbo, produced in New York, 1985; London, 1987.

the dreamer examines his pillow, produced in Waterford, Connecticut, 1985; New York, 1986.

Women of Manhattan, produced in New York, 1986.

All for Charity, produced in New York, 1987.

Italian American Reconciliation, produced in New York, 1988.

The Big Funk, produced in New York, 1990.

Beggars in the House of Plenty, produced in New York, 1991.

What Is This Everything?, produced in New York, 1992.

Kissing Christine, produced in Louisville, KY, early 1990s.

Missing Marisa, produced in Louisville, KY, early 1990s.

Psychopathia Sexualis, New York, 1998.

Where's My Money?, produced in New York, 2001.

Cellini, produced in New York, 2001.

Dirty Story, produced in New York, 2003.

Doubt, a parable, produced in New York, 2004.

Sailor's Song, produced in New York, 2004.

Screenplays

Five Corners, 1987.

Moonstruck, 1987.

The January Man, 1989.

Joe Versus the Volcano, 1990.

Alive, 1993.

Congo, 1995.

Sources

Books

Contemporary Dramatists, sixth ed., St. James Press, 1999.

Periodicals

American Theatre, November 2004, p. 22.

Entertainment Weekly, January 22, 1993, p. 40; April 1, 2005, p. 78.

Houston Chronicle, May 22, 2005, p. 6.

Maclean's, January 23, 1989, p. 45.

National Review, March 4, 1988, p. 53.

New York Observer, February 26, 2001, 17; March 24, 2003, p. 19; December 13, 2004, p. 25.

New York Times, October 14, 1982, p. C15; November 24, 1982, p. C14; June 8, 1984, p. C3; November 12, 2001, p. E5; November 8, 2004; November 24, 2004; April 1, 2005, p. E3.

New York Times Magazine, November 7, 2004, p. 31.

Times (London, England), March 29, 1984, p. 8.

Online

"John Patrick Shanley," Doollee.com, http://www.doollee.com/PlaywrightsS/ShanleyJohnPatrick.htm (August 16, 2005).

—Carol Brennan

Harry Slatkin

AP/Wide World Photos

Founder of Slatkin & Co.

Born c. 1961; married Laura; children: David, Ali (twins).

Addresses: *Office*—Slatkin & Co., 214 E. 52nd St., Flr. 4, New York, NY 10022-6207.

Career

Worked on Wall Street until early 1990s; founded Slatkin & Co., 1992; sold company to Limited Brands, 2005.

Awards: Fifi Award, Fragrance Foundation, for Best Interior Scent Collection of the Year (Prestige), for Elton Rocks Crystal Potpourri, 2004.

Sidelights

Harry Slatkin's eponymous candle and home-fragrance line was acquired by Limited Brands in 2005 for a sum reported to be in the neighborhood of $13 million. The Slatkin & Co. products joined a handful of similar premium home scents sold at Bath & Body Works and other retail chains owned by Limited Brands.

Slatkin founded the firm in 1992 after a career on Wall Street, and his wife, Laura, played an integral role in the company during its first decade in business. Slatkin had been urged to launch the line by his friend, bridal couture designer Vera Wang, and was also encouraged by another early champion,

Rose Marie Bravo, an expert on upscale retailing who had just become president of Saks Fifth Avenue. He was inspired to venture into the candle market when he realized how moribund the competition was at the time. "Everything smelled the same," he recalled in an interview with *Times* of London writer Tina Gaudoin. "I wanted smells that were playful, that transported you to another place."

Slatkin & Co. candles caught on with discerning consumers thanks to their unusual ingredients, which included wisteria, fig, and black tea. They were sold at Neiman Marcus and Bergdorf Goodman, among other posh retailers, and even attracted a high-profile clientele that included Princess Diana, Elton John, and Oprah Winfrey. Slatkin began creating special commemorative candles for ultra-exclusive charity events, such as one given to attendees at an Elton John AIDS Foundation event in 1997; a year later, Slatkin also created a special scent in honor of the British pop star's friend Diana, with a cut of the proceeds given to the Princess of Wales memorial fund. Slatkin also created candle lines co-branded with prominent tastemakers, such as fashion designer Oscar de la Renta.

Slatkin even put out a line of Kabbalah candles, which were tied to practices associated with the venerable form of mystic Judaism. A Kabbalah practitioner himself, he had first done a few special candles for fellow devotees Madonna and Demi Moore. His Kabbalah line was made up of red candles, the practice's signature color, and featured blends of centuries-old scents, such as frankincense, myrrh, and cinnamon. "In Latin, perfume means wall of smoke," he told *WWD* writer Jenny B. Fine. "Perfume was created in 4000 B.C. to keep the bad spirits away and bring the good spirits to you—so it was a natural for Kabbalah to do a line of candles."

After a decade in business, Slatkin launched a bath and body line, Slatkin Body Therapy, which debuted on Bergdorf Goodman shelves in time for the holiday 2003 season. Again, the line featured an intoxicating mix of scents, such as Black Fig and Absinthe, Bamboo and Jasmine, and Persian Lime and Mimosa. Like his candles, it quickly garnered a devoted following of nearly cult-like proportions. Black Fig and Absinthe was a particular favorite among Slatkin Body Therapy consumers, and one Texas woman even contacted him with an unusual offer so that it could become her signature scent alone. "She said she would buy everything in the inventory," Slatkin told *Harper's Bazaar* writer Kerry Diamond. "I told her I was enormously flattered but that I'd have to pass. She then asked if I could create some bottles without the name of the fragrance on them so her friends couldn't figure out what she was wearing!"

Slatkin and his wife are the parents of twins, David and Ali, born in 1999, and David was diagnosed as autistic less than two years later. In response, the Slatkins founded the New York Center for Autism, a nonprofit foundation that promotes research involving this brain disorder, which is tied to learning difficulties and diminished social skills. The Center also leads educational efforts and offers a wealth of information resources for parents. The Slatkins' foundation even played a key role in the creation of a special charter school in New York City area for autistic students. Laura Slatkin, who gave up her career at her husband's company to devote more of her energies to the Center for Autism, recalled that when David was diagnosed, they were counseled to get him into a special school as soon as possible. The Slatkins were dismayed to learn that the best ones for autistic children were in neighboring New Jersey. "My husband and I said, you know, this is not right. You should be able to educate your child in the community where you live, " she told *New York Times* journalist Emma Daly. "There should be a great school in New York City."

Slatkin and his wife also have an unusual connection to late billionaire Edmond Safra, who died in a suspicious fire in his Monte Carlo apartment in 1999. Safra's private nurse, Ted Maher, was subsequently convicted in a Monaco court for arson. Maher owned his job to the Slatkins, who had met him when he was a nurse at New York Presbyterian Hospital. After they left their camera behind in the hospital room, Maher returned it. The Slatkins were friends with a woman named Adriana Elia, who was the daughter of Lily Safra, and recommended Maher when they learned that the Safras were interesting in hiring a caretaker for the billionaire.

Sales for Slatkin's company remained strong, despite an array of competing premium lines in the candle and home-fragrance sector, and were estimated at $15 million to $20 million for 2004. In May of 2005, his company was acquired by Limited Brands, the parent company of retail clothing stores Limited and Express, and which also owns the Bath & Body Works chain, Victoria's Secret, and Henri Bendel. The deal made his New York City-based Slatkin & Co. a subsidiary of Bath & Body Works, and he remained head of his brand; he also was given a new post as president of Home Design inside the Limited Brands group, and would create items for the Bath & Body Works stores as well as other home and personal fragrance lines for the company's various retail brands. "I can create anything I want," he explained to *WWD*'s Pete Born, and also said he hoped to become "the Oprah of home."

Sources

Global Cosmetic Industry, October 2004, p. 36.
Harper's Bazaar, November 2004, p. 108.
New York Times, May 4, 2005; May 13, 2005.
People, June 6, 2005, p. 116.
Times (London, England), July 3, 2004, p. 13.
Town & Country, November 2003, p. 170.
Vanity Fair, February 2003, p. 130.
WWD, September 15, 2000, p. 49S; July 1, 2003, p. 13; June 3, 2004, p. 3; June 11, 2004, p. 8; May 13, 2005, p. 7.

—*Carol Brennan*

John W. Snow

© Kimimasa Mayama/Reuters/Corbis

United States Treasury Secretary

Born August 2, 1939, in Toledo, OH; married Carolyn; children: three. *Education:* University of Toledo, B.A., 1962; University of Virginia, Ph.D. (economics), 1965; George Washington University, L.L.B., 1967.

Addresses: *Office*—1500 Pennsylvania Ave., NW, Washington, DC, 20220.

Career

Several jobs at the U.S. Department of Transportation, including assistant secretary, deputy undersecretary, and deputy assistant secretary, 1972-76; administrator of the National Highway Traffic Safety Administration, 1976-77; visiting fellow, American Enterprise Institute, 1977; vice-president of government affairs, Chessie System Inc., 1977-80; distinguished fellow, Yale School of Management, 1978-1980; named a senior vice-president of CSX Corp., 1980; named president and CEO of CSX Transportation Inc., 1987; named president of CSX Corp., 1988; named CEO, CSX Corp., 1989; named chairman, CSX Corp., 1991; chairman, Business Roundtable, 1994-1996; U.S. Treasury secretary, 2003—.

Sidelights

John W. Snow came to the cabinet of U.S. President George W. Bush after more than a decade as the leader of railroad giant CSX, years spent effectively lobbying in Washington, and experience working in the federal government in the 1970s.

When he became secretary of the treasury, he took one of the more difficult jobs in the administration. Between 2003 to 2005, Snow had to defend free trade as the United States was struggling to compete with cheap Chinese imports and low-cost labor overseas. He also tried to help sell the president's controversial plan for reforming Social Security. After a frank statement he made about trade was used against Bush in the 2004 presidential campaign, speculation spread around Washington that Snow would be replaced. But Bush kept him on, and Snow spent 2005 as a top advocate for Bush Administration economic policies.

Snow was born in Toledo, Ohio, in 1939, graduated from the University of Toledo and earned a doctorate in economics from the University of Virginia and a law degree from George Washington University. From 1967 to 1977, he held several top jobs in the U.S. Department of Transportation, including administrator of the National Highway Traffic Safety Administration and deputy undersecretary, assistant secretary and deputy assistant secretary jobs. He left government in 1977 to work for Chessie System Inc., the railroad company that became CSX Corp. after a 1980 merger.

Snow worked his way up through several jobs in the corporation. In the 1980s, he lobbied Congress to reject the proposed merger of CSX competitor Norfolk Southern with Conrail. (It was rejected.) In 1987, he was named president and chief executive officer (CEO) of CSX's largest business group, CSX Transportation Inc. The next year, he was promoted to president of CSX itself, a sign that he would take over the company when its CEO at the time left. Sure enough, Snow was named CEO of CSX in 1989 and chairman in 1991.

As CEO of CSX, Snow earned mixed reviews. He made headlines—and stunned observers who thought he was too academic in demeanor—when he tried to take over Conrail in 1996. But despite Snow's skills at Washington lobbying, CSX ran up against the fears that the merger might reduce competition. In the end, CSX had to split up Conrail with its rival, Norfolk Southern. The deal left CSX with a large debt, and CSX had trouble integrating its share of Conrail into the company, leaving it inefficient and its stock price low.

During Snow's tenure, safety experts questioned whether CSX had done enough to improve the safety of its rail lines. But Snow moved to correct problems after they were cited, and accidents on CSX lines decreased as his tenure as CEO went on. Meanwhile, investors supported Snow's plan to narrow CSX's focus on the railroad business and gradually get rid of other investments, such as oil and real estate, that the company had acquired before he took over.

Meanwhile, Snow remained active in Republican politics and served as chairman of the Business Roundtable, a lobby of powerful corporate executives, in the mid-1990s. In late 2002, those political connections paid off when U.S. President George W. Bush nominated Snow to be treasury secretary. He replaced Paul O'Neill, who had a difficult relationship with the president and was prone to making unscripted statements about economic policy that upset stock markets. Snow was confirmed by the Senate in January of 2003 and took office in February of that year.

Snow's job as treasury secretary was difficult. He had to defend the government's monetary policy amid strong criticism from foreign governments and domestic investors. Most importantly, Snow was in charge of proclaiming the administration's support of a "strong dollar." But despite that assertion, the Bush administration declined to intervene in the international currency market (which sets exchange rates), even when the dollar was losing a lot of value. When Snow declared at an economic meeting in May of 2003 that the "strong dollar" position did not include a position on exchange rates, the dollar's value plummeted further.

Another difficult job Snow had was stating the government's economic policy toward China. In late 2003, Snow began pressuring China to let the value of its currency, the yuan, be set by international currency markets, not a rate fixed to the U.S. dollar. Such a move, the administration hoped, would cause the yuan's value to increase, also increasing the cost of Chinese products that are imported into the U.S. and compete with American goods. However, China ignored the advice, and critics explained that such a move could hurt the Chinese banking system, U.S. companies doing business in China, and U.S. consumers.

Snow also had to campaign for Bush's re-election. While doing so, he made at least one costly error. In March of 2004, he told a newspaper in the key state of Ohio that outsourcing, the practice of American companies moving jobs overseas, is part of free trade, and that free trade is good for the American economy overall. Bush's opponent, Sen. John Kerry, took that comment to mean that outsourcing is good for the U.S. economy, and used that accusation against Bush in the presidential campaign.

So after Bush was reelected, speculation ran high that Bush would replace Snow. The value of the dollar continued to fall to new lows against the euro. Critics scoffed at Snow's insistence that the U.S. was still following a strong dollar policy. Anonymous administration officials even leaked hints that Snow would be gone soon, while Republicans and investors complained that he had not figured out how to make policy pronouncements in a way that reassured the markets. But in December of 2004, Bush asked Snow to stay on into his second term. (Some reports suggested he did this only after being unable to find a replacement with whom he was comfortable.)

In 2005, Snow's job got no easier. Commentators noted that he was presiding over a decline in the importance of the treasury department. Snow went on the road in the winter to help promote the president's proposal to partially privatize Social Security by letting younger workers put some of their social security tax payments into personal investment accounts. "Why are personal accounts so important? By giving younger workers the opportunity to receive higher benefits than the current system can afford to pay, they enhance young workers' retirement security," Snow wrote in the *Wall Street Journal*. But the idea faced strong opposition and seemed stalled by the end of the year.

In April of 2005, he again told China to stop pegging the value of the yuan to the dollar, and he proposed cutting the budget deficit. "The problem is that nobody believes ... Snow's rhetoric," responded the *Washington Post* in an editorial, arguing that Snow's budget numbers were not credible because they did not include the cost of the war in Iraq or the war on terrorism. In August, Snow said the U.S. economy was improving faster than some people believed—but he felt compelled to acknowledge that the improvements were not benefiting everyone equally, and he said the administration was considering measures to better spread the economic benefits around, such as increased funding for education.

In November of 2005, on the eve of the president's trip to China, Snow also signaled a change in the diplomatic approach toward China, arguing that the U.S. needed to back off of its pressure to let currency markets set the value of the yuan. But it appeared to be a tactical diplomatic move, not a reversal in policy; observers believed the Chinese, concerned about their image, might actually let the yuan rise once they were under less public pressure to do so.

As 2005 ended, speculation continued to suggest that Snow would be asked to leave the treasury department. One prominently reported rumor, which had not been proven true as the year neared its end, had Snow being replaced as secretary by Bush chief of staff Andrew Card. *BusinessWeek* writers Richard S. Dunham and Rich Miller called Snow a "genial traveling salesman" for the Bush Administration, but said he was too pragmatic and concerned with deficits to be a perfect team player for an administration that valued tax cuts over cutting the deficit. It seemed clear that Snow would eventually leave the administration. He had reportedly told associates that he did not want to serve for Bush's entire second term, but did want to stay long enough to help the president with the debates on Social Security and tax reform.

Sources

Periodicals

BusinessWeek, October 17, 2005, p. 51.
New York Times, October 17, 1996, p. D4; December 9, 2002, p. A1; December 10, 2002, p. A30; December 25, 2002, p. C1; February 14, 2003, p. A24; May 19, 2003, p. A8; June 12, 2003, p. C13; March 31, 2004, p. C7; December 9, 2004, p. A1.
Wall Street Journal, April 8, 1987, p. 1; April 21, 1988, p. 1; December 9, 2002, p. A12; January 20, 2005, p. A15.
Washington Post, December 10, 2004, p. A1; December 12, 2002, p. A3; September 7, 2003, p. B6; January 15, 2005, p. E1; March 14, 2005, p. A17; April 19, 2005, p. A18; August 9, 2005, p. A3; September 9, 2005, p. A23; November 18, 2005, p. D6.

Online

"Being John Snow," Slate.com, http:// www.slate.com/id/2110076 (November 20, 2005).
"Profile: Secretary of the Treasury John Snow," ABCNews.com, http://abcnews.go.com/Politics/print?id=404456 (November 20, 2005).
"Secretary of the Treasury John W. Snow," The White House, http://www.whitehouse.gov/government/snow-bio.html (November 20, 2005).

—Erick Trickey

Anne Stevens

Chief Operating Officer of the Americas for Ford Motor Company

Rebecca Cook/Reuters/Landov

Born c. 1949 in Reading; PA; married Bill Stevens (a retired auto supplier manager), c. 1968; children: two. *Education:* Earned dual B.S. in mechanical and materials engineering, Drexel University, 1980; completed graduate work at Rutgers University.

Addresses: *Office*—Ford Motor Company, The American Rd., Dearborn, MI 48121.

Career

Held engineering, manufacturing, and marketing positions with ExxonMobil Corporation, c. 1981-89; joined Ford Motor Company as a marketing specialist in the plastic products division, 1990; manager in plastic and trim products operations, 1992-95; manufacturing manager, plastic and trim products operations, 1995; plant manager at Ford's Enfield, England, automotive components division, 1995-97; assistant vehicle line director of the company's small car vehicle center in Dunton, England, 1997-99; director of manufacturing business office for Ford in North America, 1999-2000; vice president for North American manufacturing, after April of 2001, and vice president for North American vehicle operations, after July of 2001; group vice president for Canada, Mexico, and South America, 2003-05; named chief operating officer of the Americas, October, 2005.

Sidelights

Anne Stevens is the highest-ranking woman in the United States automotive industry. As executive vice president and chief operating officer for Ford Motor Company's North and South American divisions, she was instrumental in drafting a reorganization plan that would help the struggling domestic automaker survive into a third century. Not long afterward, *Motor Trend* put Stevens on its annual "Power List" of the 50 most influential people in the car business. She was one of just two women to appear on it, but she also regularly makes the *Fortune* magazine rankings of the most powerful women among the ranks of corporate America.

Born around the midpoint of the twentieth century, Stevens grew up in Reading, Pennsylvania, and fell in love with car culture in her teens. She was particularly drawn to stock-car racing, but it was a different era, and women were not allowed anywhere near "the pits," the chaos-filled bays where mechanics serviced cars between laps. But Stevens disguised herself in a baggy shirt, trousers, and with her hair under a cap, and managed to get a close-up look at the dragsters. "If you looked dirty, they didn't bother you," she recalled in an interview with Micheline Maynard of the *New York Times.*

Stevens was offered a nursing school scholarship, but soon discovered she was ill-matched for a career in medicine. She dropped out, and went to work for the local telephone company. After scoring well on an aptitude test, she was given a job with the engineering department, and eventually met her future husband there. After starting a family, both went to college together, with Stevens graduating from Drexel University in 1980 with a dual degree in mechanical and materials engineering. She worked a summer job at a Ford stamping plant near Detroit, which she liked, but she had eleven job offers when she graduated, and accepted one with ExxonMobil, the oil company, which put her and her family in New Jersey.

After one of Stevens' friends died in a car accident, she began to reconsider some of her career options. She decided to enroll in a graduate business degree program at Rutgers University, where she learned about the factory-management principles of W. Edwards Deming. Deming's theories were widely used in Japan after World War II, and finally began to catch on with American manufacturers in the 1980s. When she was offered a job with Ford Motor Company in the Detroit area in 1990, she took it, and began as a marketing specialist for its plastic products division. Two years later, she was moved over to Ford's plastic and trim plant in Saline, Michigan, and by 1995 had become a full-fledged manager of a manufacturing job site. That same year, the company sent her to manage its automotive components plant in Enfield, England, where she spent the next two years. She was the first woman ever to manage one of Ford's European factories.

In 1997, Stevens advanced to the title of assistant vehicle line director with Ford's small car vehicle center in Dunton, England, which made the popular Fiesta, Ka, and Puma models for the European market. She returned to Detroit in 1999, when she was named director of the manufacturing business office for Ford in North America. At the time, she was considered to be the highest-ranking female executive among American automakers. In April of 2001, she became vice president for North American manufacturing, capping what had been an impressive decade-long rise through Ford management ranks. While other women had attained top leadership posts in the auto industry, it was rare for one to oversee a manufacturing division, an area still dominated by men who had served as plant managers once before, too.

In July of 2001, Stevens was made vice president for North American vehicle operations, which put in her charge of 29 manufacturing sites for the company. Her task was to improve plant performance, and ensure that the company's quality standards were being met across the board. Two years later, she became group vice president for Canada, Mexico, and South America, and once again, made company history: she was the first woman to hold the group vice president title at Ford. The improved performance under her watch—sales and export numbers rose in 2004, and Ford even made a profit in South America for the first time in several years—prompted the business and automotive press to cite her as a name to watch in the future.

Stevens emerged as a leader at Ford during one of the automaker's most troubled periods. Since the start of the twenty-first century, its vehicles' reputation for quality and safety had suffered, and it was steadily losing market share. Its chief executive officer, Bill Ford Jr., was the high-profile great-grandson of company founder Henry Ford, and began to take some drastic steps to steer the company clear of further financial trouble. He was said to have given Stevens a relatively free decision-making rein when she became chief operating officer of the Americas in October of 2005—a degree of autonomy not always granted in family-run companies, nor in the automotive industry in general.

Bill Ford teamed Stevens with Mark Fields, whose job title was president of the Americas, and gave them the task of coming up with a reorganization plan to save the automaker. Ford's board of directors approved it in December of 2005, and its details were announced the following month. It included a number of plant closings, the elimination of a few vehicle lines, and a reduction in the North American workforce by 28 percent over the next several years.

Named to the No. 22 spot on *Fortune* magazine's list of the 50 most powerful women in business in America in 2005, Stevens has worked to help other women at Ford follow her up the corporate ladder. She began a women's networking group when she was based in England, and later founded an informal group of female executives who met regularly at a local restaurant near Ford's World Headquarters in Dearborn. There, every few weeks, they met to talk shop, and venture their own off-the-record comments about what the company could be doing better. As Stevens admitted in an interview with *Automotive News*, writer Amy Wilson, she and her female colleagues had already "reorganized the company ... many times," at least in theory.

Sources

Automotive News, April 3, 2000, p. 3; September 11, 2000, p. 27W; September 26, 2005, p. 24; October 17, 2005, p. 48; November 21, 2005, p. 1.
New York Times, July 22, 2001, p. BU2.
Ward's Auto World, April 1996, p. 38.

—*Carol Brennan*

Jens Stoltenberg

Getty Images

Prime minister of Norway

Born March 16, 1959, in Oslo, Norway; son of Thorvald (a politician) and Karin (a politician) Stoltenberg; married Ingrid Schulerud (a diplomat); children: two. *Education:* Earned advance degree in economics from the University of Oslo.

Addresses: *Home*—Oslo, Norway. *Office*—Office of the Prime Minister, P.O. Box 8001 dep., (NO-)0030 Oslo, Norway.

Career

Part-time journalist for the *Arbeiderbladet* newspaper, 1979-81; Norwegian Labour Party, Oslo chapter, information secretary, 1981, central board member after 1985, chair, 1990-92, deputy leader, after 1992, and chair, 2002—; Labour Youth League, chair, 1985-89; executive officer, Statistics Norway, 1989-90; lecturer in economics, University of Oslo, 1989-90; Secretary at the Department of the Environment, 1990; member of parliament, 1993—; cabinet posts include minister for trade and energy, 1993-96, minister of finance, 1996-97; chair of parliamentary committee on oil and energy affairs, 1997-2000; prime minister of Norway, March 2000-September 2001, and October 2005—.

Sidelights

Norwegian politician Jens Stoltenberg ascended to the post of prime minister of his country in 2005. The election results signified a shift to the left for this Scandinavian nation of 3.4 million, which has prospered immensely thanks to its North Sea oil exports, and Stoltenberg promised to use that wealth to boost Norway's already generous network of social services. The telegenic Stoltenberg is sometimes compared to British Labour Party leader Tony Blair because of his relatively young age as head of his country's leading party of the left.

Stoltenberg was born on March 16, 1959, in Oslo, Norway's capital. His father, Thorvald, would later serve as Norway's foreign minister, the United Nations High Commissioner for Refugees, and head of the Norwegian Red Cross, while Stoltenberg's mother, Karin, would be appointed to a junior minister post in the Norwegian government. Both were members of the Norwegian Labour Party (*Det norske Arbeiderparti,* or DNA), which had been in power for much of the twentieth century thanks to consistently robust voter support for its democratic-socialist policies.

Stoltenberg joined the DNA as a teen, and studied economics at the University of Oslo. Between 1979 and 1981 he was a part-time journalist for the *Arbeiderbladet,* a national newspaper, and went on to serve as information secretary for the Oslo Labour Party in 1981. He headed the Labour Youth League after 1985, and spent a year as an executive officer for Statistics Norway, the government agency whose

American equivalent is the U.S. Census Bureau. He also taught economics at his alma mater before advancing to the post of chair of the Oslo chapter of the DNA in 1990 and state secretary at the Department of the Environment. Two years later, he became a deputy leader of the party.

Stoltenberg was first elected to Norway's *Storting*, or parliament, in 1993, representing Oslo. That same year he was named minister for trade and energy in the government of Gro Harlem Brundtland, and served for three years. He switched portfolios in 1996 to become minister of finance in the government of Brundtland's successor, Thorbjørn Jagland. After 1997, Stoltenberg served as head of the standing committee on oil and energy affairs in the *Storting,* while Kjell Magne Bondevik, a Lutheran minister and Christian People's Party member, became Norway's first non-Socialist prime minister since World War II.

Stoltenberg served his first term as prime minister after Bondevik's government resigned in March of 2000. Stoltenberg's party had tried to push for a vote on building new power stations fired by Norway's rich stores of natural gas. Bondevik and his coalition government had opposed the bill, and responded with a proposal to further restrict greenhouse gas emissions. *Storting* members voted with the DNA, which had argued the country's demand for electricity necessitated the new natural gas-fired power stations.

Stoltenberg took over the government at a time when many significant reforms were already underway. These included the controversial privatization of several industries, and his administration struggled to maintain the public's confidence. At the time, some were clamoring for a reduction in the traditionally high taxes that Norway and other Scandinavian countries levied to cover their extensive social-service programs, which included universal health care and free university education. Norway's oil revenues went into the country's Petroleum Fund, and its coffers had swelled in recent years. Stoltenberg advised a cautionary route when he presented his government's first budget to the *Storting* later in 2000, warning that it would be imprudent to spend the oil riches for short-term gains. "Spain destroyed its economy when it discovered gold in Latin America," *Financial Times* journalists Valeria Criscione and Quentin Peel quoted him as saying. "You had the Dutch disease when Holland spent all its income from gas in the 1970s, and the same in Norway in the 1980s when we spent too much. We have learned our lesson."

In parliamentary elections held on September 10, 2001, Stoltenberg's party lost heavily, taking just 24 percent of the vote in its worst showing since 1924.

Bondevik returned as prime minister to head a center-right government, and Stoltenberg concentrated on realigning the DNA to help it return to power. He won a hotly contested battle against Jagland for the party leadership in 2002, and prepared for the 2005 elections. In that contest, the DNA secured a majority, but the Socialist Left Party and the Centre Party did well at the polls, too, which necessitated the formation of a coalition government.

Sworn in as prime minister for the second time on October 17, 2005, Stoltenberg presided over a country that had continued to prosper since his first term on the job. Norway boasted a four-percent annual growth rate and had one of the lowest rates of unemployment in the world. It was usually listed at the top of the United Nations' Human Development Index, which ranked the best countries to live in the world. Thanks to rising prices per-barrel on the world oil market, the Petroleum Fund held a staggering $190 billion. Stoltenberg and the DNA proposed to spend a little more than five percent of that, or ten billion dollars, on health care, education, and senior citizen services in the coming years. "Norway has great possibilities and we have to use these for everyone in our country," he wrote in an editorial in Norway's largest newspaper, *Verdens Gang,* according to a *UPI International Intelligence* report. "That means we must spend the big money on the big issues." A more problematic debate is likely to loom over the question of European Union (EU) membership—Norway is one of the last European countries choosing to remain out of the EU, a status supported by most of the leftist parties, but Stoltenberg has backed the pro-EU side.

Stoltenberg is married to Ingrid Schulerud, a diplomat who holds a high-ranking post within the Ministry of Foreign Affairs. They met while students at the Cathedral School of Oslo, when Schulerud beat him in a student-government election. They have two children. In 2005 Stoltenberg appeared in *The Rich Country,* a documentary film that tracked his path to a second term as prime minister. His wife and children did not appear in it, but in one segment he cooks a dinner of the national delicacy, whale meat, for his parents. The prime minister is reportedly an avid online gamer, and in multiplayer contests like *Age of Empires* he uses the name *Steklov,* which the Soviet Union's secret service, the KGB, once used to identify him.

Sources

Periodicals

Economist, September 17, 2005, p. 51.
Financial Times, October 4, 2000, p. 9.
Time International, September 12, 2005, p. 18.
Times (London, England), October 18, 2001, p. 19.

UPI International Intelligence, September 8, 2005.

Variety, March 20, 2006, p. 28.

Online

"Prime Minister Jens Stoltenberg," Office of the Prime Minister, http://odin.dep.no/smk/eng lish/prime_minister/biographical_data/001001-160 093/dok-bn.html (May 21, 2006)

—*Carol Brennan*

Joss Stone

Singer and songwriter

Born Joscelyn Eve Stoker, April 11, 1987, in Ashill, Devon, England; daughter of Richard (a business owner) and Wendy Stoker.

Addresses: *Contact*—S-Curve Records, 150 Fifth Ave., New York, NY 10011. *Home*—Devon, England. *Website*—http://www.jossstone.com.

Career

Landed recording deal with S-Curve Records, 2002; singer and songwriter, 2002—.

Sidelights

Supremely gifted British singer Joss Stone burst onto the R&B music scene in 2003 with the release of her debut album *The Soul Sessions*. Though Stone was just a teenager, her extraordinary vocal capabilities propelled the album to gold certification in the United States and helped jumpstart her career. Since then, Stone has become immensely popular with a broad fan base—her looks appeal to the younger crowd, while her music captures an older audience. Established musicians are eager to sing with her. Stone has sung alongside such music legends as Mick Jagger, Donna Summer, Chaka Khan, Smokey Robinson, and Gladys Knight. Elton John even invited her to sing at one of his Oscar parties. In 2004 Stone released her second album, *Mind, Body & Soul*, which garnered three Grammy nominations, proving Stone to be much more than just a one-album novelty.

© Contographer ®/Corbis

The third of four children, Stone was born Joscelyn Eve Stoker on April 11, 1987, in Ashill, Devon, England, to Richard and Wendy Stoker. Her father owns a fruit and nut import/export business; her mother used to manage vacation cottages but now spends her time chaperoning Stone while she is on tour. Stone's parents, though not musically inclined, enjoyed collecting albums and consequently, Stone spent her early years listening to lots of music. Her parents played rock and pop, including the Beatles, but also filled the house with the music of Anita Baker, Janis Joplin, Whitney Houston, and James Brown. When Stone was ten, she became captivated with Aretha Franklin after seeing a television commercial advertising one of the Queen of Soul's CDs. Stone promptly placed the music on her Christmas list. At home, Stone sung her heart out using a hairbrush for a microphone; at school, however, Stone was so shy her music teacher had no idea she could sing, let alone belt out soulful melodies.

Initially, Stone entered the music world for economic reasons—she wanted money. Around the time she was 12, her family got into an argument with neighbors over the ownership of a field that Stone rode her horse, Freddy, on. Stone's family could not afford to buy the field, so they sold her horse. Upset that her family could not afford the field, Stone decided to take matters into her own hands and get a job—she wondered if she could make money singing.

Around 2000, Stone entered a contest to appear on the BBC-TV talent show *Star for a Night*. She did not even know a whole song, so for her tryout Stone sent in a tape of herself singing half of "Amazing Grace," half of "Jesus Loves Me" and part of "This Little Light of Mine." The tape was good enough to earn her a live audition for the show. When the big day arrived, Stone planned to sing Carole King's "(You Make Me Feel Like) A Natural Woman," but when she stepped before the judges, fear gripped her and she forgot the first line—the judges had to remind her. Despite the foible, once Stone got started, she nailed the song and earned the right to compete on the amateur talent show.

For this phase of the competition, Stone sang a Donna Summer tune, "On the Radio." Stone won the contest and was then asked to perform on a charity show, where she captured the attention of some London producers who contacted S-Curve Records chief executive officer Steve Greenberg, the man who discovered 1990s teen sensation Hanson. Intrigued by the young Brit, Greenberg flew Stone to New York in early 2002 so he could listen to her sing since she had no demo track. They downloaded karaoke tracks off the Internet and Stone added her voice—she sang "Midnight Train to Georgia" and "(Sittin' on) the Dock of the Bay." Speaking to Joe D'Angelo of MTV.com, Greenberg recalled how Stone's voice astonished him. "When I first heard her sing, I really couldn't believe that this big, soulful, nuanced, precious, wonderful, knowing voice was coming out of this 14-year-old girl," he said. "It didn't make sense." With no second thoughts, Greenberg signed her to his label.

Stone's next adventure involved traveling back to the United States to record an album. Stone, a struggling dyslexic who hated school, was happy to quit and begin pursuing a music career. Stone has said the only part of school she liked was lunchtime. Greenberg arranged for Stone to work with 1970s and '80s soul pioneer Betty Wright, who received a 1974 Grammy Award for her song "Where Is the Love?". Working with a veteran like Wright pushed Stone to sing at a new level. Wright used her connections to hook Stone up with a phenomenal cast of musicians, including Miami soul scene players Willie "Little Beaver" Hale on guitar, Benny Latimore on piano, and Timmy Thomas on organ.

Speaking to *USA Today*'s Steve Jones, Wright recalled the day she introduced Stone to the band members. Wright played Stone's vocals before the face-to-face introduction, and "they described her as 300 pounds. To have a voice like hers, she had to be a big girl. When they saw her come into the room, they didn't believe it was her."

For Stone, the introduction meant trial by fire; she had never sung with a band before. Together, they produced an album full of obscure old-school soul classics that showcased Stone's full vocal range. At times, her voice is high and pleasant, but there are also times when Stone drops her voice, treating listeners to her husky purr. A few of the songs featured on the album include Laura Lee's "Dirty Man," Sugar Billy's 1975 one-hit wonder "Super Duper Love" and Aretha Franklin's "All the King's Horses." Each song was rearranged and produced with a different feel than the original. Stone also recorded the White Stripes hit "Fell in Love With a Girl," though the song was remade as "Fell in Love With a Boy."

Stone spent less than a week recording the album, which was not intended to be a huge success. S-Curve simply wanted Stone to have something out on the market that could percolate on the underground so when Stone released her own album, she would have some name recognition. Instead, music lovers snatched up the album. It sold more than 2.5 million copies worldwide and hit the Top 10 chart in 13 countries. It was certified gold in the United States. Besides making waves on the radio, "Fell in Love With a Boy" was picked up by MTV and VH1 as part of each music channel's video rotation, causing her popularity—and record sales—to surge. Soon, television hosts requested her presence and she appeared on *The Tonight Show with Jay Leno* and *Last Call With Carson Daly*.

Besides figuring out how to record with a band, Stone had to learn to perform live. She played her first gig at a tiny Miami place called the Tobacco Road. Stone was so nervous she cried, but eventually made it out on stage. Looking back, Stone acknowledges that the name change—from Joscelyn Stoker to Joss Stone—has helped her gain the courage to perform for audiences. She had been reluctant to change her name, but found that shedding her childhood moniker also helped her shed her adolescent anxiety. "I can't be Joss Stoker when I'm singing," she told the *Daily Telegraph*'s Craig McLean, "because if I was, I'd stand by the mike [and] have my hair right over my face like this."

Becoming comfortable onstage has been Stone's biggest challenge; her trademark is to perform barefoot. When she sings, Stone's voice makes her seem like a seasoned veteran much older than her actual age. However, when a song ends, Stone often transforms back into the teenager that she is. According to Abigail Wild in the Glasgow *Herald*, a critic once noted, "As the song ends and the giggling begins, there's a moment of confusion, as if the audience can't quite believe the two noises are coming from the same mouth."

Stone's second album, *Mind, Body & Soul*, debuted in 2004. Stone says the title is fitting because in the first album, she was just giving audiences a little piece of her. It contained her voice and her emotions, but not her own songs. However, in her second album Stone says she bared all by sharing songs she had written herself, some when she was just 14.

In sum, Stone co-wrote eleven of the 14 songs with the help of seasoned songwriters such as Wright, Desmond Child, Portishead's Beth Gibbons, and Motown legend Lamont Dozier, whose son, Beau, she later dated. Their writing approach was carefree. "We'd just go in and vibe—we'd each think of something and mix it all up together," Stone told the *Toronto Sun*'s Mary Dickie. "Ideas were flying around the room. I like that way of writing. I don't like it to be cut and dried—there's too much pressure. The idea is to have fun together." Stone has said she hopes to write a third album mostly on her own.

Mind, Body & Soul, filled with smoky vocals, includes the energizing kiss-off first single "You Had Me," the brazen, up-tempo "Don't Cha Wanna Ride," the rock-soul ballad "Killing Time," and "Spoiled," a lament on the downside of good luck. "Jet Lag," sung against a thumping backbeat, describes a love so sweeping that it is physically exhausting.

The album proved Stone's initial success was more than a fluke and that she would be staying on the charts for years to come. Like *Soul Sessions*, *Mind* went gold in the United States, meaning it sold more than 500,000 copies. The album also climbed the charts in England and Stone became the youngest female solo artist to have a number one album in Britain. Just 17, Stone was nine months younger than the previous record-holder, Avril Lavigne.

In addition, Stone received three Grammy nods for the album, including best new artist, best pop vocal album, and best female pop vocal performance, the latter for the track "You Had Me." Stone did not win in any category, but the night was nonetheless memorable. During the February of 2005 awards ceremony, Stone performed a duet with Grammy Award-winning rocker Melissa Etheridge. They paid tribute to 1960s rocker Janis Joplin by singing their own rendition of her 1968 classic "Piece of my Heart."

Though her music career is just getting started, Stone keeps an eye out for the future. Speaking to *Entertainment Weekly*, Stone said she was far from finished and noted that she does not even feel like she has accomplished much yet. "I want to act a bit. Later on, I kind of want to be a midwife."

For the time being, fans hope Stone stays put in the music world. In his profile of Stone for the *Daily Telegraph*, McLean said that he believed Stone has a long music career ahead of her. He wrote that she was "a supernaturally gifted performer who can feel and even inhabit a song, summoning up an intensity that vocalists twice, even three times her age are pushed to match. When her talent fully matures, the sky's the limit."

Selected discography

The Soul Sessions, S-Curve Records, 2003.
Mind, Body & Soul, S-Curve Records, 2004.

Sources

Periodicals

Daily Telegraph (London, England), September 18, 2004, p. 4; October 5, 2004, p. 10.
Entertainment Weekly, June 24/July 1, 2005, p. 108.
Herald (Glasgow, Scotland), October 23, 2004, p. 17.
People, November 17, 2003, p. 102.
Rolling Stone, November 11, 2004, pp. 47-48.
Toronto Sun, May 29, 2005, p. S10.
USA Today, October 3, 2003, p. 8E.

Online

"Joss Stone," MTV.com, http://www.mtv.com/news/yhif/stone_joss/ (October 2, 2005).

—*Lisa Frick*

System of a Down

Rock group

Members include John Dolmayan (born July 15, 1973, in Lebanon), drums; Daron Malakian (born July 18, 1975, in Hollywood, CA; son of artists), singer, guitar; Shavo Odadjian (born April 22, 1974, in Yerevan, Armenia), bass; Serj Tankian (born August 21, 1967, in Beirut, Lebanon), keyboards, singer.

Addresses: *Record company*—Columbia Records, 550 Madison Ave., New York City, NY 10022. *Website*—http://www.systemofadown.com.

Career

Group formed in Los Angeles, CA, 1994; played at clubs such as the Roxy and the Troubador, mid-1990s; signed with American Recordings,

John Rogers/Getty Images for MTV

released debut album, *System of a Down,* 1998; released *Toxicity,* 2001; released *Steal This Album,* 2002; released *Mezmerize,* 2005; released *Hypnotize,* 2005.

Awards: Grammy Award for Best Hard Rock Performance, National Academy of Recording Arts and Sciences, for "B.Y.O.B.," 2006.

Sidelights

Armenian-American rockers System of a Down have sold ten million records since their 1998 self-titled debut. With a style best characterized as metal-meets-Middle-Eastern-melodies, the California-based quartet has opened up a new door inside what had been a tradition-bound, often formulaic genre of arena rock. Yet perhaps even more groundbreaking is the band's outspokenness, particularly regarding Armenian history and American foreign policy. "System of a Down's music expresses a social and political awareness rare in heavy metal," noted Adam Sweeting of London's *Guardian* newspaper, "railing against corporate enslavement, media propaganda and ... pornographic TV and the death of American democracy."

All four members of System of a Down are of Armenian heritage. Daron Malakian, the band's guitarist and chief songwriter, is the only one who was born in the United States. His parents emigrated from Iraq—where small communities of settlers from nearby Armenia live—in 1974, the year before he was born. Both parents were sculptors, and Malakian grew up in Hollywood, California. He attended a private school in the Los Angeles area for Armenian-American youth, as did System of a Down bassist Shavo Odadjian, who came to the United States from Armenia with his family when he was five. Both Serj Tankian, singer and keyboard player, and John Dolmayan, the band's drummer, were born in Lebanon to Armenian families, and came to California as children as well.

Tankian also attended the Armenian-American school, but was born in 1967, making him the oldest member of the band. He had an established career as chief executive officer of a software company well before the band formed. "I didn't start writing music and playing instruments until I went to college," Tankian told Greg Kot of the *Chicago Tribune.* "When I did, I realized I was famished for them. I've been playing like a madman ever since."

Malakian, by contrast, was determined to become a musician before he entered kindergarten. Blessed with a musical talent that gave him the ability to play nearly any instrument just by picking it up, he was an ardent metalhead in his teens. Around the time he finished high school, however, he suddenly discovered the music of the Beatles. "The Beatles changed my life as much as Slayer did," he admitted to Lisa Sharken in a *Guitar Player* interview. "Listening to the Beatles helped me do things like create a chorus by combining a waltz beat with a metal riff, because they weren't afraid to combine styles or mix heavy music with softer stuff."

Malakian and Tankian first joined forces in a band called Soil, and Odadjian served as Soil's manager. They coalesced as System of a Down around 1994, taking their name from a poem written by Malakian, who became the band's primary songwriter. "I was trying to write the songs that I couldn't buy at the store," he said in the *Guardian* interview. "I was trying to write the music for the band I wanted to be a fan of."

System of a Down began by playing the southern California rock-club circuit, and attracted a strong following. They graduated to such venues as Roxy, the Whiskey, and the Troubadour, all of which are known as Los Angeles-area hot spots for music-industry executives searching for new talent. But they were often told their act was simply too distinctive, as Malakian told the *Chicago Tribune*'s Kot. "We weren't white, black, or Latino. We didn't belong in any category they could market to."

Their luck changed when a show at the Viper Room, the infamous club owned by Johnny Depp where the actor River Phoenix died, was seen by legendary music producer Rick Rubin. Rubin had once been the business partner of Russell Simmons, and their Def Jam American label had launched the careers of Run D.M.C., Public Enemy, and the Beastie Boys. Rubin signed Malakian and his bandmates to his label, American Recordings, which was affiliated with Columbia Records, and offered to produce their first studio effort.

System of a Down was released in 1998, and sold an impressive 750,000 copies. Its breakout single, "Sugar," received immense radio airplay, but the final track, "P.L.U.C.K.," was one of the band's first published diatribes on political hypocrisy. All of the band members had relatives who were affected by the Armenian genocide that took place between 1915 and 1923, when the Turkish-controlled Ottoman Empire acted upon some long-standing hostilities between the Armenian and Turkish peoples. As a result of mass deportations and systematic bloodshed, as many as two million Armenians died during the period, but the genocide was never formally acknowledged by the international community. In the intervening decades, Armenians have sought recognition and apology for the massacre.

"P.L.U.C.K." addressed the Armenian tragedy in frank terms, with lyrics that railed, "A whole race Genocide/Taken away all of our pride/A whole race Genocide/Taken away." Even in the modern era, most Western nations have avoided commenting on the matter, fearing that it might damage relations with Turkey, a crucial ally at the border between Europe and the Middle East. As Tankian told the *Guardian*'s Sweeting, "It was a true genocide whose lessons should have been learned, and all our grandparents and elders are survivors of it. Hitler got pointers from it, because he saw that nobody was doing anything about it."

Following the release of their debut album, the band toured heavily over the next few years, including stints on the annual summer metal showcase known as Ozzfest. They also opened for Limp Bizkit, and were regularly grouped with that act and other practitioners of what came to be known as "nu metal," such as Korn and Linkin Park. System of a Down's politically motivated lyrics, however, shared more with another California outfit, rapcore pioneers Rage Against the Machine, and the band sought to stay true to their own vision of what they hoped to be, both for themselves and for their fans. They viewed their musical style as an amalgam of influences, from punk to rap, and as Malakian told another *Guitar Player* writer Jude Gold, "It's funny when people say our stuff sounds Armenian—and we are Armenian—but a lot of my parts are influenced by the melodic, Arabic-styled solos of [Iron Maiden guitarists] Dave Murray and Adrian Smith."

Rubin worked with them once again on their second effort, *Toxicity*, which was released on September 4, 2001. It debuted in the No. 1 spot on the *Billboard* chart, giving the band the dubious honor of being the best-selling record in the United States the same week that the country suffered its first-ever major attack on its own soil. The strong political content in some of *Toxicity*'s songs invited misinterpretation in the heated weeks following 9/11, however. There was a line in "Chop Suey" about "self-righteous suicide," which prompted bizarre rumors on music Internet sites and chat rooms in which conspiracy theorists wondered if System of a Down's members had some knowledge beforehand of the attack. Their Armenian heritage, sometimes confused with Arabic, also led to uninformed chatter that the band was being investigated by U.S. government agencies. Adding to the furor, a de-

jected Tankian wrote an essay immediately following 9/11 with the title "Understanding Oil," that floated around the Web and incited a flood of hate mail to the band from fans who accused them of being anti-American. In some markets, radio station managers even banned their songs from airplay.

With characteristic determination, System of a Down went on the road once again to support *Toxicity*, nervily calling their tour the "Pledge of Allegiance" campaign. The record eventually sold six million copies, and served to keep them somewhat distant from others in the nu-metal genre. Their next release was not a standard studio effort, but instead a collection of tracks the band and Rubin had rejected for *Toxicity*. When unfinished studio versions began showing up on System of a Down fan sites on the Internet, the band decided to release them anyway. The result was 2002's *Steal This Album*, its title a nod to the illegal file-sharing of music that was intensely debated at the time. *Entertainment Weekly*'s Evan Serpick gave it a mixed review, noting that "No matter how hard the label tries to repackage them as 'alternate tracks,' though, the fact remains: If they were that good, they would've made the original cut."

System of a Down spent much of 2004 working on a new record, a process that again yielded so many songs that they decided to release a double album, albeit one with two halves spaced six months apart. It was a somewhat unusual move, but as Malakian told Gavin Martin in London's *Times* newspaper, "if we were living in the 1960s, when people were on acid and could listen to a double album ten times in a row, they'd be released together. But we just don't have that attention span in the world of iPods."

The first installment, *Mezmerize*, was issued in May of 2005. Again, the band did not hesitate including political messages in their music, most notably on "B.Y.O.B. (Bring Your Own Bomb)," which posed the questions, "Why don't presidents fight the war?/Why do they always send the poor?" The song earned the band its first Grammy Award, for Best Hard Rock Performance, in 2006. The cover art for *Mezmerize* was done by Malakian's father, but the lyrics criticizing the U.S. war in Iraq since 2003 had an even deeper personal resonance: some of the family's relatives still live in Iraq.

The other half of the double album, *Hypnotize*, was released in November of 2005, and carried on the politically critical message. Its opening track, "Attack," featured the lyrics, "Bombs illustrate what we already know/Candles cry towards the sky/

Racing your flags along polluted coast/Dreaming of the day that/We attack." Though the band's songs were notably critical of geopolitical events of recent years, Malakian told Chris Riemenschneider of the Minneapolis *Star Tribune*, they didn't plan on naming names. "I don't believe in complaining about George Bush," he explained. "That's like getting hurt on a ride at Disneyland and complaining to Mickey Mouse about it. There are people behind the mouse."

Both 2005 releases marked a slight shift in the System of a Down line-up, with Malakian taking over lead-vocal duties on some songs from Tankian. The main songwriting duties were still shouldered by Malakian, but he relied heavily on input from others. Tankian, in particular, provided a more introspective voice, and the former software executive has published collections of his mystical poetry. He also collaborates with Tom Morello, Rage Against the Machine/Audioslave guitarist, on a nonprofit foundation they formed called Axis of Justice, which also has a website that promotes social-justice issues. The Axis group also produces a monthly radio show heard on terrestrial radio in the Los Angeles area and nationwide by subscribers of the XM satellite-radio service.

System of a Down announced they would join the 2006 Ozzfest, and in some dates where organizer Ozzy Osbourne was not scheduled to play due to health issues, they were slated to appear as the headlining act. They also said, however, that after that tour they planned to take a hiatus to pursue some individual projects. "There's no rule that says you have to make records constantly, like clockwork, to continue being who you are," Malakian told MTV's Chris Harris. "We want to live our lives, [because being in a band] really consumes a big part of your life, and sometimes you just want to stop and slow down. We started being just these guys in a band, and the next thing you know, everyone's asking for autographs. It plays with your head."

Selected discography

System of a Down, Columbia/American, 1998.
Toxicity, Columbia/American, 2001.
Steal This Album, Columbia/American, 2002.
Mezmerize, Columbia/American, 2005.
Hypnotize, Columbia/American, 2005.

Sources

Periodicals

Chicago Tribune, May 27, 2005.
Entertainment Weekly, November 29, 2002, p. 105.
Guardian (London, England), May 27, 2005, p. 7.
Guitar Player, July 2000, p. 41; January 2002, p. 86.
Rolling Stone, December 1, 2005, p. 117.
Star Tribune (Minneapolis, MN), September 23, 2005, p. 3E.
Time, November 12, 2001, p. 96.
Times (London, England), May 7, 2005, p. 18.

Online

"System Of A Down Aren't Breaking Up—They're Going On Hiatus," MTV .com, http://www.mtv.com/news/articles/1530066/20060503/system_of_a_down.jhtml?headline s=true (May 18, 2006).

—*Carol Brennan*

Hannah Teter

AP Images

Snowboarder

Born January 27, 1987, in Belmont, VT; daughter of Jeff (a foreman) and Pat (a nurse) Teter.

Addresses: *Contact*—U.S. Olympic Committee, One Olympic Pl., Colorado Springs, CO 80909.

Career

Had first snowboarding lesson at the age of eight; began competing in snowboarding competitions, 1998; won Junior World Championship in the women's halfpipe, 2002; became first woman to land a 900 in competition, 2002; turned pro during the 2002-03 season; named to the U.S. national team, 2003; won bronze in women's halfpipe at the Winter X Games, 2003; won four World Cup halfpipe events, 2003-04; won women's halfpipe competition, Winter X Games, 2004; named the U.S. Snowboard Overall Grand Prix women's halfpipe champion, 2004; won bronze in women's superpipe, World Snowboard Champions, 2005; Vans Cup Champion, 2005; won bronze in superpipe, Winter X Games, 2005; won women's halfpipe at the Chevy Grand Prix, 2005; won gold in women's halfpipe, Winter Olympics, 2006.

Awards: Female Rookie of the Year Award, *Transworld Snowboarding*, 2003; Competitor of the Year Award, North American Snowsports Journalist Association, 2004.

Sidelights

Teenage snowboarder Hannah Teter won Olympic Gold competing in the halfpipe in the 2006 Winter Games held in Turin, Italy. She had been competing in major snowboarding events for several years, primarily in halfpipe but also slopestyle, and was doing well on national and international levels. Teter was known for being risky and aggressive in her tricks as a snowboarder while also having fun. She told Jody Berger of the *Rocky Mountain News*, "That's my thing. I just go big."

Teter was born on January 27, 1987, at her parents' home in the small village of Belmont, Vermont. She was the only daughter and youngest child of Jeff and Pat Teter. Her parents were former flower children who had worked on a family farm in Missouri. A bad watermelon crop compelled the couple to move to Vermont, where they enjoyed skiing. Teter's father worked as a road foreman for the town of Mount Holly, Vermont, while her mother was an emergency room nurse.

Three of Teter's older brothers, Amen, Abe, and Elijah, got the family interested in snowboarding. (She also has another older brother named Josh who is mildly autistic, and only ski blades [ski blades are shorter than regular skiis].) Abe Teter received his first plastic snowboard when he was ten years. He and his older brother, Amen, would play with it every day in a halfpipe they built in the family's front yard. Abe Teter began competing in snowboard competitions when he was 14 years old. Elijah Teter also began competing as a snowboarder beginning in 1996.

Trying to keep up with her brothers, as she did with many activities, Teter began snowboarding herself at the age of eight with a lesson on a nearby mountain. She soon proved that she had snowboarding skills of her own and began competing in 1998. Teter participated in local events in Vermont like the Junior Jam of the U.S. Open in 1998. She soon moved into international events. By 2002, Teter was the Junior World Champion in the halfpipe. That same year, Teter became the first woman to ever land a 900 (rotating 900 degrees on the board in the air) in competition. Discussing the trajectory of her success, Teter told Justin Tejada of *Sports Illustrated for Kids*, "I just kept progressing, going from small contests to amateur contests, then all of a sudden—boom!—I was attending the big dawg contest circuit and doing extremely well."

During the 2002-03 snowboarding season, Teter turned professional, and, in 2003, made the U.S. national team for the first time. Teter was the youngest member of the U.S. national team at the time. She won medals at many major competitions beginning in 2003. That year, she won the Van Triple Crown in the halfpipe and finished second overall in slopestyle. Later that year, she won bronze in the halfpipe at the Winter X Games, after failing to complete a 900 in one of her runs, and won the halfpipe competition at U.S. Grand Prix events as well. Between 2003 and 2004, Teter won four World Cup halfpipe events, including one competition at Sapporo, Japan. The victory in Japan was an upset victory over the woman who won the 2002 Olympic gold in halfpipe, American Kelly Clark.

Teter was becoming recognized as one of the best snowboarders in the world, overtaking Clark by winning a number of events in 2004 and 2005. At the 2004 Winter X Games, Teter was the halfpipe champion. That same year, she was named the U.S. Snowboard Overall Grand Prix halfpipe champion. In 2004, Teter was named competitor of the year by the North American Snowsports Journalist Association. This marked the first time this award was presented to a snowboarder. Teter was also a finalist for the 2004 ESPY for best female action sport athlete. She garnered more high profile wins in 2005.

She won the bronze in superpipe at the World Snowboard Champions, and was the 2005 Vans Cup Champion. She also won bronze at the Winter X Games in the superpipe and won the Chevy Grand Prix in halfpipe as well.

As successful as Teter was, she remained focused as an athlete and continued to push herself to try new tricks. She told MountainZone.com, "There are so many things that lead an athlete to success ... for some it's all about effort and commitment, for others it's all about having a drive to achieve, and I feel like for me it's all about living in the moment."

While competing all over the world, Teter often traveled with her brothers Abe and Elijah, who also competed at many of the same events. Both Abe and Elijah Teter were members of the U.S. National snowboarding team and pro boarders. Her eldest brother, Amen, was the manager and agent for his younger siblings. While her brothers did well in snowboarding, she ended up eclipsing them in terms of success, primarily because she was smaller (an advantage on the halfpipe) and more talented. In addition to support, her brothers helped by giving her toughness and a mental edge over her competitors. During her travels, Teter also continued to attend school. Teter went to a school that served snowboarders and other athletes, the Okemo Mountain School in Ludlow, Vermont. When she was away from home, she did her schoolwork online and earned all A's. College was a potential destination in her future.

Early in 2006, Teter was suffering from knee problems. She decided not to compete in the Winter X Games so she could focus on the Winter Olympics. Teter made the U.S. Olympic team, competing in the women's halfpipe. Her victory was sealed in her first run, when she scored 44.6. Teter did her second run anyway, and scored even higher with a score of 46.4. As she always did, she rode while wearing her iPod, listening to positive, fast music while she won her first Olympic gold medal.

During her off-season, Teter trained by skateboarding and wakeboarding. She also worked out on a Bowflex, with a punching bag, and did strength and agility training. Teter remained committed to improving her training and her tricks to ensure she stays at the top of her game. Tracy Anderson, associate editor of *Future Snowboarding*, told Carl T. Hall of the *San Francisco Chronicle*, "She's very happy-go-lucky, always full of energy, and she's known more than any other female rider for her really big airs. She's not afraid to just roll up the wall of the halfpipe and just let it go."

Sources

Periodicals

Associated Press State and Local Wire, March 12, 2003.

Boston Globe, January 16, 2003, p. E10; March 16, 2006, p. C12.

CosmoGirl!, February 2006, p. 63.

Denver Post, February 14, 2006, p. A1.

International Herald Tribune, February 15, 2006, p. 21.

Record (Bergen County, NJ), February 7, 2004, p. S1.

Rocky Mountain News (Denver, CO), January 15, 2003, p. 20C; February 1, 2003, p. 13B.

San Francisco Chronicle, February 9, 2006, p. O6.

San Jose Mercury News, February 14, 2006.

Sports Illustrated for Kids, February 1, 2004, p. 56.

USA Today, January 28, 2005, p. 1C.

Online

"Hannah Teter," NBCOlympics.com, http://www.nbcolympics.com/athletes/5058598/detail.html?qs=;t=11;tab=Bio (May 1, 2006).

"Hannah Teter," United States Olympic Committee, http://www.usoc.org/26_26735.htm (May 1, 2006).

"The Teter Legacy," MoutainZone.com, http://snowboard.mountainzone.com/2005/teter/ (May 1, 2006).

—*A. Petruso*

Lily Tuck

AP/Wide World Photos

Author

Born in France in 1938; married and divorced first husband; married second husband (died, 2002); children: three sons. *Education:* Received degrees from Radcliffe College and the Sorbonne.

Addresses: *Agent*—Georges Borchardt, Inc., 136 E. 57th St., New York, NY 10022. *Home*—New York, NY.

Career

Published first novel, *Interviewing Matisse, or The Woman Who Died Standing Up*, 1991; published other novels, including *The News from Paraguay*.

Awards: National Book Award for Fiction, National Book Foundation, for *The News from Paraguay*, 2004.

Sidelights

Lily Tuck was the surprise winner of the 2004 National Book Award in fiction for her fourth novel, *The News from Paraguay*. Tuck's win caused ripples inside the American literary world, for she was a relatively unknown writer and the National Book Foundation committee seemed to have bypassed novels published that year by much more prominent names. The honor, whose past winners have included William Faulkner and Alice Walker, is considered the second most prestigious prize in American fiction, surpassed only by the Pulitzer.

Tuck was born in France in 1938, to which her parents had fled after Nazi dictator Adolf Hitler came to power five years before in their native Germany. When Nazi troops invaded France in 1940, her fam-

ily was forced into a second exile, and this time went to South America. Tuck was sent to schools in Lima, Peru, and Montevideo, Uruguay, while her father served in the forces of the French Foreign Legion for a time. When her parents divorced, Tuck and her mother settled in New York City.

As a young woman, Tuck earned a degree from Radcliffe College, and married at a relatively early age. Her husband was independently wealthy, and for a time they lived in Thailand in the 1960s, where he attempted to launch a business venture. She had three sons in five years, but was divorced from her husband and returned to France. She earned a master's degree in American literature from the Sorbonne, Paris's famed university, and began writing a story based on the actual case of a rather well-known American living in Thailand who had gone missing.

Tuck had known that man, Jim Thompson, personally. He was a Princeton-trained architect who settled in Thailand in the late 1940s, after a stint with the forerunner of the Central Intelligence Agency. In the 1950s and '60s, Thompson became a well-known figure in Thailand thanks to his revival of the country's ancient silk weaving industry. He disappeared one day in 1967 after going out for a hike in the highlands that bordered Malaysia. The unsolved mystery has intrigued many for decades, and various theories have usually linked his disappearance to his former career in U.S. Army intelligence.

Tuck devoted herself to the Thompson story, and then shopped the manuscript around to various publishers. "I spent seven years on it and then couldn't get it published," she told Wendy Smith in a *Publishers Weekly* interview. By 1977, she had married a second time and settled in New York City. Returning to her craft, she decided to take an intensive writing workshop run by Gordon Lish, a one-time editor at *Esquire* who had helped shape the prose of short-story master Raymond Carver. The tutelage helped, and she finished what she would feel was her most experimental novel, *Interviewing Matisse, or The Woman Who Died Standing Up*, which Knopf published in 1991. The novel consists entirely of dialogue in the form of a telephone call between two old friends, whose mutual friend has been discovered dead, at home, standing up and wearing only lingerie and rubber boots. Their conversation wends around their friendship with the dead woman and their own storied lives.

Tuck's second novel, *The Woman Who Walked on Water*, centers on a wealthy woman who abandons her family to travel with an Indian mystic. A third novel, *Siam, or The Woman Who Shot a Man*, was the first one to earn Tuck relatively good reviews in the press. Here, finally, she was able to incorporate the Jim Thompson story in a plot centering around a young American journalist who arrives in Thailand (formerly Siam) with her new husband in 1967. "Tuck uses words with economy," noted a *Publishers Weekly* contributor, "evoking the lush locale and mysterious culture of Thailand with precise details and sensory images."

Siam even earned Tuck a nomination for a PEN/Faulkner Award for Fiction in 1999. *Limbo, and Other Places I Have Lived*, a collection of short stories and her first title for HarperCollins, appeared in 2002. She was in the process of writing her fourth novel when her husband died in 2002 after 25 years of marriage; she had also been shaken by the World Trade Center attacks in her hometown, New York City, the year before. Thus *The News from Paraguay* did not reach bookstore shelves until 2004, when it scored well with critics and judges of the National Book Award alike.

The News from Paraguay is the fictional story of Eliza Lynch, a Paris courtesan of Irish birth who was the real-life mistress of Paraguay's dictator, Francisco Solano López. In Tuck's book, she is called Ella, and the story moves from their first meeting in Paris in 1854, when she is the mistress of a Russian noble and he is the son of Paraguay's president, to their later life in Paraguay and Solano's disastrous instigation of a war with Brazil that decimated the country in the 1860s.

When Tuck won the National Book Award for 2004 for her work—and with it, a $10,000 prize—she caused somewhat of a stir when she admitted in her acceptance speech she had never been to Paraguay. The Paraguayan government immediately issued an invitation, and the news of a book about Solano—still a national hero to many Paraguayans, partly for standing up to far mightier South American superpowers of his time despite his reputation for brutality—and its author's imminent visit began to attract attention in the press. Though it had not yet been published in Spanish, Paraguay's official language, Tuck's novel and its depiction of the dictator stirred a contentious public debate.

On the other side, historians noted that Solano's record as a statesman was indeed a blemished one, and that Tuck's book was a work of fiction, after all. She nearly canceled her trip, but in the end went, was feted, and was supplied with a police bodyguard just in case. "I'm glad I didn't come before I wrote the book," a *New York Times* article by Larry Rohter quoted her as saying, "because I would have been overwhelmed by all the factions and their points of view. I am a quiet person, not a politician, so I don't know if I would even have started to write if I knew all of the issues that were at stake."

Selected writings

Interviewing Matisse, or The Woman Who Died Standing Up (novel), Knopf (New York City), 1991.
The Woman Who Walked on Water (novel), Riverhead Books (New York City), 1997.
Siam, or The Woman Who Shot a Man (novel), Overlook Press (Woodstock, NY), 1999.
Limbo, and Other Places I Have Lived (short stories), HarperCollins (New York City), 2002.
The News from Paraguay (novel), HarperCollins, 2004.

Sources

New York Times, January 7, 2000, p. 49; January 29, 2002, p. E10; November 18, 2004, p. A25; November 30, 2004, p. B2; February 17, 2005, p. A4.
New York Times Book Review, February 10, 2002, p. 26.
Publishers Weekly, February 1, 1991, p. 64; January 8, 1996, p. 55; September 27, 1999, p. 67; December 10, 2001, p. 51; May 3, 2004, p. 172; June 7, 2004, p. 27.
Seattle Post-Intelligencer, March 18, 2005, p. 24.
Time, November 29, 2004, p. 146.

—Carol Brennan

Keith Urban

Singer and songwriter

Born Keith Lionel Urban, October 26, 1967, in Whangarei, North Island, New Zealand; son of Bob (a convenience store operator) and Marienne (a convenience store operator) Urban.

Addresses: *Contact*—c/o Flood Bumstead Mc-Cready & McCarthy, PO Box 331549, Nashville, TN 37206.

Career

Began playing guitar at age of six; won country music talent shows beginning at the age of eight; formed a band in Australia, 1988; moved to Nashville, TN, 1992; formed the Ranch (three-piece band), 1995; with the Ranch, signed record deal with Capitol Nashville; released *The Ranch*, 1997; released solo album, *Keith Urban*, 2000; toured with Brooks & Dunn's Neon Circus, 2001; released *Golden Road*, 2002; had two number-one singles from *Golden Road*: "Somebody Like You" and "Who Wouldn't Want to Be Me"; released *Be Here*, 2004; *Golden Road* was certified triple platinum in the United States, c. 2005.

Awards: Westpac starmaker award, Tamworth Country Music Festival, 1990; Horizon award, Country Music Association, 2001; new male vocalist award, Academy of Country Music, 2001; best male vocalist award, Academy of Country Music, 2001; album of the year award, Academy of Country Music, for *Keith Urban*, 2001; male vocalist of the year award, Country Music Association, 2004; album of the year award, Academy of Country Music, for *Be Here*, 2005; top male vocalist award, Academy of

© *Tami Chappell/Reuters/Corbis*

Country Music, 2005; album of the year award, Academy of Country Music, for *Be Here*, 2005; entertainer of the year award, Country Music Association, 2005; male vocalist of the year award, Country Music Association, 2005; best country album, Australian Recording Industry Assocation, 2005; Grammy award for best male country vocal performance, Recording Academy, for "You'll Think of Me," 2005; video of the year, Country Music Television Awards, for "Better Life," 2006; international artist achievement award, Country Music Association; Golden Guitar Award, best male vocalist and best instrumentalist.

Sidelights

Australian-raised Keith Urban became a break-out country singer in his native country before coming to the United States in the early 1990s to try his luck in Nashville, Tennessee. After briefly working with his band the Ranch, Urban found success as a country solo artist by the end of the 1990s and was poised to become an international country superstar in the early 2000s. His first three solo albums sold nearly six million copies in six years. Describing his appeal, Bruce McMahon of *Sunday Telegraph Magazine* wrote, "He is the complete package, a cowboy punk with style and substance. He's a songwriter who not only sings with conviction, but entertains and plays a mean guitar...."

Born in New Zealand in 1967, Urban was the second son of Bob and Marienne Urban. When Urban was two years old, he moved to Australia with his family, which included his older brother, Shane. Raised primarily in Caboolture, Brisbane, Australia, Urban's parents ran a convenience store. Music and American culture were part of family life. Urban's father's side of the family was musical. His father played the drums, while his paternal grandfather was a piano teacher. Both of his parents were fans of country music, exposing the young Urban to artists such as Dolly Parton, Jim Reeves, Glen Campbell, and Ricky Skaggs.

When Urban was four years old, his parents gave him a ukulele. He spent about two years learning chords and watching other people to pick up what he could. Urban graduated to guitar at the age of six, taking music lessons from a local teacher. Within a year, the young Urban wanted to be a country musician in Nashville. At the age of seven, he began performing with the Westfield Super Juniors, a group created to show off talented youngsters. Beginning at the age of eight, Urban won country music talent shows. Country music was his only real interest as a child. He felt most at home performing, but was quite quiet off stage.

By the time Urban was 14 years old, he was working with a band on a steady basis. Throughout his teen years, he played in clubs every weekend, with his parents driving him to his gigs. Of this point in his career, Urban told Sandra McLean in the *Sunday Mail*, "I had been playing for such a long time, it didn't seem odd of me to do this. I always seemed to get on well with older people. I never associated with people my own age at school. I spent a lot of time on my own." Urban quit school after the tenth grade and played in pubs throughout Queensland. When he was 17, he joined Rusty and the Ayers Rockettes and played with them for a time. Urban's family totally supported him.

Country was not his only musical influence as he aged. While still in his teens, he heard Dire Straits for the first time and memorized every note on every album by the band. Soon, this rock influence crept into Urban's country sound, primarily in his guitar solos. He also liked bands like AC/DC and Fleetwood Mac, and was particularly moved by John Mellencamp's 1987 album *Lonesome Jubilee*.

Urban formed his own three-piece band in 1988. The group played in bars in Brisbane, before touring all over Australia. Urban often sang covers of songs from a variety of genres. In 1990, he won the Westpac Starmaker Award at the Tamworth Country Music Festival in Australia, leading to his signing a record deal with EMI. In 1991, released his first record in Australia, *Keith Urban.* The album produced four number-one singles there. Urban compared his sound at the time to the Eagles—like country, but with a distinctive amount of rock and blues influence. He already had a distinctive look with spiked hair.

As Urban's career was developing in Australia, he began looking to the United States for his next move. He first visited the United States in 1990, then made songwriting trips in 1990, 1991, and 1992. Urban wanted to move there as soon as possible, but it took several years to get the visas he needed. Urban left his band behind in Australia and made his move in 1992. He knew going to Nashville was risky. He was quoted by the *Sunday Mail*'s McLean as saying, "I knew I would be a little fish in a big sea, but that's the appeal. You have so many people you can learn from and play with. I want to get to that caliber of player and writer."

For the first few years in Nashville, Urban worked on his songwriting and took on odd jobs. He also formed a new band, the Ranch, with Peter Clarke, an Australian drummer, and Jerry Flowers, an American bass player, in 1995. Though Urban liked performing with the band, Americans were a little more unsure what to make of them. As Urban described it to Angela Pulvirenti in the *Sunday Telegraph*, "Because we (Peter and I) were raised on the Australian pub scene, our performances were raw and confronting. Nashville wasn't ready for someone who sweated on his guitar and threw it around the stage."

The Ranch played all over the United States, and their exciting live show soon attracted the attention of local Nashville labels. However, it took time for their take on country music, labeled alt country, to be fully accepted. The band signed a deal with Capitol Nashville and released an album in 1997. Though the record did not receive support from the label, critics embraced it. Urban soon had a number of personal issues. He developed problems with his vocal cords which did not allow him to sing for several months. Urban also had relationship difficulties and developed a taste for cocaine in 1997 because of his lack of success and loneliness. He later went through rehab for drug addiction. Urban told Pulvirenti of the *Sunday Telegraph*, "You do it so long and you become depressed, then you become disgusted, then you become terrified you're going to die. I know it sounds ridiculously simple, but I got to the point where I knew it wasn't me, and I just stopped."

As Urban made his way through these troubles, country music was changing and he felt his new songs were not appropriate for the Ranch. Urban told Deborah Evans Price of *Billboard*, "The songs were more personal. It didn't feel like a band record this time around. And creatively, I think, the band was getting to the point where it just didn't make any sense to continue on. Jerry was writing more R&B-type songs and was really wanting to pursue his own thing, so I thought this would be the perfect time for us to part ways and move on and look back at the Ranch as being a good, fun project."

The Ranch then broke up, though they later regrouped and recorded another album in 2004 that was also not a success. After the demise of the Ranch, Urban did not have problems finding work. While working on his own solo career, he appeared on the records of other leading country artists, including the Dixie Chicks (contributing to *Fly*) and Garth Brooks (contributing to *Double Live*). Urban decided to approach his own sound differently with the support of his label, now headed by Mike Dungan, who did not push Urban to be anything but himself.

Urban soon had his own deal with Capitol Nashville. He released his first American solo album, *Keith Urban*, in 1999. Though he did not look like a traditional country artist, Urban found himself embraced by the country faithful. Urban was marketed to attract an audience similar to the Dixie Chicks as well as build on the base he already had. He had a number-one single with "But for the Grace of God," which was written with two members of the all-girl pop group the Go-Gos. Urban told Michael A. Capozzoli, Jr., of the *Chicago Sun-Times*, "There are songs on the album about losing love, but not being beaten down or downtrodden by that loss. I try to see the light, even in the darkest circumstance." The album peaked at number 17 on the Top Country Albums chart and was certified gold.

Urban received more mainstream attention by joining the Brooks & Dunn Neon Circus tour in early 2001. However, his rising star dimmed for a short amount of time when Urban had a brief relapse in his drug use and when he developed more vocal cord problems. Urban had a hemorrhage in his cords, but they healed when he took a break from singing. He rebounded by releasing a more successful album in 2002, *Golden Road*. The songs continued to reflect a positive attitude. Urban wrote or contributed to nearly all the songs on the album, and acted as its producer. He told Phyllis Stark of *Billboard*, "I have a few sides to me, like every artist does. I have the real romantic side, which is very

genuine. And I have a very rough, unpolished, raw side. I was hoping we could achieve both on this album [and] cover the gamut of my personality."

The first single from the album, "Somebody Like You," was number one for six weeks on country charts. In 2003, another track from the album, "Who Wouldn't Want to Be Me," was also a number-one song. *Golden Road* went platinum in the United States, selling more than one million copies in 2002, was still in the top 20 on *Billboard*'s "Top Country Albums" chart in 2004, and triple platinum by 2005.

By 2004, observers believed that Urban was on the verge of superstardom as one of the top country artists in the United States, if not the world. That year, he released *Be Here* on Capitol. The album was also produced by Urban, who wrote or co-wrote nine songs. *Be Here* debuted at number three on the album charts, and spent some time at number one. Urban also had a number-one song with "Days Go By." Barry Gilbert of the *St. Louis Post-Dispatch* wrote of the album, "Urban's music is propelled by muscular, memorable hooks and melodies and is supported by his guitar and banjo, which percolates right up in the mix and is becoming his signature sound.... [The songs] are overwhelmingly positive, celebrating living and loving in the moment and being accountable, without being preachy or pandering." *Be Here* was certified double platinum.

Urban reached a milestone in his career when he was named Male Vocalist of the Year by the Country Music Association in 2004. This huge honor was but one of many major awards given to Urban in 2004 and 2005. Tabloids began following Urban in this time period because of his relationship with actress Nicole Kidman, bringing Urban a whole new following. Yet Urban remained humble. Just before the release of *Be Here*, Urban told *Billboard*'s Stark, "When I look at myself, I see the guy that's still struggling." He also looked at his career in a similar light, telling Stark, "When [success] starts happening, you keep viewing yourself as the guy trying to get there. I don't think that will ever change, because there will always be new horizons."

Selected discography

Keith Urban, EMI International, 1991.
The Ranch, WEA, 1997.
Keith Urban, Capitol Nashville, 1999.
Golden Road, Capitol/EMI, 2002.
In the Ranch, Liberty, 2004.
Be Here, Capitol, 2004.

Sources

Periodicals

Billboard, September 25, 1999; October 5, 2002, p. 44; May 29, 2004; September 25, 2004.

Chicago Sun-Times, October 31, 1999, p. 9.

Ottawa Citizen, September 20, 2003, p. J1.

Plain Dealer (Cleveland, OH), June 8, 2001, p. 17; October 28, 2005, p. 8.

St. Louis Post-Dispatch, December 2, 2004, p. 8.

San Diego Union-Tribune, December 8, 2005, p. 4.

Sunday Mail (Queensland, Australia), August 19, 1990; July 21, 1991; September 17, 1995; October 31, 2004.

Sunday Telegraph (Sydney, Australia), September 29, 2002, p. 4; January 1, 2006, p. 9.

Sunday Telegraph Magazine (Sydney, Australia), November 27, 2005, p. 1.

Online

"Keith Urban," CMT.com, http://www.cmt.com/ artists/az/urban_keith/bio.jhtml (April 11, 2006).

"Keith Urban," Internet Movie Database, http:// www.imdb.com/name/nm1236707/ (April 11, 2006).

"Urban, Underwood tops at CMT Awards," CNN. com, http://www.cnn.com/2006/SHOWBIZ/ Music/04/11/cmt.awards.ap/index.html (April 11, 2006).

—A. Petruso

John Varvatos

Fashion designer

Born c. 1955; children: two. *Education:* Graduated from Eastern Michigan University.

Addresses: *Office*—26 West 47th St., New York, NY 10011.

Career

Worked in men's retail during high school and college; co-owned men's clothing store, Grand Rapids, MI; Polo Ralph Lauren, Midwest region salesperson, then sales, merchandising, and design posts in New York, NY, office, 1983-90; corporate president of menswear, Calvin Klein, 1990-93; vice chairman and executive vice president of design and merchandising, London Fog Industries, 1993-95; interim chairman, London Fog, 1994-95; vice president in charge of men's design, Polo Ralph Lauren, 1995-98; senior vice president of special projects, Nautica Enterprises, 1998; founded John Varvatos (a design company), 1999; showed first men's collection, 2000; opened the John Varvatos New York flagship store, 2000; launched John Varvatos Men's fragrance, 2004; produced first women's line, 2004; added skincare products under the name John Varvatos Skin, 2005.

Awards: Perry Ellis Award for New Menswear Designer, Council of Fashion Designers of America, 2000; Menswear Designer of the Year, Council of Fashion Designers of America, 2001, 2005.

AP/Wide World Photos

Sidelights

After years of working for leading American men's wear designers, John Varvatos launched his own line of men's wear and related lifestyle products in 2000 to positive reviews and quick sales. The Varvatos name was soon associated with quality, elegance, and practical yet interesting men's fashion. Though not as high-end as Helmut Lang or Gucci, as Ginia Bellafante wrote in the *New York Times,* "The designer's clothes seem intended for the kind of guy who has moved into a salary bracket that no longer confines him to Banana Republic." The success of his men's line led to more products being designed and sold under the Varvatos name, including cologne, skin care, and a line of women's wear.

Born around 1955, Varvatos was raised in suburban Detroit, in Allen Park, Michigan. His father was a Greek American who worked as an accountant. The household was conservative, but rock music was Varvatos' outlet. By the time he could drive, he was going to rock shows in the area.

His interest in music led to a fascination with fashion. Varvatos attempted to dress like a rock star as much as he could. By the time he was a senior in high school, he worked in a men's clothing store. Varvatos continued to work in men's retail while attending Eastern Michigan University. He also learned how to play guitar, teaching himself to play. He performed with some bands, such as Sweet Wine, a group he started with a cousin.

Though Varvatos originally intended to be a science teacher while attending college, he went into the retail business after completing college. With a friend, he opened up a men's store that was located in Grand Rapids, Michigan. One label carried by the store was Polo by Ralph Lauren. Because of Varvatos' success selling in the label's clothes, he was hired by the Ralph Lauren company in 1983 as a Midwest region salesperson.

His success at this position led to new posts within the company. He was transferred to New York City, where he worked in sales as well as merchandising and design. Of this experience, he told Josh Sims of the *Financial Times*, "It wasn't yet a designer world when I was with Ralph. But I learned more in my first year there than in my entire career since, especially in terms of business acumen.... Ralph was a real marketer and I picked that up."

Varvatos left Ralph Lauren in 1990 when he was lured to Calvin Klein. There, Varvatos served as the corporate president of men's wear, in charge of all men's wear design. He told Ariel Foxman of *Fortune*, "The challenge at Calvin Klein was the blank canvas. There was no men's wear when I got there." In addition to launching Calvin Klein's men's collection, he also developed and launched the cK brand and the extremely successful Calvin Klein underwear line.

In 1993, Varvatos joined London Fog Industries. He served as a vice chairman and executive vice president of product design and merchandising. Varvatos was hired to improve the company's image and revitalize its product lines, and did well in the position. Varvatos also briefly served as the interim chairman of the company from August 1994 until early 1995 when a permanent chairman was hired. When Varvatos resigned in early 1995, he remained a consultant with London Fog for a short amount of time.

Varvatos returned to Polo later that year. Upon his return, he was named vice president and put in charge of men's design for all of Polo Ralph Lauren brands, including Polo by Ralph Lauren and Polo Sport. As he had done at Calvin Klein, Varvatos

successfully launched a new line. He created the Polo Jeans Company line, which sold well. The experience at Polo proved educational when Varvatos started his own company.

In 1998, Varvatos left Ralph Lauren to join Nautica Enterprises as senior vice president of special projects. Part of the lure of going to Nautica was that it would financially back Varvatos's own company. (Nautica had approached him several years earlier about starting his own line, but Varvatos rejected the offer at the time.) Nautica produced men's clothing, including sportswear, active wear, and outerwear. In addition to being given the means to start his own company, Varvatos also designed Nautica's jeans and added a fashionable touch to the company's line.

Varvatos launched his company in 1999, called simply John Varvatos. His first collection of men's wear came in early 2000 for fall/winter 2000. The line included wardrobe staples that were well-crafted and well-designed, including wool suits, pants, shirts, ties, topcoats, sweaters, and sportswear. In addition, Varvatos included other accessories and footwear. From the first, Varvatos's clothing had a distinctive look; there was an eclectic touch to the collection. Varvatos told Michael Steele of *NewYorkMetro.com*, "I don't like things that are so uniform. I like people who mix things and come up with their own sense of style.... I don't want to feel like I'm wearing everything so perfectly thought-out."

There was one important aspect to Varvatos' clothing: He recognized that the rules about men's clothing did not exist in the same way any more. He could take chances and did so. Varvatos told the *Daily News*, "Color can be fun when it's used right, but business clothes are still not about that. On weekends or at dinner, you can add some color underneath the business wardrobe. But not every guy wants to wear color every day."

Varvatos showed his first collection in New York during Fashion Week. Reviewing the line, Linda Gillan Griffin of *Houston Chronicle* commented, "Varvatos ... put together a superbly British-detailed collection of thick woolen jackets, coats, suits and casual wear." While Griffin praised his use of modern fabrics in his suits and jackets, she did not like all of his pants, especially the crop-legged ones.

Varvatos' ideas and his clothes were generally well-received. His line was not just embraced by the fashion press, but by the stores which can make or break a young designer and his company. Big department stores bought Varvatos' first collection, including Bergdorf Goodman and Saks Fifth Avenue. Shortly after the launch of the fall/winter 2000 line, Varvatos opened his first store in New York City. Also called John Varvatos, this flagship store was located in Soho. He went on to open several boutique stores in the United States in the early 2000s.

Varvatos found similar success with his second collection, for spring/summer 2001. While the shape of his clothes was similar to the fall/winter 2000 line, the sweaters and jackets went from wool to a cashmere-linen blend. Varvatos was careful to include touches that would appeal to his audience, such as a pocket for a cell phone in a coat. His clothes continued to take up more space at major department stores; he added Barneys and Neiman Marcus to his existing clients.

By the launch of Varvatos' third collection, he was recognized as a growing force in the industry and his clothing was associated with quality. After selling his first two collections primarily in the United States, his fall/winter 2001 collection was the first to be sold internationally. This particular collection was regarded by critics as masculine, but accessible. Reviewing the line, Robin Givhan of the *Washington Post* wrote, "His is the sort of clothing that attracts a variety of men with its easy cuts, its luxurious fabrics, and the confident styling that is both of-the-moment and timeless."

In his subsequent collections for men, Varvatos continued to follow his own voice. He varied the cut of his clothing, especially suits, and the colors which he used. He took chances, including a series of wide-legged pants similar to a cut that was popular in the 1930s. Varvatos told Sims of *Financial Times*, "I don't follow trends. I follow my gut." Many of his risks paid off.

Success brought new challenges for Varvatos. His parent company, Nautica, was undergoing a major transition. In 2003, Nautica was bought out by VF Corp., a more mainstream apparel company that was publicly traded. The change brought some uncertainty to Varvatos' future, but he continued to evolve his brand.

Also in 2003, Varvatos began working on his first line for women. Launched for fall/winter 2004, he designed apparel, shoes, outerwear, and accessories for women. He told Sarah Taylor of *Footwear News*, "I've been thinking about a women's collection for a long time. I definitely don't want to be compared to anybody. I don't want to come out with anything unless it has our own handwriting and our own look." As soon as the line was launched, he planned to open a store that only sold his women's line.

Varvatos tried to mimic the tone of his men's line with his women's line. Though he wanted his women's line to be versatile and accessible, he was fully aware that there was more competition in women's wear. Varvatos was attracted by the possibility of doing more there because women are perceived as more open to change in fashion. However his women's wear was not an immediate success, and it took several seasons to find his own look. His women's line was not regarded as refined as his men's line, which remained better known and more lucrative.

Despite the disappointment over his women's line, Varvatos continued to expand his company. In 2004, he launched his first fragrance for men. The cologne was called John Varvatos for Men, and included input in the scent from the designer himself. The following year, he added a line of around 12 skin care products for men, called John Varvatos Skin. Both the fragrance and skin care line were first sold in the United States, then sold around the world. Varvatos also signed a new deal with Converse, the athletic footwear manufacturer, to design a line of clothing under the Chuck Taylor label. For several years, he had designed his own version of classic shoes in the Converse line.

While Varvatos took chances with these products, he also became a part-owner of the company that bore his name. In 2005, he signed a new deal with VF Corp. that gave him twenty percent of his company, which saw sales of his collection reaching $50 million by 2005. (Nautica and VF Corp. had owned all of his company under the previous deal.) Though Varvatos wanted to take ownership of his own company, he did not have the financing or financial status to do so. This deal was the best offer he received. While this was going on, he continued to expand his retail presence by opening a new New York store devoted to shoes and accessories.

Varvatos worked hard to balance the design and business sides of his company. He told Bellafante in the *New York Times*, "I'm a business person as well as a designer. Sometimes designers are brilliant creatively, but they lose touch with what's happening at the store. You have to ring the register."

Sources

Periodicals

Atlanta Journal-Constitution, February 10, 2003, p. 1E.

Chicago Sun-Times September 30, 2004, p. 57.

Cosmetics International Cosmetic Products Report, October 2003, p. 10; September 2004, p. 13.

Daily News (New York, NY), July 23, 2000, p. 12.

Esquire, October 2000, p. 74.

Financial Times (London, England), July 7, 2001, p. 11.

Footwear News, July 28, 2003, p. 66; February 2, 2004, p. 112; February 9, 2004, p. 96; April 25, 2005, p. 2.

Fortune, November 27, 2000, p. 348.

Global Cosmetic Industry, March 2003, p. 12.

Houston Chronicle, February 9, 2000, p. 1.

Los Angeles Times, June 8, 2005, p. E11.

New York Times, August 24, 1994, p. D3; September 12, 2000, p. B11; June 18, 2005, p. C2.

PR Newswire, January 12, 1995; September 10, 1998.

Washington Post, February 12, 2001, p. C1; January 23, 2005, p. D1.

Online

"Biography," John Varvatos, http://www.john varvatos.com/biography/biography.html (October 15, 2005).

"Look Like a Rock Star," *New Yorkmetro.com,* http://www.newyorkmetro.com/nymetro/shopping/fashion/features/n_9125/index.html (October 15, 2005).

—*A. Petruso*

Tabaré Vázquez

Enrique Marcarian/Reuters/Landov

President of Uruguay

Born Tabaré Ramón Vázquez Rosas, January 17, 1940; married to Maria Auxiliadora Delgado; children: four. *Education:* Received medical degree from the University of the Republic (Uruguay) as an oncology and radiology specialist, 1972.

Addresses: *Office*—Casa de Gobierno, Edificio Libertad, Avenida Luis Alberto de Herrera 3350, Montevideo 11600, Uruguay. *Website*—http://www.presidencia.gub.uy.

Career

Worked as a doctor, c. 1970-2004; joined central committee of the Socialist Party of Uruguay, 1987; elected mayor of Montevideo, 1989; took office, 1990; ran unsuccessfully for president of Uruguay, 1994 and 1999; elected president of Uruguay, 2004; inaugurated, 2005.

Sidelights

When Tabaré Vázquez was sworn in as president of Uruguay in March of 2005, he made history in his own country and signified the emergence of a new political trend in South America. A longtime member of the Socialist Party, at the head of a coalition that included former guerrillas, Vázquez became Uruguay's first leftist president, shattering a two-party system that had governed the country for 150 years. He promised justice for those abused and murdered by a military dictatorship decades earlier. He also joined a growing number of left-wing leaders that govern almost all of South America, presenting a new challenge to the foreign policy of the United States and the free-market reforms it espouses.

Vázquez was born on January 17, 1940; his father was a politically active oil worker. He attended medical school at Uruguay's University of the Republic and graduated as an oncology and radiology specialist in 1972. In 1976, he received a scholarship to study at the Gustave Roussy Institute in Paris. During his career as a doctor, he published more than a hundred papers in national and international journals. A member of Uruguay's Socialist Party, Vázquez was named to its central committee in 1987. In 1989, he ran for mayor of Montevideo, the capital of Uruguay, as the candidate of the Broad Front, a coalition of socialists, communists, moderates and former guerrillas who had fought the military dictatorship of the 1970s and early 1980s. He won the election and took office in 1990.

As mayor of Montevideo, Vázquez became extremely popular by combining socialist ideas with some projects that embraced free-market economics. The president of Uruguay, Louis Lacalle, publicly attacked Vázquez, but the comments backfired, making Lacalle less popular and rallying support for Vázquez. But when Vázquez tried to translate his popularity as mayor into a bid for the presidency of Uruguay in 1994, he lost, gaining only 31 percent of the vote.

Five years later, Vázquez tried again, during difficult economic times for Uruguay, and he surprised many observers by placing first in the first round of voting, with 40 percent. However, he had to face the second-place finisher in a runoff under Uruguay election rules (some observers believed the second-round rule was instituted to keep the Broad Front out of power). He lost the second round with 44 percent of the vote, but his party won the largest bloc of seats in the congressional elections. His strong showing caught a lot of attention in Latin America, which was beginning to question the free-market reforms that dominated its politics and economics in the 1990s.

Uruguay was once known as the Switzerland of South America because of its prosperous economy, large middle class, highly educated population, and generous welfare state. But the country's economic fortune had been eroding for many years, and the government-provided safety net was dismantled during the reforms of the 1990s. The 2002 recessions in neighboring Brazil and Argentina hurt Uruguay badly. Its economy contracted by 10 percent, leaving one-third of all Uruguayans below the poverty line. Though the Uruguayan economy expanded by more than 10 percent in 2004, the crisis of 2002 still left many voters suspicious of both of the traditional ruling parties and eager for change.

So Vázquez again ran for president in 2004 as the Broad Front candidate, promising relief for the country's poorest citizens and a foreign policy less friendly with the United States and more friendly to communist Cuba. He united socialist idealism with pragmatic economic solutions to problems, reassuring foreign investors who often worry that left-wing politicians in Latin America will take the sort of confrontational approach favored by Venezuelan president Hugo Chavez. "[While my] eyes are on utopia, my feet are on the ground," Vázquez told voters, according to Larry Rohter of the *New York Times*.

Vázquez also said he would continue to work as a doctor one day a week while president, with substantial power delegated to his staff. Critics said that during the campaign, Vázquez was vague about many of his positions in order to please both the former guerrillas and European-style social democrats in the Broad Front. "Tabaré Vázquez is a mystery," Pablo da Silveira, a university professor and political commentator, told Rohter of the *New York Times*. "No one knows what he really thinks because he has said everything and its opposite."

The last rally Vázquez held before the election, in Montevideo in October of 2004, attracted several hundred thousand people. On October 31, Vázquez won the presidency with 51 percent of the vote. His next closest rival, from a center-right party, won 34 percent, while the ruling centrist party candidate won only 10 percent. The Broad Front also won majorities in both houses of the congress. His victory shattered the two-party system that had dominated Uruguay for 150 years.

With his inauguration in March of 2005, the *New York Times* noted, three-quarters of South America's 355 million people were governed by left-wing leaders, from Argentina to Brazil to Venezuela. In general, these leaders rejected the region's free-market reforms of the 1990s (known as the Washington Consensus because the United States promoted them so heavily) as failing to address the continent's serious problems with poverty. However, most of the leaders are also pragmatists that, unlike previous generations of South American leftists, practice financial restraint and remain hospitable to foreign investors.

Hundreds of thousands of people, waving Uruguayan flags or banners with the colors of the Broad Front coalition, celebrated Vázquez' inauguration in the streets of Montevideo. "We promised change, and we will make changes, starting with the government itself, in its attitudes and its actions," Vázquez said in his inaugural address (as quoted by Rohter in the *New York Times*). He said he would immediately create economic policies "to the benefit of those who need them to achieve a life with dignity." He also promised an "independent foreign policy," and insisted, "We will tolerate no outside interference in our internal affairs," signs that Uruguay would distance itself somewhat from the United States and negotiate forcefully with its foreign creditors, such as the International Monetary Fund.

Vázquez took office exactly 20 years after Uruguay's military dictatorship ended (it ruled the country from 1973 to 1985), and he promised to investigate never-prosecuted abuses by the dictatorship, or "dark zones in the area of human rights," as he put it (according to Rohter). "For the good of all, it is possible and necessary to clarify" what happened, he said, so "the horrors of past eras never happen again." Controversial leftist Venezuelan president

Hugo Chavez attended Vázquez's inauguration and spoke at a ceremony celebrating it. Vázquez also immediately reestablished relations with Cuba upon taking office. However, Vázquez sent several signs that his government would be centrist. He chose a moderate as his economy minister, Danilo Astori, who promised repeatedly to follow the example of the pragmatic center-left president of Brazil, Luiz Inacio Lula da Silva, in seeking financial stability while pursuing social programs. Vázquez also relegated hard-line socialists and former guerrillas in his coalition to ministries with little control over economic policy. His government announced that it wanted to renegotiate Uruguay's foreign debt of about $13 billion, but remained committed to paying it, unlike the leftist government in Argentina, which has simply stopped payments on its foreign debt.

The Vázquez government immediately launched a $100 million-a-year emergency plan to fight poverty. Out of Uruguay's population of 3.4 million, 1 million are poor. But the plan focuses on the 45,000 families who cannot afford enough food, by giving them grants of about $57 a month in housing, food, health and job assistance. Also, in July of 2005, the Vázquez government began pursuing justice in one of the worst crimes committed during the military dictatorship and civil war. It filed murder charges against the former president and his foreign minister, charging them in the kidnapping and murder of two Uruguayan congressmen who fled the country to Argentina after the congress was shut down. The government also demanded that the three branches of the military respond to several accusations of human rights abuses by August of 2005, and it began excavating a military barracks where murdered prisoners were alleged to have been buried. The investigations and charges are somewhat controversial, since the country has an amnesty in place protecting the military from being prosecuted for crimes during the civil war (it was enacted in 1986 as a condition of the military handing over power). But the amnesty does not apply to civilians or to crimes committed outside Uruguay. As of October of 2005, the government faced some protests because its poverty plan was not being implemented as quickly as had been hoped, but Vázquez still enjoyed an approval rating of about 65 percent in polls. Vázquez was elected to a five-year term, so he is expected to remain as president through March of 2010. By law, he cannot seek another term.

Sources

Periodicals

Colorlines Magazine, Fall 2005, p. 41.
Economist, July 25, 1992, p. 56; March 5, 2005, p. 38.
New York Times, November 29, 1999, p. A8; October 31, 2004, p. A18; November 1, 2004, p. A11; November 2, 2004, p. A8; March 1, 2005, p. A3; March 2, 2005, p. A9; June 1, 2005, p. A4; July 31, 2005, p. A4.
NotiSur—South American Political and Economic Affairs, October 21, 2005.
Wall Street Journal, November 2, 2004, p. A20; November 5, 2004, p. A13.

Online

"Actuacion," Presidencia, Republica Oriental del Uruguay, http://www.presidencia.gub.uy/_web/pages/pres03.htm (November 13, 2005).
"Curriculum vitae," Presidencia, Republica Oriental del Uruguay, http://www.presidencia.gub.uy/_web/cab_menus/pres01.htm (November 13, 2005).
"Uruguay elects left-wing leader," BBC News, http://news.bbc.co.uk/2/hi/americas/3968755.stm (November 13, 2005).

—*Erick Trickey*

Guy Verhofstadt

Benoit Doppagne/AFP/Getty Images

Prime Minister of Belgium

Born Guy Maurice Marie-Louise Verhofstadt, April 11, 1953, in Dendermonde, Belgium; married to a professional opera singer; children: two. *Education:* Earned law degree from Rijksuniversiteit, Ghent, Belgium, 1975.

Addresses: *Home*—Ghent, Belgium. *Office*—Federal Public Service (FPS) Chancellery of the Prime Minister, Rue de la Loi-Wetstraat 16, 1000 Brussels, Belgium.

Career

Head of the Flemish Liberal Student Party, 1972-74; political secretary to the leader of the Party for Freedom and Progress (PVV), after 1977; president of the PVV, 1982-91, and of the Flemish Liberals and Democrats (VLD), 1991-97, 1999—; elected to Belgium's Chamber of Deputies, 1985, and served as vice prime minister and minister of state for the budget, 1985-88; elected to the Senate, 1999; became prime minister after VLD's victory in parliamentary elections, 1999, and 2003.

Sidelights

Guy Verhofstadt has led two Belgian governments since 1999 as prime minister and head of the center-right Flemish Liberals and Democrats party, or VLD. His rise to the top political post was a turning point in Belgium's modern electoral history, marking the first time since 1958 that the long-

dominant Christian Democrat party fell out of power. Once known for his ardently right-of-center views, Verhofstadt became more of a political moderate in the 1990s, and is credited with leading his party to its renewal of fortunes at the polls.

Verhofstadt was born in 1953, in Dendermonde, a city in Belgium's East Flanders province. As a young man, he studied law in Ghent, the largest city in East Flanders and once a thriving center of the world's wool trade in the late Middle Ages. During his years at Ghent's Rijksuniversiteit, he became involved in Liberal Party politics, and rose to become head of the Flemish Liberal Student Party in 1972, a post he held for two years. In European politics, the term "liberal" usually refers to a center-right, pro-business party. At the time, the Liberals were formally known as Belgium's *Partij voor Vrijheid en Vooruitgang,* or Party for Freedom and Progress, and commonly referred to by its initials, PVV.

Verhofstadt graduated from the Rijksuniversiteit in 1975 with his law degree, and within two years was serving as the political secretary to PVV leader Willy De Clercq. He quickly emerged as one of the most ardent supporters of free-market reforms in Belgium, which had long been dominated politically by coalition governments between the popular Christian Democrats and their main competitor for votes, the Socialists. The Belgian press even took to referring to him as "Baby Thatcher" for his support of one of Europe's most controversial political figures of that era, British Conservative Party leader Margaret Thatcher.

In 1982, at the age of 29, Verhofstadt was elected president of the PVV. Three years later, he won his first general election to the Chamber of Deputies, one of Belgium's two chambers of parliament. In the coalition government formed that same year, he was made vice prime minister and minister of state for the budget, but voters in 1988 rejected the PPV slate, and he resigned from government along with the rest of the cabinet.

Belgium is a constitutional monarchy, with a king as well as the bicameral legislature. Political parties compete in parliamentary elections that take place at least every four years, and the party that takes the majority of votes then forms a government. If no clear majority wins, then the top vote-getters form a coalition government, with members of both parties making up the cabinet. Verhofstadt's homeland is further divided along cultural and linguistic lines. About 60 percent of its population of ten million speak Dutch and live in the provinces that make up Flanders; these are known as the Flemish Belgians. The remainder, called Walloon, are French-speakers and reside in the provinces of Wallonia. Flanders has traditionally been the more prosperous part of the country, which has led to long-simmering tensions between the two sides.

After 1991 elections, Verhofstadt tried, without success, to form a government with the Christian Democrats. He then led a shakeup of his PVV: it changed its name to the *Vlaamse Liberalen en Democraten* (Flemish Liberals and Democrats, or VLD), and the reconstituted party was bolstered by defections from the Christian Democrats and the *Volksunie* party, a Flemish nationalist party. When his second attempt to form a coalition government failed in 1995, Verhofstadt resigned as head of Party and headed to Italy for a year.

Verhofstadt spent much of his Italian sojourn reading and considering Belgium's future as part of the increasingly federalized European Union, whose headquarters were in Brussels, Belgium's capital. He returned home with some newly centrist political views, which included a more pro-environment stance. Leading the VLD once again, he allied with the Socialists and the Green Party of Wallonia to take a parliamentary majority in the coming June of 1999 elections. The campaign strongly condemned the Christian Democrats for recent corruption scandals that had rocked the country. There was also a scare over dioxin, a highly toxic chemical compound, which had been found in chicken feed in Belgium; monitors working for the European Union claimed that the incumbent Belgian government had been engaged in a cover-up over the matter. Finally, the inability of Belgium's law-enforcement arm to capture a notorious pedophile and serial killer also led to a vote of no-confidence for the Christian Democrats at the polls that June.

With the electoral victory, Verhofstadt became prime minister and the first head of a Liberal government in Belgium since 1937. Showing his commitment to the environmental causes, he pushed through a plan to end the country's reliance on nuclear power by 2021, but also demonstrated his Liberal ideals by lowering taxes. In 2001, he broke with other European heads of state when he voiced support for anti-globalism activists, who had been disrupting international economic forums over the past few years. In November of that year, Verhofstadt even invited some of the leaders of the protest movement to a summit in Ghent.

In the 2003 parliamentary elections, the Greens lost most of their seats, and exited Verhofstadt's coalition government. It took some time before a new coalition government, with the second-place Socialists, was formed, and the following year was marked by several setbacks for Verhofstadt and the VLD. After five years as prime minister, he had been unable to deliver on earlier promises to revitalize Belgium's flagging economy. He was also thwarted in his bid to become the next president of the European Commission. Further adding to his troubles, the VLD was trounced in regional elections that year, and his government became embroiled in a bitter fight over permitting nighttime flights at a Brussels airport, which the global courier DHL had requested. In the middle of the long, tense negotiations to resolve this last issue, Verhofstadt's chauffeur-driven Audi struck a concrete pillar, and he was briefly hospitalized.

Verhofstadt's VLD party has traditionally favored European integration, and in November of 2005 his book, *Verenigde Staten van Europa* ("United States of Europe") was published. In it, he made the argument that public-opinion polls seemed to show that most Europeans favored a stronger federalized Europe, which would include a European defense force.

Sources

Books

Worldmark Encyclopedia of the Nations: World Leaders, Gale, 2003.

Periodicals

Europe, February 2000, p. 25.
Financial Times, December 7, 2004, p. 35.
Independent (London, England), September 23, 2004, p. 30.
New Statesman, November 25, 2002, p. 16.

—*Carol Brennan*

Sophie von Hellermann

Artist

Born in 1975, in Munich, Germany. *Education:* Studied at the Kunstakademie in Düsseldorf, Germany, 1993-98; earned graduate fine-arts degree from the Royal College of Art, London, 2001.

Addresses: *Agent*—c/o Greene Naftali Gallery, 526 West 26th St., New York, NY 10001.

Career

Co-founder of Hobbypop artists' collective, in Düsseldorf, Germany, c. 1998; first solo exhibition at the Charles Saatchi Gallery, London, England, 2001; works first shown in the United States at the Marc Foxx Gallery, Los Angeles, CA, 2001.

Sidelights

Sophie von Hellermann emerged as one of the art world's newest stars not long after she finished her graduate degree at London's Royal College of Art in 2001. Since a highly publicized solo exhibition of her paintings at art collector Charles Saatchi's London gallery, von Hellermann has won seemingly equal amounts acclaim and disdain from critics. Of one of her shows, the *Independent*'s Sue Hubbard claimed von Hellermann's "paintings look like the work of an enthusiastic ten-year-old let loose with a big brush." Hubbard asserted, "Depending on your point of view, they are either invigoratingly immediate and fresh, or merely shallow and incompetent."

Von Hellermann was born in Munich, Germany, in 1975. Her father was a nuclear physicist, and her mother an art historian. The family relocated to the British university town of Oxford when von Hellermann was nine. She entered the Kunstakademie in Düsseldorf, Germany, in 1993, and in 1999 went on to London's prestigious Royal College of Art for a graduate fine-arts degree. The earliest exhibits of her work came during her college years, including a group show in Antwerp, Belgium, in 1999, and another at the Taylor Gallery in London a year later.

During her time in Düsseldorf, von Hellermann fell in with a group of similarly young, iconoclastic German painters and musicians, and they began working collaboratively under the name "Hobbypop." They began staging multimedia art installations that drew heavily from ironic references to contemporary culture. One of their most press-worthy events was a fake exhibition of paintings signed with the names "Ulrike" and "Andreas." The works were done by von Hellermann and fellow Hobbypop artist Markus Vater, under the pretense that a pair of infamous German terrorists—Ulrike Meinhof and Andreas Baader, who carried out a left-wing, anticapitalism campaign against West German institutions before their deaths in custody in the mid-1970s—survived into middle age and took up painting. "Everyone played at being terrorists when I was young," von Hellermann explained to Alison M. Gingeras in an *Artforum* article about the group's fascination with the Baader-Meinhof gang.

Von Hellermann graduated from the Royal College of Art in 2001. The school's student show was reviewed by Adrian Searle for the *Guardian*, who offered some of the first positive comments on her style. "I like Sophie von Hellermann's very northern European paintings: their dryness, controlled looseness, and tart palette put me in mind of Edvard Munch," Searle asserted. Later that year von Hellermann generated a fair amount of art-world buzz when a gallery owned by Charles Saatchi mounted a solo show of her new paintings. Saatchi had made his fortune in advertising, and used it to acquire one of the world's best collection of modern and contemporary art in private hands. He was also known for his generous support of emerging young British artists, like Damien Hirst, whose works re-energized the London art scene in the 1990s.

Von Hellermann had two other shows in 2001, one in Cologne, Germany, and the other at the Marc Foxx Gallery in Los Angeles. In 2002, she took part in the much-discussed group show at Paris's Centre Pompidou, *Cher Peintre* ("Dear Painter"). Included in the figurative painting exhibition were works by Francis Picabia, Sigmar Polke, and John Currin, among many other already-established names. An *Artforum* review by writer Kate Bush called her work "breathlessly brushy," and the critic went on to remark, "while it is relatively easy to forge an offbeat style, it's another thing to come up with one that is conceptually dense."

A fair amount of critical derision has dogged von Hellermann's work since that Saatchi Gallery event. She paints on untreated canvases, using acrylics and large brushes, using a stain technique that requires a certain amount of speed. Her subjects often draw upon pop-culture references, such as the one-name German chanteuse Nico, who sang with the Velvet Underground and appeared in Andy Warhol's underground movies of the 1960s. After retreating into substance abuse, Nico died in 1988 in questionable circumstances on the Spanish resort island of Ibiza. Von Hellermann painted a number of works that paid homage to the iconic singer, which were shown at the Vilma Gold Gallery in London in 2004 in a show titled *On the Ground*.

In the spring of 2005, von Hellermann had her first solo show in the United States art-world epicenter of New York City, at the Greene-Naftali Gallery. The paintings from *Goddess in the Doorway*, as the exhibit was titled, honored the centenary of Albert Einstein's breakthrough theory of relativity in 1905. "I was reading about how Einstein was thinking about particles in space moving, bumping off each other," von Hellermann explained to *New York* magazine writer Karen Rosenberg, but she also said she became deeply interested in the scientist's personal life when reading a collection of letters between him and his wife. She imagined a muse of sorts for Einstein, and many of the canvases in the show feature a comely blonde figure.

Once again, critical assessment was mixed. Writing in the *New York Times*, Ken Johnson called her latest group of paintings both "beguiling and irritating," remarking they "look sketchy and underfinished, or to a sympathetic eye, fresh and spontaneous." Von Hellermann refrains from entering into a dialogue with critics over the merits of her work. When *Vogue* writer Dodie Kazanjian asked what sends her into her studio every day, she replied that "I'm always hoping that one day I'll paint the painting that's completely fresh." Kazanjian chose von Hellermann as one of several artists whose specifically commissioned works would be installed in a new gallery at the Metropolitan Opera in New York in 2006.

Selected exhibitions

Solo

Saatchi Gallery Presents Sophie von Hellermann, London, 2001.
Vusering Hites, Vilma Gold, London, 2001.
Sophie von Hellermann, Marc Foxx Gallery, Los Angeles, 2001.
Sophie von Hellermann, Linn Lühn Gallery, Cologne, Germany, 2001, 2003.
On the Ground, Vilma Gold, London, 2004.
A Perfect Spy, Vacío 9 Gallery, Madrid, Spain, 2004.
Goddess in the Doorway, Greene-Naftali Gallery, New York City, 2005.

Group

Die Serie, Galerie 102, Düsseldorf, Germany, 1998.
What You Buy is Your Problem, Fons Welters, Amsterdam, 1999.
Trouble Spot Painting, MUHKA/NICC, Antwerp, Belgium, 1999.
Spiel des Lebens, Ehemaliges Hauptpostgebaeude, Düsseldorf, Germany, 1999.
Timothy Taylor Gallery, London, 2000.
Furore, hobbypopMUSEUM at Vilma Gold, London, 2000.
Painting Gives Me Pleasure, hobbypopMUSEUM at Artagents, Hamburg, 2000.
Death to the Fascist Insect that Preys on the Life of the People, Anthony D'Offay Gallery, London, 2001.
Cher Peintre, Centre Pompidou, Paris, 2002.
Art and Mountains, The Alpine Club, London, 2003.
Mothers, Oh!, Art, London, 2004.
POSTmoDERN, Greene Naftali Gallery, New York City, 2005.

Sources

Artforum, October 2002; March 2004.

Guardian (London, England), July 10, 2001; January 17, 2004, p. 37.

Independent (London, England), January 27, 2004, p. 15.

Independent Sunday (London, England), October 21, 2001, p. 9.

New York, May 23, 2005.

New York Times, December 7, 2003; June 10, 2005, p. E44.

Vogue, April 2005, p. 224.

—*Carol Brennan*

Jeannette Walls

Journalist and author

Born c. 1960, in Phoenix, AZ; daughter of Rex (an electrician) and Rose Mary (an artist) Walls; married Eric Goldberg, 1988 (divorced, 1996); married John Taylor (a journalist), 2002. *Education:* Received degree from Barnard College, 1984.

Addresses: *Office*—MSNBC on the Internet, One Microsoft Way, Redmond, WA 98052.

Career

Author of the "Intelligencer" column for *New York* magazine, 1987-93; gossip writer for *Esquire* magazine, 1993-98; author of "Scoop," a gossip column published four times weekly on MSNBC.com, 1998—; published first book, *Dish: The Inside Story on the World of Gossip*, 2000; published *The Glass Castle: A Memoir*, 2005.

Sidelights

Reviewers of Jeannette Walls's 2005 memoir, *The Glass Castle*, often mentioned the "truth is stranger than fiction" aphorism. Walls is part of New York's media elite, the author of a widely read gossip column published four times a week on the Web site MSNBC.com. Imposingly tall and usually described as a style-savvy redhead, she rose to a position of immense power in the celebrity-news-driven culture of the late 1990s. What she had feared for much of her stellar ascent, however, was that another journalist might uncover the real scoop—that she had lived in near-unimaginable poverty in West Virginia as a child, sometimes sharing cat food

with her siblings, and that her parents had followed her north when she was in college and then willingly became members of the city's homeless population.

Walls was 17 years old when she joined her older sister in New York in 1977. The family's roots were out West: her mother, Rose Mary, was the daughter of an Arizona cattle rancher, and married an Air Force officer named Rex Walls in 1956. Children Lori, Jeannette, Brian, and Maureen followed, but neither parent was enthusiastic about holding down a regular job. The family lived hand-to-mouth, with Rex taking occasional electrician jobs and Rose Mary using her teaching degree for a year before giving it up. Rex talked about a gold-prospecting device he called The Prospector, which never made it past the blueprint stage. Rose Mary preferred painting and drawing over supervising or even providing meals for her children.

The bohemian ideals of Walls' parents, played out in various towns of the Southwest during the 1960s, might be classified as neglect and even abuse by social workers a generation later. At age three, Walls was badly burned when she tried to cook hot dogs by herself on the family stove, and underwent skin graft operations. Later, there were times when there was no food in the house, nor even lunches for them to take to school, but their parents refused to enroll them in a free-lunch program. Sometimes Walls stole food from the lunch sacks of her classmates to stave off hunger. The family usually fled from one town to another to avoid creditors, but Rex would tell the children that the bill collectors were actually government agents. "We were always supposed to pretend our life was one long and incredibly fun adventure," Walls writes in *The Glass House*, in which she also recounts one escape when her father tossed the family cat out of the window of a moving car as they departed.

Eventually Walls and her family moved to Rex's hometown of Welch, West Virginia, a hardscrabble hamlet where nearly every household lived below the poverty line. Among a townsfolk full of poor, the Walls family was the poorest. They lived in a three-room shack without running water, and with only sporadic electricity. A hole in the roof went unmended and grew, Rex's drinking became a problem, and Walls and her siblings sometimes had to scavenge for food. Despite the hardships of her home life, Walls—taught to read at an early age by her mother—excelled in school.

Walls and her older sister began planning their escape from Welch and a home where wooden electrical spools served as their only furniture when they were in their teens. When a pair of documentary filmmakers from New York City visited the town, both she and Lori were interviewed by them; in return, they grilled the New Yorkers about what life was like there. Lori fled first, and Walls dropped out of high school after her junior year in 1977 and got on a bus to join her. They shared an apartment in the South Bronx, which was not a particularly nice neighborhood even then, but the sisters considered it paradise. Despite the dangerous streets, they were thrilled to live in a place that had water, heat, and electricity.

Walls and her sister easily found service-industry jobs, and sent for their brother. Back in West Virginia, Walls had worked on the school newspaper, and when she began high school in New York, her teachers directed her toward an internship at an alternative newspaper. From there she went on to Barnard College, part of the Columbia University system. She graduated in 1984, having financed her degree with some scholarship funds, student loans, and her own earnings. In the interim, the Walls siblings had sent for their youngest sister, Maureen, at which point Rex and Rose Mary decided to move to New York City, too. Dismayed but hopeful that the city would have some sort of positive effect on their free-spirited but ambition-less parents, Walls and her sister tried to help them at first, but Lori was forced to kick them out, and after that they lived in a van. Eventually, they joined the city's burgeoning homeless population.

Walls' story also had a Cinderella element: she began dating someone from moneyed, old-New York family. She eventually moved into the family home,

in a plush Park Avenue building, and when they wed in 1988, she did not invite her parents to the ceremony and reception at the elite Harvard Club. By then she was writing the "Intelligencer" column for *New York* magazine, which was not technically a gossip column but more of a weekly monitor of Manhattan media, politics, and celebrity cultures. At the time, her parents were living in a "squat," or an off-the-books residence in an abandoned building. This was a point when the issue of homelessness was gaining a great deal of media attention, and squatting was in some cases a form of political protest. Rex proved a media-savvy ringleader, and Walls sometimes saw him being interviewed for the local television news.

Walls' husband knew her full story, but no one in her professional life did. She was increasingly successful at her job, and the cutthroat magazine atmosphere did not deter her. "A couple people lashed out at me," she recalled in an interview with Jim Windolf for *Vanity Fair*. "This woman at *New York* magazine said, 'You Barnard [graduates] don't know what it's like for the rest of us. You had everything handed to you.' ... I was flattered. I was like, 'Yes! I pulled it off!'" Her secret was nearly made public when a comic-strip writer from the *Village Voice* called and told her he had interviewed a homeless man who claimed to be her father. She begged him to keep the story quiet, but around this same time she finally confessed to a female colleague at the magazine. That woman later wrote a romance novel about a high-profile Manhattanite, redheaded like Walls, who covers up an impoverished Appalachian past.

The "Intelligencer" column was read and noticed by many, and Walls had little trouble moving on to a higher-profile job after a few years. She turned down offers from the *New York Post* and *New York Daily News* to write a daily gossip column, instead taking a job with *Esquire* in 1993. Five years later, she moved on to MSNBC.com, where her "Scoop" column ranks among the leading scandalmongers in a pack that includes syndicated veterans Liz Smith and Cindy Adams, as well as the feared Richard Johnson of *New York Post*'s "Page Six" and his *New York Daily News* counterpart, Lloyd Grove.

Walls' first book was published in 2000. *Dish: The Inside Story on the World of Gossip*, was not a tell-all on the industry, but instead recounted its history in American pop culture over the decades. It also charted the explosive rise of a celebrity-driven media industry over the past decade. Her book did offer one somewhat scandalous assertion: she "outed" Matt Drudge of *The Drudge Report*, revealing the sexual orientation of the Internet scribe who first broke the Monica Lewinsky story. In response, Drudge published Walls' home phone number on his site, but Walls said she refused to change the listing and instead answered every call.

Walls' first marriage ended after almost a decade. In 2002, she wed a fellow journalist, John Taylor, who was familiar with the confessional-memoir genre. Three years earlier, Taylor had written an account of his own failed first marriage, *Falling: The Story of One Marriage*. But Taylor did not know the full story of Walls' upbringing. Finally, on a walk through Central Park one day, Taylor told her, "'I'm tired of this. You're lying to me about something,'" Walls recalled in the *Vanity Fair* interview. "He's a good journalist. He noticed some holes in my story. And I told him. But I was ashamed. If you have that sort of past, you either exploit it or are ashamed of it, one or the other."

Taylor encouraged Walls to come clean before someone else beat her to it, and she joked that he duct-taped her to a desk in order to force her to sit down and write her next book. The result was *The Glass Castle: A Memoir,* which enjoyed tremendous publishing-industry buzz before it appeared in stores. When chapters were sent out to test the waters, editors and reviewers clamored for more, and some admitted to reading the manuscript in one sitting. The title was taken from a fantasy that Walls's father used to spin for her, that one day he would build her a fabulous, solar-powered glass castle in the desert.

Reviews commended Walls' honesty and even-handed treatment of Rex, who had died of a heart attack in 1994, and Rose Mary, who was 70 years old but still living in an unheated East Village hovel with a multitude of cats. Critiquing it for the *New York Times Book Review,* Francine Prose asserted that "Walls has a telling memory for detail and an appealing, unadorned style. And there's something admirable about her refusal to indulge in amateur psychoanalysis, to descend to the jargon of dysfunction or theorize ... about the sources of her parents' behavior."

Walls was pleased that her candid revelations about her family did not turn out as badly as she expected. During the writing process, "I kept wondering, 'Who the heck is going to care about this pathetic kid and her wacky family?'" she told *Publishers*

Weekly interviewer Bridget Kinsella. "But the response has just bowled me over." Even Rose Mary read the book and liked it, though she took issue with a few minor characterizations, such as the fact that Walls wrote that her mother was a terrible driver.

Walls still writes the "Scoop" column, which continues to break the occasional celebrity-shocker. She was the first to report, for instance, that hackers had cracked the code of the personal digital assistant device belonging to Paris Hilton, and were posting the phone numbers and text messages online. Two of Walls' siblings also fared well as adults: Lori became a successful illustrator, while her brother retired after 20 years as a New York City cop and started college. Their youngest sister, Maureen, lives a less orthodox lifestyle in California. Childless, Walls and her husband enjoy the pinnacle of success for a New York couple: a home in Manhattan, and another in the Long Island resort community of the Hamptons. She still appreciates the small luxuries, she told *Entertainment Weekly* writer Karen Valby. "I will never take for granted a thermostat. Every time I turn on the sink it's a miracle. 'Look at all that water gushing out!' I go to the grocery store and I can buy anything I want. I don't have to ask the manager if he has any bruised bananas at a discount."

Selected writings

Dish: The Inside Story on the World of Gossip, William Morrow & Company (New York City), 2000.
The Glass Castle: A Memoir, Scribner (New York City), 2005.

Sources

Books

Walls, Jeannette, *The Glass Castle: A Memoir,* Scribner (New York City), 2005.

Periodicals

Entertainment Weekly, March 18, 2005, pp. 32-36.
More, March 2005, p. 34.
New York Times Book Review, March 13, 2005, p. 1.
People, April 4, 2005, p. 45.
Publishers Weekly, February 7, 2005, p. 20.
Time, March 7, 2005, p. 78.
Vanity Fair, April 2005, p. 184.

—*Carol Brennan*

Jeremy Wariner

Kay Nietfeld/EPA/Landov

Track athlete and coach

Born January 31, 1984, in Irving, TX. *Education:* Attended Baylor University.

Addresses: *Contact*—c/o Baylor Athletic Department, 150 Bear Run, Waco, TX 76711.

Career

Began competing as a track athlete in high school, winning two Texas state championships; won U.S. junior championship in the 400 meters, 2003; won both 400 meters and 4x400 meter relay at the Big 12 Indoor Championships, 2004; won 4x400 meter-relay at Big 12 Outdoor Championships, 2004; won both 400 meters and 4x400-meter relay at the Midwest Regional Championships, 2004; won both 400 meters and 4x400-meter relay at both the NCAA Indoor and NCAA Outdoor championships, 2004; won 400 meters at the U.S. Championship, 2004; won two Olympic gold medals in the 400 meters and 4x400 meter-relay, 2004; signed professional contract, c. 2004; worked as a volunteer coach at Baylor University, Waco, TX, 2004—; won 400 meters at the U.S. championships, 2005; won 400 meters and 4x400-meter relay at the World Championships, 2005.

Awards: Jesse Owens Award, 2004.

Sidelights

Though Jeremy Wariner did not begin running track until he was a high school student in Texas, he soon became a dominant sprinter and one of the best in the nation in the 400 meters. After entering Baylor University, he struggled with injuries for a time before emerging again as a dominant force on both the collegiate and national levels. After winning two Olympic gold medals in the 2004 summer games in Athens, Greece, Wariner proved he was one of the best sprinters in the world. The six-foot tall, 165-pound sprinter wins with a fluid racing style which emphasizes his long stride, high knees, and upright posture.

Born in 1984, Wariner grew up in Arlington, Texas, the youngest of three children born to a landscape designer father and a paralegal/daycare center operator mother. Wariner was diagnosed with ADD (Attention Deficit Disorder) and took Ritalin from the age of six. Sports were important to him from an early age, though his family was not athletic. As an elementary school student, Wariner decided that he wanted to play in the outfield for a Major League Baseball team. He also played soccer, where he was faster than nearly every player on the field.

Wariner pursued his baseball dream through his freshman year at Lamar High School in Arlington. He also played basketball and football, the latter as a defensive back and wide receiver. When Wariner was not getting much playing time on the school's baseball team, he decided to try track on the suggestion of his football coach who thought he was a very fast runner. He was faster as a freshman than any of their varsity football players. Wariner found immediate success on the track. The first time he ran the 400 meters at a meet, his time was less than 50.5 seconds. This time set a school record for sophomores while he was competing on the junior varsity squad. In the next meet, he was promoted to varsity and set a school record with a time of 48.8 seconds. Running made him feel good. Wariner told Dick Patrick of *USA Today*, "I've loved running ever since I started. It's a great stress relief."

Wariner found success on a state and national level while in high school. He won two Texas state titles, in the 200 meters and 400 meters. When he was a senior at Lamar, Wariner had the best time in the United States in the 200 meters. He also had the second best time in the United States in the 400 meters. Though a track star, Wariner continued to play football in high school, doing well. He was recruited by colleges to play receiver, though he was on the thin side for the sport. While Wariner wanted to play college football, he also wanted to run track. He chose to enter Baylor University in 2002, primarily because it was the one school which would let him both run track and play football. The scholarship situation grew complicated when his scholarship offer for football was revoked because the coach had given out too many, but Wariner stuck with Baylor, primarily because of its track coach. Clyde Hart had previously worked with Michael Johnson, who dominated the 400 meters in the 1990s and won five gold medals at the Olympics. Wariner also hoped to compete in the Olympics some day.

The first season Wariner ran with Baylor, 2003, was less than successful. During the NCAA indoor season, he suffered an injury to one of his hamstrings in the finals of the 400, finishing seventh with a time of 46.21. After this setback, his outdoor season was also not what he wanted, primarily because of a foot problem. However, Wariner did have some highlights in 2003. He won the U.S. junior championship in the 400 meters with a time of 46.41. He also finished second at the Pan Am Junior Championships in the 400 meters.

In 2004, Wariner had a breakout year, culminating in triumph on the world stage. His first victories came on the collegiate level. Though he lost the 400 meters in the first outdoor meet of 2004 to Baylor teammate Darold Williamson, Wariner won nearly every race he entered after this loss. Wariner first won the 400 meters at the Big 12 Indoor Championship as well as the 4x400-meter relay, where he and

his teammates set an NCAA record with a time of 3:03.96. He repeated this victory as a member of the 4x400-meter relay in the Big 12 Outdoor Championships. Wariner went on to the Midwest Regional Championships, where he was both the 400 meters champion as well as the 4x400-meter relay champion with his Baylor teammates. Wariner dominated both events again on the NCAA Championship level, winning both races in both the Indoor Championships and the Outdoor Championships.

Competing in the 400s meters at the U.S. championships and at the U.S. Olympic trials, Wariner again won both races. At the Olympic trials, he was the youngest winner of the 400 meters in 20 years. Representing the United States at the Olympics, Wariner won two gold medals. He won the 400 meters with a time of 44 seconds, the best time in the 400 he had to date. It was a come-from-behind victory; Wariner was in second place with 100 meters to go, but stayed in his form and ran the race he wanted, winning the event. The race was an American sweep with Otis Harris finishing second and Derrick Brew ending up in third. Wariner also won gold as a member of the 4x400-meter relay team. He ran the third leg, with Baylor teammate Williamson running the anchor.

Discussing Wariner's victory in the 400, former gold medalist Johnson, who acted as an advisor to Wariner in 2004, wrote in the *Daily Telegraph*, "Jeremy's poise down the home stretch is something that, no matter how much you coach or advise athletes, they usually don't learn until later in their career. Jeremy is a special athlete because he takes instruction incredibly well. His execution of the race was something I didn't learn to do until much later in my career."

While Wariner was lauded for his victories on the track, many commentators also noted that he was one of the few whites winning in events that have been traditionally dominated by African-American runners. Wariner was the first American white track athlete to win the 400 meters in the Olympics since Mike Larrabee in the 1964 games in Tokyo, Japan. The issue of race is something that he had dealt with for many years. He told John Crumpacker of the *San Francisco Chronicle*, "I've heard it ever since high school. It doesn't matter what race or ethnicity you are, it's your ability and how you run."

After the Olympic Games, Wariner turned professional with Johnson acting as his agent. By signing a professional contract, he could no longer compete for Baylor in NCAA meets, but he could compete nationally and internationally. Wariner continued to attend Baylor and work on his degree in outdoor recreation, while training with Hart and acting as a volunteer coach for the school. Wariner set a new goal for himself. He wanted to set a world's record in the 400 meters, beating the 44.18 mark set by Johnson in the outdoor race.

In 2005, Wariner did not compete in the indoor track season, but did participate in the outdoor season. He won the U.S. Championship again in the 400 meters, after stumbling at the start of the race. At the 2005 World Championships in Helsinki, Finland, Wariner dominated the 400 meters again. He ran the fastest race of his career with a time of 43.-93. He also won the 4x400-meter relay as anchor, with teammates Andrew Rock, Derrick Brew, and Williamson, with a time of 2:56.91.

With so much success at such a young age, Wariner believed his best years as a runner were ahead of him. He hoped to compete in the Olympics in the 2008 and 2012 games, perhaps competing in additional events like the 200 meters. Wariner knew he had room to improve as a runner, and hoped to continue the decrease in his racing times. Yet he remained determined to keep his approach to racing simple. Wariner told Gary Smith of *Sports Illustrated,* "Race issues, drug issues, I just learned to let 'em go past me. When I get on the track, my mind clears, and all I hear in my head is what Coach Hart told me: Stay focused. Get out strong. Work the turn. Keep your form."

Sources

Periodicals

Daily Telegraph (London, England), August 25, 2004, p. 7.

Houston Chronicle, March 31, 2005, p. 2.

Knight Ridder/Tribune News Service, August 24, 2004.

Plain Dealer (Cleveland, OH), August 24, 2004, p. D1.

Sacramento Bee (Sacramento, CA), May 8, 2005, p. C2.

San Francisco Chronicle, August 24, 2004, p. D7.

Sports Illustrated, December 6, 2004, p. 116; July 4, 2005, p. 77.

USA Today, August 19, 2004, p. 9D.

Online

"Heavy medals," *SI.com*, http://sportsillustrated. cnn.com/2005/more/08/14/bc.eu.spt.ath. worlds.ap/index.ht ml (February 12, 2006).

"Jeremy Wariner," USA Track & Field, http://www. usatf.org/athletes/bio/Wariner_Jeremy.asp (February 12, 2006).

"Player Bio: Jeremy Wariner," Baylor Track and Field, http://baylorbears.collegesports.com/ sports/c-track/mtt/wariner_jeremy00.html (February 12, 2006).

—*A. Petruso*

Alice Waters

© Roger Ressmeyer/Corbis

Chef, restaurant owner, and author

Born April 28, 1944, in Chatham, NJ; daughter of Charles (a business psychologist and management consultant) and Margaret (a homemaker) Waters; married to Stephen Singer (a wine consultant); children: Fanny. *Education:* Attended University of California—Santa Barbara; received degree from the University of California—Berkeley, 1967; did postgraduate work at the Montessori School, London, England.

Addresses: *Office*—Chez Panisse, 1517 Shattuck Ave, Berkeley, CA, 94709-1598.

Career

Worked as a Montessori teacher, c. 1967-71; opened Chez Panisse in Berkeley, CA, 1971; expanded to Chez Panisse Café, 1980, and Cafe Fanny; published first book, *Chez Panisse Menu Cookbook,* in 1982, followed by *Chez Panisse Vegetables* and *Fanny at Chez Panisse,* among other titles; founded the "Edible Schoolyard" project at Martin Luther King Jr. Middle School in Berkeley, and the Chez Panisse Foundation, 1996.

Awards: Named one of 10 Best Chefs in the World, Cuisine et Vins du France, 1986; Best Chef in America, James Beard Foundation, 1992.

Sidelights

Alice Waters is the chef and owner of Chez Panisse, the extraordinarily successful Berkeley, California, restaurant often credited with revolutionizing American eating habits in the 1980s. Out of her kitchen came an array of unusual dishes and produce items largely unknown to American diners, and these foods trends then spread to other menus across the country and, finally, onto supermarket shelves. Waters is regularly dubbed the founder of modern American cooking, and by the early 21st century had moved on to her next mission: to improve the eating habits of American youngsters through an innovative schoolyard-garden and cooking program. "Kids really don't know anymore where food comes from," Waters told *Vogue* writer Katrina Heron, "and they are taught to think that it doesn't matter."

Waters grew up in Chatham, New Jersey, where she was born in 1944 as the second of four daughters in her family. Her father was a business psychologist and management consultant, and her mother the typical stay-at-home mom of the era. Waters recalled that her parents had a "victory garden," a holdover from the World War II era when Americans were encouraged to cultivate backyard crops to relieve food-rationing worries. From its bounty she once made a garden-goddess Halloween costume that seemed to foreshadow her future career, adorning herself with garlands of produce and even a crown made from asparagus stalks.

When it came time for college, Waters headed to California. She spent two years at the University of California's Santa Barbara school, and then transferred to the Berkeley campus further north. This branch of the university was becoming known by the time Waters arrived as a haven for politically active students. In the early 1960s, there was a ban on all political activity on campus, but a group of students challenged the rule, arguing that this violated their constitutional rights. The Berkeley Free Speech movement laid the groundwork for a wave of campus-based protests against the Vietnam War across America over the next few years. Because of this, Berkeley became known as a tolerant, counterculture-friendly community.

Waters majored in French studies, and spent her junior year abroad at the University of Paris. It was there, and on her travels across France, that she first became enthralled by French food and how Europeans seemed to savor a meal. She began reading extensively on the subject, and found English-language guides in the cooking tomes of American expatriate Richard Olney and British kitchen doyenne Elizabeth David, both of whom had been extolling the pleasures of simple French food for a number of years by then. After graduating in 1967, Waters headed back to Europe, ostensibly for postgraduate study at the Montessori School in London, but also as way to tour France and sample its cuisine once again. She recalled a restaurant in the western, Atlantic-seaboard region of Brittany, where the chef came out and announced to the diners what that night's menu would be. Waters and her fellow diners ate trout fished that day from a nearby stream, fresh raspberries, and other items of entirely local origin. She recalled the meal as simple yet overwhelmingly enjoyable, and that diners actually applauded the chef at the end. "I tasted things I couldn't believe," she told William Plummer in a *People* interview. "I just absorbed everything."

Waters returned to Berkeley, and taught at a Montessori school there. She also began writing a cooking column for a radical newspaper run by some friends, and sometimes fed its staff. Food and culinary choices were emerging as a form of personal expression among the younger generation around this time. "Travel was cheap and everyone had been everywhere," Waters explained to *New York Times* writer Lacey Fosburgh, "and when they came back home, they wanted the same kind of good foods and freshness they'd had in France or Mexico or wherever. They didn't want to patronize worn-out established restaurants. They wanted sophisticated, really interesting foods."

Waters founded her business with the idea of meeting that demand. She borrowed $10,000, and opened the doors of Chez Panisse in 1971 in an old house on Shattuck Avenue. The name "Panisse" came from a character in a trilogy of works by French filmmaker Marcel Pagnol, whose films Waters loved. As the head chef, she had to offer a prix-fixe or "fixed price" menu, which gave the diner the barest minimum of options at a set price, simply because she did not know how to juggle a wider range of dishes during a dinner rush. She also relied on local growers to bring her produce, a rather unusual idea at the time, and spent lavishly on fresh flowers for the restaurant. "It took us a long time to become profitable, because we didn't know anything about running a restaurant," she admitted to Roman Czajkowsky in *Nation's Restaurant News* some years later. "It was very rocky for the first four years."

By the end of the decade Waters was ready to expand, and the Chez Panisse Café opened in the upstairs part of the house in 1980. It offered a broader menu than the downstairs dining room, with a focus on foods from around the Mediterranean basin, and soon became a favorite of the Bay Area's young, urban professional set as well. Responding to the increasing demand, some of those who had worked with Waters left to open their own restaurants in San Francisco-Oakland nexus, and by the early 1980s she was being hailed as the pioneer who began what was being called the new California Cuisine. The *New York Times'* enormously influential food writer of the era, Craig Claiborne, was an early fan of Chez Panisse, and in a 1981 article he commended Waters and her visionary ideas; he also had to define for readers the terms clementine and calzone, so foreign were they even to his paper's audience. "Where American gastronomy is concerned, there is one commodity that is rarer than locally grown black truffles or homemade foie gras. That is a chef of international repute who was born in the United States," Claiborne wrote of Waters. "Even rarer is such a celebrated chef who is a woman."

Gourmands and restaurant critics from France visited Chez Panisse, too, and accorded it high marks. Waters' growing fame led to her first how-to guide, the *Chez Panisse Menu Cookbook* which was published in 1982. Several other titles followed over the next two decades, but Waters avoided trading in on her reputation to join the ranks of celebrity chefs. She has never had her own television show, nor signature cookware or even line of supermarket foods, though she was courted by companies making generous offers. She also declined to replicate Chez Panisse elsewhere, feeling a restaurant worked best when its chef was on site and at least supervising the kitchen and dining room, if not actively involved in the dinner rush any longer. Her last expansion effort was for a Berkeley take-out food counter she named Cafe Fanny after both her daughter and another Pagnol character.

Waters did use her prominence to promote some of her core beliefs, however. She championed local farmers' markets, for example, as well as organic foods grown without synthetic fertilizers, pesticides, or hormones. By the early 1990s, both trends were making their way cross-country, and at the start of the twenty-first century organic-produce sections were commonplace in supermarket produce aisles. Other food trends were credited to Waters and her restaurant over the years, including the oddly named greens that eventually supplanted traditional iceberg lettuce in salads, and gourmet pizza, said to have been invented one day when a chef at Chez Panisse tossed some leftover seafood onto a round of pizza dough and added a few fresh vegetables.

Waters has won a number of awards, including her profession's most prestigious honor, the Chef of the Year title from the James Beard Foundation. That same year, Chez Panisse was also honored as Restaurant of the Year for 1992 by the Foundation. By then, Waters was thinking about her next mission, which had its origins in a comment she made once to a local reporter about the middle school she went past daily on her way to her restaurant. In response, the school's principal invited her to visit, and naturally Waters asked students what they ate for lunch. She was shocked by the answers—some didn't eat anything, while others bought a meal from a fast-food concession in the lunchroom. The principal let her plant a garden on school property, and from there she began teaching the students about food, nutrition, and the usefulness of a few kitchen skills. As she explained in an interview with Paul Rauber for *Sierra*, "I didn't want just a garden. Lots of schools have gardens. I wanted it to be a garden that relates to what the children are eating at lunch. For me, the most neglected schoolroom is the lunchroom."

Waters launched her Chez Panisse Foundation in 1996, with the goal of funding similar "Edible Schoolyards" in other schools. She calls her project the School Lunch Initiative, and the program has evolved into an entire curriculum. Students grow the produce, learn kitchen skills while preparing it, and then benefit from eating healthy meals in the school cafeteria. The Edible Schoolyard was designed to lay the foundation for a lifetime of healthy eating habits, but it also had a lesson for every hour of the school day: history classes tried out ancient grains that once helped Native American populations survive, and science classes could observe the firsthand effects of thermal energy.

Waters believed her mission could counter the negative effects of a worsening American diet. The number of obese children skyrocketed in the 1990s, thanks in part to an over-reliance on convenience foods and fast-food meals. For her, it was once again a food issue but one that had links to personal moral values or political beliefs. "If you buy fast food, you're supporting a whole other vision of the world," she told Dorothy Kalins in *Town & Country*. "These companies are out there destroying natural resources and limiting biodiversity. They're teaching kids to be wasteful."

Waters and her Foundation attracted some influential supporters, including California Governor Arnold Schwarzenegger and his wife, Maria Shriver. Waters' future goal is to have an Edible Schoolyard and School Lunch Initiative program in all California public schools some day. She even replicated her idea at Yale University, where her daughter Fanny was enrolled. The Yale Sustainable Food Project was designed to provide food for one residential dining hall, but the fare quickly became known as the best food on campus, and students began to forge passes to eat there nightly. In 2004, the program expanded to other dining halls at Yale.

Waters is also an ardent supporter of the Slow Food movement, which calls itself the antithesis to "fast" food. Its members, drawn from several countries, promote locally grown or raised food, urge the adoption of biodiversity-protective agricultural policies, and work to educate consumers about food choices. Despite her long list of achievements, Waters remains modest about her influence on American cuisine. Interviewing her for *Restaurant Business*, writer Kevin Farrell asked her what she thought her most significant impact on dining habits might be. "I think the fact that you can get a halfway decent salad in many restaurants today," she replied, "is an indication that some of the things I believe have taken hold."

Selected writings

Chez Panisse Menu Cookbook, Random House, 1982.
Chez Panisse Vegetables, Morrow Cookbooks, 1996.
Fanny at Chez Panisse: A Child's Restaurant Adventures with 46 Recipes, Morrow Cookbooks, 1997.
Chez Panisse Café Cookbook, Morrow Cookbooks, 1999.
Chez Panisse Cooking, Peter Smith Pub Inc, 2001.
Chez Panisse Fruit, Morrow Cookbooks, 2002.

Sources

Nation's Restaurant News, February 13, 1984, p. 1.
Newsweek, August 27, 2001, p. 44.

New York Times, June 3, 1981; June 19, 1983.
People, November 23, 1992, p. 184.
Restaurant Business, May 1, 1987, p. 174.
Sierra, November-December 1997, p. 24.

Town & Country, January 2005, p. 136.
Vogue, April 2005, pp. 374-77.

—*Carol Brennan*

Sam Waterston

Francis Specker/Landov

Actor

Born November 15, 1940, in Cambridge, MA; son of George Chychele (a teacher) and Alice Tucker (a painter) Waterston; married Barbara Rutledge Johns (a photographer and writer; divorced); married Lynn Louisa Woodruff, January 26, 1976; children: James (from first marriage), Graham, Elisabeth, Katherine (from second marriage). *Education:* Yale, B.A., 1962; studied acting at the Sorbonne, Paris, France; studied with the American Actor's Workshop, Frank Corsaro, and Herbert Berghoff.

Addresses: *Office*—NBC, 39 Rockefeller Plaza, New York, NY 10112.

Career

Actor on stage, including: *Antigone*, 1947; appearances with the New York Shakespeare Festival, 1963-76, including *As You Like It*, 1963, *Henry IV, Part I*, 1968, *Henry IV, Part II*, 1968, *Much Ado About Nothing*, 1972, and *Hamlet*; *Oh Dad, Poor Dad, Mama's Hung You in the Closet and I'm Feelin' So Sad*, New York City, 1963; *Indians*, 1969-70; *The Trial of the Catonsville Nine*, New York City, 1971; *Much Ado About Nothing*, New York City, 1974; *Lunch Hour*, 1980-81; *A Walk in the Woods*, 1988; *Abe Lincoln in Illinois*, 1993; *Long Day's Journey Into Night*, Syracuse Stage, 2000; *Much Ado About Nothing*, Delacorte Theatre, New York City, 2004; *Benefactors*. Television appearances include: *Camera Three*, CBS, 1964; *The Glass Menagerie*, ABC, 1973; *Much Ado About Nothing*, 1974; *Friendly Fire* (movie), ABC, 1979; *Oppenheimer*, PBS, 1982; *Q.E.D.*, 1982; *Finnegan Begin Again* (movie), HBO, 1985; *Gore Vidal's Lincoln* (movie), NBC, 1988; *I'll Fly Away*, NBC, 1991-93; *Law & Order*, NBC, 1994—; *David's Mother* (movie), CBS, 1994; *Miracle at Midnight*, (movie), 1998; *Exiled: A Law and Order Movie* (movie), NBC, 1998; *A House Divided* (movie), Showtime, 2000; *The Matthew Shepard Story* (movie), 2002. Film appearances include: *The Plastic Dome of Norma Jean* (unreleased), 1965; *Fitzwilly*, 1967; *The Great Gatsby*, 1974; *Journey Into Fear*, 1976; *Dandy, the All American Fear*, 1976; *Interiors*, 1978; *Sweet William*, 1979; *Hopscotch*, 1980; *Heaven's Gate*, 1980; *The Killing Fields*, 1984; *Hannah and Her Sisters*, 1986; *September*, 1987; *Crimes and Misdemeanors*, 1989; *The Man on the Moon*, 1991; *Serial Mom*, 1994; *The Journey of August King*, 1995; *The Proprietor*, 1996; *Shadow Conspiracy*, 1997; *Le Divorce*, 2003. Television producer of *A House Divided*, Showtime, 2000; television director of *I'll Fly Away*, NBC, 1992; film producer of *The Journey of August King*, 1995. Served as spokesperson for TD Waterhouse, a brokerage firm, 2003—; also worked as a cab driver and for a theater club.

Awards: Obie Award for distinguished performance, *Village Voice*, for *Much Ado About Nothing*, 1973; Drama Desk Award for outstanding performance, for *Much Ado About Nothing*, 1973; Golden Globe Award for best actor in a leading role—drama series, Hollywood Foreign Press Association, for *I'll Fly Away*, 1992; William Shakespeare Award for Classical Theatre, The Shakespeare Theatre of Washington, D.C., 1996; Emmy Award for outstanding information series, Academy of Television Arts and Sciences, for *Time Life's Lost Civilizations—Egypt: Quest for Immortality*, 1996; Actor Award for outstanding performance by a male actor in a drama series, for *Law & Order*, 1998; Screen Actors Guild Award for *Law & Order*, 1999.

Sidelights

Though American actor Sam Waterston is probably best known for his long-running role on the television drama series *Law & Order*, he began his career on stage and film. He appeared in a number of productions with the New York Shakespeare Festival and in New York City, beginning in the 1960s. It took a little longer for Waterston to establish himself as a film actor, but after a breakthrough role in the mid-1970s, he appeared in several prominent Woody Allen films.

Born on November 15, 1940, in Cambridge, Massachusetts, Waterston was one of four children born to George, a teacher who had emigrated from England, and Alice, a painter. Waterston began his acting career on stage as a child. His stage debut came in 1947 when he was only six years old. He played the Page in a school production of *Antigone*. His father served as a director of the production.

After graduating from the Groton School, a prep school, Waterston entered Yale University. There, he studied history, French, and drama. During his junior year, Waterston studied with the American Actor's Workshop. This experience also included a stint in Paris, France, studying related stage craft at the Sorbonne. After Waterston earned his B.A. in 1962 from Yale, he began working as an actor nearly right away. His first role was in *Oh, Dad, Poor Dad*, a touring production. Waterston also studied acting in New York City with Herbert Berghoff and Frank Carsaro.

Though Waterston had some early success as an actor, he did not work on a consistent basis. He supported himself by taking jobs as a cab driver and at a theater. Despite these early difficulties, Waterston had many significant credits in stage productions, primarily in New York City. From 1963 to 1976, Waterston appeared regularly with the New York Shakespeare Festival (NYSF). His first production with NYSF came in 1963 when he played Silvius in *As You Like It*. That same year, Waterston made his Broadway debut in *Oh Dad, Poor Dad, Mama's Hung You in the Closet and I'm Feelin' So Sad*. In this comedy, he played Jonathan Rosepettle.

Over the years, Waterston appeared in a number of acclaimed stage performances. One such role was Benedict in the 1972 NYSF production of *Much Ado About Nothing*. This production later moved to Broadway and won the actor two awards. Waterston also played the title role in *Hamlet* and Prince Hal in *Henry IV, Part I* and *Henry IV, Part II*, both done by NYSF in 1968.

Waterston developed a reputation for a taking a cerebral approach to characters and craft. He told Samuel G. Freedman of the *New York Times*, "What I really like to play is people in morally ambiguous situations. That's where things get juicy. The whole area of melodrama is, 'He killed my father, and I'm gonna kill him.' But *Hamlet* is: 'Am I allowed to do this? If I kill him, does he go to heaven?'"

Waterston also had an impressive range as a stage actor. He appeared in comedies, dramas, and biographical works. In another significant production that was staged in 1988, Waterston co-starred in the two-man drama, *A Walk in the Woods*, which was based on the events surrounding an arms negotiating session between the United States and the Soviet Union. While the events the play was based on actually occurred in Geneva, Switzerland, in 1982, the names of the men involved were fictionalized. Waterston played the U.S. diplomat. After a run in New York, the production later toured the United States. Another key role for Waterston was playing former U.S. president Abraham Lincoln in a play called *Abe Lincoln in Illinois*.

As Waterston's career took off in film and television, he continued to appear in a few stage productions. On occasion, he was able to work with some of his own children, who had their own acting ambitions. In 2000, Waterston appeared with his oldest son, James, in a production of *Long Day's Journey into Night*. Four years later, Waterston appeared with his daughter, Elisabeth, in *Much Ado About Nothing*. Waterston played the play's family patriarch, Leonato, while his daughter played his character's daughter, Hero.

Waterston's film career was not as prominent as his work on stage, though he appeared in a number of well-known films. He often played supporting roles, usually average types with a dreamy side. Waterston's career in film did not start well. His first film, *The Plastic Dome of Norma Jean*, was not released after being shot in 1965. The first film in which he appeared that was released was 1967's *Fitzwilly*.

It was not until the mid-1970s that Waterston's film career gained notice. One of his first big roles came in the 1974 adaptation of *The Great Gatsby*, based on the novel by F. Scott Fitzgerald. Waterston's portrayal of Nick Carrawy in the film led to two Golden Globe Award nominations for best supporting actor and most promising newcomer.

In the late 1970s, Waterston began appearing in films directed by noted filmmaker Woody Allen. The first film he did with Allen was 1978's *Interiors*. Waterston also appeared in critically acclaimed films by Allen such 1986's *Hannah and Her Sisters* and 1989's *Crimes and Misdemeanors*. Waterston later stated that he appreciated his time with Allen.

Arguably the most important film role that Waterston took on in his career was the lead in 1984's *The Killing Fields*. The film was based on a nonfiction work by Roland Joffe. Waterston played Sidney Schanberg, a journalist, who was doing research in Cambodia. Waterston was nominated for an Academy Award for his work in the film.

Though television became Waterston's primary acting medium in the 1990s and 2000s, he continued to appear a few films. In 1994, he had a supporting role in *Serial Mom*, a dark farcical comedy directed by John Waters. Waterston played the dim husband to Kathleen Turner's murderous title character. Three years later, Waterston played the U.S. president in *Shadow Conspiracy*. In 2003, he appeared in *Le Divorce*, playing the father of two women who lived in Paris.

Waterston began his television career in 1964, when he appeared in *Camera Three*, but it did not begin in earnest until the early 1970s. In 1973, he appeared in a television production of the Tennessee Williams' play *The Glass Menagerie*. Waterston's work as Tom on that show led to his first Emmy Award nomination.

Beginning in the early 1980s, Waterston appeared in a number of television movies and miniseries, many with a biographical or true-life bent. In 1982, Waterston played Robert Oppenheimer in the PBS miniseries, *Oppenheimer*. Oppenheimer was the physicist who played a key role in the development of the nuclear bomb. Six years later, he played President Abraham Lincoln in the television movie, *Gore Vidal's Lincoln*. In 1998's *Miracle at Midnight*, Waterston played Dr. Karl Koster. Set during World War II, Koster was a Dane whose actions saved the lives of a number of Jews in the face of the Nazi threat. Waterston's work was particularly acclaimed in the 2002 television movie, *The Matthew Shepard Story*. Waterston played the father of Matthew Shepard, a young man who was murdered because of his homosexuality.

In 2000, Waterston served as both producer and co-star of a movie for the cable network Showtime. Called *A House Divided*, the somewhat controversial movie focused on the life story of Amanda America Dixon. Waterston played her father, a plantation owner. Dixon was the product of the rape he committed on one of his slaves, Julia. The owner and his family raised Dixon as white and did not tell her that one of their servants was her mother. Dixon did not learn she had a black mother until she was an adult. She left the home after learning this fact. After her father's death, she was left her father's fortune, for which she had to fight in court. Waterston was intrigued by the dynamics of the situation. He told Dusty Saunders of *Denver Rocky Mountain News*, "As a producer I was attracted to the tantalizing prospect of trying to figure out how this worked out between all these people and how they made their way in life."

Throughout his career, the one television genre Waterston was uncomfortable was series television. He had heard and believed that the hours were long and the scripts not always worthy of his time. He had an early short stint on *Q.E.D.*, playing a physicist and professor named Quentin E. Deverill. The show only lasted for eight episodes in 1982. However, Waterston went on to appear on two significant television series, both critically acclaimed.

The first show of significance was the drama *I'll Fly Away*, which ran for two seasons on NBC in the early 1990s. Though it did not have high ratings, the show did have a loyal core following. *I'll Fly Away* was also regarded by some critics as the best show on television at the time. Set in the 1950s in the southern part of the United States, Waterston's character, Forrest Bedford, was a single father who worked as his town's district attorney. Bedford was a moderate in race relations trying to move ahead politically by bowing to white supremacy for the most part. Joshua Brand, a creator and producer of the show, told Freedman of the *New York Times*, "Forrest is a flawed man, struggling to do the right thing. And when we described that to Sam, he said, 'That's what I do best.' By which he meant, 'I play people who think.'" The race issue was often brought forward by his black housekeeper/nanny named Lilly, played by Regina Taylor. Waterston was nominated three times for Emmy Awards for his work on the show.

In 1994, a year after the cancellation of *I'll Fly Away*, Waterston joined the cast of a show that was already a hit and had been on the air for five years. Called *Law & Order*, the drama looked at a case from the point of view of the police investigating the crime and the prosecutors who try these criminals. Waterston played Jack McCoy, the assistant (later executive assistant) district attorney. The character was complicated, and a few people saw parallels between the actor and the character. Waterston told Robert Fidgeon of the *Herald Sun*, "If you think I possess similar qualities to McCoy, then I graciously accept that. He's a fine man. But the truth is I accepted the role because it meant I could spend more time with my family." The show was shot in New York City.

Waterston continued to play Jack McCoy for more than ten years. However, the cast around him often changed and he was given several new partners. Waterston also appeared in a related television movie, *Exiled: A Law & Order Movie.* Waterston won at least one award for his work on the show. He was also nominated for an Emmy Award three times, though he did not win.

Of his acting career, Waterston told the *Pittsburgh Post-Gazette*, "I consider myself to be extraordinarily fortunate. There are so many other things that one can do with one's life that aren't anywhere near as much fun. And then there are so many people who have tried to do this or make it their way in other arts who are just as talented and determined as I am and haven't had anywhere near the chances I've had. So I'm lucky, lucky, lucky."

Sources

Books

Celebrity Biographies, Baseline II, 2005.

Periodicals

brandweek.com, November 10, 2003.
Denver Rocky Mountain News, July 30, 2000, p. 4.
Herald Sun, May 10, 2000, p. H4.
New Yorker, July 26, 2004, p. 90.
New York Times, January 21, 1988, p. C21; November 17, 1991, sec. 2, p. 31; September 25, 1994, sec. 2, p. 33.
Pittsburgh-Post Gazette (Pittsburgh, PA), April 24, 2000, p. D2.
Seattle Times (Seattle, WA), April 15, 1994, p. D3; January 24, 2005, p. E1.
Washington Post, September 15, 1991, p. Y9.

Online

"Sam Waterston," NBC.com, http:://www.nbc.com/Law_&_Order/bios/Sam_Waterston.html (August 8, 2005).

—*A. Petruso*

Naomi Watts

© Laura Farr/ZUMA/Corbis

Actress

Born September 28, 1968, in Shoreham, Sussex, England; daughter of Peter (a sound engineer) and Myffanwy (a store owner) Watts.

Addresses: *Home*—Los Angeles, CA.

Career

Actress in films, including: *For Love Alone*, 1986; *Flirting*, 1991; *Matinee*, 1993; *Tank Girl*, 1995; *Children of the Corn IV: The Gathering*, 1996; *Babe: Pig in the City*, 1998; *Strange Planet*, 1999; *Ellie Parker* (short), 2001; *Mulholland Drive*, 2001; *The Ring*, 2002; *21 Grams*, 2003; *Le Divorce*, 2003; *Ned Kelly*, 2003; *I Heart Huckabees*, 2004; *We Don't Live Here Anymore*, 2004; *The Assassination of Richard Nixon*, 2004; *The Ring Two*, 2005; *Ellie Parker*, 2005; *King Kong*, 2005. Television movie appearances include: *Brides of Christ*, 1991; *Home and Away*, 1991; *Bermuda Triangle*, 1996; *The Hunt for the Unicorn Killer*, 1999. Worked as a fashion model and fashion-magazine editor, 1980s.

Sidelights

Naomi Watts struggled for more than a decade in her quest to break out of the anonymous starlet talent-pool in Hollywood. The British-born actress, best known for her roles in both *Ring* horror movies as well as a breakout performance in *Mulholland Drive*, had just a few years earlier been forced to take work in embarrassing projects, including the third *Children of the Corn* sequel. In 2005,

she won a highly coveted part as the blond temptress in director Peter Jackson's big-budget remake of *King Kong*.

Watts had a childhood that seems fodder for a screenplay itself. Born on September 28, 1968, in Shoreham, England, she was the daughter of Myffanwy, called Miv, a Welsh woman who wed the sound engineer for Pink Floyd, an emerging British rock band at the time. Watts arrived in a family that already included her brother, Ben, born the year before. Their father, Peter, provided the maniacal laughter for the Pink Floyd track "Brain Damage" on the group's era-defining 1973 LP *Dark Side of the Moon*. By then, however, Watts's parents had divorced, and her mother struggled to earn a living as a stage actress. In 1976, when Watts was seven years old, her father died. She recalled the trauma as "very sudden, and very shocking and upsetting," she told Ingrid Sischy in *Interview*. "My mom was still young and did not know how she would cope with two small children."

Watts recalled her first acting thrill at the age of four or five, which came when she went to see her mother's performance in an English community theater production of *My Fair Lady*. Seated near the front row, Watts tried in vain to get her mother's attention. "I kept waving to her, and she wasn't acknowledging me," she recalled in the interview with Sischy. "I kept thinking, 'Why won't she notice?' I wanted to be up there playing with her in that world."

Later in their childhood, Watts and her brother were sent to boarding schools in England. Watts was an admittedly poor student, a daydreamer as well as a risk-taker who liked to sneak out of the dormitory at night with her fellow troublemakers. In the early 1980s, with Britain in the midst of a deep economic recession, Miv decided to move to Australia, a plan to which the 14-year-old Watts strongly objected. She eventually adjusted to the new home in Sydney, however, and as a teenager ventured into modeling. On her first-ever audition for a television commercial, she befriended another teen model named Nicole Kidman who was also trying out for the job that day in 1982. Neither of them were hired, but the two shared a taxi ride back home, since it turned out both lived in the same part of Sydney. The friendship would be an enduring and enriching one for Watts over the years, with Kidman's success inspiring Watts to try her luck in Hollywood, too.

Unlike Kidman's, Watts' career would take some lengthy detours. She first went to Japan to model, and had a terrible experience with it. "It was after that that I made the decision that I didn't want to be in front of the camera ever again," she told Sischy in *Interview.* Returning to Sydney, she managed to parley her modeling experience into a job with the marketing department of a local department store, and from there went on to serve as assistant fashion editor at an edgy Australian fashion magazine. It was while working as fashion editor at another magazine that a friend talked her into joining a weekend drama workshop, since they were short a few female participants. The stage experience reminded Watts of how much she wanted to act, and she quit her job the following Monday.

Watts' first screen credit had come with a small role in a 1986 Australian film, *For Love Alone.* It took five more years before she landed her next job, and that came thanks in part to Kidman: Watts attended the premiere of Kidman's breakout movie, *Dead Calm,* in 1989, where she met a director who offered her a part in *Flirting,* a film about a trio of boarding school students. Watts was one of the leads, alongside Kidman and another relative unknown, Thandie Newton. From there Watts was cast in an Australian mini-series about Roman Catholic nuns, *Brides of Christ* that was shown in the United States on the A&E cable channel, and after that point decided to join Kidman in Los Angeles.

By then Kidman had wed Tom Cruise, one of Hollywood's biggest stars, and the connection helped Watts land a few auditions. Her own breakout role, however, was slow to come, and she suffered a number of small roles in bad or otherwise forgotten films. These included a part as the Shopping Cart Starlet in *Matinee,* a 1993 film with John Goodman as a B-movie producer, and a supporting role in 1995's *Tank Girl,* the much-anticipated comic-book adaptation that failed at the box office. Her career seemed to stall after that, and she made ends meet by accepting roles in anything she could get, such as Grace Rhodes in *Children of the Corn IV: The Gathering,* as a voice extra in *Babe: Pig in the City* in 1998, and as the murdered woman in a television movie, *The Hunt for the Unicorn Killer,* based on a true story of anti-war activist Ira Einhorn, who was accused of murdering his ex-girlfriend in 1977 and then avoiding prosecution for the crime by hiding out in France for 16 years.

Watts was rejected for a number of parts that might have improved her chances. She was reportedly on the shortlist for unspecified parts in *Devil's Advocate*—a breakout part for Charlize Theron—*The Postman,* Kevin Costner's 1997 post-apocalypse drama, and in the 2000 box-office hit *Meet the Parents.* Finally, her agent began asking around Hollywood, querying the producers and directors who had previously considered Watts about why they had turned her down. "'They're saying that you're too intense, that you want it too much'" Watts was told, as she recalled in the *Interview* profile by Sischy. She cried upon hearing this, but then returned the Venice Beach apartment where she lived. Her mother happened to be visiting at the time, and told not to worry. "'Do not believe these people,'" were her mother's words of caution, Watts told Sischy. "'They cannot define you, they don't know you.'"

Watts listened to her mother's advice, and kept taking acting classes and trying out for parts. She won one of the lead roles in a 1999 David Lynch pilot for ABC, *Mulholland Drive,* which aimed to replicate the success of his *Twin Peaks* series a decade earlier, but the network backed out, and Lynch was forced to use a French studio's financing to reshoot it into a feature film. Released in late 2001, the odd, dark drama incited a love-it or hate-it reaction among critics, but those who had been charmed by Lynch's disturbing vision singled out Watts for her role as Betty Elms, a Canadian who comes to Hollywood and finds it even more venal than expected, but swims with it anyway. "Her performance, nailing every subversive impulse under Betty's sunny exterior, ranks with the year's finest," asserted Peter Travers in *Rolling Stone,* while *Entertainment Week-*

ly's Owen Gleiberman compared her to "a pixie Sharon Stone," and asserted that "she's an extraordinary talent."

Critics took notice once again when Watts appeared as the beleaguered mom in *The Ring,* a sci-fi/horror flick that took in $130 million at the box office in late 2002. Reportedly both Gwyneth Paltrow and Kate Winslet were interested in playing the lead character, an investigative journalist whose son comes across an evil videotape that brings unspeakable terror to those who view it. Critics were divided once again over the film's merits, but Watts won kudos for her performance. Gleiberman, reviewing it for *Entertainment Weekly,* called her "wholesomely sensual, with a rare ability to make fear look strong." Gleiberman also liked what he termed her "live-wire charisma reminiscent of the young Debra Winger. She just about vibrates in response to whomever she's on screen with, and the audience watching *The Ring* shares that tingle."

By this point, Watts's career had reached star status. She earned an Academy Award nomination for best supporting actress in 2003's *21 Grams,* as a grieving widow who convinces the hapless professor (Sean Penn) who received her slain husband's heart in a transplant to avenge his death. She no longer had to take made-for-television movies, or projects that seemed destined for a straight-to-video release. Instead she was cast as Kate Hudson's sister in *Le Divorce,* then one of the leads in *I Heart Huckabees,* in 2004, and in the well-received *We Don't Live Here Anymore,* that same year. In the last film, she was played opposite her friend Mark Ruffalo as part of an adulterous quartet.

Though she would turn 37 in 2005, Watts won the lead in a historic Hollywood remake of *King Kong,* filmed by Peter Jackson of *Lord of the Rings* fame. It was a part that had made both Fay Wray and an unknown Jessica Lange famous in its earlier screen incarnations in 1933 and 1976, though Watts was a good decade older than either of her predecessors in the role. She was cast as Ann Darrow, the actress who travels with a film crew to a remote island in search of a massive prehistoric ape. The beast's existence proves to be real, and Darrow's presence is the only thing that can calm him.

Watts gave a farewell of sorts to her long years of struggle in Hollywood with *Ellie Parker,* a full-length comedy released in 2005, but based on a 16-minute short written and directed by a friend, Scott Coffey. The shorter version earned a terrific response when it premiered at the 2001 Sundance Film Festival, with Watts as the title character, a young woman determined to succeed in Hollywood who endures an endless round of humiliating auditions. Watts certainly mined her own experiences when she made it, she told Cassie Carpenter in an article for *Back Stage West.* "Sometimes you would barely get eye contact or a handshake, and they would be sitting down looking at your resume, saying, "Can't see anything recognizable, OK, go ahead." And then the wind just goes out of you, so it's impossible to shine in those moments."

Making up for those lean years, Watts now commands a per-picture paycheck in the $6 million range thanks to her box-office draw. She was able to buy her own home in Los Angeles, where she lives solo. Once romantically linked to fellow Australian actor Heath Ledger, she endured an inordinate amount of press attention because of the eleven-year age difference between her and Ledger, whom she met on the set of *Ned Kelly.* Finally, she could view her years of rejection before achieving stardom from a more balanced perspective. "In retrospect," she theorized to Sischy in *Interview,* "all those disappointments were the perfect thing because if I'd gotten one of those parts I'd auditioned for, I would probably still be on some TV series today."

Sources

Allure, August 2003, pp. 168-171.
Back Stage West, November 20, 2003, p. 1.
Entertainment Weekly, October 19, 2001, p. 51; October 25, 2002, p. 54; February 6, 2004, p. 48; January 14, 2005, p. 62; March 25, 2005, p. 51.
InStyle, November 1, 2004, p. 406.
Interview, December 2003, p. 162.
New Yorker, November 24, 2003, p. 113; March 28, 2005, p. 82.
People, November 4, 2002, pp. 71-72.
Rolling Stone, November 8, 2001.
Time, October 21, 2002.
Variety, February 9, 2004, p. S68.
Vogue, August 2004, p. 136.
W, March 2004, p. 402.

—*Carol Brennan*

Jennifer Weiner

AP Images

Author and journalist

Born Jennifer Agnes Weiner, March 28, 1970, in De Ridder, LA; daughter of Lawrence (a psychiatrist) and Fran (a teacher) Weiner; married Adam Bonin (an attorney), October 27, 2001; children: Lucy Jane. *Education:* Princeton University, bachelor's degree (summa cum laude), 1991; trained in journalism at Poynter Institute for Media Studies.

Addresses: *E-mail*—jen@jenniferweiner.com. *Office*—c/o Atria Books, 1230 Avenue of the Americas, New York, NY 10020.

Career

Education reporter, *Centre Daily Times,* State College, PA, 1991-94; published short story "Tour of Duty" in *Seventeen,* 1992; published short story "Someone to Trust" in *Redbook,* 1993; features writer, *Lexington Herald-Leader,* Lexington, KY, 1994-95; *Philadelphia Inquirer,* Philadelphia, PA, columnist, 1994, features writer/columnist, 1995-2001, contributed weekly book column "Under Cover," 1999-2000, contributed weekly column to features section, 2000-01; hired as contributing editor and monthly columnist, *Mademoiselle* magazine, New York, NY, 1998; appeared on *Philly After Midnight* for several years; published first novel, *Good in Bed,* 2001; published and sold rights to *In Her Shoes,* 2002; *In Her Shoes* adapted into a film of the same name, 2005.

Awards: Academy of American Poets Prize, Princeton University, 1990.

Sidelights

After beginning her career as a journalist, primarily writing for the features sections of various newspapers, Jennifer Weiner came to international acclaim as the author of fiction targeted at women, so-called "chick lit." Beginning with her first book, *Good in Bed,* her four books have been published in 33 countries and sold more than five million copies. Explaining Weiner's appeal, Tracy Cochran of *Publishers Weekly* wrote, "In all of Weiner's novels, love and humor allow her characters to overcome the harshest turns, the hardest feelings…. She tells us that she loves to come up with the happiest possible endings for her characters, endings that are unabashedly about love and self-acceptance. It strikes us that this power she has to transform her experience by writing about it—this way of being relentless like a river in her dedication to her craft—is the secret to her happy ending."

Weiner was born in 1970 at an army base in Louisiana. Within two years, the family, which included her sister, Molly, moved to Simsbury, Connecticut. There, her two brothers were born, Jake and Joe. When Weiner was about 16 years old, her father, Lawrence, a psychiatrist, left the family and divorced his wife, Fran, a teacher. Weiner did not act as the family's father at all after the divorce, other than to provide financial support. Weiner completed her public school education by graduating from Simsbury High School.

In 1987, Weiner entered Princeton University. She majored in English and minored in women's studies, while taking many creative writing classes. She was also the co-founder of the Committee to Coeducate Eating Clubs. The goal of the committee was to force the two eating clubs on campus that were still male-only to allow women to join. As a senior, Weiner wrote a thesis about novels and film and how women who are pregnant are portrayed therein.

After graduating from Princeton in 1991, Weiner decided to get additional training to pursue a career in journalism. She went through a six-week course at the Poynter Institute for Media Studies in Florida. Weiner then began her journalism career in Pennsylvania at the *Centre Daily Times.* Weiner first worked as an education reporter, writing about a number of local school districts. She later moved to writing op-ed pieces about Generation X for the paper. These pieces eventually were distributed to other Knight-Ridder newspapers. Weiner also began writing features for *Centre Daily Times.* In addition, Weiner published short stories in magazines like *Seventeen* and *Redbook* in the early 1990s.

In 1994, Weiner moved to Lexington, Kentucky, to take a job as a features writer for the *Lexington Herald-Leader.* At the same time, she continued to write her Generation X columns, but they were now published by the *Philadelphia Inquirer* and distributed by the paper on a national basis. The following year, Weiner was hired by the *Inquirer* as a features writer. She then ceased to write her columns as part of her hiring. Weiner then spent several years writing profiles of famous people, in-depth stories on topics like drug abuse among teenagers, and covering various pop culture and political events.

While writing for the *Inquirer,* Weiner also branched out, writing for magazines, journals, and web sites on a freelance basis. In 1998, she became a contributing editor and column writer for *Mademoiselle* magazine. In addition, Weiner moved into television, regularly appearing on a local late night show, *Philly After Midnight.* The contributing editorship and television work lasted only a few years as the magazine was taken off the market and the show canceled.

In the meantime, Weiner's role at the *Inquirer* continued to evolve. Beginning in October of 1999, she wrote a column for the Sunday book section entitled "Under Cover." In the column, she focused on where real life and literature met. As her role at the *Inquirer* changed, she continued to work on what would become her first novel, *Good in Bed.* The novel was sold to Pocket Books in 2000 and published in 2001. Like all her novels, Weiner drew on a bit of experience in her life, though the first book was the closest to her immediate life situations.

In 2000, Weiner moved from the book section back to general features at the *Inquirer.* She wrote a column in the general interest area that appeared weekly for about a year. A year later, when *Good in Bed* was published, Weiner left the newspaper temporarily to promote the book. Receiving a number of positive reviews, the book became a best-seller in the United States, making the *New York Times* best-seller list. It also was a hit abroad, published in 15 countries.

Weiner had a goal when she wrote the book; she told Roberta O'Hara of Bookreporter.com, "I wanted to tell a Cinderella story where Cinderella gets her happy ending without dropping down to a size six because a book like that, first and foremost, would fill a gap in my own heart and my own library, and could maybe be some measure of comfort to other teenage girls who devour 'chick books' and come away feeling like they're the only ones who've ever weighed more than their boyfriends...." Cannie Shapiro, the heroine, is a plus-sized twentysomething entertainment columnist who graduated from Princeton. An ex-boyfriend writes about her body and their sex life in a national magazine, and Cannie also learns that she is pregnant with his child. The baby, a daughter named Joy, is born premature. Cannie also struggles with her weight, finding herself at her most miserable when she is at her thinnest. Despite these trials, Weiner gives Cannie a happy ending.

With the success of *Good in Bed,* and a deal already in place for her second book, Weiner left the *Inquirer* in December of 2001 to focus on writing fiction. The year 2002 proved even more fruitful for Weiner as a fiction author. Before the September publication of *In Her Shoes,* her brother, Jake, through his company BenderSpink, sold the book rights to Fox 2000, an arm of Twentieth Century-Fox. The book was as successful as *Good in Bed* in terms of sales, and was more of a critical success than the first.

The plot of *In Her Shoes* focuses on two sisters with next to nothing in common who meet a grandmother of which they were previously unaware. Rose Fuller, the older sister, is heavier, very sensible and an attorney who went to Princeton. Rose is having an affair with a partner in her law firm. Maggie, the younger sister, is thin, body image obsessed, suffering from low self-esteem, and always messing up. In the novel, Maggie betrays Rose's trust by having sex with the man she is interested in, severing their already shaky relationship. Complicating matters is their grandmother. Because their mother died when they were young, the sisters did not know their maternal grandmother, Ella. Over the course of the novel, Maggie learns she is smart and more than just a thin body, while Rose learns that she can find happiness in simpler things, like walking dogs and interacting with people on the street. Critics noted how well Weiner drew the older characters as well as the younger ones.

After the *In Her Shoes* book tour, Weiner returned home to write her next novel and deal with her own pregnancy. She had married an attorney named Adam Bonin in 2001 and the couple had their first child in 2003, a daughter named Lucy Jane. While Weiner was writing and preparing for parenthood, her brother also sold the rights to her first novel to HBO for a television series. In 2004, Weiner's next novel, *Little Earthquakes*, was published. It sold more than her previous two books and also received good reviews. The book was optioned by Universal for film.

In *Little Earthquakes*, Weiner examines the lives of four young mothers by telling part of the story from their point of view. Three are friends who meet in a prenatal yoga class: Becky, a plus sized restaurateur; Kelly, who overcame a difficult childhood to become an overachiever; and Ayinde, an African-American woman married to a National Basketball Association player. Lia, the fourth woman, is an actress of some acclaim whose son dies of sudden infant death syndrome. Lia's life becomes difficult after his death, and she follows Becky and her baby around. Some of the four have difficult mother-in-laws, which also bonds them together. Critics generally responded positively to the novel. Reviewing the book, Deborah Sussman Susser of the *Washington Post* had reservations, but wrote, "After I finished *Little Earthquakes*, I found myself missing the characters.... It may not be as realistic as literary worlds go, but it is reassuring in its warmth and predictability. And judging by the success of chick lit generally and Weiner's books specifically, a lot of us out there are willing—even eager—to suspend our disbelief long enough to enter it."

For Weiner's next book, she moved away from a strictly chick lit story to one that included a murder mystery. In *Goodnight Nobody*, the sleuth is a mother, Kate Klein, who has three children in nursery school. Klein is not happy in her personal life. She was working as a pop culture journalist for a Manhattan-based publication when her husband moved the family to the suburbs of Connecticut. Now a stay-at-home mom, Klein does not fit into the culture of the suburbs and is looking for something to do. She is drawn into her case by finding a female neighbor dead on her kitchen floor. Klein works on solving the crime during the few hours that her children are in school. Barbara Sullivan of *Buffalo News* found the novel full of unexpected depth. She wrote, "*Goodnight Nobody* has all the components of a ripping murder mystery of the Sue Grafton/Janet Evanovich variety.... But the novel also manages to take a long, hard insightful look at the relationships between mothers and their children, working moms and stay-at-home moms and what it means to be a good parent in the 21st century."

In 2005, Weiner's profile was raised even further when the film based on *In Her Shoes* was released. Adapted for the screen by Susannah Grant and directed by Curtis Hanson, the film starred Toni Collette and Cameron Diaz as the sisters and Shirley MacLaine as the grandmother. Weiner had a cameo in the film, playing a smiling woman in the Italian market in a scene shot in Philadelphia. She also visited the set several times. Of her success as an author, Weiner told Lauren Beckham Falcone of the *Boston Herald*, "Sometimes I honestly think I am on *Candid Camera*. Like everything that's happened is really a joke. It's overwhelming and more than I could have ever dreamed of."

Selected writings

Good in Bed, Pocket Books (New York City), 2001.
In Her Shoes, Atria Books (New York City), 2002.
Little Earthquakes, Atria Books, 2004.
Goodnight Nobody, Atria Books, 2005.

Sources

Periodicals

Boston Herald, July 13, 2005, p. 4.
Buffalo News (Buffalo, NY), October 9, 2002, p. D1; October 2, 2005, p. G7.
Chicago Sun-Times, November 17, 2002, p. 9.
Entertainment Weekly, September 17, 2004, pp. 38-39.
Guardian (London, England), December 28, 2002, p. 19.
Milwaukee Journal Sentinel (Milwaukee, WI), October 20, 2005, p. B10.
Newsday, September 18, 2005, p. C33.
People, September 26, 2005, pp. 125-27.
Publishers Weekly, September 13, 2004, p. 50; June 13, 2005, p. 6; September 26, 2005, p. 10.
San Francisco Chronicle, October 30, 2005, p. D1.

Toronto Sun, June 17, 2001, p. S20.
Washington Post, September 15, 2004, p. C9.

Online

"Author Profile: Jennifer Weiner," Bookreporter. com, http://www.bookreporter.com/authors/ au-weiner-jennifer.asp (January 24, 2006).

"Jennifer Weiner," Internet Movie Database, http:// www.imdb.com/name/nm1497265/ (January 24, 2006).

Jennifer Weiner Website, http://www.jennifer weiner.com/about.htm (January 24, 2006).

—*A. Petruso*

Rachel Weisz

© Michael Crabtree/Reuters/Corbis

Actress

Born March 7, 1971, in London, England; daughter of Georg (an inventor) and Edith (a psychoanalyst) Weisz; children: a son (with Darren Aronofsky, a director). *Education:* Earned degree from Cambridge University, c. 1993.

Addresses: *Agent*—Creative Artists Agency, 9830 Wilshire Blvd., Beverly Hills, CA 90212. *Home*—New York, NY, and London, England.

Career

Actress in films, including: *Death Machine,* 1995; *Chain Reaction,* 1996; *Stealing Beauty,* 1996; *Swept from the Sea,* 1997; *Bent,* 1997; *The Land Girls,* 1998; *The Mummy,* 1999; *Sunshine,* 1999; *Beautiful Creatures,* 2001; *Enemy at the Gates,* 2001; *The Mummy Returns,* 2001; *About a Boy,* 2002; *Confidence,* 2003; *The Shape of Things* (also producer), 2003; *Runaway Jury,* 2003; *Envy,* 2004; *Constantine,* 2005; *The Constant Gardener,* 2005; *The Fountain,* 2006; *The Lady from Shanghai,* 2006. Television appearances include: *Inspector Morse,* 1993; *Scarlet and Black* (movie), 1993; *Dirty Something* (movie), 1993; *White Goods* (movie), 1994; *Seventeen* (movie), 1994; *My Summer with Des* (movie) 1998. Stage appearances include: *The Year of the Family,* Finborough Theatre, London, England, 1994; *Design for Living,* Gielgud Theatre, London, 1994-95; *Suddenly Last Summer,* Comedy Theatre, London, 1999; *The Shape of Things,* Almeida Theatre, London, 2001; *The Shape of Things,* Promenade Theatre, New York, NY, 2001.

Awards: Most Promising Newcomer, London Critics' Circle, 1995; Golden Globe for best performance by an actress in a supporting role in a motion picture, Hollywood Foreign Press Association, for *The Constant Gardener,* 2006; Academy Award for best performance by an actress in a supporting role, Academy of Motion Picture Arts and Sciences, for *The Constant Gardener,* 2006; Screen Actors Guild Award for outstanding performance by a female actor in a supporting role, for *The Constant Gardener,* 2006.

Sidelights

British screen siren Rachel Weisz won her first Academy Award in 2006 for her role in *The Constant Gardener,* the well-received adaptation of the John le Carré novel. After just a decade in the business, she was one of the most sought-after actresses on both sides of the Atlantic, appearing in such works as *The Mummy, About a Boy, Enemy at the Gates,* and *Runaway Jury.* With homes in Manhattan and the Primrose Hill section of London, Weisz avoids Los Angeles, though she once attempted to settle there when her career was just beginning. "I couldn't make a life there," she admitted to Sean O'Hagan in London's *Observer* newspaper. "You're in a car all the time, and there are no seasons."

Weisz, whose surname is pronounced "vice," was born on March 7, 1971, in London. Both of her parents had come to England from elsewhere on the

Continent—her father, Georg, was a Hungarian-born inventor, and her psychoanalyst mother, Edith, was originally from Austria. Both were from Jewish families that had fled the Nazi German threat before World War II. In England, Weisz's father rose to prominence as a developer of a self-contained respirator unit and also conceived a detector for deadly landmines. The family lived in the ritzy Hampstead area of north London, home to a long list of illustrious residents, from Charles Dickens to Bjork, and Weisz was sent to the prestigious St. Paul's Girls' School in west London, where one of her classmates was another future film star, Emily Mortimer (*Scream 3, Match Point*).

Weisz pursued a career as a catalog model in her teens. That led to her discovery by a talent scout, who offered her a part in a planned Richard Gere film, *King David.* Weisz's parents disagreed on whether she should take the role, and she herself was ambivalent about it. "I didn't want to do anything that would make me different, make people at school hate me," she told Harriet Lane in an interview with the London newspaper the *Observer.* In the end, she declined the offer.

Weisz's parents divorced when she was 16, and she struggled to finish her secondary-school obligations. When she failed her exit exams, she nearly missed her chance at a college education, but a sympathetic teacher convinced administrators at Trinity Hall College, part of Cambridge University, to let her enroll anyway but on a form of academic probation. She did well once there, studying toward a degree in English, and began performing in student theater productions. With a few friends she took a train trip through Eastern Europe on one of their breaks, visiting its major cities to attend the avant-garde theater performances that were a staple of the Communist-era cultural life in the Eastern bloc. Back in Cambridge, Weisz and her cohorts founded a theater company they named Talking Tongues.

Weisz's first brush with professional success came when an improv piece her group staged, *Slight Possession,* won an award at the Edinburgh Festival in Scotland. She recalled her student-thespian days fondly many years later, telling Jasper Rees in the *Independent on Sunday* that the period was "probably the most exciting time I can ever remember. It was all ours, and that's never been repeated. We did some of the best work I've ever done, which probably about 100 people ever saw."

Not surprisingly, Weisz's parents were uneasy with her extracurricular drama activities, and had expected her to pursue a career in law. "They weren't skeptical," she explained to O'Hagan in another *Observer* interview. "They just thought I was pretty crap. They saw me in my first play and were justifiably underwhelmed." She graduated from Trinity Hall after completing her dissertation on the ghost stories of Henry James, and decided against drama school, unlike some of her Cambridge theater friends. Hoping to break into the business right away, "I did some TV, so I completely sold out," she told Rees in the *Independent on Sunday.* "All my friends at Cambridge just thought I was the lowest of the low."

Weisz did manage to land one stage role, in a 1994 drama called *The Year of the Family* at London's Finborough Theatre, but desperately hoped to win a part in an upcoming production of a Noel Coward play, *Design for Living,* at the Gielgud Theatre. Finally, the well-known director agreed to see her, but warned her agent ahead of time that she would not be cast; she was anyway, as Gilda, one of the leads in the racy farce, and the role won her the Most Promising Newcomer of 1995 award from the London Critics' Circle.

Despite her seemingly effortless early success, Weisz felt adrift, she told Suzie Mackenzie in the *Guardian.* "Not suicidal, never that, but days when I couldn't get out of bed that kind of thing." Her psychoanalyst mother had warned her against delving into therapy, but Weisz disobeyed and spent five years on the couch. "It was the hardest thing I've ever done," she said in the same interview, but worthwhile in the end. "At last I was able to get on with my life."

Weisz made her film debut in a little-seen action thriller called *Death Machine* in 1995, and went on to win a lead role alongside Keanu Reeves in *Chain Reaction* the following year. She and Reeves played beleaguered scientists on the run from evil conspirators in the film, which earned largely negative reviews—though *New York Times* critic Janet Maslin did notice that "Weisz makes a strong sidekick for Mr. Reeves' character, even if the film doesn't give her much to do."

Weisz fared somewhat better with her third film, *Stealing Beauty,* a 1996 Bernardo Bertolucci tale of American and British expatriates in Tuscany. The cast included Jeremy Irons and Liv Tyler, and Weisz stole more than one scene as a vixenish daughter of the villa. Rees, writing in the *Independent on Sunday,* asserted that Weisz's Miranda "embodied a certain type of Englishwoman: bored, laconic, plummy, fantastically at ease with herself, jaded with disdain for the foreign surroundings in which she baked her largely naked body."

Juicier film parts were offered to Weisz after that: she was cast in a nineteenth-century romance alongside Vincent Perez in *Swept from the Sea,* and then appeared in *The Land Girls* in 1998, a World War II-era drama about a trio of women serving Britain in uniform. Her first experience with Hollywood came when she was cast in the hit 1999 flick *The Mummy* opposite Brendan Fraser. Weisz liked the role of Evelyn, the earnest librarian, she told Lane in the *Observer* interview. "Evelyn's a good character," she said. "She's not just the token girl: she has a good, meaty, feisty role, and I thought the idea of a librarian on an adventure was funny."

Weisz's dark hair, porcelain skin, and vintage-style beauty seemed to make her a natural choice for period films, especially those with a Central European flavor. She appeared with Ralph Fiennes in the Hungarian family saga *Sunshine* in 1999, and was cast as a Russian adventuress alongside Jude Law in the 2001 siege-of-Stalingrad story *Enemy at the Gates.* She was reportedly rejected, however, for the lead in *Bridget Jones's Diary,* because the film's producers considered her too attractive to play the title role convincingly.

Weisz reprised her Evelyn role for *The Mummy Returns* in 2001, and next appeared as a single mother who so captivates Hugh Grant's character in *About a Boy* that he pretends to be single parent, too. Interestingly, one of the film's two directors, Chris Weitz, had also been at Trinity Hall when Weisz was there. Because their surnames were similar, he once received a piece of mail in his slot that had been meant for her, which he found absolutely thrilling, for Weisz was known as the "Trinity Hall heartbreaker," according to the *Sunday Times'* Jeff Dawson.

After 2003's *Confidence,* in which she starred alongside Ed Burns and Dustin Hoffman, Weisz appeared in the film version of playwright Neil LaBute's *The Shape of Things.* Two years earlier, she had appeared in both the London and New York stage productions in the lead, as an American art student who remakes a somewhat disheveled, introverted young man into a more appealing mate. The story was marked by LaBute's razor-sharp dialogue delivered by characters whose amorality is the plot's centerpiece. Weisz also served as one of the film's producers, which was one of the reasons, she told *Sunday Times* journalist David Eimer, that she accepted such a wide range of film roles. "If you do a big movie like *The Mummy* and it's successful, you can help finance small movies that are more your thing," she explained. "They call them 'passion projects' in America, which sounds odd, but it makes sense."

Weisz appeared in *Runaway Jury,* the 2003 adaptation of the John Grisham novel, with John Cusack and Gene Hackman, before tackling another comedy, 2004's *Envy,* that teamed her with Jack Black and Ben Stiller. Revlon recruited her to appear in its celebrity-laden ad campaigns, which put her on a roster that included such Hollywood heavyweights as Halle Berry and Julianne Moore, and in 2005 she re-connected with Reeves for the superhero action flick *Constantine.* But it was her role in another film that year that earned Weisz her first Academy Award: she was cast as the mysterious and maddening Tessa Quayle in *The Constant Gardener,* based on espionage-thriller author John le Carré's novel of the same name. The plot centers around her murder, and the quest her diplomat husband Justin (Ralph Fiennes) embarks upon to ferret out the truth. Their unlikely romance is told in flashback, as is Tessa's involvement in unmasking nefarious pharmaceutical-company misdeeds in Kenya.

The Constant Gardener won laudatory reviews as well as some industry honors. "Weisz makes it easy to believe Tessa's fearlessness," declared *Entertainment Weekly*'s Lisa Schwarzbaum. "She's as mobile, open-faced, and sexually alive as Fiennes is shuttered, and the two make a potent couple." Her Oscar win was preceded by a Golden Globe award, each in the best actress in a supporting role category, and Weisz accepted her Academy Award visibly pregnant, a development she had been forced to announce just a few weeks earlier as a guest on *The Tonight Show with Jay Leno.* She had been romantically involved with director Darren Aronofsky (*Requiem for a Dream*), since 2001, and the two were engaged to be married. Weisz gave birth to their son on May 31, 2006.

In 2006, Aronofsky was busy finishing work on *The Fountain,* a science-fiction thriller he directed that starred Weisz and Hugh Jackman. The three-part epic was set in sixteenth-century Spain, the present, and the future, and it was the first time Weisz had worked with her fiancé. Journalists often asked her if any tensions arose from being forced to combine their personal and professional lives, but Weisz ventured only that it was "great to watch someone at work," she told Eimer, the *Sunday Times* interviewer. "I don't know if he feels the same. I guess he does. I don't get any special treatment."

Sources

Entertainment Weekly, September 2, 2005, p. 58; September 16, 2005, pp. 38-40.
Guardian (London, England), March 22, 1999, p. 4; August 1, 2003, p. 6.

Independent on Sunday (London, England), March 14, 1999, p. 20.

New York Times, August 2, 1996.

Observer (London, England), June 13, 1999, p. 6; October 16, 2005, p. 16.

Sunday Times (London, England), July 27, 2003, p. 4; March 13, 2005, p. 4.

Times (London, England), February 4, 1995, p. 5.

—*Carol Brennan*

Seth Wescott

Getty Images for Adidas

Snowboard cross athlete

Born June 28, 1976, in Durham, NC; son of Jim Wescott (a college professor and coach) and Margaret Gould-Wescott (a college professor). *Education:* Attended Western State College, Gunnison, CO.

Addresses: *Contact*—U.S. Olympic Committee, One Olympic Pl., Colorado Springs, CO 80909.

Career

Began cross-country skiing at the age of three; began alpine skiing at the age of eight; began snowboarding at the age of ten; competed in alpine skiing and snowboarding events, 1986-89; focused solely on snowboarding events, beginning in 1989; focused on halfpipe events, 1996-97; began competing in snowboard cross (SBX) events, 1997; U.S. national champion in SBX, 2000-03; won silver in SBX at the Winter X Games, 2002; was third overall in World Tour rankings for SBX, 2002; ceased to compete in halfpipe after finishing tenth, 2003; won silver in SBX at the World Championships, 2003; won silver in SBX at the Winter X Games, 2004; finished second in SBX at the World Cup, 2004; finished second in SBX at the Winter X Games, 2005; won gold in SBX at the World Championships, 2005; won gold medal in SBX at Winter Olympic Games, 2006.

Sidelights

Snowboard athlete Seth Wescott moved from competing in halfpipe to the emerging sport of snowboard cross (SBX; also known in the United States as boardercross) in the late 1990s. He soon became the dominant men's SBX racer in the world, primarily competing in big races and skipping most World Cup events. After lobbying to have SBX included in the Olympics, Wescott won the gold medal in dramatic fashion at the 2006 games in Turin, Italy.

Born in 1976 in Durham, North Carolina, he is the son of Jim Westcott, and his wife, Margaret Gould-Wescott. At the time, his father was a track and field coach at North Carolina State University, while his mother was a modern dance college professor. When Wescott was two years old, his parents moved the family, which included his sister, Sarah, to their home state of Maine. Wescott was raised in Farmington, Maine, while his parents were professors at nearby colleges.

Athletics were a part of Wescott's life from an early age. He started cross-country skiing when he was three years old, playing soccer when he was six, and alpine skiing when he was eight. When he was ten years old, Westcott began snowboarding. Beginning in 1986, he competed in both alpine skiing and snowboarding events for three years. In 1989, Wescott gave up alpine skiing to focus on snowboarding, competing primarily on the halfpipe. He also played soccer and was a member of the track and field team, competing in sprints and jumps, throughout high school. Wescott graduated from the Carrabassett Valley Academy in Maine, where many winter athletes are students and their sports are part of the school's curriculum. Wescott then attended Western State College in Colorado for a year and a half.

In the mid- to late 1990s, Wescott focused on competing in snowboarding events. From 1996 to 1997, he primarily competed in men's halfpipe. Beginning in 1997, however, Wescott's athletic focus began to slowly change. SBX was emerging as a recognized snowboarding sport, and he began competing in SBX events as well, though he also competed in the halfpipe through 2003. What attracted Wescott to SBX was the fact that victories were clear-cut, unlike the halfpipe, which is a judged event. In his bio on NBCOlympics.com, Wescott was quoted as saying, "I like snowboard cross because I get rewarded for what I do."

In SBX competitions, four competitors break out of a gate and ride snowboards down a 3,000-foot course (similar to a downhill skiing course or motocross track course). They race over jumps and turns to the finish. SBX races are fast and the potential for collision is great, and crashes occur regularly. During the elimination heats, the four racers are primarily competing against the clock to get the field to 32. After that point, the four racers are competing against each other, with the winner of each race moving on to the next round until the final four remain and someone wins the final race.

As Wescott embraced SBX, he still took halfpipe seriously. He almost made the 1998 U.S. Olympic team in the halfpipe. He told Jenn Menendez of the *Portland Press Herald*, "In my eyes I did the best and most technical run ever (trying to make the 1998 team), and for whatever reason the judges didn't let me advance. I got frustrated with the halfpipe side of things." Wescott soon specialized in SBX over such frustrations, though he again tried to make the U.S. Olympic team in 2002 in halfpipe. He believed that judging is what ultimately prevented him from making the team.

Wescott began winning SBX events in the early 2000s. Between 2000 and 2003, he was the U.S. national champion in SBX. In 2001, Wescott tore his ACL (anterior cruciate ligament) during a World Cup competition in Sapporo, Japan, on a jump, but continued to compete after recovering. He won silver in SBX in 2002 at the Winter X Games. At the end of the year, Wescott was third overall in World Tour rankings for SBX.

In 2003, Wescott began training for SBX in a stimulating new way: big mountain riding in Alaska. He would ride on a helicopter, strap on his snowboard, and be dropped on a mountain that had not been ridden before. Wescott would descend down the mountain along whatever terrain he would find, including steep faces. One drop in 2003 resulted in an avalanche which moved him 750 feet. Wescott found big mountain riding exhilarating and believed the challenges he faced helped him compete in SBX better. That year, Wescott won silver in SBX at the World Championships. He finished tenth in the halfpipe in the same competition. This event marked his last competition in halfpipe. In 2004, Wescott won silver in SBX at the Winter X Games and finished second at World Cup. One victory in 2005 was particularly difficult. After finishing second in SBX at the Winter X Games, he hurt his left knee and suffered a severe cut in his right leg a week before the World Championships. Wescott still competed and though the binding on his boots became loose in the semifinals just as he left the gate, he was able to fix it while still moving and won. Wescott then won gold in SBX at the World Championships in 2005.

In addition to competing and winning SBX events, Wescott spent much of his time lobbying for the sport on an international level. He tried to develop interest in SBX in the United States and Europe by pushing the sport in the press at every opportunity. Wescott also worked to get it included in the Winter Olympics, a goal reached when the Olympic Committee agreed to include it in the 2006 games. Wescott had some reservations about how good the Olympic course would be in Turin, Italy, and took the initiative to make guidelines for the sport by becoming SBX's World Cup tour overseer for the International Federation of Skiing.

Wescott had a life outside of SBX as well. He planned on building a house on 21 acres he owned in Maine's Carrabassett Valley. In 2005, he and some friends bought a restaurant located at the base of Sugarloaf Mountain, The Rack. Wescott also planned on completing his college degree some day, probably in journalism.

Early in 2006, Wescott was named to the U.S. snowboarding team for the Winter Olympics and competed in the first-ever SBX event at the Olympics. His gold medal victory in SBX was dramatic. Wescott made the finals, but was losing to Radoslav Zidek in the medal run when Wescott passed him on a banked turn. Wescott told Eddie Pells of the *Buffalo News*, "I just knew if I was patient and confident that I'd reach the part of the course that I could work a little better, catch the speed on him. Then coming into that one turn, I drove the inside line on him like clockwork. That's how it worked out." Wescott won the race. Of his victory, he told Fran Blinebury of the *Houston Chronicle,* "This allows me to achieve a goal that I've been pretty single-mindedly focused on for the last several years. It's the end of a long road, and it fulfills a dream."

Sources

Periodicals

Atlanta Journal-Constitution, February 17, 2006, p. E7.

Boston Globe, February 6, 2003, p. E8; February 17, 2006, p. D1.

Buffalo News (Buffalo, NY), February 16, 2006, p. D1.

Houston Chronicle, February 17, 2006, p. 1.

Los Angeles Times, February 16, 2006, p. S4.

Newsweek, December 26, 2005, p. 84.

Portland Press Herald (Portland, ME), January 23, 2005, p. D3; January 29, 2006, p. D1.

Times (London, England), February 17, 2006, p. 94.

Online

"Seth Wescott/A Team—Snowboardcross," U.S. Snowboard Team, http://www.usssnowboarding.org/team_details_print.php?bio_id=34 (May 1, 2006).

"Seth Wescott," NBCOlympics.com, http://www.nbcolympics.com/athletes/5058608/detail.html?qs=;t=11;tab=Bio (May 1, 2006).

"Seth Wescott," United States Olympic Committee, http://www.usoc.org/26_38187.htm (May 1, 2006).

—A. Petruso

Kanye West

© Steve Azzara/Corbis

Rap musician and record producer

Born Kayne Omari West, June 8, 1977; son of Ray (a marriage counselor) and Donda (a professor) West. *Education:* Attended The American Academy of Art and Chicago State University.

Addresses: *Record company*—Roc-A-Fella Records, 825 Eighth Ave., New York, NY 10019. *Website*—http://www.kanyewest.com.

Career

Producer for Chicago rappers; began producing for national hip-hop acts by contributing to Jermaine Dupri's album *Life In 1472*, 1998; produced five tracks on Jay-Z's album *The Blueprint*, 2001; produced number-one hits "Stand Up" by Ludacris and "You Don't Know My Name" by Alicia Keys, 2004; released *The College Dropout*, 2004; released *Late Registration*, 2005.

Awards: Grammy Award for best rap album, Recording Academy, for *The College Dropout*, 2005; Grammy Award for best rap song, Recording Academy, for "Jesus Walks," 2005; Grammy Award for best R&B song, Recording Academy, for "You Don't Know My Name," 2005; BET Award for best male hip-hop artist, 2005; BET Award for video of the Year, 2005; MTV Video Music Award for best male video, for "Jesus Walks," 2005.

Sidelights

Kanye West began his career in music as a producer for top hip-hop artists such as Jay-Z, but he wanted more: he wanted to rap, too. Though his middle-class background and preppy dress made him seem ill-fitted for a hip-hop scene dominated by gangsta personalities, West's talent and determination led to his massive success. His debut album, *The College Dropout*, rewrote the rules of hip-hop, reviving socially conscious lyrics and mixing them with cutting-edge commercial party beats. By the time he released his second album, *Late Registration*, in August of 2005, West had become one of hip-hop's biggest stars.

West was born on June 8, 1977, to Ray, a former Black Panther who went on to become an award-winning photographer and then a marriage counselor, and Donda, an English professor. (His name, pronounced kahn-yay, means "the only one" in Swahili.) His parents divorced when he was three years old; he mostly lived with his mother, but often spent summers with his father. He lived in China for a year at the age of ten while his mother was teaching English at a university there; he would make money entertaining people by break dancing on the streets. His father taught him to be race-conscious, while his mother helped him develop a wide vocabulary through word games. "I was taught to think on my own," he told Jim Farber of the *New York Daily News*. "That's what a lot of black kids don't get."

In high school, West became friends with producer No I.D., who was working with the rapper Common before he became a star. Inspired, West got a sampling keyboard at 15, and spent a lot of time rapping and beatmaking in his bedroom. He attended Chicago's The American Academy of Art for a year on a scholarship, then transferred to Chicago State University to pursue a degree in English. But he dropped out to pursue a career in music, thwarting his mother's hopes that he would earn several degrees. "It was drummed into my head that college is the ticket to a good life," Donda West told the *Chicago Tribune*'s Greg Kot. "but some career goals don't require college. For Kanye to make an album called *College Dropout*, it was more about having the guts to embrace who you are, rather than following the path society has carved out for you. And that's what Kanye did."

Instead, West started producing songs for Chicago rappers. In 1998, he contributed to Atlanta producer and recording star Jermaine Dupri's album *Life in 1472*. He moved from Chicago to Newark, New Jersey, and then to Hoboken in that same state, close to New York City. His big breakthrough came when he composed five songs on Jay-Z's 2001 album *The Blueprint*. The songs established a key part of West's production style: he sampled classic songs and sped them up so they turned high-pitched. Usually the songs were soul music, such as the Jackson 5 and the Temptations, though he also sampled '60s rockers The Doors. West has admitted getting the idea from The RZA of the Wu-Tang Clan, but at a time when sampling had fallen out of fashion in hip-hop, it was still unusual enough to impress. He began working with other top hip-hop artists on Jay-Z's Roc-A-Fella label. Since then, West has produced songs for more than 40 artists, including Scarface, Foxy Brown, and DMX.

West was convinced he could rap as well as produce. He started working on his own album in 2001. But when he first asked Roc-A-Fella executives to let him record his own hip-hop album, they were not receptive, because he did not have the tough background or image that had become almost required of hip-hop stars. "Kanye wore a pink shirt with the collar sticking up and Gucci loafers," Damon Dash, then-CEO of Roc-A-Fella, told Josh Tyrangiel of *Time*. "We all grew up street guys who had to do whatever we had to do to get by," Jay-Z told Tyrangiel. "Then there's Kanye, who to my knowledge has never hustled a day in his life. I didn't see how it could work."

"I was mad because I was not being taken seriously as a rapper for a long time," West told Kot of the *Chicago Tribune*. "Whether it was because I didn't have a larger-than-life persona, or I was perceived as the guy who made beats, I was disrespected as a rapper." A near-tragedy ended up giving West the creative inspiration for his project. He fell asleep at the wheel of a car in Los Angeles in October of 2002 and got in a car accident that nearly killed him. He called Roc-A-Fella's CEO from the hospital, asked for a drum machine, and created the song "Through the Wire" about his accident. He recorded the mumbled vocals three weeks after the crash, while his jaw was wired shut. The song was built on a sample from Chaka Khan's "Through the Fire." It helped convince Roc-A-Fella to let him record an album. West used the song as his calling card, passing it around on mix tapes he created to show he could rap as well as produce. "Death is the best thing that can ever happen to a rapper," West quipped to Tyrangiel in *Time*. "Almost dying isn't bad either."

While working on his album, West also produced a string of hits. His triumph came in early 2004. First, two songs he produced hit number one: "Stand Up" by Ludacris and "You Don't Know My Name" by Alicia Keys. Others, including "Slow Jamz," a collaboration with Chicago rapper Twista, and Jay-Z's "Encore," also became hit singles. Then, West's album *The College Dropout* appeared and quickly became both a critical and commercial success. It sold 440,000 copies in its first week of release, and almost three million within a year and a half. "Through the Wire" became a top-rated video on MTV and MTV2.

Critics and peers fixated on West's mix of popular party music with intelligent, socially aware lyrics. Admirers, including actor/singer Jamie Foxx (who appears on "Slow Jamz") and Darryl McDaniels of the classic rap group Run-D.M.C., declared that *The College Dropout* had restored their faith in hip-hop. The *New York Daily News'* Farber called the album "one of the most informed and political rap records since the heyday of Public Enemy and the Jungle Brothers." The song "All Falls Down" questioned materialism in the black community, while "Jesus Walks," which *Village Voice* critic Hua Hsu called "a desperate masterpiece," stunned listeners with its redemptive message embracing even drug dealers, its ambivalence ("I wanna talk to God but I'm afraid 'cause we ain't spoke in so long," West raps), and its explicit defiance of the conventional wisdom that a song about God would not get played on commercial radio.

West eagerly admitted he was mixing two sides of hip-hop: the commercial side, dominated by gangsta rap, and politically aware rappers (who were less numerous and popular at the time than in early hip-hop). "My whole theory of music is message and melody," West told Neil Drumming of *Entertainment Weekly*. While other political artists are "like cod-liver oil," West said, he promised "cough medicine mixed with Kool-Aid." The *New York Daily News'* Farber noted a lack of "gangsta clichés" in West's work. "I never killed anybody, so I don't rap about it," he told Farber. "Every song [of mine] is an inspirational song, to make you feel good." To *Spin's* Chris Ryan, he explained, "I'm one of the only rappers who has both his parents and all his grandparents still alive. My father was a Black Panther. My grandparents were involved in civil-rights marches. So I have a responsibility to reflect them."

Kelefa Sanneh of the *New York Times* called *The College Dropout* "2004's first great hip-hop album" and "a concept album about quitting school, a playful collection of party songs, and a 76-minute orgy of nose-thumbing." Sanneh wrote that West "taunts everyone who didn't believe in him: teachers, record executives, police officers, even his former boss at the Gap."

West's huge ego, which gave him the confidence to defy hip-hop stereotypes and record the album, became a huge part of his public personality. "I do music for the sake of showing off," he told Ryan of *Spin,* explaining that he shows off through music like some people flaunt their cars. He complained to interviewers about one review that gave his album a grade of B+. "My CD is so good, people will have to buy second and third copies because other people will be stealing them," he bragged to the *New York Daily News'* Farber. Sometimes, West's arrogance has alienated people, especially after he walked out of the American Music Awards, furious that he lost the award for Best New Artist to country star Gretchen Wilson.

In early 2005, West won three Grammy awards: Best Rap Album for *The College Dropout*, Best Rap Song for "Jesus Walks," and Best R&B Song for co-writing Alicia Keys' "You Don't Know My Name." After *Dropout's* success, West started his own record label called Getting Out Our Dreams (G.O.O.D.), a fashion line named Pastel Clothing, and the Kanye West Foundation, which promotes music education in schools.

West reportedly spent $2 million putting his second album together, breaking his production budget. He surprised many by working with producer Jon Brion, whose previous work had been mostly with alternative singer-songwriters such as Fiona Apple and Aimee Mann. West aimed to have more musicianship on the new album: 40-piece string sets and 30-piece horn sections grace some tracks. Guests on the album included Jay-Z, Foxx, R&B singer Brandy, Adam Levine of the band Maroon 5, and the rapper Nas.

The album, *Late Registration,* was released in late August of 2005. Distributors shipped 1.6 million copies of it to stores for its release week. It was greeted with rave reviews. *Rolling Stone's* Rob Sheffield gave it five stars, declaring it "an undeniable triumph, packed front to back, so expansive it makes the debut sound like a rough draft." *Time* dubbed him "the smartest man in pop music" on its cover.

On the album, the song "Gone" is built on an Otis Redding sample and a simple piano melody. The track "Diamonds From Sierra Leone," built on a sample of Shirley Bassey's theme song from the James Bond film *Diamonds Are Forever,* protests the sale of "blood diamonds" that profit from conflicts in Africa. "Gold Digger" encourages women to stick with working-class men who are mopping floors and serving French fries. His duet with Nas, "We Major," was considered a highlight, both for the interplay between the two rappers and an exciting moment where the music fades and West starts it up again, convinced the song is so good, it can go on past seven minutes.

Again, music writers noticed a lot of contrast and mixed inspiration in West's work, and he freely admitted it. "I'm pretty calculating," he told Tyrangiel in *Time,* while standing in a church in Prague, where he was filming the "Diamonds From Sierra Leone" video. "I take stuff that I know appeals to people's bad sides and match it up with stuff that appeals to their good sides." He mentioned lyrics in "Diamonds From Sierra Leone" about a woman that he admitted were "crass," then the lyrics that follow it, about his father baptizing him. "He's trying to change this genre, and in order to do that he's got to get people to listen to his music," Run-D.M.C.'s McDaniels told *Time's* Tyrangiel. "They've gotten so used to hardness, to stupidity, that if he has to engage in a little of that to be relevant, so be it."

West also displayed his political passions with two benefit performances in the summer of 2005. First, he performed at the Live 8 concert, meant to raise awareness about poverty and debt in the Third World. Then, after Hurricane Katrina hit the Gulf Coast of the United States in late August, West joined the benefit A Concert For Hurricane Relief. It was broadcast on NBC-TV four days after the storm, when the country was still watching terrifying news footage of evacuees stranded and even dying in downtown New Orleans. West criticized the federal government's response to the crisis in remarks carried live on national television. "George Bush doesn't care about black people," he charged, according to the Associated Press, adding that the country is set up "to help the poor, the black people, the less well-off as slow as possible."

As fall of 2005 arrived, critics were writing that West seemed to be trying to personally embody pop music. Clearly eager to break more stereotypes and musical boundaries, West announced he planned to go on tour with rock band U2 and possibly also Coldplay.

Selected discography

The College Dropout, Roc-A-Fella/Island Def Jam Records, 2004.
Late Registration, Roc-A-Fella/Island Def Jam Records, 2005.

Sources

Periodicals

Associated Press, September 3, 2005.
Chicago Tribune, February 11, 2004.
Detroit Free Press, August 28, 2005, p. 2E.
Entertainment Weekly, February 27, 2004, pp. 64-65.
New York Daily News, January 27, 2004.
New York Times, February 9, 2004.
Rolling Stone, September 8, 2005, pp. 109-10.
Spin, February 9, 2004.
Time, August 29, 2005, pp. 54-61.
Village Voice, April 7, 2004.

Online

"Kanye West, Biography," *All Music Guide,* http://www.allmusic.com/cg/amg.dll?p=amg&uid=MIW040509052203&sql=11:0mz1z 81a1yv6~T1 (August 21, 2005).
"Roc-A-Fella Records Artist Kanye West," Roc-A-Fella Records, http://www.rocafella.com/Artist.aspx?v=bio&key=7 (August 21, 2005).

—*Erick Trickey*

Joss Whedon

Wolfgang Langenstrassen/dpa/Landov

Scriptwriter, television producer, and feature film director

Born Joseph Hill Whedon, June 23, 1964, in New York, NY; son of Tom Whedon (a television scriptwriter) and Lee Stearns (a teacher); married Kai Cole (an architect), late 1980s; children: two. *Education:* Wesleyan University, Connecticut, film studies degree, 1987.

Addresses: *Home*—Los Angeles, CA. *Production company*—Mutant Enemy Productions, PO Box 900, Beverly Hills, CA 90213.

Career

Scriptwriter for television, including: *Roseanne*, ABC, 1989; *Parenthood*, NBC, 1990. Screenwriter for films, including: *Buffy the Vampire Slayer*, 1992; *Speed*, 1994; *The Getaway*, 1994; *The Quick and the Dead*, 1995; *Toy Story*, 1995; *Waterworld*, 1995; *Twister*, 1996; *Alien: Resurrection*, 1997. Wrote and produced television shows, including: *Buffy the Vampire Slayer*, The WB and UPN, 1997-2003; *Angel*, The WB, 1999-2004; *Firefly*, FOX, 2002. Made feature film directorial debut with *Serenity*, 2005.

Awards: Annie Award for best individual achievement in writing, for *Toy Story*, 1996; Viewers for Quality Television Founder's Award, 2000; Saturn Award, best genre network series, for *Buffy*, 2001.

Sidelights

Joss Whedon became a hero in television's cult-pop underground world after creating the hit television show *Buffy the Vampire Slayer*. The show,

about a teenage cheerleader whose destiny is to kill vampires, demons, and other supernatural foes, earned two Emmy nominations before ending its run in 2003. Afterward, Whedon turned to other projects and showed fans another one of his ultra-cool universes when he made his feature film directorial debut with the Western sci-fi fantasy *Serenity* in 2005.

Born Joseph Hill Whedon on June 23, 1964, the future scriptwriter grew up in Manhattan alongside two older brothers and two half-brothers. That Whedon ended up in television is not surprising considering his father and grandfather both worked in the field. Whedon's father, Tom, wrote for *Benson, The Golden Girls, Electric Company*, and *Captain Kangaroo*, while his grandfather, John, wrote for classics such as *The Andy Griffith Show, The Dick Van Dyke Show*, and *The Donna Reed Show*. Whedon's mother, Lee Stearns, taught high school and aspired to write novels. His parents divorced when he was nine and his mother remarried.

Early on, Whedon's vivid imagination became his closest companion. In many interviews Whedon has noted that as a child he felt peculiar and lonely, like he did not fit in. Whedon escaped these feelings by transporting himself to parallel universes. He imagined his toys were quirky characters with special powers and he created unending storylines about their lives. Whedon also read tons of comics, including *Spider Man* and *Fantastic Four* and pored through science-fiction books.

For Whedon, teenage life at the private Riverdale High School in upstate New York proved arduous. He escaped Riverdale in 1980 when he joined his mother on her sabbatical to England and gained admission into an all-boys boarding school called Winchester College. Based in Hampshire, the elite prep school first opened in the 1300s. At Winchester, Whedon's teenage misery—and perpetual unpopularity—continued. He shared a room with a dozen other boys and spent his weekends sneaking into town to catch movies at the local theater. He stayed at Winchester even after his family returned to the United States.

Later on, Whedon resurrected the feelings from his angst-ridden teenage years in his storylines for *Buffy*, striking a chord with countless teenagers and young adults. In an interview posted on the Edinburgh International Film Festival website, Whedon described how his dark worldview developed. "I think it's not inaccurate to say that I had a perfectly happy childhood during which I was very unhappy.... And I had a very painful adolescence, because it was all very strange to me. It wasn't like I got beat up, but the humiliation and isolation, and the whole, existential 'oh God, I exist and nobody cares' thing about being a teenager, were extremely pronounced for me." Many *Buffy* plotlines were developed from his adolescence. For example, in high school, Whedon felt so invisible and insignificant that he once drew a self-portrait with a disappearing hand. In a first-season episode titled "Out of Sight, Out of Mind," Whedon told the story of a high school girl who actually disappeared because she felt so unnoticed.

After leaving Winchester in 1982, Whedon enrolled at Wesleyan University in Wesleyan, Connecticut. During this time, he escaped reality by playing Dungeons and Dragons. In 1987, Whedon completed his film studies degree and headed to Los Angeles, California, to pursue a career in independent filmmaking, moving in with his father. At this time, Whedon changed his name to Joss, which is Chinese for "luck," though he did not have any at first. Whedon worked on experimental film projects and barely scraped by, taking jobs at a local video store and working as a researcher at the Film Institute. He spent his free time pitching film ideas to area producers but failed to interest anybody.

Finally, Whedon's father persuaded him to try television. Though Whedon had been reluctant to follow in his father's and grandfather's footsteps, he realized selling a script would keep him afloat. After punching out a few scripts, Whedon decided he loved it. He sent scripts to every contact he had in Hollywood and finally landed a job as a staff writer on the ABC sitcom *Roseanne*. Whedon left a year later and worked on NBC's *Parenthood* series.

During this time Whedon completed his *Buffy* script but found studios reluctant to take a chance on such an atypical script by a writer with no name recognition. Studios did, however, begin offering him minor writing assignments because they could see he had potential and talent. Whedon did a small amount of script work on 1994's *The Getaway*, starring Kim Basinger and Alec Baldwin, as well as 1995's *The Quick and the Dead*, which featured Sharon Stone and Gene Hackman.

Meanwhile, Whedon continued pushing his *Buffy* script and in 1988 passed it off to Sandollar Productions. Around 1990, Sandollar reached a deal on the script with husband-wife filmmakers Kaz Kuzui and Fran Rubel Kuzui. The couple secured financing from 20th Century Fox and began production, with Rubel Kuzui serving as director. The 1992 film featured Kristy Swanson as Buffy, alongside Donald Sutherland, Luke Perry, Rutger Hauer, and Paul Reubens. For Whedon, it was a dream come true, though the excitement was short-lived as he watched the film come into fruition. In Whedon's mind, he had created a hip, horror-action-dark-comedy, complete with gut-wrenching emotion. Rubel Kuzui, on the other hand, had a different vision. She saw the film as a pop-culture comedy and, ignoring the horror and emotions, produced an off-the-cuff, second-rate film.

Most reviewers did not think much of the film overall, but Whedon's script received compliments. Writing on Filmcritic.com, James Brundage summed up the film this way: "The performances, admittedly, are lacking. The direction is downright bad, and the storyline really doesn't help much, but all of this is made up in spades with one of the most finely crafted formula scripts courtesy of Joss Whedon."

At this time, Whedon had plenty of prominent scriptwriting jobs coming his way. He doctored scripts for 1994's *Speed*, 1995's *Toy Story* and *Waterworld* and 1996's *Twister*. Speaking to *In Focus'* Jim Kozak, Whedon recalled that when he received the *Toy Story* script it was a mess, though it was easy to rework because the concept was so solid. "And that's the dream job for a script doctor: a great structure with a script that doesn't work. A script that's pretty good? Where you can't really figure out what's wrong, because there's something structural that's hard to put your finger on? Death. But a good structure that just needs a new body on it is the best. So I was thrilled." Whedon worked his magic and the film was nominated for an Oscar in screenplay writing. He won an Annie Award for writing from the International Animated Film Society.

Whedon also worked on 1997's *Alien: Resurrection* and penned five endings for it. Initially, the project excited him because he had been an *Alien* fan since he saw the first installment, starring Sigourney Weaver, at the age of 14. Once again, Whedon liked the script he wrote but thought the director did not capitalize on its strengths. Realizing he would never have control over the final product, Whedon began to have doubts about scriptwriting.

Meanwhile, Sandollar Productions executive Gail Berman contacted Whedon about his *Buffy* script. She remembered its edge and thought it might have great potential on television because she had not seen anything like it since. Berman persuaded Whedon to make a presentation film to give television executives a taste of what a *Buffy* series might look like. He struggled, having never directed a piece before, but his ingenuity came through. The WB picked up the show as a midseason replacement, though at first the network suggested the title be changed to *Slayer*. Whedon refused.

Because *Buffy* was a newcomer to the struggling WB network, its budget was rather small—attracting well-known talent was out of the question. In addition, the budget put a crimp on the special effects Whedon could afford. However, Whedon's dynamic energy and vision attracted a crew of unknown, yet highly talented writers and crew members. For his lead, he snagged *All My Children* star Sarah Michelle Gellar to play Buffy and the show hit the airwaves in 1997.

Writing in the *New York Times*, Joyce Millman called the show "the coolest television coming-of-age horror-fantasy-love story ever told." Traditionally, most horror stories have portrayed women as helpless, hysterical victims; Whedon's vision was different. In *Buffy*, females rule. The protagonist is Buffy Summers, a teenage girl given the unique power to quash vampires, demons, and other supernatural foes, thereby protecting humanity from the dark side. A perky, blond cheerleader, Buffy is an unlikely hero who gets the job done with the help of her misfit friends. Buffy's companions included Willow, a brainy lesbian witch plagued by wallflower tendencies and played by Alyson Hannigan. There was also the wisecracking sidekick Xander, played by Nicholas Brendon.

The show, which explored adolescence through the lens of horror, included lively language and complex characters. It quickly nabbed a massive fan base of Internet-crazed fans who created a buzz. After five years on the WB, *Buffy* moved to the United Paramount Network (UPN) for its final two seasons. During the time the show aired, from 1997 to 2003, it received two Emmy nominations. The first came in 2000 when *Buffy* received a nomination for outstanding writing for an episode called "Hush," which included 29 minutes of dialogue-free viewing.

While Whedon was still in the throes of *Buffy*, he launched a spin-off, *Angel*, in 1999. The show was darker than *Buffy* and aimed at an older audience. It starred David Boreanaz as the vampire Angel, who had formerly been a pivotal character on *Buffy*. It was canceled by the WB after five seasons, with the final episode airing in 2004. The show's cancellation caught Whedon off guard. Speaking to *Entertainment Weekly*'s Jeff Jensen, Whedon expressed his dismay. "When we hit 100 episodes, we felt we had made a stand. I felt we had hit [our stride] in our fifth year—and then we got cut down. With *Buffy*, I was ready to end…. But with *Angel*, it was like 'Healthy Guy Falls Dead From Heart Attack.'"

At one point, Whedon had three shows running on television simultaneously. In 2002, he launched *Firefly* on FOX after the network approached him and asked for new ideas. *Firefly* was another genre-blending show—it was a science-fiction Western set in 2517. The show followed the mishaps of a renegade crew aboard a futuristic spacecraft as they traveled through the galaxy simply trying to survive. FOX canceled the show after 11 of the 14 episodes aired. When it was released on DVD, sales were brisk and *Firefly* twice landed at the No. 2 spot on Amazon's daily top-seller list. When reruns aired on the Sci Fi Channel, it nabbed even more viewers, prompting movie executives to give Whedon the go-ahead to produce a feature-length film based on the series.

The film was titled *Serenity*, the name of the oddball crew's interplanetary cargo vessel. It opened second in box office ticket sales, bringing in $10.1 million its opening weekend in October of 2005. While most people cringe at the idea of Western and science fiction together, Whedon believes the two are related because Westerns typically deal with lawlessness in remote areas, a scenario that lends itself to future frontiers as well. *New York* magazine film critic Ken Tucker noted that *Serenity* "achieves a grandness—a heightened rapture—that few adventure films even have the imagination, or the idealism, to aspire to these days."

Afterward, Whedon began work on a script for a *Wonder Woman* film, set for release in 2007, though he was mum as to the film's specifics. Speaking to *In Focus'* Kozak, Whedon described his writing process and how he plays with outlines, charts, and graphs before writing a single word. "The way I work, I'm like a vulture. I circle and circle and then I dive. I usually don't actually write anything until I know exactly how it's going to turn out. I don't 'let the computer take me away.'"

Sources

Books

Havens, Candace, *Joss Whedon: The Genius Behind Buffy,* Benbella Books, 2003.

Periodicals

Entertainment Weekly, May 21, 2004, pp. 46-48.
Los Angeles Times, October 9, 2005, p. E1.
New York, October 3, 2005, p. 74.
New York Times, April 20, 2003; September 25, 2005.

Online

"Buffy the Vampire Slayer," Filmcritic.com, http://filmcritic.com/misc/emporium.nsf/84dbbfa4d710144986256c290016f76e/d9787709f4d8f3e9882567bd0002949e?OpenDocument (February 1, 2006).

"Reel Life: Joss Whedon Live Onstage Interview," Edinburgh International Film Festival, http://www.edfilmfest.org.uk/movies/show/reel_life_joss_whedon/details (February 15, 2006).

"Serenity Now!," *In Focus,* http://www.infocusmag.com/05augustseptember/whedonuncut.htm (February 15, 2006).

"Whedon seeks return of 'gritty' sci-fi," BBC News, http://news.bbc.co.uk/go/pr/fr/-/1/hi/entertainment/film/4318938.stm (February 1, 2006).

—Lisa Frick

The White Stripes

Evan Agostini/Getty Images

Rock group

Group formed in 1997 in Detroit, MI; members include Jack White (born John Anthony Gillis, July 9, 1975, in Detroit, MI; married Meg White, 1996 [divorced, 2000]; married Karen Elson, 2005), vocals, guitar; Meg White (born Megan Martha White, December 10, 1974; married Jack White, 1996 [divorced, 2000]), drums, vocals.

Addresses: *Record company*—V2 Records, 14 East 4th St., New York, NY 10012. *Website*—http://www.whitestripes.com.

Career

Jack White was a member of the Detroit-area bands Two Part Resin, The Go, 2-Star Tabernacle, Goober and the Peas, and The Hentchmen; appeared in the film *Cold Mountain*, 2003; produced compilation album *Sympathetic Sounds of Detroit*, 2001, and Loretta Lynn's album *Van Lear Rose*, 2004. Jack and Meg White formed the White Stripes, 1997; released debut album, *The White Stripes*, 1999; released *De Stijl*, 2000; released *White Blood Cells*, 2001; released *Elephant*, 2003; appeared in the film *Coffee and Cigarettes*, 2004; released *Get Behind Me Satan*, 2005.

Awards: MTV Video Music Awards for breakthrough video, best special effects, and best editing, all for "Fell In Love With A Girl," 2002; Grammy Award for best alternative music album, Recording Academy, for *Elephant*, 2004; Grammy Award for best rock song, Recording Academy, for "Seven Nation Army," 2004; Grammy Award for best country album, Recording Academy, for *Van Lear Rose* (produced by Jack White), 2005; Grammy Award for best country collaboration with vocals, Recording Academy, for "Portland, Oregon" (with Loretta Lynn), 2005.

Sidelights

With just a guitar, drums, and vocals, the White Stripes excited modern rock fans with their breakthrough album *White Blood Cells* in 2001. They were celebrated as leaders of a "garage rock" revival that made simple guitar rock with smart lyrics popular again. After multi-platinum success, Jack and Meg White, a duo who were once married but still claim to be brother and sister on stage, have stayed true to the boundaries they set for themselves when they formed their band. They still perform most of their songs with only two instruments, record entire albums in a few weeks, and try to create music that draws from blues, folk, and rock traditions while sounding raw and new.

Jack and Meg White met at a Detroit-area coffeehouse after graduating from high school. Jack, who was born John Gillis in Detroit, grew up on the city's southwest side, playing music from an early age with a friend. Meg White, shy, with a creative bent, had grown up in Grosse Pointe Woods, an upper-middle-class Detroit suburb. Meg worked as a bartender, and Jack worked as an upholsterer while playing in various local bands, including the country-rock outfit Goober and the Peas. The couple married in 1996. Jack White took his wife's last name.

The couple began playing music together in 1997, opening for more established Detroit bands at indie-rock clubs like the Gold Dollar in Detroit's impoverished Cass Corridor. Jack White, the guitarist, singer and songwriter, was clearly the driving force of the duo. Meg seemed to learn to play drums as she went along, with her husband sometimes cueing her onstage. In interviews, Jack has spun that into a positive, consistently defending her rudimentary drumming as key to the band's primitive sound. "When we started, our objective was to be as simple as possible," Jack told Norene Cashen of the *Metro Times,* a Detroit alternative weekly newspaper. "Meg's sound is like a little girl trying to play the drums and doing the best she can. Her playing on 'The Big 3 Killed My Baby' is the epitome of what I like about her drumming. It's just hits over and over again. It's not even a drumbeat—it's just accents."

Once the band released their self-titled debut album in 1999, they had already established an identity that would stay essentially the same for years. Their sound was simple, without even the bass player that usually completes a rock band lineup. Jack was organizing the band's music in threes: guitar, vocals, drums. "It came out the most on 'The Big 3 Killed My Baby,'" he told the *Metro Times'* Cashen. "It's three chords and three verses, and we accent threes together all through that. It was a number I always thought of as perfect, or our attempt at being perfect. Like on a traffic light, you couldn't just have a red and a green. I work on sculptures too, and I always use three colors." The same three colors—white, red, and black—have always graced the White Stripes' album covers, stage outfits, and even Meg's drum kit.

Parts of *The White Stripes,* released on the small label Sympathy For the Record Industry, were rooted in the experience of living in Detroit: "The Big 3 Killed My Baby" was a protest song about the negative effects Jack felt the Big Three automakers (General Motors, Ford, and Chrysler) had on Detroit, while "Lafayette Blues" mentioned the city's French street names. The local press declared the album a success. Cashen of the *Metro Times* declared that the White Stripes had succeeded where other Detroit

bands had failed: "remind[ing] us that local identity has more options than a membership card to the latest cliché … or a one-way ticket to the coast." The band's music, she added, would excite the sort of music fan "who still gets a thrill out of raw talent."

Fans and writers were also noting another part of their stage identity: Jack often claimed that he and Meg were brother and sister, instead of husband and wife—a pretense he would keep up long after the truth was exposed. "When you see a band that is two pieces, husband and wife, boyfriend and girlfriend, you think, 'Oh, I see,'" he told David Fricke in *Rolling Stone.* "When they're brother and sister, you go, 'Oh, that's interesting.' You care more about the music, not the relationship—whether they're trying to save their relationship by being in a band."

In fact, even as the White Stripes' popularity grew, their marriage was breaking up. Writer Chris Handyside began his book *Fell In Love With A Band: The Story of the White Stripes* in March of 1999, with a scene at a local music festival: Meg and Jack had become estranged, and she did not agree to play their scheduled gig until the last minute, after which an announcer told the crowd, "I've just been informed that this is not actually the White Stripes' last show." The duo's second album, *De Stijl,* was released in 2000, the same year the Whites divorced.

The band began attracting attention outside Detroit by going on two tours as opening acts for established alternative-rock bands Pavement (in 1999) and Sleater-Kinney (in 2000). They also toured Japan and Australia after *De Stijl* was released. In early 2001, *Rolling Stone* named them one of ten bands to watch that year. Writer Jenny Eliscu explained that *De Stijl* was named after "a 1920s Dutch design movement based on simple geometric shapes and primary colors," and described their sound as "scuzzy garage rock, blues and Mod-era Sixties pop."

The White Stripes recorded their next album, *White Blood Cells,* in Memphis, Tennessee, at the studio of accomplished producer Doug Easley. Several shows on their national tour either sold out or nearly sold out. Record labels began competing to sign them. On the eve of the third album's release, the *Metro Times'* Melissa Giannini caught them confronting the beginnings of fame: fans asking for autographs, phones ringing constantly with business offers, and New York audiences showing up with arms folded, waiting to see if they lived up to the hype. The album art for *White Blood Cells* showed Jack and Meg, clad in red and white, surrounded by black shadows holding cameras. "The name, *White Blood Cells*, for the album, is this idea of bacteria coming at us, or just foreign things coming at us, or media, or attention on the band," Jack told Giannini. "It just seems to us that there are so many bands from the same time or before we started that were playing and are still playing that didn't get this kind of attention that we're getting. Is the attention good or bad?"

Critics described the band as leaders of a "garage rock" movement, also including the New York City band the Strokes, that was reviving simple, catchy guitar rock. Fans began praising the White Stripes for bringing a new energy to rock music. "That's the nicest thing," Meg told Giannini, "when somebody comes up to us and says they'd been discouraged with music and that we've made them feel a new energy for it."

While *De Stijl* included a lot of bluesy songs and slide guitar playing (as well as homages to mid-'60s British rock, such as "You're Pretty Good Looking"), *White Blood Cells* had a different mix of genres—on purpose, said Jack, who was worried about being pigeonholed as a blues band. Most of the songs on *White Blood Cells* were written on piano, then sped up and recorded with guitar.

White Blood Cells became a huge hit, selling more than 500,000 copies. The catchy, ultra-fast single "Fell In Love With A Girl" became a hit in England, and its video (featuring animation that used Legos to depict Jack and Meg) was played frequently on MTV and won three MTV Video Music Awards. *Billboard*'s Chris Moore heralded the White Stripes as the leaders of a "Detroit rock revival," noting that Jack had produced a compilation of several Detroit bands, *Sympathetic Sounds of Detroit*, and often talked up other Detroit musicians in interviews.

Some critics complained about the band's carefully crafted image; half of *Time*'s 2001 piece on the band was spent exposing the fact that the Whites were a divorced couple, not brother and sister. But most critics praised the band for making blues and simple rock sound new again. "The singer's manic intensity emerged gradually as he peppered the performance with deconstructed blues riffs and inspired solos," Jay DeFoore of the *Hollywood Reporter* wrote in his review of the band's sold-out April of 2002 show at New York's Bowery Ballroom. "With one broken string perpetually dangling from his guitar, Jack resembled a mad magician conjuring up spells from discarded songs of the past."

Like many other American alternative-rock bands, the White Stripes became widely popular in Europe first. On their 2002 European tour, they played on the British TV show *Top of the Pops*; their show in Stockholm, Sweden, sold out in 13 minutes, and they discovered that French crowds knew all their songs. Later in 2002, the White Stripes were an opening act on part of the Rolling Stones' tour. They even embraced the role of trend-setters by performing four shows with The Strokes, two in Detroit, two in New York. By then, the band had left their old independent label to sign with the larger V2 Records, which re-released all three of their albums. As part of their minimalist ethic, the White Stripes kept their shows spontaneous. "We never use a set list, and we never rehearse, really," Jack told Rob Sheffield of *Rolling Stone*. "We just keep it as spontaneous as possible and keep it off the top of our heads. If it was structured, I would get bored with it."

Expectations were high as the White Stripes released their fourth album, *Elephant*, in spring of 2003. Recorded in London, reputedly at a cost of less than $10,000, *Elephant* proved to be very much in the vein of *White Blood Cells*, but more consistent: dirty guitars playing catchy riffs, mostly rock but still blues-influenced (as on the song "Ball and Biscuit"), with a few ballads mixed in and strong songwriting throughout. Meg even made a rare appearance as a vocalist on the ballad "In the Cold, Cold Night."

The album was a huge critical success, though many critics took swipes at the band's perceived pretentions before praising the music. Josh Tyrangiel of *Time* warned readers away from the liner notes of *Elephant*, in which Jack White wrote that the album was about the "death of the sweetheart," but he called the impassioned breakup song "There's No Home For You Here" and the single and lead-off track "Seven Nation Army" classics and the ballads "You've Got Her in Your Pocket" and "I Want to Be the Boy to Warm Your Mother's Heart" "soft, hymnal, and far sweeter than you would think White capable of." Lorraine Ali of *Newsweek* claimed the band had been "overrated" in the past, but deemed *Elephant* "a far better album" than *White Blood Cells*," praising Jack White's wordplay and describing his voice as "campy and high-strung one minute, smoke-wrecked and gruff the next." *Entertainment Weekly*'s Rob Brunner groused that the "half talented" band had succeeded because Jack is a good salesman, that Meg had only recently reached "near adequacy" as a drummer, and that the red-and-white color scheme had gotten old. Yet Brunner gave the album a grade of B and called Jack "a top-notch frontman, a charismatic yowler with a seemingly endless supply of brilliantly simplistic guitar riffs that often find fresh musical twists on tired rock & roll cliches."

Elephant went platinum, selling more than 1.4 million copies in the United States and four million copies worldwide. One of the album's songs, "Seven Nation Army," became one of 2003's biggest rock singles. The album won a Grammy award for Best Alternative Music Album in 2004. After *Elephant* was released, Jack ended up in celebrity gossip columns, mostly thanks to his relationship with actress Renee Zellweger. The two had met in 2002 while filming the movie *Cold Mountain* in Romania. White played a small role in the film, a romantic drama set in the Civil War (released in December of 2003), and contributed songs in a 19th-century folk style to the soundtrack. White was showing Zellweger around Detroit in July of 2003 when he broke a finger in a small car accident; the injury forced the band to cancel a few months of tour appearances. (White and Zellweger eventually broke up, and she married country music star Kenny Chesney in May of 2005, from whom she filed for divorce a few months later.) White was also in the news because he got in a bar brawl with a fellow Detroit musician, Jason Stollsteimer, lead singer of the Von Bondies, in December of 2003, reportedly over comments Stollsteimer made in an interview downplaying White's role producing the Von Bondies' first album. White eventually pleaded guilty to misdemeanor assault and battery and was fined and ordered to attend anger-management classes.

Jack and Meg appeared in the film *Coffee and Cigarettes* in 2004, an experimental collection of shorts directed by Jim Jarmusch in which the actors drank coffee, smoked cigarettes, and talked. (Jack and Meg talked about a Tesla coil, which is used in electronic equipment.) That same year, Jack produced an album for classic country-music star Loretta Lynn, *Van Lear Rose*, which went on to win a Grammy in 2005. Plus, Jack and Lynn shared a Grammy for Best Country Collaboration With Vocals for one of that album's songs.

Though critics often complained the White Stripes relied on gimmicks to get attention, the duo actually avoid typical music-business marketing strategies. The best example came in the summer of 2005. As their fifth album, *Get Behind Me Satan*, was about to debut, the White Stripes took off on a tour of Central and South America, followed by a tour of Eastern Europe, Greece, and Russia after its release. Brian Garrity of *Billboard* had to talk to Jack White about the album by phone while the band was in Chile. "I wanted to go to places where no one had ever seen us before, so we [could] get that feeling back of those live shows where we used to have to prove ourselves," White told Garrity.

While on the South American tour, on June 1, 2005, Jack married British model Karen Elson in Manaus, Brazil. The marriage reportedly took place on a ca-

noe at the spot where the Amazon River meets two other rivers. Meg was the maid of honor, according to the White Stripes' website. "This was the first marriage for both newlyweds," the site claimed.

The band experimented with its sound on *Get Behind Me Satan,* recorded at a studio Jack White built in his home. He only played electric guitar on a few tracks; others featured piano or marimba instead. Jack White told *Rolling Stone*'s Fricke that the album, and its title, represented "the end of any unhappiness I have…. Any troubles I have are well-represented: betrayal, loss, pain…."

Reviews were good to mixed. Sasha Frere-Jones of the *New Yorker* praised Jack White's talent but expressed frustration that he continued to work within arbitrary rules of simplicity. Recording the album in less than three weeks, as the White Stripes often do, resulted in a collection of sloppy songs and made the album more "smart" than "fun," Frere-Jones complained. But Chuck Arnold of *People* gave the album 3 1/2 stars and called it "weird" but "fascinating," and Lorraine Ali of *Newsweek* called it "an explosive hybrid of under-the-radar Americana, scraggly hip-hugger rock and 21st-century innovation."

In fall of 2005, the White Stripes headed out on a tour of the United States, and Jack White was preparing to release an album with a new band, The Raconteurs, which includes his friend, Detroit rock musician Brendan Benson. In October of 2005, it was announced that the White Stripes would perform on Comedy Central's *The Daily Show* in December of that year. The duo was the first band to perform on that show.

Selected discography

White Stripes, Sympathy for the Record Industry, 1999; V2, 2002.
De Stijl, Sympathy for the Record Industry, 2000; V2, 2002.
White Blood Cells, Sympathy for the Record Industry, 2001; V2, 2002.
Elephant, V2, 2003.
Get Behind Me Satan, V2, 2005.

Sources

Books

Handyside, Chris, *Fell In Love With A Band: The Story of the White Stripes,* St. Martin's Griffin, 2004.

Periodicals

Billboard, October 27, 2001, p. 1; April 27, 2002, p. 80; June 4, 2005, p. 22.
Detroit News, March 10, 2004.
Entertainment Weekly, April 4, 2003, p. 98.
Hollywood Reporter, April 8, 2002, p. 28; September 24, 2003, p. 19.
Maclean's, May 24-31, 2004.
Metro Times (Detroit, MI), May 26, 1999; May 29, 2001.
Newsweek, June 21, 2005, p. 50; June 27, 2005, p. 60.
New Yorker, June 13, 2005, p. 178.
People, June 20, 2005, p. 28; June 27, 2005, p. 41.
Rolling Stone, February 15, 2001, p. 65; April 11, 2002, p. 47; December 12, 2002, p. 88; September 8, 2005, pp. 66-72.

Time, June 16, 2001; April 14, 2003, p. 82.
USA Today, August 12, 2003, p. 3D.

Online

"News," The White Stripes, http://www.white stripes.com/news/news.html (August 21, 2005).
"The White Stripes, Biography," *All Music Guide*, http://www.allmusic.com/cg/amg.dll?p= amg&searchlink=WHITE|STRIPES& uid= MIW030509051902&sql=11:jpx1z81a1yvo~T1 (August 21, 2005).
"White Stripes, 'Daily,'" CNN.com, http://www. cnn.com/2005/SHOWBIZ/10/07/showbuzz/ index.html#2 (October 10, 2005).

—Erick Trickey

Patrick Whitney

Photo by Tina Leto/courtesy of Patrick Whitney

Director of the Institute of Design at Illinois Institute of Technology

Born Patrick Foster Whitney, c. 1952; married Cheryl Kent (an author). *Education:* Cranbrook Academy of Art, M.F.A., 1976.

Addresses: *Contact*—Illinois Institute of Technology, 3300 S. Federal Street, Chicago, IL 60616-3793. *E-mail*—whitneyid.iit.edu.

Career

Chaired the program of the 1978 US Conference of the International Council on Graphic Design Associations; principal researcher for research initiatives Global Companies in Local Markets and Designing for the Base of the Pyramid; consultant to Aetna, Texas Instruments, McDonald's, and Zebra Technologies; Steelcase/Robert C. Pew Professor of Design; director, Institute of Design, Illinois Institute of Technology, 1986—; served on the jury of the 1995 Presidential Design Awards.

Sidelights

In the world of design, Patrick Whitney is known for his ongoing dedication to innovation and revolution. Forever investigating the ways that form impacts and interacts with function, Whitney uses his position as director of the Institute of Design, housed at Illinois Institute of Technology, and Steelcase/Robert C. Pew Professor of Design to influence design students' understanding of where and how design functions in the world. Specifically, Whitney has urged both aspiring and accomplished

designers to reconsider the role of design in the 21st century. As the Institute of Design's webpage describes, "Whitney has published and lectured throughout the world about how to make technological innovations more humane, the link between design and business strategy, and methods of designing interactive communications and products." Thinking, specifically, about the ways in which changing design strategies can respond to increasingly flexible, as opposed to mass, production and increasingly global, rather than national, markets, Whitney's ideas about design lie at the intersection of art and business, education and humanitarianism. Whitney has devoted much time and energy to investigating how the design of everyday objects, such as cell phones, impacts the quality of everyday life. Described in an issue of *Forbes* as having "devoted his life to redesigning design itself—function over styling, substance over glitz," Whitney has devoted his career, generally, to reconsidering the function of form.

At the Illinois Institute of Technology's Institute of Design, Whitney has brought this revolutionary design theory both into the classroom and into the various projects on which he has worked. As the director of the Institute of Design, Whitney oversees both a thriving undergraduate program and a highly competitive graduate program. The graduate program, in particular, is a leader in its field, offering two professional degrees, the Master of Design and the Master of Design methods, and a research-oriented PhD. Professional academics and students alike come from around the world to take part in the design innovation underway at the Institute of Design. In both his administrative and professorial capacities, Whitney is very much at the center of this activity. Indeed, his personal design philosophies and professional devotion to revolutionizing the field of design meld nicely with what the Institute of Design describes on its website as its dedication to "approach[ing] design problems from many perspectives [by] employing analytic and synthetic design methods to identify current and future needs and to humanize the technology needed to solve those problems."

Beyond his work as director and professor, however, Whitney is also intricately involved in several of the research initiatives central to the Institute of Design's vitality and stellar reputation. One of the initiatives with which Whitney has worked most closely is the Global Companies in Local Markets (GCLM) research consortium. As part of this effort, which both investigates and attempts to ease the difficulties faced by companies expanding their base from local markets to global markets, Whitney examines the cultural factors that influence how specific design innovations are received within specific cultures. In their work with the GCLM, he and the researchers whom he has assembled from around the world push beyond the anthropological studies traditionally conducted by companies seeking to introduce their products and services into foreign markets. Recognizing these studies as far too general, Whitney and his GCLM colleagues investigate the aspects of daily life that affect how various goods and services are received by communities other than those for which they were originally designed.

Also at the Institute of Design, Whitney has been involved in a research initiative entitled Designing for the Base of the Pyramid. Here, again, Whitney's work centers around understanding the function of design at a global level. With Designing for the Base of the Pyramid, however, Whitney and his colleagues investigate the extent to which considering design and employing various design innovations could enhance the living condition in developing nations, and specifically in the slums of India. As Whitney and colleague Anjali Kelkar assert in an article published in *Design Management Review*, those working on this particular research initiative are "focusing specifically on wealth creation in urban slums in the developing world." Their goal, according to Whitney and Kelkar, "is to make the local

economies more sustainable, encourage the growth of small businesses, and in the long term to help transition residents toward improved living conditions." The researchers were also focusing on the ways in which increased attention to design could help facilitate this potential economic upswing. In this case, however, the design issues to which Whitney and his colleagues are most closely attending have more to do with housing and business strategy than product design and marketing. Indeed, they are using their experience to design intricate models for economic uplift.

Whitney has been an invaluable member of the Institute of Design's faculty, in particular, and research community, in general. Yet, Whitney's contributions to the world of design extend far beyond what he has accomplished at his home institution. For decades, Whitney has served on committees and panels not directly associated with the Illinois Institute of Technology's Institute of Design and shared with diverse audiences his ideas about purposeful, sustainable, and marketable design. He has, for example, served on the Distinguished Advisor Board of the Association of Computing Machinery's Special Interest Group in Computer Human Interaction, whose primary mission is to promote interest in and knowledge of human-computer interaction and human technology. Moreover, he has been a member of the White House Council on Design and was on the jury of the 1995 Presidential Design awards. Finally, Whitney set into motion his reputation as an innovator nearly ten years before he took over as director of Institute of Design by chairing the program of the 1978 US Conference of the International Council on Graphic Design Associations. This conference marked the first major effort to consider design strategies from the perspectives of users rather than the designers. As he would be throughout his career, Whitney was at the forefront of the endeavor.

Sources

Periodicals

Design Management Review, Fall 2004.
Forbes, September 6, 2004, p. 158.

Online

"Global Companies in Local Markets," Institute of Design, http://www.id.iit.edu/ideas/gclm.html (August 24, 2005).
"Patrick Whitney," Institute of Design: People: Faculty, http://www.id.iit.edu/people/faculty_bios/whitney.html (August 17, 2005).

"Profile," Institute of Design: Overview, http://www.id.iit.edu/profile/welcome.html (August 25, 2005).

"Seventh Annual CIO 100 Symposium and Awards—Speakers," CIO 100 Symposium, http://www.cio.com/conferences/speakers.html?ID=118&BIO=473008 (August 21, 2005).

—Emily Schusterbauer

Gretchen Wilson

Todd Plitt/Getty Images

Singer and songwriter

Born June 16, 1973; children: Grace.

Addresses: *Record company*—Sony Nashville, 8 Music Square West, Nashville, TN 37212. *Website*—http://www.gretchenwilson.com.

Career

Performed in bars near hometown of Pocahontas, IL; moved to Nashville, 1996; became involved with Muzik Mafia circle of performers and artists; signed to Sony Nashville label; released *Here for the Party*, featuring hit song "Redneck Woman," 2004; released *All Jacked Up*, 2005.

Awards: Horizon Award, Country Music Association, 2004; best new artist, American Music Awards, 2004; Grammy Award for best female country vocal performance, Recording Academy, for "Redneck Woman," 2005; female vocalist of the year, Country Music Association, 2005; favorite female country artist, American Music Award, 2005.

Sidelights

At a time when female vocals in country music were mostly the province of divas who wore designer clothes and aspired to pop sophistication, Gretchen Wilson put the music back in touch with its "redneck" roots—to use the term that Wilson took to the top of the country charts. Country radio in early 2004 was ruled by Wilson's hit "Redneck Woman," an anthem whose lyrics, co-written by Wilson, dedicated themselves to "redneck girls like me." That single and the album that followed, *Here for the Party*, were among the fastest-selling recordings in country music history, and some observers thought they signaled a change in direction for the genre as a whole. The album went on to to go quadruple platinum. Her 2005 follow-up, *All Jacked Up*, was a four-time Grammy nominee.

Wilson's songs were filled with images of small-town life, and she lived the life she sang about. Born on June 16, 1973, she grew up in tiny Pocahontas, Illinois, about 35 miles east of St. Louis, Missouri. In one of the songs on *Here for the Party*, she sang of her desire to make "Pocahontas proud." She may have inherited some musical talent from her father, a musician, but he left the family soon after she was born. Wilson was raised by her mother, living in a succession of rented mobile homes. Often the pair stayed one step ahead of landlords trying to collect overdue rent payments.

"I thought everybody was redneck when I was a kid," Wilson told the Minneapolis *Star Tribune*. "I thought everybody had a single mom who worked two jobs and had peanut butter and jelly three nights a week for supper." Wilson often looked after her younger brother, Josh, and she told the New York *Daily News,* there was "tension between me and my mom because we were so close in age. We were almost like sisters. By about 12, I felt like the grownup in the house." Wilson's mother often worked as a bartender, and Wilson had to drop out of high school to join her at Big O's Tavern when she was 15. She worked as a cook while her mother tended bar.

That might seem to be a rough situation for a 15-year-old girl, "but this was a tiny bar where everyone knows everyone and the whole family is there because there's nothing else to do in town," Wilson told the *Daily News.* "It was almost like a day-care center." It also gave Wilson the chance to sing the Loretta Lynn and Patsy Cline country classics she loved in front of a live audience. Sometimes she billed herself as Country Cutie. Within a few years Wilson was singing with two local bands and was appearing at venues as far afield as the suburbs of St. Louis.

In 1996, at the age of 22, Wilson left Pocahontas with $500 in her pocket, to seek fame and fortune in Nashville. She quickly had to return to bartending in order to make ends meet, but she began to find a place in the industry by singing on demo tapes—recordings of songwriters' compositions that are used to pitch a song to a particular performer. She began knocking on music label doors, trying to get signed to a recording contract herself, but she met with universal rejection. "I'd go to these showcases and the labels would say to me, 'I'm sorry, but that's just too country,'" Wilson told the *Daily News.* "How can you be too country for country?," she mused.

A relationship with her boyfriend, Mike Penner, produced a daughter, Grace, and Wilson thought of shelving her goal of stardom. But she found her way into a creative community, the Muzik Mafia, which enabled her to revive those dreams. One person who had helped her during her early days in Nashville was John Rich, formerly a member of the group Lonestar, and a Nashville nonconformist who would later form the duo Big & Rich with another songwriter, Big Kenny (Kenny Alphin). Rich was one of the organizers of the Muzik Mafia, a loosely connected group of performers who came together in Nashville clubs for weekly stage shows, spreading the location only by word of mouth.

The Muzik Mafia featured an extraordinarily diverse collection of musicians, including a six-foot-eight African-American rapping cowboy. "You never know who is going to show.... It's like Fellini in Nashville," music executive John Grady told the *Star Tribune.* Wilson fit easily into the Muzik Mafia group, and Rich encouraged her to try her hand at songwriting. He told the *New York Times* that "Gretchen's voice just pulverized me," and the two began working together on songs. One night the two were watching country music videos that featured a succession of leggy, fashionably dressed female singers. Wilson expressed the feeling that she'd never be able to carry off an image like that because she was a redneck woman. Rich picked up on the phrase, and the future hit "Redneck Woman," with its anthemic "hell yeah" refrain and its wealth of redneck detail, was finished in under an hour.

New music in hand, Wilson auditioned for the Sony label and its new president, John Grady, who had been on the job for only three weeks. She was backed by several members of the Big & Rich band. Sensing a major hit in the making, Grady signed Wilson to Sony and released "Redneck Woman" as a single. The results were immediate and startling. In April of 2004 the song reached the top ten on *Billboard* magazine's country chart in near record time, and then ascended to the top spot. The release of Wilson's CD *Here for the Party* was moved forward twice, and it sold 227,000 copies in its first week, easily topping the country album chart and challenging R&B artist Usher for the pop album top spot. It was the best opening-week performance a country album had ever achieved. Wilson gained attention from far beyond the usual country sphere, as "Redneck Woman" became the subject of a feature on National Public Radio.

Wilson's songs could not really be classified as traditional country; they had big rock beats and showcased up-to-the-minute production electronics. Yet listeners sensed Wilson's rural roots, and that was the way Wilson wanted it. "I was determined to put together a record that was real," she told the *Boston Globe.* "I talk all the time about my idols being Loretta Lynn and Tanya Tucker and Patsy Cline and people like that. And I knew when I listened to a Loretta Lynn record that I was going to hear stories that were real. I hung on every word that came out of her mouth because I knew that she had lived that."

The Wilson phenomenon continued unabated through the summer and fall of 2004, as the dance club hit "Here for the Party" nearly matched the success of "Redneck Woman." ("I may not be a 10, but the boys say I clean up good," Wilson sang confidently.) Wilson toured major arenas and prepared for major changes in her life. "I have probably made and spent a quarter of a million dollars in the last four months," she told the *Star Tribune*. "That's more money that I could ever think about four months ago. All of a sudden, I have a corporation. I have people that work for me that I don't even know." But success did not seem likely to change Wilson. "I'd still rather go fishin' and drive a four-wheeler than go to the mall any day," she told the *Daily News*. "This is just who I am." In November of 2004 Wilson won the Country Music Association's Horizon Award, given to the top new artist of the preceding year, and she was named Best New Artist at the 2004 American Music Awards, beating heavily favored rapper Kanye West. Early in 2005, she also won a Grammy Award for the song "Redneck Woman."

On September 27, 2005, Wilson's second album, *All Jacked Up*, was released. Dubbed a "feisty follow-up" by *Entertainment Weekly*'s Will Hermes, the album featured a duet with country star Merle Haggard. Other songs touched on some of Wilson's favorite things, including Jack Daniel's whiskey and the sight of the fade mark on her boyfriend's back pocket created by his chewing tobacco tin. Her song "California Girls" was a tirade against the superficiality of Hollywood denizens, including Paris Hilton. "I personally don't know why she's such a big star. What does she do? I just don't get it," Wilson told *Newsweek*. "Being 80 pounds and blonde, and living in Hollywood? Those aren't goals."

In November of that 2005, Wilson won the Country Music Association award for female vocalist of the year and the American Music Award for favorite female country artist. Proving her first album's success was not a fluke, Wilson was nominated for four Grammy Awards in 2006, including best country album, best female country vocal performance, best country collaboration with vocals (with Haggard), and best country song. Ray Waddell, writing for *Billboard*, declared, "Beyond the bombast, Wilson has personality and soul to burn, and her impact on country music is going to be felt for many albums to come."

Selected discography

Here for the Party, Sony, 2004.
All Jacked Up, Sony, 2005.

Sources

Periodicals

Billboard, October 1, 2005, p. 64.
Boston Globe, May 30, 2004, p. N1.
Daily News (New York, NY), June 13, 2004, p. 14.
Daily Telegraph (London, England), August 21, 2004, p. Arts-6.
Denver Post, August 8, 2004, p. F1.
Entertainment Weekly, September 30, 2005, p. 91.
Los Angeles Times, May 22, 2004, p. E1; September 22, 2004, p. B11.
Newsweek, October 3, 2005, p. 103.
New York Times, June 17, 2004, p. E1.
People, October 10, 2005, p. 43.
Plain Dealer (Cleveland, OH), August 16, 2004, p. D3.
St. Louis Post-Dispatch, May 9, 2004, p. F1; May 27, 2004, p. 23.
Star Tribune (Minneapolis, MN), September 3, 2004, p. E1.
USA Today, April 5, 2004, p. D4.

Online

American Music Awards, http://abc.go.com/primetime/ama05/index.html (April 6, 2006).
Billboard.com, http://www.billboard.com/bb/releases/week_2/index.jsp (April 6, 2006).
"Gretchen Wilson," *All Music Guide*, http://www.allmusic.com (April 6, 2006).
"39th Annual CMA Awards," CMA Awards, http://www.cmaawards.com/2005/nomWin/ (April 6, 2006).

—*James M. Manheim*

Edward Witten

Physicist

Born August 26, 1951, in Baltimore, MD; son of Louis W. Witten (a physicist); married Chiara Nappi (a physicist); children: Daniela, Ilana, Rafael. *Education:* Brandeis University, history degree, 1971; Princeton University, masters degree (physics), 1974, Ph.D. (physics), 1976.

Addresses: *Home*—Princeton, NJ. *Office*—Institute for Advanced Study, School of Natural Sciences, Einstein Dr., Princeton, NJ 08540.

Career

Freelance writer, early 1970s; aide, George McGovern presidential campaign, 1972; junior fellow, Harvard University, Society of Fellows, 1977-80; full professor, Princeton University, Department of Physics, 1980-87; Charles Simonyi professor of mathematical physics, Institute of Advanced Studies, Princeton, NJ, 1987—.

Member: International Centre for Peace in the Middle East, Tel Aviv, Israel; board, Americans for Peace Now; attended Emergency World Jewish Leadership Peace Conference, Jerusalem, Israel.

Awards: MacArthur Fellowship, 1982; Einstein Medal, 1985; New York Academy of Science Award for Physics and Math Science, 1985; National Science Foundation, Alan T. Waterman Award, 1986; Fields Medal, co-winner, 1990; named one of 25 most influential Americans, *Time*, 1996; named one of 100 most influential in the world, 2004; Dannie Heinemann Prize, 1998; Frederic Esser Nemmers Prize in mathematics, 2000; National Medal of Science, 2002.

Sidelights

In the world of physics, Edward Witten is a superstar, and considered by many to be the savior of the field. His participation in the discovery of the super string theory and his M-string theory has sparked much debate in the science community as physicists and mathematicians everywhere researched to prove these theories right or wrong. Because of his contributions, he has been awarded the Fields Medal and named as one of *Time*'s 25 Most Influential Americans.

Witten was born on August 26, 1951, in Baltimore, Maryland. He was highly intelligent as a toddler. His father, Louis W. Witten, a gravitational physicist, was talking physics with him at the age of four. His father told Jack Klaff of the *Guardian*, "I would talk to Ed about science the way I would talk with adults." Witten attended Baltimore Hebrew school as a child. At the age of 12 his letters denouncing the Vietnam War appeared in the local newspaper's editorial section. Although Witten was fascinated by physics, he wanted to become a journalist. He attended Brandeis University, and graduated with a degree in history.

Witten wrote articles for the *Nation* and the *New Republic*. He also worked as an aide on George McGovern's presidential campaign in 1972. With his interest in both journalism and politics waning, Witten returned to school. He entered the doctoral program at Princeton University. At first unsure of whether to study mathematics or physics, he chose physics and earned his masters degree in 1974, and his doctorate in 1976.

Witten began his career in physics as a junior fellow of the Society of Fellows at Harvard University. Later he returned to Princeton in 1980 as full professor, one of the youngest to be appointed to that position. He taught in the physics department and many of his students nicknamed him "The Martian" because of his soft-spoken voice and his style of lecturing, which included long pauses as he gathered his thoughts. Despite his nickname, many of his students had the utmost respect for Witten.

When Albert Einstein released his theory of relativity, he breathed new life into the field of physics. Einstein spent his later years expanding his theory and trying to combine relativity with quantum physics, which both contradicted each other. He died in 1955 before finding the solution. Many thought all of the major discoveries in physics and mathematics had been discovered. Three particle theorists developed string theory which theorized that nature is not made up of miniscule particles but of tiny loops and strings, which also vibrated like a violin and instead of four dimensions, there were 26. A number of physicists disproved of the concept and it was later abandoned. A couple of physicists later lowered the number down to ten.

Witten devoted his energies to further developing string theory. He told John Horgan of the *Scientific American*, "It was very clear that if I didn't spend my life concentrating on string theory, I would simply be missing my life's calling." In 1984 he and a fellow physicist wrote a paper "about anomalies that occur during radioactive decay that could only be studied in terms of topology [shape connection] and only in ten dimensions," according to *World of Mathematics*. This hypothesis cemented previous findings that stated string theory required the presence of ten dimensions. This theory also became known as the superstring theory.

Witten's papers energized both the mathematics and physics community. Soon five varying ideas were competing as *the* string theory. Witten's belief that superstring theory would change the world was so intense he wrote a record 19 papers in one year, making him the chief proponent of string theory. He ended his teaching career at Princeton, and in 1987 became the Charles Simonyi professor of mathematical physics at the Institute of Advanced Studies (IAS), where Einstein spent his last years.

With five varying ideas of string theory, string theory reached a stalemate. However, Witten worked to find which idea was indeed the one that defined string theory. His research soon discovered that all were in fact aspects of the string theory. He combined them all to form the M-string theory. He published his findings in 1995. Again Witten sparked a flurry of debate in the community. Using "the analogy of blind men examining an elephant to explain the course of string theory until 1995," Nathan Seiberg, also working at the IAS, told Alok Jha of the *Guardian*, "One describes touching a leg, one describes touching a trunk, another describes the ears. They come up with different descriptions but they don't see the big picture. There is only one elephant...."

Witten's M-theory while bringing together the five various ideas into a workable equation, also added one more dimension and suggested that the strings were membranes or branes. These branes could exist in at least three dimensions and could grow to the size of the universe. Witten also theorized that our universe could be sitting on a brane.

Witten continued to develop new theories, including working on the twistor theory, which was created in 1965. Working this theory with the new discoveries of the day led Witten to conclude that all of the extra dimensions in both string theory and his M-theory were no longer needed. However, he told Jha of the *Guardian*, "I think twistor string theory is something that only partly works."

In the area of string theory, Witten has been the most prolific contributor. Another colleague at the IAS, Juan Maldacena, told Michael Lemonick in *Time*, "Most other people have made one or two such contributions. Ed has made ten or 15." Witten and many others believe that string theory is one step toward developing the "Theory of Everything." This theory would provide the answers to nature, the Big Bang theory, and everything else.

Witten was not without detractors. With him being a theoretical physicist, his main focus was on using calculations versus running experiments. As a result, some thought he relied too heavily on mathematics rather than actual physics. Also many believed that string theory was loopy and pure conjecture, since technically, nothing has been proven.

Witten, however, has been the recipient of numerous honors and awards. He won the Einstein Medal and the New York Academy of Science Award for Physics and Math Science in 1985. In 1990 he shared the Fields Medal, the most prestigious award given in mathematics, also the closest he could get to a Nobel Prize. He also won the Dannie Heinemann

Prize in 1998. In 2000 Witten received the Frederic Esser Nemmers Prize in Mathematics and was also awarded the National Medal of Science for his contributions to mathematics and theoretical physics in 2002.

Witten is considered by many to be a genius or as close as one can get. He is married to Chiara Nappi, a physicist at Princeton University. They have three children. In addition to his many discoveries, Witten is very active in such organizations as the International Centre for Peace in the Middle East and Americans for Peace Now.

Sources

Books

American Decades, Gale Research, 1998.
World of Mathematics, Gale Group, 2002.

Periodicals

Guardian (London, England), March 19, 1997; January 20, 2005.
Science News, August 25, 1990, p. 119.
Scientific American, November 1991.
Time, June 17, 1996, p. 66; April 26, 2004, p. 110.

Online

"A Theory of Everything?," Florida State University Physics Department, http://www.physics.fsu.edu/Courses/spring99/AST3033/theory.htm (November 21, 2005).
"Institute for Advanced Studies," School of Natural Sciences, http://www.sns.ias.edu/%7Ewitten/ (November 22, 2005).

—*Ashyia N. Henderson*

Viktor Yushchenko

Sergei Supinsky/POOL/EPA/Landov

President of Ukraine

Born Viktor Andriyovich Yushchenko, February 23, 1954, in Khoruzhivka, Sums'ka Oblast, Ukraine; son of Andriy Andriyovych (a teacher) and Varvara Tymofiyovna (a teacher) Yushchenko; married and divorced first wife; married Kateryna Chumachenko (a former U.S. State Department official), 1998; children: a son and a daughter (from first marriage), a son and two daughters (from second marriage). *Education:* Earned degree in economics from Ternopil Finance and Economics Institute, 1975.

Addresses: *Office*—Ukrainian President's Public Reception Office, 12 Shovkovychna St., Kiev, Ukraine.

Career

Chief accountant assistant on a collective farm, 1975; served in Soviet Army frontier troops stationed on Turkish border, 1975-76; began at State Bank of the Soviet Union, 1976, as acting economist, became chief of the Ulyanovsk department; deputy director of administration, USSR State Bank, Ukrainian Republican Office, 1985-87; department head, deputy chairman of the Board of Directors, Ukrainian Agro-Industrial Bank, 1988-90; deputy, first deputy chairman of the board, Republican Bank "Ukraina," 1990-93; chair and governor, National Bank of Ukraine, 1993-99; appointed prime minister of Ukraine, 1999, resigned after a vote of no-confidence in February, 2001; director, Borys Yeltsin Ukrainian-Russian Institute of Management and Business, 2001-02; elected to *Verkhovna Rada* (Ukraine national assembly), March, 2002; became leader of the "Our Ukraine" parliamentary faction, 2002, and chair of the All-Ukrainian "Our Ukraine"

civil organization after 2003; elected president of Ukraine, December, 2004.

Sidelights

Viktor Yushchenko triumphed in a brutal political battle for the presidency of Ukraine in late 2004. He led a political coalition called *Nasha Ukrayina* ("Our Ukraine"), but lost a run-off election widely believed to have been rigged in favor of a candidate who had the support of Vladimir Putin, the president of Ukraine's powerful neighbor and former master, Russia. Yushchenko, by contrast, was a pro-West economist who enjoyed broad popular as well as international support, and when the run-off election results were announced in the other candidate's favor, protesters began to gather at the main square in Kiev, the Ukraine capital.

Despite the customary Ukraine subzero late autumn temperatures, Yushchenko's supporters stood firm until a second run-off election was held, after which he was declared the legitimate winner of the presidency of Ukraine, a nation of 47 million squeezed into a landmass roughly the size of Texas. Heavily industrialized and rich in natural resources, Ukraine is also caught at a unique crossroads thanks to its geographic position between Eastern Europe and Russia. Ukrainians, traditionally suspicious of their Russian neighbors after a long and bloody history between the two powers, had struggled to create a new, democratic post-Soviet government. Thus Yushchenko's victory had great significance for pro-European Ukrainians, but it also had wider implications for the political landscape of Europe. "It showed," wrote Jason Bush and Roman Olearchyk in *BusinessWeek*, "that a decade and a half after the end of the cold war, Europe is not doomed to a new continental divide that would abandon Ukraine and the other states of the old Soviet Union to authoritarian systems characterized by rigged elections and political intimidation."

Yushchenko was born in 1954 in Khoruzhivka, a town in the oblast, or province, of Sums'ka in Ukraine's north. At the time of his birth, the country was attached to the Soviet Union as one of its constituent republics. Both of his parents were teachers, and his father was a World War II veteran who had been captured and taken prisoner by Nazi German forces, and incarcerated in Auschwitz, the notorious Nazi death camp where Jews were exterminated as part of Nazi Germany's "Final Solution" to eradicate the Jews of Europe.

As a young man, Yushchenko studied economics at a college in Ternopil in Ukraine's eastern region, and after earning his degree in 1975 took a job as an agricultural accountant on one of the large collective farms of the Soviet era, when private property or free enterprise were virtually nonexistent. He served a year in the Soviet Army, and in 1976 joined the State Bank in Ulyanovsk, a city in Russia, as an economist. He eventually rose to chief of the Ulyanovsk branch, and in 1985 was appointed to a deputy director's post at the State Bank's Ukrainian headquarters. He moved in 1988 to Kiev's Agro-Industrial Bank as a manager, and when that bank was reorganized in 1990 and its name changed to "Ukrayina," he served as the deputy chairman of its supervisory board.

Much changed in Ukraine since Yushchenko had started his career back in the mid-1970s. Soviet leader Mikhail Gorbachev, who took office in 1985, ushered in a series of reforms that eventually led to a swift and relatively bloodless end of communism in the Soviet Union. Boris Yeltsin came to power in 1991, and continued the reforms already underway that were taking the Soviet Union from a state-planned socialist economy to a free-market one. Ukraine declared its independence that same year, and followed a similar economic reform program. Despite his training as a Soviet-regime banker, Yush-

chenko had little trouble adjusting to the new era, and even came to play a leading role in the transition. In 1993, he became head of the new National Bank of Ukraine.

Yushchenko was a key figure in Ukraine's successful adoption of the *hryvnia* in 1996, which replaced the Soviet ruble. He also played a part in the creation of a new regulatory system for commercial banking in the post-Soviet era. But the Ukrainian economy was still tangled with that of Russia, and when the ruble decreased in value and Russia plunged into economic turmoil in 1998, Yushchenko managed to keep the value of the hryvnia stable despite the hyperinflation and recession that resulted. Thanks to his leadership role and growing popularity, in late 1999 Yushchenko was made the country's prime minister in a surprise move by Ukrainian president Leonid Kuchma in the midst of Kuchma's own governance crisis.

Yushchenko held the office for less than two years, and was ousted in a 2001 battle between the Ukrainian government and its coal-mining and natural gas industries. Kuchma had strong alliances with the new Ukrainian oligarchs, the business moguls who bought up large stakes in the formerly state-owned industries in the 1990s, and quickly amassed immense fortunes thanks to their government deals. Yushchenko's prudent economic policies were often opposed by the oligarchs, and some of the members of the Verkhovna Rada, or Ukrainian parliament, who were beholden to the oligarchs for their own political success, conspired with the more leftist-leaning Rada members to oust Yushchenko with a no-confidence vote. His ouster prompted a massive demonstration in Kiev, and he promised his supporters that he would return to political office soon.

In 2002 Yushchenko emerged as head of a new political coalition, *Nasha Ukrayina* (Our Ukraine), that won 26 percent of the Rada seats in March legislative elections that year. Our Ukraine was created when several parties united in opposition to Kuchma's autocratic rule to challenge him. Despite winning 112 out of the 450 seats in the Rada, the coalition was essentially powerless, however, and unable to form a coalition with other opposition parties in the Rada. Meanwhile, Kuchma's government was mired in several notorious corruption scandals, and even linked to the murder of an investigative journalist who had written unfavorably about Kuchma and his cronies.

Kuchma's two-term limit as president was set to expire in 2004. His prime minister, Viktor Yanukovych, became his handpicked party successor, and Yushchenko declared himself an independent candidate for the presidency. He ran with Yuliya Tymoshenko, a successful businesswoman-turned-Rada member whom he had named to his cabinet during his 1999-2001 stint as prime minister. Tymoshenko, who founded a successful video rental chain in 1989 and then went on to run several influential oil and natural-gas concerns in Ukraine, was set to become the first female prime minister if Yushchenko's ticket won the October 31, 2004, balloting.

The run-up to the campaign was a heated one. Yushchenko campaigned on a platform that advocated more ties to Europe and the West, greater openness in governmental affairs, and a re-examination of some of the business deals that the Kuchma government had entered into that gave away the formerly state-run enterprises to the powerful Ukraine or Russian oligarchs. Yushchenko supported the idea of allowing foreign investment instead. This prompted his political opponents to denounce Yushchenko as a puppet of foreign governments, and even claim that his wife, Kateryna, was a spy. This accusation was linked to the fact that she was a Ukrainian-American from Chicago, and had once worked at the U.S. State Department before she wed Yushchenko. But the most shocking event of the 2004 election came on September 21, when Yushchenko—known for his movie-star looks—appeared before the Rada with his face covered with terrible cysts. He told his shocked audience that he had been poisoned by his political enemies.

Yushchenko had fallen ill in the first week of September, and traveled to an Austrian clinic for treatment. Doctors initially suspected some sort of trouble with his pancreas, possibly the result of a viral infection that was linked to unknown chemical substances. His face had changed almost overnight, becoming bloated and pockmarked in a condition known as chloracne. A prominent Dutch toxicologist saw news footage of Yushchenko, and asked the Austrian clinic if he could test some of Yushchenko's blood; the scientist's hunch proved correct, and it was announced that Yushchenko had been poisoned with dioxin, an extremely toxic byproduct of pesticide manufacturing and other chemical processes.

Yushchenko claimed that the poisoning had happened at a midnight dinner on September 5, when he met with senior Ukrainian officials that included the head of Security Service of Ukraine (SBU), or secret police. He fell ill the next day, but medical professionals cast doubt on this dinner as the culprit for the dioxin poisoning, noting that symptoms generally take a minimum of three days to appear. There were other possible unknown suspects, in-

cluding perhaps someone within Yushchenko's inner circle, or someone working for the organized crime syndicates that have grown immensely powerful in the post-Soviet era. He continued to campaign, despite crippling back pains from the dioxin levels.

On October 31, 2004, Yushchenko and his ticket won 39.87 percent of the ballots, with the Yanukovych slate taking 39.32 percent of the vote. Ukrainian election laws stipulate that the presidential winner is one with a 50 percent margin, and so a run-off vote was scheduled for November 21. On that day, there were allegations of voting fraud and election irregularities, including voter intimidation, cases of multiple voting, and votes for Yanukovych that came in after the polls closed. Exit polls of voters suggested that Yushchenko carried strong lead, but instead the final tally showed Yanukovych had won by three percent.

Ukrainians turned out in large numbers to protest the results. They camped out in Kiev's Independence Square, near the main government buildings, and in the public squares of other Ukrainian cities. Television cameras broadcast the Kiev vigil around the world, and it was soon dubbed the Orange Revolution for the ribbons that supporters of Yushchenko and Tymoshenko wore. The crisis prompted the Ukraine Supreme Court to examine the election results, and its judges overturned the Yanukovych victory and ordered another run-off to be held on December 26. In that one, widely monitored by teams of international observers and judged to have been conducted fairly, Yushchenko won by an eight-percent margin, or more than two million votes.

The loser, Yanukovych, did not resign from the government leadership immediately, as is customary in the country for an outgoing prime minister and his cabinet. There were some worries that a more dangerous stand-off was looming, for the Orange Revolution supporters were still camping out on Independence Square, but when they blockaded Yanukovych's cabinet offices at news of a scheduled meeting that last December week, Yanukovych finally resigned. On New Year's Eve, Yushchenko addressed a new crowd that had gathered in the Square for the holiday countdown and unofficial victory celebration. "We have been independent for 14 years," he told the joyous Ukrainians, according to a *Time International* report, "but we have not been free. Today we are independent and free."

Yushchenko was inaugurated as an independent Ukraine's third president on January 23, 2005, with Tymoshenko taking office as the country's first female prime minister. During his first months in office, he ordered a major reorganization of the corruption-riddled bureaucracy, replacing some 18,000 officials. He also moved to halt the privatization process of a few companies that had formerly been state-owned entities and then sold off to groups of private investors. In early April, he visited U.S. President George W. Bush at the White House, and spoke before Congress as well. He urged the United States to lend support to Ukraine's bid to become a member of the European Union. In September of 2005, Yushchenko fired his entire government, amid political squabbling among its members. "I am setting before the new team one task—the ability to work as one," he said, according to CNN.com.

Yushchenko is the father of three daughters and two sons, two of them adult children from a first marriage that ended in divorce. He has a son and two daughters from his 1998 marriage to Kateryna Chumachenko, who became a Ukrainian citizen after her husband took office. Yushchenko's hobbies are considered typical Ukrainian ones: mountaineering and beekeeping. He made his annual climb of Hoverla, the Ukraine's highest mountain, in July of 2005 after receiving permission from his doctors, who were still monitoring his health after the dioxin poisoning. The culprits remain at large.

Sources

Periodicals

BusinessWeek, May 30, 2005, p. 44.

Fortune International, February 7, 2005, p. 22.

New York Times, December 20, 2004, p. A1.

Time International, December 20, 2004, p. 30; January 10, 2005, p. 34.

Times (London, England), December 28, 2004, p. 28.

Online

"Viktor Yushchenko: Biography," President of Ukraine Official Website, http://www.president.gov.ua/en/content/101_e.html (August 22, 2005).

"Yushchenko fires government," CNN.com, http://www.cnn.com/2005/WORLD/europe/09/08/ukraine.yushchenko/index.html (September 8, 2005).

—*Carol Brennan*

490

Ziyi Zhang

Actress

Born Zhang Ziyi, February 9, 1979, in Beijing, China; daughter of Zhang Yuan Xiao (a government economist) and Li Zhou Sheng (a kindergarten schoolteacher). *Education:* Attended China Central Drama Academy.

Addresses: *Agent*—William Morris Agency, One William Morris Place, Beverly Hills, CA 90212.

Career

Actress in films, including: *The Road Home*, 1999; *Crouching Tiger, Hidden Dragon*, 2000; *Rush Hour 2*, 2001; *The Legend of Zu*, 2001; *Musa the Warrior*, 2001; *Hero*, 2002; *Purple Butterfly*, 2003; *House of Flying Daggers*, 2004; *2046*, 2004; *Jasmine Flower*, 2004; *Memoirs of a Geisha*, 2005.

Awards: Golden Bauhinia Award for best supporting actress, for *Crouching Tiger, Hidden Dragon*, 2001; Hong Kong Film Critics Society award for best actress, for *2046*, 2004; Hong Kong Film award for best actress, for *2046*, 2004, named one of *People* magazine's 50 most beautiful people, 2005; Hua Biao award for excellent actress, for *House of Flying Daggers*, 2005.

Sidelights

Called "a rare talent, blending delicacy and fragility with athleticism and a formidable personality," by Bill Thompson of the *Post and Courier* of Charleston, South Carolina, Ziyi Zhang has taken

Lucy Nicholson/Reuters/Landov

the movie world by storm. She came to the attention of audiences worldwide in director Ang Lee's *Crouching Tiger, Hidden Dragon,* and since then has been unstoppable. She landed the coveted title role in the movie version of the popular novel *Memoirs of a Geisha*, and it seems that there will be many more triumphs in her future.

The actress was born Zhang Ziyi on February 9, 1979, in Beijing to Zhang Yuan Xiao, a government economist, and Li Zhou Sheng, a kindergarten schoolteacher. (When she began gaining attention from American audiences, she flipped the order of her name to conform to Western style.) She has one older brother, who owns an advertising agency. Zhang grew up poor. She told Stephen Whitty of the *Star-Ledger,* "My parents' life was not easy at all. Our house in Beijing was very small, we didn't have money—it was really before the beginning of the economic boom. The generation of the '90s, those who are now in their teens, they are the ones who are really benefiting from what is going on in China now. But I'm very glad I had what I had because it allows me to appreciate a lot of things."

Zhang began taking dance lessons when she was very young. She did not wish to become a dancer, but she was very small and frail as a child and her parents, fearful for her health, insisted that she dance to build up her strength, so they enrolled her at the Beijing Dance Academy when she was eleven. Zhang discovered that dance—mainly ballet and traditional Chinese—was good not only for her body, but for her mind. She learned much of the discipline she exudes as an adult when she was a little girl. She did not really enjoy it, however, so when the time came after six years to renew her studies, she suggested to her parents that she try drama instead; they agreed. In 1996 she enrolled in the China Central Drama Academy but she felt like she did not belong. She was extremely uncertain of her skills at first, so nervous that she had difficulty acting. "I lost myself and felt pain for the whole year," Zhang was quoted by the Xinhua News Agency. "Teacher Chang was very strict with us. I usually prayed to God before going to bed to tell me how to accomplish my homework the next day." In her second year, after she struggled hard to pass her first-year exams, she finally started to get a feel for performing. She discovered such a passion for acting that second year that at the year-end performance she rushed on stage during a show where she was playing a wife greeting her husband and accidentally crashed into a large piece of glass. She was rushed to the hospital and still bears a scar on her hand, but she had finally found the desire and passion to act that she had been missing before.

She was discovered at a casting call for a shampoo commercial with *Lantern* director Zhang Yimou (no relation). The ad was never made, but Zhang Yimou was so impressed with Zhang that he cast her in his 1999 movie, *The Road Home*. This movie is Zhang's favorite role to date. She loved the sweet devotion her character showed the man she loved and really felt passion acting in it.

It was her next film, however, that brought Zhang to the attention of critics and audiences across the globe. *Crouching Tiger, Hidden Dragon*, released in 2000, was just about as far removed from her first acting experience as she could get. Ang Lee directed the film and famous Chinese actors Chow Yun-Fat and Michelle Yeoh co-starred in the film with her. Apparently it was those two acting heavyweights that were expected to make an impact on foreign audiences, but instead the ethereal and fragile beauty that Zhang showed on screen, along with her fantastic physical strength in the martial arts scenes, captured the hearts of audiences around the globe. She was also known for her incredible dedication, on and off screen. The Xinhua News Agency wrote, "Ang Lee … has said that [Zhang] is the most enterprising girl among the actresses he has cooperated with, and she would bear any hardship." The movie was a challenge for Zhang, but one that she

welcomed gladly. She told Ian Nathan in the *Times*, "I love *Crouching Tiger* very much because I didn't know I could play this strong girl, a very powerful girl. I think Ang Lee helped me to find that kind of personality. I didn't know I could do it. I am softer. I can't kick people." For most of the film Zhang's goal was just to please Lee and hear words of praise from him. After filming was completed, Lee finally expressed how pleased he was with Zhang's performance. The director was not the only one who appreciated Zhang's hard work; people flocked the theaters to see the film. Joanna Connors of the *Plain Dealer* said of the film, "Zhang, the young actress who plays Jen, has the most difficult role. Jen is full of secrets and schemes, and she switches teams so often she should file for free agency. Zhang pulls it off effortlessly, and achieves what most actors never do: She expresses her character through her movement, like a great dancer." *Crouching Tiger, Hidden Dragon* won an Academy Award, and the Toronto Film Critics Association named the movie the best film of the year and nominated Zhang for best supporting actress.

Zhang next made her American film debut with a small role in the action-comedy *Rush Hour 2*. She took the role to help improve her English-speaking skills as much as for the experience. She also learned a great deal about the differences between the American and Chinese moviemaking cultures. Zhang told Whitty of the *Star-Ledger*, "In America, making a movie you have a lot of technology and you spend a lot of money, so the conditions are very good. I have my own trailer! And we have weekends off, and the Christmas holiday! That's a big difference from China." She had a good time acting alongside fellow countryman Jackie Chan, learning English and how to cross over to American films, although she said she was not interested in moving to the United States. She told Whitty of the *Star-Ledger* that one of the reasons she would not move here was because of a lack of good roles for Asian women. "That's a problem, I think. I'm thinking there's not a lot of opportunity yet. I know we're lucky to get these films; you can't hope too much. But I don't want to play evil girl, prostitute, all the time. I'd like to play *Monster's Ball*, a movie like that. But there are not so many good scripts written just for Asians."

Her next big role was as a blind dancer named Mei in the martial arts epic *House of Flying Daggers*. She became so dedicated to giving her all in every performance that when she was training to be in the film she carried 30 kilogram bags of sand on her legs for two months. She especially had to train for a dance she performs in the movie. Bob Strauss of the *Daily News* noted her hard work. "Her greatest physical display was the Echo Game. Challenged by Inspector Leo to prove she really is a great dancer and not just another girl-for-hire at the Peony Pavilion bordello, Mei is placed within a semi-circle of mounted drums. When Leo flicks a particular drumhead with a small stone, blind Mei must strike the same surface with an extended sleeve of her silk gown." There were no special effects in that sequence and she had to train long hours to get it right. "I had to hit every drum right; sometimes it took 20 takes, your aim has to be right on. It took about two months of rehearsal," she told Strauss. In August of 2005 Zhang won the Excellent Actress title of the Hua Biao Award, the Chinese government's film award. It was her first win, although she had been nominated several times before.

Her next role was another change from the martial arts flick for which she was becoming famous. That movie was the Chinese film *2046*. The movie is about a young woman who is trying to make ends meet in 1960s Hong Kong. She does this mainly through a series of wealthy boyfriends. She ends up connecting with a writer who has himself been hurt by love and has no qualms at passing his pain on to others. Elizabeth Weitzman of the *Seattle Times* said of Zhang's performance, "The actress captures Bai Ling's vulnerable dignity and immense pain so precisely, it's difficult to reconcile the character with the Zhang who bounds into our interview wearing a denim miniskirt, tank top, and flip-flops, and who might pass for 18." G. Allen Johnson of the *San Francisco Chronicle* said it was Zhang's "most mature performance to date."

One of her biggest coups, however, came when she obtained the title role in the film adaptation of the popular novel *Memoirs of a Geisha*, directed by Rob Marshall. She perfected her English for the part, and then had to learn a Japanese accent. It was quite a challenge, but another one that she gladly accepted. The movie opened in December of 2005 in the United States and Zhang's fans were not disappointed with her first starring role in an American film.

Having reached the pinnacle of fame in Asia, if not worldwide, in September of 2005 Zhang took part in the opening festivities of Hong Kong Disneyland along with such other famous actors as Jackie Chang, Andy Hui, and Paige O'Hara. She was also named one of *People* magazine's 50 most beautiful people. She has become a spokesmodel for Maybelline cosmetics and Pantene shampoo. She was named #131 of *Express on Sunday*'s top 300 most beautiful women and she was a presenter at the Academy Awards. That same year, Zhang was invited to join the U.S. Academy of Motion Picture Arts and Sciences. She was the only Chinese star to be invited to join that year. The membership would allow her to vote for Oscar winners. Apparently Zhang has firmly established herself as an actress to watch, one who is admired and sought after.

People talk to Zhang all the time about her easy climb to the top, but Zhang always disagrees. Zhang told the Xinhua News Agency, "My success was not by chance, instead, it's paved by hard work, pain, and tears." Now that she has achieved success in the American market, she has admitted to be contemplating staying in the country. The main problem, aside from her dismay at the lack of parts for Asians, was that she really wanted to become a role model for her own countrywomen. She told the *New York Post*, "For Western women, it's much easier to be yourself. If you want to do something, you just go and do it. In an Asian context, women are still much more modest and conservative. I want, through my roles, to express the parts in the hearts of Chinese women that they feel unable to let out." It would be hard to argue that she has not begun doing just that—she has wisely chosen a number of roles portraying women as strong and self-possessed, and it is to be expected that this will continue as her career progresses into the future.

Sources

Chicago Tribune, January 6, 2005.

Daily Mail (London, England), September 29, 2000, p. 51; December 29, 2000, p. 51.

Daily News (Los Angeles, CA), August 9, 2001, p. L3; November 14, 2004, p. U7; December 3, 2004, p. U6.

Entertainment Weekly, December 22, 2000, p. 42; January 12, 2001, p. 85; June 8, 2001, p. 53; November 12, 2004, p. 56; December 10, 2004, p. 64; December 31, 2004, p. 70; April 22, 2005, p. 50; June 24, 2005, p. 61.

Esquire, December 2000, p. 130.

Evening Standard (London, England), June 28, 2005, p. 18.

Express on Sunday, March 10, 2002, p. 28.

International Herald Tribune, December 7, 2004, p. 12.

Interview, December 2000, p. 53; June 2001, p. 58; August 2001, p. 52; December 2004, p. 112; August 2005, p. 84; October 2005, p. 150.

New Statesman, January 8, 2001, p. 33; January 1, 2005, p. 83.

New York Daily News, August 4, 2005.

New York Post, November 28, 2004, p. 89; August 3, 2005, p. 49.

New York Times, May 27, 2001, p. AR9.

Orange County Register, December 9, 2004.

People, March 12, 2001, p. 88; May 14, 2001, p. 143; September 6, 2004, p. 31; December 27, 2004, p. 35; May 9, 2005, p. 170; August 15, 2005, p. 118.

Plain Dealer (Cleveland, OH), January 12, 2001, p. 4.

Post and Courier (Charleston, SC), June 2, 2005, p. F13.

Record (Bergen County, NJ), February 21, 2005, p. F1.

San Francisco Chronicle, July 28, 2002, p. 32; August 19, 2005, p. E5.

Seattle Times, August 13, 2005, p. G3.

Star-Ledger (Newark, NJ), August 7, 2005, p. 1.

Teen People, June 1, 2002, p. 99.

Time, December 4, 2000, p. 166; January 15, 2001, p. 122; December 6, 2004, p. 125; April 18, 2005, p. 124.

Times (London, England), October 9, 2004, p. 7; December 12, 2004, p. 4.

Variety, February 21, 2000, p. 37; November 8, 2004, p. 40; May 16, 2005, p. 74; June 6, 2005, p. 28.

Xinhua News Agency, August 30, 2005; September 1, 2005; October 27, 2005.

—*Catherine Victoria Donaldson*

Obituaries

Eddie Albert

Born Edward Albert Heimberger, April 22, 1906, in Rock Island, IL; died of pneumonia, May 26, 2005, in Pacific Palisades, CA. Actor. Eddie Albert is best remembered for his role as the lawyer-turned-farmer on *Green Acres,* one of the most popular television sitcoms of the 1960s. Though Albert would be indelibly linked to that role, he had a long career in Hollywood and on Broadway, became one of the first entertainment-industry celebrities to voice concern over environmental issues, and was also a decorated war hero. The well-read actor claimed he jumped at the chance to play the hapless Oliver Wendell Douglas on *Green Acres,* despite his reservations about committing to a television series. "I knew it would be successful," he told an interviewer some years later, according to his *Los Angeles Times* obituary. "It's about the atavistic urge, and people have been getting a charge out of that ever since Aristophanes wrote about the plebs and the city folk."

Albert was born in Rock Island, Illinois, in 1906, though some sources have cited the date as 1908 instead. His mother had apparently altered his birth certificate, due to the fact that she was not yet married to his father when she became pregnant. Raised in Minneapolis, Albert spent two years at the University of Minnesota before dropping out of school to join a singing group. As one of "The Threesome," he appeared on local radio broadcasts and toured the Midwest before the group went their separate ways.

Heading to New York City in the mid-1930s, Albert found work on an NBC morning radio show, and even appeared in one of the first experimental television broadcasts in the United States when the medium was still in the testing stages. He made his Broadway debut in the short-lived *O Evening Star,* but went on to a more successful run in *Brother Rat,* a comedy set at a military academy. He reprised the role for the 1938 film version, and went on to appear in a number of other Hollywood movies before the work suddenly stopped; Albert had reportedly run afoul of his studio boss, Jack Warner, over rumors of an affair between the actor and Warner's wife. To find work he was forced to go to Mexico, where he joined a friend's circus troupe and performed as a clown and trapeze artist.

When America entered World War II in late 1941, Albert enlisted in the U.S. Navy, and saw combat duty in the Pacific theater. He was awarded a Bronze Star for rescuing 142 injured Marines during the three-day Battle of Tarawa. After returning to civilian life, he wed the Mexican-American actor and dancer known as Margo, and continued some of the training-film work he had done during the last year of the war. Eddie Albert Productions, his company, made industrial and educational films, including a few sex-education ones that were considered somewhat controversial in their day.

By the early 1950s, Albert had resumed his film career, and was also working in television. He was nominated for an Academy Award for best supporting actor for his role as Gregory Peck's photographer pal in the Audrey Hepburn movie *Roman Holiday* in 1953, and also turned in a critically acclaimed performance in the 1956 war drama, *Attack.* But it was his role as the elite Manhattan lawyer Oliver Wendell Douglas in the CBS series *Green Acres* that earned him enduring fame. The show debuted in 1965 and ran for six seasons. Its storylines centered around Oliver's quest to become a gentleman farmer on a run-down piece of land near the fictional Hooterville. Oliver's extravagantly coiffed, elegantly dressed, and elaborately bejeweled wife Lisa (Eva Gabor), meanwhile, was unwilling to give up her Park-Avenue princess ways, which provided additional comic fodder for each week's episode.

After *Green Acres*, Albert was nominated for another Academy Award for his part in *The Heartbreak Kid*, a 1972 Neil Simon comedy, as the on-screen father of Cybill Shepherd. Two years later, he proved once again he could be cast against nice-guy type when he played a sadistic prison warden who torments Burt Reynolds' character in the 1974 box-office hit *The Longest Yard*. Albert spent the remainder of his career in dozens of guest roles on television and voice-over work, from *General Hospital* to a 1997 *Spider-Man* series that aired on Fox Family.

Albert was an outspoken advocate for environmental issues all the way back to the early 1970s, especially along the California coastline. He was also active in a number of humanitarian projects, such as a 1963 United Nations food program called Meals for Millions. Widowed in 1985, he was diagnosed with Alzheimer's disease a decade later, and died at home on May 26, 2005, at the age of 99. He is survived by his son Eddie Albert Jr., also an actor; his daughter Maria Zucht, and two grandchildren. "Acting was one-tenth of his life," his son said, according to E! Online. "The majority of his life was committed to helping other people." **Sources:** *Chicago Tribune*, May 28, 2005, sec. 2, p. 11; CNN.com, http://www.cnn.com/2005/SHOWBIZ/TV/05/27/obit.eddie.albert.ap/index.html (May 31, 2005); *Entertainment Weekly*, June 10, 2005, p. 25; E! Online News, http://www.eonline.com/News/Items/0,1,16652,00.html?tnews (May 31, 2005); *Los Angeles Times*, May 28, 2005, p. B20; *New York Times*, May 28, 2005, p. B21; *People*, June 13, 2005, p. 150; *Times* (London), May 31, 2005, p. 49; *Washington Post*, May 28, 2005, p. B6.

—*Carol Brennan*

Julius Axelrod

Born May 30, 1912, in New York, NY; died December 29, 2004, in Rockville, MD. Biochemist. American biochemist Julius Axelrod conducted important research in brain chemistry that spurred the development of an entirely new class of drugs. Prozac and Paxil, the brand names of more-effective depression-treating drugs that came onto the market in the late 1980s and early '90s, were the direct result of Axelrod's discoveries about certain hormones and their actions in the part of the brain that regulates moods. For this work, he was a co-recipient of the 1970 Nobel Prize.

Axelrod was born in 1912, six years after his Polish-born parents came to America and settled on Manhattan's Lower East Side. He planned to become a doctor, and graduated from Seward Park High School on Grand Street just as the Great Depression was beginning. After one year at New York University, he transferred to the City College of New York, which offered free tuition to all city residents. After earning his undergraduate degree in 1933, he was rejected by the admissions boards of several medical schools, possibly because he was Jewish; it was an era when most medical schools accepted only a limited number of Jewish enrollees every year. Instead he took a job at a lab at the New York University Medical School, and in 1935 was hired by the New York City Department of Health to test vitamin-fortified foods. There, in 1938, Axelrod lost an eye in a laboratory accident when a bottle of ammonia exploded. For the remainder of his life he wore eyeglasses with a darkened lens over the left side.

Though his impaired vision made Axelrod ineligible to serve in the U.S. military during World War II, it did not deter his scientific ambitions in the least. He worked full time, but took night classes and earned a master's degree in chemistry from New York University. His thesis on cancer tissue enzymes impressed Dr. Bernard Brodie, who would become an important mentor to him. In 1945 Axelrod was invited to join Brodie in his research lab at Goldwater Memorial Hospital on New York City's Roosevelt Island. When Brodie moved to the National Heart Institute, part of the federally funded National Institutes of Health (NIH), in 1949, the junior scientist followed him there. Urged by his colleagues, Axelrod began work on his doctorate, and earned it in 1955, when he was in his early 40s, from George Washington University. That same year he was invited to establish a pharmacology section at the NIH's Laboratory of Clinical Science within the National Institute of Mental Health.

Some of Axelrod's earliest research work dealt with pain-relieving medications, specifically the discovery of acetaminophen as a headache reliever. The drug was later made available without a prescription under the brand name Tylenol. Around 1957, he began the work that would later earn him the Nobel Prize. His research involved catecholamines, the hormone chemicals in the brain that are stored in nerve endings. They serve as neurotransmitters, or chemical messengers between nerve cells. Axelrod looked at noradrenaline, one of these catecholamine neurotransmitters. The common scientific perception was that noradrenaline was dissolved by enzymes once it was no longer active, but Axelrod's work showed that noradrenaline was instead recycled, or reuptaken, by the nerve cells. His discovery led to the engineering of a new type of drugs that worked to block that reuptake process, particularly for serotonin, a mood-regulating neurotransmitter. These new anti-depressant medications, known as "selective serotonin reuptake inhibitors" (SSRIs), first became available in 1987 with the introduction of Prozac by prescription. Prozac and its SSRI siblings, including Zoloft and Paxil, began to be used by millions and would make a profound difference in the treatment of depression and substance abuse.

For his discovery, Axelrod shared the 1970 Nobel Prize in physiology or medicine with two other scientists also working in the field, Sir Bernard Katz, an Australian at University College of London, and Ulf von Euler of Sweden's Karlinska Institute. Axelrod also did important early work on melatonin, a hormone secreted by the pineal gland that regulates sleep cycles. He officially retired in 1984, but still came into the lab three times a week. In 1996 he was named an emeritus scientist at the NIH. He suffered from heart trouble in his later years, and died in his sleep at the age of 92 on December 29, 2004, at his home in Rockville, Maryland. He was married to Sally Taub, an elementary-school teacher, in 1938, but widowed in 1992. He is survived by two sons and three grandchildren. Respected by his colleagues and popular with his graduate assistants, Axelrod was known for his modesty. He learned of his Nobel Prize win from his dentist, after forgetting to listen to the radio that morning, and when President Richard M. Nixon made a congratulatory telephone call, Axelrod used the opportunity to challenge the Nixon Administration's planned budgetary revisions in scientific funding, which had caused some consternation at the NIH. The Nobel prizewinner later said that his achievements would have been impossible for the generation of scientists who followed him, when earning a doctorate at the age of 41 would put one far behind in the professional race. "There's not room in the field of research for people like me," he asserted, according to Jon Thurber's *Los Angeles Times* obituary, quoting an earlier interview, "who matured slowly."
Sources: *Chicago Tribune*, December 30, 2004, sec. 3, p. 8; *Los Angeles Times*, January 2, 2005, p. B14; *New York Times*, December 31, 2004, p. A22; *Times* (London), January 4, 2005, p. 46.

—*Carol Brennan*

John N. Bahcall

Born John Norris Bahcall, December 30, 1934, in Shreveport, LA; died of a rare blood disorder, August 17, 2005, in New York, NY. Astrophysicist and astronomer. Princeton astrophysicist John N. Bahcall is best known for his work concerning the creation of the Hubble Space Telescope. Launched in 1990 and still orbiting the earth, Hubble has helped scientists solve many of the universe's mysteries. In addition, Bahcall is credited with unlocking answers to several other cosmological puzzles, including the mystery of what makes the sun shine. Bahcall's research in the 1960s proved once and for all that the sun is fueled by nuclear reactions.

Bahcall was born on December 30, 1934, in Shreveport, Louisiana. He played tennis in high school and had no interest in science. When Bahcall enrolled at Louisiana State University, he decided to study philosophy, figuring he might become a rabbi. A year later, Bahcall transferred to the University of California at Berkeley, having never completed a science class in his life. At Berkeley, science was required, so he opted for physics. "It was the hardest thing I have ever done in my life, but I fell in love with science," Bahcall recalled during a 2002 commencement speech, according to *Washington Post* staffer Joe Holley. "I was thrilled by the fact that by knowing physics you could figure out how real things worked, like sunsets and airplanes, and that after a while everyone agreed on what was the right answer to a question." After the course, Bahcall decided to study physics and astronomy, choosing to rely on science—not spirituality—in his quest for greater truths.

Bahcall finished his undergraduate degree at UC Berkeley in 1956, then earned graduate degrees in physics, including a master's in 1957 from the University of Chicago and a doctorate from Harvard University, which he completed in 1961. Bahcall then worked as a research fellow at Indiana University and later joined the Kellogg Radiation Laboratory at the California Institute of Technology. While there, he worked on a series of calculations concerning the sun. Bahcall believed that the sun was probably powered by nuclear reactions, and he concluded that if so, the sun should be sending subatomic particles called neutrinos toward the earth along with its light.

He started working with astrophysicist Raymond Davis Jr. of the Brookhaven National Laboratory and the pair began what would become a decades-long collaboration. Together, they concocted an experiment to collect neutrinos. They built a neutrino detector, which was really an enormous tank filled with a chlorine-based cleaning fluid and sunk into the pit of an abandoned South Dakota gold mine. For the most part, the neutrinos passed through the tank undetected, just as they passed through all other matter, including the earth. Some neutrinos, however, collided with the chlorine atoms to create radioactive atoms. Periodically, Davis and Bahcall counted the radioactive atoms.

In 1968 they reported their experiment to the scientific world, noting that they had been able to capture and study neutrinos from the sun, thus proving that the sun's light is derived from nuclear reactions. The mystery of how the sun shines had puzzled scientists for decades—and Bahcall's investigation settled the matter.

That same year, Bahcall joined the Institute for Advanced Study at Princeton University. There, he continued his investigations with neutrinos and also studied the dark matter of the universe and the evolution of stars. By 1971, he was a full faculty member—a professor of natural resources. He trained batches of astrophysicists, many of whom became leaders in the field.

Bahcall spread his passion around the globe, traveling abroad to help launch astronomy groups at Tel Aviv University and the Weizmann Institute of Science, both in Israel. During one of these trips, he met Israeli graduate student Neta Assaf. Bahcall asked her out more than ten times before she accepted a date. Though Bahcall could not speak Hebrew and Assaf was not fluent in English, their relationship flourished and they married within a year. After relocating to the United States with her new husband, Neta Bahcall became a cosmologist at Princeton. They hold the distinction of being the only astronomy couple each with memberships to the National Academy of Sciences.

By the 1970s, Bahcall had started working with Princeton astronomer Lyman Spitzer Jr. to advocate for the development of a space telescope. Spitzer had proposed the idea of a space telescope back in the 1940s but the project did not seem viable until the 1970s when technology had advanced. Bahcall and Spitzer made numerous appearances before Congress and, after winning approval, worked on the Hubble Space Telescope's development. It was finally launched in 1990 by the space shuttle Discovery and put into orbit 370 miles above the earth. Since then, the telescope has been making daily observations of space free from the distractions imposed by the earth's atmosphere.

Speaking to the *Los Angeles Times* shortly after Bahcall's death, Caltech astronomer Maarten Schmidt recalled Bahcall as a "tenacious" creature who would never give up on an idea "and it really paid

off with the Hubble Space Telescope." Bahcall remained loyal to the instrument to the end. When former National Aeronautics and Space Administration (NASA) administrator Sean O'Keefe announced that there would be no more shuttle missions to repair the telescope following the 2003 explosion of the shuttle Columbia, Bahcall put up a fight. He penned editorials and made calls on the telescope's behalf from his hospital bed as he lay dying. Eventually, NASA agreed to reconsider.

In 2002, Raymond Davis—the man Bahcall had done his neutrino collaboration with—earned the Nobel Prize in Physics for his investigations into neutrinos. Davis shared the award with University of Tokyo professor Masatoshi Koshiba, who had also worked on neutrino detection. Many physicists believed Bahcall should have been honored as well, but he never complained. Bahcall did receive numerous awards over his lifetime, including NASA's Distinguished Public Service Medal in 1992 for his work with the Hubble Space Telescope. Bahcall also received the National Medal of Science in 1998. Over the course of his career, Bahcall wrote more than 500 scientific papers and published five books related to astrophysics, astronomy, and neutrinos. His writings helped other scientists better understand the cosmos.

Bahcall died of a rare blood disorder on August 17, 2005, at New York-Presbyterian/Weill Cornell Hospital. He was 70. Survivors include his wife, sons Safi and Dan, his daughter, Orli, and his brother, Robert. **Sources:** *Los Angeles Times,* August 20, 2005, p. B16; *New York Times,* August 19, 2005, p. C14; *Times* (London, England), September 1, 2005, p. 68; *Washington Post,* August 20, 2005, p. B6.

—*Lisa Frick*

Anne Bancroft

Born Anna Maria Louise Italiano, September 17, 1931, in New York, NY; died of uterine cancer, June 6, 2005, in New York, NY. Actress. Award-winning star of stage and screen Anne Bancroft was best known for her role as the seductive Mrs. Robinson in the 1967 film, *The Graduate.* Despite a rich and varied career in which she proved herself across a number of challenging roles, Bancroft would be forever linked to the leopard-coat-clad sophisticate who preyed on a young Dustin Hoffman.

Born in 1931, Bancroft grew up in the New York City borough of the Bronx. Her father worked in the garment industry as a pattern-maker, and her mother was a telephone operator. She seemed a natural performer from an early age, and after high school took classes at the American Academy of Dramatic Arts. Soon she was working in the fledgling medium of television, and went to Hollywood in 1952, where Twentieth Century-Fox signed her to a contract. Handed a list of surnames that day, she chose "Bancroft" for her new professional name. "My goal was simply to be a movie star. I had no idea what to be an actress meant," the *Los Angeles Times* quoted her as saying. "It was just to be famous and popular and powerful and rich."

Bancroft had a strong start in her film debut, 1952's *Don't Bother To Knock,* a thriller with Marilyn Monroe. Over the next few years, however, studio executives seemed unsure how to best utilize her talents, and she drifted from film *noir* capers into B-movies. What was likely the most regrettable role of her career came in 1954's *Gorilla at Large,* in which she played a trapeze artist who commits murders while wearing an ape suit. Finally, she returned to New York in 1955, living back at home with her family and looking for television work. She also began a more intensive study of her craft, under the guidance of Herbert Berghof, a renowned workshop teacher.

A favorable recommendation from a fellow actor helped her land an audition for a new Broadway play, but its playwright and producer were reluctant to even see her because of her lack of stage inexperience. As the play's author later remembered, Bancroft "was a dark, quick, not pretty but vitally attractive girl with a sidewalk voice that greeted me instantly with 'How was the coast, lousy, huh?' and my mind blinked; she could have walked off my pages," William Gibson said, according to the London *Independent.*

Bancroft made her Broadway debut in Gibson's *Two for the Seesaw* opposite Henry Fonda in January of 1958. She played a free-spirited, bohemian New Yorker opposite Fonda's straightlaced Midwestern lawyer, and won a Tony Award for it. She next originated the role of Annie Sullivan, the determined teacher who taught a blind and deaf Helen Keller to speak, in another play by Gibson, *The Miracle Worker.* Again, she took the Tony for Best Actress, and went on to reprise the part in the film version, which also starred her stage co-star, Patty Duke. Both women then won Academy Awards for their work.

Bancroft went on to make a number of well-received films over the next few years, but it was her appearance in *The Graduate* that forever slotted her in the public eye as Mrs. Robinson, the woman who seduces the son of her husband's law partner. Her target is Benjamin Braddock, played by an unknown Dustin Hoffman, a recent college graduate whose ineptness with the opposite sex provides much of the movie's early humor. The plot takes a darker turn when Benjamin is set up on a date with Elaine, the Robinsons' daughter. Bancroft's performance, wrote Mark Harris in *Entertainment Weekly,* proved to be "one of those acting moments that is simply a permanent part of the fabric of American movies. With a voice that sounded like a liquor cabinet filtered through a cigarette holder and a stone-cold seduction technique that was all business and half bored-to-tears, Bancroft turned Mrs. Robinson, the matron who made mincemeat of Dustin Hoffman, into an alluring and fearsome comic creation."

Bancroft was nominated for another Academy Award for *The Graduate,* which launched her co-star's career. But roles for her became scarcer, and she also became choosier. The few well-written parts she took included *The Turning Point,* a 1977 drama of female friendship and resentments set in the ballet world, which earned her another Oscar nomination. She was nominated once more, this time as Best Supporting Actress, in 1985 for the film *Agnes of God.*

Bancroft wrote and directed a 1980 comedy, *Fatso,* and appeared in some of husband Mel Brooks' projects. In 1999, she won an Emmy Award for her part in the miniseries *Deep in My Heart,* which made her one of just 15 performers who had won Emmy, Oscar, and Tony awards in their career. She died of uterine cancer on June 6, 2005, at Mount Sinai Medical Center in New York City at the age of 73. Broadway dimmed its lights the next night in her honor. Survivors include Brooks, her husband of 41 years, as well as their son, Max, a television writer; her mother, Mildred, and two sisters also survive her. Mike Nichols, who directed Bancroft in *The Graduate,* lamented the loss, remarking to CNN.com that "her combination of brains, humor, frankness, and sense were unlike any other artist. Her beauty was constantly shifting with her roles, and because she was a consummate actress she changed radically for every part." **Sources:** CNN.com, http://www.cnn.com/2005/SHOWBIZ/Movies/06/07/bancroft.obit.ap/index.html (June 8, 2005); *Entertainment Weekly,* June 17, 2005, p. 18.; E! Online, http://www.eonline.com/News/Items/0,1,16709,00.html?eol.tkr (June 8, 2005); *Houston Chronicle,* June 8, 2005, p. 3; *Independent* (London), June 9, 2005, p. 58; *Los Angeles Times,* June 8, 2005, p. A1, p. A18; *New York Times,* June 8, 2005, p. A17; *People,* June 20, 2005, p. 137; *Washington Post,* June 8, 2005, p. B6.

—Carol Brennan

Saul Bellow

Born Solomon Bellows, June 10, 1915, in Lachine, Quebec, Canada; died April 5, 2005, in Brookline, MA. Author. Saul Bellow was one of the greatest American novelists of the second half of the 20th century, winner of the Nobel Prize for Literature, the Pulitzer Prize, and three National Book Awards. His self-doubting, searching heroes and anti-heroes, often enhanced versions of himself, searched for meaning before learning to live with spiritual unease. His works were serious and philosophical, yet cleverly comic, skeptical, and full of energy. He made his hometown, Chicago, the center of many of his novels, and his work reflected both his Jewish heritage and a middle-American sensibility. His 1953 breakthrough novel, *The Adventures of Augie March*, began with one of the most celebrated opening lines of 20th-century American literature: "I am an American, Chicago born—Chicago, that somber city—and go at things as I have taught myself, freestyle, and will make the record in my own way: first to knock, first admitted; sometimes an innocent knock, sometimes a not so innocent."

Bellow was born Solomon Bellows in the small town of Lachine, Quebec, to parents who immigrated from St. Petersburg, Russia. His mother, Liza, wanted him to be a rabbi or a violinist, but he claimed he was inspired to be a great novelist by reading *Uncle Tom's Cabin* by Harriet Beecher Stowe while in the hospital at age eight. The next year, his family moved to Chicago, where his father, Abraham, worked as a baker and coal deliveryman. Bellow started writing in elementary school with his friend Sydney J. Harris, who became a Chicago newspaper columnist.

Bellow went to the University of Chicago in 1933, then transferred to Northwestern University to save money. He majored in anthropology and sociology, subjects that informed the deep curiosity about the human condition reflected in his novels. He went to graduate school at the University of Wisconsin for anthropology, but dropped out and began writing biographies for the federal government's writer's project in Chicago. He moved to New York City to write fiction, and joined the merchant marine during World War II. While in the service, he finished his first novel, *Dangling Man*, published in 1944 and styled as a journal kept by a young man from Chicago who was waiting to be drafted. His second novel, *The Victim*, about anti-Semitism, came out in 1947. Both attracted some favorable reviews, but later critics and Bellow himself regarded them as early, lesser experiments.

The idea for *The Adventures of Augie March*, the novel that made Bellow famous and won him his first National Book Award, came to him while he was studying in Paris on a Guggenheim Fellowship awarded to him in 1948. He was walking through the city when he remembered a childhood friend who was always talking wildly about an exciting new scheme. He imagined a novel told in that friend's voice, and knew he had to write it. *Augie March*, released in 1953, "announced a brand-new voice in American fiction, jazzy, brash, exuberant, with accents that were both Yiddish and Whitmanian," Mel Gussow and Charles Mcgrath wrote in Bellow's *New York Times* obituary.

Bellow's next major work, 1959's *Henderson the Rain King*, told the story of a millionaire violinist and pig farmer who travels to Africa, searching in vain for a meaning in his life. Bellow said that book found him in full use of his literary powers, and that Henderson was the character who was most like himself. "Fiction is the higher autobiography," he said (as quoted by Gussow and Mcgrath in the *New York Times*), and many of his characters were thinly veiled, slightly mythologized versions of him and his friends and enemies. The title character of his 1964 novel *Herzog*, for instance, endures another man seducing his wife, much as Bellow himself found that his second wife had cheated on him with a friend of his. Not that Bellow was usually a heartbroken guy; he was more of a heartbreaker, veteran of many love affairs, married five times and divorced four.

Herzog won Bellow his second National Book Award, while 1969's *Mr. Sammler's Planet* won him his third. His last great success, the 1975 novel *Humboldt's Gift*, depicts a Pulitzer-Prize-winning writer named Charlie Citrine who is coping with the death of his mentor, the title character, based on Bellow's friend, the poet Delmore Schwartz. The novel proved prophetic: it won Bellow the Pulitzer Prize. The Nobel Prize in Literature followed in 1976.

Critics tend to view Bellow's work after the Nobel as minor compared to his earlier achievements; they felt it was less energetic and too full of laments about decay in the culture and in his beloved Chicago. His novels of the 1980s, one critic said, are interesting mostly for a softer view of relationships between men and women than his early novels, which were sometimes criticized as hostile to women. Meanwhile, in 1989, he married his last wife, Janis Freedman, a graduate student almost 50 years younger than him; they had a daughter, his fourth child, when Bellow was 83.

Bellow taught college students for most of his career, though his financial success made it unnecessary. He explained that writing can be a lonely profession, and he prized the human contact and the chance to talk about books that teaching provided. In 1993, he left the University of Chicago to teach at Boston University, sad that most of his Chicago friends had died. He published his last novel in 2000, *Ravelstein*. Again, the main character was based on a friend of his: Allan Bloom, the University of Chicago professor whose angry defense of traditional western literature and thought, *The Closing of the American Mind*, had created a sensation in the late 1980s. *Ravelstein*, too, attracted attention, thanks to its vivid portrayal of the flamboyant, openly gay Bloom and its affecting account of male friendship.

"If Bellow is not held to rank with Hemingway and Faulkner among modern American literary titans, he is very close," the London newspaper the *Independent* declared when he died. "More than either of them, he was fascinated by both the intellectual and material worlds, happy to yoke abstractions with immediate actualities.... Bellow depicted with equal richness the world of ideas and the people who create it." Bellow died on April 5, 2005, in Brookline, Massachusetts, of natural causes; he was 89. He is survived by his wife, Janis; their daughter, Naomi Rose; Gregory, Adam, and Daniel, his sons from previous marriages; and six grandchildren. **Sources:** *Entertainment Weekly*, April 15, 2005, p. 14; *Independent* (London), April 7, 2005, p. 40; *New York Times*, April 6, 2005, p. A1; *Washington Post*, April 6, 2005, p. A1.

—*Erick Trickey*

Hans Bethe

Born Hans Albrecht Bethe, July 2, 1906, in Strasbourg, Alsace-Lorraine; died of congestive heart failure, March 6, 2005, in Ithaca, New York. Physicist. Over the course of his more than 60-year career, Nobel laureate Hans Bethe published more than 300 scientific papers, averaging one significant breakthrough a decade. One of the leading theoretical physicists of the 20th century, Bethe is best known for figuring out how stars produce light and in 1967 won the Nobel Prize in Physics for this work. In addition, Bethe played a key role in the development of the atomic bomb that ended World War II, though after its use, he spent the remainder of his life calling for a halt to nuclear proliferation.

An only child, Bethe (pronounced BAY-tuh) was born into a family of academicians on July 2, 1906, in Strasbourg, Alsace-Lorraine, an area France and Germany spent decades fighting over. At the time of Bethe's birth, the city was part of Germany. Bethe's father, a Protestant, was a physiologist at the University of Strasbourg and later taught in Frankfurt. His Jewish mother was also the child of a professor. Because the family was not religious, Bethe never considered himself Jewish.

Early on, Bethe demonstrated great ability in mathematics, though his father tried to squelch his interest because he wanted Bethe to fit in with his peers and not get too far ahead. Bethe, however, swiped his father's trigonometry and calculus books and read them in secret. He studied at the University of Frankfurt, then earned a doctorate from the University of Munich in 1928, graduating summa cum laude.

Bethe first taught physics close to home in Frankfurt and Stuttgart, then ventured out to Cambridge, England, and Rome. In the early 1930s he returned to Germany to teach at Tubingen University only to find his classes filled with swastika-clad students. Within a year he was let go as Adolf Hitler invoked a policy of anti-Semitism throughout the land.

Bethe fled to Britain and later to the United States, where in 1935 he landed at Cornell University in Ithaca, New York, where he spent the remainder of his academic career. Bethe drew attention to himself shortly thereafter by publishing, with the help of various collaborators, three articles on thermonuclear reactions in the American Physical Society's *Reviews of Modern Physics*. At the time, nuclear physics was a new field of study and these papers, which became known as "Bethe's Bible," served as the primary text on the subject for decades.

One of Bethe's most amazing discoveries came after a 1938 astrophysicists conference at the Carnegie Institution in Washington, D.C. There, the question was posed: What makes stars shine? Philosophers and astronomers had sought the answer for centuries. It took Bethe six weeks to end the mystery. Relying on his knowledge of nuclear reactions and fusion, Bethe churned out a stack of pencil and paper calculations and published them in a paper called "Energy Production in Stars." In the paper, Bethe described the process by which the sun, and similar stars, merge hydrogen into helium, thus discharging energy that bursts forth as heat and light.

In 1939 Bethe married Rose Ewald, daughter of German physicist Paul Ewald of Stuttgart, whom Bethe had worked under. Two years later, he became a U.S. citizen and as World War II unfolded, he joined the war effort by working on radar technology at the Massachusetts Institute of Technology. Later, he was appointed chief theoretical physicist of the secret Manhattan Project lab in Los Alamos, New Mexico, which developed the atomic bomb.

At Los Alamos, Bethe directed teams of leading physicists in carrying out the complex calculations necessary to build the bomb. His team figured out how much plutonium would be needed and worked to figure out if such a detonation would ignite the earth's atmosphere and destroy the planet. Team members began calling him "The Battleship" because of the way he destroyed potential problems by steaming right through to an answer.

Though Bethe helped develop the A-bomb, he believed building it was morally wrong; however, he was eager to help defeat Nazism and figured if he did not help the United States develop the A-bomb, Germany would soon enough, making Hitler unstoppable. After the war Bethe returned to academia and became a vocal critic of the nuclear arms race. He helped negotiate the first nuclear test ban treaty, which essentially banned all atmospheric tests. By the 1990s Bethe was calling for a total ban on nuclear tests.

Bethe retired from teaching in 1975 but continued writing professional papers and near the end of his life was studying and writing about the collapse of stars. To the end, he never turned to computers for calculations, relying instead on a slide rule, pencil, and paper. In his free time he enjoyed skiing, mountain climbing, and traveling, especially by train. He continued advising presidents, a service he began in the Harry Truman administration and carried on through President Bill Clinton.

Most of all, Bethe was known for inspiring generations of Cornell physicists. Speaking to the *Los Angeles Times,* the late MIT physicist Philip Morrison, who worked at Los Alamos with Bethe, once said, "Of all the people who are so bright and accomplished, few are so sweet of temperament. He finds errors in such a way as you're pleased to have the help."

Bethe died of congestive heart failure on March 6, 2005, at his home in Ithaca, New York. He was 98. He is survived by his wife, Rose; his son, Henry; his daughter, Monica; and three grandchildren. **Sources:** *Independent* (London), March 9, 2005, p. 34; *Los Angeles Times,* March 8, 2005, p. A1, p. A22; *New York Times,* March 8, 2005, p. A1; *Washington Post,* March 8, 2005, p. B6.

—*Lisa Frick*

Johnny Carson

Born John William Carson, October 23, 1925, in Corning, IA; died of complications from emphysema, January 23, 2005, in Los Angeles, CA. Television show host. Johnny Carson was one of the most powerful figures in show business during his 30-year reign as the host of NBC's *Tonight Show.* From 1962 until his sign-off in May of 1992, Carson traded quips with celebrities, politicians, and ordinary Americans from his familiar desk. His show, which aired weeknights just after the local late-night newscast, was virtually the only original programming in the time slot for an entire generation in the era before cable television.

Carson was born in 1925, the middle child of three, into a farming family in Iowa. His father was a district manager for the local utility company, and the family moved to Norfolk, Nebraska, in 1933. An admittedly shy child, Carson discovered early on he had a gift for storytelling and jokes and, paradoxically, felt far more confident around others while performing. He was a working teenage magician before graduating from high school in 1943, and after serving in the U.S. Navy during World War II enrolled at the University of Nebraska. Earning his degree in just three years, Carson began his career in radio and quickly moved on to the fledgling medium of television. He met Ed McMahon, his longtime *Tonight Show* sidekick, while hosting the game show *Who Do You Trust?* in the late 1950s.

The Tonight Show began in 1953 with comedian Steve Allen as host. He was succeeded by Jack Paar in 1957, and the mix of stand-up comedy, skits, and celebrity guests proved to be a terrific success. Carson took over as host in October of 1962, and the show would eclipse all other imitators over the next decade and cause Carson to be dubbed "the king of late-night TV" in the press. His show dominated the ratings, with 15 million viewers tuning in at its peak popularity; at one point it reportedly accounted for 17 percent of the NBC network's total profits. Middle-class Americans tuned in every night to laugh at Carson's monologue, usually rife with news-of-the-day references. The tone of his jokes became a bellwether for the national mood, and during the Watergate political scandal of Richard M. Nixon's second term, Carson's jokes about the president were the opening salvo in what became a pattern of ridicule and anti-Nixon sentiment in the country; in August of 1974 Nixon became the first president ever to resign from office.

Carson chatted with some 22,000 guests during his three-decade reign, and an appearance on *The Tonight Show* was an immeasurable publicity boost to any new star. He also had an ear for talented stand-up comics, and scores of future film and television stars had their careers launched by a stint on the show or, even more of an honor, filling in for Carson at his desk during his increasingly frequent days off. Woody Allen, Rodney Dangerfield, Bill Cosby, George Carlin, Robin Williams, Steve Martin, Roseanne Barr, Ellen DeGeneres, Ray Romano, and Drew Carey all appeared early in their careers on *The Tonight Show,* and two others, David Letterman and Jay Leno, would go on to host their own immensely successful late-night shows. Both Letterman and Leno were the entire shortlist to succeed Carson when he announced his retirement, but Leno won *The Tonight Show* slot, and Letterman eventually resigned from NBC, so deep was the rebuff.

In his final years on the air, Carson earned a reported $25 million a year, and wielded enough clout even to force NBC to cut his show from 90 to 60 minutes in 1980. "More than any other individual," wrote Richard Severo and Bill Carter in the *New York Times,* Carson "shifted the nexus of power in television from New York to Los Angeles, with his decision in 1972 to move his show from its base in Rockefeller Center in New York to NBC's West Coast studios in Burbank, Calif. That same move was critical in the changeover of much of television from live to taped performances."

Some 50 million viewers tuned in for Carson's farewell as *Tonight Show* host in May of 1992. He told his studio audience as well as a record-setting number of broadcast viewers that he considered himself "one of the lucky people in the world," he said, according to CNN.com. "I found something that I always wanted to do and I have enjoyed every single minute of it."

Though Carson had often joked in his monologues about his three divorces, he was an intensely private person. He was almost never seen in public after leaving the airwaves, but traveled around the world with his fourth wife, Alexis. They sailed on his 125-foot yacht, the *Serengeti,* and attended the annual Wimbledon tennis championships in England every summer. He was an avid tennis player, and a golfer, too, whose pretend-swing closed his nightly monologue. Sometimes, upon returning from a commercial in the old live days, viewers might catch Carson stubbing out a cigarette; he was a lifelong smoker and suffered from emphysema in his later years. He died of complications from the disease on January 23, 2005, at the age of 79, at Cedars-Sinai Medical Center in Los Angeles. He is survived by his wife, Alexis, and two sons from his first marriage, Christopher and Cory; a third son, Richard, died in a car accident in 1991.

News of Carson's death prompted heartfelt tributes from around the world. Leno, his successor, said that he still felt "like a guest in his house," according to *People.* Letterman, whom Carson sent the occasional joke for the monologue, credited his career to Carson's generosity, and asserted that his mentor's talent was unparalleled. "All of us who came after," Letterman told CNN.com, "are pretenders."

Sources: CNN.com, http://www.cnn.com/2005/SHOWBIZ/TV/01/2310/carson.obit/index.html (January 24, 2005); http://www.cnn.com/2005/SHOWBIZ/TV/02/10/johnny.carson.ap/index.html (February 10, 2005); *Entertainment Weekly,* February 4, 2005, pp. 12-16; E! Online, http://www.eonline.com/News/Items/0,1,15672,00.html?eol.tkr (January 24, 2005); *Independent* (London), January 25, 2005, p. 34; *Los Angeles Times,* January 24, 2005, p. A1, pp. A14-15; *New York Times,* January 24, 2005, p. A1; February 7, 2005, p. A2; February 9, 2005, p. A2; *People,* February 7, 2005, pp. 84-92;

—Carol Brennan

Shirley Chisholm

Born Shirley Anita St. Hill, November 30, 1924, in New York, NY; died after a series of strokes, January 1, 2005, in Ormond Beach, FL. Politician. In 1968, Shirley Chisholm became the first African-American woman ever elected to serve in the United States Congress. Fiercely dedicated to her constituents and outspoken in her commitment to social justice, Chisholm served 14 years in the U.S. House of Representatives, and was one of the most well-known women in America in her time. She even made a symbolic bid for the White House in 1972, and earned a surprisingly strong show of support during her campaign.

Born in 1924 and named Shirley Anita St. Hill, Chisholm spent her first years in the Brooklyn neighborhood of Bedford-Stuyvesant, but her clipped West Indian accent came from a childhood in Barbados. Chisholm's mother, a domestic servant and seamstress, was originally from the island nation, and her Guyana-born father worked at a factory that produced burlap sacks. All four St. Hill daughters were sent to live with their maternal grandmother so that their parents might save money for their education. Chisholm returned to New York at the age of eleven, and never lost her lilting accent.

The investment by Chisholm's parents in her future was well spent. She excelled in school, and at Brooklyn College as well. Known for her strong debating skills, in another time and place she might have earned a law degree, but instead Chisholm became a nursery-school teacher when she graduated. She went on to receive a master's degree from Columbia University, and spent her pre-political career as a teacher, early-education expert, and employee of the child welfare bureau in New York City. By the late 1950s, she had become active in Democratic Party politics in her local Bedford-Stuyvesant neighborhood.

In 1964, Chisholm ran for and won a seat representing her locality in the New York State Assembly. Four years later, she made her historic bid for Congress from Brooklyn's 12th Congressional District. The district was tightly controlled by the powerful Brooklyn Democratic Party machine, and she was not the first choice to stand for the election, considered a shoo-in for any Democratic candidate since District's number of Democratic registered voters topped 80 percent. She entered the Democratic primary anyway, and bested her heavily favored opponent with the campaign slogan, "Unbought and unbossed."

The number of female or African-American legislators in the U.S. House was still disproportionately small at the time, which made Chisholm's achievement all the more remarkable. She met with a frosty reception from her fellow lawmakers, however, but began to make her own way in the Capitol. She joined two other African-American members of the House, Louis Stokes of Ohio and Missourian William L. Clay, to found the Congressional Black Caucus, which later became a potent political force in American politics. Her assignments included stints on the Veterans' Affairs, Education, and Labor committees.

Chisholm was blunt in her criticism for the policies of Republican President Richard M. Nixon, especially regarding the controversial continuance of sending American troops to Southeast Asia at the height of the Vietnam War. She also supported new civil-rights legislation as well as equal-rights protection for American women. A household name in America by 1972, Chisholm decided to make a bid for the Democratic Party presidential ticket. She admitted her chances were slim, but gained support during the campaign and made impressive showings in a few state primaries. One of the most memorable moments of the campaign, however, was her visit to the hospital room of an Alabama Democrat, George Wallace, who was also running for the party nomination. His campaign, by contrast to hers, exploited racial tensions in America, for Wallace was a noted segregationist. He became the target of an assassination attempt while campaign-ing, and the gunshot wound put him in a wheel-chair for the rest of his life. Chisholm's visit to him was an attempt to make peace, and "black people in my community crucified me" for it, she later said, according to the *New York Times*.

Chisholm's constituents forgave her, however, and she continually won reelection. She retired from political life in 1982, when she took a teaching job at Mt. Holyoke College in Massachusetts; the move was also done in order to care for her husband, Arthur Hardwick, a Buffalo, New York-area politician and business owner who had been injured in a car accident. He died in 1986, and Chisholm moved to Florida five years later, where she spent the remainder of her years. After suffering a series of strokes, she died on New Year's Day in 2005, in Ormond Beach, Florida, at the age of 80. According to the *New York Times*, she recalled that Wallace had also questioned her bold move in visiting him—though all the major candidates had stopped by his hospital room—to which she replied, "I know what they're going to say. But I wouldn't want what happened to you to happen to anyone," the *New York Times* reported her telling Wallace. "He cried and cried and cried." **Sources:** CNN. com, http://www.cnn.com/2005/ALLPOLITICS/ 01/03/obit.chis holm.ap/index.html (January 3, 2005); *Independent* (London), January 4, 2005, p. 28; *New York Times*, January 4, 2005, p. B9; *People,* January 17, 2005, p. 108; *Washington Post,* January 3, 2005, p. A4.

—Carol Brennan

Kenneth B. Clark

Born Kenneth Bancroft Clark, July 14, 1914, in the Panama Canal Zone, Panama; died of cancer, May 1, 2005, in Hastings-On-Hudson, NY. Psychologist. Dr. Kenneth Clark, a staunch supporter of integration, used four dolls—two black, two white—to document how African-American children perceived themselves. His findings were part of several key components that led to the U.S. Supreme Court ruling that its segregation doctrine was unconstitutional. This ruling ushered in a new era of integration. Judge Robert Carter, part of the legendary team of lawyers for the National Association for the Advancement of Colored People (NAACP) who argued the case in front of the U.S. Supreme Court, told the *Los Angeles Times*, "His work was really very important to us and very essential to the victory.... He was a real American icon, a very wise man." Clark continued to work tirelessly to both integrate and improve schools for all minority and poor children. While there were many gains, the changes were never at the pace or amount he expected.

Clark was born in the Panama Canal Zone on July 14, 1914. His father, Arthur Bancroft Clark, worked for the United Fruit Company as a passenger agent. His mother, Miriam Hanson Clark, felt her children would have better educational opportunities in the United States. Clark's parents disagreed over moving back. The couple soon separated, and Miriam moved her son and daughter back to New York City.

The family moved to Harlem, and Clark began attending Public School 5. He soon transferred to P.S. 139, the same school where Harlem Renaissance poet Countee Cullen taught, and author James Baldwin attended as well. When Clark entered the ninth grade, a counselor advised him to enter a vocational school. When Miriam Clark heard about this, she marched down to the school and told the counselor in no uncertain terms that she did not move back to New York so her son could work in a factory.

Instead Clark entered George Washington High School, an academically elite school in Upper Manhattan. After graduation, he enrolled at Howard University. He wanted to major in economics, but after taking a psychology class that helped him to better understand racism, he switched to psychology. Clark also persuaded his future wife, Mamie Phipps, to change her major to psychology.

Clark earned his bachelors degree in psychology in 1935, and earned his masters a year later. During that time, he worked as an assistant professor of psychology at Howard. His wife had begun doing fieldwork on the effects of racial identity on the self-esteem of black schoolchildren. He soon joined her in this effort. They published their findings in several journals.

The couple moved to Harlem and enrolled in the doctoral program at Columbia University. Clark earned his doctorate in psychology—the first black person to do so at the university—and began teaching at Hampton Institute in Virginia. He stayed for a year, and began working with Swedish economist Gunnar Myrdal and a former professor of his, Ralph Bunche, who would later win the Nobel Peace Prize. The team worked on the Carnegie study of race relations. The findings, published as *An American Dilemma* in 1944, would become required reading in many U.S. colleges and universities.

Clark and his wife continued studying the effects of discrimination. They used four dolls, two that were black and two that were white—all identical, to measure how children felt about the color of their skin. They tested dozens of children in Washington, D.C., New York, Philadelphia, Boston, Worcester, Massachusetts, and rural Arkansas. The majority, both black and white, said the white dolls were nice and they all preferred to play with them. The majority also said the black dolls were bad; most of the black children identified with the black dolls. The couple took the results and published them in a book *Prejudice and Your Child* in 1953. Clark concluded that black children thought of themselves as inferior due to society devaluing them because of the color of their skin.

Clark's research came to the attention of Robert Carter, an attorney who was trying to dismantle segregated schools in South Carolina and was also a part of the NAACP legal team. Clark used the doll test on children in Clarendon County, South Carolina. His results were the same. Carter persuaded Thurgood Marshall, the leading attorney for the NAACP, to use Clark's findings in the case. Many at the NAACP were skeptical, but Marshall agreed. When the ruling in *Brown vs. the Board of Education* came down that the "separate but equal" doctrine of segregation was unconstitutional, Chief Justice Earl Warren cited Clark's findings as having a pivotal role in the justices reaching their conclusion. He told the *Washington Post*, "The court saw the issue clearly.... A racist system inevitably destroys and damages human beings; it brutalizes and dehumanizes them, blacks and whites alike."

During this time, Clark began his tenure at City College of New York, where he taught psychology. He and his wife also began the Northside Center for Child Development, where they treated children with personality disorders. Though they received no payment from the majority of their patients, the Center was a huge success.

Clark thought the new Supreme Court ruling would bring in sweeping change across the United States, but that was not the case. During the 1950s and the 1960s, he attacked the New York City public school system for allowing segregation to continue. An investigation ensued, and supported his charges. Clark was named to head a board of education commission to see that the schools were fully integrated. When this proved unsuccessful, he pushed for the school system to be decentralized, but the schools continued to fail.

Clark founded the Harlem Youth Opportunities Unlimited (Haryou) to help in the reorganization of Harlem schools. The group also wanted to begin preschool programs and after-school remedial classes. The group gained national attention and was earmarked to receive $110 million to help. Unfortunately, in order to receive the government funds, Haryou had to join with Associated Community Teams, whose head was Congressman Adam Clayton Powell, Jr. He and Clark never saw eye to eye and the funding was lost. Though dismayed, Clark continued in his struggle to integrate the schools and bring the New York public school system up to speed. However, when it came to the education of his own children, he chose to move to Hastings-On-Hudson in Westchester County, New York, so they could receive a better education.

In the late 1960s, Clark was elected to the New York State Board of Regents, becoming the first African American elected to the board. In 1975 he retired from City College of New York to begin a human resources consulting firm with his family. He continued publishing books, including 1967's *Dark Ghetto*, 1969's *A Relevant War Against Poverty*, and 1974's *Pathos of Power*.

Clark was asked to help turn around Washington, D.C.'s school system, but when the majority of his plan was rejected, he resigned. He retired from the Board of Regents in 1986. Throughout his career Clark battled against conservatives, black separatists, and other community leaders who had given up the fight for integration. As a result of his hard work, the NAACP honored him with its highest award, the Spingarn Medal, for his contributions to bettering race relations.

Clark suffered from cancer and succumbed to the disease on May 1, 2005, in his home in Hastings-on-Hudson, New York. He was 90. His wife preceded him in death in 1983. He is survived by his daughter, Kate; his son, Hilton; three grandchildren, and five great-grandchildren. **Sources:** *Chicago Tribune*, May 2, 2005, sec. 4, p. 10; *Guardian* (London), May 6, 2005, p. 29; *Los Angeles Times*, May 3, 2005, p. B10; *New York Times*, May 2, 2005, p. A1; *Washington Post*, May 3, 2005, p. B4.

—*Ashyia N. Henderson*

Rodney Dangerfield

Born Jacob Cohen, November 22, 1921, in Babylon, NY; died from complications from heart valve replacement surgery, October 5, 2004, in Los Angeles,

CA. Comedian and actor. When most people think of Rodney Dangerfield, the first thing that comes to mind is the line that made him famous, "I don't get no respect." But what few know is the comic was well-respected by fans and other comics. He began his career in his teens, but left show business to lead a normal life. He returned to the stage years later and became one of the hottest comics around. He opened his own comedy club that would be the launching pad for numerous comedians, including Jerry Seinfeld and Jim Carrey.

Dangerfield was born Jacob Cohen on November 22, 1921, in Babylon, New York, in the borough of Long Island. His father was a comic who went by the name of Phil Roy and2 was part of a comedy juggling act that toured the vaudeville circuit. Roy abandoned his family after Dangerfield's birth. His mother, whom Dangerfield recalled as overbearing, moved him and his sister to a swanky neighborhood in Queens. Dangerfield helped out by selling ice cream on the beach, and delivering groceries after school, sometimes to his more affluent classmates.

Dangerfield's childhood years were rough. He endured anti-Semitic remarks from his teachers, and to deal with life, he began writing jokes and stuffing them in a duffel bag. He began performing his jokes on amateur night at various clubs. Dangerfield also took on the stage name of Jack Roy. He earned two dollars after doing a comedy routine at a theater in New Jersey, his first paying job.

Dangerfield also landed a stint at a resort in the Catskills, in upstate New York. He performed for ten weeks, making $12 a week plus room and board. Once he saw that he could make a living as a comedian, he legally changed his name to Jack Roy. Though he continued to land spots at various comedy clubs, Dangerfield also drove a laundry and fish truck. He also worked as a singing waiter at the Polish Falcon nightclub in Brooklyn.

Despite bringing in as much as $300 a week, Dangerfield still struggled. He met and married singer Joyce Indig, and both decided to give up show business and lead a normal life. The couple moved to New Jersey, and soon had two children, Brian and Melanie. To provide for his family, Dangerfield became an aluminum siding salesman.

The normal life was not idyllic for Dangerfield. He began battling depression, a condition he dealt with most of his life, and sought psychiatric help. He and his wife bickered constantly and finally divorced in 1962. The couple would remarry in 1963, and divorced for good in 1970.

During his "normal" life, which he described as "a very colorless existence" to *People*, Dangerfield continued to write jokes and kept them in the duffel bag. Being debt-ridden and having to live in a seedy hotel in New York helped spark his desire to return to standup. According to the *Washington Post*, he said, "It was like a need. I had to work. I had to tell jokes. I had to write them and tell them. It was like a fix. I had the habit." Fearful of rejection, he asked club owner George McFadden not to use his name. McFadden came up with Rodney Dangerfield, and his act as a down-on-his-luck everyman catapulted Dangerfield into the spotlight. From this he landed a spot on *The Ed Sullivan Show*, which many considered his big break.

Dangerfield toured the country in the 1960s doing standup in various clubs. As more and more people took notice, he appeared on several shows including *The Merv Griffin Show*, *The Dean Martin Show*, and also *The Tonight Show* with Johnny Carson. He would appear on *The Tonight Show* 70 times throughout his career.

After viewing *The Godfather*, Dangerfield began to include the line that would define his style. As he worked on the joke, "When I played hide-and-seek, they didn't even look for me," he felt he needed something more. The film and the real-life mobsters who frequented the clubs where he performed spoke of respect. So he came up with the persona of someone who never received any respect, and added the line "I don't get no respect" to his repertoire. He tested it at one performance and received a big response. The line helped Dangerfield establish a bond with his audience and his popularity grew.

In the early 1970s, Dangerfield's former wife died, and to provide his children with a stable life, he opened the comedy club Dangerfield's in Manhattan. With him as a regular headliner, the club was a success. Dangerfield was also very generous in giving unknown comedians their chance to perform on stage. "Rodney didn't care what kind of comedy you did. As long as you were a comic, you were a part of his fraternity," comedian Carrot Top relayed to *People*. Jim Carrey, Jerry Seinfeld, Adam Sandler, and Roseanne Barr were among the many comics who performed at Dangerfield's.

Thanks to his high visibility on *The Tonight Show* and a series of Miller's Lite beer commercials, Dangerfield began his acting career with a role in the film *The Projectionist*. However, the movie was a flop, and Dangerfield concentrated on his standup comedy act and club for nine years before returned to the silver screen.

In 1980 Dangerfield took a part in the comedic film *Caddyshack*, along with Chevy Chase, Bill Murray, and Ted Knight. The movie was a hit, and led to other films including *Easy Money*, which he also wrote, *Back To School*, and *Meet Wally Sparks*. Dangerfield also took on his only dramatic role as an abusive father in *Natural Born Killers* with Juliette Lewis and Woody Harrelson. In an ironic twist, many thought his performance in 1994's *Natural Born Killers* was worthy of an Oscar nomination, but his application was rejected because the Academy of Motion Picture Arts and Sciences thought he did not have enough roles that showed his mastery of his craft. According to CNN.com, he stated, "They give no respect at all—pardon the pun—to comedy." Undeterred, Dangerfield created a website and many people emailed their criticism to the academy. They relented and offered Dangerfield admission, which he declined.

In addition to his standup and acting careers, Dangerfield also performed on Broadway in *Rodney Dangerfield on Broadway!* and released a number of comedy albums which included 1984's "Rappin' Rodney," a rap parody. He won a Grammy Award in 1981 for *No Respect*. Dangerfield also starred in a number of HBO specials; he sometimes used these specials to showcase up-and-coming comedians.

Dangerfield's health began to deteriorate. He suffered from heart problems, and underwent double bypass surgery in 2000. In 2003 the comedian also had arterial brain surgery to help increase his blood flow so he could have heart valve replacement surgery. Despite ill health, Dangerfield continued performing and making appearances. He published his autobiography *It's Not Easy Bein' Me: A Lifetime of No Respect but Plenty of Sex and Drugs* in 2004. He appeared on the sitcom *Still Standing* and also planned to release another comedy album in 2005. Dangerfield had heart valve replacement surgery in August of 2004. After the operation he suffered a small stroke that was followed by infections and abdominal complications. He slipped into a coma, but later awoke long enough to kiss his wife. Dangerfield died from complications of surgery on October 5, 2004, in Los Angeles, California; he was 82. He is survived by his second wife, Joan Child; his children, Brian and Melanie; and two grandsons. **Sources:** CNN.com, http://www.cnn.com/2004/ SHOWBIZ/10/05/obit.dangerfield.ap/index.html (October 6, 2004); *Entertainment Weekly*, October 15, 2004, p. 15; E! Online, http://www.eonline.com/ News/Items/0,1,15079,00.html?eol.tkr (October 6, 2004); *Los Angeles Times*, October 6, 2004, p. B8; *New York Times*, October 6, 2004, p. A27; *People*, October 18, 2004, pp. 69-70; *Washington Post*, October 6, 2004, p. B7.

—*Ashyia N. Henderson*

Ossie Davis

Born Raiford Chatman Davis, December 18, 1917, in Cogdell, GA; died of natural causes, February 4, 2005, in Miami Beach, FL. Actor. Actor Ossie Davis, along with his wife, Ruby Dee, were pioneers in African-American theater and film. Davis had a lengthy career, with more than 120 screen credits to his name, and was known for the subtle strength of character he projected through a dignified, fatherly demeanor and his memorably baritone voice.

Born in 1917, Davis came from rural Georgia, and was the first of five children in his family. He real name was Raiford Chatman Davis, shortened to just the initials "R.C.," but when his mother registered his birth at the country records office, the clerk misheard her and wrote down "Ossie" instead; she was too intimidated, at a time of deep racial divisions in the American South, to correct it. Davis' father was a railroad construction supervisor, an unusual post for a black man to hold, and was once warned by the local chapter of the white-supremacist group, the Ku Klux Klan, to mind his place. The Davis parents encouraged their son to get an education, and by the time he finished high school he had scholarship offers from two black colleges, but could not afford to pay his share of the tuition and board. By then, the Great Depression had struck, and the family was struggling financially. Eventually Davis hitchhiked to Washington, D.C., where he stayed with relatives while attending Howard University.

Davis warmed to two subjects at Howard, literature and the theater, and decided to move to Harlem in 1939 before completing his degree. There, he joined the Rose McClendon Players, a theater group, and supported himself with menial jobs—though he admitted to sleeping on the occasional park bench when money was truly scarce. After appearing in the 1940 Broadway production of the Harlem-set On Strivers Row, Davis served in the U.S. Army during World War II as a medical-corps technician in Africa. Back in civilian life, he was cast in the title role of a 1946 Broadway play about a returning war veteran, Jeb. During rehearsals he met Dee, and the two wed in 1948. They were often cast together as husband and wife, and in later years had become the honorary grandparents for an entire generation of African-American entertainers. One of their most memorable joint roles came in the 1991 Spike Lee film, Jungle Fever, as a devout, gospel music-loving minister and his wife, who are virtually paralyzed by their son's increasing drug addiction.

Davis and his wife began their careers during a time when black actors were rarely cast in films outside of domestic-servant roles. Even in the early years of television, career-building parts were scarce, but Davis was able to land such roles as the lead in a Eugene O'Neill play, The Emperor Jones, for a 1955 Kraft Television Playhouse event. As he said many years later in an interview, "There are ways you can make yourself a more saleable commodity. I didn't pursue those ways," London Independent writer Stephen Bourne quoted him as saying. He and Dee, he continued, "did build careers for ourselves and in the process did many theatrical things ... on street corners, churches, union halls, schools. And, in doing it our way, we didn't have to sell more of ourselves than we could get back before the sun went down."

In addition to their stage and screen work, Davis and Dee were deeply committed political and civil-rights activists. They supported a host of causes, and served as the joint emcees for the 1963 March on Washington, during which Rev. Martin Luther King Jr. made his famous "I Have a Dream" speech. Davis spoke at King's 1968 funeral, and had also delivered the eulogy for slain leader Malcolm X in 1965. He reprised the latter tribute for Spike Lee's 1992 biopic, Malcolm X.

Among Davis' impressive credits were his film debut alongside Sidney Poitier in the 1950 crime thriller No Way Out, and as Poitier's successor in the role of Walter Lee in the acclaimed Broadway drama A Raisin in the Sun in 1959. He wrote the play Purlie Victorious in the early 1960s, a work that satirized race relations in the South and went on to become the Broadway musical Purlie. He also directed the 1970 film Cotton Comes to Harlem, about two African-American police officers in Harlem, which helped launch a new black film movement.

Davis and Dee, who had three children together, were rarely separated, but Davis was in Miami Beach in early February of 2005, shooting a new film titled Retirement with co-stars Peter Falk and George Segal; Dee was on location in New Zealand also shooting a film. Davis' hotel was notified when his grandson failed to reach him on February 4, 2005. He had apparently died of natural causes at the age of 87. Survivors include his children Nora, Guy, and Hasna, and seven grandchildren, but his legacy would run deeper, actor Harry Belafonte told Elaine Woo of the Los Angeles Times. Noting that the actor and activist personally knew not only Dr. King and Malcolm X., but Paul Robeson and W.E.B. Du Bois as well, Belafonte called Davis "the embodiment of all those courageous people. I think he worked very hard at passing on to subsequent generations not only a deep and rich sense of their history but encouraged them to become more noble in their demands of life, governance and society." **Sources:** CNN.com, http://www.cnn.com/2005/ SHOWBIZ/Movies/02/04/obit.davis.ap/index. html (February 4, 2005); *Entertainment Weekly*, February 18, 2005, p. 15; *Independent* (London), February 7, 2005, p. 34; *Los Angeles Times*, February 5, 2005, p. A1, p. A21; *New York Times*, February 4, 2005, p. A14; February 9, 2005, p. A2; *People*, February 21, 2005, pp. 73-74; *USA Today*, February 7, 2005, p. 2D.

—*Carol Brennan*

Sandra Dee

Born Alexandra Cymboliak Zuck, April 23, 1942, in Bayonne, NJ; died of kidney disease, February 20, 2005, in Thousand Oaks, CA. Actress. Sandra Dee was one of Hollywood's hottest box-office draws in the early 1960s. Best remembered for her role as the irrepressible Gidget in the hit teen-surfer movie of the same name, Dee and her career failed to capture the momentum of her early years as an exuberant, attractive starlet, and she retreated into a reclusive life plagued by substance abuse. Despite her decline, she would be forever remembered as an icon for an era. "The bright, chirpy Ms. Dee defined a new kind of natural, sun-soaked innocence that America, and much of the rest of the world, quickly embraced as the radiantly healthy, outdoorsy essence of Southern California living," noted Dave Kehr in her *New York Times* obituary.

Dee was born Alexandra Cymboliak Zuck on April 23, 1942, the year given by most sources, though her actual birth date, according to her son, may have been 1941. She grew up in Bayonne, New Jersey, and her father left the family before she was five years old. Her determined, sometimes overbearing mother pushed her into a career as a child model, often by lying about Dee's age. She appeared in television commercials for Coca-Cola and Coppertone, and though to her classmates at the Professional Children's School in New York City she seemed to lead a charmed life, Dee later said she had been sexually abused by her stepfather, and battled a decimating eating disorder that began in her teens and endured for decades. At times her five-feet, five-inch frame weighed just 90 pounds.

Dee made her film debut in 1957's *Until They Sail*, and had her first hit movie as *The Reluctant Debutante* the following year, the story of an American teen taking part in the London social season. She also appeared in *Imitation of Life*, a melodramatic tale in which Lana Turner played her mother, and was signed to Universal Studios for that picture because it would have cost them too much to hire Natalie Wood, one of Hollywood's newest talents, for the part. Dee next landed the signature role of *Gidget*, the 1959 hit, and would be forever associated with the easygoing, California surfer-girl character.

That same year, however, Dee took a more substantial role in the movie *A Summer Place*, which also starred Troy Donahue. The plot dealt with teen pregnancy and the dire premarital sex taboo of the era, contrasted with the hypocrisy of an adult world in which their respective mother and father are having an extramarital affair with one another. The movie was a terrific commercial success and, according to Kehr's *New York Times* tribute, was "among the earliest studio films to commodify youthful rebelliousness, though Ms. Dee was hardly an icon of adolescent revolt with her shiny helmet of flipped hair and color-coordinated outfits."

Dee enjoyed a few heady years after this point as one of Hollywood's leading box-office draws. She appeared with Rock Hudson and Gina Lollabrigida in *Come September*, a 1961 Italian romantic comedy which served as her introduction to pop star and fellow cast member Bobby Darin. The two fell in love and wed just weeks later, and the union produced one son, Dodd Darin. Dee went on to appear in two frothy teen screen hits, *Tammy Tell Me True* and *Tammy and the Doctor*, and made two movies with her husband. Both were poorly received, however, and the couple's marriage faltered. They divorced in 1967, and Dee made a few more films before disappearing from the public eye. Universal had dropped her contract after she made *A Man Could Get Killed*, a 1966 dud. "I was simply a piece of property to them," Dee later recalled in an interview, according to her *Washington Post* obituary by Joe Holley. "I begged them not to make me do the picture, but they insisted."

Her career essentially over at the age of 26, Dee made the occasional television movie, and was devastated by the more permanent loss of her ex-husband—to whom she was still reportedly devoted—when Darin died in 1973 at the age of 37. Darin's career and his ill-fated marriage to Dee was the subject of a biopic, *Beyond the Sea*, which starred Kevin Spacey as the pop crooner and Kate Bosworth as Dee. The movie was released just two months before Dee's death from kidney disease on February 20, 2005, in Thousand Oaks, California; she is survived by her son and two grandchildren. In a 1991 interview with *People* magazine, Dee had admitted to drinking a quart of scotch a day by the late 1980s and weighing just 80 pounds, but pulled herself out of it with the help of her son. She quit drinking altogether after being diagnosed with throat cancer and kidney failure in 2000. A fuller account of her story is in *Dream Lovers: The Magnificent Shattered Lives of Bobby Darin and Sandra Dee,* the 1994 biography her son wrote. Though both that and *Beyond the Sea* touched on some painful parts of her past, Dee reportedly gave her blessing to both projects. **Sources:** *Chicago Tribune,* February 21, 2005, sec. 1, p. 9; CNN.com, http://www.cnn.com/2005/SHOWBIZ/Movies/02/20/dee.obit/index.html (February 22, 2005); E! Online, http://www.eonline.com/News/Items/0,1,15968,00.html?tnews (February 22, 2005); *Los Angeles Times,* February 21, 2005, p. B8; *New York Times,* February 21, 2005, p. A19; *People,* March 7, 2005, p. 74; *Times* (London), February 22, 2005, p. 56; *Washington Post,* February 21, 2005, p. B5.

—Carol Brennan

Bob Denver

Born Robert Denver, January 9, 1935, in New Rochelle, NY; died of complications related to cancer treatment, September 2, 2005, in Winston-Salem, NC. Actor. American actor Bob Denver was best known for his iconic roles in two classic American television situation comedies, *The Many Loves of Dobie Gillis* and *Gilligan's Island.* Both shows were hits in their original runs and remained popular in syndicated reruns for many years, keeping Denver and his off-beat characters in the public eye. Denver also appeared in several other television shows, as well as film and stage roles, and had his own syndicated oldies radio show.

Born in 1935 in New York, Denver attended high school in Brownwood, Texas. After graduation, he and his family moved to California. There, Denver attended Loyola University (later known as Loyola Marymount) in Los Angeles. While a college student, Denver was drawn into acting. He was convinced to become the house manager of the university's theater, then went on to appear in five college productions. A pre-law student, Denver graduated with his political science degree.

With degree in hand, Denver decided not to pursue a law career and started acting with the local Del Ray Players. He made his professional stage debut playing a seaman in a Los Angeles production of *The Caine Mutiny Court-Martial.* Another early stage role was in William Shakespeare's *Henry IV* as Falstaff. In order to support himself, Denver also held other jobs, working as a teacher, coach, and mail carrier for a few years as his acting career developed.

By the late 1950s, Denver was being cast in roles in film and television. He had a small role in the 1959 film *A Private's Affair.* That same year, he had a screen test which led to him being cast as Maynard G. Krebs in the sitcom *The Many Loves of Dobie Gillis,* which aired from 1959 to 1963. Krebs was a beatnik who had a goatee, wore a sweatshirt, and played the bongos. The best friend of the title character, Krebs was a goofy, unusual character who had an unconventional look at life, avoided work, and served as a contrast to the more common American teenager, Gillis, played by Denver's college classmate Dwayne Hickman. Upon Denver's death, Hickman told Dennis McLellan of the *Los Angeles Times,* "He had a wonderful sense of comedy, great timing, and he had sweet personality on the screen. I loved working with him. I was proud to be his straight man."

A year after *The Many Loves of Dobie Gillis* ended its run, Denver was cast in the role with which he would be most closely identified for the rest of his life. From 1964 to 1967, Denver played Willy Gilligan, the title character, in the hit CBS sitcom *Gilligan's Island.* The show focused on the adventures of a group of misfit castaways from all strata of society who had been shipwrecked on a tropical island in the South Pacific. Gilligan had been the first mate on the ship, the S.S. Minnow, before the wreck, and much of the show's humor was derived from his naiveté and physical humor from run-ins with the ship's captain, Jonas Grumby, known as the Skipper. When the show ended, it ran nearly continuously in syndication for decades.

In addition to the syndicated reruns of the original 98 shows, Denver portrayed Gilligan in numerous other television shows. He provided the voice of Gilligan in two animated versions of the show, including 1974's *Gilligan's Planet.* He also acted as Gilligan in three television movies based on the series, 1978's *Rescue from Gilligan's Island,* 1979's *The Castaways on Gilligan's Island,* and 1981's *The Harlem Globetrotters on Gilligan's Island.* Denver even appeared as Gilligan in an episode of *Baywatch* in 1992 and a low-budget film called *Miss Cast Away.*

While Maynard G. Krebs and Gilligan were the characters with which Denver was most identified, he also had a variety of other roles. He appeared in a few films such as 1963's *Take Her, She's Mine* and 1967's *Who's Minding the Mint?*. In the late 1960s and 1970s, Denver appeared in a number of other television shows, none of which lasted for long. From 1968 to 1970, he played Rufus Butterworth in *The Good Guys.* Denver then appeared on Broadway in 1970 in the Woody Allen-penned *Play It Again, Sam.* Denver replaced Allen himself in the lead role in the play.

Back in Los Angeles, Denver returned to television in the 1973 short-lived syndicated clone of *Gilligan's Island* called *Dusty Trails.* Instead of an island, *Dusty Trails* was set on a lost wagon train. In 1975, Denver played another Gilligan-like role in *Far Out Space Nuts,* a children's program produced by Sid and Marty Krofft that only lasted a year.

In the 1970s, Denver moved from Los Angeles to Las Vegas, Nevada, where he made his home for a number of years. In addition to his Gilligan-related roles, Denver also appeared in a number of dinner theater productions. In addition, Denver wrote his memoir, 1993's *Gilligan, Maynard & Me.* In the mid-1990s, he moved to Princeton, West Virginia, with his third wife, Dreama Perry Denver. By the end of his life, he was hosting a syndicated radio program with his wife. The show, *Little Buddy Radio,* played the oldies.

In the early 2000s, Denver began suffering from ill health. He developed cancer and received treatment at North Carolina's Wake Forest University Baptist Medical Center. In May of 2005, he also had to have quadruple bypass surgery. Denver died from complications related to his cancer treatment on September 2, 2005, in Winston-Salem, North Carolina. He was 70 years old. Denver is survived by his wife of 28 years, sons Patrick and Colin, daughters Megan and Emily, and a granddaughter. **Sources:** *Chicago Tribune,* September 7, 2005, sec. 3, p. 8; CNN.com, http://www.cnn.com/2005/SHOWBIZ/TV/09/06/denver.obit.ap/index.html (September 8, 2005); *Entertainment Weekly,* September 16, 2005, p. 18; E! Online, http://www.eonline.com/News/Items/0,1,17298,00.html?fdnews (September 8, 2005); *Los Angeles Times,* September 7, 2005, p. B10; *New York Times,* September 7, 2005, p. A27; *People,* September 19, 2005, pp. 208-09; *Times* (London), September 9, 2005, p. 79; *Washington Post,* September 7, 2005, p. B6.

—*A. Petruso*

Jacques Derrida

Born July 15, 1930, in El-Biar, Algeria; died of pancreatic cancer, October 8, 2004, in Paris, France. Phi-

losopher. Algerian-born French philosopher Jacques Derrida upended the intellectual community in the 1960s when he began promoting his own school of philosophy dubbed deconstructionism, a study of the meaninglessness of meaning. Deconstructionists seek to unravel the meaning of a text by searching for ambiguities and contradictions in hopes that they will reveal hidden meanings. Once the text is "deconstructed," the meaning becomes elusive. The philosophy provoked controversy as it spread through college campuses in the 1960s, '70s, and '80s, earning Derrida both reverence and contempt for the remainder of his life.

Derrida (pronounced deh-ree-DAH) was born into a middle-class Jewish family on July 15, 1930, in El-Biar, Algeria. His father worked as a salesman. Derrida's childhood was rife with misfortune. Two brothers died young causing his mother to become overprotective. In addition, Derrida was expelled from school around the age of 12 as a result of French Algeria's newly passed anti-Semitic laws that restricted the number of Jewish children allowed in its schools. At the time Derrida was the top student at his academy. Derrida's family, which had lived in Algeria for five generations, lost its citizenship and Derrida began to think of himself as an outsider.

As a teenager Derrida took an interest in philosophy after hearing a talk about French author and philosopher Albert Camus, who promoted a philosophy known as absurdism, which held that attempts to find meaning in life were hopeless because the world was an irrational place. His curiosity piqued, Derrida began reading the works of French writer André Gide, German philosopher Friedrich Nietzsche, and French philosophers Jean Jacques Rousseau and Jean-Paul Sartre.

After being forced out of his Algerian academy, Derrida attended an informal school for Jewish children but did not take his studies seriously and was often absent. Derrida wanted to play professional soccer but finally realized he lacked the athletic prowess to succeed. He turned to academia and earned admittance to France's most prestigious college, the École Normale Supérieure in Paris. While there he met Marguerite Aucouturier, who was studying to become a psychoanalyst. They married in 1957 and had two sons.

Derrida earned his philosophy degree in 1956, then studied briefly at Harvard University before returning to Algeria to serve as a teacher in the French army. Around 1960 Derrida began teaching philosophy and logic at the Collège de Sorbonne in France. By 1965 he was teaching at the École Normale Supérieure and contributing to the leftist magazine *Tel Quel.*

In 1966 Derrida introduced his philosophy to the United States during a symposium at Johns Hopkins University. He gained more attention the following year when he published three groundbreaking works, *Writing and Difference, Speech and Phenomena* and *Of Grammatology*, which further defined his philosophy and method. Their publication touched off animated debates in intellectual circles around the globe, though Derrida's ideas were best received in the United States. The books served to further Derrida's argument that a text can never have a single, authoritative meaning in and of itself.

While this early trio of books attracted a large number of readers, his later works were read mostly by disciples of the discipline. For most people Derrida's books (some 50 in number) were hard to comprehend. At times sentences ran three pages and footnotes even longer. The language was intentionally dense. Critics charged that his books were uncomprehendable, while his followers argued they were brilliant, perfect examples of the elusiveness of meaning.

Young intellectuals—looking for a new philosophy to call their own—were drawn to deconstructionism and it flourished on college campuses into the early 1980s. Crowds gathered to hear Derrida speak. Highly charismatic and darkly Mediterranean with a crop of prematurely white hair and bristly eyebrows, Derrida commanded attention. His lectures included ingenious plays on words, rhymes, and puns. According to Jonathan Kandell in the *New York Times,* Derrida was known for making baffling proclamations, such as, "Thinking is what we already know that we have not yet begun," and "Oh my friends, there is no friend."

Derrida's deconstructionist theory took off quickly in the field of literature as scholars began deconstructing classic works of literature and philosophy, yielding revolutionary reinterpretations. In time architects hopped on board, too, and took a "deconstructionist" approach to design by disregarding such traditions as symmetry. The theory even trickled down into pop culture. In 1997, filmmaker Woody Allen released *Deconstructing Harry*, a movie that focused on breaking down and analyzing the main character's neurotic contradictions in an attempt to understand him.

By the 1970s Derrida was regularly lecturing at Yale University and in 1986 joined the staff of the University of California at Irvine. For the next 20 years he split his time between Irvine and the École des Hautes Études en Sciences Sociales in Paris.

In 1992 Britain's Cambridge University attempted to award Derrida an honorary degree, but many faculty members protested. According to the *Washington Post,* they denounced his writings as "denying the distinctions between fact and fiction, observation and imagination, evidence and prejudice." In the end Derrida won the award by a vote of 336 to 204.

Derrida's critics accused him of being a nihilist—someone who believed there was no meaning. Detractors believed the philosophy would destroy society by reducing it to a negative state of meaning. Derrida, however, charged that just because a text contained no single meaning did not mean it did not have any meaning. Derrida's detractors forever asked him to define his philosophy in straightforward terms. He most often declined and once told a *New York Times* reporter that attempting to offer a definition for deconstructionism would simply yield "something which will leave me unsatisfied."

By the early 1990s deconstructionism was no longer in vogue, though campuses continue to teach and be influenced by the theory. Derrida continued lecturing at Irvine until 2003 and continued his duties as director of studies at the École des Hautes Études en Sciences Sociales in Paris until 2004.

Derrida died of pancreatic cancer at a Paris hospital on October 8, 2004; he was 74. He was survived by his wife, Marguerite, and two sons, Pierre and Jean, as well as a son, Daniel, whom he had with philosophy teacher Sylviane Agacinski. **Sources:** *Independent* (London), October 11, 2004, p. 34; *Los Angeles Times,* October 10, 2004, p. B16; *New York Times,* October 10, 2004, p. A1; *Washington Post,* October 10, 2004, p. C11.

—Lisa Frick

Wim Duisenberg

Born Willem Frederik Duisenberg, July 9, 1935, in Heerenveen, Netherlands; died of natural causes, July 31, 2005, in Faucon, France. Banker. Wim Duisenberg was known as the "father of the Euro" across much of Europe. As the first president of the European Central Bank, Duisenberg oversaw the introduction of a common currency, called the Euro, during his five-year tenure. For a continent whose peoples had gone to war with one another almost since they learned of the others' existence, the implementation of a single currency was an historic step among European Union (EU) member-nations, and the genial, stubborn Dutch economist was eventually commended for his managerial talents in supervising the complex process.

Born in 1935, some of Duisenberg's youth was spent under the shadow of the Nazi German occupation of the Netherlands. He grew up in the town of Heerenveen, and went on to earn his doctorate in economics from the University of Groningen in 1965. After working for the International Monetary Fund in Washington, D.C., for a time, he returned home and was made advisor to the director of the Nederlandsche Bank, the country's central bank, in 1969. Over the next decade, he served as a professor of macroeconomics at the University of Amsterdam, held a seat in the Dutch parliament, spent four years as the country's Minister of Finance, and became vice chair of a privately owned bank.

In 1981, Duisenberg was made a director of the Nederlandsche Bank, and named to its presidency a year later. He stayed on the job for 15 years, during which time he emerged as one of the most ardent advocates for the adoption of a common European currency. The process began with a 1992 agreement, called Maastricht Treaty, for a planned economic and monetary union among EU signees to the accord. Several strict criteria had to be met in each country before the currency conversion could take place in each, and central banks such as the Nederlandsche Bank played important roles in achieving those goals. During Duisenberg's tenure, for example, he linked the Dutch guilder to Germany's mark, which helped Dutch financial markets and economic indicators remain stable.

Duisenberg was named to serve as the first president of the European Central Bank (ECB) in 1998, ostensibly for an eight-year term. The job came with enormous power, and analysts asserted that, as the supervisor of interest rates in the European countries known as the eurozone, Duisenberg would wield more influence than any elected leader. Yet the appointment, which European heads of state had to agree upon, was not without controversy: France was reportedly miffed that the head of their central bank was bypassed for the post, and so a deal was struck whereby Duisenberg agreed to serve just four years. The ECB would then be turned over to Jean-Claude Trichet, director of the Banque de France.

The euro was launched as an accounting currency in the world's financial markets in January of 1999. That spurred some unexpected fluctuations and economic difficulties over the next few years, and the central banks of the member countries pleaded with Duisenberg to lower interest rates to alleviate further hardships. Known for his stubbornness and independent mind, he refused to be swayed, once even telling the bankers, "I hear, but I don't listen," according to the *Los Angeles Times*. The French press devoted innumerable unflattering headlines to what they deemed his poor stewardship. Trichet, meanwhile, faced charges of fraud for his role in a scandal involving Credit Lyonnais, a state-owned bank in France that went through several upheavals in the 1990s.

Actual Euro notes and coins were introduced throughout the eurozone on January 1, 2002. This time, Duisenberg was commended for his deft management of the major event, which essentially removed all national currencies from circulation forever and affected 305 million Europeans. By then, the Euro was doing better as well, and concern about its devaluation had faded. He announced his retirement on his 68th birthday in 2003, but stayed on the job until Trichet extracted himself from his legal quandary. Duisenberg officially stepped down on October 31, 2003.

A heavy smoker, Duisenberg likely died of a heart attack in his swimming pool in Fauchon, a town in the south of France, on July 31, 2005, where he had a summer home. Survivors include second wife Gretta, a political activist whom he married in 1987, and two sons and a daughter from his first marriage to Tine Stelling. His legacy as what some termed "Mr. Europe" was unchallenged, and he himself noted that "it has been an honor and a privilege," a CNN.com report quoted him as saying on the day the Euro notes were introduced. "Europe has made history and I have been given a place at the heart of it." **Sources:** *Chicago Tribune*, August 1, 2005, sec. 4, p. 10; CNN.com, http://www.cnn.com/2003/BUSINESS/10/31/duisenberg.stepsdown/index.html (August 1, 2005); *Los Angeles Times*, August 1, 2005, p. B9; *New York Times*, August 1, 2005, p. A13; *Times* (London), August 1, 2005, p. 42; *Washington Post*, August 1, 2005, p. B4.

—*Carol Brennan*

Andrea Dworkin

Born Andrea Rita Dworkin, September 26, 1946, in Camden, NJ; died April 9, 2005, in Washington, DC. Author. Known for her unrelenting and unforgiving stance on pornography, Andrea Dworkin had as many admirers as she had enemies. Her past as a battered wife and prostitute led her to become a major opponent in the fight for equal rights for women. Her books, *Woman Hating,* and *Pornography: Men Possessing Women,* continued to bring about public awareness about the ills of pornography. Together with legal scholar Catharine MacKinnon, Dworkin worked to bring an ordinance that would allow people, women in particular, to sue the producers of porn if their lives had been negatively impacted by the products. A couple of cities in the Midwest did adopt the ordinance but it was later overturned by the U.S. Supreme Court.

Dworkin was born to Jewish parents on September 26, 1946, in Camden, New Jersey. Dworkin's mother had heart trouble, so Andrea was constantly being shuffled among her relatives. Her father worked for the Post Office and as a guidance counselor. Her father was also a Socialist who taught his daughter to be a nonconformist at an early age. When she refused to sing the Christmas carol "Silent Night," Dworkin was forced out of the school choir.

At 18, Dworkin entered Bennington College, hoping to become a Greenwich Village artist. While protesting the Vietnam War, she was arrested and sent to New York's Women's House of Detention. While there she was subjected to a humiliating body cavity search that not only scarred her physically, but also emotionally. Upon her release, she was encouraged by Grace Paley, a writer and activist, to tell the newspapers about her abuse. Her story was picked up by the *New York Times* and other major newspapers around the country. This led to a government investigation and the eventual closing of the prison. Unfortunately for Dworkin, her parents disowned her after her disclosure. She then moved to Greece. With little money, she turned to prostitution to make ends meet. After spending a year abroad, she returned to Bennington College and earned a bachelors degree in 1968.

Dworkin moved overseas again and married a Dutch radical. Her husband began abusing her, sometimes burning her with cigarettes. She sought help, but no one would come to her aid. In an article for the *Los Angeles Times,* Dworkin wrote, "I was buried alive in silence. I didn't know that such horror had ever happened to anyone else." She ran away and hid from her husband until a female friend helped her leave the country.

Dworkin returned to the United States and divorced her husband. She worked menial jobs before becoming the assistant to Muriel Rukeyser, a poet, who encouraged Dworkin to write. At 27, Dworkin released *Woman Hating,* which included her critique of pornography. She also wrote about violence against women by examining fairy tales and myths. The *Washington Post* stated that by writing *Woman Hating,* she sought to "destroy patriarchal power at its source, the family, [and] in its most hideous form, the national state." According to the *Los Angeles Times,* Dworkin also concluded that reading pornographic material with her former husband in part led to her spousal abuse. *Woman Hating* was met with praise as well as denouncement. Many thought her stance on pornography as a tool of violence against women was refreshing, while others labeled her as a man-hater. Dworkin denied that she was against men, but she did feel "heterosexual intercourse is the pure, formalized expression of contempt for women's bodies," according to London's *Independent.* She also believed that battered women should be allowed to kill their batterers.

In 1980, the star of the porn film *Deep Throat,* Linda Marchiano (also known as Linda Lovelace), wanted to sue the film producers and distributors after suffering from being coerced into the porn business. Dworkin sought the help of fellow feminist MacKinnon, who was also a Yale law professor, to represent Marchiano. The two could not find anything in the law to help Marchiano. They drafted an ordinance that would allow people to sue the producers of porn, due to pornography being a form of sex discrimination. The ordinance was supported by various factions, including radical feminists and conservatives. Among the major opponents were feminist groups, who deemed that the ordinance hindered women's rights to explore all facets of their sexuality. The cities of Minneapolis, Minnesota, and Indianapolis, Indiana, adopted the ordinances. However, it was declared unconstitutional by the U.S. Supreme Court as it violated first amendment rights.

With her strong political stance on pornography and equal rights for women, Dworkin was a popular speaker on the lecture circuit. She also continued to release books, including *Pornography: Men Possessing Women.* After the release of this book, she was asked to speak at a conference in the United Kingdom, where opposition to pornography was growing. She also lent her support to those in the United Kingdom who were bringing about awareness concerning the ills of pornography on society. Dworkin contributed to the U.K. book, *Pornography: Women Violence and Civil Liberties.*

A number of Dworkin's releases were published by U.K. publishing houses because many American companies found her rhetoric too radical to promote. She continued to release books throughout the 1980s and 1990s, including *Intercourse, Pornogra-*

phy and Civil Right: A New Day for Women's Equality, Letters From a War Zone, and *Scapegoat: The Jews, Israel and Women's Liberation*. She also released novels and poetry, including *Ice and Fire* and *Mercy*.

Dworkin continued writing until she was unable to due to a number of illnesses. She had surgery to help her weakening knees, but suffered a series of falls post-surgery. Dworkin died in her sleep on April 9, 2005, in her home in Washington D.C.; she was 58. Dworkin is survived by her life partner of 30 years and husband (though both were homosexual) of nine years, John Stoltenberg, managing editor of *AARP* magazine. **Sources:** *Contemporary Authors Online*, Thomson Gale, 2005; *Independent* (London), April 12, 2005, p. 3; April 13, 2005, p. 42; *Los Angeles Times*, April 15, 2005, p. B10; *New York Times*, April 12, 2005, p. B7; *Washington Post*, April 12, 2005, p. B6.

—*Ashyia N. Henderson*

Richard Eberhart

Born Richard Ghormley Eberhart, April 5, 1904, in Austin, MN; died after a brief illness, June 9, 2005, in Hanover, NH. Poet and educator. The works of Richard Eberhart brought him fame and honor. Two of his most famous poems, "The Groundhog," and "The Fury of Aerial Bombardment" can be found in many anthologies and collections. He won all of the most prestigious awards for poetry, including a Pulitzer Prize. In addition to writing poems, Eberhart also taught at Dartmouth College, inspiring his students to fully express themselves in poetry. Jay Parini, a professor at Middlebury College and a former colleague of Eberhart's, told the *Los Angeles Times*, "I saw so many poets come through his door and seek him out. He was a poet of real achievement."

Eberhart was born on April 5, 1904, in Austin, Minnesota. His father worked as a vice president for the George A. Hormel meatpacking company. Unlike many poets and writers, Eberhart's childhood was a happy one. The family home was a 40-acre estate, named Burr Oaks, which he would later use as a title for a volume of poetry.

Eberhart began his college education at the University of Minnesota, but after his freshman year, his mother died of cancer. His father lost the family fortune during this time as well. There was still enough money for Eberhart to complete his education, so he transferred to Dartmouth. After receiving his bachelor's degree, Eberhart worked as a crewman aboard a freighter in the South Pacific. He worked several odd jobs, including as a tutor for the son of the King of Siam, before pursuing a second bachelors degree at Cambridge University in England. He also earned a masters degree at Cambridge. He entered Harvard University for postgraduate work, but only stayed for a year. Eberhart also released his first volume of poetry, *A Bravery of Earth*. He embraced Romanticism in his poetry, but his use of short lines and irregular rhythms kept him from fully participating in the style. According to the *Chicago Tribune*, Eberhart told New Hampshire's *Concord Monitor*, "Poems ... are milestones, to see where you were then from where you are now. To perpetuate your feelings, to establish them."

Though Eberhart strongly wanted a career in poetry, it did not pay the bills, so in 1933 he joined the faculty of St. Mark's School, a boys' school, located in Massachusetts. He taught English for eight years, and some of his pupils included Robert Lowell, also later a Pulitzer Prize winner, Blair Clark, future editor of *The Nation*, and Frank Parker, an accomplished artist. In 1941, he married Helen Butcher and joined the Naval Reserve. During World War II he worked as a gunnery instructor.

After the war ended, Eberhart worked for the Butcher Polish Company, his in-laws' family business. After several years, he returned to the world of academia, first teaching at Princeton. He taught at several universities, before becoming a writer-in-residence at his alma mater, Dartmouth, where he would remain full-time until 1970, and part-time until 1981.

Eberhart also continued to release several volumes of poetry, including *Reading the Spirit, Song and Idea, Burr Oaks, Great Praises, The Quarry: New Poems, Fields of Grace*, and *Maine Poems*. Eberhart also wrote plays, and was a founder of the Poets' Theater. He also helped many aspiring poets, including Allen Ginsberg of the Beat Generation. Eberhart celebrated each new generation of poets, but he himself was considered old-fashioned and continued with his usual style throughout a career that spanned six decades. Eberhart also lectured at numerous colleges and universities, accepted several guest teaching positions, and held readings at various locations. From 1959 to 1961, he was the Consultant in Poetry for the Library of Congress (a precursor to the poet laureate position).

In the world of poetry, there are four major awards and Eberhart won all of them. In 1962 he won Yale University's Bollingen Prize for distinguished achievement in American poetry. Following the release of *Selected Poems, 1930-1965*, Eberhart was awarded the Pulitzer in 1966. In 1977, he won the National Book Award for *Collected Poems, 1930-1976*. Eberhart also received the Frost Medal from the Poetry Society of America in 1986. He was a fellow of the Academy of American Poets and a member of the National Institute of Arts and Letters.

In addition to his love of poetry, Eberhart was an avid outdoorsman. He cross-country skied until the age of 90. Every year he and his family summered in Maine, where he enjoyed boating and was usually seen ferrying friends and colleagues around. After a short illness, Eberhart died at the age of 101 in his home in Hanover, New Hampshire on June 9, 2005. He was preceded in death by his wife, and is survived by his daughter, Gretchen, and son, Richard, as well as six grandchildren. **Sources:** *Chicago Tribune*, June 13, 2005, sec. 1, p. 9; *Contemporary Poets*, 7th ed., St. James Press, 2001; *Independent* (London), June 16, 2005, p. 39; *Los Angeles Times*, June 14, 2005, p. B10; *New York Times*, June 14, 2005, p. A21.

—*Ashyia N. Henderson*

Will Eisner

Born William Erwin Eisner, March 6, 1917, in New York, NY; died on January 3, 2005, in Lauderdale Lakes, FL. Graphic novelist. Illustrator and writer Will Eisner was an important influence on the development of the graphic novel, the more literary successor to the comic book. A talented artist who worked with some of the top names in the American comics scene in the 1930s and '40s, Eisner was revered by a later generation of illustrators and authors. One of the industry's top awards is named in his honor.

Born in 1917, Eisner grew up in the New York City borough of the Bronx. His father, who had once been a stage-set painter in imperial Vienna, encouraged his son's artistic ambitions. At DeWitt Clinton High School, one of Eisner's friends was Bob Kane, who later created the *Batman* comic series. Eisner's first published comic appeared in a magazine in 1936, the year he turned 19, and soon he and another pal, Jerry Iger, had formed Eisner & Iger, a comics studio they opened in a rented space on East 41st Street. The studio was soon flourishing thanks to such series as *Sheena, Queen of the Jungle,* and artists in their roster included both Eisner's friend,

Kane, and Jack Kirby, who was a co-creator of the popular *X-Men* series years later. Their only notable misstep was rejecting the original *Superman* strip when it was first submitted to them.

Eisner was eventually offered his own strip, and so sold his half of the partnership to Iger and created *The Spirit*, a.k.a. Denny Colt. The series featured a detective returned from the afterlife who fights crime and injustice in the Manhattan-like Central City. Colt gets by without the standard superpowers, and preferred to help out the average working person beleaguered by petty crime or institutional injustice. The series launched as a syndicated newspaper cartoon in June of 1940, and ran for 12 years. "The stories employed elements of German Expressionism, interspliced with Marx Brothers-like surreal comedy, and appealed to adults and kids alike," wrote Alan Woollcombe in London's *Independent* newspaper. Eisner's strip was also one of the first to use the silent panel, with no dialogue or thought bubbles, just a close-up to show facial expression. He also wrote and drew it himself, at a time when it was rather unusual for a strip to be the work of one person. At the peak of its popularity, *The Spirit* was carried in 20 newspapers and reached five million readers every Sunday.

There was perhaps an equally large audience for Eisner's other creation, "Joe Dope." Eisner had been drafted into the U.S. Army during World War II, and while his assistants carried on *The Spirit,* he created educational cartoons for the army that showed newly enlisted service personnel how to fix vehicles and maintain weapons. Each illustrative tale, often written in comical verse form, concluded with the warning, "Don't Be a Dope! Handle Equipment Right." Back in civilian life after the war's end, Eisner returned to writing and illustrating *The Spirit,* but he ended it in 1952, when comics seemed to be waning in popularity. He parleyed his wartime work into a new company, the American Visual Corporation, which made educational cartoons for the government and for companies like General Motors.

Eisner carried on that work for many years, until in the late 1960s a new form of comics emerged out of the counterculture. Originally called "underground," the comics coming from the likes of R. Crumb and others re-inspired Eisner to return to the form, and he began working more creatively once again. The result was *A Contract With God and Other Tenement Stories* published in 1978. Its antihero is a man, Frimme Hersh, who feels abandoned by God, and becomes a slumlord in the Bronx. The work was significant because it was a comic, but in a much longer format and with heavy philosophical themes; Eisner is believed to have coined the term "graphic novel" to describe it, which within a quarter-century would become its own bookstore section.

Eisner wrote several other graphic novels, and his earlier *Spirit* series was frequently reissued in book format. He taught at the New York School of Visual Art, and authored the 1996 textbook *Graphic Storytelling*. Since 1987 the top annual honors in the comics industry have been known as the Will Eisner Awards. The various awards are handed out annually at the Comic-Con International Convention in San Diego, California, and Eisner was one of the presenters each year. He was a legendary figure in the industry, and novelist Michael Chabon based one of his characters in *The Amazing Adventures of Kavalier & Clay* (the winner of the 2001 Pulitzer Prize for fiction), on him. Eisner's graphic novel *The Plot*, completed before his death, was published in the spring of 2005.

Eisner died on January 3, 2005, at the age of 87 near Fort Lauderdale, Florida, after undergoing quadruple bypass surgery. He is survived by his wife, Ann, and son, John. "My stories are all centered around the human being, the business of survival, of struggling against the forces of life itself," Eisner said, according to the *Independent*'s Woollcombe, "My interest is not the superhero, but the little man who struggles to survive in the city." **Sources:** *Chicago Tribune*, January 5, 2005, sec. 3, p. 11; CNN. com, http://www.cnn.com/2005/SHOWBIZ/ books/01/04/obit.eisner.ap/index.html (January 5, 2005). *Independent* (London), January 6, 2005, p. 43; *Los Angeles Times*, January 5, 2005, p. B8; *New York Times*, January 5, 2005, p. C14.

—*Carol Brennan*

Fahd, King of Saudi Arabia

Born c. 1923, in Riyadh, Saudi Arabia; died after a long illness, August 1, 2005, in Riyadh. King. Saudi Arabia's King Fahd Bin Abdul Aziz Al Saud ruled over a once-barren desert kingdom whose oil riches made it one of the world's wealthiest nations. The once-errant playboy courted alliances with the West as well as other Arab nations, which placed his tightly controlled realm in an ideological buffer zone between the Muslim world and secular democracies. Under Fahd, however, Saudi society remained authoritarian and dominated by strict Islamic-law codes.

Fahd is believed to have been born in 1923, at a time when Saudi Arabia did not yet exist as a nation. The Saud royal family had emerged as a political dynasty in the 1740s in the central Arabian peninsula by forging alliances with clerics of a conservative Islamic sect known as Wahhabism. Fahd's father, Amir Abdul Aziz, led a series of military excursions that enlarged the Saud family holdings, and in 1925 his forces captured Islam's holy city, Mecca. The following year, Aziz was proclaimed king in the Mecca's Grand Mosque. Until oil was discovered in 1938, the Saudi kingdom was a poor, sparsely populated land. Its main source of revenue came from the thousands of Muslim men who made the *hajj*, or pilgrimage to Mecca, that the religion's creed deems they must do once in their lifetime.

Among Aziz's 36 sons by his 22 wives, Fahd was part of a line known as the Sudairi Seven. These were the full-blood brothers whose alliance would become the most powerful one within the Saud ruling clan. At the Princes' School in Riyadh—the Saud family seat and Saudi capital—Fahd received a rudimentary education which included learning to read the Koran and a familiarity with shari'a, or Islamic law. His first official post came when his father made him governor of Jauf, a province in the north, in the mid-1940s.

Fahd became minister for education in 1953, the same year that Aziz died and was succeeded on the throne by the oldest of Aziz's sons, Saud. The new post was one of tremendous responsibility, because it came at a time when the country's oil riches were beginning to fund a major modernization effort, but hardline clerics objected to secular education. Despite the objections, Fahd managed to establish a network of schools and even separate ones for girls. Along the way, he reportedly enhanced his own limited education with the help of private tutors. After 1962 he served as minister of the interior under his brother, King Faisal, who had succeeded Saud to the throne.

In March of 1975, Faisal was assassinated by a nephew, and Fahd's half-brother Khalid became king. Three months later, Fahd was designated crown prince, or next in the line of succession. He began to exert influence on Saudi Arabia's domestic and foreign policy, meeting with world leaders such as U.S. president Jimmy Carter, and ascended to the throne on June 13, 1982, after Khalid's death.

Fahd spent the next dozen years of his reign engaged in delicate balancing acts on several fronts. There was a division between the country's still-powerful clerics and a growing middle class, who clamored for some semblance of democratic government. Fahd made some concessions to the powerful clerics, most notably in the continuance of Saudi Arabia's strict religious codes and restrictions on women. Outside the kingdom, Saudi Arabia was the world's largest oil exporter and, as such, was courted by a succession of U.S. presidents and secretaries of state. American support for Israel, however, made many Arabs uneasy with befriending the Jewish state's most important ally. Fahd tried to placate both sides by donating generously to the Palestinian cause, while also buying millions of dollars worth of high-tech weaponry from the United States. The presence of U.S. military bases in the kingdom was troubling to some devout Saudis, who lived in a land long hostile to outsiders and intolerant of any creed save for Wahhabism.

During the first Gulf War, U.S. forces mobilized for the attack on Iraqi-occupied Kuwait at those bases inside Saudi Arabia, which offended devout Muslims worldwide. One who resented the aid given to a foreign, largely Christian army for its attack on a Muslim nation was a Saudi exile, Osama bin Laden, whose fundamentalist organization would eventually launch deadly terrorist attacks around the world, including ones on Saudi soil.

A heavyset man who had been known for his fast-living lifestyle in the capitals of Europe during his younger years, Fahd suffered from diabetes and his health declined considerably following a 1995 stroke. A half-brother, Abdullah, took over an increasing number of executive duties as Crown Prince. Fahd was hospitalized in May of 2005 for pneumonia, and died in Riyadh on August 1, at an age estimated between 82 and 84 years old. He had eight sons by three wives, and all wives and seven of the sons survive him. The kingdom he ruled, officially, for 23 years had witnessed unprecedented changes since his boyhood, but Fahd was mindful of the reasons behind its rise as a world power. In a telephone conversation secretly taped by Iraqi intelligence services, he told an official of the Qatar government that "when we were poor, when we rode donkeys and had difficulty finding a few dates to eat, no one asked about us," he said, according to his London *Times* obituary. "They only acknowledge us now because we have money." **Sources:** *Chicago Tribune*, August 2, 2005, sec. 1, p. 2; *Los Angeles Times*, August 2, 2005, p. A1, p. A8; *New York Times*, August 2, 2005, p. C16; *Times* (London), August 2, 2005, p. 41; *Washington Post*, August 2, 2005, p. A1, p. A10.

—*Carol Brennan*

Al Held

Born Alvin Jacob Held, October 12, 1928, in New York, NY; died of natural causes, July 26, 2005, in Camerata, Umbria, Italy. Artist. Al Held earned his slot in the annals of American contemporary art with his bold, geometric canvases that took abstraction to another level. His free-floating, interlocked cubes and planes invited the viewer into a vertigo-inducing landscape that seemed to stretch on into infinity. "Immense architectural structures curve and slice through these complex paintings, often enmeshing themselves in cellular structures," noted the *Times* of London. "Viewers felt that they were exploring some mysterious universe, and Held never lost his passionate belief in abstract painting's ability to create a sublime new world."

Born in 1928, Held grew up in Brooklyn, New York, and as a teenager missed so many days of high school that it was suggested he consider leaving altogether. He eventually earned a night-school diploma, and spent two years in the U.S. Navy. Back in New York City, he enrolled in classes at the Art Students League, and went on to study at the Académie de la Grande Chaumière in Paris in the early 1950s. The first solo exhibition of his work was staged there, in 1952 at the Galerie Huit. It was in New York, however, that new and exciting currents in the art scene were happening, and Held returned home. He co-founded the Brata Gallery on East Tenth Street with several other artists, and worked in construction and as a carpenter to supplement his income during these lean years.

In the 1950s, Abstract Expressionism was the dominant new style among New York-based artists, and best exemplified in the exuberant canvases of Jackson Pollock. Held's abstract work took on a more orderly, formal tone, aided by a switch from oil to acrylic paints in 1959, and he had his first solo show in New York City that same year at the Poindexter Gallery. "Finessing the gap between Minimalism and Color Field painting," wrote *New York Times* journalist Ken Johnson of the next decade of Held's career, "he produced smooth, simplified works based on enlarged letters of the alphabet. And in the late '60s and '70s he made complex black-and-white pictures of sharply outlined cubes, pyramids, and other geometric shapes floating in illusory spaces of indeterminate depth."

Some of Held's best-known works are those floating black and white cubes, a series he began in 1967. One of the largest, which stretches more than 90 feet in length, was installed at the Empire State

Plaza in Albany, New York. In the late 1970s, in an abrupt shift, he began using color again, and the geometric shapes became so precise that they were sometimes mistaken for computer-generated art. But Held worked the old-fashioned way, using masking tape and a straight edge to map out the planes on canvas that suggested otherworldly realms to the viewer. He considered his images not unlike those of religious art, once telling an interviewer that "historically, the priests and wise men believed that it was the artist's job to make images of heaven and hell believable, even though nobody had experienced these places," he said, according to his *Chicago Tribune* obituary.

Held spent 20 years teaching at Yale University's esteemed art program, and retired as a professor in 1980. Represented by the Robert Miller Gallery in New York City, which staged what would be his last exhibition of new work in 2003, Held toiled for months and sometimes years on his immense canvases, some of which were so large that they could not be installed in a standard commercial art space. His works were avidly sought by contemporary-art enthusiasts around the world, and were part of the permanent collections of many institutions, including the Metropolitan Museum of Art and the Museum of Modern Art.

Held lived in Italy for part of the year, where the gardener for his property near the Umbrian town of Todi found the 76-year-old painter dead in his swimming pool on July 26, 2005. Italian authorities ruled it a death from natural causes. Married four times, Held is survived by his companion, Pamela Gagliani, daughter Mara Held, and one grandchild. At the time of his death, Held was completing commissions for a mural inside the Jacksonville Public Library in Florida, and a mosaic for a Manhattan subway station at Lexington Avenue and 53rd Street. **Sources:** *Chicago Tribune,* July 28, 2005, sec. 3, p. 10; *Los Angeles Times,* July 29, 2005, p. B11; *New York Times,* July 29, 2005, p. A17; *Times* (London), August 22, 2005, p. 41; *Washington Post,* July 28, 2005, p. B7.

—*Carol Brennan*

Evan Hunter

Born Salvatore Albert Lombino, October 15, 1926, in New York, NY; died of cancer, July 6, 2005, in Weston, CT. Author. Evan Hunter wrote more than 50 crime-fiction novels under the pen name Ed McBain, scoring numerous bestsellers as well as a place in American letters as the creator of a new literary form. "Without ... McBain, there would probably be no *Hill Street Blues, NYPD Blue,* or *Law & Order,*" asserted Adam B. Vary in *Entertainment Weekly,* who also claimed that in the mid-1950s the writer "essentially invented the American police procedural with a single pulp paperback."

Hunter was born Salvatore Lombino in 1926 in the New York City kitchen of his Italian-immigrant parents. The metropolis would later serve as the model for his fictional city of Isola that featured so prominently in his detective stories. He began writing while serving in the U.S. Navy from 1944 to 1946. "I was on a destroyer in the peacetime Pacific, and there wasn't much else to do," the *Washington Post's* Adam Bernstein quoted him as saying. Those early efforts all met with rejection from publishers, but Hunter did score some success writing science-fiction tales for pulp magazines after he earned a degree from Hunter College in 1950. Believing that mainstream publishers dismissed his work because of his Italian-heritage name, he changed it to Evan Hunter in 1952.

Newly married and with a growing family, Hunter struggled to make ends meet while writing on the side. He worked as a pianist, vocational-education teacher, lobster salesperson, and for a literary agency. The last job opened some doors in the book business for him, but his stint as a teacher served as the basis for his first genuine success, a 1954 novel called *The Blackboard Jungle.* The story of an idealistic educator and a classroom full of streetwise urban teens, the book sold five million copies and was made into an equally successful movie starring Glenn Ford and Sidney Poitier.

Hunter's foray into crime fiction came not long afterward, when he was recruited by an editor looking for an author to write a series in the style of Erle Stanley Gardner's profitable "Perry Mason" mysteries. The first Ed McBain book was *Cop Hater,* published in 1956, and Hunter gave the story not just one but several heroes in the form of an entire police precinct in a city called Isola. *New York Times* crime-fiction reviewer Marilyn Stasio called the novel "a radical break from a form long dependent on the educated, aristocratic detective who works alone and takes his time puzzling out a case."

Cop Hater became the first title in Hunter's long-running "87th Precinct" series, which featured recurring characters such as Detective Steve Carella and his deaf-mute wife, Teddy. As the landscape of urban America changed, so did Hunter's McBain stories, reflecting an increasingly grim and violent

Isola. Other trademarks of the series were, noted Stasio, "multiple story lines; swift, cinematic exposition; brutal action scenes and searing images of ghetto violence; methodical teamwork; authentic forensic procedures; and tough, cynical yet sympathetic police officers speaking dialogue so real that it could have been soaked up in a Queens diner between squad shifts."

The McBain stories were adapted for television in a short-lived NBC series, *87th Precinct*, that ran in the early 1960s, but the formula of making an entire squad of cops the central focus was more successfully deployed in later small-screen dramas, beginning with *Hill Street Blues* in the 1980s. Hunter also worked as a screenwriter, most notably for Alfred Hitchcock's 1963 shocker *The Birds*, while other works of his inspired filmmakers such as esteemed Japanese director Akira Kurosawa, who translated his 1959 novel *King's Ransom* into the film *High and Low*. One of the novels he wrote outside the crime-fiction genre, a 1958 suburban melodrama titled *Strangers When We Meet*, was made into the 1960 film of the same title, which starred Kirk Douglas and Kim Novak.

Hunter regularly put in ten hours a day at his desk, seven days a week, until he was slowed by a heart attack in the 1980s. Later titles of his included the 1997 memoir *Hitch and Me*, recounting his collaboration with Hitchcock, and *Let's Talk*, which chronicled his bout with cancer of the larynx. The 87th Precinct stories as Ed McBain, however, remained a publishing tour de force, with the final one, *Fiddlers*, published two months after his death. Over the course of a five-decade career, Hunter sold an estimated 100 million books, and earned several honors, including the Grand Master Award for lifetime achievement from the Mystery Writers of America. He died of cancer at age 78 at his Weston, Connecticut, home on July 6, 2005. Hunter is survived by his third wife, Dragica Dimitrijevic-Hunter; sons Mark, Richard, and Ted, from his first marriage to Anita Melnick; and stepdaughter Amanda Finley. **Sources:** *Entertainment Weekly*, July 22, 2005, p. 13; *Independent* (London, England), July 8, 2005, p. 66; *New York Times*, July 7, 2005, p. B10; *Washington Post*, July 7, 2005, p. B6.

—*Carol Brennan*

John H. Johnson

Born John Harold Johnson, January 19, 1918, in Arkansas City, AR; died after a long illness, August 8, 2005, in Chicago, IL. Publisher. John H. Johnson built a media empire based on the immensely successful magazines *Ebony* and *Jet* in the years following World War II. Both were aimed at an African-American readership, and *Ebony* in particular became enormously influential in that community. Its founder would be remembered as "a pioneer in black journalism when a large part of America lived in the shadow of segregation and open racism," noted Rupert Cornwell of London's *Independent* newspaper.

Born in 1918 in Arkansas City, Arkansas, Johnson was the grandson of slaves. His father was killed in a sawmill accident, and his mother worked as a camp cook for two years to save the money for a train ticket north for them, because there was no high school for black students in Arkansas City. Johnson's stepfather joined them in Chicago, and Johnson enrolled at DuSable High School, an all-black high school known for its rigorous academic program. He was elected class president and edited the school newspaper before he graduated in 1936.

That same year, Johnson was invited to speak before the Urban League, an early civil-rights organization. The president of an insurance company that served the black community was in the audience and, impressed, offered Johnson a job and tuition for college. He took courses at the University of Chicago, and began working at Supreme Liberty Life Insurance as an editor of its company magazine, which required him to sift through black newspapers and journals to find story ideas. He never earned his college degree, but after a few years came up with the idea for a new magazine based on *Reader's Digest*, which reprinted articles in condensed form from other publications. Unable to secure a business loan, he borrowed $500 by using his mother's household furniture as collateral. He sent out a subscription offer to Supreme Life policyholders, and when 3,000 signed up, *Negro Digest* was born. The first issue came out in November of 1942, and soon boasted a circulation of 50,000.

Johnson was by then married, and it was his wife, Eunice, who suggested the title for his next magazine project, which would be based on *Life*, another widely read publication of the day and renowned for its photojournalism. He later said his goal was to "show not only the Negroes but also white people that Negroes got married, had beauty contests, gave parties, ran successful businesses, and did all the other normal things of life," *New York Times* writer Douglas Martin quoted him as saying. The name of the new magazine was *Ebony*, and the 25,000 copies printed for its premier issue in November of 1945 sold out entirely.

Johnson's magazines relied heavily on his sales skills those first years to land the advertising accounts that brought in revenue. He was determined to win business from major American companies, not just those aimed at black consumers, and his persistence revolutionized magazine publishing. The first company he convinced was Zenith, a radio manufacturer, and others quickly followed suit. Johnson "virtually invented the black consumer market," the later executive editor of *Ebony*, Lerone Bennett Jr., told *Chicago Tribune* reporters Charles Storch and Barbara Sherlock. "He was the first publisher I know of who went to Madison Avenue and persuaded them that they had to address the African-American market and use African-American markets."

In 1951, Johnson launched *Jet*, which covered the achievements of blacks in entertainment, politics, and sports. It, too, became enormously successful, and with *Ebony* was a staple in nearly every middle-class African-American household for a generation and more. As the civil rights era gathered steam, Johnson's magazines profiled the movement's leaders, covered important events, and delivered strong opinions in both its editorials and feature articles about race relations in America.

Johnson's success as an entrepreneur and visionary kept pace with the gains made by his community over the years. In 1971, he became the first black person to own a building on Chicago's famed Michigan Avenue when he moved his Johnson Publishing headquarters there. Two years later, the company launched Fashion Fair Cosmetics, a line of makeup in shades flattering to darker skin. His wife, mother, and daughter all held executive positions, but his twenty-five-year-old son John Harold Johnson Jr. died of sickle cell anemia in 1981. A year later, Johnson became the first African American to appear on *Forbes'* annual rankings of the 400 wealthiest Americans.

The recipient of numerous honors, including the 1972 Publisher of the Year award from the Magazine Publishers Association and the Presidential Medal of Freedom in 1996 from President Bill Clinton, Johnson also earned the illustrious Spingarn Medal from the National Association for the Advancement of Colored People (NAACP), and gave generously to Howard University's school of journalism. He died after a long illness on August 8, 2005, in Chicago, Illinois, at the age of 87. Survivors include his wife of 64 years, Eunice Walker Johnson, and daughter Linda Johnson Rice, president of Johnson Publishing. *Ebony* continued to remain in the No. 1 spot among African-American-aimed magazines, with a circulation of 1.6 million in 2004. **Sources:** *Chicago Tribune*, August 8, 2005; *Independent* (London), August 11, 2005, p. 33; *Jet*, August 22, 2005, p. 6; *New York Times*, August 9, 2005, p. C22.

—*Carol Brennan*

Charles Keeling

Born Charles David Keeling, April 20, 1928, in Scranton, PA; died of a heart attack, June 20, 2005, at his summer home, in Hamilton, MT. Climate scientist. When Charles Keeling made researching the rise of carbon dioxide in the atmosphere his life's work, little did he know that his findings would become the cornerstone for the alarm raised on the effects of global warming of the Earth. His research became known as the Keeling Curve; it showed the annual rise of carbon dioxide, a greenhouse gas.

Keeling was born on April 20, 1928, in Scranton, Pennsylvania. He graduated from the University of Illinois in 1948 with a degree in chemistry. In 1954 he earned his Ph.D. in chemistry from Northwestern University. Although Keeling made chemistry his career choice, he was just as passionate about music, and could have became a concert pianist.

As a postdoctoral fellow at the California Institute of Technology, Keeling constructed an instrument that would measure the level of carbon dioxide in the atmosphere. He camped for three weeks at Big Sur State Park in California with his wife and new-born son. He took daily measurements of carbon dioxide. He learned that the level of carbon dioxide in the atmosphere was 310 parts per million (ppm). Carbon dioxide had been previously measured in the ice cores in the 19th century, before the start of the Industrial Revolution. The level then was 280 ppm.

In 1956 Keeling joined the staff at the Scripps Institution of Oceanography in San Diego. He continued his research at the Mauna Loa volcano in Hawaii. A station was built two miles up the dormant volcano. The area was chosen because it was high above the pollution. His first measurement of carbon dioxide at Mauna Loa was 315 ppm. As Keeling tested each year, he noticed an increase of one ppm.

Keeling also learned that the amount of carbon dioxide fluctuated, but was at its lowest at the end of the growing season, and at its highest at the beginning of the growing season. His studies also showed that the increase in carbon dioxide levels was caused by the increased amount of fossil fuel being used in the world. Early in his research many believed that the Earth was getting warmer, a process that was called global warming. One of the reasons was the increased amount of fossil fuels being used by humans, in both industrial factories and through the use of automobiles. Many at the beginning of Keeling's research thought that despite the increase, plant life and the ocean would absorb most of the carbon dioxide. Keeling's research proved this was not the case.

After Keeling presented his findings, the government department that had funded his study cut off his funding. However, he was determined to keep going. Keeling sought others like him in the scientific community to argue on his behalf, and he pestered government officials until they caved in. Funding was restored and the only gap in Keeling's measurements were from February to May of 1964.

As many other scientists learned more about global warming, they used the Keeling Curve, a graph that showed the steady climb of carbon dioxide in the atmosphere. Many began to sound off alarms about the increase of carbon dioxide as well as the rise in other gases such as methane, ozone, and chlorofluorocarbons. With the rise in the levels of these gases, known as greenhouse gases, the Earth continued to get warmer each year. This was labeled the greenhouse effect. Keeling also learned that the growing season began one week earlier than when he first began taking measurements.

While Keeling tried to not connect his findings with the increasing amount of fuel consumption the world used, others did. "It became clear very quickly that his measured [carbon dioxide] increase was proportional to fossil fuel emissions, and that humans were the source of the change," Dr. James E. Hansen, director of NASA's Goddard Institute for Space Studies told the *New York Times*. Many debated these claims, but because of his meticulous research, few could dispute Keeling's findings. In the 1990s he finally joined in and connected his research with the amount of fossil fuel being burned by the world. His latest findings showed the amount of carbon dioxide was 380 ppm, and the growth is now two ppm a year versus one when he first began his research. Spencer Weart, director of the Center for the History of Physics of the American Institute of Physics, told the *Washington Post*, "Keeling is one of the few people who's responsible for the fact that the scientific community was awakened to the need to study global warming before it's too late."

In addition to the research Keeling did over a span of five decades, he also continued with his love of music. He founded the UC San Diego Madrigal Singers and continued to play chamber music. He was also a civic leader, and wrote the Del Mar, California, General Plan. He was also an avid outdoorsman. He camped and hiked in several places, including California, Canada, and Switzerland. Keeling was hiking near his summer home in Hamilton, Montana, when he suffered a heart attack and died on June 20, 2005, at the age of 77. He is survived by his wife, Louise; his sons Andrew, Ralph, Eric, and Paul; his daughter, Emily; and six grandchildren. **Sources:** *Chicago Tribune*, June 25, 2005, sec. 2, p. 11; *Los Angeles Times*, June 24, 2005, p. B8; *New York Times*, June 23, 2005, p. C20; *Times* (London), June 29, 2005, p. 56; *Washington Post*, June 24, 2005, p. B5.

—Ashyia N. Henderson

George Kennan

Born George Frost Kennan, February 16, 1904, in Milwaukee, WI; died March 17, 2005, in Princeton, NJ. Diplomat and historian. George Kennan was a well-known and highly regarded shaper of American foreign policy in the latter half of the twentieth century. As a State Department official posted to Moscow in the immediate aftermath of World War II, he wrote a lengthy telegram assessing the Soviet leadership, and his warnings and suggestions became the basis for U.S. strategy toward its ideological foe for the next 50 years. Kennan's *New York Times* obituary described him as "the last of a generation of diplomatic aristocrats in an old world model—products of the 'right' schools, universities and clubs, who took on the enormous challenges of building a new world order and trying to define America's place within it."

Kennan was born in 1904 in Milwaukee, Wisconsin, and his mother died several weeks later. His father, an attorney, later remarried, and as an eight year old Kennan traveled to Germany with his stepmother in order to learn the language more fluently. He went on to master German was well as several other European tongues, and finished at a military academy in Wisconsin before entering Princeton University. In 1926, a year after earning his degree, he joined the U.S. foreign service and was posted as vice-consul in Geneva, Switzerland. Over the next decade he became fluent in Russian while holding various foreign-service posts in Berlin and some cities in Baltic region. He was part of the first U.S. diplomatic mission to the Soviet Union in 1933. While posted in Berlin once again, he was detained for five months by Nazi authorities when the United States entered World War II in 1941.

Kennan returned to Moscow during a wartime period of good relations between the United States and the Soviet Union, when both sides teamed to defeat Nazi Germany. As a senior official with excellent insight into the tightly controlled world of Soviet communism, he was wary of the U.S.-Soviet alliance and what it might forebode for Europe once the war ended. In February of 1946, Kennan received an inquiry from an official at the Treasury Department wondering why the Soviets were so vehemently against creation of the World Bank and International Monetary Fund. Kennan, left in charge at the U.S. Embassy while the ambassador was on leave, took it upon himself to write an 8,000-word reply.

Forever known as the "Long Telegram," Kennan's critique of Soviet leadership arrived at the State Department and "ranks as perhaps the most influential missive ever sent to Washington by an American diplomat in the field," said Rupert Cornwell in London's *Independent*. Kennan wrote about Josef Stalin and the circle of hardliners at the Kremlin, and warned they were more than likely planning to expand Soviet-style communism across the large sector of Eastern Europe where Red Army troops were still stationed. This warning would prove entirely correct over the next few years.

Kennan was immediately recalled to Washington, and appointed to serve as director of U.S. foreign policy planning. His views were later published in an article he wrote for *Foreign Affairs*, "The Sources of Soviet Conduct," under the pseudonym "X." During that same summer of 1947, the U.S. announced a massive foreign-aid plan for Western Europe that followed many of Kennan's ideas. This became known was the Marshall Plan, after U.S. Secretary of State George C. Marshall, and focused on an infusion of financial aid to Western European countries to avert the rise of communist political elements in those countries. Kennan also advocated the creation of a political warfare unit within the Central Intelligence Agency, which later became its covert-operations directorate; it led to the positioning of hundreds of secret agents who worked undercover to destabilize unfriendly regimes and enhance U.S. interests abroad.

Kennan soon fell out of favor in Washington, thanks in part to a disagreement with John Foster Dulles, a conservative Republican foreign policy adviser, over

how best to deal with the new threat of communist China in 1949. He was appointed the U.S. ambassador in Moscow by President Harry S Truman, but was ejected by Soviet officials when he complained that the increasingly repressive Stalinist regime severely restricted the movements of Western diplomats in the capital; he likened it to his experience in Nazi detention. He left government service when Dwight D. Eisenhower was elected president.

Though Kennan's ideas became the basis for U.S. Cold War policy, he was opposed to the arms buildup that occurred, and warned of the dangers of nuclear-weapon proliferation. He spent the remainder of his career at Princeton's Institute for Advanced Study, though he did serve briefly as ambassador to Yugoslavia during in the early 1960s. He wrote extensively on the Cold War and U.S. foreign policy, and won a Pulitzer Prize as well as a National Book Award for his 1956 tome, *Russia Leaves the War*. The first of his two volumes of memoirs, published in 1967, won both honors again. In 1989, President George H.W. Bush awarded him with the nation's highest civilian honor, the Medal of Freedom. Regarded as one of his era's most knowledgeable authorities on foreign policy, he was respected at home and abroad. In the mid-1970s, he testified before a U.S. Senate committee and claimed that his suggestion to launch political warfare against the Soviets was "the greatest mistake I ever made," his *New York Times* obituary quoted him as saying.

Kennan lived much of his life in the Princeton area, with his Norwegian-born wife—whom he met in Berlin and wed in 1931—where they raised a son and three daughters. He died in Princeton on March 17, 2005, at the age of 101, survived by his wife, Annelise Sorensen Kennan, and their four children. Even at the age of 95 he still sat for interviews and voiced strongly critical opinions of U.S. foreign policy. His *Washington Post* tribute, written by J.Y. Smith, mentioned a *New York Review of Books* interview he gave in 1999, which found him as contrarian as he was in 1949. "This whole tendency," Kennan scoffed, "to see ourselves as the center of political enlightenment and as teachers to a great part of the rest of the world strikes me as unthought-through, vainglorious and undesirable." **Sources:** CNN.com, http://www.cnn.com/2005/US/03/18/obit.kennan.ap/index.html (March 21, 2005); *Independent* (London), March 19, 2005, p. 44; *New York Times*, March 18, 2005, p. A1; *Washington Post*, March 18, 2005, p. A1.

—*Carol Brennan*

Agnes Martin

Born Agnes Bernice Martin, March 22, 1912, in Macklin, Saskatchewan, Canada; died of complications from pneumonia, December 16, 2004, in Taos, NM. Artist. Agnes Martin touched many people throughout her career, despite her tendency to shut herself off from the world. She was considered one of the great painters of the Abstract Expressionist period. Her paintings of barely there colors and lines also led some critics to characterize her as a Minimalist, a categorization she rejected. Martin won numerous awards including a National Medal of the Arts and a Golden Lion for her contribution to contemporary art.

Martin was born to Scottish Presbyterian pioneers in Canada. Her father died when she was two, and her mother raised her family by purchasing old properties, renovating them, and then selling them. The family moved to Vancouver, and her maternal grandfather helped in rearing her and her brother, using the Bible and John Bunyan's *Pilgim's Progress* to mold them. Though Martin began drawing at an early age, she decided upon a teaching career. She moved to the United States to attend Western Washington College of Education, in Bellingham, Washington from 1935 to 1938. She began teaching in high schools in various states, including Washington and Delaware. She transferred to the Teachers College at Columbia University in New York. Martin earned both her bachelors and masters degrees from Teachers College. She also taught in high schools in New Mexico. During this time, Martin attended seminars taught by Krishnamurti and Zen scholar D. T. Suzuki. These teachings would profoundly affect her, both personally and professionally.

Though Martin worked as a teacher, painting was never far from her heart. She continued honing her craft, and participated in a study program at the Harwood Museum in Taos, New Mexico. She fell in love with the area, and soon resettled there. She held her first art exhibit in Taos. Her time in the town, famous for the abundance of artists who were drawn to the town via word-of-mouth or its natural setting in the mountains, was not full of pleasantries. She endured hardship after hardship as her paintings sold for very little and not as often as she would hope. Her studio also doubled as her home for a time. Also during this time, she became a United States citizen.

Martin's art came to the attention of Betty Parsons of the legendary Betty Parsons Gallery. Parsons helped the talented artist sell a few of her paintings, and offered her a solo exhibition as long as Martin would agree to move back to New York. Martin agreed and, with the help of renowned artist Ellsworth Kelly, found a loft on Coentis Slip to live in. Coentis Slip was home to a number of struggling artists—such as Robert Rauschenberg, Jasper Johns, and James Rosenquist—whose art would become commercial successes in later years. Martin's loft was in dire need of repairs and renovations; she installed her own plumbing, and also located a studio in which to paint.

In 1958 Martin held a solo exhibition at the Parsons Gallery. Influenced by Abstract Expressionist artists such Ad Reinhardt and Mark Rothko, she began creating abstract paintings in place of landscapes and portraits, which she had previously done. Her style mimicked her contemporaries, but soon she came into her own style. According to London's *Times*, Martin stated she came into her artistic maturity around 1960. Her method, according to the *Times*, included: "a square format; canvas primed with two layers of gesso; hand-drawn pencil lines; thin layers of paint, first in oils, then in acrylic which she preferred because it was much quicker to dry."

With this method Martin's art became both lucrative and critically acclaimed. She usually kept to herself and found the pressures of the New York art world overbearing. With Coentis Slip scheduled for demolition in 1967, Martin decided to leave the art world. She gave away most of her possessions, including her painting supplies, and soon embarked upon a journey across the United States and Canada. She would not paint for seven years. She resettled in New Mexico, built an adobe house by herself, and focused on writing instead.

However, Martin's work was not soon forgotten. She still held several solo exhibitions during her self-imposed exile, including a major retrospective of her work at the University of Pennsylvania's Institute of Contemporary Art in 1973. And though she felt her work was more in line with the Abstract Expressionist period, many Minimalist period artists were heavily influenced by her art and sought her out. During her "exile" she also built three more buildings on her land and kept mainly to herself, living a very simple and quiet life.

In 1974 she began painting again. She kept her home base in New Mexico, though she moved from one town to another twice. She chose to create smaller paintings versus hiring an assistant to help her move her paintings. In 1992, she moved into a retirement residence in Taos. She continued painting, but spent most of her days with friends or in quiet solitude. She had no radio or television, and she had not read a newspaper in five decades.

Martin's art reflected her quiet and simple life. According to the *Chicago Tribune,* she said, "I often paint tranquility. If you stop thinking and rest, then a little happiness comes into your mind. At perfect rest you are comfortable." According to Christopher Knight in the *Los Angeles Times,* "An acute attention to life's quiet rhythms characterized her work."

Martin held solo exhibitions in many countries, including England, France, and Japan. She also participated in a variety of group exhibitions. Her paintings are a part of collections in a variety of museums, including the Whitney Museum in New York, the Hirshhorn Museum in Washington, D.C., the Art Gallery of Ontario, and the Stedelijk Museum in Amsterdam.

In addition to her paintings, Martin also wrote several articles and books, some non-art-related. They include 1971's *On A Clear Day,* 1992's *Writings/ Schriften,* and *La Perfection inherente a la vie,* published in 1993. Martin received numerous awards and honors for her contributions to art. She was named one of "100 Women of Achievement" in 1967 by *Harper's Bazaar* and was inducted into the American Academy of Arts and Letters. She was awarded a National Medal of Arts from the National Endowment for the Arts as well as the Golden Lion at the 1997 Venice Biennale. Martin died of complications from pneumonia in her home at the Plaza de Retiro, a retirement community in Taos, New Mexico, on December 16, 2004; she was 92. She is survived by a grandnephew, Derrick Martin. **Sources:** *Chicago Tribune,* December 17, 2004, sec. 3, p. 9; *Contemporary Women Artists,* St. James Press, 1999; *Los Angeles Times,* December 17, 2004, p. B12; *New York Times,* December 17, 2004, p. C9; *Times* (London), December 18, 2004, p. 67; *Washington Post,* December 18, 2004, p. B6.

—*Ashyia N. Henderson*

Ismail Merchant

Born Ismail Noormohammed Abdul Rehman, December 25, 1936, in Bombay, India; died of complications after surgery, May 25, 2005, in London, England. Film producer. With charm and a refusal to take no for an answer, producer Ismail Merchant was responsible for making several period films that delighted audiences around the world. He and partner James Ivory also have been credited with bringing independently produced films to the forefront and helping place Miramax Films and Sony Picture Classics, two independent distributors, on the map. Merchant's films were critically acclaimed and also helped several British stars become household names. Helena Bonham Carter commented to *Entertainment Weekly's* Missy Schwartz, "[Merchant] was a life force for whom the word *impossible* had no meaning. He had endless passion, and made films because he believed in beauty."

Merchant was born on December 25, 1936. His father, Noormohamed Haji Abdul Rehman, was a successful textile merchant in Bombay, India. The young Merchant attended both Islamic and Jesuit schools during his youth. His father was a member of the Muslim League, an organization that campaigned for the creation of Pakistan. During a political rally, Merchant, at nine years old, spoke in front of 10,000 people in support of the Muslim League's leader, Mohammed Ali Jinnah. He would later use this speaking ability to persuade both actors and film companies to join his productions.

Though Merchant could have had a future in politics, he followed his second passion: cinema. Rising Indian actress Nimmi befriended the teenager, and took him to studios and movie premieres, where he met numerous industry people. This, however, was just a hobby as his parents encouraged him to focus on his education. He studied political science and English literature at St. Xavier's College in Bombay. Merchant, however, could not resist the pull of the cinema. He spent more time in the theatrical department than in his classes. He also organized campus variety shows that were hugely successful. He changed his name to Merchant, graduated, and moved to New York to attend New York University. He was able to pay his own way thanks to the success of his variety shows. Though he wanted to earn a masters degree in business administration, the lure of film was just too strong.

Merchant spent time learning about film work from various filmmakers, including Ingmar Bergman, Federico Fellini, and Satyajit Ray, an Indian filmmaker he had not heard of until he moved to New York. He joined advertising firm McCann-Erickson to find financial backers for a film. Merchant then moved to Los Angeles, where he worked for the *Los Angeles Times'* classified department.

Merchant created his first film, a short titled *The Creation of Woman.* He persuaded a theater owner to pair the 14-minute film with an Ingmar Berman film for a few days. He also screened it at the Cannes Festival in France. Because his film was shown in a theater for at least three days, it was eligible for an Academy Award nomination, which it did receive. En route to the Cannes Festival, Merchant stopped in New York to see *The Sword and the Flute*, a documentary made by James Ivory. The two men talked about the film business and Ivory expressed a love for India. A month after their first meeting they formed Merchant Ivory to create adaptations of English novels for the Indian market.

Merchant Ivory's first film was a screen adaptation of *The Householder*, a comedic book written by Ruth Prawer Jhabvala. The two men enlisted Jhabvala's help. She agreed to write the screen adaptation of her novel, though she had never written a screenplay before. Jhabvala would become the third partner in Merchant Ivory, writing the majority of the screenplays. With Ivory as the director, it was Merchant's job to hire staff, find locations and actors, and locate financial backers. Because of his charm and business acumen, Merchant Ivory films were made cheaply but had the look of lavish productions. In addition to adapting several more of Jhabvala's novels, Merchant and Ivory also looked to authors E.M. Forster, Henry James, and V.S. Naipaul.

Several of Merchant's films went on to both critical and box office success, including *Maurice, A Room with a View, Remains of the Day,* and *Howard's End.* The company became known for creating excellent period pieces, though they would later try their hand at modern comedy and drama. Merchant Ivory received 31 Academy award nominations, and won six, but they never won for Best Film or Best Director.

With Merchant's business acumen, the company helped pave the way for other independent directors to find backing during a time where sequels reigned supreme. In a 1999 interview, Ivory said, "He's a natural showman, a great publicist, and he's just very, very good at getting his way," according to the *New York Times.* Sony Picture Classics, an independent distributor, owed its rise as one of the most successful distributors to its first release, Merchant Ivory's *Howard's End.* A number of following releases were through Sony and Miramax, but when Miramax asked that several scenes be cut from the film *The Golden Bowl*, Merchant raised the funds to buy the film back, and struck a deal with Lions Gate Entertainment. He also was prone to stealing props for various sets, and even posed as the Maharajah of Jodhpur to gain entry to the Trianon Palace Hotel in Versailles, France, to film a scene even though filming was banned in the hotel.

In addition to keeping films costs low, Merchant would persuade several high-profile actors to accept fees way below their usual asking price. But the careers of Hugh Grant, Emma Thompson, and Helena Bonham-Carter received help due to their roles in the films of Merchant Ivory. To help out the actors, Merchant would allow them to use his apartments, feed them meals he personally cooked, and once even bailed an actor out of jail.

Merchant also directed his first piece in 1974, *Mahatma and the Mad Boy*, a short film. It would be 30 years since the formation of Merchant Ivory before Merchant would direct again, this time his first full-length feature, *In Custody.* He continued to direct several more films after its release.

In addition to his love of the cinema, Merchant's other passion was cooking. He was known for fixing elaborate meals for friends, colleagues, and for everyone on the set to keep morale high. He released two cookbooks, including *Passionate Meals: The New Indian cuisine for Fearless Cooks and Adventurous Eaters,* and once owned a French-Indian restaurant in Manhattan. Merchant also wrote a memoir, *My Passage From India.*

Merchant had been having stomach problems for a year when he entered a London hospital for surgery. He died on May 25, 2005, from complications a day after his operation. He was 68. He is survived by his sisters Sabherbanu Kabadia, Sahida Retiwala, Ruksana Khan, and Rashida Bootwala. Several films Merchant produced will be released posthumously, including *The White Countess* with Ralph Fiennes, and *The Goddess*, a modern version of Bollywood musicals that are very popular in India. **Sources:** *Chicago Tribune*, May 26, 2005, sec. 3, p. 9; CNN. com, http://www.cnn.com/2005/SHOWBIZ/ Movies/05/25/merchant.death.ap/ (May 25, 2005); *Entertainment Weekly*, June 10, 2005, p. 29; E! Online, http://www.eonline.com/News/Items/ 0,1,16630,00.html?eol.tkr (May 26, 2005); *Los Angeles Times*, May 26, 2005, p. B13; *New York Times,* May 26, 2005, p. A27; *Times* (London), May 26, 2005, p. 66; *Washington Post,* May 26, 2005, p. B6.

—*Ashyia N. Henderson*

Dale Messick

Born Dalia Messick, April 11, 1906, in South Bend, IN; died April 5, 2005, in Sonoma County, CA.

Comic-strip artist. Indomitable and sassy are two words that describe Dale Messick. Her can-do spirit helped her become one of the pioneering female cartoonists who opened the door in a male-dominated profession. Her comic strip, "Brenda Starr, Reporter," was read by more than 60 million readers, and became the subject of both praise and criticism. She received a lifetime achievement award from the National Cartoonists Society.

Messick was born on April 11, 1906, to Cephas, a sign painter and teacher, and Bertha, a milliner. She was the eldest child and only daughter. Messick's love of drawing began at an early age. She had little use for school, and had to repeat both the third and eighth grades. She graduated from high school but only after her parents pressured her. In addition to drawing, she also helped her mother design and sew hats, a skill which she would later use for drawing Brenda Starr's wardrobe.

Messick studied at the Art Institute of Chicago. She followed that with employment as a greeting card designer. Despite being her family's sole provider during the early years of the Great Depression, she quit after her boss lowered her salary to give a raise to another employee. She freelanced for a while, and then won a position at another greeting card company in New York. Always the daring one, instead of taking a train or driving to New York, Messick flew in a single-engine plane that took eight hours to arrive.

Though she had drawn comic strips during her school years, she began creating a comic strip with a woman as the lead in earnest. After learning from the *New York Daily News*' award-winning cartoonist C.D. Batchelor that his newspaper was looking for a new comic strip, Messick sent in her comic strip about a female bandit for consideration. It was rejected by the publisher of the *New York Daily News*, Joseph M. Patterson, who was also the head of the Chicago Tribune-New York News Syndicate. He threw away her work, but his secretary, Mollie Slott, recovered it and encouraged Messick. She told Messick to make a few changes including changing the female bandit into a reporter, and also changing her name from Dalia to Dale. She took Slott's advice, and resubmitted her work to Patterson. He did not give her a daily slot, nor did he allow her strip space in the *New York Daily News*, but he did run the strip on Sunday in other newspapers. "Brenda Starr, Reporter" debuted in June of 1940.

Messick, who had no journalism background and, according to Richard Severo in the *New York Times*, "refused to learn about it," created Brenda Starr as the woman who every woman fantasized about being. The character received her name from a 1930s debutante, Brenda Frazier, and her body, fashion sense, and persona mirrored leading Hollywood actress, Rita Hayworth, complete with matching long red hair and a curvaceous figure. In time, Messick began dying her own hair red, and took on Starr's personality by being bold, daring, and outspoken. Adoring male fans of the strip often asked for a racier sketch of Starr. Messick obliged by sending a drawing of Starr wearing only a barrel and going over Niagara Falls.

Each week Messick had Starr take on various assignments to exotic places that only male reporters were given, which ironically mimicked real-life journalism. The audacious reporter would free herself after being kidnapped, and jumped out of airplanes, landing just outside her editor's window. She filed her completed story with the newspaper's cleaning woman. Starr also talked back to her managing editor. In addition to drawing her strip, Messick also would include cut-out dolls of Starr. She also included an African-American paper doll, Lona Night, in 1948.

While many praised Messick's work as pioneering, others criticized "Brenda Starr, Reporter" for its unrealistic portrayal of the journalism profession, since most female reporters were delegated to covering social events or city council meetings. But many of her female readers, especially little girls, looked forward to reading the comic strip to see a woman do things that during the early part of the 20th century were typically assigned to men. The *Los Angeles Times*' Claudia Luther wrote that CNN anchor Charlayne Hunter-Gault said in an interview that she "wanted nothing more than for her life to have the 'mystery and romance' she associated with Brenda's big-time, big-city journalism."

At its peak, "Brenda Starr, Reporter," was included in 250 newspapers and read by more than 60 million readers. When Starr and her long-time boyfriend, the mysterious Basil St. John, finally married after 36 years in 1976, President Gerald Ford sent a congratulatory telegram. The strip also made its debut in the *New York Daily News*, but only after publisher Patterson's death.

Though Messick found success once her strip was in circulation, she still faced sexism with the Chicago Tribune-New York News Syndicate. Each time she drew in cleavage or a navel on Starr, her employer would erase them. Even during interviews, she met with opposition. Author Trina Robbins, who wrote *A Century of Women Cartoonists*, told Patricia

Sullivan in the *Washington Post*, "Throughout [Messick's] life, she met a lot of resistance from men. Even in the early 1960s, [male interviewers] played her up as a dizzy dame instead of this brilliant comics creator."

The Chicago Tribune-New York News Syndicate forced Messick to retire in the mid-1980s. "Brenda Starr, Reporter" continued, but was written by *Chicago Tribune* columnist Mary Schmich, and drawn by June Brigman. Messick, who drew a salary and did not own the rights to the strip she created, was given a small pension for her retirement. She continued drawing, and created a single-panel comic strip, "Granny Glamour". It was rejected by *AARP* magazine, but she found a home for it in a Californian publication for the elderly. She continued to draw the strip until the age of 92.

Messick, who had married and divorced twice, moved to northern California to be near her daughter, Starr, and her two grandchildren, Curt and Laura. In recognition of her work, "Brenda Starr, Reporter" was one of 20 comic strip characters—and the only female character—chosen to be on a postage stamp during the U.S. Postal Service's 100th anniversary. The strip had also been turned into a movie serial in 1945, a made-for-television movie in 1976; and a film that starred Brooke Shields in 1992.

In honor of her groundbreaking work, the National Cartoonists Society awarded Messick with the Milton Caniff Lifetime Achievement Award in 1997. She had wanted to write an autobiography, but only came up with a title, *Still Stripping at 80!*, then when she entered her ninth decade, *Still Stripping at 90!*. Her granddaughter was in the process of creating a one-woman show, "Reporter Girl," when Messick died on April 5, 2005, at her daughter's home in Sonoma County, California; she was 98. **Sources:** *Chicago Tribune*, April 8, 2005, sec. 1, p. 11; CNN.com, www.cnn.com/2005/SHOWBIZ/books/04/07/obit.dale.messick.ap/index.html (April 8, 2005); *Los Angeles Times*, April 8, 2005, p. B10; *New York Times*, April 8, 2005, p. A25; *Washington Post*, April 8, 2005, p. B6.

—*Ashyia N. Henderson*

George Mikan

Born June 18, 1924, in Joliet, IL; died of kidney failure, June 1, 2005, in Scottsdale, AZ. Professional basketball player. In the early days of basketball, George Mikan was a superstar; he literally changed the way the game of basketball is played. He also turned the position of center from a forgettable one into a key role in his short nine-year career, earning the nickname "Mr. Basketball." Matt Zeysing, historian and archivist for the Basketball Hall of Fame told the *Washington Post*, "He was a guy who changed the game.... He was the intimidator. He was the guy taking contact."

Mikan was born on June 18, 1924, in Joliet, Illinois. His parents owned a restaurant, and the family lived upstairs. By age eleven he was six feet four inches, but very clumsy. Although he wanted to play basketball in high school, the coach discouraged him because of his clumsiness and his thick glasses. Also during that time, he stepped on a basketball and broke his leg.

Mikan became interested in becoming a priest, and entered Quigley Preparatory Seminary. He still had hopes to play basketball, and had a tryout with the coach from Notre Dame. The coach told him that he should go to a smaller school so he could get individual attention. A year later, Mikan enrolled at DePaul University and tried out for the basketball team. The coach, Ray Meyer, decided to train him to try to turn him from a clumsy boy into a basketball player. Mikan practiced daily for two and a half hours. He jumped rope to gain speed and also shadow boxed. He practiced shooting the ball with one hand (called a hook shot) and then switched to throw with the other, a practice known today as the Mikan shot. Meyer paired him with a female student to learn how to dance so he could become graceful.

After all the practice, Mikan became the go-to person on the team. He led DePaul to the championship. During play, the team strategy was to have the 6'10" Mikan stand under the basket and whenever the opposing team would take a shot, he would block the ball. This was called goaltending; the National Collegiate Athletic Association created a rule against it.

After he graduated from college, Mikan began his professional basketball career with the Chicago American Gears in the National Basketball League (NBL) in 1947. He helped the Gears win two championships before the NBL folded. Mikan signed with the Minneapolis Lakers of the National Basketball Association (NBA) for $12,500. The new league would counter his easy shots by widening the free throw line from six feet to 12. In a game against the Ft. Wayne Pistons, to keep Mikan from scoring, the opposing team just held on to the ball. This resulted in the lowest scoring game in NBA history, 19-18, in the Pistons' favor. A few years later, the NBA would establish a 24-second shot clock so no team could do that again.

Unlike most centers at that time, Mikan was a force to be reckoned with on the court. Though not the best runner, he could move up and down the court. His opponents who were trying to score or keep him from scoring ended up with bruises; Mikan used his body both to defend and to score. Throughout his playing career, Mikan would break ten bones, including both legs, fingers, and his nose.

With Mikan on the team, the Minneapolis Lakers won the championship five times in eight years. The Minneapolis team began a streak that has continued into the 21st century, as the Lakers moved to Los Angeles some time later. The success of the team was placed squarely on Mikan's shoulders. The NBA would send him to whatever city the team would play a day before the game just to drum up publicity for the fledgling league. When playing against the New York Knicks, the marquee read "Geo. Mikan vs New York Knicks."

After playing for nine years, the physical play had taken a toll on his body, and the constant traveling had made Mikan a stranger to his growing family. He retired from playing basketball. However, after receiving so much fan mail urging him to return, he came back for one season. The time away had changed him, and he could not return to his previous playing form, so he retired again. This time, he opened a law practice in Minneapolis.

Mikan would return to basketball again, but as coach of the Lakers. With a record of 9-30, he resigned as coach before completing one season. In the late 1960s, Mikan accepted the position of commissioner in the new American Basketball Association (ABA). During his tenure, he allowed the use of a red, white, and blue ball.

After Mikan stepped down as ABA commissioner, he became involved in several ventures. In addition to his law firm, he became part-owner in the Chicago Cheetahs, a roller hockey team. He also started Major Leagues Sports Franchises, Inc., and was head of Apollo/Revcon, a company that sold recreational vehicles. Mikan also helped bring another NBA franchise team to the state of Minnesota. However, he was disappointed when the owners failed to give him a job in the front office. He also petitioned the NBA to give a better pension to those who played in the NBA before 1965, but his petition was tossed out.

Mikan's health had begun to fail. He suffered from diabetes and kidney ailments. To help pay for his rising medical costs, he sold most of his memorabilia. He had one leg amputated but that did not stop him from attending a ceremony in Los Angeles when the Lakers paid tribute to his team. When the Minnesota Timberwolves paid honor to his team, he attended as well. He was named the best basketball player in the first half of the 20th century. He was also named one of the top 50 greatest basketball players in history. On June 1, 2005, he died of kidney failure in a Scottsdale, Arizona, rehabilitation center. He was 80. Close friend Miami Heat center Shaquille O'Neal offered to help the family with burial costs. Mikan is survived by his wife, Patricia; his sons Larry, Terry, Patrick, and Michael; his daughters, Trisha and Maureen; and numerous grandchildren and great-grandchildren. **Sources:** *Chicago Tribune,* June 3, 2005, sec. 1, p. 1, p. 5; *Los Angeles Times,* June 3, 2005, p. B10; *New York Times,* June 3, 2005, p. A25; *SI.com,* http://sportsillustrated.cnn.com/2005/magazine/06/02/mikan.11.6.89/index.html, http://sportsillustrated.cnn.com/2005/magazine/06/02/mikan.9.22.94/index.html, http://sportsillustrated.cnn.com/2005/writers/jack_mccallum/06/02/mikan/index.htm l, http://sportsillustrated.cnn.com/2005/basketball/nba/06/02/george.mikan.ap/index. html (June 3, 2005); *Washington Post,* June 3, 2005, p. B6.

—*Ashyia N. Henderson*

Robert Moog

Born Robert Arthur Moog, May 23, 1934, in New York, NY; died of brain cancer, August 21, 2005, in Asheville, NC. Engineer and inventor. Robert Moog (pronounced mogue) was credited with creating the first practical synthesizer, the Moog synthesizer, as well as other electronic equipment related to the production, performance, and recording of popular music. His synthesizer, in particular, was considered key to the development of popular music in the 1960s and beyond. Yet Moog did not take much credit for his creation. Allan Kozinn of the New York Times quoted Moog as saying, "I don't design stuff for myself. I'm a toolmaker. I design things that other people want to use."

Born in 1934 in New York City, Moog was the son of an electronics engineer father and a piano teacher mother. As a child, Moog was forced to take piano lessons because his mother wanted him to be a concert pianist. However, Moog took after his father and was interested in building things. When he was 14 years old, he built a Theremin, the first electronic instrument in the world. A Theremin is made of vibrating radio tubes and played by moving the hands around the tubes. Moog continued to build Theremins and kits to make Theremins through high school, enabling him to pay for much of his college education.

After graduating from the Bronx High School of Science, Moog earned his undergraduate degree in physics from Queens College. In 1957, he graduated from Columbia University with a master's degree in electrical engineering. Instead of taking the expected job in corporate research, Moog continued to produce and sell about a thousand kits to make Theremins in the early 1960s. He drummed up interested in the instrument in a popular electronics magazine, *Electronics World.* Moog also continued his education at Cornell University, where he earned his Ph.D. in engineering physics in 1965.

Some of the money Moog made from his Theremin kits was used to design more electronic instruments. One of his first inventions was the portable guitar amplifier kit. His next big creation was his version of the synthesizer. The synthesizer had been originally created by RCA in 1955 and was the size of a room. The instrument could not really be used by musicians because it relied on binary code input to produce sounds. Inspired by a meeting with a music teacher/composer, Herbert Deutsch, in 1963, Moog soon built an analog synthesizer that was cheaper, smaller, and allowed users to control the pitch, timber, duration, and intensity of sounds. A year later, Moog added a piano-like keyboard to make the instrument more accessible for musicians and introduced the Moog synthesizer to the world.

Over the next few years, Moog continued to improve his synthesizer. The first models were monophonic, which means they could only play one musical line at one time. Moog made polyphonic models which could do harmony and counterpoint to musical lines. Moog also made smaller versions of the Moog synthesizer, called the Minimoog and the Micromoog, which were more portable and could be used in concerts. Moog began selling Moog synthesizers in the mid- to late 1960s, but it took several years for his company to become a success. He was a better inventor than businessman, a flaw that would come back to hurt him.

When Moog introduced his synthesizer, he was unsure if it would catch on. It was first used in television commercials by the mid-1960s, then became popular with serious musicians. The first album to use the Moog synthesizer as its sole instrument was Walter Carlos' 1968 release, *Switched-On Bach.* The album consisted of electronic versions of classic pieces by Bach, sold millions of copies, and brought the Moog synthesizer to widespread recognition. In the late 1960s and early 1970s, the synthesizer was used on various songs and albums by leading artists such as the Beatles and Emerson, Lake, and Palmer.

The Moog synthesizer remained popular until the early 1970s when electronic music was not as trendy and cheaper synthesizers created by other manufacturers flooded the market. As his instrument became less popular, Moog moved on. He lost control of his company in 1971 to entrepreneur Bill Waytena. Moog sold his remaining rights to Moog Music two years later, though he remained with the company until 1977. By that time, Moog synthesizers were still being used on film soundtracks and in certain types of music, like disco songs. Moog spent much of his time working on guitar amplifiers.

In 1978, Moog moved to North Carolina, where he set up another company, Big Briar. Moog made electronic instruments like synthesizer modules and devised different ways of inputting electronic instruments. Moog also became a research professor of music, working at the University of North Carolina at Asheville.

Moog's synthesizers had a resurgence in popularity in the 1980s and 1990s as digital synthesizers became popular. Moog's synthesizers were still in demand because the newer versions were perceived to produce sounds that were not as warm as those produced by Moog's synthesizer. Moog decided to go to court to regain his own name in conjunction with the synthesizers. He won his court battle in 2002, and again sold Moog analog synthesizers and his other inventions under the Moog Music name. His customers included high profile contemporary bands who wanted the quality of sound created by a Moog synthesizer.

Moog was honored over the years for his technical achievements. He was given the Trustee's Award from the National Academy of Recording Arts and Sciences and the Silver Medal of the Audio Engineering Society of America. In 2002, he received a Grammy Award for his lifetime of technical achievements. While Moog's name was primarily associated with synthesizers, he also continued to make Theremins throughout his life, until the year before his death.

In April of 2005, Moog was diagnosed with an inoperable brain tumor. He died at the age of 71 of brain cancer on August 21, 2005, at his home in

Asheville, North Carolina. Moog is survived by his second wife, Ileana Grams, his five children from his first marriage, Michelle, Laura, Matthew, Renee, and Miranda, one stepdaughter from his second marriage, and five grandchildren. **Sources:** *Chicago Tribune*, August 23, 2005, sec. 3, p. 9; *Los Angeles Times*, August 23, 2005, p. B10; *New York Times*, August 23, 2005, p. A21; *Times* (London), August 23, 2005, p. 47; *Washington Post*, August 23, 2005, p. B6.

—*A. Petruso*

Gaylord A. Nelson

Born Gaylord Anton Nelson, June 4, 1916, in Clear Lake, WI; died of cardiovascular failure, July 3, 2005, in Kensington, MD. Politician and environmentalist. Using his position first as a Wisconsin governor and later as a U.S. senator representing that state, Gaylord A. Nelson promoted the protection of the environment. His environmental activism reached its zenith in 1970 when he founded the first Earth Day. Nelson continued to support such causes until his death.

Nelson was born and raised in the small Wisconsin town of Clear Lake, where his father had a small medical practice. His mother worked as a registered nurse. Politics was part of Nelson's family heritage: a great-grandfather was one of the founders of Wisconsin's Republican party. Both of Nelson's parents were also active politically, as supporters of the Progressive Republicans. Nature was also important to the young Nelson. The outdoors provided entertainment for him since his family did not even own a radio until he was in high school.

After graduating from high school, Nelson went to California, where he earned a bachelor's degree from San Jose State University. He then returned to Wisconsin to attend the University of Wisconsin law school, earning his degree in 1942. When he completed his degree, World War II was still being fought. Nelson joined the U.S. Army and was given the rank of lieutenant. He was put charge of a unit that consisted of segregated African-American soldiers, and was involved in the battles around Okinawa.

When Nelson's tour of duty ended in 1946, he returned to Wisconsin. There, he founded his own law practice in Madison and married Carrie Lee Dotson, an army nurse he met during the war. Nel-

son soon began a political career as well. After losing a race for the House of Representatives as a Progressive Republican in 1946, Nelson was elected to the state senate of Wisconsin as a Democrat in 1948. Nelson was re-elected to the post in 1952 and 1956.

In 1958, Nelson ran for a new office, that of Wisconsin's governor. When he won, he was only the second Democrat to hold that position in the twentieth century. During his four years in office, Nelson decided that environmental issues were quite important but often ignored by politicians. He changed that trend in his own time in office. For example, with his Outdoor Recreation Act Program, a one-cent tax on cigarette packages raised millions of dollars which was used to buy a million acres of land to preserve.

Nelson took his environmental activism to the national level when he was elected to the U.S. Senate in 1962. During his time in the office, he came to be known as a popular, though independent-minded, senator. While particularly concerned with environmental issues, he was also one of the first senators to speak out against the Vietnam War as early as 1964, a position he held until the war's end.

Nelson's definition of what was "environmental" encompassed many concerns over the years. He worked to have the pollution produced by cars regulated and was involved with the protection of the oceans. Nelson helped to get the harmful pesticide DDT as well as Agent Orange eradicated. He also wanted family planning to be available worldwide. In 1964, Nelson sponsored the Wilderness Act. This law ensured that some acreage would be set aside by federal agencies from areas where logging and mining activities took place. Four years later, he helped get the Wild and Scenic Rivers Act passed.

The most high-profile environmental act of Nelson's political career was the founding of Earth Day. Its creation was inspired by a 1969 visit to Santa Barbara, California, shortly after an oil spill occurred on a nearby shore. Nelson enlisted the help of mayors and governors from a number of states to organize an event to heighten national awareness about environmental issues. The first Earth Day occurred on April 22, 1970, and garnered widespread public support. Nearly 20 million Americans participated in public events, both educational and practical, through schools, colleges, and communities. Upon Nelson's death, Ben Beach, a member of the Wilderness Society, told Michael Kilian of the *Chicago Tri-*

bune, "Earth Day proved the power of an idea. This simple but compelling idea truly made the world a better place."

As the power and public support of Earth Day was realized, Congress passed a significant number of environmental laws over the next decade, with Nelson often playing a role in their creation. Nelson's influence also led to the passage of the Environmental Protection Act, Endangered Species Act, and the Safe Drinking Water Act. Another piece of legislation put the Appalachian Trail under the protection of the federal government. President Richard M. Nixon even created a new federal department, the Environmental Protection Agency, several months after the first Earth Day.

In 1972, Nelson was asked to be Democratic presidential nominee George McGovern's running mate, but Nelson declined because did not want to be limited in what he could say. After being elected to three terms as U.S. senator, Nelson lost a close election to Robert W. Kasten, Jr., in 1980, the year many Republicans came to office on the coattails of new president Ronald Reagan. After being forced from office, Nelson took a position as a counselor to the Wilderness Society, a nonprofit environmental group, where he spent the last 24 years of his career.

By 1990, Nelson's Earth Day was still going strong, with 200 million people in 136 countries participating in that year's festivities. Nelson remained a dynamic environmental activist, still concerned with, among other things, population control. In 1995, he was awarded the Medal of Freedom by President Bill Clinton for his environmental activities. This is the highest honor a civilian can receive from the U.S. government. Nelson died of heart failure at his home in Kensington, Maryland, a suburb of Washington, D.C., on July 3, 2005; he was 89. He is survived by his wife, his sons Gaylord, Jr., and Jeffrey; his daughter, Tia, and four grandchildren. **Sources:** *Chicago Tribune*, July 4, 2005, sec. 1, p. 5; CNN.com, http://www.cnn.com/2005/POLITICS/07/03/obit. nelson.ap/index.html (July 7, 2005); *Los Angeles Times*, July 4, 2005, p. B11; *New York Times*, July 4, 2005, p. A12; *Times* (London), July 5, 2005, p. 54; *Washington Post*, July 4, 2005, p. A1, p. A8.

—A. Petruso

Andre Norton

Born Alice Mary Norton, February 17, 1912, in Cleveland, OH; died of congestive heart failure,

March 17, 2005, in Murfreesboro, TN. Author. Andre Norton, one of the most popular and prolific writers of fantasy and science fiction for young adults, published more than 130 novels over 70 years, attracting many young women to the genres at a time when they were considered mostly for boys. Her uplifting novels often featured characters alienated from their societies who found their true selves through epic quests.

The author was born Alice Mary Norton in Cleveland, Ohio, on February 17, 1912, to rug salesman Adalbert Freely Norton and Bertha Stemm Norton. She graduated from Collinwood High School in Cleveland, but could not afford to finish college because of the Great Depression. She took a job at the Cleveland Public Library in 1932 and took night classes at Western Reserve University. She published her first novel, *The Prince Commands,* a novel about a small, fictional European kingdom, in 1934 at the age of 22. The same year, she legally changed her name to Andre Norton, convinced by her agent that her audience would be young boys and that her books would sell better if she had a male name.

In the early 1940s, Norton moved to Maryland, where she briefly owned a bookstore, and worked in Washington, D.C. as a librarian, including at the Library of Congress. She came back to the Cleveland library system in 1942, where she worked in the children's section. Meanwhile, she wrote novels in a variety of genres, from espionage to one set in colonial Maryland. She left the Cleveland libraries in 1950 because of ill health and became a reader for Gnome Press, a science fiction publisher. She also served as science fiction editor at World Publishing.

Her breakthrough came with the publication of her science-fiction novel *Star Man's Son 2250 A.D.,* published in 1952. In the novel, Fors, a mutant rejected by his society, goes on a quest with a telepathic cat, looking for a radiation-free lost city, and begins to believe in himself after withstanding the trials of the journey. The novel came out as the science-fiction market was turning from magazines to books, and Norton's work quickly became very popular.

Norton's books have an "almost mystical sense" of romance and an "exuberant sense that the human need for life-shaping quests was innate," wrote John Clute of the London newspaper the *Independent.* Her straightforward writing style, Clute added, "exposed the sheer romantic joy of living in the galaxy-spanning civilization" that many of her works explored.

In 1963, a few years after the American publication of J.R.R. Tolkien's *The Lord of the Rings*, Norton responded with a fantasy-novel series of her own. The first novel of the series, *Witch World*, was set on a planet that could only be reached through secret gateways. The Witch World series described a complex land called Outremer, a collection of numerous small kingdoms full of magic and conflict among dynasties entangled by romance. The series, which eventually included more than two dozen novels, made Norton famous and attracted many female readers to fantasy novels. Her other popular book series included the Beast Master and Star Ka'at novels.

Norton won most of science fiction and fantasy's highest awards: the Grand Master of Fantasy award, the Nebula Grand Master award, admission into the Science Fiction and Fantasy Writers' Hall of Fame, and the World Fantasy Award for Life Achievement. The Science Fiction and Fantasy Writers of America named an award for young adult novelists for her shortly before her death; it was to be presented for the first time in 2006.

Famously private, Norton revealed little about her life outside writing. She never married and left no descendants. However, it was clear that she was in fragile health for much of her life. In 1966, Norton and her mother, who often assisted her as a proofreader and editor, moved to Winter Park, Florida, for health reasons. Thirty years later, she moved to Tennessee, first to live on a farm in Monterey, then to a home in Murfreesboro, near Nashville. She established a library for genre writers, The High Hallack Genre Writer's Research and Reference Library, southeast of Nashville, in 1999. It was full of reference material about weapons, ancient religions, history, and mythology. It remained open until around 2004.

In her later years, to fund the library and other enterprises she sponsored, Norton began collaborating with younger authors on several books, allowing them to do most of the writing while overseeing them. Clute of the *Independent* found most of these latter titles merely "respectable," adding that "they do not have the Norton glow." Norton's health declined further in 2004, and her publisher, Tor Books, rush-printed an advance copy of her last novel, *Three Hands of Scorpio,* so that she could see it before she passed away. Norton died on March 17, 2005, at her home in Murfreesboro, Tennessee, of congestive heart failure. She was 93. She said before her death that she did not want a funeral service, but wanted to be cremated along with copies of her first and last novels. **Sources:** CNN.com, http://www.cnn.com/2005/SHOWBIZ/books/03/17/obit.norton.

ap/index.html (March 21, 2005); *Guardian* (London), March 29, 2005, p. 19; *Independent* (London), March 21, 2005, p. 35; *New York Times,* March 18, 2005, p. B8;

—Erick Trickey

Jerry Orbach

Born Jerome Bernard Orbach, October 20, 1935, in New York, NY; died of prostate cancer, December 28, 2004, in New York, NY. Actor. Jerry Orbach spent a dozen years on the hit NBC crime drama *Law & Order* as Detective Lennie Briscoe. Orbach's Briscoe was the quintessential television cop—tough, with the proverbial heart of gold—and the role catapulted the veteran actor to stopped-on-the-street stardom. Yet he had enjoyed a long, Tony-winning career on Broadway for nearly a quarter-century, and went on to a modest but impressive roster of film credits. "Orbach may have been the last of a breed," wrote Ben Brantley and Richard Severo in the *New York Times*. "No male star since has matched the breadth and continuity of his career in musicals."

Born in 1935, Orbach was a native of the Bronx borough of New York City. His father was a restaurant manager, but had once been a vaudeville performer; Orbach's mother had been a radio singer at one time, and it was from her that he first learned to sing. Though he had no formal training, Orbach won a singing contest when he was still in elementary school, and gravitated toward the performing arts even more in his teens, though by then his family had departed New York City and settled in Waukegan, Illinois. After graduating from Waukegan High School in 1952, Orbach spent a year at the University of Illinois and another two at Northwestern University just north of Chicago, a school known for its excellent drama department. When he could no longer afford the tuition, he dropped out and headed to New York City. Not long after arriving in 1955, he landed his first Off-Broadway role in *The Threepenny Opera,* the Kurt Weill-Bertolt Brecht musical. He eventually took its lead role, where his rendition of the show's signature tune, "Mack the Knife," firmly established him as a new musical star on the New York scene.

Orbach's career on Broadway grew by leaps and bounds during the following decade. Early on, he became known as an able-bodied leading man who could sing, dance, and act. His handsome, rugged looks and effortless baritone helped him land top roles, such as El Gallo, the narrator in the original Off-Broadway cast of *The Fantasticks* in 1960, for which Orbach delivered the show's most memorable number, "Try to Remember"; he also appeared in a 1965 production of *Guys and Dolls* as Sky Masterson, and won a 1969 Tony Award for best actor thanks to *Promises, Promises*. Other notable Broadway parts for Orbach included Billy Flynn in the original cast of *Chicago* in 1975, and five years later he was also in the original cast of *42nd Street* when, in a legendary Broadway moment, it was announced at the end of opening night that the show's director, Gower Champion, had died. Not even the cast knew, and producer David Merrick's announcement left the entire house dumbstruck; it was Orbach who signaled that the curtain needed to come down.

Mid-career, Orbach moved into serious Hollywood film roles thanks to his portrayal of a character based on New York organized-crime figure Joey Gallo in a 1971 project, *The Gang That Couldn't Shoot Straight*, which also starred a young Robert DeNiro. In an odd twist, Orbach and his wife befriended Gallo, who lived in their New York City apartment for a time before he was slain, probably by fellow mobsters, in 1972. Orbach played a cop in 1981's acclaimed *Prince of the City*, and showed a softer side as Jennifer Grey's dad in *Dirty Dancing*, the 1987 box-office smash. An even younger audience became familiar with Orbach's baritone when he was chosen as the voice of the candlestick Lumiere in the animated Disney story, *Beauty and the Beast*.

In 1992, Orbach joined the hit television drama series *Law & Order* in its third season. The show, set amongst the professional realm of New York City detectives and prosecutors, featured a strong cast and compelling storylines, and Orbach's Det. Briscoe—a battle-scarred, wisecracking former alcoholic—was a favorite with viewers, especially real-life police officers. Orbach said that for the first time in his career he was readily recognized on the street, and sometimes police squad cars would pull over and offer him a lift if they saw him trying to hail a cab.

Unbeknownst to his fans, Orbach had been battling prostate cancer for several years. Declining health forced him to step away from *Law & Order* after its 2003-04 season, though he still appeared on a spin-off, *Law & Order: Trial by Jury*. He died on December 28, 2004, at age 69 while undergoing treatment at New York City's Memorial Sloan-Kettering Cancer Center. He is survived by his wife, Elaine; his sons Anthony and Christopher from his first marriage,

two grandchildren, and his mother, Emily. The day after his death, all lights on Broadway were dimmed in his honor. Dick Wolf, *Law & Order*'s producer, pointed out to *Entertainment Weekly* that as Briscoe, Orbach "was the longest-running character on the longest-running drama series on television. But that was merely the capstone on one of the landmark careers in American show business." **Sources:** *Chicago Tribune*, December 30, 2004, sec. 3, p. 8; *Entertainment Weekly*, January 14, 2005, p. 20; *Los Angeles Times*, December 30, 2004, p. B8; *New York Times*, December 30, 2004, p. A21; December 31, 2004, p. A2; *People*, January 17, 2005, pp. 77-78.

—Carol Brennan

Eduardo Paolozzi

Born Eduardo Luigi Paolozzi, March 7, 1924, in Edinburgh, Scotland; died April 22, 2005, in London, England. Artist. Eduardo Paolozzi, one of the founders of the 1950s British Pop Art movement, was an influential artist in post-World War II Great Britain. Paolozzi worked in a number of mediums, but was perhaps best known for his large sculptures and collages. He also created many pieces of art for public spaces in Great Britain and Germany.

Paolozzi was the son of Italian parents, but was born and raised in Scotland. The family owned an ice cream and confection production and retail business. The young Paolozzi was supposed to join the business an adult. While he was employed in the business during his formative years, he was attracted to the aesthetics of the packaging and labels as well as the look of the advertisements. From a young age, Paolozzi thought like an artist, creating scrapbooks full of images culled from comic books and magazines.

The politics of his parents' mother country soon affected his life. Because of his father's support of Benito Mussolini and the Italian dictator's fascist politics, Paolozzi was sent to a youth camp for young fascists in Italy for a few summers in the 1930s. In 1940, after Italy became a part of World War II, Paolozzi and his father were labeled enemy aliens under the Emergency Powers Act. They were forced into an internment camp for three months. Soon after, Paolozzi's father and grandfather lost their lives when a torpedo sank a transport ship, the Arandora Star, that was taking them to Canada.

After Paolozzi's stint in the camp ended, he began studying at the Edinburgh College of Art in 1943. He wanted to become a commercial artist. His studies only lasted a few months because he was drafted by the British Army's auxiliary unit, the Royal Pioneer Corps. Paolozzi served from 1943 to 1944. Upon his discharge, he resumed his studies, this time at St. Martin's School of Art in London and Slade School of Art.

When Paolozzi was 23 years old and living in London, he had his first solo exhibit. Featured at this exhibit were examples of his early work, which primarily focused on collages later recognized as some of the first examples of British Pop Art. These collages were droll and full of wit. They were created from images of popular, middle-class culture, like magazines, photos of celebrities, and pictures of mass-produced consumer products.

Before earning a degree, Paolozzi left school in 1947 and spent the next two years living in Paris, France. He spent sometime studying at the Ecole des Beux-Arts, but primarily worked on developing his art. Paolozzi came in contact with many artists who influenced his style, including several Surrealists and avant-garde artists. After his return to London in 1949, he became known for cast-bronze sculptures that were unique at the time in their unfettered interpretation of the human form. The pieces also had a crude, unfinished quality to them. As his art career was taking off, Paolozzi was married in 1951 to a textile designer named Freda Elliot. The couple had three daughters before divorcing.

In London, Paolozzi was among the organizers of the Independent Group in the early 1950s. This society of like-minded young artists worked against the prevailing Modernist aesthetic. When the group had its first public event at London's Institute of Contemporary Arts in 1952, Paolozzi showed slides of his collage work in a talk called "Bunk." Lawrence Alloway, an art critic, called their work "Pop Art," which flowered in Great Britain in the 1950s.

Paolozzi's sculptures continued to evolve through the late 1950s. His figures began having machine parts incorporated into the design, but remained distressed in appearance. By the early 1960s, his sculptures took on a new, more Pop/futuristic look as the figures became more machine- or robot-like, were made of other metals like aluminum, and often painted in striking colors.

As Paolozzi's career developed, he worked in other mediums, including mosaics, textile design, silk-screen printing, and experimental films, with significant pieces in the latter mediums produced in the late 1960s. He also continued to create collages. While a working artist, Paolozzi also began teaching in this time period. He taught at institutions including the Royal College of Art in London, England, Fachhochschule in Cologne, Germany, and the Kuenste in Munich, Germany. At these institutions, he was an instructor in textile design, sculpture, and ceramics. His teaching career was limited by his difficult personality, and ended in 1990.

While Paolozzi often showed his work in group and solo shows, including a major retrospective in 1971 at London's Tate Gallery, the 1970s and 1980s were also a time when he created many works for public places. Related to his Pop Art roots was a mosaic he created in the 1970s for a London subway station. In the 1980s, Paolozzi sculpted a head in cast iron for Euston Square in London and a self-portrait in bronze for another street. With these public works also came public acknowledgement of his importance. He was elected to the Royal Academy of Art in 1979, and knighted ten years later.

Though Paolozzi continued to produce new works, it was not until the mid- to late-1990s that he showed his work in private galleries again. One such exhibit, entitled "Spellbound: Art and Film," was held at the Hayward Gallery in 1996. It consisted of new sculpture works, primarily in plaster, that were created in response to films. Paolozzi also continued to create large pieces of public art. In 1997, he finished one of his best-known works, a bronze statue of Sir Isaac Newton based on an image inspired by William Blake. It was placed on an exterior area of the British Library.

After a near-fatal stroke in 2001, Paolozzi suffered brain damage and was wheel-chair bound. He lived for another four years before dying in his sleep at the age of 81 at a hospital in London on April 22, 2005. He is survived by his daughters Louise, Anna, and Emma. **Sources:** *Los Angeles Times,* April 30, 2005, p. B19; *New York Times,* April 27, 2005, p. A18; *Times* (London), April 23, 2005, p. 70; *Washington Post,* April 26, 2005, p. B6.

—A. Petruso

Frank Perdue

Born Franklin Parsons Perdue, in 1920, in Salisbury, MD; died after a brief illness, March 31, 2005, in Salisbury, MD. Chief Executive Officer of Perdue

Farms. Agri-business pioneer Frank Perdue was responsible for the evolution of his family's chicken business into Perdue Farms, the third-largest poultry producer in the United States. The company captured its market share largely through Perdue's innovative ideas about large-scale breeding and processing, but he also served as its advertising pitchman in a long-running series of television commercials. Thanks to his credible delivery which explained why his birds were superior to those of the competition, Perdue Farms became the first nationally known brand of chicken.

Born in 1920, Perdue was the son of Arthur W. and Pearl Perdue, two egg farmers in Salisbury, Maryland. His father had been a railroad worker, but noticed that the egg farmers who brought their in goods for shipping appeared to be a bit more prosperous than their vegetable-growing counterparts. Perdue began working on his parents' small enterprise at an early age, recalling in one interview that he helped out at time when he still had to use two hands to carry an egg. At the age of ten, he started a farm-club project with some culls, or reject hens destined for slaughter, that his father gave him. He took good care of them, and they soon began to produce as many eggs as the other hens. The venture gave Perdue pocket money of $10 to $20 a month—an impressive sum during the hardest days of the Great Depression in the 1930s.

Despite his success, Perdue had zero interest in entering the family business. He loved baseball, and played for the team at State Teachers College in Salisbury, but realized he did not possess the requisite athletic talent. After earning his two-year degree in 1939, he also realized that a lifetime of grading papers might be tedious work, and so he headed back to the egg farm to join his father full-time in the operation. They switched to raising chickens for meat rather than selling eggs after a disease outbreak decimated their flock, and began breeding New Hampshire red chickens for broiler meat. The farm earned a small fortune when meat prices climbed during World War II, and the business grew steadily over the next decade.

Perdue became president of the company in 1952, and continued to oversee the Perdue Farms expansion plan. It was his idea to make the chicken meat appear yellower—thus more appealing to consumers—by adding marigold petals to the feed bins, and he opened new and larger processing plants over the years, which speeded up the time from factory to table. He also began to deliver his packaged meats on ice, rather than fully frozen, when refrigeration technology improved.

It was Perdue's determination to launch a national advertising campaign, however, that turned the company into a nationally known brand. In the early 1970s, he met with several dozen advertising agencies before hiring one that agreed with his plan for a campaign, but he was told that the commercials required a humorous approach, and that he needed to personally convey why his packaged supermarket chicken was better than the rest. Perdue was dubious about both strategies, but agreed to make his first television commercial.

The results were positive for the first Perdue Farms commercial, which aired in 1971. Nearly 200 more followed over the next 23 years, most featuring the tag line, "It takes a tough man to make a tender chicken" and Perdue's homespun delivery. "His bald head," noted *New York Times* journalist Melanie Warner, "droopy-eyed expression and prominent nose made people smile and feel comfortable with him. They tended to trust him more than they did slick-looking announcers." An analyst of marketing trends echoed the sentiment in another article that paid tribute to Perdue. "He looked and sounded like a chicken," Bob Garfield of *Advertising Age* told *People* magazine. "He had a weird authenticity that made you want to believe there was actually something special about his broilers."

Perdue set a new trend in advertising in which the CEO served as spokesperson for the brand. A decade after he started starring in his own commercials, Lee Iacocca of the Chrysler Corporation became Perdue's most well-known imitator. Over time, Perdue's company became the number-three poultry producer in the United States, and its successful strategies were carried on by Perdue's son, Jim, who took over in 1991. By 2004, Perdue Farms posted sales of $2.8 billion in sales, and employed 19,000.

Perdue suffered from Parkinson's disease in his later years, and died after a brief illness on March 31, 2005, at the age of 84. He was married three times, and had four children and two stepchildren. All six survived him, along with third wife Mitzi Ayala Perdue. "He built a poultry empire," asserted Joe Holley, writing in the *Washington Post*, "by putting his name on chickens and standing behind them. He may have been a country boy, but he also was a shrewd businessman who helped revolutionize the industry." **Sources:** *Chicago Tribune*, April 2, 2005, sec. 1, p. 13; *Los Angeles Times*, April 2, 2005, p. B15; *New York Times*, April 2, 2005, p. B11; *People*, April 18, 2005, p. 92; *Washington Post*, April 2, 2005, p. B1, p. B6.

—*Carol Brennan*

Rainier III, Prince of Monaco

Born Rainier Louis Henri Maxence Bertrand Grimaldi, May 31, 1923, in Monte Carlo, Monaco; died of heart, lung, and kidney failure, April 6, 2005, in Monte Carlo. Prince of Monaco. The death of Prince Rainier III of Monaco marked the end of an era for Europe's oldest royal family still in power. Rainier had headed the small city-state on the French Riviera since 1949, which made him the longest-ruling monarch in Europe. The prince and his successor, Prince Albert II, remain a vestige of a long-ago era when large swaths of Europe were divided into meager territories controlled by princely dynasties.

Born in 1923, Rainier was a Grimaldi, an adventurous Genoese family who seized control of the rocky spit of land on the Mediterranean in 1297. Wedged between the borders of modern-day France and Italy, Monaco was a French protectorate after 1861, and subsequently prospered. Rainier's father was a French nobleman named Pierre, Comte de Polignac, while his mother, Princess Charlotte, was the illegitimate daughter of Monaco's Prince Louis II and a young laundress of Algerian descent. Pierre and Charlotte divorced when their son was six.

Rainier was educated at top schools in England and Switzerland, and served in the Free French Army during World War II, which fought the Nazi occupation of France. He inherited the throne in 1949 when his grandfather died. Derided as a playboy prince, with a fondness for fast cars and pretty women, Rainier proved his detractors wrong by launching initiatives to revitalize Monaco's economy, which was in dire straits at the time. Its main source of revenue had been the legendary casino, and the profits from this had sustained Monaco—largely made up of the municipality of Monte Carlo—since the nineteenth century. So rich were its coffers that Monaco even abolished taxes on income, capital gains, and inheritance in the 1880s.

In the new postwar world, however, the fortunes of Europe's elite had declined considerably, and there was little money left to gamble at the casino. Rainier struck a deal that brought in Greek shipping tycoon Aristotle Onassis to revive the casino's fortunes, and it returned to prosperity over the next few years. Rainer also worked to bring new industries and businesses to Monaco, and make it a tourist destination for the middle classes, not just the elite. His vision for Monaco's future was boosted immensely when he met the American film star Grace Kelly, and the two were wed in 1956 after a whirlwind courtship. Kelly was one of the most celebrated Hollywood stars of her era, and was both an Academy-Award winner and a fashion icon; fortunately for Rainier, she was also Roman Catholic, which the Grimaldi dynastic rules required of a royal consort. The extravagant cathedral wedding was one of the most media-saturated events of the entire decade, and the match was widely dubbed a modern-day fairy tale.

Rainier and Grace produced a daughter, Princess Caroline, within a year. Albert, the male heir, arrived in 1958, followed seven years later by a second daughter, Princess Stephanie. Princess Grace proved a well-matched consort for Rainier. She joined him in working to improve Monaco's international reputation though her cultural and philanthropic projects, and their royal household was the object of much press attention over the years for its blend of European sophistication and American ease. The fairy tale ended in September of 1982, when Grace was killed in an automobile accident on a narrow mountain road, the Moyenne Corniche, when the car she was driving plummeted down an incline; seventeen-year-old Stephanie was with her, but survived. At the somber royal funeral—once again an international television event—Rainier appeared paralyzed by grief.

Over the next two decades, Rainier kept busy with business and royal affairs, and though there was talk that he might relinquish the throne in favor of Albert, he did not. Some palace sources hinted that he was unsure if Albert was ready for the royal duties, but Albert seemed the least wayward of the three Grimaldi children. Caroline's first marriage ended somewhat scandalously in a 1980 divorce, and she then wed Italian businessman Stefano Casiraghi in 1983, with whom she had three children, the first of whom was born less than nine months from the nuptials. Casiraghi died seven years later in speedboat accident, leaving Caroline a widow at 33, and she later became involved with a German prince, Ernst-August of Hanover, who divorced his wife to marry her in 1999. Caroline was already expecting a child, her fourth, at the time of the ceremony. Stephanie, meanwhile, had various careers as pop singer, perfume mogul, and swimsuit designer before having a child with her bodyguard; they were wed in 1995, after a second child was born, but the union ended, somewhat predictably, in divorce. She later had another child with another bodyguard, then became involved with a traveling circus and married an acrobat, which also ended in divorce in 2004. Albert, meanwhile, had never married, and his bachelor status prompted the occasional speculation about his sexual orientation.

Albert took over many of his father's official duties in early 2005, when Rainier's health declined. He was at the Prince's side when he died on April 6, 2005, at the age of 81 at Monaco's Cardiothoracic Centre of heart, lung, and kidney failure. The famed Monte Carlo Casino closed its doors that day as a sign of respect for the longtime ruler, who was succeeded in his royal record by Queen Elizabeth II of Britain as Europe's longest-serving monarch. **Sources:** CNN.com, http://www.cnn.com/2005/WORLD/europe/04/06/rainier.obit.ap/index.html (April 6, 2005); *Independent* (London), April 7, 2005, p. 41; April 16, 2005, p. 3; *New York Times*, April 7, 2005, p. 1; *People*, April 25, 2005, pp. 85-88; *Philadelphia Inquirer*, April 6, 2005; *Washington Post*, April 6, 2005.

—Carol Brennan

John Raitt

Born John Emmet Raitt, January 20, 1917, in Santa Ana, CA; died of complications from pneumonia, February 20, 2005, in Pacific Palisades, CA. Actor. Broadway star John Raitt was one of the most prolific stage performers of his generation. He was a leading star in the golden era of musical theater, and was perhaps best known for his role as Billy Bigelow in *Carousel,* which he originated in 1945. The show featured a seven-minute showstopper—written specifically for Raitt—and his booming baritone—which "remains one of the most evocative marriages of music and speech in the Broadway repertoire," asserted Raitt's obituary in the *Times* of London. Raitt also gained later fame as the father of blues-rock singer Bonnie Raitt.

Raitt was born on January 29, 1917, in Santa Ana, California. His father ran a Young Men's Christian Association (YMCA) camp in Orange County, and as a high-schooler in Fullerton, California, Raitt proved to be a talented track and field athlete, which won him a scholarship to the University of Southern California. He later transferred to the University of Redlands, where he studied physical education and dabbled in theater.

During his college years Raitt became increasingly involved in theater activities, and took his first professional jobs in the Southern California area just before World War II. He was exempted from military duty during the conflict after filing for status as a conscientious objector, which his Quaker faith permitted him to do. After some roles with the Los Angeles Civic Light Opera Company and in Pasadena-area theaters, he was signed to the MGM movie studio as a contract player. *Little Nelly Kelly* and *Ziegfeld Girl,* both released in 1941, are among Raitt's screen credits, but he never rose past a minor role during this period.

Raitt's agent suggested he try his luck in New York City instead, and arranged for him to audition for *Oklahoma!* to replace Alfred Drake, the actor who originated the role of Curly, the male lead. The Richard Rodgers-Oscar Hammerstein tale of romance and the rodeo was a massive Broadway hit when it debuted in 1943, and went on to a record five-year run in its original version. At his audition, Raitt stunned Rodgers, Hammerstein, and the show's other executive personnel by delivering the entirety of Curly's repertoire. Though they decided not to cast him as *Oklahoma!*'s Broadway lead (he was hired for the touring production), they did tailor the songs in their next immediate project, *Carousel,* just for him.

Raitt spent a year touring in the road company for *Oklahoma!* before debuting in *Carousel,* which opened at Broadway's Majestic Theater in April of 1945. The show, another tale of rural American romance but set in a traveling carnival, gave Raitt the chance to deliver the famous "Soliloquy," in which his character, Billy Bigelow, muses about his future and that of his new family. His "performance," wrote Richard Severo in the *New York Times* many years later, "was so memorable that he came to epitomize (along with Alfred Drake in *Oklahoma!*) a new distinctively modern breed of Broadway leading man—rugged cowboys and blue-collar workers."

Pegged as one of the Great White Way's rising stars, Raitt had dismal luck with subsequent roles. A string of other musicals—*Magdalena, Three Wishes for Jamie,* and *Carnival in Flanders*—all tanked, but he made a comeback in 1954 with *The Pajama Game,* a romantic comedy set in a pajama factory. He was cast as its superintendent, Sid Sorokin, while Janis Paige played the union organizer with whom he falls in love. Raitt reprised the role in the 1957 film version of the musical, in which he co-starred alongside Doris Day. Other Broadway credits for Raitt included the leads in *Man of La Mancha* and *Fiddler on the Roof.*

When the popularity of the big Broadway musical faded for a time, Raitt went to work in television. However, he continued to perform live in summer-stock theater until well into the 1980s, and often took the jobs for less pay than his star status might have commanded, simply because he said he loved to perform. Once, a 1979 *Man of La Mancha* production in Massachusetts was canceled due to a hurricane threat, but Raitt still delivered its signature song, "The Impossible Dream," after clambering aboard the tour buses full of audience members that were being turned back, "so they wouldn't go back empty-handed," his *New York Times* obituary by Severo quoted him as saying.

Raitt's daughter, Bonnie, seemed to inherit his legendary drive. After building a career throughout the 1970s and '80s, she won three Grammy Awards for her 1989 LP *Nick of Time*, a mix of hard rock and blues. She sometimes brought her father out on stage during concerts to sing a duet with her. Raitt was divorced twice, and in the early 1980s married his former college-era girlfriend, Rosemary Kraemer. He died of complications from pneumonia at his home in Pacific Palisades, California, at the age of 88, on February 20, 2005. He is survived by his wife, Rosemary; his daughter, Bonnie; his sons Steven and David, also from his first marriage; two stepdaughters, and six grandchildren. "He never sold out for the quick buck," his daughter once said in an interview, according to a *Chicago Tribune* report. "If he did Vegas, he would have been a bigger star, but he didn't want to sing for drunks and hecklers." **Sources:** *Chicago Tribune*, February 21, 2005, sec. 1, p. 11; *Los Angeles Times*, February 21, 2005, p. B9; *New York Times*, February 21, 2005, p. A19; *Times* (London), April 5, 2005, p. 54; *Washington Post*, February 21, 2005, p. B6.

—*Carol Brennan*

Judith Rossner

Born Judith Perelman, March 31, 1935, in New York, NY; died of complications from diabetes and leukemia, August 9, 2005, in New York, NY. Author. Judith Rossner produced ten novels during a career that lasted more than three decades, but her name is inevitably linked with her bestselling work, *Looking for Mr. Goodbar*. The 1975 novel was made into a successful film that starred Diane Keaton and Richard Gere as, respectively, a schoolteacher and the man she takes home from a bar who stabs her to death. Rossner based the story on an actual New York City murder, and her fictionalized account "could be read as a particularly harrowing caution for the sexually adventurous," noted Douglas Martin in the *New York Times*.

Born in 1935 in New York, Rossner grew up as Judith Perelman in the Bronx. Her father was a textile merchant, and her mother, a teacher, encouraged her daughter's literary ambitions. She penned short stories during her years at Taft High School before moving on to the City College of New York, but dropped out when she married fellow student Robert Rossner in 1954. After starting a family, the couple moved to a New Hampshire commune to run a progressive school there, but eventually separated. Rossner moved back to the city and worked as a secretary to support her young son and daughter. During her spare time she managed to write her first novel, *To the Precipice*. The 1966 tale centered around a married woman who has an affair, becomes pregnant from it, and leaves her husband.

Rossner authored two subsequent works, *Nine Months in the Life of an Old Maid* in 1969 and *Any Minute I Can Split* three years later, the latter novel concerning a pregnant woman who flees to a commune and finds it anything but utopian. During the first weeks of 1973, Rossner followed a murder case that dominated New York City newspaper headlines at the time: a 28-year-old teacher of deaf children, Roseann Quinn, had jettisoned her strict Roman Catholic upbringing and was enjoying the new era of sexual freedom for unmarried women. Quinn frequented the so-called "singles bars" of the time, apparently took a man back to her West Side apartment on New Year's Eve, and was discovered stabbed to death a few days later.

Hoping to produce a salable magazine article, Rossner first proposed the story that became *Looking for Mr. Goodbar* to *Esquire* magazine, which declined to publish it when the suspect was apprehended, fearing it would complicate his legal defense. Rossner wrote a fictionalized version instead, and the film rights to it were sold even before Simon & Schuster published it. A *New York Times* review of the novel asserted that "the sureness of Judith Rossner's writing and her almost flawless sense of timing create a complex and chilling portrait of a woman's descent into hell that gives this book considerable literary merit," according to Hillel Italie in the *Boston Globe*. The title spent weeks on the best-seller lists of 1975, selling more than four million copies, and gave Rossner financial independence for life.

In some conservative circles, the book was interpreted as a morality tale warning sexually liberated women that they, too, might meet a similar end. Rossner refused to link either her character's fate or the Quinn murder to anything but loneliness. "It's astonishing what some women will put up with just to have a warm body," she remarked a few years later, according to Mary Rourke in the *Los Angeles Times* "Some of the brightest women I know are obsessed with the search. It's very sad." The

1977 film was a box-office and critical hit, but Rossner was unhappy with the translation of her story to the big screen and commented that it would have turned out worse without the talented Keaton in the lead.

Rossner produced several more novels, none of which replicated the phenomenon of *Looking for Mr. Goodbar*. A 1983 title, *August,* was a modest success, but afterward she was struck with viral encephalitis, which caused short-term memory loss and made writing profoundly difficult. After taking some years off, she returned in 1990 with *His Little Women*, a modern-day spin on the classic Louisa May Alcott novel *Little Women*. In her final years Rossner suffered from diabetes and leukemia, and died on August 9, 2005, at the age of 70 at New York University Medical Center. A second marriage ended in divorce; she is survived by her third husband, Stanley Leff; her son, Daniel Rossner; her daughter, Jean Rossner, and three grandchildren, as well as a sister.

Remembered as a writer who deftly captured women's apprehensions over their expected roles as wives and mothers during a period of significant social change, Rossner was pragmatic about the notion of female solidarity. "All women are great friends until they're in competition for a man or a job," she once replied when asked about the feminist movement, according to her *Washington Post* obituary by Adam Bernstein, "and then they're not such great friends." **Sources:** *Boston Globe,* August 11, 2005; *Independent* (London), August 22, 2005, p. 48; *Los Angeles Times,* August 11, 2005, p. B10; *New York Times,* August 11, 2005, p. C17; *Washington Post,* August 11, 2005, p. B5.

—Carol Brennan

Artie Shaw

Born Arthur Jacob Arshawsky, May 23, 1910, in New York, NY; died December 30, 2004, at his home in Newbury Park, CA. Clarinetist and bandleader. Artie Shaw's "innovations, musical depth, and swinging style placed him firmly in the pantheon of 20th century big band and jazz musicians," according to Claudia Luther in the *Los Angeles Times*. He was a brilliant clarinetist and one of the famous bandleaders of the World War II era. Quite an experimental musician, he eventually quit the jazz scene when he realized he would have to play music other people's way if he wanted to remain popu-

lar. He took up writing and spent the rest of his life as an author, although he never gained the fame writing that he did as a musician.

Shaw was born Arthur Jacob Arshawsky on May 23, 1910, to two dressmakers. His mother was originally from Austria, and his father was originally from Russia. He was born in New York City and lived there, in a predominately Jewish neighborhood, until the age of seven when his family moved to New Haven, Connecticut.

He took to music early, playing the ukulele before he was introduced to the saxophone at age 13. He worked at a deli to earn the money to buy the instrument. His first band was the Peter Pan Novelty Orchestra, which Shaw put together in high school. The band played at local events and eventually auditioned with a dance band led by Johnny Cavallaro. Cavallaro was impressed with Shaw's skills, but did not hire him because he did not know how to sight read music.

Disappointed, Shaw went away, learned how to sight read, and was back in a month; he was hired on the spot at the age of 15. Shaw soon quit school to play in the band full time—it was at this point that he changed his name to Art Shaw. It was Cavallaro who started Shaw on the clarinet, and he liked it so much that he eventually gave up the saxophone. Shaw traveled around a lot during this time and it was while he was doing so that he met Billie Holiday, who would later sing with Shaw's band. Shaw was considered by many to be the first white bandleader to break the color barrier and hire a black singer.

Shaw was hired on as a staff musician at CBS, and because he was finally a bit stable monetarily, Shaw began educating himself. He liked it so much that he had thoughts of quitting music and becoming a writer instead. He even bought a house in Pennsylvania where he spent a year trying to write a book about a jazz musician. He eventually gave it up and went back to music, although he would never forget the dream to write.

After he moved back to New York City he formed a band to play between performances at the Imperial Theatre. He had been studying classical music, so he put together a rather odd assortment of musicians for jazz music—a string quartet, a rhythm section, and himself on clarinet. Then he composed a number, "Interlude in B-Flat," for the band to perform. It was an instant success, with the crowd clamoring for an encore. Shaw, completely stunned by the crowd's reaction, had not prepared anything else for the band to play, so they played the Interlude again. Because of this success Shaw put together his first orchestra, which opened at the Lexington Hotel in 1935. Despite the reaction of the first audience, this orchestra did not fare so well, as the fashion at the time was for jazz music.

Shaw formed a new band—this one more traditionally arranged—and named it Artie Shaw and His Orchestra. The band's first hit was in 1938 with Cole Porter's "Begin the Beguine." It was recorded as a B-side to "Indian Love Call," which was expected to be Shaw's first big hit. Instead, "Begin the Beguine" was the song that rocketed Shaw into the land of celebrity.

According to the *Los Angeles Times'* Luther, "Shaw never seemed to enjoy his fame. At one point, he was making $30,000 a week and getting tens of thousands of fan letters. But he was also what he called 'catnip for all those mobs of overexcited girls.'" He became openly disdainful of his fans, even going so far as to call them jitterbugging morons in an interview with the *New York Post*, according to Luther. He quit all of it in 1939 and declared that he was retiring and moving to Mexico. His retirement, however, did not last long. While he was in Mexico he heard a piece of music that he immediately recorded when he went back to the United States. It was called "Frenesi" and became his second huge hit.

In 1941 Shaw enlisted in the Navy and went overseas to fight in World War II. He served on a minesweeper before forming another band. He was hospitalized in 1944 for exhaustion and was soon after honorably discharged. By the time he was back in America the big band era was ending and Shaw, after a few relatively unsuccessful stints at forming new bands, finally gave it all up.

In 1954 Shaw quit the music scene, disgusted with the desire for only popular songs and nothing that might stretch and challenge the current scene. When asked why he had done such a thing, Shaw was quoted in the *Los Angeles Times* as having said, "It was like having a gangrenous arm—I had to cut it off to survive."

Shaw was an avid reader and spent more than half his life after he quit playing music professionally writing, although critics often complained that he quit a career that he was amazing at to do something at which he was mediocre—his writing was never very successful. He published his autobiography, *The Trouble With Cinderella* in 1952, and later published two books of novellas. He spent a long time working on a novel, but had not finished it by the time he died.

Shaw, however, was not forgotten. In 1985 Brigitte Berman won an Academy Award for her documentary about Shaw, *Time Is All You've Got*. Also, his albums were reissued many times and Shaw had the pleasure of watching new generations come to his music time and time again. His album *Self Portrait*, released in 2003, was nominated for a Grammy as the best historical album. At the same time he agreed to donate two of his clarinets to the Smithsonian.

Shaw was married twice before he became famous. He went on to marry Hollywood legend Lana Turner in 1940; they soon divorced and Shaw married Elizabeth Kern, the daughter of songwriter Jerome Kern. The couple had one son, Steven. They also divorced and Shaw married Hollywood beauty Ava Gardner in 1945; they divorced in 1946. His last three marriages were to author Kathleen Winsor from 1946 to 1948; Doris Dowling from 1952 to 1956, with whom he had a son, Jonathan; and actress Evelyn Keyes, whom he married in 1957 and later divorced. Shaw died at home in Newbury Park, California, of natural causes on December 30, 2004, at the age of 94. **Sources:** *Independent* (London), January 1, 2005, p. 32; *Los Angeles Times*, December 31, 2004, p. A1, p. A20-21; *New York Times*, December 31, 2004, p. A24; *USA Today*, January 3, 2005, p. 5D.

—*Catherine Victoria Donaldson*

Jaime Sin

Born Jaime Lachica Sin, August 3, 1928, in New Washington, the Philippines; died of multiple organ failure, June 21, 2005, in the Philippines. Cardinal. Cardinal Jaime Sin helped his country, the Philippines, become a true democracy by supporting its "People Power" protests of 1986. When dictator Ferdinand Marcos claimed he had won a rigged presidential election, Sin asked Filipinos to take to the streets of Manila, the country's capital, to protect two top military officials who defied Marcos. One million people answered Sin's call, pressuring Marcos to resign. In his almost 30 years as archbishop of Manila, Sin served as his nation's moral and political conscience. He led the protests that caused a second president to resign in 2001 amid corruption charges.

Sin was born in the central Philippines to a Chinese merchant and his Filipino wife. He was their 14th child in a family of 16. He became a priest in 1954, when he was 26, and was ordained a bishop in 1967 and an archbishop in the provincial archdiocese of Jaro in 1972. He was made archbishop of Manila in 1974 and a cardinal in 1976. He became a leading voice of conscience to Catholics throughout Southeast Asia, especially the heavily Catholic Philippines, on issues from poverty to government corruption and human-rights violations.

Marcos, the Philippines' longtime president, instituted martial law around the time Sin became archbishop of Manila. Eventually Marcos replaced martial law with his direct personal rule. So Sin became, in the words of the *Times* of London, Marcos' "most saintly critic." At first, Sin's policy toward the Marcos government was known as critical collaboration. Sin would criticize the regime but not encourage extreme confrontation or revolt. A conservative at heart, Sin feared that sudden social upheaval could become a revolution that would also hurt the church. He feared following the path of South Vietnam, where Buddhist monks had weakened the ruling regime by confrontational protest, making it easier for Communists to seize power. "I must be a minister of reconciliation as well as a prophet of denunciation," he once said, according to the *Times*.

However, Sin became a more aggressive critic of Marcos after opposition leader Benigno Aquino was assassinated in 1983. He encouraged Filipinos to challenge the government to reform. When Aquino's widow, Corazon Aquino, challenged Ferdinand Marcos in a presidential election in 1986, Sin warned Marcos that keeping power through electoral fraud would be "unforgivable," according to the *Washington Post*. When Marcos rigged the election in February of 1986 and claimed to have narrowly beaten Aquino, Sin and other Catholic bishops encouraged the "people power" movement that supported Aquino by calling the Marcos regime illegitimate and suggesting that Filipinos use "peaceful and non-violent means," according to the *Times*, to pressure Marcos to leave office. At one point, Sin even led his congregation in a chant of Corazon Aquino's name during a Mass.

When Defense Minister Juan Ponce Enrile and Fidel Ramos, vice chief of staff of the military, decided to break with Marcos, they called Sin and said they would support Aquino's claim to the presidency. So Sin went on the radio and asked Filipinos to go into the streets to protect Enrile and Ramos from being attacked by Marcos loyalists. A million people joined the protests. Soon after, the United States

government, until then a Marcos ally, withdrew its support, and Marcos went into exile. After Aquino became president, Sin announced that he was in critical solidarity with the government, instead of critical collaboration.

Sin continued to speak out against government corruption, which had flourished under Marcos but did not end when he left. "We got rid of Ali Baba, but the 40 thieves remained," Sin once said, according to the *Chicago Tribune*. In 1999, the cardinal criticized the new president, Joseph Estrada, an infamous womanizer and gambler of whom the church disapproved, for limiting press freedom and making secret deals with "cronies of the Marcos dictatorship," according to the *Times*. When allegations surfaced in 2000 that Estrada had taken millions of dollars in gifts from illegal gambling, Sin called on him to resign. The Filipino House of Representatives impeached Estrada, but the impeachment trial broke down when the prosecutors resigned after the Senate refused to unseal some evidence. Sin spoke to a huge crowd at a religious shrine, declaring, "We know in our hearts that the president is guilty," according to the *Times*, and praying for him to resign. Soon, Estrada did.

A few months later, poor people who had supported Estrada because of his efforts to fight poverty rioted and stormed into the presidential palace. Sin responded by apologizing that the Catholic Church in the Philippines had often neglected the poor. In 2003, just before soldiers attempted a coup against President Gloria Macapagal Arroyo, Sin urged Filipinos to guard against those who would try to overthrow the country's democratic government. The coup failed.

Sin always supported democracy, but his conservative stances on social issues (which fit with those of his church) led to disagreements with the government, especially when Ramos became president in the 1990s and promoted birth control. Sin was also known as a strong opponent of abortion. The Catholic leadership in the Vatican, meanwhile, was reportedly uncomfortable at times with Sin's close involvement in politics. It also disapproved of his attempts to establish a dialogue with communist China. But Sin was motivated by an interest in the Catholic Church in China, and his visits to the country in the 1980s allowed him to report to Pope John Paul II about his first-hand encounters with Chinese Catholics. Sin also opposed the United States' decision to go to war with Iraq in 2003 and criticized the Philippine government for supporting the invasion.

"Sin was an engaging man of great personal warmth, with a keen, dry sense of humor," the *Times* noted after he died. The cardinal often showed his humor by contrasting his name and his work. He would greet visitors to his residence by saying, "Welcome to the House of Sin," and when he was briefly mentioned as a potential successor to Pope John Paul II, he said it would not happen because "my name is bad," according to the *Washington Post*.

Sin retired from the post of archbishop of Manila in November of 2003 when he reached the church's mandatory retirement age of 75. "I have given my very best to God and country," Sin said, according to the *Washington Post*. "I beg pardon from those I might have led astray or hurt. Please remember me kindly." In April of 2005, when Pope John Paul II died and Catholic cardinals worldwide were called to Rome to choose the next pope, Sin's poor health, including kidney and heart problems, kept him from attending.

Sin died of multiple organ failure on June 21, 2005, a few days after coming down with a fever. He was 76. After his death, Arroyo remarked that she was often guided by Sin's "wisdom and profound love for the poor and oppressed," according to the *New York Times*. "A great liberator of the Filipino people and a champion of God passed away," Arroyo said. **Sources:** *Chicago Tribune*, June 21, 2005, sec. 2, p. 12; *Los Angeles Times*, June 21, 2005, p. B10; *New York Times*, June 21, 2005, p. A21; *Times* (London), June 22, 2005, p. 57; *Washington Post*, June 21, 2005, p. B6.

—*Erick Trickey*

Jimmy Smith

Born James Oscar Smith, December 8, 1928, in Norristown, PA; died February 8, 2005, in Scottsdale, AZ. Jazz musician. When many people think of jazz, most think of the saxophone, the drums, or the piano. Though jazz great Fats Waller made the organ popular, it faded into the background in the early 20th century until Jimmy Smith brought it back. Smith also brought a new style of play to the organ, and it became a mainstay in jazz music and catapulted Smith to legendary status.

Smith was born into a musical family on December 8, 1928, though many references give his birth year as 1925. His father taught him to play the piano, and young Jimmy won a contest playing the stride piano at age 12. Smith dropped out of school after completing the eighth grade. He made a living playing the piano and also worked with his father as a

dancer. Smith joined the Navy at age 15, and played in a segregated band during his tour of duty. After his discharge, he used his GI Bill to attend Philadelphia's prestigious Hamilton School of Music and the Ornstein School, where he studied piano and double bass.

Smith joined a R&B band called the Soundtones, but also worked in construction and later for the Pennsylvania Railroad during the day. He heard Wild Bill Davis—who pioneered the organ trio format—playing one night and asked him how long it would take to learn to play the organ. Davis told him it would take years to master the pedals alone. Smith borrowed money and bought a Hammond B3 organ. He practiced during the day, and played at various clubs at night. He mastered the pedals in months, and soon began playing in various venues in the area, and debuted at the legendary Small's Paradise in New York.

Using a pedal style created by organist Bill Doggett to bring out the percussive sound, Smith also worked to use his left hand to bring out a saxophone-like sound and modal tones usually associated with the piano, and his right hand to play the melodies and improvisations. In an article he wrote for the *Hammond Times*, excerpted in the *New York Times* by Ben Ratliff, Smith stated, "While others think of the organ as a full orchestra, I think of it as a horn.... I wanted that single-line sound like a trumpet, a tenor or an alto saxophone." He took part in trios and also big bands, and soon word spread about his style of play that combined the blues, R&B, and gospel. Though the Philadelphia area was known for an aggressive organ style that combined blues with bebop, Smith became the king of the new style as he was the only one who could masterfully handle the pedals on the organ. "It was organ city but Jimmy was the king because he knew how to use his feet more effectively than any of us," jazz organist Jimmy McGriff told London's *Times*. Thanks to him, the growing popularity of the organ saw the creation and subsequent spread of organ rooms (trendy bars and clubs that featured organ trios) along the East Coast.

Smith and his band played at the Newport Jazz Festival in 1957. This brought him to the attention of the Blue Note record label. His first release, *A New Sound, A New Star: Jimmy Smith at the Organ*, debuted with much fanfare. At times he was billed as the Incredible Jimmy Smith. He recorded more than 30 albums with Blue Note in a short period of time. Smith also collaborated with numerous musicians, including guitarist and college professor Kenny Burrell, saxophonist Stanley Turrentine, and trumpeter Lee Morgan. His releases included *The Sermon, The Cat*, and *Bashin'*.

Smith switched to the Verve record label in 1962. He continued to release new albums throughout the 1960s and the early part of the 1970s. He also worked with legendary guitarist Wes Montgomery. Smith began touring extensively, but slowed down when he and his family moved to Los Angeles in 1980. He opened the Jimmy Smith Supper Club. For several years, Smith toured and also performed at his club, which closed down a few years after it opened.

In the 1990s, Smith began releasing new albums, signing with the Concord jazz label. He also began to tour again. He worked with fellow organist Joey DeFrancesco, often performing with him at a local club on Sunday afternoons. Word soon spread, and the two began attracting large crowds. Smith and his wife soon moved to Scottsdale, Arizona, in 2004. He was also named a "Jazz Master" by the National Endowment of the Arts in 2004. Smith and De-Francesco recorded an album together, *Legacy*, and began preparation to go on tour. Before this could occur, Smith died at home in his sleep of natural causes on February 8, 2005, at the age of 76. His album was released posthumously. He was preceded in death by his wife, Lola, months earlier, and is survived by two daughters, a son, and a stepson. DeFrancesco told Jon Thurber in the *Los Angeles Times*, "Jimmy was one of the greatest and most innovative musicians of our time." **Sources:** *Chicago Tribune*, February 10, 2005, sec. 3, p. 10; *Contemporary Musicians*, vol. 54, Gale Group, 2005; *Los Angeles Times*, February 10, 2005, p. B10; *New York Times*, February 10, 2005, p. C17; *Times* (London), March 31, 2005, p. 58; *Washington Post*, February 11, 2005, p. B8.

—*Ashyia N. Henderson*

Susan Sontag

Born Susan Rosenblatt, January 16, 1933, in New York, NY; died of leukemia, December 28, 2004, in New York, NY. Author. Essayist and critic Susan Sontag was one of the most widely known figures in American intelligentsia in the late twentieth century. Known as equally for her provocative pronouncements as for her photogenic beauty, Sontag was a leading figure in the cultural debates that swept through her era.

Sontag had a rather bleak childhood. She was born Susan Rosenblatt in 1933 in New York City, but her mother had returned to the United States only to deliver her and then leave the infant with relatives. Sontag's parents were fur traders in China, and neither she nor her younger sister ever met their father, who died in 1938. When their mother returned to the United States and reclaimed the pair, they moved to Tucson, Arizona, because Sontag suffered from asthma, and from there to Los Angeles. Sontag eventually took the surname of her stepfather, a former U.S. Army officer.

Sontag was a voracious reader even as a child, and boasted a formidable intellect by the time she reached her teens. Promoted ahead in school three times, she graduated from North Hollywood High School at the age of 15, entered the University of California at Berkeley for one semester, and then transferred to the prestigious University of Chicago. By then she was a stunning young woman, tall and with long dark hair and dark eyes, and at the age of 17 she married one of her professors just ten days after their first meeting. Dr. Philip Rieff was 28 at the time, and the two had a son together. Before she turned 26, Sontag finished at Chicago, earned a master's degree from Harvard University, and studied at the universities of Oxford and the Sorbonne.

Moving to New York City in the late 1950s after she and Rieff divorced, Sontag wrote for *Commentary* magazine and taught at various New York City colleges. Her debut novel, *The Benefactor*, was published in 1963, but both that and a subsequent work of fiction, 1967's *Death Kit*, earned poor reviews. She had far more success with her essays on cultural topics, such as her famous 1964 piece, "Notes on Camp." In it, she defended various aspects of low culture and kitsch, asserting that such works as *Snow White* serve to, in the end, energize more mainstream cultural patterns. The work established Sontag as a maverick on the fringes of American intellectualism, where the fashion was to deride all forms of popular culture, even film. Sontag participated eagerly in the new wave of music, art, and scenester-ism herself, attending rock concerts and appearing in a couple of Andy Warhol films during the artist's experimental-filmmaking era. "Her work, with its emphasis on the outre, the jagged, and the here and now," noted Margalit Fox in the *New York Times*, "helped make the study of popular culture a respectable academic pursuit."

Sontag continued to shock the established order throughout her career. A 1966 collection of essays, *Against Interpretation* argued that criticism may inhibit creativity. Often drawing upon European theorists, such as Roland Barthes, Jean-Paul Sartre, and Elias Canetti, Sontag was said to have introduced the ideas of both Barthes and Canetti to American readers at a time when their works were not yet widely available in English translation. Her other major work, *Illness and Metaphor* came out of her bout with cancer in the mid-1970s, and a 1977 book, *On Photography*, argued that the medium may serve to deaden the senses of the viewer to the suffering of others, in part by allowing him or her to satisfy a curiosity about atrocious acts from a safe distance. That work won her a National Book Critics Circle Award. A 2000 novel, *In America*, received a National Book Award.

Sontag served as president of the prestigious writers' organization PEN for a time, and was a committed human-rights activist for much of her career. She remained outspoken, even in the wake of the September 11, 2001, attacks on New York City and the Pentagon. In an oft-quoted essay she wrote for the *New Yorker*, she chastised the U.S. political leadership for calling the al-Qaeda hijackers "cowards." "Where is the acknowledgment that this was not a 'cowardly' attack on 'civilization' or 'liberty' or 'humanity' or 'the free world' but an attack on the world's self-proclaimed superpower, undertaken as a consequence of specific American alliances and actions?" she fumed in it, according to her *Los Angeles Times* obituary by Steve Wasserman.

In her later years Sontag was the companion of photographer Annie Leibovitz. Her son, David, became a book editor in New York City at Farrar, Straus, & Giroux, and edited some of his mother's volumes. Sontag was undergoing treatment for acute myelogenous leukemia when she died at the age of 71 on December 28, 2004, at New York's Memorial Sloan-Kettering Cancer Center. **Sources:** CNN.com, http://www.cnn.com/2004/SHOWBIZ/books/12/28/obit.sontag.ap/index.html (December 28, 2004); *Entertainment Weekly*, January 14, 2005, p. 18; *Independent* (London), December 30, 2004, p. 36; *Los Angeles Times*, December 29, 2004, p. A1, pp. A24-25; *New York Times*, December 29, 2004, p. A1.

—*Carol Brennan*

Kenzo Tange

Born September 4, 1913, Imabari, Shikoku Island, Japan; died of a heart ailment, March 22, 2005, in Tokyo, Japan. Architect. Kenzo Tange was considered a genius for the buildings he designed throughout his career. His design to create the Hiroshima Peace Memorial Park was chosen, and his career took off. His design for the main stadium at the 1964 Olympics in Tokyo showcased his work to the international community. He designed more buildings in his lifetime than legendary architect Frank Lloyd Wright. Tange was awarded architecture's highest honor, the Pritzker Prize, in 1987.

Tange was born on September 4, 1913, in Imabari, on the Shikoku Island in Japan. As a teenager, he saw a failed design of Le Corbusier (whose own purist designs ushered in the Modernist era in architecture) which sparked his interest in architecture. He attended Tokyo University, graduating with a degree in architecture in 1938. He worked for four years in the office of Kunio Maekawa, who was a disciple of Corbusier.

Tange entered graduate school at Tokyo University in 1942. Four years later, he became an assistant professor in the Architecture Department. He also created the Tange Laboratory. He would go on to teach and influence a number of Japanese architects, including Takashi Asada, Fumihiko Maki, Koji Kamiya, and Kisho Kurokawa. Maki would later also win the Pritzker Prize in 1993.

After the devastation from the United States' bombing of Hiroshima, where a reported 140,000 people lost their lives and many more were negatively impacted, the country of Japan decided to rebuild the area. Tange's design for the Hiroshima Peace Memorial Park was chosen in 1949. This was a busy time for him as he also presented his ideas for the park at the International Congress of Modern Architecture in London, England. Tange was among such luminaries as Walter Gropius, Jose Luis Sert, and Le Corbusier, whose style he adopted into much of his work.

For the Hiroshima Peace Memorial Park, Tange combined traditional Japanese architecture with Le Corbusier's Modernist design. He created a concrete and glass pavilion on stilts, and also included a massive arch that evoked the funereal houses for Haniwa statues honoring ancient Japanese nobility. The park was completed in 1956, and became the spiritual core for the new Hiroshima.

Wanting to change post-war Japan into a prosperous, booming country despite its size, Tange continued to design, and following the completion of the Hiroshima Peace Memorial Park, he designed the Kagawa Prefectural Office in 1958. During this time he designed a number of buildings including Tokyo City Hall, the Rikkyo University Library (also in Tokyo), and Kurashiki City Hall. Tange also opened his own architecture firm, Kenzo Tange + Urtec. The company later became Kenzo Tange Associates.

Tange is perhaps best known for his design of the main stadium used in the 1964 Tokyo Olympics. The Yoyogi National Stadium combined traditional and modern Japanese architecture. Made up of paired structures, the stadium's roofs were suspended on slung metal cables; the result resembled ancient temples. Many lauded Tange for the surreal beauty of the stadium. At the same time, he designed and built the Santa Maria Cathedral in Tokyo. He also released his 1960 Tokyo plan that would involve building new civic buildings, a park, and two towers. He introduced designs to extend the expanding city out over the bay using bridges, viaducts, and floating parking. Tange also designed buildings in other countries. He took part in the reconstruction of the Skopje in Yugoslavia. He designed and built the Kuwait International Airport and the Overseas Union Bank in Singapore, as well as its National Library. He worked on projects in other countries including Nigeria, Italy, and Saudi Arabia. Of his work in the United States, he played a role in Baltimore, Maryland's construction of its Inner Harbor. He also designed the addition to the Minneapolis Art Museum, and the American Medical Association Building in Chicago.

Tange had continued to teach at Tokyo University, becoming a full professor of urban engineering. He retired in 1974 as a professor emeritus. He continued to teach, but mostly in North America at numerous illustrious colleges and universities, including Harvard, Princeton, the University of Alabama, the University of Toronto, and Massachusetts Institute of Technology.

Tange's constant adaptation of his building designs was praised by many, and he was awarded the Pritzker Prize in 1987. According to the *Washington Post*, the jury that chose him for the honor "called him a leading theoretician of architecture...." In his acceptance speech, which was quoted in London's *Independent*, he said, "I do not wish to repeat what I have done. I find that every project is a springboard to the next, always advancing forward from the past to the ever-changing future...." According to the *New York Times*, the jury declared, "Tange arrives at shapes that lift our hearts because they seem to emerge from some ancient and dimly remembered past and yet are breathtakingly of today."

Tange returned to Tokyo City Hall and redesigned it. Today the building is home to 13,000 bureaucrats. The building's twin-tower structure was nicknamed "Notre Dame de Tokyo," and rose high above other skyscrapers in the city. Tange suffered from a heart ailment and died on March 22, 2005, in Tokyo, Japan; he was 91. He was preceded in death by a daughter, and is survived by his wife, Takako, and son, Noritaka. **Sources:** *AIArchitect,* http://www.aia.org/aiarchitect/thisweek05/tw0401/0401tangeobit.htm (May 20, 2005); *Independent* (London), March 26, 2005, p. 48; *New York Times,* March 23, 2005, p. C16, April 11, 2005, p. A2; *Washington Post,* March 24, 2005, p. B6.

—*Ashyia N. Henderson*

Jay Van Andel

Born June 3, 1924, in Grand Rapids, MI; died of Parkinson's disease, December 7, 2004, in Ada, MI. Entrepreneur. Amway, the company co-founded by Jay Van Andel, grew into one of the most impressive—and controversial—success stories in American entrepreneurship. Van Andel was the architect of Amway's alluring direct-marketing strategy of selling consumer goods through a network of personal contacts, though the company sometimes attracted unfavorable attention from consumer-watchdog groups. Along with longtime business partner Richard DeVos, Van Andel was one of Michigan's most prominent business leaders, and a generous contributor to Republican Party and conservative political causes.

Van Andel was born in 1924 in Grand Rapids, a city in western Michigan that in the late nineteenth century had become a mecca of sorts for Dutch immigrants who belonged to an evangelical Protestant sect, the Christian Reformed Church. At the city's Christian High School, Van Andel met DeVos, and teamed with him to start a flight school after returning from service in the Army Air Corps during World War II. They opened a drive-in restaurant that made butter-fried hamburgers from their mothers' recipes, but later sold both businesses and bought a schooner to sail the Caribbean. They had planned to launch a sea-going business with it, but the vessel was wrecked near Cuba and they returned to Grand Rapids.

Back home, Van Andel and DeVos set up an import business, and also sold a food supplement called Nutrilite for its manufacturer. Using what they learned from selling that to friends and family, they founded Amway in the basement of Van Andel's house in 1959 with L.O.C., an all-purpose household cleaner. Their company moniker was short for "the American way," and relied on a multilevel direct marketing scheme. New sales recruits would buy a shipment of the products, and sell them to others at a markup price as an independent distributor. The key to success, however, was to recruit others to join the growing sales force; in return, independent distributors would receive a percentage of the profits from what their recruits sold.

Van Andel wrote all the sales and marketing materials himself in the early days of Amway, which grew to include self-help books and motivational tapes. These, too, would be sold to new recruits by the independent distributors, and the range of Amway-brand products grew to include nearly every consumer product, from soap to vitamins. Amway's blend of free-enterprise basics and motivational selling was not without its detractors, and some dissatisfied members claimed the company operated what was essentially a large-scale scam. It was investigated by the U.S. Federal Trade Commission for a number of years, but the founders' connections to a Grand Rapids-born Republican who went to the White House in 1974, Gerald R. Ford, helped it avoid further inquiries. Amway failed to elude an investigation by the Canadian government, however, which in 1983 brought tax-evasion charges against it for misstating the value of goods that crossed the U.S.-Canadian border. Amway paid a fine that totaled $58 million, the largest ever levied in Canadian history.

Amway expanded internationally, and gained a particularly large number of members in China and other Asian countries during the 1990s. The company eventually changed its name to Alticor and was thought to be valued at $6.2 billion by 2004. Van Andel retired as company chair in 1995, and continued to devote himself to philanthropic causes. Both he and DeVos gave generously to various Grand Rapids cultural institutions, and among the many projects that bear the Van Andel name is the Van Andel Institute, dedicated to education and medical research. He also funded an Arizona facility hoping to prove, through scientific methods, that the world was created by a supreme being in six days, as the Christian Bible asserts. He was also an enthusiastic donor to Republican Party coffers, and during the 2004 presidential campaign donated $2 million to Progress for America, an organization which produced a series of television ads that questioned the values and experience of Democratic White House hopeful John Kerry.

Van Andel was married to Betty Hoekstra of Grand Rapids in 1952, with whom he had four children. She died in January of 2004 on a private island the family owned in the British Virgin Islands, and later that year Van Andel spent his final weeks there, too. He returned to Michigan and died at his home in Ada, Michigan, on December 7, 2004, age 80, after suffering from Parkinson's disease for a number of years. His is survived by his sons Steve and Dave, his daughters Nan and Barb, and ten grandchildren. His personal fortune was estimated by *Forbes* at $2.9 billion. "For me, the greatest pleasure comes not from the endless acquisition of material things, but from creating wealth and giving it away," he wrote in his 1998 autobiography, *An Enterprising Life,* according to Adam Bernstein in the *Washington Post.* "The task of every person on earth is to use everything he's given to the ultimate glory of God." **Sources:** *Grand Rapids Press,* December 8, 2004, p. A7; *Los Angeles Times,* December 8, 2004, p. B8; *New York Times,* December 8, 2004, p. A29; *Washington Post,* December 8, 2004, p. B6.

—*Carol Brennan*

Luther Vandross

Born Luther Ronzoni Vandross, April 20, 1951, in New York, NY; died July 1, 2005, in Edison, NJ. Singer and songwriter. In the 1980s as R&B music turned from vocals to the slick styling of studio production that was rampant in the 1990s and the beginning of the 21st century, Luther Vandross used his natural talent to stand above the pack. He sold more than 25 million records, and many will remember the crooner for his vocals and lyrics. Music producer Kenneth "Babyface" Edmonds told *Entertainment Weekly*'s Tom Sinclair that Vandross "had one of the most unique, most magical voices of all time. That was Luther's gift: He made you fall in love with his voice."

Vandross was born in New York City on April 20, 1951. His father, Luther, and his mother, Mary Ida, raised him and his older siblings in a house filled with love and music. When Vandross was eight years old, his father died from diabetes. When Vandross was older, one of his sisters was a part of the group the Crests, who released the popular song "16 Candles."

In high school, Vandross' grades suffered as he pursued his love of music. His favorite singers were all women: Aretha Franklin, Dionne Warwick, and Cissy Houston, mother of pop superstar Whitney Houston. Vandross formed his own music group Listen My Brother, with several friends, including Carlos Alomar. Vandross sold one of his compositions, "Everybody Rejoice (A Brand New Day)." It was used in the Broadway production of *The Wiz,* and for the movie version of the musical. His friend, Alomar, had become a guitarist for rocker David Bowie, and introduced the two. Bowie was impressed with Vandross' voice and compositions. He asked the singer to help arrange his album, *Young Americans.* Vandross also went on tour with Bowie, who also requested that he open for him. Though it was daunting for Vandross, it gave him the exposure that would help him throughout his career.

Working with Bowie brought Vandross to the attention of other singers and songwriters. He was soon singing backup and penning songs for the likes of Bette Midler, Carly Simon, Donna Summer, and Barbra Streisand. But Vandross longed for his own solo career. He formed a disco group named Luther, and released two albums for Cotillion Records. Neither record did well, and Vandross was soon singing backup again. He also wrote and sang jingles for Kentucky Fried Chicken, 7Up, and the U.S. Army.

What made the search for a record deal difficult was Vandross' insistence on having total creative control, something unheard of in the 1970s and the 1980s. He sunk his money into a home studio and put together his first album, *Never Too Much.* He was able to sign a deal with Epic Records and released his album in 1981. The album was a success and the title track soared to the top of the R&B charts.

With each new release, Vandross's popularity grew. His songs of romance and his vocal arrangements captivated audiences from around the world. His albums successfully climbed the R&B charts, each going platinum by selling a million plus records, but mainstream success was very elusive. Vandross was reluctant to identify himself as an R&B singer because he felt his music transcended genres. According to the *Los Angeles Times* he said in an interview, "I consider my music to be universal. My music is based solely on feelings, not analysis." When he released his first compilation album, *The Best of Love,* he was finally able to do well on the pop charts. The song, "Here and Now," received a Grammy Award, and became a wedding anthem.

Vandross collaborated with many singers, including Janet Jackson, Mariah Carey, and his all-time favorite, Dionne Warwick. He continued writing for other people. In the 1990s he began a battle with Sony, the parent company of Epic Records, to be released from his contract. Toward the end of the decade he got his wish, and later signed with legendary music executive Clive Davis, who had just started a new label, J Records.

While Vandross had much success, his battle with his weight played out in the spotlight. As with his father, grandfathers, and his three siblings, Vandross had diabetes as well as hypertension. Throughout his career, his weight constantly fluctuated between 190 to 340 pounds. As Vandross was preparing to release an album that many deemed his most personal, *Dancing With My Father,* he suffered a stroke on April 16, 2003, which many thought was brought on by his diabetes. As his family and friends rallied around him, Vandross began the daily struggle to recover, all but disappearing from the public eye. His album was released and debuted at number one. The title track would also reach the top of the charts. Another single, "The Closer I get to You," a duet with Beyoncé Knowles, was number one on the charts, and helped Vandross win four Grammys. (Over the span of his career, he won a total of eight Grammy Awards.) A tribute to him was performed by several in the industry, and he accepted his award via a taped message, thanking his fans and all those who had supported him over the years.

One year after his stroke, Vandross appeared on *The Oprah Winfrey Show,* to give an update on his progress. Throughout his recovery, many of his friends and colleagues would stop by, some to reminisce, and others brought the gift of singing, including Patti Labelle, who sang his hit single, "If Only For One Night," for him. While family and close friends knew Vandross' ordeal was slow going, they all thought he would make a full recovery. Many in the music world were shocked to learn that he passed away on July 1, 2005. He was 54. Fans and friends came together for many tributes to the man some called "The Pavarotti of Pop." Vandross is survived by his mother. **Sources:** *Chicago Tribune,* July 2, 2005, sec. 1, pp. 1-2; CNN.com, http://www.cnn.com/2005/SHOWBIZ/Music/07/01/vandross.obit/index.html (July 5, 2005); *Entertainment Weekly,* July 15, 2005, p. 20; E! Online, http://www.eonline.com/News/Items/0,1,16867,00.html (July 5, 2005); *Los Angeles Times,* July 2, 2005, p. B18; *New York Times,* July 2, 2005, p. B14; *People,* July 18, 2005, pp. 80-84; August 29, 2005, pp. 115-16; *Times* (London), July 4, 2005, p. 50.

—Ashyia N. Henderson

Ezer Weizman

Born Ezer Weizmann, June 15, 1924, in Tel Aviv, Israel; died of respiratory infections, April 24, 2005, in Caesarea, Israel. Politician. For 50 years, as Israel's air force chief, defense minister, and president, as a leader and a political maverick, a warrior and peacemaker, Ezer Weizman provoked his country with his bold, brash personality. Like many Israeli politicians, Weizman first became famous by leading Israel to a military victory in a war with its Arab neighbors, then became an advocate of peace later in life. But Weizman's transformation was even more dramatic than most: he helped plot a bold pre-emptive attack on Egypt in 1967, then helped forge a peace treaty with Egypt eleven years later. In politics, he was an unreliable ally, pushing prime ministers on the right to negotiate with Israel's Arab foes and pressing left-wing prime ministers to be cautious of them. "A commander should have some kind of personal hallmark, which sets him apart from everyone else," he wrote in *On Eagles' Wings*, his memoir, according to the *Washington Post*. His outspokenness and unpredictability became his signature.

Weizman was born in 1924 into one of the most prominent Jewish families in what is now Israel. His uncle, Chaim Weizmann, became the first president of Israel, and many of his aunts, uncles and other relatives were leaders in charities and schools across the country. His father, Yehiel Weizmann, was an agronomist who taught at the Technicon, a prominent school. Weizman dropped the second "n" from his last name to distinguish himself from his famous uncle.

During World War II, when Israel was part of the British mandate of Palestine, Weizman volunteered to join Britain's Royal Air Force with the help of his uncle, president of the United Jewish Organization. He flew a fighter plane in Egypt and India, returning home in 1946. A year later, Weizman helped organize the beginnings of what became Israel's air force and he flew missions against Egyptian forces during Israel's war for independence in 1948 and early 1949. After the country was founded, he helped build up the air force, purchasing modern fighters from Europe. Rising quickly through the ranks, he became commander of the air force from 1958 until 1966, and personally led the training of many Israeli fighter pilots.

In 1967, as deputy chief of staff of the military, he helped plan the pre-emptive strike in the Six-Day War that practically destroyed Egypt's air force. In two hours, 300 Israeli fighter planes attacked 600 Egyptian planes on the ground, destroying 200, and they destroyed 200 more in a few hours of air combat. Commentators said Weizman's raid won the Six-Day War in its first six hours. The raid made him hugely popular in Israel.

After the war, the outspoken Weizman pushed for Israel to annex Arab areas in the West Bank and East Jerusalem. His outspokenness hurt his military career; it became clear he would not become the military chief of staff. He resigned from the army in 1969 and joined the conservative party Gahal, which led to him becoming minister of transportation for a short time. Throughout the 1970s, he engaged in a respectful power struggle with fellow conservative leader Menachem Begin. Weizman worked with Begin to build up the new Likud party and managed Begin's winning campaign for prime minister in 1977. Weizman became defense minister in Begin's cabinet.

Both men negotiated a historic peace treaty with Egyptian president Anwar Sadat. Begin and Sadat won the Nobel Peace Prize for the 1978 deal, but Weizman did much of the secret shuttle diplomacy that kept the negotiations going. His friendly approach to Sadat and Egyptian negotiators at Camp David, the American president's retreat, helped make the talks there a success.

The stark change from hawk to peacemaker was evident in his two books, *On Eagles' Wings*, written in the mid-1970s, and *The Battle For Peace* from 1981. In the first, he argued Israel should annex the West Bank and Gaza Strip, but in the second, he defended the peace accord and seemed sympathetic to Sadat's argument that the West Bank and Gaza Strip belonged to the Palestinian Arabs who lived there. Some attributed Weizman's change of heart to the serious wound his son, Shaul, sustained in 1970 during the War of Attrition between Israel and Egypt, but Weizman dismissed such speculation as amateur psychology. (Shaul died in a car accident in 1991.)

In 1980, when tensions with Begin grew into open hostility, Weizman left the cabinet. He formed a new party, Yahad (which means Together), hoping to create a moderate force in Israel's parliament, the Knesset. Yahad did not do well in the election, but still became influential because Likud and the left-wing party, Labor, had almost the same amount of strength in the Knesset. He joined the cabinet of prime minister Yitzhak Shamir, but Shamir fired him in 1990 for meeting with a member of the Palestine Liberation Organization (PLO) when negotiating with that group was illegal. Other members of the cabinet convinced Shamir to reinstate him, but he left again in 1992 to protest the government's refusal to negotiate with the Palestinians.

The Knesset elected Weizman president in 1993. Although the presidency is supposed to be mostly ceremonial, Weizman often expressed his opinions on how the prime ministers were doing. He disagreed with the Oslo peace accords of 1993 and pushed Labor prime ministers Yitzhak Rabin and Shimon Peres to stop negotiating with the Palestinians after suicide bombings. But when hard-liner Benjamin Netanyahu became prime minister in 1996, Weizman took the opposite approach, expressing unhappiness with Netanyahu, inviting Yasser Arafat to his home, and asking the United States to help Arafat and Netanyahu resolve their differences.

Weizman also took a broad view of his ceremonial responsibilities as president, visiting prisoners, refugees, and wounded soldiers returning from Lebanon and traveling to small, remote towns in Israel three days a week to display the Israeli flag. He stepped down before his second term as president ended, under pressure from an investigation into $300,000 in unreported gifts he had received from a French businessman and an Israeli businessman when he was a government minister in the 1980s and early 1990s. Weizman once claimed politics had never been his biggest ambition. "The thing I wanted more than anything in my life was to be commander of the air force," he said when asked in 1980 if he wanted to be prime minister, according to the *Independent*. "That was my piece of cake. Everything else is a little bit of cream." Weizman died of respiratory infections at his home in Caesarea, a resort town on the sea in Israel, on April 24, 2005. He was 80. He is survived by his wife, Re'uma Shamir Schwartz, and his daughter, Michal. **Sources:** *Independent*, April 26, 2005, p. 36; *New York Times*, April 25, 2005, p. B8; *Washington Post*, April 25, 2005, p. B5.

—*Erick Trickey*

William C. Westmoreland

Born William Childs Westmoreland, March 26, 1914, in Spartanburg, SC; died July 18, 2005, in Charleston, SC. Military general. William C. Westmoreland was a four-star general who led American troops during a significant portion of the Vietnam War. While the general's leadership in Vietnam was controversial, he had a long, distinguished career in the U.S. Army. Years after the war's end, he filed a high-profile lawsuit against CBS for a documentary which claimed Westmoreland had manipulated intelligence reports during the Vietnam War.

Westmoreland was born in 1914 in Spartanburg, South Carolina. The military was part of his life from the time he was a teenager. He went to school at the Citadel for one year before entering West

Point. By the time he graduated in 1936, he was the top student in his class and earned the Pershing Sword as the most militarily proficient cadet. Westmoreland then joined the U.S. Army, serving in field artillery at the rank of first captain.

During World War II, Westmoreland served with distinction. First, he was a battalion commander in North Africa and Sicily. The unit Westmoreland commanded was awarded a presidential citation for their heroic actions when they came under fire in Tunisia. He later led troops in conflicts in France, Germany, and Belgium. Westmoreland faced particularly brutal times when his division was able to capture and hold the last standing bridge on the Rhine River, the bridge at Remagen. Westmoreland and his men had to defend the bridge from enemy troops for two weeks; this gave the Allies time to build their own bridge. Their actions helped end World War II in Europe.

After serving as a paratrooper commander during the Korean War, Westmoreland's career took a different direction. While still serving in the Army, he went to the Harvard Business School in a management program. After completing the course, Westmoreland worked in the Pentagon as the head of the office of manpower. From 1955 to 1958, he served under Chief of Staff Maxwell Taylor as the secretary to the Army General Staff. Westmoreland then spent two years as the commander of the 101st Airborne Division. In 1960, he was named the superintendent of West Point. Three years later, Westmoreland, by then a lieutenant general, was ordered to go to Vietnam.

After a few months of serving as a deputy to U.S. Commander General Paul Harksins, Westmoreland was put in charge of U.S. troops in South Vietnam as the head of Military Assistance Command, Vietnam. He was also promoted to four-star general. Westmoreland assured the American public that the United States would win the war. One way he hoped to accomplish this goal was by increasing the number of American troops in the country. When Westmoreland took over in 1964, there were about 15,000 to 20,000 American "military advisors" in Vietnam; by 1968, there were about a half million American soldiers in Vietnam. Westmoreland measured success in Vietnam by the number of enemy troops killed by the massive number of American troops. The general believed that if the enemy was killed at a rate that would be faster than they could be replaced, the so-called "war of attrition," victory would be imminent.

Westmoreland's strategies lost support over his tenure in Vietnam. The increase in troops did not translate into success for the Americans in Vietnam, and led to the scorn of the American public as more and more American soldiers lost their lives. Despite being named *Time* magazine's Man of the Year in 1965, Westmoreland became the object of many Americans' discontent about the lack of progress in the war. He had a controversial appearance in front of Congress in 1967 in which Westmoreland was to defend the war, but instead labeled critics of the war unpatriotic. His troubles continued in 1968 when the Tet Offensive by the North Vietnamese caught the Americans and South Vietnamese off guard and resulted in a significant loss of territory. Though the land was eventually regained, it came at great cost and led to more American discontent over the war.

U.S. President Lyndon B. Johnson had always limited what Westmoreland could do in the war. Westmoreland was not in charge of the South Vietnamese Army nor the bombing raids of North Vietnam. Late in his tenure, Westmoreland pushed for more troops and expansion of the war into Cambodia and Laos. In 1968, Westmoreland asked for 200,000 more troops, but instead was recalled to Washington and reassigned. He was named the Army's chief of staff, but was rarely consulted on matters related to the war by U.S. President Richard M. Nixon. He retired from the U.S. Army in 1972, and moved back to his home state of South Carolina.

Westmoreland turned to public speaking, including many stops on college campuses which were often scenes of protest. In 1974, he tried to launch a political career, running for the Republican nomination for the governor's office in South Carolina. This bid was unsuccessful. Westmoreland published his memoir in 1976, *A Soldier Reports,* in which he continued to defend his decisions in Vietnam. Westmoreland insisted that the U.S. Army had not lost the war, only the South Vietnamese, because the United States dropped out.

In 1982, Westmoreland re-emerged in the news because of a controversial documentary on CBS entitled *The Uncounted Enemy: A Vietnam Deception.* The documentary claimed that Westmoreland personally changed and repressed intelligence information on the North Vietnamese and their troop numbers in the last two years that he was in charge in Vietnam. The documentary also claimed that Westmoreland's goal was to hoodwink the American public into thinking the war could be won. Westmoreland sued CBS for libel to the tune of $120 million. The case was settled out of court four months after it went to trial in 1984. CBS also admitted there were errors in the documentary.

Westmoreland died at the age of 91 on July 18, 2005, in Charleston, South Carolina, at a retirement home. He is survived by his wife, Katherine Stevens Van Deusen; his son, James Ripley; two daughters, and six grandchildren. **Sources:** *Economist,* July 30, 2005, p. 79; *Independent* (London), July 20, 2005, p. 34; *New York Times,* July 20, 2005, p. A20; *Washington Post,* July 19, 2005, p. A1.

—A. Petruso

Simon Wiesenthal

Born Szymon Wiesenthal, December 31, 1908, in Buczacz, Galicia (now part of Ukraine); died of kidney disease, September 20, 2005, in Vienna, Austria. Nazi war crimes investigator and human-rights activist. Simon Wiesenthal survived the Holocaust but lost his mother and many other family members during the ordeal in which six million European Jews were annihilated. After his release from a Nazi concentration camp in 1945, Wiesenthal dedicated his life to hunting down Nazi war criminals and is credited with bringing more than 1,100 offenders to justice. Because of his devotion to the task, he was nicknamed the "deputy for the dead."

Szymon Wiesenthal (later known as Simon) was born on December 31, 1908, in Buczacz, Galicia, which was part of the Austro-Hungarian Empire and now part of Ukraine. His father, Hans, was a sugar wholesaler and an officer in the Austrian Army; he died in combat in 1915. For a Jewish boy, Buczacz was not the safest place to live. Area Jews faced persecution from the Cossacks—peasants who served in the czar's cavalry and lived in communal settlements around Ukraine. When Wiesenthal was ten years old, a Cossack gashed his leg open with a saber as he crossed the street. Wiesenthal faced anti-Semitism again when he was denied admission to the Polytechnic Institute in the Ukrainian city of Lvov because of limits on Jewish enrollment. Instead, he studied architectural engineering at the Technical University in Prague, Czechoslovakia, graduating in 1932.

In 1936, Wiesenthal married his high school sweetheart, Cyla Müller, and opened an architectural practice in Lvov. Within a few years the Soviet Union's Red Army overran the city and began purging Jewish professionals. Wiesenthal's stepfather was arrested and his stepbrother shot. Forced to close his office, Wiesenthal found work in a bedspring factory.

In 1941, invading German soldiers displaced the Russian officers and gathered up the city's Jews for execution. Wiesenthal watched as a soldier shot half the group, gulping swigs of liquor in between executions. Wiesenthal's life was spared when the church bells rang and the soldiers retreated for evening mass. He and his wife were taken to a labor camp where he was given the job of painting swastikas on captured locomotives. In 1942, Wiesenthal's mother was executed. That same year, his wife, who was blonde and could pass for a Pole, was smuggled out of the area by the Polish underground and taken to Warsaw. Later recaptured, she was sent to western Germany to make machine guns for the Nazis.

During the Holocaust, Wiesenthal spent time in a dozen concentration camps and narrowly escaped alive. On April 20, 1943, Wiesenthal was among a group of men selected for execution in honor of German dictator Adolf Hitler's birthday. During the proceedings, an official decided someone needed to paint a swastika banner for the occasion and chose Wiesenthal for the honors, thus sparing his life again. In October of 1943, Wiesenthal persuaded an official to help him escape. Within a few months, though, he was returned to the Janowska camp on the outskirts of Lvov. Wiesenthal tried to kill himself but was revived for interrogation.

By the mid-1940s, the Germans had begun retreating toward Austria as Allied forces advanced. Many prisoners died during the journey, but Wiesenthal survived and on May 5, 1945, U.S. troops rolled into Austria, liberating Wiesenthal and other survivors. His 6-foot frame weighed less than 100 pounds. As soon as Wiesenthal regained his strength, he began gathering evidence for the War Crimes Unit of the U.S. Army in Austria. By the year's end, Wiesenthal was reunited with his wife, whom he feared dead. The next year, their daughter, Paulinka, was born.

While many survivors went back to their careers and tried to move on, Wiesenthal refused to forget the atrocities he had witnessed. He spent the remainder of his life tracking down war criminals, believing his survival gave him an obligation to pursue justice—through the proper channels—for those who had died. Wiesenthal opened the Jewish Documentation Centre to gather information on war criminals and cultivate relationships with contacts around the globe. Located in Austria, the center became a repository of concentration camp testimony.

Following the war, many war criminals fled Europe and tried to blend in by living ordinary lives. Many did not escape Wiesenthal's sleuthing. He was a clever detective, known for his extraordinary memory, and fluent in Polish, German, English, Yiddish, and Russian. Wiesenthal's work led to the arrest of several high-profile war criminals, including Franz Stangl, who was hiding in Brazil. Stangl, a Polish death camp commandant, was extradited to West Germany for trial and died in prison there. Wiesenthal also tracked down Gestapo aide Karl Silberbauer, who had arrested Anne Frank and her family.

Once, Wiesenthal tipped off a *New York Times* reporter, who hunted down Valerian D. Trifa, who had led a massacre of Jews in Romania. At the time, Trifa was working as an archbishop of the Romanian Orthodox Episcopate in Michigan. He was deported to Portugal, where he died. Wiesenthal also located concentration camp guard Hermine Braunsteiner, who had escaped to the United States in the 1950s, married and settled in the New York City borough of Queens. She was infamous for shooting small children and selecting women for the gas chambers. She received a life term.

Many times, Wiesenthal was criticized for his efforts, particularly for his publicity stunts, yet he always downplayed critics. According to the *Washington Post,* he once remarked, "I'm doing this because I have to do it. I am not motivated by a sense of revenge. Perhaps I was for a short time in the very beginning." Wiesenthal went on to note that he had to do it so people do not forget. "If all of us forgot, the same thing might happen again, in 20 or 50 or 100 years." Besides criticism, Wiesenthal faced real danger, too. In 1982, his Vienna house was firebombed, though he escaped unharmed and refused to move. German and Austrian neo-Nazis were later charged.

Wiesenthal wrote several books about his efforts, including 1967's *The Murderers Among Us* and 1989's *Justice, Not Vengeance.* His life was also the topic of a 1989 HBO movie, *Murderers Among Us: The Simon Wiesenthal Story,* based on his memoirs. Wiesenthal also promoted human rights. Later in life, he urged war criminal trials for those responsible for genocide in the former Yugoslavia. He also lectured and gave countless interviews, many times denouncing far-right politics. He also reminded world leaders of their duty to combat racism.

Over his lifetime, Wiesenthal was bestowed with many honors, including the establishment of the Simon Wiesenthal Center in Los Angeles, which is dedicated to Jewish defense, education, and commemoration. Other honors include the U.S. Congressional Gold Medal in 1980, the Presidential Medal of Freedom in 2000, and honorary British knighthood in 2004.

Wiesenthal's wife predeceased him in 2003. On September 20, 2005, Wiesenthal died of a kidney ailment in Vienna. Survivors include his daughter and three grandchildren. **Sources:** CNN.com, http://www.cnn.com/2005/US/09/20/obit.wiesenthal/index.html (September 20, 2005); *Economist,* September 24, 2005, p. 102; *Independent* (London), September 21, 2005; *New York Times,* September 21, 2005, p. A1, p. C18; *People,* October 3, 2005, p. 87; *Washington Post,* September 21, 2005, p. A1, p. A18.

—Lisa Frick

Robert Wise

Born Robert Earl Wise, September 10, 1914, in Winchester, IN; died of heart failure, September 14, 2005, in Los Angeles, CA. Director. In a career that spanned five decades, film director Robert Wise never limited himself to working in a single genre, and made movies that ranged from sci-fi to film noir. But his legacy will be forever linked with the Academy Awards he won for *West Side Story* and *The Sound of Music* in the 1960s, two of the most successful interpretations of Broadway shows ever made. In nearly all of his projects, "Wise invariably gave audiences strong, intelligent stories with fine casts, made in a style that was flawlessly lucid," wrote Michael Wilmington in the *Chicago Tribune.*

Born in 1914 in Winchester, Indiana, Wise hoped for a career in sports journalism when he entered Franklin College. It was the Great Depression, however, and his tuition money ran out, so he headed for Los Angeles. His brother was already there, working in the finance office of the RKO studios, and helped Wise find a job as a studio porter. He moved up the RKO ladder to the sound department and eventually became a film editor. He earned his first nomination for an Academy Award in editing for Orson Welles' 1941 classic *Citizen Kane.*

Welles was a major industry figure at the time, and hired Wise to work on his next project, *The Magnificent Ambersons.* Studio bosses demanded its 148-minute running time be cut when preview audiences walked out, and because Welles was out of the country at the time, gave Wise the job of fixing it. The first scenes he directed came when he had to shoot some transitions to make up for excised segments, and he managed to cut the 1942 release to 88 minutes. Welles was outraged, and claimed that Wise had ruined his picture. "In terms of a work of art, I grant you Orson's original film was better,"

Wise conceded years later, according to the *Times* of London. "But we were faced with the realities of what the studio was demanding."

Studio executives next called on Wise to salvage *The Curse of the Cat People* after the project's original director was fired and the film already behind schedule. After 1944, he worked steadily, turning out one or two movies a year, some of them minor classics, and some of which he also produced. The 1947 noir classic *Born to Kill* endured as a critics' favorite, as did his 1949 boxing story *The Set-Up* and *The Day the Earth Stood Still,* a 1951 sci-fi parable. Starlet Susan Hayward won an Academy Award for Best Actress in 1958 when Wise directed her in the death-row saga *I Want to Live!.*

Wise won two Oscars of his own in 1961 for *West Side Story,* the film adaptation of a Broadway musical based on *Romeo and Juliet.* He shared the Best Director Academy Award with choreographer Jerome Robbins, and took another for Best Picture. That track record made him an obvious choice to helm another musical adaptation, *The Sound of Music,* the 1965 Julie Andrews vehicle that became one of the top-grossing films of all time. Andrews would be forever linked to the role of a rebellious nun assigned to serve as governess for a motherless Austrian brood. She turns them into singing sensations, wins the heart of their stern father, and they all flee the Nazi threat in Europe in what was loosely based on the story of the real-life von Trapp family.

Wise's later projects included a 1971 virus-peril thriller *The Andromeda Strain, The Hindenburg,* one of the standard mid-1970s disaster flicks; the first *Star Trek* film, and the little-seen *Rooftops* from 1989, his last theatrical project. A well-known figure in Hollywood, he served a stint as president of the Directors Guild of America and another as president of the Academy of Motion Picture Arts and Sciences. In 1966 he was honored with the Academy's Irving G. Thalberg Memorial Award for his lifetime achievement as a producer, and in 1988 the Directors Guild of America bestowed on him their highest tribute, the D.W. Griffith Award. A new generation of directors had discovered his classics, among them Martin Scorsese, who said that his 1980 picture *Raging Bull* had been influenced by *The Set-Up.*

Wise celebrated his ninety-first birthday in the late summer of 2005, but had a heart attack later that week. He died of heart failure at the University of California—Los Angeles Medical Center on September 14, 2005. Widowed in 1975, Wise had a son from his first marriage, Robert E. Wise, and is also survived by his second wife, Millicent, and stepdaughter, Pamela Rosenberg. **Sources:** *Chicago Tribune,* September 16, 2005, sec. 3, p. 9; *Entertainment Weekly,* September 30, 2005, p. 21; *Los Angeles Times,* September 15, 2005, p. B10; *New York Times,* September 16, 2005, p. A25; *Times* (London), September 16, 2005, p. 74; *Washington Post,* September 16, 2005, p. B7.

—*Carol Brennan*

Cumulative Nationality Index

This index lists all newsmakers alphabetically under their respective nationalities. Indexes in softbound issues allow access to the current year's entries; indexes in annual hardbound volumes are cumulative, covering the entire *Newsmakers* series.

Listee names are followed by a year and issue number; thus **1996**:3 indicates that an entry on that individual appears in both 1996, Issue 3, and the 1996 cumulation. For access to newsmakers appearing earlier than the current softbound issue, see the previous year's cumulation.

Arlen, Harold
  Obituary **1986**:3
Arman **1993**:1
Armstrong, C. Michael **2002**:1
Armstrong, Henry
  Obituary **1989**:1
Armstrong, Lance **2000**:1
Arnaz, Desi
  Obituary **1987**:1
Arnold, Tom **1993**:2
Arquette, Patricia **2001**:3
Arquette, Rosanna **1985**:2
Arrau, Claudio
  Obituary **1992**:1
Arrested Development **1994**:2
Arthur, Jean
  Obituary **1992**:1
Ash, Mary Kay **1996**:1
Ashanti **2004**:1
Ashcroft, John **2002**:4
Ashe, Arthur
  Obituary **1993**:3
Aspin, Les
  Obituary **1996**:1
Astaire, Fred
  Obituary **1987**:4
Astin, Sean **2005**:1
Astor, Mary
  Obituary **1988**:1
Atkins, Robert C.
  Obituary **2004**:2
Atwater, Lee **1989**:4
  Obituary **1991**:4
Aucoin, Kevyn **2001**:3
Aurre, Laura
  Brief Entry **1986**:3
Austin, 'Stone Cold' Steve **2001**:3
Autry, Gene
  Obituary **1999**:1
Avedon, Richard **1993**:4
Axelrod, Julius
  Obituary **2006**:1
Axthelm, Pete
  Obituary **1991**:3
Aykroyd, Dan **1989**:3 **1997**:3
Azaria, Hank **2001**:3
Azinger, Paul **1995**:2
Babbitt, Bruce **1994**:1
Babilonia, Tai **1997**:2
Bacall, Lauren **1997**:3
Backstreet Boys **2001**:3
Backus, Jim
  Obituary **1990**:1
Bacon, Kevin **1995**:3
Badgley, Mark and James Mischka **2004**:3
Badu, Erykah **2000**:4
Baez, Joan **1998**:3
Bahcall, John N.
  Obituary **2006**:4
Bailey, F. Lee **1995**:4
Bailey, Pearl
  Obituary **1991**:1
Baird, Bill
  Brief Entry **1987**:2
Baiul, Oksana **1995**:3
Baker, Anita **1987**:4
Baker, James A. III **1991**:2
Baker, Kathy
  Brief Entry **1986**:1
Bakker, Robert T. **1991**:3
Bakula, Scott **2003**:1

Baldessari, John **1991**:4
Baldrige, Malcolm
  Obituary **1988**:1
Baldwin, Alec **2002**:2
Baldwin, James
  Obituary **1988**:2
Ball, Alan **2005**:1
Ball, Edward **1999**:2
Ball, Lucille
  Obituary **1989**:3
Ballard, Robert D. **1998**:4
Ballmer, Steven **1997**:2
Bancroft, Anne
  Obituary **2006**:3
Banks, Dennis J. **1986**:4
Banks, Jeffrey **1998**:2
Banks, Tyra **1996**:3
Barad, Jill **1994**:2
Baraka, Amiri **2000**:3
Baranski, Christine **2001**:2
Barber, Red
  Obituary **1993**:2
Barbera, Joseph **1988**:2
Barkin, Ellen **1987**:3
Barkley, Charles **1988**:2
Barks, Carl
  Obituary **2001**:2
Barksdale, James L. **1998**:2
Barnes, Ernie **1997**:4
Barney **1993**:4
Barr, Roseanne **1989**:1
Barrett, Craig R. **1999**:4
Barry, Dave **1991**:2
Barry, Lynda **1992**:1
Barry, Marion **1991**:1
Barrymore, Drew **1995**:3
Barshefsky, Charlene **2000**:4
Baryshnikov, Mikhail Nikolaevich **1997**:3
Basie, Count
  Obituary **1985**:1
Basinger, Kim **1987**:2
Bassett, Angela **1994**:4
Bateman, Jason **2005**:3
Bateman, Justine **1988**:4
Bates, Kathy **1991**:4
Battle, Kathleen **1998**:1
Bauer, Eddie
  Obituary **1986**:3
Baumgartner, Bruce
  Brief Entry **1987**:3
Baxter, Anne
  Obituary **1986**:1
Bayley, Corrine
  Brief Entry **1986**:4
Beal, Deron **2005**:3
Beals, Jennifer **2005**:2
Beals, Vaughn **1988**:2
Beame, Abraham
  Obituary **2001**:4
Bean, Alan L. **1986**:2
Beattie, Owen
  Brief Entry **1985**:2
Beatty, Warren **2000**:1
Beck **2000**:2
Becker, Brian **2004**:4
Bedford, Deborah **2006**:3
Beene, Geoffrey
  Obituary **2005**:4
Beers, Charlotte **1999**:3
Begaye, Kelsey **1999**:3
Bell, Art **2000**:1

Bell, Ricky
  Obituary **1985**:1
Bellamy, Carol **2001**:2
Belle, Albert **1996**:4
Bellow, Saul
  Obituary **2006**:2
Belluzzo, Rick **2001**:3
Belushi, Jim **1986**:2
Belzer, Richard **1985**:3
Ben & Jerry **1991**:3
Benatar, Pat **1986**:1
Bening, Annette **1992**:1
Bennett, Joan
  Obituary **1991**:2
Bennett, Michael
  Obituary **1988**:1
Bennett, Tony **1994**:4
Bennett, William **1990**:1
Benoit, Joan **1986**:3
Benson, Ezra Taft
  Obituary **1994**:4
Bentsen, Lloyd **1993**:3
Bergalis, Kimberly
  Obituary **1992**:3
Bergen, Candice **1990**:1
Berger, Sandy **2000**:1
Berkley, Seth **2002**:3
Berle, Milton
  Obituary **2003**:2
Berle, Peter A.A.
  Brief Entry **1987**:3
Berlin, Irving
  Obituary **1990**:1
Berman, Gail **2006**:1
Berman, Jennifer and Laura **2003**:2
Bern, Dorrit J. **2006**:3
Bernardi, Herschel
  Obituary **1986**:4
Bernardin, Cardinal Joseph **1997**:2
Bernhard, Sandra **1989**:4
Bernsen, Corbin **1990**:2
Bernstein, Elmer
  Obituary **2005**:4
Bernstein, Leonard
  Obituary **1991**:1
Berresford, Susan V. **1998**:4
Berry, Chuck **2001**:2
Berry, Halle **1996**:2
Bethe, Hans
  Obituary **2006**:2
Bettelheim, Bruno
  Obituary **1990**:3
Bezos, Jeff **1998**:4
Bialik, Mayim **1993**:3
Bias, Len
  Obituary **1986**:3
Biden, Joe **1986**:3
Bieber, Owen **1986**:1
Biehl, Amy
  Obituary **1994**:1
Bigelow, Kathryn **1990**:4
Bikoff, James L.
  Brief Entry **1986**:2
Billington, James **1990**:3
Birch, Thora **2002**:4
Bird, Brad **2005**:4
Bird, Larry **1990**:3
Bishop, Andre **2000**:1
Bissell, Patrick
  Obituary **1988**:2
Bixby, Bill
  Obituary **1994**:2

Black, Carole **2003**:1
Black, Cathleen **1998**:4
Black, Jack **2002**:3
Black Eyed Peas **2006**:2
Blackmun, Harry A.
  Obituary **1999**:3
Blackstone, Harry Jr.
  Obituary **1997**:4
Blaine, David **2003**:3
Blair, Bonnie **1992**:3
Blakey, Art
  Obituary **1991**:1
Blanc, Mel
  Obituary **1989**:4
Blass, Bill
  Obituary **2003**:3
Bledsoe, Drew **1995**:1
Blige, Mary J. **1995**:3
Bloch, Erich **1987**:4
Bloch, Henry **1988**:4
Bloch, Ivan **1986**:3
Block, Herbert
  Obituary **2002**:4
Bloodworth-Thomason, Linda **1994**
  :1
Bloomberg, Michael **1997**:1
Blume, Judy **1998**:4
Bly, Robert **1992**:4
Blyth, Myrna **2002**:4
Bochco, Steven **1989**:1
Boehner, John A. **2006**:4
Boggs, Wade **1989**:3
Bogosian, Eric **1990**:4
Bohbot, Michele **2004**:2
Boiardi, Hector
  Obituary **1985**:3
Boies, David **2002**:1
Boitano, Brian **1988**:3
Bolger, Ray
  Obituary **1987**:2
Bollinger, Lee C. **2003**:2
Bolton, Michael **1993**:2
Bombeck, Erma
  Obituary **1996**:4
Bonds, Barry **1993**:3
Bonet, Lisa **1989**:2
Bonilla, Bobby **1992**:2
Bon Jovi, Jon **1987**:4
Bonner, Robert **2003**:4
Bono, Sonny **1992**:2
  Obituary **1998**:2
Bontecou, Lee **2004**:4
Boone, Mary **1985**:1
Booth, Shirley
  Obituary **1993**:2
Bopp, Thomas **1997**:3
Borofsky, Jonathan **2006**:4
Bose, Amar
  Brief Entry **1986**:4
Bosworth, Brian **1989**:1
Bosworth, Kate **2006**:3
Botstein, Leon **1985**:3
Boudreau, Louis
  Obituary **2002**:3
Bowe, Riddick **1993**:2
Bowles, Paul
  Obituary **2000**:3
Bowman, Scotty **1998**:4
Boxcar Willie
  Obituary **1999**:4
Boxer, Barbara **1995**:1
Boyer, Herbert Wayne **1985**:1

Boyington, Gregory 'Pappy'
  Obituary **1988**:2
Boyle, Gertrude **1995**:3
Boyle, Lara Flynn **2003**:4
Boyle, Peter **2002**:3
Boynton, Sandra **2004**:1
Bradford, Barbara Taylor **2002**:4
Bradley, Bill **2000**:2
Bradley, Todd **2003**:3
Bradley, Tom
  Obituary **1999**:1
Bradshaw, John **1992**:1
Brady, Sarah and James S. **1991**:4
Brady, Tom **2002**:4
Braff, Zach **2005**:2
Brando, Marlon
  Obituary **2005**:3
Brandy **1996**:4
Braun, Carol Moseley **1993**:1
Bravo, Ellen **1998**:2
Bravo, Rose Marie **2005**:3
Braxton, Toni **1994**:3
Brazile, Donna **2001**:1
Breathed, Berkeley **2005**:3
Bremen, Barry **1987**:3
Bremer, L. Paul **2004**:2
Brennan, Edward A. **1989**:1
Brennan, Robert E. **1988**:1
Brennan, William
  Obituary **1997**:4
Brenneman, Amy **2002**:1
Breyer, Stephen Gerald **1994**:4 **1997**
  :2
Bridges, Lloyd
  Obituary **1998**:3
Brinkley, David
  Obituary **2004**:3
Bristow, Lonnie **1996**:1
Brite, Poppy Z. **2005**:1
Brockovich-Ellis, Erin **2003**:3
Brody, Adrien **2006**:3
Brokaw, Tom **2000**:3
Bronfman, Edgar, Jr. **1994**:4
Bronson, Charles
  Obituary **2004**:4
Brooks, Albert **1991**:4
Brooks, Diana D. **1990**:1
Brooks, Garth **1992**:1
Brooks, Gwendolyn **1998**:1
  Obituary **2001**:2
Brooks, Mel **2003**:1
Brower, David **1990**:4
Brown, Bobbi **2001**:4
Brown, Dan **2004**:4
Brown, Dee
  Obituary **2004**:1
Brown, Edmund G., Sr.
  Obituary **1996**:3
Brown, J. Carter
  Obituary **2003**:3
Brown, James **1991**:4
Brown, Jerry **1992**:4
Brown, Jim **1993**:2
Brown, John Seely **2004**:1
Brown, Judie **1986**:2
Brown, Les **1994**:3
Brown, Les
  Obituary **2001**:3
Brown, Paul
  Obituary **1992**:1
Brown, Ron
  Obituary **1996**:4

Brown, Ron **1990**:3
Brown, Willie **1996**:4
Brown, Willie L. **1985**:2
Browner, Carol M. **1994**:1
Browning, Edmond
  Brief Entry **1986**:2
Bryant, Kobe **1998**:3
Brynner, Yul
  Obituary **1985**:4
Buchanan, Pat **1996**:3
Buck, Linda **2004**:2
Buckley, Betty **1996**:2
Buckley, Jeff
  Obituary **1997**:4
Buffett, Jimmy **1999**:3
Buffett, Warren **1995**:2
Bullock, Sandra **1995**:4
Bundy, McGeorge
  Obituary **1997**:1
Bundy, William P.
  Obituary **2001**:2
Bunshaft, Gordon **1989**:3
  Obituary **1991**:1
Burck, Wade
  Brief Entry **1986**:1
Burger, Warren E.
  Obituary **1995**:4
Burk, Martha **2004**:1
Burnett, Carol **2000**:3
Burnison, Chantal Simone **1988**:3
Burns, Charles R.
  Brief Entry **1988**:1
Burns, Edward **1997**:1
Burns, George
  Obituary **1996**:3
Burns, Ken **1995**:2
Burns, Robin **1991**:2
Burr, Donald Calvin **1985**:3
Burroughs, William S.
  Obituary **1997**:4
Burroughs, William S. **1994**:2
Burrows, James **2005**:3
Burstyn, Ellen **2001**:4
Burton, Tim **1993**:1
Burum, Stephen H.
  Brief Entry **1987**:2
Buscaglia, Leo
  Obituary **1998**:4
Buscemi, Steve **1997**:4
Busch, August A. III **1988**:2
Busch, August Anheuser, Jr.
  Obituary **1990**:2
Busch, Charles **1998**:3
Busch, Kurt **2006**:1
Bush, Barbara **1989**:3
Bush, George W., Jr. **1996**:4
Bush, Jeb **2003**:1
Bush, Millie **1992**:1
Bushnell, Candace **2004**:2
Bushnell, Nolan **1985**:1
Buss, Jerry **1989**:3
Butcher, Susan **1991**:1
Butler, Brett **1995**:1
Butler, Octavia E. **1999**:3
Butterfield, Paul
  Obituary **1987**:3
Bynes, Amanda **2005**:1
Caan, James **2004**:4
Caen, Herb
  Obituary **1997**:4
Caesar, Adolph
  Obituary **1986**:3

Cage, John
  Obituary **1993**:1
Cage, Nicolas **1991**:1
Cagney, James
  Obituary **1986**:2
Cain, Herman **1998**:3
Calhoun, Rory
  Obituary **1999**:4
Caliguiri, Richard S.
  Obituary **1988**:3
Callaway, Ely
  Obituary **2002**:3
Calloway, Cab
  Obituary **1995**:2
Calloway, D. Wayne **1987**:3
Cameron, David
  Brief Entry **1988**:1
Cammermeyer, Margarethe **1995**:2
Campanella, Roy
  Obituary **1994**:1
Campbell, Bebe Moore **1996**:2
Campbell, Ben Nighthorse **1998**:1
Campbell, Bill **1997**:1
Canfield, Alan B.
  Brief Entry **1986**:3
Cannon, Nick **2006**:4
Cantrell, Ed
  Brief Entry **1985**:3
Caplan, Arthur L. **2000**:2
Capriati, Jennifer **1991**:1
Caras, Roger
  Obituary **2002**:1
Caray, Harry **1988**:3
  Obituary **1998**:3
Carcaterra, Lorenzo **1996**:1
Card, Andrew H., Jr. **2003**:2
Carell, Steve **2006**:4
Carey, Drew **1997**:4
Carey, Mariah **1991**:3
Carey, Ron **1993**:3
Carlin, George **1996**:3
Carlisle, Belinda **1989**:3
Carlson, Richard **2002**:1
Carmona, Richard **2003**:2
Carnahan, Jean **2001**:2
Carnahan, Mel
  Obituary **2001**:2
Carney, Art
  Obituary **2005**:1
Carpenter, Mary-Chapin **1994**:1
Carradine, John
  Obituary **1989**:2
Carson, Ben **1998**:2
Carson, Johnny
  Obituary **2006**:1
Carson, Lisa Nicole **1999**:3
Carter, Amy **1987**:4
Carter, Benny
  Obituary **2004**:3
Carter, Billy
  Obituary **1989**:1
Carter, Chris **2000**:1
Carter, Gary **1987**:1
Carter, Jimmy **1995**:1
Carter, Joe **1994**:2
Carter, Nell
  Obituary **2004**:2
Carter, Ron **1987**:3
Carter, Rubin **2000**:3
Carter, Vince **2001**:4
Caruso, David **1994**:3
Carver, Raymond

  Obituary **1989**:1
Carvey, Dana **1994**:1
Case, Steve **1995**:4 **1996**:4
Casey, William
  Obituary **1987**:3
Cash, Johnny **1995**:3
Cash, June Carter
  Obituary **2004**:2
Cassavetes, John
  Obituary **1989**:2
Cassidy, Mike **2006**:1
Castelli, Leo
  Obituary **2000**:1
Castillo, Ana **2000**:4
Catlett, Elizabeth **1999**:3
Cattrall, Kim **2003**:3
Caulfield, Joan
  Obituary **1992**:1
Cavazos, Lauro F. **1989**:2
Caviezel, Jim **2005**:3
Cerf, Vinton G. **1999**:2
Chabon, Michael **2002**:1
Chaing Kai-Shek, Madame
  Obituary **2005**:1
Chamberlain, Wilt
  Obituary **2000**:2
Chamberlin, Wendy **2002**:4
Chancellor, John
  Obituary **1997**:1
Chaney, John **1989**:1
Channing, Stockard **1991**:3
Chapman, Tracy **1989**:2
Chappell, Tom **2002**:3
Chappelle, Dave **2005**:3
Charles, Ray
  Obituary **2005**:3
Charron, Paul **2004**:1
Chase, Chevy **1990**:1
Chast, Roz **1992**:4
Chastain, Brandi **2001**:3
Chatham, Russell **1990**:1
Chaudhari, Praveen **1989**:4
Chavez, Cesar
  Obituary **1993**:4
Chavez, Linda **1999**:3
Chavez-Thompson, Linda **1999**:1
Chavis, Benjamin **1993**:4
Cheadle, Don **2002**:1
Cheatham, Adolphus 'Doc'
  Obituary **1997**:4
Cheek, James Edward
  Brief Entry **1987**:1
Chenault, Kenneth I. **1999**:3
Cheney, Dick **1991**:3
Cheney, Lynne V. **1990**:4
Cher **1993**:1
Chia, Sandro **1987**:2
Chihuly, Dale **1995**:2
Chiklis, Michael **2003**:3
Child, Julia **1999**:4
Chisholm, Shirley
  Obituary **2006**:1
Chittister, Joan D. **2002**:2
Chizen, Bruce **2004**:2
Cho, Margaret **1995**:2
Chouinard, Yvon **2002**:2
Christopher, Warren **1996**:3
Chu, Paul C.W. **1988**:2
Chung, Connie **1988**:4
Chyna **2001**:4
Cisneros, Henry **1987**:2
Claiborne, Liz **1986**:3

Clancy, Tom **1998**:4
Clark, J. E.
  Brief Entry **1986**:1
Clark, Jim **1997**:1
Clark, Kenneth B.
  Obituary **2006**:3
Clark, Marcia **1995**:1
Clark, Mary Higgins **2000**:4
Clarke, Richard A. **2002**:2
Clarke, Stanley **1985**:4
Clarkson, Kelly **2003**:3
Clarkson, Patricia **2005**:3
Clavell, James
  Obituary **1995**:1
Clay, Andrew Dice **1991**:1
Cleaver, Eldridge
  Obituary **1998**:4
Clemens, Roger **1991**:4
Clements, George **1985**:1
Cleveland, James
  Obituary **1991**:3
Cliburn, Van **1995**:1
Clinton, Bill **1992**:1
Clinton, Hillary Rodham **1993**:2
Clooney, George **1996**:4
Clooney, Rosemary
  Obituary **2003**:4
Close, Glenn **1988**:3
Clyburn, James **1999**:4
Cobain, Kurt
  Obituary **1994**:3
Coburn, James
  Obituary **2004**:1
Coca, Imogene
  Obituary **2002**:2
Cochran, Johnnie **1996**:1
Coco, James
  Obituary **1987**:2
Codrescu, Andreá **1997**:3
Coen, Joel and Ethan **1992**:1
Coffin, William Sloane, Jr. **1990**:3
Cohen, William S. **1998**:1
Colasanto, Nicholas
  Obituary **1985**:2
Colby, William E.
  Obituary **1996**:4
Cole, Johnetta B. **1994**:3
Cole, Kenneth **2003**:1
Cole, Natalie **1992**:4
Coleman, Dabney **1988**:3
Coleman, Sheldon, Jr. **1990**:2
Coles, Robert **1995**:1
Collier, Sophia **2001**:2
Collins, Albert
  Obituary **1994**:2
Collins, Billy **2002**:2
Collins, Cardiss **1995**:3
Collins, Eileen **1995**:3
Collins, Kerry **2002**:3
Colwell, Rita Rossi **1999**:3
Combs, Sean 'Puffy' **1998**:4
Commager, Henry Steele
  Obituary **1998**:3
Como, Perry
  Obituary **2002**:2
Condit, Phil **2001**:3
Condon, Richard
  Obituary **1996**:4
Conigliaro, Tony
  Obituary **1990**:3
Connally, John
  Obituary **1994**:1

Kirk, David **2004**:1
Kissinger, Henry **1999**:4
Kissling, Frances **1989**:2
Kistler, Darci **1993**:1
Kite, Tom **1990**:3
Klass, Perri **1993**:2
Klein, Calvin **1996**:2
Kline, Kevin **2000**:1
Kloss, Henry E.
  Brief Entry **1985**:2
Kluge, John **1991**:1
Knievel, Robbie **1990**:1
Knight, Bobby **1985**:3
Knight, Philip H. **1994**:1
Knight, Ted
  Obituary **1986**:4
Knight, Wayne **1997**:1
Knowles, John
  Obituary **2003**:1
Koch, Bill **1992**:3
Koch, Jim **2004**:3
Kohnstamm, Abby **2001**:1
Koogle, Tim **2000**:4
Koons, Jeff **1991**:4
Koontz, Dean **1999**:3
Koop, C. Everett **1989**:3
Kopits, Steven E.
  Brief Entry **1987**:1
Koplovitz, Kay **1986**:3
Kopp, Wendy **1993**:3
Koppel, Ted **1989**:1
Kordich, Jay **1993**:2
Koresh, David
  Obituary **1993**:4
Kornberg, Arthur **1992**:1
Kors, Michael **2000**:4
Kostabi, Mark **1989**:4
Kostova, Elizabeth **2006**:2
Kovacevich, Dick **2004**:3
Kozinski, Alex **2002**:2
Kozol, Jonathan **1992**:1
Kramer, Larry **1991**:2
Kramer, Stanley
  Obituary **2002**:1
Krantz, Judith **2003**:1
Kravitz, Lenny **1991**:1
Krim, Mathilde **1989**:2
Kroc, Ray
  Obituary **1985**:1
Krol, John
  Obituary **1996**:3
Kroll, Alexander S. **1989**:3
Krone, Julie **1989**:2
Kruk, John **1994**:4
Krzyzewski, Mike **1993**:2
Kubler-Ross, Elisabeth
  Obituary **2005**:4
Kubrick, Stanley
  Obituary **1999**:3
Kudrow, Lisa **1996**:1
Kulp, Nancy
  Obituary **1991**:3
Kunitz, Stanley J. **2001**:2
Kunstler, William **1992**:3
Kunstler, William
  Obituary **1996**:1
Kuralt, Charles
  Obituary **1998**:3
Kurzban, Ira **1987**:2
Kurzweil, Raymond **1986**:3
Kushner, Tony **1995**:2
Kutcher, Ashton **2003**:4

Kwoh, Yik San **1988**:2
Kyser, Kay
  Obituary **1985**:3
Lachey, Nick and Jessica Simpson
  2004:4
LaDuke, Winona **1995**:2
Laettner, Christian **1993**:1
Lafley, A. G. **2003**:4
LaFontaine, Pat **1985**:1
Lagasse, Emeril **1998**:3
Lahiri, Jhumpa **2001**:3
Lahti, Christine **1988**:2
Laimbeer, Bill **2004**:3
Lake, Ricki **1994**:4
Lalas, Alexi **1995**:1
Lamb, Wally **1999**:1
Lamour, Dorothy
  Obituary **1997**:1
L'Amour, Louis
  Obituary **1988**:4
Lancaster, Burt
  Obituary **1995**:1
Land, Edwin H.
  Obituary **1991**:3
Lander, Toni
  Obituary **1985**:4
Landers, Ann
  Obituary **2003**:3
Landon, Alf
  Obituary **1988**:1
Landon, Michael
  Obituary **1992**:1
Landrieu, Mary L. **2002**:2
Landry, Tom
  Obituary **2000**:3
Lane, Burton
  Obituary **1997**:2
Lane, Diane **2006**:2
Lane, Nathan **1996**:4
Lang, Eugene M. **1990**:3
Lange, Jessica **1995**:4
Lange, Liz **2003**:4
Langer, Robert **2003**:4
Langevin, James R. **2001**:2
Langston, J. William
  Brief Entry **1986**:2
Lanier, Jaron **1993**:4
Lansbury, Angela **1993**:1
Lansdale, Edward G.
  Obituary **1987**:2
Lansing, Sherry **1995**:4
Lanza, Robert **2004**:3
LaPaglia, Anthony **2004**:4
Lardner Jr., Ring
  Obituary **2001**:2
Larroquette, John **1986**:2
Larson, Jonathan
  Obituary **1997**:2
LaSalle, Eriq **1996**:4
Lauder, Estee **1992**:2
Lauper, Cyndi **1985**:1
Lauren, Ralph **1990**:1
Lawless, Lucy **1997**:4
Lawrence, Martin **1993**:4
Laybourne, Geraldine **1997**:1
Lazarus, Charles **1992**:4
Lazarus, Shelly **1998**:3
Lear, Frances **1988**:3
Leary, Denis **1993**:3
Leary, Timothy
  Obituary **1996**:4
LeBlanc, Matt **2005**:4

Lederman, Leon Max **1989**:4
Lee, Brandon
  Obituary **1993**:4
Lee, Chang-Rae **2005**:1
Lee, Henry C. **1997**:1
Lee, Jason **2006**:4
Lee, Pamela **1996**:4
Lee, Peggy
  Obituary **2003**:1
Lee, Spike **1988**:4
Leguizamo, John **1999**:1
Lehane, Dennis **2001**:4
Leibovitz, Annie **1988**:4
Leigh, Janet
  Obituary **2005**:4
Leigh, Jennifer Jason **1995**:2
Lelyveld, Joseph S. **1994**:4
Lemmon, Jack **1998**:4
  Obituary **2002**:3
Lemon, Ted
  Brief Entry **1986**:4
LeMond, Greg **1986**:4
Leno, Jay **1987**:1
Leonard, Elmore **1998**:4
Leonard, Sugar Ray **1989**:4
Lepore, Nanette **2006**:4
Lerner, Michael **1994**:2
Lerner, Sandy **2005**:1
Leslie, Lisa **1997**:4
Letterman, David **1989**:3
Levin, Gerald **1995**:2
Levine, Arnold **2002**:3
Levine, James **1992**:3
Levinson, Barry **1989**:3
Levitt, Arthur **2004**:2
Lewis, Edward B.
  Obituary **2005**:4
Lewis, Edward T. **1999**:4
Lewis, Henry
  Obituary **1996**:3
Lewis, Huey **1987**:3
Lewis, John
  Obituary **2002**:1
Lewis, Juliette **1999**:3
Lewis, Loida Nicolas **1998**:3
Lewis, Ray **2001**:3
Lewis, Reggie
  Obituary **1994**:1
Lewis, Reginald F. **1988**:4
  Obituary **1993**:3
Lewis, Richard **1992**:1
Lewis, Shari **1993**:1
  Obituary **1999**:1
LeWitt, Sol **2001**:2
Lewitzky, Bella
  Obituary **2005**:3
Leyland, Jim **1998**:2
Liberace
  Obituary **1987**:2
Libeskind, Daniel **2004**:1
Lichtenstein, Roy **1994**:1
  Obituary **1998**:1
Lieberman, Joseph **2001**:1
Lightner, Candy **1985**:1
Liguori, Peter **2005**:2
Lilly, John C.
  Obituary **2002**:4
Liman, Arthur **1989**:4
Limbaugh, Rush **1991**:3
Lin, Maya **1990**:3
Lincoln, Blanche **2003**:1
Lindbergh, Anne Morrow

Obituary **2001**:4
Lindros, Eric **1992**:1
Lindsay, John V.
    Obituary **2001**:3
Lines, Ray **2004**:1
Ling, Bai **2000**:3
Ling, Lisa **2004**:2
Lipinski, Tara **1998**:3
Lipkis, Andy
    Brief Entry **1985**:3
Lipsig, Harry H. **1985**:1
Lipton, Martin **1987**:3
Lisick, Beth **2006**:2
Lithgow, John **1985**:2
Little, Benilde **2006**:2
Little, Cleavon
    Obituary **1993**:2
Liu, Lucy **2000**:4
LL Cool J **1998**:2
Lobell, Jeanine **2002**:3
Locklear, Heather **1994**:3
Lodge, Henry Cabot
    Obituary **1985**:1
Loewe, Frederick
    Obituary **1988**:2
Lofton, Kenny **1998**:1
Logan, Joshua
    Obituary **1988**:4
Lohan, Lindsay **2005**:3
Long, Nia **2001**:3
Long, Shelley **1985**:1
Longo, Robert **1990**:4
Lopes, Lisa
    Obituary **2003**:3
Lopez, George **2003**:4
Lopez, Jennifer **1998**:4
Lopez, Nancy **1989**:3
Lord, Bette Bao **1994**:1
Lord, Jack
    Obituary **1998**:2
Lord, Winston
    Brief Entry **1987**:4
Lords, Traci **1995**:4
Lott, Trent **1998**:1
Louganis, Greg **1995**:3
Louis-Dreyfus, Julia **1994**:1
Louv, Richard **2006**:2
Love, Courtney **1995**:1
Love, Susan **1995**:2
Loveless, Patty **1998**:2
Lovett, Lyle **1994**:1
Lovley, Derek **2005**:3
Lowe, Edward **1990**:2
Lowe, Rob **1990**:4
Lowell, Mike **2003**:2
Loy, Myrna
    Obituary **1994**:2
Lucas, George **1999**:4
Lucci, Susan **1999**:4
Luce, Clare Boothe
    Obituary **1988**:1
Lucid, Shannon **1997**:1
Lucke, Lewis **2004**:4
Ludlum, Robert
    Obituary **2002**:1
Lukas, D. Wayne **1986**:2
Lupino, Ida
    Obituary **1996**:1
Lutz, Robert A. **1990**:1
Lynch, David **1990**:4
Lyne, Susan **2005**:4
Lynn, Loretta **2001**:1

Mac, Bernie **2003**:1
MacCready, Paul **1986**:4
MacDonald, Laurie and Walter
    Parkes **2004**:1
MacDowell, Andie **1993**:4
MacFarlane, Seth **2006**:1
Mack, John J. **2006**:3
MacKinnon, Catharine **1993**:2
MacMurray, Fred
    Obituary **1992**:1
MacNelly, Jeff
    Obituary **2000**:4
MacRae, Gordon
    Obituary **1986**:2
Macy, William H. **1999**:3
Madden, Chris **2006**:1
Madden, John **1995**:1
Maddux, Greg **1996**:2
Madonna **1985**:2
Maglich, Bogdan C. **1990**:1
Magliozzi, Tom and Ray **1991**:4
Maguire, Tobey **2002**:2
Maher, Bill **1996**:2
Mahony, Roger M. **1988**:2
Maida, Adam Cardinal **1998**:2
Mailer, Norman **1998**:1
Majerle, Dan **1993**:4
Malkovich, John **1988**:2
Malloy, Edward 'Monk' **1989**:4
Malone, John C. **1988**:3 **1996**:3
Malone, Karl **1990**:1 **1997**:3
Maltby, Richard, Jr. **1996**:3
Mamet, David **1998**:4
Manchin, Joe **2006**:4
Mancini, Henry
    Obituary **1994**:4
Mankiller, Wilma P.
    Brief Entry **1986**:2
Mann, Sally **2001**:2
Mansfield, Mike
    Obituary **2002**:4
Mansion, Gracie
    Brief Entry **1986**:3
Manson, Marilyn **1999**:4
Mantegna, Joe **1992**:1
Mantle, Mickey
    Obituary **1996**:1
Mapplethorpe, Robert
    Obituary **1989**:3
Maraldo, Pamela J. **1993**:4
Maravich, Pete
    Obituary **1988**:2
Marchand, Nancy
    Obituary **2001**:1
Marcus, Stanley
    Obituary **2003**:1
Marier, Rebecca **1995**:4
Marin, Cheech **2000**:1
Marineau, Philip **2002**:4
Maris, Roger
    Obituary **1986**:1
Mark, Mary Ellen **2006**:2
Marky Mark **1993**:3
Marriott, J. Willard
    Obituary **1985**:4
Marriott, J. Willard, Jr. **1985**:4
Marsalis, Branford **1988**:3
Marsalis, Wynton **1997**:4
Marshall, Penny **1991**:3
Marshall, Susan **2000**:4
Marshall, Thurgood
    Obituary **1993**:3

Martin, Agnes
    Obituary **2006**:1
Martin, Billy **1988**:4
    Obituary **1990**:2
Martin, Casey **2002**:1
Martin, Dean
    Obituary **1996**:2
Martin, Dean Paul
    Obituary **1987**:3
Martin, Judith **2000**:3
Martin, Lynn **1991**:4
Martin, Mary
    Obituary **1991**:2
Martin, Steve **1992**:2
Martinez, Bob **1992**:1
Marvin, Lee
    Obituary **1988**:1
Mas Canosa, Jorge
    Obituary **1998**:2
Master P **1999**:4
Masters, William H.
    Obituary **2001**:4
Matalin, Mary **1995**:2
Mathews, Dan **1998**:3
Mathis, Clint **2003**:1
Matlin, Marlee **1992**:2
Matlovich, Leonard P.
    Obituary **1988**:4
Matthau, Walter **2000**:3
Matthews, Dave **1999**:3
Mattingly, Don **1986**:2
Matuszak, John
    Obituary **1989**:4
Mauldin, Bill
    Obituary **2004**:2
Maxwell, Hamish **1989**:4
Mayes, Frances **2004**:3
Maynard, Joyce **1999**:4
McAuliffe, Christa
    Obituary **1985**:4
McCain, John S. **1998**:4
McCall, Nathan **1994**:4
McCarron, Chris **1995**:4
McCarthy, Carolyn **1998**:4
McCarthy, Jenny **1997**:4
McCartney, Bill **1995**:3
McCartney, Linda
    Obituary **1998**:4
McCloskey, J. Michael **1988**:2
McCloskey, James **1993**:1
McCloy, John J.
    Obituary **1989**:3
McColough, C. Peter **1990**:2
McConaughey, Matthew David **1997**:1
McCourt, Frank **1997**:4
McCrea, Joel
    Obituary **1991**:1
McDermott, Alice **1999**:2
McDonald, Camille **2004**:1
McDonnell, Sanford N. **1988**:4
McDonough, William **2003**:1
McDormand, Frances **1997**:3
McDougall, Ron **2001**:4
McDuffie, Robert **1990**:2
McElligott, Thomas J. **1987**:4
McEntire, Reba **1987**:3 **1994**:2
McFarlane, Todd **1999**:1
McFerrin, Bobby **1989**:1
McGillis, Kelly **1989**:3
McGinley, Ted **2004**:4
McGowan, William **1985**:2

McGowan, William G.
  Obituary **1993**:1
McGrath, Judy **2006**:1
McGraw, Phil **2005**:2
McGraw, Tim **2000**:3
McGraw, Tug
  Obituary **2005**:1
McGreevey, James **2005**:2
McGruder, Aaron **2005**:4
McGuire, Dorothy
  Obituary **2002**:4
McGwire, Mark **1999**:1
McIntyre, Richard
  Brief Entry **1986**:2
McKee, Lonette **1996**:1
McKenna, Terence **1993**:3
McKinney, Cynthia A. **1997**:1
McKinney, Stewart B.
  Obituary **1987**:4
McLaughlin, Betsy **2004**:3
McMahon, Jim **1985**:4
McMahon, Vince, Jr. **1985**:4
McMillan, Terry **1993**:2
McMillen, Tom **1988**:4
McMurtry, James **1990**:2
McMurtry, Larry **2006**:4
McNamara, Robert S. **1995**:4
McNealy, Scott **1999**:4
McNerney, W. James **2006**:3
McRae, Carmen
  Obituary **1995**:2
McSally, Martha **2002**:4
McVeigh, Timothy
  Obituary **2002**:2
Meadows, Audrey
  Obituary **1996**:3
Meier, Richard **2001**:4
Meisel, Steven **2002**:4
Mellinger, Frederick
  Obituary **1990**:4
Mello, Dawn **1992**:2
Mellon, Paul
  Obituary **1999**:3
Melman, Richard
  Brief Entry **1986**:1
Meltzer, Brad **2005**:4
Mengers, Sue **1985**:3
Menninger, Karl
  Obituary **1991**:1
Menuhin, Yehudi
  Obituary **1999**:3
Merchant, Ismail
  Obituary **2006**:3
Merchant, Natalie **1996**:3
Meredith, Burgess
  Obituary **1998**:1
Merkerson, S. Epatha **2006**:4
Merrick, David
  Obituary **2000**:4
Merrill, James
  Obituary **1995**:3
Merritt, Justine
  Brief Entry **1985**:3
Messick, Dale
  Obituary **2006**:2
Messing, Debra **2004**:4
Metallica **2004**:2
Meyers, Nancy **2006**:1
Mfume, Kweisi **1996**:3
Michelman, Kate **1998**:4
Michener, James A.
  Obituary **1998**:1

Mickelson, Phil **2004**:4
Midler, Bette **1989**:4
Mikan, George
  Obituary **2006**:3
Mikulski, Barbara **1992**:4
Milano, Alyssa **2002**:3
Milbrett, Tiffeny **2001**:1
Milburn, Rodney Jr.
  Obituary **1998**:2
Milland, Ray
  Obituary **1986**:2
Millard, Barbara J.
  Brief Entry **1985**:3
Miller, Andre **2003**:3
Miller, Ann
  Obituary **2005**:2
Miller, Arthur **1999**:4
Miller, Bebe **2000**:2
Miller, Bode **2002**:4
Miller, Dennis **1992**:4
Miller, Merton H.
  Obituary **2001**:1
Miller, Nicole **1995**:4
Miller, Rand **1995**:4
Miller, Reggie **1994**:4
Miller, Roger
  Obituary **1993**:2
Miller, Sue **1999**:3
Mills, Malia **2003**:1
Mills, Wilbur
  Obituary **1992**:4
Milosz, Czeslaw
  Obituary **2005**:4
Minner, Ruth Ann **2002**:2
Minnesota Fats
  Obituary **1996**:3
Minsky, Marvin **1994**:3
Misrach, Richard **1991**:2
Mitchell, Arthur **1995**:1
Mitchell, George J. **1989**:3
Mitchell, John
  Obituary **1989**:2
Mitchell, Joni **1991**:4
Mitchelson, Marvin **1989**:2
Mitchum, Robert
  Obituary **1997**:4
Mizrahi, Isaac **1991**:1
Moakley, Joseph
  Obituary **2002**:2
Moby **2000**:1
Mohajer, Dineh **1997**:3
Molinari, Susan **1996**:4
Monaghan, Tom **1985**:1
Mondavi, Robert **1989**:2
Monica **2004**:2
Monk, Art **1993**:2
Monroe, Bill
  Obituary **1997**:1
Monroe, Rose Will
  Obituary **1997**:4
Montana, Joe **1989**:2
Montgomery, Elizabeth
  Obituary **1995**:4
Moody, John **1985**:3
Moody, Rick **2002**:2
Moog, Robert
  Obituary **2006**:4
Moon, Warren **1991**:3
Moonves, Les **2004**:2
Moore, Archie
  Obituary **1999**:2
Moore, Clayton

Obituary **2000**:3
Moore, Demi **1991**:4
Moore, Julianne **1998**:1
Moore, Mandy **2004**:2
Moore, Mary Tyler **1996**:2
Moore, Michael **1990**:3
Moose, Charles **2003**:4
Moreno, Arturo **2005**:2
Morgan, Dodge **1987**:1
Morgan, Robin **1991**:1
Morita, Noriyuki 'Pat' **1987**:3
Moritz, Charles **1989**:3
Morris, Dick **1997**:3
Morris, Doug **2005**:1
Morris, Kathryn **2006**:4
Morris, Mark **1991**:1
Morrison, Sterling
  Obituary **1996**:1
Morrison, Toni **1998**:1
Morrison, Trudi
  Brief Entry **1986**:2
Morrow, Rob **2006**:4
Mortensen, Viggo **2003**:3
Mosbacher, Georgette **1994**:2
Mos Def **2005**:4
Mosley, Walter **2003**:4
Moss, Cynthia **1995**:2
Moss, Randy **1999**:3
Motherwell, Robert
  Obituary **1992**:1
Mott, William Penn, Jr. **1986**:1
Mottola, Tommy **2002**:1
Mourning, Alonzo **1994**:2
Moyers, Bill **1991**:4
Moynihan, Daniel Patrick
  Obituary **2004**:2
Mulcahy, Anne M. **2003**:2
Muldowney, Shirley **1986**:1
Mulkey-Robertson, Kim **2006**:1
Mullis, Kary **1995**:3
Mumford, Lewis
  Obituary **1990**:2
Muniz, Frankie **2001**:4
Murdoch, Rupert **1988**:4
Murphy, Brittany **2005**:1
Murphy, Eddie **1989**:2
Murray, Arthur
  Obituary **1991**:3
Murray, Bill **2002**:4
Musburger, Brent **1985**:1
Muskie, Edmund S.
  Obituary **1996**:3
Mydans, Carl
  Obituary **2005**:4
Nader, Ralph **1989**:4
Nance, Jack
  Obituary **1997**:3
Napolitano, Janet **1997**:1
Natsios, Andrew **2005**:1
Nauman, Bruce **1995**:4
Navratilova, Martina **1989**:1
Neal, James Foster **1986**:2
Nechita, Alexandra **1996**:4
Neeleman, David **2003**:3
Neiman, LeRoy **1993**:3
Nelson, Gaylord A.
  Obituary **2006**:3
Nelson, Harriet
  Obituary **1995**:1
Nelson, Rick
  Obituary **1986**:1
Nelson, Willie **1993**:4

Stallings, George A., Jr. **1990**:1
Stallone, Sylvester **1994**:2
Staples, Roebuck 'Pops'
    Obituary **2001**:3
Stargell, Willie
    Obituary **2002**:1
Starr, Kenneth **1998**:3
Steel, Danielle **1999**:2
Steel, Dawn **1990**:1
    Obituary **1998**:2
Steele, Shelby **1991**:2
Stefani, Gwen **2005**:4
Steger, Will **1990**:4
Steig, William
    Obituary **2004**:4
Steiger, Rod
    Obituary **2003**:4
Stein, Ben **2001**:1
Steinberg, Leigh **1987**:3
Steinbrenner, George **1991**:1
Steinem, Gloria **1996**:2
Stella, Frank **1996**:2
Stempel, Robert **1991**:3
Stephanopoulos, George **1994**:3
Sterling, Bruce **1995**:4
Stern, David **1991**:4
Stern, Howard **1988**:2 **1993**:3
Stern, Isaac
    Obituary **2002**:4
Stevens, Anne **2006**:3
Stevens, Eileen **1987**:3
Stevenson, McLean
    Obituary **1996**:3
Stewart, Dave **1991**:1
Stewart, Jimmy
    Obituary **1997**:4
Stewart, Jon **2001**:2
Stewart, Martha **1992**:1
Stewart, Payne
    Obituary **2000**:2
Stewart, Potter
    Obituary **1986**:1
Stewart, Tony **2003**:4
Stiles, Julia **2002**:3
Stiller, Ben **1999**:1
Stine, R. L. **2003**:1
Stockton, John Houston **1997**:3
Stofflet, Ty
    Brief Entry **1987**:1
Stokes, Carl
    Obituary **1996**:4
Stone, I.F.
    Obituary **1990**:1
Stone, Irving
    Obituary **1990**:2
Stone, Oliver **1990**:4
Stone, Sharon **1993**:4
Stonesifer, Patty **1997**:1
Strait, George **1998**:3
Strange, Curtis **1988**:4
Strauss, Robert **1991**:4
Streep, Meryl **1990**:2
Street, Picabo **1999**:3
Streisand, Barbra **1992**:2
Stritch, Elaine **2002**:4
Stroh, Peter W. **1985**:2
Stroman, Susan **2000**:4
Strug, Kerri **1997**:3
Studi, Wes **1994**:3
Styne, Jule
    Obituary **1995**:1
Suarez, Xavier

Brief Entry **1986**:2
Sui, Anna **1995**:1
Sullivan, Leon
    Obituary **2002**:2
Sullivan, Louis **1990**:4
Sulzberger, Arthur O., Jr. **1998**:3
Summitt, Pat **2004**:1
Sun Ra
    Obituary **1994**:1
Sununu, John **1989**:2
Susskind, David
    Obituary **1987**:2
Swaggart, Jimmy **1987**:3
Swank, Hilary **2000**:3
Swanson, Mary Catherine **2002**:2
Swayze, John Cameron
    Obituary **1996**:1
Sweeney, John J. **2000**:3
Swift, Jane **2002**:1
Swoopes, Sheryl **1998**:2
System of a Down **2006**:4
Szent-Gyoergyi, Albert
    Obituary **1987**:2
Tafel, Richard **2000**:4
Tagliabue, Paul **1990**:2
Tan, Amy **1998**:3
Tandy, Jessica **1990**:4
    Obituary **1995**:1
Tannen, Deborah **1995**:1
Tanny, Vic
    Obituary **1985**:3
Tarantino, Quentin **1995**:1
Tarkenian, Jerry **1990**:4
Tartakovsky, Genndy **2004**:4
Tartikoff, Brandon **1985**:2
    Obituary **1998**:1
Tartt, Donna **2004**:3
Taylor, Jeff **2001**:3
Taylor, Lawrence **1987**:3
Taylor, Lili **2000**:2
Taylor, Maxwell
    Obituary **1987**:3
Taylor, Paul **1992**:3
Taylor, Susan L. **1998**:2
Tellem, Nancy **2004**:4
Tenet, George **2000**:3
Terry, Randall **1991**:4
Tesh, John **1996**:3
Testaverde, Vinny **1987**:2
Teter, Hannah **2006**:4
Thalheimer, Richard
    Brief Entry **1988**:3
Tharp, Twyla **1992**:4
Thiebaud, Wayne **1991**:1
Thomas, Clarence **1992**:2
Thomas, Danny
    Obituary **1991**:3
Thomas, Dave **1986**:2 **1993**:2
    Obituary **2003**:1
Thomas, Debi **1987**:2
Thomas, Derrick
    Obituary **2000**:3
Thomas, Edmond J. **2005**:1
Thomas, Frank **1994**:3
Thomas, Helen **1988**:4
Thomas, Isiah **1989**:2
Thomas, Michael Tilson **1990**:3
Thomas, Michel **1987**:4
Thomas, Thurman **1993**:1
Thompson, Fred **1998**:2
Thompson, Hunter S. **1992**:1
Thompson, John **1988**:3

Thompson, John W. **2005**:1
Thompson, Lonnie **2003**:3
Thompson, Starley
    Brief Entry **1987**:3
Thomson, James **2002**:3
Thornton, Billy Bob **1997**:4
Thurman, Uma **1994**:2
Thurmond, Strom
    Obituary **2004**:3
Tiffany **1989**:1
Tillman, Robert L. **2004**:1
Tillstrom, Burr
    Obituary **1986**:1
Tilly, Jennifer **1997**:2
Tisch, Laurence A. **1988**:2
Tito, Dennis **2002**:1
TLC **1996**:1
Tom and Ray Magliozzi **1991**:4
Tomei, Marisa **1995**:2
Tompkins, Susie
    Brief Entry **1987**:2
Tone-Loc **1990**:3
Toomer, Ron **1990**:1
Toone, Bill
    Brief Entry **1987**:2
Torme, Mel
    Obituary **1999**:4
Torre, Joseph Paul **1997**:1
Totenberg, Nina **1992**:2
Tower, John
    Obituary **1991**:4
Townsend, Kathleen Kennedy **2001**:3
Trask, Amy **2003**:3
Traub, Marvin
    Brief Entry **1987**:3
Travis, Randy **1988**:4
Travolta, John **1995**:2
Treybig, James G. **1988**:3
Tribe, Laurence H. **1988**:1
Tritt, Travis **1995**:1
Trotman, Alex **1995**:4
Trotter, Charlie **2000**:4
Troutt, Kenny A. **1998**:1
Trudeau, Garry **1991**:2
Truitt, Anne **1993**:1
Trump, Donald **1989**:2
Tsongas, Paul Efthemios
    Obituary **1997**:2
Tucci, Stanley **2003**:2
Tuck, Lily **2006**:1
Tucker, Chris **1999**:1
Tucker, Forrest
    Obituary **1987**:1
Tully, Tim **2004**:3
Tune, Tommy **1994**:2
Ture, Kwame
    Obituary **1999**:2
Turlington, Christy **2001**:4
Turner, Janine **1993**:2
Turner, Kathleen **1985**:3
Turner, Lana
    Obituary **1996**:1
Turner, Ted **1989**:1
Turner, Tina **2000**:3
Turturro, John **2002**:2
Tutwiler, Margaret **1992**:4
Twitty, Conway
    Obituary **1994**:1
Twombley, Cy **1995**:1
Tyler, Anne **1995**:4
Tyler, Liv **1997**:2

Williams, Vanessa L. **1999**:2
Williams, Venus **1998**:2
Williams, Willie L. **1993**:1
Williamson, Marianne **1991**:4
Willis, Bruce **1986**:4
Willson, S. Brian **1989**:3
Wilson, August **2002**:2
Wilson, Brian **1996**:1
Wilson, Carl
  Obituary **1998**:2
Wilson, Cassandra **1996**:3
Wilson, Edward O. **1994**:4
Wilson, Flip
  Obituary **1999**:2
Wilson, Gretchen **2006**:3
Wilson, Jerry
  Brief Entry **1986**:2
Wilson, Owen **2002**:3
Wilson, Pete **1992**:3
Wilson, William Julius **1997**:1
Winans, CeCe **2000**:1
Winfield, Paul
  Obituary **2005**:2
Winfrey, Oprah **1986**:4 **1997**:3
Winger, Debra **1994**:3
Winick, Judd **2005**:3
Winokur, Marissa Jaret **2005**:1
Winston, George **1987**:1
Winter, Paul **1990**:2
Wise, Robert
  Obituary **2006**:4
Witherspoon, Reese **2002**:1
Witkin, Joel-Peter **1996**:1
Witten, Edward **2006**:2
Wolf, Naomi **1994**:3
Wolf, Stephen M. **1989**:3
Wolfe, Tom **1999**:2
Wolff, Tobias **2005**:1
Wolfman Jack
  Obituary **1996**:1
Womack, Lee Ann **2002**:1
Wong, B.D. **1998**:1
Wood, Elijah **2002**:4
Woodard, Lynette **1986**:2
Woodcock, Leonard
  Obituary **2001**:4
Woodruff, Robert Winship
  Obituary **1985**:1
Woods, James **1988**:3
Woods, Tiger **1995**:4
Woodson, Ron **1996**:4
Woodwell, George S. **1987**:2
Worth, Irene
  Obituary **2003**:2
Worthy, James **1991**:2
Wright, Steven **1986**:3
Wright, Will **2003**:4
Wrigley, William, Jr. **2002**:2
Wu, Harry **1996**:1
Wyle, Noah **1997**:3
Wynette, Tammy
  Obituary **1998**:3
Wynn, Keenan
  Obituary **1987**:1
Wynn, Stephen A. **1994**:3
Wynonna **1993**:3
Xzibit **2005**:4
Yamaguchi, Kristi **1992**:3
Yamasaki, Minoru
  Obituary **1986**:2
Yankovic, 'Weird Al' **1985**:4
Yankovic, Frank

  Obituary **1999**:2
Yard, Molly **1991**:4
Yeager, Chuck **1998**:1
Yearwood, Trisha **1999**:1
Yetnikoff, Walter **1988**:1
Yoakam, Dwight **1992**:4
Yokich, Stephen P. **1995**:4
York, Dick
  Obituary **1992**:4
Young, Coleman A.
  Obituary **1998**:1
Young, Loretta
  Obituary **2001**:1
Young, Robert
  Obituary **1999**:1
Young, Steve **1995**:2
Youngblood, Johnny Ray **1994**:1
Youngman, Henny
  Obituary **1998**:3
Zagat, Tim and Nina **2004**:3
Zahn, Paula **1992**:3
Zamboni, Frank J.
  Brief Entry **1986**:4
Zamora, Pedro
  Obituary **1995**:2
Zanker, Bill
  Brief Entry **1987**:3
Zanuck, Lili Fini **1994**:2
Zappa, Frank
  Obituary **1994**:2
Zech, Lando W.
  Brief Entry **1987**:4
Zellweger, Renee **2001**:1
Zemeckis, Robert **2002**:1
Zerhouni, Elias A. **2004**:3
Zetcher, Arnold B. **2002**:1
Zevon, Warren
  Obituary **2004**:4
Ziff, William B., Jr. **1986**:4
Zigler, Edward **1994**:1
Zinnemann, Fred
  Obituary **1997**:3
Zinni, Anthony **2003**:1
Zito, Barry **2003**:3
Zucker, Jeff **1993**:3
Zucker, Jerry **2002**:2
Zuckerman, Mortimer **1986**:3
Zwilich, Ellen **1990**:1

ANGOLAN
Savimbi, Jonas **1986**:2 **1994**:2

ARGENTINIAN
Barenboim, Daniel **2001**:1
Bocca, Julio **1995**:3
Duhalde, Eduardo **2003**:3
Herrera, Paloma **1996**:2
Maradona, Diego **1991**:3
Pelli, Cesar **1991**:4
Sabatini, Gabriela
  Brief Entry **1985**:4
Timmerman, Jacobo
  Obituary **2000**:3

AUSTRALIAN
Allen, Peter
  Obituary **1993**:1
Anderson, Judith
  Obituary **1992**:3
Bee Gees, The **1997**:4
Blanchett, Cate **1999**:3

Bond, Alan **1989**:2
Bradman, Sir Donald
  Obituary **2002**:1
Clavell, James
  Obituary **1995**:1
Freeman, Cathy **2001**:3
Gibb, Andy
  Obituary **1988**:3
Gibson, Mel **1990**:1
Helfgott, David **1997**:2
Hewitt, Lleyton **2002**:2
Hughes, Robert **1996**:4
Humphries, Barry **1993**:1
Hutchence, Michael
  Obituary **1998**:1
Irwin, Steve **2001**:2
Jackman, Hugh **2004**:4
Kidman, Nicole **1992**:4
Klensch, Elsa **2001**:4
Ledger, Heath **2006**:3
Luhrmann, Baz **2002**:3
McMahon, Julian **2006**:1
Minogue, Kylie **2003**:4
Murdoch, Rupert **1988**:4
Norman, Greg **1988**:3
Powter, Susan **1994**:3
Rafter, Patrick **2001**:1
Rush, Geoffrey **2002**:1
Summers, Anne **1990**:2
Travers, P.L.
  Obituary **1996**:4
Tyler, Richard **1995**:3
Urban, Keith **2006**:3
Webb, Karrie **2000**:4

AUSTRIAN
Brabeck-Letmathe, Peter **2001**:4
Brandauer, Klaus Maria **1987**:3
Djerassi, Carl **2000**:4
Drucker, Peter F. **1992**:3
Falco
  Brief Entry **1987**:2
Frankl, Viktor E.
  Obituary **1998**:1
Hrabal, Bohumil
  Obituary **1997**:3
Jelinek, Elfriede **2005**:3
Lamarr, Hedy
  Obituary **2000**:3
Lang, Helmut **1999**:2
Lorenz, Konrad
  Obituary **1989**:3
Perutz, Max
  Obituary **2003**:2
Porsche, Ferdinand
  Obituary **1998**:4
Pouillon, Nora **2005**:1
Puck, Wolfgang **1990**:1
Strobl, Fritz **2003**:3
von Karajan, Herbert
  Obituary **1989**:4
von Trapp, Maria
  Obituary **1987**:3
Wiesenthal, Simon
  Obituary **2006**:4

BANGLADESHI
Nasrin, Taslima **1995**:1

BELARUSSIAN
Lukashenko, Alexander **2006**:4

BELGIAN
Clijsters, Kim **2006**:3
Henin-Hardenne, Justine **2004**:4
Hepburn, Audrey
Obituary **1993**:2
Verhofstadt, Guy **2006**:3
von Furstenberg, Diane **1994**:2

BOLIVIAN
Sanchez de Lozada, Gonzalo **2004**:3

BOSNIAN
Izetbegovic, Alija **1996**:4

BRAZILIAN
Cardoso, Fernando Henrique **1996**:4
Castaneda, Carlos
Obituary **1998**:4
Collor de Mello, Fernando **1992**:4
Fittipaldi, Emerson **1994**:2
Ronaldo **1999**:2
Salgado, Sebastiao **1994**:2
Senna, Ayrton **1991**:4
Obituary **1994**:4
Silva, Luiz Inacio Lula da **2003**:4
Xuxa **1994**:2

BRITISH
Adamson, George
Obituary **1990**:2
Baddeley, Hermione
Obituary **1986**:4
Beckett, Wendy (Sister) **1998**:3
Branson, Richard **1987**:1
Chatwin, Bruce
Obituary **1989**:2
Cleese, John **1989**:2
Cummings, Sam **1986**:3
Dalton, Timothy **1988**:4
Davison, Ian Hay **1986**:1
Day-Lewis, Daniel **1989**:4 **1994**:4
Dench, Judi **1999**:4
Egan, John **1987**:2
Eno, Brian **1986**:2
Ferguson, Sarah **1990**:3
Fiennes, Ranulph **1990**:3
Foster, Norman **1999**:4
Gift, Roland **1990**:2
Goodall, Jane **1991**:1
Hamilton, Hamish
Obituary **1988**:4
Harrison, Rex
Obituary **1990**:4
Hawking, Stephen W. **1990**:1
Hockney, David **1988**:3
Hoskins, Bob **1989**:1
Hounsfield, Godfrey **1989**:2
Howard, Trevor
Obituary **1988**:2
Ireland, Jill
Obituary **1990**:4
Knopfler, Mark **1986**:2
Laing, R.D.
Obituary **1990**:1
Lawrence, Ruth
Brief Entry **1986**:3
Leach, Robin
Brief Entry **1985**:4
Lennox, Annie **1985**:4 **1996**:4
Livingstone, Ken **1988**:3
Lloyd Webber, Andrew **1989**:1

Macmillan, Harold
Obituary **1987**:2
MacMillan, Kenneth
Obituary **1993**:2
Maxwell, Robert **1990**:1
Michael, George **1989**:2
Milne, Christopher Robin
Obituary **1996**:4
Moore, Henry
Obituary **1986**:4
Murdoch, Iris
Obituary **1999**:4
Norrington, Roger **1989**:4
Oldman, Gary **1998**:1
Olivier, Laurence
Obituary **1989**:4
Philby, Kim
Obituary **1988**:3
Rattle, Simon **1989**:4
Redgrave, Vanessa **1989**:2
Rhodes, Zandra **1986**:2
Roddick, Anita **1989**:4
Runcie, Robert **1989**:4
Obituary **2001**:1
Saatchi, Charles **1987**:3
Steptoe, Patrick
Obituary **1988**:3
Stevens, James
Brief Entry **1988**:1
Thatcher, Margaret **1989**:2
Tudor, Antony
Obituary **1987**:4
Ullman, Tracey **1988**:3
Wilson, Peter C.
Obituary **1985**:2
Wintour, Anna **1990**:4

BRUNEI
Bolkiah, Sultan Muda Hassanal **1985**:4

BULGARIAN
Christo **1992**:3
Dimitrova, Ghena **1987**:1

BURMESE
Suu Kyi, Aung San **1996**:2

CAMBODIAN
Lon Nol
Obituary **1986**:1
Pol Pot
Obituary **1998**:4

CAMEROONIAN
Biya, Paul **2006**:1

CANADIAN
Altman, Sidney **1997**:2
Arbour, Louise **2005**:1
Atwood, Margaret **2001**:2
Balsillie, Jim and Mike Lazaridis
2006:4
Barenaked Ladies **1997**:2
Black, Conrad **1986**:2
Bouchard, Lucien **1999**:2
Bourassa, Robert
Obituary **1997**:1
Bourque, Raymond Jean **1997**:3
Burr, Raymond

Obituary **1994**:1
Campbell, Kim **1993**:4
Campbell, Neve **1998**:2
Campeau, Robert **1990**:1
Candy, John **1988**:2
Obituary **1994**:3
Carrey, Jim **1995**:1
Cavanagh, Tom **2003**:1
Cerovsek, Corey
Brief Entry **1987**:4
Cherry, Don **1993**:4
Chretien, Jean **1990**:4 **1997**:2
Christensen, Hayden **2003**:3
Coffey, Paul **1985**:4
Copps, Sheila **1986**:4
Cronenberg, David **1992**:3
Cronyn, Hume
Obituary **2004**:3
Crosby, Sidney **2006**:3
Dewhurst, Colleen
Obituary **1992**:2
Dion, Celine **1995**:3
Eagleson, Alan **1987**:4
Ebbers, Bernie **1998**:1
Egoyan, Atom **2000**:2
Erickson, Arthur **1989**:3
Fonyo, Steve
Brief Entry **1985**:4
Foster, David **1988**:2
Fox, Michael J. **1986**:1 **2001**:3
Frank, Robert **1995**:2
Frye, Northrop
Obituary **1991**:3
Fuhr, Grant **1997**:3
Garneau, Marc **1985**:1
Gatien, Peter
Brief Entry **1986**:1
Giguere, Jean-Sebastien **2004**:2
Gilmour, Doug **1994**:3
Graham, Nicholas **1991**:4
Granholm, Jennifer **2003**:3
Green, Tom **1999**:4
Greene, Graham **1997**:2
Greene, Lorne
Obituary **1988**:1
Gretzky, Wayne **1989**:2
Haggis, Paul **2006**:4
Haney, Chris
Brief Entry **1985**:1
Harris, Michael Deane **1997**:2
Hayakawa, Samuel Ichiye
Obituary **1992**:3
Hennessy, Jill **2003**:2
Hextall, Ron **1988**:2
Hull, Brett **1991**:4
Jennings, Peter Charles **1997**:2
Johnson, Pierre Marc **1985**:4
Jones, Jenny **1998**:2
Juneau, Pierre **1988**:3
Jung, Andrea **2000**:2
Karsh, Yousuf
Obituary **2003**:4
Keeler, Ruby
Obituary **1993**:4
Kent, Arthur **1991**:4 **1997**:2
Kielburger, Craig **1998**:1
Kilgore, Marcia **2006**:3
Korchinsky, Mike **2004**:2
Lalonde, Marc **1985**:1
Lang, K.D. **1988**:4
Lanois, Daniel **1991**:1
Lavigne, Avril **2005**:2

Lemieux, Claude **1996**:1
Lemieux, Mario **1986**:4
Leávesque, Reneá
   Obituary **1988**:1
Levy, Eugene **2004**:3
Lewis, Stephen **1987**:2
Mandel, Howie **1989**:1
Markle, C. Wilson **1988**:1
Martin, Paul **2004**:4
McKinnell, Henry **2002**:3
McLachlan, Sarah **1998**:4
McLaren, Norman
   Obituary **1987**:2
McLaughlin, Audrey **1990**:3
McTaggart, David **1989**:4
Messier, Mark **1993**:1
Morgentaler, Henry **1986**:3
Morissette, Alanis **1996**:2
Moss, Carrie-Anne **2004**:3
Mulroney, Brian **1989**:2
Munro, Alice **1997**:1
Myers, Mike **1992**:3 **1997**:4
O'Donnell, Bill
   Brief Entry **1987**:4
Ondaatje, Philip Michael **1997**:3
Parizeau, Jacques **1995**:1
Peckford, Brian **1989**:1
Peterson, David **1987**:1
Pocklington, Peter H. **1985**:2
Pratt, Christopher **1985**:3
Raffi **1988**:1
Randi, James **1990**:2
Reisman, Simon **1987**:4
Reitman, Ivan **1986**:3
Reuben, Gloria **1999**:4
Rhea, Caroline **2004**:1
Richard, Maurice
   Obituary **2000**:4
Roy, Patrick **1994**:2
Rypien, Mark **1992**:3
Sainte-Marie, Buffy **2000**:1
Sakic, Joe **2002**:1
Shaffer, Paul **1987**:1
Shields, Carol
   Obituary **2004**:3
Short, Martin **1986**:1
Strong, Maurice **1993**:1
Sutherland, Kiefer **2002**:4
Tilghman, Shirley M. **2002**:1
Trudeau, Pierre
   Obituary **2001**:1
Twain, Shania **1996**:3
Vander Zalm, William **1987**:3
Vardalos, Nia **2003**:4
Vickrey, William S.
   Obituary **1997**:2
Villeneuve, Jacques **1997**:1
Weir, Mike **2004**:1
Whitehead, Robert
   Obituary **2003**:3
Williams, Lynn **1986**:4
Wilson, Bertha
   Brief Entry **1986**:1
Wood, Sharon
   Brief Entry **1988**:1
Young, Neil **1991**:2
Yzerman, Steve **1991**:2

CENTRAL AFRICAN
Bozize, Francois **2006**:3

CHADIAN
Deby, Idriss **2002**:2

CHILEAN
Arrau, Claudio
   Obituary **1992**:1
Lagos, Ricardo **2005**:3
Pinochet, Augusto **1999**:2

CHINESE
Chaing Kai-Shek, Madame
   Obituary **2005**:1
Chan, Jackie **1996**:1
Chen, Joan **2000**:2
Chen, T.C.
   Brief Entry **1987**:3
Deng Xiaoping **1995**:1
   Obituary **1997**:3
Fang Lizhi **1988**:1
Gao Xingjian **2001**:2
Gong Li **1998**:4
Hatem, George
   Obituary **1989**:1
Hou Hsiao-hsien **2000**:2
Hu Jintao **2004**:1
Hu Yaobang
   Obituary **1989**:4
Hwang, David Henry **1999**:1
Jiang Quing
   Obituary **1992**:1
Jiang Zemin **1996**:1
Lee, Ang **1996**:3
Lee, Henry C. **1997**:1
Li, Jet **2005**:3
Lord, Bette Bao **1994**:1
Lucid, Shannon **1997**:1
Ma, Pony **2006**:3
Tan Dun **2002**:1
Weihui, Zhou **2001**:1
Wei Jingsheng **1998**:2
Woo, John **1994**:2
Wu, Harry **1996**:1
Wu Yi **2005**:2
Yao Ming **2004**:1
Ye Jianying
   Obituary **1987**:1
Yen, Samuel **1996**:4
Zhang, Ziyi **2006**:2
Zhao Ziyang **1989**:1

COLOMBIAN
Botero, Fernando **1994**:3
Garcia Marquez, Gabriel **2005**:2
Juanes **2004**:4
Leguizamo, John **1999**:1
Pastrana, Andres **2002**:1
Schroeder, Barbet **1996**:1
Shakira **2002**:3
Uribe, Alvaro **2003**:3

CONGOLESE
Kabila, Joseph **2003**:2
Kabila, Laurent **1998**:1
   Obituary **2001**:3
Mobutu Sese Seko
   Obituary **1998**:4

COSTA RICAN
Arias Sanchez, Oscar **1989**:3

COTE D'IVOIRIAN
Gbagbo, Laurent **2003**:2

CROATIAN
Ivanisevic, Goran **2002**:1
Mesic, Stipe **2005**:4
Tudjman, Franjo **1996**:2
Tudjman, Franjo
   Obituary **2000**:2

CUBAN
Acosta, Carlos **1997**:4
Canseco, Jose **1990**:2
Castro, Fidel **1991**:4
Cruz, Celia
   Obituary **2004**:3
Cugat, Xavier
   Obituary **1991**:2
Estefan, Gloria **1991**:4
Garcia, Andy **1999**:3
Garcia, Cristina **1997**:4
Goizueta, Roberto **1996**:1
   Obituary **1998**:1
Gutierrez, Carlos M. **2001**:4
Palmeiro, Rafael **2005**:1
Saralegui, Cristina **1999**:2
Zamora, Pedro
   Obituary **1995**:2

CYPRIAN
Chalayan, Hussein **2003**:2
Kyprianou, Spyros
   Obituary **2003**:2

CZECH
Albright, Madeleine **1994**:3
Hammer, Jan **1987**:3
Hasek, Dominik **1998**:3
Havel, Vaclav **1990**:3
Hingis, Martina **1999**:1
Hrabal, Bohumil
   Obituary **1997**:3
Jagr, Jaromir **1995**:4
Klima, Petr **1987**:1
Kukoc, Toni **1995**:4
Maxwell, Robert
   Obituary **1992**:2
Porizkova, Paulina
   Brief Entry **1986**:4
Reisz, Karel
   Obituary **2004**:1
Serkin, Rudolf
   Obituary **1992**:1
Stoppard, Tom **1995**:4
Trump, Ivana **1995**:2
Zatopek, Emil
   Obituary **2001**:3

DANISH
Borge, Victor
   Obituary **2001**:3
Hau, Lene Vestergaard **2006**:4
Kristiansen, Kjeld Kirk **1988**:3
Lander, Toni
   Obituary **1985**:4
Rasmussen, Anders Fogh **2006**:1

DJIBOUTI
Guelleh, Ismail Omar **2006**:2

Redgrave, Lynn **1999**:3
Reisz, Karel
  Obituary **2004**:1
Richards, Keith **1993**:3
Ritchie, Guy **2001**:3
Roth, Tim **1998**:2
Saatchi, Maurice **1995**:4
Sacks, Oliver **1995**:4
Schlesinger, John
  Obituary **2004**:3
Scott, Ridley **2001**:1
Seal **1994**:4
Sentamu, John **2006**:2
Seymour, Jane **1994**:4
Smith, Paul **2002**:4
Smith, Zadie **2003**:4
Springer, Jerry **1998**:4
Springfield, Dusty
  Obituary **1999**:3
Stewart, Patrick **1996**:1
Sting **1991**:4
Stone, Joss **2006**:2
Stoppard, Tom **1995**:4
Strummer, Joe
  Obituary **2004**:1
Sullivan, Andrew **1996**:1
Taylor, Elizabeth **1993**:3
Taylor, Graham **2005**:3
Thompson, Emma **1993**:2
Tilberis, Elizabeth **1994**:3
Trotman, Alex **1995**:4
Uchida, Mitsuko **1989**:3
Ustinov, Peter
  Obituary **2005**:3
Ware, Lancelot
  Obituary **2001**:1
Watson, Emily **2001**:1
Watts, Naomi **2006**:1
Weisz, Rachel **2006**:4
Westwood, Vivienne **1998**:3
Wiles, Andrew **1994**:1
Wilkinson, Tom **2003**:2
Wilmut, Ian **1997**:3
Winslet, Kate **2002**:4

FIJI ISLANDER
Mara, Ratu Sir Kamisese
  Obituary **2005**:3
Singh, Vijay **2000**:4

FILIPINO
Aquino, Corazon **1986**:2
Lewis, Loida Nicolas **1998**:3
Macapagal-Arroyo, Gloria **2001**:4
Marcos, Ferdinand
  Obituary **1990**:1
Natori, Josie **1994**:3
Ramos, Fidel **1995**:2
Salonga, Lea **2003**:3
Sin, Jaime
  Obituary **2006**:3

FINNISH
Halonen, Tarja **2006**:4
Kekkonen, Urho
  Obituary **1986**:4
Ollila, Jorma **2003**:4
Torvalds, Linus **1999**:3

FRENCH
Adjani, Isabelle **1991**:1
Agnes B **2002**:3
Arnault, Bernard **2000**:4
Baulieu, Etienne-Emile **1990**:1
Becaud, Gilbert
  Obituary **2003**:1
Besse, Georges
  Obituary **1987**:1
Binoche, Juliette **2001**:3
Bourgeois, Louise **1994**:1
Brando, Cheyenne
  Obituary **1995**:4
Calment, Jeanne
  Obituary **1997**:4
Cardin, Pierre **2003**:3
Cartier-Bresson, Henri
  Obituary **2005**:4
Chagall, Marc
  Obituary **1985**:2
Chirac, Jacques **1995**:4
Colbert, Claudette
  Obituary **1997**:1
Cousteau, Jacques-Yves
  Obituary **1998**:2
Cousteau, Jean-Michel **1988**:2
Cresson, Edith **1992**:1
Delors, Jacques **1990**:2
Deneuve, Catherine **2003**:2
Depardieu, Gerard **1991**:2
Derrida, Jacques
  Obituary **2006**:1
Dubuffet, Jean
  Obituary **1985**:4
Duras, Marguerite
  Obituary **1996**:3
Fekkai, Frederic **2003**:2
Gaultier, Jean-Paul **1998**:1
Godard, Jean-Luc **1998**:1
Grappelli, Stephane
  Obituary **1998**:1
Guillem, Sylvie **1988**:2
Indurain, Miguel **1994**:1
Klarsfeld, Beate **1989**:1
Kouchner, Bernard **2005**:3
Lacroix, Christian **2005**:2
Lefebvre, Marcel **1988**:4
Louboutin, Christian **2006**:1
Malle, Louis
  Obituary **1996**:2
Mercier, Laura **2002**:2
Millepied, Benjamin **2006**:4
Mitterrand, Francois
  Obituary **1996**:2
Nars, Francois **2003**:1
Petrossian, Christian
  Brief Entry **1985**:3
Picasso, Paloma **1991**:1
Ponty, Jean-Luc **1985**:4
Prost, Alain **1988**:1
Rampal, Jean-Pierre **1989**:2
Reza, Yasmina **1999**:2
Rothschild, Philippe de
  Obituary **1988**:2
Rykiel, Sonia **2000**:3
Simone, Nina
  Obituary **2004**:2
Starck, Philippe **2004**:1
Tautou, Audrey **2004**:2
Thom, Rene

  Obituary **2004**:1
Thomas, Michel **1987**:4
Ungaro, Emanuel **2001**:3
Villechaize, Herve
  Obituary **1994**:1
Xenakis, Iannis
  Obituary **2001**:4

GABONESE
Bozize, Francois **2006**:3

GERMAN
Barbie, Klaus
  Obituary **1992**:2
Becker, Boris
  Brief Entry **1985**:3
Bethe, Hans
  Obituary **2006**:2
Beuys, Joseph
  Obituary **1986**:3
Blobel, Gunter **2000**:4
Boyle, Gertrude **1995**:3
Brandt, Willy
  Obituary **1993**:2
Breitschwerdt, Werner **1988**:4
Casper, Gerhard **1993**:1
Dietrich, Marlene
  Obituary **1992**:4
Etzioni, Amitai **1994**:3
Fischer, Joschka **2005**:2
Frank, Anthony M. **1992**:1
Graf, Steffi **1987**:4
Grass, Gunter **2000**:2
Gursky, Andreas **2002**:2
Hahn, Carl H. **1986**:4
Hess, Rudolph
  Obituary **1988**:1
Honecker, Erich
  Obituary **1994**:4
Kiefer, Anselm **1990**:2
Kinski, Klaus **1987**:2
  Obituary **1992**:2
Klarsfeld, Beate **1989**:1
Klemperer, Werner
  Obituary **2001**:3
Klum, Heidi **2006**:3
Kohl, Helmut **1994**:1
Krogner, Heinz **2004**:2
Lagerfeld, Karl **1999**:4
Max, Peter **1993**:2
Mengele, Josef
  Obituary **1985**:2
Mutter, Anne-Sophie **1990**:3
Newton, Helmut **2002**:1
Nuesslein-Volhard, Christiane **1998**:1
Pfeiffer, Eckhard **1998**:4
Pilatus, Robert
  Obituary **1998**:3
Polke, Sigmar **1999**:4
Rey, Margret E.
  Obituary **1997**:2
Richter, Gerhard **1997**:2
Sander, Jil **1995**:2
Schily, Otto
  Brief Entry **1987**:4
Schrempp, Juergen **2000**:2
Schroder, Gerhard **1999**:1
Schumacher, Michael **2005**:2
Tillmans, Wolfgang **2001**:4
Von Hellermann, Sophie **2006**:3

Sinopoli, Giuseppe **1988**:1
Staller, Ilona **1988**:3
Tomba, Alberto **1992**:3
Versace, Donatella **1999**:1
Versace, Gianni
  Brief Entry **1988**:1
  Obituary **1998**:2
Zanardi, Alex **1998**:2
Zeffirelli, Franco **1991**:3

JAMAICAN
Marley, Ziggy **1990**:4
Tosh, Peter
  Obituary **1988**:2

JAPANESE
Akihito, Emperor of Japan **1990**:1
Ando, Tadao **2005**:4
Aoki, Rocky **1990**:2
Arakawa, Shizuka **2006**:4
Doi, Takako
  Brief Entry **1987**:4
Hirohito, Emperor of Japan
  Obituary **1989**:2
Honda, Soichiro
  Obituary **1986**:1
Hosokawa, Morihiro **1994**:1
Isozaki, Arata **1990**:2
Itami, Juzo
  Obituary **1998**:2
Katayama, Yutaka **1987**:1
Koizumi, Junichiro **2002**:1
Kurosawa, Akira **1991**:1
  Obituary **1999**:1
Kutaragi, Ken **2005**:3
Masako, Crown Princess **1993**:4
Matsuhisa, Nobuyuki **2002**:3
Mitarai, Fujio **2002**:4
Miyake, Issey **1985**:2
Miyazaki, Hayao **2006**:2
Miyazawa, Kiichi **1992**:2
Mori, Yoshiro **2000**:4
Morita, Akio **1989**:4
Morita, Akio
  Obituary **2000**:2
Murakami, Takashi **2004**:2
Nagako, Empress Dowager
  Obituary **2001**:1
Nara, Yoshitomo **2006**:2
Nomo, Hideo **1996**:2
Obuchi, Keizo **1999**:2
Obuchi, Keizo
  Obituary **2000**:4
Oe, Kenzaburo **1997**:1
Sasakawa, Ryoichi
  Brief Entry **1988**:1
Shimomura, Tsutomu **1996**:1
Suzuki, Ichiro **2002**:2
Suzuki, Sin'ichi
  Obituary **1998**:3
Takada, Kenzo **2003**:2
Takei, Kei **1990**:2
Takeshita, Noburu
  Obituary **2001**:1
Tanaka, Tomoyuki
  Obituary **1997**:3
Tange, Kenzo
  Obituary **2006**:2
Taniguchi, Yoshio **2005**:4
Toyoda, Eiji **1985**:2
Uchida, Mitsuko **1989**:3
Yamamoto, Kenichi **1989**:1

JORDANIAN
Abdullah II, King **2002**:4
al-Abdullah, Rania **2001**:1
Hussein I, King **1997**:3
  Obituary **1999**:3

KAZAKHSTANI
Nazarbayev, Nursultan **2006**:4

KENYAN
Kibaki, Mwai **2003**:4
Maathai, Wangari **2005**:3
Moi, Daniel arap **1993**:2

KOREAN
Chung Ju Yung
  Obituary **2002**:1
Kim Dae Jung **1998**:3
Kim Il Sung
  Obituary **1994**:4
Kim Jong Il **1995**:2
Lee Jong-Wook **2005**:1
Pak, Se Ri **1999**:4
Roh Moo-hyun **2005**:1

LATVIAN
Baryshnikov, Mikhail Nikolaevich
1997:3

LEBANESE
Berri, Nabih **1985**:2
Jumblatt, Walid **1987**:4
Sarkis, Elias
  Obituary **1985**:3

LIBERIAN
Doe, Samuel
  Obituary **1991**:1

LIBYAN
Qaddhafi, Muammar **1998**:3

LITHUANIAN
Landsbergis, Vytautas **1991**:3

MACEDONIAN
Trajkovski, Boris
  Obituary **2005**:2

MADAGASCAN
Ravalomanana, Marc **2003**:1

MALAWI
Banda, Hastings **1994**:3

MALAYSIAN
Choo, Jimmy **2006**:3
Ngau, Harrison **1991**:3
Yeoh, Michelle **2003**:2

MEXICAN
Alvarez Bravo, Manuel
  Obituary **2004**:1
Catlett, Elizabeth **1999**:3
Colosio, Luis Donaldo **1994**:3
Esquivel, Juan **1996**:2
Felix, Maria
  Obituary **2003**:2

Fox, Vicente **2001**:1
Garcia, Amalia **2005**:3
Graham, Robert **1993**:4
Hayek, Salma **1999**:1
Kahlo, Frida **1991**:3
Paz, Octavio **1991**:2
Salinas, Carlos **1992**:1
Santana, Carlos **2000**:2
Tamayo, Rufino
  Obituary **1992**:1
Zedillo, Ernesto **1995**:1

MONACO
Albert, Prince of Monaco **2006**:2
Rainier III, Prince of Monaco
  Obituary **2006**:2

MOROCCAN
King Hassan II
  Obituary **2000**:1

MOZAMBICAN
Chissano, Joaquim **1987**:4
Dhlakama, Afonso **1993**:3
Machel, Samora
  Obituary **1987**:1

NAMIBIAN
Nujoma, Sam **1990**:4

NEPALI
Shah, Gyanendra **2006**:1

NEW ZEALANDER
Campion, Jane **1991**:4
Castle-Hughes, Keisha **2004**:4
Crowe, Russell **2000**:4
Frame, Janet
  Obituary **2005**:2
Jackson, Peter **2004**:4
Kleinpaste, Ruud **2006**:2
Shipley, Jenny **1998**:3

NICARAGUAN
Astorga, Nora **1988**:2
Cruz, Arturo **1985**:1
Obando, Miguel **1986**:4
Robelo, Alfonso **1988**:1

NIGERAN
Abacha, Sani **1996**:3
Babangida, Ibrahim Badamosi **1992**:4
Obasanjo, Olusegun **2000**:2
Okoye, Christian **1990**:2
Olajuwon, Akeem **1985**:1
Sade **1993**:2
Saro-Wiwa, Ken
  Obituary **1996**:2

NIGERIAN
Olopade, Olufunmilayo **2006**:3

NORWEGIAN
Brundtland, Gro Harlem **2000**:1
Cammermeyer, Margarethe **1995**:2
Olav, King of Norway
  Obituary **1991**:3
Stoltenberg, Jens **2006**:4

PAKISTANI

Bhutto, Benazir **1989**:4
Zia ul-Haq, Mohammad
Obituary **1988**:4

PALESTINIAN

Arafat, Yasser **1989**:3 **1997**:3
Freij, Elias **1986**:4
Habash, George **1986**:1
Husseini, Faisal **1998**:4
Nidal, Abu **1987**:1
Sharon, Ariel **2001**:4
Terzi, Zehdi Labib **1985**:3

PANAMANIAN

Blades, Ruben **1998**:2

PERUVIAN

Fujimori, Alberto **1992**:4
Perez de Cuellar, Javier **1991**:3
Testino, Mario **2002**:1

POLISH

Begin, Menachem
Obituary **1992**:3
Eisenstaedt, Alfred
Obituary **1996**:1
John Paul II, Pope **1995**:3
Kieslowski, Krzysztof
Obituary **1996**:3
Kosinski, Jerzy
Obituary **1991**:4
Masur, Kurt **1993**:4
Niezabitowska, Malgorzata **1991**:3
Rosten, Leo
Obituary **1997**:3
Sabin, Albert
Obituary **1993**:4
Singer, Isaac Bashevis
Obituary **1992**:1
Walesa, Lech **1991**:2

PORTUGUESE

Saramago, Jose **1999**:1

PUERTO RICAN

Alvarez, Aida **1999**:2
Del Toro, Benicio **2001**:4
Ferrer, Jose
Obituary **1992**:3
Julia, Raul
Obituary **1995**:1
Martin, Ricky **1999**:4
Novello, Antonia **1991**:2
Trinidad, Felix **2000**:4

ROMANIAN

Basescu, Traian **2006**:2
Ceausescu, Nicolae
Obituary **1990**:2
Codrescu, Andreá **1997**:3

RUSSIAN

Brodsky, Joseph
Obituary **1996**:3
Gorbachev, Raisa
Obituary **2000**:2
Gordeeva, Ekaterina **1996**:4
Grinkov, Sergei
Obituary **1996**:2

Kasparov, Garry **1997**:4
Kasyanov, Mikhail **2001**:1
Konstantinov, Vladimir **1997**:4
Kournikova, Anna **2000**:3
Lapidus, Morris
Obituary **2001**:4
Lebed, Alexander **1997**:1
Primakov, Yevgeny **1999**:3
Putin, Vladimir **2000**:3
Safin, Marat **2001**:3
Sarraute, Nathalie
Obituary **2000**:2
Schneerson, Menachem Mendel
1992:4
Obituary **1994**:4
Sharapova, Maria **2005**:2
Titov, Gherman
Obituary **2001**:3

RWANDAN

Kagame, Paul **2001**:4

SALVADORAN

Duarte, Jose Napoleon
Obituary **1990**:3

SAUDI

Fahd, King of Saudi Arabia
Obituary **2006**:4

SCOTTISH

Coldplay **2004**:4
Connery, Sean **1990**:4
Ferguson, Craig **2005**:4
Ferguson, Niall **2006**:1
McGregor, Ewan **1998**:2
Mina, Denise **2006**:1
Paolozzi, Eduardo
Obituary **2006**:3
Ramsay, Mike **2002**:1
Rowling, J.K. **2000**:1

SENEGALESE

Senghor, Leopold
Obituary **2003**:1

SOMALIAN

Iman **2001**:3

SOUTH AFRICAN

Barnard, Christiaan
Obituary **2002**:4
Blackburn, Molly
Obituary **1985**:4
Buthelezi, Mangosuthu Gatsha **1989**
:3
Coetzee, J. M. **2004**:4
de Klerk, F.W. **1990**:1
Duncan, Sheena
Brief Entry **1987**:1
Fugard, Athol **1992**:3
Hani, Chris
Obituary **1993**:4
Makeba, Miriam **1989**:2
Mandela, Nelson **1990**:3
Mandela, Winnie **1989**:3
Matthews, Dave **1999**:3
Mbeki, Thabo **1999**:4
Oppenheimer, Harry
Obituary **2001**:3

Paton, Alan
Obituary **1988**:3
Ramaphosa, Cyril **1988**:2
Sisulu, Walter
Obituary **2004**:2
Slovo, Joe **1989**:2
Suzman, Helen **1989**:3
Tambo, Oliver **1991**:3
Theron, Charlize **2001**:4
Treurnicht, Andries **1992**:2
Woods, Donald
Obituary **2002**:3

SOVIET

Asimov, Isaac
Obituary **1992**:3
Chernenko, Konstantin
Obituary **1985**:1
Dalai Lama **1989**:1
Dubinin, Yuri **1987**:4
Dzhanibekov, Vladimir **1988**:1
Erte
Obituary **1990**:4
Federov, Sergei **1995**:1
Godunov, Alexander
Obituary **1995**:4
Gorbachev, Mikhail **1985**:2
Grebenshikov, Boris **1990**:1
Gromyko, Andrei
Obituary **1990**:2
Karadzic, Radovan **1995**:3
Milosevic, Slobodan **1993**:2
Molotov, Vyacheslav Mikhailovich
Obituary **1987**:1
Nureyev, Rudolf
Obituary **1993**:2
Sakharov, Andrei Dmitrievich
Obituary **1990**:2
Smirnoff, Yakov **1987**:2
Vidov, Oleg **1987**:4
Yeltsin, Boris **1991**:1
Zhirinovsky, Vladimir **1994**:2

SPANISH

Almodovar, Pedro **2000**:3
Banderas, Antonio **1996**:2
Blahnik, Manolo **2000**:2
Calatrava, Santiago **2005**:1
Carreras, Jose **1995**:2
Cela, Camilo Jose
Obituary **2003**:1
Chillida, Eduardo
Obituary **2003**:4
Cruz, Penelope **2001**:4
Dali, Salvador
Obituary **1989**:2
de Pinies, Jamie
Brief Entry **1986**:3
Domingo, Placido **1993**:2
Juan Carlos I **1993**:1
Lopez de Arriortua, Jose Ignacio
1993:4
Miro, Joan
Obituary **1985**:1
Moneo, Jose Rafael **1996**:4
Montoya, Carlos
Obituary **1993**:4
Samaranch, Juan Antonio **1986**:2
Segovia, Andreás
Obituary **1987**:3
Wences, Senor
Obituary **1999**:4

SRI LANKAN
Bandaranaike, Sirimavo
Obituary **2001**:2
Ondaatje, Philip Michael **1997**:3
Wickramasinghe, Ranil **2003**:2

SUDANESE
Turabi, Hassan **1995**:4

SWEDISH
Bergman, Ingmar **1999**:4
Cardigans, The **1997**:4
Carlsson, Arvid **2001**:2
Garbo, Greta
Obituary **1990**:3
Hallstrom, Lasse **2002**:3
Lindbergh, Pelle
Obituary **1985**:4
Lindgren, Astrid
Obituary **2003**:1
Olin, Lena **1991**:2
Palme, Olof
Obituary **1986**:2
Persson, Stefan **2004**:1
Renvall, Johan
Brief Entry **1987**:4
Sorenstam, Annika **2001**:1

SWISS
del Ponte, Carla **2001**:1
Federer, Roger **2004**:2
Frank, Robert **1995**:2
Vasella, Daniel **2005**:3
Vollenweider, Andreas **1985**:2

SYRIAN
al-Assad, Bashar **2004**:2
Assad, Hafez
Obituary **2000**:4
Assad, Hafez al- **1992**:1
Assad, Rifaat **1986**:3

TAHITIAN
Brando, Cheyenne
Obituary **1995**:4

TAIWANESE
Chen Shui-bian **2001**:2
Ho, David **1997**:2
Lee Teng-hui **2000**:1

TANZANIAN
Nyerere, Julius
Obituary **2000**:2

THAI
Thaksin Shinawatra **2005**:4

TRINIDADIAN
Ture, Kwame
Obituary **1999**:2

TUNISIAN
Azria, Max **2001**:4

TURKISH
Ocalan, Abdullah **1999**:4

UGANDAN
Amin, Idi
Obituary **2004**:4
Museveni, Yoweri **2002**:1

UKRAINIAN
Baiul, Oksana **1995**:3
Yushchenko, Viktor **2006**:1

URUGUAYAN
Vazquez, Tabare **2006**:2

UZBEKISTANI
Karimov, Islam **2006**:3

VENEZUELAN
Herrera, Carolina **1997**:1
Perez, Carlos Andre **1990**:2

VIETNAMESE
Dong, Pham Van
Obituary **2000**:4
Le Duan
Obituary **1986**:4
Le Duc Tho
Obituary **1991**:1

WELSH
Bale, Christian **2001**:3
Dahl, Roald
Obituary **1991**:2
Hopkins, Anthony **1992**:4
Jenkins, Roy Harris
Obituary **2004**:1
Jones, Tom **1993**:4
Macdonald, Julien **2005**:3
William, Prince of Wales **2001**:3
Zeta-Jones, Catherine **1999**:4

YEMENI
Saleh, Ali Abdullah **2001**:3

YUGOSLAVIAN
Filipovic, Zlata **1994**:4
Kostunica, Vojislav **2001**:1
Pogorelich, Ivo **1986**:4
Seles, Monica **1991**:3

ZAIRAN
Mobutu Sese Seko **1993**:4
Obituary **1998**:1

ZAMBIAN
Chiluba, Frederick **1992**:3

ZIMBABWEAN
Mugabe, Robert **1988**:4

Cumulative Occupation Index

This index lists all newsmakers alphabetically by their occupations or fields of primary activity. Indexes in softbound issues allow access to the current year's entries; indexes in annual hardbound volumes are cumulative, covering the entire *Newsmakers* series.

Listee names are followed by a year and issue number; thus **1996**:3 indicates that an entry on that individual appears in both 1996, Issue 3, and the 1996 cumulation. For access to newsmakers appearing earlier than the current softbound issue, see the previous year's cumulation.

ART AND DESIGN

Adams, Scott **1996**:4
Adams-Geller, Paige **2006**:4
Addams, Charles
Obituary **1989**:1
Adler, Jonathan **2006**:3
Agnes B **2002**:3
Allard, Linda **2003**:2
Alvarez Bravo, Manuel
Obituary **2004**:1
Anderson, Laurie **2000**:2
Ando, Tadao **2005**:4
Arman **1993**:1
Armani, Giorgio **1991**:2
Ashwell, Rachel **2004**:2
Aucoin, Kevyn **2001**:3
Avedon, Richard **1993**:4
Azria, Max **2001**:4
Badgley, Mark and James Mischka
2004:3
Baldessari, John **1991**:4
Banks, Jeffrey **1998**:2
Barbera, Joseph **1988**:2
Barks, Carl
Obituary **2001**:2
Barnes, Ernie **1997**:4
Barry, Lynda **1992**:1
Bean, Alan L. **1986**:2
Beene, Geoffrey
Obituary **2005**:4
Beuys, Joseph
Obituary **1986**:3
Bird, Brad **2005**:4
Blahnik, Manolo **2000**:2
Blass, Bill
Obituary **2003**:3
Bohbot, Michele **2004**:2
Bontecou, Lee **2004**:4
Boone, Mary **1985**:1
Borofsky, Jonathan **2006**:4
Botero, Fernando **1994**:3
Bourgeois, Louise **1994**:1
Bowie, David **1998**:2
Boynton, Sandra **2004**:1
Breathed, Berkeley **2005**:3
Brown, Bobbi **2001**:4
Brown, J. Carter

Obituary **2003**:3
Bunshaft, Gordon **1989**:3
Obituary **1991**:1
Calatrava, Santiago **2005**:1
Cameron, David
Brief Entry **1988**:1
Campbell, Ben Nighthorse **1998**:1
Campbell, Naomi **2000**:2
Cardin, Pierre **2003**:3
Cartier-Bresson, Henri
Obituary **2005**:4
Castelli, Leo
Obituary **2000**:1
Catlett, Elizabeth **1999**:3
Cavalli, Roberto **2004**:4
Chagall, Marc
Obituary **1985**:2
Chalayan, Hussein **2003**:2
Chast, Roz **1992**:4
Chatham, Russell **1990**:1
Chia, Sandro **1987**:2
Chihuly, Dale **1995**:2
Chillida, Eduardo
Obituary **2003**:4
Choo, Jimmy **2006**:3
Christo **1992**:3
Claiborne, Liz **1986**:3
Clemente, Francesco **1992**:2
Cole, Kenneth **2003**:1
Cooper, Alexander **1988**:4
Crumb, R. **1995**:4
Dali, Salvador
Obituary **1989**:2
Davis, Paige **2004**:2
DeCarava, Roy **1996**:3
de Kooning, Willem **1994**:4
Obituary **1997**:3
de la Renta, Oscar **2005**:4
Diebenkorn, Richard
Obituary **1993**:4
Diller, Elizabeth and Ricardo
Scofidio **2004**:3
Dolce, Domenico and Stefano
Gabbana **2005**:4
Donghia, Angelo R.
Obituary **1985**:2
Duarte, Henry **2003**:3

Dubuffet, Jean
Obituary **1985**:4
Dunham, Carroll **2003**:4
Ecko, Marc **2006**:3
Eisenman, Peter **1992**:4
Eisenstaedt, Alfred
Obituary **1996**:1
Eisner, Will
Obituary **2006**:1
Ellis, Perry
Obituary **1986**:3
Engelbreit, Mary **1994**:3
Erickson, Arthur **1989**:3
Erte
Obituary **1990**:4
Eve **2004**:3
Fekkai, Frederic **2003**:2
Ferretti, Alberta **2004**:1
Field, Patricia **2002**:2
Finley, Karen **1992**:4
Fisher, Mary **1994**:3
Ford, Tom **1999**:3
Foster, Norman **1999**:4
Frank, Robert **1995**:2
Frankenthaler, Helen **1990**:1
Freud, Lucian **2000**:4
Frieda, John **2004**:1
Gaines, William M.
Obituary **1993**:1
Galliano, John **2005**:2
Gaultier, Jean-Paul **1998**:1
Gehry, Frank O. **1987**:1
Giannulli, Mossimo **2002**:3
Gober, Robert **1996**:3
Golden, Thelma **2003**:3
Goody, Joan **1990**:2
Gorder, Genevieve **2005**:4
Gordon, Michael **2005**:1
Gould, Chester
Obituary **1985**:2
Graham, Nicholas **1991**:4
Graham, Robert **1993**:4
Graves, Michael **2000**:1
Graves, Nancy **1989**:3
Greenberg, Robert **2003**:2
Groening, Matt **1990**:4
Guccione, Bob **1986**:1

Brief Entry **1987**:2
Trudeau, Garry **1991**:2
Truitt, Anne **1993**:1
Twombley, Cy **1995**:1
Tyler, Richard **1995**:3
Ungaro, Emanuel **2001**:3
Valvo, Carmen Marc **2003**:4
Varvatos, John **2006**:2
Venturi, Robert **1994**:4
Versace, Donatella **1999**:1
Versace, Gianni
  Brief Entry **1988**:1
  Obituary **1998**:2
von Furstenberg, Diane **1994**:2
Von Hellermann, Sophie **2006**:3
Vreeland, Diana
  Obituary **1990**:1
Wagner, Catherine F. **2002**:3
Walker, Kara **1999**:2
Wang, Vera **1998**:4
Warhol, Andy
  Obituary **1987**:2
Washington, Alonzo **2000**:1
Waterman, Cathy **2002**:2
Watterson, Bill **1990**:3
Wegman, William **1991**:1
Westwood, Vivienne **1998**:3
Whitney, Patrick **2006**:1
Wilson, Peter C.
  Obituary **1985**:2
Winick, Judd **2005**:3
Wintour, Anna **1990**:4
Witkin, Joel-Peter **1996**:1
Yamasaki, Minoru
  Obituary **1986**:2

BUSINESS
Abraham, S. Daniel **2003**:3
Ackerman, Will **1987**:4
Adams-Geller, Paige **2006**:4
Adler, Jonathan **2006**:3
Agnelli, Giovanni **1989**:4
Ailes, Roger **1989**:3
Akers, John F. **1988**:3
Akin, Phil
  Brief Entry **1987**:3
Albrecht, Chris **2005**:4
Allaire, Jeremy **2006**:4
Allaire, Paul **1995**:1
Allard, Linda **2003**:2
Allen, Bob **1992**:4
Allen, John **1992**:1
Alter, Hobie
  Brief Entry **1985**:1
Alvarez, Aida **1999**:2
Ames, Roger **2005**:2
Amos, Wally **2000**:1
Ancier, Garth **1989**:1
Andreessen, Marc **1996**:2
Annenberg, Walter **1992**:3
Antonini, Joseph **1991**:2
Aoki, Rocky **1990**:2
Arad, Avi **2003**:2
Aretsky, Ken **1988**:1
Arison, Ted **1990**:3
Arledge, Roone **1992**:2
Armstrong, C. Michael **2002**:1
Arnault, Bernard **2000**:4
Ash, Mary Kay **1996**:1
Ashwell, Rachel **2004**:2
Aurre, Laura
  Brief Entry **1986**:3

Ballmer, Steven **1997**:2
Balsillie, Jim and Mike Lazaridis **2006**:4
Banks, Jeffrey **1998**:2
Barad, Jill **1994**:2
Barksdale, James L. **1998**:2
Barrett, Craig R. **1999**:4
Bauer, Eddie
  Obituary **1986**:3
Beals, Vaughn **1988**:2
Becker, Brian **2004**:4
Beene, Geoffrey
  Obituary **2005**:4
Beers, Charlotte **1999**:3
Ben & Jerry **1991**:3
Benetton, Luciano **1988**:1
Berlusconi, Silvio **1994**:4
Berman, Gail **2006**:1
Bern, Dorrit J. **2006**:3
Besse, Georges
  Obituary **1987**:1
Bezos, Jeff **1998**:4
Bieber, Owen **1986**:1
Bikoff, James L.
  Brief Entry **1986**:2
Black, Carole **2003**:1
Black, Cathleen **1998**:4
Black, Conrad **1986**:2
Bloch, Henry **1988**:4
Bloch, Ivan **1986**:3
Bloomberg, Michael **1997**:1
Bohbot, Michele **2004**:2
Boiardi, Hector
  Obituary **1985**:3
Bolkiah, Sultan Muda Hassanal **1985**:4
Bond, Alan **1989**:2
Bose, Amar
  Brief Entry **1986**:4
Boyer, Herbert Wayne **1985**:1
Boyle, Gertrude **1995**:3
Boynton, Sandra **2004**:1
Brabeck-Letmathe, Peter **2001**:4
Bradley, Todd **2003**:3
Branson, Richard **1987**:1
Bravo, Ellen **1998**:2
Bravo, Rose Marie **2005**:3
Breitschwerdt, Werner **1988**:4
Brennan, Edward A. **1989**:1
Brennan, Robert E. **1988**:1
Bronfman, Edgar, Jr. **1994**:4
Brooks, Diana D. **1990**:1
Brown, John Seely **2004**:1
Brown, Tina **1992**:1
Buffett, Jimmy **1999**:3
Buffett, Warren **1995**:2
Burnison, Chantal Simone **1988**:3
Burns, Robin **1991**:2
Burr, Donald Calvin **1985**:3
Busch, August A. III **1988**:2
Busch, August Anheuser, Jr.
  Obituary **1990**:2
Bushnell, Nolan **1985**:1
Buss, Jerry **1989**:3
Cain, Herman **1998**:3
Callaway, Ely
  Obituary **2002**:3
Calloway, D. Wayne **1987**:3
Campeau, Robert **1990**:1
Canfield, Alan B.
  Brief Entry **1986**:3
Carter, Billy

Obituary **1989**:1
Case, Steve **1995**:4 **1996**:4
Cassidy, Mike **2006**:1
Chalayan, Hussein **2003**:2
Chappell, Tom **2002**:3
Charron, Paul **2004**:1
Chenault, Kenneth I. **1999**:3
Chizen, Bruce **2004**:2
Choo, Jimmy **2006**:3
Chouinard, Yvon **2002**:2
Chung Ju Yung
  Obituary **2002**:1
Claiborne, Liz **1986**:3
Clark, Jim **1997**:1
Cole, Kenneth **2003**:1
Coleman, Sheldon, Jr. **1990**:2
Collier, Sophia **2001**:2
Combs, Sean 'Puffy' **1998**:4
Condit, Phil **2001**:3
Cooper, Alexander **1988**:4
Cooper, Stephen F. **2005**:4
Coors, William K.
  Brief Entry **1985**:1
Copeland, Al **1988**:3
Covey, Stephen R. **1994**:4
Cox, Richard Joseph
  Brief Entry **1985**:1
Craig, James **2001**:1
Craig, Sid and Jenny **1993**:4
Crandall, Robert L. **1992**:1
Crawford, Cheryl
  Obituary **1987**:1
Cray, Seymour R.
  Brief Entry **1986**:3
  Obituary **1997**:2
Cummings, Sam **1986**:3
D'Alessio, Kitty
  Brief Entry **1987**:3
David, George **2005**:1
Davis, Crispin **2004**:1
Davison, Ian Hay **1986**:1
DeBartolo, Edward J., Jr. **1989**:3
de la Renta, Oscar **2005**:4
Dell, Michael **1996**:2
DeLuca, Fred **2003**:3
Deming, W. Edwards **1992**:2
  Obituary **1994**:2
de Passe, Suzanne **1990**:4
Devine, John M. **2003**:2
Diemer, Walter E.
  Obituary **1998**:2
DiFranco, Ani **1997**:1
Diller, Barry **1991**:1
Disney, Lillian
  Obituary **1998**:3
Disney, Roy E. **1986**:3
Dolby, Ray Milton
  Brief Entry **1986**:1
Dolce, Domenico and Stefano Gabbana **2005**:4
Donahue, Tim **2004**:3
Doubleday, Nelson, Jr. **1987**:1
Downey, Bruce **2003**:1
Drexler, Millard S. **1990**:3
Drucker, Peter F. **1992**:3
Duisenberg, Wim
  Obituary **2006**:4
Dunlap, Albert J. **1997**:2
Dupri, Jermaine **1999**:1
Dyson, James **2005**:4
Eagleson, Alan **1987**:4
Eaton, Robert J. **1994**:2

Renvall, Johan
  Brief Entry **1987**:4
Robbins, Jerome
  Obituary **1999**:1
Rogers, Ginger
  Obituary **1995**:4
Stroman, Susan **2000**:4
Takei, Kei **1990**:2
Taylor, Paul **1992**:3
Tharp, Twyla **1992**:4
Tudor, Antony
  Obituary **1987**:4
Tune, Tommy **1994**:2
Varone, Doug **2001**:2
Verdi-Fletcher, Mary **1998**:2
Verdon, Gwen
  Obituary **2001**:2
Whelan, Wendy **1999**:3

EDUCATION
Abramson, Lyn **1986**:3
Alexander, Lamar **1991**:2
Bakker, Robert T. **1991**:3
Bayley, Corrine
  Brief Entry **1986**:4
Billington, James **1990**:3
Bollinger, Lee C. **2003**:2
Botstein, Leon **1985**:3
Bush, Millie **1992**:1
Campbell, Bebe Moore **1996**:2
Casper, Gerhard **1993**:1
Cavazos, Lauro F. **1989**:2
Cheek, James Edward
  Brief Entry **1987**:1
Cheney, Lynne V. **1990**:4
Clements, George **1985**:1
Cole, Johnetta B. **1994**:3
Coles, Robert **1995**:1
Commager, Henry Steele
  Obituary **1998**:3
Curran, Charles E. **1989**:2
Davis, Angela **1998**:3
Delany, Sarah
  Obituary **1999**:3
Deming, W. Edwards **1992**:2
  Obituary **1994**:2
Dershowitz, Alan **1992**:1
Dove, Rita **1994**:3
Drucker, Peter F. **1992**:3
Eberhart, Richard
  Obituary **2006**:3
Edelman, Marian Wright **1990**:4
Edwards, Harry **1989**:4
Etzioni, Amitai **1994**:3
Feldman, Sandra **1987**:3
Ferguson, Niall **2006**:1
Fernandez, Joseph **1991**:3
Folkman, Judah **1999**:1
Fox, Matthew **1992**:2
Fulbright, J. William
  Obituary **1995**:3
Futrell, Mary Hatwood **1986**:1
Futter, Ellen V. **1995**:1
Ghali, Boutros Boutros **1992**:3
Giamatti, A. Bartlett **1988**:4
  Obituary **1990**:1
Goldhaber, Fred
  Brief Entry **1986**:3
Gray, Hanna **1992**:4
Green, Richard R. **1988**:3
Gregorian, Vartan **1990**:3
Gund, Agnes **1993**:2

Hackney, Sheldon **1995**:1
Hair, Jay D. **1994**:3
Harker, Patrick T. **2001**:2
Hayakawa, Samuel Ichiye
  Obituary **1992**:3
Healy, Bernadine **1993**:1
Healy, Timothy S. **1990**:2
Heaney, Seamus **1996**:2
Heller, Walter
  Obituary **1987**:4
Hennessy, John L. **2002**:2
Hill, Anita **1994**:1
Hill, J. Edward **2006**:2
Hillegass, Clifton Keith **1989**:4
Horwich, Frances
  Obituary **2002**:3
Hunter, Madeline **1991**:2
Janzen, Daniel H. **1988**:4
Jones, Edward P. **2005**:1
Jordan, King **1990**:1
Justiz, Manuel J. **1986**:4
Kandel, Eric **2005**:2
Kemp, Jan **1987**:2
Kerr, Clark
  Obituary **2005**:1
King, Mary-Claire **1998**:3
Kopp, Wendy **1993**:3
Kozol, Jonathan **1992**:1
Lagasse, Emeril **1998**:3
Lamb, Wally **1999**:1
Lang, Eugene M. **1990**:3
Langston, J. William
  Brief Entry **1986**:2
Lawrence, Ruth
  Brief Entry **1986**:3
Laybourne, Geraldine **1997**:1
Leach, Penelope **1992**:4
Lee, Chang-Rae **2005**:1
Lerner, Michael **1994**:2
Levine, Arnold **2002**:3
MacKinnon, Catharine **1993**:2
Malloy, Edward 'Monk' **1989**:4
Marier, Rebecca **1995**:4
McAuliffe, Christa
  Obituary **1985**:4
McCall Smith, Alexander **2005**:2
McMillan, Terry **1993**:2
Morrison, Toni **1998**:1
Mumford, Lewis
  Obituary **1990**:2
Nemerov, Howard
  Obituary **1992**:1
Nye, Bill **1997**:2
O'Keefe, Sean **2005**:2
Owens, Delia and Mark **1993**:3
Pagels, Elaine **1997**:1
Paglia, Camille **1992**:3
Paige, Rod **2003**:2
Parizeau, Jacques **1995**:1
Peter, Valentine J. **1988**:2
Riley, Richard W. **1996**:3
Rodin, Judith **1994**:4
Rosendahl, Bruce R.
  Brief Entry **1986**:4
Rowland, Pleasant **1992**:3
Scheck, Barry **2000**:4
Schuman, Patricia Glass **1993**:2
Shalala, Donna **1992**:3
Sherman, Russell **1987**:4
Silber, John **1990**:1
Simmons, Adele Smith **1988**:4
Simmons, Ruth **1995**:2

Simon, Lou Anna K. **2005**:4
Singer, Margaret Thaler
  Obituary **2005**:1
Smoot, George F. **1993**:3
Sowell, Thomas **1998**:3
Spellings, Margaret **2005**:4
Spock, Benjamin **1995**:2
  Obituary **1998**:3
Steele, Shelby **1991**:2
Swanson, Mary Catherine **2002**:2
Tannen, Deborah **1995**:1
Thiebaud, Wayne **1991**:1
Thomas, Michel **1987**:4
Tilghman, Shirley M. **2002**:1
Tribe, Laurence H. **1988**:1
Tyson, Laura D'Andrea **1994**:1
Unz, Ron **1999**:1
Van Duyn, Mona **1993**:2
Vickrey, William S.
  Obituary **1997**:2
Warren, Robert Penn
  Obituary **1990**:1
West, Cornel **1994**:2
Wexler, Nancy S. **1992**:3
Whitney, Patrick **2006**:1
Wiesel, Elie **1998**:1
Wigand, Jeffrey **2000**:4
Wiles, Andrew **1994**:1
Wilson, Edward O. **1994**:4
Wilson, William Julius **1997**:1
Wolff, Tobias **2005**:1
Wu, Harry **1996**:1
Zanker, Bill
  Brief Entry **1987**:3
Zigler, Edward **1994**:1

FILM
Abbott, George
  Obituary **1995**:3
Adjani, Isabelle **1991**:1
Affleck, Ben **1999**:1
Aiello, Danny **1990**:4
Albert, Eddie
  Obituary **2006**:3
Alda, Robert
  Obituary **1986**:3
Alexander, Jane **1994**:2
Alexander, Jason **1993**:3
Allen, Debbie **1998**:2
Allen, Joan **1998**:1
Allen, Woody **1994**:1
Alley, Kirstie **1990**:3
Almodovar, Pedro **2000**:3
Altman, Robert **1993**:2
Ameche, Don
  Obituary **1994**:2
Anderson, Judith
  Obituary **1992**:3
Andrews, Julie **1996**:1
Aniston, Jennifer **2000**:3
Apatow, Judd **2006**:3
Applegate, Christina **2000**:4
Arad, Avi **2003**:2
Arden, Eve
  Obituary **1991**:2
Arkoff, Samuel Z.
  Obituary **2002**:4
Arlen, Harold
  Obituary **1986**:3
Arnaz, Desi
  Obituary **1987**:1
Arnold, Tom **1993**:2

Reeves, Steve
    Obituary **2000**:4
Reilly, John C. **2003**:4
Reiner, Rob **1991**:2
Reiser, Paul **1995**:2
Reisz, Karel
    Obituary **2004**:1
Reitman, Ivan **1986**:3
Remick, Lee
    Obituary **1992**:1
Reuben, Gloria **1999**:4
Reubens, Paul **1987**:2
Ricci, Christina **1999**:1
Richards, Michael **1993**:4
Riddle, Nelson
    Obituary **1985**:4
Ringwald, Molly **1985**:4
Ritchie, Guy **2001**:3
Ritter, John **2003**:4
Robards, Jason
    Obituary **2001**:3
Robbins, Jerome
    Obituary **1999**:1
Robbins, Tim **1993**:1
Roberts, Doris **2003**:4
Roberts, Julia **1991**:1
Rock, Chris **1998**:1
Rodriguez, Robert **2005**:1
Rogers, Ginger
    Obituary **1995**:4
Rogers, Roy
    Obituary **1998**:4
Roker, Roxie
    Obituary **1996**:2
Rolle, Esther
    Obituary **1999**:2
Rollins, Howard E., Jr. **1986**:1
Ross, Herbert
    Obituary **2002**:4
Roth, Tim **1998**:2
Rourke, Mickey **1988**:4
Rowan, Dan
    Obituary **1988**:1
Rudner, Rita **1993**:2
Rudnick, Paul **1994**:3
Ruehl, Mercedes **1992**:4
RuPaul **1996**:1
Rush, Geoffrey **2002**:1
Russo, Rene **2000**:2
Ryan, Meg **1994**:1
Ryder, Winona **1991**:2
Sagal, Katey **2005**:2
Salonga, Lea **2003**:3
Sandler, Adam **1999**:2
Sarandon, Susan **1995**:3
Savage, Fred **1990**:1
Savalas, Telly
    Obituary **1994**:3
Schlesinger, John
    Obituary **2004**:3
Schneider, Rob **1997**:4
Schroeder, Barbet **1996**:1
Schumacher, Joel **2004**:3
Schwarzenegger, Arnold **1991**:1
Schwimmer, David **1996**:2
Scorsese, Martin **1989**:1
Scott, George C.
    Obituary **2000**:2
Scott, Randolph
    Obituary **1987**:2
Scott, Ridley **2001**:1
Sedgwick, Kyra **2006**:2

Seidelman, Susan **1985**:4
Sevigny, Chloe **2001**:4
Seymour, Jane **1994**:4
Shaffer, Paul **1987**:1
Shanley, John Patrick **2006**:1
Sharkey, Ray
    Obituary **1994**:1
Shawn, Dick
    Obituary **1987**:3
Sheedy, Ally **1989**:1
Sheen, Martin **2002**:1
Shepard, Sam **1996**:4
Shields, Brooke **1996**:3
Shore, Dinah
    Obituary **1994**:3
Short, Martin **1986**:1
Shue, Andrew **1994**:4
Shyamalan, M. Night **2003**:2
Silverman, Jonathan **1997**:2
Silvers, Phil
    Obituary **1985**:4
Silverstone, Alicia **1997**:4
Sinatra, Frank
    Obituary **1998**:4
Singleton, John **1994**:3
Sinise, Gary **1996**:1
Siskel, Gene
    Obituary **1999**:3
Slater, Christian **1994**:1
Smirnoff, Yakov **1987**:2
Smith, Kevin **2000**:4
Smith, Will **1997**:2
Smits, Jimmy **1990**:1
Snipes, Wesley **1993**:1
Sobieski, Leelee **2002**:3
Soderbergh, Steven **2001**:4
Sondheim, Stephen **1994**:4
Sorkin, Aaron **2003**:2
Sorvino, Mira **1996**:3
Sothern, Ann
    Obituary **2002**:1
Southern, Terry
    Obituary **1996**:2
Spacek, Sissy **2003**:1
Spacey, Kevin **1996**:4
Spade, David **1999**:2
Spader, James **1991**:2
Spheeris, Penelope **1989**:2
Spielberg, Steven **1993**:4 **1997**:4
Stack, Robert
    Obituary **2004**:2
Staller, Ilona **1988**:3
Stallone, Sylvester **1994**:2
Steel, Dawn **1990**:1
    Obituary **1998**:2
Stefani, Gwen **2005**:4
Steiger, Rod
    Obituary **2003**:4
Stevenson, McLean
    Obituary **1996**:3
Stewart, Jimmy
    Obituary **1997**:4
Stewart, Patrick **1996**:1
Stiles, Julia **2002**:3
Stiller, Ben **1999**:1
Sting **1991**:4
Stone, Oliver **1990**:4
Stone, Sharon **1993**:4
Stoppard, Tom **1995**:4
Streep, Meryl **1990**:2
Streisand, Barbra **1992**:2
Strummer, Joe

    Obituary **2004**:1
Studi, Wes **1994**:3
Styne, Jule
    Obituary **1995**:1
Susskind, David
    Obituary **1987**:2
Sutherland, Kiefer **2002**:4
Swank, Hilary **2000**:3
Tanaka, Tomoyuki
    Obituary **1997**:3
Tandy, Jessica **1990**:4
    Obituary **1995**:1
Tarantino, Quentin **1995**:1
Tautou, Audrey **2004**:2
Taylor, Elizabeth **1993**:3
Taylor, Lili **2000**:2
Theron, Charlize **2001**:4
Thiebaud, Wayne **1991**:1
Thompson, Emma **1993**:2
Thompson, Fred **1998**:2
Thornton, Billy Bob **1997**:4
Thurman, Uma **1994**:2
Tilly, Jennifer **1997**:2
Tomei, Marisa **1995**:2
Travolta, John **1995**:2
Tucci, Stanley **2003**:2
Tucker, Chris **1999**:1
Tucker, Forrest
    Obituary **1987**:1
Turner, Janine **1993**:2
Turner, Kathleen **1985**:3
Turner, Lana
    Obituary **1996**:1
Turturro, John **2002**:2
Tyler, Liv **1997**:2
Ullman, Tracey **1988**:3
Union, Gabrielle **2004**:2
Urich, Robert **1988**:1
    Obituary **2003**:3
Usher **2005**:1
Ustinov, Peter
    Obituary **2005**:3
Vanilla Ice **1991**:3
Van Sant, Gus **1992**:2
Vardalos, Nia **2003**:4
Varney, Jim
    Brief Entry **1985**:4
    Obituary **2000**:3
Vaughn, Vince **1999**:2
Ventura, Jesse **1999**:2
Vidal, Gore **1996**:2
Vidov, Oleg **1987**:4
Villechaize, Herve
    Obituary **1994**:1
Vincent, Fay **1990**:2
Voight, Jon **2002**:3
Walker, Nancy
    Obituary **1992**:3
Wallis, Hal
    Obituary **1987**:1
Warhol, Andy
    Obituary **1987**:2
Washington, Denzel **1993**:2
Wasserman, Lew
    Obituary **2003**:3
Waters, John **1988**:3
Waterston, Sam **2006**:1
Watson, Emily **2001**:1
Watts, Naomi **2006**:1
Wayans, Damon **1998**:4
Wayans, Keenen Ivory **1991**:1
Wayne, David

Vandross, Luther
  Obituary 2006:3
Van Halen, Edward 1985:2
Vanilla Ice 1991:3
Vaughan, Sarah
  Obituary 1990:3
Vaughan, Stevie Ray
  Obituary 1991:1
Vega, Suzanne 1988:1
Vollenweider, Andreas 1985:2
von Karajan, Herbert
  Obituary 1989:4
von Trapp, Maria
  Obituary 1987:3
Walker, Junior
  Obituary 1996:2
Washington, Grover, Jr. 1989:1
Wasserman, Lew
  Obituary 2003:3
Weintraub, Jerry 1986:1
Wells, Mary
  Obituary 1993:1
West, Dottie
  Obituary 1992:2
West, Kanye 2006:1
White, Barry
  Obituary 2004:3
White Stripes, The 2006:1
Williams, Joe
  Obituary 1999:4
Williams, Pharrell 2005:3
Williams, Vanessa L. 1999:2
Willis, Bruce 1986:4
Wilson, Brian 1996:1
Wilson, Carl
  Obituary 1998:2
Wilson, Cassandra 1996:3
Wilson, Gretchen 2006:3
Winans, CeCe 2000:1
Winston, George 1987:1
Winter, Paul 1990:2
Womack, Lee Ann 2002:1
Wynette, Tammy
  Obituary 1998:3
Wynonna 1993:3
Xenakis, Iannis
  Obituary 2001:4
Xzibit 2005:4
Yankovic, 'Weird Al' 1985:4
Yankovic, Frank
  Obituary 1999:2
Yearwood, Trisha 1999:1
Yoakam, Dwight 1992:4
Young, Neil 1991:2
Zappa, Frank
  Obituary 1994:2
Zevon, Warren
  Obituary 2004:4
Zinnemann, Fred
  Obituary 1997:3
Zwilich, Ellen 1990:1

**POLITICS AND
GOVERNMENT--FOREIGN**
Abacha, Sani 1996:3
Abdullah II, King 2002:4
Adams, Gerald 1994:1
Ahern, Bertie 1999:3
Akihito, Emperor of Japan 1990:1
al-Abdullah, Rania 2001:1
al-Assad, Bashar 2004:2
Albert, Prince of Monaco 2006:2

Albright, Madeleine 1994:3
Amin, Idi
  Obituary 2004:4
Annan, Kofi 1999:1
Aquino, Corazon 1986:2
Arafat, Yasser 1989:3 1997:3
Arens, Moshe 1985:1
Arias Sanchez, Oscar 1989:3
Aristide, Jean-Bertrand 1991:3
Assad, Hafez
  Obituary 2000:4
Assad, Hafez al- 1992:1
Assad, Rifaat 1986:3
Astorga, Nora 1988:2
Babangida, Ibrahim Badamosi 1992
  :4
Balaguer, Joaquin
  Obituary 2003:4
Banda, Hastings 1994:3
Bandaranaike, Sirimavo
  Obituary 2001:2
Barak, Ehud 1999:4
Barbie, Klaus
  Obituary 1992:2
Basescu, Traian 2006:2
Begin, Menachem
  Obituary 1992:3
Berger, Oscar 2004:4
Berlusconi, Silvio 1994:4
Berri, Nabih 1985:2
Bhutto, Benazir 1989:4
Biya, Paul 2006:1
Blair, Tony 1996:3 1997:4
Bolkiah, Sultan Muda Hassanal 1985
  :4
Bouchard, Lucien 1999:2
Bourassa, Robert
  Obituary 1997:1
Bozize, Francois 2006:3
Brandt, Willy
  Obituary 1993:2
Brundtland, Gro Harlem 2000:1
Buthelezi, Mangosuthu Gatsha 1989
  :3
Campbell, Kim 1993:4
Cardoso, Fernando Henrique 1996:4
Castro, Fidel 1991:4
Ceausescu, Nicolae
  Obituary 1990:2
Cedras, Raoul 1994:4
Chaing Kai-Shek, Madame
  Obituary 2005:1
Chambas, Mohammed ibn 2003:3
Chen Shui-bian 2001:2
Chernenko, Konstantin
  Obituary 1985:1
Chiluba, Frederick 1992:3
Chissano, Joaquim 1987:4
Chretien, Jean 1990:4 1997:2
Ciampi, Carlo Azeglio 2004:3
Collor de Mello, Fernando 1992:4
Colosio, Luis Donaldo 1994:3
Copps, Sheila 1986:4
Cresson, Edith 1992:1
Cruz, Arturo 1985:1
Dalai Lama 1989:1
Deby, Idriss 2002:2
de Hoop Scheffer, Jaap 2005:1
de Klerk, F.W. 1990:1
Delors, Jacques 1990:2
Deng Xiaoping 1995:1
  Obituary 1997:3

de Pinies, Jamie
  Brief Entry 1986:3
Devi, Phoolan 1986:1
  Obituary 2002:3
Dhlakama, Afonso 1993:3
Doe, Samuel
  Obituary 1991:1
Doi, Takako
  Brief Entry 1987:4
Dong, Pham Van
  Obituary 2000:4
Duarte, Jose Napoleon
  Obituary 1990:3
Dubinin, Yuri 1987:4
Duhalde, Eduardo 2003:3
Fahd, King of Saudi Arabia
  Obituary 2006:4
Ferguson, Sarah 1990:3
Finnbogadóttir, Vigdiás
  Brief Entry 1986:2
Fischer, Joschka 2005:2
Fox, Vicente 2001:1
Freij, Elias 1986:4
Fujimori, Alberto 1992:4
Galvin, Martin
  Brief Entry 1985:3
Gandhi, Indira
  Obituary 1985:1
Gandhi, Rajiv
  Obituary 1991:4
Gandhi, Sonia 2000:2
Garcia, Amalia 2005:3
Garneau, Marc 1985:1
Gbagbo, Laurent 2003:2
Ghali, Boutros Boutros 1992:3
Gorbachev, Mikhail 1985:2
Gorbachev, Raisa
  Obituary 2000:2
Gowda, H. D. Deve 1997:1
Gromyko, Andrei
  Obituary 1990:2
Guelleh, Ismail Omar 2006:2
Habash, George 1986:1
Habibie, Bacharuddin Jusuf 1999:3
Halonen, Tarja 2006:4
Hani, Chris
  Obituary 1993:4
Harriman, Pamela 1994:4
Harris, Michael Deane 1997:2
Havel, Vaclav 1990:3
Herzog, Chaim
  Obituary 1997:3
Hess, Rudolph
  Obituary 1988:1
Hirohito, Emperor of Japan
  Obituary 1989:2
Honecker, Erich
  Obituary 1994:4
Hosokawa, Morihiro 1994:1
Hu Jintao 2004:1
Hume, John 1987:1
Hussein, Saddam 1991:1
Husseini, Faisal 1998:4
Hussein I, King 1997:3
  Obituary 1999:3
Hu Yaobang
  Obituary 1989:4
Izetbegovic, Alija 1996:4
Jenkins, Roy Harris
  Obituary 2004:1
Jiang Quing
  Obituary 1992:1

Jiang Zemin **1996**:1
Johnson, Pierre Marc **1985**:4
Juan Carlos I **1993**:1
Juliana
  Obituary **2005**:3
Jumblatt, Walid **1987**:4
Juneau, Pierre **1988**:3
Kabila, Joseph **2003**:2
Kabila, Laurent **1998**:1
  Obituary **2001**:3
Kagame, Paul **2001**:4
Kamel, Hussein **1996**:1
Karadzic, Radovan **1995**:3
Karimov, Islam **2006**:3
Karzai, Hamid **2002**:3
Kasyanov, Mikhail **2001**:1
Kekkonen, Urho
  Obituary **1986**:4
Khatami, Mohammed **1997**:4
Khomeini, Ayatollah Ruhollah
  Obituary **1989**:4
Kibaki, Mwai **2003**:4
Kim Dae Jung **1998**:3
Kim Il Sung
  Obituary **1994**:4
Kim Jong Il **1995**:2
King Hassan II
  Obituary **2000**:1
Kohl, Helmut **1994**:1
Koizumi, Junichiro **2002**:1
Kostunica, Vojislav **2001**:1
Kouchner, Bernard **2005**:3
Kufuor, John Agyekum **2005**:4
Kyprianou, Spyros
  Obituary **2003**:2
Lagos, Ricardo **2005**:3
Lalonde, Marc **1985**:1
Landsbergis, Vytautas **1991**:3
Lebed, Alexander **1997**:1
Le Duan
  Obituary **1986**:4
Le Duc Tho
  Obituary **1991**:1
Lee, Martin **1998**:2
Lee Jong-Wook **2005**:1
Lee Teng-hui **2000**:1
Leávesque, Reneá
  Obituary **1988**:1
Levy, David **1987**:2
Lewis, Stephen **1987**:2
Livingstone, Ken **1988**:3
Lon Nol
  Obituary **1986**:1
Lukashenko, Alexander **2006**:4
Macapagal-Arroyo, Gloria **2001**:4
Machel, Samora
  Obituary **1987**:1
Macmillan, Harold
  Obituary **1987**:2
Major, John **1991**:2
Mandela, Nelson **1990**:3
Mandela, Winnie **1989**:3
Mara, Ratu Sir Kamisese
  Obituary **2005**:3
Marcos, Ferdinand
  Obituary **1990**:1
Martin, Paul **2004**:4
Masako, Crown Princess **1993**:4
Mas Canosa, Jorge
  Obituary **1998**:2
Mbeki, Thabo **1999**:4
McGuinness, Martin **1985**:4

McLaughlin, Audrey **1990**:3
Megawati Sukarnoputri **2002**:2
Megawati Sukarnoputri **2000**:1
Mesic, Stipe **2005**:4
Milosevic, Slobodan **1993**:2
Mitterrand, Francois
  Obituary **1996**:2
Miyazawa, Kiichi **1992**:2
Mobutu Sese Seko
  Obituary **1998**:4
Mobutu Sese Seko **1993**:4
  Obituary **1998**:1
Moi, Daniel arap **1993**:2
Molotov, Vyacheslav Mikhailovich
  Obituary **1987**:1
Mori, Yoshiro **2000**:4
Mubarak, Hosni **1991**:4
Mugabe, Robert **1988**:4
Mulroney, Brian **1989**:2
Museveni, Yoweri **2002**:1
Musharraf, Pervez **2000**:2
Nagako, Empress Dowager
  Obituary **2001**:1
Nazarbayev, Nursultan **2006**:4
Netanyahu, Benjamin **1996**:4
Nidal, Abu **1987**:1
Niezabitowska, Malgorzata **1991**:3
Nujoma, Sam **1990**:4
Nyerere, Julius
  Obituary **2000**:2
Obando, Miguel **1986**:4
Obasanjo, Olusegun **2000**:2
Obuchi, Keizo **1999**:2
Obuchi, Keizo
  Obituary **2000**:4
Ocalan, Abdullah **1999**:4
Olav, King of Norway
  Obituary **1991**:3
Palme, Olof
  Obituary **1986**:2
Papandreou, Andrea
  Obituary **1997**:1
Parizeau, Jacques **1995**:1
Pastrana, Andres **2002**:1
Paton, Alan
  Obituary **1988**:3
Patten, Christopher **1993**:3
Paz, Octavio **1991**:2
Peckford, Brian **1989**:1
Peres, Shimon **1996**:3
Perez, Carlos Andre **1990**:2
Perez de Cuellar, Javier **1991**:3
Peterson, David **1987**:1
Philby, Kim
  Obituary **1988**:3
Pinochet, Augusto **1999**:2
Pol Pot
  Obituary **1998**:4
Preával, Reneá **1997**:2
Primakov, Yevgeny **1999**:3
Princess Margaret, Countess of
  Snowdon
  Obituary **2003**:2
Putin, Vladimir **2000**:3
Qaddhafi, Muammar **1998**:3
Queen Elizabeth the Queen Mother
  Obituary **2003**:2
Rabin, Leah
  Obituary **2001**:2
Rabin, Yitzhak **1993**:1
  Obituary **1996**:2

Rafsanjani, Ali Akbar Hashemi **1987**
  :3
Rahman, Sheik Omar Abdel- **1993**:3
Rainier III, Prince of Monaco
  Obituary **2006**:2
Ram, Jagjivan
  Obituary **1986**:4
Ramos, Fidel **1995**:2
Rao, P. V. Narasimha **1993**:2
Rasmussen, Anders Fogh **2006**:1
Ravalomanana, Marc **2003**:1
Reisman, Simon **1987**:4
Robelo, Alfonso **1988**:1
Robinson, Mary **1993**:1
Roh Moo-hyun **2005**:1
Saleh, Ali Abdullah **2001**:3
Salinas, Carlos **1992**:1
Sanchez de Lozada, Gonzalo **2004**:3
Sarkis, Elias
  Obituary **1985**:3
Saro-Wiwa, Ken
  Obituary **1996**:2
Savimbi, Jonas **1986**:2 **1994**:2
Schily, Otto
  Brief Entry **1987**:4
Schroder, Gerhard **1999**:1
Shah, Gyanendra **2006**:1
Sharon, Ariel **2001**:4
Shipley, Jenny **1998**:3
Silva, Luiz Inacio Lula da **2003**:4
Simpson, Wallis
  Obituary **1986**:3
Sisulu, Walter
  Obituary **2004**:2
Slovo, Joe **1989**:2
Staller, Ilona **1988**:3
Stoltenberg, Jens **2006**:4
Strauss, Robert **1991**:4
Suu Kyi, Aung San **1996**:2
Suzman, Helen **1989**:3
Takeshita, Noboru
  Obituary **2001**:1
Tambo, Oliver **1991**:3
Terzi, Zehdi Labib **1985**:3
Thaksin Shinawatra **2005**:4
Thatcher, Margaret **1989**:2
Trajkovski, Boris
  Obituary **2005**:2
Treurnicht, Andries **1992**:2
Trimble, David **1999**:1
Trudeau, Pierre
  Obituary **2001**:1
Tudjman, Franjo **1996**:2
Tudjman, Franjo
  Obituary **2000**:2
Turabi, Hassan **1995**:4
Uribe, Alvaro **2003**:3
Vajpayee, Atal Behari **1998**:4
Vander Zalm, William **1987**:3
Vazquez, Tabare **2006**:2
Verhofstadt, Guy **2006**:3
Wahid, Abdurrahman **2000**:3
Walesa, Lech **1991**:2
Wei Jingsheng **1998**:2
Weizman, Ezer
  Obituary **2006**:3
Werner, Ruth
  Obituary **2001**:1
Wickramasinghe, Ranil **2003**:2
William, Prince of Wales **2001**:3
Wilson, Bertha
  Brief Entry **1986**:1

Wu Yi **2005**:2
Ye Jianying
    Obituary **1987**:1
Yeltsin, Boris **1991**:1
Yushchenko, Viktor **2006**:1
Zedillo, Ernesto **1995**:1
Zeroual, Liamine **1996**:2
Zhao Ziyang **1989**:1
Zhirinovsky, Vladimir **1994**:2
Zia ul-Haq, Mohammad
    Obituary **1988**:4
Chirac, Jacques **1995**:4

POLITICS AND GOVERNMENT--U.S.
Abraham, Spencer **1991**:4
Abrams, Elliott **1987**:1
Abzug, Bella **1998**:2
Achtenberg, Roberta **1993**:4
Agnew, Spiro Theodore
    Obituary **1997**:1
Ailes, Roger **1989**:3
Albright, Madeleine **1994**:3
Alexander, Lamar **1991**:2
Alioto, Joseph L.
    Obituary **1998**:3
Allen Jr., Ivan
    Obituary **2004**:3
Alvarez, Aida **1999**:2
Archer, Dennis **1994**:4
Ashcroft, John **2002**:4
Aspin, Les
    Obituary **1996**:1
Atwater, Lee **1989**:4
    Obituary **1991**:4
Babbitt, Bruce **1994**:1
Baker, James A. III **1991**:2
Baldrige, Malcolm
    Obituary **1988**:1
Banks, Dennis J. **1986**:4
Barry, Marion **1991**:1
Barshefsky, Charlene **2000**:4
Beame, Abraham
    Obituary **2001**:4
Begaye, Kelsey **1999**:3
Bennett, William **1990**:1
Benson, Ezra Taft
    Obituary **1994**:4
Bentsen, Lloyd **1993**:3
Berger, Sandy **2000**:1
Berle, Peter A.A.
    Brief Entry **1987**:3
Biden, Joe **1986**:3
Boehner, John A. **2006**:4
Bonner, Robert **2003**:4
Bono, Sonny **1992**:2
    Obituary **1998**:2
Boxer, Barbara **1995**:1
Boyington, Gregory 'Pappy'
    Obituary **1988**:2
Bradley, Bill **2000**:2
Bradley, Tom
    Obituary **1999**:1
Brady, Sarah and James S. **1991**:4
Braun, Carol Moseley **1993**:1
Brazile, Donna **2001**:1
Bremer, L. Paul **2004**:2
Brennan, William
    Obituary **1997**:4
Brown, Edmund G., Sr.
    Obituary **1996**:3
Brown, Jerry **1992**:4
Brown, Ron

Obituary **1996**:4
Brown, Ron **1990**:3
Brown, Willie **1996**:4
Brown, Willie L. **1985**:2
Browner, Carol M. **1994**:1
Buchanan, Pat **1996**:3
Bundy, McGeorge
    Obituary **1997**:1
Bundy, William P.
    Obituary **2001**:2
Bush, Barbara **1989**:3
Bush, George W., Jr. **1996**:4
Bush, Jeb **2003**:1
Caliguiri, Richard S.
    Obituary **1988**:3
Campbell, Ben Nighthorse **1998**:1
Campbell, Bill **1997**:2
Card, Andrew H., Jr. **2003**:2
Carey, Ron **1993**:3
Carmona, Richard **2003**:2
Carnahan, Jean **2001**:2
Carnahan, Mel
    Obituary **2001**:2
Carter, Billy
    Obituary **1989**:1
Carter, Jimmy **1995**:1
Casey, William
    Obituary **1987**:3
Cavazos, Lauro F. **1989**:2
Chamberlin, Wendy **2002**:4
Chavez, Linda **1999**:3
Chavez-Thompson, Linda **1999**:1
Cheney, Dick **1991**:3
Cheney, Lynne V. **1990**:4
Chisholm, Shirley
    Obituary **2006**:1
Christopher, Warren **1996**:3
Cisneros, Henry **1987**:2
Clark, J. E.
    Brief Entry **1986**:1
Clinton, Bill **1992**:1
Clinton, Hillary Rodham **1993**:2
Clyburn, James **1999**:4
Cohen, William S. **1998**:1
Collins, Cardiss **1995**:3
Connally, John
    Obituary **1994**:1
Conyers, John, Jr. **1999**:1
Cornum, Rhonda **2006**:3
Cuomo, Mario **1992**:2
D'Amato, Al **1996**:1
Daschle, Tom **2002**:3
Dean, Howard **2005**:4
DeLay, Tom **2000**:1
Dinkins, David N. **1990**:2
Dolan, Terry **1985**:2
Dole, Bob **1994**:2
Dole, Elizabeth Hanford **1990**:1
Dukakis, Michael **1988**:3
Duke, David **1990**:2
Ehrlichman, John
    Obituary **1999**:3
Elders, Joycelyn **1994**:1
Engler, John **1996**:3
Ervin, Sam
    Obituary **1985**:2
Estrich, Susan **1989**:1
Falkenberg, Nanette **1985**:2
Farmer, James
    Obituary **2000**:1
Farrakhan, Louis **1990**:4
Faubus, Orval

Obituary **1995**:2
Feinstein, Dianne **1993**:3
Fenwick, Millicent H.
    Obituary **1993**:2
Ferraro, Geraldine **1998**:3
Fish, Hamilton
    Obituary **1991**:3
Fitzgerald, A. Ernest **1986**:2
Fleischer, Ari **2003**:1
Florio, James J. **1991**:2
Flynn, Ray **1989**:1
Foley, Thomas S. **1990**:1
Forbes, Steve **1996**:2
Foster, Vincent
    Obituary **1994**:1
Frank, Anthony M. **1992**:1
Frank, Barney **1989**:2
Franks, Tommy **2004**:1
Frist, Bill **2003**:4
Fulbright, J. William
    Obituary **1995**:3
Galvin, John R. **1990**:1
Garrison, Jim
    Obituary **1993**:2
Gates, Robert M. **1992**:2
Gebbie, Kristine **1994**:2
Gephardt, Richard **1987**:3
Gergen, David **1994**:1
Gingrich, Newt **1991**:1 **1997**:3
Giuliani, Rudolph **1994**:2
Glenn, John **1998**:3
Goldwater, Barry
    Obituary **1998**:4
Gore, Albert, Jr. **1993**:2
Gore, Albert, Sr.
    Obituary **1999**:2
Gramm, Phil **1995**:2
Granholm, Jennifer **2003**:3
Greenspan, Alan **1992**:2
Griffiths, Martha
    Obituary **2004**:2
Haldeman, H. R.
    Obituary **1994**:2
Hall, Gus
    Obituary **2001**:2
Harriman, Pamela **1994**:4
Harriman, W. Averell
    Obituary **1986**:4
Harris, Katherine **2001**:3
Harris, Patricia Roberts
    Obituary **1985**:2
Hastert, Dennis **1999**:3
Hatch, Orin G. **2000**:2
Hayakawa, Samuel Ichiye
    Obituary **1992**:3
Heinz, John
    Obituary **1991**:4
Heller, Walter
    Obituary **1987**:4
Helms, Jesse **1998**:1
Hills, Carla **1990**:3
Hiss, Alger
    Obituary **1997**:2
Holbrooke, Richard **1996**:2
Hughes, Karen **2001**:2
Hull, Jane Dee **1999**:2
Hundt, Reed Eric **1997**:2
Hyde, Henry **1999**:1
Inman, Bobby Ray **1985**:1
Jackson, Jesse **1996**:1
Jackson, Jesse, Jr. **1998**:3
Jackson, Thomas Penfield **2000**:2

Whitman, Christine Todd **1994**:3
Whitmire, Kathy **1988**:2
Wilder, L. Douglas **1990**:3
Williams, Anthony **2000**:4
Williams, G. Mennen
  Obituary **1988**:2
Wilson, Pete **1992**:3
Yard, Molly **1991**:4
Young, Coleman A.
  Obituary **1998**:1
Zech, Lando W.
  Brief Entry **1987**:4
Zerhouni, Elias A. **2004**:3
Zinni, Anthony **2003**:1

RADIO

Albert, Marv **1994**:3
Albom, Mitch **1999**:3
Ameche, Don
  Obituary **1994**:2
Autry, Gene
  Obituary **1999**:1
Backus, Jim
  Obituary **1990**:1
Barber, Red
  Obituary **1993**:2
Becker, Brian **2004**:4
Bell, Art **2000**:1
Blanc, Mel
  Obituary **1989**:4
Campbell, Bebe Moore **1996**:2
Caray, Harry **1988**:3
  Obituary **1998**:3
Carson, Johnny
  Obituary **2006**:1
Cherry, Don **1993**:4
Codrescu, Andreá **1997**:3
Cosell, Howard
  Obituary **1995**:4
Costas, Bob **1986**:4
Crenna, Richard
  Obituary **2004**:1
Day, Dennis
  Obituary **1988**:4
Denver, Bob
  Obituary **2006**:4
Dr. Demento **1986**:1
Donnellan, Nanci **1995**:2
Durrell, Gerald
  Obituary **1995**:3
Edwards, Bob **1993**:2
Fleming, Art
  Obituary **1995**:4
Ford, Tennessee Ernie
  Obituary **1992**:2
Gobel, George
  Obituary **1991**:4
Goodman, Benny
  Obituary **1986**:3
Gordon, Gale
  Obituary **1996**:1
Graham, Billy **1992**:1
Granato, Cammi **1999**:3
Grange, Red
  Obituary **1991**:3
Greene, Lorne
  Obituary **1988**:1
Gross, Terry **1998**:3
Harmon, Tom
  Obituary **1990**:3
Harvey, Paul **1995**:3
Harwell, Ernie **1997**:3

Hill, George Roy
  Obituary **2004**:1
Hollander, Joel **2006**:4
Hope, Bob
  Obituary **2004**:4
Houseman, John
  Obituary **1989**:1
Hughes, Cathy **1999**:1
Imus, Don **1997**:1
Ives, Burl
  Obituary **1995**:4
Karmazin, Mel **2006**:1
Kasem, Casey **1987**:1
Keyes, Alan **1996**:2
King, Larry **1993**:1
Kyser, Kay
  Obituary **1985**:3
Leávesque, Reneá
  Obituary **1988**:1
Limbaugh, Rush **1991**:3
Magliozzi, Tom and Ray **1991**:4
Milligan, Spike
  Obituary **2003**:2
Nelson, Harriet
  Obituary **1995**:1
Olson, Johnny
  Obituary **1985**:4
Osgood, Charles **1996**:2
Paar, Jack
  Obituary **2005**:2
Paley, William S.
  Obituary **1991**:2
Parks, Bert
  Obituary **1992**:3
Parsons, Gary **2006**:2
Porter, Sylvia
  Obituary **1991**:4
Quivers, Robin **1995**:4
Raphael, Sally Jessy **1992**:4
Raye, Martha
  Obituary **1995**:1
Reagan, Ronald
  Obituary **2005**:3
Riddle, Nelson
  Obituary **1985**:4
Roberts, Cokie **1993**:4
Saralegui, Cristina **1999**:2
Schlessinger, Laura **1996**:3
Seacrest, Ryan **2004**:4
Sedaris, David **2005**:3
Sevareid, Eric
  Obituary **1993**:1
Shore, Dinah
  Obituary **1994**:3
Smith, Buffalo Bob
  Obituary **1999**:1
Smith, Kate
  Obituary **1986**:3
Stern, Howard **1988**:2 **1993**:3
Swayze, John Cameron
  Obituary **1996**:1
Tom and Ray Magliozzi **1991**:4
Totenberg, Nina **1992**:2
Wolfman Jack
  Obituary **1996**:1
Young, Robert
  Obituary **1999**:1

RELIGION

Abernathy, Ralph
  Obituary **1990**:3
Altea, Rosemary **1996**:3

Applewhite, Marshall Herff
  Obituary **1997**:3
Aristide, Jean-Bertrand **1991**:3
Beckett, Wendy (Sister) **1998**:3
Benson, Ezra Taft
  Obituary **1994**:4
Bernardin, Cardinal Joseph **1997**:2
Berri, Nabih **1985**:2
Browning, Edmond
  Brief Entry **1986**:2
Burns, Charles R.
  Brief Entry **1988**:1
Carey, George **1992**:3
Chavis, Benjamin **1993**:4
Chittister, Joan D. **2002**:2
Chopra, Deepak **1996**:3
Clements, George **1985**:1
Cleveland, James
  Obituary **1991**:3
Coffin, William Sloane, Jr. **1990**:3
Cunningham, Reverend William
  Obituary **1997**:4
Curran, Charles E. **1989**:2
Daily, Bishop Thomas V. **1990**:4
Dalai Lama **1989**:1
Dearden, John Cardinal
  Obituary **1988**:4
Dorsey, Thomas A.
  Obituary **1993**:3
Eilberg, Amy
  Brief Entry **1985**:3
Farrakhan, Louis **1990**:4
Fox, Matthew **1992**:2
Fulghum, Robert **1996**:1
Graham, Billy **1992**:1
Grant, Amy **1985**:4
Hahn, Jessica **1989**:4
Harris, Barbara **1989**:3
Harris, Barbara **1996**:3
Healy, Timothy S. **1990**:2
Henry, Carl F.H.
  Obituary **2005**:1
Huffington, Arianna **1996**:2
Hume, Basil Cardinal
  Obituary **2000**:1
Hunter, Howard **1994**:4
Irwin, James
  Obituary **1992**:1
Jackson, Jesse **1996**:1
John Paul II, Pope **1995**:3
Jumblatt, Walid **1987**:4
Kahane, Meir
  Obituary **1991**:2
Khomeini, Ayatollah Ruhollah
  Obituary **1989**:4
Kissling, Frances **1989**:2
Koresh, David
  Obituary **1993**:4
Krol, John
  Obituary **1996**:3
Lefebvre, Marcel **1988**:4
Levinger, Moshe **1992**:1
Mahesh Yogi, Maharishi **1991**:3
Mahony, Roger M. **1988**:2
Maida, Adam Cardinal **1998**:2
Malloy, Edward 'Monk' **1989**:4
McCloskey, James **1993**:1
Mother Teresa **1993**:1
  Obituary **1998**:1
Obando, Miguel **1986**:4
O'Connor, Cardinal John **1990**:3
O'Connor, John

Obituary **2000**:4
Osteen, Joel **2006**:2
Perry, Harold A.
   Obituary **1992**:1
Peter, Valentine J. **1988**:2
Rafsanjani, Ali Akbar Hashemi **1987**:3
Rahman, Sheik Omar Abdel- **1993**:3
Rajneesh, Bhagwan Shree
   Obituary **1990**:2
Reed, Ralph **1995**:1
Reese, Della **1999**:2
Robertson, Pat **1988**:2
Robinson, V. Gene **2004**:4
Rogers, Adrian **1987**:4
Runcie, Robert **1989**:4
   Obituary **2001**:1
Schneerson, Menachem Mendel **1992**:4
   Obituary **1994**:4
Scott, Gene
   Brief Entry **1986**:1
Sentamu, John **2006**:2
Sharpton, Al **1991**:2
Shaw, William **2000**:3
Sin, Jaime
   Obituary **2006**:3
Smith, Jeff **1991**:4
Spong, John **1991**:3 **2001**:1
Stallings, George A., Jr. **1990**:1
Swaggart, Jimmy **1987**:3
Taylor, Graham **2005**:3
Turabi, Hassan **1995**:4
Violet, Arlene **1985**:3
Wildmon, Donald **1988**:4
Williamson, Marianne **1991**:4
Youngblood, Johnny Ray **1994**:1

SCIENCE

Abramson, Lyn **1986**:3
Adams, Patch **1999**:2
Adamson, George
   Obituary **1990**:2
Agatston, Arthur **2005**:1
Allen, John **1992**:1
Altman, Sidney **1997**:2
Atkins, Robert C.
   Obituary **2004**:2
Axelrod, Julius
   Obituary **2006**:1
Bahcall, John N.
   Obituary **2006**:4
Bakker, Robert T. **1991**:3
Ballard, Robert D. **1998**:4
Barnard, Christiaan
   Obituary **2002**:4
Baulieu, Etienne-Emile **1990**:1
Bayley, Corrine
   Brief Entry **1986**:4
Bean, Alan L. **1986**:2
Beattie, Owen
   Brief Entry **1985**:2
Berkley, Seth **2002**:3
Berle, Peter A.A.
   Brief Entry **1987**:3
Berman, Jennifer and Laura **2003**:2
Bethe, Hans
   Obituary **2006**:2
Bettelheim, Bruno
   Obituary **1990**:3
Blobel, Gunter **2000**:4
Bloch, Erich **1987**:4

Boyer, Herbert Wayne **1985**:1
Bristow, Lonnie **1996**:1
Brown, John Seely **2004**:1
Buck, Linda **2004**:2
Burnison, Chantal Simone **1988**:3
Carlsson, Arvid **2001**:2
Carson, Ben **1998**:2
Cerf, Vinton G. **1999**:2
Chaudhari, Praveen **1989**:4
Chu, Paul C.W. **1988**:2
Coles, Robert **1995**:1
Collins, Eileen **1995**:3
Colwell, Rita Rossi **1999**:3
Comfort, Alex
   Obituary **2000**:4
Conrad, Pete
   Obituary **2000**:1
Cousteau, Jacques-Yves
   Obituary **1998**:2
Cousteau, Jean-Michel **1988**:2
Cram, Donald J.
   Obituary **2002**:2
Cray, Seymour R.
   Brief Entry **1986**:3
   Obituary **1997**:2
Crick, Francis
   Obituary **2005**:4
Davis, Noel **1990**:3
DeVita, Vincent T., Jr. **1987**:3
Diemer, Walter E.
   Obituary **1998**:2
Djerassi, Carl **2000**:4
Douglas, Marjory Stoneman **1993**:1
   Obituary **1998**:4
Downey, Bruce **2003**:1
Duke, Red
   Brief Entry **1987**:1
Durrell, Gerald
   Obituary **1995**:3
Earle, Sylvia **2001**:1
Fang Lizhi **1988**:1
Fano, Ugo
   Obituary **2001**:4
Fauci, Anthony S. **2004**:1
Fields, Evelyn J. **2001**:3
Fiennes, Ranulph **1990**:3
Fisher, Mel **1985**:4
Folkman, Judah **1999**:1
Fossey, Dian
   Obituary **1986**:1
Foster, Tabatha
   Obituary **1988**:3
Fraser, Claire M. **2005**:2
Futter, Ellen V. **1995**:1
Gale, Robert Peter **1986**:4
Gallo, Robert **1991**:1
Garneau, Marc **1985**:1
Geller, Margaret Joan **1998**:2
Gerba, Charles **1999**:4
Gerberding, Julie **2004**:1
Gilbert, Walter **1988**:3
Gilruth, Robert
   Obituary **2001**:1
Glenn, John **1998**:3
Gold, Thomas
   Obituary **2005**:3
Goldman-Rakic, Patricia **2002**:4
Goodall, Jane **1991**:1
Gould, Gordon **1987**:1
Gould, Stephen Jay
   Obituary **2003**:3
Grandin, Temple **2006**:1

Greene, Brian **2003**:4
Hagelstein, Peter
   Brief Entry **1986**:3
Hair, Jay D. **1994**:3
Hale, Alan **1997**:3
Hammond, E. Cuyler
   Obituary **1987**:1
Haseltine, William A. **1999**:2
Hatem, George
   Obituary **1989**:1
Hau, Lene Vestergaard **2006**:4
Hawking, Stephen W. **1990**:1
Healy, Bernadine **1993**:1
Hill, J. Edward **2006**:2
Ho, David **1997**:2
Horner, Jack **1985**:2
Horowitz, Paul **1988**:2
Hounsfield, Godfrey **1989**:2
Hoyle, Sir Fred
   Obituary **2002**:4
Irwin, James
   Obituary **1992**:1
Jacobs, Joe **1994**:1
Janzen, Daniel H. **1988**:4
Jarvik, Robert K. **1985**:1
Jemison, Mae C. **1993**:1
Jorgensen, Christine
   Obituary **1989**:4
Kandel, Eric **2005**:2
Keeling, Charles
   Obituary **2006**:3
Keith, Louis **1988**:2
Kessler, David **1992**:1
Kevorkian, Jack **1991**:3
King, Mary-Claire **1998**:3
Klass, Perri **1993**:2
Kleinpaste, Ruud **2006**:2
Koop, C. Everett **1989**:3
Kopits, Steven E.
   Brief Entry **1987**:1
Kornberg, Arthur **1992**:1
Krim, Mathilde **1989**:2
Kubler-Ross, Elisabeth
   Obituary **2005**:4
Kwoh, Yik San **1988**:2
Laing, R.D.
   Obituary **1990**:1
Langer, Robert **2003**:4
Langston, J. William
   Brief Entry **1986**:2
Lanza, Robert **2004**:3
Leakey, Mary Douglas
   Obituary **1997**:2
Leakey, Richard **1994**:2
Lederman, Leon Max **1989**:4
LeVay, Simon **1992**:2
Levine, Arnold **2002**:3
Lewis, Edward B.
   Obituary **2005**:4
Lilly, John C.
   Obituary **2002**:4
Lorenz, Konrad
   Obituary **1989**:3
Love, Susan **1995**:2
Lovley, Derek **2005**:3
Lucid, Shannon **1997**:1
Maglich, Bogdan C. **1990**:1
Marsden, Brian **2004**:4
Masters, William H.
   Obituary **2001**:4
McIntyre, Richard
   Brief Entry **1986**:2

Menninger, Karl
Obituary **1991**:1
Minsky, Marvin **1994**:3
Montagu, Ashley
Obituary **2000**:2
Moog, Robert
Obituary **2006**:4
Morgentaler, Henry **1986**:3
Moss, Cynthia **1995**:2
Mullis, Kary **1995**:3
Ngau, Harrison **1991**:3
Nielsen, Jerri **2001**:3
Novello, Antonia **1991**:2
Nuesslein-Volhard, Christiane **1998**:1
Nye, Bill **1997**:2
O'Keefe, Sean **2005**:2
Olopade, Olufunmilayo **2006**:3
Ornish, Dean **2004**:2
Owens, Delia and Mark **1993**:3
Patton, John **2004**:4
Pauling, Linus
Obituary **1995**:1
Penrose, Roger **1991**:4
Perutz, Max
Obituary **2003**:2
Peterson, Roger Tory
Obituary **1997**:1
Pinker, Steven A. **2000**:1
Plotkin, Mark **1994**:3
Pople, John
Obituary **2005**:2
Porco, Carolyn **2005**:4
Porter, George
Obituary **2003**:4
Pough, Richard Hooper **1989**:1
Profet, Margie **1994**:4
Prusiner, Stanley **1998**:2
Quill, Timothy E. **1997**:3
Radecki, Thomas
Brief Entry **1986**:2
Redenbacher, Orville
Obituary **1996**:1
Redig, Patrick **1985**:3
Richter, Charles Francis
Obituary **1985**:4
Rifkin, Jeremy **1990**:3
Rizzoli, Paola **2004**:3
Rock, John
Obituary **1985**:1
Rosenberg, Steven **1989**:1
Rosendahl, Bruce R.
Brief Entry **1986**:4
Rosgen, Dave **2005**:2
Sabin, Albert
Obituary **1993**:4
Sacks, Oliver **1995**:4
Sagan, Carl
Obituary **1997**:2
Sakharov, Andrei Dmitrievich
Obituary **1990**:2
Salk, Jonas **1994**:4
Obituary **1995**:4
Schank, Roger **1989**:2
Schenk, Dale **2002**:2
Schroeder, William J.
Obituary **1986**:4
Schultes, Richard Evans
Obituary **2002**:1
Sears, Barry **2004**:2
Shepard, Alan
Obituary **1999**:1
Shimomura, Tsutomu **1996**:1

Shirley, Donna **1999**:1
Sidransky, David **2002**:4
Singer, Margaret Thaler
Obituary **2005**:1
Skinner, B.F.
Obituary **1991**:1
Smoot, George F. **1993**:3
Soren, David
Brief Entry **1986**:3
Spelke, Elizabeth **2003**:1
Spergel, David **2004**:1
Spock, Benjamin **1995**:2
Obituary **1998**:3
Steger, Will **1990**:4
Steptoe, Patrick
Obituary **1988**:3
Sullivan, Louis **1990**:4
Szent-Gyoergyi, Albert
Obituary **1987**:2
Thom, Rene
Obituary **2004**:1
Thompson, Lonnie **2003**:3
Thompson, Starley
Brief Entry **1987**:3
Thomson, James **2002**:3
Toone, Bill
Brief Entry **1987**:2
Tully, Tim **2004**:3
Vagelos, P. Roy **1989**:4
Venter, J. Craig **2001**:1
Vickrey, William S.
Obituary **1997**:2
Vitetta, Ellen S. **2005**:4
Waddell, Thomas F.
Obituary **1988**:2
Weil, Andrew **1997**:4
Wexler, Nancy S. **1992**:3
Whipple, Fred L.
Obituary **2005**:4
Whitson, Peggy **2003**:3
Wigand, Jeffrey **2000**:4
Wigler, Michael
Brief Entry **1985**:1
Wiles, Andrew **1994**:1
Wilmut, Ian **1997**:3
Wilson, Edward O. **1994**:4
Witten, Edward **2006**:3
Woodwell, George S. **1987**:2
Yeager, Chuck **1998**:1
Yen, Samuel **1996**:4
Zech, Lando W.
Brief Entry **1987**:4

SOCIAL ISSUES
Abbey, Edward
Obituary **1989**:3
Abernathy, Ralph
Obituary **1990**:3
Ali, Muhammad **1997**:2
Allred, Gloria **1985**:2
Amory, Cleveland
Obituary **1999**:2
Anastas, Robert
Brief Entry **1985**:2
Andrews, Lori B. **2005**:3
Arbour, Louise **2005**:1
Aristide, Jean-Bertrand **1991**:3
Baez, Joan **1998**:3
Baird, Bill
Brief Entry **1987**:2
Baldwin, James
Obituary **1988**:2

Ball, Edward **1999**:2
Banks, Dennis J. **1986**:4
Bayley, Corrine
Brief Entry **1986**:4
Beal, Deron **2005**:3
Bellamy, Carol **2001**:2
Ben & Jerry **1991**:3
Bergalis, Kimberly
Obituary **1992**:3
Berresford, Susan V. **1998**:4
Biehl, Amy
Obituary **1994**:1
Blackburn, Molly
Obituary **1985**:4
Block, Herbert
Obituary **2002**:4
Bly, Robert **1992**:4
Bradshaw, John **1992**:1
Brady, Sarah and James S. **1991**:4
Bravo, Ellen **1998**:2
Breathed, Berkeley **2005**:3
Bristow, Lonnie **1996**:1
Brockovich-Ellis, Erin **2003**:3
Brooks, Gwendolyn **1998**:1
Obituary **2001**:2
Brower, David **1990**:4
Brown, Jim **1993**:2
Brown, Judie **1986**:2
Burk, Martha **2004**:1
Bush, Barbara **1989**:3
Cammermeyer, Margarethe **1995**:2
Caplan, Arthur L. **2000**:2
Caras, Roger
Obituary **2002**:1
Carter, Amy **1987**:4
Carter, Rubin **2000**:3
Chavez, Cesar
Obituary **1993**:4
Chavez-Thompson, Linda **1999**:1
Chavis, Benjamin **1993**:4
Clark, Kenneth B.
Obituary **2006**:3
Cleaver, Eldridge
Obituary **1998**:4
Clements, George **1985**:1
Clinton, Hillary Rodham **1993**:2
Coffin, William Sloane, Jr. **1990**:3
Cole, Johnnetta B. **1994**:3
Coles, Robert **1995**:1
Connerly, Ward **2000**:2
Coors, William K.
Brief Entry **1985**:1
Corwin, Jeff **2005**:1
Cozza, Stephen **2001**:1
Crisp, Quentin
Obituary **2000**:3
Cruzan, Nancy
Obituary **1991**:3
Davis, Angela **1998**:3
Dees, Morris **1992**:1
DeMayo, Neda **2006**:2
Devi, Phoolan **1986**:1
Obituary **2002**:3
Dickinson, Brian **1998**:2
Dorris, Michael
Obituary **1997**:3
Douglas, Marjory Stoneman **1993**:1
Obituary **1998**:4
Downey, Morton, Jr. **1988**:4
Duncan, Sheena
Brief Entry **1987**:1
Dworkin, Andrea

Eagleson, Alan **1987**:4
Earnhardt, Dale
 Obituary **2001**:4
Earnhardt, Dale, Jr. **2004**:4
Ederle, Gertrude
 Obituary **2005**:1
Edwards, Harry **1989**:4
Elway, John **1990**:3
Epstein, Theo **2003**:4
Esiason, Boomer **1991**:1
Evans, Janet **1989**:1
Ewing, Patrick **1985**:3
Fabris, Enrico **2006**:4
Faldo, Nick **1993**:3
Favre, Brett Lorenzo **1997**:2
Federer, Roger **2004**:2
Federov, Sergei **1995**:1
Fehr, Donald **1987**:2
Ferrari, Enzo **1988**:4
Fielder, Cecil **1993**:2
Fiennes, Ranulph **1990**:3
Firestone, Roy **1988**:2
Fittipaldi, Emerson **1994**:2
Flood, Curt
 Obituary **1997**:2
Flutie, Doug **1999**:2
Foreman, George **2004**:2
Foss, Joe **1990**:3
Freeman, Cathy **2001**:3
Fuhr, Grant **1997**:3
Furyk, Jim **2004**:2
Galindo, Rudy **2001**:2
Garcia, Joe
 Brief Entry **1986**:4
Gardner, Randy **1997**:2
Garnett, Kevin **2000**:3
Gathers, Hank
 Obituary **1990**:3
Gault, Willie **1991**:2
Gerulaitis, Vitas
 Obituary **1995**:1
Giamatti, A. Bartlett **1988**:4
 Obituary **1990**:1
Gibson, Althea
 Obituary **2004**:4
Gibson, Kirk **1985**:2
Giguere, Jean-Sebastien **2004**:2
Gilmour, Doug **1994**:3
Glaus, Troy **2003**:3
Gomez, 'Lefty'
 Obituary **1989**:3
Gooden, Dwight **1985**:2
Gordeeva, Ekaterina **1996**:4
Gordon, Jeff **1996**:1
Graf, Steffi **1987**:4
Granato, Cammi **1999**:3
Grange, Red
 Obituary **1991**:3
Graziano, Rocky
 Obituary **1990**:4
Greenberg, Hank
 Obituary **1986**:4
Gretzky, Wayne **1989**:2
Griffey, Ken Jr. **1994**:1
Grinkov, Sergei
 Obituary **1996**:2
Gruden, Jon **2003**:4
Gumbel, Greg **1996**:4
Gwynn, Tony **1995**:1
Hagler, Marvelous Marvin **1985**:2
Hamilton, Scott **1998**:2
Hamm, Mia **2000**:1

Hamm, Paul **2005**:1
Hanauer, Chip **1986**:2
Hardaway, Anfernee **1996**:2
Harkes, John **1996**:4
Harmon, Tom
 Obituary **1990**:3
Hart, Carey **2006**:4
Harwell, Ernie **1997**:3
Hasek, Dominik **1998**:3
Hawk, Tony **2001**:4
Hayes, Woody
 Obituary **1987**:2
Helton, Todd **2001**:1
Hempleman-Adams, David **2004**:3
Henderson, Rickey **2002**:3
Henin-Hardenne, Justine **2004**:4
Hernandez, Willie **1985**:1
Hershiser, Orel **1989**:2
Hewitt, Lleyton **2002**:2
Hextall, Ron **1988**:2
Hill, Grant **1995**:3
Hill, Lynn **1991**:2
Hingis, Martina **1999**:1
Hogan, Ben
 Obituary **1997**:4
Hogan, Hulk **1987**:3
Holtz, Lou **1986**:4
Holyfield, Evander **1991**:3
Howard, Desmond Kevin **1997**:2
Howser, Dick
 Obituary **1987**:4
Hughes, Sarah **2002**:4
Hull, Brett **1991**:4
Hunter, Catfish
 Obituary **2000**:1
Indurain, Miguel **1994**:1
Inkster, Juli **2000**:2
Irvin, Michael **1996**:3
Irwin, Hale **2005**:2
Ivanisevic, Goran **2002**:1
Iverson, Allen **2001**:4
Jackson, Bo **1986**:3
Jackson, Phil **1996**:3
Jagr, Jaromir **1995**:4
Jenkins, Sally **1997**:2
Jeter, Derek **1999**:4
Johnson, Earvin 'Magic' **1988**:4
Johnson, Jimmy **1993**:3
Johnson, Kevin **1991**:1
Johnson, Keyshawn **2000**:4
Johnson, Larry **1993**:3
Johnson, Michael **2000**:1
Johnson, Randy **1996**:2
Jones, Jerry **1994**:4
Jones, Marion **1998**:4
Jordan, Michael **1987**:2
Joyner, Florence Griffith **1989**:2
 Obituary **1999**:1
Joyner-Kersee, Jackie **1993**:1
Kallen, Jackie **1994**:1
Kanokogi, Rusty
 Brief Entry **1987**:1
Kasparov, Garry **1997**:4
Kelly, Jim **1991**:4
Kemp, Jack **1990**:4
Kemp, Jan **1987**:2
Kemp, Shawn **1995**:1
Kerrigan, Nancy **1994**:3
Kidd, Jason **2003**:2
King, Don **1989**:1
Kiraly, Karch
 Brief Entry **1987**:1

Kite, Tom **1990**:3
Klima, Petr **1987**:1
Knievel, Robbie **1990**:1
Knight, Bobby **1985**:3
Koch, Bill **1992**:3
Konstantinov, Vladimir **1997**:4
Kournikova, Anna **2000**:3
Kroc, Ray
 Obituary **1985**:1
Krone, Julie **1989**:2
Kruk, John **1994**:4
Krzyzewski, Mike **1993**:2
Kukoc, Toni **1995**:4
Laettner, Christian **1993**:1
LaFontaine, Pat **1985**:1
Laimbeer, Bill **2004**:3
Lalas, Alexi **1995**:1
Landry, Tom
 Obituary **2000**:3
Lemieux, Claude **1996**:1
Lemieux, Mario **1986**:4
LeMond, Greg **1986**:4
Leonard, Sugar Ray **1989**:4
Leslie, Lisa **1997**:4
Lewis, Lennox **2000**:2
Lewis, Ray **2001**:3
Lewis, Reggie
 Obituary **1994**:1
Leyland, Jim **1998**:2
Lindbergh, Pelle
 Obituary **1985**:4
Lindros, Eric **1992**:1
Lipinski, Tara **1998**:3
Lofton, Kenny **1998**:1
Lopez, Nancy **1989**:3
Louganis, Greg **1995**:3
Lowell, Mike **2003**:2
Lukas, D. Wayne **1986**:2
MacArthur, Ellen **2005**:3
Madden, John **1995**:1
Maddux, Greg **1996**:2
Majerle, Dan **1993**:4
Malone, Karl **1990**:1 **1997**:3
Mantle, Mickey
 Obituary **1996**:1
Maradona, Diego **1991**:3
Maravich, Pete
 Obituary **1988**:2
Maris, Roger
 Obituary **1986**:1
Martin, Billy **1988**:4
 Obituary **1990**:2
Martin, Casey **2002**:1
Mathis, Clint **2003**:1
Mattingly, Don **1986**:2
Matuszak, John
 Obituary **1989**:4
McCarron, Chris **1995**:4
McCartney, Bill **1995**:3
McGraw, Tug
 Obituary **2005**:1
McGwire, Mark **1999**:1
McMahon, Jim **1985**:4
McMahon, Vince, Jr. **1985**:4
Messier, Mark **1993**:1
Mickelson, Phil **2004**:4
Mikan, George
 Obituary **2006**:3
Milbrett, Tiffeny **2001**:1
Milburn, Rodney Jr.
 Obituary **1998**:2
Miller, Andre **2003**:3

Cumulative Subject Index

This index lists all newsmakers by subjects, company names, products, organizations, issues, awards, and professional specialties. Indexes in softbound issues allow access to the current year's entries; indexes in annual hardbound volumes are cumulative, covering the entire *Newsmakers* series.

Listee names are followed by a year and issue number; thus **1996**:3 indicates that an entry on that individual appears in both 1996, Issue 3, and the 1996 cumulation. For access to newsmakers appearing earlier than the current softbound issue, see the previous year's cumulation.

ACT-UP
See: AIDS Coalition to Unleash
Power

Adolph Coors Co.
Coors, William K.
Brief Entry **1985**:1

Adoption
Clements, George **1985**:1

Advertising
Ailes, Roger **1989**:3
Beers, Charlotte **1999**:3
Freeman, Cliff **1996**:1
Kroll, Alexander S. **1989**:3
Lazarus, Shelly **1998**:3
McElligott, Thomas J. **1987**:4
Ogilvy, David
Obituary **2000**:1
O'Steen, Van
Brief Entry **1986**:3
Peller, Clara
Obituary **1988**:1
Proctor, Barbara Gardner **1985**:3
Riney, Hal **1989**:1
Saatchi, Charles **1987**:3
Saatchi, Maurice **1995**:4
Sedelmaier, Joe **1985**:3
Vinton, Will
Brief Entry **1988**:1
Whittle, Christopher **1989**:3

AFL-CIO
See: American Federation of Labor
and Congress of Industrial
Organizations

African National Congress [ANC]
Buthelezi, Mangosuthu Gatsha **1989**
:3
Hani, Chris
Obituary **1993**:4
Mandela, Nelson **1990**:3
Mbeki, Thabo **1999**:4
Sisulu, Walter
Obituary **2004**:2
Slovo, Joe **1989**:2
Tambo, Oliver **1991**:3

Agriculture
Davis, Noel **1990**:3

AIDS
See: Acquired Immune Deficiency
Syndrome

**AIDS Coalition to Unleash Power
[ACT-UP]**
Kramer, Larry **1991**:2

AIM
See: American Indian Movement
Peltier, Leonard **1995**:1

A.J. Canfield Co.
Canfield, Alan B.
Brief Entry **1986**:3

ALA
See: American Library Association

Albert Nipon, Inc.
Nipon, Albert
Brief Entry **1986**:4

Alcohol abuse
Anastas, Robert
Brief Entry **1985**:2
Bradshaw, John **1992**:1
Lightner, Candy **1985**:1
MacRae, Gordon
Obituary **1986**:2
Mantle, Mickey
Obituary **1996**:1
Welch, Bob **1991**:3

ALL
See: American Life League

Alternative medicine
Jacobs, Joe **1994**:1
Weil, Andrew **1997**:4

Alvin Ailey Dance Theatre
Jamison, Judith **1990**:3

AMA
See: American Medical Association

Amazon.com, Inc.
Bezos, Jeff **1998**:4

**American Academy and Institute of
Arts and Letters**
Brooks, Gwendolyn **1998**:1
Obituary **2001**:2
Cunningham, Merce **1998**:1
Dickey, James
Obituary **1998**:2
Foster, Norman **1999**:4
Graves, Michael **2000**:1
Mamet, David **1998**:4
Roth, Philip **1999**:1
Vonnegut, Kurt **1998**:4
Walker, Alice **1999**:1
Wolfe, Tom **1999**:2

American Airlines
Crandall, Robert L. **1992**:1

American Ballet Theatre [ABT]
Bissell, Patrick
Obituary **1988**:2
Bocca, Julio **1995**:3
Englund, Richard
Obituary **1991**:3
Feld, Eliot **1996**:1
Ferri, Alessandra **1987**:2
Godunov, Alexander
Obituary **1995**:4
Gregory, Cynthia **1990**:2
Herrera, Paloma **1996**:2
Kaye, Nora
Obituary **1987**:4
Lander, Toni
Obituary **1985**:4
Parker, Sarah Jessica **1999**:2
Renvall, Johan
Brief Entry **1987**:4
Robbins, Jerome

Obituary **1999**:1
Tudor, Antony
Obituary **1987**:4

American Book Awards
Alexie, Sherman **1998**:4
Baraka, Amiri **2000**:3
Child, Julia **1999**:4
Erdrich, Louise **2005**:3
Kissinger, Henry **1999**:4
Walker, Alice **1999**:1
Wolfe, Tom **1999**:2

American Civil Liberties Union [ACLU]
Abzug, Bella **1998**:2
Glasser, Ira **1989**:1

American Express
Chenault, Kenneth I. **1999**:3
Weill, Sandy **1990**:4

**American Federation of Labor and
Congress of Industrial Organizations
[AFL-CIO]**
Chavez-Thompson, Linda **1999**:1
Sweeney, John J. **2000**:3

American Indian Movement [AIM]
Banks, Dennis J. **1986**:4

American Library Association [ALA]
Blume, Judy **1998**:4
Heat-Moon, William Least **2000**:2
Schuman, Patricia Glass **1993**:2
Steel, Danielle **1999**:2

American Life League [ALL]
Brown, Judie **1986**:2

American Medical Association [AMA]
Bristow, Lonnie **1996**:1
Hill, J. Edward **2006**:2

**Amer-I-can minority empowerment
program**
Brown, Jim **1993**:2

American Museum of Natural History
Futter, Ellen V. **1995**:1

American Music Awards
Ashanti **2004**:1
Badu, Erykah **2000**:4
Boyz II Men **1995**:1
Brooks, Garth **1992**:1
Cole, Natalie **1992**:4
Franklin, Aretha **1998**:3
Jackson, Alan **2003**:1
Jackson, Michael **1996**:2
Jay-Z **2006**:1
Jewel **1999**:2
Keys, Alicia **2006**:1
Loveless, Patty **1998**:2
McEntire, Reba **1987**:3 **1994**:2
Newton-John, Olivia **1998**:4
Parton, Dolly **1999**:4
Spears, Britney **2000**:3
Strait, George **1998**:3

Hardaway, Anfernee **1996**:2
Jackson, Phil **1996**:3
Johnson, Earvin 'Magic' **1988**:4
Johnson, Kevin **1991**:1
Johnson, Larry **1993**:3
Jordan, Michael **1987**:2
Kemp, Shawn **1995**:1
Kidd, Jason **2003**:2
Knight, Bobby **1985**:3
Krzyzewski, Mike **1993**:2
Kukoc, Toni **1995**:4
Laettner, Christian **1993**:1
Laimbeer, Bill **2004**:3
Leslie, Lisa **1997**:4
Lewis, Reggie
  Obituary **1994**:1
Majerle, Dan **1993**:4
Malone, Karl **1990**:1 **1997**:3
Maravich, Pete
  Obituary **1988**:2
McMillen, Tom **1988**:4
Mikan, George
  Obituary **2006**:3
Miller, Andre **2003**:3
Miller, Reggie **1994**:4
Mourning, Alonzo **1994**:2
Mulkey-Robertson, Kim **2006**:1
Olajuwon, Akeem **1985**:1
O'Malley, Susan **1995**:2
O'Neal, Shaquille **1992**:1
Palmer, Violet **2005**:2
Riley, Pat **1994**:3
Robinson, David **1990**:4
Rodman, Dennis **1991**:3 **1996**:4
Stern, David **1991**:4
Stockton, John Houston **1997**:3
Summitt, Pat **2004**:1
Swoopes, Sheryl **1998**:2
Tarkenian, Jerry **1990**:4
Thomas, Isiah **1989**:2
Thompson, John **1988**:3
Vitale, Dick **1988**:4 **1994**:4
Wallace, Ben **2004**:3
Webber, Chris **1994**:1
Wilkens, Lenny **1995**:2
Woodard, Lynette **1986**:2
Worthy, James **1991**:2
Yao Ming **2004**:1

Beatrice International
  Lewis, Reginald F. **1988**:4
    Obituary **1993**:3

Benetton Group
  Benetton, Luciano **1988**:1

Benihana of Tokyo, Inc.
  Aoki, Rocky **1990**:2

Berkshire Hathaway, Inc.
  Buffett, Warren **1995**:2

Bethlehem, Jordan, city government
  Freij, Elias **1986**:4

Bicycling
  Armstrong, Lance **2000**:1
  Indurain, Miguel **1994**:1
  LeMond, Greg **1986**:4
  Roberts, Steven K. **1992**:1

Bill T. Jones/Arnie Zane & Company
  Jones, Bill T. **1991**:4

Billiards
  Minnesota Fats
    Obituary **1996**:3

Biodiversity
  Wilson, Edward O. **1994**:4

Bioethics
  Andrews, Lori B. **2005**:3
  Bayley, Corrine
    Brief Entry **1986**:4
  Caplan, Arthur L. **2000**:2

Biogen, Inc.
  Gilbert, Walter **1988**:3

Biosphere 2
  Allen, John **1992**:1

Biotechnology
  Gilbert, Walter **1988**:3
  Haseltine, William A. **1999**:2

Birds
  Berle, Peter A.A.
    Brief Entry **1987**:3
  Pough, Richard Hooper **1989**:1
  Redig, Patrick **1985**:3
  Toone, Bill
    Brief Entry **1987**:2

Birth control
  Baird, Bill
    Brief Entry **1987**:2
  Baulieu, Etienne-Emile **1990**:1
  Djerassi, Carl **2000**:4
  Falkenberg, Nanette **1985**:2
  Morgentaler, Henry **1986**:3
  Rock, John
    Obituary **1985**:1
  Wattleton, Faye **1989**:1

Black Panther Party
  Cleaver, Eldridge
    Obituary **1998**:4
  Newton, Huey
    Obituary **1990**:1
  Ture, Kwame
    Obituary **1999**:2

Black Sash
  Duncan, Sheena
    Brief Entry **1987**:1

Blockbuster Video
  Huizenga, Wayne **1992**:1

Bloomingdale's
  Campeau, Robert **1990**:1
  Traub, Marvin
    Brief Entry **1987**:3

Boat racing
  Aoki, Rocky **1990**:2
  Conner, Dennis **1987**:2
  Copeland, Al **1988**:3

Hanauer, Chip **1986**:2
Turner, Ted **1989**:1

Bodybuilding
  Powter, Susan **1994**:3
  Reeves, Steve
    Obituary **2000**:4
  Schwarzenegger, Arnold **1991**:1

Body Shops International
  Roddick, Anita **1989**:4

Boston Bruins hockey team
  Bourque, Raymond Jean **1997**:3

Bose Corp.
  Bose, Amar
    Brief Entry **1986**:4

Boston Celtics basketball team
  Ainge, Danny **1987**:1
  Bird, Larry **1990**:3
  Lewis, Reggie
    Obituary **1994**:1
  Maravich, Pete
    Obituary **1988**:2

Boston, Mass., city government
  Flynn, Ray **1989**:1
  Frank, Barney **1989**:2

Boston Properties Co.
  Zuckerman, Mortimer **1986**:3

Boston Red Sox baseball team
  Boggs, Wade **1989**:3
  Clemens, Roger **1991**:4
  Conigliaro, Tony
    Obituary **1990**:3
  Damon, Johnny **2005**:4
  Epstein, Theo **2003**:4
  Henderson, Rickey **2002**:3
  Ramirez, Manny **2005**:4
  Vaughn, Mo **1999**:2
  Williams, Ted
    Obituary **2003**:4

Boston University
  Silber, John **1990**:1

Bowling
  Anthony, Earl
    Obituary **2002**:3
  Weber, Pete **1986**:3

Boxing
  Abercrombie, Josephine **1987**:2
  Ali, Laila **2001**:2
  Armstrong, Henry
    Obituary **1989**:1
  Bowe, Riddick **1993**:2
  Carter, Rubin **2000**:3
  Danza, Tony **1989**:1
  De La Hoya, Oscar **1998**:2
  Douglas, Buster **1990**:4
  Foreman, George **2004**:2
  Graziano, Rocky
    Obituary **1990**:4

Brown, Willie L. **1985**:2
Roybal-Allard, Lucille **1999**:4
Wilson, Pete **1992**:3

Camping equipment
Bauer, Eddie
  Obituary **1986**:3
Coleman, Sheldon, Jr. **1990**:2

Canadian Broadcasting Corp. [CBC]
Juneau, Pierre **1988**:3

Cancer research
DeVita, Vincent T., Jr. **1987**:3
Folkman, Judah **1999**:1
Fonyo, Steve
  Brief Entry **1985**:4
Gale, Robert Peter **1986**:4
Hammond, E. Cuyler
  Obituary **1987**:1
King, Mary-Claire **1998**:3
Krim, Mathilde **1989**:2
Love, Susan **1995**:2
Rosenberg, Steven **1989**:1
Szent-Gyoergyi, Albert
  Obituary **1987**:2
Wigler, Michael
  Brief Entry **1985**:1

Cannes Film Festival
Brando, Marlon
  Obituary **2005**:3
Egoyan, Atom **2000**:2
Hou Hsiao-hsien **2000**:2
Mirren, Helen **2005**:1
Smith, Kevin **2000**:4

Carnival Cruise Lines
Arison, Ted **1990**:3

Car repair
Magliozzi, Tom and Ray **1991**:4

Cartoons
Addams, Charles
  Obituary **1989**:1
Barbera, Joseph **1988**:2
Barry, Lynda **1992**:1
Blanc, Mel
  Obituary **1989**:4
Chast, Roz **1992**:4
Disney, Roy E. **1986**:3
Freleng, Friz
  Obituary **1995**:4
Gaines, William M.
  Obituary **1993**:1
Gould, Chester
  Obituary **1985**:2
Groening, Matt **1990**:4
Judge, Mike **1994**:2
MacFarlane, Seth **2006**:1
MacNelly, Jeff
  Obituary **2000**:4
Mauldin, Bill
  Obituary **2004**:2
Messick, Dale
  Obituary **2006**:2
Parker, Trey and Matt Stone **1998**:2
Schulz, Charles
  Obituary **2000**:3

Schulz, Charles M. **1998**:1
Spiegelman, Art **1998**:3
Tartakovsky, Genndy **2004**:4
Trudeau, Garry **1991**:2
Watterson, Bill **1990**:3

Catholic Church
Beckett, Wendy (Sister) **1998**:3
Bernardin, Cardinal Joseph **1997**:2
Burns, Charles R.
  Brief Entry **1988**:1
Clements, George **1985**:1
Cunningham, Reverend William
  Obituary **1997**:4
Curran, Charles E. **1989**:2
Daily, Bishop Thomas V. **1990**:4
Dearden, John Cardinal
  Obituary **1988**:4
Fox, Matthew **1992**:2
Healy, Timothy S. **1990**:2
Hume, Basil Cardinal
  Obituary **2000**:1
John Paul II, Pope **1995**:3
Kissling, Frances **1989**:2
Krol, John
  Obituary **1996**:3
Lefebvre, Marcel **1988**:4
Mahony, Roger M. **1988**:2
Maida, Adam Cardinal **1998**:2
Obando, Miguel **1986**:4
O'Connor, Cardinal John **1990**:3
O'Connor, John
  Obituary **2000**:4
Peter, Valentine J. **1988**:2
Rock, John
  Obituary **1985**:1
Sin, Jaime
  Obituary **2006**:3
Stallings, George A., Jr. **1990**:1

CAT Scanner
Hounsfield, Godfrey **1989**:2

Cattle rustling
Cantrell, Ed
  Brief Entry **1985**:3

Caviar
Petrossian, Christian
  Brief Entry **1985**:3

CBC
See: Canadian Broadcasting Corp.

CBS, Inc.
Cox, Richard Joseph
  Brief Entry **1985**:1
Cronkite, Walter Leland **1997**:3
Moonves, Les **2004**:2
Paley, William S.
  Obituary **1991**:2
Reasoner, Harry
  Obituary **1992**:1
Sagansky, Jeff **1993**:2
Tellem, Nancy **2004**:4
Tisch, Laurence A. **1988**:2
Yetnikoff, Walter **1988**:1

CDF
See: Children's Defense Fund

Center for Equal Opportunity
Chavez, Linda **1999**:3

Centers for Living
Williamson, Marianne **1991**:4

Central America
Astorga, Nora **1988**:2
Cruz, Arturo **1985**:1
Obando, Miguel **1986**:4
Robelo, Alfonso **1988**:1

Central Intelligence Agency [CIA]
Carter, Amy **1987**:4
Casey, William
  Obituary **1987**:3
Colby, William E.
  Obituary **1996**:4
Deutch, John **1996**:4
Gates, Robert M. **1992**:2
Inman, Bobby Ray **1985**:1
Tenet, George **2000**:3

Centurion Ministries
McCloskey, James **1993**:1

Cesar Awards
Adjani, Isabelle **1991**:1
Deneuve, Catherine **2003**:2
Depardieu, Gerard **1991**:2
Tautou, Audrey **2004**:2

Chanel, Inc.
D'Alessio, Kitty
  Brief Entry **1987**:3
Lagerfeld, Karl **1999**:4

Chantal Pharmacentical Corp.
Burnison, Chantal Simone **1988**:3

Charlotte Hornets basketball team
Bryant, Kobe **1998**:3
Johnson, Larry **1993**:3
Mourning, Alonzo **1994**:2

Chef Boy-ar-dee
Boiardi, Hector
  Obituary **1985**:3

Chess
Kasparov, Garry **1997**:4
Polgar, Judit **1993**:3

Chicago Bears football team
McMahon, Jim **1985**:4
Payton, Walter
  Obituary **2000**:2

Chicago Bulls basketball team
Jackson, Phil **1996**:3
Jordan, Michael **1987**:2
Kukoc, Toni **1995**:4
Pippen, Scottie **1992**:2

Chicago Blackhawks
Hasek, Dominik **1998**:3

Chicago Cubs baseball team
Caray, Harry **1988**:3
  Obituary **1998**:3
Sosa, Sammy **1999**:1

Chicago, Ill., city government
Washington, Harold
Obituary **1988**:1

Chicago White Sox baseball team
Caray, Harry **1988**:3
Obituary **1998**:3
Leyland, Jim **1998**:2
Thomas, Frank **1994**:3
Veeck, Bill
Obituary **1986**:1

Child care
Hale, Clara
Obituary **1993**:3
Leach, Penelope **1992**:4
Spock, Benjamin **1995**:2
Obituary **1998**:3

Children's Defense Fund [CDF]
Clinton, Hillary Rodham **1993**:2
Edelman, Marian Wright **1990**:4

Chimpanzees
Goodall, Jane **1991**:1

Choreography
Abdul, Paula **1990**:3
Ailey, Alvin **1989**:2
Obituary **1990**:2
Astaire, Fred
Obituary **1987**:4
Bennett, Michael
Obituary **1988**:1
Cunningham, Merce **1998**:1
Dean, Laura **1989**:4
de Mille, Agnes
Obituary **1994**:2
Feld, Eliot **1996**:1
Fenley, Molissa **1988**:3
Forsythe, William **1993**:2
Fosse, Bob
Obituary **1988**:1
Glover, Savion **1997**:1
Graham, Martha
Obituary **1991**:4
Jamison, Judith **1990**:3
Joffrey, Robert
Obituary **1988**:3
Jones, Bill T. **1991**:4
Lewitzky, Bella
Obituary **2005**:3
MacMillan, Kenneth
Obituary **1993**:2
Mitchell, Arthur **1995**:1
Morris, Mark **1991**:1
Nureyev, Rudolf
Obituary **1993**:2
Parsons, David **1993**:4
Ross, Herbert
Obituary **2002**:4
Takei, Kei **1990**:2
Taylor, Paul **1992**:3
Tharp, Twyla **1992**:4
Tudor, Antony
Obituary **1987**:4
Tune, Tommy **1994**:2
Varone, Doug **2001**:2

Christian Coalition
Reed, Ralph **1995**:1

Christic Institute
Sheehan, Daniel P. **1989**:1

Chrysler Motor Corp.
Eaton, Robert J. **1994**:2
Iacocca, Lee **1993**:1
Lutz, Robert A. **1990**:1

CHUCK
See: Committee to Halt Useless
College Killings

Church of England
Carey, George **1992**:3
Runcie, Robert **1989**:4
Obituary **2001**:1

Church of Jesus Christ of Latter-Day Saints
See: Mormon Church

CIA
See: Central Intelligence Agency

Cincinatti Bengals football team
Esiason, Boomer **1991**:1

Cincinnati Reds baseball team
Davis, Eric **1987**:4
Rose, Pete **1991**:1
Schott, Marge **1985**:4

Cinematography
Burum, Stephen H.
Brief Entry **1987**:2
Markle, C. Wilson **1988**:1
McLaren, Norman
Obituary **1987**:2

Civil rights
Abernathy, Ralph
Obituary **1990**:3
Abzug, Bella **1998**:2
Allen Jr., Ivan
Obituary **2004**:3
Allred, Gloria **1985**:2
Aquino, Corazon **1986**:2
Baldwin, James
Obituary **1988**:2
Banks, Dennis J. **1986**:4
Blackburn, Molly
Obituary **1985**:4
Buthelezi, Mangosuthu Gatsha **1989**:3
Chavez, Linda **1999**:3
Chavis, Benjamin **1993**:4
Clements, George **1985**:1
Connerly, Ward **2000**:2
Davis, Angela **1998**:3
Dees, Morris **1992**:1
Delany, Sarah
Obituary **1999**:3
Duncan, Sheena
Brief Entry **1987**:1
Farmer, James
Obituary **2000**:1
Faubus, Orval
Obituary **1995**:2
Glasser, Ira **1989**:1

Griffiths, Martha
Obituary **2004**:2
Harris, Barbara **1989**:3
Healey, Jack **1990**:1
Hoffman, Abbie
Obituary **1989**:3
Hume, John **1987**:1
Jordan, Vernon, Jr. **2002**:3
King, Bernice **2000**:2
King, Coretta Scott **1999**:3
Kunstler, William **1992**:3
Makeba, Miriam **1989**:2
Mandela, Winnie **1989**:3
Marshall, Thurgood
Obituary **1993**:3
McGuinness, Martin **1985**:4
Pendleton, Clarence M.
Obituary **1988**:4
Ram, Jagjivan
Obituary **1986**:4
Shabazz, Betty
Obituary **1997**:4
Sharpton, Al **1991**:2
Shcharansky, Anatoly **1986**:2
Simone, Nina
Obituary **2004**:2
Slovo, Joe **1989**:2
Stallings, George A., Jr. **1990**:1
Steele, Shelby **1991**:2
Sullivan, Leon
Obituary **2002**:2
Suzman, Helen **1989**:3
Ture, Kwame
Obituary **1999**:2
Washington, Harold
Obituary **1988**:1
West, Cornel **1994**:2
Williams, G. Mennen
Obituary **1988**:2
Williams, Hosea
Obituary **2001**:2
Wu, Harry **1996**:1

Civil War
Foote, Shelby **1991**:2

Claymation
Park, Nick **1997**:3
Vinton, Will
Brief Entry **1988**:1

Cleveland Ballet Dancing Wheels
Verdi-Fletcher, Mary **1998**:2

Cleveland Browns football team
Brown, Jim **1993**:2

Cleveland Cavaliers basketball team
Wilkens, Lenny **1995**:2

Cleveland city government
Stokes, Carl
Obituary **1996**:4

Cleveland Indians baseball team
Belle, Albert **1996**:4
Boudreau, Louis
Obituary **2002**:3
Greenberg, Hank
Obituary **1986**:4

Lofton, Kenny **1998**:1
Veeck, Bill
  Obituary **1986**:1

Cliff's Notes
  Hillegass, Clifton Keith **1989**:4

Climatology
  Thompson, Starley
    Brief Entry **1987**:3

Clio Awards
  Proctor, Barbara Gardner **1985**:3
  Riney, Hal **1989**:1
  Rivers, Joan **2005**:3
  Sedelmaier, Joe **1985**:3

Cloning
  Lanza, Robert **2004**:3
  Wilmut, Ian **1997**:3

Coaching
  Bowman, Scotty **1998**:4
  Brown, Paul
    Obituary **1992**:1
  Chaney, John **1989**:1
  Hayes, Woody
    Obituary **1987**:2
  Holtz, Lou **1986**:4
  Howser, Dick
    Obituary **1987**:4
  Jackson, Phil **1996**:3
  Johnson, Jimmy **1993**:3
  Knight, Bobby **1985**:3
  Leyland, Jim **1998**:2
  Lukas, D. Wayne **1986**:2
  Martin, Billy **1988**:4
    Obituary **1990**:2
  McCartney, Bill **1995**:3
  Paterno, Joe **1995**:4
  Schembechler, Bo **1990**:3
  Shula, Don **1992**:2
  Tarkenian, Jerry **1990**:4
  Walsh, Bill **1987**:4

Coca-Cola Co.
  Goizueta, Roberto **1996**:1
    Obituary **1998**:1
  Keough, Donald Raymond **1986**:1
  Woodruff, Robert Winship
    Obituary **1985**:1

Coleman Co.
  Coleman, Sheldon, Jr. **1990**:2

Colorado Avalanche hockey team
  Lemieux, Claude **1996**:1

Colorization
  Markle, C. Wilson **1988**:1

Columbia Pictures
  Pascal, Amy **2003**:3
  Steel, Dawn **1990**:1
    Obituary **1998**:2
  Vincent, Fay **1990**:2

Columbia Sportswear
  Boyle, Gertrude **1995**:3

Comedy
  Alexander, Jason **1993**:3
  Allen, Steve
    Obituary **2001**:2
  Allen, Tim **1993**:1
  Allen, Woody **1994**:1
  Anderson, Harry **1988**:2
  Arnold, Tom **1993**:2
  Atkinson, Rowan **2004**:3
  Barr, Roseanne **1989**:1
  Bateman, Jason **2005**:3
  Belushi, Jim **1986**:2
  Belzer, Richard **1985**:3
  Benigni, Roberto **1999**:2
  Berle, Milton
    Obituary **2003**:2
  Bernhard, Sandra **1989**:4
  Black, Jack **2002**:3
  Bogosian, Eric **1990**:4
  Borge, Victor
    Obituary **2001**:3
  Brooks, Albert **1991**:4
  Brooks, Mel **2003**:1
  Burns, George
    Obituary **1996**:3
  Burrows, James **2005**:3
  Busch, Charles **1998**:3
  Butler, Brett **1995**:1
  Candy, John **1988**:2
    Obituary **1994**:3
  Carey, Drew **1997**:4
  Carney, Art
    Obituary **2005**:1
  Carrey, Jim **1995**:1
  Carvey, Dana **1994**:1
  Chappelle, Dave **2005**:3
  Chase, Chevy **1990**:1
  Cho, Margaret **1995**:2
  Clay, Andrew Dice **1991**:1
  Cleese, John **1989**:2
  Cook, Peter
    Obituary **1995**:2
  Cosby, Bill **1999**:2
  Crystal, Billy **1985**:3
  Dangerfield, Rodney
    Obituary **2006**:1
  DeGeneres, Ellen **1995**:3
  Diamond, Selma
    Obituary **1985**:2
  Dr. Demento **1986**:1
  Fallon, Jimmy **2003**:1
  Farley, Chris
    Obituary **1998**:2
  Fey, Tina **2005**:3
  Ford, Faith **2005**:3
  Foster, Phil
    Obituary **1985**:3
  Foxworthy, Jeff **1996**:1
  Foxx, Jamie **2001**:1
  Foxx, Redd
    Obituary **1992**:2
  Franken, Al **1996**:3
  Gleason, Jackie
    Obituary **1987**:4
  Gobel, George
    Obituary **1991**:4
  Goldberg, Whoopi **1993**:3
  Gordon, Gale
    Obituary **1996**:1
  Gregory, Dick **1990**:3
  Hackett, Buddy
    Obituary **2004**:3

Hall, Arsenio **1990**:2
Hill, Benny
  Obituary **1992**:3
Hope, Bob
  Obituary **2004**:4
Hughley, D.L. **2001**:1
Humphries, Barry **1993**:1
Irwin, Bill **1988**:3
Jones, Jenny **1998**:2
Kinison, Sam
  Obituary **1993**:1
Lawrence, Martin **1993**:4
Leary, Denis **1993**:3
Leguizamo, John **1999**:1
Leno, Jay **1987**:1
Letterman, David **1989**:3
Lewis, Richard **1992**:1
Lisick, Beth **2006**:2
Lopez, George **2003**:4
Mac, Bernie **2003**:1
Mandel, Howie **1989**:1
Martin, Steve **1992**:2
McCarthy, Jenny **1997**:4
Miller, Dennis **1992**:4
Milligan, Spike
  Obituary **2003**:2
Morita, Noriyuki 'Pat' **1987**:3
Murphy, Eddie **1989**:2
Murray, Bill **2002**:4
Myers, Mike **1992**:3 **1997**:4
O'Brien, Conan **1994**:1
O'Donnell, Rosie **1994**:3
Parker, Trey and Matt Stone **1998**:2
Paulsen, Pat
  Obituary **1997**:4
Penn & Teller **1992**:1
Peterson, Cassandra **1988**:1
Pryor, Richard **1999**:3
Reiser, Paul **1995**:2
Reubens, Paul **1987**:2
Rhea, Caroline **2004**:1
Richards, Michael **1993**:4
Rivers, Joan **2005**:3
Rock, Chris **1998**:1
Rogers, Ginger
  Obituary **1995**:4
Rowan, Dan
  Obituary **1988**:1
Rudner, Rita **1993**:2
Sandler, Adam **1999**:2
Schneider, Rob **1997**:4
Seinfeld, Jerry **1992**:4
Shandling, Garry **1995**:1
Shawn, Dick
  Obituary **1987**:3
Short, Martin **1986**:1
Silvers, Phil
  Obituary **1985**:4
Skelton, Red
  Obituary **1998**:1
Smigel, Robert **2001**:3
Smirnoff, Yakov **1987**:2
Spade, David **1999**:2
Tucker, Chris **1999**:1
Wayans, Keenen Ivory **1991**:1
Williams, Robin **1988**:4
Wilson, Flip
  Obituary **1999**:2
Wright, Steven **1986**:3
Yankovic, 'Weird Al' **1985**:4
Youngman, Henny
  Obituary **1998**:3

Bernstein, Elmer
  Obituary **2005**:4
Bochco, Steven **1989**:1
Boyle, Peter **2002**:3
Brooks, Mel **2003**:1
Burnett, Carol **2000**:3
Burnett, Mark **2003**:1
Burrows, James **2005**:3
Carney, Art
  Obituary **2005**:1
Carter, Chris **2000**:1
Carter, Nell
  Obituary **2004**:2
Chase, Chevy **1990**:1
Chiklis, Michael **2003**:3
Child, Julia **1999**:4
Clarkson, Patricia **2005**:3
Coca, Imogene
  Obituary **2002**:2
Coco, James
  Obituary **1987**:2
Cooke, Alistair
  Obituary **2005**:3
Copperfield, David **1986**:3
Corwin, Jeff **2005**:1
Cosby, Bill **1999**:2
Cronkite, Walter Leland **1997**:3
Davis, Bette
  Obituary **1990**:1
De Cordova, Frederick **1985**:2
De Matteo, Drea **2005**:2
De Vito, Danny **1987**:1
Dewhurst, Colleen
  Obituary **1992**:2
Fey, Tina **2005**:3
Field, Patricia **2002**:2
Field, Sally **1995**:3
Finney, Albert **2003**:3
Flanders, Ed
  Obituary **1995**:3
Fosse, Bob
  Obituary **1988**:1
Foster, Jodie **1989**:2
Frankenheimer, John
  Obituary **2003**:4
Franz, Dennis **1995**:2
Freleng, Friz
  Obituary **1995**:4
Gandolfini, James **2001**:3
Gellar, Sarah Michelle **1999**:3
Gless, Sharon **1989**:3
Gobel, George
  Obituary **1991**:4
Goldberg, Gary David **1989**:4
Goldberg, Leonard **1988**:4
Gossett, Louis, Jr. **1989**:3
Grammer, Kelsey **1995**:1
Grodin, Charles **1997**:3
Guest, Christopher **2004**:2
Haggis, Paul **2006**:4
Hanks, Tom **1989**:2 **2000**:2
Hartman, Phil **1996**:2
  Obituary **1998**:4
Heche, Anne **1999**:1
Helgenberger, Marg **2002**:2
Henning, Doug
  Obituary **2000**:3
Hoffman, Dustin **2005**:4
Hopkins, Anthony **1992**:4
Howard, Trevor
  Obituary **1988**:2
Huffman, Felicity **2006**:2

Janney, Allison **2003**:3
Jennings, Peter Charles **1997**:2
Johnson, Don **1986**:1
Jones, Tommy Lee **1994**:2
Joyce, William **2006**:1
Kavner, Julie **1992**:3
Kaye, Danny
  Obituary **1987**:2
Keeshan, Bob
  Obituary **2005**:2
Knight, Ted
  Obituary **1986**:4
Koppel, Ted **1989**:1
Kuralt, Charles
  Obituary **1998**:3
LaPaglia, Anthony **2004**:4
Larroquette, John **1986**:2
Lemmon, Jack **1998**:4
  Obituary **2002**:3
Letterman, David **1989**:3
Levinson, Barry **1989**:3
Levy, Eugene **2004**:3
Lewis, Shari **1993**:1
  Obituary **1999**:1
Liberace
  Obituary **1987**:2
Lucci, Susan **1999**:4
MacFarlane, Seth **2006**:1
Malkovich, John **1988**:2
Mantegna, Joe **1992**:1
McFarlane, Todd **1999**:1
Meredith, Burgess
  Obituary **1998**:1
Merkerson, S. Epatha **2006**:4
Messing, Debra **2004**:4
Midler, Bette **1989**:4
Miller, Arthur **1999**:4
Mirren, Helen **2005**:1
Moore, Julianne **1998**:1
Moore, Mary Tyler **1996**:2
Murray, Bill **2002**:4
Myers, Mike **1992**:3 **1997**:4
North, Alex **1986**:3
O'Brien, Conan **1994**:1
O'Connor, Carroll
  Obituary **2002**:3
O'Connor, Donald
  Obituary **2004**:4
Olmos, Edward James **1990**:1
Olson, Johnny
  Obituary **1985**:4
Page, Geraldine
  Obituary **1987**:4
Paulsen, Pat
  Obituary **1997**:4
Pryor, Richard **1999**:3
Randall, Tony
  Obituary **2005**:3
Redgrave, Vanessa **1989**:2
Ritter, John **2003**:4
Rivera, Geraldo **1989**:1
Rivers, Joan **2005**:3
Roberts, Doris **2003**:4
Rock, Chris **1998**:1
Rolle, Esther
  Obituary **1999**:2
Rollins, Howard E., Jr. **1986**:1
Romano, Ray **2001**:4
Rose, Charlie **1994**:2
Saralegui, Cristina **1999**:2
Schulz, Charles M. **1998**:1
Scott, George C.

  Obituary **2000**:2
Seymour, Jane **1994**:4
Silvers, Phil
  Obituary **1985**:4
Sinatra, Frank
  Obituary **1998**:4
Sorkin, Aaron **2003**:2
Springer, Jerry **1998**:4
Stack, Robert
  Obituary **2004**:2
Stein, Ben **2001**:1
Stiller, Ben **1999**:1
Streep, Meryl **1990**:2
Susskind, David
  Obituary **1987**:2
Tharp, Twyla **1992**:4
Tillstrom, Burr
  Obituary **1986**:1
Vieira, Meredith **2001**:3
Vonnegut, Kurt **1998**:4
Walker, Nancy
  Obituary **1992**:3
Walters, Barbara **1998**:3
Ward, Sela **2001**:3
Waterston, Sam **2006**:1
Weitz, Bruce **1985**:4
Wilson, Flip
  Obituary **1999**:2
Winfield, Paul
  Obituary **2005**:2
Witt, Katarina **1991**:3
Woods, James **1988**:3
Young, Robert
  Obituary **1999**:1

Encore Books
  Schlessinger, David
    Brief Entry **1985**:1

Energy Machine
  Newman, Joseph **1987**:1

Entrepreneurs
  Akin, Phil
    Brief Entry **1987**:3
  Allen, John **1992**:1
  Alter, Hobie
    Brief Entry **1985**:1
  Aoki, Rocky **1990**:2
  Arison, Ted **1990**:3
  Aurre, Laura
    Brief Entry **1986**:3
  Bauer, Eddie
    Obituary **1986**:3
  Ben & Jerry **1991**:3
  Berlusconi, Silvio **1994**:4
  Black, Conrad **1986**:2
  Bloomberg, Michael **1997**:1
  Boiardi, Hector
    Obituary **1985**:3
  Bose, Amar
    Brief Entry **1986**:4
  Branson, Richard **1987**:1
  Buffett, Warren **1995**:2
  Burr, Donald Calvin **1985**:3
  Bushnell, Nolan **1985**:1
  Campeau, Robert **1990**:1
  Clark, Jim **1997**:1
  Covey, Stephen R. **1994**:4
  Craig, Sid and Jenny **1993**:4
  Cray, Seymour R.
    Brief Entry **1986**:3

Martin, Ricky **1999**:4
Martin, Steve **1992**:2
McCartney, Paul **2002**:4
McEntire, Reba **1987**:3 **1994**:2
McFerrin, Bobby **1989**:1
McLachlan, Sarah **1998**:4
Menuhin, Yehudi
  Obituary **1999**:3
Metallica **2004**:2
Midler, Bette **1989**:4
Miller, Roger
  Obituary **1993**:2
Mitchell, Joni **1991**:4
Monica **2004**:2
Moog, Robert
  Obituary **2006**:4
Morissette, Alanis **1996**:2
Murphy, Eddie **1989**:2
Nelson, Willie **1993**:4
Newton-John, Olivia **1998**:4
Orbison, Roy
  Obituary **1989**:2
Osbournes, The **2003**:4
OutKast **2004**:4
Palmer, Robert
  Obituary **2004**:4
Parton, Dolly **1999**:4
Pass, Joe
  Obituary **1994**:4
Pink **2004**:3
Pride, Charley **1998**:1
Prince **1995**:3
Pryor, Richard **1999**:3
Puente, Tito
  Obituary **2000**:4
Raitt, Bonnie **1990**:2
Rattle, Simon **1989**:4
Reznor, Trent **2000**:2
Riddle, Nelson
  Obituary **1985**:4
Rimes, LeeAnn **1997**:4
Sade **1993**:2
Santana, Carlos **2000**:2
Selena
  Obituary **1995**:4
Shakira **2002**:3
Silverstein, Shel
  Obituary **1999**:4
Simon, Paul **1992**:2
Sinatra, Frank
  Obituary **1998**:4
Smith, Will **1997**:2
Solti, Georg
  Obituary **1998**:1
Sondheim, Stephen **1994**:4
Stefani, Gwen **2005**:4
Sting **1991**:4
Streisand, Barbra **1992**:2
System of a Down **2006**:4
Torme, Mel
  Obituary **1999**:4
Tosh, Peter
  Obituary **1988**:2
Travis, Randy **1988**:4
Turner, Tina **2000**:3
Twain, Shania **1996**:3
U **2002**:4
Urban, Keith **2006**:3
Usher **2005**:1
Vandross, Luther
  Obituary **2006**:3
Vaughan, Stevie Ray

  Obituary **1991**:1
Washington, Grover, Jr. **1989**:1
West, Kanye **2006**:1
White, Barry
  Obituary **2004**:3
White Stripes, The **2006**:1
Williams, Joe
  Obituary **1999**:4
Williams, Pharrell **2005**:3
Williams, Robin **1988**:4
Wilson, Flip
  Obituary **1999**:2
Wilson, Gretchen **2006**:3
Winans, CeCe **2000**:1
Wynonna **1993**:3
Yankovic, Frank
  Obituary **1999**:2
Yearwood, Trisha **1999**:1
Zevon, Warren
  Obituary **2004**:4

Grand Ole Opry
  Snow, Hank
    Obituary **2000**:3

Grand Prix racing
  Prost, Alain **1988**:1

Green Bay Packers football team
  Favre, Brett Lorenzo **1997**:2
  Howard, Desmond Kevin **1997**:2
  Sharpe, Sterling **1994**:3
  White, Reggie **1993**:4

Greenpeace International
  McTaggart, David **1989**:4

Greens party (West Germany)
  Schily, Otto
    Brief Entry **1987**:4

GRP Records, Inc.
  Grusin, Dave
    Brief Entry **1987**:2

Gucci
  Ford, Tom **1999**:3

Gucci Shops, Inc.
  Gucci, Maurizio
    Brief Entry **1985**:4
  Mello, Dawn **1992**:2

Gun control
  Brady, Sarah and James S. **1991**:4

Gulf + Western
  Diller, Barry **1991**:1

Gymnastics
  Hamm, Paul **2005**:1
  Retton, Mary Lou **1985**:2
  Strug, Kerri **1997**:3

Hampshire College
  Simmons, Adele Smith **1988**:4

Handicap rights
  Brady, Sarah and James S. **1991**:4
  Dickinson, Brian **1998**:2

H & R Block, Inc.
  Bloch, Henry **1988**:4

Hanna-Barbera Productions
  Barbera, Joseph **1988**:2
  Hanna, William
    Obituary **2002**:1

Hard Candy
  Mohajer, Dineh **1997**:3

Harlem Globetrotters basketball team
  Woodard, Lynette **1986**:2

Harley-Davidson Motor Co., Inc.
  Beals, Vaughn **1988**:2

Hartford, Conn., city government
  Perry, Carrie Saxon **1989**:2

Hasbro, Inc.
  Hassenfeld, Stephen **1987**:4

Hasidism
  Schneerson, Menachem Mendel
  1992:4
    Obituary **1994**:4

Hasty Pudding Theatricals
  Beatty, Warren **2000**:1
  Burnett, Carol **2000**:3
  Hanks, Tom **1989**:2 **2000**:2
  Peters, Bernadette **2000**:1

Hearst Magazines
  Black, Cathleen **1998**:4
  Ganzi, Victor **2003**:3

Heisman Trophy
  Flutie, Doug **1999**:2
  Howard, Desmond Kevin **1997**:2
  Jackson, Bo **1986**:3
  Testaverde, Vinny **1987**:2
  Williams, Ricky **2000**:2

Helmsley Hotels, Inc.
  Helmsley, Leona **1988**:1

Hemlock Society
  Humphry, Derek **1992**:2

Herbalife International
  Hughes, Mark **1985**:3

Hereditary Disease Foundation
  Wexler, Nancy S. **1992**:3

Herut Party (Israel)
  Levy, David **1987**:2

HEW
  See: Department of Health,
    Education, and Welfare

Hewlett-Packard
  Fiorina, Carleton S. **2000**:1
  Hewlett, William
    Obituary **2001**:4

Packard, David
Obituary **1996**:3

HGS
See: Human Genome Sciences, Inc.

HHR
See: Department of Health and
Human Services

High Flight Foundation
Irwin, James
Obituary **1992**:1

Hitchhiking
Heid, Bill
Brief Entry **1987**:2

Hobie Cat
Alter, Hobie
Brief Entry **1985**:1
Hasek, Dominik **1998**:3

Hockey
Bourque, Raymond Jean **1997**:3
Cherry, Don **1993**:4
Coffey, Paul **1985**:4
Crosby, Sidney **2006**:3
Eagleson, Alan **1987**:4
Federov, Sergei **1995**:1
Fuhr, Grant **1997**:3
Giguere, Jean-Sebastien **2004**:2
Gilmour, Doug **1994**:3
Granato, Cammi **1999**:3
Gretzky, Wayne **1989**:2
Hextall, Ron **1988**:2
Hull, Brett **1991**:4
Jagr, Jaromir **1995**:4
Klima, Petr **1987**:1
Konstantinov, Vladimir **1997**:4
LaFontaine, Pat **1985**:1
Lemieux, Claude **1996**:1
Lemieux, Mario **1986**:4
Lindbergh, Pelle
Obituary **1985**:4
Lindros, Eric **1992**:1
Messier, Mark **1993**:1
Pocklington, Peter H. **1985**:2
Richard, Maurice
Obituary **2000**:4
Roy, Patrick **1994**:2
Sakic, Joe **2002**:1
Yzerman, Steve **1991**:2
Zamboni, Frank J.
Brief Entry **1986**:4

Honda Motor Co.
Honda, Soichiro
Obituary **1986**:1

Hong Kong government
Lee, Martin **1998**:2
Patten, Christopher **1993**:3

Horror fiction
Barker, Clive **2003**:3
Brite, Poppy Z. **2005**:1
Harris, Thomas **2001**:1
King, Stephen **1998**:1

Koontz, Dean **1999**:3
Stine, R. L. **2003**:1

Horse racing
Day, Pat **1995**:2
Desormeaux, Kent **1990**:2
Krone, Julie **1989**:2
Lukas, D. Wayne **1986**:2
McCarron, Chris **1995**:4
Mellon, Paul
Obituary **1999**:3
O'Donnell, Bill
Brief Entry **1987**:4
Pincay, Laffit, Jr. **1986**:3
Secretariat
Obituary **1990**:1
Shoemaker, Bill
Obituary **2004**:4

Houston Astros baseball team
Lofton, Kenny **1998**:1
Ryan, Nolan **1989**:4

Houston Oilers football team
Moon, Warren **1991**:3

Houston Rockets basketball team
Olajuwon, Akeem **1985**:1
Yao Ming **2004**:1

Houston, Tex., city government
Watson, Elizabeth **1991**:2
Whitmire, Kathy **1988**:2

HUD
See: Department of Housing and
Urban Development

Hustler Magazine
Flynt, Larry **1997**:3

Hugo Awards
Asimov, Isaac
Obituary **1992**:3

Human Genome Sciences, Inc. [HGS]
Haseltine, William A. **1999**:2

Huntington's disease
Wexler, Nancy S. **1992**:3

Hyatt Legal Services
Bloch, Henry **1988**:4
Hyatt, Joel **1985**:3

Hydroponics
Davis, Noel **1990**:3

IACC
See: International Anticounterfeiting
Coalition

IBM Corp.
See: International Business
Machines Corp.

Ice cream
Ben & Jerry **1991**:3

Ice skating
Arakawa, Shizuka **2006**:4
Baiul, Oksana **1995**:3
Gordeeva, Ekaterina **1996**:4
Grinkov, Sergei
Obituary **1996**:2
Hamilton, Scott **1998**:2
Hughes, Sarah **2002**:4
Kerrigan, Nancy **1994**:3
Lipinski, Tara **1998**:3
Thomas, Debi **1987**:2
Witt, Katarina **1991**:3
Yamaguchi, Kristi **1992**:3
Zamboni, Frank J.
Brief Entry **1986**:4

Imani Temple
Stallings, George A., Jr. **1990**:1

Immigration
Kurzban, Ira **1987**:2
Lewis, Loida Nicolas **1998**:3
Mahony, Roger M. **1988**:2

Imposters
Bremen, Barry **1987**:3

Inacomp Computer Centers, Inc.
Inatome, Rick **1985**:4

Indiana Pacers basketball team
Miller, Reggie **1994**:4

Indiana University basketball team
Knight, Bobby **1985**:3

Indonesia
Wahid, Abdurrahman **2000**:3

Insurance
Davison, Ian Hay **1986**:1
Hilbert, Stephen C. **1997**:4

Integrated circuit
Noyce, Robert N. **1985**:4

Intel Corp.
Barrett, Craig R. **1999**:4
Grove, Andrew S. **1995**:3
Noyce, Robert N. **1985**:4

Interarms Corp.
Cummings, Sam **1986**:3

**International Anticounterfeiting
Coalition [IACC]**
Bikoff, James L.
Brief Entry **1986**:2

International Brotherhood of Teamsters
Carey, Ron **1993**:3
Hoffa, Jim, Jr. **1999**:2
Presser, Jackie
Obituary **1988**:4
Saporta, Vicki
Brief Entry **1987**:3

**International Business Machines Corp.
[IBM Corp.]**
Akers, John F. **1988**:3
Chaudhari, Praveen **1989**:4
Gerstner, Lou **1993**:4

Liberal Party (Canada)
Chretien, Jean **1990**:4 **1997**:2
Peterson, David **1987**:1

Liberal Party (South Africa)
Paton, Alan
Obituary **1988**:3

Library of Congress
Billington, James **1990**:3
Dickey, James
Obituary **1998**:2
Van Duyn, Mona **1993**:2

Likud Party (Israel)
Netanyahu, Benjamin **1996**:4

Lillian Vernon Corp.
Katz, Lillian **1987**:4

Limelight clubs
Gatien, Peter
Brief Entry **1986**:1

Lincoln Savings and Loan
Keating, Charles H., Jr. **1990**:4

Linguistics
Tannen, Deborah **1995**:1

Literacy
Bush, Millie **1992**:1
Kozol, Jonathan **1992**:1

Little People's Research Fund
Kopits, Steven E.
Brief Entry **1987**:1

Little Caesars pizza restaurants
Ilitch, Mike **1993**:4

Live Aid
Bono **1988**:4
Dylan, Bob **1998**:1
Geldof, Bob **1985**:3
Graham, Bill **1986**:4
Obituary **1992**:2

L.L. Bean Co.
Gorman, Leon
Brief Entry **1987**:1

Lloyd's of London
Davison, Ian Hay **1986**:1

Loews Corp.
Tisch, Laurence A. **1988**:2

Log Cabin Republicans
Tafel, Richard **2000**:4

Lone Ranger
Moore, Clayton
Obituary **2000**:3

Los Angeles city government
Bradley, Tom
Obituary **1999**:1
Riordan, Richard **1993**:4

Los Angeles Dodgers baseball team
Hershiser, Orel **1989**:2
Nomo, Hideo **1996**:2
Welch, Bob **1991**:3

Los Angeles Express football team
Young, Steve **1995**:2

Los Angeles Kings hockey team
Gretzky, Wayne **1989**:2

Los Angeles Lakers basketball team
Bryant, Kobe **1998**:3
Buss, Jerry **1989**:3
Chamberlain, Wilt
Obituary **2000**:2
Johnson, Earvin 'Magic' **1988**:4
Riley, Pat **1994**:3
Worthy, James **1991**:2

Los Angeles Museum of Contemporary Art
Isozaki, Arata **1990**:2

Los Angeles Raiders football team
Gault, Willie **1991**:2
Upshaw, Gene **1988**:1

Los Angeles Sparks basketball team
Leslie, Lisa **1997**:4

Louisiana Legislature
Duke, David **1990**:2

Louisiana state government
Roemer, Buddy **1991**:4

Luis Vuitton
Arnault, Bernard **2000**:4

LPGA
See: Ladies Professional Golf Association

MADD
See: Mothers Against Drunk Driving

Magic
Anderson, Harry **1988**:2
Blackstone, Harry Jr.
Obituary **1997**:4
Blaine, David **2003**:3
Copperfield, David **1986**:3
Henning, Doug
Obituary **2000**:3
Jay, Ricky **1995**:1
Randi, James **1990**:2

Maine State Government
Muskie, Edmund S.
Obituary **1996**:3

Major League Baseball Players Association
Fehr, Donald **1987**:2
Selig, Bud **1995**:2

Malawi Congress Party [MCP]
Banda, Hastings **1994**:3

Marriott Corp.
Marriott, J. Willard
Obituary **1985**:4
Marriott, J. Willard, Jr. **1985**:4

Martial arts
Chan, Jackie **1996**:1
Lee, Brandon
Obituary **1993**:4
Li, Jet **2005**:3

Maryland state government
Schaefer, William Donald **1988**:1

Massachusetts state government
Dukakis, Michael **1988**:3
Flynn, Ray **1989**:1
Frank, Barney **1989**:2
Moakley, Joseph
Obituary **2002**:2

Mathematics
Hawking, Stephen W. **1990**:1
Lawrence, Ruth
Brief Entry **1986**:3
Penrose, Roger **1991**:4
Pople, John
Obituary **2005**:2
Thom, Rene
Obituary **2004**:1
Wiles, Andrew **1994**:1

Mattel, Inc.
Barad, Jill **1994**:2
Eckert, Robert A. **2002**:3
Handler, Ruth
Obituary **2003**:3

Max Factor and Company
Factor, Max
Obituary **1996**:4

Maximilian Furs, Inc.
Potok, Anna Maximilian
Brief Entry **1985**:2

Mazda Motor Corp.
Yamamoto, Kenichi **1989**:1

McDonald's Restaurants
Kroc, Ray
Obituary **1985**:1

McDonnell Douglas Corp.
McDonnell, Sanford N. **1988**:4

MCI Communications Corp.
Cerf, Vinton G. **1999**:2
McGowan, William **1985**:2
McGowan, William G.
Obituary **1993**:1

MCP
See: Malawi Congress Party

Medicine
Adams, Patch **1999**:2
Baulieu, Etienne-Emile **1990**:1
Bayley, Corrine
  Brief Entry **1986**:4
Carson, Ben **1998**:2
Crichton, Michael **1995**:3
DeVita, Vincent T., Jr. **1987**:3
Duke, Red
  Brief Entry **1987**:1
Elders, Joycelyn **1994**:1
Foster, Tabatha
  Obituary **1988**:3
Gale, Robert Peter **1986**:4
Gallo, Robert **1991**:1
Hatem, George
  Obituary **1989**:1
Healy, Bernadine **1993**:1
Hill, J. Edward **2006**:2
Hounsfield, Godfrey **1989**:2
Jacobs, Joe **1994**:1
Jarvik, Robert K. **1985**:1
Jemison, Mae C. **1993**:1
Jorgensen, Christine
  Obituary **1989**:4
Keith, Louis **1988**:2
Kevorkian, Jack **1991**:3
Klass, Perri **1993**:2
Koop, C. Everett **1989**:3
Kopits, Steven E.
  Brief Entry **1987**:1
Kwoh, Yik San **1988**:2
Langston, J. William
  Brief Entry **1986**:2
Lorenz, Konrad
  Obituary **1989**:3
Morgentaler, Henry **1986**:3
Novello, Antonia **1991**:2
Olopade, Olufunmilayo **2006**:3
Radocy, Robert
  Brief Entry **1986**:3
Rock, John
  Obituary **1985**:1
Rosenberg, Steven **1989**:1
Rothstein, Ruth **1988**:2
Sabin, Albert
  Obituary **1993**:4
Sacks, Oliver **1995**:4
Schroeder, William J.
  Obituary **1986**:4
Spock, Benjamin **1995**:2
  Obituary **1998**:3
Steptoe, Patrick
  Obituary **1988**:3
Sullivan, Louis **1990**:4
Szent-Gyoergyi, Albert
  Obituary **1987**:2
Vagelos, P. Roy **1989**:4
Weil, Andrew **1997**:4
Wigler, Michael
  Brief Entry **1985**:1

Men's issues
Bly, Robert **1992**:4
McCartney, Bill **1995**:3

Mercedes-Benz
See: Daimler-Benz AG

Merck & Co.
Vagelos, P. Roy **1989**:4

Metromedia, Inc.
Kluge, John **1991**:1

Miami Dolphins football team
Shula, Don **1992**:2

Miami, Fla., city government
Suarez, Xavier
  Brief Entry **1986**:2

Michigan state government
Engler, John **1996**:3
Williams, G. Mennen
  Obituary **1988**:2

**Microelectronics and Computer
Technologies Corp.**
Inman, Bobby Ray **1985**:1

Microsoft Corp.
Ballmer, Steven **1997**:2
Belluzzo, Rick **2001**:3
Gates, Bill **1993**:3 **1987**:4
Stonesifer, Patty **1997**:1

Middle East
Arafat, Yasser **1989**:3 **1997**:3
Arens, Moshe **1985**:1
Assad, Hafez al- **1992**:1
Begin, Menachem
  Obituary **1992**:3
Berri, Nabih **1985**:2
Freij, Elias **1986**:4
Ghali, Boutros Boutros **1992**:3
Hussein, Saddam **1991**:1
Hussein I, King **1997**:3
  Obituary **1999**:3
Jumblatt, Walid **1987**:4
Khatami, Mohammed **1997**:4
Khomeini, Ayatollah Ruhollah
  Obituary **1989**:4
Levy, David **1987**:2
Nidal, Abu **1987**:1
Rafsanjani, Ali Akbar Hashemi **1987**
  :3
Redgrave, Vanessa **1989**:2
Sarkis, Elias
  Obituary **1985**:3
Schwarzkopf, Norman **1991**:3
Terzi, Zehdi Labib **1985**:3

Military
Abacha, Sani **1996**:3
Arens, Moshe **1985**:1
Aspin, Les
  Obituary **1996**:1
Babangida, Ibrahim Badamosi **1992**
  :4
Boyington, Gregory 'Pappy'
  Obituary **1988**:2
Cammermeyer, Margarethe **1995**:2
Cedras, Raoul **1994**:4
Cornum, Rhonda **2006**:3
Doe, Samuel
  Obituary **1991**:1
Dzhanibekov, Vladimir **1988**:1
Fitzgerald, A. Ernest **1986**:2
Franks, Tommy **2004**:1
Galvin, John R. **1990**:1
Garneau, Marc **1985**:1
Hess, Rudolph
  Obituary **1988**:1
Hope, Bob

Obituary **2004**:4
Hussein, Saddam **1991**:1
Inman, Bobby Ray **1985**:1
Jumblatt, Walid **1987**:4
Lansdale, Edward G.
  Obituary **1987**:2
Le Duan
  Obituary **1986**:4
Le Duc Tho
  Obituary **1991**:1
Marier, Rebecca **1995**:4
McCain, John S. **1998**:4
McSally, Martha **2002**:4
North, Oliver **1987**:4
Paige, Emmett, Jr.
  Brief Entry **1986**:4
Pinochet, Augusto **1999**:2
Powell, Colin **1990**:1
Rickover, Hyman
  Obituary **1986**:4
Schwarzkopf, Norman **1991**:3
Shalikashvili, John **1994**:2
Taylor, Maxwell
  Obituary **1987**:3
Ventura, Jesse **1999**:2
Westmoreland, William C.
  Obituary **2006**:4
Willson, S. Brian **1989**:3
Yeager, Chuck **1998**:1
Ye Jianying
  Obituary **1987**:1
Zech, Lando W.
  Brief Entry **1987**:4
Zia ul-Haq, Mohammad
  Obituary **1988**:4

Milwaukee Brewers baseball team
Sheffield, Gary **1998**:1
Veeck, Bill
  Obituary **1986**:1

Minimalist art
Richter, Gerhard **1997**:2

Minnesota state government
Ventura, Jesse **1999**:2
Wellstone, Paul
  Obituary **2004**:1

**Minnesota Timberwolves basketball
team**
Garnett, Kevin **2000**:3
Laettner, Christian **1993**:1

Minnesota Vikings football team
Moss, Randy **1999**:3
Payton, Walter
  Obituary **2000**:2

Miramax
Weinstein, Bob and Harvey **2000**:4

Miss America Pageant
Wells, Sharlene
  Brief Entry **1985**:1
Williams, Vanessa L. **1999**:2

Miss Manners
Martin, Judith **2000**:3

Mister Rogers
Rogers, Fred **2000**:4

Brief Entry **1986**:1
Petrossian, Christian
    Brief Entry **1985**:3
Pouillon, Nora **2005**:1
Puck, Wolfgang **1990**:1
Shaich, Ron **2004**:4
Thomas, Dave **1986**:2 **1993**:2
    Obituary **2003**:1
Waters, Alice **2006**:3
Zagat, Tim and Nina **2004**:3

Retailing
Adams-Geller, Paige **2006**:4
Bern, Dorrit J. **2006**:3
Bravo, Rose Marie **2005**:3
Charron, Paul **2004**:1
Choo, Jimmy **2006**:3
Drexler, Millard S. **1990**:3
Ecko, Marc **2006**:3
Ginsberg, Ian **2006**:4
Lepore, Nanette **2006**:4
Marcus, Stanley
    Obituary **2003**:1
Persson, Stefan **2004**:1
Prevor, Barry and Steven Shore **2006**
    :2

Reuben Awards
Gould, Chester
    Obituary **1985**:2
Schulz, Charles
    Obituary **2000**:3

Revlon, Inc.
Bosworth, Kate **2006**:3
Duffy, Karen **1998**:1
Perelman, Ronald **1989**:2

Rhode Island state government
Violet, Arlene **1985**:3

Richter Scale
Richter, Charles Francis
    Obituary **1985**:4

Ringling Brothers and Barnum & Bailey Circus
Burck, Wade
    Brief Entry **1986**:1
Feld, Kenneth **1988**:2

RJR Nabisco, Inc.
Horrigan, Edward, Jr. **1989**:1

Robotics
Kwoh, Yik San **1988**:2

Rock Climbing
Hill, Lynn **1991**:2

Rockman
Scholz, Tom **1987**:2

Roller Coasters
Toomer, Ron **1990**:1

Rolling Stone magazine
Wenner, Jann **1993**:1

Rotary engine
Yamamoto, Kenichi **1989**:1

Running
Benoit, Joan **1986**:3
Joyner, Florence Griffith **1989**:2
    Obituary **1999**:1
Knight, Philip H. **1994**:1
Zatopek, Emil
    Obituary **2001**:3

Russian Federation
Putin, Vladimir **2000**:3
Yeltsin, Boris **1991**:1

SADD
See: Students Against Drunken Driving

Sailing
Alter, Hobie
    Brief Entry **1985**:1
Conner, Dennis **1987**:2
Koch, Bill **1992**:3
Morgan, Dodge **1987**:1
Turner, Ted **1989**:1

St. Louis Blues hockey team
Fuhr, Grant **1997**:3
Hull, Brett **1991**:4

St. Louis Browns baseball team
Veeck, Bill
    Obituary **1986**:1

St. Louis Cardinals baseball team
Busch, August A. III **1988**:2
Busch, August Anheuser, Jr.
    Obituary **1990**:2
Caray, Harry **1988**:3
    Obituary **1998**:3
McGwire, Mark **1999**:1
Pujols, Albert **2005**:3

St. Louis Rams football team
Warner, Kurt **2000**:3

San Antonio Spurs basketball team
Duncan, Tim **2000**:1
Robinson, David **1990**:4

San Antonio, Tex., city government
Cisneros, Henry **1987**:2

San Diego Chargers football team
Barnes, Ernie **1997**:4
Bell, Ricky
    Obituary **1985**:1
Unitas, Johnny
    Obituary **2003**:4

San Diego Padres baseball team
Dravecky, Dave **1992**:1
Gwynn, Tony **1995**:1
Kroc, Ray
    Obituary **1985**:1
Sheffield, Gary **1998**:1

San Francisco city government
Alioto, Joseph L.
    Obituary **1998**:3
Brown, Willie **1996**:4

San Francisco 49ers football team
DeBartolo, Edward J., Jr. **1989**:3
Montana, Joe **1989**:2
Rice, Jerry **1990**:4
Walsh, Bill **1987**:4
Young, Steve **1995**:2

San Francisco Giants baseball team
Bonds, Barry **1993**:3
Dravecky, Dave **1992**:1

SANE/FREEZE
Coffin, William Sloane, Jr. **1990**:3

Save the Children Federation
Guyer, David
    Brief Entry **1988**:1

SBA
See: Small Business Administration

Schottco Corp.
Schott, Marge **1985**:4

Schwinn Bicycle Co.
Schwinn, Edward R., Jr.
    Brief Entry **1985**:4

Science fiction
Anderson, Poul
    Obituary **2002**:3
Asimov, Isaac
    Obituary **1992**:3
Butler, Octavia E. **1999**:3
Kelley, DeForest
    Obituary **2000**:1
Lucas, George **1999**:4
Norton, Andre
    Obituary **2006**:2
Sterling, Bruce **1995**:4

Sculpture
Beuys, Joseph
    Obituary **1986**:3
Bontecou, Lee **2004**:4
Borofsky, Jonathan **2006**:4
Botero, Fernando **1994**:3
Bourgeois, Louise **1994**:1
Chia, Sandro **1987**:2
Chillida, Eduardo
    Obituary **2003**:4
Christo **1992**:3
Dubuffet, Jean
    Obituary **1985**:4
Dunham, Carroll **2003**:4
Gober, Robert **1996**:3
Graham, Robert **1993**:4
Graves, Nancy **1989**:3
Kaskey, Ray
    Brief Entry **1987**:2
Kelly, Ellsworth **1992**:1
Kiefer, Anselm **1990**:2
Lin, Maya **1990**:3
Moore, Henry
    Obituary **1986**:4
Murakami, Takashi **2004**:2
Nevelson, Louise
    Obituary **1988**:3
Ono, Yoko **1989**:2
Paolozzi, Eduardo

Submarines
  Rickover, Hyman
    Obituary **1986**:4
  Zech, Lando W.
    Brief Entry **1987**:4

Sun Microsystems, Inc.
  McNealy, Scott **1999**:4

Sunbeam Corp.
  Dunlap, Albert J. **1997**:2

Suicide
  Applewhite, Marshall Herff
    Obituary **1997**:3
  Dorris, Michael
    Obituary **1997**:3
  Hutchence, Michael
    Obituary **1998**:1
  Quill, Timothy E. **1997**:3

Sundance Institute
  Redford, Robert **1993**:2

Sunshine Foundation
  Sample, Bill
    Brief Entry **1986**:2

Superconductors
  Chaudhari, Praveen **1989**:4
  Chu, Paul C.W. **1988**:2

Supreme Court of Canada
  Wilson, Bertha
    Brief Entry **1986**:1

Surfing
  Curren, Tommy
    Brief Entry **1987**:4
  Johnson, Jack **2006**:4

SWAPO
  See: South West African People's
  Organization

Swimming
  Ederle, Gertrude
    Obituary **2005**:1
  Evans, Janet **1989**:1
  Van Dyken, Amy **1997**:1

Tampa Bay Buccaneers football team
  Bell, Ricky
    Obituary **1985**:1
  Gruden, Jon **2003**:4
  Johnson, Keyshawn **2000**:4
  Testaverde, Vinny **1987**:2
  Williams, Doug **1988**:2
  Young, Steve **1995**:2

Tandem Computers, Inc.
  Treybig, James G. **1988**:3

Teach for America
  Kopp, Wendy **1993**:3

Tectonics
  Rosendahl, Bruce R.
    Brief Entry **1986**:4

Teddy Ruxpin
  Kingsborough, Donald
    Brief Entry **1986**:2

Tele-Communications, Inc.
  Malone, John C. **1988**:3 **1996**:3

Televangelism
  Graham, Billy **1992**:1
  Hahn, Jessica **1989**:4
  Robertson, Pat **1988**:2
  Rogers, Adrian **1987**:4
  Swaggart, Jimmy **1987**:3

Temple University basketball team
  Chaney, John **1989**:1

Tennis
  Agassi, Andre **1990**:2
  Ashe, Arthur
    Obituary **1993**:3
  Becker, Boris
    Brief Entry **1985**:3
  Capriati, Jennifer **1991**:1
  Clijsters, Kim **2006**:3
  Courier, Jim **1993**:2
  Davenport, Lindsay **1999**:2
  Federer, Roger **2004**:2
  Gerulaitis, Vitas
    Obituary **1995**:1
  Gibson, Althea
    Obituary **2004**:4
  Graf, Steffi **1987**:4
  Henin-Hardenne, Justine **2004**:4
  Hewitt, Lleyton **2002**:2
  Hingis, Martina **1999**:1
  Ivanisevic, Goran **2002**:1
  Kournikova, Anna **2000**:3
  Navratilova, Martina **1989**:1
  Pierce, Mary **1994**:4
  Riggs, Bobby
    Obituary **1996**:2
  Roddick, Andy **2004**:3
  Sabatini, Gabriela
    Brief Entry **1985**:4
  Safin, Marat **2001**:3
  Sampras, Pete **1994**:1
  Seles, Monica **1991**:3
  Sharapova, Maria **2005**:2
  Williams, Serena **1999**:4
  Williams, Venus **1998**:2

Test tube babies
  Steptoe, Patrick
    Obituary **1988**:3

Texas Rangers baseball team
  Rodriguez, Alex **2001**:2
  Ryan, Nolan **1989**:4

Texas State Government
  Bush, George W., Jr. **1996**:4
  Richards, Ann **1991**:2

Therapeutic Recreation Systems
  Radocy, Robert
    Brief Entry **1986**:3

Timberline Reclamations
  McIntyre, Richard
    Brief Entry **1986**:2

Time Warner Inc.
  Ho, David **1997**:2
  Levin, Gerald **1995**:2
  Ross, Steven J.
    Obituary **1993**:3

TLC Beatrice International
  Lewis, Loida Nicolas **1998**:3

TLC Group L.P.
  Lewis, Reginald F. **1988**:4
    Obituary **1993**:3

Today Show
  Couric, Katherine **1991**:4
  Gumbel, Bryant **1990**:2
  Norville, Deborah **1990**:3

Tony Awards
  Abbott, George
    Obituary **1995**:3
  Alda, Robert
    Obituary **1986**:3
  Alexander, Jane **1994**:2
  Alexander, Jason **1993**:3
  Allen, Debbie **1998**:2
  Allen, Joan **1998**:1
  Bacall, Lauren **1997**:3
  Bailey, Pearl
    Obituary **1991**:1
  Bancroft, Anne
    Obituary **2006**:3
  Bates, Alan
    Obituary **2005**:1
  Bennett, Michael
    Obituary **1988**:1
  Bloch, Ivan **1986**:3
  Booth, Shirley
    Obituary **1993**:2
  Brooks, Mel **2003**:1
  Brynner, Yul
    Obituary **1985**:4
  Buckley, Betty **1996**:2
  Burnett, Carol **2000**:3
  Carter, Nell
    Obituary **2004**:2
  Channing, Stockard **1991**:3
  Close, Glenn **1988**:3
  Crawford, Cheryl
    Obituary **1987**:1
  Crawford, Michael **1994**:2
  Cronyn, Hume
    Obituary **2004**:3
  Dench, Judi **1999**:4
  Dennis, Sandy
    Obituary **1992**:4
  Dewhurst, Colleen
    Obituary **1992**:2
  Fagan, Garth **2000**:1
  Ferrer, Jose
    Obituary **1992**:3
  Fiennes, Ralph **1996**:2
  Fierstein, Harvey **2004**:2
  Fishburne, Laurence **1995**:3
  Flanders, Ed
    Obituary **1995**:3
  Fosse, Bob
    Obituary **1988**:1
  Foster, Sutton **2003**:2
  Gleason, Jackie
    Obituary **1987**:4

Cumulative Newsmakers Index

This index lists all newsmakers included in the entire *Newsmakers* series.

Listee names are followed by a year and issue number; thus **1996**:3 indicates that an entry on that individual appears in both 1996, Issue 3, and the 1996 cumulation.

McRae, Carmen 1920(?)-1994
  Obituary **1995**:2
McSally, Martha 1966(?)- **2002**:4
McTaggart, David 1932(?)- **1989**:4
McVeigh, Timothy 1968-2001
  Obituary **2002**:2
Meadows, Audrey 1925-1996
  Obituary **1996**:3
Megawati Sukarnoputri 1947- **2002**:2
Megawati Sukarnoputri 1947- **2000**:1
Mehta, Zubin 1938(?)- **1994**:3
Meier, Richard 1934- **2001**:4
Meisel, Steven 1954- **2002**:4
Mellinger, Frederick 1924(?)-1990
  Obituary **1990**:4
Mello, Dawn 1938(?)- **1992**:2
Mellon, Paul 1907-1999
  Obituary **1999**:3
Melman, Richard
  Brief Entry **1986**:1
Meltzer, Brad 1970- **2005**:4
Menchu, Rigoberta 1960(?)- **1993**:2
Meneghel, Maria da Graca
  See Xuxa
Mengele, Josef 1911-1979
  Obituary **1985**:2
Mengers, Sue 1938- **1985**:3
Menninger, Karl 1893-1990
  Obituary **1991**:1
Menuhin, Yehudi 1916-1999
  Obituary **1999**:3
Merchant, Ismail 1936-2005
  Obituary **2006**:3
Merchant, Natalie 1963- **1996**:3
Mercier, Laura 1959(?)- **2002**:2
Mercury, Freddie 1946-1991
  Obituary **1992**:2
Meredith, Burgess 1909-1997
  Obituary **1998**:1
Merkerson, S. Epatha 1952- **2006**:4
Merrick, David 1912-2000
  Obituary **2000**:4
Merrill, James 1926-1995
  Obituary **1995**:3
Merritt, Justine
  Brief Entry **1985**:3
Mesic, Stipe 1934- **2005**:4
Messick, Dale 1906-2005
  Obituary **2006**:2
Messier, Mark 1961- **1993**:1
Messing, Debra 1968- **2004**:4
Metallica **2004**:2
Meyers, Nancy 1949- **2006**:1
Mfume, Kweisi 1948- **1996**:3
Michael, George 1963- **1989**:2
Michelangeli, Arturo Benedetti 1920- .....
  1988:2
Michelman, Kate 1942- **1998**:4
Michener, James A. 1907-1997
  Obituary **1998**:1
Mickelson, Phil 1970- **2004**:4
Midler, Bette 1945- **1989**:4
Mikan, George 1924-2005
  Obituary **2006**:3
Mikulski, Barbara 1936- **1992**:4
Milano, Alyssa 1972- **2002**:3
Milbrett, Tiffeny 1972- **2001**:1
Milburn, Rodney Jr. 1950-1997
  Obituary **1998**:2
Milland, Ray 1908(?)-1986
  Obituary **1986**:2

Millard, Barbara J.
  Brief Entry **1985**:3
Millepied, Benjamin 1977(?)- **2006**:4
Miller, Andre 1976- **2003**:3
Miller, Ann 1923-2004
  Obituary **2005**:2
Miller, Arthur 1915- **1999**:4
Miller, Bebe 1950- **2000**:2
Miller, Bode 1977- **2002**:4
Miller, Dennis 1953- **1992**:4
Miller, Merton H. 1923-2000
  Obituary **2001**:1
Miller, Nicole 1951(?)- **1995**:4
Miller, Percy
  See Master P
Miller, Rand 1959(?)- **1995**:4
Miller, Reggie 1965- **1994**:4
Miller, Robyn 1966(?)-
  See Miller, Rand
Miller, Roger 1936-1992
  Obituary **1993**:2
Miller, Sue 1943- **1999**:3
Milligan, Spike 1918-2002
  Obituary **2003**:2
Mills, Malia 1966- **2003**:1
Mills, Wilbur 1909-1992
  Obituary **1992**:4
Milne, Christopher Robin 1920-1996
  Obituary **1996**:4
Milosevic, Slobodan 1941- **1993**:2
Milosz, Czeslaw 1911-2004
  Obituary **2005**:4
Milstead, Harris Glenn
  See Divine
Mina, Denise 1966- **2006**:1
Minghella, Anthony 1954- **2004**:3
Minner, Ruth Ann 1935- **2002**:2
Minnesota Fats 1900(?)-1996
  Obituary **1996**:3
Minogue, Kylie 1968- **2003**:4
Minsky, Marvin 1927- **1994**:3
Mintz, Shlomo 1957- **1986**:2
Miro, Joan 1893-1983
  Obituary **1985**:1
Mirren, Helen 1945- **2005**:1
Misrach, Richard 1949- **1991**:2
Mitarai, Fujio 1935- **2002**:4
Mitchell, Arthur 1934- **1995**:1
Mitchell, George J. 1933- **1989**:3
Mitchell, John 1913-1988
  Obituary **1989**:2
Mitchell, Joni 1943- **1991**:4
Mitchell, Joseph 1909-1996
  Obituary **1997**:1
Mitchelson, Marvin 1928- **1989**:2
Mitchum, Robert 1917-1997
  Obituary **1997**:4
Mitterrand, Francois 1916-1996
  Obituary **1996**:2
Mixon, Oscar G.
  See Walker, Junior
Miyake, Issey 1939- **1985**:2
Miyake, Kazunaru
  See Miyake, Issey
Miyazaki, Hayao 1941- **2006**:2
Miyazawa, Kiichi 1919- **1992**:2
Mizrahi, Isaac 1961- **1991**:1
Moakley, Joseph 1927-2001
  Obituary **2002**:2
Mobutu Sese Seko 1930-1998
  Obituary **1998**:4

Mobutu Sese Seko 1930-1997 .... **1993**:4
  Obituary **1998**:1
Moby 1965- **2000**:1
Mohajer, Dineh 1972- **1997**:3
Moi, Daniel arap 1924- **1993**:2
Molina, Alfred 1953- **2005**:3
Molinari, Susan 1958- **1996**:4
Molotov, Vyacheslav Mikhailovich
  1890-1986
  Obituary **1987**:1
Monaghan, Thomas S.
  See Monaghan, Tom
Monaghan, Tom 1937- **1985**:1
Mondavi, Robert 1913- **1989**:2
Moneo, Jose Rafael 1937- **1996**:4
Monica 1980- **2004**:2
Monk, Art 1957- **1993**:2
Monroe, Bill 1911-1996
  Obituary **1997**:1
Monroe, Rose Will 1920-1997
  Obituary **1997**:4
Montagu, Ashley 1905-1999
  Obituary **2000**:2
Montana, Joe 1956- **1989**:2
Montand, Yves 1921-1991
  Obituary **1992**:2
Montgomery, Elizabeth 1933-1995
  Obituary **1995**:4
Montoya, Carlos 1903-1993
  Obituary **1993**:4
Moody, John 1943- **1985**:3
Moody, Rick 1961- **2002**:2
Moog, Robert 1934-2005
  Obituary **2006**:4
Moon, Warren 1956- **1991**:3
Moonves, Les 1949- **2004**:2
Moore, Archie 1913-1998
  Obituary **1999**:2
Moore, Clayton 1914-1999
  Obituary **2000**:3
Moore, Demi 1963(?)- **1991**:4
Moore, Dudley 1935-2002
  Obituary **2003**:2
Moore, Henry 1898-1986
  Obituary **1986**:4
Moore, Julianne 1960- **1998**:1
Moore, Mandy 1984- **2004**:2
Moore, Mary Tyler 1936- **1996**:2
Moore, Michael 1954(?)- **1990**:3
Moose, Charles 1953(?)- **2003**:4
Moreno, Arturo 1946- **2005**:2
Morgan, Claire
  See Highsmith, Patricia
Morgan, Dodge 1932(?)- **1987**:1
Morgan, Robin 1941- **1991**:1
Morgentaler, Henry 1923- **1986**:3
Mori, Yoshiro 1937- **2000**:4
Morissette, Alanis 1974- **1996**:2
Morita, Akio 1921- **1989**:4
Morita, Akio 1921-1999
  Obituary **2000**:2
Morita, Noriyuki 'Pat' 1932- **1987**:3
Morita, Pat
  See Morita, Noriyuki 'Pat'
Moritz, Charles 1936- **1989**:3
Morris, Dick 1948- **1997**:3
Morris, Doug 1938- **2005**:1
Morris, Kathryn 1969- **2006**:4
Morris, Mark 1956- **1991**:1
Morris, Nate
  See Boyz II Men